Lecture Notes in Computer Science 3820

Commenced Publication in 1973
Founding and Former Series Editors:
Gerhard Goos, Juris Hartmanis, and Jan van Leeuwen

Laurence T. Yang Xingshe Zhou
Wei Zhao Zhaohui Wu Yian Zhu
Man Lin (Eds.)

Embedded Software and Systems

Second International Conference, ICESS 2005
Xi'an, China, December 16-18, 2005
Proceedings

Springer

Volume Editors

Laurence T. Yang
Man Lin
St. Francis Xavier University
Department of Computer Science
Antigonish, NS, B2G 2W5, Canada
E-mail: {lyang,mlin}@stfx.ca

Xingshe Zhou
Yian Zhu
Northwestern Polytechnical University
No. 127 West Youyi Road, P.O. Box 404
Xi'an City, Shaanxi Province, 710072, China
E-mail: {zhouxs,zhuya}@nwpu.edu.cn

Wei Zhao
Texas A&M University, Department of Computer Science
College Station, TX 77843-1112, USA
and
National Science Foundation, Division of Computer and Network Systems
4201 Wilson Blvd, Arlington, VA 22230, USA
E-mail: w-zhao@tamu.edu

Zhaohui Wu
Zhejiang University
College of Computer Science
Hangzhou, Zhejiang Province, 310027, China
E-mail: wzh@zju.edu.cn

Library of Congress Control Number: Applied for

CR Subject Classification (1998): C.3, C.2, C.5.3, D.2, D.4, H.4

ISSN 0302-9743
ISBN-10 3-540-30881-4 Springer Berlin Heidelberg New York
ISBN-13 978-3-540-30881-2 Springer Berlin Heidelberg New York

Springer is a part of Springer Science+Business Media

springeronline.com

Printed in Germany

Typesetting: Camera-ready by author, data conversion by Scientific Publishing Services, Chennai, India
Printed on acid-free paper SPIN: 11599555 06/3142 5 4 3 2 1 0

Preface

Welcome to the proceedings of the 2005 International Conference on Embedded Software and Systems (ICESS 2005) held in Xian, China, December 16-18, 2005.

With the advent of VLSI system level integration and system-on-chip, the center of gravity of the computer industry is now moving from personal computing into embedded computing. Embedded software and systems are increasingly becoming a key technological component of all kinds of complex technical systems, ranging from vehicles, telephones, aircraft, toys, security systems, to medical diagnostics, weapons, pacemakers, climate control systems, etc.

The ICESS 2005 conference provided a premier international forum for researchers, developers and providers from academia and industry to address all resulting profound challenges; to present and discuss their new ideas, research results, applications and experience; to improve international communication and cooperation; and to promote embedded software and system industrialization and wide applications on all aspects of embedded software and systems.

Besides the main conference, we also featured the following four workshops to extend the spectrum of the main conference:

- Scheduling Techniques for Real-Time Systems
- IXA/IXP Application in Embedded Systems
- The Modeling and Security of Ubiquitous Systems
- Intelligent Storage System and Technology

There was a very large number of paper submissions (360) for the ICESS 2005 main conference, not only from Asia and the Pacific, but also from Europe, and North and South America. All submissions were reviewed by at least three program or technical committee members or external reviewers. It was extremely difficult to select the papers for the conference because there were so many excellent and interesting submissions. In order to allocate as many papers as possible and keep the high quality of the conference, we finally accepted 140 papers and 31 papers for the main conference and for the workshops, respectively. There were 63 main conference papers and 8 workshop papers selected in the LNCS proceedings. We believe that all of these papers and topics not only provided novel ideas, new results, work in progress and state-of-the-art techniques in this field, but also promoted cutting-edge research and future cooperation, and stimulated future research activities in the area of embedded software and systems.

The exciting conference program was the result of the hard and excellent work of program vice-chairs, external reviewers, and program and technical committee members under a very tight schedule. We were also grateful to the members of the local organizing committee for supporting us in handling so many organizational tasks. Last but not least, we hoped you enjoyed the conference's technical and social program, and the natural and historic attractions of the ancient city of Xian.

October 2005

Laurence T. Yang, Xingshe Zhou, Wei Zhao,
Zhaohui Wu, Yian Zhu and Man Lin

Organization

ICESS 2005 was organized by Northwestern Polytechnical University, China in collaboration with St. Francis Xavier University, Canada.

Sponsors

National Natural Science Foundation of China
Important Software Committee of National 863 Program
China Computer Federation
Northwestern Polytechnical University, China
Springer, Lecture Notes in Computer Science (LNCS)

Executive Committee

General Chairs:	Zhaohui Wu, Zhejiang University, China
	Wei Zhao, Texas A&M University and NSF, USA
Program Chairs:	Laurence T. Yang, St. Francis Xavier University, Canada
	Xingshe Zhou, Northwestern Polytechnical University, China
Program Vice-chairs:	Huiyang Zhou, University of Central Florida, USA
	Walid Taha, Rice University, USA
	Yann-Hang Lee, Arizona State University, USA
	Naehyuck Chang, Seoul National University, Korea
	Luis Gomes, Universidade Nova de Lisboa, Portugal
	Mohammed Y. Niamat, The University of Toledo, USA
	Susumu Horiguchi, Tohoku University, Japan
	Elhadi Shakshuki, Acadia University, Canada
	Wenjing Lou, Worcester Polytechnic Institute, USA
	Pin-Han Ho, University of Waterloo, Canada
	Hong-Va Leong, Hong Kong Polytechnic University, China
	Qun Jin, Waseda University, Japan
	Arjan Durresi, Louisiana State University, USA
	Marios D. Dikaiakos, University of Cyprus, Cyprus
Workshop Chairs:	Yian Zhu, Northwestern Polytechnical University, China
	Man Lin, St. Francis Xavier University, Canada
Panel Chairs:	Joseph K. Ng, Hong Kong Baptist University, China
	Xu Cheng, Peking University, China

Conference Secretary:	Yuying Wang, Northwestern Polytechnical University, China
Publication Chair:	Tony Li Xu, St. Francis Xavier University, Canada
Local Executive Committee:	Zhanhuai Li (Chair) Hong Tang, Yubo Wang, Mingxing Sun, Yumei Zhang

Program/Technical Committee

Raza Abidi	Dalhousie University, Canada
Esma Aimeur	Université de Montréal, Canada
H. Amano	Keio University, Japan
Leonard Barolli	Fukuoka Institute of Technology, Japan
Darcy Benoit	Acadia University, Canada
Marian Bubak	Cyfronet University of Krakow, Poland
Jun Cai	University of Waterloo, Canada
Jiannong Cao	Hong Kong Polytechnic University, China
Keith Chan	Hong Kong Polytechnic University, China
Karam Chatha	Arizona State University, USA
Xiangqun Chen	Peking University, China
Phoebe Chen	Deakin University, Australia
Jing Chen	National Cheng Kung University, Taiwan
Yu Chen	Tsinghua University, China
Zhanglong Chen	Fudan University, China
Xiuzhen Cheng	George Washington University, USA
Xu Cheng	Peking University, China
Jen-Yao Chung	IBM, USA
Debatosh Debnath	Oakland University, USA
Yunwei Dong	Northwestern Polytechnical University, China
Stephen Edwards	Columbia University, USA
Tomoya Enokido	Rissho University, Japan
Thomas Fahringer	University of Innsbruck, Austria
Farzan Fallah	Fujitsu Laboratory in America, USA
Ling Feng	University of Twente, The Netherlands
Hakan Ferhatosmanoglu	Ohio State University, USA
Joao Miguel Fernandes	Universidade do Minho, Portugal
Antonio Ferrari	Universidade de Aveiro, Portugal
Jose Manuel Ferreira,	Universidade do Porto, Portugal
Yue Gao	Hopen Software Eng. Co. Ltd., China
Mukul Goyal	University of Wisconsin Milwaukee, USA
Rick Ha	University of Waterloo, Canada
Naiping Han	Chinasoft Network Technology Co. Ltd., China
Anwar Haque	Bell Canada, Canada
Takahiro Hara	Osaka University, Japan
Martin Hofmann	University of Munich, Germany
Seongsoo Hong	Seoul National University, Korea

Program/Technical Committee (continued)

Zhigang Hu	IBM T.J. Watson Research Center, USA
Michael C. Huang	University of Rochester, USA
Xinming Huang	University of New Orleans, USA
Liviu Iftode	Rutgers University, USA
Clinton L. Jeffery	New Mexico State University, USA
Hai Jiang	University of Waterloo, Canada
Xiaohong Jiang	Tohoku University, Japan
Roumen Kaiabachev	Rice University, USA
Masashi Kastumata	Nippon Institute of Technology, Japan
Vlado Keselj	Dalhousie University, Canada
Ismail Khalil Ibrahim	Johannes Kepler University of Linz, Austria
Cheeha Kim	Pohang University of Science and Technology, Korea
Jihong Kim	Seoul National University, Korea
Jung Hwan Kim	University of Toledo, USA
Kwanho Kim	Samsung Electronics, Korea
Sung Won Kim	Yeungnam University, Korea
Aris Kozyris	National Technical University of Athens, Greece
C.M. Krishna	University of Massachusetts, USA
Morihiro Kuga	Kumamoto University, Japan
Younggoo Kwon	Sejong University, Korea
Anchow Lai	Intel, USA
Wai Lam	Chinese University of Hong Kong, China
Hsien-Hsin Lee	Georgia Tech, USA
Chin-Laung Lei	National Taiwan University, Taiwan
Qun Li	College of William and Mary, USA
Tao Li	University of Florida, USA
Minghong Liao	Harbin Institute of Technology, China
Xinhau Lin	University of Waterloo, Canada
Yen-Chun Lin	Taiwan University of Science and Technology, Taiwan
Antonio Liotta	University of Essex, UK
Chunlei Liu	Troy University, USA
Xiang Long	Bei Hang University, China
Yung-Hsiang Lu	Purdue University, USA
Jing Ma	University of New Orleans, USA
Wenchao Ma	Microsoft Research Asia, China
Zakaria Maamar	Zayed University, UAE
Ricardo Machado	Universidade do Minho, Portugal
Paulo Maciel	Federal University of Pernambuco, Brazil
Evangelos Markatos	ICS-FORTH and University of Crete, Greece
Grant Martin	Tensilica, USA
Janise McNair	University of Florida, USA

Program/Technical Committee (continued)

Teo Yong Meng	National University of Singapore, Singapore
Yan Meng	Stevens Institute of Technology, USA
Tulita Mitra	National University of Singapore, Singapore
S.M.F.D. Syed Mustapha	University of Malaysia, Malaysia
Soraya K. Mostefaoui	University of Fribourg, Switzerland
Tomasz Muldner	Acadia University, Canada
Horacio Neto	Instituto Superior Tecnico, Portugal
Naoki Nishi	NEC, Japan
WenSheng Niu	Aeronautics Computing Research Institute, China
Sebnem Ozer	Motorola Inc., USA
Gordon Pace	University of Malta, Malta
Jens Palsberg	University of California at Los Angeles, USA
Seung-Jong Park	Louisiana State University, USA
Ian Philp	Los Alamos National Lab, USA
Massimo Poncino	University of Verona, Italy
Sunil Prabhakar	Purdue University, USA
Elliott Rachlin	Honeywell, USA
Omer Rana	Cardiff University, UK
Minghui Shi	University of Waterloo, Canada
Timothy K. Shih	Tamkang University, Taiwan
Basem Shihada	University of Waterloo, Canada
Youngsoo Shin	KAIST, Korea
Dongkun Shin	Samsung Electronics, Korea
Kimura Shinnji	Waseda University, Japan
Sandeep Shukla	Virginia Tech, USA
Valery Sklyarov	Universidade de Aveiro, Portugal
Prasanna Sundararajan	Xilinx Inc, USA
Wonyong Sung	Seoul National University, Korea
Abd-Elhamid M. Taha	Queen's University, Canada
Makoto Takizawa	Tokyo Denki University, Japan
Jean-Pierre Talpin	INRIA, France
Kian-Lee Tan	National University of Singapore, Singapore
Xinan Tang	Intel Corp., Intel Compiler Lab., USA
Zahir Tari	RMIT, Australia
P.S. Thiagarajan	National University of Singapore, Singapore
Xuejun Tian	Aichi Prefectural University, Japan
Hiroyuki Tomiyama	Nagoya University, Japan
Ali Saman Tosun	University of Texas at San Antonio, USA
Nur A. Touba	University of Texas at Austin, USA
Andre Trudel	Acadia University, Canada
Lorna Uden	Staffordshire University, UK

Program/Technical Committee (continued)

Alexander P. Vazhenin	University of Aizu, Japan
Jari Veijalainen	University of Jyvaskyla, Finland
Salvatore Vitabile	University of Palermo, Italy
Sarma Vrudhula	Arizona State University, USA
Wenye Wang	North Carolina State University, USA
Xiaoge Wang	Tsinghua University, China
Ying-Hong Wang	Tamkang University, Taiwan
Weng-Fai Wong	National University of Singapore, Singapore
Eric Wong	University of Texas at Dallas, USA
Jing Wu	CRC, Canada
Dong Xie	IBM China Research Lab, China
Yuan Xie	Pennsylvania State University, USA
Lin Xu	National Natural Science Foundation, China
Dong Xuan	Ohio State University, USA
Ryuichi Yamaguchi	Matsushita Co., Japan
Jie Yang	Spirent Communications, Inc., USA
Jun Yang	University of California, Riverside, USA
Chi-Hsiang Yeh	Queen's University, Canada
Y. Yokohira	Okayama University, Japan
Muhammed Younas	Oxford Brookes University, UK
Hsiang-Fu Yu	National Center University, Taiwan
Demetrios Zeinalipour-Yazti	University of California at Riverside, USA
Surong Zeng	Motorola Inc., USA
Guozhen Zhang	Waseda University, Japan
Daqing Zhang	Agent for Science, Technology and Research, Singapore
Shengbing Zhang	Northwestern Polytechnical University, China
Zhao Zhang	Iowa State University, USA
Wei Zhang	Southern Illinois University, USA
Youtao Zhang	University of Texas at Dallas, USA
Baihua Zheng	Singapore Management University, Singapore
Jun Zheng	University of Ottawa, Canada
Kougen Zheng	Zhejiang University, China
Dakai Zhu	University of Texas at San Antonio, USA

Additional Reviewers

Iouliia Skliarova	Universidade de Aveiro, Portugal
Mário Véstias	INESC-ID, Portugal
Anikó Costa	Universidade Nova de Lisboa, Portugal
António Esteves	Universidade do Minho, Portugal
Raimundo Barreto	Universidade do Amazonas, Brazil

Workshop on Scheduling Techniques for Real-Time Systems

Introduction

Welcome to the proceedings of the 2005 International Workshop on Scheduling Techniques for Real-Time Systems (IWSRT 2005) held in conjunction with ICESS 2005 in Xi'an, China, December 16-18, 2005. Traditionally, scheduling has been an important aspect of real-time systems in ensuring soft/hard timing constraints. As real-time computing becomes complicated and has more limitations (e.g., power consumption), the demand for more sophisticated scheduling techniques becomes increasingly apparent.

The purpose of this workshop was to bring together researchers from both universities and industry to advance real-time scheduling techniques and its applications. IWSRT 2005 focused on the current technological challenges of developing scheduling algorithms:

- Power aware scheduling for real time systems
- Heuristic scheduling for real-time systems
- Parallel real-time scheduling
- Scheduling for distributed real-time systems
- Schedulability test, analysis and verification
- QoS scheduling for multimedia applications

From the many submissions, six papers were included in the workshop program. The workshop consisted of short presentations by the authors and encouraged discussion among the attendees. We hope that IWSRT 2005 provided a relaxed forum to present and discuss new ideas and new research directions, and to review current trends in this area. The success of the workshop was the result of the hard work of the authors and the program committee members. We were grateful for everyone's efforts in making the conference a success. Special thanks go to the members of the ICESS 2005 organizing committee for their support and help in many organizational tasks. We hoped you enjoyed the workshop program and the attractions of the ancient city of Xi'an.

Workshop Chairs

Man Lin, St. Francis Xavier University, Canada
Fan Zhang, Hong Kong University of Science and Technology, China
Dakai Zhu, University of Texas at San Antonio, USA

Program/Technical Committee

Samarjit Chakraborty	National University of Singapore, Singapore
Deji Chen	Emerson Process Management, USA
Yuanshun Dai	Indiana University-Purdue University, USA
Zonghua Gu	Hong Kong University of Science and Technology, Chir
Hai Jin	Huazhong University of Science and Technology, China
Rodrigo de Mello	University of Sao Paulo, Brazil
Xiao Qin	New Mexico Institute of Mining and Technology, USA
Gang Quan	University of South Carolina, USA
Chi-Sheng Shih	National Taiwan University, Taiwan
Shengquan Wang	Texas A&M, USA

Workshop on IXA/IXP Application in Embedded Systems

Introduction

The 2005 International Workshop on IXA/IXP Application in Embedded Systems (IWIXA) was held in conjunction with the International Conference on Embedded Software and Systems (ICESS 2005), December 16-18, 2005, at Northwestern Polytechnical University, Xi'an, P.R. China. The workshop aimed to provide a stimulating environment for IXA/IXP researchers and developers to share their experience in order to promote the understanding of the latest trends in Network Processors and their application development in embedded systems. The workshop invited new and original submissions addressing theoretical and practical topics in the following fields (but not limited to these topics):

- Internet eXchange Architecture (IXA) in embedded systems
- Network Processors and IXP
- The IXA/IXP Network Processors-based applications
- New Network Technology
- IXA/IXP-related training and experiments

The workshop received 21 paper submissions. After careful review, 11 papers were accepted for the workshop program. The workshop committee was grateful to all authors for their interesting contributions.

Workshop Chair

Naiqi Liu, University of Electronic Science and Technology, China

Workshop Coordinator

Jeffrey Cao, Intel, China

Program/Technical Committee

Luo Lei	University of Electronic Science and Technology, China
Hang Lei	University of Electronic Science and Technology, China
Guangjun Li	University of Electronic Science and Technology, China

Workshop on the Modeling and Security of Ubiquitous Systems

Introduction

Rapid progress in computer hardware technology has made computers compact (e.g. laptop, palmtop), powerful, and more affordable. Furthermore, recent advances in wireless data communications technology have spawned an increasing demand for various types of services. As a result, we are witnessing an explosive growth for research and development efforts in the field of ubiquitous communication and computing systems.

The global growth of interest in the Internet and in high-quality audio, and video conferencing and VOD, coupled with a growing high-bandwidth structure, will lead to a rapidly expanding market for ubiquitous multimedia services. The popularity of mobile services should eventually affect the market for ubiquitous networks. For this reason, mobile based technologies, such as mobile synchronization, QoS assurance, mobile IP-based multimedia technologies and the security of mobile information systems, need to be studied and developed for future services offered to subscribers in future mobile information systems. This ubiquitous information technology will allow users to travel within an office building, from office to home, around the country and the world with a portable computer in their hands. Disconnection will no longer be a network fault, but a common event intentionally caused by the user in order to preserve a consequence of mobility.

The workshop on Modeling and Security in Ubiquitous Information Systems contained a collection of high-quality papers on this subject. In addition to this, we received a few more papers, as a result of the call-for-papers for this topic. Each paper went through a rigorous, peer review process as required by the conference. Based upon the review committee's decision, four papers were selected for their original contributions as well as their suitability to the topic of this workshop.

Many people have contributed to the creation of this workshop. Thanks are due to the members of Howon University's Mobile Networks Laboratory and the members of Kyonggi University's Security Laboratory for their support. Special thanks go to the members of the review committee for their excellent cooperation. Their hard work, comments and suggestions really helped to improve the quality of the papers. We would like to take this opportunity to thank everyone who made this workshop possible: the authors, the ICESS 2005 organizing committee and the publisher.

Workshop Chair

Dong Chun Lee, Howon University, Korea

Program/Technical Committee

Bernard Burg	HP Labs., USA
Kijoon Chae	Ewha Womans University, Korea
Ying Chen	IBM China Research Lab., China
Anthony Chung	Depaul University, USA
Alex Delis	New York Polytechnic University, USA
Maggie Dunham	Southern Methodist University, USA
Adrian Friday	Lancaster University, UK
ReX E. Gantenbein	Wyoming University, USA
Takahiro Hara	Osaka University, Japan
Yong-Sok Her	Kyushu University, Japan
Hang Dai Hoon	Kyung Won University, Korea
Jadwiga Indulska	Queensland University, Australia
Christian S. Jensen	Aalborg University, Denmark
Hai Jin	Huazhong University of Science and Technology, China
Myuhang-Joo Kim	Seoul Women's University, Korea
Sang-Ho Kim	Korea Information Security Agency, Korea
Masaru Kitsuregawa	Tokyo University, Japan
Shonali Krishnaswamy	Monash University, Australia
Tae Won Kang	Agency for Defense Development, Korea
Taekyoung Kwon	Sejong University, Korea
Young Bin Kwon	Chung-Ang University, Korea
Alexandros Labrinidis	Pittsburgh University, USA
Jeong Bae Lee	Sun Moon University, Korea
Wang-Chien Lee	Pennsylvania State University, USA
Hui Lei	IBM T. J. Watson Research Center, USA
Jong-In Lim	Korea University, Korea
Seng Wai Loke	Monash University, Australia
Hanqing Lu	Chinese Academy of Science, China
Sanjay Kumar Madria	Missouri-Rolla University, USA
Se Hyun Park	Chung-Ang University, Korea
Oscar Pastor	Valencia University, Spain
Evaggelia Pitoura	Ioannina University, Greece
Andreas Pitsillides	Cyprus University, Cyprus
Indrajit Ray	Colorado State University, USA
Peter Reiher	University of California at Los Angeles, USA
Claudia Roncancio	ENSIMAG/LSR, France
Seref Sagiroglu	Gazi University, Turkey
Ming-Chien Shan	HP, USA
Theodore E. Simos	Peloponnese University, Greece
SungWon Sohn	Electronics and Telecommunications Research Institute, Korea
Ki-Sung Yoo	Korea Institute of Science and Technology Information, Korea

Workshop on Intelligent Storage Systems and Technology

Introduction

With the present explosive growth in information, the demand for storage systems is increasing rapidly. To satisfy such mounting demand, storage systems are required to be more scalable, reliable, secure and manageable than they are currently. There is a clear and recent trend in which some intelligence is moved from host machines to storage devices and implemented in the embedded controller. The 2005 International Workshop on Intelligent Storage Systems and Technology (ISST 2005) brought together storage systems researchers and practitioners to explore new directions in the design, implementation, evaluation, and deployment of storage systems. ISST 2005 was one of the workshops held in conjunction with the 2nd International Conference on Embedded Software and Systems (ICESS 2005) held in Xian, China, December 16-18, 2005.

We were extremely grateful to the program committee members who worked under a very tight schedule to complete the rigorous review process for the large number of submissions received by ISST 2005. Their hard work lead to the selection of the 10 papers presented at the workshop.

Workshop Chairs

Dan Feng, Huazhong University of Science and Technology, China
Hong Jiang, University of Nebraska-Lincoln, USA

Program/Technical Committee

Liang Fang	National University of Defense Technology, China
Jizhong Han	Chinese Academy of Sciences, China
Ben Xubin He	Tennessee Technological University, USA
Xiao Qin	New Mexico Institute of Mining and Technology, USA
Fang Wang	Huazhong University of Science and Technology, China
Frank Zhigang Wang	Cranfield University, UK
Song Wu	Huazhong University of Science and Technology, China
Changsheng Xie	Huazhong University of Science and Technology, China
Lu Xu	Chinese Academy of Science, China
Ke Zhou	Huazhong University of Science and Technology, China
Yifeng Zhu	University of Maine, USA

Table of Contents

Track 3: Real-Time Systems

Track 6: Testing and Verification

Track 7: Reconfigurable Computing

Track 8: Agent and Distributed Computing

Track 11: Pervasive/Ubiquitous Computing and Intelligence

Track 12: Multimedia and Human-Computer Interaction

Track 13: Network Protocol, Security and Fault-Tolerance

Track 14: Workshop Selected Papers

Keynote Speech

Are Lessons Learnt in Mobile Ad Hoc Networks Useful for Wireless Sensor Networks?

Lionel Ni

Department of Computer Science,
Hong Kong University of Science and Technology,
Clear Water Bay, Kowloon, Hong Kong

Abstract. Many researchers consider wireless sensor networks (WSNs) as special case of Mobile Ad Hoc Networks (MANETs). Although WSNs do share some similarities with MANETs, WSNs are very different from MANETs and have many unique research issues. I argue that lessons learnt from research in MANETs are of little use when studying WSNs. This talk will address the major differences between MANETs and WSNs. The focus of this talk will be on new challenging research issues in WSNs, such as ID management, adaptive route - an exciting research area.

L.T. Yang et al. (Eds.): ICESS 2005, LNCS 3820, p. 1, 2005.

Compiler-Directed Scratchpad Memory Management

Jingling Xue

Programming Languages and Compilers Group,
School of Computer Science and Engineering,
University of New South Wales,
Sydney, NSW 2052, Australia

Abstract. On-chip memory, in the form of (hardware-managed) cache, (software-managed) scratchpad memory (SPM) or some combination of both, is widely used in embedded systems. Most high-end embedded systems have both cache and SPM on-chip since each addresses a different need. Caches allow easy integration and are often effective but are unpredictable. SPMs are more energy-efficient than caches since they do not need complex tag-decoding logic. In addition, SPMs provide absolutely predictable performance but the programmer or compiler must schedule explicit data/instruction transfers between the SPM and off-chip main memory in an embedded system. In today's industry, this task is largely accomplished manually. The programmer often spends a lot of time on partitioning data and/or instructions and inserting explicit data/instruction transfers required between the SPM and main memory. Such a manual approach is time-consuming and error-prone. Obtaining satisfactory solutions for large application programs by hand can be challenging. Furthermore, hand-crafted code is not portable since it is usually customised for one particular architecture.

This talk introduces a compiler approach, called *memory coloring*, that we have recently developed to automatically allocating the arrays in a program to an SPM. The arrays are frequently used in embedded applications such as image processing and signal processing. The novelty of this approach lies in partitioning an SPM into a pseudo register file, splitting the live ranges of arrays to create potential data transfer statements between the SPM and off-chip main memory, and finally, adapting an existing graph-colouring algorithm for register allocation to assign the arrays in the program into the register file. This compiler-directed approach is efficient due to the practical efficiency of graph-colouring algorithms. We have implemented this work in the SUIF/machSUIF compiler framework. Preliminary results over benchmarks show that this compiler-directed approach represents a promising solution to automatic SPM management.

L.T. Yang et al. (Eds.): ICESS 2005, LNCS 3820, p. 2, 2005.

Heterogeneous Multi-processor SoC: An Emerging Paradigm of Embedded System Design and Its Challenges

Xu Cheng

Department of Computer Science,
Peking University, Beijing, China

Abstract. The recent years have witnessed a variety of new embedded applications. Typical examples include mobile multimedia gadgets, digital televisions, high-end cell phones, wireless network applications, etc. The salient features of these applications include more comprehensive functionalities, higher performance demand, and low-power consumption. These requirements render the traditional single processor-based embedded systems no longer an appropriate realization for such applications. On the other hand, the continual advance of VLSI technologies enables more and more transistors to be integrated on a single chip. The International Technology Roadmap for Semiconductors predicts that chips with a billion transistors are within reach. As a result, the push (application demands) and pull (VLSI technology) forces together give birth to the multi-processor system-on-chips (MPSoCs).

Heterogeneous MPSoCs are different from traditional embedded systems in many aspects and they ask for new design and implementation methodologies. Heterogeneous MPSoCs are not merely a hardware design. The complexity and heterogeneity of the system significantly increase the complexity of the HW/SW partitioning problem. Meanwhile, evaluating the performance and verifying its correctness is much more difficult compared to traditional single processor-based embedded systems. Constructing a simulator to simulate the system's behavior and evaluate its performance takes more effort compared to conventional embedded systems. The verification of the system also becomes challenging.

Programming a heterogeneous MPSoC is another challenge to be faced. This problem arises simply because there are multiple programmable processing elements and since they are heterogeneous, software designer needs to have expertise on all of these processing elements and needs to take a lot of care on how to make the software running as a whole.

There are a lot more issues that do not appear or easier to tackle on traditional embedded systems, trade-offs between performance and low-power will dominate the design life time. However, the incoming challenges also brought us many opportunities either to industry and academic research.

L.T. Yang et al. (Eds.): ICESS 2005, LNCS 3820, p. 3, 2005.

Trace-Based Runtime Instruction Rescheduling for Architecture Extension

YuXing Tang, Kun Deng, HongJia Cao, and XingMing Zhou

School of Computer, National University of Defense Technology, China 410073
{tyx, kundeng, hjcao, xmzhou}@nudt.edu.cn

Abstract. The update of embedded processor may introduce new function unit, new coprocessor, or even new additional DSP. In many cases, software application can't be fully rebuilt to utilize these new resources. This paper describes a novel framework, called Runtime Instruction Rescheduling (RIR), to solve this problem. RIR can find hot spots in binary codes, build a large instruction window to generate trace, reschedule and optimize instructions in traces. Different scheduling policies have been simulated. Shown from detailed simulation, RIR helps the old binary codes benefit from new hardware resources.

1 Introduction

Advance computer system may change quickly in architecture, especially in high-end embedded or mainframe area. Extended instruction-set, new function unit or even a new coprocessor may be added in the new and powerful system. For example, TI's new TMS320DM310 has a DSP and an additional imaging accelerator except for the arm core [1].

Researchers have presented link-time instruction scheduling to optimize binary codes [2] for new architecture. Rebuilding all applications maybe a good way to take the full advantages of system updating. But full rebuilding may not be applicable in many cases. Lacking of complete source codes may cause trouble in software rebuilding. The widely used binary library will prevent application developer from transforming them freely.

In this paper, we present a novel framework for ***R****untime* ***I****nstruction* ***R****escheduling* (RIR). RIR can detect hot spots during the dynamic execution. Without recompiling or recoding, RIR will select suitable instructions for scheduling and inject the results into the new executing engine. The scheduling is based on trace [3] and trace cache [9], which is suitable for various instruction scheduling and aggressive optimizing [3][8][10]. Profile-guided loop unrolling and function inline are the main optimizing methods. Detailed simulations demonstrate that RIR is a good choice to accelerate already-compiled application during system updating.

The rest of this paper is organized as follows. Section 2 presents related works. Section 3 introduces the framework for runtime instruction rescheduling. Section 4 describes the details of experiments. Section 5 presents the simulation results, and then concludes the paper and discusses future work in Section 6.

L.T. Yang et al. (Eds.): ICESS 2005, LNCS 3820, pp. 4 – 15, 2005.

2 Related Works

Instruction scheduling is one of the main research topics in compiler and microarchitecture design. Early researches focused on static compilation. J.Fisher [3] introduced trace compaction for global code optimization.

Crusoe [5] used software to schedule CISC instructions to be executed in a VLIW core. Researchers in UIUC [4][8] presented two runtime frameworks for superscalar processor to optimize hot spot in runtime. Also Dynamo [6] exhibits promising result for runtime optimization based on software.

Recent years, many projects of dynamic optimization or binary translation have been proposed to scheduling code during architecture migration [2][4][5][6]. Most researches use simple threshold of trace-begin and trace-end to control the trace selection [6][10] or only use fill unit for optimization [16]. And all available optimizing and scheduling will perform in small piece of code. Simple-threshold methodology simplifies the trace control logic and keeps the cost low. But unalterable scheduling can't adapt to complex and various runtime situations well. Sometimes the optimization has to be conservative [7][11]. RIR uses continuous trace profiling [15] and multi-level mechanism to solve this problem.

Loop unrolling and software pipelining may be the most effective way to exploit ILP [12]. Many optimizing algorithms and scheduling methods are focus on loop. But it is difficult to select the number of unrolling iterations in runtime. Most of the time, unrolling must be conservative to avoid the trace fail [12]. Aggressive strategy needs a tiny kernel loop, which is familiar in scientific computing [13]. The method in RIR tries to unroll the loop in general application, and implement the SMD scheduling in dynamic unrolled loop body.

3 Runtime Instruction Rescheduling

3.1 Control Flow of RIR

The framework of Runtime Instruction Rescheduling (RIR) is designed to solve the mismatch problem between hardware and software. As described in fig.1, unchanged binary image is injected into the new architecture. In early iterations, these instructions won't take advantages from the new hardware resources added by system updating.

Off the processor datapath, profiling is used to grasp execution behavior [11]. Those frequently executed code will form an instruction window for runtime scheduling. In following iterations, scheduled code will be executed by the new resource.

Compared with traditional solutions of recompiling source codes, RIR may have following advantages.

- **No burden for software developer.** Rescheduling is transparent to all software application. Software can be accelerated without recompiling source code.

- **Speed up old compiled code.** RIR can reschedule old instructions, select suitable new instructions as substitution, and use the new function units to speed up the execution.
- **Minor changes in architecture.** A layer of special software completes most work of RIR, introducing only small microarchitecture changes. Meanwhile RIR software can perform more aggressive scheduling than hardware.
- **Scheduling according to software's real behavior.** Runtime scheduling will be directed by real-time profiling information. Thus scheduling can adapt to dynamic behavior of execution.

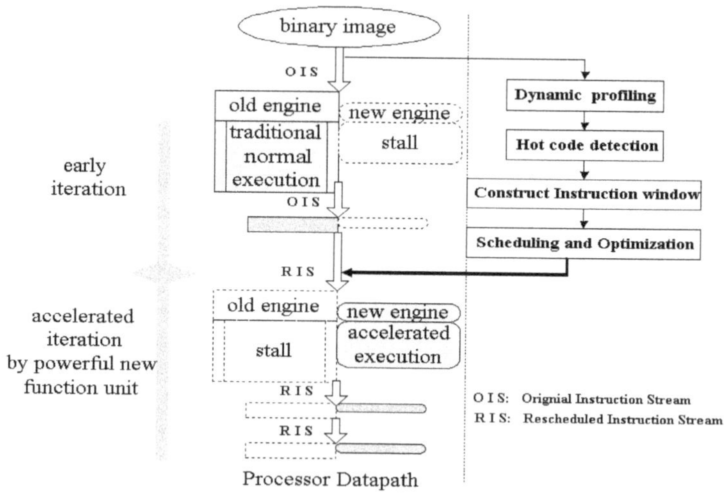

Fig. 1. Execution flow of RIR (the shaded parts present active executing engine during different iterations)

3.2 Trace-Based RIR

Trace is the basic scheduling unit in RIR. Guided by dynamic profiling [15], those frequently executed sequential codes are formed into hot trace. Scheduling in trace will stride over the boundary of branch. If the control exits from the middle of trace, compensating code or roll back is need to keep right execution. We call this as *trace fail*, otherwise *trace hit*. The large instruction window of long hot trace will enable aggressive schedule and optimization, but it is easier to fail than small trace. Now RIR use checkpoint mechanism. When trace failed, processor state would be recovered to the beginning of trace, and lower level trace or even unscheduled code would be executed instead.

As shown in Fig.2a, ABDEG is the hot path. This path will be extracted from original Control Flow Graphic (CFG) (Fig.2b). The rescheduled trace will be executed more efficiently (Fig.2c).

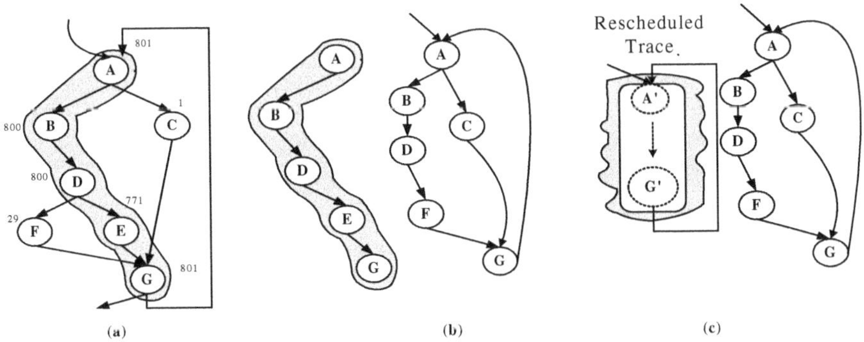

Fig. 2. CFG transfer in RIR hot trace

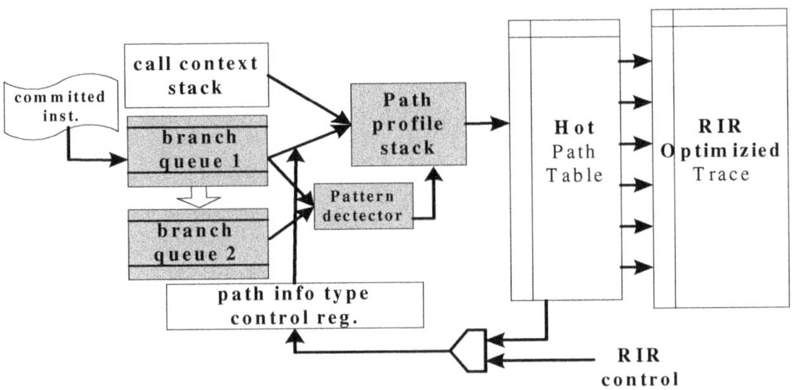

Fig. 3. Main hardware components in RIR

Fig.3 presents the main hardware components of RIR. An instruction queue is used to buffer the committed branches from pipeline. Combined with another queue, these two queues are used to detect the dynamic pattern to direct optimization (section 3.3 for detail). As the profiler in [15], a path stack is used to discover execution path from the stream of branches. The Least Frequently Used (LFU) policy serves the purpose of keeping frequently executed path in hot path table. Dynamic optimization routines must transform the instructions in every hot path into an optimized trace. An index function connects the hot paths and optimized RIR traces, as a link between original code and transformed code.

The kernel of RIR is the heuristic algorithm for trace generation, described as following:

1) Dynamic profiling records the information of basic blocks, such as branch type, branch bias level, target address, branch taken times.
2) Detect trace-begin condition. (various thresholds and metrics for different control instruction and pattern)

3) Collect instruction to form trace. Each basic block is added to trace according to its performance potential. This potential is calculated by the block size, bias level, and possible optimization.
4) Detect trace-end condition. Predict possible performance gain from whole trace, and the cost of useful global schedule and optimization.
5) Perform advised trace scheduling and optimizing.

Distinguish from simple threshold trace method, after a trace has been generated, trace profiling will be use to detect the usefulness of every trace. Trace will be organized and transformed in predefined levels. The frequently executed and successful low-level trace will become the candidate to form a high-level trace. The trace in higher level may have more exploited ILP, and apply more aggressive optimizing then the trace in lower level.

3.3 Multi-level Trace Strategy

RIR use the instruction pattern and execution time to control the generation and level changing of trace. Instruction pattern, especially the pattern of branch instruction, is useful to select a suitable scheduling and optimizing method. Table 1 gives currently concerned instruction Pattern in RIR.

Table 1. Instruction pattern and possible optimizing choice

Instruction Pattern	Description
Biased direct conditional branch	Biased block may be joined to a large trace
Backward direct conditional branch + backward branch	Possible internal loop, branch occurs time can tell the unrolling times
Biased indirect branch	If the number of branch target is limited and biased, it can be treat as an direct branch
Small function call	the size of function and the frequency will induce the optimization of inline

As shown in Fig.4, two branch queues are connected to detect the execution pattern. The first is known as buffer queue, because it is also used to buffer the branch for path stack (Fig.3). RIR will check the tail of buffer queue for backward branch. For possible unrolling loop, the target of backward branch should in the second branch queue. Illustrated in fig.4, when the call instruction moves to the tail of pattern queue, RIR will search for corresponding return in both queue. The address of branch instruction and its target address will help RIR calculate path size (loop size or function size).

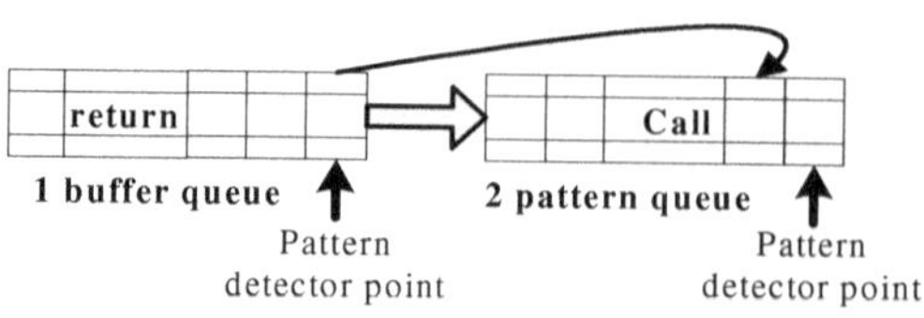

Fig. 4. Pattern detect in branch queue

Direct unconditional branch will not be treated as the boundary of basic block. According the type of end branch, the profiling will record additional information, such as block size, continuous branch times or function size. All these information are used to select the most suitable scheduling method and predict the gain and cost before optimization.

RIR classifies the optimizing and scheduling into different levels. Low-level optimization can be applied to all trace, with low cost and little gain. High-level optimization can only applied to peculiar instruction stream. But high-level trace will get huge performance improvement, and cost more storage and time. Current RIR has three levels:

1. Copy propagation, constant propagation. Because of the ISA and data dependency, such optimization still can be applied in runtime.
2. Conservative loop unrolling. Instructions in the unrolled loop may be scheduled or substituted to use the hardware resources more efficiently and effectively.
3. Aggressive loop unrolling and function inline. The hot loop will be unrolled more times than in level-2.

Actually different embedded system may choose different optimization and classification. In order to compare with traditional simple threshold control and single-pass optimization, this paper uses loop unrolling and function inline as main optimization.

Similar to PARROT's gradual optimization [10], all trace in RIR will be in low-level firstly. Then those hot traces will be recognized after several successful executions. Hot traces will be rescheduled and re-optimized into high-level trace. If a high-level trace jumps out from the middle and fails frequently, it will be degraded into low-level.

Compared with popular simple trace management, multi-level trace has more opportunity to apply different optimization. Trace generation will be quicker and earlier than ever, because it is easy to construct a low-level trace. Trace profiling will direct the unrolling times, and then help to construct a precise instruction window for runtime scheduling. Continuous profiling makes RIR adaptive to changeful and complex runtime behavior. The trace length limits in traditional method should be loosed. Abutting trace cache lines can be combined to store a long trace, because optimizing such as loop unrolling can spill the length limits.

4 Simulation

Highly recomposed SimpleScalar toolset v3.0d is used to evaluate the design of RIR. The main processor is an embedded RISC core, much like MIPS 4Kp embedded core. The baseline architecture parameters are in Table 2. The architectural extensions are given in Fig.5. In this simulation, the SIMD unit is selected as the new hardware resource added during architectural migration.

SIMD unit has similar function as AltiVec, MMX or SSE [14]. It can execute multiply or add instruction for the packed data. Previously, recompiling is needed to take the advantage of SIMD extension. RIR eliminate this rebuilt demand. Old application, which has been built and compiled without the knowledge of new extension, will also benefit from SIMD under the framework of RIR. Multiple iterations of internal loop may be executed in parallel in SIMD unit. RIR can substitute suitable instructions into SIMD instructions.

Table 2. Baseline architecture overview

Instruction	Mips32 style instruction, quad word memory access
L1 Icache	8kB, 32 byte lines, 2-way set associative, 1 cycles for hit
L1 Dcache	8kB, 32 byte lines, 4-way set associative, 1 cycles for hit
Pipeline	5 stage, 4 issue out-of-order
RIR Trace cache	1024 internal operation storage
Fetch width	4 instruction per cycle
Issue width	4 instruction per cycle
Mis-prediction	3 cycle for pipeline flush
Reorder buffer	16 entry and other 8 entry for load/store
Function Units and latency (total/issue)	4 Int ALU (1/1), 1 Int Mult (2/1) / Div (20/19), 4 memory (1/1), 4 FP Add (2/1), 1 FP Mult (4/1) / Div (12/12) / Sqrt (24/24)

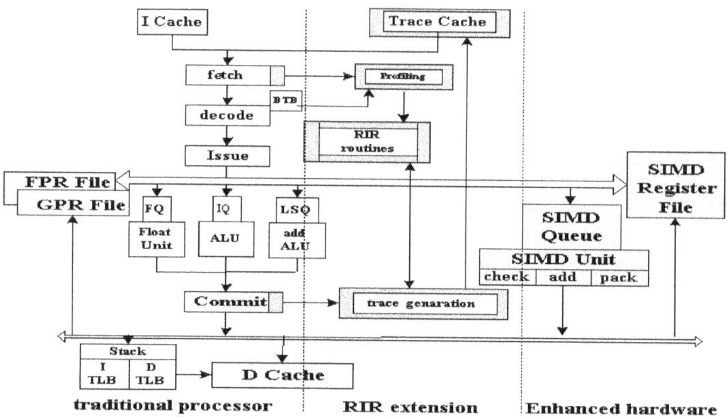

Fig. 5. Simulated Microarchitecture. Deep shaded parts present the extensions of RIR. Grayish parts present the new SIMD function unit added during architectural migration.

Dynamic profiling monitors instruction-fetch and gathers information from branch unit. Those frequently executed codes will trigger trace generation. ROM or flash memory is used to store RIR routines. They act just as normal system traps. A special memory space named trace cache is used to store the scheduled traces.

Figure 6 presents a piece of code from one dimension FFT. At the beginning of loop, the small variable *i* will direct internal *if* to perform the addition of *a_rl* not *b_im*. The right side of figure 6 is the assembly code of internal loop. Frequent instructions are in heavy black.

Figure 7 gives the level-1(a), level-2(b) and level-3(c) trace in RIR. Actually level-1 trace equals to the result of popular simple threshold trace control. Several heuristic

```
for (i = 0; i<ex; i++){
    lenb /=2, timb = 0;
    for (j = 0; j<numb; j++){
      w=0;
      for(k = 0; k < lenb; k++){

            j1 = timb + k;
            j2 = j1 + lenb;
            if (i < ex/2)
                  a_rl[j1] = a_rl[j1] + a_rl[j2];
            else
                  b_im[j1] = b_im[j1] + b_im[j2];

            w += numb;
      }timb +=(2*lenb);
    }numb *=2;
}
```

```
LoopK          slt     R2, R3, R4
               bne     R2, R0, LoopJ_END
               add     R11,R5,R3
               add     R12,R4,R11
               sra     R10, R9, 1
               slt     R10, R1, R10
               bne     R10, R0 ELSE1
               lw      R16, R11(R7)
               lw      R17, R12(R7)
               add     R16, R16, R17
               sw      R11(R7), R16
               j       Loop_Kend
ELSE1:         lw      R18, R11(R8)
               lw      R19, R12(R8)
               add R18, R18, R19
               sw      R11(R8), R11
LoopK_END: add     R6, R6, R20
               add     R3, R3, 1
               j       LoopK
LoopJ_END:
```

Fig. 6. The example code from FFT

```
LoopK        slt   R2, R3, R4
             bne   R2, R0, LoopJ_END
             add   R11,R5,R3
             add   R12,R4,R11
             lw    R16, R11(R7)
             lw    R17, R12(R7)
             add   R16, R16, R17
             sw    R11(R7), R16
             j     Loop_Kend
             add   R6, R6, R30
LoopK_END:   add   R3, R3, 1
      j            LoopK
```

(a) level-1: threshold control to select frequent instuctions

```
LoopK  slt   R2, R3, R4
       bne   R2, R0, LoopJ_END
       add   R11,R5,R3        add   R21,R5, R20
       add   R12,R4,R11       add   R22,R4, R21
       lw    R16, R11(R7)     lw    R26, R21(R7)
       lw    R17, R12(R7)     lw    R27, R22(R7)
       add   R3, R3, 2        add   R20, R3, 1
       add   R6, R6, R30      add   R6, R6, R30
       add   R16, R16, R17    add   R26, R26, R27
       sw    R11(R7), R16     sw    R21(R7), R26
       j LoopK
LoopJ_END:
```

(b) level-2 unroll the loop twice

```
LoopK  slt     R2, R3, R4
       bne     R2, R0, LoopJ_END
       lwvh    v1, R11(R7)    lwvl v1, R21(R7)
       lwvh    v2, R12(R7)    lwvl v2, R22(R7)
       add     R3, R3, 2      add R20, R3, 1
       add     R11,R5,R3      add R21,R5, R20
       add     R12,R4,R11     add R22,R4, R21
       addvE   v1, V1, V2     mulad R6,R6,R30,2
       swvh    R11(R7), v1    swvh R21(R7), v2
       j LoopK
LoopJ_END
```

(c) level-3 deep scheduling and SIMD optimization

Fig. 7. Multi-level trace optimized from the code of figure 6

threshold algorithms may unroll the internal loop conservatively, and then construct level-2 trace. Elaborate RIR implements aggressive SIMD scheduling in level-3 trace to accelerate trace further.

Level-1 trace (fig.7a) will be constructed firstly. Level-1 trace contains the frequent instructions, but no further scheduling or optimization. Then RIR may unroll the internal loop (fig.7b), and perform register renaming and scheduling to execute the two iterations in a single level-2 trace. Aggressive SIMD scheduling and instruction substitute can be seen in level-3 trace. Level-3 trace benefits from SIMD extension much more, because of the special SIMD instructions.

Four policies of trace generation have be simulated:

1) Baseline (trace cache but no RIR and optimization). Naive trace generation, which under the control of simple threshold. The main performance contribution is from code layout of trace, not from dynamic optimization.
2) RIR+inline. Function inline is another fertile resources to enlarge trace size.

3) RIR+unroll. Most dynamic optimizations concentrate on the loops, because unrolled loops are easy to be optimized by software pipelining or SIMD (Vector) unit. The unrolling times will under the control of RIR framework.
4) RIR+full optimization. Predict gain and cost during trace generation. A set of scheduling and optimizing algorithms, such as constant propagation, remove branches, and strength reduction etc, are used as the same way of unroll and inline.

Six benchmarks (gzip, vpr, gcc, parser, bzip2 and art) come from SPEC CPU2000, the other 7(jpeg, mpeg, gsm, pgp, mesa and epic) are from MediaBench. All compiled with "-finline-functions, -funroll-loops, -O2" flag.

5 Results

In fig.8, we try to construct large trace aggressively, but without the guide of RIR. Large trace will fail more frequently (lower hit rate) than small one. The optimizing and scheduling were done in vain if trace fails.

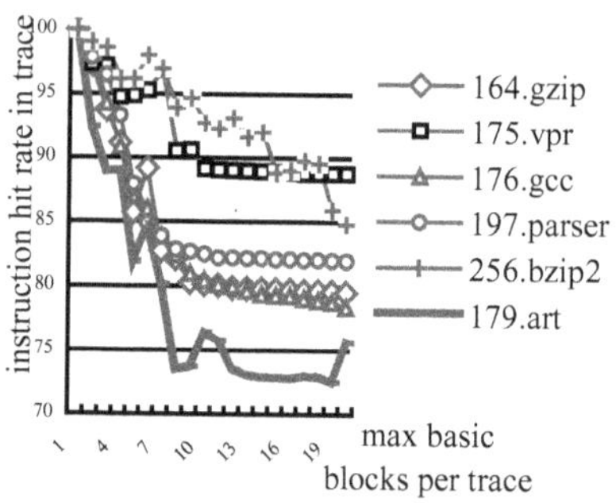

Fig. 8. Hit rates in different trace size limits

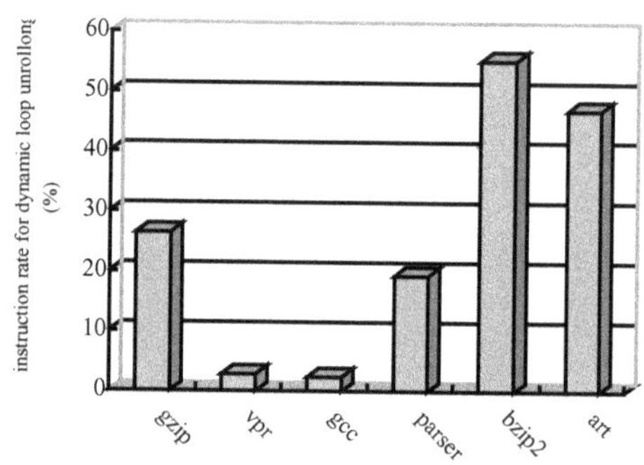

Fig. 9. Dynamic unrolling in unrolled benchmar

As illustrated in fig.9, RIR+unrolling is used to discover the usability of dynamic loop unrolling. Note all benchmarks have unrolled the loops statically by compiler. Every benchmark can benefit from RIR+unrolling. However, not all benchmarks can gain enough from loop unrolling. In the dynamic scheduling of bzip2, 55.172% of execution may hit in the dynamic unrolled loop. Gcc and vpr are the worst, less than 2% execution cycles hit in dynamic unrolled loop.

Fig.10 presents the hit rates for different trace policies with the same average trace size (23 instructions per trace). The results are normalized to baseline (the leftmost bar). Because more available optimizations result in the generation of more useful large traces, proposed RIR has the highest hit rate. RIR achieve higher performance in mediabench than spec2000, because the media applications are easier to be optimized by loop unrolling, function-inline and other scheduling methods.

In Fig.11, we put those scheduled traces into SIMD unit to check the real performance. Speedup rates are normalized to normal execution (**no** rescheduling for SIMD). Although the improvement of hit rate in gcc is low (Fig.10), it still can get benefits from SIMD acceleration. Bzip2 gets the largest improvement from high hit rate of large trace.

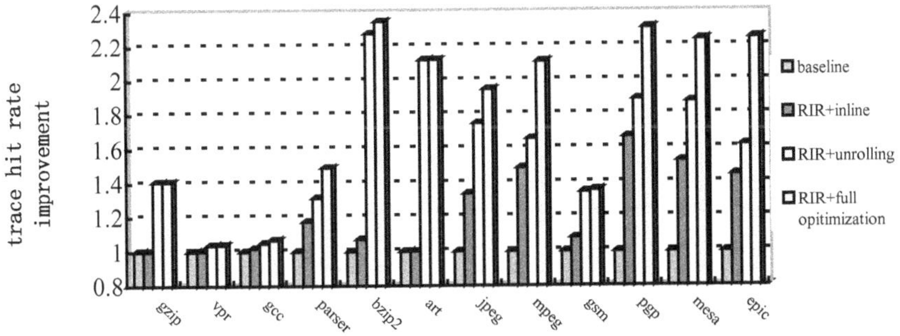

Fig. 10. *Normalized* trace hit rate for different policies

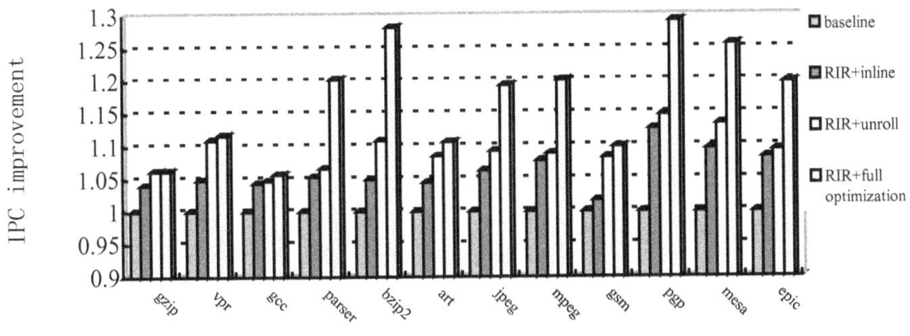

Fig. 11. Speedup by SIMD unit executing rescheduled trace

Proposed RIR is always better than pure unroll and pure inline under multi-level trace control. Although current RIR only integrate simple scheduling and optimizing, average speedup to none-SIMD execution is 17%. This improvement comes from RIR trace generation and scheduling for fast SIMD unit.

Fig.12 presents the percentage of trace in different level during the simulation of fig.11. *Normal* means the instruction is not fetched from trace cache. As shown in fig.12, most of the instructions come from trace cache. (Notes: High-level traces are upgraded from low-level trace.) Because we give a strict limit to level-3 optimization, level-3 traces in gzip and art are less than 1%. Recalling fig.8, the trace hit rate of these two benchmark will decrease quickly if we try to construction large trace aggressively but blindly. RIR framework will apply optimization and scheduling more precisely.

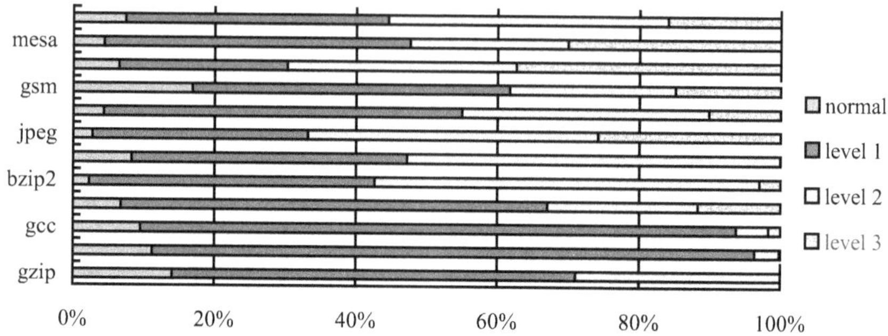

Fig. 12. The rate of trace in different level during dynamic execution

Path profiler, pattern detector, hot path table and trace storage may consume additional hardware resource for advance embedded processor. These silicon areas also can be used for larger L1 cache. In Fig.13, baseline architecture use 8KB L1 I cache and 8KB L2 D cache. The 4k T-cache means that the trace cache can contain 4k internal operations (16KB). RIR use a 3k t-cache to store the optimized trace, the rest silicon are used for other RIR hardware in fig.3. Simulation shows that RIR may achieve better performance than I cache enlargement or pure trace cache mechanism. Scheduling code into additional new hardware resource (SIMD unit) improves the execution further more.

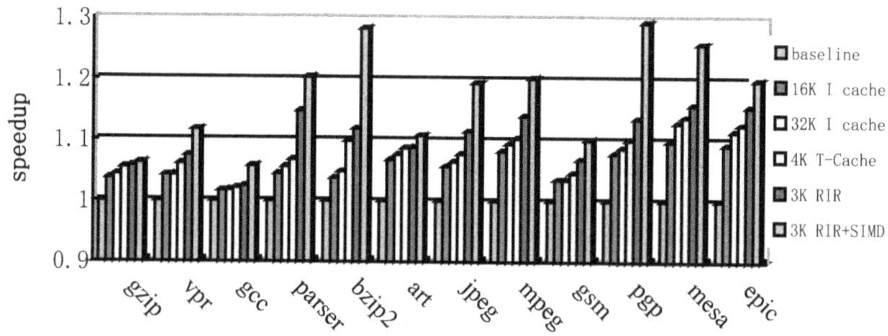

Fig. 13. IPC improvement for large I cache, large T-cache, RIR and RIR+SIMD

6 Conclusion

Runtime Instruction Rescheduling can help old compiled code benefit from new extension of system architecture. No source code rewriting, object rebuilding or binary instrumentation is needed. Future RIR will be enhanced to save power by shutting down main processor when trace is executed in accelerating resources. More aggressive optimization will be implemented and evaluated. Aggressive optimization may need the storage space for intermediate language or SSA code [17]. Code expansion and storage cost should be giver further attention.

References

1. D. Talla, R. Austen, D. Brier, et al. TMS320DM310 – A Portable Digital Media Processor. Proceeding of 15th Symposium on High Performance Chips. 2003
2. Lian Li, Jingling Xue. A Trace-based Binary Compilation Framework for Energy-Aware Computing. Proceedings of the 2004 ACM SIGPLAN/SIGBED conference on Languages, compilers, and tools (LCTES '04), pages 95-106, 2004
3. J.A. Fisher. Trace Scheduling: A Technique for Global Microcode Compaction. IEEE Transaction on Computer. Pages 478-490,July 1981
4. M M. Merten, A. Trick, R. Barnes, E. Nystrom, C. George, J. Gyllenhaal, and W. W. Hwu. An Architectural Framework for Runtime Optimization. IEEE Transactions on Computers, pages 567-589, June 2001
5. James C Dehnert, Brian K Grant, John P Banning, et al. The Transmeta Code Morphing Software: Using Speculation, Recovery, and Adaptive Retranslation to Address Real-life Challenges. Proceedings of the 2003 International Symposium on Code Generation and Optimization]. Pages 15-24, 2003.
6. Vasanth Balsa, E. Duesterwald, S. Banerjia. Dynamo: A Transparent Dynamic Optimization System. Proceedings of the ACM SIGPLAN '00 Conference on Programming Language Design and Implementation, pages 1-12 , 2000.
7. Thomas M. Conte, Kishore N. Menezes, Mary Ann Hirsch. Accurate and Practical Profile-Driven Compilation Using the Profile Buffer. Proceedings of the 29th Annual International Symposium on Microarchitecture, pages 36-45, 1996
8. Sanjay J. Patel and Steven S. Lumetta. Replay: A Hardware Framework for Dynamic Optimization. IEEE Transactions on Computers, Vol.50 NO. 6 pages 590-608, 2001
9. E. Rotenberg, S. Bennett, and J.E. Smith. Trace Cache: A low latency approach to high bandwidth instruction fetching. Proceedings of 29th International Symposium on Microarchitecture, pages 24-35, 1996.
10. R. Rosner, Y. Almog, M. Moffie, N. Schwartz, A. Medelson. Power Awareness through Selective Dynamically Optimized Traces, Proceedings of the 31st annual international symposium on Computer architecture (ISCA-31), pages 162-173, 2004.
11. Marc Berndl, Laurie Hendren. Dynamic profiling and trace cache generation, Proceedings of the international symposium on code generation and optimization: feedback-directed and runtime optimization, pages 276-285, 2003.
12. Vicki H. Allan, Reese B. Jones, Randall M. Lee, Stephen J. Allan. Software Pipeline, ACM computing Surveys (CSUR), vol.27 issue 3, Pages 367-432, 1995.
13. J.R. Ellis. Bulldog: A Compiler for VLIW Architecture. MIT Press, Cambridge, MA, 1986.
14. Intel Corp. IA-32 Intel Architecture Software Developer's Manual volume 1: Basic Architecture, No.25366515, 2004.
15. Kapil Vaswani, Matthew J.Thazhuthaveetil, Y.N.SriKant. A Programmable Hardware Path Profiler. Proceedings of the International Symposium on Code Generation and Optimization, pages 217-228, 2004.
16. Manoj Franklin, Mark Smotherman. A Fill-unit Approach to Multiple Instruction Issue. Proceedings of 27th annual international symposium on Microarchitecture, pages 162-171, 1994
17. Brian Matthew Fahs. An Analysis of A Novel Approach to Dynamic Optimization. M.S. Thesis of the University of Illinois at Urbana-Champaign, 2003

Bioinformatics on Embedded Systems: A Case Study of Computational Biology Applications on VLIW Architecture

Yue Li and Tao Li

Intelligent Design of Efficient Architectures Laboratory (IDEAL),
Department of Electrical and Computer Engineering,
University of Florida, Gainesville, Florida 32611
yli@ecel.ufl.edu, taoli@ece.ufl.edu
http://www.ideal.ece.ufl.edu/

Abstract. Bioinformatics applications represent the increasingly important workloads. Their characteristics and implications on the underlying hardware design, however, are largely unknown. Currently, biological data processing ubiquitously relies on the high-end systems equipped with expensive, general-purpose processors. The future generation of bioinformatics requires the more flexible and cost-effective computing platforms to meet its rapidly growing market. The programmable, application-specific embedded systems appear to be an attractive solution in terms of easy of programming, design cost, power, portability and time-to-market. The first step towards such systems is to characterize bioinformatics applications on the target architecture. Such studies can help in understanding the design issues and the trade-offs in specializing hardware and software systems to meet the needs of bioinformatics market. This paper evaluates several representative bioinformatics tools on the VLIW based embedded systems. We investigate the basic characteristics of the benchmarks, impact of function units, the efficiency of VLIW execution, cache behavior and the impact of compiler optimizations. The architectural implications observed from this study can be applied to the design optimizations. To the best of our knowledge, this is one of the first such studies that have ever been attempted.

1 Introduction

The study of genetics has remarkably advanced our knowledge of the fundamental of life: in 1865, G. Mendel first discovered the phenomena of genetic inheritance, whereas now, life sciences have matured to the extent of making cloning of living beings a reality. Today, to understand biological processes and, in turn, advances in the diagnosis, treatment, and prevention of genetic diseases, researchers rely on the advanced laboratory technologies (e.g., electrophoresis and mass spectrometry, micro array transcript analysis) [1] to study all the genes as well as their activity levels and complex interactions in an organism.

As genomic science moves forward, having accessible computational tools with which to extract and analyze genomic information is essential. The field of bioinformatics, defined as the computationally handling and processing of genetic

L.T. Yang et al. (Eds.): ICESS 2005, LNCS 3820, pp. 16–29, 2005.

information, has experienced an explosive growth in the last decade. Since the human genome [2] has been deciphered, it has become evident that bioinformatics will become increasingly important in the future. Today, bioinformatics has become an industry and has gained acceptance among number of markets especially in pharmaceutical, biotechnology, industrial biotechnology and agricultural biotechnology. A number of recent market research reports estimate the size of the bioinformatics market is projected to grow to $243 billion by 2010 [3].

Clearly, computer systems which provide high-performance, cost-effective genetic data processing play a vital role in the future growth of the bioinformatics market. Many major IT companies (e.g., IBM, Microsoft, SGI, and Apple) have announced products specific to bioinformatics applications [4, 5], while dozens of start-up companies devoted to bioinformatics have arisen [6, 7]. Most of these solutions continue to address the needs of bioinformatics by developing complex and expensive high-end systems equipped with general-purpose processors. Costly and time-consuming, these approaches can also result in hardware and software architectures that are not optimized for the price, power, size and flexibility requirements of the future bioinformatics computing.

As their popularities and market continue to grow, future bioinformatics and computational biology are likely to adopt the application-specific processors and systems to win the increased competition between manufacturers. It has been widely accepted that embedded systems have become powerful enough to meet the computational challenge from many application domains [8]. On the other hand, using programmable, application-specific processors can provides much more flexible solutions than an approach based on ASICs and is much more efficient than using general-purpose processors in terms of cost, power, portability and the time-to-market.

To achieve high-performance, genetic information processing needs to exploit instruction level parallelism (ILP). General-purpose processor architectures, such as aggressive, out-of-order execution superscalar, detect parallelisms at runtime using highly complex hardware. In contrast, VLIW architectures use the compilers to detect parallelisms and reduce hardware implementation cost. Consequently, the VLIW is increasingly popular as the architecture paradigms for the programmable, application-specific embedded processors [9].

The first step towards the cost-effective genetic data processing platforms is to characterize the representative bioinformatics applications on the target architecture. Such studies can help in understanding the design issues of the new generation of programmable, application-specific processors to meet the needs of bioinformatics market as well as the software/hardware tradeoffs that can be made to fine tune the systems. This paper evaluates several representative bioinformatics software on the VLIW based embedded systems. The workloads we used include the popular DNA/protein sequence analysis, molecular phylogeny inference and protein structure prediction tools. We investigate various architectural features, such as the basic workload characteristics, impact of function units, the efficiency of VLIW execution, cache behavior and the effectiveness of compiler optimizations. The architectural implications observed from this study can be applied to the design optimizations. To the best of our knowledge, this is one of the first such studies that have ever been attempted.

The rest of the paper is organized as follows. Section 2 provides brief reviews of biology background and bioinformatics study areas. Section 3 describes the workloads, the architectures modeled, and the simulation methodology. Section 4 presents the characterization of bioinformatics benchmarks and the architectural implications. Section 5 concludes the paper.

2 Bioinformatics Background

This section provides an introductory background for biology and describes the major areas of bioinformatics.

2.1 DNA, Gene and Proteins

All living organisms use DNA (deoxyribonucleic acid) as their genetic material. The DNA is essentially a double chain of simpler molecules called nucleotides, tied together in a helical structure famously known as the double helix. There are four different kinds of nucleotides: adenine (A), guanine (G), cytosine (C) and thymine (T). Adenine (A) always bonds to thymine (T) whereas cytosine (C) always bonds to guanine (G), forming base pairs. A DNA can be specified uniquely by listing its sequence of nucleotides, or base pairs. In bioinformatics, the DNA is abstracted as a long text over a four-letter alphabet, each representing a different nucleotide: A, C, G and T. The genome is the complete set of DNA molecules inside any cell of a living organism that is passed from one generation to its offspring.

Proteins are the molecules that accomplish most of the functions of the living cell. A protein is a linear sequence of simpler molecules called amino acids. Twenty different amino acids are commonly found in proteins, and they are identified by a letter of the alphabet or a three-letter code. Like the DNA, proteins are conveniently represented as a string of letters expressing its sequence of amino acids. A gene is a contiguous stretch of genetic code along the DNA that encodes a protein.

2.2 Bioinformatics Tasks

In this subsection, we illustrate the major interests in the bioinformatics, including sequence analysis, phylogeny inference, and protein 3D structure prediction.

2.2.1 Sequence Analysis and Alignments

Sequence analysis, the study of the relationships between the sequences of biological data (e.g., nucleotide and protein), is perhaps the most commonly performed tasks in the bioinformatics. Sequence analysis can be defined as the problem of finding which parts of the sequences are similar and which parts are different. By comparing their sequences, researchers can gain crucial understanding of the biological significance and functionality of genes and proteins: high sequence similarity usually implies significant functional or structural similarity while sequence differences hold the key information of diversity and evolution.

```
Sequence A GAATTCAGT-A
           | | || || |
Sequence B GGA-TC-GTTA
```

Fig. 1. Alignment of two sequences (The aligned sequences match in seven positions)

The most commonly used sequence analysis technique is sequence alignment. The idea of aligning two sequences (of possibly different sizes) is to write one on top of the other, and break them into smaller pieces by inserting gaps ("-") in one or the other so that identical subsequences are eventually aligned in a one-to-one correspondence. In the end, the sequences end up with the same size. Figure 1 illustrates an alignment between the sequences A = "GAATTCAGGTA" and B= "GGATCGTTA". The objective is to match identical subsequences as far as possible. In the example, the aligned sequences match in seven positions.

```
Sequence A   -AGGTCAGTCTA-GGAC
Sequence B   --GGACTGA----GGTC
Sequence C   GAGGACTGGCTACGGAC
```

Fig. 2. Multiple DNA sequence alignment

When using a given sequence to find similar sequences in a database, one very often obtains many sequences that are significantly similar to the query sequence. Comparing each and every sequence to every other in separate processes may be possible when one has just a few sequences, but it quickly becomes impractical as the number of sequences increases. Multiple sequence alignment compares all similar sequences in one single step: all sequences are aligned on top of each other in a common coordinate system. In this coordinate system, each row is the sequence for one DNA or protein, and each column is the same position in each sequence. Figure 2 illustrates a multiple alignment among the sequences A = "AGGTCAGTCTAGGAC", B= "GGACTGAGGTC", and C="GAGGACTGGCTACGGAC".

2.2.2 Molecular Phylogeny Analysis

Biologists estimate that there are about 5 to 100 million species of organisms living on earth today. Evidence from morphological, biochemical, and gene sequence data suggests that all organisms on earth are genetically related. Molecular phylogeny is the inference of lines of ancestry for organisms based on DNA or protein sequences of those organisms. The genealogical relationships of living things can be represented by an evolutionary tree. In the evolutionary trees, the relationships among the species are represented, with the oldest common ancestor as the trunk or "root" of the tree. The real problem is that of determining just how close or distant the relationship is. Bioinformatics phylogeny analysis tools provide crucial understanding about the origins of life and the homology of various species on earth.

2.2.3 Protein Structure Prediction

A protein sequence folds in a defined three-dimensional structure, for which, in a small number of cases, the coordinates are known. The determination of the three-dimensional structures of the proteins is of great significance for many questions in biology and medicine. For example, knowing how a protein is arranged in the cell membrane helps us to understand how they work and can lead to understanding not only the cause, but also eventually to the cure for virus infections, such as the common cold. Bioinformatics protein analysis tools translate the chemical composition of proteins into their unique three-dimensional native structure.

3 Experimental Methodology

This section describes the workloads and the methodology we used in this study.

3.1 Simulation Framework

Our experimental framework is based on the Trimaran system designed for research in instruction-level parallelism [10]. Trimaran uses the IMPACT compiler [11] as it's front-end. The IMPACT compiler performs C parsing, code profiling, block formation and traditional optimizations [12]. It also exploits support for speculation and predicated execution using superblock [13] and hyperblock [14] optimizations. The Trimaran back-end ELCOR performs instruction selection, register allocation and machine dependent code optimizations for the specified machine architecture. The Trimaran simulator generator generates the simulator targeted for a parameterized VLIW microprocessor architecture.

3.2 Bioinformatics Workloads

To characterize the architectural aspects of the representative bioinformatics software, we use six popular bioinformatics tools in this study. This subsection provides a brief description of the experimented workloads.

Fasta: *Fasta* [15] is a collection of popular bioinformatics searching tools for biological sequence databases. These tools perform a fast protein comparison or a fast nucleotide comparison using a protein or DNA sequence query to a protein or DNA sequence library.

Clustal W: *Clustal W* [16] is a widely used multiple sequence alignment software for nucleotides or amino acids. It produces biologically meaningful multiple sequence alignments of divergent sequences. It calculates the best match for the selected sequences, and lines them up so that the identities, similarities and differences can be seen.

Hmmer: *Hmmer* [17] employs hidden Markov models (profile HMMs) for aligning multiple sequences. Profile HMMs are statistical models of multiple sequence alignments. They capture position-specific information about how conserved each column of the alignment is, and which residues are likely.

Phylip: *Phylip* (PHYLogeny Inference Package) [18] is a package of the widely used programs for inferring phylogenies (evolutionary trees). Methods that are available in the package include parsimony, distance matrix, maximum likelihood, bootstrapping, and consensus trees. Data types that can be handled include molecular sequences, gene frequencies, restriction sites and fragments, distance matrices, and discrete characters. In this study, we use *dnapenny*, a program that performs branch and bound to find all most parsimonious trees for nucleic acid sequence.

POA: *POA* [19] is sequence alignment tool. POA uses a graph representation of a multiple sequence and can itself be aligned directly by pairwise dynamic programming, eliminating the need to reduce the multiple sequence to a profile. This enables the algorithm to guarantee that the optimal alignment of each new sequence versus each sequence in the multiple sequence alignment will be considered.

Predator: *Predator* [20] predicts the secondary structure of a protein sequence or a set of sequences based on their amino acid sequences. Based on the amino acid sequence and the spatial arrangement of these residues the program can predict regions of alpha-helix, beta-sheets and coils.

Table 1. Benchmark description

Program	Description	Input Dataset
fasta	compare a protein/DNA sequence to a protein/DNA database	human LDL receptor precursor protein, *nr* database (the primary database from NCBI)
clustalw	progressively align multiple sequences	317 *Ureaplasma's* gene sequences from the *NCBI Bacteria* genomes database
hmmer	align multiple proteins using profile HMMs	a profile HMM built from the alignment of 50 globin sequences, uniprot_sprot.dat from the *SWISS-PROT* database
dnapenny	find all most parsimonious phylogenies for nucleic acid sequences	ribosomal RNAs from bacteria and mitochondria
poa	sequence alignment using Partial Order Graph	317 *Ureaplasma's* gene sequences from the *NCBI Bacteria* genomes database
predator	predict protein secondary structure from a single sequence or a set of sequences	100 *Eukaryote* protein sequences from NCBI genomes database

Table 1 summarizes the experimented workloads and their input data sets. We use the highly popular biological databases, including *nr* (the primary database from The National Center for Biotechnology Information (NCBI) [21]) and *SWISS-PROT* (an annotated biological sequence database from the European Bioinformatics Institute (EBI) [22]). The two multiple sequences alignment tools (*clustalw* and *POA*) use the same input data set: the 317 *Ureaplasma's* gene sequences from the *NCBI Bacteria* genomes database [23]. The input for the protein structure prediction tool predator is the 100 *Eukaryote* protein sequences from the NCBI genomes database.

3.3 Machine Configuration

The simulated machine architecture comprises a VLIW microprocessor core and a two-level memory hierarchy. The VLIW processor exploits instruction level parallelism with the help of compiler to achieve higher instruction throughput with minimal hardware. The core of the CPU consists of 64 general purpose registers, 64 floating point registers, 64 predicate registers, 64 control registers and 16 branch registers. There is no support for register renaming like in a superscalar architecture. Predicate registers are special 1-bit registers that specify a true or false value. Comparison operations use predicate registers as their target register. The core can execute up to eight operations every cycle, one each for the eight functional units it has. There are 4 integer units, 2 floating point units, 1 memory unit and 1 branch unit. The memory unit performs load/store operations. The branch unit performs branch, call and comparison operations. The level-one (L1) memory is organized as separate instruction and data caches. The processor's level-two (L2) cache is unified. Table 2 summarizes the parameters used for the processor and memory subsystems.

Table 2. Machine configuration

VLIW Core	
Issue Width	8
General Purpose Registers	64, 32-bit
Floating-Point Registers	64, 64-bit
Predicate Registers	64, 1-bit (used to store the Boolean values of instructions using predication)
Control Registers	64, 32-bit (containing the internal state of the processor)
Branch Target Registers	16, 64-bit (containing target address and static predictions of branches)
Number of Integer Units	4, most integer arithmetic operations: 1 cycle, integer multiply 3 cycles, integer divide 8 cycles
Number of Floating Point Units	2, floating point multiply 3 cycles, floating point divide 8 cycles
Number of Memory Units	1
Number of Branch Units	1, 1 cycle latency
Memory Hierarchy	
L1 I-Cache	8KB, direct map, 32 byte/line, cache hit 1 cycle
L1 D-Cache	8KB, 2-way, 32 byte/line, cache hit 1 cycle
L2 Cache	64KB, 4-way, 64 byte/line, L2 hit 5 cycles, 35 cycles external memory latency

4 Results

This section presents a detailed characterization of the VLIW processor running the bioinformatics software. Unless specified, all the applications are compiled with the IMPACT compiler with the maximum –O4 option to produce optimized code for the VLIW processor. All benchmarks are run to the completion of 1 billion instructions. We examine benchmark basic characteristics, the efficiency of VLIW execution, the impact of function units, cache behavior and the impact of compiler optimizations.

4.1 Benchmark Basic Characteristics

Figure 3 shows the dynamic operations mix of the examined bioinformatics tools. The dynamic operations are broken down into seven categories: branches, loads, stores, integer (ialu) and floating point (falu) operations, compare-to-predicate (cmpp) operations and prepare-to-branch (pbr) operations. Prepare-to-branch operations are used to specify the target address and the static prediction for a branch ahead of the branch point, allowing a prefetch of instructions from the target address. Compare-to-predicate operations are used to compute branch conditions, which are stored in predicate registers. Branch operations test predicates and perform the actual transfer of control.

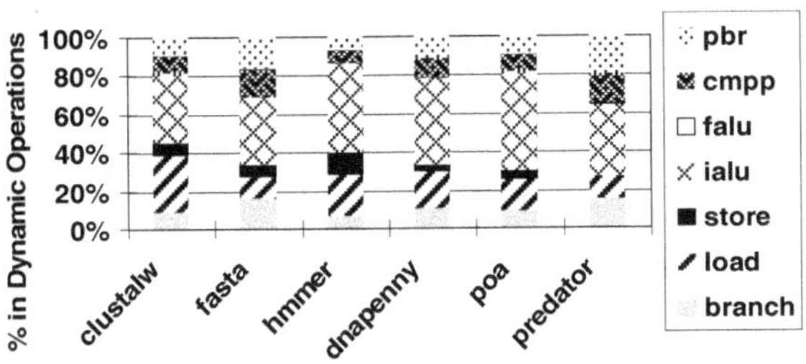

Fig. 3. Dynamic Operations Mix

As can be seen, load and integer operations dominate the dynamic operations in the studied bioinformatics programs. Overall, loads and integer computations account for more than 60% of dynamic operations. Only 5% of operations executed are stores. Stores occur only when updating the dynamic data structures such as HMM (e.g. on *hmmer*) and alignment score matrices (e.g. on *clustalw*, *fasta* and *POA*). Branches constitute 12% of operations executed. Additionally, there are 11% compare-to-predicate and 13% of prepare-to-branch operations in the dynamics operations. The experimented workloads all contain negligible (less than 0.1%) floating point operations, suggesting that floating point units are under-utilized. Therefore, the bioinformatics embedded processors may remove the costly and power-hungry floating point units and use software emulation for the floating point execution.

4.2 ILP

Figure 4 shows the number of dynamic operations completed each cycles on the VLIW machine. To quantify the baseline ILP performance, we use the classic compiler optimizations and assume the perfect caches. As can be seen, although the VLIW machine can support 8 operations every cycle, on the average, only 1.3

operations are completed per cycle. The processor baseline OPC (operations per cycle) ranges from 1.27 (*clustalw*) to 1.45 (*predator*). This indicates that control and data dependencies between operations limit the available ILP. Using conventional code optimizations and scheduling methods, VLIW processors can not attain the targeted ILP performance on the studied bioinformatics software.

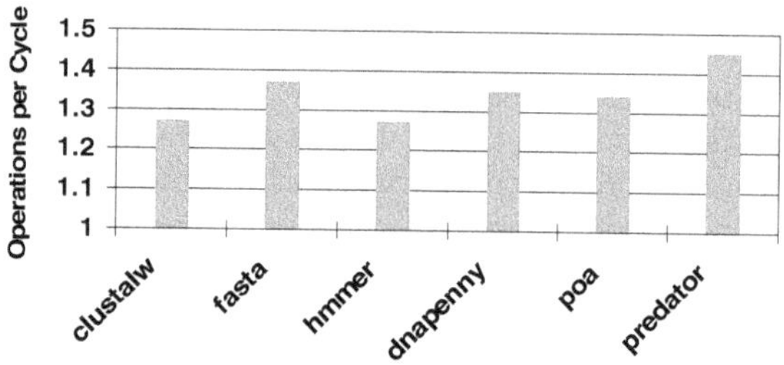

Fig. 4. Baseline ILP

4.3 Impact of Function Units

On the VLIW processors, the number and type of function units affects the available resources for the compiler to schedule the operations. The presence of several instance of certain function unit allows the compiler to schedule several operations using that unit at the same time. Figure 3 shows that the integer and memory operations dominate the bioinformatics software execution. We investigate the impact of the integer and memory units on the benchmark performance in this subsection.

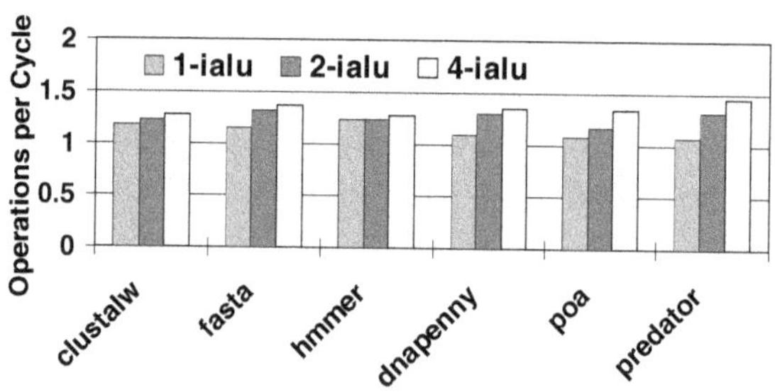

Fig. 5. Impact of Integer Units

We vary the number of integer units from 1 to 4 while keeping other architectural parameters at their default values. Figure 5 shows the impact of integer units on the ILP performance. As can be seen, increasing the number of integer units provides a consistent performance boost on the integer computation intensive benchmarks, since it permits greater exploitation of ILP by providing larger schedulable resources. When the number of integer units increase from 1 to 4, the processor ILP performance increases from 2.4% (*hmmer*) to 35.5% (*predator*), with an average of 16%.

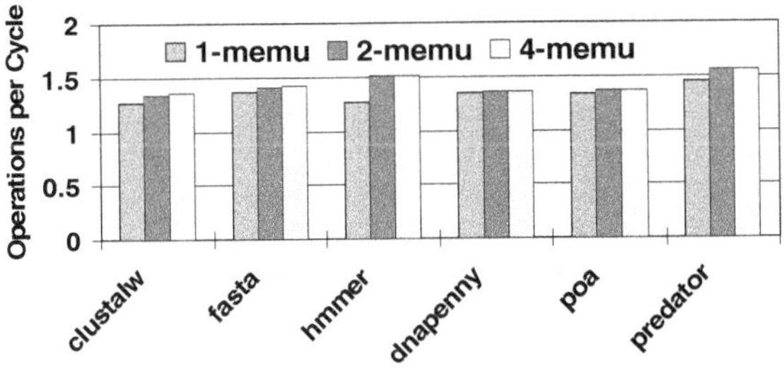

Fig. 6. Impact of Memory Units

We also perform experiments varying the number of memory units. Similarly, when we vary the memory units, the setting of other machine parameters are fixed. Figure 6 shows the impact of the memory units on the performance. We find that adding more memory units does not effectively improve performance on the majority of workloads. Increasing the memory units from 1 to 2 provides a performance gain ranging from 1% (*dnapenny*) to 19% (*hmmer*). Further increasing the memory units from 2 to 4 yields negligible performance improvement. The traditional compiler optimizations lack the capability of scheduling the instructions across the basic block boundaries, making the added memory units underutilized.

4.4 Cache Performance

This section studies the cache behavior of bioinformatics applications. Figure 7 shows the variation in the cache miss rates with cache associativity. We vary the cache associativity from 1 to 4, keeping the sizes of the L1 I-cache, L1 D-cache and L2 cache fixed at their default values. Cache misses are further broken down into conflict, capacity and compulsory misses. As can be seen, direct map instruction caches yield high miss rates on nearly all of the studied benchmarks. The conflict misses due to the lack of associativity dominate the cache misses. The instruction cache miss rates drop significantly with the increased associativity: the 4-way set associative, 8KB L1 I-cache shows a miss rate of less than 1%. This indicates that bioinformatics applications usually have small code footprints. A small, highly associative instruction cache can attain good performance on the bioinformatics applications.

Compared with instruction misses, data misses are difficult to absorb, even with the high cache associativity. Figure 7 (b) shows that on the 8-way L1 data cache, the miss ratios exceed 12% on benchmarks *fasta*, *hmmer* and *POA*. Unlike the instruction misses, the data cache misses are dominated by the capacity misses. This is because sequence alignment programs normally work on large data sets with little data reuse. Figure 7 (c) shows that the L2 misses on five out of six programs are dominated by the capacity misses, suggesting that most of the L2 misses are caused by data references. Increasing the L2 cache associativity does not seem to be very helpful.

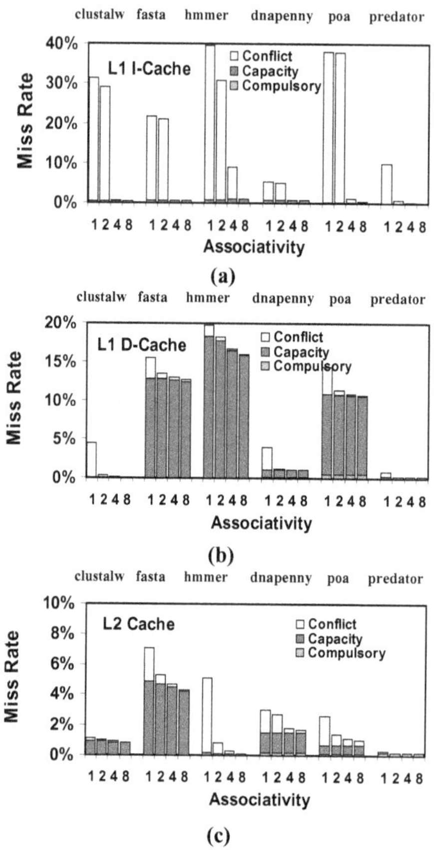

Fig. 7. Impact of Cache Associativity

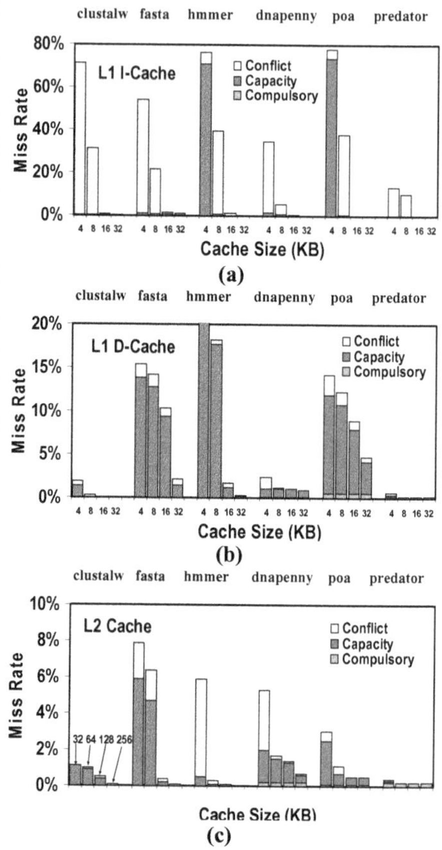

Fig. 8. Impact of Cache Size

We also perform experiments varying the size of the caches. When we vary the L1 instruction cache, the sizes of L1 data cache and L2 cache are fixed. The associativity of the L1 I-cache, L1 D-cache and L2 cache are set to be direct-map, 2-way and 4-way. Figure 8 plots the cache miss rates for a range of varied cache sizes. As can be seen, on a direct-map instruction cache, increasing the cache sizes from 8K to 16K can nearly eliminates all the cache misses. For data references, a 32K L1 cache can achieve good hit ratios across all the benchmarks. The large working sets of *fasta*, *hmmer* and *POA* cause substantial traffic to the L2 cache. The entire working sets can be captured by a L2 cache with a size of 256K Byte. Larger input data would increase the working set requiring larger caches.

4.5 Compiler Optimizations

A compiler for VLIW processors must expose sufficient instruction-level parallelism (ILP) to effectively utilize the parallel hardware. This subsection examines the impact of compiler optimizations on the bioinformatics software execution.

We first investigate the impact of basic compiler optimizations on the benchmark performance. The IMPACT compiler provides a set of classic optimizations such as constant propagation, copy propagation, constant folding, and strength reduction. These optimizations do not necessitate any additional microarchitectural support. On the IMPACT compiler, level 0 option does not contain any optimization. Level 1 option contains local optimizations. Level 2 option contains local and global optimizations. Level 3 option contains local, global and jump optimizations. Level 4 option contains local, global, jump and loop optimizations.

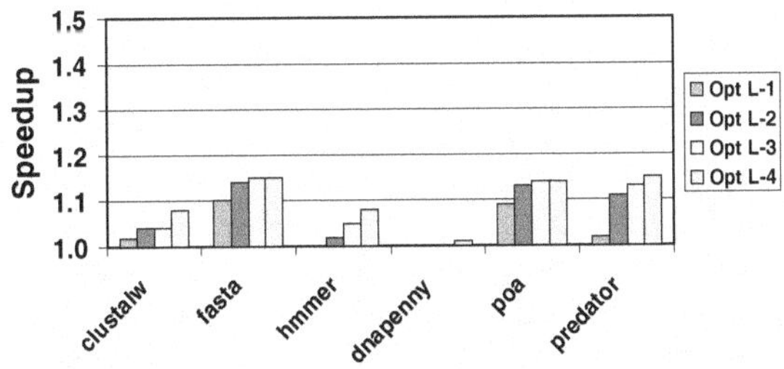

Fig. 9. Impact of Basic Compiler Optimizations

Figure 9 shows the effectiveness of using classic compiler optimizations. The program execution time (presented in terms of speedup) is normalized to that with no compiler optimizations. As can be seen, the basic compiler optimizations provide a speedup ranging from 1.0X to 1.15X. The classic compiler optimizations yield limited ILP performance improvement.

More aggressive compiler optimization technique can be used to further exploiting ILP. The IMPACT compiler provides two types of such optimizations: superblock and hyperblock optimizations. The superblock optimizations [13] form superblocks, add loop unrolling and compiler controlled speculation, in addition to the basic block optimizations. Compiler controlled speculation allows greater code motion beyond basic block boundaries, by moving instructions past conditional branches. Hyperblock optimizations [14] add predicated execution (conditional execution/if-conversion) to superblock optimizations. Predicated execution can eliminate all non-loop backward branches from a program.

Figure 10 shows the speedups of program execution due to superblock and hyperblock optimizations. The data is normalized to that of using the basic compiler optimization. Figure 10 shows that compared to the basic block optimizations, the superblock optimizations further yield speedups ranging from 1.1X to 1.8X. The hyperblock optimization results in speedups ranging from 1.1X to 2.0X. On the average, superblock and hyperblock optimizations improve performance by a factor of 1.3X and 1.5X. These speedups present an opportunity for improving the efficiency of VLIW execution on the bioinformatics applications.

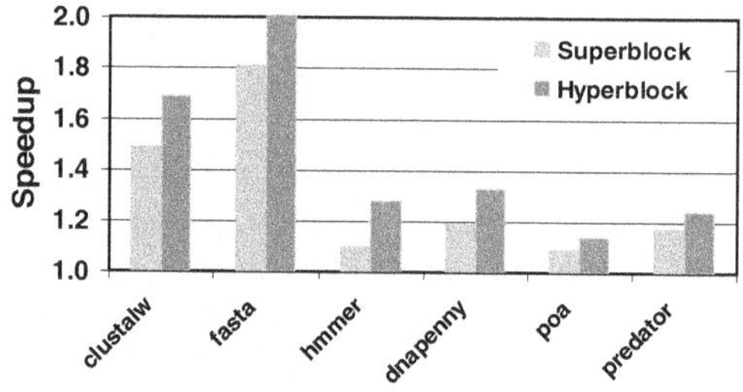

Fig. 10. Impact of Aggressive Compiler Optimizations

5 Conclusions

In the near future, bioinformatics and computational biology are expected to become one of the most important computing workloads. Bioinformatics applications usually run on the high-end systems with general purpose processors like superscalar. The rapidly growing market and the increasingly intensive competition between manufactures require the cost-effective bioinformatics computing platforms. The programmable, application-specific embedded processors and systems appear to be an attractive solution in terms of cost, power, size, time-to-market and easy of programming.

In order to design the complexity/cost effective processors and specialize hardware and software for the genetic information processing needs, a detailed study of the representative bioinformatics workloads on the embedded architecture is needed. This paper studies how the VLIW and compiler perform to extract the instruction level parallelism on these emerging workloads. The workloads we used include the popular DNA/protein sequence analysis, molecular phylogeny inference and protein structure prediction tools. Characteristics including operation frequencies, impact of function units, cache behavior, and compiler optimizations are examined for the purposes of defining the architectural resources necessary for programmable bioinformatics processors.

The major observations are summarized as follows: Loads and integer operations dominate bioinformatics applications execution. Floating point unit is underutilized. The baseline ILP performance is limited on the studied bioinformatics applications due to the data and control dependences in the instruction flow. A small, set-associative instruction cache can handle instruction footprints of bioinformatics applications efficiently, suggesting that bioinformatics applications have good locality and small instruction footprints. For the L1 data cache, capacity misses dominate the cache miss, suggesting that the bioinformatics applications have poor data locality. Therefore, in the L1 data cache design, increasing capacity is more efficient than increasing associativity. Classic compiler optimizations provide a factor of 1.0X to 1.15X performance improvement. More aggressive compiler optimizations such as superblock and hyperblock optimizations provide additional 1.1X to 2.0X performance enhancement, suggesting that they are important for the VLIW machine to sustain the desirable performance on thc bioinformatics applications.

In the future, we plan to explore new architectural and compiler techniques for VLIW processors to support bioinformatics workloads. We also plan to expend our study to include other bioinformatics applications such as molecular dynamics, gene identification, protein function assignment, and microarray data analysis.

References

[1] D. E. Krane and M. L. Raymer, Fundamental Concepts of Bioinformatics, ISBN: 0-8053-4633-3, Benjamin Cummings, 2003.
[2] The Human Genome Project Information, http://www.ornl.gov/sci/techresources/Human_Genome/home.shtml
[3] Bioinformatics Market Study for Washington Technology Center, Alta Biomedical Group LLC, www.altabiomedical.com, June 2003.
[4] SGI Bioinformatics Performance Report, http://www.sgi.com/industries/sciences/chembio/pdf/bioperf01.pdf
[5] The Apple Workgroup Cluster for Bioinformatics, http://images.apple.com/xserve/cluster/pdf/Workgroup_Cluster_PO_021104.pdf
[6] BioSpace, http://www.biospace.com/
[7] Genomeweb Daily News, http://www.genomeweb.com/
[8] A. S. Berger, Embedded Systems Design - An Introduction to Processes, Tools, & Techniques, ISBN 1-57820-073-3 CMP Books, 2002
[9] P. Faraboschi, J. Fisher, G. Brown, G. Desoli, F. Homewood, Lx: A Technology Platform for Customizable VLIW Embedded Processing, In the Proceedings of the International Symposium on Computer Architecture, 2000
[10] The Trimaran Compiler Infrastructure, http://www.trimaran.org
[11] W.W. Hwu et.al. The IMPACT project, http://www.crhc.uiuc.edu/IMPACT
[12] A.V. Aho, R. Sethi, J.D. Ullman. Compilers: Principles, Techniques and Tools, Pearson Education Pte. Ltd., 2001.
[13] W.W. Hwu and S. A. Mahlke, The Superblock: An Effective Technique for VLIW and Superscalar Compilation, In the Journal of Supercomputing, page 224-233, May 1993.
[14] S. A. Mahlke, D. C. Lin, W. Y. Chen, R. E. Hank, R. A. Bringmann, Effective Compiler Support for Predicated Execution Using the Hyperblock, In the International Symposium on Microarchitecture, 1994.
[15] D. J. Lipman and W. R. Pearson, Rapid and Sensitive Protein Similarity Searches, Science, vol. 227, no. 4693, pages 1435-1441, 1985.
[16] J. D. Thompson, D.G. Higgins, and T.J. Gibson, Clustal W: Improving the Sensitivity of Progressive Multiple Sequence Alignment through Sequence Weighting, Positions-specific Gap Penalties and Weight Matrix Choice, Nucleic Acids Research, vol. 22, no. 22, pages 4673-4680, 1994.
[17] S. R. Eddy, Profile Hidden Markov Models, Bioinformatics Review, vol. 14, no. 9, page 755-763, 1998.
[18] J. Felsenstein, PHYLIP - Phylogeny Inference Package (version 3.2), Cladistics, 5: 164-166, 1989.
[19] C. Lee, C. Grasso and M. F. Sharlow, Multiple Sequence Alignment using Partial Order Graphs, Bioinformatics, vol. 18, no. 3, pages 452-464, 2002.
[20] D. Frishman and P. Argos, 75% Accuracy in Protein Secondary Structure Prediction, Proteins, vol. 27, page 329-335, 1997.
[21] NCBI, http://www.ncbi.nlm.nih.gov/
[22] The UniProt/Swiss-Prot Database, http://www.ebi.ac.uk/swissprot/
[23] The NCBI Bacteria genomes database ftp://ftp.ncbi.nih.gov/genomes/Bacteria/.

The Design Space of CMP vs. SMT for High Performance Embedded Processor

YuXing Tang, Kun Deng, and XingMing Zhou

School of Computer, National University of Defense Technology, China 410073
{tyx, kundeng, xmzhou}@nudt.edu.cn

Abstract. In embedded world, many researchers have begun to examine Simultaneous Multithreading (SMT) and Chip Multiprocessing (CMP) for various demands. SMT and CMP both make a chip to achieve greater throughput. But the power, chip size and thermal features are also important for embedded system. In this paper we compare the design space of both architecture. As simulation results shown, although extending wide-issue processor into SMT has the advantage of small design changes, high hardware resource efficiency and high throughput, CMP presents better scalability in raw performance and power metric under heavy multithreaded workload than SMP. CMP integrates several similar processor in a single chip, so it can't uses the chip area efficiently like SMT. And the chip area limits will prevent the CMP from equipping a large L2 cache, which will hurt the performance of memory-bound application. The evaluation also points out the design problem and possible solution for power, chip size and thermal efficiency in CMP and SMT.

1 Introduction

New developments and new standards in embedded processors, such as mobile entertainment, high bandwidth network and multimedia application, call for a significant increase in raw performance while at the same time the market demands low power, small chip size and good thermal feature. Multimedia, mobile and communication workloads are inherently multithreaded. Using multithreading architecture to improve the whole performance rather than a single program makes SMT and CMP attractive for high-end embedded processor.

In today's processor design, the execution time of single processor is not the only metric. The whole throughput, power, energy, size, security and fault-tolerate become emergent metrics. The high IPC of SMT and CMP make them possible to compromise for power, chip size and thermal feature. More hardware resources promise SMT and CMP a wide design space for different metrics.

Having been developed for over 10 years, SMT and CMP architecture have many new choices. Not limited by D.M.Tullsen's extension in superscalar [2], there are SMT based on VLIW and scalar core. Integrating two or three high-end cores or dozens of simple cores, and using homogeneous or heterogeneous core for integration, these are still unresolved questions in CMP design.

In this paper we compare the simulation results of SMT and CMP under different hardware and workloads configuration. The main design metrics and targets include

L.T. Yang et al. (Eds.): ICESS 2005, LNCS 3820, pp. 30 – 38, 2005.

raw performance (IPC), power, chip area and temperature. Different metrics may correlate with each other. For example, low power often means some sacrifice in performance. This paper also discusses some interrelationships among main metrics.

2 Related Works

Hardware multithreading (MT) begin to enter the main stream of processor design [1][4]. Comparing to MultiScalar or other MT architectures that change programming mode or hurt the compatibility, SMT and CMP are the two most popular MT architectures in academic and industry.

2.1 SMT

D.M. Tullsen proposed to extend a wide-issue superscalar processor into multithreading context [2]. The original SMT was designed to improve the utilization of superscalar hardware with tiny additional cost. SMT needs to add thread tag in single thread (ST) architecture, and maintain a hardware context for every simultaneous thread, including general register file, PC register and other state registers.

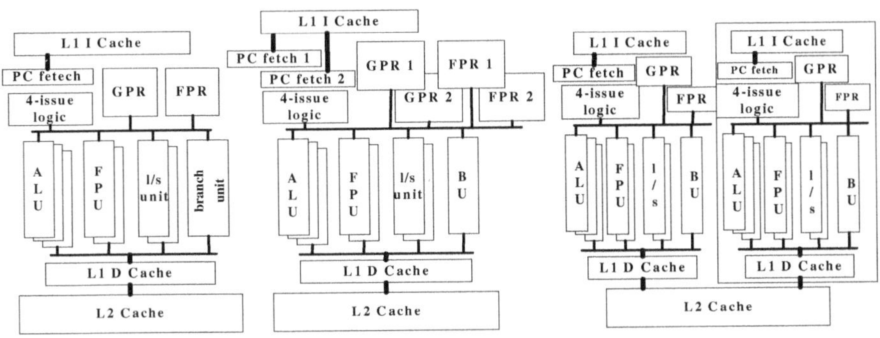

Fig. 1. ST superscalar, SMT and CMP architecture overview

2.2 CMP

L. Hammond et.al [3] argued that wire delay and complexity would prevent super wide-issue (>4) processor to exploit more ILP. Their CMP use relatively simple processor cores to exploit only moderate mounts of ILP within a single thread, while executing multiple threads in parallel across these cores. Generally, the multiple processor cores have their own L1 cache, but share L2 Cache. In early design, the processor core in CMP is much simpler than SMT.

Alpha21364 and Hyper-threading have proved that it is an efficient and effective way to implement SMT in existing design. S. Kaxiras et.al present the implementation of SMT VLIW core for mobile phone workloads [8]. CMP have been used for many years for network processor. Figure.1 presents the architecture different among single thread superscalar, SMT and CMP processor.

Early in 1997, architecture researchers have compared SMT and CMP performance for possible billion-transistor architecture. Early researches focused on raw performance (IPC) and execution time [2][3]. In 2001, S. Kaxiras et al [8] studied the power consumption of CMP and SMT in DSP design. R. Sasanka et al [5][6] compare the energy efficiency of SMT and CMP in multimedia workloads. Yingmin Li et al [9] further compare the different thermal feature of SMT and CMP. This paper surveys the comparing of SMT vs. CMP in performance, power, chip size and thermal under different processor configuration and workloads.

3 Methodology and Workloads

SPEC2K is the most frequently used benchmarks for CPU design. For multithreading test, several benchmarks will be united to construct a workload. MediaBench is more suitable for the validation of embedded processor. In desktop, hand-hold and mobile market, there are huge number of multithreaded media processing. For N person's net-meeting, one video/audio encoder and N-1 decoders are needed to run in parallel in each terminal. In following experiments, the benchmarks have been classified into 4 types, according to their IPC in 4-issu out-of-order RISC processor (Table 2.) deriving from MIPS 4Kp embedded core.

Table 1. Benchmarks and workloads classification

Type	Benchmark	Remark
Spec-H	175.vpr, 176.gcc, 252.eon, 256.bzip2	IPC > 1
Spec-L	164.gzip, 181.mcf, 197.parser	IPC < 1
Media-H	GSM, MPEG2-d, jpeg, epic	IPC > 2
Media-L	H.263-e, MPEG2-e, G.721	IPC < 2

Multimedia applications are easier to exploit ILP than SPEC, but H.263 and mpeg2 encoder has the IPC of 1.6 and 1.5 respectively, far below mpeg2-decoder from mediabench (IPC=3.2). The average IPC of gzip , mcf and parser is lower than 1. mcf suffers from high L2 cache miss rate, and delivers the worst IPC of 0.38. To evaluation SMT and CMP performance in low ILP media applications, we added H.263 and mpeg encoder into Media-L, although they are not included in official MediaBench.

Table 2. Baseline single thread architecture

Issue width	4 instruction per cycle
Function unit	3-AlU, 2-FPU, 1-branch unit, 2 load/store units
Branch predictor	4K entry bimod
Register file	32 GPR, 32 FPR
L1 Icache/Dcache	8KB, 2-way, 32B blocks, 1-cycle/hit
L2 Cache	128KB, 4-way, 44B blocks, 8-cycle/hit

The benchmarks in these 4 types will mixed together to form multithread workloads. Several threads from SPEC-L can test the efficiency of multithread architecture when ILP in each thread is difficult to be exploited. The composing of workload uses the method in [5][9]. 4 simulation frameworks, SMTSIM, MP-Simplesim, Wattch and Hotspot, have been used in following simulation. In simulation, *SMTx* means that ***x*** threads run simultaneously in ***1*** processor of SMT style; *CMP*x means that there are ***x*** processing core in ***1*** chip, each core execute ***1*** thread.

4 Compare the Raw Performance

4.1 Performance Under Same Processor Core

In the test of figure.2 and figure.3, similar processor core (Table 2) has been used in SMT and CMP. SMT has the same total issue width as CMP, as well as L1 and L2 cache size.

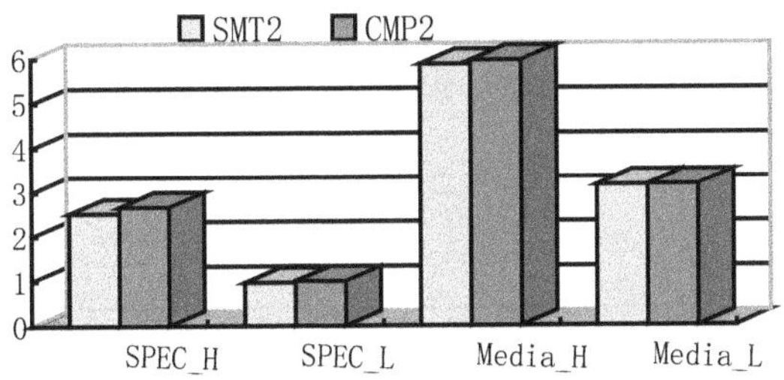

Fig. 2. IPC of SMT vs. CMP in same core under 2-thread workloads

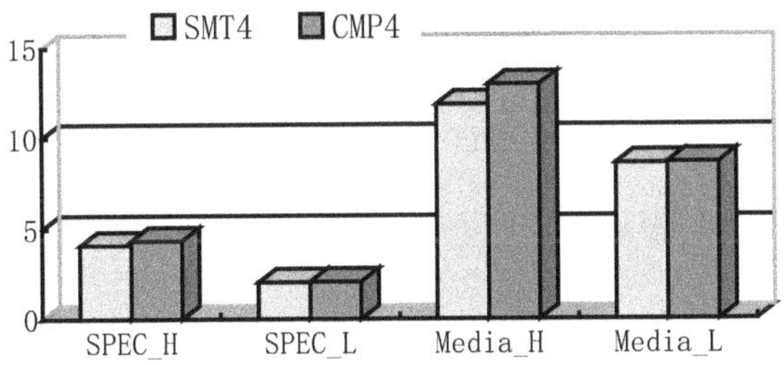

Fig. 3. IPC of SMT vs. CMP in same core under 4-thread workloads

For better hardware utilization, SMT2 have the same configuration of function units as ***a single*** processor core in CMP. SMT4 extends the issue bandwidth into 16 instruction/cycle, and double the function units into SMT2.

As shown from results, CMP have better performance than SMT when they are using the same processor core. Especially for SPEC-H and Media-H, because of the low competition in hardware, CMP show better scalability than SMT.

4.2 Performance When CMP Use Simple Core

To control the hardware cost of implementation, CMP may integrate several simpler cores than SMT or ST processor. In the evaluation of figure.4 and figure.5, CMP2/CMP4 use 2-issue superscalar processor, which has only 1-ALU and 1-FPU. But SMT and CMP have the same size of L1 and L2 cache.

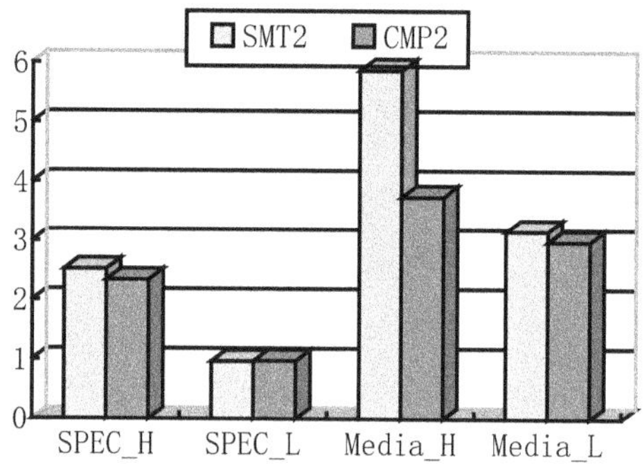

Fig. 4. IPC of SMT vs. CMP in different core under 2-thread workloads

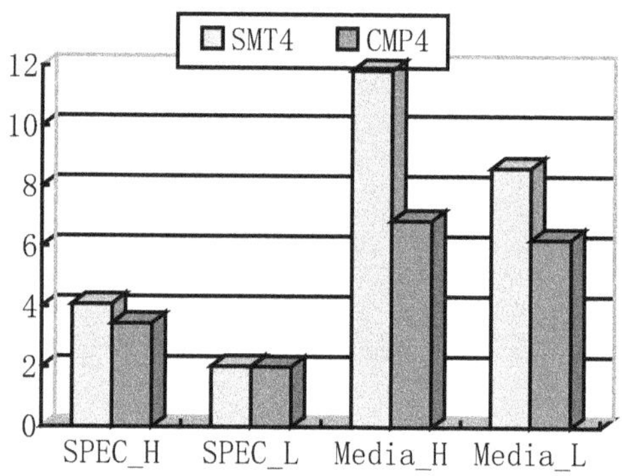

Fig. 5. IPC of SMT vs. CMP in different core under 4-thread workloads

For SPEC2000 benchmarks, the performance of CMP2 is close to SMT4. SMT achieves tiny superior in SPEC-H. However, for media benchmarks, CMP is limited by its issue bandwidth, and its performance is much lower than SMT.

4.3 Performance with Limitation in Chip Size

The results from figure.2 to figure.5 indicate that CMP should integrate several high-performance cores. But these cores will occupy more chip area. Keeping both the CMP and SMT use the same chip size, CMP has to sacrifice its L2 cache size for additional core. Section 6 discusses chip area in detail. In figure.6 and figure.7, SMT and CMP use the same high performance core. But SMT2 and SMT4 have 256KB and 512KB L2 cache respectively, but CMP2 and CMP4 are 128KB and 245KB respectively.

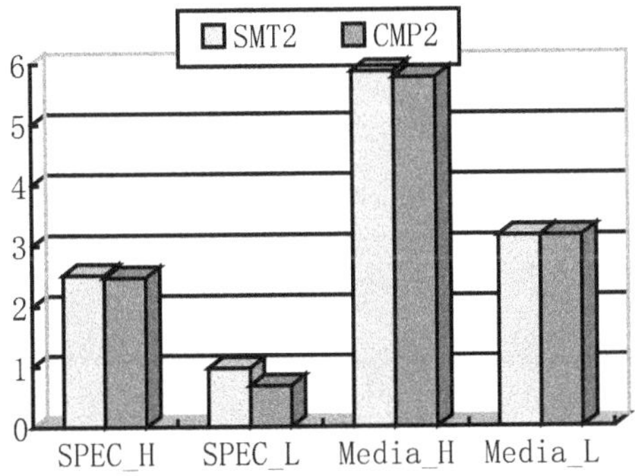

Fig. 6. IPC of SMT vs. CMP in limited chip size under 2-thread workloads

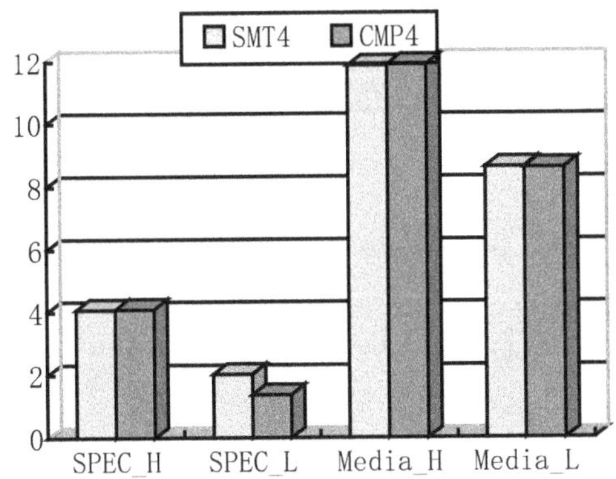

Fig. 7. IPC of SMT vs. CMP in limited chip size under 4-thread workloads

Except for SPEC-L, small L2 cache has little impact for CMP. This may because that most benchmarks are cpu-bound, and have high hit rate in cache. Mcf in SPEC-L is memory-bound. CMP suffer from the limited size of l2 cache in SPEC-L. SMT is superior for memory-bound application because it has the ability to implement large L2 cache.

5 The Power of CMP and SMT

Formula 1 has been widely used to calculate the power of processor. The value of Power-Rate is to examine whether the throughput increasing brings further power dissipation

$$Power = V^2 * F * \sigma * C \tag{1}$$

$$Power\text{-}Rate = Power / IPC = V^2 * F * \sigma * C / IPC \tag{2}$$

V is the supply voltage of processor. F presents the operating frequency. σ is the active factor of hardware components, which between 0 and 1. C is the load capacity of circuit. We derive V, E and C from ITRS data [11]. After the simulation under Wattch [10] framework, we get the value of σ.

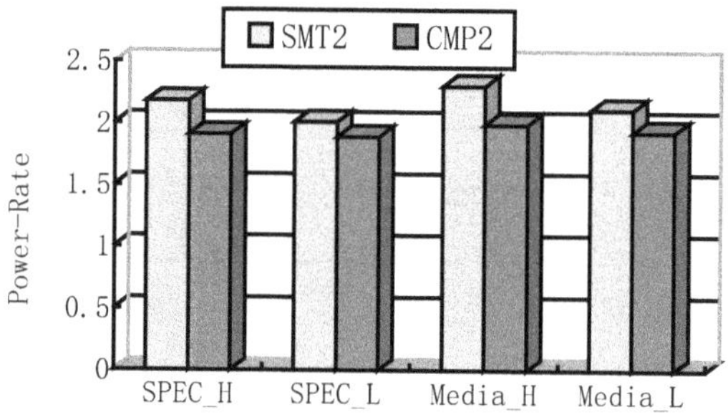

Fig. 8. Power Rate of SMT vs. CMP in 2-thread workloads

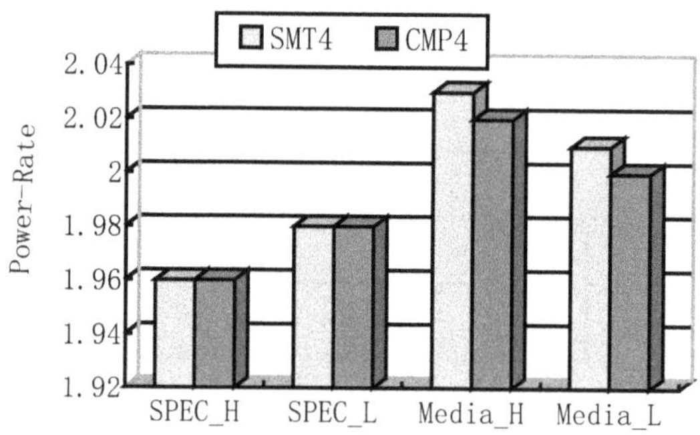

Fig. 9. Power Rate of SMT vs. CMP in 4-thread workloads

Figure.8 and Figure.9 illustrate that CMP is better than SMP in low power design. The competition in SMT's register port and result bus makes the active factor σ high. Furthermore, CMP is more suitable to use DVS (Dynamic Voltage Scalar) mechanism for low power, because it has more separated hardware components for scheduling than SMT. This means lots for handhold equipments which execute multimedia application. They may use DVS to decrease the operating frequency in order to increase battery time. The tests in [6] and [8] also indicate that CMP can achieve lower voltage and dissipation than SMT by DVS, even under the real-time demands of multimedia.

6 Chip Size for SMT and CMP

Certainly CMP needs more chip area than SMT when they use the same processor core. The chip size of CMP increases linearly with the number of cores (threads). The increased interconnection, such as result bus and shared I/O port, impacts the chip size of SMT. In previous research [1], SMT has the same function unit configuration as single thread processor for high utilization. Actually, in 4-way and 8-way SMT, more function units are needed than 2-way SMT. They will occupy more chip area, but this increasing is lower than CMP.

Based on the method in [8] and the die area date of MIPS R4000, Table 3 shows the predicated data of chip area for SMT and CMP. Without the consideration of memory system (cache and TLB), SMT need a little more than half of the CMP's silicon area.

Table 3. The chip area for Multithread architecture

Component area	ST	2-way MT	4-way MT	8-way MT
Function unit	47%	47%	70%	94%
Register File	21%	42%	84%	168%
Fetch-Issue logic	24%	24%	48%	86%
Reorder buffer	8%	16%	32%	64%
Further interconnection	0%	7%	14%	56%
SMT chip size	100%	136%	248%	468%
CMP chip size	100%	200%	400%	800%

Although SMT is simple in microarchitecture, it is more complex in layout and physical implementation than CMP. The further interconnection part in Table 3 includes this exponential cost.

7 Thermal Feature

With the help of HotSpot and Wattch framework, we can identify the components which have the highest competition and deliver most heat. SMT's temperature increases in sharing and competed unit, while CMP's temperature increases globally by heavy workloads. Comparing with ST architecture, the α value of SMT is 78% higher in register allocation and decode-issue logic. In reorder buffer, the α value of SMT is 89% higher than single thread architecture. The highest temperature of SMT component may be 20℃ higher than average. But for CMP which has the same average temperature, it has no outstanding high temperature parts.

For the high competition in register file, SMT can apply bank structure to limit the competition. [9] was proposed to limit the fetch bandwidth or register read/writer ability, in order to decrease the utilization of key components. Cluster methodology can decrease the competition, but it will increase the delay of pipeline. The read/write of cache is also the main reason of high temperature, multi-bank structure will be helpful.

8 Conclusion

From the purpose to use existing superscalar design, SMT has the advantage of small chip size, high resource utilization and easy-to-implement. But the different thread in SMT will compete the shared resources, such as issue logic and function unit. Under heavy threaded workloads, CMP is more attractive in power and thermal feature limited design. In future advance embedded processor, SMT may become a basic design choice like superscalar. Using several SMT cores to construct CMP has been proved to be a promising design, as well as integrating heterogeneous cores in CMP. The performance, power, chip size and thermal feature of these designs should be checked in future works.

References

1. Doug Burger, James R.Goodman. Billion-Transistor Architectures: There and Back Again. IEEE Computer. Vol.37, No.3, pp.22-27, March 2004.
2. D.M. Tullsen. S.J. Eggers, and H.M. Levy. Simultaneous Multithreading: Maximumizing On-Chip Parallelism. In Proceedings of ISCA 22nd, pp.392-403, 1995.
3. L. Hammond, B.A. Nayfeh, and K. Olukotum. A Single-Chip Multiprocessor. In IEEE Computer Special Issue on Billion-Transistor Processors, September 1997.
4. Theo Ungerer, Borut Robic A Survey of Processors with Explicit Multithreading. ACM Computing Surveys, Vol.35, No.1, pp.29-63, March 2003.
5. R. Sasanka, S. V. Adve, E. debes, and Y.K. Chen. Energy Efficiency of CMP and SMT Architectures for Multimedia workloads. In UIUC CS Technical Report UIUCDCS-R-2003-2325, 2003.
6. R. Sasanka, S. V. Adve, E. debes, Y.K. Chen, and E. Debes. The Energy Efficiency of CMP vs. SMT for Multimedia workloads. In ICS, 2004.
7. J.Burns and J.L. Gaudiot. Area and System Clock Effects on SMT/CMP Processors. In PACT, 2000.
8. S. Kaxiras. G. Narlikar, A.D. Berenbaum, and Z. Hu. Comparing Power Consumption of and SMT and a CMP DSP for mobile phone Workloads. In CASES, 2001.
9. Yingmin Li, D. Brooks, Zhigang Hu, K. Skadron. Performance, Energy, and Thermal Considerations for SMT and CMP Architectures. In HPCA, 2005.
10. D. Brooks, V. Tiwari, M. Martonosi. Wattch: A Framework for Architectureal-Level Power Analysis and Optimizations. In ISCA27, 2000.
11. SIA. International Technology Roadmap for Semiconductors. 2004

Reconfigurable Microarchitecture Based System-Level Dynamic Power Management SoC Platform

Cheong-Ghil Kim, Dae-Young Jeong, Byung-Gil Kim, and Shin-Dug Kim

Supercomputing Lab, Dept. of Computer Science, Yonsei University,
134 Shinchon-Dong, Seodaemun-ku, Seoul, Korea 120-749
{cgkim, dangbang, fokus, sdkim}@parallel.yonsei.ac.kr

Abstract. Power-aware design is one of the most important areas to be emphasized in multimedia mobile systems, in which data transfers dominate the power consumption. In this paper, we propose a new architecture for motion compensation (MC) of H.264/AVC with power reduction by decreasing the data transfers. For this purpose, a reconfigurable microarchitecture based on data type is proposed for interpolation and it is mapped onto the dedicated motion compensation IP (intellectual property) effectively without sacrificing the performance or the system latency. The original quarter-pel interpolation equation that consists of one or two half-pel interpolations and one averaging operation is designed to have different execution control modes, which result in decreasing memory accesses greatly and maintaining the system efficiency. The simulation result shows that the proposed method could reduce up to 87% of power caused by data transfers over the conventional method in MC module.

Keyword: H.264/AVC, motion compensation, quarter-pel interpolation, low-power, memory access, multimedia SoC, system architecture.

1 Introduction

The demand of low-power and high-speed computing architecture for mobile systems has been increased dramatically due to the dominant popularity of multimedia processing and video compression. And the system-on-chip (SoC) technology integrating many components onto a single chip allows designing embedded systems within a short period; furthermore grows into SoC platform technology targeting a class of applications [9]. In this era, data and video coding is very important function because of small storage of mobile devices and limited bandwidth of wireless internet. H.264/AVC [10], the latest video coding standard, is the most remarkable codec at the present time since it can make high-quality motion pictures transmitted at low bit rates. Therefore, H.264/AVC is used for many multimedia applications, such as teleconferencing, mobile video communication, education applications, and digital multimedia broadcasting (DMB). As a key multimedia application, H.264/AVC requires complex operations to achieve high-quality and high-density compression compared with earlier ones. The primitive operation of H.264/AVC decoder is motion compensation (MC) which requires extensive computations accompanied with heavy memory accesses [11].

L.T. Yang et al. (Eds.): ICESS 2005, LNCS 3820, pp. 39 – 49, 2005.

In general, multimedia applications involve data-dominant algorithms which require large amounts of data and complex arithmetic processing. It means that the data transfer and memory organization will have a dominant impact on the power and area cost of the realization [1]. In multimedia systems, this is why architectural and algorithmic level approaches for low power could get the biggest result compared with other level of abstractions such as technology, layout, circuit, and gate [2]. Therefore, an efficient implementation method of the algorithms to reduce power consumption is required at the system-level by designing application specific memory organization and control flow. The paper [3] recalls the importance of this idea by showing that I/O energy can be as high as 80% of the total energy consumption of the chip, and to tackle this problem, there have been several methods on low power video and signal processing applications [4-7].

This research proposes a new computing architecture for motion compensation with low-power in H.264/AVC codec. It can achieve large savings in the system power of a crucial part of H.264/AVC decoder by decreasing memory accesses without sacrificing the performance or the system latency. For this purpose, we devise two techniques; one is merging two different stages, half-pel interpolation and averaging, into one; the other is reordering execution sequences of the interpolation. These are mapped onto SIMD (single instruction multiple data)-style architecture equipping with small intermediate memory, which result in much fewer memory accesses while executing interpolation stages.

In the next section, we describe the motion compensation algorithm in H.264/AVC. Section 3 introduces the basic architecture of SoC platform. In Section 4, the proposed method for quarter-pel interpolation is described. In Section 5, the power model and the simulation results are introduced. Finally, the paper ends with conclusions in Section 6.

2 Motion Compensation in H.264/AVC

Video coding is achieved by removing redundant information from the raw video sequence. In general, pixel values are correlated with their neighbors both within the same frame and between consecutive frames, which is known as spatial and temporal redundancy, respectively. Those redundancies can be reduced by motion estimation and compensation which are often based on rectangular blocks (*MxN* or *NxN*). A *16x16* pixel area is the basic data unit for motion compensation in current video coding standards, which is called as a macroblock.

2.1 Block-Based ME/MC and H.264/AVC

H.264 is based on the block-based motion estimation and compensation and similar with previous standards; however, it can achieve significant gains in coding efficiency over them. This may come from the enhanced key features to motion estimation and compensation; (a) variable block-size motion compensation with small block sizes, (b) quarter-pel motion estimation accuracy, and (c) multiple reference pictures selection. However, it is inherently accompanying with increased complexities. Fig. 1 shows MC kernel which contains nested loops using 6-tab FIR filter. And there are several conditional branches at the last loop.

```
for ( j = 0 ; j < block_size ; j++ )          // block_size = 4
   for ( i = 0 ; i < block_size ; I++ )
      for (result = 0, x = -2 ; x < 4 ; x++)
      // 6_tab FIR filter
       resut += imgY[max(0,min(y,y_pos+j))[max(0,max(x,x_pos+i+x))*COEF[x+2];
```

Fig. 1. Fractional pixel interpolation in inter motion compensation

2.2 Half-pel / Quarter-pel Interpolation in H.264/AVC

In H.264, quarter-pel interpolation is presented for motion estimation accuracy. The quarter-pel interpolation that make 1/4 pixels to offer more detail images is made up with conventional half-pel interpolations that make 1/2 pixels and averaging operation that calculate the average of half pixel and integer pixel. As shown in Fig. 2, the quarter-pel and half-pel interpolations support for a range of block sizes (from 16x16 down to 4x4) and quarter resolution motion vectors.

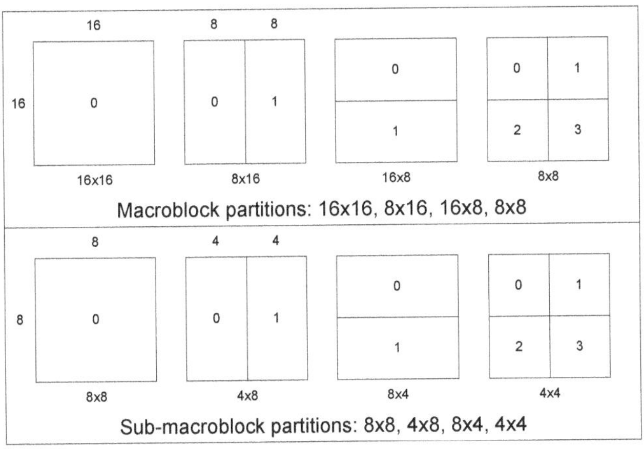

Fig. 2. Macroblock partitions

The motion vector consists of two coordinates, x and y. If the motion vector of current macroblock has two half values, half-pel interpolation is needed alone. But, if motion vector has one or two quarter values, both half-pel interpolations and averaging are needed. The half-pel interpolation needs six adjacent pixel values which lie on a straight line to decide the middle value of two adjacent pixels, as shown in Fig. 3(a). Gray rectangles are integer-pels and white rectangles with strips are half-pels. The equation of half-pel interpolation is presented as:

$$b = [(E - 5F + 20G + 20H - 5I + J)/32] \tag{1}$$

Several addition, multiply, and shift instructions are required to compute b. Although the equation looks like very simple, it has to be repeated many times and requires a lot of data transfers.

As shown in Fig. 3(b), in averaging stage, the value is calculated with the average of integer-pel value and half-pel value which are already computed in half-pel interpolation stage. The equation of averaging is presented as:

$$a = (G + b) / 2 \tag{2}$$

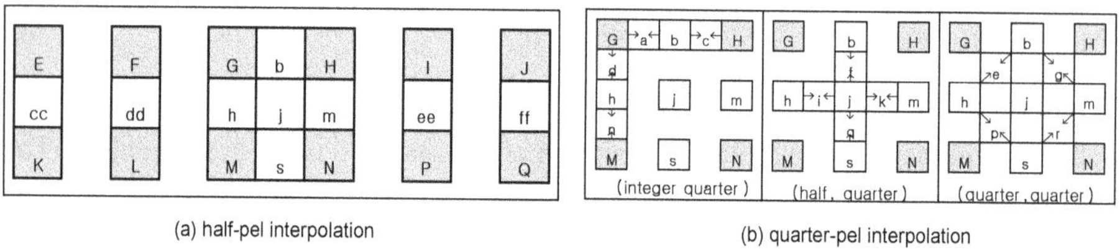

Fig. 3. Interpolation of half-pel and quarter-pel positions

From memory access point of view, the system has to bring the referenced macroblock from off-chip memory to local memory while executing each interpolation. Moreover, local memory access is also required since the interim values have to be stored in the half of quarter-pel interpolation execution. Table 1 shows the number of repeated interpolation executions on each video resolution. The result shows that the number of half-pel interpolations is twice as many as that of quarter-pel interpolations. However, each quarter-pel interpolation consists of one or two half-pel interpolation stage and averaging stage. Therefore, quarter-pel interpolations need more performance than half-pel interpolations, and quarter-pel interpolations are most complex parts in motion compensation. Table 2 shows how many values are needed from the memory by macroblock sizes. Memory access is generated frequently and there's no specific locality

Table 1. Interpolation count by resolution

Resolution	Max. half-pel interpolation count per frame	Max. quarter-pel interpolation count per frame
QCIF(176*144)	50688	25344
CIF(352*288)	202752	101376
VGA(640*480)	614400	307200
1080i(1920*1080)	4147200	2073600

Table 2. The number of memory access by macroblock sizes

Macroblock size	Necessary memory accesses for quarter-pel interpolation	Max. count of memory accesses per frame in VGA resolution
16X16	4921	5905200
16X8, 8X16	2456	5894400
8X8	1368	6566400
8X4, 4X8	684	6566400
4X4	412	7910400

among memory accesses. Therefore, memory accesses are occurring on each interpolation. This is a significant problem in H.264/AVC decoding scheme since memory access not only extends the execution time, but also causes the oligopoly of the internal bus that other memory requests from other system parts cannot be accepted.

3 Basic System Architecture

As depicted in Fig. 4 the basic architecture is composed of several IP cores dedicated for target applications and components at system level. There is a 32-bit RISC-based main processor which executes all decoding operations performs interface and transfers data with other modules including DSP, memory subsystem, and on-chip system bus. In addition various I/O peripherals can be configured through system bus. All memories are independent from each and can be accessed concurrently.

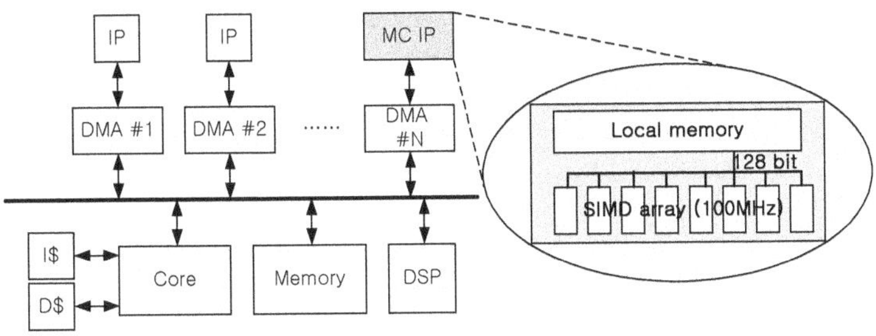

Fig. 4. Overall system architecture

The target application discussed here is motion compensation of H.264/AVC; the shaded module shown in the above figure is MC IP consisting of several processing elements (PEs) operating on SIMD mode and small intermediate memory which is application specific and shared by all PEs. Therefore, each PE can read the used data from local shared memory instead of accessing to large external memory which consumes energy heavily. Each PE can operate in parallel without data waiting cycles since operations of them are independent and the data is fed from a shared local memory through internal 128-bit wide bus at every cycle.

And memory hierarchy is consisted of off-chip memory and local memory. We assume that off-chip memory has 1M byte capacity and local memory is 1K byte. It is sufficient to store 6 frames on off-chip memory and interim values of motion compensation on local memory. Result values of entropy coding that is first decoding stage of H.264 are saved in off-chip memory. Motion compensation stage gets these values from off-chip memory and use local memory as interim reservoir. If all interpolation execution is over, then send results to off-chip memory again. So it is impossible to reduce off-chip memory access unless compensation accuracy is diminished. Only possible decrease of memory access is on local memory with reduced interim load/store.

4 Proposed Methodology of Quarter-pel Interpolation

The proposed quarter-pel interpolation consists of two techniques resulting in the reduction of memory accesses. One is merging two interpolation stages into one for the (integer, quarter) interpolation shown in Fig. 5. This figure presents the flow diagrams of the conventional and proposed quarter-pel interpolation in conjunction with the pixel representation shown in Fig. 3. The other is reordering the execution sequences for the (half, quarter) or (quarter, quarter) interpolation as shown in Fig. 6. The proposed two methods are internally taking advantage of the temporal locality to remove the redundant memory accesses.

4.1 The (Integer, Quarter) Case

The quarter-pel interpolation requires half-pel interpolations to be executed for an entire macroblock. Then it can go further for either averaging stage directly or averaging stage following one more execution of half-pel interpolations in another direction. The decision is made by motion vector value types. In case of the motion vector of (integer, quarter), (half, half) values are not necessary (*j* in Fig. 3), so only one half-pel interpolation is needed. Otherwise, another half-pel interpolation is required for *j* as the case of (half, quarter) or (quarter, quarter).

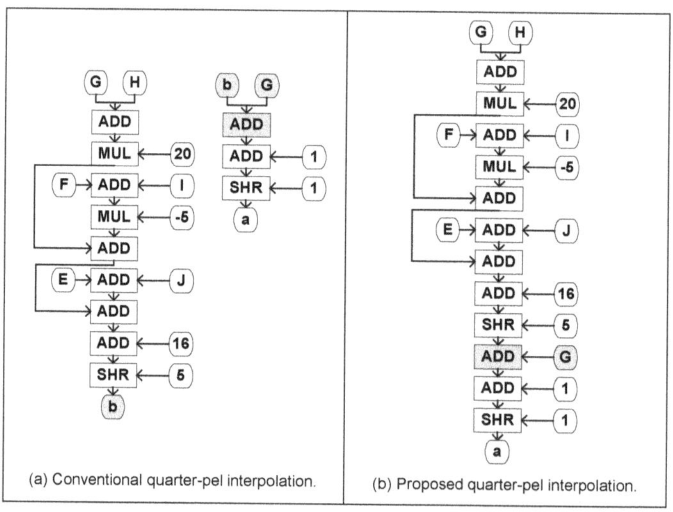

(a) Conventional quarter-pel interpolation.

(b) Proposed quarter-pel interpolation.

Fig. 5. Detailed view of two different interpolations

The conventional quarter-pel interpolation is composed of two stages executed separately. However, in case of motion vector (integer, quarter), two stages are not necessarily executed separately. Therefore, we propose a method of merging two interpolation processes into one. And the modified equation is obtained as below:

$$a = [([(E - 5F + 20G + 20H - 5I + J)/32] + G)/2] \qquad (3)$$

The shaded blocks shown in Fig. 5 are representing the result of the proposed modification mapped on the SIMD module. In this way, memory accesses can be reduced by removing interim loads/stores with simple controls. The effect will be mentioned in detail in Section 5.

4.2 The (Half, Quarter) / (Quarter, Quarter) Case

For this stage, we devise a new execution flow by reordering conventional 17 steps as shown in Fig. 7(b), and then it is mapped onto the array effectively to reduce local memory accesses. In the figure, the left section shows the conventional flow; the right section does the proposed one; the arrows signify the reordering positions; at the bottom the counts show the number of reads/writes of each flow. In this Figure, reducing method of folded memory access is not contained because mix of two methods is very complex, so hard to understand. The reordered executions are summarized as below:

1. *Execute 5 row interpolations to make old half pixels in horizontal direction, and store the results.*
2. *Execute 1 row interpolation to make new half pixels.*
3. *Load the interim results and necessary pixel values, and execute proposed interpolations (Eq.3) in vertical direction with loaded pixels and pixel executed on stage 2.*
4. *Repeat step 2 and 3.*

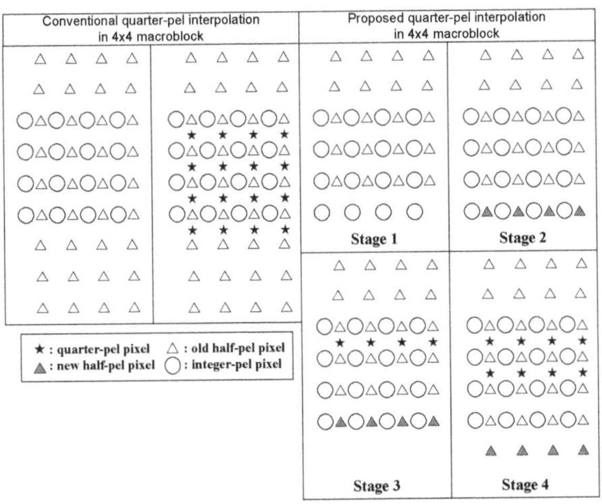

Fig. 6. Rearrangement of interpolation executions

Conventional quarter-pel interpolation method is shown in the left of Fig. 6. First, all horizontal interpolations are executed to make interim values for vertical interpolations; and then, all vertical interpolations which need the interim values are executed. Consequently, there are unnecessary memory accesses that can be reduced. The proposed interpolation method shown in the right of Fig. 6 can minimize unnecessary interim memory accesses by changing the order of interpolation sequence. Stage 1 in Fig. 6 is the part that cannot be modified, so this stage is same as the conventional interpolation. Stage 2 makes one row half pixels as the interpolation results that are going to be needed for vertical half-pel interpolations requiring 6 variables in column. These 6 variables in column are interpolated in stage 3. And stage 3 utilizes the merging method generated in Section 4.1, so can make quarter pixels though there is no interim memory access. Because the 5 variables in column are not required to be loaded in vertical half-pel interpolation by utilizing temporal locality mentioned in Section 4.3, six variables for horizontal half-pel interpolation to make black triangle and one variable for quarter-pel interpolation to make black star are loaded for each interpolation in stage 4.

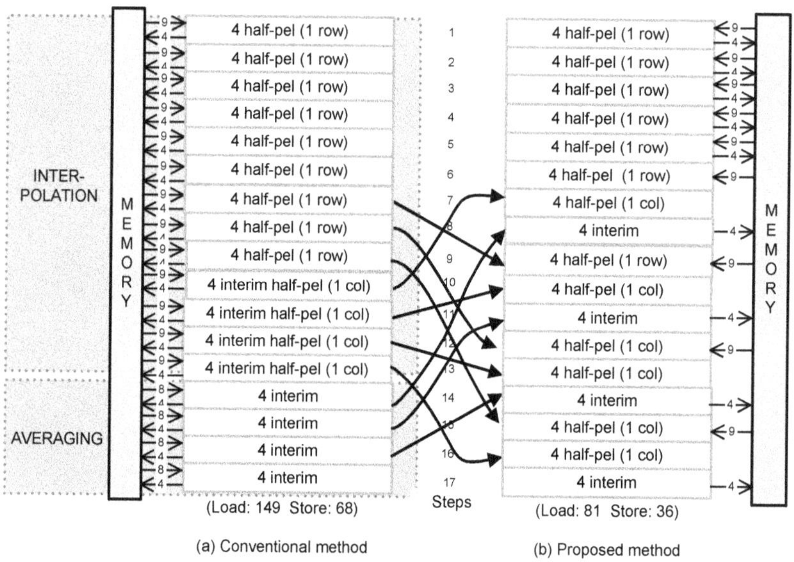

Fig. 7. Reordering sequence and memory access counts

4.3 The Temporal Locality in Interpolation Stages

The temporal data locality of interpolation stages are utilized to achieve reductions of interim loads/stores by keeping variables read in the previous interpolation stages. As shown in Fig 8, first interpolation needs pixels starting from A to F; second interpolation from B to G, and so on. In this case, there are needless folded memory accesses that may increase power consumption. Those accesses could be removed in this stage, which can be realized not by hardware configuration but by code optimization. Fig. 9 shows the result of code regeneration, in which all conventional interpolation codes are merged and folded data loads are removed. This method is utilized in overall interpolation stages.

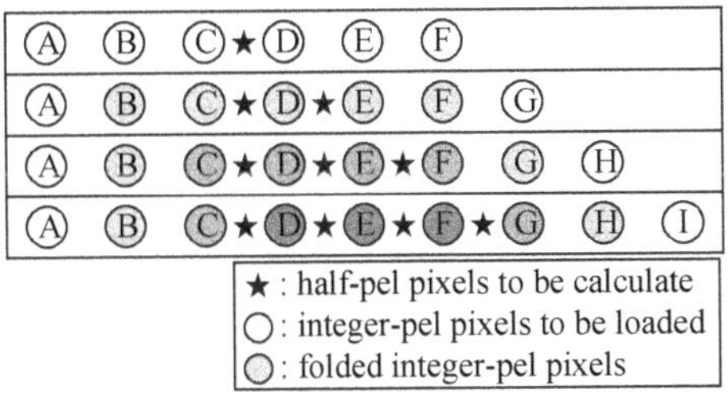

Fig. 8. Folded memory accesses between interpolations

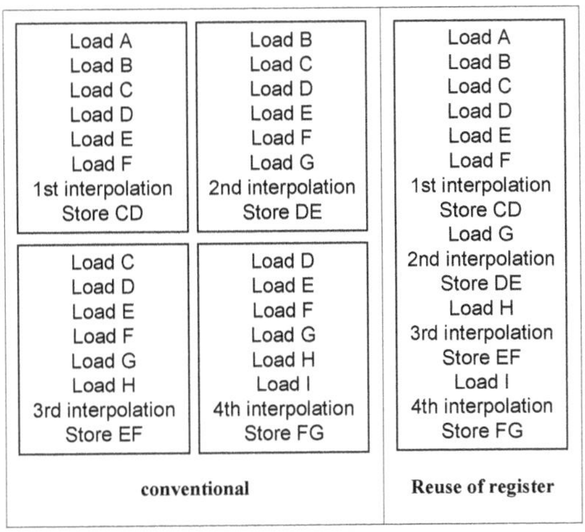

Fig. 9. Difference between conventional method and reuse of register method

5 Power Model and Performance Evaluation

To obtain power estimation from high level system description, we used the methodology similar with [1], such that we conduct a relative comparison that selects the most promising candidates. The application discussed here is H.264/AVC, a data-intensive application in which power due to memory transfer is dominant, and both conventional and proposed algorithms are mapped onto the same target architecture. Therefore, we can neglect the power consumption in operators, controls and so on. In this way, our emphasis is on the achieved power reduction that comes from decreasing data transfer in another word memory accesses.

The power of data transfer is a function of the size of the memory, the frequency of access, and the technology [1]. Here, the technology can be a memory type which will be excluded on the assumption of on-chip, and then the simple power model function can be expressed as below:

$$P_{Transfers} = E_{Tr} \times \frac{\#\,Transfers}{Second} \tag{4}$$

$$E_{Tr} = f(\#\,words\ ,\#\,bits\ ) \tag{5}$$

In [8] a function *f* is proposed to estimate the energy per transfer E_{Tr} in terms of the number of words and with width in bits. Total system power can be considered linearly proportional to the numbers of data transfer. Supposing we compare the power reduction ratio between two different operational models on the same system, we have to know the required energy for one data transfer and the total number of data transfers of input video streams for two operation models. Based on the power model of [8] the energy for one read to a memory of 256×256 words of eight bit is estimated to be 1.17μJ. We selected 4 input video streams; salesman, carphone, container, and mthr_dotr. Their fame size is QCIF and 178 frames of each video stream are used. For the simulation, an algorithm mapping method was used and programmed the two operational models with C^{++} based on the hardware architecture shown in Fig. 4.

The result shows that the proposed method can reduce memory accesses greatly by changing control flows of quarter-pel interpolation. It did not bring out the performance degradation and system latency because there is no deleting operation. In all input video streams, the proposed method attained up to 87% of reduced local memory accesses, which resulted in decreasing power consumption at the same ratio.

As referenced above, these proposed methods are only for local memory access reduction. In Fig. 10, because both off-chip and local memory accesses are shown, only about 46% of memory accesses are reduced. But, our result shows local memory access reduction only.

Video image	Interpolation method	Off-chip memory read count	Off-chip memory write count	Local memory READ count	Local memory WRITE count	Consumed energy to READ from local memory (μ Joule)	READ power saving ratio (1-proposed /conventional)	Consumed energy to WRITE from local memory (μ Joule)	WRITE power saving ratio of (1-proposed /conventional)
salesman	conventional	9972288	4432128	1466940	900780	26.19	87.93%	16.08	86.94%
	proposed	9972288	4432128	177216	117760	3.16		2.10	
carphone	conventional	10008000	4448000	5951480	3795928	106.25	86.85%	67.77	88.15%
	proposed	10008000	4448000	782231	449780	13.97		8.03	
container	conventional	9505152	4224512	930084	483892	16.60	97.65%	8.64	98.03%
	proposed	9505152	4224512	21951	9720	0.39		0.17	
mthr_dotr	conventional	9828288	4368128	3447044	2070564	61.54	88.61%	36.97	90.70%
	proposed	9828288	4368128	392697	192820	7.01		3.44	

Fig. 10. Simulation results

6 Conclusion

We have presented a new architecture for motion estimation of H.264/AVC with power reduction by decreasing data transfers. In data intensive applications such as H.264/AVC, data transfers dominate the power consumption. For this objective, we used a microarchitecture level configurability according to the value of motion vectors, which allow the system to operate on different control flows while executing quarter-pel interpolation. As a result, we can achieve power reduction at system-level significantly. The simulation result shows that the proposed interpolation method could reduce up to 87% of power consumption compared with conventional method on the target architecture without scarifying performance.

Acknowledgement

This work was supported by the Korea Research Foundation Grant. (KRF-2004-041-D00545)

References

1. Smith, R., Fant, K., Parker, D., Stephani, R., Ching-Yi, W.: System-Level Power Optimization of Video Codecs on Embedded Cores: A Systematic Approach. Processing of Journal of VLSI Signal, 18 (1998) 89-109.
2. Kakerow, R.: Low Power Design Methodologies for Mobile Communication Computer Design. Proceedings of 2002 IEEE International Conference on VLSI in Computers and Processors, Sep. (2002) 8-13.
3. Musoll, E., Lang, T., Cortadella, J.: Exploiting the Locality of Memory References to Reduce the Address Bus Energy. Proceeding of 1997 International Symposium on Low Power Electronics and Design, Aug. (1997) 202-207.
4. Kim, H., Park, I. C.: High-Performance and Low-Power Memory-Interface Architecture for Video Processing Applications. IEEE Transactions on Circuits and Systems for Video Technology, Vol. 11, Issue 11, Nov. (2001) 1160-1170.
5. Kapoor, B.: Low Power Memory Architectures for Video Applications. Proceedings of the 8th Great Lakes Symposium on VLSI, Feb. (1998) 2-7.
6. Brockmeyer, E., Nachtergaele, L., Catthoor, F.V.M., Bormans, J., De Man, H.J.: Low Power Memory Storage and Transfer Organization for the MPEG-4 Full Pel Motion Estimation on a Multimedia Processor. IEEE Transactions on Multimedia, Vol. 1, Issue 2, June (1999) 202-216.
7. Nachtergaele, L., Catthoor, F., Kapoor, B., Janssens, S., Moolenaar, D.: Low Power Storage Exploration for H.263 Video Decoder. Workshop on VLSI Signal Processing IX, 30 Oct.-1 Nov. (1996) 115-124.
8. Landman, P.: Low-Power Architectural Design Methodologies. PhD thesis, U.C. Berkeley, Aug. (1994).
9. Vahid, F., Givargis T.: Platform Tuning for Embedded Systems Design. Computer, Vol. 34 N. 3, Mar. (2001) 112-114.
10. ISO/IEC 14496–10:2003: Coding of Audiovisual Objects-Part 10: Advanced Video Coding, 2003, also ITU-T Recommendation H.264: Advanced Video Coding for Generic Audiovisual Services.
11. Sato, K.; Yagasaki, Y.: Adaptive MC Interpolation for Memory Access Reduction in JVT Video Coding. Proceedings of Seventh International Symposium on Signal Processing and Its Applications, Vol. 1, July (2003) 77-80.

A Methodology for Software Synthesis of Embedded Real-Time Systems Based on TPN and LSC

Leonardo Amorim[1], Raimundo Barreto[1], Paulo Maciel[1], Eduardo Tavares[1], Meuse Oliveira Jr[1], Arthur Bessa[2], and Ricardo Lima[3]

[1] CIn - UFPE
{lab2, rsb, prmm, eagt, mnoj}@cin.ufpe.br
[2] FUCAPI
arthur.bessa@fucapi.br
[3] DSC - UPE
ricardo@dsc.upe.br

Abstract. This paper shows an approach for software synthesis in embedded hard real-time systems starting from Live Sequence Charts (LSC) scenarios as specification language. As the name suggests, LSCs specify liveness, that is, things that must happen. Therefore allowing the distinction between possible and necessary behavior as well as the specification of possible anti-scenarios. Embedded software has become much harder to design due to the diversity of requirements and high complexity. In such systems, correctness and timeliness verification is an issue to be concerned. The software synthesis method takes a specification (in this case composed by LSC scenarios) and automatically generates a program source code where: (i) functionalities and constraints are satisfied; and (ii) operational support for task's execution is provided. This paper adopts a time Petri net (TPN) formalism for system modeling in order to find feasible pre-runtime schedules, and for synthesizing predictable and timely scheduled code. Embedded software synthesis has been receiving much attention. However, few works deal with software synthesis for hard real-time systems considering arbitrary precedence and exclusion relations.

1 Introduction

Due to the increasing complexity and diversity of requirements, embedded software has become much harder to design. Since several applications demand safety properties, the correctness and timeliness verification is an important issue to be concerned. The adoption of formal and/or semi-formal modeling methods in early phases of embedded system design may significantly contribute for the success of the project, since they allow verification of properties and validating the system's requirements.

Message Sequence Chart (MSCs) for long has been adopted by the International Telecommunication Union [1] and nowadays also adopted in the UML [2] as a language of sequence diagrams. Sequence charts provide a visual representation of inter relationship between processes, tasks, environments and object instances of a given specification. MSCs can be used for testing scenarios that will be further checked against the

L.T. Yang et al. (Eds.): ICESS 2005, LNCS 3820, pp. 50–62, 2005.

behavior of the final system. Nevertheless, MSCs do not provide means for designers to represent what may, must and may not happen (anti-scenarios).

Live Sequence Charts (LSCs) [3] is a language based on scenarios, which specify liveness, that is, things that must happen, as well as anti-scenarios, that is, things that must not happen during the whole system's execution.

Software synthesis consists of two main activities [4]: (i) task handling, and (ii) code generation. Task handling takes into account tasks scheduling, resource management, and inter-task communication. Code generation is responsible for static generation of source code for each individual task. The scheduling approach adopted is a *pre-runtime* method and it is throughly described in [5], where schedules are computed entirely off-line. Pre-runtime schedules can reduce context switching, their execution are predictable, and exclude the need of complex operating systems.

Xu and Parnas [6] present an algorithm that finds an optimal pre-runtime schedule on a single processor for real-time process segments with release, deadline, and arbitrary exclusion and precedence relations, but real-world experimental results are not presented. Abdelzaher and Shin [7] extended Xu and Parnas' work in order to deal with distributed real-time systems. The scheduler synthesis proposed by Altisen et.al. [8] synthesizes all *dynamic on-line scheduling* satisfying a given property. However, they do not directly address the state explosion problem. Sgroi et al. [9] propose a software synthesis method based on quasi-static scheduling using free-choice Petri nets, which does not deal with real-time constraints. Hsiung [10] presents a formal software synthesis based on Petri nets, mixing quasi-static scheduling, and dynamic fixed-priority scheduling. However, it does not show how to add preemption.

2 Proposed Method Overview

This section presents an overview of the proposed synthesis method. The method described hereafter, takes into account single processor architecture only. The aim of this paper is to present an approach for software synthesis in embedded hard real-time systems starting from LSC scenarios, for specifying constraints and inter-task relations. After that, the tasks' modeling is performed by adopting an *transition-annotated* TPN, that is, a TPN with code associated with transitions. Afterward, the model is employed for synthesizing a feasible schedule (one that satisfies all constraints), and generates a scheduled code in accordance with the found schedule.

Figure 1 depicts a diagram of the phases composing the proposed methodology. In this figure, the requirement analysis phase should provide the behavioral and constraints specification. Besides, the hardware infrastructure should also be carefully considered. The modeling phase deals with the translation from specification into the respective TPN model. In order to allow portability, the TPN model is expressed in PNML (Petri Net Markup Language) format [11]. The scheduling synthesis phase uses a pre-runtime scheduling method. Starting from the TPN model, a schedule is entirely computed during design time. The algorithm is based on depth-first search method. The code generation phase aims to generate the respective scheduled code, considering the previously computed schedule, constraints and processor architecture. More details about the methodology are presented in the following sections.

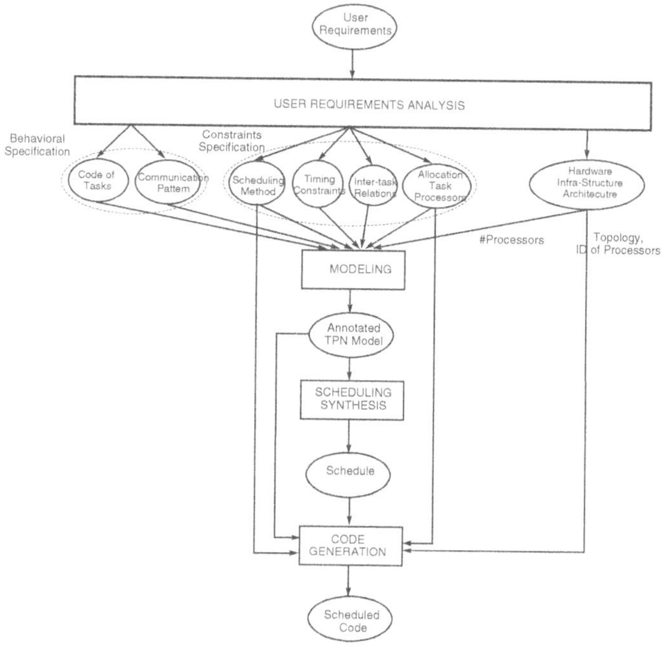

Fig. 1. Proposed Software Synthesis Methodology Phases

3 Computational Model

Computational model syntax is given by a time Petri net [12], and its semantics by a timed labeled transition system. A time Petri net (TPN) is a bipartite directed graph represented by a tuple $\mathcal{P}= (P, T, F, W, m_0, I)$. P (places) and T (transitions) are non-empty disjoint sets of nodes. The edges are represented by $F \subseteq (P \times T) \cup (T \times P)$. $W : F \rightarrow \mathbb{N}$ represents the weight of the edges. A TPN marking m_i is a vector $m_i \in \mathbb{N}^{|P|}$, and m_0 is the initial marking. $I : T \rightarrow \mathbb{N} \times \mathbb{N}$ represents the timing constraints, where $I(t) = (EFT(t), LFT(t))\ \forall t \in T, EFT(t) \leq LFT(t)$, $EFT(t)$ is the Earliest Firing Time, and $LFT(t)$ is the Latest Firing Time.

A code-labeled time Petri net (CTPN) is an extension of the TPN, which is represented by $\mathcal{P}_c = (\mathcal{P}, \mathcal{C})$. $\mathcal{P}$ is the underlying TPN, and $\mathcal{C}$:$T \nrightarrow \mathcal{SC}$ is a partial function that assigns transitions to behavioral source code, where $\mathcal{SC}$ is a set of source codes. It is worth observing that $\mathcal{C}$ is a partial function, therefore, some transitions may have no associated source code.

A set of enabled transitions is denoted by: $ET(m_i) = \{t \in T \,|\, m_i(p_j) \geq W(p_j, t)\}$, $\forall p_j \in P$. The time elapsed, since the respective transition enabling, is denoted by a clock vector $c_i \in \mathbb{N}^{|ET(m_i)|}$. The dynamic firing interval ($I_D(t)$) is dynamically modified whenever the respective clock variable $c(t)$ is incremented, and t does not fire. $I_D(t)$ is computed as follows: $I_D(t) = (DLB(t), DUB(t))$, where $DLB(t) = max(0, EFT(t) - c(t))$, $DUB(t) = LFT(t) - c(t)$, $DLB(t)$ is the Dynamic Lower Bound, and $DLB(t)$ is the Dynamic Upper Bound.

Let $\mathcal{P}$ be a TPN, M be the set of reachable markings of $\mathcal{P}$, and C be the set of clock vectors. The set of states S of $\mathcal{P}$ is given by $S \subseteq (M \times C)$, that is a state is defined by a marking, and the respective clock vector.

$FT(s)$ is the set of fireable transitions at state s defined by: $FT_P(s) = \{t_i \in ET(m) \mid \pi(t_i) = \min(\pi(t_k)) \wedge DLB(t_i) \leq \min(DUB(t_k)), \forall t_k \in ET(m)\}$. The *firing domain* for t at state s, is defined by the interval: $FD_s(t) = [DLB(t), \min(DUB(t_k))]$.

The semantics of a TPN $\mathcal{P}$ is defined by associating a timed labeled transition system (TLTS) $\mathcal{L}_\mathcal{P} = (S, \Sigma, \rightarrow, s_0)$: (i) S is the set of states of $\mathcal{P}$; (ii) $\Sigma \subseteq (T \times \mathbb{N})$ is a set of actions labeled with (t, θ) corresponding to the firing of a firable transition (t) at time (θ) in the firing interval $FD_s(t), \forall s \subset S$; (iii) $\rightarrow \subseteq S \times \Sigma \times S$ is the transition relation; (iv) s_0 is the initial state of $\mathcal{P}$.

Let $\mathcal{L}_\mathcal{P}$ be a TLTS derived from a TPN $\mathcal{P}$, and $s_i = (m_i, c_i)$ a reachable state. $s_{i+1} = \mathtt{fire}(s_i, (t, \theta))$ denotes that firing a transition t at time θ from the state s_i, a new state $s_{i+1} = (m_{i+1}, c_{i+1})$ is reached, such that: (1) $\forall p \in P,\ m_{i+1}(p) = m_i(p) - W(p,t) + W(t,p)$; (2) $\forall t_k \in ET(m_{i+1})$: (i) $C_{i+1}(t_k) = 0$ (if $(t_k = t) \vee (t_k \in ET(m_{i+1}) - ET(m_i))$), or (ii) $C_{i+1}(t_k) = C_i(t_k) + \theta$, otherwise.

Let $\mathcal{L}_\mathcal{P}$ be a TLTS derived from a TPN $\mathcal{P}$, s_0 its initial state, $s_n = (m_n, c_n)$ a final state, and $m_n = M^F$ is the desired final marking.

$$s_0 \overset{(t_1,\theta_1)}{\longrightarrow} s_1 \overset{(t_2,\theta_2)}{\longrightarrow} s_2 - - \rightarrow s_{n-1} \overset{(t_n,\theta_n)}{\longrightarrow} s_n$$

is defined as a *feasible firing schedule*, where $s_i = \mathtt{fire}(s_{i-1}, (t_i, \theta_i)),\ i > 0$, if $t_i \in FT(s_{i-1})$, and $\theta_i \in FD_{s_{i-1}}(t_i)$.

The modeling methodology guarantees that the final marking M^F is well-known since it is explicitly modeled.

4 Specification Model

LSC language fills out the gaps of the previous sequence diagram models, distinguishing things that can happen of things that must happen. Sequence of events that can happen in an execution of the system can be specified using existential chart that works as a system test case. On the other hand, sequence of events that should happen for all and any execution of the system should be modeled using universal charts. Each universal chart possesses a pre-condition (prechart) that, if successfully executed, forces the execution of the scenario specified in the chart body. If the pre-condition is not satisfied, a violation occurs.

In LSC language, the system is modeled using object oriented notions and terminologies. A system is composed by objects that represents class instances. Every object in the application is associated with a set of properties and a set of methods. Each property is based on a type, from which its value can be selected.

The specification model is composed by: (i) a set of periodic preemptable tasks with bounded discrete time constraints; and (ii) inter-task relations, such as precedence and exclusion relations.

Let $\mathcal{T}$ be the set of tasks in a system. A periodic task is defined by $\tau_i = (ph_i, r_i, c_i, d_i, p_i)$, where ph_i is the initial phase; r_i is the release time; c_i is the worst case computation time required for execution of task τ_i; d_i is the deadline; and p_i is the period. A sporadic task is defined by τ_k = (c_k, d_k, min_k), where min_k is the minimum period between two activations of task τ_k. A task is classified as sporadic if it can be randomly activated, but the minimum period between two activations is known. Preruntime scheduling can only schedule periodic tasks. However, Mok [13] has proposed a translation from sporadic to periodic tasks.

A task τ_i *precedes* task τ_j, if τ_j can only start executing after τ_i has finished. A task τ_i *excludes* task τ_j, if no execution of τ_j can start while task τ_i is executing. If it is considered a single processor, then task τ_i could not be preempted by task τ_j.

All timing constraints are expressed in task time units (TTUs), where each TTU has a correspondence with some multiple of a specific timing unit (millisecond, second, etc). In this paper, a TTU is the smallest indivisible granule of a task, during which a task cannot be preempted by any other task. A TTU is also called a preemption point.

In order to provide the specification model, LSC scenarios could be used as an intuitive and user-friendly way for specifying timing constraints and inter-task relations scenarios. Before modeling scenarios which represent task's time constraints and inter-task relations, it is necessary to create data types to represent a task and the processor, so the following steps should be taken: Create a new class for representing a task, labeled "Task", without properties and methods; Create the desired number of "Task" instances; Create a new class for representing the processor, labeled "Proc", which contains a *String* property, called "task", with an "execute" prefix and a method, called "grant", with one "STRING" parameter; Create one instance of "Proc" class.

After creating data types and the corresponding instances, it must be created a scenario for each task, in which, its time constraints are defined. Individually, these scenarios do not specify any inter-task relation, hence tasks can execute concurrently. The following steps should be taken to specify such scenarios: Create an universal chart for each task and inserts the "grant" method call in the prechart section. The method parameter should be a sequence of characters that specifies task's time constraints. Time constraints should be separate by comma in the following way: "ph,r,c,d,p", where *ph* is the initial phase, *r* is the release time, *c* is the worst time of computation, *d* is the deadline and *p* is the period; In the chart body section of the created universal chart, inserts the message "execute task(par)" (*self* message of *Proc* instance), where *execute* is the property's prefix, *task* is the property created above and *par* is a parameter, which value is the task name. When this message occurs, it changes the value of "task" property of "Proc" instance.

Figure 2 depicts two LSC charts, one for task *T0* and other for task *T1*. *T0* and *T1* are "Task" instances and *Proc* is an "Proc" instance. If prechart (denoted by a dashed border line) is successfully executed, then the chart body (denoted by a solid border) should be satisfied by the system. So, these scenarios say that every time task *T0* or *T1* requests the processor and the processor grants the permission to these tasks to execute, these tasks must be executed, and they can execute concurrently, because no relation between them is specified.

In order to establishes some inter-task relations, additional scenarios must be created for each kind of relation (precedence and exclusion). A precedence relation establishes an order in the execution, which could be modeled in the following way: Create an

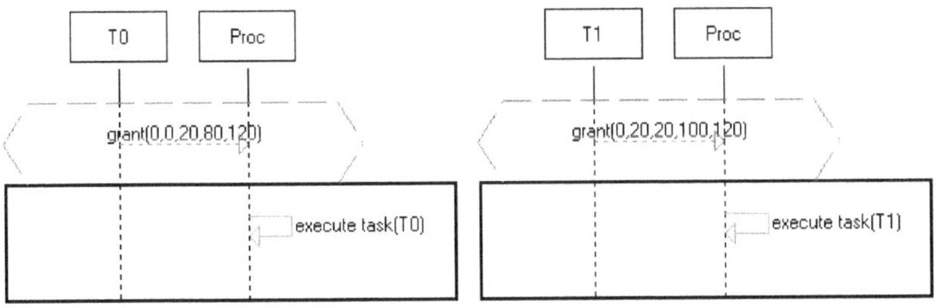

Fig. 2. Time constraints scenarios for tasks *T0* and *T1*

universal chart and inserts the message "execute task(t1)" in the prechart section, where *t1* precedes the task specified in the chart body section (next step); In the chart body section, inserts the "grant" method, which is called from the task that must be executed after the task specified previous.

Figure 3 depicts a precedence relation between task *T0* and *T1*, where *T0* precedes *T1*. As described previously, each task has a scenario, in which, its time constraints are defined. In Figure 2, whenever task *T0* requests the processor, the processor should execute this task. However, in Figure 3 a precedence relation between task *T0* and *T1* is specified, so when *T0* finishes its execution, task *T1* must requests the processor (see Figure 3) and then executes (see Figure 2).

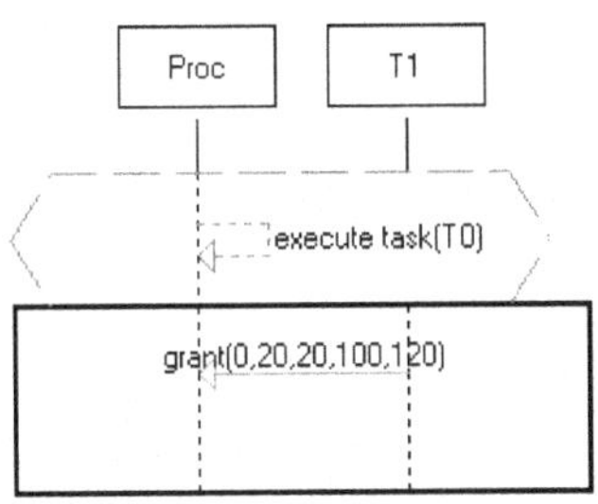

Fig. 3. Precedence relation between tasks *T0* and *T1*

An exclusion relation prohibits the execution of some task while another task is executing. An exclusion relation could be modeled using anti-scenarios (prohibitive) in the following way: Create an universal chart and inserts an LSC condition that checks if the value of "task" property of "Proc" instance is equals to the task that excludes the other (specified next); After creating the above condition, inserts the "grant" method, which is called from the task and it is excluded by the task specified previously; In the chart body section, inserts a *hot* condition with *FALSE* value. This condition will never be evaluated to a true value, so when it executes, a requirement violation occurs and the chart must be aborted. Figure 4 depicts an anti-scenario modeling, where task *T1* excludes task *T2*. Whenever task *T1* is executing and task *T2* requests the processor,

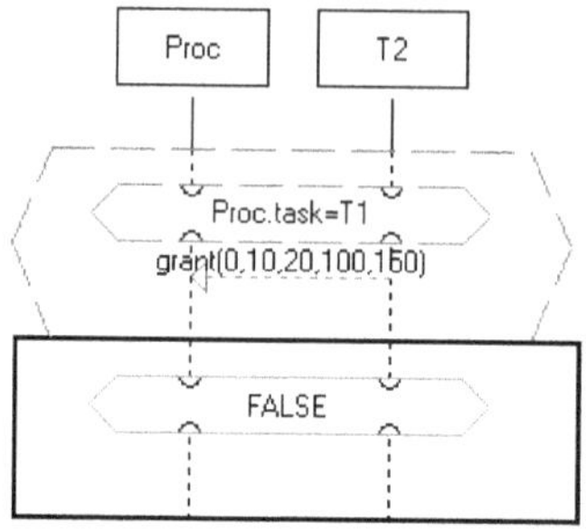

Fig. 4. Exclusion relation between task *T1* and task *T2*

a requirement violation occurs, because the *hot* condition in the chart body always evaluates to a false value, forcing the chart to be aborted.

In order to automate software synthesis process, we developed an *LSC2SS* engine with the purpose to parse LSC inscriptions and creates the respective Petri Net model.

5 System Model for Scheduling Generation

This section shows how to model the tasks of the system, and inter-task relations, such as precedence and exclusion relations, starting from LSC scenarios. Due to lack of space, this section presents just a summary. The interested reader is referred to [5]. Time Petri net (TPN) is a mathematical formalism that allows modeling of several features present in most concurrent and real-time systems, such as, precedence and exclusion relations, communication protocols, multiprocessing, synchronization mechanisms, and shared resources. The proposed modeling applies composition rules on building blocks models. These blocks are specific for the scheduling policy adopted, that is, pre-runtime scheduling policy. One of these specific situations is that pre-runtime algorithm schedules tasks considering a schedule period that corresponds to the least common multiple (called P_S) between all periods in the task set. Within this new period, there are several *tasks instances* of the same task, where $\mathcal{N}(\tau_i) = P_S/p_i$ gives the instances of task τ_i.

In the proposed modeling, the considered building blocks are (Figure 5): (a) Fork; (b) Join; (c) Periodic Task Arrival; (d) Deadline Checking; (e) Non-preemptive Task Structure; (f) Preemptive Task Structure; and (g) Processors. These blocks are summarized below:

a) Fork Block. The fork block is responsible for starting all tasks in the system. Therefore, this block models the creation of n concurrent tasks.

b) Join Block. The join block execution states that all tasks in the system have concluded their execution in the schedule period. It is worth noting that a marking in place p_{end} represents the desirable final marking (or M^F). In this case, $M(p_{end}) = 1$ indicates that a feasible firing schedule was found.

c) Periodic Task Arrival Block. This block models the periodic invocation for all task instances in the schedule period (P_S). Transition t_{ph_i} models the initial phase of the

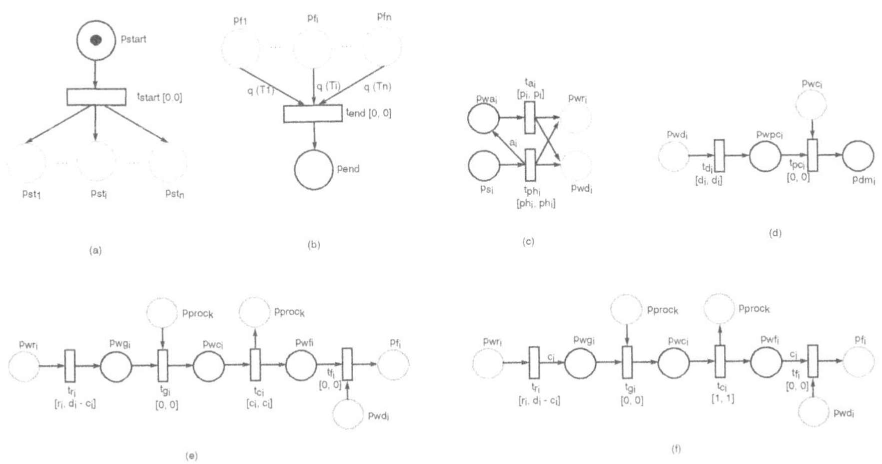

Fig. 5. Proposed Building Blocks

task first instance. Similarly, transition t_{a_i} models the periodic arrival (after the initial phase) for the remaining instances. It is worth noting the weight ($\alpha_i = \mathcal{N}(\tau_i) - 1$) of the arc ($t_{ph_i}, p_{wa_i}$), where this weight models the invocation of all remaining instances after the first task instance.

d) Deadline Checking Block. Some works (e.g. [8]) extended the Petri net model for dealing with deadline checking. The proposed modeling method uses elementary net structures to capture deadline missing. Obviously, deadline missing is an undesirable situation when considering hard real-time systems. Therefore, the scheduling algorithm must eliminate states that represent undesirable situations like this one.

e) Non-preemptive Task Structure Block. Considering a non-preemptive scheduling method, the processor is just released after the entire computation to be finished. Figure 5(e) shows that time interval of computation transition has bounds equal to the task computation time (i.e., $[c_i, c_i]$).

f) Preemptive Task Structure Block. This scheduling method implies that a task are implicitly split into all possible subtasks, where the computation time of each subtask is exactly equal to one task time unit (TTU). This method allows running other conflicting tasks, in this case, meaning that one task preempts another task. This is modeled by the time interval of computation transitions ([1,1]), and the entire computation is modeled through the arc weights.

g) Processor Block. The processor modeling consists of a single place p_{proc_i}, where its marking states how many processors are available. If $m(p_{proc}) > 1$, it is considered a multiprocessor architecture with unified memory access (UMA).

6 Software Synthesis Approach

This section presents the software synthesis approach. It shows methods for scheduling synthesis and code generation phases.

```
1  scheduling-synthesis(S,M^F,TPN)
2  {
3    if (S.M = M^F) return TRUE;
4    tag(S);
5    PT = pruning(firable(S));
6    if (|PT| = 0) return FALSE;
7    for each (⟨t,θ⟩ ∈ PT) {
8      S'= fire(S, t, θ);
9      if (untagged(S') ∧
10        scheduling-synthesis (S',M^F,TPN)){
11        add-in-trans-system (S,S',t,θ);
12        return TRUE;
13     }
14   }
15   return FALSE;
16 }
```

Fig. 6. Schedule Synthesis Algorithm

6.1 Pre-runtime Scheduling Synthesis

The algorithm proposed (Fig. 6) is a depth-first search method on a TLTS. So, the TLTS is partially generated on-the-fly. The *stop criterion* is obtained whenever the desirable final marking M^F is reached. Considering that, (i) the Petri net model is guaranteed to be bounded, and (ii) the timing constraints are bounded and discrete, this implies that the TLTS is finite and thus the proposed algorithm always finishes.

The only way the algorithm returns TRUE is when it reaches a desired final marking (M^F), implying that a feasible schedule was found (line 3). The state space generation algorithm is modified (line 5) to incorporate the state space pruning. `PT` is a set of ordered pairs $\langle t, \theta \rangle$ representing for each firable transition (post-pruning) all possible firing time in the firing domain. The *tagging scheme* (lines 4 and 9) ensures that no state is visited more than once. The function `fire` (line 8) returns a new generated state (S') due to the firing of transition t at time θ. The feasible schedule is represented by a timed labeled transition system that is generated by the function `add-in-trans-system` (line 11). When the system does not have a feasible schedule, the whole reduced state space is analyzed.

6.2 Scheduled Code Generation

This section aims to present the approach for C-code generation starting from the scheduling found. The code is generated by traversing the TLTS (feasible firing schedule), and detecting the time where the tasks are to be executed.

The proposed method for code generation includes not only the code of tasks (implemented by C functions), but also includes a timer interrupt handler, and a small dispatcher. Such dispatcher is adopted to automate several controls needed to the execution of tasks. Timer programming, context saving, context restoring, and tasks calling are examples of such additional controls. The timer interrupt handler always transfers the control to the the dispatcher, which will evaluate the need for performing either context saving or restoring, and calling the specific task.

Figure 7 shows a simplified version of the proposed dispatcher. The data structures include a table containing the respective information: (i) start time; (ii) a flag indicating if either it is a new task instance or a preemption resuming; (iii) task id; and (iv) a function pointer. This table is stored in an array of type `SchItem` (Fig. 8). There are some shared variables that stores information about the size of the schedule (`SCHEDULE_SIZE`), information of the task currently executing (`struct SchItem item`), a pointer to the task function (`taskFunction`), and so on.

```
void dispatcher()
{
  struct SchItem item=sch[schIndex];
  globalClock = item.starttime;

  if(currentTaskPreempted) {
    // context saving
  }
  if(item.isPreemptionReturn) {
    // context restoring
  }
  else {
    taskFunction=item.functionPointer;
  }
  schIndex=((++schIndex)%SCHEDULE_SIZE);
  progrTimer(sch[schIndex].starttime);
  activateTimer();
}
```

Fig. 7. Dispatcher

```
void taskT1() {...}
void taskT2() {...}

#define SCHEDULE_SIZE 7

struct SchItem sch[SCHEDULE_SIZE] =
{
  {0, false, 1, (int *)taskT1},
  {3, false, 2, (int *)taskT2},
  {8, false, 2, (int *)taskT2},
  {11,false, 1, (int *)taskT1},
  {14,false, 2, (int *)taskT2},
  {17,false, 1, (int *)taskT1},
  {20,false, 2, (int *)taskT2}
};
```

Fig. 8. Generated code example

7 Case Study

In order to show the practical fesiability of the proposed methodology, this section presents a real-world case study, namely, Heated Humidifier. The purpose of this system is insertion of water vapor in the gaseous mixture used in a sort of electro-medical systems. For maintaining such vapor, the system must warm up the water in a recipient

Table 1. Heated-Humidifier Specification

Task	r	c	d	p
A (temp-sensor-start)	0	1	1,500	10,000
B (temp-sensor-handler)	11	1	1,500	10,000
C (PWM)	0	8	1,500	10,000
D (pulse-generator)	0	4	4	50
E (temp-adjust-part1)	0	1	5,000	10,000
F (temp-adjust-part2)	1501	2	5,000	10,000
Inter-task Relations				
A PRECEDES B				
B PRECEDES C				
E PRECEDES F				

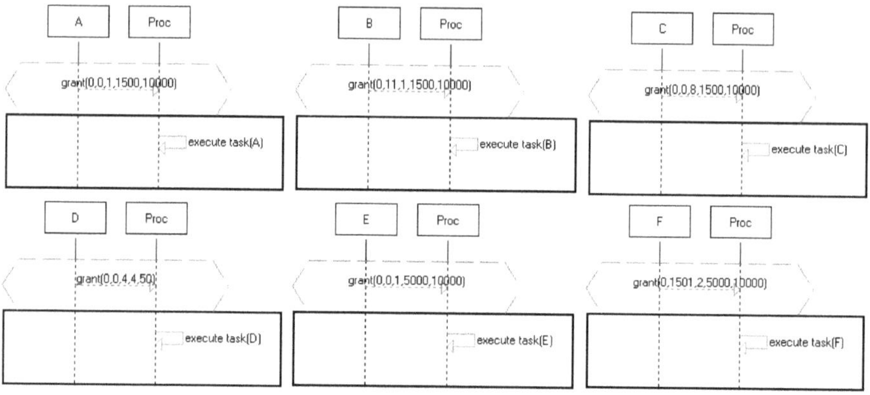

Fig. 9. Tasks' time constraints scenarios

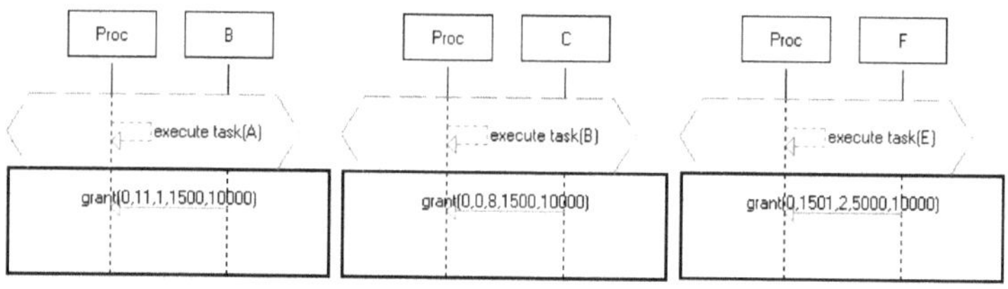

Fig. 10. Precedence relation scenarios

and maintain the water temperature in a prescribed value. This equipment is very useful in hospital's critical care units (CCUs).

Table 1 shows part of the specification model. Considering the 8051-family architecture, the overhead of the interrupt and dispatcher is equal to 20μs (2 TTUs). The values are expressed in *task time units* (TTUs), where each TTU (Section 4) is equal to 10μs. Figure 9 shows timing constraints scenarios for each task specified, and Figure 10 shows the LSC scenarios for the three precedence relation. These LSC scenarios was modeled according to the rules presented in Section 4. As Figure 10 presents, before requesting the processor (chart body), the task with higher priority must be first executed (prechart). Whenever the "grant" message is executed in these scenarios, the same event is fired in the corresponding scenario specified in Figure 9, therefore enabling the current task to be executed.

In order to avoid the *key bouncing*, the key reading for temperature adjustment is divided in two tasks. If task E indicates that a key is pressed, after a specific minimal time (generally 15ms), the task F must confirm such key pressing. The same solution is applied for reading the temperature sensor. The first task (task A) is responsible for starting the A/D conversion. After elapsing a specific time (generally 100μs), the second task (task B) may start reading the temperature and updating a shared variable. A feasible schedule was found in 0.486 seconds, verifying 6022 states, which is the minimum number of states to be verified. Figure 11 shows part of the heated-humidifier generated code.

```
void taskT1() {...}    void taskT2() {...}
void taskT3() {...}    void taskT4() {...}
void taskT5() {...}    void taskT6() {...}
#define SCHEDULE_SIZE 505
struct SchItem sch[SCHEDULE_SIZE] =
{
  {0,   false, 4, (int *)taskT4},
  {24,  false, 1, (int *)taskT1},
  {50,  false, 4, (int *)taskT4},
  {74,  false, 5, (int *)taskT5},
  {100,false, 4, (int *)taskT4},
  {124,false, 2, (int *)taskT2},
  {150,false, 4, (int *)taskT4},
  {174,false, 3, (int *)taskT3},
  {200,false, 4, (int *)taskT4},
        :
        :
}
```

Fig. 11. Heated-Humidifier Code

8 Conclusions

This paper proposed a method for software synthesis of embedded hard real-time systems, where the specification of constraints and inter-task relations is based on LSC, and the proposed scheduling model is based on TPNs.

LSC is a language based on scenarios, more powerful that its predecessors (UML sequence diagram for instance), since it provides means for describing scenarios, things that must happen and may happen, as well as anti-scenarios, that is, things that must not happen during the whole system's execution.

Predictability is an important concern when considering time-critical systems. Pre-runtime scheduling approach is used in order to guarantee that all critical tasks meet their deadlines. Despite the analysis technique (i.e. state space exploration) is not new, to the best of our present knowledge, there is no similar work that uses formal methods for modeling time-critical systems, considers arbitrary precedence/exclusion relations, for finding pre-runtime schedules, and generates timely and predictable scheduled code.

Analysis of properties in large dimension nets is not trivial. Therefore, methods that allow transforming models while preserving system properties has been largely studied. Usually, these transformations are reductions that are applied to larger models in order to obtain smaller ones while preserving properties. This is a further work to be investigated.

References

[1] ITU-T: Message Sequence Chart (MSC). (Geneva, 1996)

[2] OMG: Unified Modeling Language (UML) documentation. (2005) http://www.omg.org.

[3] Harel, D., Marelly, R.: Come, Lets Play: Scenario-Based Programming Using LSCs and Play-Engine. (2003)

[4] Cornero, M., Thoen, F., Goossens, G., Curatelli, F.: Software synthesis for real-time information processing systems. Code Generation for Embedded Processors (1995) 260–279

[5] Barreto, R., Tavares, E., Maciel, P., Neves, M., Oliveira Jr., M., Amorim, L., Bessa, A., Lima, R.: A time petri net-based approach for software synthesis considering dispatcher overheads, IEEE Computer Society Press. Rio de Janeiro, Brazil (2005)

[6] Xu, J., Parnas, D.: Scheduling processes with release times, deadlines, precedence, and exclusion relations. IEEE Trans. Soft. Engineering **16** (1990) 360–369

[7] Abdelzaher, T., Shin, K.: Combined task and message scheduling in distributed real-time systems. IEEE Trans. Parallel Distributed Systems **10** (1999) 1179–1191
[8] Altisen, K., Göbler, G., Pnueli, A., Sifakis, J., Tripakis, S., Yovine, S.: A framework for scheduler synthesis. IEEE Real-Time System Symposium (1999) 154–163
[9] Sgroi, M., Lavagno, L., Watanabe, Y., Sangiovanni-Vincentelli, A.: Synthesis of embedded software using free-choice petri nets. DAC'99 (1999)
[10] Hsiung, P.A.: Formal synthesis and code generation of embedded real-time software. In CODES (2001)
[11] Weber, M., Kindler, E.: The petri net markup language. Petri net Technology Communication Systems. Advances in Petri Nets. (2002)
[12] Merlin, P., Faber, D.J.: Recoverability of communication protocols. IEEE Trans. Comm. **24** (1976) 1036–1043
[13] Mok, A.K.: Fundamental Design Problems of Distributed Systems for the Hard-Real-Time Environment. PhD Thesis, MIT (1983)

Ahead of Time Deployment in ROM of a Java-OS

Kevin Marquet, Alexandre Courbot, and Gilles Grimaud

IRCICA/LIFL, University of Lille I, France
INRIA Futurs, POPS research group
{Kevin.Marquet, Alexandre.Courbot, Gilles.Grimaud}@lifl.fr

Abstract. This article shows how it is possible to place a great part of a Java system in read-only memory in order to fit with the requirements of tiny devices. Java systems for such devices are commonly deployed off-board, then embedded on the target device in a ready-to-run form. Our approach is to go as far as possible in this deployment, in order to maximize the amount of data placed in read-only memory. Doing so, we are also able to reduce the overall size of the system.

1 Introduction

Deploying a Java system dedicated to be embedded into a tiny device such as a sensor involves producing a ready-to-run binary image of it. This binary image is later burnt into a persistent memory of the device, usually Read-Only Memory (ROM), to produce the initial state of the system on the device.

In addition to ROM, tiny devices include several types of writable memories such as RAM, EEPROM, or Flash memory. All these memories have different access times, physical space requirements, and financial costs. For instance, ROM is very cheap and takes few physical space on the silicon, which usually makes it this memory the most significant one in terms of quantity; but it cannot be erased. Writable memories on the other hand are a rare ressource because of their cost and physical footprint.

The memory mapping of data into these different memories is computed off-board, when producing the binary image. A correct placement of the system data at that time is critical for embedded systems. In a domain where the software and hardware productions are tightly tied, placing more data in ROM can divide the final cost of the device and makes the other writable memories available for run-time computations.

Our approach is to go as far as possible in the off-line deployment of the system to maximize ROM usage while decreasing the overall size of the system. We operate at different steps of the deployment process. For each step, we measure the amount of data that can safely be placed in ROM, as well as the overall size of the system, thus obtaining an evolution of these two measurements all along the deployment. Our experiments have been performed on the Java In The Small (JITS[1]) Java-OS toolkit.

L.T. Yang et al. (Eds.): ICESS 2005, LNCS 3820, pp. 63–70, 2005.

The remainder of this paper is organized as follows. Section 2 presents some work related to this paper. Section 3 then introduces the issues related to the placement in ROM of an embedded Java system. The deployment scheme of a JITS system is then briefly described in section 4. In particular, we detail the steps that are important for maximizing ROM placement and reducing the size of the final system. Section 5 details our results, by showing the amount of data it is possible to put in ROM and the size of the system for every deployment step. Finally, we conclude on our results.

2 Related Work

Embedding Java systems into tiny devices while minimizing their size has been studied using different approaches. Rayside [2] and Tip [3]'s approach is to extract the minimal necessary subset to run an application from a Java library. They use abstract interpretation to determine classes, fields and methods that may be used by the application and discard the rest. JITS uses a similar mechanism to extract the needed parts of the library and core system according to the threads that are being deployed. Squawk [4] is a CLDC-compliant implementation of the Java virtual machine targeted at next-generation smart cards. It uses an indirection table containing the references of all objects. This implies a run-time performance reduction, and the use of a part of the writable memory to store this table. Java 2, Micro Edition [5] is a stripped-down specification of the Java platform for small devices. It includes JavaCodeCompact, a class pre-loader and pre-linker that allows classes to be linked with the virtual machine.

These works doesn't take into account the specifics of the *physical type* of memory that tiny devices use. In particular, such devices generally include a high quantity of read-only memory. This important parameter is at the heart of our deployment approach.

3 Placing Data in ROM

A tiny device of the range of the smart card includes different kinds of memories. Their respective cost and physical footprint properties lead to the following proportions: about hundreds of kilobytes of ROM, dozens of kilobytes of persistent, writable memory and kilobyte(s) of RAM. Larger, more expensive devices can embed more memory - but these proportions are usually respected.

In a traditional Java Virtual Machine (JVM), the loading of applications is clearly defined: classes must be loaded, linked, and initialized [6]. In the case of an embedded Java-OS, these phases can be made partly during the off-line deployment, in order to embed a partially deployed system [7]. This results in a faster start up of the system, but it is also possible to take advantage of various steps during the deployment to increase the amount of data placed into ROM, as well as reducing the size of the system. Indeed, some Java objects involved in the deployment process reach their definitive form during these steps, and can then be considered as immutable. Others are just useful to initialize the system and can be removed.

As placing objects in ROM prevents any further modifications of them, it is impossible to place an object that the system needs to change at run-time in a read-only memory. This leads to the definition of immutability of an object [8], in relationship to the semantics of the program: *an object is immutable if it is never modified by the code of the program.* Our approach is to detect all immutable objects and to place them in ROM.

Among the objects that are needed at run-time, some are always immutable. Their immutability does not depend on the deployment process. For instance, the `String` objects and their associated character arrays are objects that can never be modified. Other objects are created during the loading process and are either not modified or even not used at run-time.

The next section describes the deployment process of JITS. It details how it is possible, for each step of the deployment process, to increase the number of objects in ROM and to decrease the size of the overall system.

4 Deploying Embedded Java

Before being embedded into a small device, a Java-OS is deployed off-board. All the initializations that have not been made during this phase are performed when the device starts up, in order to place the system in a state where it is ready to run applications. While these operations are made at run-time in a traditional JVM (section 4.1), they can also be performed during the offline deployment of the embedded Java-OS in order to improve the size of the system and the amount of data in ROM (section 4.2).

4.1 Java Class Loading Process

A Java platform initializes itself before being able to run applications. In particular, classes must go through different loading states described by the Java virtual machine specification [6] before being ready to use.

Loading. During this phase, the class structure is read (from a stream on a file or a network connection for instance) and the internal structures for classes, methods and fields are created. All the external references are still symbolic. Classes are marked as `LOADED` after this step.

Linking. The linking step transforms the external symbolic references into direct ones. This step can either be performed once and for all (all the symbolic references are resolved, which involves loading the classes that are referenced) or just-in-time during runtime (each reference is linked when the bytecode interpreter meets it for the first time). During this phase, methods are modified in order to replace the non-linked bytecodes with linked counterparts.

Initializing. Before being ready to run, the static statements of the classes must be executed. Once this phase is performed, the class is granted state `READY`.

This class loading scheme is tightly linked to the upper-level application deployment process.

4.2 Application Deployment Process

The pre-deployment phase of JITS is able to perform the class loading process. At each step, useless objects can be removed and some others considered as immutable. All these steps are performed by a tool called *romizer*). As the JITS *romizer* initializes the system before producing a binary image of it, it differs from JavaCodeCompact (JCC, [9]), the J2ME deployment tool, which only loads and links Java classes and lets the initializations be made at run-time.

Loading. After this step, apart from objects that are always immutable such as strings, very few objects can be placed in ROM. Bytecodes contained in the code associated to a method are subject to modification during linking. However, if the code associated to a method does not contain any mutable bytecode, this code is immutable. In the same way, few objects can be considered useless after this step. Only the objects used to read the class from the streams can be removed, as well as all the information that has been extracted from them. The associated useless classes can be removed as well. A previous study [10] has shown that the constant pools of the classes can be compacted during this phase.

Linking. After the linking phase, all external references from the bytecode are resolved, and more parts of the code can thus be considered immutable. All methods are linked which makes them immutable as well. The `LINKED` state also constitutes another important stage regarding the lifetime of classes: at this state, all objects referenced by classes can be placed in ROM excepted the static zones which can be modified at run-time. The classes themselves can be considered immutable if their states is stored outside of them.

Initializing. In addition to the loading and linking phases, the JITS romizer is able to execute the static statements of the classes. This avoids spending time to execute the static statements at run-time but also allows to placethe immutable objects attached to a static field in read-only memory. Although there are few objects that are concerned by this in the Java libraries, applications are more subject to use them.

Applications Initialization. Once the static statements are executed, our tool instantiates the threads that will begin to run when the device starts up. Doing this during deployment brings one benefit: it is possible to make a static abstract interpretation [11] of the code in order to detect the parts of the deployed system that will be used at run-time. Our approach at this level is the same as in [2] and [12]. We extract a subset of the system containing only the libraries needed for the system. From the `run` method of the selected threads, we perform a depth-through analysis of the code in order to list all the classes, methods and fields used, discarding the others. Our static analysis makes use of constant value propagation in order to compute a precise control flow graph and detect more unused objects. In addition to the removal of these objects, it is possible to remove their references in the static zones in order to compress them.

The use of a specific installation process such as Java Card or OSGI would allow even better results, mainly placing more objects in read-only memory. Indeed, the installation functions allow to go further in the deployment process. However, we intend to provide a Java platform that is able to load and execute traditional Java applications and not only applications in a specific format.

System Projection. In order to transform the off-board deployed system into its binary image, the romizer builds the dependency graph of all the objects of the system. All the objects it contains are walked through in order to assign them a destination memory. This computation is made thanks to the the properties of objects (such as types and values) that are retrieved from the graph of objects. This permits for instance to identify all objects whose type is `Class` and whose field value `state` is `READY` as objects that are immutable. This computation also provides the relationships between objects. For example, all the objects attached to the `staticZone` field of an instance of `Class` must be described in the memory mapping as objects that must be placed in writable memory. Building the graph of objects is also an elegant way to discard useless objects. Indeed, the references to these objects are broken, thus making them unreachable and garbage collectable when the graph is built.

All along the loading process, some objects become immutable and others become useless. Next section shows the evolution of the amount of data in ROM and the overall size of the system at each step of the deployment.

5 Results

This section measures the benefits of deploying the system off-board. The size of the system and the amount of data in ROM are measured after each step of the deployment. The parts of the OS written in native code are not included in our measurements, although it will eventually be executed from a read-only memory. Three applications are measured. The first one is a basic *Hello World* application which shows the memory footprint of a minimal application. The second one is Sun's *AllRichards* which executes seven versions of the Richard scheduling algorithm. This application is interesting because it includes a high number of classes (76). Finally, the well-known *Dhrystone* benchmark is measured, showing quite different results because it uses several static data structures.

Details concerning the impact on the run-time features are also discussed.

5.1 Loading

In addition to objects that are immutable as soon as they are instantiated (strings), the majority of objects become immutable once the classes are loaded. Excepted objects that are immutable as soon as they are created (as strings), the majority of objects become immutable once the classes are loaded. All methods containing a bytecode that will be changed during the linking phase are mutable. However, parts of code that do not contain such bytecodes can be placed in

ROM after this step; 9% are concerned for AllRichards. The compaction of the constant pools allows to reduce their initial size by about 160 Kilobytes.

Table 1 gives the size of the system and the size of data it is possible to place in read-only memory if the system were to be embedded just after this step.

Table 1. System sizes (in Kilobytes) after loading phase

Benchmark	**Size (KB)**	**in ROM (KB)**	**% in ROM**
HelloWorld	308	181	59%
AllRichards	411	185	45%
Dhrystone	315	170	54%

5.2 Linking

We have seen that the linking phase is important. After this step, all classes (17 Kilobytes for *AllRichards*) and methods (60 Kilobytes for *AllRichards*) can be placed in ROM. As bytecodes are mutated, a greater number of bytecode arrays become immutable (33 Kilobytes over 87 Kilobytes). In addition, other entries in the constant pools become useless, allowing to re-compact them. This leads to the measuqrements given in table 2.

Table 2. System sizes (in Kilobytes) after linking phase

Benchmark	**Size (KB)**	**in ROM (KB)**	**% in ROM**
HelloWorld	242	181	78%
AllRichards	319	258	81%
Dhrystone	247	194	79%

5.3 Initializing Static Fields

Initializing the static fields turns the classes into state `READY`. Once the classes are in this state, all bytecodes can be replaced by their linked counterparts, leading all fractions of code (87 Kilobytes) to be immutable. The benefits of this phase also include to avoid these initializations when the device starts up. Table 3 presents the measurements we have done when all the classes are in the state `READY`. These results takes account of the sizes of the objects allocated by the

Table 3. System size (in Kilobytes) after initialization phase

Benchmark	**Size (KB)**	**in ROM (KB)**	**% in ROM**
HelloWorld	245	236	96%
AllRichards	323	307	95%
Dhrystone	318	238	75%

static statements. In particular, the overall size of the system for *Dhrystone* is greater than at the previous step because this application allocates 64Kilobytes of static arrays that will be modified at run-time.

5.4 Threads Deployment

Deploying threads allows to dramatically reduce the size of the system, as presented in table 4. In particular, only 6440 bytes of classes, 14 Kilobytes bytes of methods and 18 Kilobytes of code remains for *AllRichards*.

Table 4. System size (in bytes) after threads creation and analysis

Benchmark	Size (KB)	in ROM (KB)	% in ROM
HelloWorld	11326	9795	86%
AllRichards	74134	68315	92%
Dhrystone	86558	14316	16%

6 Conclusion

This article addresses the issue of placing parts of a Java-OS in ROM, which is necessary for tiny devices. At each step of the deployment of the system, it is possible to place a number of objects in ROM in order to decrease the necessary quantity of modifiable memory. It is also possible to remove objects that have become useless in order to reduce the overall size of the embedded system.

The mechanisms involved in these optimizations take advantage of the particular deployment process of a Java-OS. We gave results concerning the size of

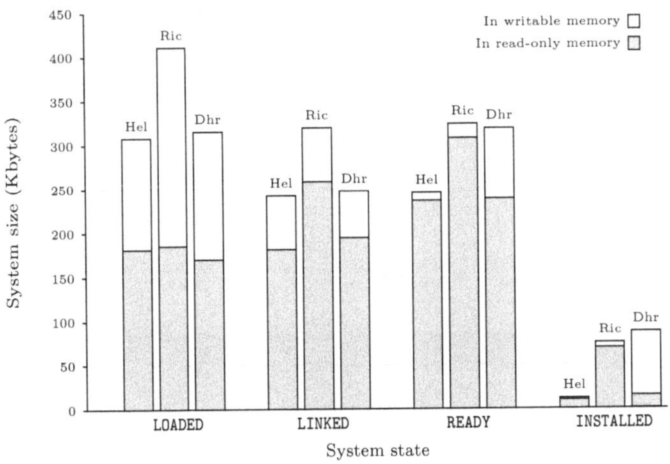

Fig. 1. Memory footprint and repartition across the different states of the system

data it is possible to place in ROM and the overall size of the system. Figure 1 summaries the evolution of these two measurements. It shows that the more the system is initialized off-board, the higher the proportion of objects in ROM is.

References

1. "Java In The Small." http://www.lifl.fr/RD2P/JITS/.
2. D. Rayside and K. Kontogiannis, "Extracting java library subsets for deployment on embedded systems," *Sci. Comput. Program.*, vol. 45, no. 2-3, pp. 245–270, 2002.
3. F. Tip, P. F. Sweeney, C. Laffra, A. Eisma, and D. Streeter, "Practical extraction techniques for java," *ACM Trans. Program. Lang. Syst.*, vol. 24, no. 6, pp. 625–666, 2002.
4. N. Shaylor, D. N. Simon, and W. R. Bush, "A java virtual machine architecture for very small devices," in *LCTES '03: Proceedings of the 2003 ACM SIGPLAN conference on Language, compiler, and tool for embedded systems*, pp. 34–41, ACM Press, 2003.
5. S. Microsystems, "Java 2 plateform, micro edition (j2me)."
6. T. Lindholm and F. Yellin, *The Java Virtual Machine Specification.* Addison-Wesley, 1996.
7. D. Mulchandani, "Java for embedded systems," *IEEE Internet Computing*, vol. 2, no. 3, pp. 30–39, 1998.
8. I. Pechtchanski and V. Sarkar, "Immutability specification and its applications," in *JGI 'O2: Proceedings of the 2002 joint ACM-ISCOPE conference on Java Grande*, pp. 202–211, ACM Press, 2002.
9. S. Microsystems, "The k virtual machine (kvm) white paper. technical report," 1999.
10. C. Rippert, A. Courbot, and G. Grimaud, "A low-footprint class loading mechanism for embedded java virtual machines," in *In Proc. of PPPJ'04.*, ACM Press, 2004.
11. P. Cousot and R. Cousot, "Abstract interpretation: a unified lattice model for static analysis of programs by construction or approximation of fixpoints," in *POPL '77: Proceedings of the 4th ACM SIGACT-SIGPLAN symposium on Principles of programming languages*, pp. 238–252, ACM Press, 1977.
12. F. Tip, P. F. Sweeney, and C. Laffra, "Extracting library-based java applications," *Commun. ACM*, vol. 46, no. 8, pp. 35–40, 2003.

The Research on How to Reduce the Number of EEPROM Writing to Improve Speed of Java Card*

Min-Sik Jin**, Won-Ho Choi, Yoon-Sim Yang, and Min-Soo Jung***

Dept of Computer Engineering, Kyungnam University, Masan, Korea
{comsta6, hoya9499, ysyang, msjung}@kyungnam.ac.kr

Abstract. Java Card technology enables smart cards and other devices with very limited memory to run small applications, called applets. It provides users with a secure and interoperable execution platform that can store and update multiple applications on a single device. This Java Card technology is now a mature and accepted standard smart card standards and SIM technology. However, the main concern of Java Card is now its low execution speed caused by the hardware limitation. In this paper, we propose several ideas about how to improve an execution speed of Java Card. The key idea of our approach is that an EEPROM writing operation is more expensive than that of RAM. We suggest how to use RAM as much as possible; Transaction_In_RAM(TrIR), Resolution_In_RAM and Java Object-buffer.

1 Introduction

Java Card technology [1, 2, 3] enables smart cards and other devices with very limited memory to run small applications, called applets, that employ Java technology such as a platform independence and a dynamic downloading(post-issuance). For these reasons, Java Card technology is an accepted standard for smart card and SIM technology [15]. SIM cards are basically used to authenticate the user and to provide encryption keys for digital voice transmission. However, when fitted with Java Card technology, SIM cards can provide transactional services such as remote banking and ticketing, and also service a post-issuance function to manage and install applications in cards after the cards issued [1, 3, 15].

A Java Card is essentially an Integrated Circuit Card(ICC) with an embedded Java Card Virtual Machine. The Central Processing Unit(CPU) can access three different types of memory: a persistent read-only memory(ROM) which usually contains a basic operating system and the greatest part of the Java Card runtime environment, a persistent read-write memory(EEPROM) which can be used to store code or data even when the card is removed from the reader, and a volatile read-write memory(RAM) in which applications are executed [4, 7].

* This work is supported by Kyungnam University Research Fund, 2005.

** Ph.D Student of Kyungnam University.

*** Professor of Kyungnam University.

L.T. Yang et al. (Eds.): ICESS 2005, LNCS 3820, pp. 71 – 84, 2005.

The major point of criticism with regard to Java for smart cards is its low execution speed. The execution speed of Java bytecode executed by an interpreter is 10 to 20 times slower than program code written in C. Besides of slow speed in terms of Java language, in a traditional Java Card, we first found inefficient parts that are making it more slowly. It is related to many EEPROM writing. The speed of EEPROM write operation is mainly 10000 times slower than that of RAM write operation. It causes a drop in execution speed of Java Card [4].

The first reason of many EEPROM write operations in Java Card is for processing a transaction. Java Card always stores all old values at the referenced location into a transaction buffer in EEPROM during a transaction [1, 3]. We finally found that more than 80% of the number of total EEPROM write operations occurs to process a transaction. The second reason of many EEPROM write operations is for resolution of indirect references during the download of new application called post-issuance. The Java Card installer performs the process of these resolutions that changes many indirect references to real physical addresses of API in Java Card [2]. The third reason is about a single EEPROM write operation with a page-buffer [14].

For these reasons, in this paper, we suggest three ideas to improve the speed of Java Card; the **Transaction_In_RAM(TrIR)** that logs new value, not old value in RAM, new Java Card Installer with the **Resolution_In_RAM** technology that resolves indirect references into direct reference in RAM during the post-issuance and **new Object-buffer** based on a high locality of Java Card objects that are stored in heap area.

This paper is organized as follows. Section 2 describes about Java Card, Java Card memory model, Java Card installer as related works in detail. Section 3 gives a design about how to improve an execution speed of Java Card with Transaction_In_RAM and Resolution_In_RAM technologies that are introduced in this paper by using comparing to those of traditional Java Card. Section 4 explains about algorithms for the implementation of these technologies. Section 5 gives the performance results about each technology separately and also the result after integrating both algorithms. Finally, we present the conclusion and the future work in section 6.

2 The Java Card Environment

2.1 Java Card Memory System

Current and upcoming smart card hardware provides very limited storage capabilities. The memory resources typically consist of Read Only Memory (ROM), Random Access Memory (RAM) and Electrically Erasable Programmable Read Only Memory (EEPROM). EEPROM is used to store long-lived data. In contrast, RAM loses its contents after a power loss and is thus only available for temporary storage.

As illustrated in figure 1, a typical Java Card system places the JCRE code(virtual machine, API classes, and other software) in ROM. Applet code can also be stored in ROM. RAM is used for temporary storage. The Java Card runtime stack is allocated in RAM. Intermediate results, method parameters, and local variables are put on the stack. Native methods, such as those performing cryptographic computations, also save intermediate results in RAM. Longer-lived data such as downloaded applet classes are stored in EEPROM [1, 3, 4, 7].

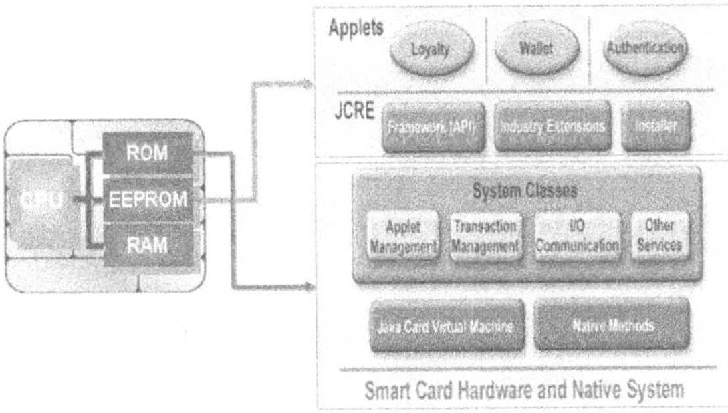

Fig. 1. Java Card Memory Model that is consisted of three areas and its contents

The applet instance and associated persistent objects of an application must survive a session. Therefore they are placed in the non volatile storage on a card, usually EEPROM. EEPROM provides similar read and write access as RAM does. However, The difference of both memory is that writing operations to EEPROM are typically more than 1,000 times slower than to RAM and the possible number of EEPROM writing over the lifetime of a card is physically limited [4].

Table 1. Comparison of memory types used in Smart Card microcontrollers [4]

Type of memory	Number of possible write/erase cycles	Write time per memory cell	Typical cell size
RAM	Unlimited	≈70 ns	≈1700 μm2
EEPROM	100,000~1,000,000	3-10 ms	≈400 μm2

2.2 Java Card Installer for Post-issuance

Applet installation refers to the process of loading applet classes in a CAP file, combining them with the execution state of the Java Card runtime environment, and creating an applet instance to bring the applet into a selectable and execution state [1, 2].

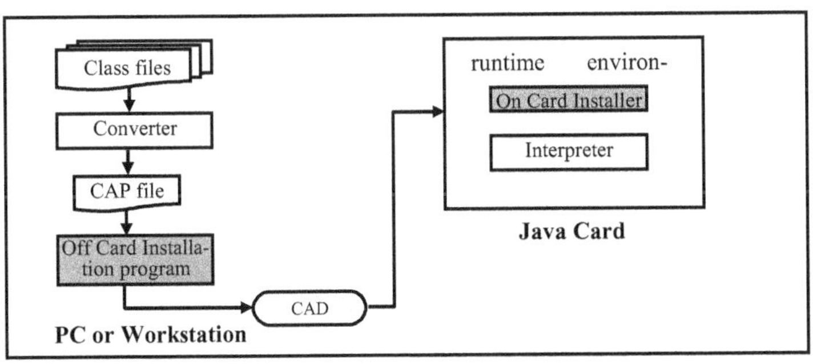

Fig. 2. Java Card Installer and off-card installation program [3]

On the Java Card platform, the loading and installable unit is a CAP file. A CAP file consists of classes that make up a Java package. To load an applet, the off-card installer takes the CAP file and transforms it into a sequence of APDU commands, which carry the CAP file content. By exchanging the APDU commands with the off-card installation program, the on-card installer writes the CAP file content into the card's persistent memory and links the classes in the CAP file with other classes that reside on the card. The installer also creates and initializes any data that are used internally by the JCRE to support the applet. As the last step during applet installation, the installer creates an applet instance an registers the instance with the JCRE.

3 EEPROM Writing of a Typical Java Card

3.1 EEPROM Writing Mechanism

The EEPROM has an internal 128~256 bytes page organization. If the page size is 128bytes, users can write any size of data from 1 to 128 bytes. However when users want to write data that are larger than 128 bytes or overlapped between two pages, users should do memory write management. It may need to call write routine twice, if it is overlapped between two pages, even its size is not more than 128bytes [12, 14].

When Java Card first writes a data in the EEPROM address range, the data is in fact written into the page-buffer. A typical EEPROM update(erase & write) routine will generate the high voltage twice. At that time the data, stored in the page-buffer is transferred into the non-volatile EEPROM cells. After the operation, the page buffer will be cleared automatically.

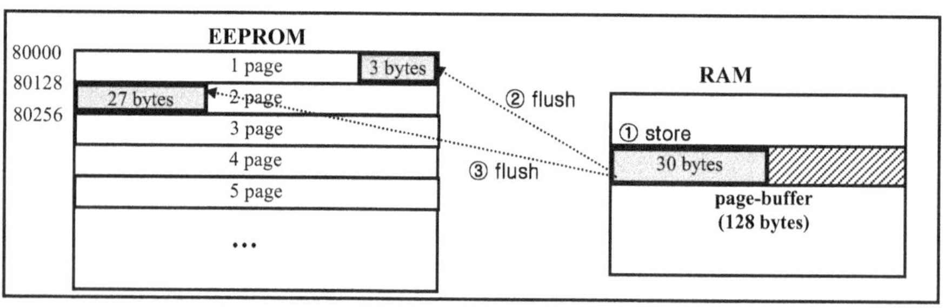

Fig. 3. Writing operation of EEPROM that is organized by 128 bytes by using the page-buffer in RAM

As illustrated in figure 3, if the system writes consecutive 30 bytes (80100~80129), first, The data to be written is transferred to the page-buffer. The data stored in page-buffer on RAM can be available 1-byte up to 128-byte because EEPROM is organized 128-byte. For this reason, only 3 bytes first are written into 1 page area. And then the remainder in the page-buffer is written into 2 page area in EEPROM.

3.2 Basic Java Card Transaction Model Using Old Value Logging

A transaction is a set of modifications performed atomically, which means that either all modifications are performed or none are performed. This is particularly for smart cards, because the card reader powers them: when you unexpectedly remove the card from the reader (this is called "tearing"), it's possible that you're interrupting a critical operation that needed to run to completion. This could put the card in an irrecoverable state and make it unusable.

To prevent this, the Java Card platform offers a transaction mechanism. As soon as a transaction is started, the system must keep track of the changes to the persistent environment(EEPROM). The Java Card must save old value of EEPROM address that will be written into a particular area(T_Buffer) in EEPROM. In other words, If a transactional computation aborts, the Java Card must be able to restore old_value from the T_Buffer in EEPROM to its previous position.

In case of commit, the check_flag byte of the T_Buffer must just be marked invalid and the transaction is completed. In case of abort, the saved values in the buffer are written back to their former locations when the Java Card is re-inserted to CAD.

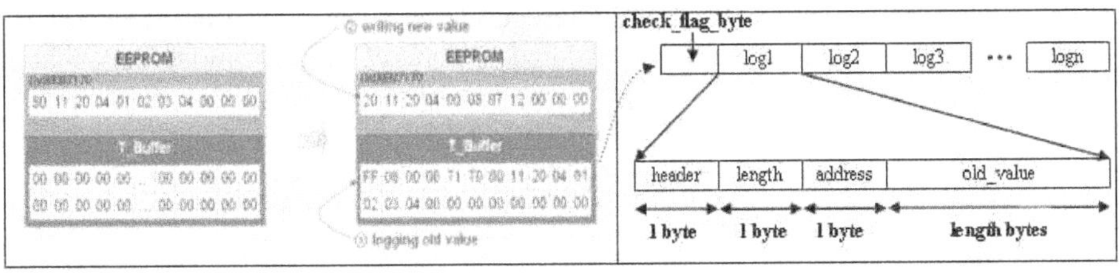

Fig. 4. How to store old values in T_Buffer on EEPROM and the inner structure of T_buffer has a lot of logs and each log consists of 4 parts; header, length, address and old_value

As illustrated figure 4, one object is created by new instruction during the execution. Before this object(20 11 20 04 00 08 87 12) is stored in its address, 0x00087170, old value(80 11 20 04 01 02 03 04) of this address should first be stored in T_Buffer with three additional fields that is mentioned earlier. Finally, new value is stored at the referenced location. In the typical Java Card, all referenced old values are stored T_Buffer area during a transaction. If a transaction is committed without any problems, All old values that T_Buffer has are ignored with a mark as a garbage. However, if a failure occurs before a transaction, the participating fields in the transaction are restored to their original contents from the T_Buffer.

Table 2. The number of EEPROM writing per each area of whole EEPROM during the downloading and executing of each applet

EMV Applet		Wallet Applet	
EEPROM area	the number of writing	EEPROM area	the number of writing
StaticField	1,681	staticfield	752
Heap	1,659	Heap	1,121
T_buffer	**10,121**	**T_buffer**	**8,478**
Total	**13,461**	**Total**	**10,351**

Table 2 below shows the number of EEPROM writing per each area of whole EEPROM. T_buffer area writing is about 75 to 80 percent of total number. The reason why the writing number of this area is higher than other areas is a transaction mechanism of a traditional Java Card to guarantee an atomicity. In a traditional Java Card, this transaction mechanism makes the Java Card more slow and inefficient.

3.3 Basic Java Card Installer with the Resolution in EEPROM

The CAP file has a compact and optimized format, so that a Java package can be efficiently stored and executed on Java Card. Among several components in the CAP file, the constantpool_component and method_component include various types of constants including method and field references which are resolved when the program is linked or downloaded to the Java Card.

As mentioned earlier, the constant pool component has lots of constants that must be resolved during the downloading of CAP file. Before constants are resolved to real addresses, these are consisted of tokens. Namely, the token of each constant is resolved to real address of Java Card API. After the resolution of constants, Java Card performs the resolution of indirect references into constants that are already resolved if bytecodes in methodcomponent have indirect references as an operand. This linking operation of the methodcomponent is executed when a referencelocationcomponent is finally sent to Java Card.

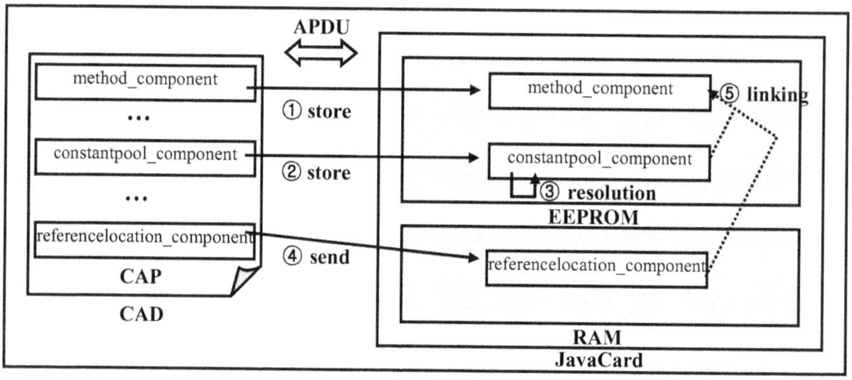

Fig. 5. The procedure for downloading a CAP file with resolution in EEPROM in a traditional Java Card

Figure 5 above shows the procedure for downloading a CAP file. First, both method_component and constantpool_component are saved in heap area in EEPROM. Second, the installer performs the resolution for constants of constantpool_component that is already downloaded. Next, the referencelocation_component is sent to RAM. This component has lists of offsets that must be replaced into constant in constant_poolcomponent among bytecodes in the method_component. Finally, the installer replaces bytecodes in method_component into resolved constants by using the offset data of referencelocation_component [1, 3].

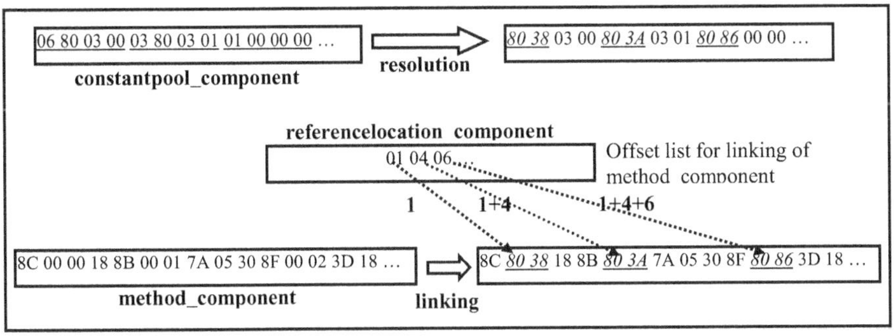

Fig. 6. The raw method_component and resolved constantpool_component saved in EEPROM and the linking result of method_component from constantpool and referencelocation

Consequently, the size of referencelocation means the number of bytecodes that must be replaced in method_component. While referencelocation_component is downloading, Java Card continually changes an operand of bytecodes in method_component as the size of referencelocation. It makes Java Card Installer more slow.

3.4 A Traditional Java Card with One Page-Buffer

As mentioned earlier, a Java Card can write between 1 byte and 128 consecutive bytes with this page buffer into EEPROM. For example, If EEPROM addresses of objects that will be written by a Java Card are sequentially 0x86005 and 0x86000, although both addresses are within 128 bytes, Java Card will first writes one object data in 0x86005 through the page-buffer, and then, after the page-buffer is clear, another object data will be written in 0x86000.

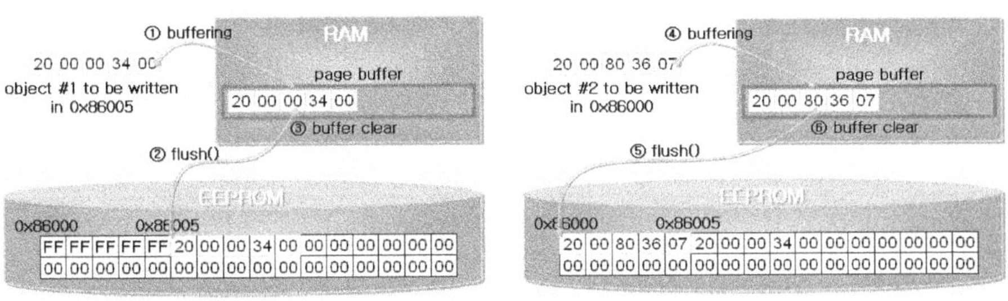

Fig. 7. How to write objects to EEPROM of the traditional Java Card using an inefficient page-buffer algorithm

Above figure 7 shows the page-buffer algorithm of a traditional Java Card. this page-buffer is just to write consecutive data to EEPROM. It dose not have the function for caching.

4 Our Changed Java Card with a Reduced EEPROM Writing

4.1 Our Transaction_In_RAM(TrIR) Technology

As mentioned in the related works, smart cards including a Java Card support a transaction mechanism by saving old_values in EEPROM. The number of EEPROM writing in order to support the transaction is about 75 to 80 percent of the total number of EEPROM writing. EEPROM writing is typically more than 1,000 times slower than writing to RAM. It makes also Java Card much more slow and inefficient.

We suggested new TrIR technology using RAM, not EEPROM in this paper. If such tearing such as power loss happens in the middle of a transaction, all data after transaction began should be ignored. If T_Buffer area to save old_values places in RAM, in case of power loss, RAM is automatically reset. It means the preservation of old_values.

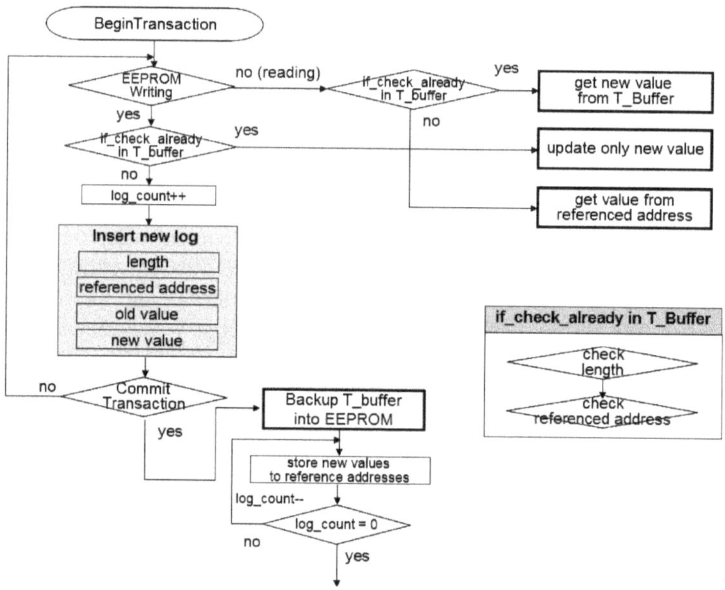

Fig. 8. The algorithm of our TrIR technology that stores new value and old value into T_buffer in RAM

Figure 8 shows the algorithm of our TrIR technology that stores new value and old value into T_buffer in RAM. Our T_Buffer stores new value and old value in T_Buffer on RAM. The last operation of our algorithms is to move all new values in T_Buffer to referenced addresses. If tearing such as power loss happens during this operation, new data that are already changed at target addresses are invalid. For this reason, our T_Buffer has also old values in addition to new values. As soon as a transaction commits, T_Buffer is moved a backup area in EEPROM to prevent this situation.

Table 3. The comparison of between old value logging and new value logging [17]

Old value logging(a traditional JCVM)	New value logging(our algorithm)
- fast read accesses a the up-to-date values are always stored at the referenced location - the original value for a given location must be saved in T_Buffer. - committing a transaction is cheap as the new value are already in place - abort a transaction is expensive as the saved values have to be written back to the original locations.	- a slow read access as the up-to-date values for a location must be searched in the T_Buffer - write operations always have to update the T_Buffer as any new store operation has to be recorded there - committing a transaction is expensive as the new values have to be written to their target locations. - aborting a transaction is cheap as the original values are still in place.

In our algorithm, Read performance lags always behind as T_Buffer must be scanned-typically linearly-for a formerly written value. The situation can be better in case of the much more expensive write operation. As mentioned earlier, writing costs is more expensive than reading costs and EEPROM writing costs also is much more expensive than RAM writing costs. The total number of EEPROM writing to support a transaction is reduced by 50%.

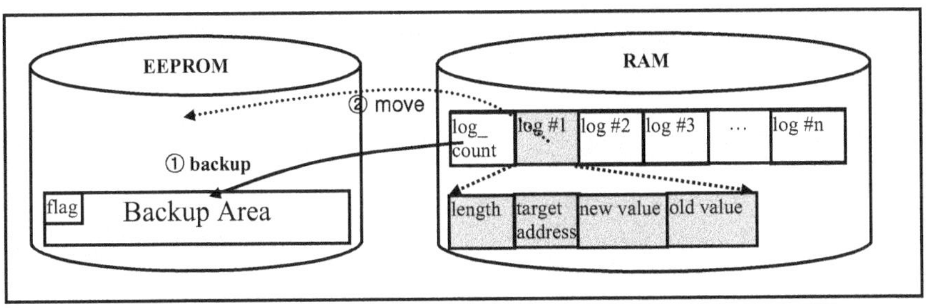

Fig. 9. Backup Area in EEPROM and new structure of T_Buffer that consists of 4 fields: length, target address, new value and old value

4.2 Our Resolution_In_RAM Technology

Our changed installer is very simple. The key idea of our Installer is to use RAM as much as possible by resolving indirect references [5] in RAM, not EEPROM. The important difference of both memory types is that writing to RAM is typically more than 1000 times faster than that to EEPROM.

Our changed installer has more flexible than a traditional one. Especially, the size of method_component is not always fixed. It means that the size of component can exceed the remaining size of RAM. For this reason, when downloading a referencelocation_component, first of all, the installer checks the total size of a method_component to calculate proper block-size for resolution. Figure 5 show The resolution and linking procedure of our changed installer using a RAM Area. The operation of ⑤ to ⑦ repeats until the end of referencelocation_component.

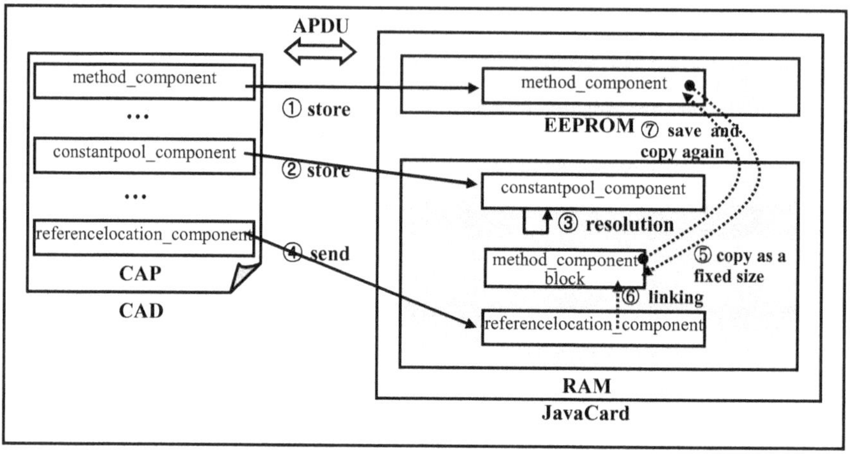

Fig. 10. The resolution and linking procedure of our changed installer using a RAM Area

4.3 Our Object-Buffer Based on Java Card Objects with a High Locality

When an applet is executed on Java Card, if the information such as objects and class data that the applet writes are close to each other, the total number of EEPROM writing would be reduced by adding a caching function to the page-buffer. First of all, to do this, the writing address of objects and data created by Java Card must have a high locality. It causes the number of EEPROM writing to reduce and also makes a hitting rate of caching function more high.

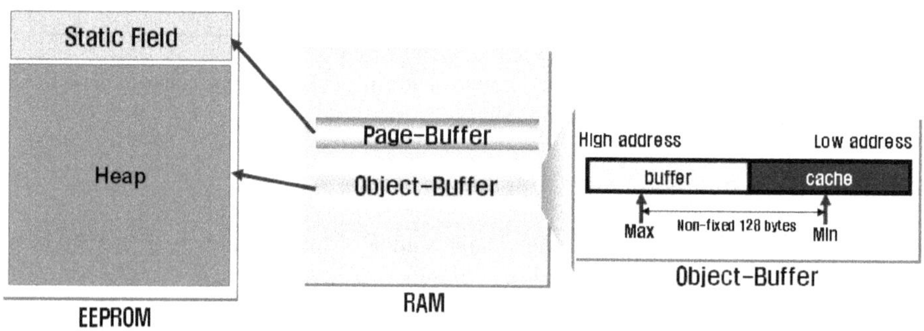

Fig. 11. Heap-buffer that consists of 2 part; the buffer and cache. The data between Min and Max can be written to EEPROM at a time.

In chapter 3, we explained how to write data in EEPROM by using one page buffer in a traditional Java Card in the low level. We also discovered that all objects and data that the Java Card creates during the execution have a high locality. It means that an additional caching function makes the number of EEPROM writing go down. For these reasons, we developed new Java Card with two page buffer in RAM; one is the existing page buffer for non-heap area, another (Object-buffer) is for heap area in EEPROM. The heap area is where objects created by Java Card are allocated.

In our changed Java Card, the existing page buffer is the very same that of a traditional Java Card in terms of a size and a function. The existing page buffer can write between 1 byte and up to 128 consecutive bytes to non-heap area at a time. However, our Object-buffer is for only heap area in EEPROM. The object-buffer of 256 bytes consists of 2 parts; 128 bytes for a buffer, 128 bytes for a cache.

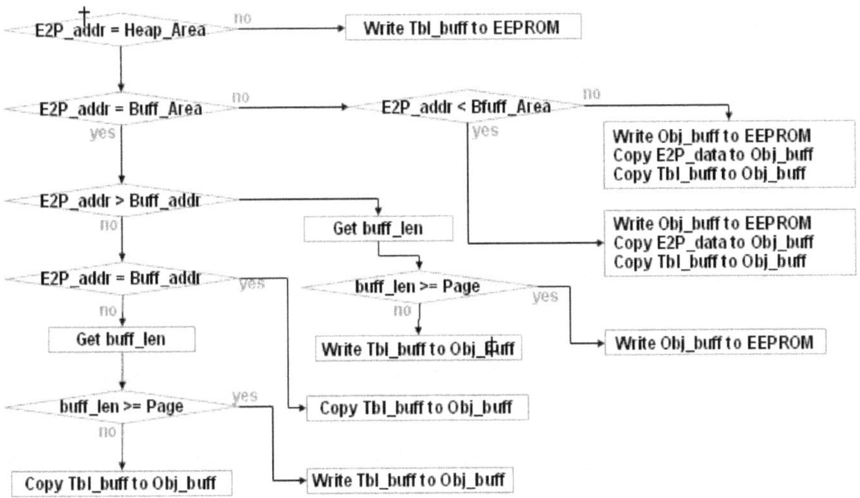

Fig. 12. The Object-buffer algorithm that checks continually the Min and Max points to write the object-buffer to EEPROM when Java Card writes data to heap area. (†E2p_addr : the EEPROM address that data will be written, ‡ heap_buff(Obj_buff) : our new heap buffer with caching and buffering function for just heap area in EEPROM).

Figure 12 above shows the main algorithm using the Object-buffer and page-buffer The writing of non heap-area is performed with the existing page buffer. The writing of heap-area is executed with the Object-buffer. When the Java Card writes data related to Java Card objects into heap area of EEPROM, the first operation is to get 128 bytes lower than the address that will be written and to copy them to the cache area of the Object-buffer. Next, the buffer area(128-byte) of the Object-buffer is cleared. Two points, Max and Min have the highest and lowest points that are written after Java Card get new 256 bytes to the Object-buffer. the gap between them continually is checked in order to write the heap buffer to EEPROM. Max and Min are non-fixed points to raise the efficiency of the heap buffer. The reason why the gap between Max and Min is 128 bytes is that our target chip, CalmCore16, supports the EEPROM writing of 128 bytes at a once.

5 Evaluation of Our Approach

The key of our approach is to improve an execution speed of the Java Card by reducing the number of EEPROM writing. The main idea is also that EEPROM writes are typically more than 1,000 times slower than writes to RAM. One of the analyzed results of a traditional Java Card is that Java Card logs old values in T_Buffer area on EEPROM during a transaction and has one low-level page-buffer to write data to EEPROM regardless of the high locality of Java objects and has an installer using a resolution in EEPROM. For this reason, we developed new TrIR technology, new heap-buffer and new installer.

①	②	③

JCSystem.begin_transaction();
byte a = new byte[5];
JCSystem.commit_transaction();
	JCSystem.begin_transaction();
	byte a1 = new byte[5];
	byte a2 = new byte[5];
	...
	byte a5 = new byte[5]
	JCSystem.commit_transaction();
		JCSystem.begin_transaction();
		byte a1 = new byte[5];
		byte a2 = new byte[5];
		...
		byte a10 = new byte[5]
		JCSystem.commit_transaction();

	①	②	③
Traditional	41.720 ms	150.475 ms	301.295 ms
Our approach(TrIR)	26.163 ms	83.173 ms	130.278 ms

Fig. 13. The comparison of an execution speed between a traditional Java Card and our changed Java Card with the TrIR technology using the different number of the *new* operator

Below Table 4 and Figure 14 below shows the comparison between a traditional Java Card and our changed Java Card in regard to the number of EEPROM writing and the execution speed. During the dynamic downloading of applets called a post-issuance, the speed of downloading, installation and execution is also reduced by 44%. Consequentially, the reduced EEPROM writing caused Java Card to improve an execution speed.

One applet consists of over 11 components that include all information of one applet package. We also produced downloading results about each component. Basically, when Java Card installer downloads one applet, the component that takes a long time is the referencelocation component. The reason is that both are related to the resolution of indirect references during the downloading. Our approach almost reduced the downloading time of the referencelocation by 50%.

Table 4. The comparison between a traditional Java Card and our changed Java Card with regard to an execution speed. (Experiment is made with CalmCore16 MCU [14], SAMSUNG MicroController for smart card).

Applets	Original	Our approach	Reduced Rate
Channel Demo	76140	35645	53%
JavaLoyalty	72703	42495	42%
JavaPurse	232109	123944	47%
ObjDelDemo	159420	94898	40%
PackageA	90530	53498	41%
PackageB	74859	42342	43%
PackageC	32734	17322	47%
Photocard	64608	38934	40%
RMIDemo	57328	33243	42%
Wallet	57140	32156	44%
EMV small Applet	61766	35476	43%
EMV Large Applet	119812	64834	46%
Average			44%

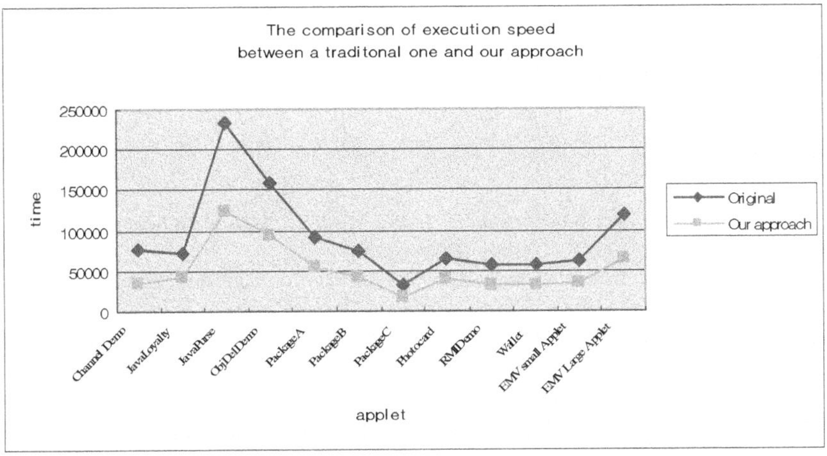

Fig. 14. The comparison between a traditional Java Card and our changed Java Card with regard to an execution speed

Components	Traditional	Our Approach	Reduce
Initialize	1485	1688	-203
Select Install	6281	3812	2469
CAP Begin	1234	485	749
Header	3562	2156	1406
Directory	3969	2344	1625
Import	2875	1640	1235
Applet	3250	1922	1328
Class	2203	1484	719
Method	11266	8541	2625
StaticField	2297	1469	828
ConstantPool	6781	4984	1797
ReferenceLocation	9141	4719	4422
CAP End	625	422	203
Create Applet	2171	1672	499
Total	57140	37438	19702

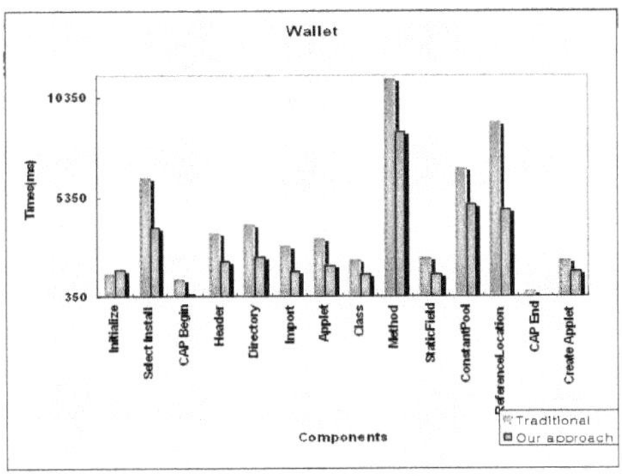

Fig. 15. The comparison between a traditional Java Card and our changed Java Card in regard to Wallet applet's downloading and execution speed per each component

6 Conclusion and Future Work

Java Card technology is already a standard for smart cards and SIM cards [11, 15]. A Java language is basically slower than other languages. The card platforms also have a heavy hardware limitation. In spite of a Java's slow speed, the reasons why Java Card technology is selected as a standard are a post-issuance and a platform independence. When Java Card downloads new application, a post-issuance generally spends a lot of time [10, 11].

In this paper, we have proposed the method to reduce the number of EEPROM writing with new TrIR mechanism, new installer and new Object-buffer based on the high locality of Java Card objects. It also makes the downloading time and execution time of Java Card more fast. With our approach, the number of EEPROM writing and the downloading speed reduced by 80% and 44% separately. It also enables an application to be downloaded more quickly in the case of an application sent to a mobile phone via the GSM network (SIM).

References

1. Sun Microsystems, Inc. JavaCard 2.2.1 Virtual Machine Specification. Sun Microsystems, Inc. URL: http://java.sun.com/products/javacard (2003).
2. Sun Microsystems, Inc. JavaCard 2.2.1 Runtime Environment Specification. Sun Microsystems, Inc. URL: http://java.sun.com/products/javacard (2003).
3. Chen, Z. Java Card Technology for Smart Cards: Architecture and programmer's guide. Addison Wesley, Reading, Massachusetts (2001).
4. W.Rankl,. W.Effing,. : Smart Card Handbook Third Edition, John Wiley & Sons (2001).
5. James Gosling, Bill Joy, Guy Steele, and Gilad Bracha. : The Java Language Specification, Second Edition. Addison-Wesley, http://java.sun.com/docs/books/jls/index.html (2001).
6. Marcus Oestreicher, Ksheerabdhi Krishna. : USENIX Workshop on Smartcard Technology, Chicago, Illinois, USA, May 10–11, 1999.
7. M. Oestreicher and K. Ksheeradbhi, "Object Lifetimes in JavaCard," Proc. Usenix Workshop Smart Card Technology, Usenix Assoc., Berkeley, Calif., (1999) 129–137.
8. Michael Baentsch, Peter Buhler, Thomas Eirich, Frank Höring, and Marcus Oestreicher, IBM Zurich Research Laboratory, Java Card From Hype to Reality (1999).
9. Pieter H. Hartel , Luc Moreau. : Formalizing the safety of Java, the Java virtual machine, and Java card, ACM Computing Surveys (CSUR), Vol..33 No.4, (2001) 517-558.
10. M.Oestreicher, "Transactions in JavaCard,", Proc. Annual Computer Security Applications Conf., IEEE Computer Society Press, Los Alamitos, Calif., to appear, Dec. 1999.
11. Kim, J. S., and Hsu, Y.2000. Memory system behavior of Java programs: methodlogy and analysis. In Proceedings of the ACM Java Grande 2000 Conference, June.
12. http://www.gemplus.com. : OTA White Paper. Gemplus (2002).
13. The 3rd Generation Partnership Project. : Technical Specification Group Terminals Security Mechanisms for the (U)SIM application toolkit. 3GPP (2002).
14. MCULAND, http://mculand.com/e/sub1/s1main.htm.
15. X. Leroy. Bytecode verification for Java smart card. Software Practice & Experience, 2002 319-340.
16. SAMSUNG, http://www.samsung.com/Products/Semiconductor.
17. SIMAlliance, http://www.simalliance.org.
18. Beckert, B., Mostowski, W.: A program logic for handling Java Card's transaction mechanism. In Pezze, M., ed.: Fundamental Approaches to Software Engineering, FASE'2003. Volume 2621 of Lecture Notes in Computer Science. (2003) 246-260.
19. Oestreicher, M.: Transactions in Java Card. In: 15th Annual Computer Security Applications Conf. (ACSAC), Phoenix, Arizona, IEEE Computer. Soc, Los Alamitos, California (1999) 291-298.

A Packet Property-Based Task Scheduling Policy for Control Plane OS in NP-Based Applications

Shoumeng Yan, Xingshe Zhou, Fan Zhang, and Yaping Wang

School of Computer Science, Northwestern Polytechnic University, Shaanxi Xi'an 710072
yansm@mail.nwpu.edu.cn

Abstract. In NP-based networking elements, there are various kinds of packet traffic between data plane and control plane, which have different priorities and are handled by different tasks running on control plane OS. The critical packets need to be processed in time, otherwise the system, even the network, may enter some unstable states. Thus, the packets should be processed according to their priorities, i.e., packet-processing tasks for more important packets should be executed sooner if they are both in ready state. From the perspective of control plane OS design, packet-processing tasks should be scheduled based on some properties of packets waiting to be processed. This paper proposes a packet property-based task scheduling policy to alleviate the problem. The design and implementation are described and the performance results are discussed. The results show that this scheduling policy can achieve our design goal properly.

1 Introduction

Increasing requirements of network rates and sophisticated networking services make the traditional networking devices based on GPP or ASIC become a bottleneck of networking applications. As a solution, Network Processor (NP), which has high processing rate and flexible programming ability, is adopted in the design of networking application systems more and more widely. NP generally consists of multiple packet processing engines and a general purpose processor. Networking elements like routers and switches often involve two cooperating planes: one is used for fast packet processing (data plane), and the other is used for exception handling, data plane configuration and routing/signaling protocol processing (control plane). As for a NP-based solution, works in the two planes are often accomplished by the processing engines and general processor individually. There is no operating system running on the processing engines because data plane functions are usually less complex but more performance critical. However, for its complexity, control plane is often equipped with an embedded operating system.

It is evident that there are various kinds of packet flows between the two planes, especially from data plane to control plane, and each of which may have a unique priority. Accordingly, on the control plane operating system, there are many different handling tasks for these packets respectively, such as routing protocol daemons. These tasks usually have a loop logic as "calling receiving system call[1]→packet

[1] Receiving system calls include select, receive, and send etc.

L.T. Yang et al. (Eds.): ICESS 2005, LNCS 3820, pp. 85 – 95, 2005.

handling→calling receiving system call". In general, control plane tasks can run slower than data plane ones. But, it does not mean that the control plane functions are not time critical. In some routing protocols [1], for example, if packets for keeping alive between neighbors cannot be responded in time, router may be declared down, and which cause a network wide recalculation of the topology. **For these critical packets, we can expect naturally the related handling tasks should start to run as soon as possible after packets arrive. Furthermore, if there are multiple packets having arrived at the same time, their handling tasks should be executed in a suitable order according to priorities of these packets.**

However, commonly used control plane OS, e.g., VxWorks and Linux, are lack of capability to guarantee that. Now, we consider what happens in Linux with a packet handling task. If the receiving buffer of a task is empty, the receiving system call will block the task until some packet arrives and make buffer non-empty. After that, the task will enter ready state. However, it does not mean the task will be scheduled to run immediately although the scheduling policy in Linux tries to give a higher priority to the task that are blocked before being waken up. The reason is that there may exist many other packet handling tasks, or even other I/O tasks having been waken up just now. As Linux does not differentiate packet handling tasks with ordinary I/O tasks and does not distinguish among packet handling tasks, a task for the most critical packet may not necessarily be able to acquire CPU and the packet processing may be delayed. This delay could be tens of milliseconds (We name this delay as **scheduling delay**.). If other delays in packet journey are also taken into account, we will find there maybe a quite long latency since a packet is sent out until the packet is handled. In many occasions mentioned above, this delay may be too long to be acceptable.

To alleviate this condition, we suggest associating task scheduling with packet attributes and propose a packet property-based task scheduling policy for control plane OS in NP-based devices. The scheduling policy is able to derive a suitable priority of the handling tasks according to attributes of the packets they are handling currently. Thus, it can make more critical packets get processed sooner and suffer shorter delay. From its open source property and its broad application in network devices, Linux is chosen as the basis of our study.

The rest of this paper is organized as follows. Section 2 reports related works. Section 3 gives an overview of relevant implementation in Linux. Section 4 proposes the design of the packet property-based task scheduling policy and discusses the implementation of individual components. In section 5, performance evaluation is presented. Section 6 discusses an improved method and section 7 summarizes the paper.

2 Related Works

Because commonly used operating systems like Linux are not designed for network processing purposely, they are lack of scheduling support for packet processing. Previous researches mainly focus on general real-time performance improvement techniques such as preemptive kernel [2, 3, 4], high-resolution timer [5, 6], and scheduling policies [7] based on task attributes, e.g., period or deadline of task. Works in preemptive kernel and high-resolution timer are not in conflict with our packet property-based scheduling policy because they are for the same goal but address different aspects of the problem. In fact, they can be good supporting mechanisms for our scheduling policy. As for scheduling policies based on task attributes, we think they are not suitable for network processing environments. In such environments, it is difficult to determine task attributes like period and deadline because packet arrival has an asynchronous and even random fashion. Thus, these scheduling policies are difficult to be applied in network processing systems.

AEM [8], an asynchronous event mechanism in Carrier Grade Linux [11], also aims at shortening the delay that events suffered. If a packet is viewed as an event, AEM can be applied for our goal. However, AEM requires all the tasks are programmed with a completely new programming model. Considering the abundance of applications currently running on Linux, there will be a huge amount of porting work to be done. On the contrary, our scheduling policy does not require any modification to existing applications.

3 An Overview of Relevant Implementation in Linux

Because our study is based on Linux, we now present an overview of relevant implementation in Linux to give readers some related knowledge. The kernel under investigation is 2.4.22.

3.1 Kernel Behavior After Packet Arrival

When a packet arrives, the protocol stack will firstly determine whether its destination is local or remote. If the packet is for a remote host, *ip_forward* routine is called to forward the packet. Otherwise, if the packet is for local delivery, *sock_queue_rcv_skb* routine is called to append the packet to a socket receiving buffer. Then, in *sock_queue_rcv_skb* routine, *data_ready*, a function pointer to *sock_def_readable*, is called. If the handling task for the packet is sleeping on its socket, it is awakened by *wake_up_interruptible* routine invocated in *sock_def_readable*. Finally, *wake_up_interruptible* puts the task into the ready list through calling *try_to_wake_up*, which will call *reschedule_idle* routine next. If *reschedule_idle* routine finds that priority of current process is less than the awakened one, it will set *need_schedule* flag to inform the scheduler to do reschedule.

3.2 The Scheduler

In Linux, a scheduling cycle is called an *epoch*. At the beginning of each epoch, the scheduler allocates a time slice, of which default value is about 60ms, to each task including the ones in sleeping state. The time slice of current task is decreased at each timer interrupt. When the time slice of each ready task becomes zero, current epoch is terminated and the scheduler allocates time slice for all the tasks again.

The scheduling policy is implemented in the *schedule* routine, which is used to determine which task should acquire CPU. The routine is called when the time slice of current task is exhausted, when current task returns to user space from system call or after interrupt handling, when current task goes to sleep, or when a new task is put into the ready list. *schedule* routine calculates priority or weight of each task via invocation of the *goodness* routine and selects the task with biggest priority to run. The algorithm of *goodness*() is as follows:

if counter!=0, weight = 20 + counter− nice;
else weight = 0.

Here, *counter* records the remaining number of ticks of task time slice, of which initial value is about 6. If a task is occupying CPU, its *counter* will decrease with time. *nice* can be used by user to improve or reduce the priority of a process, which has the following relation with the initial value of *counter*: *initial value of counter = (20-nice)/4 + 1.* Generally, *nice* ranges between -20 and 19. Thus, we can infer that the initial value of *counter* should ranges between *1* and *11*. Moreover, when *nice* is -*20*, *counter* gets *11*. As we know, the default value of *nice* is *0*, and thus the default value of *counter* is *6*.

If time slice of all the ready tasks is exhausted, *schedule* will reallocate time slice for all the tasks according to the following formula.

counter = (counter/2) + (20 - nice)/4 + 1

After the reallocation, all ready tasks have time slice equal to *initial value of counter*. For each sleeping task, the time slice is equal to the summation of *initial value of counter* and half the remaining time slice. Thus, in effect, the weight of sleeping tasks is improved to make them more competitive after they are awakened. But, the improvement is limited and not beyond two times of *(20-nice)/4+1* [9]. When *nice* is equal to *-20*, *counter* has maximum value of *22*, which is recorded as ***CounterLimit***. As we has explained above, this priority improvement for sleeping tasks is not enough and can not guarantee that packet handling task is scheduled to run right after packet arrives. Thus, we design a packet property-based scheduling policy to address the problem.

4 Task Scheduling Policy Based on Packet Property

4.1 Concept of the Design

The proposed scheduling policy will discriminate not only between packet handling tasks and other tasks such as IO handling tasks, but also among packet handling tasks according to property of packets being processed. The scheduling framework is illustrated in Fig. 1 and discussed as follows.

After a packet arrives, a property table is looked up with packet metadata as input to find the priority of the packet.

If lookup succeeds, i.e., there exists a matched item in the table, priority of the handling task for that packet is calculated according to the packet priority. In our policy, the calculated priority of handling tasks will be higher than other tasks and the higher the priority of its packet, the higher the priority of the handling task. This guarantees the handling tasks for more crucial packets can get more advantaged position in competition for CPU and thus have a shorter scheduling delay to process the packets in time.

If lookup fails, it means the system does not regard that packet as critical. Hence, in our policy, the related handling task is treated as normal task and will be scheduled with the original policy of Linux.

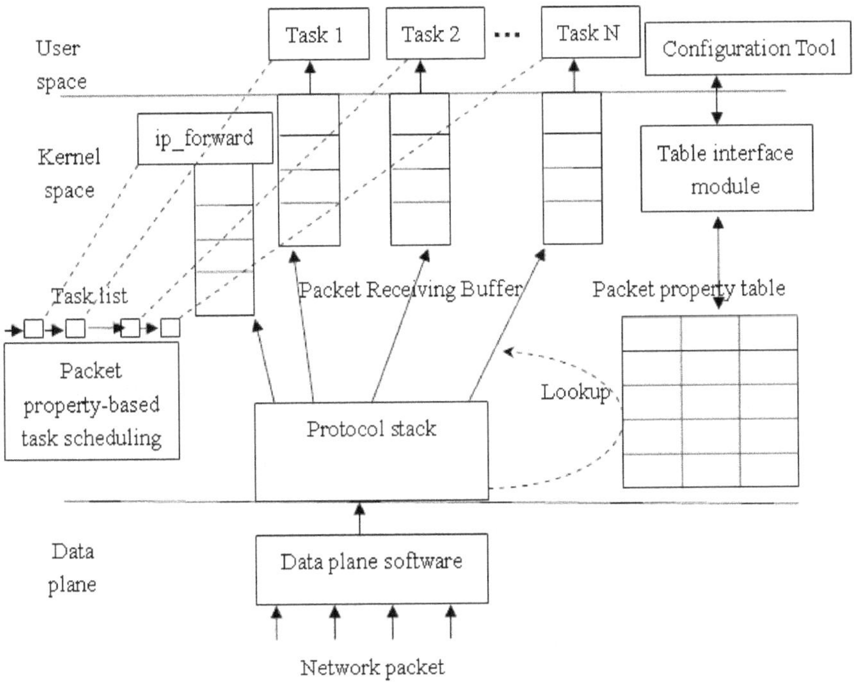

Fig. 1. Packet Property-based Task Scheduling Framework

It has to be noted that in general, this policy will not let handling tasks with higher priorities to starve ones with lower priorities because packet handling usually takes a very short time. However, for fear that some handling tasks enter an abnormal state in some conditions, e.g., enters a dead loop due to programming bugs, we design a guaranteeing mechanism to detect the ill-behaved tasks and degrade them to normal tasks. This mechanism is presented in detail in section 6.

Our packet property-based task scheduling policy is transparent to applications. That means the existing applications need no modification and development of new applications can also pay no attention to it. In fact, an application can be not aware of the underlying scheduling policy at all, but can benefit from it.

4.2 Packet Property Table and Packet Priority Determining Algorithm

Our scheduling framework relies on a packet property table which consists of many packet property records. Each record has some packet attribute fields and a priority field. The Kernel will look up the table to determine priority of handling task before waking it up. In theory, properties of packet can be any combination of its metadata or payload. But, for simplicity, we now only consider the metadata of packet. A record can have the following format.

(ip_protocol, dst_ip, dst_port, src_ip, src_port, packet_priority)

Here, *ip_protocol* is *protocol* field in IP header of packet, which need to be set if you want to give some protocol certain priority. *dst_ip* is the destination IP address of packet, which has direct relation to a physical port of certain line card. If you want to give a priority to packets from certain data plane physical port, you should set *dst_ip* field. *dst_port* is the destination port of packet. *src_ip* and *src_port* is source IP address and source port of packet respectively. *packet_priority* is the priority you want to give the matched packets, which should be greater than zero.

Not all the fields of a property record must be set except for *packet_priority* field. Some fields may be simply left as blank, which means these fields can match anything. Packet property table is maintained by system administrator with configuration tool illustrated in Fig. 1. On the other hand, the table can be set by applications using programming API.

When we have the packet property table, we can determine packet priority by looking up the table in appropriate occasion. Obviously, packet priority should be decided before it is put into a socket receiving buffer. Thus, according to the discussion in section 3.1, we should add the implementation of packet priority determining algorithm in *sock_queue_rcv_skb* routine.

In essence, packet priority determining algorithm is a process of table lookup, i.e., looking up the packet property table with packet metadata and obtaining the *packet_priority* field of the matched record. To accelerate the lookup, we design two data structure, i.e., a fast cache and a hash table. Thus, the algorithm is a two level lookup process as follows.

(1) After a packet arrives, a fast cache matching process is started through comparison between packet metadata and cache content. If succeed, goto (3.)

(2) If fast cache matching fails, a hash key is calculated based on packet metadata and the key is used to search the hash table. When a conflict in hash process is encountered, we use a chain to solve the conflict.

(3) A successful fast cache matching or hash table searching returns the packet_priority field of the resulting record.

(4) If above fast cache matching and hash table searching both fails, we know that there is no matched record for the packet. Thus, zero is returned. A zero value indicates that the system regard the packet as an unimportant packet and the related handling task is treated as a normal Linux task.

Up to now, priority of packet is determined (We should add a field in Linux *sk_buff* struct to record the result). Then, the packet is to be put into one socket receiving buffer (a linked list). The packet is not simply appended at the tail of the list but it is inserted at a suitable position to guarantee the list has a descendent order by *packet_priority* from head to tail. Because handling task always take packet from list head, the sorted linked list structure in effect can guarantee that **at least for the same task , the higher the packet priority is, the sooner the packet is served.**

4.3 Task Priority Determining Algorithm

Now that we have packet priority determined, we can then determine task priority. According to the description in section 3.2, we implement the task priority determining algorithm in *goodness* routine. Thus, we have a new *goodness* routine as follows.

(1) *If packetProFlag is TRUE, goto (2). Otherwise, goto (3).*
(2) *weight = 20 + CounterLimit + packet_priority – nice.*
(3) *If Counter is not zero, weight = 20 + counter –nice. Otherwise, weight = 0.*

Here, *packetProFlag*, a new field in task_struct of Linux, indicates whether a task is for packet handling or not.

In the new goodness routine, we can see, packet handling tasks will obtain advantageous position compared with common Linux tasks because ***CounterLimit*** is greater than counter. As for different packet handling tasks, the priorities of them are determined by priorities of the packets being processed now. This means handling tasks for more critical packets will win the competition for CPU. Thus, it is true **for many different tasks that the higher the packet priority is, the sooner the packet is served.** Considering the conclusion in section 4.2, we in fact guarantee that **for all packets in all socket receiving buffers the higher the packet priority is, the sooner the packet is served.**

4.4 Manipulating the Packet Handling Task Flag

In the new implementation of *goodness*, we have introduced a *packetProFlag* variable. In this section, we will discuss when and how to set or clear the flag for each task. When a packet arrives, there are two cases for its handling task.

Case 1: Handling task is now being blocked to wait for packet
According to analysis in section 3.1, the handling task is sleeping on a socket in this case. We can set its *packetProFlag* in *sock_def_readable* just before kernel wakes up it by *wake_up_interruptible* invocation. The process can be depicted as follows. Firstly, *packet_priority* field in *sk_buff* structure of packet is copied to the field with same name but in *task_struct* of related task. If *packet_priority* is greater than zero, i.e., there exists matched record for the packet in property table, *packetProFlag* is set to TRUE. Otherwise, it is set to FALSE. Hereafter, *goodness* will be called by Linux kernel to compare the priority of the task that is just awakened with that of current task. If the awakened task has higher priority than current task, kernel will set *need_schedule* flag to TRUE. This then triggers a kernel reschedule procedure. We can infer that if current task is a common Linux task but not packet handling task, its priority will always be lower than the awakened task and thus the awakened packet handling task will be scheduled to run in time.

Case 2: Handling task is now not being blocked to wait for packet
In this case, the handling task is now processing other packet while a new packet is arriving. The new packet will be put into socket receiving buffer by kernel, and when the task issues another receiving system call, it will return immediately because it can get packet from the buffer. We can modify the implementation of the receiving system calls and add codes to manipulate the *packetProFlag*. In our new receiving system call implementations, *packet_priority* field in *sk_buff* structure of packet is copied to the field with same name but in *task_struct* of current task. As in case 1, if *packet_priority* is greater than zero, *packetProFlag* is set to TRUE. If not, it is set to FALSE. At the same time, *need_schedule* is set to TRUE, which triggers the kernel to do reschedule. After the reschedule, if current task is still the task with highest priority, it keeps to run. Otherwise, it means there must be a task just awakened by a packet with higher priority and current task has to be preempted out.

4.5 Redesign of *ip_forward*

From the analysis in section 3.1, we know that kernel protocol stack will invoke *ip_forward* routine to forward the packets for remote host. In current implementation of Linux, this forwarding routine executes in a soft interrupt environment and thus has a higher priority than packet handling task. However, in control plane OS for network processor, many packets for local delivery have higher priority than packets to be forwarded in fact. Thus, forwarding should not always be preferred and the design of forwarding process should be retrofitted. Our proposal is to give *ip_forward* an incarnation of Linux kernel thread, which makes it get out of soft interrupt environment. Besides, we add a forwarding buffer for the *ip_forward* kernel thread mimicking the socket receiving buffer of packet handling task. The kernel protocol stack will put the packet to be forwarded to the forwarding buffer. As a kernel thread, *ip_forward* will loop to check the forwarding buffer. If the buffer is empty, it will be blocked. If not, it will read a packet from the buffer and forward it out. Thus, in essence, *ip_forward* thread now has a common structure with packet handling task and can be regarded as a packet handling task. That is to say, the packet property-based scheduling policy can be applied to this thread too. We can set various records in the packet property table for different data flows to be forwarded. In this way, *ip_forward* can introduce some flavor of QoS through giving different treatment to packets belonging to different data flow, which is obviously better than the original FIFO implementation.

4.6 Packet Property Table Configuration Tool and API

In addition to modifications to kernel presented above, we also provide system users a table configuration tool to manipulate the packet property table. As illustrated in Fig. 1, the tool consists of two components: a table interface kernel module and a user space tool. The kernel module implements table reading and writing functions and provide IOCTL interfaces through a character device to user space applications. The user space tool fulfills table manipulating commands from system administrator through issuing IOCTL calls to the character device. The system administrator can construct suitable table records in system wide based on his knowledge of the system using the configuration tool. The IOCTL interfaces can be used as the programming API by developers of packet handling application to set task wide records in the packet property table.

If user does not want to give some packets importance any more, he can simply remove related records. This make the handling tasks behave as normal Linux tasks when such packets arrive. Thus, we can say our proposed scheduling policy is very flexible in real application.

5 Performance Evaluations

Packet property-based scheduling will make packet handling tasks get higher priorities than normal Linux tasks and their priorities are proportional to importance of the packets they are handling. As a result, such a scheduling policy should make packet handling tasks for more critical packets experience shorter scheduling delay.

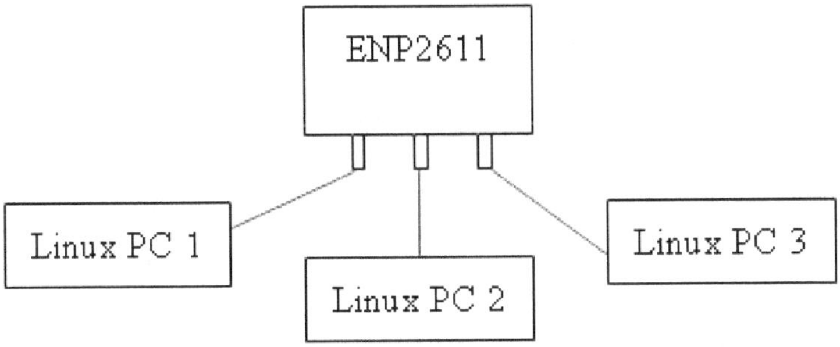

Fig. 2. Experiment Platform

And as for total delay packets experienced, the conclusion should also be true because scheduling delay is part of the total delay. Thus, in our experiments, delays that packets experienced are measured.

Our experiment platform is illustrated as Fig. 2. There is an ENP2611 [10] network processor board and three Linux/PCs. They are connected through gigabit fiber channel. On each PC, there runs a *UDP client* program which sends a packet of 500 bytes to ENP2611 board with predefined interval (i.e., 30ms for PC1, 40ms for PC2, and 50 ms for PC3). On control plane of ENP2611, i.e., the XScale processor, there runs three *UDP servers* which receive packets from the three *UDP clients* individually and send back the received packets immediately as acknowledgements. Besides, there are 20 or 40 background common tasks (*bckgrd*) which possess a loop logic as "computing for 10ms→sleeping for 200ms→computing for 10ms". According to original scheduling policy of Linux, sleeping periodically will make *bckgrd* tasks get relatively high priority after being awakened. Thus, they are very advantageous competitors for CPU in original Linux.

We give packets from the three *UDP clients* different priorities individually through setting property table, i.e., give low priority to packets with 30ms interval, medium priority to packets with 40ms interval, and high priority to packets with 50ms interval. We measure the time since *UDP clients* sent packet out until they received the reply for common Linux case and extended Linux case. In each experiment, we let each *UDP client* send out 100,000 packets.

The results are shown in Table 1. For constraints of paper length, we only present in the table the delay data of packets with high priority. As for packets for low and medium priority, our results show that they experience a little longer delay than packets with high priority, but the *bckgrd*s have no influence on them. This proves that packet handling task has advantage over common Linux task.

From table 1, we can see that on original Linux, packets of high importance was still delayed for so large a time span that it is cannot tolerable in some cases mentioned in section 1. The long delay is because that original Linux does not differentiate among packets and not differentiate between packet handling tasks and common I/O processing tasks (In our experiments, *bckgrd* simulates the behavior of I/O processing task.). However, in the extended Linux, the average packet round trip time and round trip time of most packets both stay at a very lower level. Also, the results for packets with high priority are not influenced by the number of *bckgrd* and other packets with lower priority.

Table 1. Experimental Results

	Packet Number with RoundTripTime< 200us	Packet Number with RoundTripTime>10ms	Average RoundTripTime
Original Linux (20 bckgrd)	93,578	2,019	178us
Extended Linux (20 bckgrd)	99,958	5	89us
Original Linux (40 bckgrd)	91,244	3,019	271us
Extended Linux (40 bckgrd)	99,957	4	91us

6 An Improved Algorithm

In general, our scheduling policy will not let handling tasks with higher priority to starve ones with lower priority because packet handling usually takes a very short time. However, in some abnormal cases, e.g., a packet handling task enters a dead loop due to programming bugs, the task will not go to sleep and thus not relinquish the CPU until packet with higher priority arrives. If no packet with higher priority arrives for a long period, other tasks will be starved. To attack such a problem, it is necessary to have a guaranteeing mechanism to detect the ill-behaved tasks and get it out of the abnormal conditions in time. In our design, a variable called *packetProCounter* denoting the maximum time slice a packet handling task can have, is introduced for each packet handling task. This variable can have different value from *counter* variable of common task but will be decreased at the same time when *counter* is decreased (Usually, the decrease is done when timer interrupt occurs). When the handling task is scheduled to run due to it has the packet with highest priority, the *packetProCounter* variable is initialized. And later, its value is decreased when each timer interrupt occurs. Here, we have an expectation that the task should go to sleep before the maximum time slice is exhausted. Thus, if the packet handling task still runs when *packetProCounter* becomes zero, the kernel knows that there should be something wrong with the task. In this case, the kernel will degrade this packet handling task to a common Linux task (The kernel simply sets its packetProFlag to FALSE.). Thus, this ill-behaved task will no longer have advantages over other tasks and will not starve other tasks any more.

With this mechanism integrated, we have an improved algorithm for *goodness* as follows.

(1) *If* packetProFlag *is TRUE, goto (2). Otherwise, goto (3).*
(2) *If* packetProCounter *is not zero, weight=20+CounterLimit+packet_priority-nice; Otherwise,* weight=*0 and packetProFlag is set to FALSE.*
(3) *If* counter *is not zero, weight=20+counter-nice; Otherwise,* weight=*0.*

7 Conclusions

This paper proposes a packet property-based task scheduling policy for control plane operating system of NP-based network elements. This policy determines priority of packet handling task based on properties of the packets it in charge of. With this scheduling policy, we can make packets get processed in an appropriate order and keep the system or even the network away from some related unstable states. The experimental results show that the scheduling policy can achieve our design goal properly. Because the research is for network processing system purposely, the scheduling policy is only for packet handling now. But, with minor extensions, we believe the policy can also be used to handle other events. In the future, we will extend current work and form a more general event property-based task scheduling policy.

Acknowledgements

This work is supported by the 863 project of China (No. 2003AA1Z2100) and the Scientific and Technological Innovation Foundation for Youth teachers of NPU (No. M016213). We gratefully acknowledge the financial and technical support from the committee of the 863 project. We also wish to thank the anonymous reviewers for their constructive comments.

References

1. RFC 2328 - OSPF Version 2, http://www.faqs.org/rfcs/rfc2328.html
2. MontaVista, Powering the embedded revolution, http://www.mvista.com.
3. Shui Oikawa and Raj Rajkumar, Linux/RK: A portable resource kernel in Linux. In IEEE Real-Time Systems Symposium, December 1998.
4. Yu-Chung and Kwei-Jay Lin. Enhancing the real-time capability of the Linux kernel. In IEEE Real Time Computing Systems and Applications, October 1998.
5. Mohit Aron and Peter Druschel, Soft timers: Efficient microsecond software timer support for network processing, ACM Transactions on Computer Systems, August 2000.
6. KURT Linux, http://www.ittc.ku.edu/kurt/
7. Linux Kernel Scheduler Enhancements, http://tik.cs.hut.fi/~knuppone/kernel/
8. AEM – The Linux Asynchronous Event Machanism, http://aem.sourceforge.net/
9. D. Bovet and M. Cesati, Understanding the Linux Kernel, O'Reilly & Associates, 2001.
10. Radisys, ENP2611 Data Sheet, Radisys, 2003
11. Carrier Grade Linux, http://www.osdl.org/lab_activities/carrier_grade_linux/

RBLS: A Role Based Context Storage Scheme for Sensornet*

Qin Huaifeng and Zhou Xingshe

School of Computer Science, Northwestern Polytechnical University
qinhf@mail.nwpu.edu.cn
zhouxs@nwpu.edu.cn

Abstract. To addressing the self adaptation problem arises from large scale densely deployed sensornet, we argue that integrating the principle of context aware with sensornet is feasible. To build such a context aware sensornet, proper context describing and storing mechanisms must be provided. In this paper, we propose RBLS, a Role Based Local Storage scheme. RBLS is designed simple and energy efficient. Aimed at providing context storage support for sensornet, RBLS stores contexts at node's local space and dynamically allocates extra spaces according to the roles a node holding. A "snapshot" is used by RBLS to record a neighbor's private contexts. We evaluate the performance of RBLS against a primitive scheme. Simulation results are included in this paper.

1 Introduction

Advances in MEMS technology, wireless communications, and digital electronics have enabled the development of low-cost, low-power, multifunctional sensor nodes that integrating the ability of sensing, computing, and communication[1]. The low per node cost will enable the development of densely distributed sensor networks for a wide range of applications. While single sensor node can perform signal processing and computation, its ability is limited. Nodes in these dense networks will coordinate to accomplish sensing task. These large number of wireless connected sensor nodes composed a distributed ad hoc network which we call sensornet. Usually, sensornet is deployed in remote and hostile environment where manual configuration is not always possible. To achieve scalable, robust and long-lived goal, nodes of sensornet must be self adaptable. Learning the lesson from context aware computing, we proposed the idea of context aware sensornet (CASN) [2]. Nodes of CASN are able to adjust their behaviors according to the relevant situation, that is, be context aware.

One of the challenge arises from CASN is the representation of context. To efficiently using context, context aware systems should provide permanent or temporal context storage schemes. As most of the traditional context aware systems are built upon well defined infrastructure, they care little about context storage problem. There are many off the shelf database products can be selected by these systems to store context. However, the situation of CASN is different. In CASN, there is no mature data storage technology can be directly applied. The limited memory size and battery energy of sensor node worsen the problem of context storage in CASN.

* The paper is supported by Doctorate Foundation of Northwestern Polytechnical University (No.200348).

L.T. Yang et al. (Eds.): ICESS 2005, LNCS 3820, pp. 96 – 106, 2005.

Different from traditional context aware system, we consider that CASN is node centric. That is, the situations of the node and the neighbor but not the situations of the human are important to CASN. Limited by the radio range, to communicating with other nodes hops away, one node must depend on its neighbors to relay the packets. Therefore, node's neighbors are the immediate objects a node can interact with. We believe that the contexts of the neighbors' have important impact on node's decision of adjusting its behaviors while other peer nodes' context may have no effect on it. Also, there are some global contexts which are meaningful to the node. For example, the location of the sink node can contribute to selecting next hop node in a context aware routing algorithm. But we argue that accessing global context is not frequently happened in CASN. Be node centric, query of context is initiated within sensornet by the sensor node but not by the user of the sensornet. Again, this kind of query is frequently initiated between pairs of adjacent nodes. Considering the costs of communication, storing contexts on a centric point (within or outside the sensornet) is inefficient and energy consumptive. Therefore storing node's context locally is more suitable and can results in significant energy savings [3].

In a summary, context storage problem of CASN exhibit following features:

- A node can act as both the producer of the context and the consumer of the context.
- There are global contexts in CASN.
- Contexts of neighbors have important impact on node's behavior.
- Partial query and local storage is the primary query & storage mode of CASN.

Considering the features above, in this paper, we proposed a role based local storage scheme, which we call RBLS (Role Based Local Storage). RBLS is designed simple and energy efficient. It is a distributed storage scheme. There is no single centric storage point provided in RBLS. Sensornet scale up or adding new context has gentle effects on the overhead of RBLS.

In this paper, we present the motivation and the algorithms of RBLS. The remainder of this paper is organized as follows. Section 2 reviews some related research work. Section 3 describes our previous. Then in section 4 we present our approach of RBLS. Section 5 gives a simulation result and conclusions are in Section 6.

2 Backgrounds and Related Work

Computers in traditional context aware systems are designed to adapt its behavior according to the context of user. However, be node centric, each node of CASN is expected to adjust its behaviors according to the situation of other peer nodes. A node can get services from other nodes. It can also provide services to other nodes. However, sensor node is indistinctive from one to another. This makes it difficult to program specific actions for specific node. To distinguish these indistinctive nodes, we proposed a sensor society model to modeling sensornet[2]. A sensornet can be modeled as *sensoc*:

Sensoc=(SAgent, SCL, SRole, SRule, f)

- *SAgent* is a non-empty set of society member.
- *SCL* is the communication language of society.

- *SRole* is a non-empty set of society role names.
- *SRule* is the sets of social rule all members should obey.
- *f(SAgent* $\times$ *T)* $\rightarrow$ *SRole* This function indicates that at time *t*, each member of the society should be assigned at least one role.

Each role is associated with certain services. By modeling sensornet using sensor society, each node of sensornet is assigned at least one role. It is assumed that all the nodes have the common knowledge of sensor society. Therefore, a node can match the required services based on the roles held by its neighbors. Consequently, a pair of nodes can act properly according to the roles they are holding. "Role" is an important concept in CASN. It is also useful to settle the cooperative relationship between nodes. When considering the enable technologies of CASN, we find that "role" plays important role.

Referring Dey's definition of context[4], we defined context of CASN as: *Context of CASN is any information that can be used to characterize the situation of the entity that is involved in sensornet actions. Entities of CASN include sensor nodes, sensing task and sensing data.* This definition is given under the background of sensornet. Based on this definition, context of CASN is categorized into node context (including role context), task context and sensing data context. To use context effectively, context must be represented properly. However, restricted by node's limited resource, existing context represent technologies such as ontology based method can not be applied in CASN. Referring ontology's concept of knowledge sharing, we proposed a Micro Sensornet Ontology (μSONG). μSONG provides simple and flexible way to expressing context. It is also helpful when reasoning high level context in CASN[1].μSONG provides: (1) a set of CASN context vocabulary; (2) formalized context describing method; (3) semi-formalized relationship describing method.

Another important work of context representation is providing permanent or temporal context storage scheme. While most of the traditional context aware systems care little about context storage problem, resource restricted feature of sensornet extrude the problem distinctively.

Most of the traditional context aware researches apply off the shelf database products to store permanent context. However, those database products are too big to be adopted by CASN.

Data management is one of the hottest research topics of sensornet. Many researches have studied the data storage problems of sensornet, such as[3;5-9], etc. However, considering the application backgrounds of sensornet, how to manage data streams originated from thousands of sensor nodes in energy efficient manner and report the events occurred in target regions to the user timely is crucial to these researches. As boosted by the need of the specific application, technologies derived from these researched are usually application specific and need specific supporting infrastructure. Queries are usually initiated outside the sensornet by sensornet user. As data type, data scale and data accessing modes of these two kinds of schemes are different, a special designed light weighted context storage scheme for CASN is required.

---

[1] Detailed introduction of μSONG is beyond the scope of this paper. We will discuss it in another paper.

3 Our Approach of Context Storage

In this section, we first show a primitive way of context storage. Then referring to this primitive scheme, we discuss our role based context storage scheme.

3.1 A Primitive Way

As discussed before, considering the context accessing mode of CASN, storing context on node is reasonable. A node provides context to its neighbor, but it also gets context from its neighbors. A context storage scheme should facilitate the context storing and accessing between nodes.

A primitive context storage scheme is allocating all the required spaces in one time. Considering the node be a context provider, the scheme allocates spaces for each context listed in μSONG vocabulary. Let's tag the region allocated as *S*. Now, considering the node be a context consumer, a simple way to get neighbors' contexts is copying their contexts to node's local space. At the first time, node copies the whole *S* from its neighbor, after that, it only updates neighbor's changing contexts. Therefore, the available contexts a node can get are the collections of contexts its neighbors provided. When a node gets global context from one of its neighbor, it updates the corresponding context it provided and inform the change to its neighbors. Then neighbors of this node also get this global context.

Let's use s denoting the size of μSONG vocabulary, use $t(i)$ denoting the space required by *i-th* context. Supposing each node has n neighbors. Then using this primitive storage scheme, the spaces required by a node can be expressed as:

$$(n+1)\times\sum_{i=1}^{s}t(i) \tag{1}$$

The advantages of this primitive scheme lie in that it is simple to implement and it can ease the localized processing of context. However, its disadvantage is also distinct. First, the contexts a node can provide are uncertain during life of the node. Allocating spaces for all the contexts listed in μSONG vocabulary wastes node's precious memory space. Second, as many nodes can provide same global context, copying all the contexts from a node's neighbors may result storing redundant contexts. Finally, if s and n are large enough, totally spaces required by a node will very big. Besides this, required spaces will increase rapidly when sensornet grown bigger or new context added in.

3.2 Node's Local Contexts

Obviously, a node does not necessarily providing all the contexts in μSONG vocabulary. To study the minimized contexts set node is required to provide, we decompose the contexts residing on the nodes. Fig.1 shows the contexts residing on n nodes.

Fig.1 divided contexts into two parts. The one is basic context which is used to characterize the situation of the node. Some situations or properties of the node are common for all the nodes, such as node's ID and node's location, etc. Basic context is used for these common situations. The knowledge of basic context is sharing among nodes. Therefore if node *A* wants to query the basic context of node *B*, *A* needs not to ask if *B* can provide it. *A* can directly query required context by name.

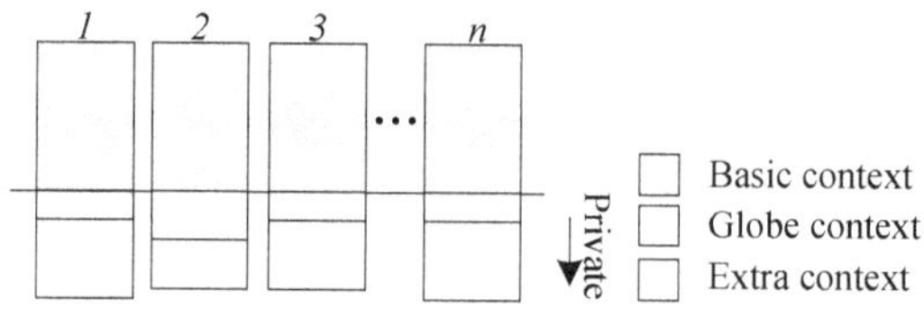

Fig. 1. Node's local contexts

Except basic context, other contexts residing on the node are categorized into private context. A node has no previous knowledge of its neighbor's private context. Therefore if node *A* wants to query the private context of node *B*, the first thing it need to do is confirm that *B* can provide specific context. Private context includes global context and extra context. Supposing global context is diffused through the sensornet from one node to another, different node may have different global context. When node undertakes specific processing, it may get extra contexts and provides them consequently. For example, to execute sensing task, a node may get and provide task contexts.

The number of node's private context is uncertain. Therefore, dealing the uncertainty of node's private context is important to designing reasonable context storage scheme.

3.3 Role Based Local Storage Scheme

Based on the analysis above, we proposed a localized context storage scheme - Role Based Local Storage (RBLS). The motivation of RBLS is storing minimal contexts on node. Therefore, RBLS avoids allocating storage space for all the contexts in one time. Also, RBLS does not support totally copy neighbor's contexts to local space.

We argue that the difference of nodes' private context is actually resulted from the different roles nodes holding. For example, if the role *Sensor* is held by the node that execute sensing task and the role *Router* is held by the node that help forwarding sensing data, the contexts required by these tow roles may different. A *Sensor* node may require specific task contexts to decide the types of sensor, the frequency of sampling, the duration of sensing task, etc. While a *Router* node may need the location context of target node. These specific required contexts are node's private contexts.

In our sensor society model, Post Condition (PoC) of holding role explicitly expresses the extra information required by the node who holding this role. If we use a CRD (Context Requirement Descriptor) expressing the extra contexts required by holding specific role, then the extra contexts required (and thus provided) by a node is determinable at runtime.

Working process of RBLS can be simply described as below. Initially, RBLS allocates context storage spaces for basic context. Then based on the roles held by node, RBLS calculates CRD and allocates extra context storage spaces for the node. When the node lost specific role, context spaces that no longer required are freed by RBLS.

Because RBLS does not support totally copy neighbor's contexts to local space, when a node wants to query context from its neighbors, it must know which neighbor can provide required context. To address this problem, RBLS records a "snapshot" of neighbors' private context. RBLS maintains "snapshot" for each of its neighbor.

Node's neighbor table is used to store "snapshot". Node Id in neighbor table can index neighbor quickly. Node *C* in Fig.2 has 3 neighbors (*B*, *C* and *D*). As shown in Fig.2, node *C* maintains a neighbor table which stores the "snapshots" of neighbors' private context.

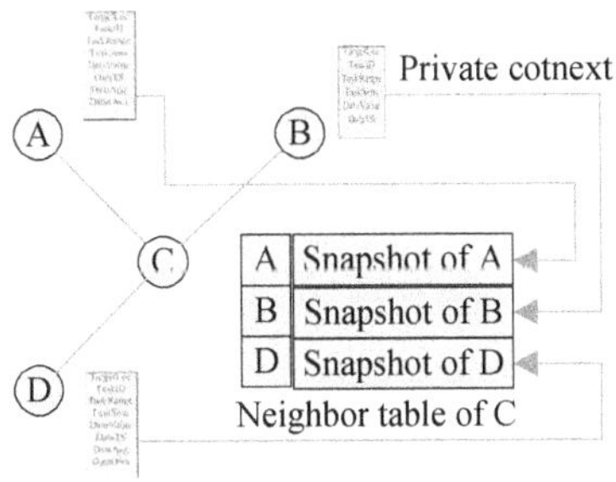

Fig. 2. Snapshots of neighbors'

Supposing the number of node's basic context is *l*, and the number of node's private context is *k*. The space required to store "snapshot" of *i-th* neighbor is marked as $t^{'}(i)$. Then using RBLS, the space required by the node which has *n* neighbors can be expressed as:

$$\sum_{i=1}^{l} t(i) + \sum_{j=1}^{k} t(j) + \sum_{\gamma=1}^{n} t^{'}(\gamma) \tag{2}$$

Because $l + k \leq s$, we get:

$$\sum_{i=1}^{l} t(i) + \sum_{j=1}^{k} t(j) + \sum_{\gamma=1}^{n} t^{'}(\gamma) \leq \sum_{i=1}^{s} t(i) + \sum_{\gamma=1}^{n} t^{'}(\gamma)$$

$$\leq \sum_{i=1}^{s} t(i) + n \max_{1 \leq \gamma \leq n} \left\{ t^{'}(\gamma) \right\}$$

Referring formula (1), we can conclude that if the formula below is valid then RBLS is better than previous primitive scheme. Therefore, the method used to record private context's "snapshot" has strong effect on the performance of RBLS.

$$\max_{1 \leq \gamma \leq n} \left\{ t^{'}(\gamma) \right\} \ll \sum_{i=1}^{s} t(i) \tag{3}$$

3.4 Implementation Issues

In this subsection, we discuss implementation issues related to RBLS.

- **Build CRD**

Removing basic context from μSON vocabulary, we get a set of private context. Let's denote this set as *P*. *P* has *p* members. We use bitmap represent CRD. That is, CRD is a p bits bitmap and each bit of CRD corresponds with a member of P. Setting a bit of CRD to 1 indicates that corresponding context in P is required by role and vice versa.

Bitmap can efficiently reduce the size of CRD. However, if p is large, the size of CRD is also big. For example, if $p=256$, then each role will require 32 bytes to declare its extra contexts requirement. To reduce the size of CRD, bitmap must be compressed. By repartitioning P, we get 4 subsets, i.e. global context, task context, sensing data context and free context. These 4 subsets are marked as P_{Globe}, P_{Task}, P_{Data} and P_{Free} and corresponding size are p_{Globe}, p_{Task}, p_{Data} and p_{Free}. Similar to basic context, P_{Task} includes minimal contexts for characterizing sensing task, while P_{Data} includes minimal contexts for characterizing sensing data. All the other contexts that can not be included in P_{Globe}, P_{Task} and P_{Data} are categorized into P_{Free}. We argue that if a role require task contexts, all the members in P_{Task} are required. Carried the idea farther, as sensing data is the product of executing sensing task, we infer that if a role require task contexts, members in $P_{Task} \cup P_{Data}$ are all necessary. Therefore, as shown in Fig. 3, a p bits bitmap can be compressed to a $p_{Globe}+1+p_{Free}$.

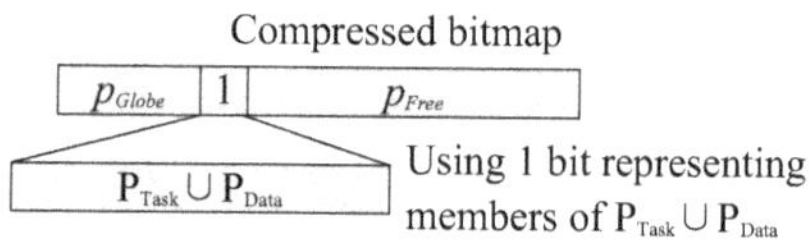

Fig. 3. Bitmap compression

Each node maintains a CRD. Each role is assigned a CRD when definition. To identify them, role's CRD is marked as rCRD. CRD is recalculated when node's holding roles changed. In a summary there are 3 kind of role changing situation: getting new role, getting extra role, and losing role. CRD is recalculated according to one of these 3 situations. Shifting role from one to another is seen as the process of losing one role first then getting another role. During this process, CRD is calculated twice.

- **Allocating spaces for private context**

A node got new role may require extra contexts and need additional storage spaces. While a node lost role may result freeing unnecessary context space. Different from calculating CRD, RBLS does not trigger space reallocating action at each point of role changing. In fact, RBLS reallocates spaces based on calculated CRD. And this is happened when the whole role changing process is finished.

To handle the spaces allocated, RBLS also maintains a CAB (Context Allocation Bitmap) to mark the spaces allocated for. CAB is in fact a copy of CRD. However, after CRD changed, RBLS can compare CAB with CRD to find the contexts that no longer require by the node and correctly free corresponding spaces.

When reallocating spaces for private context, RBLS first frees no longer required spaces then allocates spaces for newly added contexts. When freeing spaces, RBLS calculates the value of $CAB \wedge \neg CRD$. The bits that set to "1" in result indicate that corresponding contexts are no longer required. Fig. 4(a) shows the process of finding contexts that no longer required. To ease illustrating, 8 bits bitmaps are used. Again, when allocating additional spaces, RBLS calculates the value of $\neg CAB \wedge CRD$. The bits that set to "1" in result indicate that corresponding contexts require allocating new spaces. Fig. 4(b) shows the process of finding contexts that require allocating new spaces.

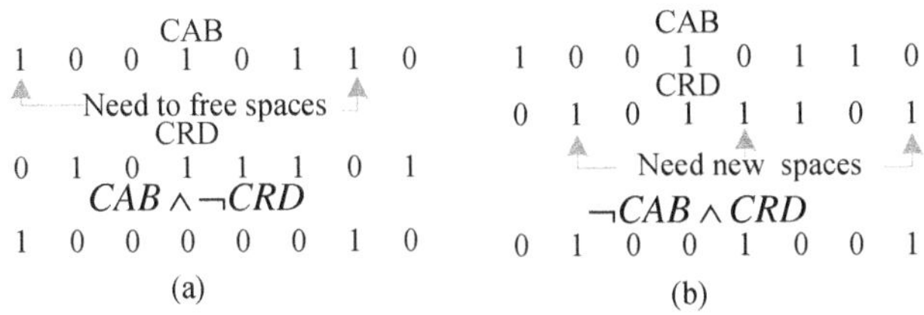

Fig. 4. Free vs. Allocating

- **About "snapshot"**

One good feature of CRD is that it also records the private context node provided. It can be proved that using CRD as snapshot can satisfy the restriction of inequality (3).

Because $s\min\limits_{1\le i\le s}\{t(i)\} < \sum\limits_{i=1}^{s} t(i)$ is valid, to satisfy $\max\limits_{1\le\gamma\le n}\{t'(\gamma)\} \ll \sum\limits_{i=1}^{s} t(i)$, we need to prove that the inequity $\max\limits_{1\le\gamma\le n}\{t'(\gamma)\} \ll s\min\limits_{1\le i\le s}\{t(i)\}$ is valid. As CRD is used as "snapshot", it can be inferred that $\max\limits_{1\le\gamma\le n}\{t'(\gamma)\} = p_{Globe} + 1 + p_{Free}$.

Because $p_{Globe} + 1 + p_{Free} < s$, we only need to prove that $s \ll s\min\limits_{1\le i\le s}\{t(i)\}$ is valid. It is equal to $1 \ll \min\limits_{1\le i\le s}\{t(i)\}$. Obviously, this inequality is valid.

A node gets complete CRDs from its neighbors when building neighbor table at initialization phase. Later, if neighbor's CRD changed, "snapshot" of the neighbor must be synchronized. To reduce packet size, when synchronizing "snapshot", CRD does not always being sent completely. RBLS adopts a zone based way to update "snapshot". As Fig. 3 shown, there are 3 zones in CRD. If the change of CRD occurs only in one of these 3 zones, neighbor can sent only the CRD fragment of that zone to the node. This avoids resending whole CRD every time.

Table 1. CRD zone codes

00	Updating whole CRD	01	Updating *PGlobe* zone only
10	Updating *PTask* ∪ *PData* zone only	11	Updating *PFree* zone only

3.5 Long Term Storage

Long term storage is provided in CASN. However, it is not "long" enough to store history contexts days or months ago. As CASN is node centric, most of the contexts are node's situation related. It is a fact that to adjust node's the behavior, contexts minutes ago is much meaningful than contexts days ago. Therefore, CASN only stores history contexts a short time ago. FIFO queues are used to manage history context. Historic contexts belong to same context are queued into same queue.

4 Simulation Results

We have coded an implementation of RBLS by adding new library into TinyOS[10]. We also evaluate the performance of RBLS using TOSSIM[11].TOSSIM is a simulator for wireless sensor networks. It can capture network behavior at a high fidelity while scaling to thousands of nodes. We employ a grid topology which has same distance between two nodes. Radio range used in TOSSIM is 50 feet. This means each mote transmits its signal in a disc of radius 50 feet. The radio model we used in our simulation is "lossy" model. The "lossy" radio model means that a bit transmitted by a node has a certain chance of being flipped. The probabilities of bit error between pairs of nodes can be generated using LossyBuilder tool which provided with TOSSIM. In our simulation, a node sends CRD to its neighbor respectively. If the neighbor receives CRD, it echoes a respond. Node will send CRD repeatedly until all the neighbor responded or it reaches max retry times.

There are 37 contexts in our simulation. In these contexts, 15 contexts belong to basic contexts; 10 belong to task context; 5 belong to sensing data context; 2 belong to global context and 5 belong to free context. Therefore, there are totally 22 contexts can be used as private context. These 22 contexts can be described using an 8 bit CRD. To simplify the scenario, we assumed that each context occupied 6 bytes space. There are 3 roles (R_1, R_2, and R_3) defined in our simulation. The CRD of *R1* is zero which means that R_1 does not require extra contexts. The CRD of R_2 is 00101000. The CRD of R_3 is 10011100. Each node is originally assigned a role R_1. Node's holding role can shift from one to another. Role shifting actions happen at least once every half-hour. Simulation time is 5 hours after all nodes is initialized.

In our first test, we measured the spaces required by single node that holds R_1 using RBLS and primitive scheme respectively. We vary the number of node's neighbor. Fig.5 (Test#1) shows the result. The result shows that when node's neighbors increased, spaces required by node using primitive scheme increased sharply. However, when using RBLS, space augment was not so remarkable. In our second test, we measured the spaces required by a node when it holds different roles. In this test, node has no neighbor. Fig.5 (Test#2) shows the result. The result reveals that role shifting has no effect on the performance of primitive scheme. However, at each point, using RBLS consumes fewer spaces than using primitive scheme.

Our third test measured the max messages transmitted by node using RBLS. Node density in this test is 4 nodes/35 feet^2. We vary the network size. Fig.5 (Test#3) shows the result. As shown in figure, network size has no significant influence on the performance of RBLS. This result coincides with our expectation. As we mentioned before, node's situation is influenced by the nodes in neighborhood. Therefore result in Fig.5 (Test#3) is reasonable.

In our last test, we measured maintaining costs of RBLS and primitive scheme. We use a moderate network size (100 nodes) and vary the deploy density of sensornet. Fig.5 (Test#4) shows max messages transmitted by node having max neighbors. Simulation result shows that max messages transmitted increase sharply when node density is high. We think this can ascribe to our CRD updating mode. Because a node sends CRD to its neighbor respectively, when node's neighbor increased with the increase of node density, the node must send more messages. Interesting, when the distance between two nodes is close to 50 feet, messages transmitted increased too. We believe this is because bit error rate is increased sharply when the deploy distance close to 50 feet. As a result, node must always resend messages time and times again. Reducing node's retry times may optimize the performance. Results from Fig.5 (Test#4) reveal that maintaining costs of RBLS is much lower than that of primitive scheme.

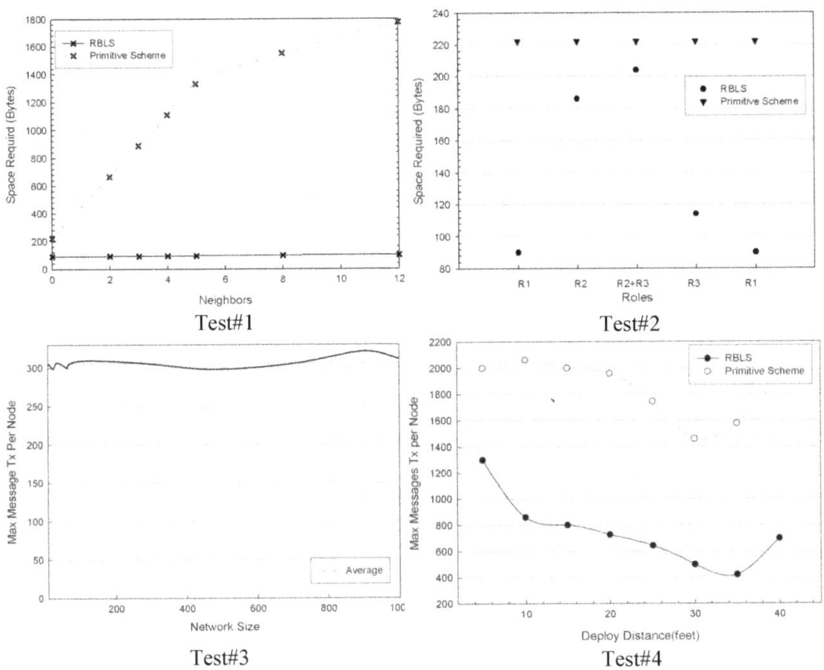

Fig. 5. Simulation result of RBLS

5 Conclusion and Future Work

This paper presented the design and evaluation of RBLS, a context storage scheme for sensornet. Our analysis reveals that dealing the uncertainty of node's private context is important to designing reásonable context storage scheme. We argue that the difference of nodes' private context is actually resulted from the different roles they are assigned. Extra contexts required (and thus provide) by a node can be determined by the roles held by it. RBLS takes advantage of this feature and allocates context storage space dynamically.

In a summary, RBLS is a simple and energy efficient context storage scheme. Our simulation results show that maintaining costs of RBLS is very small comparing to that of primitive scheme. Another good feature of RBLS is that the size of sensornet has no significant effects on its performance. The simulation results show that the number of messages transmitted increases rapidly when node density increased. However, when node density increased, redundant nodes are also increased. We believe that the performance of RBLS can be improved by dynamically turn some redundant nodes off.

A cache may useful for some frequently queried contexts. Currently, we are working to enable RBLS support cache. We expect this feature can improve the performance of RBLS farther. RBLS is one of the enable technologies of CASN. Based on it, we are intending to develop a context managing component to providing transparent context accessing services to CASN applications and other CASN services.

References

[1] I.F.Akyildiz et al., "Wireless Sensor Networks: a survey," *Computer Networks*, vol. 38, no. 4, pp. 393-422, 2002.

[2] Qin Huaifeng and Zhou Xingshe, "Integrating Context Aware with Sensor Network," to appear in *Proceedings of the 1st International Conference on Semantics, Knowledge and Grid (SKG2005)*, 2005.

[3] Deepak Ganesan, Deborah Estrin, and John Heidemann, "DIMENSIONS: Why do we need a new Data Handling architecture for Sensor Networks?," in *Proceedings of the ACM Workshop on Hot Topics in Networks*, pp.143-148, 2002. ACM Press.

[4] Anind K.Dey and Gregory D.Abowd, "Towards a Better Understanding of Context and Context-Awareness," in *Workshop on The What, Who, Where, When, and How of Context-Awareness, as part of the 2000 Conference on Human Factors in Computing Systems (CHI 2000)*, Hague, Netherlands, Apr.2000.

[5] Benjamin Greenstein et al., "DIFS: A Distributed Index for Features in Sensor Networks," in *Proceedings of the First IEEE International Workshop on Sensor Network Protocols and Applications*, May.2003.

[6] Yong Yao and Johannes Gehrke, "The Cougar Approach to In-Network Query Processing in Sensor Networks," *SIGMOD Record*, vol. 31, no. 3, pp. 9-18, 2002.

[7] Samuel Madden et al., "TAG: a Tiny Aggregation Service for Ad-Hoc Sensor Networks," in *Proceedings of the Fifth Symposium on Operating Systems Design and Implementation (OSDI)*, pp.131-146, Boston, MA, USA, Dec.2002.

[8] Xin Li et al., "Multi-dimensional Range Queries in Sensor Networks," in *Proceedings of the First International Conference on Embedded Networked Sensor Systems*, 2003.

[9] Sylvia Ratnasamy et al., "GHT: A Geographic Hash Table for Data-Centric Storage," in *Proceedings of the First ACM International Workshop on Wireless Sensor Networks and Applications (WSNA 2002)*, pp.78-87, Sep.2002.

[10] TinyOS, *http://www.tinyos.net/*, 2005.

[11] Philip Levis et al., "TOSSIM: Accurate and scalable simulation of entire TinyOS applications," in *Proceedings of the First ACM Conference on Embedded Networked Sensor Systems (SenSys 2003)*, Nov.2003.

CDP: Component Development Platform for Communication Protocols

Hong-Jun Dai, Tian-Zhou Chen, Chun Chen, and Jiang-Wei Huang

College of Computer Science, Zhejiang University, Hangzhou 310027, P.R. China
{Dahogn, tzchen, chenc, hjw}@zju.edu.cn

Abstract. Complexity of software systems has significantly grown with social dependence on computer system, especially for mobile and internet. So we present component-based communication protocol architecture. In this architecture, Component Development Platform (CDP) is the kernel software. CDP is one of the rapid communication components' development tools. It is the collection of views and plug-ins to form a series of tools and it takes much flexibility and configuration ability. For the customization of component-based communication protocols, code analysis tools make a good abstract from original practical source codes to visual structure model too. This becomes the feasible guidance and roadmap to develop the components and component-based communication protocols.

1 Introduction

Complexity of software systems has significantly grown with social dependence on computer system. Especially communications become prevalent with more complexity, such as mobile and internet. To deal with these, software systems model with component-based architecture such as COM, CORBA and EJB [7]. Many tools for complex systems have widely used to aid programmers such as IDE and CASE tools.

On the other hand, embedded communication systems have universally used for mobile and internet, for example, wireless mobile telephones and internet routers. It is different with common applications because of the limitation of processor speed or memory capability [2, 3]. This brings different component-based architecture to software development, test and maintenance. It is in great need of convenient tools.

Communications are maintained by communication protocols. The protocols are more complex because of the consideration of synchronization, mutex etc [4]. For embedded systems, there are many kinds of embedded operating systems (EOS). Protocols need transport among various EOS. Furthermore, system support for communications may be partial and fixed because of the hardware limitation, so protocols may transplant according to device too. The transport equals to protocol implementation.

The utilization of component-based communication protocols is a good solution to reduce the repetitive implementation of protocols [6]. This also brings more flexible functionality. We present component-based communication protocol architecture (CCPA) [1] to develop, test, store, assemble and load the components. In this

L.T. Yang et al. (Eds.): ICESS 2005, LNCS 3820, pp. 107 – 116, 2005.

architecture, component development platform is the kernel software. Good development tools can lead to high efficiency.

CDP is an IDE to develop and test the communication components. The protocols for given hardware and EOS are made up with these components. IDE may be not necessary for software development. Usually we can use a series of tools in order, with a name tool-chain. So developers need to read many documents, which describe the developing process from beginning to end. For example, the organization of the projects, the usage of cross-platform compilers and build tools, the test and quality assurance of the products, the storage of the products [5]. Each step uses the specific tool, this makes the development so complex. If CDP exists, we can link all these tools together and use them within this IDE.

For a long time, we have paid much attention to design and implement components. Common compilers such as gcc (g++), JDK, and common commercial IDE such as Visual C++, Borland C++ Builder, are generally used for the protocol development. There is few optimization and customization for the development of communication protocols. We can find the features of this kind of development.

There is a strong resemblance among various protocol implementations. The transport is only suitable for hardware or EOS. We can analyze the existing stable source codes to abstract the unalterable parts. In CCPA, we rewrite these source codes as components, so the analysis should point to the loose coupling points. CDP then provides a guidance to assemble and describe the components.

To reduce the complexity of embedded software development, the process to compile and debug is seldom on chip. We use tool chains target to the embedded systems. There are so many kinds of tool chains that the parameters may be different. We can analyze the common parameters to abstract a list of popular switches. CDP provides a uniform interface to programmers suitable for these tool chains.

The components we get are used to assemble protocols. These need to be more stable and robust, so the components must test strictly. The tests base on two aspects: component itself and assembly global reliability. Not only the quality of components but also the usage into protocols should validate. CDP provides the virtual environments to test components.

On all accounts, CDP is a customized IDE for component-based communication protocol development. The paper first explains CCPA briefly in Part 2, and then introduces the CDP framework as a whole in Part 3. Code analysis abstract is the kernel of the paper and it is illuminated in Part 4. Part 5 gives the implementations with multiple views, various plug-ins and how to link cross-platform compilers.

2 CCPA Overview

CDP is a part of CCPA. CCPA modularizes the implementation of protocols component-based. It is the architecture for the development, storage and utilization of particular components for different EOS. Based on CCPA, We devise multiple light-weight protocol components that are customized for application requirements and device characteristics. We can analyze the existing source codes of the protocols, develop and test qualified components target to different EOS. The stable and certified components store into a library for further reuse. Only necessary components load into devices automatically or manually, keep partly active according to the current network and environment status. The protocols in active can be remote controlled without the communication shutting down.

CCPA includes a set of correlative software systems, such as Component Development Platform (CDP), Component Library (CL), Component Assembly Platform (CAP), and Operating System Support Environment (OSSE). Component Description Language (CDL) joins these software systems together and encapsulates the components description accurately. A general scenario of the architecture illuminates with figure 1.

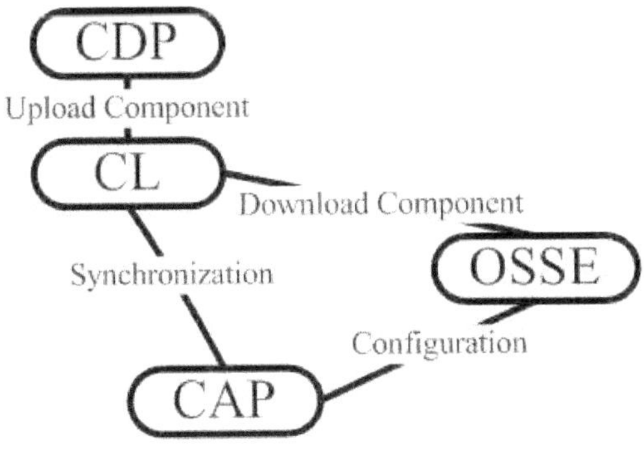

Fig. 1. CCPA Basic Deployment

CDP generates the components suitable for EOS. It uses the certain cross platform tool-chains customized for target EOS. The built binary components need to check the quality and reusability. Only qualified components are regarded as stable and stored into CL. CL is not merely a binary data base for component storage. It does much quality assurance, exchange and component transfer work. OSSE executes on EOS or joins into EOS kernel. It supports the component-based protocols and protocol stacks. It can self-adapt with the application requirements and network environment, or can manually controlled by CAP remotely. OSSE loads or unloads the components while keeps the communication services active.

3 CDP Framework

CDP includes many units, which are shown in figure 2. Code editor is an enhanced text notepad basically. For convenient programming, code assist tools associate tightly to provide the highlight of the reserved words and auto fill-in of source codes according to the build-in templates. These templates support C, C++ and Java etc. Code analysis tools analyze the invoke methods and relations in source codes. Code wizards generate the templates of source codes framework which are universal to given programming model. This avoids the iterative boring work to write the changeless framework codes.

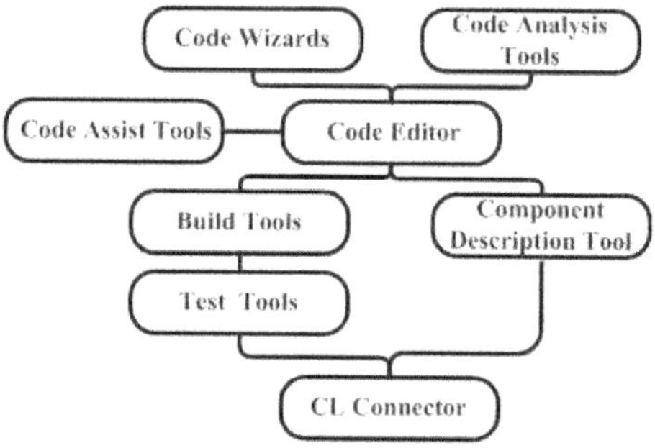

Fig. 2. Main units in CDP structure

Build tools are used to link existing tool-chains to compile and link, through which the source codes compile into binary components executable to target EOS. Test tools check the quality and reusability of the binary component. It can invoke the components on the simulation systems of the target devices and EOS. Press test and integrality test of the component all can finish on these simulation systems. Component description tools create the CDL files. Sometimes, it is graphic interface which fills in the items according to the prompt facilities. This avoids the users to know the details of CDL, because CDL is only the basis of the platform information exchange, it can be merely understood by software. CL Connector transfers the components and the corresponding CDL files to CL. Only the components which have passed the test can upload to CL.

As an IDE, CDP is implemented with Model-View-Control (MVC) patterns. We design many views to help the visual programming. For more flexibility of CDP organization, each unit maintains in figure 2 implements as plug-in. A plug-in may encapsulate the data models and views, it provides extern interface with XML file descriptions. Each unit has more than one plug-in. We can load useful plug-ins according to the project requirements. Only the framework of CDP is unchangeable.

4 Code Analysis Abstract

Almost all the common protocols have at least one version of their robust C language implementation, because of more efficiency and flexibility. We give the example using C description too. These source codes are almost used procedural-based programming concept. This means the main structure of the codes is that function calls another function or function is invoked by another function. There is always a "main" function found as program entry. We present an ideal model of procedural-based programming like this:

There are no global variables, "goto" statements and macros to substitute functions. The "main()" function is the unique root of the program. All the functions invoke other functions hierarchically. All the variables are also all local variables which only exert within the functions. This means no matter how many source codes, the structure of the program can be abstracted as a tree and be expressed as tree data structure. The example codes are shown in program 1 and the tree views are shown in Figure 3.

```
static int udpv6_sendmsg(...)
{
          ...
          udpv6_destroy_sock(sin6);
          ...
          udp_v6_flush_pending_frames(sin6);
          ...
          udpv6_close(sk);
          ...
          return 0;
}
static int udpv6_destroy_sock(...)
{
          lock_sock(sk);
          udp_v6_flush_pending_frames(sk);
          release_sock(sk);
          inet6_destroy_sock(sk);
          return 0;
}
static void udp_v6_flush_pending_frames(...)
{
          ...
          if (up->pending) {
            ...
            ip6_flush_pending_frames(sk);
         }
}
static void udpv6_close(...)
{
          inet_sock_release(sk);
}
```

Program 1. A segment of ideal source codes

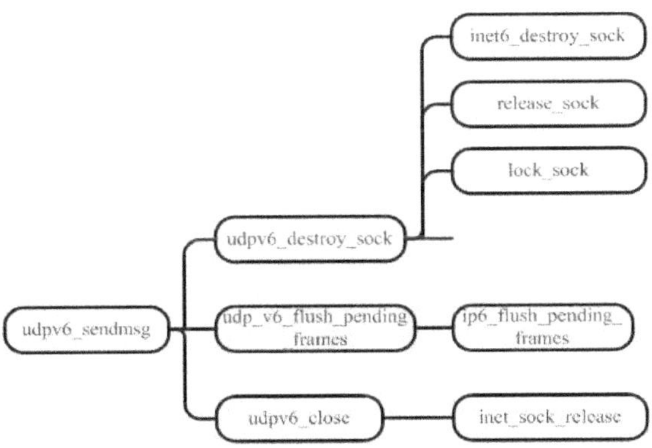

Fig. 3. The tree abstract

An integral tree can be cut into several small trees according to the explicit hierarchy and few associations exist between the small trees. We can separate the program tree of above ideal model into several sub-programs too. Each sub-program can compose a component easily. If all the sub-programs are all component-based, the full functions of programs can assemble through linking all these components.

This ideal model has a certain distance to common C program. On the other hand, some difference can be found between common C programs and original communication protocol programs. First, protocols are utilization-oriented that programs normally divide into many units logistically according to various implementation focuses. Functions frequently invoke each other inside the unit and seldom invoke the functions outside its unit. Second, efficiency is the most important for protocol implementation while programming style becomes the secondary, so there are many "goto" statements, global variables and macro definitions in source codes. Although it is hard to read, it exists actually. Third, many basic protocols are related to device or EOS. They are optimized for special hardware, many assembly language codes appear in the function and functions invoke static library directly.

We find a feasible way to compromise between the ideal model and practical original programs. Because the analysis of Code Analysis Tools (CAT) in CDP is only a generic computer-aided way and there is no need to be too much precise, it is acceptable to do abstract work to only get the structure of the programs and relations of calling functions. We can even simplify the practical programs before abstract. We constitute the following basic rules.

Global variable is a static entity that acts throughout the program. The lifetime begins as soon as program starts and ends until program terminates. We consider global variables as functions because they have the same scope. We even pre-process the global variables in programs with function encapsulation: the initializations and value assignments are regarded as functions "init(), get(),set()".

Macros are the most complicated. But they are widely used in C as constants or templates. We classify them into two types according to the functionality: simple type and complex type. Simple type means macro is only the alias of constant or string, such as "#define TCP_TWKILL_QUOTA 100" or "#define INTEGER int". Other macros are defined as complex type. They even may be used as substitution of functions or expression segments. They may be used as templates in C++. We care few about simple type macros because they only can be considered as value substitution. We can substitute them back during pre-process. In contrast, almost nothing can be done with the complex type macros because of too much complexity. We usually leave them unchanged or mark them out.

For procedural-based program, there is a unique starting point which is "main()" function or a specific function. From this entry, the running process steps forward statement-by-statement. These statements normally are declaration statements, assignment statements, branch statements and loop statements.

Local variables are common in functions. Declaration statements and assignment statements mainly act on them. Because we care more about the structure analysis, parameters of local variables can be certain ignored. We omit all the local variables definitions and value assignments by constants during analysis, because which variables and which values pass into a function are unconcerned indeed. Concretely, if a local variable is assigned by function return value, only function invoke is considered. If a global variable is assigned by a local variable, it is regarded as a "set()" function invoke of the global variable. If the local variable is a function pointer, it needs to be considered as function invoke too when the pointer is initialized or assigned value. All the other types of local pointer variables are all omitted.

There are two main types of processing statements: branch statement and loop statement. In the ordinary course, branch statements include "if...else..., switch...case..." and loop statements include "for..., do...while..., while..." in C language. These statements divide programs into units according to its scope and construct the structure of the program.

Loop statement units often can be marked as a whole in the analysis because the loop unit can hardly be separated alone. We may build a component to contain the loop unit or abstract a component in the loop units, but the loop is coherent and it is no use to only pack the segment process of the loop statements.

Branch statements are important for our analysis because there often may be loose couple point of the program. It may be potential logical division designed by the original source code programmers. The logical division sometimes shows the division of the utilization-oriented unit which can form a functional component easily.

There is a special statement: "goto" statement, which is so powerful that the processing step can jump directly to the specified location. Although the program becomes artistic and comprehensible, this leads too much complexity and always destroys the procedural structure of the program. The "goto" statement is considered as a kind of function invoke from the "goto" statement point to the pointed label. The result of goto may be branch structure or loop structure. If it is a kind of branch, the division may take place here too.

After the abstract above, the result approaches the ideal model shown in Figure 3. The basic relations of the programs are invoking relations among the functions and the branch or loop statements point to the possible associations among the segments. This kind of code analysis tools has approximated original programs as the tree model, which can be used to guild the division of suitable components.

5 Implementation Details

We use CDP for a kind of enterprise router protocol development. The main interface is shown in figure 4. We design the entire units of the CDP framework (shown in figure 2) as plug-ins and form the entire visible contents with views.

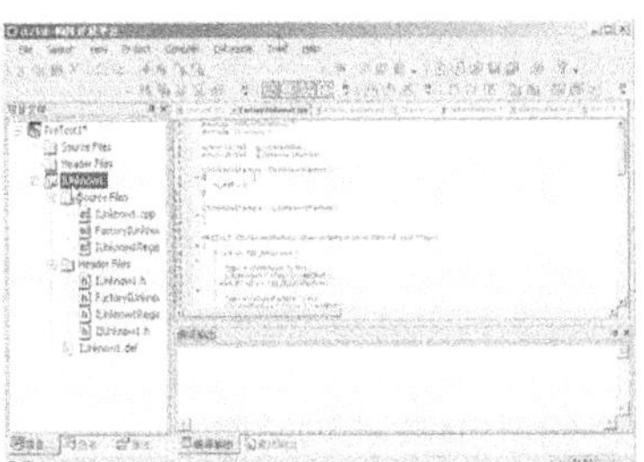

Fig. 4. CDP main interface

5.1 CDP Views

In CDP, we design many views to help the display of the analysis and guild the development of the component. Views are all the visible contents of CDP. Each view shows the unit function or the analysis result. There are mainly four types of views: code management views, code analysis views, task views and component description views. These views also have associations with all kinds of plug-ins.

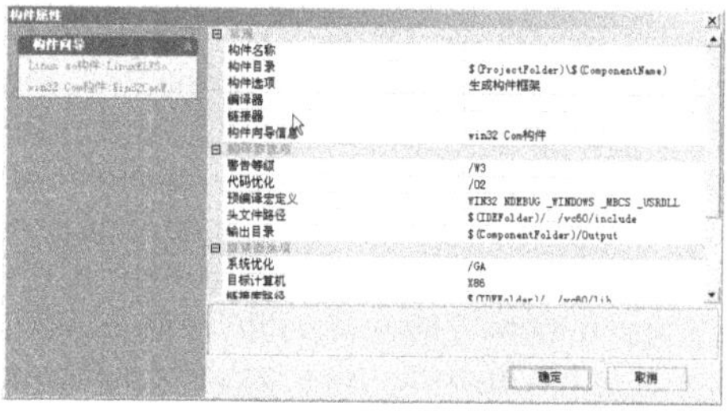

Fig. 5. Code wizard view

Code management views include code editor view, project management view, and code wizard view. As seen in figure 4, code editor view, which is the main body of IDE, lies in right-middle and project management view lies in left. Code assist tools color the source codes with different highlights and mark all the pairs of brackets back and forth. Project management view forms the total source files as a tree and classifies with different folders according to the component division and file type. A project can build more than one component and each folder has its own source file, head files, configuration files. One of code wizard view is shown in figure 5. We can set many common options of the compilers by the click of the switches. These settings decide the generation and optimization of the build tools for component source codes.

Code analysis views have two types: accurate analysis views and abstract views. Accurate views show the results of lexical analysis and grammar analysis by analysis tools. Macros, global variables and functions are the main atoms of the codes and each atom has its view to list all of their elements. Some tools even can provide a mechanism to translate all the simple type macros back into actual values automatically.

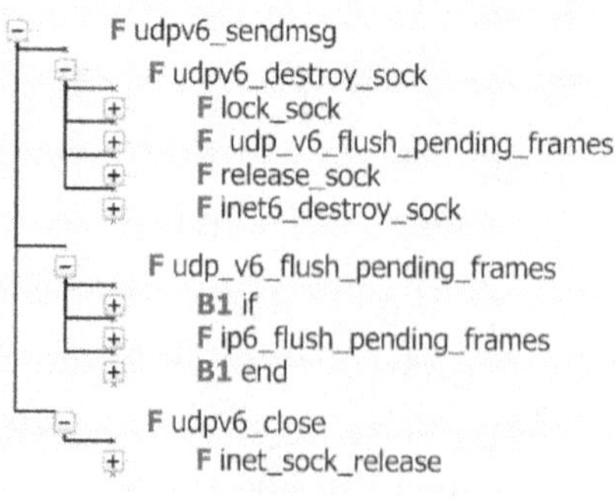

Fig. 6. Abstract view of Program 1

Abstract view is the display of the analysis according to the abstract and simplification principles as illustrated in Part 4. This is a tree view and marks Macros (M), global variables (G), functions (F), branch statements (B), loop statements (L) for the guidance. This view helps us to divide components according to this hierarchy tree. We even can easily click and drag the mouse to reform and construct the components through visualization. Figure 6 shows the abstract view of Program 1.

Tasks views mainly include the feedbacks and the results of the build tools. The search results of the code editor and the planning tasks made by users, the trace information during the build process and the debug state of the running debug tools are shown here too. Task views including result views lies in the right-bottom of CDP as shown in figure 4. The user also can define own planning tasks and reminders tasks too.

Component description views are used to generate CDL files. CDL files do not only describe the generated component's characters but also define the communication protocols. Because CDL is merely used between software so that it is not necessary to be known by CDP users, the component description views are not the text editor of CDL but the graphic interface. It provides much convenience that users only fill in the blanks according to the prompts. There is auto translation to generate CDL files.

5.2 CDP Plug-Ins

Except the framework of CDP, all the other units, even including code editors, are plug-ins. This means all the units including code editor are replaceable too. Plug-in is not a component but a set of components, it is the basic unit of functional implementation. There is often more than one plug-in for one function unit. This makes much flexibility and configuration ability. All of the plug-ins obey open programming standards, describe by format-fixed files which are organized by XML. They store in the same directory from where the CDP framework can load all of the plug-ins automatically. This is something like the popular open source project, such as Eclipse Project.

Many plug-ins are visual tools, they control both display contents and functions of the views. Some other plug-ins are the link and pipes of other tools, such as test plug-in is the link of the corresponding simulate systems according to the EOS or hardware types of components. Usually plug-ins are partly installed, for examples, build tools plug-in has tight association with different tool-chains. For a certain kind of EOS or devices, it only loads a series of tool chains. If the program needs compile components for Intel XScale architecture with embedded Linux, we only load arm-Linux-gcc (arm-Linux-g++) tool-chains.

CDP executes on Windows OS. To use tool-chains on Linux, we have configured Cygwin to support the tool-chains. Cygwin environment is built previously. All the work has done in advance to form the basic foundation to mask the OS.

5.3 Cross-Platform Build Tools

Generally CDP is an IDE used on common PC whose OS is Windows or Linux. The source codes are edited and managed on PC, but the generative components are used in EOS. The cross-platform compilers must be used to compile the source codes. We analyze the most popular compilers and design a uniform graphic interface to switch most commonly used compiler options.

We can find comparability among different tool-chains. For example, while using GCC series cross-platform compilers, GCC has own option switch and corresponding patches for different CPU. It has wonderful mechanism to coordinate the used standard library and the dynamic library in the compiling process. The trace of the build process and the debug of the program are the simple link to tools such as GDB for target Linux.

6 Conclusions

CDP is one of the rapid communication components development tools. It is the collection of views and plug-ins to form a series of tools such as code editor, code wizards, code analysis tools, code assist tools, build tools, component description tool, test tools and CL connector. This takes much flexibility and configuration ability so that many existing tools and tool-chains can link into CDP conveniently. Furthermore, for the customization of component-based communication protocols, code analysis tools make a good abstract from original practical source codes to visual structure model. This is the feasible guidance and roadmap to construct the components. As a complex development process of communication protocols, CDP does much computer-aided analysis and development work.

References

1. Dai, H.J, Chen, T.Z., Chen, C: CCPA: Component-based communication protocol architecture for embedded systems. Journal of Zhejiang University: Science. 6A (2005) 79–86
2. Ascia, G., Catania, V., Palesi, M.: A GA-based design space exploration framework for parameterized system-on-a-chip platforms. IEEE Transactions on Evolutionary Computation. Vol. 8 (2004) 329–346
3. Lim, K., Wan, L., Guidotti, D.: System-on-a-package (SOP) module development for a digital, RF and optical mixed signal integrated system. Electronic Components and Technology, 2004. ECTC '04. Proceedings. Vol.2 (2004) 1693–1697
4. Subramanian, V., Tront, J.G., Bostian, C.W., Midkiff, S.F.: Design and implementation of a configurable platform for embedded communication systems. Parallel and Distributed Processing Symposium, 2003. Proceedings. International. (2003) 22–26
5. Perkusich, A., Almeida, H.O., de Araujo, D.H.: A software framework for real-time embedded automation and control systems. Emerging Technologies and Factory Automation, 2003. Proceedings. ETFA '03. IEEE Conference. Vol. 2 (2003) 181–184
6. Volgyesi, P., Ledeczi, A.: Component-based development of networked embedded applications. Euromicro Conference, 2002. Proceedings. (2002) 68–73
7. Xia, C., Michael, R., Lyu, K.F.: Component-based software engineering: technologies, development frameworks, and quality assurance schemes. Seventh Asia-Pacific Software Engineering Conference (2000)

TrieC: A High-Speed IPv6 Lookup with Fast Updates Using Network Processor

Xianghui Hu[1], Bei Hua[1], and Xinan Tang[2]

[1] Department of Computer Science and Technology,
University of Science and Technology of China, Hefei, P.R. China 230027
xhhu@mail.ustc.edu.cn, bhua@ustc.edu.cn
[2] Intel Compiler Lab, USA
xinan.tang@intel.com

Abstract. Address lookup is one of the main bottlenecks in Internet backbone routers, as it requires the router to perform a longest-prefix-match when searching the routing table for a next hop. Ever-increasing Internet bandwidth, continuously growing prefix table size and inevitable migration to IPv6 address architecture further exacerbate this situation. In recent years, a variety of high-speed address lookup algorithms have been proposed, however most of them are inappropriate to IPv6 lookup. This paper proposes a high-speed IPv6 lookup algorithm TrieC, which achieves the goals of high-speed address lookup, fast incremental prefix updates, high scalability and reasonable memory requirement by taking great advantage of the network processor architecture. Performance of TrieC is carefully evaluated with several IPv6 routing tables of different sizes and different prefix length distributions on Intel IXP2800 network processor(NPU). Simulation shows that TrieC can support IPv6 lookup at OC-192 line rate. Furthermore, if TrieC is pipelined in hardware, it can achieve one IPv6 lookup per memory access.

Keywords: Network processor, IPv6 lookup, parallel programming, embedded system design, routing, prefix expansion.

1 Introduction

Due to the rapid growth of the Internet bandwidth and continuously increasing size of the routing tables, IP address lookup becomes one of the most challenging tasks in backbone routers. By the inevitable migration to the next generation IPv6 128-bit address space, IPv6 lookup becomes even more demanding.

Traditional routers generally use application specific integrated circuits (ASIC), FPGA, or general-purpose processor (GPP) as a building block. ASIC provides guaranteed high-performance with low power, but lack of flexibility makes it unable to keep up with the rapid changes in network protocols. FPGA offers certain flexibility but it costs more to build and its power consumption is very high. On the other hand, GPPs can meet the requirements of flexibility, short development period and low cost, but often fail to meet the performance requirements because they are not specially optimized for network processing. For example, the efficiency of the GPP cache system relies on data's temporal locality, which is not a common case in

L.T. Yang et al. (Eds.): ICESS 2005, LNCS 3820, pp. 117 – 128, 2005.

today's high-speed and aggregated networks. As a consequence, network processor unit(NPU) emerges as a promising candidate for networking building block. It retains both the high performance of ASIC and flexibility advantage of GPP through parallel and programmable architecture. At present, many companies including Intel, Freescale, Agrere, AMCC and EZchip have developed programmable NPUs. Many system companies including Cisco, Alcatel, HUAWEI, and ZTE use NPUs to build switches and routers.

This paper presents an efficient IPv6 address lookup scheme called TrieC, which achieves O(1) search time with fast incremental updates and reasonable memory requirement by taking great advantage of the characteristics of NPU, especially of Intel IXP network processor. Although our experiment was done on Intel IXP2800, the same performance can be achieved on other similar NPUs. The main contributions of the paper are as follows:

- A new IPv6 address lookup algorithm (TrieC) is proposed with the features of high speed, fast prefix incremental updates, high scalability and reasonable memory requirement.
- A modified compact prefix expansion (MCPE) technique is designed to use less memory for address search and prefix incremental update than traditional prefix expansion.
- An architecture awareness algorithm implementation aiming at IXP2800 NPU is elaborated, which: 1) takes advantage of the special instruction set of IXP 2800, especially the bit counting and CRC instruction to make the search of the compressed tables fast; 2) distributes IPv6 routing table in four SRAM channels to support simultaneously data accesses; and 3) partitions the tasks appropriately on three IXP2800 Microengines(MEs) to achieve IPv6 lookup at OC-192 line rate.

The rest of the paper is organized as follows. Section 2 describes issues of existing approaches in IP address lookup, especially in the IPv6 circumstances. Section 3 explains the design and mechanism of TrieC. Section 4 discusses how to implement incremental prefix updates efficiently. Section 5 introduces the optimized implementation on IXP2800. Section 6 shows simulation results and performance analysis. Finally, section 7 concludes.

2 Related Work

The most popular data structure for longest prefix match is trie[6-8]. In order to reduce memory accesses in trie, various kinds of techniques such as prefix expansion and multibit trie[12] have been proposed. Multi-bit trie expands a set of arbitrary length prefixes to a predefined set of prefixes by prefix expansion. Its search time is linear with the multi-bit tree levels and its update time depends on both prefix length and maximum node size. However, its worst-case memory requirement is $O(2^k*N*W/k)$, where k, N and W are search stride, number of prefixes and maximum prefix length respectively. Basic-24-8-DIR[13] is a hardware implementation using prefix expansion for IPv4 lookup with maximum two memory accesses, but it needs more than 32Mbytes memory and even more memory or dual memory bank for routing updates.

Waldvogel et al.[9] use binary search on hash table organized by prefix length. The scheme requires log_2W memory accesses, where W is the maximum prefix length, in the worst case. However, it requires very long preprocessing time to compute markers noting the existence of longer prefixes, hence the update time is $O(N*log_2W)$ and the whole routing table must be reconstructed. Multiway range tree [11] reduces search time and update time to $O(k*log_kN)$ through modifying binary search by prefix length, it also analyzes the feasibility for IPv6 address lookup. However, its memory requirement is $O(k*N*log_kN)$.

Lapson et al.[10] introduce multicolumn search for IPv6 addresses that avoided the multiplicative factor of W/M inherent in basic binary search by doing binary search in columns of M bits, and moving between columns using pre-computed information. However, in the worst case, it needs approximate 15 memory accesses for IPv6 address lookup because of $O(log_k2N+W/M)$ search time.

Additionally, TCAM-based, CPU caching[5], reconfigurable fast IP lookup engine[14], binary decision diagrams[20] etc. are all hardware-based IP lookup schemes. Their advantages are high lookup speed, whereas their disadvantages like specific hardware support, high power consumption, complicated prefix update and high cost limit their application to a certain degree.

Obviously, the main problem of existing lookup schemes is that they cannot combine high-speed lookup, fast updates and acceptable memory storage for IPv6 address lookup at the same time.

This paper presents our solution of an IPv6 lookup scheme-TrieC based on the modified compact prefix expansion (MCPE) technique and fixed-level multibit trie structure. High performance search is achieved through fixing the levels of TrieC tree, and fast incremental update is achieved by storing the unexpanded prefix length in MCPE nodes. Moreover, memory requirement is reduced to a reasonable capacity due to compressed MCPE technique.

3 Algorithm Design and Mechanism

3.1 Basic Idea

In trie structure, prefix information is stored along the path from the root to the leaf node of the tree. To reduce the path length and thus memory access times, prefix expansion technique is applied to increase the routing table size in a fixed stride so that the resulted expanded table could be visited in the same stride index. The proposed scheme is based on the following observations:

1. 2^{n-m} redundant next-hop information must be stored if an m-bit prefix is expanded to 2^n n-bit prefixes, where n is equal to or greater than m, using prefix expansion.
2. Statistics of existing IPv6 routing tables and the IPv6 addresses allocation policies indicate that the percentage of the prefixes whose lengths are equal to or greater than 48-bit is approximate only 5%.
3. Only aggregatable global unicast addresses, whose format prefix (FP) field is always set to 001, need to be searched in the allocated IPv6 address space. Additionally, the lower 64 bits of IPv6 address are allocated to interface ID, so the core router can ignore them.[1-3]

Therefore, the basic idea of TrieC is to ignore the highest three bits, build a four-level compressed multibit trie tree using the stride 21-8-8-8 for the prefixes whose lengths are longer than 3bits and shorter than 49bits, then use hash to search the other prefixes whose lengths are longer than 48bits and shorter than 65bits.

3.2 Modified Compact Prefix Expansion

The modified compact prefix expansion (MCPE) technique is motivated by the fact that there is a lot of redundant next-hop information in traditional prefix expansion. For example, if the IPv6 prefix (2002:4*::/18,A) and (2002:5*::/20,B) are expanded to 24-bit prefixes using the traditional prefix expansion, 64(=2^{24-18}) new prefixes are formed as shown in Fig.1(a). Obviously, the same next-hop index repeats many times. A repeats 48 times totally, and B repeats 16 times.

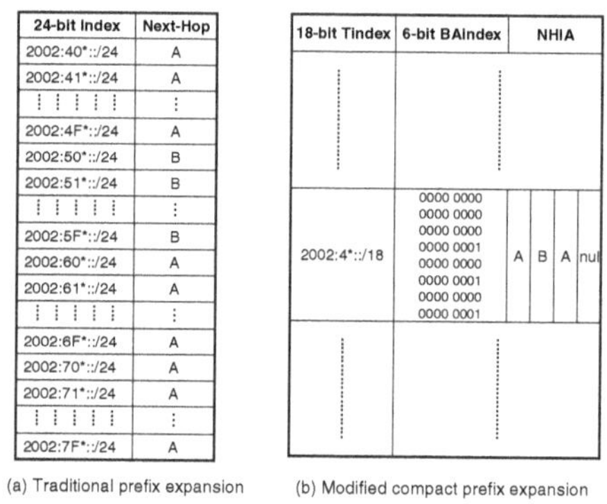

Fig. 1. Traditional prefix expansion vs. modified compact prefix expansion (MCPE)

The main idea of MCPE is to store consecutively identical next-hop index only once in a next-hop index array (NHIA). The NHIA in Fig.1(b) has three entries (A, B, A); the highest 18 bits of 24-bit prefix are used as the index to search a Tindex table and the next 6 bits are used as another index to search a bit-vector BitAtlas in a BAindex table. The 64-bit BitAtlas is organized as follows: if the next-hop information denoted by bit I is the same as that denoted by bit I-1, bit I is set to 0; otherwise, bit I is set to 1, indicating that different next-hop information must be added into NHIA. In Fig. 2 (b), bit 0 is 1 since it starts a new NHIA entry; bit 16 is 1 since its NHIA is B that is different from previous entry A; bit 32 is 1 since its NHIA is A again which is different from previous entry B.

Now assume we want to search the next-hop information relating to IPv6 address 2002:6A*::/24. Firstly, we use the highest 18 bits as Tindex to find out the MCPE entry 2002:4*::/18, then we use the next 6 bits '101010' as BAindex to find the bit offset in BitAtlas, which is 42. Since total three bits are set in BitAtlas from offset 0 to offset 42, the third element 'A' in NHIA is the lookup result.

The TrieC table in Fig.1 is called TrieC18/6. Similarly, TrieCm/n is designed to represent $2^{(m+n)}$ uncompressed (m+n)-bit prefixes. Using MCPE technique, the TrieC tree eliminates redundant information and preserves the high-speed index access characteristic of traditional prefix expansion technique.

3.3 Data Structure

Our stride series for TrieC algorithm is 24-8-8-8-16. The data structures include three types of tables: TrieC15/6 table (ignored highest three bits 001), TrieC4/4 table, and Hash-16 table. TrieC15/6 table is the first-level table that stores all the prefixes whose lengths fall into [1:24]-bit. TrieC4/4 tables are from the second to the fourth level of TrieC trees, whose prefix lengths belong to [25:32]-bit, [33:40]-bit, and [41:48]-bit respectively. Hash16 table stores all the prefixes whose lengths belong to [49:64]-bit.

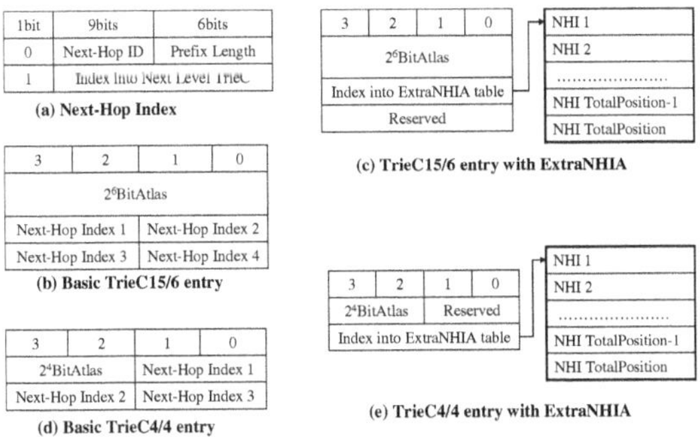

Fig. 2. Data structures of TrieC scheme

The next-hop index (NHI) structure, which stores the lookup result including the next-hop IP address and the output interface, is shown in Fig. 2(a). The original prefix length is stored in NHI due to the requirement of incremental prefix updates. Each NHI entry is 2 bytes, with the most significant bit setting to 0 indicating that the remaining bits consist of a next-hop ID in NHI[14:6], and an unexpanded prefix length in NHI[5:0], while a "1" in this bit indicating that the remaining 15 bits contain a pointer to the next level TrieC node.

The TrieC15/6 table contains 2^{15} entries, which is called TrieC15/6_entry, and has two types of structures: Basic and ExtraNHIA. The basic structure supports up to four NHIs and ExtraNHIA supports more NHIs, in which:

1. TrieC15/6_entry [127:64]: stores a 64-bit vector BitAtlas. The least significant bit is always set to one because each IP address absolutely matches the default route. TotalEntropy that is the total number of bits set in the bit vector represents the size of array NHIA or ExtraNHIA. For a bit position P, the number of bits set in BitAtlas[P:0] named PositionEntropy[P] gives the NHI index in array NHIA or ExtraNHIA. For each P, the equation PositionEntropy[P]<=TotalEntropy always holds.
2. TrieC15/6_entry[63:0]: stores up to 4 NHIs or a pointer to ExtraNHIA array. If TotalEntropy of BitAtlas field is no greater than 4, TrieC15/6_entry[63:0] stores NHI1, NHI2, NHI3 and NHI4 orderly as shown in Fig. 2(b). Otherwise, TrieC15/6_entry[63:32] stores a 32-bit pointer that points to ExtraNHIA array as shown in Fig. 2(c).

Similarly, each TrieC4/4 table has 2^4 entries and each entry is 8 bytes. The structures of basic and ExtraNHIA TrieC4/4 entry are shown in Fig. 2 (d) and (e). The unique difference among all TrieC4/4 tables is that if the flag bit of NHI in the fourth level of TrieC tree is set to one, the Hash16 table must be searched. The Hash16 table uses cyclic redundancy check (CRC) as a hash function that is known as a semi-perfect hash function. The structure of a Hash16 entry is (prefix, next-hopID) pair.

3.4 Lookup Mechanism

Fig. 3 gives a routing table search algorithm based on compressed TrieC tables. We will use an example to show how these tables are searched.

```
IPv6_Lookup_TrieC (IN DstIP, OUT Next-HopID)
{
    Current_Block = TrieC15_6;
    Tindex  = DstIP [124:110];
    Bit_Vec  = GetBitVec (Current_Block, Tindex);
    BAindex = DstIP [109:104];
    NHI = GetNHI(Bit_vec, BAindex);
    if (NHI.flag = 0) return NHI.Next-HopID;
    else
    {// search TrieC4/4 tables, base[i] is base of (i+1)th-level TrieC tree
        Current_Block = TrieC4/4 at Base[0]+NHI[14:0];
        for (i=1;i<=3;i++)
        {
            Tindex  = DstIP[103-8*(i-1):100-8*(i-1)];
            Bit_vec = GetBitVec (Current_Block, Tindex);
            BAindex= DstIP[99-8*(i-1):96-8*(i-1)];
            NHI = GetNHI (Bit_Vec, BAindex);
            If (NHI.flag = 0) return NHI.Next-HopID;
            else
            {
              if (i!=3) Current_Block=TrieC4/4 at Base[i]+NHI [14:0]<<4;
              else break;  //search longer prefix in Hash16
            }
        }
        if (Hash (DstIP [79:64])) return Next-HopID;
        else return Default-Next-HopID;
    }
}// IPv6_Lookup_TrieC
```

Fig. 3. Pseudo code to search TrieC multi-level tree for IPv6 address

Assume that the following routes are already in the TrieC table: (2002:4C60::/18,A), (2002:4C6F::/28,B). The first route requires an entry in TrieC15/6 that corresponds to the 24-bit prefixes from 2002:40*::/24 to 2002:7F*::/24. The second route further needs a second level TrieC4/4 to be used because its length is 28-bits.

Suppose we are looking up the destination IPv6 Address 2002:4C6A::200C, Fig. 4 shows the detailed lookup process. Firstly, DstIP[124:110] that is '000000000001001' is used as the Tindex to find the entry 2002:4*::/18 in TrieC15/6; then DstIP[109:104] that is '001100' is used as the BAindex to find the bit offset that is 12 in BitAtlas; two bits set from offset 0 to offset 12 makes PositionEntropy=2, thus the second entry in NHIA is located; a '1' in NHI[15] indicates that NHI[14:0] contains a pointer to the next level TrieC4/4, so NHI[14:0]<<4+DstIP[103:100] is used as the Tindex to the next level TrieC4/4, and then DstIP[99:96] is used as the BAindex to find out the PositionEntropy that is 1, which then locates the desired next-hop ID, which is B.

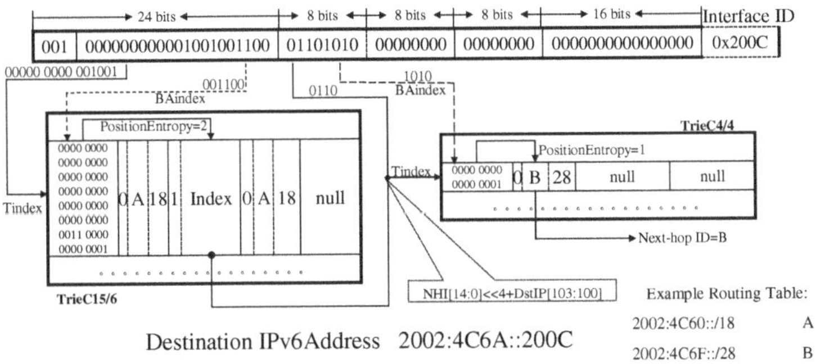

Fig. 4. IPv6 address lookup example of the TrieC scheme

4 Routing Updates

New routing information must be exchanged among routers as network topology changes. The frequency of routing updates could be as high as a few hundred times per second. Since the routing table cannot be accessed during update, routing updates must be executed fast and efficiently.

The operation of adding a new prefix, NewRoute(new_prefix/new_length, new_next-hop), can be classified into two categories according to the value of new_length: BitAtlas affected and BitAtlas unaffected. The range of the prefix length corresponding to the former is called TableRange[start_length, end_length] and the range corresponding to the latter is called BitAtlasRange[start_length, end_length]. For instance, the TableRange and BitAtlasRange of TrieC15/6 table are [4,18] and [19,24] respectively.

Consider the updates in a TableRange. Because a NewEntry matches $2^{(\text{TableRange.end\_length-new\_length})}$ TrieC entries and their whole BitAtlas fields, we only need update the NHIs of matched entries. If an old NHI satisfies: flag=0, PrefixLength<=NewEntry.new_length and Next-HopID $\neq$ NewEntry.new_next-hop, it is replaced by the NewEntry. Otherwise, we need search and update the next level of TrieC tree. In the case of BitAtlasRange, NewEntry exactly matches one TrieC entry and $2^{(\text{BitAtlasRange.end\_length-new\_length})}$ bits in the BitAtlas field of the matched entry. For each matched bit, we only need update the bit and its corresponding NHI if PrefixLength<=NewEntry.new_length and Next-HopID $\neq$ NewEntry.new_next-hop. Otherwise, we need search and update the next level of TrieC tree.

The process of adding new prefixes (2002:E7B::/17,C) and (2002:279::/23,D) into the example routing table is shown as Fig. 5. The prefix (2002:E7B::/17,C) matches two TrieC15/6 entries with the Tindex '000000000001000' and '000000000001001'. Only the first NHI(null) of the former TrieC15/6 entry is replaced by NHI(0,C,17) because the NHI(null) matches the update condition. In Fig. 5(b), the prefix

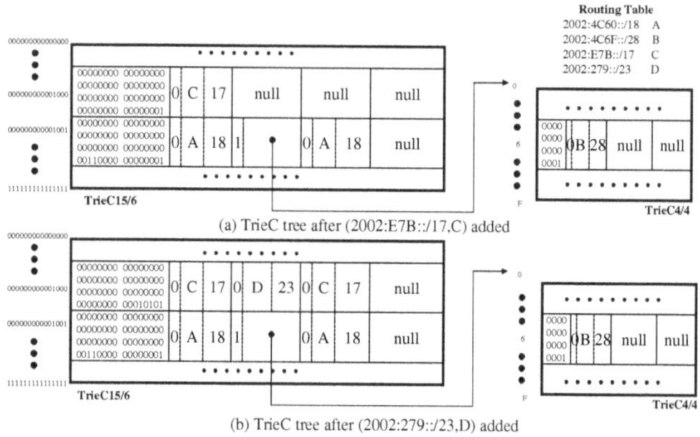

Fig. 5. Routing updates of the example IPv6 routing table

(2002:279::/23,D) matches only one TrieC15/16 entry, whose Tindex is '000000000001000', and two bits in the BitAtlas field of this entry. Because the NHI corresponding to these two bits matches the update condition, i.e., NHI.Prefix-Length=17<new_length=23 and NHI.Next-HopID=C ≠ new_next-hop=D, both of these two bits are set to one and the corresponding NHIs are updated.

5 Optimization on IXP2800 Network Processor

Intel IXP2800 NPU is a programmable network processor that comprises a single XScale processor, sixteen Microengines(MEs), four SRAM controllers, three RDRAM controllers and high-speed bus interfaces. Each ME has eight hardware-assisted threads of execution. All threads in a particular ME execute the same code stored on that ME. Complete descriptions of the hardware architecture and software framework are available from the IXP2800 manuals[19]. We implemented TrieC algorithm in MicroengineC language and simulated it on Intel Developer DevWorkbench 4.1[19], which offers a cycle-accurate simulator of IXP2800 network processor.

Through analysis, we identified the following operations as time-consuming ones: calculation of TotalEntropy and PositionEntropy, SRAM memory accesses, and CRC hash operation. The efficiency of those operations affects the performance of TrieC greatly. We will show how to optimize these operations by taking advantage of the characteristics of IXP2800 network processor.

Firstly, the main workload of entropy calculation in TrieC is to count the number of bit set in bit-vector BitAtlas. The naive implementation of checking each bit and counting the number of bit set seen so far it is very slow and needs a few hundred shift, ALU and branch instructions. Intel IXP2800 network processor has a built-in instruction POP_COUNT that can calculate the number of bit set in a 32-bit register in three clock cycles. Such tremendous reduction of the number of instructions lays a solid foundation for TrieC to achieve line rate.

On IXP2800 NPU, each SRAM access takes more than 100 cycles, hiding memory latency becomes another important step towards high-performance. We hid the memory-access latencies by means of:

- **Parallelized access:** IXP2800 NPU contains four independent SRAM controllers and each channel supports up to 64Mbytes SRAM. We partitioned the TrieC tables, and then distributed them properly into four SRAM channels. TrieC15/6 table and hash16 table were stored in SRAM channel 0, because their sizes were smaller than that of each TrieC4/4. The second, third and fourth level TrieC4/4 tables were stored in SRAM channel 1, 2 and 3 respectively, so that they could be accessed in parallel.
- **Vectoring access:** On IXP2800 NPU, adjacent SRAM locations can be fetched in one instruction to the array of SRAM transfer registers, which allows for a significant reduction in the number of SRAM access. As the maximal length of each SRAM access instruction can be up to 64-bytes, we carefully designed the data structures of Tries15/6 and TriesC4/4 such that the sizes of TrieC15/6 entry and TrieC4/4 entry were less than 64-bytes and thus each table entry could be fetched in one SRAM access.

Finally, each ME has a CRC Unit, which operates in parallel with the execution of data path and supports one time CRC operation within the period of each two consecutive instructions. By using the CRC unit to perform hash calculation, TrieC speeded up the search of hash16 table.

6 Simulation and Performance Analysis

Since IPv6 is not yet widely deployed, existing IPv6 tables, which normally have less 1000 prefixes[16][17], are small and unlikely to reflect future IPv6 network growth. Currently, randomly generated tables are often used for IPv6 research and development. To reflect the IPv6 address distribution as objectively as possible, we used three different ways to generate nine IPv6 routing tables whose prefix length distributions are shown in Tab. 1. Group A was generated from the CERNET[17], 6Bone, 6Net and Telstra BGP IPv6 routing tables[16], reflecting the existing IPv6 prefix length distribution. Group B was generated from the non-random generator IPv6 table proposed by M Wang et. al[18], reflecting the ideal IPv6 routing tables. Group C was calculated as the arithmetical average of A and B, reflecting the future IPv6 tables.

Table 1. Prefix length and entries used in simulation

	Prefix Number								
	N=200000			N=300000			N=400000		
Length	A	B	C	A	B	C	A	B	C
1-24	8439	110	4274	12660	165	6413	16878	220	8549
25-32	138821	14806	76814	208231	22209	115220	277641	29612	153627
33-40	11029	31080	21053	16543	46620	31582	22056	62160	42109
41-48	29224	142640	85932	43836	213960	128899	58448	285280	171864
49-64	12487	11360	11923	18731	17040	17886	24975	22720	23847

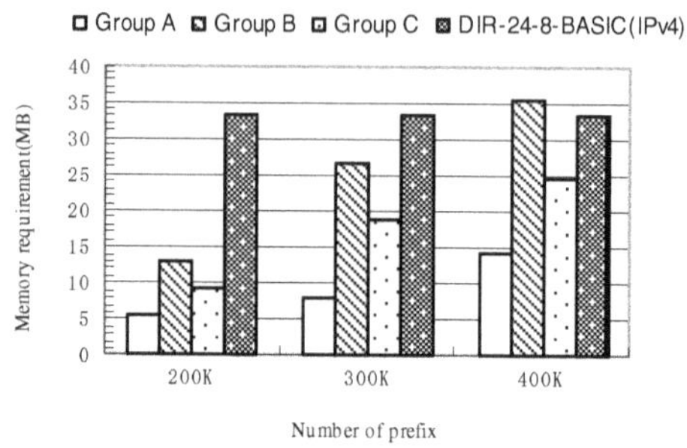

Fig. 6. Memory requirements of nine IPv6 routing tables vs. of DIR-24-8-BASIC(IPv4)

For each group, we generated three different sizes of tables with 200K, 300K and 400K entries. All the prefix values are generated randomly.

Memory requirements of the nine IPv6 tables are shown in Fig. 6. Obviously, memory requirements increase along with table sizes. Note that the memory requirement of table B-400K is approximate 35Mbytes,which is slightly higher than 33Mbyes of DIR-24-8-BASIC for IPv4, but is significantly lower than the estimated memory requirement of multibit-trie, which is approximately more than 820Mbytes at 8-bit strides for 400K entries. With such high a compression rate, the entire routing tables can be stored in SRAM.

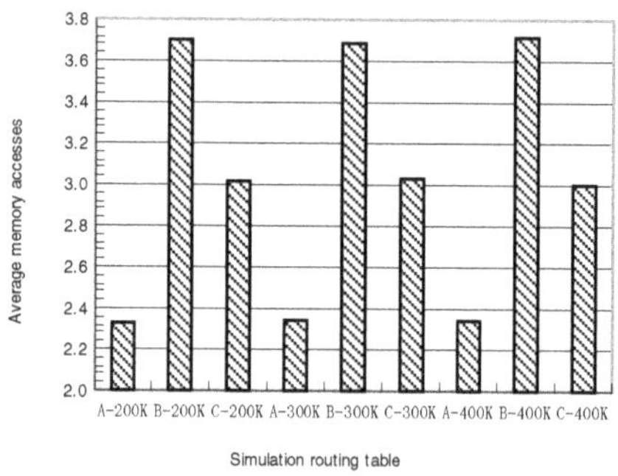

Fig. 7. Average memory accesses of nine IPv6 routing tables

In the worst case, TrieC needs eight memory accesses and one hash operation. It is clear from Fig. 7 that there is no any relation between average memory accesses and size of IPv6 routing table; the average memory accesses depend only on the prefix length distribution of the table. For example, the average memory accesses of the three tables belonging to group-B are all close to four, because the percentages of the prefixes whose lengths between 41-48 bits in these tables are all higher than 70%. On average, the number of memory access of these nine IPv6 tables is far less than eight, which indicates that the percentage of the ExtraNHIA nodes is extremely low. Simulation results demonstrated it, and found that the percentage was only about 3.6%.

Table 2. Minimal threads number required to meet OC-192 line rate on IXP2800 NPU

Routing table	Minimal Threads number	Lookup rate (Mlps.)	
		Single-thread	Multi-threads
Group A	9	3.72	23.84
Group B	17	1.81	21.36
Group C	11	2.55	21.32
Worst case	19	1.54	21.18

Assume that the minimal packet size is 60-bytes, then approximate 20.83Mlps lookup rate is required to support OC-192 line rate. Tab. 2 gives the minimal number of threads required to reach the line rate speed for each group, in which on average 9, 17 and 11 threads are needed for group A, B and C respectively. Considering that there are 16 MEs on IXP2800, and TrieC just consumed less than three MEs of entire ME budget; therefore, there is still enough room for other networking application such as classification and traffic management to meet their line rate requirements.

Finally, we compare the performance of TrieC with some existing outstanding schemes in Tab. 3.

Table 3. Comparison of search, update, space complexities and scalability for IPv6

Scheme	Search time	Update time	Memory requirement	IPv6
Patricia trie	O(W)	O(W)	O(N*W)	N
Multibit trie	O(W/k)	$O(W/k+2^k)$	$O(2^k*N*W/k)$	N
Binary search	$O(\log_2 W)$	$O(N*\log_2 W)$	$O(N*\log_2 W)$	Y
Multiway search	$O(\log_K 2N)$	O(N)	O(N)	Y
DIR-24-8-BASIC	O(1)	Dual bank memory	33MB@IPv4	N
TrieC	O(1)	O(W/k)	O(N*W/k)	Y

7 Conclusion

This paper proposes an IXP2800-based high performance IPv6 lookup algorithm (TrieC) that features high-speed address lookup, fast routing table update, high scalability, and reasonable memory requirement. A modified compact prefix expansion (MCPE) technique that supports faster address search and prefix incremental update with less memory requirement than traditional prefix expansion is designed to build a four-level TrieC tree for IPv6 address lookup. Techniques such as distributed routing table allocation in four SRAM channels, functional pipelining, BitAtlas field calculation speedup, parallelized SRAM accesses, consolidating adjacent SRAM accesses and hardware CRC hash unit are used to optimize the proposed scheme on IXP2800 network processor. These optimizaiton techniques can also be applied to other similar NP architectures. Performance of TrieC is evaluated with nine IPv6 routing tables of different sizes and different prefix length distributions on Intel IXP2800 network processor. Simulation shows that TrieC implemented on IXP2800 can support IPv6 lookup at OC-192 line rate. Furthermore this algorithm can be easily implemented in a pipelined architecture (ASIC) and achieve one IPv6 lookup per SRAM access.

References

1. R. Hinden, S. Deering, RFC2373 IP Version 6 Addressing Architecture
2. R. Hinden, S. Deering, RFC2374 IPv6 Aggregatable global unicast address format,
3. S. Deering, R. Hinden, RFC2460 Internet Protocol, Version 6 (IPv6) Specification
4. Internet Performance Measurement and Analysis Project, http://www.merit.edu/~ipma
5. M. A. Ruiz-Sanchez, E.W. Biersack, and W. Dabbous, "Survey and taxonomy of IP address lookup algorithms," IEEE Network, vol. 15, pp.8–23, Mar.-Apr. 2001
6. Morrison, "PATRICIA-Practical Algorithm to Retrieve Information Coded in Alphanumeric," J. ACM, vol. 15, no. 4, pp. 514–534, Oct. 1968
7. W. Doeringer, G. Karjoth and M. Nassehi, "Routing on Longest Matching Prefixes," IEEE Trans. on Networking, vol. 4, no. 1, pp.86-97, Feb. 1996
8. N. Yazdani and P. S. Min, "Fast and scalable schemes for the IP address lookup problem," in Proc. IEEE Conf. High Performance Switching and Routing, 2000, pp. 83–92.
9. M. Waldvogel, G. Varghese, J. Turner, and B. Plattner, "Scalable high speed IP routing lookups," Proc. ACM SIGCOMM '97, vol. 27, no. 4, pp. 25–36, Oct. 1997.
10. B. Lampson, V. Srinivasan, and G. Varghese, "IP lookups using multiway and multicolumn search," in Proc. IEEE INFOCOM'98, San Francisco, CA, 1998, pp. 1248–1256.
11. Subhash Suri; Varghese, G.; Warkhede, P.R., "Multiway Range Trees: Scalable IP Lookup with Fast updates", Global Telecommunications Conference, 2001.GLOBECOM'01. IEEE Volume 3, 25-29 Nov. 2001 pp. 1610-1614 vol.3
12. V. Srinivasan, G. Varghese, "Fast address lookups using controlled prefix expansion", Proc. ACM Sigmetrics'98, June 1998 pp. 1–11.
13. P. Gupta, S. Lin, and N. McKeown, "Routing lookups in hardware at memory access speeds," in Proc. IEEE INFOCOM'98, vol. 3, San Francisco, USA, 1998, pp. 1240-1247.
14. E. Taylor, J. W. Lockwood, T. S. Sproull, J. S. Turner, and D. B. Parlour, "Scalable IP lookup for programmable routers," in Proc. IEEE INFOCOM'2002, vol. 2, New York, 2002, pp. 562-571.
15. Raj Jain, "A Comparison of Hashing Schemes for Address Lookup in Computer Networks", Communications, IEEE Transactions on Volume 40, Issue 10, Oct. 1992 pp. 1570-1573
16. http://bgp.potaroo.net/index-v6.html
17. http://bgpview.6test.edu.cn/bgp-view/index.shtml
18. M Wang, S Deering, T Hain, L Dunn, "Non-random Generator for IPv6 Tables", High Performance Interconnects, Proceedings 12th Annual IEEE Symposium on 25-27 Aug. 2004 pp. 35-40
19. http://www.intel.com/design/network/products/npfamily/ixp2xxx.htm
20. Sangireddy, R.; Somani, A.K.; "High-speed IP routing with binary decision diagrams based hardware address lookup engine", Selected Areas in Communications, IEEE Journal on Volume 21, Issue 4, May 2003 pp. 513-521

Separate Compilation for Synchronous Modules

Jia Zeng and Stephen A. Edwards*

Department of Computer Science, Columbia University,
New York, USA

Abstract. Synchronous models are useful for designing real-time embedded systems because they provide timing control and deterministic concurrency. However, the semantics of such models usually require an entire system to be compiled at once to analyze the dependencies among modules. The alternative is to write modules that can respond when the values of some of their inputs are unknown, a tedious and error-prone process.

We present a compilation technique that allows a programmer to describe synchronous modules without having to consider undefined inputs. Our algorithm transforms such a description into code that does as much as it can with undefined inputs, allowing modules to be compiled separately and assembled later.

We implemented our technique in a compiler for the Esterel language and present results that show the technique does not impose a substantial overhead.

1 Introduction

The synchronous model of computation [1] has emerged as a successful, practical way to assemble models of concurrent embedded systems because of its deterministic concurrency and its precise control over time. Each process in a synchronous model operates in lock-step with a global clock, and communication between modules is implicitly synchronized to this clock. Provided the processes execute fast enough, processes can precisely control the time (i.e., the clock cycle) when something happens.

In addition to domains including avionics [2] and hardware design [3], the synchronous model has been used for constructing processor simulations [4, 5]. Especially in this latter setting, heterogeneous synchronous models [6], which can assemble and run synchronous components with no knowledge about their contents, is preferable because it allows separate compilation of components (e.g., cache models, branch prediction units) and even allows them to be written in different programming languages.

In the heterogeneous synchronous model [6], a system is assembled from a collection of concurrently-running blocks that communicate through instantaneous "wires" each connected from a single block's output port to one or more input ports on other blocks. That the blocks be able to respond when not all their input wires are defined is the main requirement for being able to run such blocks without knowledge of their contents. Furthermore, a block must be well-behaved when presented with unknown inputs, e.g., if a block decides output o has value v even though input i is undefined, it may not change its mind, e.g., change the output to w once i becomes defined. But if blocks

* Edwards and his group are supported by an NSF CAREER award, a grant from Intel corporation, an award from the SRC, and from New York State's NYSTAR program.

L.T. Yang et al. (Eds.): ICESS 2005, LNCS 3820, pp. 129–140, 2005.

do obey these rules, such a system can adopt a Ptolemy-like philosophy [7] in which systems can be assembled from black-box components and executed efficiency with precise, deterministic semantics.

Although it is possible to write such well-behaved synchronous blocks in a general-purpose language such as C, it is a tedious and error-prone process. The alternative, which we propose here, is for the programmer to write blocks only taking into account their behavior when all their inputs are applied and have the compiler interpolate the correct behavior of the block when only some of the inputs are applied. While it would be correct to make the blocks strict, i.e., to respond with no information about any output unless all the inputs are defined, but this is not very helpful.

In this paper, we propose an algorithm that does this interpolation on programs written in the synchronous concurrent, imperative language Esterel [8]. Constructs in Esterel only explicitly address the behavior when all inputs are known (i.e., the user cannot control them to respond in a certain way to unknown values), but their semantics are clear when not all inputs are known.

Our work generates code from Esterel that responds to unknown inputs. The enables separate compilation and the assembly of modules written in other languages.

2 Related Work

Digital logic simulators often perform a similar two- to three-valued interpolation. In hardware description languages such as Verilog or VHDL, users often compose systems out of apparently two-valued logic functions such as AND or OR. The simulator, however, interprets them as three-valued functions and performs the simulation in the extended domain. It has long been known, however, that this tends to greatly slow the simulation and attempts have been made to circumvent it where possible (e.g., by detecting when two-valued-only simulation is possible and doing it when possible). Overcoming this speed penalty is a primary goal of our work.

Our intermediate representation bears some resemblance to binary decision diagrams (BDDs—see, e.g., Bryant's survey [9]), but differ enough to make their manipulation very different. Compared to the most common type of BDD, the ROBDD (reduced, ordered BDD), our programs may test variables in different orders and multiple times along a path. Although certain styles of BDDs (e.g., free BDDs) relax this restriction, our formalism is even less like most BDDs because it can communicate within itself, i.e., assign and later test the value of the variable assigned, whereas BDDs typically only make assignment at their leaves. As a result, most BDD algorithms, which are able to assume disciplined variable orderings and a single type of node, are inapplicable for our application. Others, however, have used BDDs to synthesize software [10].

Our algorithm is like a partial evaluation of a three-valued simulator on programs represented as graphs, which resembles many other techniques for generating sequential code from concurrent models [11]. Our algorithm, as a side-effect, orders the nodes under forks and generates a purely sequential program. While this is probably undesirable for certain systems, more clever techniques, such as Zeng et al. [12] could probably be woven into ours to more efficiently generate sequential code.

3 GRC: Graph Code

We represent the programs we are compiling using a variant of the Graph Code (GRC) format due to Potop-Butucaru [13]. GRC is like a traditional control-flow graph augmented with concurrency and nodes for controlling it. However, loops are prohibited (cross-cycle loops are allowed). The result is a compact, precise way to represent Esterel programs [8], which we compile with our technique, although the same representation could be used for other synchronous, imperative languages.

A GRC program is a rooted directed acyclic graph $G = (N, r, c, V, O, S, t)$ where N is the set of nodes, $r \in N$ is the distinguished root node, $c : N \to (N \cup \{\text{null}\})^*$ is a function that returns the vector of control successors of a node (Successors are ordered, e.g., if $c(n) = (n_1, n_2, n_3)$, then node n can pass control to its first successor n_1, its second successor n_2, or n_3). A null successor represents no successor, used, for example, when there is a *then* branch from a predicate, but no *else* branch.

The finite set V denotes variables. $O \subset V$ are the output variables. $V \setminus O$ are the input variables. S denotes the set of possible states of the program.

Each node has a type given by the function $t : N \to$ {assign-v-to-one, assign-v-to-zero, predicate-on-v, fork, switch, enter, terminate-at-l, sync }. When executed, an assign-v-to-one node sets the variable v to 1 (v is a variable in V). Predicate-on-v tests variable v and sends control to one of its successors; switch is similar but tests program state instead of a variable; enter changes the program state. A fork node sends control to all its successors, which must eventually re-converge at a sync node. All predecessors of a sync must be terminate-at-l nodes, which indicate the exit level of their respective threads. A sync node passes control to the successor whose number corresponds to the highest-numbered terminate node that passed control to it.

The assign-v-to-zero nodes are only added to the graph during our construction. As its name suggests, an assign-v-to-zero node sets the variable v to 0. In two-valued execution, a variable's default value is 0, making such nodes unnecessary. But in the

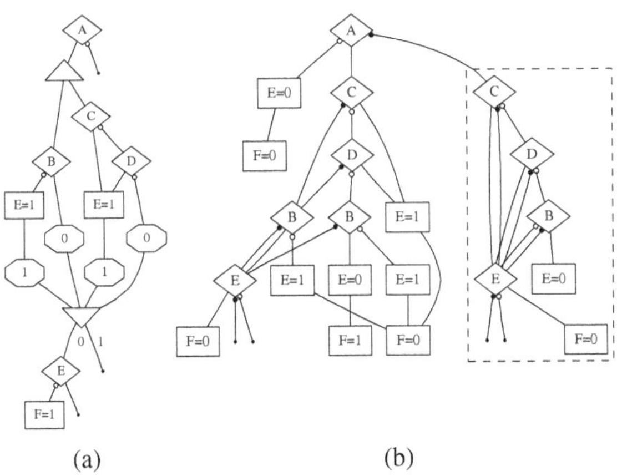

Fig. 1. (a) A two-valued GRC. Arcs with bubbles are taken when a variable is 0. (b) Its three-valued projection produced by our algorithm. Arcs with solid bubbles are taken when a variable's value is unknown. Figure 6 shows the construction of the nodes in the dotted region.

three-valued execution that is the result of our procedure, variables default to the undefined value and therefore require assign-v-to-zero nodes.

Figure 1 depicts such a program graphically. All arcs point downward. The type of each node is indicated by its shape. Assignments are boxes, predicates are diamonds, forks are triangles, terminates are octagons, and syncs are upside-down triangles. The label on a predicate or assignment node indicates the variable tested or set. For predicate nodes, the first (false-valued) arc is indicated with a bubble at its source. The label on a terminate indicates the exit level of the corresponding thread. For sync node, each arc is labeled with a number which matches the exit level. A dashed line denotes a data dependency (as shown in Figure 6a: $6 \to 10$, $9 \to 10$, $10 \to 14$, $15 \to 16$).

A two-valued execution of a GRC program (which contains no assign-to-zero nodes by definition) starts with an initial program state and an assignment of values to input variables (i.e., either $v = 0$ or $v = 1$ for all $v \in V \setminus O$). Then it derives a subset S of the nodes as follows. S includes the root node; every successor node of each fork, assignment, enter, or terminate node in S; and for every predicate node n in S that refers to variable v, the first (true) successor is in S if v is an input variable with value 1 or the graph includes an assignment-to-one node for v, and the second (false) successor of n otherwise. For a sync node, all of its predecessors' (terminate nodes) exit levels are checked, and S includes the sync's successor under the branch whose label is the same as the highest exit number. The value of each output variable is 1 if the set includes an assignment-v-to-one node to variable v and 0 otherwise.

Consider executing the graph in Figure 1a using the node numbers from Figure 6a and with the assignments A=1, B=1, C=0, and D=1. Node 1 is in S since it is the root, and since A=1, node 2 is also. This adds nodes 3 and 8. Since B=1, node 12 is in S but node 9 and node 11 are not, and since C=0, node 4 is in S, and since D=1, node 6 and 7 are in S but node 5 is not. Since node 7 and node 12 are included, and node 7's exit level (1) is higher than node 12 (0), sync node 13's branch 1 is executed. That excludes node 14 and 15 from S. In the end, $S = \{1,2,3,4,6,7,8,12,13\}$ so E=1 and F=0.

The above procedure requires the value of every input variable to be known when the program starts; we want to relax this. In particular, if we know the values of only certain inputs, we would like to conclude whatever we can about as many outputs as possible provided they are consistent with any future values for the unassigned inputs.

One way to answer this question is to execute the GRC program using three-valued logic, i.e., adding a third value that represents unknown or undefined (we write it $\bot$) to the usual 0s and 1s. This introduces another set of nodes to the simulation procedure: those that might run if additional input is provided later. This is a more complicated procedure that does not reduce to the usual sequential execution behavior of imperative programs, unlike the two-valued simulation of GRC defined above, which can be transformed into sequential code using a fairly inexpensive procedure [12].

4 Our Construction Algorithm

Our main contribution is the algorithm described here that takes a GRC program and constructs a fast sequential program that evaluates the graph in the three-valued domain, i.e., it allows some of the input variables to be undefined. Our algorithm works in four

```
procedure Main(G)
   Add data dependencies
   s = topological sort of the augmented graph
   ComputeRelavantVars()
   Set val[v] = ⊥ for all variables
   Set ctrl[n,i] = ⊥ for all nodes & successors
   Set term[n,i] = ⊥ for all sync & exit lvls
   Construct(root of G, val, ctrl, term)
```

(a)

```
procedure ComputeRelavantVars()
   for i = 1,...,N do     schedule is s_1,...,s_N
      Set relevant_arcs[s_i] = ∅
      Set relevant_vars[s_i] = ∅
      for each j = i,...,N do
         for each arc s_k → s_j with k < i do
            add s_k → s_j to relevant_arcs[s_i]
         if s_j tests or set any variable v then
            add v to relevant_vars[s_i]
```

(b)

Fig. 2. (a) The Main procedure and (b) ComputeRelevantVars

phases (see Figure 2a). Given a GRC program, we add nodes and arcs to represent data dependencies, compute a topological order of this annotated graph, compute information about the subgraph under each node that will tell us what information we can forget during a simulation of the program, and finally construct a sequential program by performing this simulation. We try to keep the size of the generated program under control; we do this by allowing as much reconvergence as possible in the generated code, i.e. by identifying (and reusing) equivalent states during the simulation.

4.1 Adding Data Dependencies

The algorithm starts by adding data dependencies. For each output variable v, this process adds an assign-v-to-zero node and then adds arcs from each assign-v-to-one node to this new node, and arcs from this new node to each predicate-on-v node that tests v. The result is that there is now a path from each assign-v-to-one node for a variable to each node that tests that variable, hence ensuring the topological sort respects data dependencies. Furthermore, it introduces an assign-v-to-zero node that will appear in the schedule when it is possible to determine that a particular variable may be zero. Figure 6a shows the effect of applying this procedure on Figure 1a.

4.2 Summarizing Dependency Information

Keeping the size of the generated graph under control is the main trick in our algorithm. Although it would be correct to consider the value of each variable and control arc when considering which subgraphs can be shared during code generation, this would be very inefficient and always produce an exponentially-large tree as a result. Instead, we attempt to model the state of a simulation using as little information as possible because we want to consider a maximum number of states to be identical so code for them can be shared.

Our insight is this: at a particular point in the schedule, we only care about nodes that appear later in the schedule since by definition we must have already executed anything earlier, and only two things matter about them: the variables they test and the state of control arcs that lead from nodes earlier in the schedule to later nodes.

Consider building a subgraph for the nodes starting at 8 in Figure 6a, and assume the node numbers correspond to their position in the schedule. At this point, the simulation will have established values for variables A, C, and D, but we do not directly care about any of them since code for them has already been generated and we will not test any of them later. However, we do care about whether node 10 will be executed, which can be affected by node 6, and whether node 13 was triggered by its predecessors, since we will be generating code for nodes 10 and 13 (they appear after 8 in the schedule).

As a result, we consider identical any simulation states that differ only on variables A, C, or D. We also consider the control flowing in to nodes 8, 10, and 13.

The ComputeRelavantVars procedure (Figure 2b) builds two sets that exactly capture this notion of which variables and control states we care about during the construction. By stepping through the nodes of the graph in scheduled order, ComputeRelavantVars computes relevant_arcs[s_i], the set of all arcs that go from nodes before s_i in the schedule s to nodes after s_i, and relevant_vars[s_i], the set of all variables that are either tested or set in the nodes after s_i. Note that because s is a topological order, nodes after s_i in the schedule necessarily include the subgraph under s_i.

In Figure 6a, if $s = (1,2,3,4,5,6,7,8,9,10,11)$, ComputeRelavantVars finds relevant_arcs[8] = {2→8, 6→10, 5→13, 7→13}, relevant_vars[6] = $\{B,E,F\}$. Both relevant_vars and relevant_arcs are global and are not modified after ComputeRelavantVars.

4.3 Construct

The Construct procedure (Figure 3) simulates the three-valued behavior of the GRC program and, as a side-effect, constructs our objective: a graph that reproduces its behavior. In addition to the node n that is being synthesized, it takes three arrays: val[v] is the value (0, 1, or $\perp$) of each variable; ctrl$[n,i]$, $i = 0,1,\ldots$ is the state (again, 0, 1, or $\perp$) of each control arc leaving each node; and term$[n,i]$ is the state of each termination level $i = 0 \ldots M$ reaching each sync node n (M is the maximum possible exit level reaching n).

Construct begins by checking for an end condition: for the last node in the schedule s, the "node following it" is simply null. It then computes two partial functions (associative arrays): var_state, which contains the value of each relevant variable, i.e., those set or tested by any node that comes after n in the schedule (computed earlier by ComputeRelavantVars); and node_state, which computes the execution state (1=will run, 0=will not run, or $\perp$=might run) of all the relevant nodes, i.e., predecessors of n plus all those with incoming arcs that come before n in the schedule (again, computed earlier by ComputeRelavantVars).

Together, the node itself and the two partial state functions constitute the total state on which the subgraph to be built for n. The procedure then looks to see whether a subgraph with identical state has already been built and returns it if it exists.

Otherwise, the real work starts. First, the node following n in the schedule is identified as m, since it will be recursed on later. The procedure assumes the node n is a flow-through type (e.g., assign-v-to-one or a fork) and sets all its control successors to have the same activation condition as the node itself. These assignments will be modified below when necessary, especially for predicate and switch nodes.

There are two main cases: once the node is known not to run, this information is propagates as far as possible by the PropagateZeros procedure. Nodes that set each such variable to zero are created, assembled into a chain. Finally the subgraph that executes the nodes after n is connected to the end of this chain after a recursive call to Construct.

```
function Construct(n, val, ctrl, term)
  if n is null then
    return null                                          bottom of the program
  Clear node_state                                       partial function on nodes
  node_state[n] = 1 if n is the root node, ⊥ otherwise
  for each arc p -i-> q in relevant_arcs[n] do
    node_state[q] = node_state[q] OR ctrl[p, i]
  var_state = val                                        partial function on variables
  for each v not in relevant_vars[n] do
    var_state[v] = DONTCARE
  if BuiltNode[⟨n, var_state, node_state⟩] exists then
    return BuiltNode[⟨n, var_state, node_state⟩]
  m = node following n in s                              on which to recurse
  for each successor n_i of n do                         assume flow-through
    ctrl[n,n_i] = node_state[n]
  if node_state[n] = 0 then                              node known not to run
    PropagateZeros(n, node_state, ctrl, val)
    Create chain (v_1 = 0) → (v_2 = 0) → ··· → (v_k = 0) for each variable v_i such that
    val[v_i] = 0
    Add an arc from (v_k = 0) → Construct(m, val, ctrl,term)
    n′ = the first node in the chain: "(v_1 = 0)"
  else                                                   node_state[n] is ≠ 0
    n′ = NULL
    case n.type of
    Assign-v-to-one :
      if node_state[n] = 1 and val[v] = ⊥ then
        n′ = Copy(n)                                     assign-v-to-one that executes
        val[v] = 1;
    Enter :
      if node_state[n] = 1 then
        n′ = Copy(n)                                     Enter that executes
    Terminate-at-l :
      c = SyncMap[n]                                     the sync node related with n
      term[c][l] = term[c][l] OR node_state[n]
    Sync :
      BuildSync(n,ctrl,term)
    Switch or predicate-on-v :
      n′ = BuildCondition(n,m,val,ctrl,term)
      goto End
    n″ = Construct(m, val, ctrl,term)
    Link(n′,n″)
  End: BuiltNode[⟨n,var_state,node_state⟩] = n′
  return n′
```

Fig. 3. The Construct Function

```
function BuildCondition(n,m,val,ctrl,term)
  if n is predicate-on-v and val[v] is known then
    ctrl[n,val[v]] = node_state[n]                      active branch
    ctrl[n,1−val[v]] = 0                                inactive branch
    n′ = Construct(m, val, ctrl,term)
  else                              switch or predicate with unknown variable
    n′ = Copy(n)
    for each successor n_i of n do
      ctrl[n,i] = node_state[n]                         active branch
      for each successor n_j of n other than n_i do
        ctrl[n,j] = 0                                   inactive branch
        if v is not NULL then                           predicate value is ⊥
          val[v] = i
      Add an arc n′ → Construct(m, val, ctrl,term)
    if n is a predicate then
      for each successor n_i of n do
        val[v] = ⊥
        ctrl[n,i] = node_state[n]                       active branches
      Add an arc n′ → Construct(m, val, ctrl,term)
  return n′
```

Fig. 4. The BuildCondition Function

The other case, when the node might or is known to run (node_state = $\perp$ or 1), is handled quite differently. Dealing with assign-v-to-one and enter nodes is simple: If it is known to run, it is simply copied to the new graph. Furthermore, for an assign-v-to-one node, the value of v is set to 1 so that it will be propagated to later constructions.

Conditional nodes (predicate-on-v and switch) are more complicated. To deal with them, the BuildCondition function is called (Figure 4). If the processed node n is a predicate-on-v and v's value is known, the branches under n are set to active and inactive depending on the value.

Otherwise, if the node is a switch or a predicate-on-v whose variable v is unknown, the algorithm constructs an identical conditional node in the generated program and considers all possibilities: one of the branches—corresponding to a possible condition—is set active, and the others are made inactive (their control state is set to zero). For switch, the possible conditions correspond to each of its successors. For a predicate node, the possible conditions are related to the variable's value, which can be true, false, or unknown when the generated program runs. In the last condition, all branches are set active. For each condition, the variable value is saved appropriately in val array and then Construct is called on the next node in sequence with the new state.

Terminate and sync nodes deal with exit levels and are handled separately. For every sync node, its related threads' exit levels are preserved by the term array. When a terminate-at-l node is met at the end of a thread, if it is known to be executed, it sets the term array element of the exit level l to be 1 for the corresponding sync; if its control value is $\perp$ and no other thread exited at the same level, the element in the term array is set to $\perp$. The sync node computes the highest possible exit level(s) by looking at the term array, then passes its control value to the corresponding branch. This algorithm simulates the two-valued behavior. BuildSync in Figure 5a simulates sync's behavior.

```
function BuildSync(n,ctrl,term)
  unknown_ctrl = false
  findmax = false
  for each i in term[n], max to min do
    if term[n][i] is 0 then
      ctrl[n][i] = 0;
    else
      if findmax is false then
        findmax = true
        if term[n][i] is ⊥ then
          unknown_ctrl = true
      if unknown_ctrl is true then
        ctrl[n][i] = ⊥
      else
        ctrl[n][i] = node_state[n]
      if term[n][i] is 1 then
        break
  return ctrl
```

(a)

```
function PropagateZeros(n, node_state, ctrl, val)
  if n is null then
    return
  node_state' = node_state
  for each arc t -i-> n do
    node_state'[n] = node_state'[n] OR ctrl[t,i]
  if node_state'[n] is 0 then
    for each successor n_i of n do
      ctrl[n,i] = 0
    if n.type is Assign-v-to-zero then
      val[v] = 0
  m = node following n in s
  PropagateZeros(m, node_state', ctrl, val)
```

(b)

Fig. 5. (a) The BuildSync Function and (b) the PropagateZeros function

For all these types, Construct is called on the next node m and saves the root of returned subgraph to n''. Switches and predicates are exceptional: they have different new states built to meet all possible conditions, so Construct is called for every condition.

Finally, n' is the new node as the root of the subgraph constructed on n. To make it possible to later identify its state, this fact is recorded in BuildNode. n' is returned to the caller, which probably adds an arc leading to it.

We use a few simple helper functions (not shown). Link(n,m) connects arcs: if n is null, it returns m; otherwise, a control arc $n \longrightarrow m$ is added and n is returned. Copy(n) creates a new node in the generated program with the same type and variable as node n.

4.4 State

The Construct procedure maintains a collection of subgraphs in the generated program, each corresponding to a particular node in the original program and the state that it implicitly assumes the original program was in before reaching the subgraph. Such a state is a triple: $\langle n, \text{var\_state}, \text{node\_state} \rangle$. n is the node leading the subgraph constructed, var_state is a partial assignment of values to variables the subgraph cares about, and node_state is an analogous assignment of values to control arcs relevant to the subgraph. Specifically, those that pass into the subgraph from outside: arcs within the subgraph, by definition, will be evaluated as part of the subgraph.

4.5 Monotonicity

The code generated by our algorithm is monotonic. When adding data dependencies (Section 4.1), an assign-v-to-zero node is linked after all assign-v-to-one and before all predicate-on-v nodes. This ensures assign-to-one nodes appear first in the topological order, followed by the assign-to-zero node, and finally all predicates that test v.

A $v = 0$ assignment is made only when none of the assign-v-to-one nodes could or did execute (see Figure 3 line 17-18 and Figure 5b), so the code will never change a variable's value from 1 to 0. It is also impossible for the generated code to change v's value from 0 to 1 because the topological ordering of nodes places assign-to-ones before assign-to-zeros. The *val* array records variables' values throughout the Construct function. So when a predicate-on-v node is met (see Figure 3 line 36-38 and Figure 4), val[v] is checked first. If v's value is known, the only active branch will be set, and the val[v] will not be touched but just passed to later construction (see Figure 4 line 2-5).

4.6 The Example

Figure 6 illustrates some of the algorithm's behavior on Figure 1. A, B, C, and D are input variables; E and F are outputs. Figure 6a was derived from Figure 1 by adding data dependencies. Figure 6b shows the graph after assuming A=⊥, C=0, D=0, and B=0 and arriving at node 14. The label on each arc indicates its value in the ctrl array. Figure 6c is similar, but it assumes A=⊥, C=1 and B=⊥ (predicate-on-D is known not to run in this configuration, so D's value is irrelevant). Our algorithm determines that the code generated for these two states is the same and can be shared.

Specifically, at node 14, variables E and F are relevant (and unknown in both Figures 6b and 6c) and the state of node 14 is relevant. In both cases, the state of 14 is ⊥, which is equal to the ctrl value of incoming arc 13→14.

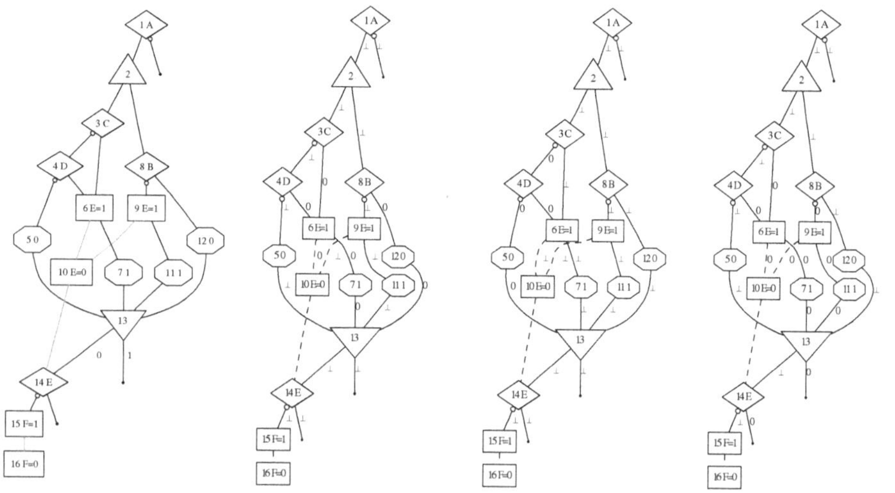

A=⊥ C=0 D=0 B=0 A=⊥ C=1 D=⊥ B=⊥ A=⊥ C=0 D=0 B=1

(a) (b) (c) (d)

Fig. 6. (a) After adding data dependence nodes and arcs to Figure 1a. (b), (c), (d) Possible simulation states upon reaching node 14. Cases (b) and (c) are equivalent since the relevant variables (E and F) and state of node 14 (the one with incoming arc(s) from outside of the subgraph) are the same. Case (d) is different. Cases (b) and (c) share the node that tests E, whereas case (d) creates the E=0 node in the dashed box in Figure 1b.

Table 1. Experimental Results

Example	Lines	Average cycle times		
		Esterel V5	SCFG	3-Valued
comexp	88	1.67s	0.61s	0.80s
iwls3	70	1.04s	0.35s	0.26s
3vsim2	48	0.68s	0.32s	0.46s
multi3	120	1.39s	0.45s	0.47s

In these two states, node 10 may still run in the future, so no code is generated to set E to 0, E is therefore also unknown, so it is tested, and F=0 may later be able to run. The code generated for these states is the test of E followed by the assignment of F to 0 in the dashed region of Figure 1b. Paths from the test of C (i.e., when C is 0—Figure 6b) and the test of B (i.e., when B is $\perp$—Figure 6c) converge on this subgraph because the algorithm has identified these states as equivalent.

By contrast, assuming A=$\perp$, C=0, D=0 and B=1 gives the state in Figure 6d. Here it is known that node 10 (assign 0 to E) will run because none of its predecessors will (this is reversed from the usual rule because such nodes are specially designed to detect when a variable is set to 0). This leads to different code of the other two cases, i.e., the assignment of 0 to E attached to the true branch under the test of B in Figure 1b.

5 Experimental Results and Conclusions

We compared the speed of the code generated by our algorithm to that from the Esterel V5 compiler, which translates the Esterel program into a logic circuit and generates code to simulate it, and to the code generated by the algorithm described by Zeng et al. [12], which generates sequential code by adding guard variables. To obtain the average cycle times in Table 1, we ran the generated C code from all three compilers (compiled with gcc `-O3`) for 10 million cycles on a 2.5 GHz Pentium 4 running Linux.

Table 1 shows our results. While the theoretical complexity of our algorithm is exponential, the experiments we ran show it appears to not be an issue in practice.

The code generated by the other two compilers (V5 and SCFG) only perform two-valued computation. Because our compiler adds code for three-valued computation, it generates slower code. However, the experimental results suggest that the slow-down is fairly mild and in some cases, our compiler actually generates faster code. We suspect it is because our compiler uses a different technique to sequentialize the concurrent code.

Together, these experiments suggest that our algorithm is practical, at least for modest-sized programs. There are certainly additional opportunities for optimization. In particular, we intend to integrate this technique with our earlier technique for producing efficient sequential code from (concurrent) program dependence graphs [12].

Although our algorithm was originally designed to generate monotonic three-valued programs from two-valued ones to work with the heterogeneous synchronous model of computation, it may have other applications. The general idea of partially simulating networks and recording the results as a branching program resembles some approaches for generating efficient simulators for gate-level circuit descriptions [14, 15].

While these approaches insisted on a BDD-like representation, our technique suggests the possibility of selectively "forgetting" inputs, which should give an interesting tradeoff between efficiency and code size.

References

1. Benveniste, A., Caspi, P., Edwards, S.A., Halbwachs, N., Guernic, P.L., de Simone, R.: The synchronous languages 12 years later. Proceedings of the IEEE **91** (2003) 64–83 Invited.
2. Berry, G., Bouali, A., Fornari, X., Ledinot, E., Nassor, E., De Simone, R.: Esterel: A formal method applied to avionic software development. Science of Computer Programming **36** (2000) 5–25
3. Arditi, L., Bouali, A., Boufaied, H., Clave, G., Hadj-Chaib, M., Leblanc, L., de Simone, R.: Using Esterel and formal methods to increase the confidence in the functional validation of a commercial DSP. In: Proceedings of the ERCIM Workshop on Formal Methods for Industrial Critical Systems (FMICS), Trento, Italy (1999)
4. Vachharajani, M., Vachharajani, N., August, D.I.: The Liberty structural specification language: A high-level modeling language for component reuse. In: Proceedings of the ACM SIGPLAN Conference on Program Language Design and Implementation (PLDI). (2004)
5. Penry, D.A., August, D.I.: Optimizations for a simulator construction system supporting reusable components. In: Proceedings of the 40th Design Automation Conference, Anaheim, California (2003) 926–931
6. Edwards, S.A., Lee, E.A.: The semantics and execution of a synchronous block-diagram language. Science of Computer Programming **48** (2003) 21–42
7. Buck, J.T., Ha, S., Lee, E.A., Messerschmitt, D.G.: Ptolemy: A mixed-paradigm simulation/prototyping platform in C++. In: Proceedings of the C++ At Work Conference, Santa Clara, California (1991)
8. Berry, G., Gonthier, G.: The Esterel synchronous programming language: Design, semantics, implementation. Science of Computer Programming **19** (1992) 87–152
9. Bryant, R.E.: Binary decision diagrams and beyond: Enabling technologies for formal verification. In: Proceedings of the IEEE/ACM International Conference on Computer Aided Design (ICCAD), San Jose, California (1995) 236–243
10. Chiodo, M., Giusto, P., Jurecska, A., Lavagno, L., Hsieh, H., Suzuki, K., Sangiovanni-Vincentelli, A., Sentovich, E.: Synthesis of software programs for embedded control applications. In: Proceedings of the 32nd Design Automation Conference, San Francisco, California, Association for Computing Machinery (1995) 587–592
11. Edwards, S.A.: Compiling concurrent languages for sequential processors. ACM Transactions on Design Automation of Electronic Systems **8** (2003) 141–187
12. Zeng, J., Soviani, C., Edwards, S.A.: Generating fast code from concurrent program dependence graphs. In: Proceedings of Languages, Compilers, and Tools for Embedded Systems (LCTES), Washington, DC (2004) 175–181
13. Potop-Butucaru, D.: Optimizations for faster execution of Esterel programs. In: Proceedings of Memocode, Mont St. Michel, France (2003) 227–236
14. Murgai, R., Hirose, F., Fujita, M.: Logic synthesis for a single large look-up table. In: International Workshop on Logic Synthesis. (1995) 6–11–6–19
15. Ashar, P., Malik, S.: Fast functional simulation using branching programs. In: Proceedings of the IEEE/ACM International Conference on Computer Aided Design (ICCAD), San Jose, California (1995) 408–412

Implementation of Hardware and Embedded Software for Stream Gateway Interface Supporting Media Stream Transmissions with Heterogeneous Home Networks

Young-choong Park[1], Seung-ok Lim[1], Kwang-sun Choi[1], Kawng-mo Jung[1], and Dongil Shin[2,*]

[1] Korea Electronics Technology Institute, #8th FL, Good Friend Bank B/D 270-2, Seohyun-Dong, Pundang-Gu Sungnam-Si, KyungGi-Do, Korea
{ycpark, solim, kwchoi, jungkm}@keti.re.kr

[2] Department of Computer Engineering, Sejong University, 98 Gunja-dong, Kwangjin-Gu, Seoul, Korea
dshin@sejong.ac.kr

Abstract. In modern information society, we are confronted by an alteration paradigm called the information technology (IT) revolution. Recently, along with advances in various computing technologies, new concepts, such as a convergence phenomenon among information devices, have given rise to ubiquitous and pervasive computing around the world. Also, the realization of the home network, which is one of the core solutions for future computing, has become an important issue. This paper describes the architecture of the next generation home network interface hardware, which will support various home networks and media services through a media stream transmission in heterogeneous home networks. For the transmission of media streams, such as MPEG-2 TS and DVD, we designed and implemented hardware and embedded software for the stream gateway interface which supports media stream transmission with heterogeneous home networks.

1 Introduction

In the 21st century, we are confronted by an alteration paradigm called the information technology (IT) revolution. Recently, along with advances in various computing technologies, new concepts, such as a convergence phenomenon among information devices, have given rise to ubiquitous and pervasive computing around the world. Emerging ubiquitous computing technology aims to "enhance computer use by making many computers available throughout the physical environment. Computing power and communication capability is embedded in every appliance, including digital-TVs, air-conditioners, sensors, and so forth, and users can access the ubiquitously present appliances anywhere and anytime via home networks like IEEE1394, WLAN, PLC, UWB and Zigbee[1]-[4].

Many researchers consider a home network to be one of the core infrastructures for the realization of ubiquitous computing. In the past decade, there have been numerous

* Corresponding author.

L.T. Yang et al. (Eds.): ICESS 2005, LNCS 3820, pp. 141 – 149, 2005.

research efforts in home networks. The research and development needed for home networks has existed for a long time but have not been used because of difficulties in market formation from the lack of a killer application, a scramble for the technology, and an absence of commercial technology. However, through the development of a national communication infrastructure and the spread of an acknowledgement of our home life, many researchers have proposed a detailed solution to the interspersed problems. Thus, in two or three years, the technology related to a home network will be a popular issue in the IT area.

In this paper, we discuss how we designed, implemented and tested the stream gateway interface (SGI) of a home station (HS) for media stream transmission, to handle a media stream such as MPEG-2 TS, DVD, or VoD in a heterogeneous home network. This interface will be referred to as HS_SGI. Also, we explain the transmission of the media stream by HS_SGI.

This paper is organized as follow: in Section 2, we explain several requirements and system architectures for the next generation home platform (NGHP) through related work on the future home network. In section 3, we describe the HS_SGI architecture in detail. Sections 4 and 5 present the implementation and test of the HS_SGI, respectively. Finally, we conclude with a brief summary and a description of future work in Section 6.

2 Related Work

In the heterogeneous home network environment, the key element is interoperability among the heterogeneous home network devices, multimedia processing for home digital services and linking with the ubiquitous computing technology for the coming ubiquitous home. There are several research studies that have been done to ensure the above key elements.

Schulzrinne *et al.* describes the requirements of a globally-scalable ubiquitous computing system and is developing such a system based on Session Initiation Protocol (SIP), with Bluetooth devices for location sensing and Service Location Protocol (SLP) for service discovery. Also they introduce context-aware location information to augment device discovery and user communication called the Columbia InterNet Extensible Multimedia Architecture (CINEMA) infrastructure for multimedia collaboration[1].

Moon, *et al.* presents universal home network middleware (UHNM) architecture, which guarantees seamless interoperability among the heterogeneous home network middleware for future homes and provides high-level abstraction and zero-configuration, as well as makes new services available without a great effort.

Bae, *et al* proposes a new scheme for the home server platform for providing home digital services by connecting a home network and the internet. This scheme is an integrated form of a home multimedia server, a home control server and a home information server and has an interface between access networks and home networks, various kinds of wired and wireless home network devices, and multimedia processing modules[3].

As shown in the above studies, there are many research studies in the areas of home gateways and servers for multimedia transmission in heterogeneous home networks. This indicates the development of the NGHP in these environments.

The NGHP is taking shape as an integration station that combines the set-top gateway and multi-service gateway. It is becoming a digital convergence media gateway with the abilities of the set-top, broadband modem, home networking and IP streaming. It also has the set-top box function of providing services such as HDTV, Contents Protection, PVR, Web browsing and Interactive TV, along with the transmission of data, voice and entertainment. In order to have the aforementioned functions, there are several requirements for the NGHP:

- universal networking platform based on open architecture
  NGHP needs data communication between the heterogeneous network and the communication platform for an open architecture supporting many to many communications.
- multimedia data Switching architecture
  Since various kinds of stream sources, such as audio, video, control, data and voice are present in the Internet world, the switching architecture needs features such as data-capability, real-time, delay and a mechanism that can switch between channels.
- QoS architecture based on next-generation services
  Since various kinds of multimedia data are present in a home, NGHP should classify and process the heterogeneous traffic.
- common connectivity standardization
  NGHP needs the modularization of the gateway internal function and network interface and the common connectivity standardization to be able to connect universally.

The architecture of the NGHP considering the above proposed features is illustrated in Fig. 1.

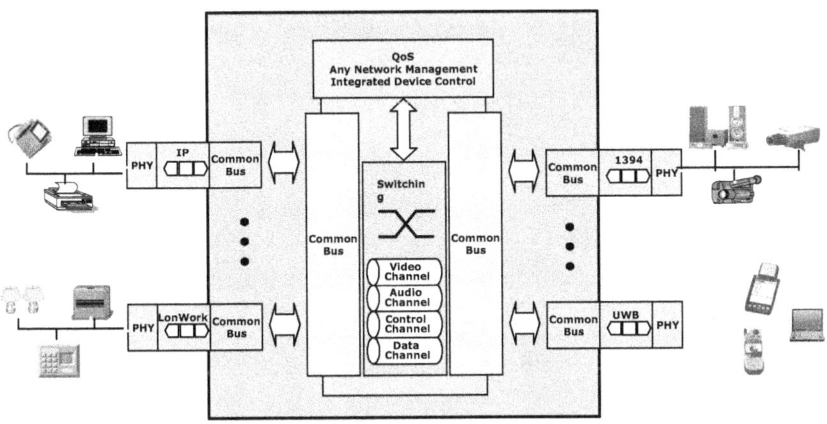

Fig. 1. Architecture of the NGHP

3 Architecture of the HS_SGI

In this section, we describe the hardware and software of the SGI module specified for the transmission of the media stream in NGHP.

Fig. 2 shows the internal architecture of the SGI module. The core hardware architecture consists of the following sub-modules: the LVDS Prot Interface, SGI field programmable gate array (FPGA), CPU Module and Common Bus Interface. The LVDS Port Interface is in charge of providing the MPEG-2 TS packets to the processing module by connecting to the MPEG Test System. We have implemented the HS_SGI Hardware Module using the internal architecture of the SGI hardware of Fig. 2 and made the test board based on it as shown in Fig. 3.

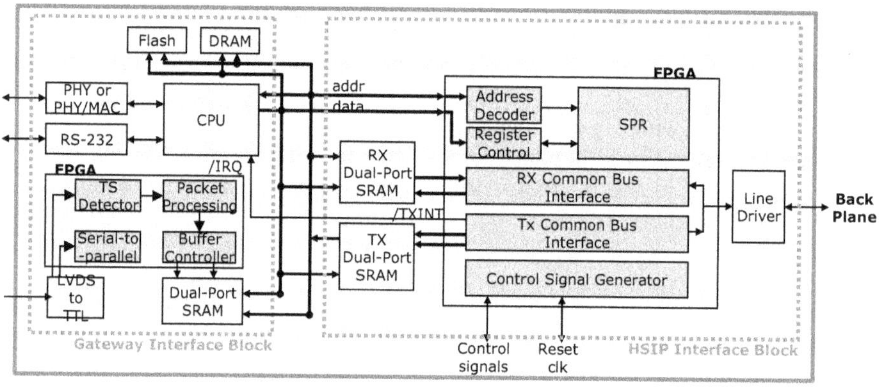

Fig. 2. Internal Architecture of SGI

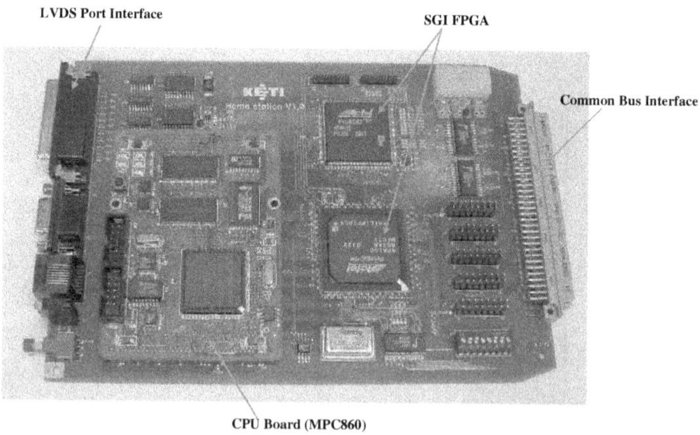

Fig. 3. HS SGI Hardware Module

We have exemplified the SGI Algorithm to operate the module. Fig. 4 shows the operation process of the SGI Algorithm. The system initialization process begins by booting the SGI module. The SGI Module confirms whether the MPEG-TS packet is transferred through the loading of the Polling LVDS module by checking the Rx DPSRAM. After it makes sure of the input of the MPEG-2 TS packet from the MPEG Test System, the Input data is transmitted to the Common Protocol (CP) header generator and the BDP(Buffer Description Protocol) for sending the input data to the HGI (Home Gateway Interface) Module through the Common Bus. After it checks the

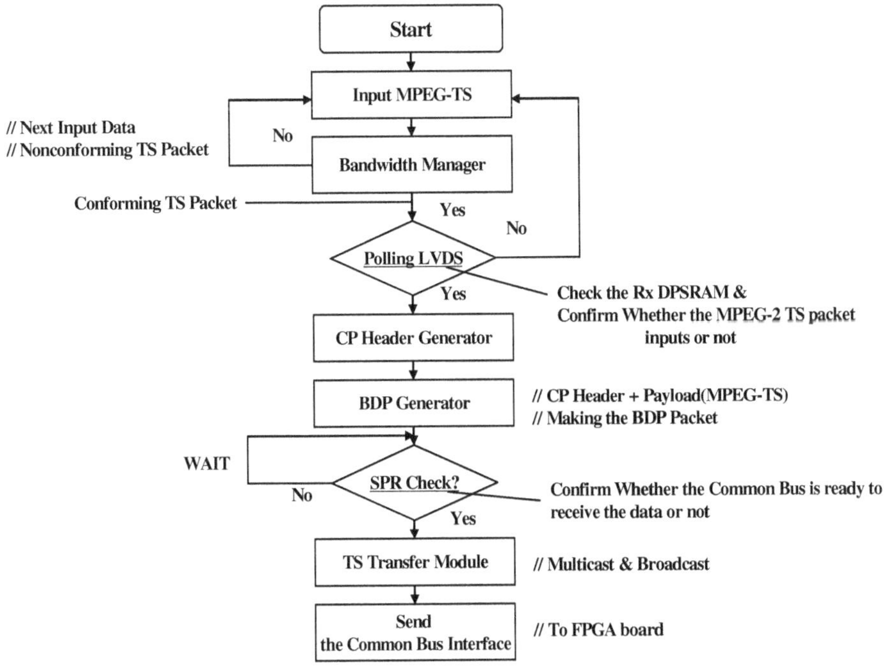

Fig. 4. SGI Algorithm

Special Purpose Register (SPR), which is able to check whether the data is sent to the Common Bus, Packets are stored in the Tx DPSDRAM and input packets are transmitted to the Common Bus via the TS Transfer Module. Through a repetition of this series of steps, input packets are sent to the HGI from the SGI by forwarding the input packets to the HGI Module via the Common Bus.

We are implementing the parts of the bandwidth manager[4] and the TS transfer module mentioned above for a one to one test system. After this, we are going to complement these modules for the processing of a media stream in a many to many test system[6,7]. Until now, we have described the SGI Algorithm for efficiently processing a media stream. In section 4 Implementation of the HS_SGI, we delineate the detailed operating procedure for transmitting media data using this algorithm[5].

4 Implementation and Testing of the HS_SGI

4.1 Implementation of the HS_SGI

In this section, we discuss how we embodied the above SGI design in practice and tested a module to verify the sending of media data via the data scenario ("SGI->HSIP->HGI"). MPEG-2 TS packets produced from the AD953 MPEG Test System are transmitted to the SGI Module via the LVDS interface. The embedded SGI FPGA in the SGI internal module and a CPU board using an MPC860 manages the processing of Module transmission.

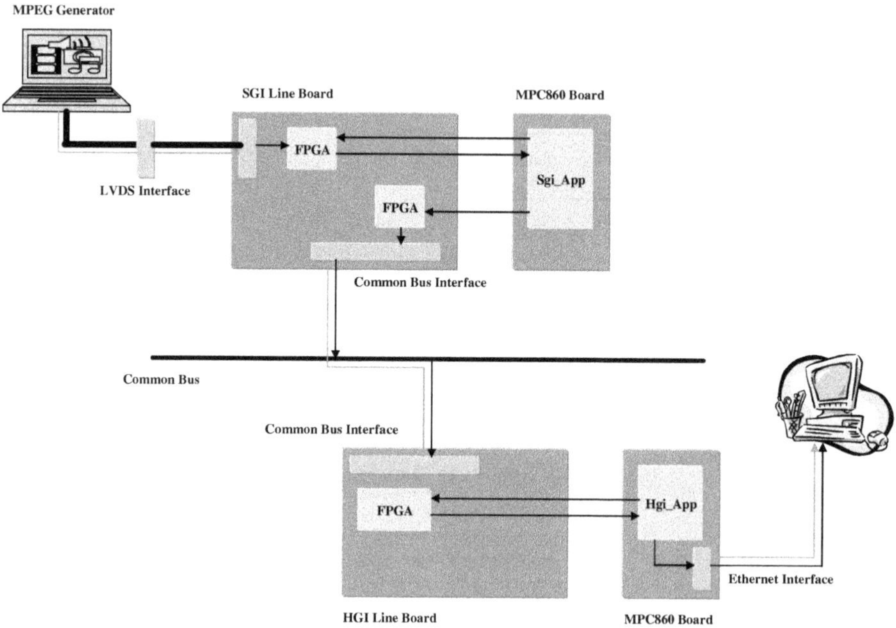

Fig. 5. Data Transmission Architecture between SGI and HGI

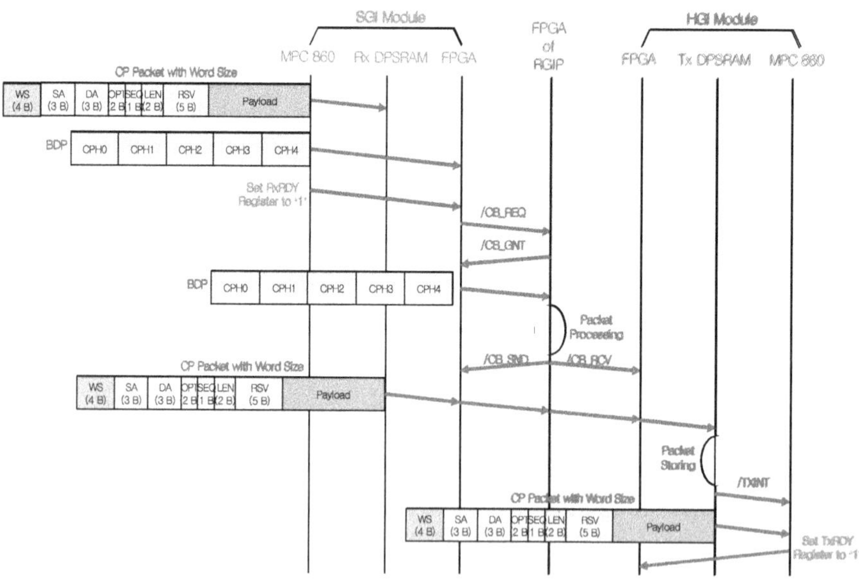

Fig. 6. SGI Data Transfer Flow

Fig. 6 shows the detailed operating procedure using the SGI module. The data produced from the MPEG TS generator is encapsulated as CP packets in the application software of the MPC 860 dotter board, which is the CPU board of the HS SGI board, and stored in the Rx DPSRAM. Thus it creates a BDP using the address of the Rx DPSRAM that is stored in the header information and the data of the CP packet and the created BDP is sent to the FPGA of the HS SGI, after setting the RxRDY register to '1'. When the RxRDY register is set to '1', the HS SGI FPGA sends a Common Bus Request (CB_REG) signal to the HSIP's FPGA. And HSIP's FPGA sends Common Bus Grant (CB_GNT) signal, which means the Bus Admission, to the HS SGI. In order to get the bus admission into the common bus arbitration method, the HS SGI can send the data via the common bus.

The HS SGI receives the CB_GNT signal from the HSIP's FPGA when it is sent via the common bus. After packet processing, the HSIP's FPGA sends the Common Bus Send (CB_SND) signal and the Common Bus Receive (CB_RCV) signal to the HS SGI and the HS HGI respectively. CB_SND means the packet sending signal and CB_RCV means the packet receiving signal. The HS SGI transmits the CP packets stored in the Rx DPSRAM to the Tx DPSRAM of the HS HGI based on the CB_SND and CB_RCV. The HS HGI generates the TXINT signal and transmits the packet in the Tx DPSRAM of the HS HGI to the application software of the MPC 860 board. After setting the TxRDY register to '1', the HS SGI's FPGA is able to receive the data.

4.2 Test of the HS_SGI

Fig. 7 shows the test-bed for data transmission between the heterogeneous interfaces. It shows that packets being sent to the HGI board from the SGI board in our

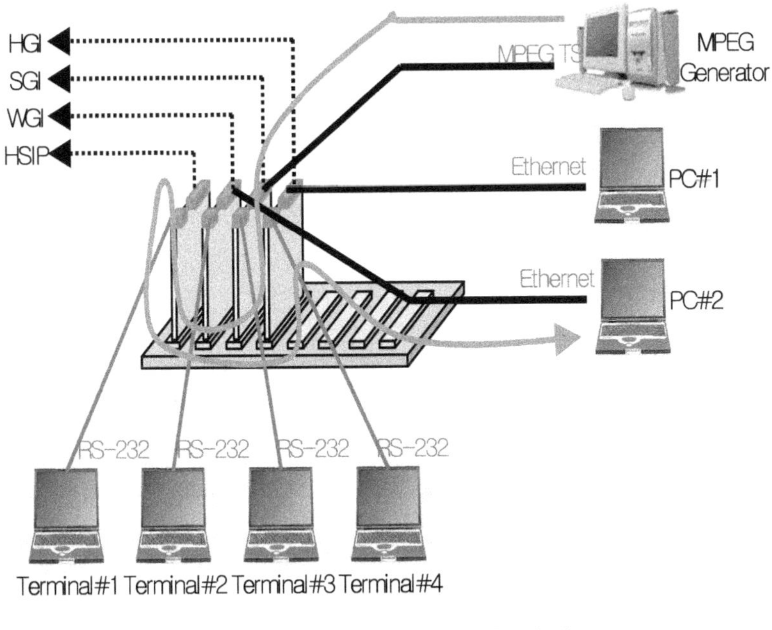

Fig. 7. Data Transmission Test-bed

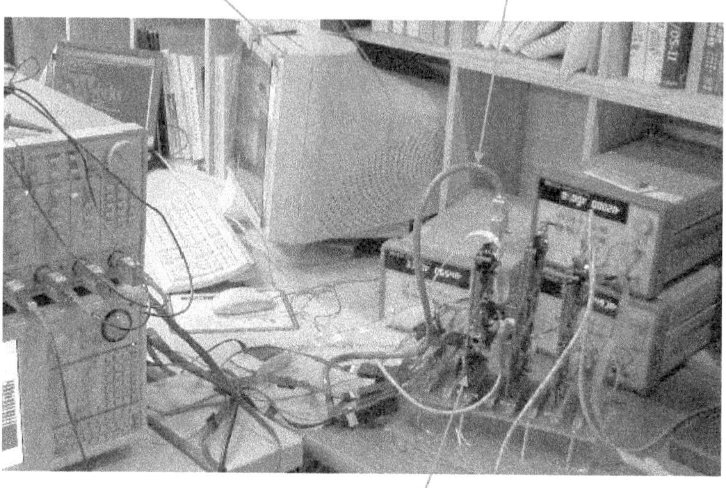

Fig. 8. HS SGI Test Suite

home station. The MPEG-2 TS packets produced from an MPEG Generator are sent to the HGI board, where they are sent to PC#2, which is connected to the HGI interface via Home Station Internal Protocol (HSIP) and HGI. We have implemented the core module using VxWorks as an operating system and tested the core module with several end-devices using various operating systems, such as Linux and Windows.

Fig. 8 shows the test sight of the home station in our lab. It presents a media stream transmission sight through the SGI module of the home station.

5 Conclusion and Future Work

In this paper, we have discussed the design and implementation of the SGI module for the next-generation HS for the transmission of a media stream like MPEG-2 TS packets. Also, the operation of transmission of multimedia data over an HS_SGI has been explained. Since we developed the prototype related to an HS_SGI, we have the ability to develop advanced functions related to the SGI module, such as a bandwidth manager, multicast, broadcast and so forth.

In the near future, based on the diffusion of ubiquitous computing technology and home network technologies, users will require the ability to ubiquitously access present appliances from anywhere and at anytime. Thus, the end-to-end connectivity between appliances inside the home is possible where all the information transported will be multimedia data.

References

[1] H. Schulzrinne, X. Wu, S. Sidiroglou, S. Berger, "Ubiquitous Computing in Home Networks", *IEEE Communications Magazine*, November.

[2] K. Moon, Y. Lee, Y. Son and C. Kim, "Universal Home Network Middleware Guaranteeing Seamless Interoperability among the Heterogeneous Home Network Middleware", *IEEE Transaction on Consumer Electronics*, Vol. 49, No. 3, August, 2003

[3] C. Bae, J. Yoo, K. Kang, Y. Choe and J. Lee, "Home Server for Home Digital Service Environments", *IEEE Transaction on Consumer Electronics*, Vol. 49, No. 4, November, 2003

[4] A. Croll, E. Packman, "Managing Bandwidth: deploying QoS In Enterprise Networks", *Prentice Hall PTR*

[5] N. Chaddha, "A Software Only Scalable Video Delivery System for Multimedia Applications over Heterogeneous Network", *Image Processing*, 1995. *Proceeding., International Conference* on, Vol. 3, 23~26, Oct 19, 1995

[6] Bichot Guillaume, Ramaswamy Kumar, Burklin Helmut, and Stahl Thomas, "Methods for bridging a HAVi sub-network and a UPnP sub-network and device for implementing said methods", *Thomson Multimedia*, 2002

[7] Eiji Tokunaga, Hiro Ishikawa, Makoto Kurahashi, Yasunobu Morimoto, and Tatsuo Nakajima, "A Framework for Connecting Home Computing Middleware", *ICDCSW'02*, 2000

On Using Locking Caches in Embedded Real-Time Systems*

A. Martí Campoy[1], E. Tamura[2], S. Sáez[1], F. Rodríguez[1], and J.V. Busquets-Mataix[1]

[1] Departamento de Informática de Sistemas y Computadores, Universidad Politécnica de Valencia, Camino de Vera s/n, 46022 Valencia, Spain
{amarti, ssaez, prodrig, vbusque}@disca.upv.es
[2] Grupo de Automática y Robótica, Pontificia Universidad Javeriana – Cali, Colombia
eutamo@doctor.upv.es

Abstract. Cache memories are crucial to obtain high performance on contemporary processors. However, they have been traditionally avoided in embedded real-time systems due to their lack of determinism. Unfortunately, most of the techniques to attain predictability on caches are complex to apply, precluding their use on real applications. This work reviews several techniques developed by the authors to use cache memories in "real" embedded real-time systems, with the ease of use in mind. Those techniques are based on a locking cache, which offers a very predictable behaviour. Both static and dynamic use are proposed as well as the algorithms and methods required to make the schedulability analysis using two different scheduling policies. Also proposed is a genetic algorithm that finds, within acceptable computational cost, the sub-optimal set of instructions that must be preloaded in cache. Finally, a set of statistical analyses compares the locking cache versus a conventional one.

Keywords: Cache memories, embedded real-time systems, genetic algorithms, predictability, schedulability analysis, performance evaluation, execution time, response time.

1 Introduction

Embedded systems are composed of a combination of hardware and software components which perform specific functions in host systems, which range from domestic appliances to space explorers. The vast majority of processing elements manufactured worldwide are used in such systems. In some cases, embedded systems need to satisfy stringent timing requirements. Hence, they also may be Real-Time systems, in which the correctness of the system depends not only

* Work partially supported by Ministerio de Educación y Ciencia, Dirección General de Investigación under project DPI2003-08320-C02-01.

L.T. Yang et al. (Eds.): ICESS 2005, LNCS 3820, pp. 150–159, 2005.

on the logical result of computations, but also on the time at which the results are produced.

Embedded Real-Time Systems is a very exciting and expanding field, whose applications are found in command and control systems, process control, automated manufacturing. In every case, they typically control the environment in which they operate and they need to guarantee the response times. To cope with the increasing complexity, many embedded real-time systems use modern microprocessors, which provide a higher throughput. Contemporary microprocessors include cache memories in their memory hierarchy to increase system performance. General-purpose systems benefit directly from this architectural improvement, but for embedded real-time systems, their inclusion raises the complexity when analysing task set schedulability. In fact, using cache memories presents two problems. The first problem lies in estimating the Worst Case Execution Time, *WCET*, due to intra-task or intrinsic interference. Intra-task interference occurs when a task removes its own instructions from the cache due to conflict and capacity misses. When the task tries to execute those removed instructions, cache misses increase the execution time of the task. This way, the delay caused by the cache memory interference must be included in the WCET calculation. The second problem is to estimate the task response time due to inter-task or extrinsic interference. Inter-task interference occurs in preemptive multitask systems when a task displaces the working set of any other task from the cache. When the preempted task resumes execution, a burst of cache misses increases its execution time. This effect, called cache-refill penalty or cache-related preemption delay must be considered in the schedulability analysis, since it situates task execution time over the precalculated WCET. Modelling cache behaviour is very complex, like described in several proposals [3], [8], [7], [6], [2]. Thus, several alternatives to conventional caches have been proposed. One of these alternatives is the use of locking caches.

2 Locking Cache Basics

Several processors include a cache memory with the ability to lock its contents, thus precluding its replacement when the processor fetches new instructions. The use of locking caches in embedded real-time systems offers several advantages:

- Intrinsic interference is eliminated, and extrinsic interference is bounded and can be estimated in advance. This makes cache behaviour very predictable, allowing a simple analysis, even when other architecture improvements are used, since memory access delays are constant. This is an improvement over other alternatives like SMART [5] and others that do not fully remove interferences and still demand complex analyses.
- Necessary hardware is nowadays present in several commercial processors, and only minor hardware modifications are mandatory in order to get the best performance.
- In several cases, the use of locking caches presents about the same or better performance than that obtained when using a conventional cache.

- The use of locking cache is transparent to programmers, since he/she does need to neither include any special instructions nor use additional tools to write the applications.

The only disadvantage when using locking caches is that system performance depends on selecting the instructions loaded and locked in cache. This selection must be carefully accomplished and presents some degree of complexity.

3 Static Use of Locking Caches

The main goal of using statically locking caches is its full predictability and thus, the simplicity when estimating execution and response times [10]. In this case, the locking cache is loaded with a well-known set of instructions before the execution begins, and the cache remains unmodified during system operation. Although locking caches are present in several processors, some minor modifications in these architectures are needed in order to get full predictability and the best possible performance:

- Cache can be totally locked or unlocked. When cache is locked, there are no new tag allocations.
- Cache can be loaded using a cache-fill instruction, selecting the memory block to load it.
- There exists a one-cache-line size buffer to temporarily store those instructions not selected to be loaded into cache, thus improving its sequential access. The penalty incurred for executing instructions to be loaded in this buffer is the same as those executing from cache.

The WCET of tasks may be easily estimated using the timing analysis presented in [13]. The effect introduced by the cache inclusion is then reduced to know which instructions are loaded and locked in cache and which not. Thus, since there are no replacements in cache memory and the set of instructions to be locked is selected by the system designer, the WCET is easily estimated.

Regarding response time of tasks, it can be estimated using Cached Response Time Analysis, *CRTA*, [2], an extension to Response Time Analysis, *RTA*, [1] for fixed priority, *FP*, scheduled systems. CRTA is based in an iterative equation (1) where the cache effect is incorporated in parameter γ_j. This parameter represents the time required to refill the cache after each preemption. When a locking cache is used statically, only the temporal buffer changes during preemptions, so in the worst case the value of γ_j is the time needed to reload the temporal buffer, one cache miss.

$$w_i^{n+1} = C_i + B_i + \sum_{\forall\, j \in hp(i)} \left\lceil \frac{w_i^n}{T_j} \right\rceil \times (C_j + \gamma_j)\,. \qquad (1)$$

When the priority of tasks is dynamically assigned, as it happens with an Earliest Deadline First, *EDF*, scheduler, the schedulability analysis is accomplished using the Initial Critical Instant, *ICI*, analysis proposed in [12]. This schedulability test does not consider any cache penalty due to preemptions, so the effect of cache memories must be included in this analysis. Two questions arise when cache effect wants to be considered: the time needed to reload the cache; and the number of preemptions a task suffers. The first question has an easy answer. When a locking cache is statically used, only the temporal buffer must be reloaded. The second question is more difficult to answer in systems with dynamic priorities. It is quite easier however to determine the number of preemptions a task originates when an EDF scheduler is used: these preemptions can only occur on task arrivals. Therefore, a task generates a preemption when it arrives or does not generate any preemption at all.

Since the ICI test is not based upon the individual times of tasks but rather upon the global system utilisation, the cache penalty (reload of temporal buffer) can be accounted for to the preempting task, instead of incorporating this delay in the preempted task. Thus, equations (2) and (3) show the resulting ICI test equations, where the only modification is to add the time needed to reload the temporal buffer (T_{miss}) to the WCET of each task. By making use of functions $G(t)$ and $H(t)$ it is possible to derive the value of the initial critical instant, R, by resolving the recurrence formula given in equation (4) until $R_{i+1} = R_i$.

$$G(t) = \sum_{i=1}^{n}(C_i + T_{miss}) \times \left\lceil \frac{t}{P_i} \right\rceil . \qquad (2)$$

$$H(t) = \sum_{i=1}^{n}(C_i + T_{miss}) \times \left\lfloor \frac{t + P_i - D_i}{P_i} \right\rfloor . \qquad (3)$$

$$R_{i+1} = G(R_i), R_0 = 0 . \qquad (4)$$

4 Dynamic Use of Locking Caches

Dynamic use of locking cache is proposed with a single objective: getting better performance than that obtained through the static use, and at the same time, keeping a high degree of predictability [11]. The operation of dynamic use is quite similar to the one proposed in the static use: loading and locking in a cache memory a previously selected set of instructions. However, in dynamic use, the cache contents change in well known instants of time: every time a task begins or resumes execution, the cache memory is flushed and reloaded with a set of instructions belonging to the new scheduled task. Once the instructions are loaded, the cache is locked until a new task is dispatched for execution. This way, each task may use all the available cache space in order to improve its execution time, in clear contrast with static use, where all tasks must share the cache. In order to operate as desired, hardware and software requirements must be met. First, the processor must offer instructions to unlock and flush the cache. In addition, the operating system must store the list of instructions (addresses) to load in cache for each task; finally, the scheduler must include a small loop to load the cache every time a new task is scheduled. In this scenario, WCET is estimated in the same way that when cache is statically used, since intra-task interference does not exist. However, the estimation of response time of tasks must consider the effect of reload cache after preemptions, and computing this effect is not easy because tasks may suffer two kinds of interference: direct interference or indirect interference. Direct interference means that a task increases its response time because it is forced to reload its own instructions that were previously removed during preemption. Indirect interference means that a task increases its response time because executing any other higher priority tasks increases its response time, due to its own extrinsic interference.

The value of direct-extrinsic interference is the time a task needs to load and lock its instructions in the cache. The value of indirect-extrinsic interference is the time other higher priority task needs to load and lock its instructions in the cache. Since response time analysis must consider the worst-case scenario in order to provide an upper bound of tasks' response time, the maximum possible increment of time must be taken into account for each preemption. Equations (5) and (6) show the cache refill penalty and CRTA equation respectively. $time\_to\_load_z$ is the time a task needs to load its instructions, and γ_j^i is the cache refill penalty for a task τ_i preempted by a task τ_j.

$$\gamma_j^i = \max_{j<z\leq i} (time\_to\_load_z) . \tag{5}$$

$$w_i^{n+1} = C_i + B_i + \sum_{\forall\, j \in hp(i)} \left\lceil \frac{w_i^n}{T_j} \right\rceil \times (C_j + \gamma_j^i) . \tag{6}$$

When a dynamic scheduler as EDF is used, the sequence in which the tasks are activated is unknown. This means that a task may be preempted by any other task in the system, but it also means that the preempting task may be preempted at the same time by any other task. That is, the number of tasks that may produce indirect interference has no limit. This way, the value of cache-refill penalty due to indirect interference may be the time to reload the cache of any task in the system but the preempted. Thus, the cache refill penalty for any task will be the maximum from the *time_to_load* of all system's tasks, every time, and every preemption. Since the time needed to reload the cache may significantly vary between tasks, considering this scenario will produce a high overestimation when computing the response time of tasks and the system utilisation. Therefore, dynamic use of locking cache is not suitable for dynamic schedulers, due to the impossibility of getting accurate analysis results.

5 Selecting Contents for the Locking Cache

The increase of performance due to the use of cache memories is very significant; hence, embedded real-time systems must take advantage of it. The architecture of a locking cache guarantees determinism, but not performance. In order to achieve both goals, i.e., a fully predictable cache and a performance similar to that provided by a conventional cache, the instructions to be locked must be carefully selected. It is not easy however to find an algorithm that select blocks to load and lock in cache in a straight way. In preemptive, multitasking systems, the execution time of tasks depend on the execution time of higher priority tasks. In addition, indirect interference in dynamic use causes that the response time of tasks depends on the time needed to reload the cache contents. This way, cache contents must be selected considering not the isolated tasks, but all of the tasks interacting in the system. Exhaustive search, including branch and bound, presents an intractable computational cost, since the number of possible solutions is huge. In addition, since the problem is not monotonic, algorithms like hill climbing are not useful. Genetic algorithms, proposed in [4], performing a randomly directed search, can be used in this problem, finding a sub-optimal solution within an acceptable computational time. Two versions of a genetic algorithm [9], one for static and the other for dynamic use, have been developed. The algorithm evaluates a set of possible solutions using a fitness function to sort them. New solutions are created by combining the best individuals of the previous generation, and the process is repeated a fixed number of times. Since the block is the minimum unit of information that can be transferred from main memory to cache, the algorithm provides the set of blocks to be locked, rather than its individual instructions. It also brings an estimation of the WCET of each task executing in a locked cache with the chosen set of blocks, and the response time of all tasks considering the estimated WCET using the locking cache as given by equations (1) and (6). The main disadvantage of the genetic algorithm is its temporal cost, whose execution takes between four and six hours and it may take up to twelve hours when solving some problems. But, on the other hand, it offers an interesting advantage, because several fitness functions may be used to sort the solutions, thus guiding the algorithm to improve the performance in the way that the system designer is most interested on: minimising system utilisation, maximising task slacks, or tuning the response time of tasks.

6 Experimental Results

Predictability and performance of locking cache have been evaluated using a large set of experiments. Around 30 systems have been used. Each experiment is composed of a set of tasks, ranging from three to eight tasks. Tasks used in experiments are artificially created to stress the proposed cache scheme. A simple tool is used to create tasks. The tool requires the main parameters of every task, such as the number of loops and nesting level, its size, loops size, the number of if-then-else structures and their respective sizes. Task period is hand-defined to make the system schedulable, and the task deadline is equal to its period. The workload of any task may be a single loop, if-then-else structures, nested loops, streamlined code, or any mix of these. The code size for a task may be large (up to 32 Kbytes) or short (lower than 1 Kbyte). More than two hundred experiments had been accomplished. Each experiment is simulated using direct-mapped, two-set associative, four-set associative and fully associative caches, with cache sizes ranging from 1 Kbyte to 64 Kbytes. For all cases, line size is 16 bytes (four instructions) and in most of the cases, the task set footprint is bigger than the cache size; furthermore, in some cases, just one task may require more space than the cache can provide. Fetching any instruction from main memory takes 10 cycles, while fetching any instruction from cache (or temporal buffer) takes just 1 cycle. For each experiment, the response time of each task is estimated using the genetic algorithm, then simulated in a locking cache using the blocks selected by the genetic algorithm, and finally it is simulated in a conventional cache to evaluate performance and predictability.

First results concern predictability and accuracy of analysis methods. For a Fixed Priority Scheduler, FPS, response time of tasks (RT_e) as estimated by the genetic algorithm is compared with the response time of tasks obtained by simulating its execution with a locking cache (RT_{sl}). For the EDF scheduler, the system utilisation (U_e) as estimated by the genetic algorithm is compared with the system utilisation obtained by simulating its execution with a locking cache (U_{sl}).

Figure 1 show the cumulative frequency polygons of error between the estimated and simulated results. For an FPS, the error (or overestimation) is defined as $e_{fps} = (RT_e/RT_{sl}) - 1$; in the case of EDF the following formula is used: $e_{edf} = (U_e/U_{sl}) - 1$.

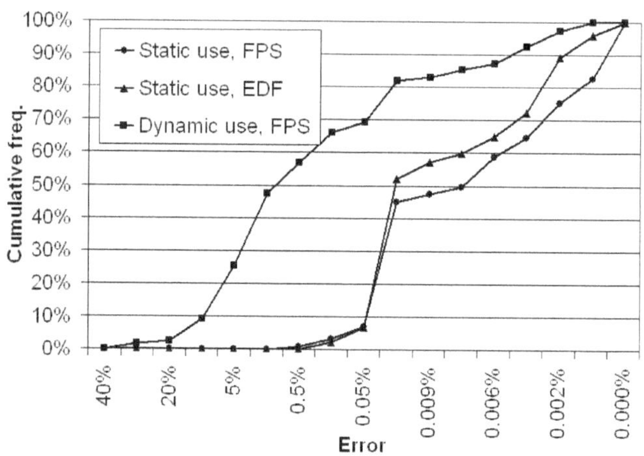

Fig. 1. Cumulative frequency polygon of error between estimated and simulated response time

From Figure 1 it can be seen that for static use and FP scheduler, the error is less than 1% in the whole set of experiments. Furthermore, in more than 90% of the cases, the error is lower than 0.05% and it is below than 0.01% in around 50% of the cases. The results obtained when using a statically locked cache with an EDF scheduler look very similar to those achieved with the FP scheduler. However, it is possible to observe a slightly greater error; it is 0.01% in around 40% of the cases. This is due to the excessively conservative assumption that states that every task causes a preemption when it is activated. Yet, since cache refill penalty is extremely low, error increases in an almost negligible way. Figure 1 also shows the dynamic use of locking cache with an FP scheduler and shows an overestimation, which is higher than that in the two previous cases since taking into account the worst case is inherent to indirect preemptions. In 10% of the cases, error fluctuates between 10% and 30% but it falls down to 1% for more than 50% of the cases. Certainly, there exists a high variability in the error obtained.

Figure 2 illustrate results concerning performance and show the cumulative frequency polygons of gain/loss of performance, P, when comparing utilisation using a conventional (simulated) cache, U_c, and the utilisation using a locking cache as estimated by the genetic algorithm, U_e. Here, $P = U_c/U_e$. A result less than one indicates that the utilisation using the locking cache is higher than the utilisation using the conventional cache, thus losing performance. On the other hand, results higher than one mean that the use of locking caches offers, not just determinism, but also a performance gain.

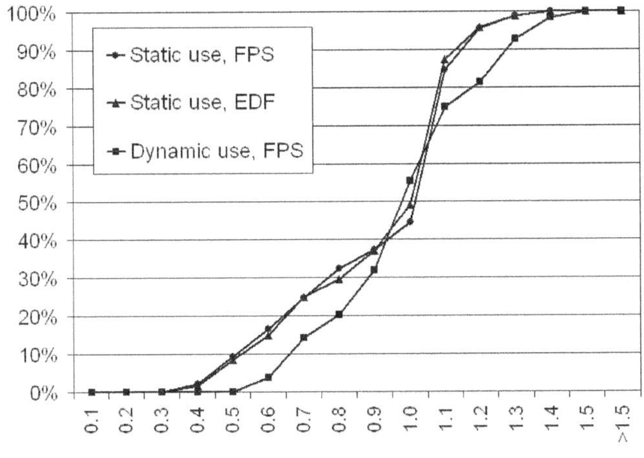

Fig. 2. Cumulative frequency polygon of gain/loss of performance of locking cache in front of conventional cache

In Figure 2, it is also possible to note that for static use and FP scheduler in more than 60% of the cases, there are no significant losses in performance (those in which the ratio is above 0.9). The same conclusions can be drawn from Figure 2 for static use and EDF scheduler. As can be seen in Figure 2, in the case of the dynamic use and FP scheduler, about 70% of the experiments do not demonstrate significant losses in performance; besides that, in 20% of the cases, there is a significant gain in performance (above 1.2) when dynamic use is employed.

7 Conclusions and Future Work

The use of locking caches in embedded real-time systems has proved to be very useful, since it exhibits a highly predictable behaviour, thus facilitating the schedulability analysis and, at the same time, offering a performance analogous to that provided by a conventional cache, which on the other hand, is hard to incorporate into the real-time system analysis.

Moreover, dynamic use of locking cache beats any previous proposal using cache memory in an embedded real-time system:

- In contrast to alternative proposals to conventional caches, the locking cache completely removes intrinsic interference while extrinsic interference is tightly bounded. Other approaches have some level of unpredictability, thus requiring more complex models and analyses to estimate both the execution and the response times.
- Even though using locking cache poses performance losses in some cases when compared to using conventional caches, none of the existing proposals is able to offer a tightly precise estimation, thus resulting also in a performance loss in practical terms.

Albeit it might seem that there are no further possibilities in using locking caches in embedded real-time systems, there still exist some paths to follow. In all of them, the main goal is to increase the performance of the locking cache. This can be done as follows:

- By reducing the time required reloading cache contents in dynamic use of locking cache. This has a twofold effect. First, minimising the time required to reload cache obviously minimises the execution times. In addition, the overestimation of the response times is minimised, which in practical terms is equivalent to a performance increase, since the designer may fine-tune the system in a better way. This reduction can be accomplished by means of a memory hierarchy like those proposed in [14] in which the cache memory can be locked on a per-line basis and include flags to reflect the line lock status for the blocks pertaining to the current executing task. The memory hierarchy also needs an extra, dedicated SRAM to store the locking state information for the whole task set plus some simple, easy to add hardware for proper operation.
- In addition, since it has been found that the performance of the outcome of the genetic algorithm can be very dependant on the fitness function used, the genetic algorithm may provide different fitness functions to satisfy the system designer needs by allowing him/her to optimise the utilisation, the slack, or by trying to find a trade-off solution in between.
- Finally, the genetic algorithm is being parallelised to be executed in a Linux cluster with a message-passing environment by using the homogeneous "island" approach, in which several loosely-related sub-populations are processed by different processing elements to speed up the calculations.

References

1. Audsley, A.N., Burns, A., Richardson, M., Tindell, K.: Applying new scheduling theory to static priority pre-emptive scheduling. Software Engineering Journal, **8** (1993) 284-292

2. Busquets-Mataix, J.V., Wellings, A.J., Serrano-Martin, J.J., Ors-Carot, R., Gil, P.: Adding instruction cache effect to an exact schedulability analysis of preemptive real-time systems. In: Proc. of the Eighth Euromicro Workshop on Real-Time Systems. IEEE Computer Society Press, Los Alamitos (1996) 271-276
3. Healy, C.A., Arnold, R.D., Mueller, F., Harmon, M.G., Walley, D.B.: Bounding pipeline and instruction cache performance. IEEE Trans. Comput. **48** (1999) 53-70
4. Holland, J. H.: Adaptation in Natural and Artificial Systems. MIT Press, Cambridge (1992)
5. Kirk, D.B.: SMART (Strategic Memory Allocation for Real-Time) cache design. In: Proc. of the 10th IEEE Real-Time Systems Symposium. IEEE Computer Society Press, Los Alamitos (1989) 229-237
6. Lee, C.-G., Hahn, J., Seo, Y.-M., Min, S.L., Ha, R., Hong, S., Park, C.Y., Lee, M. C., Kim, S.: Enhanced analysis of cache-related preemption delay in fixed-priority preemptive scheduling. In: Proc. of the 18th IEEE Real-Time Systems Symposium (RTSS '97). IEEE Computer Society Press, Los Alamitos (1997) 187-198
7. Li, Y.-T.S., Malik, S., Wolfe, A.: Cache modeling for real-time software: beyond direct mapped instruction caches. In: Proc. of the 17th IEEE Real-Time Systems Symposium (RTSS '96). IEEE Computer Society Press, Los Alamitos (1996) 254-263
8. Lim, S.-S., Bae, Y.H., Jang, G.T., Rhee, B.-D., Min, S.L., Park, C.Y., Shin, H., Park, K., Moon, S.-M., Kim, C.S.: An accurate worst case timing analysis for RISC processors. IEEE Trans. Softw. Eng. **21** (1995) 593-604
9. Martí Campoy, A., Pérez Jiménez, A., Perles Ivars, A., Busquets Mataix, J.V.: Using genetic algorithms in content selection for locking-caches. In: Proc. of the IASTED International Symposia Applied Informatics. Acta Press, Innsbruck (2001) 271-276
10. Martí Campoy, A., Perles Ivars, A., Busquets Mataix, J.V. Static Use of Locking Caches in Multitask Preemptive Real-Time Systems. Proceedings of the IEEE/IEE Real-Time Embedded Systems Workshop (Satellite of the 22nd IEEE Real-Time Systems Symposium), London, UK, December 2001.
11. Martí Campoy, A., Perles Ivars, A., Busquets Mataix, J.V. Dynamic Use of Locking Caches in Multitask, Preemptive Real-Time Systems. Proceedings of the 15th Triennial World Congress of the International Federation of Automatic Control, Elsevier Science, Barcelona, Spain. July 2002.
12. Ripoll, I., Crespo, A., Mok, A.: Improvement in feasibility testing for real-time tasks. Journal of Real-Time Systems. **11** (1996) 19-40
13. Shaw, A.C.: Reasoning about time in higher-level language software. IEEE Trans. Softw. Eng. **15** (1989) 875-889
14. Tamura, E., Rodríguez, F., Busquets-Mataix, J.V., Martí Campoy, A.: High Performance Memory Architectures with Dynamic Locking Cache for Real-Time Systems. In: Proc. of the Work-In-Progress session of the 16th Euromicro Conference on Real-Time Systems. Available as Technical Report from the University of Nebraska-Lincoln, Department of Computer Science and Engineering (TRUNL-CSE-2004-0010), (2004) 1-4

Trace Acquirement from Real-Time Systems Based on WCET Analysis*

Ji Meng-Luo, Wang Xin, and Qi Zhi-Chang

Department of Computer Science and Technology,
National University of Defense Technology, 410073 Changsha, China
Jimengluo@Yahoo.com.cn

Abstract. Embedded real-time systems often operate under strict timing constraints. In order to test a real-time system thoroughly, we should instrument the system under test with assertions. Thus, the timing behaviors of such a system will change more or less. In this paper, we present two methods to weaken or even remove the timing related impact of the inserted assertions. Firstly, a new monitoring schema is presented which has less time intrusive than software motoring and can test the target system completely. This schema is a mixture of hardware monitoring and software monitoring. Secondly, in order to weaken the time intrusiveness of assertions as much as possible, we present a WCET analysis based time correction method. This method can compute the accurate execution time of assertions and corrects the recorded time of interested events.

1 Introduction

Embedded real-time systems such as avionics are often complex and safety-critical. Their functionality must be thoroughly validated before they are deployed in actual environment. So it is a contemporary challenge for testing such safety-critical real-time systems.

In order to assure their correctness and safety, timing constraints are specified during the design process. In the testing process, test oracles are generated from these timing constraints. Test oracle is a method to verify whether the system under test has behaved correctly on a particular execution [1]. It can not only automatically check if the system under test is acted correctly, but also promotes the efficiency of software testing, and relieves programmers from the tedious work of checking testing results. Obviously, it is inevitable that the traces of real-time systems must be acquired during the process of real-time systems testing.

The inputs of test oracles are traces of real-time systems. Either the hardware monitor or the software monitor is used to acquire the traces of real-time systems. While hardware monitors detect and collect the occurrences of the events outside the system under test, software monitors insert assertions (set of instructions, also called software probes [2]) into the systems under test to detect and collect the occurrences

* This work was supported by the National Natural Science Foundation of China under Grant No. 60303013 and the National Grand Fundamental Research 973 Program of China under Grant No.2005CB321804.

L.T. Yang et al. (Eds.): ICESS 2005, LNCS 3820, pp. 160 – 171, 2005.

of the events inside the systems. Hardware monitors will not change the timing behaviors of the systems under test, but they can't collect all the information needed. For example, hardware monitors cannot detect local variables. Contrariwise, the execution of assertions introduced by a software monitor will disturb the timing behaviors of the application tasks in the systems under test. In the research of test oracle, most effort is on the issues about how to automatically generate executable oracles from real-time specifications, but few of them concerns the acquirement of run-time traces from real-time systems.

In this paper, we discuss the methods of acquiring run-time traces from real-time systems, and present a schema, which is a trade-off between hardware monitors and software monitors, to thoroughly collect run-time traces and introduce as less timing intrusiveness as possible. We quantify the additional time needed to schedule testing task and all the application tasks of the system under test. Then, we present a new method to calculate the execution time of the assertions by the techniques of Worst Case Execution Time (WCET) analysis and correct the timing behaviors recorded by assertions.

The remainder of this paper is organized as follows. Section 2 discusses the advantages and disadvantages of different real-time monitor schema and quantify the time of the intrusiveness caused by the software monitor and inserted assertions. In section 3, we present a method to calculate the execution time of different types of assertions and a method to correct the time recorded by the assertions. We discuss the related works and present a conclusion in section 4 and section 5.

2 Test Oracle and Real-Time Monitoring

2.1 Test Oracle and Monitoring

Test oracle is used to check whether the system under test has behaved correctly on a particular execution based on its specifications. A test oracle consists of two parts; the first part is the oracle information (sometimes is called test oracle directly) that specifies what are the correct actions (behaviors) for the system under test, i.e. designates properties that the system must be satisfied. The second part is the oracle execution process that validates the correctness of the traces acquired from system under test according to the oracle information. It is often the case for the real-time systems that reactivity and timing relations are very complex, so it is an error-free and efficient way to use formal methods and automated techniques during generating test oracles. Fig. 1 shows the role of test oracles in the software testing. Obviously, the acquirement of run-time traces from real-time systems is a premise for the test oracle to work.

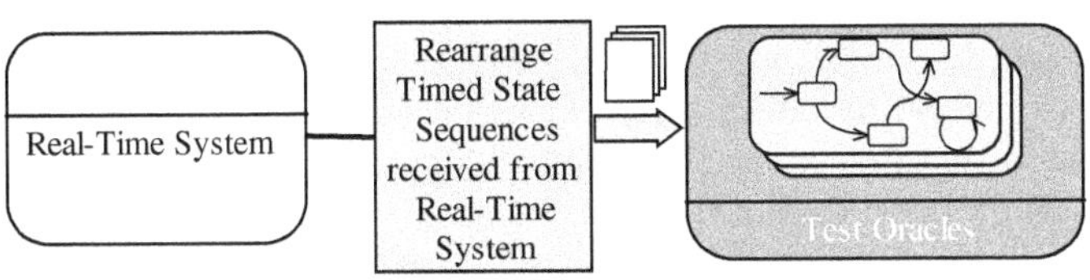

Fig. 1. The role of test oracles in software testing

The main job of test oracle is to monitor the execution of the system under test, and validate whether or not the traces of the system under test satisfy their specifications. Jahanian [3] classifies the monitoring into two modes: *synchronous* and *asynchronous*.

In synchronous monitoring, the software probes (assertions) are inserted into the program and explicitly check the satisfiability of the constraints at a particular point during the execution of the program by directly manipulating the event histories that shared by the cooperating tasks. Thus, handling of any violations against the constraints is carried out synchronously on the threads of the executing tasks. In this mode, the test oracle is executed as a part of the application. Because the execution time of test oracle is immense (it is exponential) [3], the timing behaviors of the application tasks are changed greatly.

Alternatively, in asynchronous monitoring, the monitor, which handles the exceptions asynchronously, is a separate task. The conformance of the run-time sequences of system under test with the specification is checked and handled separately from the application tasks. The program that checks the conformance is called *monitor software*, as shown in Fig.2.

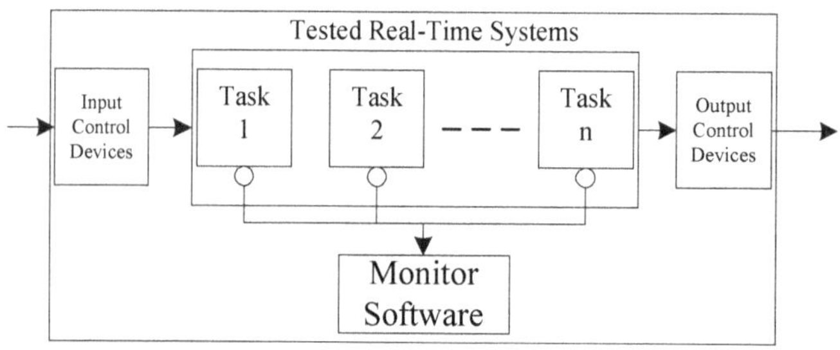

Fig. 2. Asynchronous monitoring

The monitor software is an individual task in the system under test, so it is necessary for a hard real-time system to schedule monitor software as a task with the application tasks together. The application will possibly become unavailable because of the immense resource consuming of the test oracle. So it is a natural choice to place the monitor software out of the system under test. In this manner, in order to flexibly control the events, it is better to split the monitor software into two part, the simple one is called *monitor client* which stays in the system under test and is scheduled with application tasks, and another one is still called *monitor software* which runs on a individual system and takes the main jobs of the original monitor software. The role of monitor client and monitor software is shown in Fig. 3.

Additionally, monitors can be classified into hardware monitors and assertion monitors. Hardware monitors [2] [4] use special hardware (such as specialized coprocessors) to detect and collect event occurrences by snooping and matching bus signals of the systems under test. This method allows non-intrusive monitoring, but it is not sufficient to monitor all the needed changes of events especially when there exist some state changes that are invisible out of the system under test.

Assertion monitor is a kind of software monitors [5] [6] [7] that insert the assertions (software probes) into the systems under test to detect and collect the event data.

Although this kind of monitoring can detect all the event behaviors, the software probes will introduce timing intrusiveness to the target system. Timing predictability is a fundamental requirement of real-time systems. When assertion monitor is used to acquire the system states, the timing intrusiveness introduced by assertions must be quantified.

Based on the above characteristics of monitoring, we present a specification- and system character-dependent trace acquirement schema.

2.2 Specification- and System Character-Dependent Trace Acquirement Schema

Specification- and system character-dependent trace acquirement schema uses different ways to get the traces of an event in system under test relying on whether the monitored event in specifications is external or internal and whether the event occurrence is periodic or sporadic.

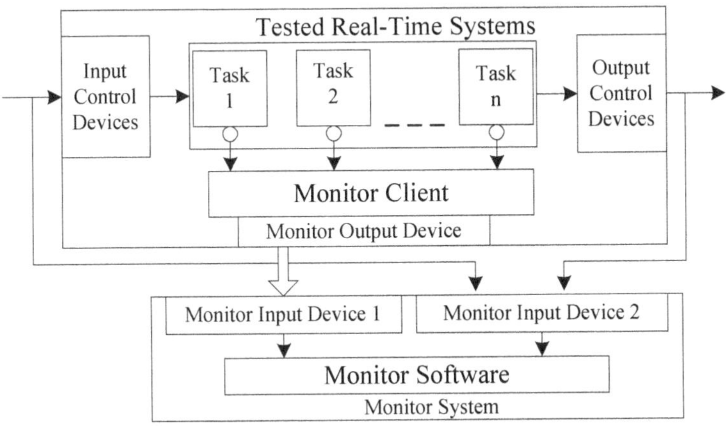

Fig. 3. Mixture monitoring of software and hardware monitoring

As showed in Fig. 3, we adopt a mixture asynchronous monitoring schema, which is a mixture of hardware and software monitoring and place the monitor out of the system under test.

In fig.3, the *monitor client* and the *monitor software* are as mentioned in previous section. Monitor client collects data from the application tasks under test and sends the collected data to monitor system. Monitor client is simple and little-resource-consuming. Monitor input device 1 receives the data from monitor client. Monitor input device 2 collects data from the input and output of the system under test. Monitor software deals with the collected data from input device 1 and 2, and checks the conformance of the run-time sequences of the system under test with the specification.

In the mixture schema, assertions are only inserted after the statements that may change the internal states. When an internal state is changed, its value and occurring time will be sent to monitor client and output to the monitor software. When an external event value is changed, monitor software will capture its state and occurring time.

The advantage of this mixed monitoring include: ① all the states can be monitored; ② Monitor client spends less time because the function of test oracle is moved to software monitor out of the system under test. This schema is suitable for hard real-time system.

2.3 Quantify the Intrusiveness of Asynchronous Monitoring

No matter how simple the inserted assertions are, the timing behaviors of the system under test would be influenced more or less. So when designing the real-time system, apart from the time saved for application tasks, we should save enough spare time for testing. The quantity of the spare time saved for testing is:

$$TimeForTest = WCET(MonitorClient) + \sum_{i \in Tasks} (WCET_{Instr}(i) - WCET_{Uninstr}(i)) \qquad (1)$$

where *Tasks* is the set of application tasks, $WCET_{Instr}(i)$ and $WCET_{Uninstr}(i)$ are the WCET of *i*-th task after and before insertion of assertions, respectively, *WCET(MonitorClient)* is the WCET of the monitor client who is mentioned in previous section.

Apart from the spare time saved for testing, the timing order of the events in original system would be changed by the insertion of assertions. For instance, a specification specifies that *event B* is required to occur before *event A* within $1ms$, i.e. $\Box(A \rightarrow \Diamond_{[0,1]} B)$. If *event A* occurred at moment 10 and *event B* occurred at moment 11 during the first normal running of the real-time system, the specification was satisfied. But *event A* would occur at moment 13 and *event B* occur at moment 12 during the second running of the real-time system after assertions for *event A* and *event B* have been inserted, the specification would no longer be satisfied. This is a typical run-time error due to the insertion of assertions.

To guarantee that the timing order of the real-time system would not be affected by the inserted assertions, the offset time caused by the assertions should be removed from the time they recorded. The affect of the assertions to the original application tasks include two part: one is the execution time of the assertions themselves that would prolong the execution time of the application task, another is the different execution time of the application tasks, which is changed by the existence of the assertions in the system under test, for example, the instruction address of the application tasks would be changed due to the insertion of assertions, and as a result, its cache behavior would be changed.

3 Time Analysis and the Correctness of Inserted Assertions

3.1 WCET Analysis

In order to guarantee each task to be completed within its deadline, we must analyze each task's Worst-Case Execution Time (WCET). WCET analysis is an important area in real-time research area [8], which focuses on computing upper bounds of the processor execution time of code segment for a given application. WCET analysis must fulfill safety and tightness. Safety means that the WCET estimate must not be under the worst case. Tightness of the computed WCET bounds can save the time that must be reserved for each task and, as a result, reduce the cost of the system.

A WCET analysis process for C program is showed in Fig. 4 and is depicted in detail in [9]. The *parser* translates a C source code program into an immediate code that contains the structure information of the program. Based on the program structure information, the *program flow analyzer* extracts flow information for WCET analysis. These flow information contains the call graph of functions, recursive calls, bounds of loops, whether the branches of a *if* statement contain a loop exit statement (e.g. break and return statement), and so on.

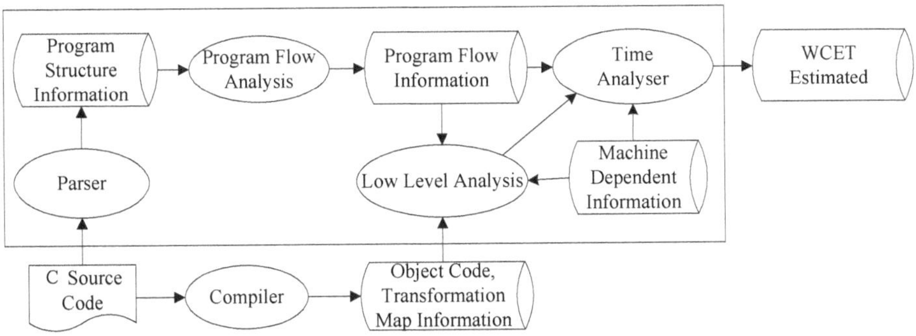

Fig. 4. WCET analysis process for C source code

The C *compiler* translates the C source code into the object code and generates mapping information between the source code and the object code. Based on above information, the program flow information and the specific machine information, *low-level analysis* calculates the execution time of each instruction and/or each basic block [10]. The specific machine information includes the configuration of the computer and the timing characteristic of each instruction. *Time analyzer* computes the upper bounds of the processor execution time of pieces of code for a given task based on the program flow information and the timing behaviors of each basic block that we need.

3.2 Changed Time Analysis for the System Under Test

An instrumentation point *CS* is a place in program where an assertion can be inserted. As an assertion is a set of statements, for the syntax correctness, *CS* must be a place before some statement. Suppose an inserted assertion is *DS*, *CS* is before S_1, the statements after instrumentation would be $DS; S_1$.

A checking point *JS* is a place in program at which we measure the time impact of the inserted assertions. Suppose the beginning place of the program is *KS* (*KS* is not always the first statement of the program, it is the first statement of the application task to be scheduled [11]), and the statements after instrumentation is $DS; S_1$, normally *JS* is just before S_1, but in some cases it maybe in or even after S_1.

For any checking point *JS*, the difference between the time after instrumentation and before the instrumentation is

$$TimeChanged(JS) = Time_{Instr}(KS \rightarrow JS) - Time_{Uninstr}(KS \rightarrow JS) \tag{2}$$

where $KS \rightarrow JS$ denotes the program path from *KS* to *JS*, $Time_{Instr}(KS \rightarrow JS)$ and $Time_{Uninstr}(KS \rightarrow JS)$ denotes the execution time running from *KS* to *JS* after and before the instrumentation, respectively.

Because the program after instrumentation is composed of the original program and the inserted assertions, so there exists

$$TimeChangedInstr(JS) = DSTime(JS) + ChangedUninstr(JS) \tag{3}$$

where

$$DSTime(JS) = \sum_{\substack{DS_i \in KS \rightarrow JS \\ DS_i \in DSSet}} DS_i \tag{4}$$

$$ChangedUninstr(JS) = \sum_{\substack{S_i \in KS \rightarrow JS \\ S_i \notin DSSet}} (Time_{Instr}(S_i) - Time_{Uninstr}(S_i)) \tag{5}$$

denote the execution time of inserted assertions and the changed time of the original program due to instrumentation, respectively. And *DSSet* denotes the set of assertions.

Equation (3) shows that the difference time $TimeChangedInstr(JS)$ of *JS* is composed of two parts: one is the execution time of inserted assertions and another is the difference time of the original program before and after instrumentation, and the latter is related to the former. Similarly, the precision of the computation of $TimeChangedInstr(JS)$ is also determined by the two parts mentioned above.

For simple *CISC* processors (i.e. the execution time of two instructions is equal to the sum of the execution time of each instruction), the inserted assertions have no impact on the execution time of the original program statements, so $TimeChangedInstr(JS)$ =0. But this is not the case for modern RISC processors.

According to the timing property, Engblom [12] classifies the characteristics of modern processor to two classes: global and local. Cache and branch prediction are global and pipeline is local, for instance. For the instrumented statements $DS;S_1$, the pipeline information of S_1 is changed due to the insertion of *DS* [13], so the execution time of S_1 is changed accordingly. The memory address of S_1 may change due to the insertion of *DS*, so the cache behaviors and the timing behavior of S_1 will change at last.

In this paper, we only concern the timing behaviors of inserted assertions. We suppose here that $TimeChanged(JS)$ can always be calculated accurately for checking point *JS*. There are several cases: either the processor is a simple *CISC* processor, or $Time_{Instr}(KS \rightarrow JS)$ and $Time_{Uninstr}(KS \rightarrow JS)$ can be calculated accurately by the WCET analysis technique for the program structure (e.g. the analysis for cache of pipeline by Healy [14] [15]), or although there is an offset of the time analysis, but the difference between $Time_{Instr}(KS \rightarrow JS)$ and $Time_{Uninstr}(KS \rightarrow JS)$ is accurate because they have the same offset.

3.3 Construction of Assertion

Assertions are inserted in the source code of a real-time system. There are two modalities for the construction of assertions: the initial assignment assertions and the normal assertions. Initial assignment assertions assign the initial values to every state at the beginning of the program. The initial values are determined by the specifications. Normal assertions are inserted before the statements that would change the internal state (variable) of the system. Altogether, there are four types of assertion: conditional assertion, for all assertion, exist assertion and the other, as showed in Table 1.

Table 1. Four types of assertion

	Conditional	For all	Exist	Other
Meaning	for judging the change of state	for the formulas contains more than one variable		initialize
Statement Structure	S_1;...;if (E) $\{S_{t1};...;S_{tn}\}...;S_n$;	S_1;...;for (E') {if (E) $\{S_{t_1};...;S_{t_j}$; break;$\}S_{o_1}...;S_{o_m}\}...;S_n$;		$S_1;S_2;...;S_n$;
Initial		√	√	√
Normal	√	√	√	

For example, a constraint □[0, 100](∀i∈1..20(A[i] != *Emergency*)) in a specification, whose meaning is that any component of array A can not be in *Emergency* state within 100 unit, is a *for all* assertion. And a constraint □[0, 100](∃i∈1..20(A[i] == *Emergency*)) , which means that there exists a component of array A which will be in *Emergency* state within 100 time unit, is an *exist* assertion. These two assertions have a same statement structure: S_1;...;for (E') {if (E) $\{S_{t_1};...;S_{t_j}$; break;$\}S_{o_1}...;S_{o_m}\}...;S_n$;, where S is a program statement, E and E' are the codes of conditional expression.

3.4 Execution Time Analysis of the Inserted Assertions

From the point of execution time analysis, the statement shapes showed in Table 1 can be decomposed into three kinds of statement sequences: sequential statements, conditional statement and loop statement.

Sequential statements $S_1;S_2$

For a simple *CISC* processor, its execution time is

$$Time(S_1;S_2) = Time(S_1) + Time(S_2) \tag{6}$$

For a pipelined processor, its execution time can be analyzed by using the reserved table [16][14], i.e. after the concatenation of the reserved table of S_1 and S_2, the execution time of S_1;S_2 is the cycles from the first stage of the first instruction to the last stage of the last instruction.

When there is a cache miss, the penalty time should be added. Healy presented a more accurate calculation for pipeline and instruction cache processor [15].

Conditional statement *if (E) then S1; else S2;*

The execution time of a conditional statement can be calculated as two sequential statements when the evaluation result of conditional expression E is known:

$$Time\ (if\ (E)\ then\ S1;\ else\ S2;) := \begin{cases} Time(E;S1) & \text{if } E\text{=TRUE} \\ Time(E;S2) & \text{if } E\text{=FALSE} \end{cases} \tag{7}$$

where E is the code of conditional expression as mentioned before, $Time(E;\ S1;)$ is the execution time of the conditional expression E and the statement S_1. $Time(E;\ S2;)$ is similar.

Loop statement for (E') {if (E) $\{S_{t_1};...;S_{t_j};$ break;$\}S_{o_1}...;S_{o_m}$}

Suppose the iterations of loop is n>0, then

$Time$ (for (E') {if (E) $\{S_{t_1};...;S_{t_j};$ break;$\}S_{o_1}...;S_{o_m}$ })=

$$\begin{cases} Time(E';E;S_{o_1}...;S_{o_m})*(n-1)+Time(E';E;S_{t_1}...;S_{t_j}) & \text{if } E \text{ evaluated to TRUE once} \\ Time(E';E;S_{o_1}...;S_{o_m})*n+Time(E') & \text{if } E \text{ never evaluated to TRUE} \end{cases} \tag{8}$$

Equation (7) shows that the computation needs to know the evaluation result of the conditional expression E, and moreover, equation (8) needs to know not only the evaluation result of the conditional expression E but also the iterations of the loop. All these information can be acquired through monitor. For example, by inserting some identification statement at a statement entry, monitor can determine the execution path of an inserted assertion.

3.5 Time Computation and Correction of the System Under Test

For any checking point $JS, TimeChanged(JS)$, which is the changed time after the instrumentation, not only rely on the inserted assertion but also the original program. In previous section, we suppose that $TimeChanged(JS)$ can be calculated accurately. For accurate computation of the execution time of a program, loop iterations are the first to be known. Here we discuss how to deal with loop structure of a program in the system under test, the other structures are discussed in [17] [16] [14].

Because of the existence of monitor, the result of $TimeChanged(JS)$ is not required to know in advance. So we can take a more accurate time analysis method than the methods presented in WCET analysis literatures such as [18] and [19]. For example, we can let monitor extract the loop iterations exactly through inserting loop identification at the entry of loop. In the following, we suppose that the loop is at i-th iteration, where i>0. And for any checking point JS, we use $Time(KS \rightarrow JS)$ to denote $Time_{Instr}(KS \rightarrow JS)$ and $Time_{Uninstr}(KS \rightarrow JS)$, where KS is the beginning place of the program.

It is natural to consider that KS is outside of any loops. If not, when JS and KS are in the same level of a loop, it is obvious that $Time(KS \rightarrow JS) = Time(P_{KS \rightarrow S})$, where $P_{KS \rightarrow S}$ denotes the statement sequence from KS to JS.

Suppose *JS* is at a level deeper than *KS*, i.e. *JS* is in a loop for $(E)\ S$, then

$$Time_i(KS \rightarrow JS) = Time(P_{KS \rightarrow WKS}) + (i-1) * Time(E;S) + Time(E;P_{WKS \rightarrow JS}) \tag{9}$$

where *WKS* is the beginning location of statement *S*, $P_{KS \rightarrow WKS}$ denotes the statement sequence from *KS* to *WKS* , and $P_{WKS \rightarrow JS}$ denotes the statement sequence from *WKS* to *KS*.

Using WCET analysis, the monitor can determine $Time(P_{KS \rightarrow WKS})$, $Time(E;S)$ and $Time(E;P_{WKS \rightarrow JS})$ by equation (6)(7)(8), according to the values of conditional expressions of the conditional statements and loop statements and the iterations of loop.

From equation (9), we also have

$$Time_i(KS \rightarrow JS) = Time_{i-1}(KS \rightarrow JS) + Time(E;P_{WKS \rightarrow JS}) \tag{10}$$

Other kind of loop statements (such as while and do...while) and multiple level loop statements can be handled in the similar way.

The occurring time of an event would be changed due to the insertion of assertions, so the timing order of the events from a real-time system would be changed. Through the above computation, we can correct the recorded event time. And as a result, the event timing order is corrected.

Suppose the monitoring time for assertion A is T_A , the corrected time $T_{A'}$ should be

$$T_{A'} = T_A - TimeChanged(JS) \tag{11}$$

4 Related Work

Hardware monitoring approaches are proposed in [2] [4]. These approaches use special hardware (such as specialized co-processor) to detect and collect event occurrences by snooping and matching bus signals of the systems under test. These methods allow for non-intrusive monitoring to the system under test, but are not sufficient to monitor all needed events such as local variables changed in program. Software monitoring [5] [6] [7] approaches insert software probes into the systems under test for event detection and event data collection. Although these methods can detect all event activities, but software probes introduce large timing interference for the systems under test.

F. Jahanian[20] [3] emphasized the quantification of timing intrusiveness of software probes on the behaviors of application tasks and proposed to view monitoring activities as time-constrained tasks and to include them in the scheduling analysis of the systems under test.

Peters [21] designed a monitor for real-time systems which combines software monitor and hardware monitor. The hardware monitor, who is called system monitor in his literature, observes by using specific input devices. Peters' work was similar to ours but does not discuss the problems of timing intrusiveness to the systems under test.

5 Conclusion

In this paper we discuss the timing behaviors of different kind of monitor in real-time test oracle. We propose an asynchronous monitor schema that is a mixture of hardware monitor and software monitor. The proposed schema has as little intrusiveness as possible and can test the target system thoroughly. The only drawback of the schema is its complication.

To test a real-time system completely, the system under test must be instrumented with assertions. The inserted assertions will affect the timing behaviors of the target system. Based on the WCET analysis tool, we accurately calculate the execution time of assertions and correct the event time records.

While the schema is especially suitable for hard real-time system because of its complication, the time corrected method can be applied to both hard and soft real-time system.

References

1. Baresi, L., Young, M.: Test Oracles. Report No. CIS-TR01-02, Dept. of Computer and Information Science, University of Oregon. (2001) http://www.cs.uoregon.edu/-michal/pubs/oracles.html
2. Liu, A.C., Parthasarathi, R.: Hardware Monitoring of a Multiprocessor System. IEEE Micro. 9(5) (1989)44-51
3. Jahanian, F.: Run-time monitoring of real-time systems. In: Son, S.H. (eds.): Advances in Real-time Systems, Prentice-Hall (1995)435-460
4. Tsai, J.J.P., Fang, K.-Y., Chen, H.-Y.: A Noninvasive Architecture to Monitor Real-Time Distributed Systems. Computer, 23(3) (1990)11-23
5. Dodd, P.S., Ravishankar, C.V.: Monitoring and Debugging Distributed Real-Time Programs.,Software–Practice and Experience, 22(10) (1992)863-877
6. Joyce, J., Lomow, G., Slind, K., Unger, B.: Monitoring Distributed Systems. ACM Trans. Computer Systems, 5(2) (1987)121-150
7. Tokuda, H., Kotera, M., Mercer, C.W.: A Real-Time Monitor for a Distributed Real-Time Operating System. Proc. ACM Workshop Parallel and Distributed Debugging, (1988)68-77
8. Puschner, P., Burns, A.: Guest Editorial: A Review of Worst-Case Execution-Time Analysis. Real-Tim Systems,18(2-3) (2000)115-128
9. Ji, M.L., Li, J., Wang, X., Qi, Z.C.: An Automatic WCET Analysis Tool Based on Abstract Interpretation. Computer Engineer, to be printed in 8(2006)
10. V. A, Alfred, Sethi, R., Ullman, J.D.: Compilers, Principles, Techniques, and Tools. Addison-Wesley, (1997)
11. Hu, E.Y.S., Bernat, G., Wellings, A.: Addressing Dynamic Dispatching Issues in WCET Analysis for Object-Oriented Hard Real-Time Systems. Proceedings of the 5th IEEE International Symposium on Object-Oriented Real-Time Distributed Computing. Washington D.C., USA. (2002)109--116
12. Engblom, J.: Processor Pipelines and Static Worst-Case Execution Time Analysis. PhD thesis, Acta Universitatis Upsaliensis, Uppsala, Sweden. (2002)
13. Engblom, J., Jonsson, B.: Processor pipelines and their properties for static WCET analysis. In Proc. 2nd Embedded Software Conference: Alberto, S.V.L., Sifakis, J. (Eds.): Embedded Software, LNCS 2491 Springer Verlag, Grenoble, France (2002) 334-348
14. Healy, C.A., Arnold, R.D., Mueller, F., Whalley, D.B., Harmon, M.G.: Bounding Pipeline and Instruction Cache Performance. IEEE Transactions on Computers, 48(1) (1999)

15. Healy, C.A., Whalley, D.B.: Automatic Detection and Exploitation of Branch Constraints for Timing Analysis. IEEE Transactions on Software Engineering, (2002)763-781
16. Lim, S.S., Bae, Y.H., Jang, G.T., Rhee, B.D., Min, S.L., Park, C.Y., Shin, H., Park, K., Moon, S.M., Kim, C.S.: An accurate worst case timing analysis for RISC processors. IEEE Transactions on Software Engineering, 21(7) (1995)593–604
17. Shaw, A.C.: Reasoning about time in higher level language software. IEEE Transactions on Software Engineering, 15(7) (1989)875–889
18. Healy, C.A., Sjödin, M., Whalley, D.B.: Bounding Loop Iterations for Timing Analysis. In Proc. IEEE Real-Time Technology and Aplications Symposium, (1998)12–21
19. Gustafsson, J., Ermedahl, A.: Automatic derivation of path and loop annotations in object-oriented real-time programs. Parallel and Distributed Computing Practices, (1998)1(2)
20. Jahanian, F., Rajkumar, R., Raju, S.C.V.: Runtime Monitoring of Timing Constraints in Distributed Real-Time Systems. Real-Time Systems, 7(3) (1994)247–273
21. Peters, D.K., Parnas, D.L.: Requirements-based Monitors for Real-Time Systems. IEEE Transactions on Software Engineering, 28(2) (2002)146-158

Elimination of Non-deterministic Delays in a Real-Time Database System

Masaki Hasegawa[1], Subhash Bhalla[1], and Laurence T. Yang[2]

[1] Graduate School of Computer Science and Engineering,
University of Aizu, Aizu-wakamatsu,
Fukushima 965-8580, Japan

[2] Department of Computer Science, St. Francis Xavier University,
Antigonish, NS, B2G 2W5, Canada

Abstract. In a real-time database system, the conventional method of transaction method can not be used. In these methods, the deadlock detection is based on (a) use of delay to cause and watch deadlocks, (b) high overheads of periodic checking (c) Non-deterministic nature of the delays, and lastly, (d) difficulties to scale up the existing solutions (centralized). The proposal is based on enhanced local processing and peer-to-peer (P2P) communication for distributed transaction process. The earlier procedures incorporate additional steps for handling wait-for states and deadlocks. This activity is carried out by methods based on wait-for-graphs or probes. These methods introduce a centralized computation at source (for each occurrence of a delay). The proposal introduces asynchronous operations in transaction processing. As a result the detection processes do not wait for occurrences of delays (time-out). These start the delay elimination process instantaneously. The technique incurs low overheads and eliminates the possibility of occurrence of waiting.

1 Introduction

The distributed computing paradigm emphasizes the use of distributed resources in a decentralized manner. However, the distributed systems perform services such as deadlock detection in a localized (centralized) manner. That is, on each occurrence of a wait-for state, a probe or effort to make a transaction wait-for graph (TWFG) is initiated [4, 9, 10, 14, 15, 16]. This leads to high computation overheads [3, 13].

In the present proposal, a peer-to-peer (P2P) message algorithm attempts to perform detection of wait-for states, by using a P2P model of message communication by using local wait-for precedences [13] (Figure 1 and Figure 2).

1.1 Transaction Processing Using Message to Waiting Peer

We consider performance enhancements using the following.

1. **Local processing:** In a P2P system, it is possible to reduce inter-site communication by considering the available wait-for information in close proximity (next in waiting) of a transaction manager(TM) at its (local) data manager (DM) [13];

L.T. Yang et al. (Eds.): ICESS 2005, LNCS 3820, pp. 172–185, 2005.

2. **Asynchronous Processing:** Many occurrences of wait-for situations can be avoided by informing a peer (data manager or transaction manager), in advance. For example,

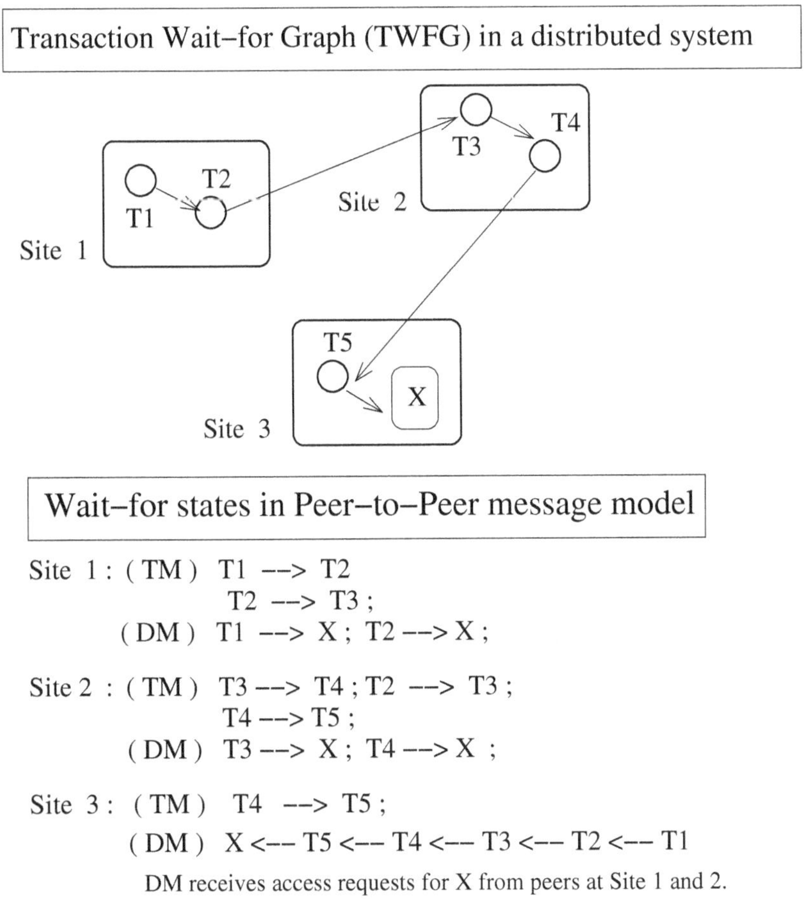

Fig. 1. Equivalent Wait-for states in P2P Computing

- at each event when a peer transaction holding locks, enters a wait stage, it informs the waiting peer transaction of the change in its TWFG.

Most of the earlier research techniques do not consider any co-operation between a TM and DMs [16, 9, 10]. The following is a summary of the proposal made by the present study.

- In place of a global activity to form TWFGs the transaction activity focuses on available information by introducing asynchronous operations, local computations, and parallel computations (see Example 1 and Example 2);

- Commonly occurring precedences as per the order of arrival of transactions can be ignored; The other type of precedences in which a later transaction gets the precedence to execute before older transaction, are termed as 'odd precedences'. Their presence is essential to form any deadlock. Therefore,
  - Deadlock is removed by handling few odd precedences in a P2P manner. Many odd edge precedences can be reversed as soon as these occur without a need to wait for the occurrence of a deadlock.
  - Odd precedence can be substituted by an orderly precedence through an exchange one pair of messages (with no losses) in all the cases of static locking. These can be substituted with similar effects in most cases of dynamic locking.
  - Multiple odd precedences within a TWFG can be processed in parallel to reduce delays; Such local computations can reduce the number of odd precedences and thus reduce inter-site communication overheads;
- For prevention of repeated roll-backs the time-stamp priority can be assigned to a transaction.

These possibilities are briefly described in the following sections. The next section presents details of the mechanism using examples. An analysis of the automatic detection model is presented in Section 3. Section 4 considers higher level wait-for conditions such as multi-level deadlocks. In section 5, the remaining cases that need exchange of a message are examined with the help of a performance evaluation study. The section 6 presents a discussion of the results. The last section presents summary and conclusions.

2 Asynchronous Steps in Transaction Management

2.1 Increased Local Processing Activity in P2P Computing

Deadlock detection is difficult in a distributed environment. Existing algorithms detect deadlocks by constructing a transaction-wait-for-graph (TWFG - a directed graph whose nodes represent transactions and arcs represent the wait-for relationships). The performance studies indicate that a major component of cost of running the detection algorithms is wasteful (occurs in the absence of a deadlock) [15].

The present study proposes an asynchronous detection scheme. It also uses transaction wait-for information. For example, let us assume that transaction T_1 is executing at a site (site 1). On receiving a denial of request that data item is locked by T_2 ($T_1 \rightarrow T_2$), it attempts to find the deadlock forming edge ($T_2 \rightarrow T_1$) from local information. If transaction T_2 is waiting at site 1 for T_1, it indicates a deadlock (Figure 2). Scheduling can be carried out by using such partial graphs without use of lock tables [7, 15, 11, 12, 2, 3]. The change permits increased interaction between a transaction manager(TM) and local and other data managers DMs. The graphs are referred to as local access graphs (LAGs). A LAG of T_i at site S_k contains conflicting edges of all transactions T_j such that, both T_i and T_j have a conflict on some data items resident at S_k (DM5 at Site3 in Figure 1).

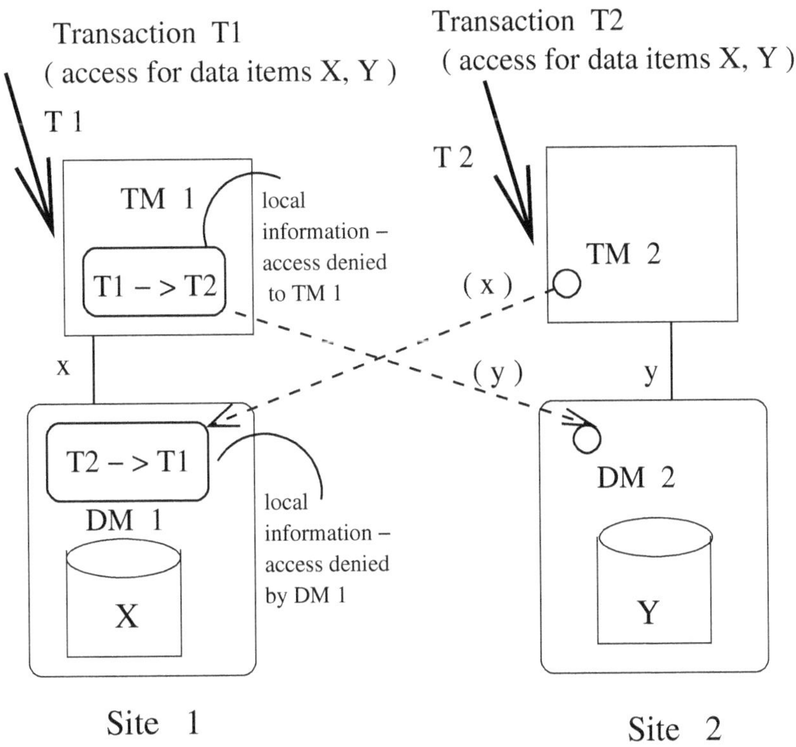

Fig. 2. Deadlock detection process with no inter-site messages

Thus, the possibility of deadlocks is eliminated by local computations. Please consider the following examples. In static locking, all lock requests are granted prior to start of transaction execution. In a distributed database system, in some cases the static locking schemes are preferable to dynamic ones as these allow concurrent transmission of all lock requests. Also, the execution proceeds with no delays, after the grant of locks.

Example 1 : Static Locking (no message exchange for deadlock detection) Consider a distributed system with 2 sites. Assume that two transactions T_1 and T_2 arrive at the same time (time t) and request data items x and y (Figure 2). Initially, TM at site 1 (TM_1) receives the lock for data item 'x'. It sends a message to DM at site 2 (DM_2) for grant of lock for item 'y' (at time t+1). The request is denied. TM_1 receives the message (at time t+2) (Table 1).

The following tests need to be performed at the local site before sending a lock request and after receiving a reject message.

1. examination of all pending locking requests at the local DM (find conflicting transactions, if any).
2. examine the received reject message and search among pending requests at local DM to detect a deadlock .

Table 1. Allocation of data accesses in static locking

Site	Time t	Time t+1	Time t+2
Site 1	TM_1:T_1 needs (x,y) lock x request DM_2 for y	DM_1: T_2 needs (x,y) send reject message $T_2 \rightarrow T_1$	TM_1 receives reject message $T_1 \rightarrow T_2$
Site 2	TM_2: T_2 needs (x,y) lock y request DM_1 for x	DM_2:T_1 needs (x,y) sends reject message $T_1 \rightarrow T_2$	TM_2 receives reject message $T_2 \rightarrow T_1$ abort T_2

In the given example both sites detect a deadlock during the second test.

Example 2 : Dynamic Locking (no message exchange for deadlock detection) Assume that two transactions T_1, and T_2 arrive at the same time and request data items $T_1(x)$ and $T_2(y)$. After few steps of execution more requests for data are generated ($T_1(y)$ and $T_2(x)$). Each site performs the above (two) tests locally.

Table 2. Allocation of data accesses in dynamic locking

Site	Time t	Time t+1	Time t+2
Site 1	TM_1:T_1 locks (x) TM_1:T_1 needs (y) request DM_2 for y		TM_1 : receives reject message $T_1 \rightarrow T_2$
Site 2	TM_2: T_2 locks y	DM_2 : TM_1 needs (x,y) DM_2 send reject message $T_1 \rightarrow T_2$	TM_2 : T_2 also needs (x) request causes deadlock $T_2(x,y) \rightarrow T_1(x,y)$ unlock y, grant $T_1(y)$

Site 2 (on the basis of test 1) detects a deadlock during time t+2 before issuing a request for item 'x'. Transaction T_2 releases y to remove the conflict at the local DM (exchange of precedence). The examples 1 and 2 show ideal conditions (please refer to section on 'Two Site Model' for an analysis).

3 Automatic Detection of Wait-For Condition

Definition 1: (Odd edge, Even edge): Given that, two transactions T_i and T_j have a conflict over data item 'x'. Let T_i be an older transaction with $T_j > T_i$. If T_j waits and accesses data items after T_i, it forms a naturally occurring precedence. The event $T_j \rightarrow T_i$ is termed as an 'even edge'. The occurrence of a reverse wait-for precedence $T_i \rightarrow T_j$ is an antagonistic edge, called an 'odd edge'.

Definition 2: A deadlock occurs when a cyclic wait-for graph is formed. It contains at least one even edge and at least one odd edge.

Definition 3: If two transactions T_i and T_j form a deadlock ($T_j \rightarrow T_i$ and $T_i \rightarrow T_j$), it is termed as a '2-level deadlock'. A deadlock involving 'n' transactions is termed as a n-level deadlock.

3.1 One Site Model

In case of one computation site having two transactions, the deadlock can be detected locally (without inter-site communication). The TM and DM have information about all the wait-for states. By choosing appropriate data structure (section 16.1.4, [17]), it is possible to detect the deadlock, as soon as soon as it occurs. The lock table maintains a list of data items being requested with a linked list of transactions that seek the data items. The data manager also maintains an index of transaction identifiers, so that it is possible to determine-

1. set of locks held by a given transaction;
2. set of other items in the intent list (locks not granted, but waiting) of a given transaction; and
3. set of known transactions in the wait-for graph of a given transactions;

The above index lists are updated as soon as a wait-for condition arises.

3.2 Two Site Model

In a distributed database with 2 sites, if transactions or data items are at the same site, The TM or DM has all the information to detect deadlock (One Site Model, as above). When transactions and data items are separated (Figure 2), messages are needed in some cases. For example, in Example 1 both sites detect the deadlock.

But, in another case(Figure 3), T1 locks Y(at site2, other site), T2 locks X(at site1, other site). T1 needs X, and T2 needs Y. Then TM1 receives information that T1 waits for T2 from DM1. TM2 receives information that T2 waits for T1 from DM2. To detect deadlock, a message is needed in this case (a message from

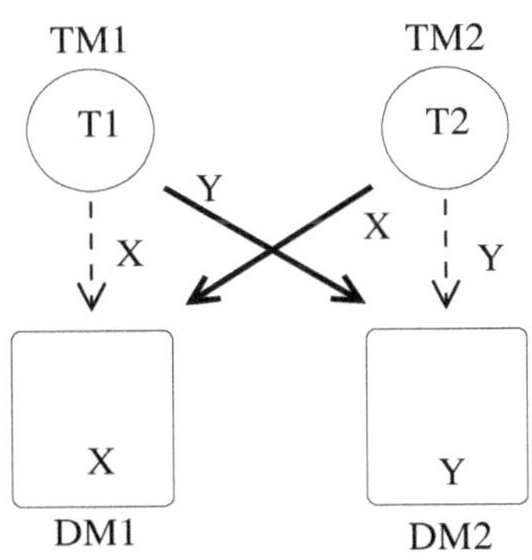

Fig. 3. Two system sites-case 2

DM1 to its peer (at T2) about the occurrence of an odd precedence.). Also, if T2 informs its peer DM2 about occurrence of an odd precedence, DM2 locally informs TM1. A cyclic wait-for condition (deadlock) is detected. The possibilities of occurrences of data items X,Y and transactions T1 and T2 at sites 1 and 2 are listed in Table 3.

Table 3. Enumeration of cases of occurrence of Transaction and data items

Case	X	Y	T1	T2
1	1	1	1	1
2	1	1	1	2
3	1	1	2	1
4	1	1	2	2
5	1	2	1	1
6	1	2	1	2
7	1	2	2	1
8	1	2	2	2

In cases 1-5 and 8, the deadlocks are detected by local computations (either, all transactions are co-located, or all data items are co-located). In cases 6 and 7, possibilities of occurrence of Example 1 (and Example 2) cover 50 % cases (with no message exchange). This leaves about 12.5 % chances of occurrences of cases that need an additional message. (In practice, this number may be less, if at the time of refusing a grant of lock, the DM1 also informs T2 about the wait-for condition of T1. However, in this study, we consider exchange of wait-for edges and not wait-for graphs).

We examine the permutations by which the data or transactions can be at the same site to support conflict detection (see section 4.2). For a general case, binomial distribution of probability (of message exchange cases) for 2 level deadlocks is given by P_n, given n sites in equation (1) (Figure 4) [13].

$$P_n = \frac{n(n-1)^2 + (n-1)(n-2)(n-3)}{2n^3} \tag{1}$$

3.3 Multi-site Model

With increase in the number of sites, the number of cases with no message exchange, are given by equation 1 (above), (Figure 4.). A similar analysis for 3-level deadlocks, shows the number of cases with no message exchange, as shown by (Figure 4.).

3.4 Deadlock Detection by Exchange of Messages

The remaining cases of deadlocks, are detected by incorporating minimal exchange of messages.

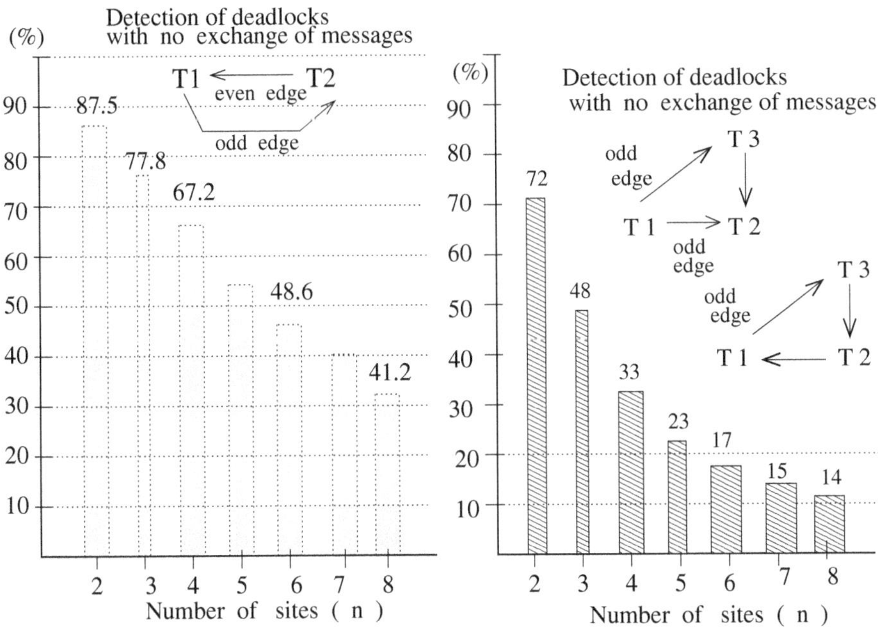

Fig. 4. Proportion of no message exchange cases (2 level and 3 level deadlocks)

Remaining 2 Level Deadlocks. Each transaction has an associated set of DMs that have granted or are considering lock grant requests from the transaction's TM site. As soon as a transaction faces a wait-for condition, its TM informs its peer group (its DM sites and other waiting TMs) about its wait-for condition by virtue of a message. Similarly, as soon as a wait-for condition occurs at a DM, it informs its peers (the transactions that form the wait-for condition), about the occurrence of a wait-for condition. In contrast, conventional techniques wait for delays to occur and then start a deadlock detection process. We have studied the possibilities of message exchanges, and delays, in the Performance Consideration section.

Theorem 1. If an odd edge occurs at data manager site DM_i, then DM_i informs, both transactions T_i and T_j that form the odd edge. A 2-level deadlock will be detected as soon as it occurs.

Proof. The event $T_j \rightarrow T_i$ will be detected by either, T_j or T_i. Both transactions also know about the occurrence of the $T_i \rightarrow T_j$. This is a sufficient condition for deadlock detection.

Remaining 3 Level Deadlocks. If a wait-for edge occurs at data manager site DM_i, DM_i informs, both transactions T_i and T_j that form the wait-for edge.

Theorem 2. In case of two participating sites, A 3-level deadlock will be detected as soon as it occurs.

Proof. In case of two-sites, there are two cases:

Case I: (all three transactions occur at one site) A deadlock will be detected by local computations of wait-for conditions of T_i, T_j and T_k.

Case II: (Two transactions T_i and T_j occur at one site, and third transaction T_k occurs at the second site) A deadlock will be detected by local computations of wait-for conditions at the site with two transactions T_i and T_j, as both transaction have the information about the preceding and successive transaction.

Similarly, in the case of 3 sites, in the worst case, the transactions are separated and are at different sites. At least one of the transactions share additional wait for information with a co-located DM.

4 Remaining Multi-level Deadlocks

4.1 Asynchrony in Processing Steps: Edge Substitution

The sites prepare the wait-for graphs (also called local access graphs (LAGs)) and carry out the following odd edge elimination locally [13]. As a point of departure from the existing practice, the DM does not serve the TM in the first-come-first serve order, but according to transaction order. This steps prevents occurrences of a few wait-for edges and delays due to deadlocks.

Theorem 3: If an odd edge occurs at data manager site DM_i, then, there are two possibilities.

1. The preceding transaction is executing transaction (which will terminate in finite time). If the preceding transaction enters a wait state, it is aborted.
2. The preceding transaction is a waiting transaction, the odd edge is reversed and substituted with an even edge.

This prevents occurrence of n-level deadlock.

This is a sufficient condition for deadlock detection and elimination. This step prevents conflicts by virtue of improved local computations. Thus, by adoption of edge substitution through additional message exchanges many aborts do not occur.

5 Advance Message Communication

For the detection of a deadlock (multi-level wait-for state), asynchronous operations are supported, as per the following description. Advanced wait-for information messages are sent by a waiting TM to the concerned DMs. Each transaction has an associated set of DMs that have granted or are considering lock grant requests from the transaction's TM site. As soon as a transaction faces a wait-for condition, its TM informs its peer group (its DM sites and other waiting TMs) about its wait-for condition by virtue of a message. In contrast, conventional techniques wait for delays to occur and then start a deadlock detection process. We have studied the possibilities of message exchanges, and the delays that are possible. In many cases, it is possible to detect the global occurrence of a deadlock with no additional messages. The following asynchronous exchanges of messages have been examined.

1. Odd-Messages : A blocked transaction, checks if the waiting order is proper (that is, it is waiting for an older transaction). Otherwise, it informs the its peer sites (waiting TMs, or data access site DMs) about its wait-for condition.
2. Even-Messages : A blocked transaction, checks if the waiting order is proper (it is waiting for an older transaction). It informs its peer sites, about its wait-for condition.
3. All-Messages : A blocked transaction, informs its peer sites, about changes in its present TWFG.

5.1 Performance Considerations

Simulation Model. A comparison of performance of a similar edge interchange approach with respect to conventional techniques has been presented in [3]. Intuitively, many transactions gain quick response on account of local processing. Many advanced steps carried out on account of asynchronous computing prevent delays for later transactions. Our simulation study in this report considers the performance of the following four types of asynchronous messages as separate cases.

1. No messages are sent (example 1 and example 2),
2. **even message**: A site at which an even edge occurs, sends a message to its peer sites (e.g. when T2 → T1, the site (TM of T2) sends messages to data sites of T2 and to other waiting TMs),
3. **odd message**: A site in which an odd edge occurs sends a message to its peer sites,
4. **both messages**: A site at which a wait-for state (an even or an odd edge) occurs sends a message to its peer sites.

Under these conditions, we study the formation of deadlocks and their detection. We use an independent algorithm which detects all deadlocks. Thus, we find the number of all deadlocks and the percentage of deadlocks which the algorithm could detect. Table 4 shows parameters of the simulation model. During

Table 4. Data for the simulation model

No. of sites	2-20
Total No. of data items in all sites	10000
Range of transaction size	12 - 30 (data items)
Total No. of transaction	40000
No. of active transaction	5 (range 1 - 10)

Table 5. Percentage deadlocks detected in first cycle of wait-for messages

Number of Sites /messages	2	3	4	5	6	7	8	9	10
Even edges	98	97	96	97	94	96	93	93	93
Odd edges	99	98	97	97	95	94	94	95	94
All edges	100	100	100	100	100	100	100	100	100

Table 6. Average number of messages per transaction (MPL level = 5)

Number of Sites /messages	2	3	4	5	6	7	8	9	10
Even edges	0.9	1.25	1.6	1.85	2.2	2.5	2.7	2.9	3.1
Odd edges	0.8	1.0	1.2	1.35	1.45	1.5	1.65	1.7	1.8
All edges	1.0	1.4	1.9	2.35	2.75	3.2	3.5	3.75	4.0

simulation, the number of messages (NM) of each type and number of deadlocks (ND) are counted.

The possibility of using asynchronous operations method is demonstrated by the following tables. These show the percentage of deadlocks detected by local processing and message communication (one message to a peer (next in waiting) site for conveying edge information). Table 5 and Table 6 show that odd edge detection method incurs fewer overheads and detects more deadlocks. However, detection of all deadlocks, requires sending both types of messages.

Figure 5 shows the proportion of 2 level or 3 level deadlocks within all occurrences of wait-for states.

All 2 level deadlocks can be detected. Similarly, 3 or more level deadlocks in 1 or 2 sites can be detected with few or no message communication.

5.2 Related Studies

In conventional systems, the idea to wait for an occurrence of deadlock and subsequent removal leads to large delays due to synchronized transaction processing activity which causes blocking [6, 8]. Similar delays exist in case of databases with respect to synchronization activity and point out the need for improvements in techniques [1, 6, 5]. Currently, there are few proposals in this area of research [6, 8]. The proposed P2P approach introduces, asynchronous conflict detection. It enhances local and parallel computations.

A few wait-for edge removal approaches have been proposed earlier. In the algorithm [15], the deadlocks are eliminated by reordering the lock requests. The algorithm must also be run regularly to detect deadlocks.

In case of a conventional distributed system, TWFGs can be large and analyzing these for cycles, each time a transaction has to wait, can be time consuming. Based on this observation there have been earlier studies in *time-stamp based deadlock prevention.* These consider aborting the waiting transactions. Two approaches are commonly followed, namely, the *Wait-Die* approach and

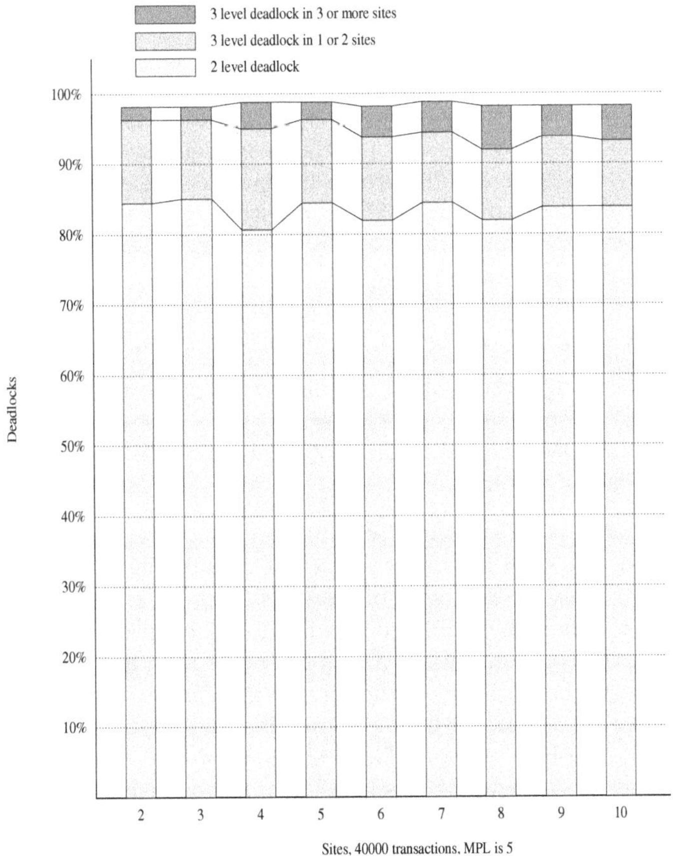

Fig. 5. Proportion of multi-level wait-for states with deadlocks

the *Wound-Wait* approach. Both approaches depend on the occurrence of wait-for status and do not consider the absence or occurrence of a deadlock to decide about the abort. These approaches are similar to the *locking based approaches* with no waiting policy. These reduce waiting delays but incur more wasted processing on account of many restarts [14].

For implementation of P2P computing, the proposed approach is similar to the Wound-Wait approach. However, in place of transaction abort, it attempts to correct the transaction order asynchronously, if it is possible. It considers confirmation (or reversal) of precedence as soon as an odd precedence occurs. Similarly, in the case of data items that are sought by many transactions (*hot spots*) the wait-for precedences are sorted.

Similar to the wound-wait schemes, older transactions succeed in getting data access before newer transaction in case of a conflict. A few remaining transactions restart with their old time-stamp. Eventually each transaction becomes the oldest in the system and is sure to complete (*no starvation*).

6 Summary and Conclusions

The proposal considers enhancements to local processing by considering improved co-operation between peer sites (next in waiting). This mechanism results in removing wait-for delays caused by earlier synchronization activity. Thus, the time-out delays are removed. The proposal depends on use of the asynchronous techniques, such as TM to TM (P2P) computing (edge substitution) and advancing message communication (instantly informing a known wait-for graph to next in the waiting peer sites).

For the server side enhancements, the proposal recommends,

- A wait-for edge (partial wait-for graphs) as a unit for message exchange (in place of a 'wait' or 'lock grant' message).
- The TMs and DMs improve sharing of local (and P2P) information and use improved data structures.

As a result, by asynchronously sending wait-for (even and odd) messages, the system can detect all deadlocks in 1 cycle considering up to 3 server sites. In any system, most of the cases of deadlocks are covered by 2 level and 3 level deadlocks. These are eliminated as a result of local processing. Considering the overheads, the communication of wait-for edges is an asynchronous activity and causes no synchronization overheads. On the contrary, it removes timeout delays. The two proposals, the edge substitution and abort of odd precedences, (as techniques), are P2P activity. These eliminate delays caused by multi-level deadlocks (more than 3 level deadlocks). The proposal attempts to provide true distributed computing environment to achieve higher level of performance. The simulation study confirms the analytical inferences derived for the automatic detection for the wait-for model.

References

1. D. Agrawal, A. El Abbadi, and R.C. Steinke, "Epidemic Algorithms in Replicated Databases," *Proceedings of the 16th Symposium on Database Systems (PODS)*, 1997.
2. S. Bhalla, "Executing Serializable Transactions within a Hard Real-Time Database System," *5th International Conference on High Performance Computing, (HiPC 98)*, Dec. 1998, published by IEEE computer society, pp. 408-415.
3. S. Bhalla, "The Performance of an Efficient Distributed Synchronization and Recovery Algorithm," *Journal of Supercomputing*, Kluwer Academic publisher, vol. 19, No. 2, pp. 199-219, June 2001.
4. P.A.Bernstein, V.Hadzilacos and N.Goodman, Concurrency control and recovery in database systems, Addison-W
5. Y. Breitbart, R. Komondoor, R. Rastogi, S. Seshadri, and A. Silberschatz, "Update Propagation protocols For Replicated Databases," *Proceedings of the SIGMOD Conference on Management of Data, SIGMOD record*, vol. 28, No. 2, June 1999.
6. L. Do, P. Ram, and P. Drew, "The Need for Distributed Asynchronous Transcations," *SIGMOD Record*, vol. 28, No. 2, June 1999.

7. M.H.Eich and S.H. Garad, "The performance of flow graph locking," *IEEE Transactions on Software Engineering*, vol.16, no.4, pp.477-483, April 1990.
8. J. Gray, P. Helland, P. O'Neil and D. Shasha, "The Dangers of Replication and a Solution," *Proceedings of 1996 Annual SIGMOD conference, SIGMOD Record*, June 1996, pp. 173-182.
9. N. Krivokapic, A. Kemper and E. Gudes, "Deadlock Detection in Distributed Database Systems : a New Algorithm and a Comparative Analysis", *VLDB Journal*, vol. 8, no. 2, pp. 79-100, Oct. 1999.
10. A. Kshemkalyani and M. Singhal, "On Characterization and Correctness of Distributed Deadlock Detection," *Journal of Parallel and Distributed Computing*, vol. 22, no. 1, pp. 44-59, July 1994.
11. P.K.Reddy, and S.Bhalla, "Deadlock prevention in a distributed database system," *SIGMOD Record*, vol. 22, no. 3, pp. 40-46, September 1993.
12. P.K. Reddy, and S. Bhalla, "A Non-Blocking Transaction Data Flow Graph Based Protocol for Replicated Databases," *IEEE Transactions on Knowledge and Data Engineering*, vol. 7, no. 5, pp. 829-834, October 1995.
13. P.K. Reddy, and S. Bhalla, "Asynchronous Operations in Distributed Concurrency Control", *IEEE Transactions on Knowledge and Data Engineering*, vol. 15, No. 3, May 2003.
14. I.K. Ryu and A. Thomasian, "Performance Analysis of Dynamic Locking with the No-Waiting Policy," *IEEE Transactions on Software Engineering*, vol. 16, no. 7, July 1990.
15. S.C.Shyu, V.O.K.Li, and C.P.Weng, "An abortion free distributed deadlock detection/resolution algorithm," *Proc. IEEE 10th International Conference on Distributed Computing Systems*, pp.1-8, June 1990.
16. M.Singhal, "Deadlock detection in distributed systems," *IEEE Computer*, pp.37-47, November 1989.
17. A. Silberschatz, H.F. Korth, and S. Sudarshan, "Database Systems Concepts", Mc-Graw Hill Book Company, 4th edition, 2002.

Solving Real-Time Scheduling Problems with Model-Checking

Zonghua Gu

Department of Computer Science,
Hong Kong University of Science and Technology

Abstract. Real-time scheduling is a well-studied field with mature techniques such as Rate Monotonic Analysis. In this paper, we investigate an alternative approach to solving real-time scheduling problems with model-checking. We use the modeling formalism Hybrid Automata and the model-checker HyTech for this purpose, and illustrate advantages and limitations of this approach as compared to the conventional real-time scheduling techniques. In particular, we can use model-checking for analysis of best-case response time of tasks in addition to the worst-case response time, and we can take advantage of HyTech's parametric analysis capability to derive task parameters such as the critical scaling factor.

1 Introduction

Real-time scheduling is a well-studied field with mature techniques such as *Rate Monotonic Analysis* (RMA)[1] [1] that are widely applied in industry. RMA addresses the class of systems where each task is assigned a *fixed priority*. A set of recursive equations are used to calculate the *Worst-Case Response Time* (WCRT) of each task, that is, the longest possible time the task takes to finish its execution, taking into account interference and blocking times caused by higher-priority tasks and shared variables. If a task's WCRT is less than its deadline, then the task is *schedulable*; if all tasks in the taskset are schedulable, then the entire taskset is schedulable. There are other scheduling techniques for *dynamic-priority* systems, such as the *Earliest-Deadline First* (EDF) algorithm, but we focus on fixed-priority systems in this paper, which can be analyzed with the RMA algorithm.

Model-checking is an automated formal verification technique that relies on exhaustive state-space exploration to prove or disprove system properties. This field started with untimed system models and properties, e.g., SMV and Spin, and was later extended to address real-time and hybrid systems, e.g., Uppaal [2] and HyTech [3]. RMA is typically used to determine if the system is schedulable, while model-checking is typically used to verify concurrency properties, as well as system-level timing properties such as freshness, correlation and separation constraints.

[1] *Abbreviations:* BCET–Best-Case Execution Time; BCRT–Best-Case Response Time; HA–Hybrid Automata; RMA–Rate Monotonic Analysis; TA–Timed Automata; WCET–Worst-Case Execution Time; WCRT–Worst-Case Response Time.

L.T. Yang et al. (Eds.): ICESS 2005, LNCS 3820, pp. 186–197, 2005.

In this paper, we use model-checking to address the real-time scheduling analysis problem. Specifically, we use the *Hybrid Automata* (HA) formalism as defined in the model-checker HyTech [3]. There are a number of reasons for adopting the model-checking approach:

- RMA has certain assumptions and restrictions that make it non-applicable to certain scheduling problems, for example, certain types of Ada tasking models [4]. Since model-checking relies on exhaustive state-space exploration instead of analytical derivation, it can handle arbitrary tasksets.
- RMA analysis focuses almost exclusively on WCRT analysis, while it is also desirable to analyze the system's *Best-Case Response Time* (BCRT) when *task jitter* is important, defined as the difference between the WCRT and BCRT of a task.
- The *parametric analysis* capability of model-checkers such as HyTech enables us to perform reverse queries on the system taskset to answer questions such as: how should we modify the taskset parameters in order to satisfy certain system-level timing constraints?

This paper is structured as follows: We first discuss the motivation for calculating BCRT in Section 2. We then provide a brief introduction to Hybrid Automata and the HyTech model-checker in Section 3. We then discuss modeling of real-time scheduling with Hybrid Automata in Section 4, and apply our techniques to an application example in Section 5. We draw conclusions and discuss future work in Section 6.

2 Motivation for Bast-Case Response Time

There are a number of reasons for needing the BCRT in addition to the more typical WCRT of a task. First, some systems may have requirements imposed by the external environment on maximum allowable task jitter. It may not be enough to guarantee that a task completes before its deadline. The task also has to complete *after* a certain time to achieve optimal performance. Second, when analyzing precedence-constrained task-chains, the upstream task's jitter is often a large contributing factor to the downstream task's response time. Due to lack of BCRT analysis techniques, the BCRT is typically assumed to be zero in order to be on the safe side. This results in task jitter that is often much larger than the actual value. This in turn yields overly pessimistic scheduling results for these types of systems, causing low system utilization and wasted system resources.

As an example, consider the taskset in Figure 1. Tasks T_1, T_2 and T_4 are triggered by periodic signals from the outside environment(e_1 with period 10, e_2 with period 30, e_4 with period 50, respectively), and T_3 is triggered by a message sent by T_2 over the network upon its completion. We assume network delays are negligible compared to task execution times. Within the boxes are shown the task's [BCET, WCET] pair and its priority. Even though the external trigger is strictly periodic, the upstream task T_2 has variable response times, which translates into the release jitters of the downstream task T_3. This has

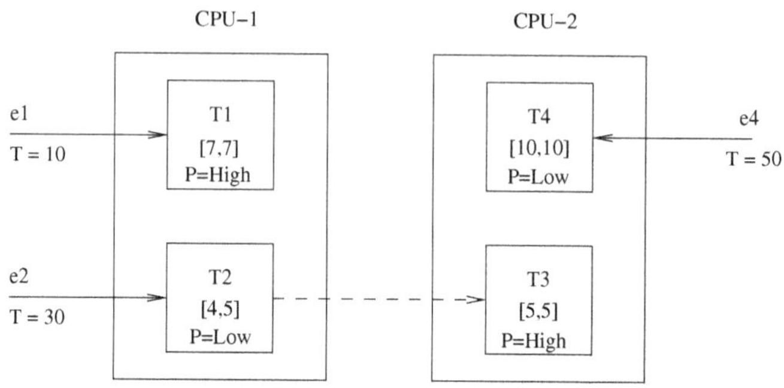

Fig. 1. Taskset with 4 tasks and 2 processors

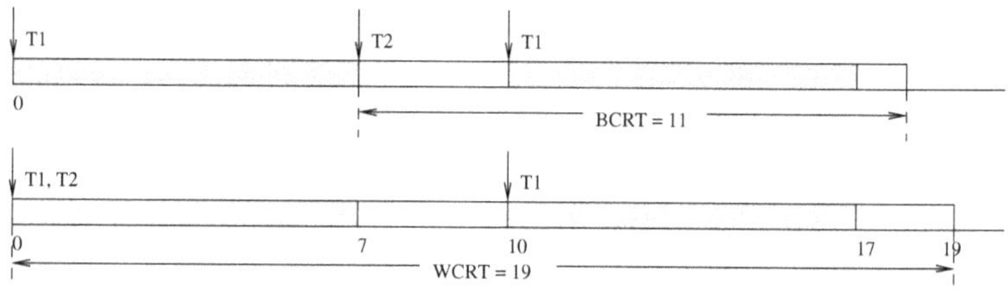

Fig. 2. Calculation of T_3's release jitter

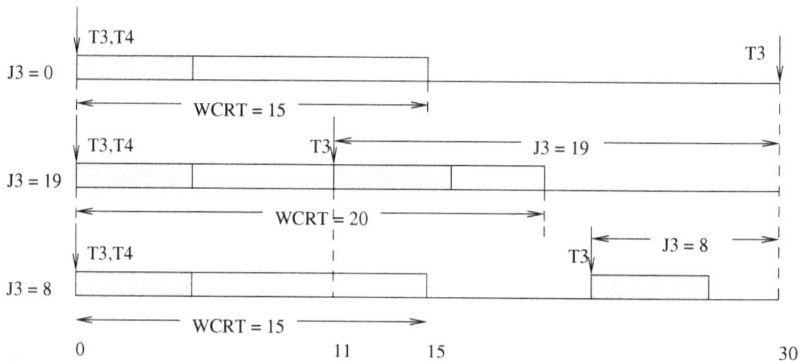

Fig. 3. The effects of high-priority T_3's release jitter on low-priority T_4's response time

a detrimental effect on a lower-priority task T_4. In Figure 2, downward arrows indicate task release. BCRT of T_2 is achieved when it is released at time 7 and executes for its BCET 4. WCRT of T_2 is achieved when it is released at time 0 and executes for its WCET 5. The release jitter of T_3 is therefore $J_3 = \text{WCRT}_2 - \text{BCRT}_2 = 19 - 11 = 8$. The top part of Figure 3 shows the case where $J_3 = 0$. T_4 is preempted only once and has a WCRT of 15. The middle part shows the case where $J_3 = 19$, that is, we consider $\text{WCRT}_2 = 19$ and $\text{BCRT}_2 = 0$ in the absence of appropriate BCRT analysis techniques. Here excessive release jitter of T_3 results in a pessimistic estimate of T_4's WCRT (20). The bottom part shows the case where $J_3 = 8$, the true release jitter of T_3. Here T_4 achieves a WCRT of 15. This example shows the importance of obtaining BCRT for accurate estimation of release jitters.

This point can be seen clearly from the RMA equations for calculating WCRT of a task T_i:

$$w_i^{n+1} = C_i + B_i + \sum_{\forall j \in hp(i)} \lceil \frac{J_j + w_i^n}{P_j} \rceil C_j \quad (1)$$

$$R_i = w_i + J_i \quad (2)$$

R_i WCRT of task T_i.
w_i intermediate variable for calculating R_i.
$hp(i)$ set of tasks that can preempt T_i.
C_l WCET of T_l.
P_j period of T_j.
B_j blocking term, i.e., worst-case delay caused by shared-resource synchronization with lower-priority tasks.
J_j worst-case jitter for T_j.

The jitter J_j is equal to the maximum variation of the response time of the task that precedes T_j. Let's call it T_k with BCRT_k and WCRT_k. Then $J_j = \text{WCRT}_k - \text{BCRT}_k$. Without effective techniques for calculating BCRT, we assume that $\text{BCRT}_k = 0$, hence $J_j = \text{WCRT}_k$. However, if we can have a more accurate estimation of BCRT_k, then we can have a smaller jitter J_j, and in turn, a smaller WCRT_i for T_i. Using HyTech, we can derive accurate BCRT and WCRT values for all tasksets that can be modeled with HA. Next, we discuss the details of our modeling approach.

3 Introduction to Hybrid Automata and HyTech

A *hybrid dynamical system* has both real-valued and boolean-valued variables. A system trajectory is a sequence of flows and jumps: during flows, the boolean part of the state stays constant and the real part of the state evolves over time; at jumps, the entire state changes instantaneously. We describe hybrid dynamical systems using *Hybrid Automata* (HA). A HA annotates the control graph of a finite automaton with conditions on real-valued variables. Each node of the graph represents an operating mode of the system, and is annotated with differential inequalities that prescribe the possible evolutions (flows) of the real variables while the system remains in the given mode. Each edge of the graph represents a switch in operating mode, and is annotated with a condition that prescribes the possible changes (jumps) of the real variables when the system executes the mode switch. HyTech [3] is a model-checker for *Linear Hybrid Automata* (LHA), where the dynamics of the continuous variables are defined by linear differential inequalities of the form $A\dot{\mathbf{x}} \sim b$, where $\mathbf{x}$ is the vector of first derivatives of the variables $\mathbf{x}$. Since the only real-valued variable involved in real-time scheduling

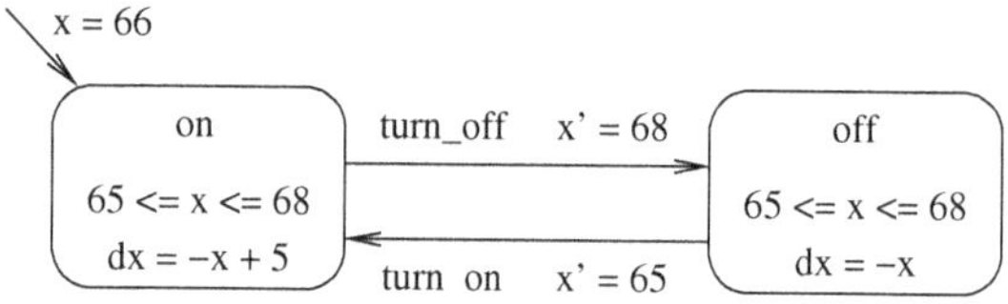

Fig. 4. The thermostat automaton

is time, which always increases linearly, all real-time scheduling problems can be encoded with LHA, hence are amenable to analysis using HyTech.

Figure 4 shows the HA model for a thermostat, taken from [3]. It has two operating modes: the heater is on (mode `on`), or off (mode `off`). Initially, the heater is on and the temperature x is 66 degrees. When the heater is on, the temperature rises at the rate of $-x+5$ degrees per minute; when the heater is off, the temperature falls at the rate of $-x$ degrees per minute. The heater can be turned off when the temperature reaches 68 degrees, and it can be turned on when the temperature falls to 65 degree. This is due to the edge conditions $x = 68$ and $x = 65$, which assert when a mode switch *may* occur. To force mode switches, such as forcing the heater to be turned off when the temperature reaches 68 degrees, we annotate the operating modes with so-called *invariant conditions* (in addition to the annotation with differential equations): the system can remain in a mode only as long as the corresponding invariant condition is satisfied. Thus, the invariant conditions $65 \leq x \leq 68$ of both operating modes prescribe that a mode switch *must* occur before the temperature leaves the operating interval of $[65, 68]$ degrees.

Though not shown in the example, *events* permit the synchronization of jumps between concurrent hybrid automata. Events has a *broadcast* synchronization semantics, as opposed to the conventional *pairwise* synchronization semantics in processes algebras, with explicit notation of input and output channels like `e?` and `e!`. In HA, event labels do not have input or output direction, but all automata with the same event label must synchronize and make a transition simultaneously. An *urgent* event is denoted by having `asap` in front of the event label. Jumps enabled by urgent events must be taken as soon as possible without delay.

A major strength of HyTech is its ability to perform parametric analysis. Often a system is described using parameters, and the designer is interested in knowing which values of the parameters are required for correctness. For example, we can set the rate condition in the `on` state of the Thermostat automaton to be $dx = -x + \alpha$, and then determine the necessary range of the parameter α in order to satisfy the requirement that the heater is active less than 2/3 of the first 60 minutes. In comparison, UPPAAL [2], a model-checker for Timed Automata, does not have parametric analysis capabilities, and one must resort to a trial-and-error approach based on binary search to obtain similar results.

Real-time modeling formalisms can be either *discrete-time*, where time progresses in discrete steps, or *dense-time*, where time is a continuous variable. Using discrete-time formalisms such as Verus [5], we can easily model *preemp-*

tive scheduling, where a higher-priority task can preempt a lower-priority task during its execution, by explicitly keeping a discrete counter that keeps track of the lower-priority task's accumulated execution time. In order to model preemptive scheduling with a dense-time formalism without a *stopwatch* mechanism, where a clock can be stopped and restarted, e.g., *Timed Automata* (TA) [2], we can simulate discrete-time semantics by only allowing state transitions at discrete, periodic clock-ticks [6]. As we adopt finer clock-tick granularity, modeling accuracy increases, but the system state space grows exponentially. This severely limits the smallest clock-tick interval we can adopt. Even though scheduling of the real system is driven by clock-ticks of the operating system and hardware, we have to adopt a clock-tick interval in the TA model that is much larger than that of the operating system and hardware. Therefore, the model built with this technique is only a coarse approximation of the real system behavior. Another shortcoming is that we can only model integer time, so we have to convert non-integer numbers into integers. For example, a task with execution time 7.3 and period 10.1 can be converted into another task with execution time 73 and period 101 with a proportional increase in all other system timing parameters, or as a conservative approximation, a task with execution time 8 and period 10. However, the latter approach breaks down for time intervals, for example, the set of discrete time values [4, 5, 6] is not a correct abstraction of the continuous time interval [4.3, 5.8], but the continuous time interval [4.0, 6.0] is. HA is a dense-time formalism with a stopwatch mechanism, which allows us to keep track of how long a lower-priority task has been executing before being preempted by a higher-priority task. This allows us to construct a more accurate model of preemptive scheduling than using discrete-time formalisms. Even though the stopwatch mechanism makes reachability analysis of HA undecidable in the general case, some authors[4] have shown that the HA model is actually decidable for most practical scheduling problems. We did not run into any decidability problems for our application examples. Also, HA has no problem dealing with fractional numbers as long as they are rational. Therefore, we use HA in this paper to model and analyze real-time scheduling problems.

4 Task Modeling with Hybrid Automata

Figure 5 shows a periodic task modeled with HA, and Figure 6 shows an automaton that works together with the task automaton. As shown in Figure 5, A task initially goes into `wait` state. When it gets triggered it goes into `waitready` state and then immediately goes into `ready` state after issuing a `check_request`, and setting `rt_pri = pri`, i.e., setting its runtime priority to its nominal priority. This triggers the auxiliary automaton in Figure 6 to go from `waiting` to `check_all`. This enables the channel `check` and forces all the task automata currently in states `ready` and `run` into the `checking` state. Each task checks to see if it's the highest priority task. If yes, then it goes to the `run` state; if not, it goes to the `ready` state. `runtime` is a stopwatch that keeps track of the task's execution time by increasing at rate 1 in the `run` state, and stopping in

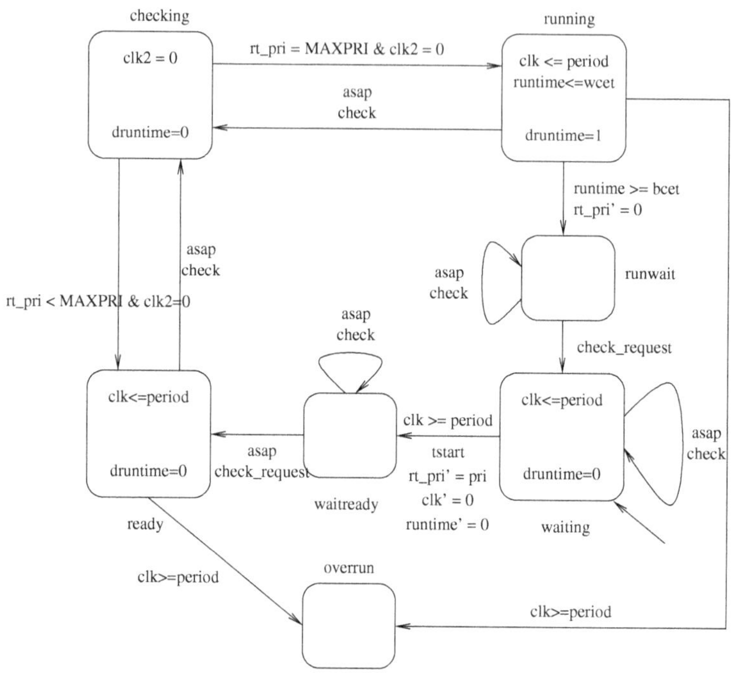

Fig. 5. An automaton modeling a periodic task

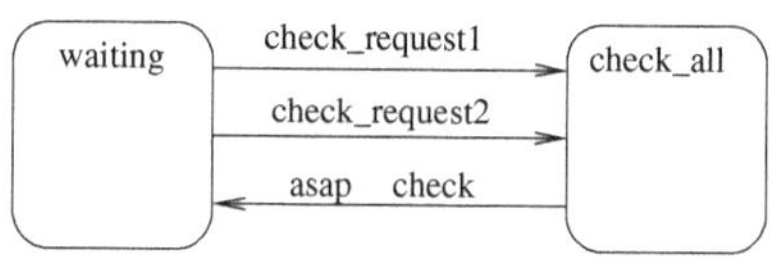

Fig. 6. An auxiliary automaton used in conjunction with the task automata in Figure 5

the `ready` state. When the task has been running for [BCET, WCET], it can choose to finish its execution and go back to the `wait` state after issuing another `check_request`, which in turn triggers another round of checking among all ready tasks.

Figure 7 shows two observer automata used to check the WCRT and BCRT. HyTech checks for reachability of the *violation* states in order to detect task response times falling outside of the range of [BCRT, WCRT]. When a task is triggered, the task automaton issues event `tstart`, and forces the observer automaton to go from `idle` state to `waiting` state. At the same time, `clk` is reset to 0, a real-time clock variable that always increases at a uniform rate. We consider the two observer automata separately:

- If the task finishes within a specified upper bound WCRT, then the task automaton issues event `tfin` before `clk` reaches WCRT, and the observer automaton for WCRT goes back to the `idle` state. Otherwise, it goes into the

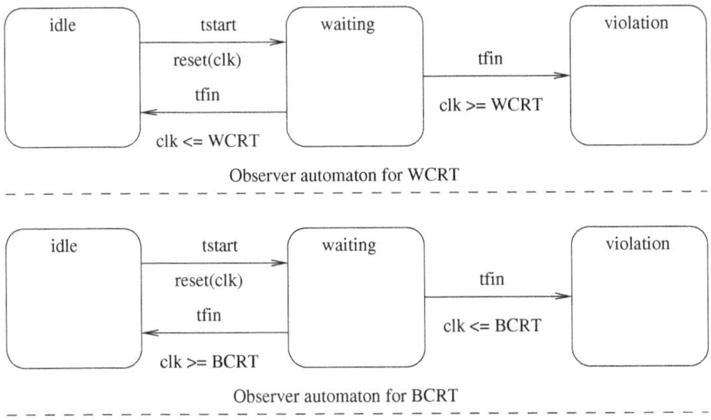

Fig. 7. Observer automata for checking WCRT and BCRT

`violation` state, and the model-checker detects a violation of the specified WCRT (deadline).
- If the task finishes after a specified lower bound BCRT, then the task automaton issues event `tfin` after `clk` reaches WCRT, and the observer automaton for BCRT goes back to the `idle` state. Otherwise, it goes into the `violation` state, and the model-checker detects a violation of the specified BCRT.

Note that we will need one pair of observer automata for each task that we want to check BCRT and WCRT for. Due to the broadcast synchronization semantics, the pair of observer automata will be both triggered concurrently with the task automaton under observation, hence the model-checker can report violations of either BCRT or WCRT within the same model-checking session.

5 Application Examples

Table 1 shows a taskset consisting of two precedence-constrained task-chains: $J_{11} \rightarrow J_{12} \rightarrow J_{13} \rightarrow J_{14}$ and $J_{21} \rightarrow J_{22} \rightarrow J_{23}$. It took HyTech about 4 hours to

Table 1. A taskset taken from [7]. CS stands for *critical section.*

Task Name	Priority	Release Time	BCET	WCET	Longest CS	WCRT	BCRT
J_{11}	2	0	10	40	0	50	10
J_{12}	4	20	5	10	0	60	25
J_{13}	2	75	20	30	10	130	95
J_{14}	4	130	15	50	0	240	145
J_{21}	3	30	10	10	0	50	40
J_{22}	3	60	5	40	20	110	65
J_{23}	1	120	20	70	60	250	140

check each WCRT or BCRT parameter. As discussed in [7], when all jobs have their maximum execution times we may not observe the worst-case completion times of all the jobs, and vice-versa. So non-trivial extensions to the techniques discussed in [7] will be needed if we want to obtain the BCRTs analytically.

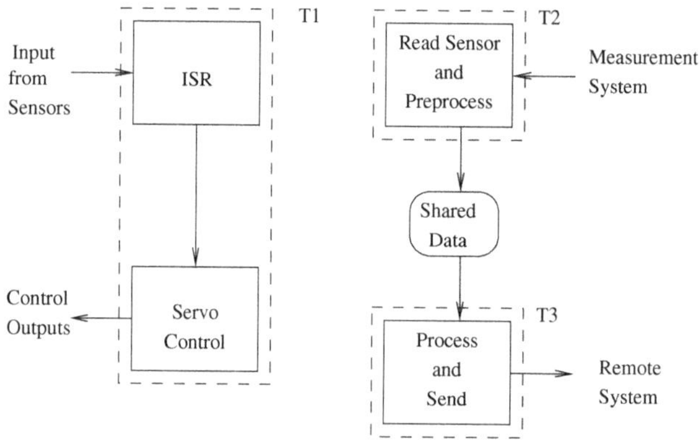

Task	$period_i$	C_{i1}	C_{i2}	C_{i3}	D_i	P_{i1}	P_{i2}	P_{i3}	WCRT	BCRT
T_1	40	1	5	-	40	10	7	-	18	6
T_2	100	10	5	5	100	4	8	4	72	20
T_3	50	8	12	-	50	5	8	-	31	20

Fig. 8. One example taskset

We use another application example to demonstrate the parametric analysis capabilities of HyTech. Figure 8 shows a taskset considered by Harbour, Klein and Lehoczky in [8]. This is a single-processor system. (The original example in [8] has five tasks, but we reduced it to three for clarity purposes.) Task T_1 reads inputs from the servo sensors and performs the control action. Task T_2 reads the distance sensors, does some preprocessing, writes it to the shared data area. Task T_3 does some further processing and sends the results to a remote system. All three tasks are periodic. Each task consists of sequentially-executing subtasks of varying priorities. For example, task T_1 is composed of two subtasks, Interrupt Service Routine (ISR) (priority=10, WCET=1) and Servo Control(priority=7, WCET=5).

In [8], this taskset was analyzed with extended RMA techniques to obtain the WCRT of each end-to-end task. However, no general techniques are available for calculating the BCRT for this task model. Using HyTech and taking advantage of its parametric analysis capability, we have obtained the BCRT values, as shown in Figure 8. In this case the BCRT is equal to the WCET, since for each task it happens to be possible to find a best-case phasing such that it suffers no preemption, but that is not true in general.

We can query the model-checker for a variety of other timing properties of the taskset. Suppose T_2 writes its outputs at the end of its execution, and T_3

reads its inputs at 0.1ms after it starts execution, then the time interval between the two events is the possible age of the shared data between T_2 and T_3, i.e., the minimum and maximum length of time that the data stays in the shared data area before its consumption by T_3. We may want to put an upper bound on this value in order to make sure that T_3 does not consume a piece of data that is too stale. Using HyTech, we can determine the time interval to be $[4.1, 18.1]$, when the phasing between all 3 tasks is 0, i.e., T_1, T_2 and T_3 all start their first job at the exact same instant. This information is not readily available from conventional real-time scheduling analysis techniques.

We can also answer other questions such as:

- If we would like to achieve a WCRT of 68 instead of 72 for T_2 by reducing the WCET of all subtasks by an equal speedup factor $f_{speedup}$, what is the minimum $f_{speedup}$? The answer is 1.05, i.e., the WCET of each subtask needs to be uniformly reduced by a factor of 1.05. To achieve the same goal, if we can only modify one subtask T_{32} to reduce its WCET by δt while leaving all other task parameters unchanged, what is the minimum δt? The answer is 3, i.e., the WCET of T_{32} has to be reduced from 12 to 9.
- Suppose the taskset is schedulable as given, what is the *critical scaling factor* $f_{slowdown}$ for the taskset while still maintaining schedulability? The answer is 1.45, that is, we can afford to increase the WCET of each subtask uniformly by a factor of 1.45 while still keeping the system schedulable. We may want to do this in order to move the application to a slower processor.

Without the parametric analysis capability of HyTech, the designer would have to resort to a trial-and-error approach, i.e., guessing a value and plugging it into the RMA equations to see if it works, possibly using binary search. Since the RMA equations are recursive, it is not straightforward to derive an analytical relationship that can be used to solve for the needed parameters. This is one of the main advantages of model-checking with HyTech over RMA.

6 Conclusions and Future Work

In this paper, we have considered application of model-checking to solving real-time scheduling problems. In particular, we have used the Hybrid Automata formalism and its corresponding model-checker HyTech. To reiterate, our model-checking approach to real-time scheduling analysis has several advantages over RMA. First, we can deal with arbitrary tasksets within a uniform modeling framework. For example, the two tasksets considered in Section 5 have different characteristics and must be solved with different real-time scheduling techniques, but we can model and analyze both of them within the HyTech framework. Second, we can calculate both WCRT and BCRT of a task to obtain a more accurate estimate of its release jitter, and in turn, obtain less pessimistic WCRT values for the downstream tasks. Third, we can use parametric analysis to query the model-checker for a variety of timing properties, which can only be done via a trial-and-error approach with RMA.

However, state-space explosion severely limits the utility of the model-checking approach, especially when continuous time variables are involved as in Hybrid Automata or Timed Automata. Even the 5-task system in [8] causes a memory exhaustion error in HyTech. Most model-checkers provide a set of guidelines for tweaking the models in order to improve scalability, such as reducing the number of clocks, manually composing a set of automata instead of letting the tool compose them, abstraction techniques to eliminate or minimize the irrelevant parts of the model, etc. If the designer has followed all of the guidelines and still cannot check the model successfully, then the only remaining suggestion is to "use the biggest and fastest machine you can get" (quote from an online user's group). Significant progress in model-checking technology will have to be made before it can be directly applied to realistic-sized systems.

As users of the model-checking technology instead of developers, we do not plan to address the state-space explosion problem directly. However there are a number of practical techniques at the application-level that can help with the scalability issue. One possible approach is to use RMA to obtain the [BCRT, WCRT] pair of a task, which is in turn used as the transition time intervals for a system-level Timed Automata model. Then the model can be checked for system-level timing properties, assuming that the system schedulability is guaranteed by RMA. Another possibility is to use a model-checker to check for the [BCRT, WCRT] of an upstream task, and then use the derived jitter value in the RMA equation for the downstream task. However this approach breaks down if the task graph has a loop, i.e., the downstream task can in turn affect the upstream task's release jitter. In that case we can either model-check the entire end-to-end task system, or use the holistic schedulability analysis technique [9]. As part of our future work, we plan to investigate techniques for improving scalability by combining the use of real-time scheduling theory and model-checking. We also plan to extend our modeling framework to address dynamic priority systems as well as mixed systems where some tasks are scheduled with static priorities while others are scheduled with dynamic priorities.

References

1. M. H. Klein, T. Ralya, B. Pollak, and R. Obenza, *A Practitioner's Handbook for Real-Time Analysis: Guide to Rate Monotonic Analysis for Real-Time Systems.* Kluwer Academic Publishers, 1993.
2. (2005) The UPPAAL website. [Online]. Available: http://www.uppaal.com
3. T. Henzinger, P. Ho, and H. Wong-Toi, "HYTECH: A model checker for hybrid systems," *Software Tools for Technology Transfer*, pp. 110–112, 1997.
4. S. Vestal, "Modeling and verification of real-time software using extended linear hybrid automata," in *Proc. the Spin Workshop*, 1998, pp. 12–25.
5. S. Campos, E. Clarke, W. Marrero, and M. Mineam, "The Verus tool: A quantitative approach to the formal verification of real-time systems," in *Proc. International Conference on Computer-Aided Verification (CAV), LNCS 1254*, 1997, pp. 452–455.
6. G. Madl and S. Abdelwahed, "Model-based analysis of distributed realtime embedded system composition," in *ACM Conference on Embedded Software (EMSOFT)*, September 2005.

7. J. Sun, M. K. Gardner, and J. W. Liu, "Bounding completion times of jobs with arbitrary release times, variable execution times and resource sharing," *IEEE Trans. Software Eng.*, vol. 23, pp. 603–615, 1997.
8. M. Harbour, M. H. Klein, and J. Lehoczky, "Timing analysis for fixed-priority scheduling of hard real-time systems," *IEEE Trans. Software Eng.*, vol. 20, no. 2, pp. 13–28, 1994.
9. K. Tindell and J. Clark, "Holistic schedulability analysis for distributed hard real-time systems," *Microprocessing and Microprogramming - Euromicro Journal (Special Issue on Parallel Embedded Real-Time Systems)*, vol. 40, pp. 117–134, 1994.

Efficient FPGA Implementation of a Knowledge-Based Automatic Speech Classifier

Sabato M. Siniscalchi[1,3], Fulvio Gennaro[1], Salvatore Vitabile[2,4], Antonio Gentile[1,4], and Filippo Sorbello[1,4]

[1] Dipartimento di Ingegneria Informatica, Universitàdi Palermo, V.le delle Scienze (Edif. 6), 90128 Palermo, Italy
[2] Dipartimento di Biotecnologie Mediche e Medicina Legale, Universitàdi Palermo, Via del Vespro, 90127 Palermo, Italy
[3] Center for Signal and Image Processing, School of Electrical and Computer Engineering, Georgia Institute of Technology, Atlanta, Georgia 30332, USA
[4] Istituto di CAlcolo e Reti ad alte prestazioni – Consiglio Nazionale delle Ricerche, V.le delle Scienze (Edif. 11), 90128 Palermo, Italy

Abstract. Speech recognition has become common in many application domains, from dictation systems for professional practices to vocal user interfaces for people with disabilities or hands-free system control. However, so far the performance of Automatic Speech Recognition (ASR) systems are comparable to Human Speech Recognition (HSR) only under very strict working conditions, and in general far lower. Incorporating acoustic-phonetic knowledge into ASR design has been proven a viable approach to rise ASR accuracy. Manner of articulation attributes such as vowel, stop, fricative, approximant, nasal, and silence are examples of such knowledge. Neural networks have already been used successfully as detectors for manner of articulation attributes starting from representations of speech signal frames. In this paper an optimized digital Knowledge-based Automatic Speech Classifier for real-time applications is implemented on FPGA using six attribute scoring Multi-Layer Perceptrons (MLP). Digital MLP key features are a virtual neuron architecture and use of sinusoidal activation functions for the hidden layer. Implementation results on FPGA show that use of sinusoidal activation functions decrease hardware resource usage of more than 50% for slices, FFs, LUTs and more than 35% for FPGA RAM blocks when compared with the standard sigmoid-based neuron implementation. Furthermore, neuron virtualization allows for a significant decrease of concurrent memory access, resulting in improved performance for the entire attribute scoring module.

1 Introduction

Artificial Neural Networks (ANN) have been proposed as solution for design of medical expert systems, handwritten character recognition [2], automatic road signs recognizers [3], and so on. An Multi-layer perceptron (MLP) neural network on a SIMD architecture was presented in [1]. The implementation exploits the SIMPil processor precision giving the same performance of the software implementation. A real-time road signs recognition system was designed by means of the same architecture in [3].

L.T. Yang et al. (Eds.): ICESS 2005, LNCS 3820, pp. 198 – 209, 2005.

In [5], Porrmann at al. propose an artificial neural networks implementation on reconfigurable hardware accelerator which requires a high resource rate. Operations are implemented in fixed point and the internal numerical precision is a trade-off between hardware resources, calculation time and approximation quality. In [4], Huelsbergen proposes a representation for dynamic graphs in reconfigurable hardware and its application to some fundamental graph algorithms. The bottleneck of this approach is the high level of required connections. In [7] a standard MLP implementation for speech recognition on FPGA is proposed. The paper presents the results of both serial and parallel MLP implementation. VHDL and Handel-C languages are then compared. The used hidden activation function is the sigmoid one with 8-bit discretization for inputs, for weights, and for post-synaptic values. For the pre-synaptic values a 23 bits accumulator is used.

Although there exists plenty of literature about the hardware implementation of an ANN, this problem is still an open research issue. In this paper a real-time *manner of articulation* classifier based upon an optimized MLP with sinusoidal activation function is presented. The manner of articulation attributes are *vowel, stop, fricative, approximant, nasal,* and *silence*. They are speech features that show strong relation to human speech production [7], and robustness to speech variations [10] as well. These six events are extracted directly by short time MFCCs, and represent the direct input to six detectors, which are afterward combined to generate the classification score. The manner of articulation system is part of the Automatic Speech Attribute Transcription (ASAT) project [11], and a software neural network-based architecture for these manner of articulation attributes was already implemented in [14]. The main idea of the ASAT project is that the performance of conventional *knowledge-ignorant* modeling approaches can be improved integrating the knowledge sources available in a large body of speech science literature. In [10] it is showed that the idea of a direct incorporation of acoustic-phonetic knowledge into ASR design rises its accuracy. These "knowledge-based" features (also referred to as **speech attributes** in the same work) are used to augment the front-end module of a conventional ASR system by means of a set of feature detectors able to capture the speech attributes. The idea of using ANNs as backbone of the ASAT project is due because neural networks can learn a mapping from an input space to an output space realizing a compromise between recognition speed, recognition rate and hardware resources. The generalization capability of neural networks is acquired during the training phase and the generalization degree achieved is strictly related to the training set characteristics.

In addition, a digital Knowledge-based Automatic Speech Classifier for real-time applications has been implemented on FPGA using six attribute scoring Multi-Layer Perceptrons. Each one of the MLP detector classifies input speech frames into a single attribute category. The performance is evaluated on continuous phone recognition using the TIMIT database [12]. The MLP design incorporates a virtual neuron architecture and sinusoidal activation functions for the hidden layer. Neuron virtualization allows for a significant decrease of concurrent memory access, whilst use of sinusoidal activation functions optimizes hardware resource employment.

The rest of the paper is organized as follows. Section 2 describes the general framework of the *knowledge extraction* module. The digital implementation of the six MLP detectors is shown in section 3. Section 4 presents the experimental set-up and results with comparison to the baseline architecture. Concluding remarks are given in the last section of the paper to summarize its main contributions.

2 Knowledge Extraction Module

The Knowledge Extraction (KE) module uses a frame-based approach to provide K manner of articulation attributes A_i, where i=1,2, … K, from an input speech signal $s(t)$. In this paper the manner classes were chosen as in [5], and are listed in Table 1. The KE module, depicted in Figure 1, is composed of two fundamentals blocks: the feature extraction module (FE), and the attribute scoring module (SC). The FE module consists of a bank of K feature extraction blocks FE_i, where i=1,2, … K, and it maps a speech waveform into a sequence of speech parameter vectors $\mathbf{Y}_i$, i=1,2, … K. Actually, each of the FE_i is fed by the same speech waveform $s(t,)$ and for each speech-frame it computes a thirteen MFCC feature vector $\mathbf{X}_i$ (12 MFCCs + Energy). The frame length is of 30 msec overlapped by 20 msec. Finally, FE_i produces as output a 117-feature vector $\mathbf{Y}_i$ combining the actual frame with the eight surrounding frames, 4 frames before and after, so that each speech parameter vector represents

Table 1. Manner of articulation attribute definition

Articulation Manner	Class Elements	Anti-Class Elements
Vowel	IY, IH, EH, EY, AE, AA, AW, AY, AH, AO, OY, OW, UH, UW, ER, AX, IX	JH, CH, S, SH, Z, ZH, F, TH, V, DH, B, D, G, P, T, K, DX, M, N, NG, EN, L, R, W, Y, HH, EL, SIL
Fricative	JH, CH, S, SH, Z, ZH, F, TH, V, DH	IY, IH, EH, EY, AE, AA, AW, AY, AH, AO, OY, OW, UH, UW, ER, AX, IX, B, D, G, P, T, K, DX, M, N, NG, EN, L, R, W, Y, HH, EL, SIL
Stop	B, D, G, P, T, K, DX	IY, IH, EH, EY, AE, AA, AW, AY, AH, AO, OY, OW, UH, UW, ER, AX, IX, JH, CH, S, SH, Z, ZH, F, TH, V, DH, M, N, NG, EN, L, R, W, Y, HH, EL, SIL
Nasal	M, N, NG, EN	IY, IH, EH, EY, AE, AA, AW, AY, AH, AO, OY, OW, UH, UW, ER, AX, IX, JH, CH, S, SH, Z, ZH, F, TH, V, DH, B, D, G, P, T, K, DX, L, R, W, Y, HH, EL, SIL
Silence	SIL	IY, IH, EH, EY, AE, AA, AW, AY, AH, AO, OY, OW, UH, UW, ER, AX, IX, JH, CH, S, SH, Z, ZH, F, TH, V, DH, B, D, G, P, T, K, DX, M, N, NG, EN, L, R, W, Y, HH, EL

nine frames. The SC module is composed of six feed-forward neural networks, and its goal is to attach a score, referred to as *knowledge score* (KS_i), to each vector $\mathbf{Y}_i$. The input of each network is a 9 frames of 12 MFCCs + energy, so that the input layer is of 117 nodes. The output layer has two nodes, one for the desired class, and one for the anti-class. Actually, the value obtained for the desired class for case i is defined to be the KS_i.

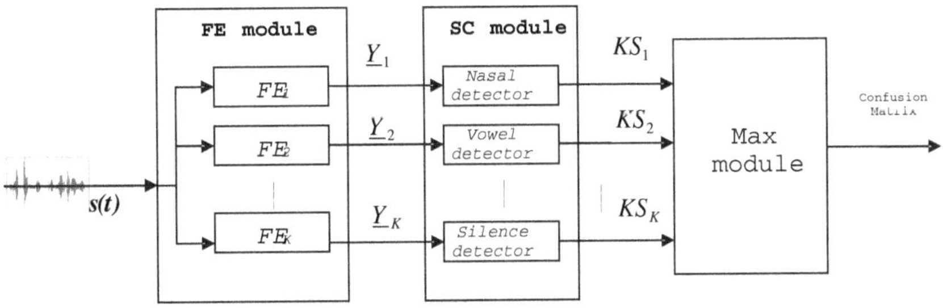

Fig. 1. Knowledge Extraction Module, adapted from [5]. The detectors are based on a MLP neural network.

3 Multi-layer Perceptron Digital Design

In [15] an efficient MLP digital implementation for road signs recognition and high energy physics experiments classification has been proposed. This initial design has been adapted and optimized for automatic speech classification and is presented in this section.

A single MLP digital architecture is used to implement each of the detectors described in Figure 1. As depicted in Figure 2, this architectural design aims to satisfy

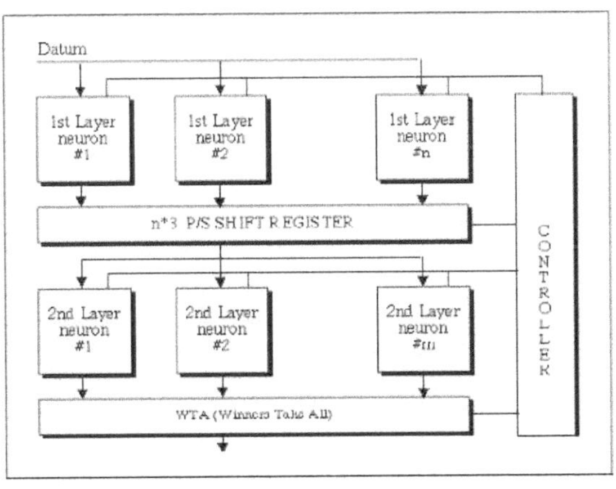

Fig. 2. Functional block diagram of the MLP architecture

high design modularity, high density of neurons on device, high recognition rate and speed. As a results, (a) data input acts in a serial way; (b) data processing acts in parallel among the neurons and serially within each neuron; (c) second layer processing is pipelined with first layer processing. The Winners Takes All (WTA) circuit selects, among a set of *m* numbers, the greatest activation level units.

The basic digital neural network elements, as multipliers and accumulators, are designed following the standard solutions. Single neuron architecture is depicted in Figure 4. The output activation function is a linear function, whilst sinusoidal activation function is employed as activation function of the hidden layer. Fixed point arithmetic with two's complement representation is used for the chip implementation of the MLP. Principal constrains of this project are the compromise between the neural network accuracy and the bit depth for input and weight data, and the compromise between the neural network accuracy and the bit depth for the pre-synaptic value and the post-synaptic value of the hidden activation function.

4 The Digitized Sinusoidal Activation Function

Conventional MLP digital implementations use 8 bits for inputs, weights and post-synaptic discretization [7], and a bit depth discretization related to the application domain. In what follows, some formulas have been developed in order to obtain the digitized value from floating point neural network training. These formulas are referred to input (I_{dj}) and weight (W_{di}) digitized values.

$$I_{dj} = I_j \left(\frac{\text{Input Levels - 1}}{\text{Input Range}} \right), \quad W_{di} = W_i \left(\frac{\text{Input Levels - 1}}{\text{Weights Range}} \right). \tag{1}$$

Concerning the sinusoidal activation function, the number of input level, the input and the output range affect the sinusoid period. For the sinusoidal function, considering its periodicity in order to obtain a module with a minimum pre-synaptic value, the above said influence is expressed by the following formula.

$$\Pi_d = \pi \times \left(\frac{\text{Weight Levels Sin - 1}}{\text{Weights Range Sin.}} \times \frac{\text{Input Levels - 1}}{\text{Input Range}} \right). \tag{2}$$

Where Π_d is the digitized π value shown in the Figure 3.

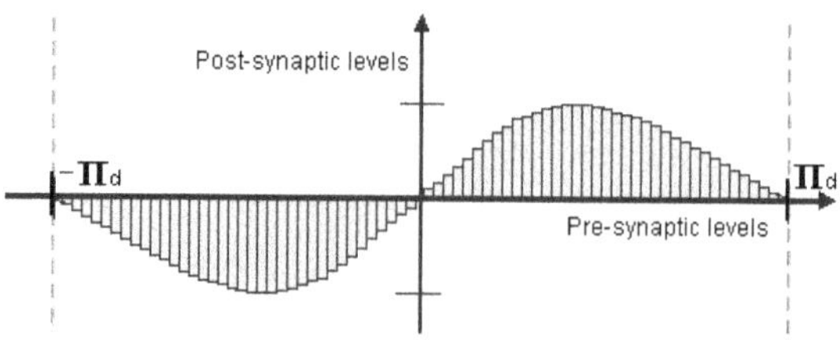

Fig. 3. The digitized sinusoidal function; Π_d is the digitized π value

The relative accumulator dimension (AD), expressed as number of bits, must at least represent Π_d. This dimension does not depend upon the number of inputs. Figure 4 gives the neuron architecture used in the hardware approach, with the accumulator that is the fundamental used resource.

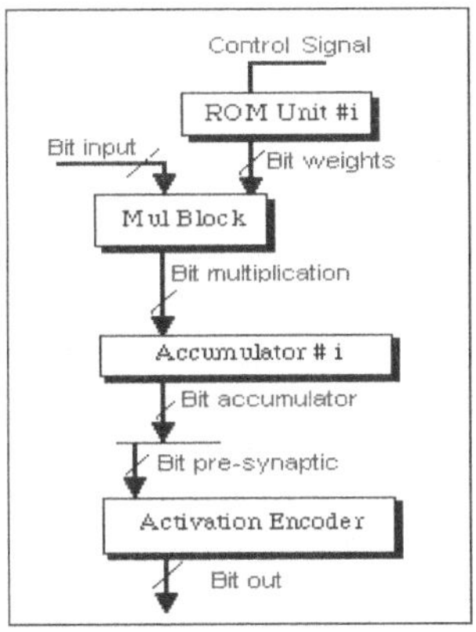

Fig. 4. The neuron architecture in the hardware approach

The number of bits used during the floating point to fixed point conversion related to network inputs, hidden layer weights, pre-synaptic values, and post synaptic values are critical issues during the digitalization phase.

Following the approach proposed in [7], a digital MLP classifier for speech recognition has been implemented on a Xilinx VirtexII XC2V3000-4 FPGA. Table 2 lists the required resources for a full precision parallel MLP implementation with 117 inputs, 100 hidden neurons having the standard sigmoid activation function, and 2 output neurons having the linear activation function. Also in this implementation 8-bit bit depth for inputs, for weights, and for post-synaptic values were used. For the pre-synaptic values a 23 bits accumulator was used. The slight difference between the two implementations can be ascribed to the different Xilinx FPGA families used here and in [7].

Table 2. FPGA required resources for a 117-100-2 neural network implementation on a Xilinx VirtexII XC2V3000-4. The standard sigmoid based implementation uses 8 bits for inputs, 8 bits for weights, 23 bits for pre-synaptic values and 8 bits for post-synaptic. The sinus based implementation (ID=B) uses 3 bits for inputs, 5 bits for weights, 5 bits for prc-synaptic values and 3 bits for post-synaptic valus.

Hidden Activation function	Slices	FFs	LUTs	RAMs
Sigmoid	5506 (38%)	3725 (12%)	10058 (35%)	94 (98%)
Sinus (ID=B)	2539 (17.5%)	1533 (4.9%)	4112 (14.3%)	60 (62.5%)

Table 3. Network configurations using sinusoidal activation functions. Relative result accuracy is also given for the case of the nasal detector.

ID	Hidden Activation function	Input bits	Weight bits	Pre-Synaptic bits	Post-Synaptic bits	Accuracy
A	Sinus	3	4	4	3	94%
B	Sinus	3	5	5	3	99,5%
C	Sinus	4	5	5	4	100%

To evaluate the effectiveness of the sinusoidal hidden activation function, a set of experimental tests have been performed to obtain the optimum number of bit for inputs, weights, pre-synaptic functions, and post-synaptic functions. Some of the tested configurations for the case of the nasal detector are reported in Table 3. These values are normalized respect to percentage of accuracy of the software version, which is 88,65%.

Although it is possible to reach the same level of accuracy of the software implementation (C case), the sinus based MLP was implemented following B configuration to get a trade-off between used resource and accuracy. The used resources of related neural network implementation are listed in Table 2. The aforementioned study was conducted for the other five detectors.

The difference between the two implementations can be ascribed to the sinusoidal activation function that determines an high FPGA resources saving of above 50% for slices, FFs, LUTs and of above 35% for FPGA RAM blocks. Resources saving is related to the chosen hidden activation function that needs a lower accumulator dimension since it can be optimized with a smaller number of bits. FPGA RAMs block saving is related to the smallest number of bits used for weights discretizing.

5 The Virtual Neuron Architecture

As pointed out in a real classification tasks require a large number of neurons, consequently a FPGA based neural prototypes use external RAM memory to store neuron weights.

The virtual neuron implementation makes efficient the mapping of a neural network into hardware devices since it leads to a significant decreasing of concurrent memory access. Since each neural network is large in size and input data are processed once, memory subsystem is typically the bottleneck. The *virtual neuron* based implementation allows to exploit a serial-parallel architecture since data input acts in a serial way, data processing acts in parallel among the virtual neurons and serially within each neuron first layer processing is pipelined with second layer processing. The proposed architecture is composed by N hidden neurons, M output neurons, h hidden virtual neurons, k output virtual neurons and h FIFO buffers between hidden and output layer. In Figure 5 the hardware neural architecture is shown. The approach is based on the instantiation of h and k *virtual neurons*, where h is a sub-multiple of the hidden layer neurons and k is a sub-multiple of the output layer neurons. At network start-up, the h virtual entities take the first h input data and their relative weights from RAM.

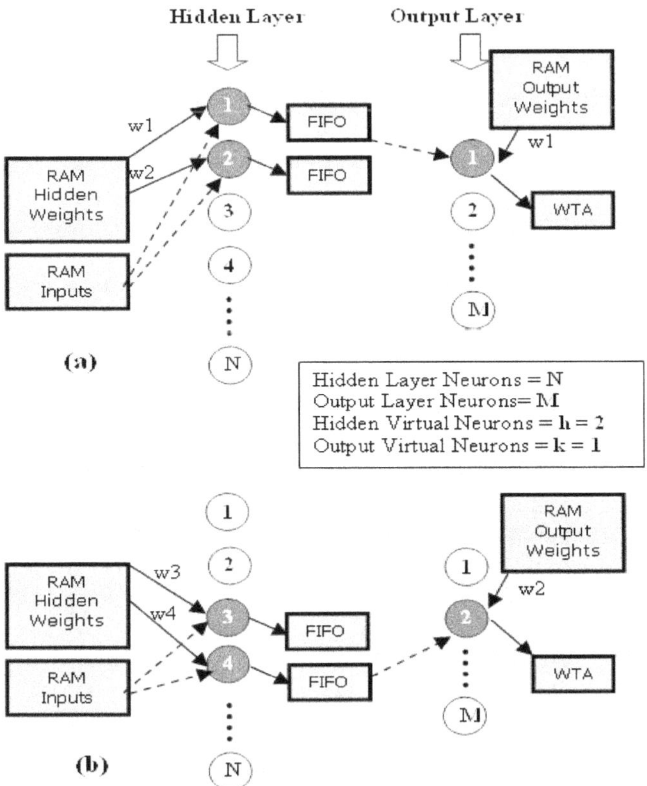

Fig. 5. The proposed neural architecture shown two first layer virtual neurons and one second layer virtual neuron; in (a) the first processing step is shown; in (b) the second processing step is shown

After the first cycle, the obtained partial results are stored in the shift-register accumulator of each virtual neuron (on internal FIFO buffer). Successively, the next group of h virtual neurons, representing the real neurons of first layer ranging from $h+1$ to $2h$, are considered. Therefore, the same processing on input data and relative weights is repeated. The process ends when the last block of real neurons of first layer, between $N-h$ and N neuron, is processed. Finally, the bias value previous and the chosen activation function are applied to the FIFO list. The obtained results are stored in h external FIFO lists, one for each virtual neuron. These values represent the input data for the second layer. The external FIFO lists are used for pipeline implementation. In fact, after the pipeline latency time, second layer processing starts while the execution of first layer is still running.

For second layer the same elaboration is performed using the k *virtual neurons*: data stored in the external FIFO buffers are the input values for the output layer. The second layer weights are stored in the external RAM, too.

Finally, the WTA circuit selects, among all output values of the second layer, the higher output in 1 clock cycle. With serial inputs the total execution time of hidden and output layer is $T=ts1+ts2$. Considering the pipeline, this time is $T=max(ts1, ts2)$;

where *ts1* and *ts2* are respectively the execution time of hidden layer and output layer (including T_{WTA}).

6 Experiments and Results

The evaluation of the proposed Manner of Articulation Extraction module was performed on the TIMIT Acoustic-Phonetic Continuous Speech Corpus database [12], which is a well-known speech corpus in the speech recognition field. This database is composed of a total of 6300 sentences; it has a one-channel, 16-bit linear sampling format, and it was sampled at 16000 samples/sec. The MLP detectors were trained on 3504 randomly selected utterances, and to be consistent with [10] and [9] the four phones "cl", "vcl", "epi", and "sil" were treated as a single class, thus reducing the TIMIT phone set to a set of 45 context-independent (CI) phones. The front-end module is in the process of being implemented following the guidelines given in [13]. Instead the max module is a simple comparator circuit. The MLP module is the focus of this work, and a detailed description is given in what follows.

Each of the six detectors is a three-layer network the input of which is a window of nine frames, that is, 117 parameters. The nodes of hidden layers are 100. The output layer contains two units, and a simple linear activation function is used. Finally, the max module applies a max function to the KS_i outputs in order to compute the overall confusion matrix. As previously stated, the detectors work in a frame-based paradigm, so that their performance was evaluated in term of frame error rate. Each frame

Table 4. Software (Hardware) phoneme percentages accuracies for the manner of articulation attributes using sinusoidal activation function

%	Vowel	Fricative	Stop	Nasal	App.	Silence
Vow.	**91,00 (89,85)**	1,38	1,53	1,26	4,64	0,19
Fric.	3,16	**88,06 (87,02)**	5,53	1,02	0,89	1,24
Stop	6,32	7,41	**81,03 (79,89)**	1,71	1,57	1,96
Nas.	9,65	2,44	3,25	**81,45 (81,04)**	2,20	0,90
App.	30,82	2,88	3,26	2,74	**59,11 (58,07)**	1,19
Sil.	1,10	1,09	1,88	0,61	0,58	**94,74 (94,21)**

was classified according to the neural network with the largest value. The global confusion matrix for the manner of articulation attributes is given in Table 4. The (p, q)-th element of the confusion matrix measures the rate of the p-th attribute being classified into the q-th class. In addition, the results of the digitalized attribute scoring module are given in parenthesis.

The digital version Knowledge-based Automatic Speech Classifier is implemented on Celoxica RC203 board [6] equipped with a Xilinx VirtexII XC2V3000-4 FPGA. Neural architectures were described using the VHDL language and were synthesized using the Xilinx ISE 6.3 tools.

In Figure 6, the relations between execution time and hardware resources using sinusoidal functions for the configuration B topology are shown. The execution time as well as the hardware resources decreases with the hidden layer virtual neurons number in inversely proportional way. In addition, the pair (for the configuration B) topology has been considered to calculate the used hardware resources for their implementation on FPGA. The execution time is compared with the execution time of the related software implementation on a standard Pentium IV, 2Mhz with 1Gbyte of RAM.

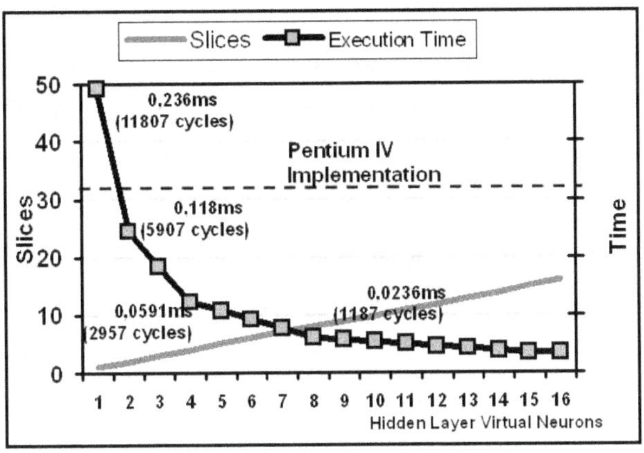

Fig. 6. The relation between execution time and used resource vs the number of virtual hidden neurons

The number of hidden virtual neurons for each of the MLPs has been fixed to 10, representing the best trade-off between execution time and allocated resource. The above MLP digital implementation requires 1187 cycles and, consequently, 0,0236ms for its execution.

Table 5 illustrates the synthesis report for a single MLP architecture implementation using the Xilinx ISE 6.3 tools as well as the allocated resources for the entire scoring module. It is easy to see that the chosen configuration for each MLP allows the implementation of the 6 detectors in a single FPGA. The same results could not have been accomplished if 8 bits for each of the neural network parameters had been used.

Table 5. Synthesis report for a single MLP architecture as well as for the entire scoring module using the sinusoidal activation function

	Slices	FFs	LUTs	RAMs
Single MLP architecture	802 (5.6%)	654 (2.3%)	1359 (4.7%)	10 (10.5%)
Entire scoring module	4830 (33.7%)	4058 (14.1%)	8234 (28.7%)	60 (62.5%)

7 Conclusion

In this paper a Knowledge-based Automatic Speech Classifier was implemented using six attribute scoring Multi-Layer Perceptrons. The entire scoring module was synthesized on a single FPGA chip. Each MLP features a virtual neuron architecture and uses sinusoidal activation functions for the hidden layer. Implementation results on FPGA show that use of sinusoidal activation functions decrease hardware resource usage of more than 50% for slices, FFs, LUTs and of more than 35% for FPGA RAM when compared with the standard sigmoid-based neuron implementation. Furthermore, neuron virtualization allows for a significant decrease of concurrent memory access, resulting in improved performance for the entire attribute scoring module. The obtained scoring module execution time gives ample room to implement a real-time speech classifier.

References

1. S. Vitabile, A. Gentile, G. Dammone, F. Sorbello. "MLP Neural Network Implmentation on a SIMD Architecture", Lecture Notes in Computer Science 2486, Springer-Verlag, pp. 99-108, 2002.
2. F. Sorbello, G.A.M. Gioiello, S. Vitabile, "Handwritten Character Recognition using a MLP", Knowledge-Based Intelligent Techniques in Character Recognition, Chapter 5, pp. 91-119, CRC Press Publishers, 1999.
3. S. Vitabile, A. Gentile, F. Sorbello, "Real-Time Road Signs Recognition on a SIMD Architecture", WSEAS Transactions on Circuits and Systems, Issue 3, Volume 3, May 2004, pp. 664-669, ISSN: 1109-2734.
4. L. Huelsbergen, "A Representation for Dynamic Graphs in Reconfigurable Hardware and its Application to Fundamental Graph Algorithms", 8th International Symposium on Field Programmable Gate Arrays, ISBN 1-58113-193-3.
5. M. Porrmann, U. Witkowski, H. Kalte, U. Ruckert, "Implementation of Artificial Neural Hardware Accelerator", 10th Euromicro Workshop on Parallel, Distributed and Network-based Processing, pp.243-250, January 9-11, 2002, Spain.
6. RC203 Software Manual http://www.celoxica.com/support/documentation
7. E.M. Ortigosa, P.M. Ortigosa, A. Canas, E. Ros, R. Agis, and J. Ortega, "FPGA Implementation of Multi-layer Perceptrons for Speech Recognition", LNCS Vol. 2778, Springer-Verlag, pp. 1048 – 1052.
8. K. Kirchhoff. "Combining Articulatory and Acoustic Information for Speech Recognition in Noisy and Reverberant Environments", Proc. of the International Conference on Spoken Language Processing, Sydney, Australia, pp. 891-894

9. K. F. Lee and H. W. Hon, "Speaker-independent phone recognition using hidden Markov models", IEEE Trans. On Acoust., Speech and Signal Process., Vol. 37, No. 11, pp. 1641-1648, 1989.
10. J. Li, Y. Tsao and C.-H. Lee, "A Study on Knowledge source integration for candidate rescoring in automatic speech recognition," Proc. of ICASSP05.
11. Lee, C.-H., "From knowledge-ignorant to knowledge-rich modeling: a new speech research paradigm for next generation automatic speech recognition," Proc. ICSLP, 2004.
12. J. S. Garofolo, L. F. Lamel, W. M. Fisher, J. G. Fiscus, D. S. Pallett, and N. L. Dahlgren, "DARPA TIMIT Acoustic-Phonetic Continuous Speech Corpus," U.S. Dept. of Commerce, NIST, Gaithersburg, MD, February 1993.
13. J.-C. Wang et al, Chipdesign of MFCC extraction for speech recognition, INTEGRATION, the VLSI journal 32 (2002) 111–131)
14. S. M. Siniscalchi, J. Li, G. Pilato, G. Vassallo, M. A. Clements, A. Gentile, F. Sorbello, "Application of E-αNets to Feature Recognition of Manner of Articulation in Knowledge-based Automatic Speech Recognition," Proceeding of the Italian Workshop on Neural Nets (WIRN 2005), Springer-Verlag.
15. S. Vitabile, V. Conti, F. Gennaro, F. Sorbello (2005). "Efficient MLP Digital Implementation on FPGA", 8°EUROMICRO Conference on Digital System Design (DSD 2005), pp. 218-222, IEEE Computer Society Press.

A Topology Control Method for Multi-path Wireless Sensor Networks*

Zhendong Wu[1], Shanping Li[1], and Jian Xu[2]

[1] College of Computer Science, Zhejiang University, Hangzhou, China 310027
zhendongwu@hotmail.com
shan@cs.zju.edu.cn
[2] Department of Computer Science, Dianzi University, Hangzhou, China 310018
Jian.xu@hziee.edu.cn

Abstract. Future sensor networks will be consisted of large number of untethered and unattended sensors. Energy efficiency and load balance will be two important design issues for these networks. Some researches [2] [3] have found that topology control, which changes the set of neighbors of some nodes in the networks, can be used to improve the energy efficiency and load balance. In this paper, we take link reliability and multi-path into consideration when designing topology control algorithms. Based on an analytical link loss model [8], the relationship of energy efficiency, load balance and number of neighbors is analyzed. We found that there is a contradiction in improving energy efficiency and load balance at the same time. A layered topology control method LELBM (Layered Energy-efficient and Load Balance Method) is proposed to adjusting network's topology for increasing energy efficiency and meanwhile getting good load balance. Analysis and simulation show that this method can significantly improve the network's performance.

Keywords: Sensor Networks, Topology Control, Load balance, Energy efficiency, Multi-path.

1 Introduction

Future sensor networks will be consisted of large number of untethered and unattended sensors. Energy efficiency and load balance will be important design considerations for these networks [1]. Many topology control algorithms, which assign different transmit powers to different nodes to meet a globe topology property, have been proposed to increase the energy efficiency [2] [3]. The experiments showed that a good designed topology would increase the energy efficiency significantly [2] [3]. But, in 802.11 [4] environment, which are widely used in MANET(mobile ad hoc networks), the sensors will use a confirmed transmit power. So we need some new topology control algorithms that do not change sensors' transmit powers.

Recent studies [5] [6] have shown that wireless links in real sensor networks are unreliable. This unreliability exposes one of greedy forwarding algorithm's weaknesses, which is the node we chosen may have "poor links" with the current node.

* This paper is supported by National Natural Science Foundation of China (No. 60473052).

L.T. Yang et al. (Eds.): ICESS 2005, LNCS 3820, pp. 210 – 219, 2005.

The "poor links" may result in a high rate of packet drops and energy wastage. It brings us the idea that a good topology should take link reliability into consideration.

Base on the reliability consideration, we introduce the concept of multi-path into sensor network. Multi-path is favorite alternative for both circuit switched and packet switched networks, as it provides an easy mechanism to distribute traffic and balance network load, as well as considerate fault tolerance. So using multi-path will be a good choice for sensor networks due to its limited energy and unreliable links.

In this paper, we adjust the network's topology through changing the set of neighbors of some nodes at the condition of fixed transmit power. Two strategies are found to select the set of neighbors for optimizing energy efficiency, balancing energy load respectively. For making two strategies work together, we provide a layered method LELBM (Layered Energy-efficient and Load Balance Method). Simulations show that using LELBM, we get a good load balance and energy efficiency.

The rest of the paper is organized as follows. In section 2, we introduce the related work. In section 3, we describe the statistical link-loss model and metrics of our work. In section 4, we propose two strategies and a method for making them work together. In section 5, we introduce the results of our simulations. In section 6, we present our conclusions.

2 Related Works

We are inspired by previous work in topology control [2] [3], energy-efficient forwarding strategy [1] [7], multi-path algorithm [13] [14] [15] [16].

Ramanathan R et al [2] and Alaa M et al [3] found that energy efficiency could be improved through adjusting the transmit powers of nodes in a multi-hop wireless network. These algorithms work well in one type sensor networks that the transmit powers of nodes can be adjusted. Then, in 802.11 environment, which uses a confirmed transmit power, these algorithms can't work.

GEAR [1] selected the lower consumed energy nodes as the next hops. One drawback of this algorithm is it has not considered link reliability, so it would not get very good performance in real sensor networks because of the unreliable links. Seada et al. [7] provided an energy-efficient forwarding strategy. It assumes that the number of the neighbors is unchanged and the source-destination path can be described as a chain topology. This assumption is a little too ideal. Normally, the number of the neighbors is changed from source to destination. Especially in multi-path environment, the number of neighbors is more important for correct routing and load balance. We studied the relationship of the energy efficiency, load balance and the number of neighbors, and give a method to choose neighbors.

Multi-path algorithms, such as [13] [14] [15] [16], have not taken energy efficiency into consideration.

3 Model and Metrics

3.1 Model

To take link reliability into consideration, we need a link loss model. We take advantage of link layer model in paper [8] to do our link reliability analysis. From it we can derive:

$$PRR(d) = (1 - \frac{1}{2}\exp^{-\frac{r(d)}{2}\frac{1}{0.64}})^{\rho 8 f} \quad (1)$$

Where PRR is the packet reception rate, d is the transmitter-receiver distance, r is the signal to noise ratio (SNR), ρ is the encoding ratio and f is the frame length. Figure 1 show instances of the link layer model where the different regions can be observed, where 'm' means meters. It shows the existence of a large "transitional region" where the link quality has high variance, including both good and highly unreliable links [8].

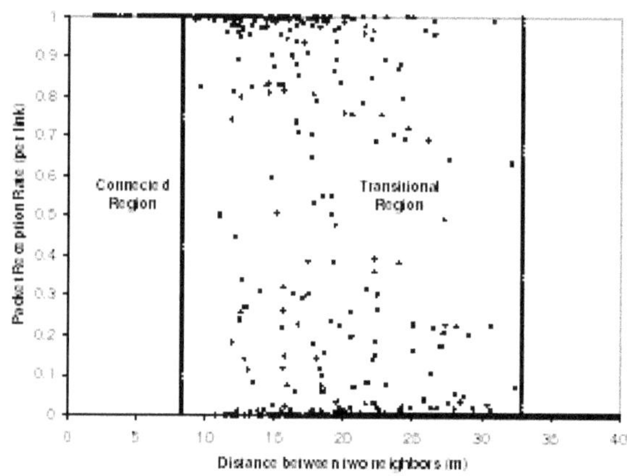

Fig. 1. Samples from a realistic analytical link loss model

We can conclude from this model that there is a trade-off between PRR and d. It means that higher value of d will result in lower value of PRR in the neighbor node. Obviously, lower values of PRR will cause more energy wastage due to more retransmissions operation. But high value of PRR does not equal to energy efficiency. In condition of fixed transmit-power, lower values of d (higher values of PRR) will also result in more energy wastage because of more transmission operations. So, it worths studying how to choose neighbor set in different link reliability for better network's energy efficiency.

In conclusion, our work is based on the following assumptions:

(I) Nodes know the neighbor's location, the neighbor's n (the number of neighbors) and the link's PRR of their neighbors.
(II) Nodes are randomly distributed.

3.2 Metrics

In order to evaluate the energy efficiency and the load balance in multi-path, we use the following metrics:

- Delivery Rate (r): Percentage of packets sent by the source which reached the sink

- Energy Efficiency (Eeff): The energy spent by the network for sending one byte from the source to the sink successfully.
- Mean Energy Consume (Emean):

$$\text{Emean} = \frac{\text{the sum of the energy spent}}{N} \tag{2}$$

- Energy Variance (Evar): we use this metric to evaluate the load balance of a network. When the value is lower, the load balance is better. If the value is very high, it means some nodes will exhaust their energy soon, and result in the useful system lifetime decline.

$$\text{Evar} = \frac{1}{N}\left[(E_1 - \text{Emean})^2+(E_2 - \text{Emean})^2+\ldots+(E_N - \text{Emean})^2\right] \tag{3}$$

The N is the sum of the nodes.

We assign Psrc to be the number of packets sent by the source, Etx and Erx the amount of energy required by a node to transmit and receive a packet, and Ere the energy used to read only the header of the packet. We have:

$$\text{Etotal} = \text{Etx} + \text{Erx} + (n - 1)\,\text{Ere} \tag{4}$$

The Etotal is the total amount of energy consumed by the network for each transmitted packet. The n is a variant, the number of neighbors.

Subsequently, Eeff is given by:

$$Eeff = \frac{(Psrc \cdot r \cdot L)}{(Psrc \cdot Etotal \cdot k)} = \frac{(r \cdot L)}{(Etotal \cdot k)} \tag{5}$$

The L is the length of each packet. For analyzing easily, in our analysis model, we require L be a constant (L = 1024 or 512), and it is a reasonable assumption in WLAN. The k is the total hops from source to sink.

According to these metrics, if we want to improve energy efficiency and load balance simultaneously, then we should increase Eeff and decrease Evar at the same time.

4 LELBM: A Topology Control Method for Multi-path

In this section, we study how to increase Eeff firstly, and then how to decrease Evar secondly, and finally how to make them work simultaneously.

4.1 Increasing Energy Efficiency

According to equation (5), Eeff $= \frac{(r \cdot L)}{(Etotal \cdot k)}$, Where L is constant. To get better energy efficiency, we need increase (r/k) and reduce Etotal.

In our model, all packets sent by the source would reach the sink, unless the link lost the packet. The PRR(d) describes the probability of packet sending in one hop. In reality, the nodes are not uniformly distributed. However, they are in the large scale in networks, so we can assume the longer and shorter distance will be counteracted. Then we get a reasonable assumption that the nodes are uniformly distributed in the region, we can compute the total hops from the source to the sink when the d is confirmed.

$$\text{Total hops} = (\text{dsrc} - \text{dsink}) / (d) \tag{6}$$

Then the (r/k) is:

$$(r/k) = \frac{PRR(d)^{((\text{dsrc}-\text{dsink})/d)}}{(\text{dsrc} - \text{dsink})/d} \tag{7}$$

$$ln(r/k) = (\text{dsrc} - \text{dsink})\frac{\ln PRR(d)}{d} + ln d - ln(\text{dsrc} - \text{dsink}) \tag{8}$$

Here, dsrc – dsink is a constant when the source and destination are confirmed. Thus, in order to increase (r/k), we need to maximize the value of $(\text{dsrc} - \text{dsink})\frac{\ln PRR(d)}{d}$ + *ln*d.

Now, we need reduce Etotal. According to equation (4) and our assumptions, Etx, Erx and Ere are constant in one scene. Moreover, in 802.11, the length of packet is 512byte or 1024byte normally, and the header of the packet is about 50byte. Then (t is a constant):

$$\text{Erx} \approx (10\sim20)\ \text{Ere},\ \text{Etx} = t\text{Erx}; \tag{9}$$

$$\text{Etotal} \approx (1+t)\text{Erx} + (n-1)\text{Ere} \approx (15(1+t) + n - 1)\text{Ere} \tag{10}$$

So a small n is hoped for reducing Etotal. The n is the number of neighbors. Sum up, we get:

$$\text{Eeff} \approx \frac{\frac{L}{k} PRR(d)^{\frac{dsrc-d\sin k}{d}}}{(15(1+t)+n-1)Ere} \tag{11}$$

$$\text{lnEeff} \approx [\text{lnL} - \text{lnEre} - \ln(\text{dsrc} - \text{dsink})] + (\text{dsrc} - \text{dsink})\frac{\ln PRR(d)}{d} + \ln d - \ln(15t+14+n) \tag{12}$$

Equation (12) shows the relationship of the energy efficiency and the number of neighbors. It can be concluded from the equation (12) that we can improve energy efficiency by increasing the value of $(\text{dsrc} - \text{dsink})\frac{\ln PRR(d)}{d}$ + *ln*d and decreasing the n.

4.2 Improving Load Balance

In order to get a good load balance, we need decrease Evar to get a low value. It can be deduced from the equation (3) that if all items (Ei) close to Emean, we can get a good load balance. In multi-path conditions, according to equation (4), the energy consumption of every node that belongs to the same route is Etx and Erx, and for the node does not belong to the route is Ere. If there are some nodes to participate many routes transmission simultaneously, the load balance will not be good. Moreover, if there are some nodes that consume all Eres of each route, which means that the selected paths are too close, the load balance will not be good either. So in multi-path conditions, node-disjoint routes and some appropriate distance away from two routes are expected for good load balance. Because a larger n can provide more opportunities for choosing appropriate nodes satisfy two conditions above, a large n is expected for good load balance.

It is a contradiction to decrease the n for improving energy efficiency while to increase n to get good load balance. To deal with this condition, we should find an appropriate number of neighbors (n) for energy efficiency and load balance both side.

The work of K.Chintalapudi et al [11], concerning the relationship of the network's service quality and the number of neighbors, shows that an average degree of 11-12 nodes within the ranging neighborhood is needed for good network's service quality. It means that for good load balance the n (number of neighbors) need greater than 12 ($n \geq 12$), but once the number (n) satisfied this suggestion, it should be the less the better.

4.3 Working Together

From above, we can get two strategies for topology control. Next, we will demonstrate a specific method LELBM to make them work together.

LELBM use a layered method to generate a topology for energy efficiency and load balance. The mainly benefit to use this layered method is that it can make two strategies (one for energy efficiency, one for load balance) work together. In order to avoid nodes with weak links, we blacklist a set of neighbors based on a certain criteria, and then route in the remaining neighbors. For example, the criteria could like this: the PRR is lower 20%, or the number of neighbors is lower 12. Of course, there is a risk that greedy routing fails when a node has no neighbors closer to the destination in the remaining neighbors. But, in a dense network, this situation will happen scarcely, so this approach is reasonable.

LELBM:

First, we blacklist a set of neighbors that the PRR is lower one value. We use V1 denotes the set of the remaining neighbors.

Second, we choose a set of neighbors that have the highest value of (dsrc – dsink)$\dfrac{\ln PRR(d)}{d}$ + lnd in the V1. We use V2 denotes the set we chosen.

Third, we choose a set of neighbors that ($n \geq 12$) in the V2. We use V3 denotes the set we chosen.

All nodes with their neighbor set V3 construct a topology for energy efficiency and load balance.

5 Simulations and Comparisons

LELBM is designed to improve energy efficiency and load balance, so we primarily measure the performance of network's energy efficiency and load balance. Moreover, we are interested in how this comparative measure scales with network density. We evaluate how LELBM that equipped with multi-path routing algorithm [16] compares with GPSR [9] that not used topology control.

5.1 Simulation Environment

We simulated LELBM in ns2 [10], using the wireless extensions developed at Carnegie Mellon (CMU). Because the CMU have not realized the link layer model derived in [8], we slightly modify the simulation code of CMU (in wireless-phy.cc). At the same time, we install our own route agent to ns2.

In the simulations where we compare LELBM with GPSR, we initialize the Shared Media interface with parameters to make it work like the 914MHz Lucent WaveLAN DSSS radio interface. Our simulations are for networks of 50 nodes with 802.11 WaveLAN radios, with a nominal 250-meter range. The nodes are initially placed at random in a rectangular region. Through adjusting the size of the region, we get different node density. 10 CBR flows in 1k/s are used in our simulation. We present the link layer model derived in [8] in a simpler style as Table 1.

Table 1. A simple link layer model

d (distance)	0~50	50~100	100~150	150~200	200~250
PRR(d)	100%	90%	70%	50%	30%

We evaluate LELBM and GPSR using three metrics: delivery rate, average consumed energy (it reflects the energy efficiency of a network), and Energy Variance (Evar).

5.2 Delivery Rate

Figure 2 shows the number of packets the source delivers successfully for various densities (Neighbors/Range). The delivery rate of "weak links" is very low, so "weak links" will deeply affect the delivery rate of whole route. It can be derived from Figure 2 that GPSR has more "weak links" than LELBM because of the lower delivery rate.

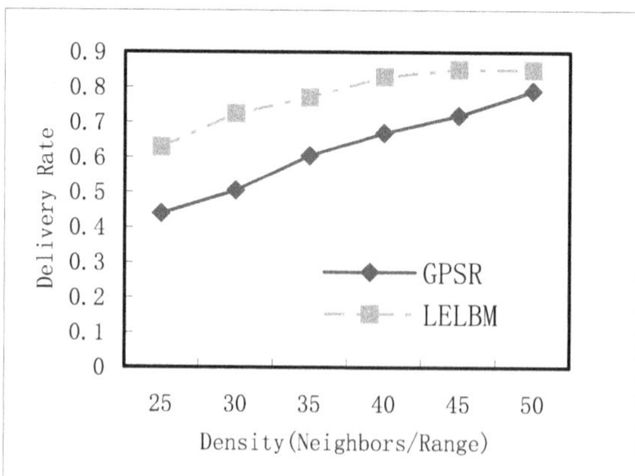

Fig. 2. Delivery rate

5.3 Average Consumed Energy

Figure 3 shows how much energy is consumed for various densities (Neighbors/Range). Obviously, LELBM has better energy efficiency than GPSR. In simulation, we find that when there are "weak links" in GPSR, LELBM can observably improve the link's performance through choosing "good links". So, the more "weak links" GPSR has, the better performance LELBM has comparing with GPSR. However, with increase of node density, there are less "weak links" in GPSR. So when the density is 50, the consumed energy of LELBM and GPSR are almost the same. What's more, the number of nodes in our simulation is 50, which equal to the highest density we used. If the number of nodes we used is greater than 50, the energy consumed of LELBM would still less than GPSR.

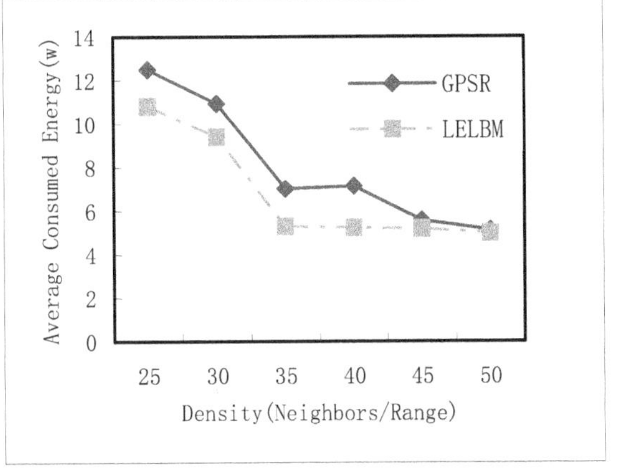

Fig. 3. Average Consumed Energy

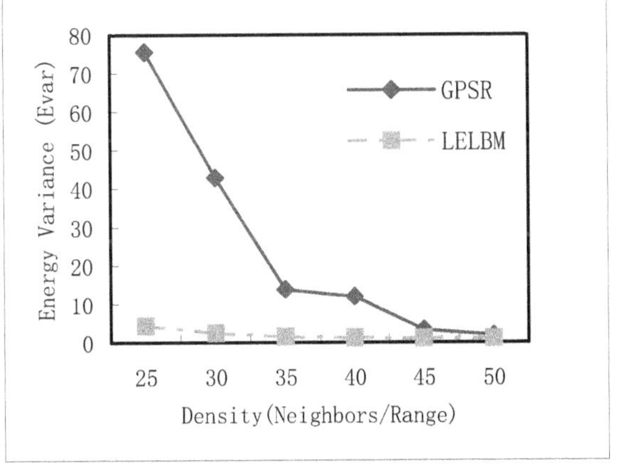

Fig. 4. Energy Variance (Evar)

5.4 Energy Variance

Figure 4 shows energy variance at different densities. When the density of the network is not high (n < 40), the load balance get notably improvement in LELBM. "Weak links" causes repeated resending, and result in too much energy consumption. LELBM help us replace the "weak links" by "good links", in which resending is not frequent. Moreover multi-path also balances the energy load. So, in all densities we tested, the energy variance (Evar) changed smoothly. It's a very good property.

6 Conclusions

We have presented a topology control method LELBM with two energy efficiency and load balance concerned strategies for multi-path wireless sensor networks. We have studied the relationship of the energy efficiency, load balance and the number of neighbors to get LELBM. Our method achieves considerably better energy efficiency and load balance than GPSR, which do not used topology control algorithms. In order to get better performance, we will try to figure out the tradeoff between the energy efficiency and load balance in future work.

References

1. Yan Yu, Ramesh Govindan, and Deborah Estrin. Geographical and energy aware routing: A recursive data dissemination protocol for wireless sensor networks. Technical report, May 2001.
2. Ramanathan R, Rosales-Hain R. Topology control of multihop wireless networks using transmit power adjustment. In: Proc. of the IEEE INFOCOM. Tel-Aviv: IEEE,2000. 404~413.
3. Alaa M, Marwan K. Power controlled dual channel (PCDC) medium access protocol for wireless ad hoc networks. In: Proc. of the IEEE INFOCOM. San Francisco: IEEE,2003. 470~480.
4. IEEE 802.11. Wireless LAN medium access control (MAC) and physical layer (PHY) specifications 1999.
5. D. Ganesan, B. Krishnamachari, A. Woo, D. Culler, D. Estrin and S. Wicker. "Complex Behavior at Scale: An Experimental Study of Low-Power Wireless Sensor Networks". UCLA CS Technical Report UCLA/CSD-TR 02-0013, 2002.
6. A. Woo, T. Tong and D. Culler. "Taming the Underlying Issues for Reliable Multhop Routing in Sensor Networks". ACM SenSys, November 2003.
7. K. Seada, M. Zuniga, A. Helmy, B. Krishnamachari. "Energy-Efficient Forwarding Strategies for Geographic Routing in Lossy Wireless Sensor Networks". *SenSys'04,* November 3–5, 2004, Baltimore, Maryland, USA.
8. M. Zuniga and B. Krishnamachari, "Analyzing the Transitional Region in Low Power Wireless Links", IEEE Secon 2004.
9. B. Karp and H. Kung. "Greedy Perimeter Stateless Routing." In Proceedings of the Sixth Annual ACM/IEEE International Conference on Mobile Computing and Networking (Mobicom 2000), 2000.
10. NS2. URL http://www.isi.edu/nsnam/ns/

11. K.Chintalapudi, R.Govindan, G.Sukhatme, A.Dhariwal, "Ad-Hoc Localization Using Ranging and Sectoring ," in *Proceedings of IEEE Infocom*, 2004.
12. W.R.Heinzelman, A.Chandrakasan and H.Balakrishnan. Energy-Efficient Communication Protocol for Wireless Microsensor Networks. In Proceedings of the 33rd Hawaii international Conference on System Sciences – 2000.
13. F. Ye, G. Zhong, S. Lu, and L. Zhang. GRAdient Broadcast: A Robust Data Delivery Protocol for Large Scale Sensor Networks. To appear in *ACM Wireless Networks (WINET)*, Vol. 11, No. 2, March 2005.
14. A Nasipuri, R Castaneda, S DAS. Performance of Multipath Routing for On-Demand Protocols in Mobile Ad Hoc Networks[J]. ACM/Kluwer Mobile Networks and Applications(MONET) Journal, 2001,6(4): 339-349.
15. Kai Wu, Janelle Harms. Performance study of a multipath routing method for wireless mobile Ad hoc Networks[A]. Cincinnati, Ohio Aug: Proceedings of IEEE/ACM 9th International Symposium on Modeling, Analysis and simulation(MASCOTS 01). New York: ACM Press, 2001.99-107
16. D. Ganesan, R. Govindan, S. Shenker, and D. Estrin, "*Highly resilient, energy efficient multipath routing in wireless sensor networks*," in Mobile Computing and Communications Review (MC2R), 2002.

Dynamic Threshold Scheme Used in Directed Diffusion

Ning Hu[1], Deyun Zhang[1], and Fubao Wang[2]

[1] School of Electronics and Information Engineering, Xi'an Jiaotong University, Xi'an, Shannxi 710049, China
{huning, dzhang}@xanet.edu.cn
[2] Institute of Broadband Network, Northwest Polytechnical University, Xi'an, Shannxi 710072, China
wangfb@nwpu.edu.cn

Abstract. Since sensor nodes are generally constrained in on-board energy supply, saving energy is crucial in extending the lifetime of the wireless sensor networks. In this paper, we present a dynamic threshold scheme used in the data propagation phase of Directed Diffusion, which can decrease the traffic between nodes and therefore prolongs the longevity of wireless sensor networks. The sensor node sends data to the sink only when the sampling value reaches the hard threshold and the difference between the current sample value and the last sent value is greater than the soft threshold, which reduces data traffic to conserve energy. The soft threshold will be adjusted by using the historical values to make the proportion of sending due to timeout equal to the expected value. Whether the values of a sensed attribute change drastically or not, the data sent will continue at a reasonable rate, which adapts the sensor network to the changeful circumstance. Simulation results show that the improved Directed Diffusion based on dynamic threshold can prolong the network lifetime about 35% compared with the original system and can reacting immediately to drastic change in the values of a sensed attribute.

1 Introduction

Advances in MEMS-based sensor technologies and low-power communication technologies have made it possible to manufacture small sensors with sensing, processing, and wireless communication capabilities in a cost effective and low energy consumption fashion. These micro sensor nodes scattered in the sensed area can be organized as ad hoc network dynamically, witch forms a wireless sensor network. They sample independently and send the sampled value to the sink – information collected point. The wireless sensor networks have the advantages of fault tolerance, easy deployment and accurate sensing, which can be applied in many fields, such as battlefield surveillance, environment monitoring and biological detection [1][2]. Since sensor networks are based on the dense deployment of disposable and low-cost sensor nodes, destruction of some nodes by hostile actions does not affect a military operation as much as the destruction of a traditional sensor, which makes sensor networks concept a better approach for battlefields.

The wireless senor networks have been hot research area at recent years, in which information aggregation and data routing with low energy consumption become the important research area. Since the sensor networks often work in the unattended circumstance, which battery replacement is impossible, the nodes must use all kinds of

L.T. Yang et al. (Eds.): ICESS 2005, LNCS 3820, pp. 220–229, 2005.

energy-saving methods to decrease the energy consumption and prolong the longevity of the sensor network. So energy-saving is a critical problem to be considered first.

Some routing protocols have been proposed for Ad-Hoc network [10]. But these protocols defined for wireless ad hoc networks are not well suited for wireless sensor networks because what they take into account firstly is not energy saving, so the research results can not be applied to wireless sensor networks directly. Further researches have to be done to use energy efficiently.

The inspiration in this paper is from TEEN [6]. The idea is applying the threshold scheme to the data propagation of Directed Diffusion, which can decrease traffic for reducing the energy consumption. Data transmission based on threshold is to transmit sensed data if the data value exceeds predefined thresholds. Using static thresholds would be efficient if the changes in the environment are usual and the threshold values are well predicted. Nevertheless, when the thresholds are not appropriate for the network, sensor nodes can run out of energy in a short time because of frequent transmissions or users can not get enough information about the current status of the network because of rare transmissions. So the dynamic threshold generation algorithm has been further presented to adjust threshold with the proportion of sending due to timeout, which keeps the data traffic a reasonable level.

2 Related Works

Researchers have suggested some energy-aware routing protocols from the aspect of reducing the data traffic in the wireless sensor networks.

A data-center routing protocol, SPIN [3], is introduced by Kulik. Nodes running SPIN assign a high-level descriptor to completely describe their collected data (called meta-data) and perform meta-data negotiations before any data is transmitted. This assures that there is no redundant data sent throughout the network. There are three phases defined in SPIN to exchange data between nodes. The nodes received data firstly broadcast ADV message containing meta-data, and their neighbors being interested in this data send REQ message to request the specific data, then the nodes owning the data send DATA message that carry the actual data.

The most well known protocol is Directed Diffusion [4], where a sink queries the sensors in an on-demand fashion by disseminating an interest, i.e., a list of attribute-value pairs for the desired data, in order to build reverse paths from all potential sensing sources to the sink. This reverse path vector is named a "gradient". As the interest is propagated hop-by-hop throughout the network, paths are established between sink and sources. Directed Diffusion uses the reinforcement mechanism to select a high quality path for the data flow among multiple paths available. Each node only forwards a packet to a specific next hop neighbor along the reinforced path, which can eliminate redundant transmissions to save energy.

Clustering is another good idea to save energy by data aggregation. LEACH [5] is such a clustering-based protocol, which forms clusters of the sensor nodes based on the received signal strength and use local cluster heads as routers to the sink. All the data processing such as data fusion and aggregation are local to the cluster and cluster heads perform data aggregation in order to save energy. Cluster heads change randomly over time in order to balance the energy dissipation of nodes.

The threshold scheme is introduced firstly in TEEN [6], which is another hierarchical routing protocol. A cluster head sends its members a hard threshold, which is the minimum possible value of an attribute to trigger a sensor node to switch on its transmitter and transmit to the cluster head and a soft threshold, which further reduces the number of transmissions if there is little or no change in the value of sensed attribute. APTEEN [7] is a hybrid protocol that uses both periodic and event based data gathering. In addition to TEEN, a set of parameters are announced by cluster heads. These are Attributes (user interests - physical parameters), Schedule (TDMA schedule - a slot for each node) and Count Time. Thresholds are used in the same way with TEEN; moreover, when a sensor node does not sense a value exceeding thresholds for a period equal to the count time, it transmits the sensed value. This avoids that there is no data to be sent in long time. Simulation of TEEN and APTEEN has shown that these two protocols outperform LEACH. The main drawbacks of the two approaches are the overhead and complexity of forming clusters in multiple levels, implementing threshold-based functions and dealing with attribute-based naming of queries.

Location-based routing scheme can eliminate the number of transmission significantly by diffusing query message only to that particular region. GEAR [8] is such a protocol that restricts the number of interests in Directed Diffusion by only considering a certain region rather than sending the interests to the whole network. It forwards the packet to the target region. When the packet has reached the region, it can be diffused in that region by either recursive geographic forwarding or restricted flooding.

GAF [9] divides the network area into fixed zones and form a virtual grid. In each virtual grid, nodes will select one sensor node to stay awake for a certain period of time and then they go to sleep. It can substantially increase the network lifetime as the number of nodes increases.

3 Motivation

Many works have been done to save energy of the sensor node, but those are not enough to achieve our objects of energy consumption. Some trivial information is not necessary for kinds of applications. We think that there are also lots of works remain to do and many existing protocols can be further improved. We also believe that sensor networks should provide the end user with the ability to control the trade-off between energy efficiency, accuracy and response times dynamically. Moreover, the sensor network system should also react immediately to drastic changes in the value of a sensed attribute when the circumstance has changed. So, in our research, we have focused on improving a popular data-center routing protocol – Directed Diffusion, which can fulfill these requirements.

4 Improved Directed Diffusion Base on Dynamic Threshold

Since wireless sensor networks are application-oriented, this paper takes example for temperature monitoring to describe the improved Directed Diffusion based on dynamic threshold. When the temperature value sampled by sensors of the sensor network varies drastically or becomes too high, the wireless sensor network can provide more detail information by sending more data to the sink, by which user can get enough information to cope with these abnormal events.

In this paper, we only introduce the Directed Diffusion routing protocol sketchily. You can get the detail description by consulting document [4].

4.1 Parameters Related

There are two thresholds used in our scheme, which is similar to those presented in TEEN [6]. We have further proposed an algorithm to adjust the threshold dynamically when the circumstance changes. This dynamic threshold adjusting algorithm is simple enough to easy implement in sensor nodes and has low overhead, which is very suitable to the systems of resource limited.

Hard Threshold (H_T): This is a threshold value for the sensed attribute, beyond which the data sampled by sensor node can be sent to the sink.

Soft Threshold (S_T): This is a small change in the value of the sensed attribute which triggers the node to switch on its transmitter and transmit.

Sending Timeout ($T_{timeout}$): It is the maximum time period between two successive reports sent by a node.

4.2 Task Description

Interest is a task description for data matching the attributes. In directed diffusion, task descriptions are named by, for example, a list of attribute-value pairs that describe a task [4]. The temperature monitoring task might be described as:

```
type = temperature // task type
interval = 0.5s // sampling interval
startAt = 00:10:00 // start time of the task
expiresAt = 01:30:00 // end time of the task
hardThreshold = 35℃ // hard threshold
softThreshold = 2℃ // initial value of the soft threshold
timeout = 2.5s // maximal sending interval
slideWindow = 5s // size of the set storing historical records
alpha = 0.4 // the proportion of sending data due to timeout
```

This task description constitutes an interest, which represents following scenes: This temperature monitoring task starts after 10 minutes and lasts 80 minutes, samples current temperature every 0.5 seconds. The sampled data is sent to the sink only when the current sample value is higher than 35℃ and the difference between this sample value and last sent value is greater than the soft threshold (its initial value is equal to 2℃ and may adjust dynamically later). To avoid no data transmitted to the sink too long time, the sensor node forces to send the current sample value when there is no data to be sent beyond 2.5 seconds.

4.3 Interest Propagation and Gradients Establishment

The improved Directed Diffusion based on dynamic threshold works the same as the original Directed Diffusion does in both interest propagation and gradients establishment. Main process about these aspects is described as follows.

The sink broadcasts interests through its neighbors. Interest diffuses throughout the network hop-by-hop, and is broadcast by each node received it to its neighbors. Each node received the interest caches it and builds an interest entry, which contains several gradient fields. Each gradient field presents a gradient that is a reply link to a neighbor from which the interest was received. So there might be multiple paths to reach the sink from this node. A node also might receive data from several neighbors, which makes it have a change to do in-network data aggregation. The process of interest propagation and gradient establishment continues until gradients are setup from the sources back to the sink. The whole gradient field has been established by far.

The path along which data are received firstly will be reinforced, through which data can be transmitted at higher rate. Any node that has data to send selects a path according to a local policy to transmit the data to its neighbor. The sink has to resend periodically the interest throughout the sensor network to maintain the gradients

4.4 Data Propagation and Dynamic Threshold Generation

After the gradients establishment completes, the source can send data to the sink along these gradients. The node will send data only when both the following conditions are true:

1. The current value of the sensed attribute is greater than the hard threshold.
2. The difference between the current value of the sensed attribute and the data value last sent is greater than the soft threshold.

A series of data sent by one sensor node can be regarded as a data stream, which is a set that contains infinite elements. Each element can be represented as $< v, t >$, where v is the sample value and t is its corresponding transmission time. The recent elements constitute a slide window on the data stream, by which the soft threshold is calculated to adapt to the drastic changes in the value of a sensed attribute.

We assume that the data enter the slide window in time sequence. So the data in slide window can be represented as

$$< v_l, t_l >, < v_{l+1}, t_{l+1} >, \cdots, < v_{u-1}, t_{u-1} >, < v_u, t_u > \tag{1}$$

where $l < u$ and $t_u - t_l = T$ at any time. That is to say, only sample value in the slide window will be stored in sensor node.

The elements of which data are sent due to timeout constitute a subset.

$$S^* = \{ < v_i, t_i > | \, |v_i - v_{i-1}| < S_T \; or \; v_i < H_T, l < i \le u \} \tag{2}$$

To decrease the energy consumption, it should try its best to increase the sending interval. At the same time, enough data have to be sent when sample values change drastically. This can be achieved by controlling the proportion of sending due to timeout in the slide window. During interval of T, the proportion of sending due to timeout is calculated as follows.

$$P^* = \frac{|S^*|}{u-l+1} \tag{3}$$

Assuming that the proportion of sending due to timeout is set to α in advance, the algorithm of adjusting soft threshold is as follows:

(1) If $P^* > \alpha$, then set $S_T^{'} = 0.9 * S_T$;

(2) If $P^* < \alpha$, then set $S_T^{'} = 1.1 * S_T$;

(3) If $P^* = \alpha$, then set $S_T^{'} = S_T$.

Parameter α in this algorithm used to let user designate an expected value, which is the goal value to let the proportion of sending data due to timeout achieve by adjusting soft threshold. This gives the user a chance to control the trade-off between energy efficiency, accuracy and response times. Choosing α depends on the statistical character of the data generation.

The algorithm described above means that the soft threshold should be decreased when the sending interval is too long, be increased when the sending interval is too short, and have no change when the sending interval is equal to the expected value.

5 Performance Evaluation

To evaluate the performance of our improved protocol, we have implemented it based on Intanagonwiwat's code on the ns-2 simulator [11]. Our goals in the simulation are as follows:

1. Compare the performance of the improved Directed Diffusion and the original Directed Diffusion on the basis of the longevity of the network.
2. Study how the related parameters, such as the size of the slide window (T), the expected proportion of sending due to timeout (α), and the characters of the sample value of source, effect on the soft threshold (S_T).

5.1 Simulation Environment

The simulation has been performed on a network of 50 nodes, which dispersed in a rectangular area with 160x160m. Five sources and one sink have been chosen randomly in those nodes. The value of a sensed attribute subjects to normal distribution, where EX is equal to 30 and DX is equal to 10. These sources send data packet whose size is 64 bytes at the interval of 0.5s. The sink generates interest message whose size is 36 bytes at the interval of 5s.

The ns-2 simulator implements a 1.6 Mb/s 802.11MAC layer. To more closely mimic realistic sensor network radios [12], we altered the ns-2 radio energy model such that the idle-time power dissipation was about 0.035W, or nearly 10% of its receive power dissipation (0.395W) and about 5% of its transmit power dissipation (0.660W). Each node has a radio range of 40 m. The initial energy is set to 100J. The simulation ends when the energy of all nodes is exhausted.

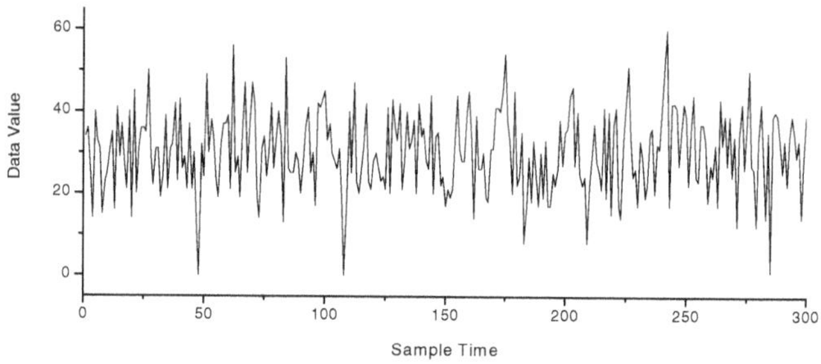

Fig. 1. Data generated by source subjecting to normal distribution (EX=30, X=10)

Figure 1 show us the data generated by source subjecting to normal distribution, where EX is equal to 30 and DX is equal to 10. It impresses on us the values of the sensed attribute changing drastically in our given data source. In our study, we will generate more smooth data based on it.

5.2 Results

We simulate the original Directed Diffusion, the improved Directed Diffusion based on hard threshold and the improved Directed Diffusion based on both hard and soft threshold at the same simulation scene described above. Other parameters correlating with the simulation is set as follows: α is set to 0.4, the size of slide window is set to 10 sending periods (5s), hard threshold is set to 35, soft threshold is initially set to 2 and sending timeout is set to 5 sending periods (2.5s).

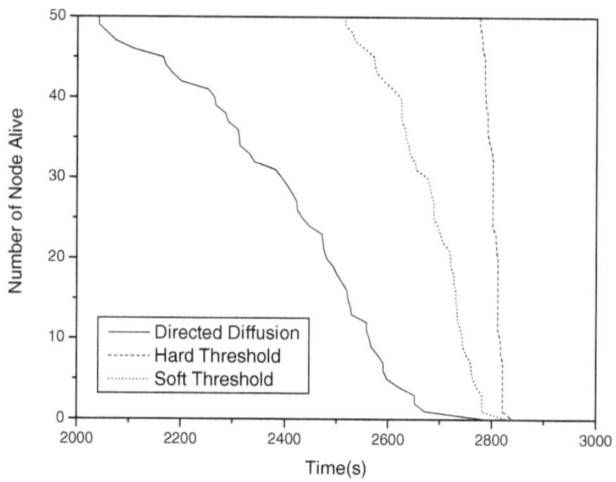

Fig. 2. Comparison of the number of nodes alive

Figure 2 shows that the threshold scheme can actually decrease the energy consumption and prolong the longevity of the wireless sensor network. The current sensed value little differing from the value last sent will not be transmitted, which decreases the traffic. So the energy dissipation in a node, especially one belongs to the sharing path from several sources to the sink, is reduced. The longevity of the node first died prolongs 35% compared with that in the original system.

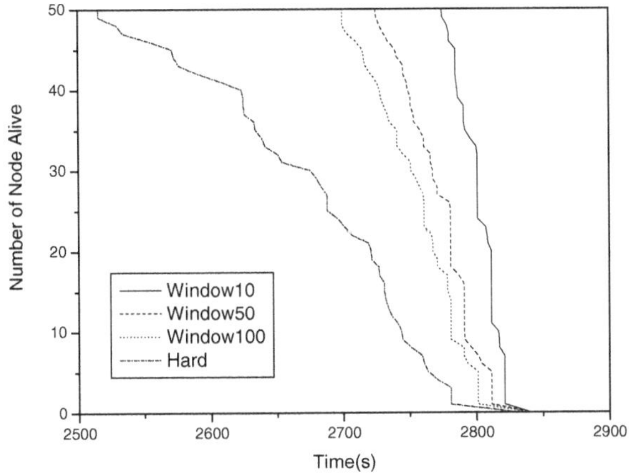

Fig. 3. Effect of window size upon node longevity

Since adjusting soft threshold depends on sending history recorded in the slide window, whose size will effect on the node longevity. Figure 3 shows that the more large the window size, the more short the node longevity. This because large window is not sensitive to little change of sensed value and soft threshold is not adjusted in time with changing in the value of the sensed attribute.

Simulation also shows that the energy consumption changes little with different α if the statistical character of the data generation has no change.

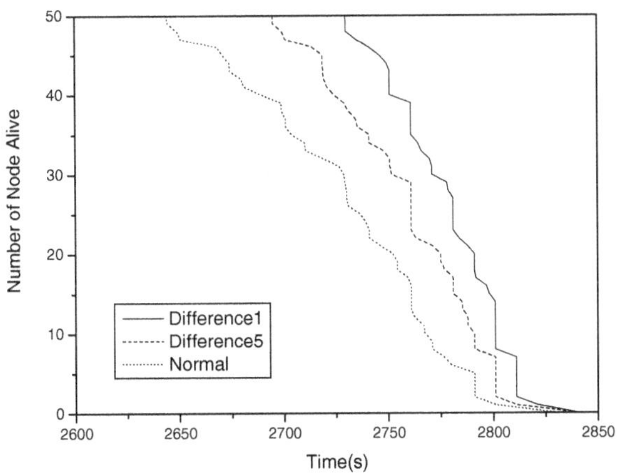

Fig. 4. Effect of data character upon node longevity ($\alpha = 0$)

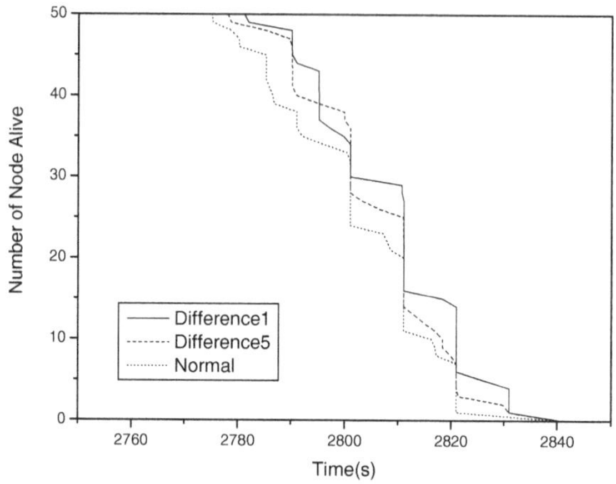

Fig. 5. Effect of data character upon node longevity ($\alpha = 0.4$)

The sampling value little differing from last sent data will not be sent when soft threshold scheme has been introduced. Data character - the difference between adjacent sampling values, will have an effect on actual sending rate of a node, which affects the node longevity. Figure 4 shows the effect of data character upon the node longevity under the condition of timeout sending is not allowed (here the soft threshold will become very little). The three curves in figure 4 separately represent different data characters - sampling value subjects to normal distribution (EX=30, DX=10), and two other sources in which the difference of adjacent sampling values is no more than 1 or 5 (they are generated based on that normal distribution and inserted values to make the change more smooth). Simulation result shows the more smooth data changes, the more node longevity is long. Small variety in sampling value results in few data value reaching soft/hard threshold, which decreases the energy consumption for transmitting or receiving.

Figure 5 shows how the data characters affect the node longevity when α is set to 0.4. Since 40% data being allowed to transmit due to timeout, part of the data changing smoothly will also be sent to sink. The soft threshold can be adjusted dynamically with the change of the data character, so the data sending rates of three sources are quite similar, which results in node longevity of these sources being close to each other. This can be proved by our simulation.

6 Conclusions

This paper introduces soft/hard threshold scheme into data propagation phase of Directed Diffusion, which prolongs the node longevity through reducing the traffic between potential sources and the sink. Hard threshold can filter out unimportant data sampled by sensor and soft threshold farther discards the trivial data, which decreases the energy consumption of the sensor node. The ability of adapting to the drastic change in the source character is introduced by dynamic soft threshold. Whether the values of a sensed attribute change drastically or not, the data sent will continue at a reasonable rate, which adapts the sensor network to the changeful circumstance. Simulation results show that the improved Directed Diffusion based on dynamic threshold can prolong the lifetime of the wireless sensor networks.

References

[1] D. Estrin, R. Govindan, J. Heidemann, et al., "Next Century Challenges: Scalable Coordination in Sensor Networks," in the Proceedings of the 5th Annual ACM/IEEE International Conference on Mobile Computing and Networking (MobiCom'99), Seattle, WA, August 1999.

[2] I. F. Akyildiz, W. Su, Y. Sankarasubramaniam, et al., "Wireless Sensor Networks: A Survey," Computer Networks, vol. 38, pp. 393-422, March 2002.

[3] J. Kulik, W. R. Heinzelman, and H. Balakrishnan, "Negotiation-based Protocols for Disseminating Information in Wireless Sensor Networks," Wireless Networks, vol. 8, pp. 169-185, March-May 2002.

[4] C. Intanagonwiwat, R. Govindan, and D. Estrin, "Directed Diffusion for Wireless Sensor Networking," IEEE/ACM Transactions on Networking, vol. 11, pp. 2-16, February 2003,

[5] W. Heinzelman, A. Chandrakasan and H. Balakrishnan, "Energy-Efficient Communication Protocol for Wireless Microsensor Networks," in the Proceedings of the 33rd Hawaii International Conference on System Sciences (HICSS '00), Maui, Hawaii, January 2000.

[6] A. Manjeshwar and D. P. Agrawal, "TEEN: A Protocol for Enhanced Efficiency in Wireless Sensor Networks," in the Proceedings of the 1st International Workshop on Parallel and Distributed Computing Issues in Wireless Networks and Mobile Computing, San Francisco, CA, April 2001.

[7] A. Manjeshwar and D. P. Agrawal, "APTEEN: A Hybrid Protocol for Efficient Routing and Comprehensive Information Retrieval in Wireless Sensor Networks," in the Proceedings of the 2nd International Workshop on Parallel and Distributed Computing Issues in Wireless Networks and Mobile computing, Ft. Lauderdale, FL, April 2002.

[8] Y. Yu, D. Estrin, and R. Govindan, "Geographical and Energy-Aware Routing: A Recursive Data Dissemination Protocol for Wireless Sensor Networks," UCLA Computer Science Department Technical Report, UCLA-CSD TR-01-0023, May 2001.

[9] Y. Xu, J. Heidemann, and D. Estrin, "Geography-informed Energy Conservation for Ad Hoc Routing," in the Proceedings of the 7th Annual ACM/IEEE International Conference on Mobile Computing and Networking (MobiCom'01), Rome, Italy, July 2001.

[10] E. M. Royer, C. K. Toh, "A Review of Current Routing Protocols for Ad-Hoc Mobile Wireless Networks," IEEE Personal Communications Magazine, vol. 6, pp. 46–55, April 1999.

[11] UCB/LBNL/VINT, "Network Simulator-ns," http://www.isi.edu/nsnam/ns/.

[12] W. J. Kaiser, "WINS NG 1.0 transceiver power dissipation specifications," Sensoria Corporation, San Diego, CA.

Compiler-Directed Energy-Aware Prefetching Optimization for Embedded Applications*

Juan Chen[1], Yong Dong[2], Huizhan Yi[3], and Xuejun Yang

School of Computer, National University of Defense Technology,
Changsha 410073, P.R. China
[1]{juanchen@nudt.edu.cn}, [2]{luckpeople@163.com},
[3]{huizhanyi@nudt.edu.cn}

Abstract. High energy consumption has become a limiting factor for battery-operated embedded systems. Most low-power compiler optimization techniques take the approach of minimizing the energy consumption while meeting small performance loss. In addition, it is possible that the available *energy budget* is not sufficient to meet the optimal performance objective. In such situation, energy-constrained optimization is more significant. In this paper, we explore two kinds of energy-aware prefetching optimizations: prefetching optimization with minimizing energy consumption and energy-constrained prefetching optimization. We exploit energy saving opportunities through reducing memory stalls and CPU stalls caused by too early or too late prefetching. We build models for these two kinds of energy-aware prefetching optimization approaches and use a group of array-dominated applications to validate our approach.

1 Introduction

High energy consumption has become a limiting factor to develop designs for battery-operated embedded systems due to exorbitant cooling, packing and power costs. **Dynamic Voltage Scaling (DVS)** is a major low-power technique [1][2][3][4][5][10][11][12]. In this article, we consider two kinds of energy-aware prefetching optimizations: the first is minimizing energy consumption within small performance loss; the second one is optimizing performance within the available energy budget (E_{budget}). Assume energy required to meet the optimal performance without energy constraint is E_{bound}. In scarce-energy settings where $E_{budget} < E_{bound}$, energy-constrained optimization may cause some performance loss.

Software prefetching improves performance by effectively hiding memory access latency through overlapping memory access with computation [6]. However, software prefetching does not always implement perfect data prefetching because it requires prefetch instructions are inserted at the right places. Prefetching too early or too late may cause memory or CPU stalls. By reducing memory frequency or CPU frequency or both, we can save energy consumption.

There usually exist two imperfect prefetch optimization cases: **CPU-bound case** and **memory-bound case**. In CPU-bound case, prefetching operation is too early or

* This work was supported by the National High Technology Development 863 Program of China under Grant No. 2002AA1Z2101 and No. 2004AA1Z2210.

L.T. Yang et al. (Eds.): ICESS 2005, LNCS 3820, pp. 230–243, 2005.

memory access latency is too short so that the prefetched data is provided before actually being used. Although memory access latency is completely hidden, prefetching too early makes memory access completes ahead of the actual data access. We refer to this time interval as *memory stalls*. The second case is memory-bound case, where memory access dominates the whole time and CPU stalls cannot be avoided due to prefetching too late or too long memory access latency. Figure 1 illustrates the behavior of prefetching.

With DVS, we utilize CPU stalls and memory stalls to reduce memory frequency or CPU frequency or both so as to minimize energy consumption or meet scarce energy budget. In CPU-bound case, the major method is to adjust memory frequency to eliminate memory stalls combined with small CPU frequency scaling. In memory-bound case, the major method is to reduce CPU frequency to eliminate CPU stalls while adjusting small memory frequency. Furthermore, it is necessary to adjust both of their frequencies instead of one of them for energy savings.

In this research effort, we introduce the notion *time* to characterize the performance benefits from prefetching—*time* denotes the program execution time with software prefetching optimization. In energy-constrained prefetching optimization, *time* is minimized. In energy optimization problem, performance (*time*) loss is limited within some degree.

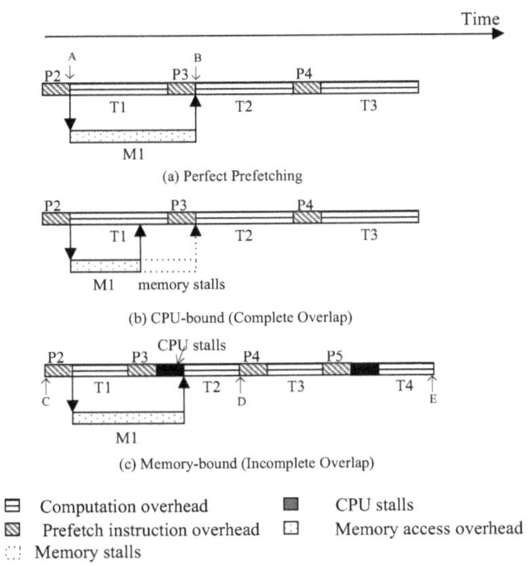

Fig. 1. Prefetching Optimization. P2, P3, P4, P5 represent prefetchinstrution overhead for the second, third, fourth and fifth iteration, respectively. M1 represents memory access overhead caused byprefetching. T1, T2, T3 and T4 represent computation overhead in thefirst, second, third and fourth iteration. Note: here iteration denotes theoutmost iteration.

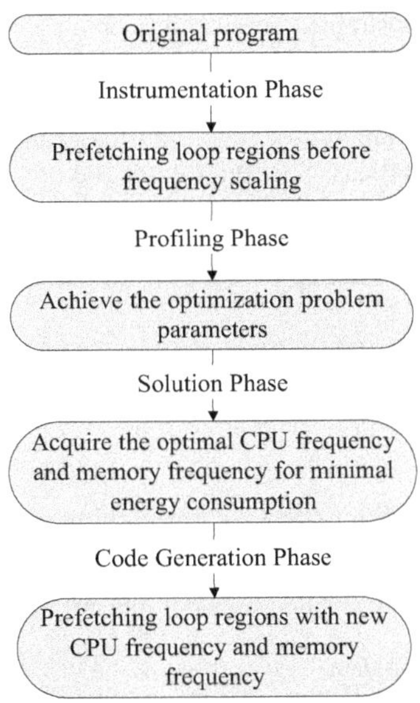

Fig. 2. Compilation Framework

The prototype implementation consists of four phases. It starts by instrumenting the original program at selected program locations (instrumentation phase). The instrumented code is then simulated, drawing out some profiled data (profiling phase). Once the profiling is done, all the parameters of this optimization problem are determined. The next work is to obtain the optimal CPU and memory frequencies through solving the above optimization problem (solution phase). Finally, the frequency-setting calls are inserted at the appropriate situations so that the selected region is executed at the appropriate frequency and the rest of the program be executed at the highest frequency (code generation phase). The first three phases have been implemented and we are working for code generation phase. The whole compilation framework is shown in Figure 2.

In this article, we evaluate the impact of different parameters on optimization results and draw some conclusions. Finally, we use a group of array-dominated applications to validate our conclusions.

For the research on software prefetching techniques [6][7][8], Todd [6] provided a comprehensive analysis on software prefetching. Ricardo Bianchini et al. [9] presented analytical models of the performance benefits of multithreading and prefetching. Xiaobo Fan et al. [5] believed the best voltage/frequency for minimizing power consumption should be obtained by including memory power in the decision. We exploited memory stalls and CPU stalls existing in imperfect prefetching to reduce CPU or memory voltage/frequency for energy savings. We have done some initial research on energy-constrained prefetching optimization [15]. In this article, we present a comprehensive analysis on energy-aware prefetching optimization from two different perspectives.

The remainder of this paper is organized as follows. In section 2, we build energy-aware prefetching optimization model. Section 3 provides experimental results and analysis. Section 4 gives the conclusions and Future Works.

2 Energy-Aware Prefetching Optimization

2.1 Overview

The prototypical loop that we optimize with prefetching looks like:

```
for ( i = 0 ; i < N ; i ++)  Compute ( i ) ;
```

After software prefetching optimization, the above loop is changed into:

```
// iteration 0, prefetch b blocks
prefetch ( 0, b );
for ( i = 0 ; i < N - step ; i += step ) {
    // prefetch b blocks for iterations i+step to i+2*step-1
    prefetch  ( i + step , b);
    // compute iterations i to i + step - 1
    for ( j = 0 ; j < step ; j ++ )  Compute ( i * step + j );
}
for ( j = 0 ; j < step ; j++ )  Compute ( i * step + j ) ;
```

In the above prefetching loop, several prefetch instructions are inserted. The major parameters involved in modeling the energy behavior of the above prefetching loop are the number of the cache blocks prefetched for each prefetching instruction, b; the number of prefetching instructions per iteration, N_b; the energy overhead of each prefetched cache block, E_b; the time overhead of each prefetched cache block, C_p; the total latency of cache misses per iteration, C_m; and the computation between two consecutive prefetch instructions, C_c. Table 1 summarizes these parameters.

Prefetching allows greater flexibility when trying to overlap memory access and computation, since the compiler or user can schedule the prefetches according to the memory access latency and the amount of work per iteration of each loop in the program. This intelligent scheduling of prefetches adjusts b and the iteration *step* size appropriately as the above code segment shows.

The optimal number of blocks to prefetch at a time depends on the available cache space; blocks prefetched into the cache may be replaced before being used. Another limitation is the number of prefetched blocks that can fit in a prefetch/transaction buffer. With these constraints, the amount of useful work that can be overlapped with memory access may be insufficient to hide memory latency completely. To analyze this problem, we simplify it as Figure 1 shows.

Figure 1 illustrates the behavior of the prefetching loop. The execution alternates between prefetch instruction and computation intervals. Each prefetch accessing cache blocks are to be used one computation block ahead. While it is possible to have loops that prefetch more than one computation block ahead, we can always transform such loops into an equivalent loop that prefetches a single computation block ahead.

In Figure 1(a), **P2** denotes prefetch instruction operation, where calculates the data address to be prefetched (b, N_b, E_b are involved). **M1** executes memory access operations caused by prefetch instruction (C_m, f_m are involved). **T2** accesses the prefetched data at point **B** (C_c, f_c are involved). Figure 1(a) shows perfect prefetching behavior. Memory accesses caused by prefetch are fully overlapped with computation, where no CPU stall or memory stall exists. If prefetech instructions cannot be inserted at the right places, two kinds of imperfect prefetchings occur as shown in Figure 1(b) and Figure 1(c). In terms of CPU-bound or memory-bound case, we adjust memory frequency f_m and CPU frequency f_c to save energy consumption. In this article, we present two energy-aware prefetching optimization problems as follows.

Problem 1: given a loop L optimized with software prefetching and a DVS-enabled CPU and memory system, find optimal CPU frequency f_c and memory frequency f_m, then minimize energy consumption while permitting small performance loss.

Problem 2: given a loop L optimized with software prefetching and a DVS-enabled CPU and memory system, find optimal CPU frequency f_c and memory frequency f_m, then the performance objective is optimal while meeting a given energy budget.

2.2 Energy and Performance Analytical Models

2.2.1 Energy Model

The total energy consumption $E_{total} = E_p + E_c + E_m$, where E_p represents the energy consumption of prefetching instructions. We assume the number of prefetched cache block per iteration is B, which is the product of b and N_b. Thus the energy consumption for N loop iterations $E_p = E_b \cdot b \cdot N_b \cdot N$

E_c represents the energy consumption of CPU computation. Due to continuously variable CPU frequency, $P_c(f_c)$ is denoted the CPU power dissipation for CPU frequency of f_c. C_c / f_c represents CPU computation time. Then CPU energy consumption during N loop iterations $E_c = P_c(f_c) \cdot C_c / f_c \cdot N$.

E_m represents memory energy consumption. Due to continuously variable memory frequency, $P_m(f_m)$ represents the memory power dissipation for memory frequency of f_m. C_m / f_m represents memory access time. Then the memory access energy consumption for N iterations $E_m = P_m(f_m) \cdot C_m / f_m \cdot N$

Thus, we can get $E_{total} = E_b \cdot b \cdot N_b \cdot N + P_c(f_c) \cdot C_c / f_c \cdot N + P_m(f_m) \cdot C_m / f_m \cdot N$.

In CMOS systems, dynamic power dissipation varies linearly with frequency and quadratically with supply voltage as given by the equation $P \propto \alpha C V^2 f$, where α is the switching activity factor, C is the load capacitance, V is the supply voltage and f is the clock frequency. The relationship between supply voltage V and frequency f is $f \propto (V - V_{th})^{\beta} / V$, where V_{th} represents threshold voltage, and β is a proportional factor between 1 and 2. It is reasonable to assume frequency f is linearly proportion with voltage V so as to draw the following formula:

$$P = \alpha \cdot C \cdot f^3 \tag{1}$$

In terms of formula (1), $P_c(f_c) = \alpha_1 \cdot C_1 \cdot f_c^3$ and $P_m(f_m) = \alpha_2 \cdot C_2 \cdot f_m^3$. So we can get:

$$E_{total} = E_b \cdot b \cdot N_b \cdot N + k_1 \cdot f_c^2 \cdot C_c \cdot N + k_2 \cdot f_m^2 \cdot C_m \cdot N \tag{2}$$

where $k_1 = \alpha_1 \cdot C_1$ and $k_2 = \alpha_2 \cdot C_2$.

2.2.2 Performance Model

In the previous section, we have defined performance objective—*time*. *Time* calculates the execution time for prefetching loop. To calculate this value, two cases need to be considered. In CPU-bound case (Figure 1(b)), the total execution time of prefetching loop is calculated by prefetching instruction and CPU computation as follows.

$$T_{total} = N \cdot \left(\frac{b \cdot N_b \cdot C_p}{f_c} + \frac{C_c}{f_c}\right) \quad cond1$$

In memory-bound case, CPU stall occurs every other prefetching operation as Figure 1(c) shows. The time interval from **C** to **D** and the time interval from **D** to **E** are identical. We can conclude that the total execution cycles are *N/2* times as many as the execution cycles during **C** to **D**. Since the execution cycles during **C** to **D** are $\left(\frac{b \cdot N_b \cdot C_p}{f_c} + \frac{C_m}{f_m} + \frac{C_c}{f_c}\right)$, and we assume $N \bmod 2 = 0$, thus the total execution time is

$$T_{total} = \frac{N}{2} \cdot \left(\frac{b \cdot N_b \cdot C_p}{f_c} + \frac{C_m}{f_m} + \frac{C_c}{f_c}\right) \quad cond2$$

where *cond1* and *cond2* represent CPU-bound case and memory-bound case, respectively. That is,

$$cond1 \ \ represents \ \ \frac{C_m}{f_m^0} \le \frac{b \cdot N_b \cdot C_p}{f_c^0} + \frac{C_c}{f_c^0}, \quad cond2 \ \ represents \ \ \frac{C_m}{f_m^0} > \frac{b \cdot N_b \cdot C_p}{f_c^0} + \frac{C_c}{f_c^0}$$

where f_c^0 and f_m^0 represent initial CPU and memory frequencies, respectively. We can easily judge which case one application belongs to in terms of profiled data and initial frequency value. Then, the total execution time is calculated in terms of the individual case as follows.

$$T_{total} = \begin{cases} N \cdot (\frac{b \cdot N_b \cdot C_p}{f_c} + \frac{C_c}{f_c}) & cond1 \\ \frac{N}{2} \cdot (\frac{b \cdot N_b \cdot C_p}{f_c} + \frac{C_m}{f_m} + \frac{C_c}{f_c}) & cond2 \end{cases} \quad (3)$$

Replace f_c and f_m with f_c^0 and f_m^0 in equation (3), the initial time T_{total}^0 is easily calculated.

2.3 Energy-Aware Prefetching Optimization

For energy optimization problem, β of performance loss is satisfied. Inequality (5-1) and (5-2) show two performance constraints under CPU-bound case and memory-bound case, respectively. Inequality (6-1) and (6-2) guarantee CPU-bound case (memory-bound case) still belongs to CPU-bound case (memory-bound case) during voltage/frequency scaling. For energy-constrained optimization problem, performance objectives have the different presentations under two cases due to equation (3). The meanings of all the parameters and variables are listed in Table 1.

Energy optimization problem

$$\min(E_b \cdot b \cdot N_b \cdot N + k_1 \cdot f_c^2 \cdot C_c \cdot N + k_2 \cdot f_m^2 \cdot C_m \cdot N) \quad (4)$$

$$\begin{cases} N \cdot (\frac{b \cdot N_b \cdot C_p}{f_c} + \frac{C_c}{f_c}) \le (1+\beta) \cdot N \cdot (\frac{b \cdot N_b \cdot C_p}{f_c^0} + \frac{C_c}{f_c^0}) & cond1 \quad (5\text{-}1) \\ \frac{N}{2} \cdot (\frac{b \cdot N_b \cdot C_p}{f_c} + \frac{C_m}{f_m} + \frac{C_c}{f_c}) \le (1+\beta) \cdot \frac{N}{2} \cdot (\frac{b \cdot N_b \cdot C_p}{f_c^0} + \frac{C_m}{f_m^0} + \frac{C_c}{f_c^0}) & cond2 \quad (5\text{-}2) \end{cases}$$

$$\begin{cases} C_m / f_m - (b \cdot N_b \cdot C_p + C_c) / f_c \le 0 & cond1 \quad (6\text{-}1) \\ C_m / f_m - (b \cdot N_b \cdot C_p + C_c) / f_c > 0 & cond2 \quad (6\text{-}2) \end{cases}$$

$$f_c' \le f_c \le f_c'' \quad (7)$$

$$f_m' \le f_m \le f_m'' \quad (8)$$

Energy-constrained optimization problem

$$\begin{cases} \min(N \cdot (\frac{b \cdot N_b \cdot C_p}{f_c} + \frac{C_c}{f_c})) & cond1 \quad (9\text{-}1) \\ \min(\frac{N}{2} \cdot (\frac{b \cdot N_b \cdot C_p}{f_c} + \frac{C_m}{f_m} + \frac{C_c}{f_c})) & cond2 \quad (9\text{-}2) \end{cases}$$

$$E_b \cdot b \cdot N_b \cdot N + k_1 \cdot f_c^2 \cdot C_c \cdot N + k_2 \cdot f_m^2 \cdot C_m \cdot N \le E_{budget} \quad (10)$$

$$\begin{cases} C_m / f_m - (b \cdot N_b \cdot C_p + C_c) / f_c \le 0 & cond1 \quad (11\text{-}1) \\ C_m / f_m - (b \cdot N_b \cdot C_p + C_c) / f_c > 0 & cond2 \quad (11\text{-}2) \end{cases}$$

$$f_c' \le f_c \le f_c'' \quad (12)$$

$$f_m' \le f_m \le f_m'' \quad (13)$$

3 Experiments

We assume CPU and memory frequency vary continuously and satisfy $P_c = (7.72e-27) \cdot f_c^3$ and $P_m = (1.09e-24) \cdot f_m^3$ in terms of equation (1). Parameter k_1 and k_2 are estimated according to Transmeta's Crusoe TM5900 processor parameters [13]. The power specifications for TM5900 CPU and DDR are shown in Table 2.

Table 1. System parameters and program parameters for our optimization problems

System Paramter	Meaning	Value
E_b	Energy consumption by a cache block prefetched	10 pJ
b	The number of cache block prefetched by a prefetching instruction	4
C_p	A prefetched cache block computation time	1 cycles
k_1	The coefficient for $P_c = k_1 \cdot f_c^3$	7.72e-27
k_2	The coefficient for $P_m = k_2 \cdot f_m^3$	1.09e-24
f_c^0	Initial CPU frequency	1000 MHz
f_m^0	Initial memory frequency	133 MHz
$f_c^{'}$	The lower bound of continous CPU frequency	433 MHz
$f_c^{''}$	The upper bound of continuous CPU frequency	1000 MHz
$f_m^{'}$	The lower bound of continuous memory frequency	83 MHz
$f_m^{''}$	The upper bound of continuous memory frequency	133 MHz
Program Parmeter	**Meaning**	**Value**
N	Prefetching loop iteration counts	Program specified
C_c	Computation time in once iteration (cycles)	Profiled
C_m	Memory access time in once iteration (cycles)	Profiled
N_b	The number of prefetching instructions in one iteration	Optimization specified
β	Performance loss degeree (100%)	User specified
E_{budget}	Energy budget	specified

Table 2. Clock frequency, supply voltage, and power dissipation for TM5900 CPU and DDR. Come from Transmeta Crusoe TM5700/5900 Data Book.

CPU Fre (MHz)	CVDD (V)
1000	1.25
900	1.20
800	1.10
667	1.00
567	0.90
433	0.80

(a) The relationship between CPU frequency and voltage

State	CPU Fre (MHz)	CVDD (V)	Power (W)
Normal	1000	1.25	6.50
Auto Halt (ACPI C1)	433	0.80	0.35
Quick Start (ACPI C2)	433	0.80	0.30
Deep Sleep (ACPI C3)	-	0.80	0.15-0.40
DSX	-	0.625	0.10-0.25

(b) The relationship between CPU frequency, voltage and power

Current (A)	Power (W)
1	2.5
0.5	1.25
0.2	0.5
0.048	0.12

(c) The relationship between DDR current and power. DDR frequency is 83MHz-133MHz.

We use SimpleScalar tool set [14] to profile some necessary parameters such as C_c and C_m. Modified SimpleScalar tool set [14] models a 1 GHz 4-way issue dynamically-scheduled processor. This simulator models all aspects of the processor including the instruction fetch unit, the branch predictor, register renaming, the functional unit pipelines, and the reorder buffer. This modified SimpleScalar tool set enables software prefetching through adding a prefetch instruction to the ISA of the processor model. In addition, our simulator also models the memory system in detail. A split 8-Kbyte direct-mapped L1 cache with 32-byte cache blocks, and a unified 256-Kbyte 4-way set-associative L2 cache with 64-byte cache blocks are assumed. Such cache configuration can meet our input data sets.

As Table 1 shows, there are 11 system parameters and 6 program parameters. In this section, we analyze the impact of four program parameters on two kinds of optimization problems. The parameter analysis is divided into two groups: C_c and C_m; β and E_{budget}.

3.1 C_c and C_m

(1) *Problem 1*

For two kinds of energy-aware optimizations, we simulate the impact of C_c and C_m on these two objectives. In *Problem 1*, minimizing energy consumption is our objective. Assume initial energy consumption before frequency scaling is E_{ini}, and the minimum energy consumption after frequency scaling is E_{min}, the energy saving percentage is represented by formula (14).

$$Energy\ saving = \frac{E_{ini} - E_{\min}}{E_{ini}} \times 100\% \tag{14}$$

Figure 3 gives the energy saving percentages under different C_c and C_m values.

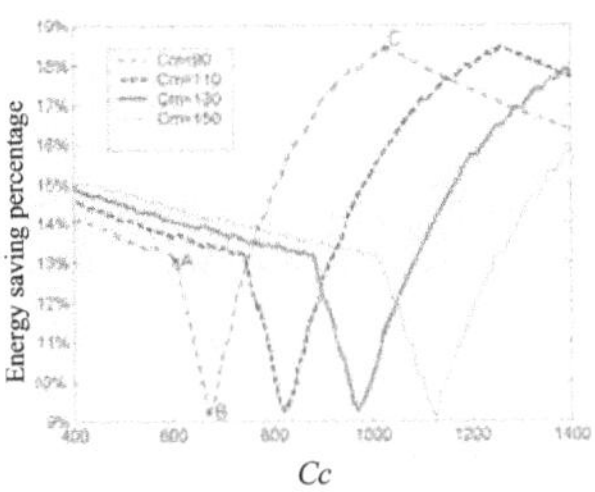

Fig. 3. Energy saving percentage as *Cc* and*Cm* vary

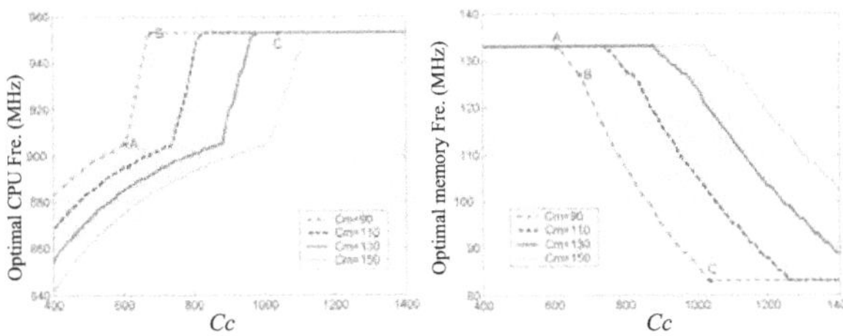

(a) Optimal CPU Fre. as *Cc* and *Cm* vary (b) Optimal memory Fre. as *Cc* and *Cm* vary

Fig. 4. Optimal CPU and memory frequencies as *Cc* and *Cm* vary

Focus on the curve where $C_m = 90$, we notice three points (**A, B, C**) on this curve, among which the minimum energy saving is obtained at point **B**. That is because point **B** is the dividing point for memory-bound case and CPU-bound case: the left points of **B** belong to memory-bound cases; the right points of **B** belong to CPU-bound cases. More approach to point **B**, CPU stalls or memory stalls are smaller so that less energy savings can be obtained. On the contrary, farther away from point **B**, CPU stalls or memory stalls are bigger so as to achieve more energy savings. Thus, the whole curve looks like a '**V**' shape and point **B** lies in the minimum of '**V**' shape.

Figure 4 presents the varying curves of CPU and memory frequencies under the same conditions. The point **A, B** and **C** are the same with those in Figure 3.

(2) *Problem 2*

In *Problem* 2, performance optimization is our objective. Figure 5 shows time variance as C_c and C_m vary. From point **Ai** to **Bi** (i=1, 2, 3, 4), the change trends occur an exception. That is because the points before **Ai** belong to memory-bound cases and the points after **Bi** belong to CPU-bound cases and the calculation formulas for these two cases are different.

Figure 6 gives the optimal CPU and memory frequency settings as C_c and C_m vary. From these two curves, the optimal CPU frequency value is non-decreasing as C_c increases while the optimal memory frequency value is non-increasing as C_c increases under a fixed C_m value. The C_c value and C_m value at points **Ai** and **Bi** (i=1, 2, 3, 4) are the same with those in Figure 5. Therefore, we can contrast Figure 6 with Figure 5.

From the above analyses, we can conclude that:

- C_c and C_m determine CPU-bound case or memory-bound case. More approach to the dividing point, less energy saving is obtained in *Problem 1*. The optimal CPU frequency and memory frequency variances have different characteristics;
- For *Problem 2*, under fixed C_m value, performance decreases as C_c increases. A little exception occurs around the dividing point.

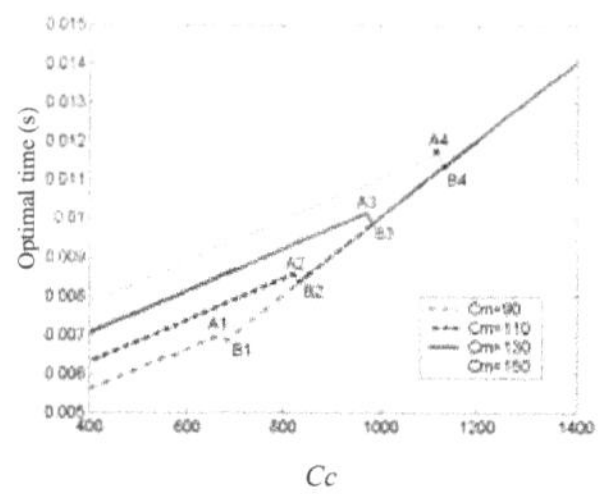

Fig. 5. Time variances as *Cc* and *Cm* vary. Here α = *90%*

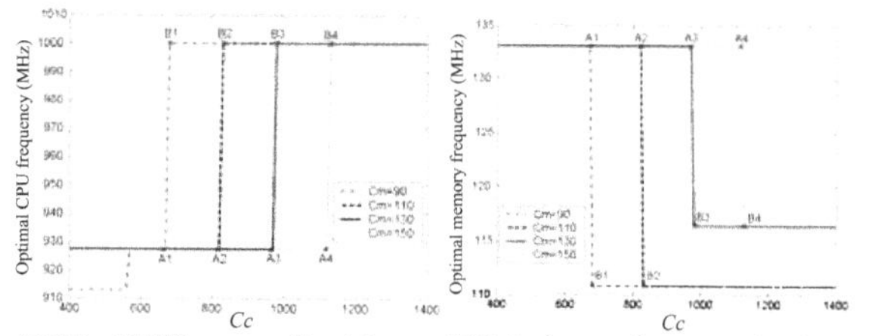

(a) Optimal CPU frequency as *Cc* and *Cm* vary (b) Optimal memory frequency as *Cc* and *Cm* vary

Fig. 6. Optimal CPU and memory frequency settings as *Cc* and *Cm* vary. here α=*90%*

3.2 β and E_{budget}

(1) *Problem 1*

Interestingly, the objective in *Problem 1* is just the constraint in *Problem 2*; the objective in *Problem 2* is just the constraint in *Problem 1*. In the previous section 5.2.1, we have analyzed two objectives variances as C_c and C_m vary. In this section, we will discuss

1) the impact of β on energy objective in *Problem 1*;
2) the impact of E_{budget} on performance objective in *Problem 2*.

Figure 7 shows energy saving percentage under different β values. Four curves represent $\beta = 0$, $\beta = 5\%$, $\beta = 10\%$, $\beta = 15\%$, respectively. Obviously, as β increases, more energy saving can be obtained. We also notice that when $\beta = 0$, different properties for CPU-bound case and memory-bound case are showed: In CPU-bound case, energy saving can be achieved without performance loss while in memory-bound case, no energy saving can be achieved without performance loss. That can be explained by Figure 8. If we adjust CPU frequency through prolonging the time of T1 from Figure 8(a) to Figure 8(b), then the time of T2, T3 and T4 are all prolonged. So performance penalty cannot be avoided. Later energy-constrained parameter analyses also explain this from the other perspective.

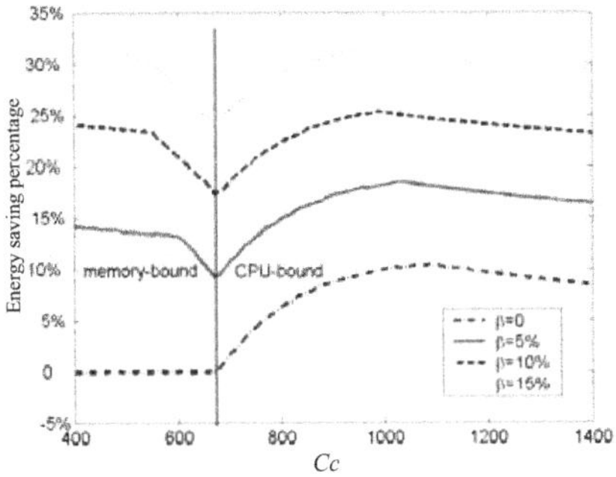

Fig. 7. Energy saving variance as β varies. here *Cm*=90.

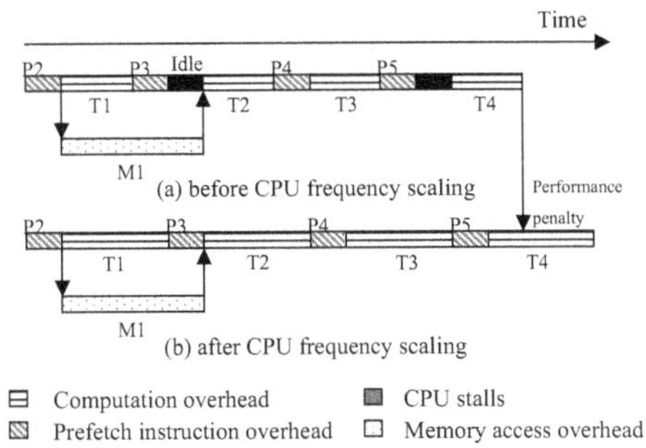

Fig. 8. No energy saving can be obtained without performance penalty in memory-bound case

(2) *Problem 2*

For *Problem 2*, we only consider scarce-energy settings, where $E_{budget} < E_{bound}$. To describe the degree of energy scarce, we define α as the ratio of energy budget to energy bound as follows.

$$E_{budget} = \alpha \cdot E_{bound}$$

As α increases, energy budget is more approach to energy bound and performance is more approach to the optimal value. All of these varying trends are shown in Figure 9(a) and Figure 10(a), where blue solid lines represent execution time (inverse proportion to performance) under different α values and black dot lines represent the optimal performance when energy bound is reached. Performance is approach to the optimal performance value as α increases.

For CPU-bound case as Figure 9(a) shows, when $\alpha = 91.1\%$, performance has reached the optimal value instead of $\alpha = 100\%$. In contrast, for memory-bound case shown in Figure 10(a), performance doesn't achieve the optimal level until $\alpha = 100\%$. This shows that in CPU-bound case, the optimal performance can be reached under less energy budget (less than energy bound). While in memory-bound case, the optimal performance must be reached with energy bound. This conclusion is consistent with the conclusion of *Problem 1*. That is, in CPU-bound case, energy saving can be obtained with no performance loss while in memory-bound case, no energy saving can be obtained with no performance loss.

To illustrate the optimal CPU frequency setting and memory frequency setting, we also show the optimal CPU and memory frequency under the same conditions in Figure 9(b)-(c) and Figure 10(b)-(c). In CPU-bound case (Figure 9(b)-(c)), CPU frequency keeps at 1GHz while memory frequency is climbing and it reaches the highest point until $\alpha = 100\%$. In terms of objective (9-1), the performance value in CPU-bound is determined by CPU frequency. Therefore, when CPU frequency reaches the highest value, performance reaches the optimal value. After that, memory frequency increase only consumes unnecessary energy. That is why the energy saving can be obtained with no performance loss for CPU-bound case.

In contrast, in memory-bound case, performance is determined by both CPU frequency and memory frequency in terms of objective (9-2). Only when both of them reach the highest values, the performance reaches the optimal. That explains why no energy saving can be obtained with no performance loss.

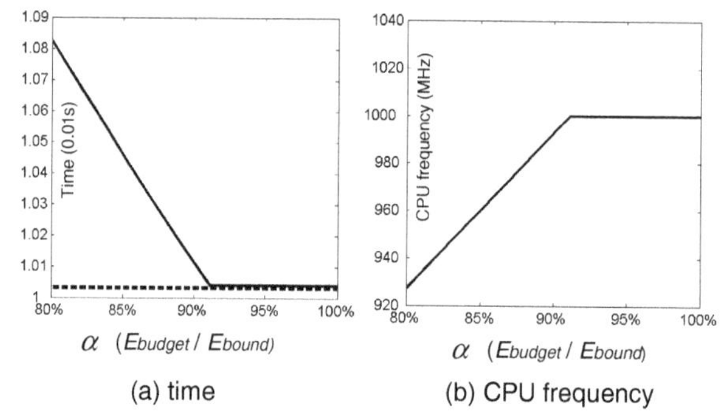

Fig. 9. The impact of *Ebudget* on the optimization results when CPU-bound case.*Cc*=1000, *Cm*=90

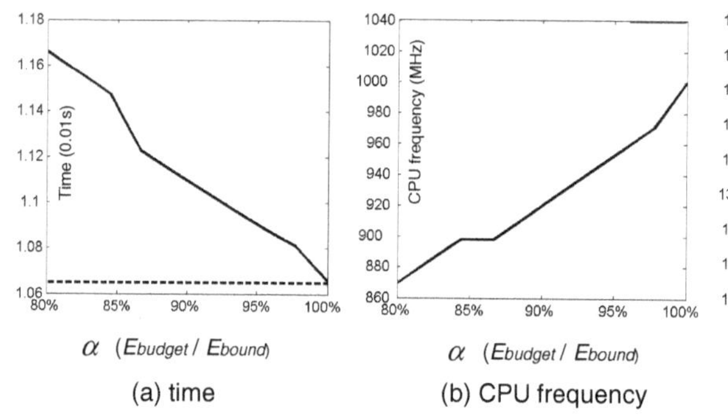

Fig. 10. The impact of E_{budget} on the optimization results when memory-bound case.*Cc*=1000, *Cm*=150

From the above analyses on β and E_{budget}, we can conclude that:

- For *Problem 1*, when CPU-bound case, energy saving can be obtained without performance loss while in memory-bound case, no energy saving can be achieved with no performance loss;
- For *Problem 2*, when CPU-bound case, the optimal performance can be reached under less energy budget (less than energy bound). While in memory-bound case, the optimal performance must be reached with energy bound.

3.3 Experimental Results

After the detailed parameter analyses, we choose a set of array-dominated applications to validate the effectiveness of our energy optimization approach. They include Matmult, Stencil, Syr2k, Adi, and 2D Jacobi. Matmult represents matrices product, Stencil is a stencil computing program for five dots, Syr2k is Rank-2K update computation program for solving zonal symmetry matrix from BLAS, Adi derives from the core base benchmark of Livermore, and 2D Jacobi performs a 2D Jacobi relaxation. These benchmarks description is given in Table 3.

Table 3. The description of benchmarks

Benchmarks	The number of Array	Size
Matmult	3	1024*1024
Stencil	2	1024*1024
Syr2k	3	1024*1024
Adi	6	1024*1024*3
2D Jacobi	2	1024*1024

3.3.1 Minimizing Energy Consumption

Energy saving for each benchmark under different β values is shown in Figure 11. The experimental results accurately reflect our analytical results. Adi and 2D Jacobi, which belong to CPU-bound cases, achieve 10.1% and 1.1% energy savings with no performance loss, respectively. Other benchmarks all belong to memory-bound cases and no energy saving can be achieved without performance loss. Table 4 shows the detailed data about CPU frequency, memory frequency and energy savings.

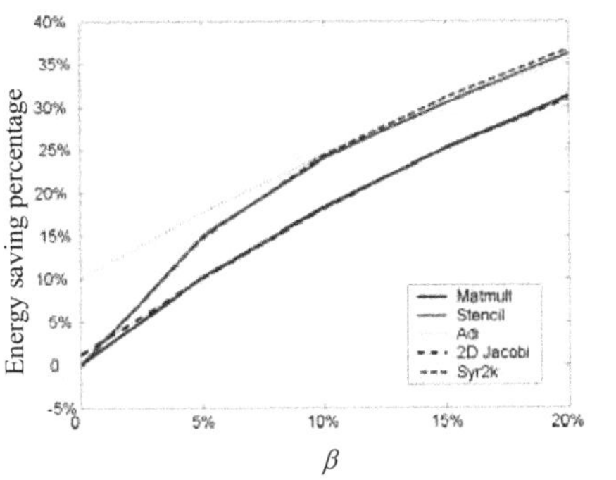

Fig. 11. Energy saving percentage for each benchmark

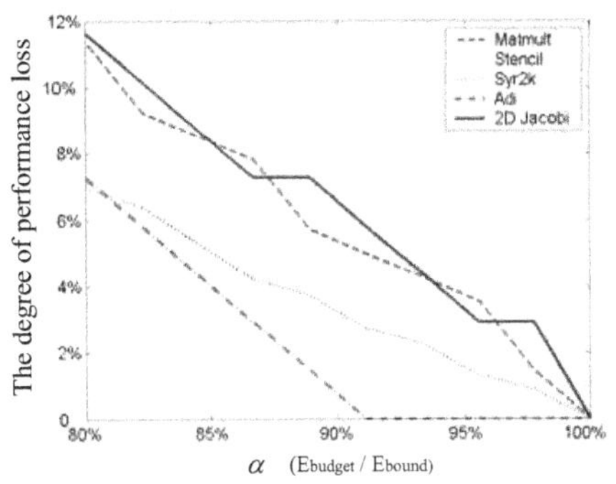

Fig. 12. The degree of performance loss for each benchmark

3.3.2 Energy-Constrained Optimization Problem

Assume execution time (inverse proportion to performance) under energy constraint is *Time* and execution time without energy constraint is *InitialTime*, the degree of performance loss can be calculated by formula (15).

$$Performance\ Loss\ (100\%) = \frac{\frac{1}{InitialTime} - \frac{1}{Time}}{\frac{1}{InitialTime}} \times 100\% \tag{15}$$

As α value varies, the performance loss for each benchmark is shown in Figure 12. Experimental results validate our analytical conclusions. Benchmark Adi reaches the optimal performance with 91.1% of energy bound. Table 5 gives the detailed experimental data for the optimal CPU and memory frequency settings.

Table 4. Optimal CPU and memory frequency settings and energy savings for each benchmark with variable β

Type	Benchmarks	β	CPU frequency (MHz)	Memory frequency (MHz)	Energy Savings
memory-bound case	Matmult	0	1000	133	0
		5%	940	129	10.17%
		10%	896	123	18.37%
		15%	860	117	25.16%
		20%	825	112	31.20%
	Stencil	0	1000	133	0
		5%	830	133	15.03%
		10%	709	133	24.02%
		15%	669	128	30.50%
		20%	649	122	36.15%
	Syr2k	0	1000	133	0
		5%	856	133	14.75%
		10%	747	133	24.40%
		15%	688	130	31.07%
		20%	656	125	36.67%
CPU-bound case	Adi	0	1000	83	10.11%
		5%	953	83	17.77%
		10%	910	83	24.45%
		15%	870	83	30.39%
		20%	834	83	35.51%
	2D Jacobi	0	1000	130	1.10%
		5%	953	124	10.14%
		10%	910	118	18.20%
		15%	870	113	25.17%
		20%	834	109	31.03%

Table 5. Optimal CPU and memory frequency settings and performance loss for each benchmark with variable α

Type	Benchmarks	α	CPU frequency (MHz)	Memory frequency (MHz)	Performance Loss
memory-bound case	Matmult	82.2%	898	122	9.3%
		86.7%	927	122	7.8%
		91.1%	942	127	5.0%
		95.6%	971	127	3.6%
		100%	1000	133	0
	Stencil	82.2%	782	133	6.3%
		86.7%	840	133	4.4%
		91.1%	898	133	2.7%
		95.6%	942	133	1.5%
		100%	1000	133	0
	Syr2k	82.2%	811	133	6.4%
		86.7%	869	133	4.2%
		91.1%	913	133	2.7%
		95.6%	956	133	1.3%
		100%	1000	133	0
CPU-bound case	Adi	82.2%	942	88.6	5.8%
		86.7%	971	88.6	2.9%
		91.1%	1000	88.6	0
		95.6%	1000	111	0
		100%	1000	133	0
	2D Jacobi	82.2%	898	122	10.2%
		86.7%	927	122	7.3%
		91.1%	942	127	5.8%
		95.6%	971	127	2.9%
		100%	1000	133	0

4 Conclusions and Future Works

Energy consumption is more and more important for battery-powered embedded systems due to the need for longer battery life and portability. Compiler-directed optimization techniques are more and more concerned. In our article, we combined two kinds of energy-aware prefetching optimization approaches: one is minimizing energy consumption within some performance loss; the other is energy-constrained optimization approach. We implement these two optimizations mainly through simultaneously adjusting CPU and memory frequencies. For CPU-bound case and memory-bound case, frequency scaling shows the different characteristics. We analyze the impact of several parameters on optimization results and draw some conclusions. Finally, a group of array-dominated applications are used to validate our analytical conclusions. In the future, we will consider more actual model, i.e. Considering N discrete voltage/frequency levels instead of continuous voltage/frequency scaling. Thus, more exact and actual model should be built.

References

1. Gang Qu. What is the Limit of Energy Saving by Dynamic Voltage Scaling? In the Proceedings of International Conference on Computer-Aided Design (ICCAD'01), Nov 4-8, 2001, San Jose, CA, USA. pp:560-563.
2. H. Saputra, M. Kandemir, N. Vijaykrishnan, M. J. Irwin, J. S. Hu, C-H. Hsu, U. Kremer. Energy-Conscious Compilation Based on Voltage Scaling. In LCTES'02-SCOPES'02, June 19-21, 2002, Berlin, Germany.
3. Fen Xie, Margaret Martonosi and Sharad Malik. Compile-Time Dynamic Voltage Scaling Settings: Opportunities and Limits. In the Proceedings of ACM SIGPLAN 2003 Conference on Programming Language Design and Implementation (PLDI'03), June 9-11, 2003, San Diego, California, USA.
4. Woo-Cheol Kwon and Taewhan Kim. Optimal Voltage Allocation Techniques for Dynamically Variable Voltage Processors. In the Proceedings of 2003 Design Automation Conference (DAC'03), June 2-6, 2003, Anaheim, California, USA.
5. Xiaobo Fan, Carla S. Ellis and Alvin R. Lebeck. The Synergy between Power-aware Memory Systems and Processor Voltage Scaling. In Proceedings of the Workshop on Power-Aware Computer Systems (PACS'03), Dec 2003.
6. Todd C. Mowry. Tolerating Latency Through Software-Controlled Data Prefetching. Ph.D. thesis, Stanford University, Computer System Laboratory, March 1994.
7. Shimin Chen, Phillip B. Gibbons and Todd C. Mowry. Improving Index Performance through Prefetching. In Proceedings of the 2001 SIGMOD International Conference on Management of Data. pp: 235-246.
8. Abdel-Hameed Badawy, Aneesh Aggarwal, Donald Yeung, and Chau-Wen Tseng. The Efficacy of Software Prefetching and Locality Optimizations on Future Memory Systems. Journal of Instruction-Level Parallelism. June 2004.
9. Ricardo Bianchini and Beng-Hong Lim. Evaluating the Performance of Multithreading and Prefetching in Multiprocessors. Journal of Parallel and Distributed Computing (JPDC), special issue on Multithreading for Multiprocessors, August 1996.
10. C. Hsu, U. Kremer, and M. Hsiao. Compiler-Directed Dynamic Voltage/Frequency Scheduling for Energy Reduction in Microprocessors. In International Symp. On Low Power Electronics and Design (ISLPED'01), pages 275-278, August 2001.
11. Chung-Hsing Hsu. Compiler-Directed Dynamic Voltage and Frequency Scaling for CPU Power and Energy Reduction. Ph. D. Dissertation. New Brunswick, New Jersey. October 2003.
12. J. Pouwelse, K. Langendoen, and H. Sips. Dynamic Voltage Scaling on a Low-Power Microprocessor. In the Seventh Annual International Conference on Mobile Computing and Networking 2001, pp: 251-259.
13. Crusoe Processor Model TM5700/TM5900 Data Book. http://www.transmeta.com/crusoe_docs/tm5900_databook_040204.pdf
14. D. Burger and T. M. Austin, "The SimpleScalar Tool Set, Version 2.0". CS TR 1342, University of Wisconsin-Madison, June 1997.
15. Juan Chen, Yong Dong, Hui-zhan Yi, Xue-jun Yang. Energy-Constrained Prefetching Optimization in Embedded Applications. To be appeared in the Proceedings of the 2005 IFIP International Conference on Embedded and Ubiquitous Computing (EUC '05). Nagasaki City, Japan, 6-9 December 2005.

A Dynamic Energy Conservation Scheme for Clusters in Computing Centers*

Wenguang Chen[1], Feiyun Jiang[1], Weimin Zheng[1], and Peinan Zhang[2]

[1] Dept. of Computer Science and Technology, Tsinghua University, Beijing, China
[2] Intel China Research Center, Beijing, China

Abstract. HPC clusters are widely used to execute parallel tasks. With the increasing number of nodes and frequency of processors, they consume huge amount of energy. The heat generated by clusters also imposes very heavy load for cooling infrastructures. The utilization of some clusters is not always high, indicating that there is a huge space to conserve energy consumption with more intelligent energy management scheme. Although there has been some energy conservation schemes proposed for web clusters, they are not applicable to HPC clusters. In this paper we propose a dynamic energy conservation scheme for HPC clusters. The scheme is to turn some cluster nodes on and off dynamically according to the current and historical workload. The goal is to reduce the energy consumption of clusters with minimal performance loss. We evaluate our scheme by simulation and show that it can effectively conserve energy consumption.

Keywords: Energy Conservation, Cluster, Parallel Computing.

1 Introduction

HPC clusters are widely used to execute parallel tasks. Energy consumption is becoming a key design issue for HPC clusters now. Because off-the-shelf hardware prices constantly decrease, clusters are more affordable to be purchased than before. However, the operational cost of clusters is even higher than before. The reasons are: (1)The energy consumed by clusters increases because of higher processor frequency and larger number of nodes.(2) The heat generated by clusters also increases greatly. For a cluster with medium to large number of nodes, it requires significant investment on equipments and energy consumption of cooling systems.

On the other hand, utilization of some HPC clusters is just 50% or even lower[1]. Although most modern processors and systems can be put into power saving mode by voltage-scaling techniques [5], idle nodes in HPC clusters still consume quite huge amount of energy. Chase et.al. found that conventional servers used at least 60% of their peak power in idle state[10], which indicates that more energy can be conserved by more intelligent power management scheme for HPC clusters.

* This project is partially supported by Intel Corp.

L.T. Yang et al. (Eds.): ICESS 2005, LNCS 3820, pp. 244–255, 2005.

Some energy conservation schemes have been proposed for web server clusters [10, 11, 12, 17]. Although web servers clusters and HPC clusters share the common term *cluster*, there are substantial difference between them regarding their workload. A job submitted to HPC clusters normally requires multiple processors and much more execution time. So the energy conservation scheme designed for web server clusters could not be applied to HPC clusters trivially.

In this paper we characterize workload logs of several HPC clusters. Then we propose a simple yet effective scheme to conserve energy consumption for HPC clusters. In our scheme, not all idle nodes are turned off immediately, some spare nodes are reserved for future tasks. When the workload becomes heavy, some nodes will be turned on in advance for future jobs. In this way, we can conserve energy consumption with minimal performance loss.

This paper is organized as follows. Section 2 describes related work. Section 3 shows the origin of the workloads used in this research, then characterizes the workload in various aspects. Different energy management schemes are presented in section 4. Section 5 describes the experimental results and Section 6 closes the paper with a summary.

2 Related Work

Power-efficient design are receiving increasing attention recently. The research work on this area can be characterized with three levels: chip level, single system level and multiple-system level.

Chip level power-efficient design[2, 3] is motivated by the requirement of providing long battery life time for portable electronic appliances. The design needs to explore tradeoff between power and conventional design constraints, i.e., performance and area.

Above the chip level, single-system level techniques such as dynamic power management(DPM)[4] and dynamic voltage scaling(DVS)[5] have been applied extensively with good results. In computer systems, DRAM is a big source to consume energy. So memory energy optimization has also been researched[6, 7]. In addition to the hardware only approach, some software/hardware integrated methods have also been proposed[7, 8, 9].

Some operating systems, such as Microsoft Windows 2000 and Microsoft Windows server 2003 could support the hibernate mode or sleep mode which uses very little power. However, these features are mainly designed for notebook and desktop computers, and could not be applied to either HPC clusters or web server clusters directly. In Microsoft's document on configuring server clusters, it is suggested that "Do not use APM/ACPI Power saving features"[18].

At the multiple-system level, there has been some research work on conserving energy consumption for server clusters, e.g., data center with many WWW servers. Node vary-on/vary-off(VOVO) scheme for web server clusters has been proposed in [10, 11]. In this scheme, CPU demand of servers is monitored. When it exceeds a certain threshold, e.g. 90%, more nodes will be turned on. When the CPU demand becomes lower than a certain threshold, some nodes should be turned off. Elnozahy et.al evaluates five policies for cluster-wide power management in server farms[12]. The policies employ various combinations of dynamic voltage scaling and node vary-on/vary-off(VOVO). The best results are obtained by using a coordinated voltage scaling policy in conjunction with VOVO. Rajamani et.al identified the key system and workload factors that impact power management policies for server clusters. They also proposed two improvement over the simple threshold policies: spare servers and history-based schemes. The spare servers scheme was used to deal with the observed spikes in workload[17].

Although the above power management schemes works well for server clusters, they are essentially variation of utilization threshold -based schemes and could not be used in HPC clusters trivially.

In HPC clusters, a single job is sufficient to push the CPU utilization to almost 100% in cluster nodes allocated to it. What's more, memory, I/O and network bandwidth in allocated cluster nodes are also used heavily with a single job only. Allocating multiple jobs to the same node would cause resource conflict and damage the performance seriously. Thus, it is a common practice that different jobs do not share cluster node in HPC clusters. So the CPU utilization threshold-based power management scheme could not be applied to HPC clusters trivially.

In this paper, we propose to use spare nodes to conserve energy consumption of HPC clusters. Although the idea of spare nodes has also been proposed by Rajamani et.al. [17] for server clusters, it was proposed as an improvement of threshold based schemes. While in this paper, we use the spare nodes scheme only in the context of HPC cluster. We propose an algorithm to determine the number of spare nodes dynamically and verify its effectiveness by simulating various HPC cluster workloads.

Choi et.al proposed an disk storage power management approach for the server systems which accesses remote active storage devices instead of turning on local storage devices[16]. It is another dimension of the problem and was orthogonal to ours.

3 Collecting Information

Since our key goal is to propose an energy conservation scheme for HPC clusters, we need information on the workload experienced by production systems. Unfortunately, there is no standard benchmarks for workload in HPC clusters. We got 3 workload logs from supercluster.org[1], which were generated by production cluster systems with the Maui scheduler[19]. In fact, there are totally 5 workloads there, but only 3 of them are downloadable. They are described in Table 1.

Table 1. Workload used in this research

Site/Machine Name	Procs	jobs	Period
CHPC/Icebox	266	20000	Mar. 2000-Mar 2001
OSC/Linux Cluster	178	80000	Jan. 2000-Nov. 2001
MHPCC/Tsunami	224	4100	Mar. 1998-Apr. 1998

There are many fields in the log files, such as *submission time, nodes requested, dispatch time, start time, completion time* and *wall clock limit* etc. In our research, we just take the following fields into account:

- Submission time $t_{submission}$: The time when job was submitted.
- Nodes of requested $p_{requested}$: The number of processors requested.
- Start time t_{start}: The time when job began execution.
- Completion time $t_{completion}$: The time when job completed execution.

These systems have different architectures. For example, the MHPCC/Tsunami is an IBM SP2 machine, which is indeed a clusters of SMPs, i.e., we can not turn-off one processor for this machine. The OSC/Linux Clusters is also a cluster with both quad-processor nodes and dual-processor nodes. In this paper, however, we will first assume that all nodes are just single processor nodes for simplicity, so each processor can be turned on or turned off independently. The effect of multi-processor nodes will be discussed later in this paper.

3.1 System Utilization

To identify the potential benefits of energy conservation on these workloads, we need to know the utilization of each system. Table 2 demonstrates the average number of active processors in each system, and calculates utilization accordingly.

In all systems, the system utilization is below 50%, which indicates that more than 50% processors are idle in average. It is obvious that if we can turn the inactive processors off, we will be able to save a lot of energy.

Table 2. Utilization of Our Reference Systems

Site/Machine Name	Average Number of Active Processors	Total Number of Processors	Utilization
CHPC/Icebox	102.9	266	38.7%
OSC/Linux Cluster	75.4	178	42.4%
MHPCC/Tsunami	67.9	224	21.5%

3.2 Distribution of Job Size

The job size is the number of processors requested by a job. Both Downey and Cirne have reported that the uniform-log distribution provides a good fit for the job size in supercomputer workload[13, 14]. This was the case for our reference workloads. Table 1 shows the cumulative distribution function of job size of our reference workloads. It should be noticed that the size of more than 90% jobs is less than 16. Comparing with around 200 processors in each system, most of jobs only have very small size.

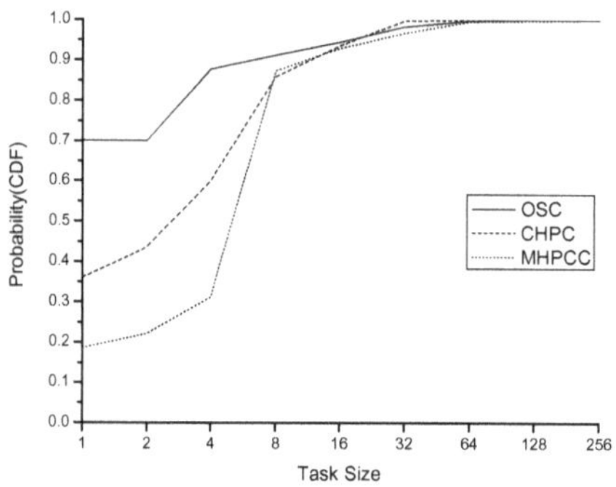

Fig. 1. Size of Jobs CDF

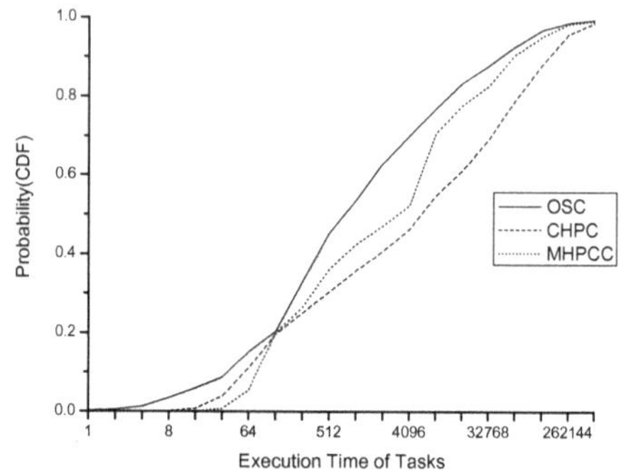

Fig. 2. Time of Jobs CDF

3.3 Distribution of Job Execution Time

As noticed by Downey[14], the uniform-log distribution provides a good fit for the job execution time in our 3 reference workloads. Figure 2 plots the observed job execution time. It should be noticed that for all of our 3 reference workloads, more than 30% of tasks are tasks whose execution time is less than 1024 seconds. For the OSC workload, the ratio is even higher than 50%. Because a normal system boot up time is about 200 seconds, which is comparable with the "short" tasks' time. The distribution of job execution time indicates that using naive energy management scheme,which would cost some time to bring idle systems up, will damage the the system performance considerably.

4 Schemes of Energy Management for Computing Clusters

In this section, we define some schemes of energy management for computing clusters. In order to describe them more clearly, we define some notations first.

- $n_{queue}(t)$: The number of nodes that required by tasks in queue at time t
- $n_{idle}(t)$: The number of idle nodes in cluster at time t
- $n_{act}(t)$: The number of active nodes in cluster at time t.
- $n_{off}(t)$: The number of nodes which is in the power-off state at time t in cluster
- $n_{turning\_off}(t)$: The number of nodes that are being turning off
- $n_{turning\_on}(t)$: The number of nodes that are being turning on
- $n_{arvl}(t_1, t_2)$: The number of nodes that are required by tasks which arrive between time t_1 and t_2
- $n_{cmpl}(t_1, t_2)$: The number of nodes that are required by tasks which complete between time t_1 and t_2
- t_{off} : Time required to turn off a node

- t_{on} : Time required to turn on a node
- n_{cluser} : The number of total nodes in the cluster.

It should be noted that at any given time t,

$$n_{cluster} = n_{act}(t) + n_{idle}(t) + n_{down}(t) + n_{turning\_off}(t) + n_{turning\_on}(t)$$

4.1 Always-On Scheme

This is the scheme used by current computing clusters. Nodes in cluster are not turned off and on in normal situations at all. They are always on, which could be described as

$n(t)_{off} = 0$ for any time t.

4.2 Naive Scheme

Under this scheme,

$n(t)_{idle} = 0$ for any time t.

In another word, the nodes in clusters are turned off as soon as they becomes idle if there is no task in queue. Similarly, a certain number of nodes will be turned on as soon as there is a coming request for the number of nodes.

4.3 Optimal Scheme

In this scheme, we assume a perfect knowledge of the arrival time of tasks, which enable us to avoid situations where tasks wait for required nodes to start up. In this scheme, the total completion time of all tasks is the same as the always-on scheme, i.e. a node is turned off only if it will not damage the system's performance.

Because there's no way for us to get the perfect knowledge of the arrival times of tasks in practical, the scheme shows the upper bound of amount of energy that can be conserved without damaging the performance of parallel clusters .

The scheme includes strategies for completion and arrival of tasks.

- On completion of tasks
  At time t, when a task which requires m nodes has just completed, let
  $t' = t + t_{off} + t_{on}$,
  then
  $n_{tbt\_off}(t) = m + n_{idle}(t) + n_{compl}(t, t') + n_{turning\_on}(t) - n_{queue}(t) - n_{arrl}(t, t')$
  if $n_{tbt\_off}(t) > 0$, it is the number of nodes to be turned off at time t. Otherwise, we do nothing at time t.
- On arrival of tasks
  If a task will arrive at time t which requires m nodes, let
  $t' = t - t_{off} - t_{on}$,
  then
  $n_{tbt\_on}(t') = m + n_{queue}(t') + n_{arrl}(t', t) - n_{idle}(t') - n_{compl}(t', t) - n_{turning\_on}(t')$
  if $n_{tbt\_on}(t') > 0$, it is the number of nodes to be turned on at time t'. Otherwise, we do nothing at time t'.

4.4 N-Redundant Scheme

Since no perfect knowledge of the arrival times of tasks are available in practice, we need to find a good approach to deal with the dynamic arrival of tasks. We proposed a simple yet effective scheme $n - redundant$.

The $n-redundant$ scheme is motivated by the analysis on job size distribution in section 4.2, which indicates that most jobs are with small sizes. So only a small number of redundant active nodes would meet the requirement of most jobs.

In general, we use $n(t)$ to denote the maximum number of idle nodes at time t.

The $n - redundant$ scheme is to hold at most $n(t)$ idle nodes whenever possible, i.e.

$n_{idle}(t) \leq n(t)$ for any time t.

In n-redundant schemes, the maximum number of idle nodes is $n(t)$, so the energy that may be consumed by other idle nodes are conserved. On the other hand, the performance of the system is not damaged greatly by latency introduced by power-on time, since the $n(t)$ idle nodes can be used immediately for arrival of tasks.

We still use the actions taken on completion and arrival of parallel tasks to describe the $n - redundant$ scheme.

- On completion of tasks

  At time t, when a task which requires m nodes has just completed, first recompute the value of $n(t)$(the algorithm to compute $n(t)$ will be discussed in the next section), then let

  $n_{tbt\_off}(t) = m + n_{idle}(t) + n_{turning_on} - n_{queue}(t) - n(t)$ where n(t) is the maximum number of

  if $n_{tbt\_off}(t) > 0$, it is the number of nodes to be turned off at time t. Otherwise, we do nothing at time t.
- On arrival of tasks

  If a task arrives at time t which requires m nodes, then

  $n_{tbt\_on}(t) = m + n_{queue}(t) + n - n_{idle}(t) - n_{turning_on}$

  if $n_{tbt\_on}(t) > 0$, it is the number of nodes to be turned on at time t. Otherwise, we do nothing at time t.

4.5 Determine the Value $n(t)$ for the N-Redundant Scheme

In the $n - redundant$ scheme, it is very important to determine the value of $n(t)$. Since the redundant nodes are used to obtain better performance for short tasks, we should use statistics of size of short tasks to determine it. We define the threshold ts, so that all tasks with execution time less than or equal to ts will be considered as short tasks, whose performance will be damaged significantly by the latency of system boot-up.

To calculate the $n(t)$, we maintain a task queue qq which contains the most recently quitted short tasks. The size of the queue is m, so at most recent m quitted tasks will be stored in qq. The $n(t)$ remains unchanged unless there is a quitted job. When a job quits at time t, we need to update the value of $n(t)$. We choose the number of redundant nodes n as the minimum integer such that $p\%$ or more short tasks in qq are of size less than or equal to n. The algorithm is trivial based on the above definition and omitted due to limited space. The value n is stored in a global variable. The complexity of the algorithm is $O(N)$, where N is the number of nodes in the HPC cluster.

Table 3 shows the typical value n for the 3 clusters according to the rule described above. It could be observed that the value is relatively small comparing with the number of nodes in clusters.

Table 3. Determine the number of redundant nodes for each workloads

Site/Machine Name	Number of Short tasks	n
CHPC/Icebox	7014	12
OSC/Linux Cluster	43235	16
MHPCC/Tsunami	1744	10

5 Experimental Results

5.1 Performance Metrics

In order to evaluate the system performance for different energy conservation schemes, we need to define a proper performance metric.

Feitelson et.al. have suggested the "bounded-slowdown" metric to avoid the extreme effects introduced by very short tasks[15]. For bounded-slowdown, a threshold value τ is used to filter the short tasks, its definition is

$bounded - slowdown = max\{\frac{t_c - t_s}{max\{t_c - t_r, \tau\}}, 1\}$

It is obvious that the behavior of this metric depends on the choice of τ. In this paper, we choose 20 seconds for it. The reason for this value is that we believe that it represents the typical time for a user to submit a very short job to parallel clusters and get the result. Users will not be very sensitive when the response time of the job is already less than 20 seconds, no matter how short the job is.

5.2 Experimental Results

We implemented a simulator to evaluate the performance of our proposed energy conservation scheme. The simulator uses the traces of maui scheduler as its input, which is described in Section 3. It implements the FCFS (First Come, First Serve) scheduler.

We simulated various energy conservation schemes for the 3 selected workloads by comparing their average bounded-slowdown and consumed energy.

Fig 3 shows the bounded-slowdown of different schemes on systems with different boot time. We simulated boot time from 25 seconds to 250 seconds. The typical boot time is around 150s for current Linux servers, yet 250s boot time is also observed on some servers. The simulation result shows that the $always - on$ and opt schemes almost always get the same bounded-slowdown for all the three workloads and they almost remain constant when the boot time changes. The $naive$ scheme changes with the boot time sharply and obtains much worse bounded-slowdown performance than $always - on/opt$ schemes when the boot time is 150 seconds or larger. Even when the boot time is only 50s, there is still considerable performance difference between the $naive$ scheme and the $always - on/opt$ scheme. The $n - redundant$ scheme, however, changes with the boot time much more mildly, it's performance is only slightly (5%) worse than $always - on/opt$ scheme's when the boot time is less than 150s. The simulation result encourages the server/OS manufacturers to provide servers/OS with fast boot time, which could be used by both the $n-redundant$ scheme and the $naive$ scheme to reduce the performance lost. When the boot time could be reduced to less than 25 seconds, $naive$ scheme becomes more favorable.

Figure 4 shows the experimental results on energy consumption of different schemes. Because the energy consumption of different schemes change only slightly with the boot time, we just show the data when the boot time is set to 150 seconds. Since we don't really experiment on real systems, we use the aggregate active $processor * hour$ of a cluster as the metric for energy conservation. It could be illustrated that the $always - on$ scheme consumes the most energy. The $naive$ scheme and the opt scheme performs the best in this metric because they almost don't waste any energy. The $n - redundant$ conserves more than 40% energy than the $always - on$ scheme. The figure also indicates that the $n - redundant$ scheme can conserve more than 80% of *conservable* energy consumption by comparing the $n - redundant$ scheme to the opt scheme.

6 Conclusion and Future Work

In this paper, we proposed an energy conservation scheme $n - redundant$ for clusters in computing centers which execute parallel tasks. It is compared with $naive$ schemes and *optimal* schemes. Experimental results demonstrated that the $n - redundant$ scheme is efficient in energy conservation while maintain the performance well: it can reserve 40% energy consumption of with performance loss around 5%.

The simulation results also shows that if servers could support fast boot time, the energy conservation scheme could be more efficient. We are investigating the situations when server supports several level of low power states with different power consumption and enter/exit time.

We are integrating the $n - redundant$ scheme with the OpenPBS cluster scheduler now. Then it will be installed in several production clusters to test the performance of the scheme in real workloads.

Other future work includes: In addition to calculate the number of idle nodes, we could go one step further to determine which nodes should be turned on and off wisely by considering the topology of the cluster. This would get two more potential benefits: 1) By allocating neighbor nodes in clusters to parallel tasks,

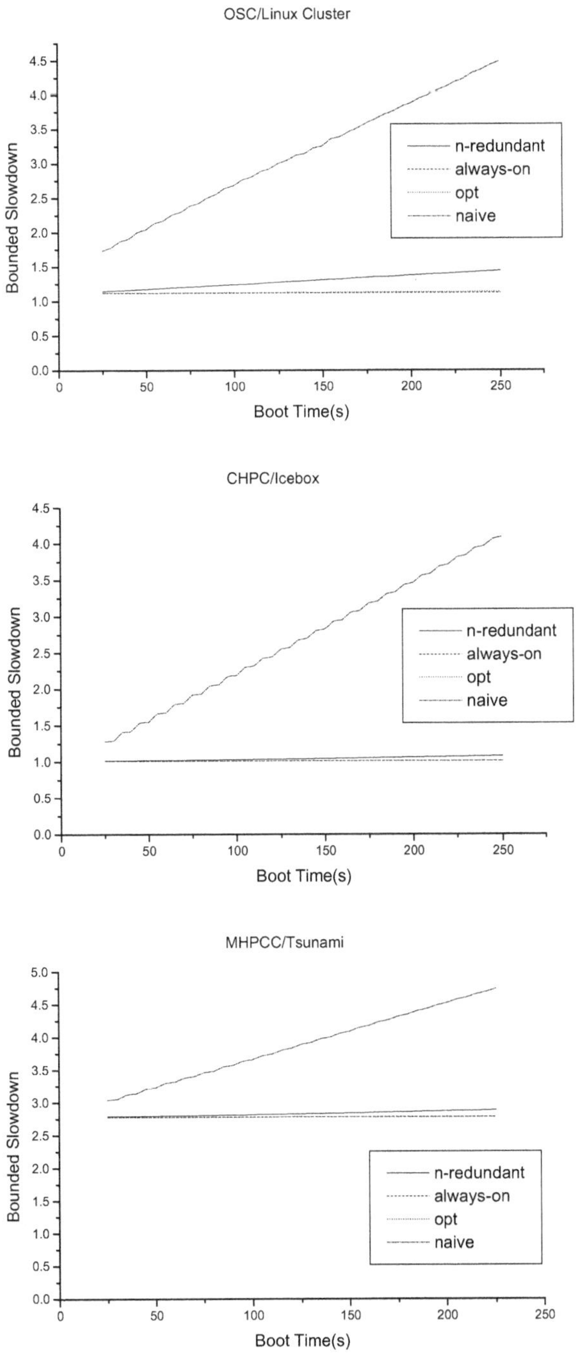

Fig. 3. Bounded-slowdown with different strategies

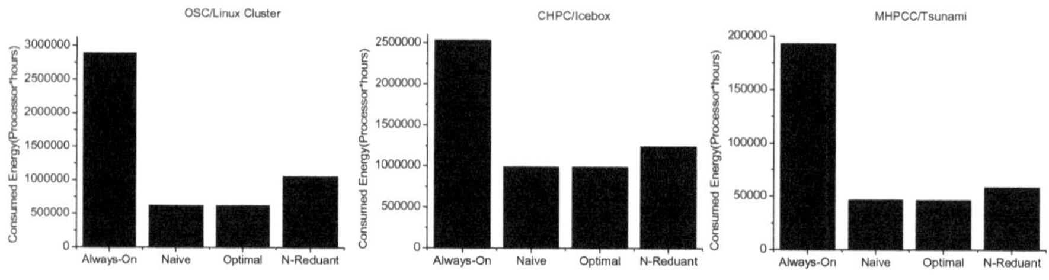

Fig. 4. Energy Consumed with different strategies

communication overhead of the parallel tasks could be reduced. 2) When the nodes connected by a switch are all in power-off state, the switch itself can also be turned-off and more energy could be conserved.

References

1. Supercluster.org: http://www.supercluster.org/research/traces/
2. Chandrakasan A. and Brodersen R.: Low-Power Digital CMOS Design. Klumer, 1995
3. Nebel W. and Mermet J., eds.: Low-Power Design in Deep Submicron Electronics, Kluwer, 1997
4. Eui-Young, C., Luca, B., Alessandro, B., Yung-Hsiang, L. and Giovanni D.M.: Dynamic Power Management for Nonstationary Service Requests, IEEE Transaction on Computers, **51**(11),(2002),1345-1361
5. Pering, T., Burd, T., and Brodersen, R.: The simulation and evaluation of Dynamic Voltage Scaling Algorithms. Proc. Int'l Symp. Low Power Electronics and Design, pp. 76-81, Aug. 1998
6. Kirubanandan, N., Sivasubramaniam, A., Vijaykrishnan, N., Kandemir, M. and Irwin M. J.:Memory Energy Characterization and Optimization for SPEC2000 Benchmarks, Proc. IEEE 4th Annual Workshop on Workload Characterization, pp. 193-201, 2001
7. Delaluz, V.,Kandemir, M.,Vijaykrishnan, N., Sivasubramaniam, A. Irwin, M.J.: DRAM Energy Management Using Software and Hardware Directed Power Mode Control, Proc. 7th Int'l Symp. on High Performance Computer Architecture, pp. 159-170, 2001
8. Pouwelse, J., Langendoen, K. and Sips, H.: Application-Directed Voltage Scaling, IEEE Transactions on Very Large Scale Integration Systems,**11**(5),(2003),812-826
9. Vijaykrshnam, N.,Kandemir, M., Irwin, M.J., Kim, H.S. and Ye, W. :Energy-driven Integrated Hardware-Software Optimizations using SimplePower, Proc. 27th Annual Int'l Symp. on Computer Architecture, pp 95-106, 2000
10. Chase, J.S., Anderson D.C., Thakar, P.N., Vahdat A.M. and Doyle R.P.:Managing Energy and Server Resources in Hosting Centers,Proc, Eighteenth ACM Symp. on Operating systems principles, pp 103-116, 2001
11. Pinheiro, E., Bianchini, R., Carrera, E.V. and Heath T.: Load Balancing and Unbalancing for Power and Performance in Cluster-Based Systems. Technical Report DCS-TR-440, Department of Computer Science, Rutgers University, May 2001

12. Elnozahy, E.N., Kistler, M. and Rajamony R.: Energy-Efficient Server Clusters, Proc. Second Workshop on Power Aware Computing Systems, 2002
13. Walfredo, C. and Francine B.: A Comprehensive Model of the Supercomputer Workload, Proc. IEEE 4th Workshop on Workload Characterization, pp 140-148, 2001
14. Downey, A.: Using Queue Time Predictions for Processors Allocation. Proc. Job Scheduling Strateies for Parallel Processing 1997 , LNCS **1291**, Springer-Verlag, 1997
15. Feitelson D. G., Rudolph L., Schwiegelshohn U., Sevcik K.C. and Wong P.: Theory and practice in parallel job scheduling. Proc. Job Scheduling Strateies for Parallel Processing 1997 , LNCS **1291**, Springer-Verlag, 1997
16. Choi J. H. and Franke H.: Storage Power Management for Cluster Servers Using Remote Disk Access. Proc. Euro-Par 2004, LNCS **3149**, pp. 460-467, Springer-Verlag, 2004
17. Rajamani K. and Lefurgy C.:On Evaluating Request-Distribution Schemes for Saving Energy in Server Clusters, Proc. IEEE International Symposium on Performance Analysis of Systems and Software (ISPASS'03), pp111-122,March 2003.
18. Microsoft Company, Inc, Best practices for configuring and operating server clusters, http://www.microsoft.com/technet/prodtechnol/windowsserver2003/library/ServerHelp/2798643f-427a-4d26-b510-d7a4a4d3a95c.mspx, Jan 2005
19. Bode B., Halstead D. M., Kendall R. and Lei Z. The Portable Batch Scheduler and the Maui Scheduler on Linux Clusteres, Proceedings of the 4th Annual Linux Showcase and Conference, Atlanta, October 10-14, 2000, Atlanta, Georgia, USA

Realization of Video Object Plane Decoder on On-Chip Network Architecture

Huy-Nam Nguyen, Vu-Duc Ngo, and Hae-Wook Choi

System VLSI Lab Laboratory, SITI Research Center, School of Engineering,
Information and Communications University (ICU),
Yusong P.O. Box 77, Taejon 305-714, Korea
{huynam, duc75, hwchoi}@icu.ac.kr

Abstract. System-on-chip (SoC) designs provide integrated solutions to challenging design problems in the telecommunications, multimedia, and so on. Present and future SoC are designed using pre-existing components which we call cores. Communication between the cores will become a major bottleneck for system performance as standard hardwired bus-based communication architectures will be inefficient in terms of throughput, latency and power consumption. To solve this problem, a packet switched platform that considers the delay and reliability issues of wires so called Network-on-Chip (NoC) has been proposed. In this paper, we present interconnected network topologies and analyze their performances with a particular application under bandwidth constrains. Then we compare the performances among different ways of mapping the cores onto a Mesh NoC architecture. The comparison between Mesh and Fat-Tree topology is also presented. These evaluations are done by utilizing NS-2, a tool that has been widely used in the computer network design.

1 Introduction

Traditionally, on-chip global communication has been addressed by shared-bus structures and ad-hoc direct interconnection. These architectures are not scalable on large SoC de-signs [1]. Future SoC will contain a multitude of different intellectual property (IP) blocks. Though sub-micron technology creates good chances to reduce the gate delays, the global wire delays significantly increase due to interconnect width and thickness or remain constant by including repeaters [2]. This matter leads to high power consumption. In order to support the communication between these blocks in a structured way, a scalable communication architecture that supports the trend of SoC integration consists of an on-chip packet switched network, generally known as Network-on-Chip (NoC) [3]. By using this design approach, the need of global wire can be omitted. The wires are now used only as the connections between switches. Also, we do not any longer worry about global synchronization due to decoupling of the processing nodes. Hence, Network-on-Chip designs have addressed the distinctive challenges of providing an efficient, reliable interaction among System-on-chip components.

L.T. Yang et al. (Eds.): ICESS 2005, LNCS 3820, pp. 256–264, 2005.

The two promising Network-on-Chip topologies are Mesh and Fat-Tree [6], [7]. Their performance evaluation with respect to physical constrains was introduced by Petrini et al. [4]. The comparison showed clearly that the Fat-Tree topology [5] has superior performance to that of Mesh topology.

In several application domains, such as multimedia processing, the bandwidth requirement between the cores in SoCs is increasing. As an example of such a media processing application, the block diagram of Video Object Plane Decoder [8] is introduced in Fig. 1. In order to implement this VOP decoder and verify all above mentions in terms of NoC architecture, we need to carry out the high level NoC topology in the scenario of on chip network implementation. Choosing simulation tool and defining the physical constraints for it are now at the beginning stage. Among network simulation tools, NS-2 [9], with its capabilities of describing network topologies, network protocol, packet scheduling schemes, routing algorithm, and also traffic generation methods, emerges to be the suitable solution.

In [6] and [7], the author proposed the Mesh and Fat-Tree architectures for NoC design. However, the performances of these architectures are not yet mentioned in terms of high level of topology evaluation. The mapping of cores onto NoC architecture presents new challenges when compared to the mapping in parallel processing because of the traffic requirements on the links of a NoC are known for a particular application, thus the bandwidth constrains in the NoC architecture need to be satisfied by the mapping [10]. The cores onto NoC architectures mapping problem is addressed in [10], [11]. In [11], a branch-and-bound algorithm is used to map cores onto a mesh-based architecture satisfying the bandwidth constraints and minimizing the total energy consumption.

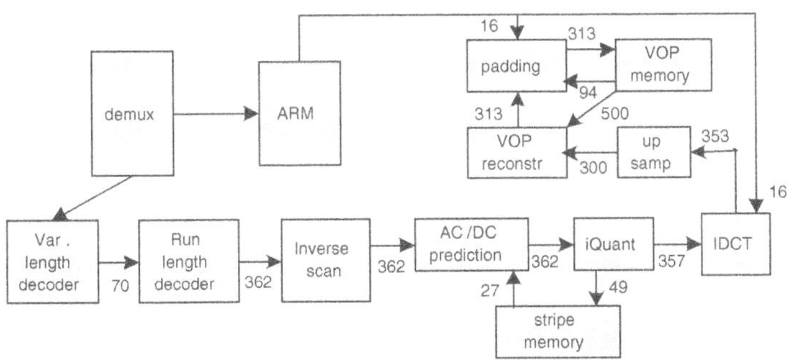

Fig. 1. Block Diagram of Video Object Plane Decoder (VOPD)

In this paper, we take the advantage of NS-2 to simulate and verify the performance of our proposed interconnection architecture for a particular NoC's application. Because of particular application, VOPD with the communication bandwidth in Fig. 1, we can manually choose the mapping modes and compare the performances among these architectures and these mapping modes as well with the relevant bandwidth between cores.

2 Interconnection Architectures for Realizing VOPD

2.1 Mesh Architecture

The $k - ary\ d - dimensional$ Mesh architecture is built by its dimension d and radix k. The total number of switches is k^d. The k^d switches are organized in an $d{-}dimensional$ grid such that there are k switches located in each dimension and wrap-around connections. Since the number of cores (IPs)that can be connected to one switch is $d{-}1$ so the total number of mounted cores is clearly calculated by

$$N_{Mesh} = k^d(d-1). \tag{1}$$

Denote b as the unidirectional bandwidth, the total bandwidth of the network can be obtained by

$$B_{Mesh} = 2k^d b. \tag{2}$$

Mesh architecture offers a simple connection scheme and the number of the mounted IPs is relatively high compared to the total bandwidth. Therefore the Shortest Path routing is mostly applied on Mesh but the performance of Mesh architecture is not high. Fig. 2 shows the example of 4-ary 2-dimensional Mesh architecture.

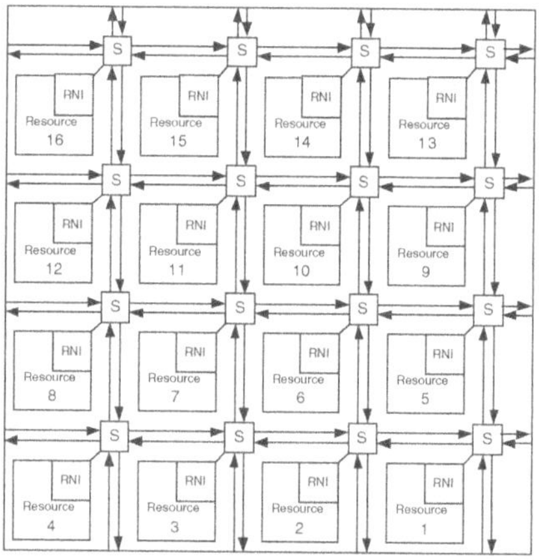

Fig. 2. 4-ary 2-dimensional Mesh topology

2.2 Fat-Tree Architecture

Fat-Tree is an indirect interconnection network based on a complete binary tree that gets as thicker as it approaches the root. So The bandwidth of the Fat-Tree increases as it goes closer to the root. A set of processors are located at the leaves of the Fat-Tree and each edge of the tree corresponds to a bi-directional channel between parent and child. These above feature make Fat-Tree sufficiently applicable with advanced routing algorithm as Distance Vector

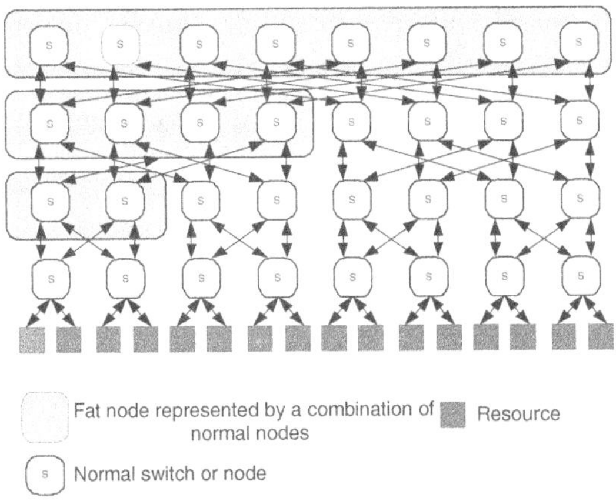

Fig. 3. 4-ary 2-dimensional Fat-Tree topology

instead of Shortest Path routing. The number of cores that can be mounted on one certain Fat-Tree depends on the depth of the tree. As this depth increases, the number of mounted cores and therefore the total capacity of the network raise. This leads Fat-Tree architecture have better performance compared with Mesh architecture. With $k - ary\ d - dimensional$ Fat-Tree architecture, which is shown in Fig.3 (case of $k = 4$, $d = 2$), the number of mounted IPs and the number of switches are respectively calculated as follow

$$N_{Fat-Tree} = k^d, \tag{3}$$

$$S_{Fat-Tree} = k^{d-1}d, \tag{4}$$

Therefore the total bandwidth is presented by

$$B_{Fat-Tree} = 2k^d db. \tag{5}$$

3 VOPD Implementation Based on NS-2

The network simulator, NS2, with its capabilities of describing network topologies, network protocols, routing algorithms, packet scheduling schemes, as well as traffic generation methods, has been broadly using in the field of computer network design and simulation. Moreover, NS2 provides also the routing strategies and the basic network transmission protocols, such as UDP and TCP. By using the built-in NS-2, we can work out above mentioned obstacles.

With increased processing speed of cores and the integration of many applications onto a single device, the bandwidth demands will scale up to much larger values. In Video Object Plane decoder shown in Fig. 1, each block corresponds to a core and the edges connecting the cores are labelled with bandwidth demands of the communication between them. The bandwidth demands are hundreds of

Table 1. Application of On chip network constraints to NS2

On chip network model	Applied NS2 constraints
Connections	Rs2Rt and Rt2Rs
Transmission protocols	UDP
Packet size	8 bytes
Buffer size	8, 16, 32 (packets)
Queuing schemes	FQ or SFQ
Routing strategy	Static
Routing schemes	Shortest Path
Traffic generator	Exponential

Mbytes/s. There are 12 blocks (or 12 cores) need to be considered. Hence, to implement this decoder, the 16 switches NoC architecture is needed. It is 4x4 Mesh architecture or 4 - ary 2 - dimensional Fat-Tree. In this context, we carry out the simulation for a random mapping as well as the suboptimal mapping of the IPs onto the NoC architectures in the sense of data rate constraint. The communication protocol used by NS-2 is defined in Table 1.

In particular, the VOPD must be implemented as the heterogeneous NoC architecture. Therefore, the demands of communication bandwidth originated from each core are different. This leads us to use fair queuing schemes such as Fair Queuing (FQ) or Stochastic Fair Queuing (SFQ) instead of Drop Tail queuing despite of their overhead in terms of complexity. This complexity can be compensated by using UDP protocol and static routing strategy.

4 Simulation Results and Discussion

In this paper, we simulate to compare the performances offer by the two architectures, Mesh and Fat-Tree, using the similar options of routing, queuing as

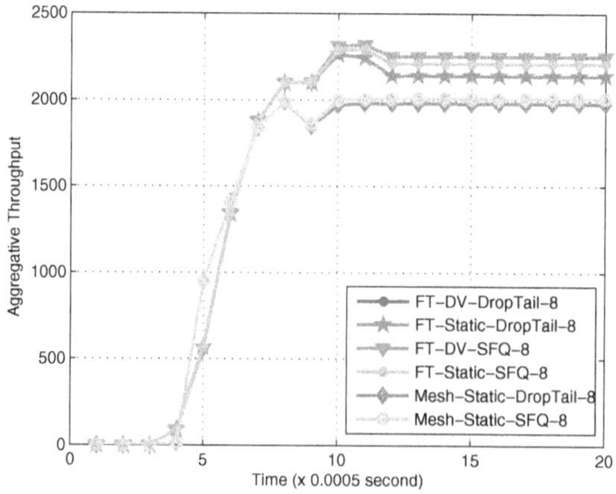

Fig. 4. Throughput Comparison of Fat-Tree (FT) and Mesh topologies

well as buffer sizes to verify the better architecture which is Fat-Tree. With 4x4 Mesh and 4 - ary 2 - dimensional Fat-Tree, data rate of each resource up to 200Mbps, the simulation result is shown in Fig. 4. As we can see, the Fat-Tree topology with the embedded routing algorithm of Distance Vector and SFQ queuing algorithm gains highest throughput. In the stable period, this design achieves approximately 250Mbps higher than that of Mesh architecture using Shortest Path routing and DropTail queuing schemes [12].

With certain application that is VOPD as mentioned, we use NS-2 with the communication protocols described in Table. 1 to simulate 12-block VOPD for the 4x4 Mesh architecture. We compare the performances between random mapping and suboptimal mapping with different bisection bandwidths. At first, we just simply map the 12 VOPD blocks randomly onto 4x4 Mesh architecture (Fig. 5). The AC/DC prediction block is mapped onto switch 0, ARM block is mapped onto switch 1, IDCT block is mapped onto switch 2, and so on. The corresponding data rates (in Mbps)of the connections between each two relative

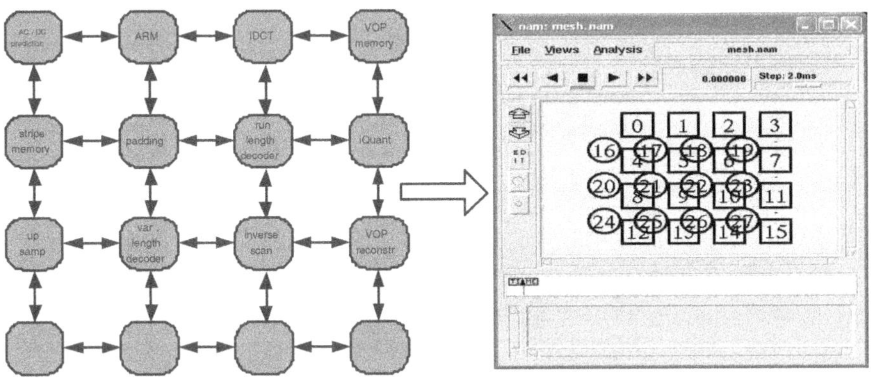

Fig. 5. Random Mapping of VOPD blocks onto Mesh Architecture

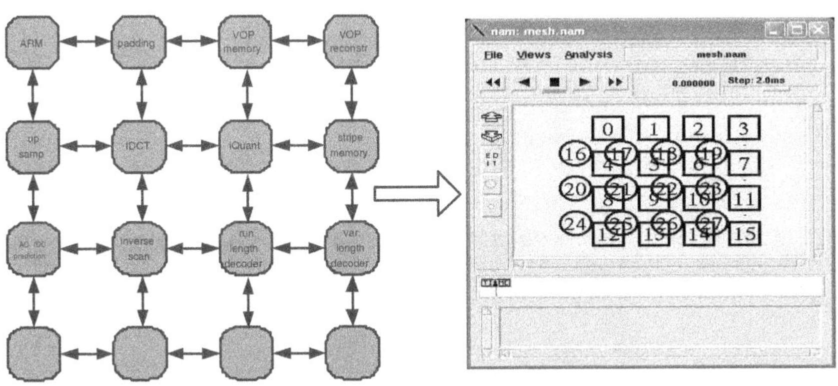

Fig. 6. Suboptimal Mapping of VOPD blocks onto Mesh Architecture

blocks were presented in Fig. 1. The simulations are done with different values of the defined bisection bandwidth and the results indicate that with higher bisectional bandwidth, the number of drop packets is smaller. This means that aggregated throughput of each IP (block) increase. Particularly, when the 1000 Mbps bisectional bandwidth is applied to the connections between every two adjacent switches, the throughput of each IP is saturated and is satisfy the bandwidth requirement.

However, the saturated bisectional bandwidth above is high due to non-optimal mapping of the IPs onto NoC architecture. This random (or non-optimal) mapping not only results in high complexity and used area but also increases the unnecessary usage of switches' power. Therefore, due to the high requirement of data transaction, the two IPs which transfer large amount of data to each others should be allocated next to each others as shown in Fig. 6. This so called subop-

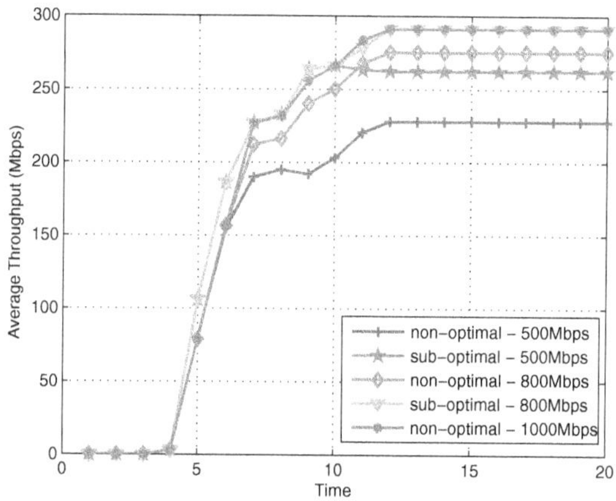

Fig. 7. Throughput comparison of Mapping Modes with different Bisection Bandwidth

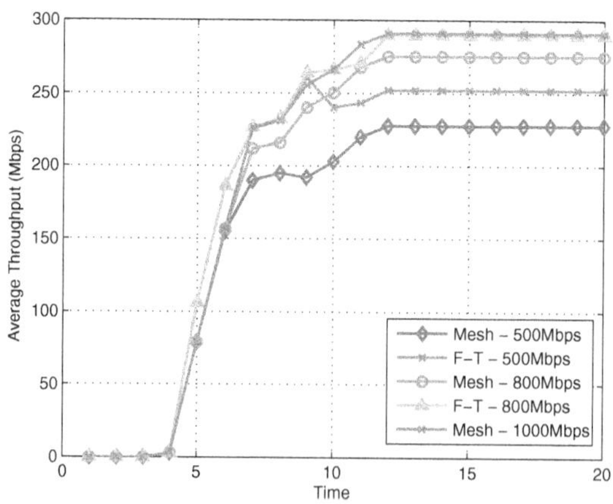

Fig. 8. Throughput Comparison between Fat-Tree (F-T) and Mesh Architecture with Different Bisection Bandwidth

timal mapping will decrease the load in links between switches so it will decrease the data conflict as well as packet drop. Fig. 7 shows that with the bisectional bandwidth of 800 Mbps we can obtain the saturated throughputs. It is significantly better than previous non-optimal mapping with saturated bandwidth of nearly 1 Gbps.

The last experiment is carried out to show the superior performance of Fat-Tree architecture compare to Mesh architecture when applying them to VOPD application. Fig. 8 depicts the throughput of the two architectures with bisectional bandwidth of 500 Mbps, 800 Mbps and 1000 Mbps. It is shown that that the Fat-Tree provides better performance in term of throughput. When the 800 Mbps bisectional bandwidth is applied to connections between every two adjacent switches in Fat-Tree case, the throughput of each IP also reach the saturated point. It is the same as the case of suboptimal Mesh.

5 Conclusion

In this paper, we use NS-2 tool to simulate and carry out the high level simulation of NoC based on Mesh and Fat-Tree topologies and achieve the best combination for our design is Fat-Tree topology with the embedded routing algorithm of Distance Vector and SFQ queuing algorithm. By allocating the Video Object Plane Decoder's blocks onto the Mesh NoC architecture and comparing the performance of the non-optimal mapping and sub-optimal mapping we obtain a fast mapping mode satisfying the bandwidth constraints of a Mesh NoC. With the same mapping and the same condition, we reaffirm the superior of Fat-tree architecture to Mesh architecture. For the time being, we just mention the performance in term of throughput. Other parameters such as latency or area are beyond of this paper. We will analyze them in the other works.

References

1. P. Guerrier, A. Grenier,"A generic architecture for on-chip packet-switched interconnection ", Design automation and test in Europe conference, pp. 250-256, Aug. 2000.
2. M. A. Horowitz et al.,"The future of wires," Proceeding of IEEE, Vol. 89, Issue. 4 , pp. 490-504, Apr 2001
3. L. Benini and G. De Micheli,"Networks On Chips: A new SoC paradigm," IEEE computer, Jan. 2002.
4. F. Petrini and M. Vanneschi, "Network performance under Physical Constrain," Proceedings of International Conference on Parallel Processing, pp.34 - 43, Aug 1997.
5. C. E. Leiserson,"Fat Trees: Universal networks for hardware efficient supercomputing," IEEE Transactions on Computer, C-34, pp. 892-90,1 Oct 1985.
6. H. Kariniemi, J. Nurmi, "New adaptive routing algorithm for extended generalized fat trees on-chip," Proceedings of International Symposium on System-on-Chip, pp. 113 - 118, Nov 2003.

7. P. P. Pande, C. Grecu, A. Ivanov, R. Saleh, "Design of a switch for network on chip applications," Proceedings of the 2003 International Symposium on Circuits and Systems, pp. V-217 - V-220 vol. 5, May 2003.
8. E. B. Van der Tol, E. G. T. Jaspers, "Mapping of MPEG-4 Decoding on a Flexible Architecture Platform", SPIE 2002, pp. 1-13, Jan, 2002.
9. Ns2: www.isi.edu/nsnam/ns/.
10. S. Murali and G. De Micheli, "Bandwidth Constrained Mapping of Cores onto NoC Architectures," Proc. Conf. DATE 2004.
11. J. Hu and R. Marculescu, "Energy-Aware Mapping for Tile-Based NoC Architecture under Performance Constraints," Proc. Asia and South Pacific Design Automation Conf. 2003, pp. 233-239, Jan. 2003.
12. Yi-Ran Sun, S. Kumar, A. Jantsch, "Simulation and Evaluation for a Network on Chip Architecture Using NS-2," Proceeding of 20th IEEE Norchip Conference, Nov 2002.

Network on Chip for Parallel DSP Architectures

Yuanli Jing, Xiaoya Fan, Deyuan Gao, and Jian Hu

Aviation Microelectronic Center, Northwestern Polytechnical University,
710072, Xi'an, China
jingyl2002@yahoo.com.cn

Abstract. Network-on-Chip is a new methodology of System-on-Chip design. It can be used to improve communication performance among many computing nodes of parallel DSP architectures. Simulations based on the 16-node 2D-mesh DragonFly DSP architecture show that the routing distance of 72.9% inter-node communication is 1. A fast local router is proposed to improve the performance of this communication. Experiments on our simulator show that overall inter-node communication delay is decreased by 59.4%.

1 Introduction

High-end and Large-scale DSP applications need more computing nodes to be integrated into a chip. Advances in semiconductor technology make this trend possible. By the end of the decade, SoCs, using 50-nm transistors operating below one volt, will grow to 4 billion transistors running at 10 GHz, according to the International Technology Roadmap for Semiconductors. The major challenge designers of these systems must overcome will be to provide for functionally correct, reliable operation of the interacting components. On-chip physical interconnections will present a limiting factor for performance and, possibly, energy consumption [1].

As the feature size of process technology continues to shrink, the performance of interconnect has not scaled as rapidly as the transistor switching speeds. Critical paths are becoming dominated by interconnection delays, especially when the logic is spread across the chip.

A scalable communication architecture that supports the trend of SoC integration consists of an on-chip packet-switched micro-network of interconnects, generally known as Network-on-Chip (NoC) [1][2][3]. The scalable and modular nature of NoCs and their support for efficient on-chip communication potentially leads to NoC-based multiprocessor systems characterized by high structural complexity and functional diversity [4].

The DragonFly is a multiprocessor system for DSP applications, based on Network-on-Chip methodology. Its network is delicately designed to achieve low delay with high channel utilization.

2 DragonFly DSP Architecture

The DragonFly DSP architecture integrates 16 DSP nodes, 8 I/O processing units (IOP) and 8 DRAMs (Fig.1.a). These DSP nodes, IOPs and DRAMs are interconnected by two-dimension mesh.

L.T. Yang et al. (Eds.): ICESS 2005, LNCS 3820, pp. 265–274, 2005.

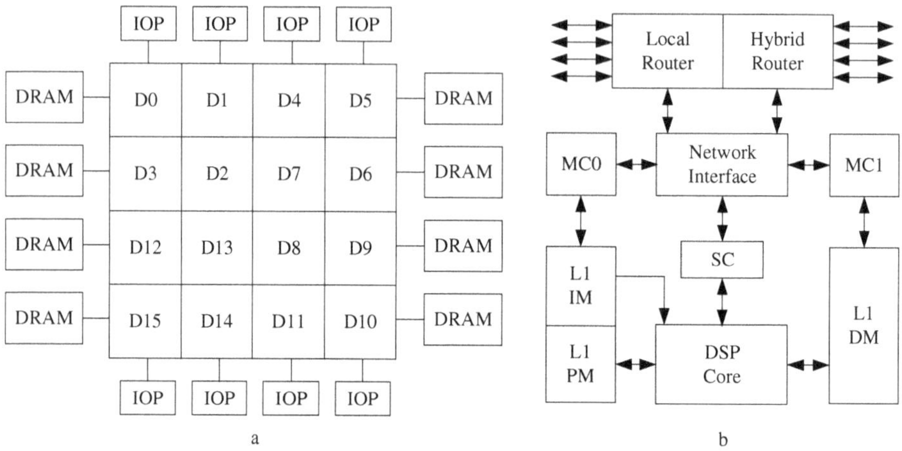

Fig. 1. DragonFly DSP architecture (a) and DragonFly DSP node (b)

Each DSP node contains (Fig. 1b):

(1) A four-stage, in-order, single-issue, pipelined DSP core with three computing units: ALU, MAC, shifter [5].
(2) One level-1 instruction memory (L1 IM); Two independent level-1 data memory blocks (L1 DM, L1 PM) to support double data accesses simultaneously [5].
(3) Two memory controllers (MC) for remote memory access: MC0 for IM and PM, MC1 for DM; One system controller (SC) for passing system control messages, such as synchronization and system interrupt.
(4) Network interface for packet buffering and translation between packet and original message to or from MC and SC.
(5) One fast local router for only inter-neighbor routing and one slow hybrid router for both local and remote routing.

3 Network-on-Chip Subsystem

The original DragonFly DSP node contains only a hybrid router for packet routing. Statistical results of the simulation that statically maps 6 benchmarks to 16-node 2D-mesh DragonFly show that average 72.9% inter-node communication is between neighbors, that is to say, its routing distance is 1 (Table 1).

Table 1. Routing distance (h) distribution for benchmarks

	FIR	FFT	MM	CONV	ADPCM	SSA
h=1	56.8%	80%	57%	65.7%	93%	85%
h>1	43.2%	20%	43%	34.3%	7%	15%

Based on this communication locality, a double-router network is proposed to improve performance of inter-neighbor routing by a fast local router and the original hybrid router is used for both local and remote routing. Performance analysis below will show the improvement by this double-router network.

3.1 Performance Analysis

Agarwal's contention model [6] for buffered, direct networks is used to evaluate performance of our different NoC architectures. This model can estimate average delay for *k*-ary *d*-cube networks, in which there is no flow control and deadlock. The average delay of *n* bytes packet in *k*-ary *d*-cube networks is

$$T(n,k,d,w,\rho)=(\frac{n}{w}+h_{ave}\cdot\Delta)+h_{ave}\cdot W(n,k,d,w,\rho)\ . \tag{1}$$

and

$$W(n,k,d,w,\rho)=\frac{n}{w}\cdot\frac{\rho}{1-\rho}\cdot\frac{h_{ave}-1}{h_{ave}^{2}}(1+\frac{1}{d})\ ,\ h_{ave}=d(\frac{k-1}{2})\ . \tag{2}$$

Here, w is network bandwidth; h_{ave} is average routing distance; ρ is channel utilization and $\triangle$ is router delay.

Suppose there is no flow control and deadlock in two networks and their total bandwidth is same. The 16-node 2D-mesh network is a 4-ary 2-cube, that is to say, $k=4$, $d=2$. Other parameters for double-router network and single-router network is depicted in Table 2.

Table 2. Parameters for two networks

Routers	Parameters
Local router (LR)	$h_{ave}=1,\ \Delta=1,\ w=w_L$
Hybrid router (HR)	$h_{ave}=4,\ \Delta=2,\ w=w_H,\ \rho=\rho_H$
Single hybrid router (SR)	$h_{ave}=3,\ \Delta=2,\ w=w_H+w_L,\ \rho=\frac{4}{3}\cdot\frac{w}{w_H}\cdot\rho_H$

The average delay of *n* bytes packet in local router (LR), hybrid router (HR) and single hybrid router (SR) is T_L, T_H, T_S.

$$T_L(n,w_L)=\frac{n}{w_L}+1\ . \tag{3}$$

$$T_H(n,w_H,\rho_H)=\frac{n}{w_H}+8+\frac{9}{8}\cdot\frac{n}{w_H}\cdot\frac{\rho_H}{1-\rho_H}\ . \tag{4}$$

$$T_S(n,w,\rho)=\frac{n}{w}+6+\frac{n}{w}\cdot\frac{\rho}{1-\rho}\ . \tag{5}$$

Suppose w = 12 bytes, $w_L : w_H = 1:1, 2:1, 4:1$ and n = 6,12,24 bytes respectively. According to equations (3)(4)(5), performance comparisons for different routers are given in Table 3, Table 4 and Table 5. It can be concluded that

(1) T_S increases more faster than T_H as ρ increases and T_L isn't affected by ρ. That is to say, single-router network is more sensitive to channel utilization than double-router network.

(2) T_S increases more faster than T_H and T_L as n increases. That is to say, single-router network is more sensitive to packet size than double-router network.

(3) T_S is greater than T_H after ρ goes beyond certain point. That is to say, double-router network guarantees lower delay under higher channel utilization than single-router network.

Table 3. Packet average delay under different channel utilization (ρ) for three routers. Packet size is 6 bytes.

ρ	T_S	T_L(1:1)	T_L(2:1)	T_L(4:1)	T_H(1:1)	T_H(2:1)	T_H(4:1)
0.1	6.56	2	1.75	1.63	9.04	9.54	10.54
0.3	6.71	2	1.75	1.63	9.14	9.64	10.63
0.5	7	2	1.75	1.63	9.26	9.74	10.73
0.7	7.67	2	1.75	1.63	9.4	9.86	10.83
0.9	11	2	1.75	1.63	9.57	9.99	10.94

Table 4. Packet average delay under different channel utilization (ρ) for three routers. Packet size is 12 bytes.

ρ	T_S	T_L(1:1)	T_L(2:1)	T_L(4:1)	T_H(1:1)	T_H(2:1)	T_H(4:1)
0.1	7.11	3	2.5	2.25	10.09	11.09	13.09
0.3	7.43	3	2.5	2.25	10.29	11.27	13.27
0.5	8	3	2.5	2.25	10.52	11.48	13.46
0.7	9.33	3	2.5	2.25	10.80	11.72	13.66
0.9	16	3	2.5	2.25	11.15	11.98	13.88

Table 5. Packet average delay under different channel utilization (ρ) for three routers. Packet size is 24 bytes.

ρ	T_S	T_L(1:1)	T_L(2:1)	T_L(4:1)	T_H(1:1)	T_H(2:1)	T_H(4:1)
0.1	8.22	5	4	3.5	12.18	14.17	18.17
0.3	8.86	5	4	3.5	12.57	14.55	18.53
0.5	10	5	4	3.5	13.04	14.96	18.91
0.7	12.67	5	4	3.5	13.60	15.47	19.32
0.9	26	5	4	3.5	14.29	15.96	19.76

In Table 2, it is supposed that LR's $\triangle$ is half of HR's $\triangle$. In fact, the router delay $\triangle$ is dependent on router micro-architecture. Optimized micro-architecture will decrease delay of the local router greatly.

3.2 Hybrid Router Micro-architecture

The hybrid router adopts the micro-architecture of virtual-channel router proposed by Li-Shiuan Peh [7][8] (Fig. 2). There are p input controllers, each with routing logic, and virtual channel (vc) state and buffers for the v virtual channels per physical channel. The architectures of the global virtual-channel allocator and switch allocator vary with *pi*, *po* and v. The crossbar switch design is unaffected by v, and varies only with *pi*, *po* and w.

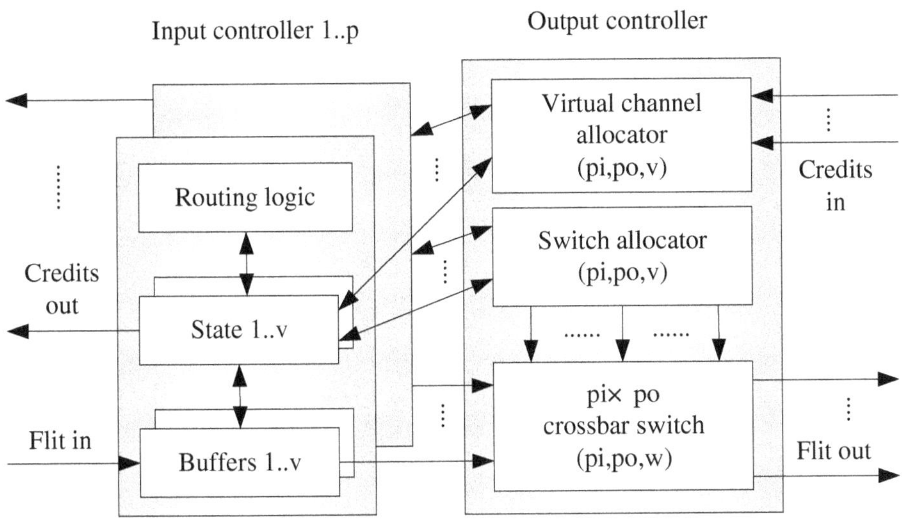

Fig. 2. Canonical micro-architecture of a virtual-channel router [7]

The flow of flits through the states of routing, virtual-channel allocation, switch allocation and switch traversal in a virtual-channel router is depicted in Fig. 3. Here, consider a two-flit packet, a head flit followed by a tail flit, flowing through a virtual-channel router. In the virtual-channel router, there is a separate input queue and a separate copy of the channel state (*vc state*) for each virtual channel. When the head flit of this packet arrives at the *input controller* of the injection channel, its virtual-channel identifier (VCID) field is decoded and the entire flit buffered in the appropriate flit queue. For instance, the packet in our example is injected into input virtual channel 0 (*vi*=0) of the injection channel, and buffered accordingly into queue 0. At this point, virtual channel 0 enters the *routing* state, and the destination field of the flit is sent to the *routing logic*, which returns the output virtual channels *{vo}* (not physical channels) the packet may use. In this example, we assume the routing logic returns *{vo=e0, e1}* for the eastern output port [8].

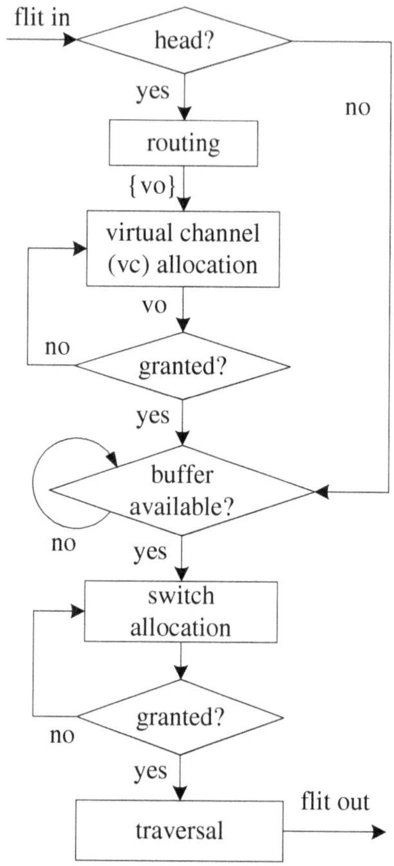

Fig. 3. Flow of a flit through routing, virtual channel allocation, switch allocation and switch traversal in a virtual-channel router [8]

Upon receipt of the output virtual channels, the state for *vi* is set to *virtual-channel allocation*. Input virtual channel *vi* then sends its requests for desired output virtual channels to the *global virtual-channel allocator*, which collects all the requests from each virtual channel of the input controllers and returns available output virtual channels to successful requestors. When *vi* is allocated an output virtual channel, say, output virtual channel 1 (*vo=e1*) of the eastern port, the head flit consults the buffer count for *vo* and if there is a buffer available to hold the flit, it sends requests for the eastern output port to the *global switch allocator*. Instead of reserving output ports for the entire duration of a packet, the switch allocator of a virtual-channel router allocates crossbar passage to flits of different packets on a cycle-by-cycle basis. Once this head flit secures passage through to the eastern output port, it leaves for the *crossbar switch* and on to the next hop, with its VCID field overwritten with *vo*. The buffer count for *vo* is then decremented. At the same time, a credit containing *vi* is returned to the previous hop, prompting the injection channel's buffer count for virtual channel 0 to be incremented [8].

When the subsequent tail flit arrives, it is put into the buffer queue of input virtual channel 0, as its VCID field is 0. It then inherits the output virtual channel *vo* reserved by its head flit, and submits a request to the global switch allocator for the eastern output port if there are buffers available to hold it. Once it is granted crossbar passage, it informs the virtual-channel allocator to release the reserved *vo*, and leaves for the next hop, with its VCID field also updated to *vo*=1 [8].

3.3 Local Router Micro-architecture

The routing delay of hybrid router is high. Its static circuit delay (no load) is at least 4 cycles - routing, virtual channel allocation, switch allocation and switch traversal - and there are three kinds of dynamic contention delay (with load), respectively for virtual channel allocation, buffer allocation and switch allocation (Fig.2). Local router aims at routing inter-neighbor packets of the DragonFly architecture with stable one-cycle delay. Its micro-architecture is optimized for this target.

In local router, there are routing paths only between neighbor ports and local port(s), without neighbor-to- neighbor paths. That is to say, the local router is deadlock-free because no routing loop can exist; so virtual channel is not necessary any more for eliminating deadlock [9]. Suppose it has *n* neighbor ports and one local port. The local router is partitioned into two independent routers: router A for neighbors-to-local path and router B for local-to-neighbors path (Fig. 4).

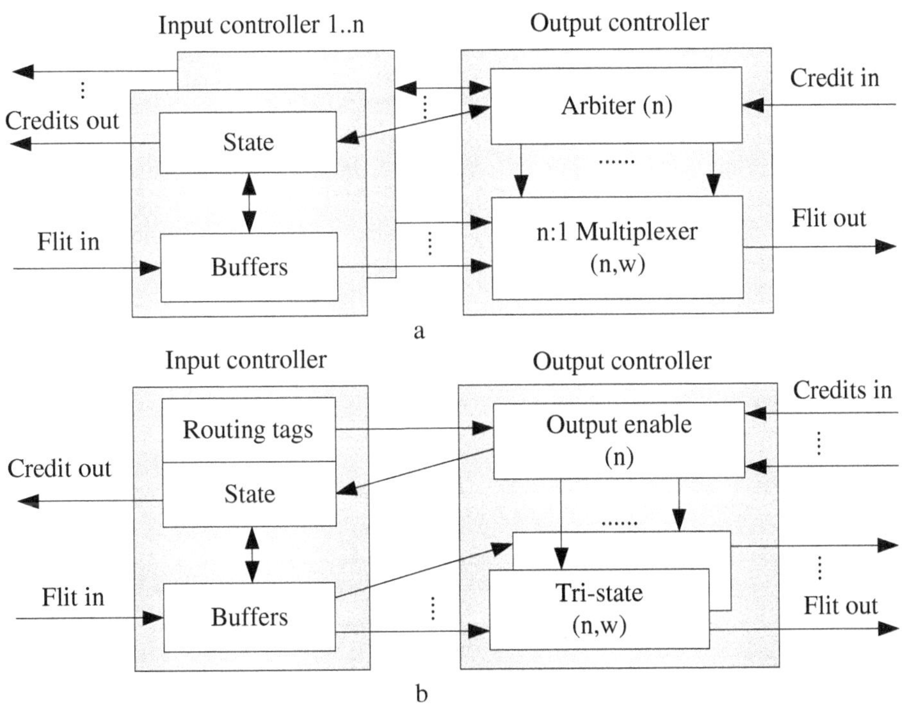

Fig. 4. Canonical micro-architecture of a local router. (a) Router A for n neighbor ports to 1 local port; (b) Router B for 1 local port to n neighbor ports.

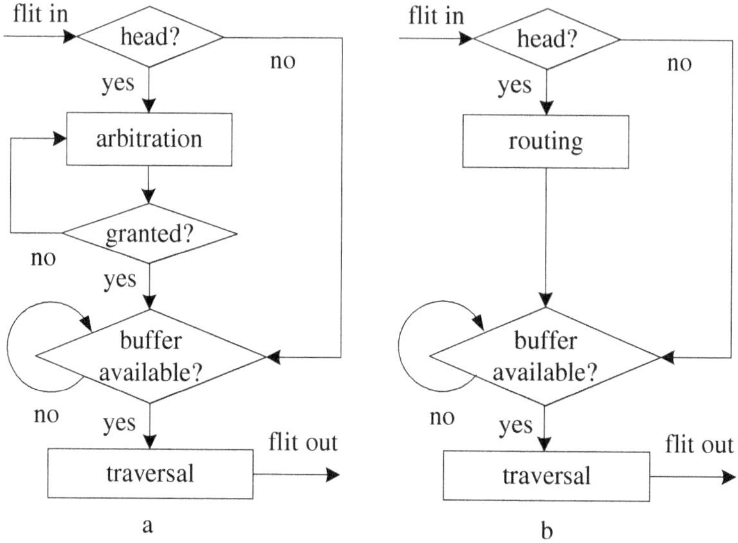

Fig. 5. Flow of a flit through the router A (a) and the router B (b)

Flow of a flit through the local router is similar to that of the hybrid router. A flit in router A goes through output arbitration and multiplexer traversal, without routing and virtual channel allocation (Fig. 5a). A flit in router B goes through routing and tri-state traversal, without switch allocation and virtual channel allocation (Fig.5b). The local router becomes faster than the hybrid router by eliminating two static routing states and one dynamic contention delay for virtual channel allocation.

The local router can support more local ports to increase parallelism of local communication and decrease its routing delay further. Suppose it has $n = m \cdot k$ neighbor ports and m local ports. Partition neighbor ports into m clusters and k neighbor ports in each cluster share a different local port. If $n = m$, the local router becomes extremely parallel and fast, and flits in it just request the available buffers and traverse it when granted.

4 Simulation

The simulator is our 16-node 2D-mesh DragonFly (Fig. 1). It supports two different networks: single-router or double-router. The size of its memory subsystem is configurable. The simulator configuration is listed in Table 6.

Table 6. Simulator configuration

	Single-router	Double-router
DSP node	16	16
L1 memory	16K*16	16K*16
DRAM	2M*8	2M*8
Channel width	64 bits	32 bits for each router

Table 7. Benchmarks Description

Benchmark	Description
FIR	Finite Impulse Response
FFT	Fast Fourier Transform
MM	Matrix Multiple
CONV	2D Image Convolution
ADPCM	Adaptive Differential PCM Coder/Decoder
SSA	Signal Spectrum Analysis

Benchmarks include four typical DSP algorithms and two complex DSP applications (Table 7). The communication locality is greatly affected by how benchmarks are mapped. Two rules are followed:

(1) Load balance. The DragonFly architecture aims at maximizing parallelism of DSP applications. Load balance among so many nodes is the primary rule for mapping.
(2) Communication minimization. Map those loads with more inter-node communication to closer nodes as possible as it is.

5 Conclusion and Future Work

The simulation results (Table.8) show that DRN's average delay is 40.6% of SRN's. That is to say, the proposed local router decreases original network delay by 59.4%. This result is consistent with performance comparisons depicted in Tables.3-5, because average 72.9% inter-node communication is transferred through the fast local router.

The DRN is introduced on the basis of 16-node 2D-mesh DragonFly DSP architecture. It can be used to speed up communication in many NoC applications where communication locality is high.

Table 8. Communication delays on 6 benchmarks for single-router network (SRN) and double-router network (DRN)

	FIR	FFT	MM	CONV	ADPCM	SSA
SRN	7200	36864	34560	8352	5964	97748
DRN	2800	16096	12840	3628	4491	37619

Area of DRN 's data-path is similar to that of SRN, because their overall bandwidth is same. A little more area is needed for DRN 's additional control logic. Two independent small routers of DRN may consume less power than one large router of SRN, especially when dynamic power management (DPM) techniques are used. Our future work will focus on area and power analysis of SRN and DRN.

References

[1] Benini. L.; De Micheli. G., "Networks on chips: a new SoC paradigm," *IEEE Computer*, Vol.35, Jan 2002, pp.70-78.

[2] Kumar, S.; Jantsch, A.; Soininen, J.-P.; Forsell, M.; Millberg, M.; Oberg, J.; Tiensyrja, K.; Hemani, A.; "A network on chip architecture and design methodology," *VLSI on Annual Symposium, IEEE Computer Society ISVLSI*, 2002, pp.105 –112.

[3] J. Hu and R. Marculescu, "Exploiting the Routing Flexibility for Energy/Performance Aware Mapping of Regular NoC Architectures," Proceeding of DATE Conference. 2003, Mar. 2003.

[4] Bertozzi, D.; Jalabert, A.; Srinivasan Murali; Tamhankar, R.; Stergiou, S.; Benini, L.; De Micheli, G.; "NoC synthesis flow for customized domain specific multiprocessor systems-on-chip", *IEEE Transactions on Parallel and Distributed Systems,* vol.16, no.2, Feb 2005, pp.113-129.

[5] Jing Yuanli. "DSP Processor Architectures," *MS dissertation*, March, 2002.

[6] Agarwal. A. "Limits on Interconnection Network Performance," *IEEE Transactions on Parallel and Distributed Systems,* Vol.2, 1991, pp.398-412.

[7] Li-Shiuan Peh; Dally, W.J.;" A delay model for router microarchitectures," *IEEE Micro*, Vol.21, Issue 1, Jan.-Feb. 2001, pp.26-34

[8] Li-Shiuan Peh, "Flow control and micro-architectural mechanisms for extending the performance of interconnection networks," *PhD dissertation*, 2001, pp.76-89.

[9] Culler D.E., Singh J.P., Gupta A. "Parallel Computer Architecture: A Hardware/Software Approach (Second Edition)," August 1998.

A New Methodology of Integrating High Level Synthesis and Floorplan for SoC Design*

Yunfeng Wang[1], Jinian Bian[1], Xianlong Hong[1], Liu Yang[1], Qiang Zhou[1], and Qiang Wu[2]

[1] Tsinghua University, Beijing, China 100084
{wangyf00, yliu02}@mails.tsinghua.edu.cn
{bianjn, hxl-dcs, zhouqiang}@tsinghua.edu.cn
[2] Hunan University, Changsha, China 410082
wuqiang@hnu.cn

Abstract. As silicon CMOS technology is scaled into the nanometer regime, a whole system can be integrated into one chip. At the same time, the computer-aided design technology is challenged by two major features: the ever-increasing design complexity of gigascale integration and complicated physical effects inherent from the nanoscale technology. In this paper, a new methodology of integrating High Level Synthesis and Floorplan together is presented. The whole design flow is divided into two phases: a fast searching space scan procedure and a detailed solution optimize procedure. The searching space of integrating HLS and Floorplan is first "smoothed" by a "Behavior Information based Cluster Algorithm", and then a fast scan of this smoothed searching space is proceeded. The result of the first phrase will be used as the start point of the detailed optimize procedure. The experimental result show that the methodology is efficient.

1 Introduction

As silicon CMOS technology is scaled into the nanometer regime, a whole system can be integrated into one chip. Also, the computer-aided design technology is challenged by two major features: the ever-increasing design complexity of gigascale integration and complicated physical effects inherent from the nanoscale technology.

It has been presented that, for a 50M-gates design (available on CMOS technology), more than 7M lines VHDL codes are needed at RT Level [9]. This will be a big challenge for manual design. A higher level abstraction of circuit model, such as high level synthesis, is needed to manage this huge functional complexity. It has been presented that High Level Synthesis can ten times reduce the number of lines of source codes [11] [10]. High Level Synthesis, will greatly enhance the design efficiency.

* This work is mainly supported by NSFC 90407005 and partially supported by NSFC 90207017 and NSFC 60236020.

L.T. Yang et al. (Eds.): ICESS 2005, LNCS 3820, pp. 275–286, 2005.

At the same time, with the proceed of manufacture technology, the feature size of integrated circuits has been proceed into deep sub-macron level. As CMOS technology scales down deeply, designing of devices and chips will encounter the fundamental electrical and material limits[8]. Emerging physical problems for design quality in nanometer technology is needed. In the nanometer regime, interconnects has demonstrates over 70% of the total delay of a circuit, are undoubtedly a major factor in determining the chip performance. A manufacture-aware design phases of EDA flow is needed to manage this deep sub-macron physical effects.

In traditional design flow of integrated circuits, high-level synthesis does scheduling and allocation, and then Floorplan determines the actual positions of modules in a physical design. Since Floorplan is separated from high level synthesis, no interconnect information can be supplied to synthesis process, and no behavior information is left in Floorplan procedure. This communication-less flow will cause serious problems. Because these two phases of design flow are based on different delay estimation model, the result of high-level synthesis may be totally wrong for floor-planning, especially in timing aspect. An efficient and physically-based methodology to represent closer coupling between a process technology and circuit/system design must be devised. The relentless pursuit of cost reduction per function has made the interaction inevitable. Thus, traditional assumptions for weak coupling and so called "divide and conquer" approach no longer holds in searching for a self-consistent design solutions based on nanometer technology[1]. To solve this problem, a co-operation between the two phases is necessary

Several researchers has addressed the problem of integrating HLS and Floorplan together. J. P. Weng presented 3D algorithm in [2], which was known as the one of the earliest research of this problem. P.Prabhakaran presented a simultaneous scheduling, allocation and floorplan algorithm in [7]. Recently, an algorithm for unifying HLS and physical design is provided by M. Rim [6]. However, the HLS and Floorplan are still separated in these algorithms, and the "complexity explosion" problem can not be avoid. S. Tarafdar presented a data-centric HLS and Floorplan algorithm in [4]. But the algorithm in [4] is a constructive algorithm. As we known, most times, a simulated annealing approach may find a better result in this kind of problems.

In this paper, a new methodology which combine High Level Synthesis and Floorplanning together is presented. The main idea of the methodology is to combine the High Level Synthesis phase and Floorplanning phase into one phase, which do scheduling, allocation and floorplanning at same time, in order to provide a self-consistent design solution.

However, because High Level Synthesis and Floorplan are both NP-HARD problems, the simple combination of this two phrases will cause a "complexity explosion". To solve this problem, the whole flow of this new methodology is divided into two phrases: a fast scan of a "smoothed" searching space of integrating HLS and Floorplan, and a detailed optimization phrase. In the first phrase, the searching space is first smoothed by a behavior information based cluster algorithm, and then a fast scan of this "smoothed" searching space is proceeded. And then, a rather detailed High Level Synthesis and Floorplan phrase is used to search an optimized solution on the original searching space.

The paper is organized as following: in section 2, the problem formulation and the representation of the solution is presented; in section 3, the first phrase of the methodology is introduced in detail, including the behavior information based functional units cluster algorithm; in section 4, the detail optimize algorithm is described; the experimental result and the conclusion is given out in the last section.

2 Problem Formulation and Representation of the Solution

2.1 Problem Formulation

The inputs to our approach are a CDFG(Control Data Flow Graph)[5] and resource constraints. The total delay of the circuit can be calculated by following equation:

$$D = d \times s \tag{1}$$

where D is the total delay of the circuit, d is the delay of each control step, s is the number of control steps. d is calculated as following:

$$d = \max\{d_i\}; i = 1, 2, \dots \tag{2}$$

where d_i is the delay of the i_{th} control step. d_i can be calculated as following:

$$d_i = \max d_f + d_w \tag{3}$$

where d_f is the delay of one active functional unit in the i_{th} control step, and d_w is the delay of corresponding interconnect wires. d_w can be calculated as following:

$$\begin{aligned} d_w &= \frac{R \cdot C}{2} \\ R &= r \cdot l \\ C &= c \cdot l \end{aligned} \tag{4}$$

where r is the unit-resistance of interconnect wires, and c is the unit-capacitance of interconnect wires. l is the length of each interconnect wire.

The target of our approach is to optimize D in equation 1 under resource constraints.

2.2 Representation of the Solution

A two-dimension grid is used to present the result of scheduling and allocation, as shown in Figure 1, which was first presented in [3]. The rows of the grid

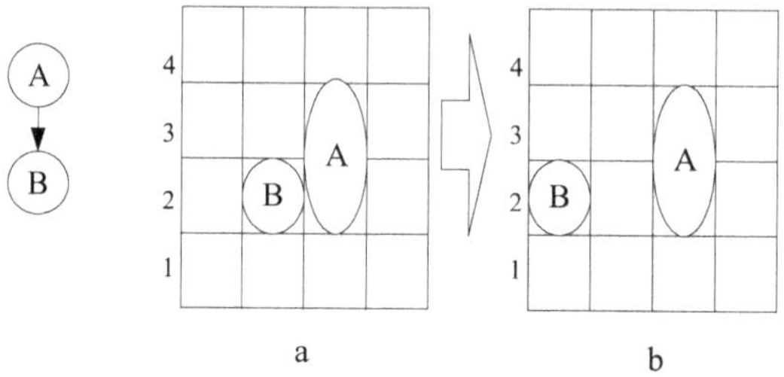

Fig. 1. Using Two Dimension Grid to Represent the Result of High Level Synthesis

stand for control-steps of scheduling; while the columns stand for the functional units to be used in the circuit. The result of scheduling and allocation can be considered as the placement of the two-dimension grid.

As shown as in Figure 1 (a), operation B is placed in row 2 and column 2, means that operation B is scheduled to control step 2 and allocated to functional unit 2. When operation B is moved into row 2 and column 1, as shown in figure 1 (b), means the operation B is re-allocated to functional unit 1.

A Corner Block List (CBL) representation is used to represent the result of Floorplan. CBL use 3 strings (S, L, T) to represent the result of Floorplan. A typical CBL is shown as Figure 2.

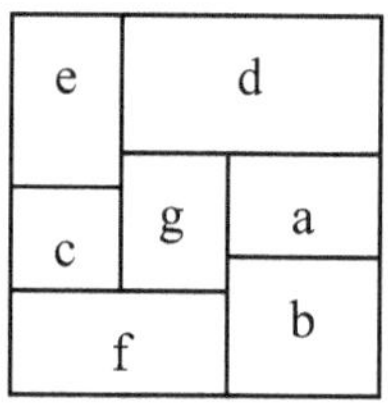

Corner Block List:
S=(fcegbad)
L=(001100)
T=(0 0 10 10 0 10)

Fig. 2. Use CBL to represent the result of Floorplan

CBL representation is a topology based non-slicing Floorplan representation method. The detailed information about CBL is presented in [12].

3 Fast Scanning on a Smoothed Searching Space

3.1 Basic Process of the First Phrase

A simulated annealing approach is used in this "fast searching space scan" phrase. For each iteration of simulated annealing approach, a new solution of High Level Synthesis is retrieved. And then, a behavior information based functional unit clustering algorithm is used to cluster functional units into several groups. The functional units which are clustered into one group will be considered as a single "big" functional unit in Floorplan process. This will highly reduce the computational complexity of Floorplan, and the original searching space is also smoothed by this clustering process. The whole flow of this first phrase can be illustrated as Figure 3.

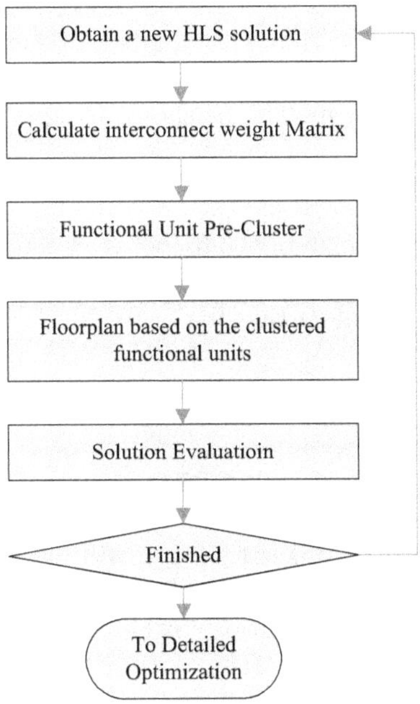

Fig. 3. Optimization Procedure in the First Phrase

As shown in Figure 3, any time a new HLS solution is obtained, a functional unit clustering process will be used to cluster functional units before Floorplan. This functional unit clustering procedure will highly reduce the complexity of Floorplan. Also, this procedure will reduce the accurateness of interconnect information, but it's not fatal in this phrase. The interconnect information between clustered functional units is enough for such a fast scan. A detailed optimize procedure will be proceeded based on the result of this phrase.

In the first phrase of our methodology, the new solution of HLS is retrieved by following actions:

- Reschedule an operation to a valid control step
- Reallocate an operation to an currently empty functional unit
- Reallocate two operations by exchange their functional units

These actions will be selected randomly to be proceeded in each iteration.

3.2 Behavior Information Based Functional Unit Clustering

The functional unit clustering algorithm is based on the weight of each interconnect wire. In traditional design flow, the behavior information is lost in Floorplan phrase. Interconnect optimization in Floorplan can only base on the physical weight of each interconnect wire. A new algorithm is presented in this section. This algorithm calculates the weight of interconnect wires based on behavior information.

An interconnect weight matrix M is used to proceed functional unit clustering. For convenience, let's assume that the number of functional units is n, and assume that the number of operations in CDFG is m.Then, the interconnect weight matrix will be a $n \times n$ matrix, as shown in equation 5.

$$M = |a_{i,j}|; \quad i \in [1, n], j \in [1, n] \tag{5}$$

where $a_{i,j}$ means the interconnect weight between functional unit i and functional unit j. Registers are considered as a special kind of functional unit too. The value of $a_{i,j}$ can be calculate by equation 6

$$a_{i,j} = \sum_k WO_k \cdot W_{o_k,i} \cdot W_{o_l,j} \cdot W_{o_k,o_l}; \quad k \in [1, m], \quad l \in [1, m] \tag{6}$$

where m is the number of operations in CDFG. $W_{o_k,i}$ will be 1 if the k_{th} operation is allocated to functional unit i, 0 if not. $W_{o_l,j}$ will be 1 if the l_{th} operation is allocated to functional unit j, 0 if not. W_{o_k,o_l} will be 1 if there is a direct data flow between the k_{th} operation and the l_{th} operation (storing variables into register is considered a special operation), other wise 0. WO_k can be calculated by equation 7.

$$WO_k = \frac{D_{cs}}{D_{cs} - D_o} \tag{7}$$

In equation 7, D_{cs} means the delay of a control step, and D_o is the functional unit delay of this operation.

As shown in Figure 4 (a), operation A and operation B are both allocated to functional unit $FU1$, and their outputs are both stored in register $Reg1$. It

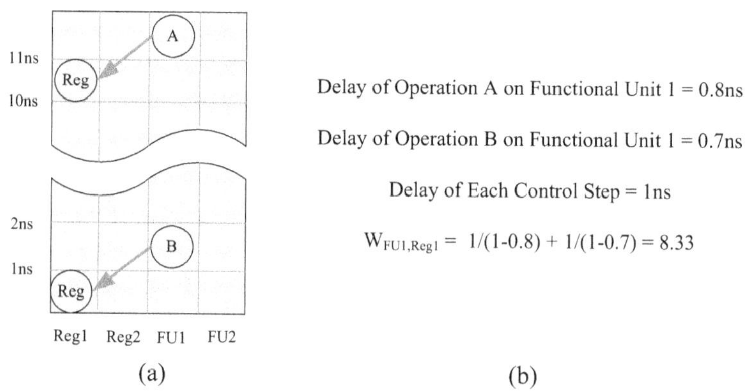

Fig. 4. Interconnect Weight between Two Functional Units

easy to know that there will be only one group of interconnect wires between functional unit $FU1$ and register $Reg1$ in physical design. The weight of this interconnect, $W_{FU1,Reg1}$, will be calculated as Figure 4 (b). This weight not only represents the density of physical interconnects between two functional units, but also represents the density of behavior interconnects between two functional units.

For each time a new HLS solution is obtained, this matrix will be calculated. The sum of each line of this matrix is calculated also. The functional unit with the maximum value-sum will be considered the most "heavy traffic" functional unit. This functional unit and all its neighbor functional units (who has interconnects with this functional unit) will be clustered together. The weight between these functional units will be updated to 0, and then another functional unit cluster is calculated by the same algorithm until there is no functional unit left.

As we described above, for each iteration of the simulated annealing algorithm: 1) a new HLS solution is obtained; 2) the interconnect weight matrix is calculated, and functional unit clustering is then proceeded; 3) Floorplan based on clustered functional units. The cost will be evaluated based on this Floorplan result. When the simulated annealing algorithm is finished, a detailed optimization process is proceeded.

4 Detail Optimization

When the first phrase is finished, an initial result of High Level Synthesis and Floorplan is obtained. This result includes a two-dimension grid described in section 2.2, and a initial Floorplan. A detail optimization procedure is then proceeded based on this result. Because the initial Floorplan is based on pre-clustered functional units, it will be unwrapped firstly. A simulated annealing approach is used to proceed this detail optimization procedure. For each iteration of simulated annealing algorithm, a new High Level Synthesis result is firstly retrieved based on the floorplan information, and then a new floorplan is obtained if necessary. Because the searching space of this phrase has been constrained in a relative "small" scale, the floorplan according to this new High Level Synthesis result will not change too much. An incremental Floorplan is used to retrieve the new floorplan result. The design flow of the second phrase can be shown as Figure 5.

A heuristic algorithm is used to get a new High Level Synthesis result based on the floorplan information. The basic idea of this algorithm can be shown as Figure 6.

The initial result of synthesis is shown as Figure 6 (a), and the result of floorplan based on this result is shown as Figure 6 (f). From Figure 6 (f), it is found that operation A is allocated to functional unit f_2, which is too far from reg_4 to satisfy the delay constraint. It is also found that f_3 is just the very position for operation A. The following action will be taken to optimize the solution: 1) The operation allocated to f_3 (operation C in this case) will be taken out of the grid. Then, operation A is re-allocated to f_3, as shown in Figure 6 (b).

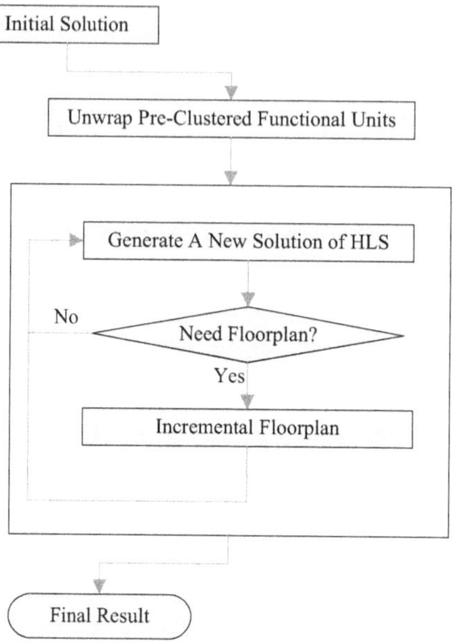

Fig. 5. Detailed Optimization

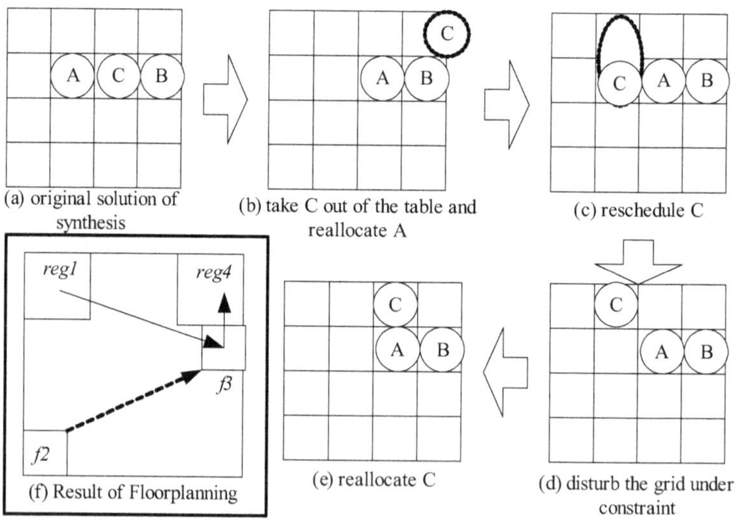

Fig. 6. High Level Synthesis Optimization Based on Floorplan Information

This action can be repeated several times to find a better solution. 2) Operation C is allocated to another functional unit. If it is possible to allow operation C to execute in more control steps, then re-schedule it, as shown in Figure 6 (c). 3) Disturb the grid under constraints by rescheduling some operations under constraints, as shown in Figure 6 (d). 4) Repeat these procedures to find a better solution.

The basic idea and the entire searching procedure has been described above. In detail, a virtual force-balance algorithm is used to obtain a new High Level Synthesis result.

For each operation O in the grid, the local path set S of this operation can be defined as following:

$$\begin{aligned} S &= < f \times R > \\ R &= \{r_1, r_2, \ldots\} \end{aligned} \tag{8}$$

where f is the functional unit where operation O is allocated. R is the set of registers which has direct data flow with operation O, as shown in Figure 7.

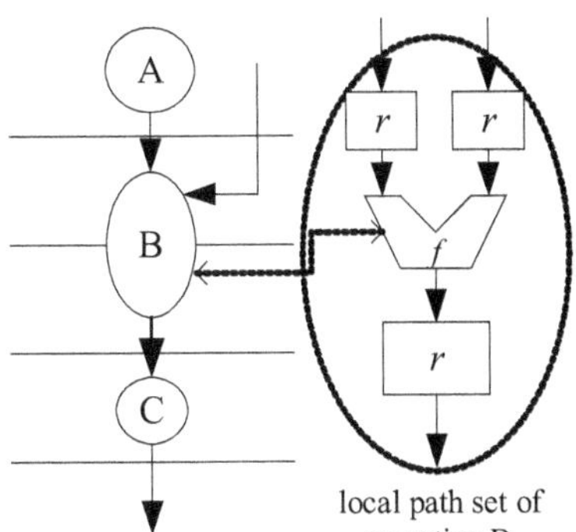

Fig. 7. Local Path Set

For each operation O in the grid, assume that the operation is allocated to functional unit f. A virtual force acted on the operation O is calculated by following equation:

$$\boldsymbol{F_o} = \sum_i \boldsymbol{F_{o,r_i}} \tag{9}$$

where $\boldsymbol{F_{o,r_i}}$ is the force caused by the i_{th} register in the "local path set" of operation O.

$$\boldsymbol{F_{o,r_i}} = \boldsymbol{P_{r_i}} - \boldsymbol{P_f} \tag{10}$$

where $\boldsymbol{P_f}$ is the position of functional unit f, $\boldsymbol{P_{r_i}}$ is the position of the i_{th} register in the local path set of operation O. In this case, the best position for operation op on a chip is the functional unit where the virtual force acted on O is minimized.

While the best situation of the circuit is that all its operations are on their best position or nearly best position. According to the grid representation, the

```
For each control step (cstep) in grid {
  For each kind of operation begin in this cstep {
    Select an operation O of this kind of operation which begin
      execute in this cstep randomly.
    Set the iterative count to be zero.
    Calculate the best column for O in this cstep.
    Take O out of the grid.
    While ( count is less than max-count and
      the best column of O is not empty in this cstep)
      if (the best column in this cstep is locked by an operation O') {
        Calculate the next best column for O in this cstep.
      } else {
        Take O' out of the grid.
        Put O into the best column in this cstep.
        Set O = O'.
        Calculate the best column of O in this cstep.
        count ++
      }
    }
    if ( the best column of O in this cstep is not empty) {
      Calculate the best empty column for O in this cstep.
      Put O into the best column in this cstep
    }
  }
```

Fig. 8. Reallocation/Rescheduling Algorithm based on Floorplan

best column for operation O in a grid is the column represents the best functional unit for O on the chip. The re-allocation algorithm is described as Figure 8.

The re-allocation procedure was called alternatively to find a good solution. If a better result is not found in finite iterations, one operation will be re-scheduled, or an additional functional unit resource will be added. No matter new resources are added or not, an incremental Floorplan procedure will be called when a new High Level Synthesis result is retrieved.

As we can see from the description above, this new HLS solution will not change the original searching space of Floorplan too much. An incremental Floorplan will find a stable Floorplan result rapidly.

5 Experimental Result and Conclusion

The methodology is implemented and tested by C++, on Sun Sparc, Solaris. The value of unit-resistance and unit-capacitance is presented in table 1. Table 2 presents the experimental result under 250nm technology, and Table 3 presents the experimental result under 160nm technology. Table 2 and Table 3 have a same structure. column 1 presents the example name, column 2 presents the final number of control step of each circuit. column 3 gives out the used area ratio of the chip. The original delay of each control step and optimized delay of each control step is presented in column 4 and column 5.

The experimental result shows that the performance of the final circuit can be optimized 24% at most under 160ns technology.

Table 1. Parameter List

	Description	Value
r	Wire resistance per unit length (ω/ m)	0.075
c	Wire capacitance per unit length (fF/ m)	0.118

Table 2. Experimental Result under 250nm Technology

Sample Name	No. of CS	Area Ratio	Orig. Delay of each CS	Opt. Delay of each CS	Opt. Ratio
fir11	14	95.63%	3.4	2.7	79.41%
iir7	18	93.75%	2.4	2.0	83.33%
ellipf	17	91.21%	2.7	2.2	81.48%

Table 3. Experimental Result under 160nm Technology

Sample Name	No. of CS	Area Ratio	Orig. Delay of each CS	Opt. Delay of each CS	Opt. Ratio
fir11	14	95.63%	1.7	1.3	76.47%
iir7	18	94.47%	1.9	1.6	84.21%
ellipf	17	94.62%	2.5	1.9	76%

We can draw a conclusion from the experimental result: in this paper, a new methodology (including its supporting algorithms) is presented to integrate HLS and Floorplan together; and the experimental result show that the methodology is efficient.

The detailed algorithms of functional unit clustering based on behavior information and the algorithm of the detailed optimization algorithm is also provided in this paper, in order to support the methodology. However, the basic idea of this methodology is the most important contribution of this paper. In traditional methodology of EDA, the computational complexity is too high to find a good result by simultaneously optimization of HLS and Floorplan. The motivation of the first phrase of this methodology is to reduce the complexity of integrating HLS and Floorplan, and avoid uncomplete search of the solution space. A behavior information based functional unit cluster algorithm is used to smooth the searching space.

The main contributions of this paper are: 1) provides a new methodology to integrate HLS and Floorplan together; 2) provides a behavior information based functional unit cluster algorithm; 3) provides a detailed optimization algorithm. The algorithms and the methodology are tested by examples, and the experimental result show that the methodology is efficient.

References

1. Jeong-Taek Kong, *CAD for Nanometer Silicon Design Challenges and Success* IEEE Transactions on Very Large Scale Integration(VLSI) Systems, Vol. 12, No. 11, November 2004
2. J.P.Weng and A.C.Parker, *3D Scheduling: High Level Synthesis with Floorplanning* 28th ACM/IEEE Design Automation Conference, pp. 668-673, 1991.
3. H. Jang and Barry M. Pangrle, *A Grid-Based Approach for Connectivity Binding with Geometric Costs* ICCAD-93, pp. 94-99, 1993.
4. S.Tarafdar, M.Leeser et al., *A Data-Centric Approach to High-Level Synthesis*, IEEE Transactions on Computer-Aided Design of Integrated Circuits and Systems, Vol.19, No.11, November 2000
5. Qiang Wu, Yunfeng Wang, Jinian Bian, Weimin Wu and Hongxi Xue, *A Hierarchical CDFG as Intermediate Representation for Hardware/Software Codesign*, Proceeding of ICCCAS'02, Chengdu, China, 2002.
6. William E. Dougherty and Donald E. Thomas, *Unifying Behavior Synthesis and Physical Design* Design Automation Conference, 2000. Proceedings 2000. 37th , June 5-9, 2000 pp. 756 - 761
7. P.Prabhakaran and P.Banerjee, *Simultaneous Scheduling, Binding and Floorplanning in High-level synthesis*, Proceedings of the IEEE International Conference on VLSI Design, pp. 428-434, 1998.
8. The International Technology Roadmap for Semiconductor, 2003
9. R. Goering, *Panelists ponder why U.S. lags in ESL design*, EE Times, Feb. 17, 2005
10. K. Wakabayashi, *C-based behavioral synthesis and verification analysis on industrial design examples*, Proceedings of the Asian and South Pacific Design Automation Conference, pp. 344-348, Jan. 2004.
11. K. Wakabayashi and T.Okamoto, *C-based SoC design flow and EDA tools: an ASIC and system vendor perspective*, IEEE Transactions on Computer-Aided Design of Integrated Circuits and Systems, vol. 19(12), pp.1507-1522, Dec. 2000.
12. Hong Xianlong, Huang Gang et al., *Corner Block List: An Effective and Efficient Topological Representation of Non-slicing Floorplan*, Proceeding of ICCAD 2000, pp. 8-12

Designing On-Chip Network Based on Optimal Latency Criteria

Vu-Duc Ngo, Huy-Nam Nguyen, and Hae-Wook Choi

System VLSI Lab Laboratory, SITI Research Center, School of Engineering,
Information and Communications University (ICU),
Yusong P.O. Box 77, Taejon 305-714, Korea
{duc75, huynam, hwchoi}@icu.ac.kr

Abstract. A new chip design paradigm, so called Network on Chip, has been introduced based on the demand of integration of many heterogeneous semiconductor intellectual property (IP) blocks. The Network on Chip design not only requires the good performance but also the minimization of several physical constraints such as the network latency, the used area as well as the power consumption of design. This paper analyzes the average latency of heterogeneous Network on Chip architectures in which the shortest path routing algorithm is applied. This average latency includes the queuing latency and the wire latency, and is calculated for general cases of allocating IPs onto the fixed generic switching architectures such as 2-D Mesh and Fat-Tree. With different allocation schemes of IPs, the network has different average latencies. Hence, this article presents an optimal search that adopts the Branch and Bound algorithm to find out the optimal mapping scheme to achieve the minimal network latency. This algorithm automatically map the desired IPs onto the target Network on Chip architecture with the criteria of lowest network latency. Some experiments of On Chip Multiprocessor Network application are simulated. The results show that the network latency is significantly saved with the optimized allocation scheme for the several cases of generic architectures of On Chip Multiprocessor Network application.

1 Introduction

The idea of designing a mass integration of System on Chip (SoC) IPs such as processors, DSPs, as well as memory array was proposed in [1], so called Network on Chip (NoC). This new design methodology allows us overcome the hardest problem of SoC design which is the non-scalable global wires that used to connect all the IPs. This complex system of wires, the main factor that leads to the propagation delay exceeding the system's clock period [5], is replaced by the packet based switching core and the communication protocols which are defined on it. The packet based interconnection network allows us flexibly choose the network architectures, network protocols, etc. Obviously, these merits lead to the improvement of the system's performance as well as modularity.

L.T. Yang et al. (Eds.): ICESS 2005, LNCS 3820, pp. 287–298, 2005.

The NoC, somewhat, resembles the parallel computer network. From the view point of the parallel computer network, Agrawal [2] analyzed the limit of the interconnection network in terms of the network latency. However, in this context, the author strictly assumed that the network is homogenous. The work showed the relation between the network performance and the variation of the required bandwidth as well as the latency. Recently, the authors in [6, 7, 8] had different approaches for the NoC design. They proposed the algorithms to automatically map IPs onto the target NoC architecture so as to optimize the power consumption. These papers used the same energy model for the power consumption, the energies of one bit data consumed by switches and wires were assumed to be constant. However, from our knowledge, these mentioned energies depend much on the processing capability of switch and the flying time on wire [4, 12], respectively. Due to the fact that the NoC architecture is totally heterogeneous in terms of the differences in switch capabilities and wire connections, the desired IPs are naturally different from one to the others such as DSP, RAM, USB, and processor, etc. These lead us to model the latencies on the switches and wires to calculate the network latency and then to optimize it by the optimal mapping scheme of IPs onto the target NoC architecture.

For most of the applications, the satisfaction of the latency is one of the most important factors that need to be strongly considered. In other words, it must be extremely tight. Recently, an On Chip Multiprocessor Networks (OCMN) is proposed by Ye et al. [3]. This application is expected to be mostly suitable for NoC design due to its requirements of high computation and connectivity as well. In this paper, we do analysis on the issue of NoC latency with different generic architectures. Because the fact is that the longer the packet is travelling around network in the single chip the more power is consumed. Consequently, the fundamental issue that needs to be solved is: Which switching core should each IP core be mounted to in order to minimize the network latency. To do so, we first derive the closed form equation of the network latency including queuing and wire latencies for the case of random mapping of IPs onto a pre-selected NoC architecture to which the shortest path routing algorithm is applied. The latencies of these random mappings would be varied due to the following realities:

- The routing table of applied routing algorithm would be changed in accordance with the change of mapping IPs onto pre-selected NoC architecture.
- The queuing and wire latencies would be changed in accordance with the content of the routing table.

We then utilize the optimal search algorithm, so called the Branch and Bound algorithm, to automatically map the desired IPs onto the NoC architecture along with guaranteeing that the network latency is minimized. The novelty of our work in this paper can be summarized as follows:

- We design the NoC with the minimum network latency criteria with the IPs being allocated automatically onto a pre-selected architecture as the outcome of an optimal search
- The generic NoC architecture is considered in our latency derivation as well as optimization.

The rest of this article is organized as follows. The model of the NoC architecture and its queuing as well as wire latency are analyzed in Section 2. The Branch and Bound algorithm and the optimization of the latency constraint of the On Chip Multiprocessor Networks application are introduced in Section 3. Finally, we conclude our contribution and mention about our future work in Section 4.

2 Analysis of the On-Chip Network Latency

The network latency is composed by two components, queuing latency and wire latency. The queueing latency stands for the latency that occurs inside the network node (a combination of one switch and one mounted IP). While, the wire latency presents the latency occurs along the wires that connect every two neighbor switches. In this section, we analyze the mentioned latencies one by one.

2.1 Queuing Latency

Let us define the network node to be a combination of one switch and one mounted IP as illustrated in Fig.1. This subsection derives the queuing latency of the network. First, let us define the network node as $M/M/1$ model. The average number of packets at the simple network node shown by Fig.1, N_p, is presented by

$$N_p = \frac{\lambda}{\mu - \lambda}, \tag{1}$$

where λ denotes the arrival rate of the packet to the switch, while μ represents the mean of the processing time of the network node. Applying the Little theorem for this simple network node, the queuing latency is obtained by

$$T_{Queue} = \frac{N_p}{\lambda} = \frac{1}{\mu - \lambda}. \tag{2}$$

In this context, we consider a real complex network case depicted in the Fig. 2. Without loosing generality, we can define the set $\mathbf{C_j}$ as the set of the incoming

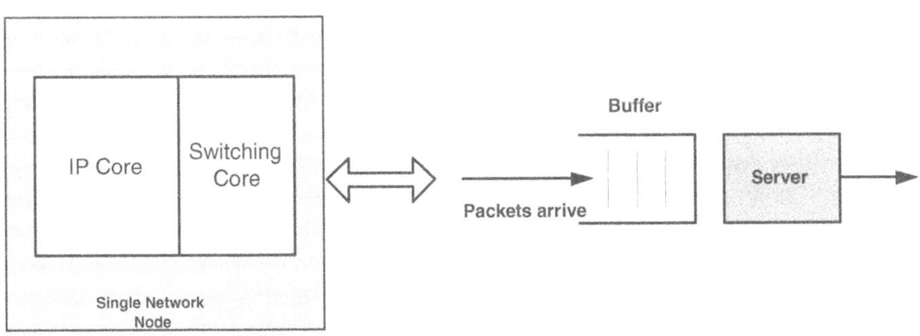

Fig. 1. Single network node and queuing model

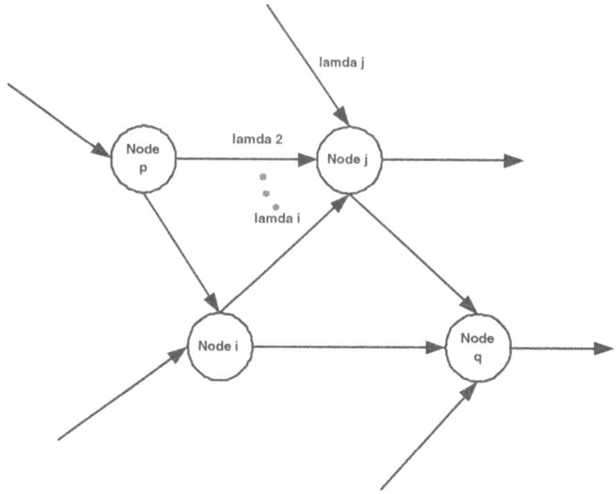

Fig. 2. Complex network model

routes of the jth network node. For an ith individual route that belongs to $\mathbf{C_j}$, the average number of packets is $N_p^i = \lambda_i T_i$. Since the routes are i.i.d, we apply the Little theorem to calculate the complex network node as the following equation

$$T_{Queue}^{j} = \frac{\sum_{i \in \mathbf{C_j}} \lambda_i T_i}{\sum_{i \in \mathbf{C_j}} \lambda_i} = \frac{\sum_{i \in \mathbf{C_j}} \lambda_i \frac{1}{\mu_j - \lambda_i}}{\sum_{i \in \mathbf{C_j}} \lambda_i}. \quad (3)$$

Here we should note that the set $\mathbf{C_j}$ includes the jth route which stands for the route where the data from the jth IP is generated toward the jth switch, the λ_i is the corresponding arrival rate of ith routes, and μ_j is the mean of the processing time of the jth network node. The route latency is considered as the sum of the latency of several given nodes that belong to this route.
Thus, the latency of ith route (R_i) is

$$T_{Queue}^{R_i} = \sum_j \frac{\sum_{i \in \mathbf{C_j}} \lambda_i \frac{1}{\mu_j - \lambda_i}}{\sum_{i \in \mathbf{C_j}} \lambda_i} \times \delta_{ij}, \quad (4)$$

where

$$\delta_{ij} = \begin{cases} 1, & if j^{th} node \in R_i, \\ 0, & otherwise. \end{cases} \quad (5)$$

For certain mapping scheme of the pre-connected IPs onto a pre-selected NoC architecture, the routing table will be determined accordingly to the used routing algorithm (with an given application, the connections between IPs are predetermined). By the known routing table, the network latency in terms of the queuing latency is simply calculated.

2.2 Wire Latency

The wire latency, so called time-of-flight, basically implies the on-chip interconnection latency. It is calculated based on how electrically it is modelled and designed. From [4], the on-chip interconnection can be modelled by RC, or RLC models. The power dissipation increases analogously with the time-of-flight of the signal. Among these mentioned models, the most popular one that we apply in this article is RLC described by Fig.3. The wire latency of RLC model, or the time of flight of signal through the interconnection, is represented by

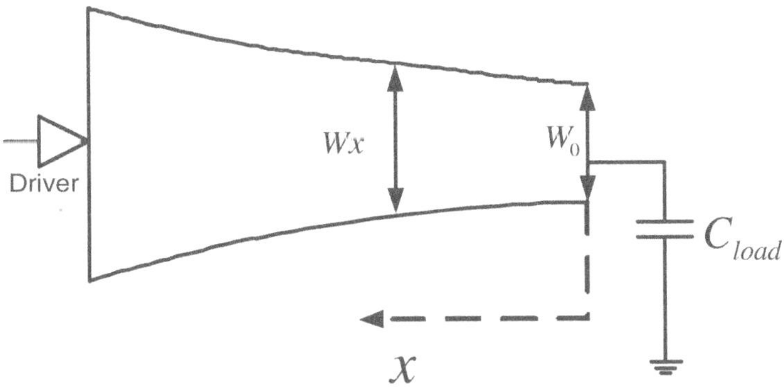

Fig. 3. General tapped RLC line model

$$T_{Wire} = \sqrt{L_{line} C_{line}}, \tag{6}$$

where L_{line} and C_{line} are the interconnection inductance and capacitance, respectively. However, the values of interconnection inductance and capacitance are depended on the physical shape of the designed interconnection. In terms of the interconnection width, they are calculated as follow

$$L_{line} = \frac{L_0}{W(x)}; C_{line} = C_0 W(x) + C_f, \tag{7}$$

where L_0 is the wire inductance per area unit, C_0 is the wire capacitance per area unit, C_f is the fringing capacitance per unit of length, and $W(x)$ denotes the line width as the function of x. For a given shape function $W(x)$, the wire latency of an interconnection that used to connect the two neighbor switches finally is

$$T_{Wire} = \sqrt{\int_0^l \frac{L_0}{W(x)} \int_0^x [C_0 W(y) + C_f] dy dx}, \tag{8}$$

where l is the wire's length. Hence, it is clearly seen that the different lengths of wires result in different values of wire latencies.

To find out the optimum shape function $W(x)$ that minimize the wire delay with the given value of l, we differentiate the right hand side of (8) and set the differentiated equation to be 0 then solve it. The relation of $W(x)$ with the other parameters consequently is obtained as follows

$$W(x) = W_0 e^{\frac{2L_0 C_0}{c} x}, \tag{9}$$

where $c = \frac{2C_f L_0 l}{W_0}$. Therefore, we can conclude that the optimum shape function of the RLC interconnection model must follow the general exponential function. The above discussion shows how to calculate the wire latency of signal flying over one hop (one hop is defined as the interconnection that connects two neighbor switches). The route latency in terms of wire latency is calculated as the sum the wire latencies over all the hops that belong to the mentioned route.

Thus,

$$T_{Wire}^{R_i} = \sum_j \sqrt{\int_0^{l_j} \frac{L_0}{W(x)} \int_0^x [C_0 W(y) + C_f] dy dx} \times \delta_{ij} \tag{10}$$

where $T_{Wire}^{R_i}$ is the ith route latency, and

$$\delta_{ij} = \begin{cases} 1, & if j^{th} wire \in R_i, \\ 0, & otherwise. \end{cases} \tag{11}$$

Consequently, the wire latency of the entire network is the sum of the wire latencies of all the routes that belong to the routing table.

2.3 Network Latency

This subsection finalizes the equations that are used to calculate the network latency. In the previous subsections, we already obtained individually the closed form formulas of the queuing latency and the wire latency for one given route.

Based on the the predetermined connection between IPs and the shortest path routing table of a certain mapping scheme of IPs onto the NoC architecture considered in this article, the network latency in terms of the wire and queuing latencies is calculated by

$$T_{Net} = \sum_{i=1}^{m} [T_{Wire}^{R_i} + T_{Queue}^{R_i}], \tag{12}$$

where m is the fixed number of routes belonging to the routing table.

Finally,

$$T_{Net} = \sum_{k=1}^{m} \left[\sum_j \frac{\sum_{i \in \mathbf{C_j}} \lambda_i \frac{1}{\mu_j - \lambda_i}}{\sum_{i \in \mathbf{C_j}} \lambda_i} \delta_{kj} \right] + \sum_{k=1}^{m} \left[\sum_n \sqrt{\int_0^{l_n} \frac{L_0}{W(x)} \int_0^x [C_0 W(y) + C_f] dy dx} \times \delta_{kn} \right], \tag{13}$$

where the δ_{kj} and δ_{kn} are equal to 1 if the jth node and the nth wire belong to the kth route, respectively, otherwise they are equal to 0. Straightforwardly, T_{Net} is the function of mapping IPs onto NoC architecture due to the fact that the mapping scheme changes the given route between the 2 certain IPs changes accordingly. It follows that the network nodes and the wires belonging to this route are different compared to those of the other mapping schemes. Finding the minimum value of the cost function T_{Net} returns the $NP - hard$ problem. To solve it, this article utilizes the Branch and Bound algorithm for the latency metric. This algorithm automatically maps the IPs onto the target NoC architecture to obtain the minimum latency.

3 Optimal Mapping Based on Minimum Latency Criteria

As discussed in the previous sections, the latency of the NoC depends very much on how the mapping scheme of the IPs onto the fixed NoC architecture is established. Simply described, for certain application, we identify that onto which switch should IP be mapped so that the of network latency is minimized under the assumption of the shortest routing algorithm is applied. To do so, we have some definitions as follows:

Definition 1. An IPs Implementation Graph (IIG) $\mathcal{G} = G(V, \lambda)$ is a directed graph where

- Each vertex v_i represents a certain IP.
- Each directed arc λ_{ij} represents the arrival rate of the data packets generated from the ith IP toward j^{th} IP.

Definition 2. An Switching Architecture Graph (SAG) $\mathcal{G}' = G(U, R)$ is a directed graph where

- Each vertex u_i presents a certain switch core, the corresponding μ_j denotes its switch's mean of processing time.
- Each directed arc r_{ij} represents the route from u_i to u_j in the routing table.

Now we can state our mapping problem as follows:

Given an IIP and a SAG graphs that satisfy

$$Size(IIG) \leq Size(SAG), \tag{14}$$

and after mapping, the arc $T(r_{ij})$, as the cost function, denotes the route latency that calculated by the summation of the RHS of the equations (4) and (10). The $Size()$ function denotes the number of vertexes on the graph. The shortest path routing is applied in this context and the cost function of found path is the accumulated latency after every hop.

Find a mapping scheme *map()* from IIP onto ASG which:

$$min\Big\{T_{Net} = \sum_{r_{ij} \in R_T} T(r_{ij})\Big\}, \tag{15}$$

where R_T denotes the routing table, or

$$min\left\{T_{Net} = \sum_{k=1}^{m}\left[\sum_{j}\frac{\sum_{i\in \mathbf{C_j}}\lambda_i\frac{1}{\mu_j-\lambda_i}}{\sum_{i\in \mathbf{C_j}}\lambda_i}\delta_{kj}\right] + \sum_{k=1}^{m}\right.$$
$$\left.\left[\sum_{n}\sqrt{\int_0^{l_n}\frac{L_0}{W(x)}\int_0^{x}\left[C_0W(y)+C_f\right]dydx \times \delta_{kn}}\right]\right\}, \tag{16}$$

such that:

$$\begin{cases} map(v_i) = u_j, \\ \forall v_i \in V, \exists u_j \in U, \\ \forall v_i \neq v_j, map(v_i) \neq map(v_j). \end{cases} \tag{17}$$

Without loosing generality, we assume that $Size(IIG) = p \leq Size(SAG) = q$. The example of mapping of 11 IPs onto the 4×4 Mesh architecture is shown in Fig. 4.

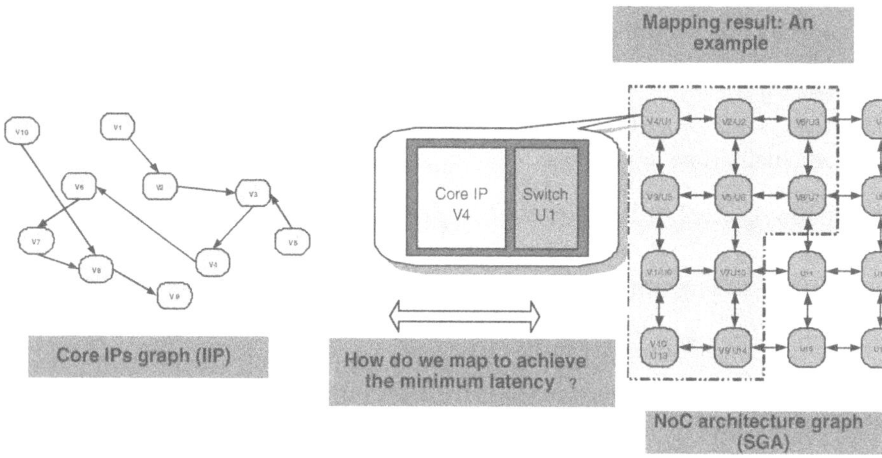

Fig. 4. A mapping example

Since the number of ways of choosing p switches among q switches of the target NoC architecture for p IPs is C_q^p, and also we can have $p!$ permutational cases of p given IPs. It follows that if we apply the simple Min-Max algorithm to find out the minimum network latency accordingly with the optimum mapping scheme, the complexity can be measured by

$$Complexity = O\big(p! \times C_q^p\big). \tag{18}$$

This order of complexity returns the NP-hard search. In order to reduce the complexity while working out the automatically optimal mapping as well as the minimum network latency, we apply the wellknown search algorithm, so called Branch and Bound (BnB) [10]. The adding, removing and sorting path operations of BnB algorithm for figuring out the optimal path (equivalent to finding out the optimal mapping) of this mentioned case are based on the accumulated latency at each network node. The BnB algorithm is shortly presented by the piece of random code depicted in Fig. 5. The *Optimum_mapping_cost* is the minimum latency metric and the *new_path's cost* is the accumulated latency of one route. This route must belong to the shortest path routing table. The optimal mapping's latencies of Mesh and Fat-Tree architectures of OCMN in terms of topology sizes are respectively depicted in Fig. 6 and Fig. 7.

```
Sort the IPs by their arrival rates
Optimum_mapping_cost = + infinity
1. QUEUE  <--  path only containing the root_node;

2. WHILE     (QUEUE is not empty
                        AND first path does not reach goal
(Optimum_mapping_cost)) {
      For each unoccupied switche node {

           create new_path (to a children node);

           allocate routing paths (with respect to shortest
            path routing table);

           calculate the accumulated cost as the
            accumulation of network node latency;
           if (new path's cost < Optimum_mapping_cost){
                      Optimum_mapping_cost = new_path's
                 cost;

                      Optimum_mapping = new-path; }
           add the new_path to the QUEUE;
      }

3. IF Optimum_mapping_cost reached
           THEN success;
           ELSE failure;
```

Fig. 5. The BnB algorithm

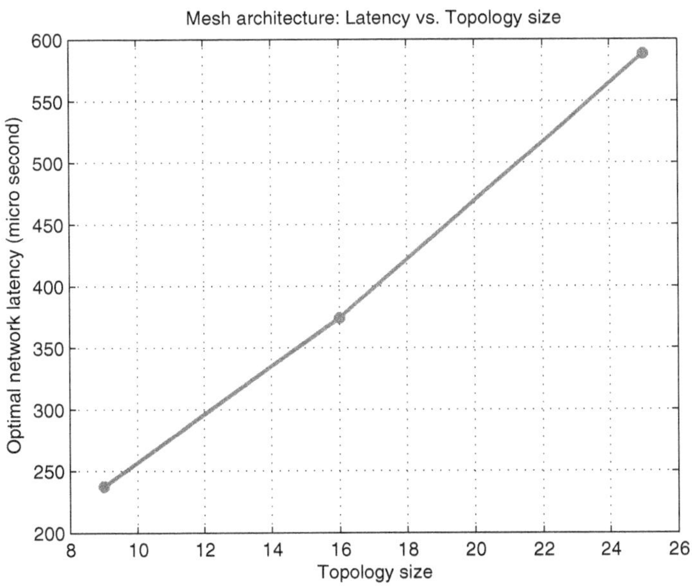

Fig. 6. Optimal network latency of Mesh architecture

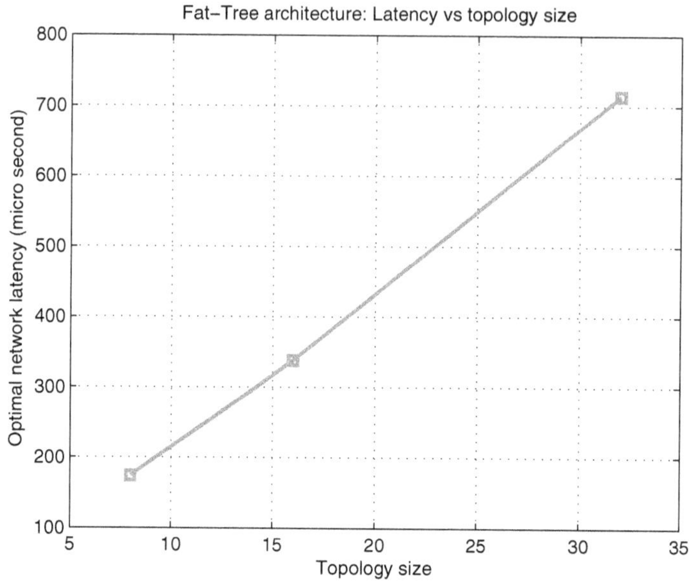

Fig. 7. Optimal network latency of Fat-Tree architecture

Table 1. Mesh architecture of OCMN

Architecture	RM Latency	BnB latency	Latency saved
3 × 3 Mesh	374μs	237.5μs	36.5%
4 × 4 Mesh	627μs	374μs	40.3%
5 × 5 Mesh	836μs	588μs	29.6%

Table 2. Fat-Tree architecture of OCMN

Architecture	RM Latency	BnB latency	Latency saved
8 Fat-Tree	258μs	174μs	32.4%
16 Fat-Tree	516μs	338μs	25.6%
32 Fat-Tree	924μs	714μs	22.7%

As can be seen in this figure, the bigger size or the higher number of mounted IPs and switches is, the more latency occurs. The number of mounted IPs and also the number of switches of Mesh architecture are 9, 16, and 25, respectively. For the Fat-Tree architecture, we simulate three topologies with number of IP are 8, 16, and 32, respectively. The simulation results of this work in terms of latency savings for the Mesh and Fat-Tree architectures of OCMN are depicted in Table 1 and Table 2. As we can see in these table, the most latency saving in case of Mesh architecture is 40.3% compared to Random Mapping (RM) scheme corresponding to 4×4 Mesh, and the most latency saving in case of Fat-Tree architecture is 32.4% compared to RM scheme corresponding to 8 Fat-Tree. We denote the RM schemes are the mapping schemes that IPs are mounted onto switches randomly. Hence, the network latency metrics are randomly achieved. In these experiments, we apply the $0.18\mu m$ technology for the RLC wire model and Markovian models for IPs and switches.

4 Conclusion and Future Work

In this paper, we analyzed the heterogenous NoC network latency in terms of the queuing and wire latencies. We also applied the Branch and Bound algorithm to automatically map the desired IPs onto the pre-selected NoC architecture in order to obtain the minimum latency. We carried out the experiments for generic Mesh and Fat-Tree architectures of OCMN application. The results showed that the optimal network latencies corresponding to optimal mapping of IPs onto NoC architecture are significantly saved in comparison with the random mapping latency. In the future, we have plan to figure out the relationship between the latency and the power in the sense of both analytical analysis as well as simulation for the RTL level of IPs and NoC architectures.

References

1. L. Benini and G. DeMicheli, "Networks On Chips: A new SoC paradigm", IEEE computer, Jan, 2002.
2. A. Agarwal, "Limit on interconnection network performance", Parallel and Distributed Systems, IEEE Transactions on Volume 2, Issue 4, Oct. 1991 pp. 398 - 412.
3. T. Ye, L. Benini and G. De Micheli," Packetization and Routing Analysis of On-Chip MultiProcessor Networks", JSA Journal of System Architecture, Vol. 50, February 2004, pp. 81-104.
4. M. A. El-Moursy and E. G. Friedman, "Desing Methodologies For On-Chip Inductive Interconnection", Chapter. 4, Interconnect-Centric Design For Advanced SoC and NoC, Kluwer Academic Publishers, 2004.
5. R. Ho, et al, "The future of wires," Proceedings of the IEEE, pp. 490 - 504, April 2001.
6. J. Hu, R. Marculescu, "Exploiting the Routing Flexibility for Energy Performance Aware Mapping of Regular NoC Architectures", in Proc. Design, Automation and Test in Europe Conf, March 2003.
7. J. Hu, R. Marculescu, "Energy-Aware Communication and Task Scheduling for Network-on-Chip Architectures under Real-Time Constraints, in Proc. Design, Automation and Test in Europe Conf, Feb. 2004.
8. S.Murali and G.De Micheli, Bandwidth-Constrained Mapping of Cores pnto NoC Architectures, , DATE, International Conference on Design and Test Europe, 2004, pp. 896-901.
9. T. Tao Ye, L. Benini, G. De Micheli, "Packetization and Routing for On-Chip Communication Networks," Journal of System Architecture, special issue on Networks-on-Chip.

10. T. H. Cormen, et al, "Introduction to algorithms," Second Edition, The MIT press, 2001.
11. D. Bertozzi, L. Benini and G.De Micheli, "Network on Chip Design for Gigascale Systems on Chips," in R. Zurawski, Editor, Industrial Technology Handbook, CRC Press, 2004, pp. 95.1-95.18 on Chips, Morgan Kaufmannn, 2004, pp. 49-80.
12. L. Benini and G. De Micheli, "Networks on Chip: A new Paradigm for component-based MPSoC Design," in A. Jerraja and W.Wolf Editors, "Multiprocessor Systems on Chips", Morgan Kaufmannn, 2004, pp. 49-80.
13. D. Bertsekas and R. Gallager, "Data Networks," Chapter 5., Second Edition, Prentice-Hall, Inc., 1992.
14. A. Jalabert, S. Murali, L. Benini, G. De Micheli, "xpipesCompiler: A Tool for instantiating application specific Networks on Chip", Proc. DATE 2004.
15. M. Dall'Osso, G. Biccari, L. Giovannini, D.Bertozzi, L. Benini, "Xpipes: a latency insensitive parameterized network-on-chip architecture for multiprocessor SoCs", 21st International Conference on Computer Design, Oct. 2003, pp. 536 - 539.
16. C. E. Leiserson, "Fat Trees: Universal networks for hardware efficient supercomputing," IEEE Transactions on Computer, C-34, pp. 892-90,1 Oct 1985.

Microprocessor Based Self Schedule and Parallel BIST for System-On-a-Chip

Danghui Wang, Xiaoya Fan, Deyuan Gao, Shengbing Zhang, and Jianfeng An

Aviation Microelectronic Center, Northwestern Polytechnical University,
Xi'an, P.R. China 710072
{wangdh, zhangsb, anjf}@mail.nwpu.edu.cn
{fanxy, gaody}@nwpu.edu.cn

Abstract. The purpose of this paper is to develop a flexible test method with high efficiency for core-based system-on-a-chip (SOC). The novel feature of the approach is the use of an embedded microprocessor/memory pair to test the remaining components of SOCs. The characteristics are: (1) Several IP cores can be tested in parallel; (2) The order of test tasks need not to be queued during test integration, but scheduled by test program. It is called microprocessor based self schedule and parallel BIST for SOC (MBSSP-BIST). By analyzing the bandwidth of test data, the feasibility of MBSSP-BIST is proved. Finally, several SOCs in ITC'02 benchmark are used to verify the approach and the results show that MBSSP-BIST can improve test efficiency significantly.

1 Introduction

Recent development in semiconductor technology have made it possible to design an entire system onto a single chip, commonly known as the System-On-a-Chip (SOC)[1]. A related practice which is evolving is the use of predefined logic called Cores or Macros[2]. A Core is a highly complex logic block which is fully defined in terms of its behavior, also predictable and reusable[2]. System designers can purchase cores from core-vendors and integrate them with their own user-defined logic(UDL)[3] to implement SOCs. It is referred to these designs as core-based systems.

Core-based SOCs have significant advantages. Because most of system is on the same chip, SOCs can operate faster with less power. SOCs reduce the number of discrete components used, thereby reducing the total size and cost of the end-product. Furthermore, using embedded cores in SOCs has the potential of greatly reducing the time-to-market because of the design re-use involved.

Testing core-based systems is a major challenge. The major factor is that the accessibility of the cores and blocks is greatly reduced. Furthermore, the system designer might have a restricted knowledge of the core internals due to the protection of Intellectual Property(IP) of the cores.

Unlike the way smaller designs are tested, SOCs cannot be tested as a single unit because such a test solution would give a poor fault-coverage and the overall test generation is impractical, and often impossible. A better way to test SOCs is testing

L.T. Yang et al. (Eds.): ICESS 2005, LNCS 3820, pp. 299–309, 2005.

each of the cores separately, with other tests to determine whether the system functions as a whole.

Researchers have focused on several aspects of the SOC testing, such as Test Access Mechanism(TAM)[4][5][6], Test Wrapper design[7][8][9], Test Scheduling and optimization[10][11][12][13], etc. All these researches are based on the testing method that uses the Automation Test Equipment(ATE) directly. According to ITRS01, the ATE performance is improving at a much slower rate than the speed of the device. This implies an increasing yield loss due to external testing since ground-banding to cover tester errors results in a loss of more and more otherwise good chips. Furthermore, high-speed testers are very costly and might not be available for some high performance chips.

Built-in self-test(BIST) and design-for-testability(DFT) have been regarded as possible solutions. BIST solutions eliminate the need for high speed testers and offer the ability to apply and analyze at-speed test signals on chip with greater accuracy than that of the tester. However, the addition of DFT hardware incurs non-trivial area, performance, and design time overhead, and thus slowing down the time-to-market. In addition, existing structural BIST techniques cause abnormal power consumption due to the high-switching random patterns applied in the test mode. Therefore, new BIST techniques have to be developed.

2 Related Works

In IP core based SOCs, examples of IPs are microprocessors, DSPs, PCI, MPEG and JPEG cores. In addition, memory cells such as RAM/ROM may be embedded in SOC. User defined logic(UDL) consists of all other logic entities added by the user to customize the circuit. The embedded microprocessors or DSPs can realize complicate functions, and can be used to test other parts of the SOCs.

Kwang Ting Chen et al proposed an "embedded software-based self-test for SOC design"[14]. They constructed an SOC based on PCI bus. The SOC contains a microprocessor. Test program can be downloaded into the embedded memory first, then microprocessor runs in functional mode and executes the test program. The test program contains test pattern generation, test pattern application and test response analysis. In this method, IP testing and connection testing can be done with the microprocessor on the SOC, and this can eliminate the requirement of the high-speed, high accuracy ATE.

Like Kwang Ting Chen, Papachristou et al also uses a microprocessor as test controller. In this research, IP core vendor is responsible for test pattern generation. IP testing is divided into three steps: (1)Download phase, the compressed test data are organized into frame format and downloaded into the embedded memory through DMA interface. (2) Test pattern application, the embedded microprocessor reads test data from memory, decompresses them and then applies the decompressed data on the IP under test. Once an IP testing begins, the IP occupies the microprocessor and memory until its testing is over. (3) Test response analysis, when a test pattern is applied on the IP core, test controller reads the response and compares it with the anticipated response to see if there are errors in the circuit.

Compared to the conventional structural BIST, the above two methods improve test efficiency, and have the following characteristics: (1)Resource reuse; (2) Test costs reduction; (3) Test accuracy improvement; (4) Functional test and at-speed test.

In the methods, all the IPs in an SOC are tested serially. When an IP test task occupies the test controller, embedded memory and data bus, it will not release these resources until its test task is finished, even if these resources are idle during its test procedure. This obviously reduces the usage efficiency of these test resources.

In the methods, the order of all the test tasks are queued in the test integration procedure. But the different test order can result in different test time[15], so test integration engineers have to schedule the test order elaborately, and this is an aspect of test schedule, and is also an NP complete problem which can be solved by all kinds of heuristic algorithms. These algorithms have high complexity and long computation time, which reduce the test development efficiency and prolong the test development.

This paper proposes a test method named "Microprocessor Based Self Schedule and Parallel BIST" for SOC, which does not need to order the test tasks manually and can test different IPs in parallel.

3 Basic Method

In order to improve the usage of the microprocessor, memory and system bus, different steps of IP test can be overlapped, this method results in parallel testing of different IPs.

Because of the programmability of the embedded microprocessor, if a test task (IP1) does not need shared test resources for a period of time before its test procedure finishes, these test resources can be assigned to other test tasks. In this period, IP1 tests itself under the control of its local test resources, such as scan chain controller or BIST controller etc. This can overlap the test steps of different test tasks as fig.1.

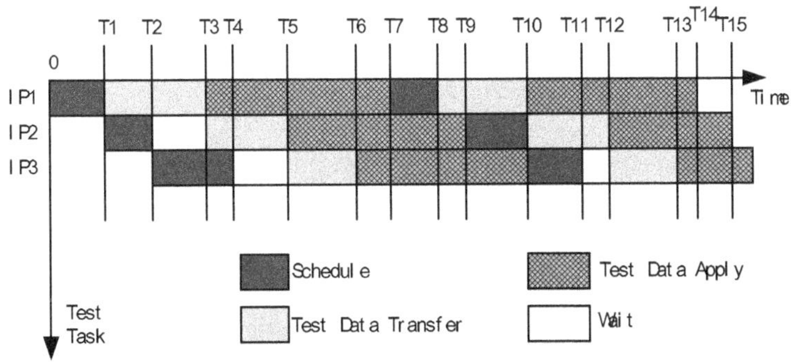

Fig. 1. Parallel Test

In Fig.1, during period 0~T1, microprocessor is used to schedule for IP1, data bus is used to transfer test data for IP1 during period T1~T3, the local DFT circuit of IP1 is working and applying test data during period T3~T7. In the same way, IP2 is scheduling during T1~T2, transferring test data during T3~T5, and applying test data during T5~T9. From the figure, it can be seen that during period T5~T6, IP1 and IP2 are tested in parallel, and IP1, IP2 and IP3 are tested in parallel during T6~T7.

Because there exist many memories in SOCs, the test state of every IP core can be stored in memories. Software which runs on the microprocessor can record the execution of every test task and every test resource, and can decide which test task will be served in the next period. This test schedule is controlled by the test program which is stored in the embedded memories, rather than controlled by the test integration engineers during test integration period. This method has the characteristic of self schedule.

In fig.2, at the T7 moment, IP1 cannot execute its test procedure because there is either no test data to consume or no space to store test response, IP1 has to send a request to test controller. But at this moment, test controller is serving for IP2, IP1 has to send the request repeatedly. IP3 sends a request at T8 moment. At T9 moment, IP2's request has been finished and the test controller becomes idle, IP1 and IP3 are both sending request at this moment. The arbiter program in the test program selects one of the IPs of IP1 and IP3 according to their request types and the states of the shared resources. In fig.2, IP3 is selected at the T9. At the T12 moment, the test task of IP2 is finished, the test controller selects IP4 from waiting queue and actives it.

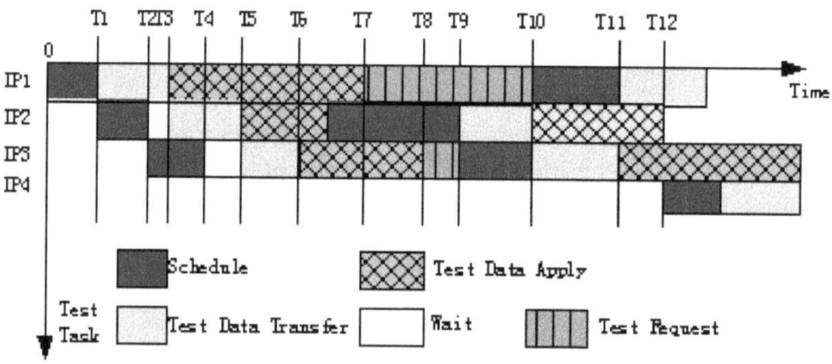

Fig. 2. Self Schedule

The test method is called "Microprocessor Based Self Schedule and Parallel Built-in-Self-Test" (MBSSP-BIST).

The conceptual architecture of MBSSP-BIST is shown in fig.3. Test program and test data are stored in External Tester, which can be a cheap, low-speed ATE or a computer system. When the test procedure begins, test data and test program are downloaded into embedded memories through Memory/IO Interface. Microprocessor is working in functional mode, fetching instructions and executing test program. At the appropriate moment, microprocessor transfers test data from memories to the wrapper of IP through system bus. The IP under test is tested by the control circuit located in wrapper, and the test response is stored into the buffer in the wrapper. Microprocessor reads test response from buffer and analyzes it at the appropriate moment.

From fig.3, it can be seen that there are several buffers on the path from external tester to IP under test. These buffers can act as pipeline buffers and support parallel test. In this architecture, the required hardware almost exists in the architecture of SOC test which uses ATE directly. As a path that transfers data in/out of SOCs, Memory/IO interface is a dedicated unit for all SOCs, memory and microprocessor(or DSP) almost exist in all SOCs. System bus can be reused in test mode. IP wrapper must be added in structural test. So in MBSSP-BIST, little hardware has to be added.

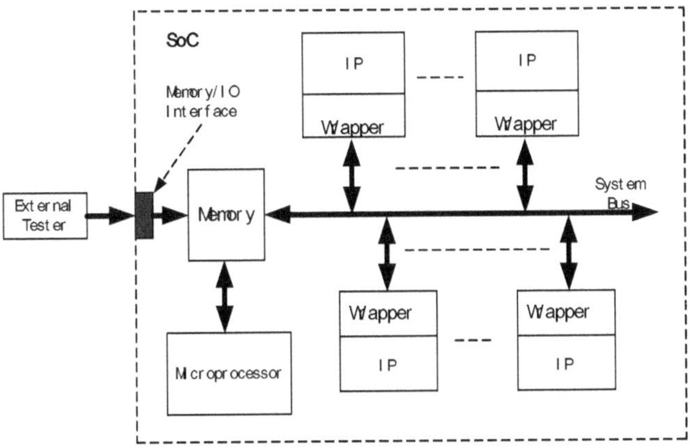

Fig. 3. Conceptual Architecture

Because there are memories used as data buffers, the real test speed can be higher than that of the External Tester.

4 Feasibility Analysis

When testing an SOC with ATE directly, test data transfer from external tester to circuit under test (CUT) through TAM, the bandwidth of tester is equal to the bandwidth of the CUT consuming, so the test speed is under restriction of the tester's speed and the TAM width.

Assuming the frequency of the memory/IO interface is $f_{Mem/IO}$, the width of the data is $W_{Mem/IO}$, the speed of test data transferring from external tester to SOCs is $V_{Mem/IO} = f_{Mem/IO} \times W_{Mem/IO}$. In the same way, test data consumption speed is $V_{internal} = f_{internal} \times W_{internal}$, where $f_{internal}$ is the test frequency of IP, and $W_{internal}$ is the test data consumed in one cycle.

In order to describe the problem, 2 conceptions are defined:

Definition 1: Test Data Flux on Interface is the amount of test data transferred through Memory/IO interface to SOC under test, and is identified as $M_{Mem/IO}$.

Definition 2: Equality Test Data Flux is the real amount of test data applied on the circuit under test, and is identified as $M_{equality}$. It determines the time that test data can be consumed. For scanned circuits, $M_{equality}$ equals to the amount of test data transferred through Scan-in and Scan-out port of the scan chains. For BISTed circuits which use pseudo-random method, $M_{equality}$ is the amount of test data that are generated by the longest LFSR.

From these 2 definitions, the test data transfer time $T_{transfer}$ and the test data consumed time $T_{consume}$ can be defined as follows:

$$T_{transfer} = M_{mem/IO} / V_{Mem/IO} = M_{Mem/IO} / (f_{Mem/IO} \times W_{Mem/IO}) \tag{1}$$

$$T_{consume} = M_{equality} / V_{internal} = M_{equality} / (f_{internal} \times W_{internal}) \tag{2}$$

The relationship of these 2 values can be used to prove that the parallel test is reasonable. The ratio of the two values is:

$$\begin{aligned} & T_{consume} / T_{transfer} \\ &= [M_{equality} / (f_{internal} \times W_{internal})] / [M_{Mem/IO} / (f_{Mem/IO} \times W_{Mem/IO})] \\ &= (M_{equality} / M_{Mem/IO}) \times (f_{Mem/IO} / f_{internal}) \times (W_{internal} / W_{Mem/IO}) \end{aligned} \tag{3}$$

For any IP core, $(M_{equality} / M_{Mem/IO}) \geq 1$, when $f_{internal} = f_{Mem/IO}$, ATE tests the IP core directly. $W_{Mem/IO}$ is the data bus width of the SOC, which is generally 32 bits at the current manufacturing techniques. $W_{internal}$ is the amount of test data consumed by the circuit in one cycle, and it equals to the number of scan chains when the DFT method of the circuit is scan. From the analysis of the benchmark circuits in ITC'02, it can be seen that most of the IP cores have less than four scan chains [16]. For a single IP , the speed of the memory/IO interface is fast enough to provide test data, and because of $W_{Mem/IO} > W_{internal}$, the value of expression (3) is larger than 1, it is possible for multiple IP cores to be connected on test bus to realize parallel test, but the frequency of the ATE and test are equal.

When $f_{internal} > f_{Mem/IO}$, $f_{Mem/IO} / f_{internal} < 1$, because $W_{internal} / W_{Mem/IO} > 1$ and $M_{equality} / M_{Mem/IO} \geq 1$, the value of expression (3) is possibly larger than 1, and possibly less than 1. From the analysis result of ITC'02 Benchmark, it can be seen that the value of $W_{internal} / W_{Mem/IO}$ is about 8, so the value of expression (3) will not be less than 1 if $f_{Mem/IO} / f_{internal}$ is not less than 1/8, which is reasonable under the current technique.

Furthermore, the value of $M_{equality} / M_{Mem/IO}$ can be discussed. According to the types of DFT and the application method of test patterns, IP cores can be classed into the following types: (1) Cores with decompressed and deterministic test patterns. These cores have the characteristic that $(M_{Mem/IO})_{\det er\min istic} = (M_{equality})_{\det er\min isitic}$. (2) Cores with compressed and deterministic test patterns. The compressed ratio is K, that is, $(M_{Mem/IO})_{compressed} / (M_{equality})_{compressed} = K$. (3)Cores with structural BIST. When testing these cores, only the BIST circuits need to be activated. When BIST finishes, BIST results are read and analyzed. In this case, test data transferring through memory/IO interface is only the length of 2 instructions, and the amount of test data applied to the CUT is the test data generated by the DFT circuit. $(M_{Mem/IO})_{BISTed} = 2 \times instruction\_length$ bits, where *instruction_length* is generally 32 bits, $(M_{Mem/IO})_{BISTed} = 64$ bits. In BISTed circuit, it is the most popular to generate test patterns with LFSR, an n bits LFSR can generate $(2^n - 1) \times n$ bits test data. Because all the LFSRs in a IP can work in parallel, $(M_{equality})_{BISTed} = (2^n - 1) \times n$ bits, where $n = \max(l_i)$, and l_i is the length of ith LFSR. (4)Cores with pseudo-random test pattern generated by software. In this case, software simulates LFSR to generate test patterns, $(M_{Mem/IO})_{P\_BISTed} = instruction\_nubmer \times instruction\_length$ bits, $(M_{equality})_{P\_BISTed} = (2^n - 1) \times n$ bits. In any microprocessor, a software program which simulates LFSR has instructions less than several hundred.

Suppose in an SOC, the number of cores of these 4 types are $j_{\det er\min istic}, j_{compressed}$, j_{BISTed} and j_{P_BISTed}, the total amount of test data to be downloaded through memory/IO interface is:

$$M_{Mem/IO} = \sum_{i=1}^{j_{\det er\min istcic}} [(M_{Mem/IO})_{\det er\min istic}]_i + \sum_{i=1}^{j_{compressed}} [(M_{Mem/IO})_{compressed}]_i + \sum_{i=1}^{j_{BISTed}} [(M_{Mem/IO})_{BISTed}]_i + \sum_{i=1}^{j_{P\_BISTed}} [(M_{Mem/IO})_{P\_BISTed}]_i \tag{4}$$

The amount of test data applied on the CUT is :

$$M_{equality} = \sum_{i=1}^{j_{\det er\min istcic}} [(M_{equality})_{\det er\min istic}]_i + \sum_{i=1}^{j_{compressed}} [(M_{equality})_{compressed}]_i + \sum_{i=1}^{j_{BISTed}} [(M_{equality})_{BISTed}]_i + \sum_{i=1}^{j_{P\_BISTed}} [(M_{equality})_{P\_BISTed}]_i \tag{5}$$

So, we have expressions (6) (on the next page). In expressions (6), the two parts of the denominator $\sum_{i=1}^{j_{BISTed}} [(M_{Mem/IO})_{BISTed}]_i$ and $\sum_{i=1}^{j_{P\_BISTed}} [(M_{Mem/IO})_{P\_BISTed}]_i$ is much small compared to test data applied to the CUT, so they can be ignored approximately. In this way, expression (6) changes to expression (7).

$$(M_{equal} / M_{Mem/IO}) = \{ \sum_{i=1}^{j_{deterministic}} [(M_{equality})_{deterministic}]_i + \sum_{i=1}^{j_{compressed}} [(M_{equality})_{compressed}]_i + \sum_{i=1}^{j_{BISTed}} [(M_{equality})_{BISTed}]_i + \sum_{i=1}^{j_{P\_BISTed}} [(M_{equality})_{P\_BISTed}]_i \} \div \{ \sum_{i=1}^{j_{deterministic}} [(M_{Mem/IO})_{deterministic}]_i + \sum_{i=1}^{j_{compressed}} [(M_{Mem/IO})_{compressed}]_i + \sum_{i=1}^{j_{BISTed}} [(M_{Mem/IO})_{BISTed}]_i + \sum_{i=1}^{j_{P\_BISTed}} [(M_{Mem/IO})_{P\_BISTed}]_i \} \tag{6}$$

expression (7) is as follows:

$$(M_{equality} / M_{Mem/IO}) = \{ \sum_{i=1}^{j_{deterministic}} [(M_{equality})_{deterministic}]_i + \sum_{i=1}^{j_{compressed}} [(M_{equality})_{compressed}]_i + \sum_{i=1}^{j_{BISTed}} [(M_{equality})_{BISTed}]_i + \sum_{i=1}^{j_{P\_BISTed}} [(M_{equality})_{P\_BISTed}]_i \} \div \sum_{i=1}^{j_{deterministic}} [(M_{Mem/IO})_{deterministic}]_i + \sum_{i=1}^{j_{compressed}} [(M_{Mem/IO})_{compressed}]_i \tag{7}$$

For cores with compressed and deterministic test patterns, it is assumed that the compressed ratio for i^{th} core is K_i. For cores with decompressed and deterministic test patterns, their compressed ratio can be considered 1, so expression (7) changes as follows:

$$(M_{equality} / M_{Mem/IO}) = \{ \sum_{i=1}^{j_{compressed}} [(M_{equality})_{compressed}]_i + \sum_{i=1}^{j_{BISTed}} [(M_{equality})_{BISTed}]_i + \sum_{i=1}^{j_{P\_BISTed}} [(M_{equality})_{P\_BISTed}]_i \} \div \sum_{i=1}^{j_{compressed}} K_i \times [(M_{equality})_{compressed}]_i \tag{8}$$

Because $K_i \le 1$, expression (9) can be deduced (On the next page):

From $(f_{Mem/IO} / f_{internal}) \times (W_{internal} / W_{Mem/IO}) > 1$, by replacing the appropriate parts in expression (3), the following result can be obtained: $T_{consume} / T_{transfer} > 1$

In order to eliminate the inaccuracy of ATE, more and more IP cores take BIST or pseudo-BIST as their DFTs, and this results in the last part of the numerator in expression (8) larger and larger, the denominator smaller and smaller, and the value of $M_{equality} / M_{Mem/IO}$ larger and larger , which causes $T_{consume} / T_{transfer}$ to become larger and larger.

$$(M_{equality} / M_{Mem/IO}) \geq 1 + \frac{\sum_{i=1}^{j_{BISTed}} [(M_{equality})_{BISTed}]_i + \sum_{i=1}^{j_{P\_BISTed}} [(M_{equality})_{P\_BISTed}]}{\sum_{i=1}^{j_{compressed}} K_i \times [(M_{equality})_{compressed}]_i} \quad (9)$$

For certain number of IP cores, several test tasks can run parallel if $T_{consume} / T_{transfer} > 1$. If the value of $T_{consume} / T_{transfer}$ is larger than the number of IP cores under test, all the cores can be tested at-speed. If the value of $T_{consume} / T_{transfer}$ is less, some of IP cores under test can be tested at-speed, and this is valuable if some IPs must detect delay faults.

5 Experiment Results

An experiment environment is constructed to verify the MBSSP-BIST according fig.3. In the experiment, a microprocessor based on Intel 486DX4 is used as test controller, the circuits in ITC'02 are used as IP cores. They are connected through a 32-bit data bus. The width of data bus is also extended to 64 bits. Some logic that is only for test purpose is added to the processor and a kind of IP test wrapper is designed. A test control program is designed to control the test procedure according to the basic method of MBSSP-BIST in section 3.

The test time of every SOC is shown in Table1.

Table 1. Experiment for ITC'02

SOC	TAM Width	[17][1]	[17][2]	[17][3]	M-BIST[4]
D695	32	87400	67680	49927	40841
	64	38006	27804	24688	20699
P22810	32	657574	590661	518722	422453
	64	630646	319212	270676	211385
P34392	32	1923386	1468967	121589 6	992425
	64	1278277	633937	610760	534613
P93791	32	3905079	2575413	1974419	1667646
	64	1532709	1127242	1076828	947649

Notes: 1. Only one Scan Enable Pin.
2. A Scan Enable Pin per TAM.
3. Pin-Constrained TR-Architect.
4. MBSSP-BIST.

In this case, test control signals[17] are considered. The test time is given in test clock cycles. From the experiment, it can be deduced that MBSSP-BIST also improves the efficiency of TAM bandwidth. The improved ratio is shown as Table 2.

Table 2. The Improved Ratio of ITC'02

SOC	TAM Width	[17][1]	[17][2]	[17][3]
D695	32	53.68%	40.19%	18.92%
	64	45.54%	25.55%	16.16%
P22810	32	35.76%	28.48%	18.56%
	64	66.48%	33.78%	21.90%
P34392	32	48.40%	24.44%	18.38%
	64	58.18%	15.67%	12.47%
P93791	32	57.30%	35.25%	15.54%
	64	38.17%	15.93%	12.00%

From Table 2, it can be seen that MBSSP-BIST improves by about 12.00%~21.90% compared to other methods when the test frequency equals to that of external tester. In MBSSP-BIST, because the test frequency can be higher than that of external tester, the test efficiency will be improved more notably.

6 Conclusion

In this paper, a test method named MBSSP-BIST is proposed. Based on the microprocessor and memories embedded on SOCs, every test task of IP cores can be done as software program of microprocessor. Using this test method, test integration engineers need not schedule the IP test order, this work is done by the test program during test procedure. This can greatly reduce the work of test integration engineers and improve test development efficiency. Since the test procedure is divided into several phases and can be overlapped, and since the SOC test speed is not limited to the tester's speed, the overall testing time is reduced.

References

[1] VISA. VSI Alliance Test Access Architecture Version1.0(TST 21.0). http://www.vsi.org. (2001. 9)

[2] K. Dc, "Test Methodology for Embedded Cores Which Protects Intellectual Property", VLSI Test Sym. (1997). 2-9,

[3] N. Touba and B. Pouya, "Testing Embedded Cores Using Partial Isolation Rings", VLSI Test Sym. (1997). 10-16,

[4] Mounir Benabdenbi, Walid Maroufi, Meryem Marzouki: CAS-BUS:a Test Access Mechanism and a Toolbos Environment for Core-based System Chip Testing. Journal of Electronic Test: Theory and Application. (2002)

[5] Erik Jan Marinissen, Robert Arendsen, Gerard Bos, Hans Dingenmanse, Maurice Lousberg, and Clements Wouters: A Structured And Scalable Mechanism for Test Access to Embedded Reusable Cores. Proceedings IEEE International Test Conference(ITC), (1998), PP284-293

[6] I. Ghosh, S. Dey, N.K. Jha: A Fast and Low-Cost Testing Technique for Core-Based System-Chips. IEEE Transactions on Computer-Aided Design of Integrated Circuits and Systems. Vol. 19, NO.8 (2000), 863-877,

[7] Yervant Zorian: System-on-Chip: Embedded Test in Practice. The 12th Asia Test Symposium Tutorial. (2003)
[8] E.J. Marinissen, R. Kapur, M. Lousberg, T. Mclaurin, M. Ricchetti, Y. Zorian: On IEEE P1500's Standard for Embedded Core Test. Journal of Electronic Testing: Theory and Application, Volume 18(2002), 365-283.
[9] S. Koranne: A Novel Reconfigurable Wrapper for Testing of Embedded Core-Bsed SOCs and its AsSOCiated Scheduling Algorithm, Journal of Electronic Testing: Theory and Application, Volume18,issues 4-5(2002)
[10] E. Larsson, Z. Peng: Testing Scheduling and Scan-Chain Division Under Power Constraint. IEEE Proc. Asia Test Symposium,(2001),259-264,
[11] M. Sugihara, H. Date, H. Yasuura: A Novel Test Methodology for Core-Based System LSIs and a Testing Time Minimization Problem. IEEE Proc. International Test Conference(1998),465-472
[12] W. Jiang, B.Vinnakota, Defect-Oriented Test Scheduling. IEEE Transactions on VLSI Systems, Volume 9, Issue 3(2001),427-438
[13] T. J. Chakraborty, Test Scheduling for Core-Based Systems. Computer-Aided Design, Volume11 (2000). 391 – 394
[14] Angela Krstic, Li Chen, Wei-Cheng Lai, Kwang-Ting Cheng, Sujit Dey: Embedded Software-Based Self-Test for Programmable Core-Based Designs. IEEE Design & Test of Computer, Volume 19, Issue 4(2002), 18-27
[15] C. A. Papachristou, F. Martin, M. Nourani: Microprocessor Based Testing for Core-Based System on Chip. Proceeding of Design and Automaton Conference(1999), 586-591
[16] IEEE P1500 Standard for Embedded Core Test. http://grouper.ieee.org/group/1500. (2003)
[17] Wei Zou, Sudhakar M. Reddy, Irith Pomeranz, Yu Hhuang: SOC Test Scheduling Using Simulated Annealing. Proceedings of the 21st IEEE VLSI Test Symposium(2003), 325-330.

Self-correction of FPGA-Based Control Units

Iouliia Skliarova

University of Aveiro, Department of Electronics and Telecommunications, IEETA,
3810-193 Aveiro, Portugal
iouliia@det.ua.pt
http://www.ieeta.pt/~iouliia/

Abstract. This paper presents a self-correcting control unit design using Hamming codes for finite state machine (FSM) state encoding. The adopted technique can correct single-bit errors and detect two-bit errors in the FSM register within the same clock cycle. The main contribution is the development of a parameterizable VHDL package and the respective error-correcting modules, which can easily be added to an FSM specification using any state assignment strategy and having any number of inputs, outputs and states. Besides of application to FSM error correction, the developed tools can easily be adapted to other applications where error detection and correction is required.

Keywords: Self-correcting finite state machines, Hamming codes, specification in VHDL.

1 Introduction

Concurrent error detection and correction is very important in many high-reliability applications. Nowadays, FPGA are increasingly being used for such applications, working in hazardous operating environments. In such circumstances, radiation or overheating can cause either a temporary or a permanent fault in a system prohibiting that it functions correctly.

A control part of the system is the most critical part since it plays the central role in correct functioning of the whole system. Therefore, providing the control units with the properties of self-checking and self-correction is very important.

A number of synthesis techniques have been proposed aimed at design of control units with concurrent error detection [1-3]. These techniques permit a circuit to be synthesized that is capable of providing the identification of an erroneous behavior as soon as it is observable. In this paper, we propose using error-correcting codes that allow for changing the illegal system state to the correct state.

For such purposes, a VHDL package has been developed that includes functions required for generating error-correcting codes and a number of VHDL modules have been designed that make use of these functions and can be employed for constructing a self-correcting control circuit. Besides of specifying self-correcting control units, the developed tools can directly be used for providing error correction and detection properties in other application domains, such as communication systems (data networks, memory caches, etc.).

L.T. Yang et al. (Eds.): ICESS 2005, LNCS 3820, pp. 310–319, 2005.

This paper is organized in 5 sections. Section 2 that follows this introduction is devoted to an overview of the adopted error-correcting codes. Section 3 proposes a general structure of self-correcting control unit and includes the detailed description of the developed VHDL functions and modules. The results of experiments are reported in section 4. Finally, concluding remarks are given in section 5.

2 Error Correction

The control units are usually modeled with the aid of *Finite State Machines* (FSMs). An FSM can be defined as a 6-tuple $M = (S, X, Y, \varphi, \psi, s_0)$, where $S=\{s_0,\ldots,s_{M-1}\}$ is a finite set of states, $X=\{x_0,\ldots,x_{L-1}\}$ is a finite set of inputs, $Y=\{y_0,\ldots,y_{N-1}\}$ is a finite set of outputs, φ: $S \times X \rightarrow S$ is the next state function, ψ: $S \times X \rightarrow Y$ is the output function, and $s_0 \in S$ is the initial state.

The hardware model of FSM is shown in fig. 1. The FSM consists of a combinational circuit (that produces the primary outputs and calculates the next state based on the input values and the present state) and a register (a number of flip-flops or latches) that stores the present FSM state. If the FSM register experiences a fault, it could place the FSM in either a legal (but not correct) state or an illegal state. To allow for recovering from such erroneous state transitions, Hamming codes [4] can be used for state encoding. Hamming codes have a minimum distance of 3 (between different code words) and can therefore be employed for correcting any single-bit fault.

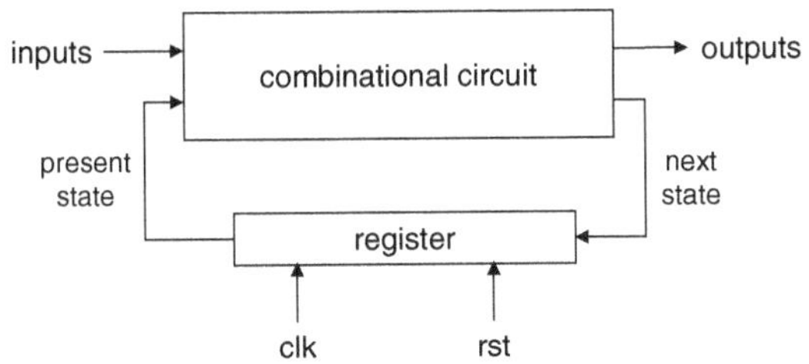

Fig. 1. Hardware model of FSM

Hamming codes can easily be constructed for any FSM encoding scheme, such as one-hot, Gray, etc. For d data bits, the Hamming method requires adding p parity bits, such that $d \leq 2^p-1-p$, thus yielding $(d+p)$-bit codes. The bit positions in a Hamming code can be numbered from 1 through $d+p$. In this case, those bit positions whose number is a power of 2 are parity bits, and the remaining positions are data bits.

Fig. 2 illustrates how a 10-bit state code can be augmented with parity bits. Each parity bit is grouped with a subset of those data bits whose numbers have a 1 in the same bit when expressed in binary. For instance, parity bit p_0 with position 1_{10} ($000\mathbf{1}_2$) is grouped with data bits with positions 3 ($001\mathbf{1}_2$), 5($010\mathbf{1}_2$), 7($011\mathbf{1}_2$), 9($100\mathbf{1}_2$), 11($101\mathbf{1}_2$), and 13 ($110\mathbf{1}_2$) as illustrated by dashed arrows in the upper part of fig. 2. Then, such a value is assigned to each parity bit as to guarantee that the respective group produces even parity (has an even number of 1s).

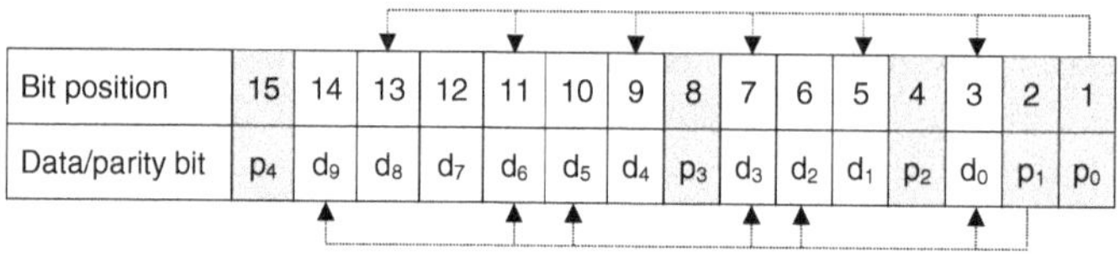

Fig. 2. Hamming code data and parity bits

A distance-3 Hamming code can easily be modified to obtain a distance-4 code by adding one more parity bit (overall parity bit p_4 in fig. 2) chosen so that the parity of all the bits including the new one is even. This new code can detect double errors that are not correctable.

For error correction, all the parity groups are checked. The possible error types and the respective actions to take are summarized in table 1. If one or more parity groups have odd parity and the overall parity bit is 0, then a double-bit error has occurred, which is not correctable. If all the parity groups have even parity then the state code is assumed to be correct. Otherwise, if one or more groups have odd parity and the overall parity bit is 1, then a single-bit error is supposed to have occurred. In this case, a syndrome (the pattern of groups that have odd parity) is created indicating the bit position whose value is assumed to be wrong and consequently has to be complemented. The syndrome can be calculated by XOR-ing the parity bits read out of the FSM register with the new parity bits generated from the data stored in the register. For example, if the FSM register outputs the code 000000000000100, then the new parity bits p_0 (with position 1) and p_1 (with position 2) will have odd parity corresponding to the position 3 ($0001_2 \oplus 0010_2 = 0011_2$) whose value has to be complemented producing the correct state code 000000000000000.

Table 1. Error detection and correction

Syndrome	Overall parity bit	Error type and actions to take
$= 0$	0	no error
$= 0$	1	overall parity bit error; no problem for correct FSM operation
$\neq 0$	0	double-bit error; not correctable
$\neq 0$	1	single-bit error; correctable by calculating the syndrome and inverting the respective bit position

3 Self-correcting FSM

3.1 Hardware Model

The hardware model of self-correcting FSM is presented in fig. 3. The *Parity Encoder* block creates the parity bits to store with the FSM state bits in the FSM register. The parity bits can trivially be calculated by XOR-ing the relevant FSM state bits.

The *Code Corrector* block receives the present state from the FSM register and corrects it if required. For such purposes the syndrome is generated by calculating the new parity bits and XOR-ing them with the parity bits read out of the register. Then, a correction mask is produced based on the result of the syndrome.

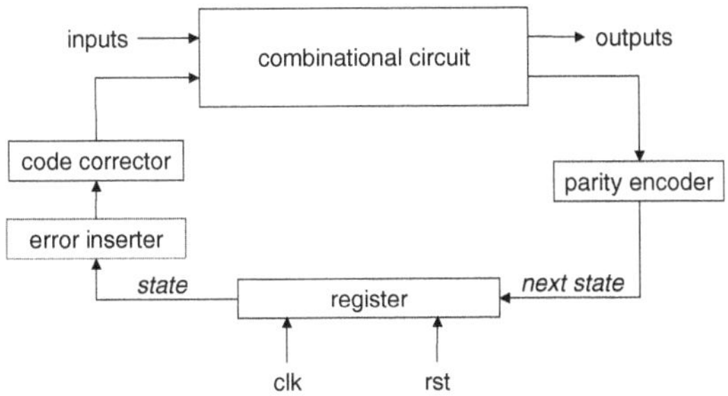

Fig. 3. Hardware model of self-correcting FSM

When either no error is detected or a double error is detected, all the bits of the mask are set to 0. Otherwise the mask is generated so as to conceal all the state bits except for the erroneous bit. Finally, the mask is XOR-ed with the data read out of the FSM register. As a result, when no single-bit errors are detected, the FSM state passes through the *Code Corrector* without any changes, whereas when a single-bit error is detected the corrupted bit is inverted to the correct value. It is important that error correction is performed within the same clock cycle.

To allow for diagnosis, *Error Inserter* block is used to introduce single or multiple bit errors to the FSM state (see fig. 3).

3.2 Specification in VHDL

To facilitate the VHDL description of the blocks introduced in section 3.1, a package `parity_types` was developed, which includes the following functions:

- `Function` **`calculate_parity`** `(constant state : in std_logic_vector; constant n : in natural) return std_logic` – this function receives two parameters: an FSM state and a number of a parity group, and calculates the required parity bit value for this parity group;
- `Function` **`calculate_mask`** `(constant syndrome : in std_logic_vector; constant n : in natural) return std_logic_vector` – this function receives a syndrome and the number of bits used for FSM state encoding and generates the mask used for correcting single-bit errors;

These functions are described in VHDL as indicated in fig. 4 for FSMs using at most 11 bits for state encoding and consequently requiring at most 4 parity bits (not counting the overall parity bit). This restriction is due to the space limitations. In order to support more bits for state encoding only two constant arrays `parity_table` and mask_table (and the respective data types) have to be modified; the functions themselves do not require any changes to be introduced.

```
library IEEE;
use IEEE.STD_LOGIC_1164.all;
use IEEE.STD_LOGIC_UNSIGNED.all;

package parity_types is

  type PAR is array (natural range 0 to 3) of std_logic_vector(10 downto 0);
  type MASK is array (natural range 0 to 15) of std_logic_vector(10 downto 0);

   constant parity_table   : PAR := (0 => "10101011011",  1 => "11001101101",
                                      2 => "11110001110",  3 => "11111110000");

   constant mask_table   : MASK := ( 0 => "00000000000",   1 => "00000000000",
                                      2 => "00000000000",   3 => "00000000001",
                                      4 => "00000000000",   5 => "00000000010",
                                      6 => "00000000100",   7 => "00000001000",
                                      8 => "00000000000",   9 => "00000010000",
                                     10 => "00000100000",  11 => "00001000000",
                                     12 => "00010000000",  13 => "00100000000",
                                     14 => "01000000000",  15 => "10000000000");

  function calculate_parity (constant state : in std_logic_vector;
                             constant n : in natural) return std_logic;
  function calculate_mask   (constant syndrome : in std_logic_vector;
                             constant n : in natural) return std_logic_vector;
end parity_types;


package body parity_types is

function calculate_parity (constant state : in std_logic_vector;
                           constant n : in natural) return std_logic is
    variable masked : std_logic_vector(state'high downto 0);
    variable result : std_logic;
  begin
      masked := state and parity_table(n)(state'high downto 0);
      result := '0';

      for i in masked'range loop
            result := result xor (masked(i));
      end loop;

      return result;
  end function calculate_parity;


function calculate_mask (constant syndrome : in std_logic_vector;
                         constant n : in natural) return std_logic_vector is
    variable mask : std_logic_vector(n downto 0);
    variable address : natural range mask_table'range;
  begin
      address := conv_integer(syndrome);
      mask := mask_table(address)(n downto 0);
      return mask;
  end function calculate_mask;

end parity_types;
```

Fig. 4. VHDL package defining functions and data types required for parity calculation and error correction

In the developed package two data types are declared. The first data type `PAR` is an array of four 11-bit standard logic vectors. A constant `parity_table` of type `PAR`, for every parity group (from 0 to 3), marks by 1s the FSM state bits that have to be used for calculating the parity of the group. For example, in order to calculate the parity bit p_0 state bits 0, 1, 3, 4, 6, 8, and 10 have to be analyzed, resulting in a vector 10101011011. The remaining FSM state bits, denoted by 0s in the constant `parity_table`, are not relevant for the considered parity groups. The function `calculate_parity` firstly masks out with the aid of the constant `parity_table` not relevant state bits and stores the result in the variable `masked`. Then, in a loop statement, all the relevant state bits are XOR-ed together calculating in such a way a value to be assigned to the respective parity bit. This value is kept in a variable `result` and is returned from the function. Note that the number of state bits to be analyzed is not fixed and is selected with the attribute `high` applied to the FSM state. Consequently, the function can be used for calculating the parity bit values for FSM states encoded with an arbitrary number of bits.

The second data type `MASK` is an array of sixteen 11-bit standard logic vectors. A constant `mask_table` of type `MASK` stores for each possible syndrome to be calculated in the *Code Corrector* block, the relevant mask that has to be applied to the FSM state in order to correct possible errors. For example, if the generated syndrome is equal to 0011_2, the mask 00000000001 indicates that state bit 0 is in error and has to be complemented. The function `calculate_mask` firstly converts a received syndrome from standard logic vector to a natural value with the aid of function `conv_integer` (defined in package `std_logic_unsigned` of `ieee` library). Then, the calculated value is used for accessing one of the vectors declared in the constant `mask_table`, which is subsequently returned from the function.

With the aid of the developed package, the *Parity Encoder* and the *Code Corrector* block can de described in VHDL as shown in the code below.

The *Parity Encoder* block is parameterizable with the aid of two generic constants (n and m) which indicate respectively the number of bits used for FSM state encoding and the number of the required parity bits. Inside the block, the value to be assigned to each parity bit is calculated with the aid of a generate statement which permits the function `calculate_parity` to be invoked the required number (m) of times. The resulting parity bit values are written to the output parity vector.

The *Code Corrector* block is similarly parameterizable with the aid of two generic constants (n and m) which indicate the number of bits used for FSM state encoding and the number of the required parity bits, respectively. Inside the block, first of all the new parity bits are calculated with the aid a generate statement invoking the `calculate_parity` function m times. After that a syndrome is generated by XOR ing the previously calculated parity vector (read out of the FSM register) with the newly calculated parity vector. Based on the syndrome, a mask is produced with the aid of the function `calculate_mask`. Finally, the mask is applied to the FSM state read from the FSM register allowing a possible error to be corrected.

It is very important that the developed functions and modules are parameterizable (with the aid of attributes and generic constants [5]) and can therefore be used for providing error correction ability for any number of data bits (currently at most 120 data bits are supported). Consequently, the proposed modules can directly be employed for any FSM with any number of states and using any state encoding technique (as far as the number of state bits does not exceed the currently imposed 120-bit limitation) and also for other applications.

```
library IEEE;          use IEEE.STD_LOGIC_1164.ALL;
library corr_codes;    use corr_codes.parity_types.all;

entity encoder is
    generic(n : natural := 11; m : natural := 3);
    port ( state : in std_logic_vector(n downto 0);
           parity : out std_logic_vector(m downto 0));
end encoder;

architecture Behavioral of encoder is
begin
    calc_parity: for i in 0 to m generate
           parity(i) <= calculate_parity(state, i);
    end generate;
end Behavioral;

-------------------------------------

library IEEE;          use IEEE.STD_LOGIC_1164.ALL;
library corr_codes;    use corr_codes.parity_types.all;

entity corrector is
    generic (n : natural := 11; m : natural := 3);
    port ( state : in std_logic_vector(n downto 0);
           in_parity : in std_logic_vector(m downto 0);
           corr_state : out std_logic_vector(n downto 0));
end corrector;

architecture Behavioral of corrector is
    signal new_parity : std_logic_vector(m downto 0);
    signal syndrome : std_logic_vector(m downto 0);
    signal mask : std_logic_vector(n downto 0);
begin
    calc_parity: for i in 0 to m generate
           new_parity(i) <= calculate_parity(state, i);
    end generate;

    syndrome <= in_parity xor new_parity;
    mask <= calculate_mask(syndrome, state'high);
    corr_state <= mask xor state;
end Behavioral;
```

The complete self-checking FSM can be constructed from the designed modules as shown in fig. 5 for a simple sequence detector having one input, one output, and 5 states and using Gray state encoding technique. The respective state diagram and state/output table are shown in fig. 6. The developed parameterizable modules and the `parity_types` package were put in a library `corr_codes`.

```
library IEEE;
use IEEE.STD_LOGIC_1164.ALL;

entity sec1_gray is
    Port ( clk, reset : in std_logic;
           X : in std_logic;
           Y : out std_logic);
end sec1_gray;

architecture mixed of sec1_gray is
    signal state, next_state, corr_state : std_logic_vector(2 downto 0);
    signal parity, next_parity : std_logic_vector(2 downto 0);
begin

FSM_register: process(clk, reset)
begin
      if reset = '0' then
         state <= (others => '0');  parity <= (others => '0');
      elsif rising_edge(clk) then
         state <= next_state;
         parity <= next_parity;
      end if;
end process FSM_register;

--error inserter, not shown here for the sake of clarity

par_encoder: entity corr_codes.encoder(behavioral)
     generic map (n => state'high, m => parity'high)
     port map(state => next_state, parity => next_parity);

corrector: entity corr_codes.corrector(behavioral)
     generic map (n => state'high, m => parity'high)
     port map(state => state, in_parity => parity, corr_state => corr_state);

combinational_circuit: process (corr_state, X)
begin
   case corr_state is
     when "000" => --S0
            Y <= '0';
            if (X = '0') then next_state <= "000"; --S0
            else next_state <= "001"; end if;      --S1
     when "001" => --S1
            Y <= '0';
            if (X = '0') then next_state <= "000"; --S0
            else next_state <= "011"; end if;      --S2
     when "011" => --S2
            Y <= '0';
            if (X = '0') then next_state <= "010"; --S3
            else next_state <= "011"; end if;      --S2
     when "010" => --S3
            Y <= '0';
            if (X = '1') then next_state <= "110"; --S4
            else next_state <= "000"; end if;      --S0
     when "110" => --S4
            Y <= '1';
            if (X = '1') then next_state <= "011"; --S2
            else next_state <= "000"; end if;      --S0
     when others => next_state <= "000";           --S0
            Y <= '0';
   end case;
end process combinational_circuit;

end mixed;
```

Fig. 5. VHDL code describing a Moore self-correcting FSM with the aid of the developed modules

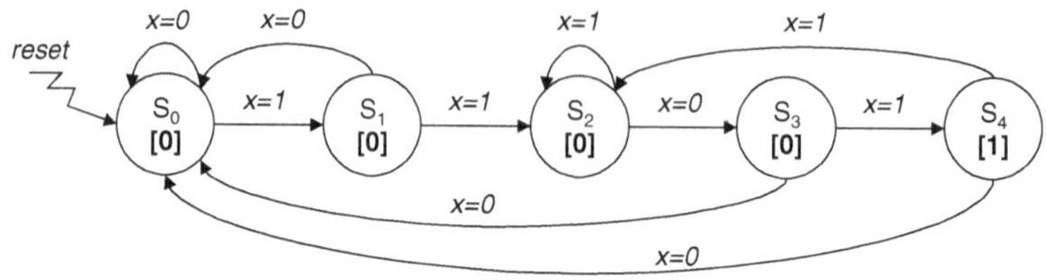

present state	next state		y
	x = 0	x = 1	
000 (S_0)	000	001	0
001 (S_1)	000	011	0
011 (S_2)	010	011	0
010 (S_3)	000	110	0
110 (S_4)	000	011	1

Fig. 6. State diagram and state/output table of a simple 4-bit sequence detector

4 Experiments

Obviously, the introduced error correction facility leads to area overhead and overall performance degradation. To estimate the influence of the added modules on the required FSM resources and the resulting clock frequency, two FSMs (*sec1* and *sec2*) have been selected.

Each FSM was synthesized using the Xilinx Synthesis Technology (XST) tool [6] targeted to Spartan-IIE xc2s300e –6 speed grade FPGA. For each FSM three types of state encoding have been examined (one-hot, binary, and Gray). After that each FSM was modified so as to provide for single-bit error correction as described in section 3, and the resulting VHDL descriptions were also synthesized. The obtained results expressed in terms of the required FPGA slices and the maximum attainable clock frequency, are presented in table 2. The synthesis process for both cases (i.e. for FSMs with and without error correction facilities) was optimized for speed.

Table 2. The results of experiments

FSM	inputs	outputs	states	state encoding	without error correction		with error correction	
					FPGA slices	performance	FPGA slices	performance
sec1	1	1	5	binary	2	285 MHz	7	133 MHz
				Gray	2	270 MHz	10	97 MHz
				one-hot	4	245 MHz	20	83 MHz
sec2	4	3	17	binary	18	123 MHz	39	65 MHz
				Gray	17	142 MHz	30	65 MHz
				one-hot	16	183 MHz	112	45 MHz

The worst results, in terms of both the increase in the number of FPGA slices and the performance degradation, were received for one-hot state encoding technique. This can be explained by the fact that one-hot state encoding technique requires more bits to represent FSM states and therefore always obligates more parity bits to be introduced than in the case of compact binary or Gray state encoding techniques. For example, *sec1* FSM has 5 states, which can be encoded with 3 bits (binary or Gray codes) supplemented by 3 parity bits (not counting the overall parity bit), whereas in the case of one-hot state encoding, 5 data bits and 4 parity bits are required. Augmenting the total number of bits from 6 (3+3) to 9 (5+4) leads obviously to increasing the complexity of both *Parity Encoder* and *Code Corrector* blocks and consequently increments the latency and the resource consumption of the whole control circuit.

From table 2 we can also see that as the FSM complexity increases, the error correction logic overhead becomes less noticeable and can be tolerated for high-reliability applications.

5 Conclusion

This paper proposed a design methodology for implementation of self-correcting control circuits derived from a VHDL specification. The entire approach has been presented, focusing the attention on the developed parameterizable VHDL package and the error-correcting modules, which can easily augment any VHDL FSM description with a single-bit error correction facility. The results obtained for a number of control circuits have been presented, which show that the inevitable area and performance overhead can be tolerated for high-reliability applications.

References

1. Bolchini, C., Montandon, R., Salice, F., Sciuto, D.: Design of VHDL based Totally Self-Checking Finite-State Machine and Data-Path Descriptions. IEEE Trans. on Very Large Scale Integration (VLSI) Systems, vol. 8, no. 1 (2000) 98-103
2. Zeng, C., Saxena, N., McCluskey, E.J.: Finite State Machine Synthesis with Concurrent Error Detection. In: Proc. Int. Test Conf. (1999) 672-679
3. Levin, I., Sinelnikov, V.: Self-Checking of FPGA-based Control Units. In: Proc. of the 9th Great Lakes Symposium on VLSI (1999) 292-295
4. Wakerly, J.F.: Digital Design. Principles and Practices. 3rd ed. Prentice Hall (2000)
5. Ashenden P.J.: The Designer's Guide to VHDL. Morgan Kaufmann Publishers, Inc. (1996)
6. ISE, FPGAs. [Online]. Available: www.xilinx.com

Detecting Memory Access Errors with Flow-Sensitive Conditional Range Analysis

Yimin Xia, Jun Luo, and Minxuan Zhang

School of Computer Science, National University of Defense Technology,
Changsha 410073, P.R. China
ymxia@nudt.edu.cn

Abstract. Accessing an out-of-bounds memory address can lead to nondeterministic behaviors or elusive crashes. Static analysis can detect memory access errors from program source codes without runtime overhead, but existing techniques are either very imprecise or exponential cost. This paper proposes a precise and effective method to detect memory access errors. Firstly, it generates a state for each statement with a flow-sensitive, inter-procedural algorithm. A state includes not only range constraints like the traditional range analysis, but also occurrence conditions of the range constraints. Secondly, it solves states of memory access statement to evaluate the sizes of accessed memory bounds. The costs of state generation and state resolution are polynomial. We have implemented a prototype of the analysis method. Applied to 7 popular programs, the prototype found 40 memory access errors with a high precision of 80%.

1 Introduction

Memory corruption errors can lead to serious consequence. Type unsafe languages, such as C and C++, do not check memory accesses at runtime, and such errors will lead to software's nondeterministic behaviors or elusive crashes. Type safe languages, such as Java, check memory accesses at runtime and raise an exception when it detects a memory access error. If one of these exceptions is unhandled by the programmer, the program will be aborted. In 1996, the explosion of Ariane 501 shortly after launch was due to an overflow in an arithmetic conversion. This failure cost over $500 millions to the European space program. CERT advisories show that almost 50% of security attacks on computer systems were related to buffer overruns[1, 2]. Classical verification techniques based on development process, code reviewing and testing were unable to detect that defect.

In recent years, static analysis techniques have been used to detect memory access errors from source codes. Previous works have focused on path-sensitive analysis[2, 3] and flow-insensitive analysis[4, 5]. Path-sensitive analysis is accurate but expensive. It tracks every branch in the control-flow of a program in which the execution state differs along the two branch paths may result in an exponential complexity. The flow-insensitive analysis is rapid but its result is very imprecise because it does not consider statement orders and branch conditions.

In this paper, we propose a conditional, symbolic range analysis to detect memory access errors. Range analysis computes the potential bound of each access that may

L.T. Yang et al. (Eds.): ICESS 2005, LNCS 3820, pp. 320–331, 2005.

be attained for any program input. Traditional range analysis[8, 9] only considers constraints between value ranges of variables, which lead to too conservative analysis and imprecise results. However, conditional range analysis considers occurrence conditions of range constraints, which can improve the precisions of range resolution evidently.

The major contributions of this paper can be summarized in the following:

1. A fundamental, new insight for range analysis. Except generating range constraints from assignment statements, we also track conditions of range constraints from branch statements, assertion statements and assignment statements. When we judge whether a memory access would be out-of-bounds, the conditions of range constraints can prevent most false alarms and improve the precision of range analysis.
2. A flow-sensitive, inter-procedural algorithm for constraint states generation. The algorithm propagates range constraints and condition constraints along the control flow of a program, and merge constraints at join points. Because all states are independent of paths, the algorithm avoids states explosion of full path-sensitive analysis, as well as it has better precision than traditional range analysis.
3. An algorithm for constraint resolution. For the state of a memory access statement, the algorithm first uses a linear programming solver to compute tightest ranges of constraint variables, and then solve the inequality group that includes tightest ranges of constraint variables, constraint conditions in the state and a out-of-bounds condition for the statement.
4. A prototype of our analysis method. We applied the prototype to 7 popular programs. The experimental results show it is accurate and effective: it can analyze ten thousands lines of code in a minute with the precision of 80%.

The rest of the paper is organized as follows: In Section 2, an example for our algorithm is given. In Section 3, we present the algorithm for state generation. In Section 4, we present the algorithm for state resolution. In Section 5, the experimental results are discussed. We discuss related work in Section 6 and conclude at last.

2 Example

In this section, we use an example to explain how memory access errors can be detected using conditional range analysis. Consider the simplified snippet of code shown in Figure 1 and suppose we are interested in determining the safety of memory access `argv[optind++]` in line 6 and `spec_fd[fd]` in line 13. We compare two range analysis methods as follows.

Ranges are expressed as lower and upper bounds on program variable. A range constraint has the form $\gamma(e_1) \supseteq \gamma(e_2)$, where function γ maps a variable expression to its value range, e_1 and e_2 are variable expressions. Though the following analysis is flow-sensitive and context-sensitive that generates a state for each statement, these methods can also be path-sensitive or flow-insensitive.

Traditional range analysis: The traditional range analysis ignores conditions of range constraints, so the value range of *optind* and *fd* are regarded as $[0, +\infty]$. As a result, a false alarm about *optind* is reported.

```
struct spec_fd_t {
   int len,pos;
   unsigned char *buf;
} spec_fd[3];

int main(argc, argv) {
  env = add_envopt(&argc, &argv, OPTIONS_VAR);
  if (env != NULL)
     args = argv;
  while (optind < argc) {
     ifd = open(argv[optind++], O_RDONLY | O_BINARY,
RW_USER);
     len = spec_read(ifd, buf, size);
  }
...
}

int spec_read(int fd, unsigned char *buf, int size) {
  if (fd > 3)
     return -1;
  if(spec_fd[fd].pos >= spec_fd[fd].len)
     return EOF;
...
}
```

Fig. 1. Running Example

Conditional range analysis: A state in conditional range analysis is composed by range constraints and conditions of the range constraints. The value range of *env* in line 5 is $[0, +\infty]$ and its condition is (*optind<argc*). The condition (*optind<argc*) guarantees the safety of memory access `argv[optind++]` in line 6, and avoids a false alarm. The condition of line 13 is ($fd \leq 3$), which cannot guarantee that *fd* is less than 3. But *fd* is a parameter, we analyze its call statement in line 7, which has range constraints $\{\gamma(\text{env})\supseteq[0,+\infty], \gamma(\text{ifd})\supseteq[0,+\infty], \gamma(\text{fd})\supseteq \gamma(\text{ifd})\}$ and conditions {`optind < argc, fd≤3`}. Because the range constraints and its condition cannot guarantee that `fd` is less than 3, and no parameter of `main` is relation to the constraints and conditions, an alarm about `fd` in line 13 is emitted.

3 State Generation

In this section, we first give the definition of state, then present the algorithm of state generation, and analyze the algorithm at last.

Since memory addresses are accessed through pointers, a pointer analysis should be processed before state generation. Many pointer analysis algorithms, such as Steensgaard[20], DAS[21], can used to determine the set of each pointer point-to and the alias set of each pointer.

Definition 1: Locations $\mathcal{L}$ = {v| v is a variable in the program} ∪ {*malloc*$_i$| *i* is a program point where *malloc* instruction is called}

For a location $l \in \mathcal{L}$, we have the following constraint variables:

- *l.val* represents potential values stored in *l*, including primitive type (int, long, char, etc.) values and locations;
- *l.assize* represents the allocation size of *l*;
- *l.len* represents the accessed length by a load or store instruction to *l*;
- *l.offset* represents potential offsets from the base address to the addresses of locations that are pointed by *l.val*.

In this paper, we write *V* to represent the set of constraint variables, write Ω to represent the value set of constraint variables, function *loc* maps the name of a variable to its location, and function *pt* maps the name of a pointer to the location set it points to. We also assume that programs are in static single assignment (SSA) form. A program is in SSA form when every variable within it has at most one defining statement.

3.1 State Definition

A state represents range constraints between constraint variables and value constraints between constraint variables, and the latter is the necessary condition for the former occurrence.

Definition 2: $\mathcal{P} =< P, \sqsubseteq_p >$ is a lattice, where:

1. $P = \{t \mid t = \sum_{i=1}^{n} a_i v_i + b,\ a_i, b \in Z, v_i \in \Omega\} \cup \{uninit, unknown\}$ is the value set of linear expressions of constraint variables, where *Z* is the set of integer, *uninit* represents the value of uninitialized constraint variables, and *unknown* represents the value of non-linear constraint expressions;
2. $p_1 \sqsubseteq_p p_2$ if $p_1 = uninit$, or $p_2 = unknown$ or $p_1 - p_2 \le 0$;
3. *Unknown* is the top element of $\mathcal{P}$ and *uninit* is the bottom element of $\mathcal{P}$.

The value of a constraint variable is *uninit* if either the program variables that it correspond to have not been initialized in the source code, or program statements that affect the value of the program variables have not been captured by our analyzer. The latter case may arise when the constraint generator does not have a model for a library function that affects the value of the constraint variable.

A range can represent the set of potential values that a constraint variable attains at runtime. Ranges are symbolically expressed as lower and upper bounds on constraint variables. The computing of an range expression can be safely approximated by the following equations:

$$\gamma(uninit) = \varnothing \tag{1}$$

$$\gamma(unknown) = [-\infty\ , +\infty] \tag{2}$$

$$\gamma(c) = [c\ ,\ c],\ \text{where}\ c \in Z \tag{3}$$

$$[inf_1,\ sup_1] + [inf_2,\ sup_2] = [inf_1 + inf_2,\ sup_1 + sup_2] \tag{4}$$

$$[inf_1,\ sup_1] - [inf_2,\ sup_2] = [inf_1 - sup_2,\ sup_1 - inf_2] \tag{5}$$

$$\gamma(\sigma(x_1,\ldots,x_n)) = \begin{cases} \sigma(\gamma(x_1),\ldots,\gamma(x_n)) & if\ \ \sigma(x_1,\ldots,x_n) \in P \\ [-\infty, +\infty] & otherwise \end{cases} \tag{6}$$

Define 3: A state $S = [\ R,\ C\ ]$, where:

1. $R = \{\ \gamma(x) \supseteq \gamma(\sigma(x_1,\ldots,x_n)) \mid x, x_1,\ldots,x_n \in V\ \}$ is a set of inclusion relations between the value ranges of constraint variables and the value range of constraint variable expressions.
2. $C = \{\ \sigma(x_1,\ldots,x_n) \uparrow 0 \mid \sigma(x_1,\ldots,x_n) \in P,\ \uparrow \in \{<, \leq, =, \geq, >\}\ \}$ is a set of condition constraints that represent relations between values of constraint variables.

3.2 Algorithm

The control flow graph of a procedure is $G = \langle N, E, start, exit\rangle$ with a set of nodes N and a set of edges $E \subseteq N \times N$. A node $n \in N$ represents a statement or a predicate in the procedure and a edge $e = (m, n) \in E$ indicates transfer of control between nodes m, $n \in N$. Respectively, *start* and *exit* are the unique start node and the unique exit node in the procedure.

A program is represented by a super graph $G^* = (N^*, E^*)$, where G^* consists of a collection of control flow graphs G_1, G_2, … . The other nodes of control flow graphs represent the statements and predicates of procedures in the usual way, except that a procedure call statement is represented by two nodes, a *call* node and a *return* node. The sets of all *start*, *exit*, *call* and *return* nodes in the super graph will be denoted by *Start*, *Exit*, *Call* and *Return*, respectively. In addition to the ordinary intraprocedural edges that connect the nodes of the individual flow graphs, for each procedure call represented by *call* node c and *return* node r, G^* has an intraprocedural edge from c to r.

We write $S(n)$ to represent the state of node n, $R(S)$ to represent the range constraints of state S, $C(S)$ to represent the condition constraints of state S, and S^* to represent the set of states associated with statements in a program. Each edge is assigned to a transfer function $Trans$: $E^* \times S^* \rightarrow S^*$. For a edge $e \in E^*$ and a input state $S_{in} \in S^*$, $Trans(e, S_{in})$ generates a output state S_{out} with following rules:

1. $R(S_{out}) = R(S_{in}) \cup \{\gamma(x) \supseteq \gamma(f(x_1,\ldots,x_n))\}$ if the source node of edge e has a side effect of $x \mapsto f(x_1,\ldots,x_n)$, otherwise $R(S_{out}) = R(S_{in})$.
2. The condition constraints $C(S_{out}) = C(S_{in}) \cup Cond(e)$, where
   - if the source node of e is a branch statement, such as *if* and *while* in language C, $Cond(e)$ is the transfer condition of e.
   - if the source node of e is an assertion statement, $Cond(e)$ is the assertion of the assertion statement.

- if the source node of *e* has a side effect, *Cond*(*e*) is the addition constraint between constraint variables. For example, the addition constraint of $x \mapsto y+5$ is $x > y$.

The pseudo code of state generation is presented in Figure 2. This is a worklist algorithm that updates constraints of statements until no further updates are possible.

```
global
    Worklist: 2^{E*}
    SS: N* → S*

procedure Propagate(G* = ⟨N*, E*⟩)
begin
    for each m ∈ N* do SS(m) := (∅,∅)
    Worklist := E*

    while Worklist ≠∅ do
       Remove a node e from Worklist
       d = dst(e)
       R(SS(d)) = ⊓_{r, p∈pre(d)} R(Trans((p,d), SS(p)))
       C(SS(d)) = ⊓_{c, p∈pre(d)} C(Trans((p,d), SS(p)))
       switch(d)
         case d ∈ Exit:
           Worklist := Worklist ∪ retSite(procOf(d))
         case d ∈ Call:
           for each actual parameter ap in d and its corresponding formal parameter
    fp do
              R(SS(d)) = R(SS(d)) ∪ {γ(fp) ⊇ γ(ap)}
         case d ∈ Return:
              R(SS(d)) = R(SS(d)) ∪ R(SS(exit(calledProc(d))))
    if SS(m) has changed then Worklist := Worklist ∪ {(d, n) | n∈ succ(d)}
end
```

Fig. 2. Algorithm for state generation

The algorithm uses the following functions:

- *calledProc*: maps a *call* node or a *return* node to the name of the called procedure.
- *procOf:* maps a node to the name of its enclosing procedure.
- *retSite*: maps the name of a procedure to *return* nodes that return from the procedure.

The meet operator of range constraints $R \sqcap_r R'$ is set union $R \cup R'$. The meet operator of condition constraints $C \sqcap_c C'$ is computed as follows:

1. Build two variable relation graphs $G_v = (N_v, E_v)$ and $G_v' = (N_v', E_v')$. The vertices of G_v and G_v' are the constraint variables in C and C' respectively. For each condition constraint $x \uparrow y$ in C (or C'), where $\uparrow \in \{<, \leq, =, \geq, >\}$, we add the labeled edge $x \xrightarrow{\uparrow} y$ in G_v (or G_v');
2. Form a variable relation graph $G_v'' = (N_v'', E_v'')$, where $N_v'' = N_v \cup N_v'$, $E_v'' = \{ x \xrightarrow{\uparrow} y \mid x \xrightarrow{\uparrow} y \in E_v$ and $x \xrightarrow{\uparrow} y \in E_v' \}$
3. Delete redundant edges of G_v'': if there is a path $x \xrightarrow{\uparrow,*} z \xrightarrow{\uparrow} y$, delete edge $x \xrightarrow{\uparrow} y$, where $x \xrightarrow{\uparrow,*} z$ represents a path from x to z;
4. Generate the result: $C \sqcap_c C' = C \cup C' \cup \{ x \xrightarrow{\uparrow} y \mid x \xrightarrow{\uparrow} y \in E_v'' \}$.

3.3 Algorithm Analysis

The algorithm guarantees all statements not in the *Worklist* satisfy equations $SS(s) = (\sqcap_{r,p \in pre(s)} R(Trans((p,s), SS(p))), \sqcap_{c,p \in pre(s)} C(Trans((p,s), SS(p))))$. At the end, *Worklist* is empty, so the algorithm is correct.

At each iteration, the set of range constraints of a statement is increased and the set of condition constraints of a statement is reduced, so the meet operator and transfer functions are monotone. We use widening/narrowing operators to ensure termination and accelerate convergence [6].

Let $|N|$ and $|E|$ be the number of nodes and edges in the super graph of a program respectively. Assume each statement in a loop can be computed by widening/narrowing at most M times, and the maximum depth of loop nests is K, the node number to be processed is at most $O(M^K|E|)$. Let the time of transfer function be J, the time of meet operator of range constraints be H, the time of meet operator of condition constraints be Q. The complexity of state generator is $O(M^k|E|\,(J+H+Q))$.

4 State Resolution

After state generation, each statement is concerned with a set of linear range constraints and a set of linear condition constraints. For the state s of a statement st, range constraints $R(s)$ defines a constraint system $\wedge_{1 \leq i \leq n} RC_i$, where each $RC_i \in R(s)$. The solution of $\wedge_{1 \leq i \leq n} RC_i$ represents possible value ranges of constraint variables. Each constraint variable has a solution $[-\infty, +\infty]$, but it is too conservative and no any use. Linear program[7] can provide the minimal ranges of constraint variables for a set of range constraints, which is enough precise for our analysis.

A linear program is an optimization problem that can be expressed as follows:

Objective function: cx

Constraint condition: $Ax \geq b$

Where constraint matrix A is an $m \times n$ matix, cost coefficient c and right-hand-side vector b are vectors of constants, decision variable x is a vector of variables.

A linear program is said to be *feasible* if one can find finite values for all the variables that satisfy all the constraints. A solution is said to be *optimal* if it maximizes (or minimizes) the value of the objective function. A linear program is said to be *unbounded* if a solution exists, but no solution optimizes the objective function.

Since the bounds of memory regions are integer, the problem of memory access error detection is called mixed integer programming that is a NP-complete problem, and several approximation of optimal solution can be attained in polynomial time[22].

4.1 Constraint Reduce

Though linear program can solve a set of linear range constraints, it does not attain optimal solution for all cases. If there is a uninitialized constraint variable or a dependency cycle between constraint variables, the linear program may be unbounded or infeasible.

A constraint variable is uninitialized if either the program variables that it correspond to have not been initialized in the source code, or program statements that affect the value of the program variables have not been captured by the analyzer. To remove uninitialized constraint variables from the set of linear range constraints *R*, we search constraint variables whose ranges do not include any constant or any range of constraint variable, and remove these constraint variables from *R*. Repeat this process until no constraint variable can be removed.

To break dependency cycles in the set of range constraints *R*, we form a dependency graph $G_d = (N_d, E_d)$, whose vertices are constraint variables in *R*. If there is a constraint $\gamma(x) \supseteq \gamma(f(x_1,\ldots,x_n)) \in R$, we add a directed edge $x_i \rightarrow x$, $1 \le i \le n$. Search strongly connected components (SCCs) in G_d with DFS algorithm, we can find dependency cycles in *R*. We delete incoming edges of the node that has the least outcoming edges in a SCC of G_d, and set the node's range to $[-\infty, +\infty]$. At last, we transfer G_d to a acyclic graph G_d' and transfer *R* to a new set of range constraints *R'*.

4.2 Algorithm

For a memory access through pointer *p* in statement *st*, the *out-of-bounds conditions* are *loc(p).offset* < 0 and *pt(p).asize* - *loc(p).offset* - *pt(p).len* < 0. If one of out-of-bounds conditions is satisfied under state *S(st)*, the dereference of *p* is said a memory access error. The precision of a detection algorithm to a program is $\frac{|W|}{|T|}$, where $|W|$ is the number of real errors, $|T|$ is the number of total warnings.

The pseudo code of state solution is presented in Figure 3, where ε is an out-of-bounds condition and *S* is the state of memory access statement. If any out-of-bounds condition is analyzed at most once in a procedure, the algorithm can be terminable. Because any nontrivial property about the language recognized by a Turing machine is undecidable[23], no one can have a solution of a nontrival property that is both sound and complete. To avoid generating too many false positives, our alogirthm ignores undecidable solutions that may lose some vulnerabilities.

procedure Solve(ε, S)
begin

1 Remove uninitialized constraint variables from $R(S)$ to $R'(S)$;
2 Break dependency cycles in $R'(S)$, to attain a acyclic dependency graph G'_d and a new set of range constraints $R''(S)$;
3 $VS \leftarrow \{v| v\in \varepsilon$ or there is a path from v to v', where $v'\in \varepsilon\}$
4 Use $R'(st)$ as the constraint condition, and apply linear program to solve minimal rangs of constraint variables in VS;
5 Solve the inequality group, which includes condition constraints $C(S)$, minimal rangs of constraint variables in VS and ε:
  5.1 If the inequality group exist a solution, the ε is unsafe and the analyzer reports a warning;
  5.2 If the inequality group exists a solution and there is any parameter of the current procedure in VS, the analyzer resolves ε in the state of *call* nodes that call the enclosing procedure of the current statement.

end

Fig. 3. Algorithm for state solution

5 Experiments

We have designed a static analysis tool, called MOC, to implement our algorithms. The architecture of MOC is shown in Figure 4. MOC uses the front-end of LLVM[10] to transform C/C++ source programs into static single assignment (SSA) form[11]. MOC applies Steensgaard algorithm, a whole program flow-insensitive context-insensitive pointer analysis algorithm, to analyzing pointer alias.

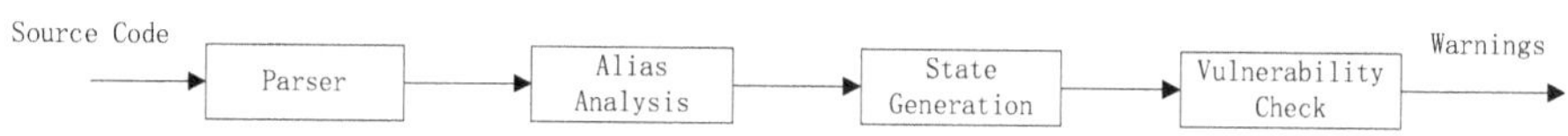

Fig. 4. The architecture of MOC

We applied MOC to two group experiments. These experiments were taken on a 2.2GHz Pentium 4 machine with 512MB of memory running Linux. The first group experiments measure some programs in SPEC2000 package, and the result is summarized in Table 1. The column LOC displays the number of source lines in the original source, the column FN displays the number of source function. The TW reports the number of total warnings, and the FA reports the number of false alarms.

Programs in SPEC2000 have been developed many years and they are high quality systems as benchmarks to measure compilers. MOC reported 43 bugs in 4 applications of SPEC2000, and had an average precision of 84%. Many bugs in 186.crafty can be easily exploited by supplying an especially command line argument to the program.

Table 1. The experimental results for SPECK2000

Program	LOC	FN	time (s)	TW	FA	Precision
164.gzip	17444	40	1.6	3	0	100%
186.crafty	21182	104	14.6	31	5	84%
197.parser	11421	299	23.4	4	0	100%
256.bzip2	4675	61	1.8	5	2	60%
Total	54722	504	41.4	43	7	84%

The second group experiments compared MOC with [3]. The latter presents an algorithm that identifies buffer overruns using path and context-sensitive analysis with the demand-driven technique. Table 2 is the experimental results, where bold font is MOC and italic is [3]. The speeds of MOC are higher clearly. Especially, MOC only spends 0.4 second to analyze `lhttpd`, and [3] spends 99 seconds. It shows our analysis is much faster than path-sensitive analysis.

Table 2. The results of contrast experiment

Program	LOC	FN	time (s)		TW		FA		Precision	
bftpd 1.0.11	2946	47	**1.4**	*2.3*	**2**	*1*	**0**	*0*	**50%**	*100%*
gzip 1.2.4	8162	93	**0.9**	*2.0*	**1**	*1*	**0**	*0*	**100%**	*100%*
lhttpd 0.1	888	21	**0.4**	*99*	**2**	*1*	**1**	*0*	**100%**	*100%*
Total	11996	161	**2.7**	*103.3*	**5**	*3*	**1**	*0*	**80%**	*100%*

6 Relation Work

Dynamic analysis techniques[13~16] can detect out-of-bounds memory access in runtime, but fail to eliminate errors from source code. Several static analysis techniques have been proposed to detect memory access errors from source code, and thus help the developer to eliminate errors before the source code is deployed.

CSSV[17] and Splint[18] are annotation driven tools. These tools use user-supplied annotations, such as pre- and post-conditions of a function, to aid static analysis. Since annotations burden users, these tools are limited to existing code bases.

BOON[4] and [5] model strings as abstract data types and transform the buffer overrun detection problem into a range analysis problem. With flow-insensitive and context-insensitive analysis, they are efficient, but their false positive rates are very high.

CGS[19] checks out-of-bounds array accesses in multithreaded C programs. CGS analyzes programs using flow-insensitive analysis, except the numerical invariants of loops. It also makes context-sensitive analysis for functions that have a pointer in their signature, and context-insensitive analysis for others. The false alarm rate of CGS is low for multithreaded C programs, but unknown for others. CGS depends specializing algorithms to analyze loops in different software, which limits its impact in the software industry.

ARCHER[2] and Xie et. al.[3] make path-sensitivity analysis to detect memory errors. Since path-sensitive analysis follows the actual program paths, the false alarm rates of these tools are very low. However, the exponential cost limits their scale to large code bases.

7 Conclusion

In this paper, we propose a conditional symbolic range analysis to detect memory access errors statically. First, we use a flow-sensitive, inter-procedural algorithm to generate a state for each statement in a program, and a state includes a set of range constraints and a set of conditions. Then, we solve states of memory access statements to evaluate the sizes of accessed memory bounds with linear program, and determinate access errors in a program with inequality group resolutions. We implement a prototype. The experimental results show that it is precise and effective.

References

1. CERT/CC. Advisories. http://www.cert.org/advisories.
2. Yichen X., Andy C., Dawson E.: ARCHER: Using Symbolic, Path-sensitive Analysis to Detect Memory Access Errors. European Software Engineering Conference and the ACM SIGSOFT Symposium on the Foundations of Software Engineering (ESEC/FSE), Helsinki, Finland, 2003.
3. V. Benjamin Livshits, Monica S. L.: Tracking Pointers with Path and Context Sensitivity for Bug Detection in C Programs. ESEC/FSE, Helsinki, Finland, 2003.
4. D. Wagner, J. Foster, E. Brewer, A. Aiken.: A first step towards automated detection of buffer overrun vulnerabilities. The Symposium on Network and Distributed Systems Security, USA, 2000.
5. Vinod G., Somesh J., David C., David M., David V.: Buffer Overrun Detection using Linear Programming and Static Analysis. ACM conference on computer and communications security, USA, 2003.
6. P. Cousot, R. Cousot.: Abstract interpretation: a unified lattice model for static analysis of programs by construction or approximation of fixpoints. ACM Symposium on PLDI, USA, 1977.
7. R. Wunderling.: Paralleler und Objektorientierter Simplex-Algorithmus. PhD thesis, Konrad-Zuse-Zentrum fur Informationstechnik Berlin, TR, 1996.
8. W. Blume, R. Eigenmann.: Symbolic range propagation. The 9th International Parallel Processing Symposium, USA, 1995.
9. Suan H.Y., Susan H.: Pointer-Range analysis. Static Analysis Symposium, Italy, 2004.
10. Chris L., Vikram A.: LLVM: A Compilation Framework for Lifelong Program Analysis & Transformation. 2nd IEEE / ACM International Symposium on Code Generation and Optimization, USA, 2004.
11. LLVM Language Reference Manual, http://llvm.cs.uiuc.edu/docs.
12. R. Hastings, B. Joyce.: Purify: Fast detection of memory leaks and access errors. The Winter USENIX Conference, USA, 1992.
13. R. Jones, P. Kelly.: Backwards-compatible bounds checking for arrays and pointers in C programs. The International Workshop on Automatic Debugging, Sweden, 1997.
14. Greg M.: Bounds Checking Projects. http://gcc.gnu.org/projects/bp/main.html

15. Olatunji R., Monica S.L.: A Practical Dynamic Buffer Overrun Detector, Network and Distributed System Security Symposium, USA, 2004.
16. John W., Mariam K.: A Comparison of Publicly Available Tools for Dynamic Buffer Overrun Prevention, Network and Distributed System Security Symposium, USA, 2003.
17. Nurit D., Michael R., Mooly S.: CSSV: Towards a Realistic Tool for Statically Detecting All Buffer Overruns in C. ACM Conference on PLDI, USA, 2003.
18. David E., David L.: Improving Security Using Extensible Lightweight Static Analysis. IEEE Software, Jan/Feb 2002.
19. Arnaud V., Guillaume B.: Precise and Efficient Static Array Bound Checking for Large Embedded C Programs. ACM Conference on PLDI, USA, 2004.
20. Steensgaard B.: Points-to Analysis in Almost Linear Time. ACM Conference on PLDI, USA, 1996.
21. Manuvir D.: Unification-based pointer analysis with directional assignments. ACM Conference on PLDI, USA, 2000.
22. Thomas H.C., Charles E.L., Ronald L.R., Clifford S.: Introduction to algorithms, the MIT press, 2001.
23. H.G. Rice.: Classes of Recursively Enumerable Sets and their Decision Problems. Transactions of the American Mathematical Society No. 89, pp. 25-29, 1953.

Deductive Probabilistic Verification Methods of Safety, Liveness and Nonzenoness for Distributed Real-Time Systems

Satoshi Yamane

Dept. of Information Engineering, Kanazawa University,
Kanazawa City, Japan
Tel:+81.76.234.4856, Fax:+81.76.234.4900
syamane@is.t.kanazawa-u.ac.jp

Abstract. Recently, model-checking and probabilistic timed simulation verification methods of probabilistic timed automata have been developed. In this paper, we propose probabilistic timed transition systems by generalizing probabilistic timed automata, and propose deductive verification rules of probabilistic real-time linear temporal logic over probabilistic timed transition systems. As our proposed probabilistic timed transition system is a general computational model, we have developed general verification methods.

1 Introduction

Distributed real-time systems are of vital economic importance and are literally becoming ubiquitous. They have already become an integral component of safety critical systems involving aviation, telecommunications, and process control applications. Today, timed automaton [1] is the standard tool for specifying and verifying real-time systems by model-checking methods [2]. On the other hand, in order to express the relative likelihood of the system exhibiting certain behavior, M. Kwiatkowska has developed probabilistic timed automata and their model-checking method [3]. Moreover, the verification method of probabilistic timed simulation of probabilistic timed automata has been developed [4]. In this paper, we develop probabilistic timed transition systems by generalizing probabilistic timed automata, and develop deductive verification rules over probabilistic timed transition systems. Our probabilistic timed transition system is a general computational model with discrete probability distributions. By probabilistic timed transition systems, we can construct general verification methods. Here we mention related works about temporal verifications of both probabilistic and real-time systems as follows:

1. In 1982, A. Pnueli has developed a proof principle for liveness properties based on the general idea of well-founded descent [5]. But the work [5] constitutes only a partial solution to the general problem of verifying probabilistic concurrent programs, since it only presents an isolated proof principle for liveness properties. Several subsequent works have tried to extend it into

L.T. Yang et al. (Eds.): ICESS 2005, LNCS 3820, pp. 332–345, 2005.

more comprehensive proof systems [6, 7, 8] as follows: (1)First, M. Sharir has developed the system based on generalization of branching time temporal logic [6]. (2)Next, D. Lehmann has developed the system [7]. Lehmann's system is essentially a linear time system which follows a linear history but may refer to untaken alternatives [7]. (3)Moreover, an alternative approach based on the standard linear temporal logic is presented by A. Pnueli [8]. In 1986, A. Pnueli has adopted the linear approach suggested in the work [8] and extended it to multiprocess concurrent programs, i.e., to programs for n processes for n processes for unspecified but $n \geq 2$. A. Pnueli's proof system is first applied to the free philosophers algorithm. But A. Pnueli has not considered real-time aspects.

2. In 1991, H.A. Hansson has developed bisimulation verification of discrete time probabilistic process algebra, and model-checking of discrete time probabilistic temporal logic [10]. Namely, H.A. Hansson has extended classical process algebra with discrete time and probability. But H.A. Hansson has not considered dense time models.
3. A notable contribution to the area of the verification of probabilistic systems operating in dense time was offered by R. Alur, C. Courcoubetis and D.L. Dill [11, 12], who provided a model checking technique for a variant of Generalized Semi-Markov Processes against timed properties in 1991. But they have not developed deductive verification systems.
4. N. Lynch and F. Vaandrager have developed several kinds of timed simulation proof methods their timed automata [13] in 1991. Their timed automata [13] can serve as a semantic model, and their proposed proof methods are constructed on this semantic model. Our proposed model includes their timed automata. Moreover, we consider probabilistic behaviors, but they have not considered probabilistic behaviors.
5. R. Segala has developed the model of probabilistic timed automata, which is a dense time model, but is used in the context of manual simulation and bisimulation verification techniques in 1995 [14]. But R. Segala has not developed deductive temporal verification systems.
6. In 1996, Y. Kesten, Z. Manna and A. Pnueli have developed clocked transition systems by generalizing timed automata, and verification rules of real-time temporal logic [15]. But they have not considered probabilistic behaviors.
7. In 1999, M. Kwiatkowska has developed probabilistic timed automata with discrete probability distributions, and their model-checking method [3]. After that, S. Yamane has developed some simple timed simulation verification of probabilistic timed automata [4]. Moreover, M. Kwiatkowska has applied probabilistic timed automata into specification of IEEE 1394 FireWire Root Contention Protocol [16]. But they have not developed deductive verification systems.

In this paper, we develop probabilistic timed transition systems by generalizing probabilistic timed automata, and deductive verification rules such as safety and liveness properties, nonzenoness of probabilistic real-time temporal logic. The verification of liveness properties requires adjustments of the proof rules developed for untimed systems [17, 18], reflecting the fact that progress in the real time systems is ensured by the progress of time and not by fairness. By our proposed method, we can construct a general computational model and verification methods. Our proposed method does not refer to the region graph. In general, deductive verification method is completely general but typically requires significant human guidance, whereas model checking though restricted to a limited range of properties of small finite state systems, is largely automatic. Recently, in LICS2003 [19], M. Kwiatkowska mentions that the proof system of probabilistic timed automata is an important open problem. To the best of our knowledge, deductive verification systems of probabilistic real-time temporal logic over probabilistic timed transition systems have never been developed before now.

2 Real-Time Systems with Discrete Probabilities

In this section, we propose probabilistic timed transition systems by generalizing probabilistic timed automata [3].

2.1 Probabilistic Timed Transition Systems

First, we define discrete probability distributions as follows:

Definition 1. (Discrete probability distribution)
We denote the set of discrete probability distributions over a finite set Q by $\mu(Q)$. Therefore, each $p \in \mu(Q)$ is a function $p : Q \rightarrow [0, 1]$ such that $\sum_{q \in Q} p(q) = 1$. Supp(p) denotes the support of p, i.e. the set of elements $q \in Q$ with $p(q) > 0$. ∎

Next, we define probabilistic timed transition systems as follows:

First, we consider a finite set of system variables. System variables are typed, where the type of a variable, such as boolean, integer, etc., indicates the domain over which the variables ranges. We define a state s to be a type-consistent interpretation, assigning to each variable u a value $s[u]$ over its domain. We denote by Σ the set of all states.

Definition 2. (Probabilistic timed transition system)
A probabilistic timed transition system **PTS** $= (V, \Theta, prob, \Pi)$ *consists of :*

1. *V : A finite set of system variables.*
   The set $V = L \cup D \cup C$ is partitioned into $L = \{l_1, \ldots, l_o\}$ the set of location variables, $D = \{u_1, \ldots, u_n\}$ the set of discrete variables, and $C = \{t_1, \ldots, t_m\}$ the set of clocks. Clocks always have the type real. The discrete variables can be of any type. The location variable has the location value. We introduce a special clock $T \in C$, representing the master clock, as one of the system variables. We define $s_{L \cup D}$ to be a type-consistent interpretation, assigning to each variable $u \in L \cup D$ a value $s_{L \cup D}[u]$ over its domain. Each variable $u \in L \cup D$ is time-invariant. We denote by $\Sigma_{L \cup D}$ the set of all

type-consistent interpretations of location and discrete variables. Moreover, we define s_C *to be a type-consistent interpretation, assigning to each variable* $c_i \in C$ *a value* $s_C[c_i]$ *over its domain. Each variable* $c_i \in C$ *is time-variant. We denote by* Σ_C *the set of all clock values.*

2. Θ *: The initial condition. A satisfiable assertion characterizing the initial states. It is required that*

$$\Theta \rightarrow t_1 = \ldots = t_m = T = 0,$$

i.e., the clocks are reset to zero at all initial states.

3. Π *FThe time-progress condition.*

An assertion over V. *The assertion is used to specify a global restriction over the progress of time.*

4. *prob : A finite set of transitions.*

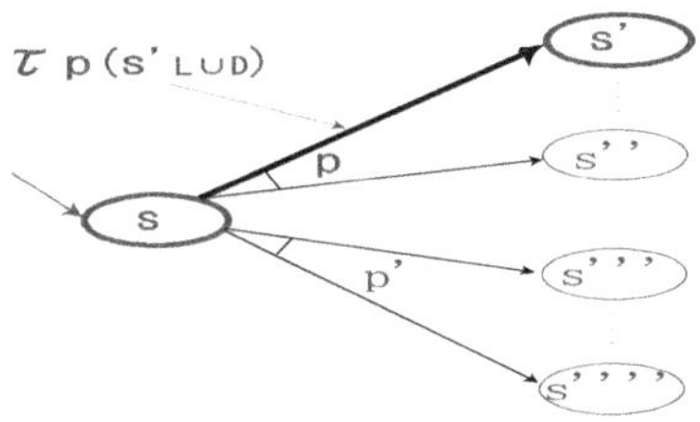

Fig. 1. A transition of Probabilistic timed transition system

(a) *Each transition* $\tau_{p(s\prime_{LUD})} \in \mathcal{T}$ *is a function*

$$prob : \Sigma_{LUD} \rightarrow 2^{TICK \times \mu(\Sigma_{LUD})},$$

mapping each $s_{LUD} \in \Sigma_{LUD}$ *into both a set of* $TCIK$ *and a set of discrete probability distributions* $\mu(\Sigma_{LUD})$ *as shown in figure 1. If we consider* $s_{LUD} \in \Sigma_{LUD}$ *and* $(tick, p) \in prob(s_{LUD})$*, a probabilistic transition from a state* s *to a state* $s\prime$ *with probability* $p(s\prime_{LUD})$ *occurs, where* $tick \in TICK$, $p \in \mu(\Sigma_{LUD})$ *and* $s_{LUD} \in \Sigma_{LUD}$.

(b) *Now we define a set of* $TCIK$ *as follows:*
Transition $tick \in TICK$ *is a special transition intended to represent the passage of time. Its transition relation is given by:*

$$\rho_{tick} : \exists \triangle > 0.\Omega(\triangle) \wedge L\prime = L \wedge D\prime = D \wedge C\prime = C + \triangle$$

where $\Omega(\triangle)$ *is given by*

$$\Omega(\triangle) : \triangle > 0 \wedge \forall t \in [0, \triangle).\Pi(L, D, C + t).$$

Let $L=\{l_1, \ldots, l_o\}$ *be the set of location variables of* **PTS**, $D=\{u_1, \ldots, u_m\}$ *be the set of discrete variables of* **PTS** *and* $C = \{t_1, \ldots, t_k, T\}$ *be the set of its clocks. Then, the expression* $C\prime = C + \triangle$ *is an abbreviation for*

$$t_1\prime = t_1 + \triangle \wedge \ldots \wedge t_k\prime = t_k + \triangle \wedge T\prime = T + \triangle$$

and $\Pi(L, D, C+t)$ is an abbreviation for

$$\Pi(l_1, \ldots, l_o, u_1, \ldots, u_m, t_1+t, \ldots, t_k+t, T+t).$$

(c) *The function associated with a transition $\tau_{p(s\prime_{L \cup D})}$ is represented by an assertion $\rho_{\tau_{p(s\prime_{L \cup D})}}(V, V\prime)$, called the transition relation, which relates a state $s \in \Sigma$ to its $\tau_{p(s\prime_{L \cup D})}$-successor $s\prime \in \tau_{p(s\prime_{L \cup D})}(s)$ by referring to both unprimed and primed versions of the system variables. An unprimed version of a system variable refers its value in s, while a primed version of the same variable refers to its value in $s\prime$.* ■

Next, we define a path of a probabilistic timed transition system as follows:

Definition 3. (Path)
Paths in a probabilistic timed transition system arise by resolving both the nondeterministic and probabilistic choices. A path of the probabilistic timed transition system is a non-empty finite or infinite sequence:

$$\omega = s_0 \stackrel{tick_0, p_0}{\longrightarrow} s_1 \stackrel{tick_1, p_1}{\longrightarrow} s_2 \stackrel{tick_2, P_2}{\longrightarrow} s_3 \stackrel{tick_3, p_3}{\longrightarrow} s_4 \ldots\ldots$$

where $s_i \in \Sigma$, $s_i \in \tau_{p_{i-1}(s_{i\,L \cup D})}(s_{i-1})$ or $C_i = C_{i-1} + \triangle_{i-1}$. Here C_i denotes C at s_i and C_{i-1} denotes C at s_{i-1}. $\omega(k)$ denotes the k-th state of ω. The location and discrete values of the last state of ω is denoted by $last(\omega)$. $Path_{fin}$ is the set of finite paths, and $Path_{fin}(s)$ is the set of paths in $Path_{fin}$ such that $\omega(0) = s$. $Path_{ful}$ is the set of infinite paths and $Path_{ful}(s)$ is the set of paths in $Path_{ful}$ such that $\omega(0) = s$. Also, $Path_{fin}(s_{L \cup D})$ is the set of paths in $Path_{fin}$ such that $\omega(0) = s$. Moreover, $Path_{ful}(s_{L \cup D})$ is the set of paths in $Path_{ful}$ such that $\omega(0) = s$.

A path ω of **PTS** *is a finite or infinite sequence of states satisfying:*

1. *Initiation: $s_0 \models \Theta$*
2. *Consecution:*
   (1) *Case of probabilistic transitions: $s_i \in \tau_{p_{i-1}(s_{i\,L \cup D})}(s_{i-1})$.*
   (2) *Case of tick transition: $C_i = C_{i-1} + \triangle_{i-1}$, where C_i denotes C at s_i and C_{i-1} denotes C at s_{i-1}.*

Moreover, in some case, a path ω of **PTS** *is an infinite sequence of states satisfying:*

3. *Time Divergence: The sequence $s_0[T]$,$s_1[T]$,..,$s_i[T]$,... grows beyond any bound. That is, as i increases, the value $s_i[T]$ of T at s_i increases beyond any bound.* ■

2.2 Adversary

We now introduce adversaries of probabilistic timed transition systems as functions which resolve all the nondeterministic choices of the system [3]. The concept of adversaries has been proposed by A. Pnueli [5] and M. Vardi [20]. Moreover, M. Kwiatkowska has applied it into probabilistic timed automata with discrete probability distributions [3]. In this paper, we use M. Kwiatkowska's definitions.

Definition 4. (Adversary of a probabilistic timed transition system) *An adversary of a probabilistic timed transition system* **PTS** $= (V, \Theta, prob, \Pi)$ *is a function* A *mapping every finite path* ω *of* **PTS** *to* $(tick, p) \in prob(s_{L \cup D})$ *such that* $A(\omega) \in prob(last(\omega))$*, where* $last(\omega)$ *denotes the last location and discrete values of* ω*,* $s_{L \cup D} \in \Sigma_{L \cup D}$*,* $tick \in TICK$*,* $p \in \mu(s_{L \cup D})$*.* ■

For an adversary A of a probabilistic timed transition system **PTS** $= (V, \Theta, prob, \Pi)$, we define $Path^A_{fin}$ to be the set of finite paths. With each adversary A we associate a sequential Markov chain, which can be viewed as a set of paths in **PTS**. Formally, if A is an adversary of the probabilistic timed transition system **PTS**, then $\mathbf{MC}^A = (Path^A_{fin}, \mathbf{P}^A)$ is a Markov chain where:

$$\mathbf{P}^A(\omega, \omega\prime) = \begin{cases} p(s_{L \cup D}) \; if \quad A(\omega) = (tick, p) \quad and \quad \omega\prime = \omega \overset{tick,p}{\longrightarrow} s \\ \qquad 0 \; otherwise. \end{cases}$$

For any probabilistic timed transition system and adversary A, let $\mathcal{F}_{path}{}^A$ be the smallest σ-algebra on $Path_{ful}{}^A$ which contains the sets:

$$\{\omega | \omega \in Path_{ful}{}^A \text{ and } \omega\prime \text{ is a prefix of } \omega \;\} \text{ for all } \omega\prime \in Path_{ful}{}^A.$$

We now define a measure $Prob^A$ on the σ-algebra $\mathcal{F}_{path}{}^A$, by first defining the following function on the set of finite paths $Path_{ful}{}^A$.

Definition 5. $(Prob_{fin}{}^A)$
Let A *be an adversary of the probabilistic timed transition system* **PTS**. *Let* $Prob_{fin}{}^A : Path^A_{fin} \to [0, 1]$ *be the mapping inductively defined on the length of paths in* $Path_{fin}{}^A$ *as follows:*

1. *If* $|\omega| = 0$*, then* $Prob_{fin}{}^A(\omega) = 1.0$.
2. *If* $|\omega| \neq 0$*, then if* $\omega = \omega\prime \overset{tick,p}{\longrightarrow} s$ *for some* $\omega\prime \in Path_{fin}{}^A$*, then* $Prob^A_{fin}(\omega) = Prob^A_{fin}(\omega\prime) \cdot \mathbf{P}^A(\omega\prime, \omega)$*, where* $\mathbf{P}^A(\omega\prime, \omega) = p(s_{L \cup D})$. ■

Definition 6. $(Prob^A)$
The measure $Prob^A$ *on* $\mathcal{F}_{path}{}^A$ *is the unique measure such that:*

$$Prob^A(\{\omega | \omega \in path^A_{ful} \text{ and } \omega\prime \text{ is a prefix of } \omega \;\}) = Prob_{fin}{}^A(\omega\prime). \quad ■$$

A common restriction imposed in the study of real-time systems is that of nonzenoness. A probabilistic timed transition system is defined to be nonzeno if every finite path can be extended into an infinite path. Here a state is called accessible if it appears in a path of a probabilistic timed transition system. Nonzenoness requires that a state s is accessible iff it appears in some path of a probabilistic timed transition system.

3 Probabilistic Real-Time Linear Temporal Logic

In this section, we introduce probabilistic real-time linear temporal logic. To specify properties of probabilistic timed transition systems, we use the language of temporal logic, as presented in the book [17].

First, we define syntax of probabilistic real-time linear temporal logic. Here we only use the following:

Definition 7. (Syntax of probabilistic real-time linear temporal logic) *Syntax of probabilistic real-time linear temporal logic is inductively defined as follows:*

1. *q is any first-order formula.*
2. *$[\Box q]_{\sqsupseteq\lambda}$, where q is any first-order formula, and $\lambda \in [0,1]$, $\sqsupseteq$ is $\geq$ or $>$.*
   $[\Box q]_{\sqsupseteq\lambda}$ means that q always holds true satisfying $\sqsupseteq \lambda$.
3. *$[\Box(q \rightarrow \Diamond r)]_{\sqsupseteq\lambda}$, where q and r are any first-order formula.*
   $[\Box(q \rightarrow \Diamond r)]_{\sqsupseteq\lambda}$ means that q entails eventually r satisfying $\sqsupseteq \lambda$. ■

Next, we define semantics of probabilistic real-time linear temporal logic as follows:

Definition 8. (Semantics of probabilistic real-time linear temporal logic)
Given a probabilistic timed transition system **PTS** *and a set $\mathcal{A}$ of adversaries, then for any state s of* **PTS**, *probabilistic real-time linear temporal logic formula ϕ, the satisfaction relation $s \models_{\mathcal{A}} \phi$ is defined inductively as follows:*

1. *$s \models_{\mathcal{A}} q$*
   $\Longleftrightarrow s \models q$, where $s \models q$ means that an assertion q holds true on state s.
2. *$s \models_{\mathcal{A}} [\Box q]_{\sqsupseteq\lambda}$*
   $\Longleftrightarrow Prob^A(\{\omega | \omega \in Path_{ful}{}^A(s)$, and, $\omega(i) \models_{\mathcal{A}} q$ for $\forall i$ $\}) \sqsupseteq \lambda$ for all $A \in \mathcal{A}$.
3. *$s \models_{\mathcal{A}} [\Box(q \rightarrow \Diamond r)]_{\sqsupseteq\lambda}$*
   $\Longleftrightarrow Prob^A(\{\omega | \omega \in Path_{ful}{}^A(s)$, and, $\omega(i) \models_{\mathcal{A}} q$ and for some $j \geq i$ $\omega(j) \models_{\mathcal{A}} r$ for every i $\}) \sqsupseteq \lambda$ for all $A \in \mathcal{A}$. ■

Next, we define concepts of q-state, state valid and valid as follows: (1)Given a probabilistic timed transition system **PTS**, a set $\mathcal{A}$ of adversaries, an assertion q, a state s of **PTS**, if q holds on s, then s is a q-state. (2)Given a probabilistic timed transition system **PTS**, a set $\mathcal{A}$ of adversaries, an assertion q, if it holds over all accessible states for every $A \in \mathcal{A}$, then an assertion q is called state valid. In this paper, we say that a state s is accessible if it appears in some path of **PTS**. (3)Given a probabilistic timed transition system **PTS**, a set $\mathcal{A}$ of adversaries, a temporal formula ϕ, if it holds over all the paths of **PTS** for every $A \in \mathcal{A}$, then a temporal formula ϕ is called valid.

4 Verifying Safety Property

In this section, we present methods for verifying safety property ($[\Box q]_{\sqsupseteq\lambda}$) of probabilistic timed transition systems. We construct methods for verifying safety property of probabilistic timed transition systems by extending Z. Manna's and

A. Pnueli's verification methods of reactive systems [17] and real-time systems [15].

First, we define the deductive verification rule of safety property.

For every adversary A of $\mathbf{PTS} = (V, \Theta, prob, \Pi)$, a path of the probabilistic timed transition system is a non-empty finite or infinite sequence:

$$\omega = s_0 \stackrel{tick_0, p_0}{\longrightarrow} s_1 \stackrel{tick_1, p_1}{\longrightarrow} s_2 \stackrel{tick_2, p_2}{\longrightarrow} s_3 \stackrel{tick_3, p_3}{\longrightarrow} s_4 \stackrel{tick_4, p_4}{\longrightarrow} s_5 \ldots\ldots$$

where $s_i \in \Sigma$, $s_i \in \tau_{p_{i-1}(s_{L \cup D i})}(s_{i-1})$ or $C_i = C_{i-1} + \triangle_{i-1}$. The transition relation ρ_{tick_i} is given by :

$$\rho_{tick_i} : \exists \triangle_i > 0. \Omega(\triangle_i) \wedge L\prime = L \wedge D\prime = D \wedge C\prime = C + \triangle_i,$$

where $\Omega(\triangle_i)$ is given by

$$\Omega(\triangle_i) : \triangle_i > 0 \wedge \forall t \in [0, \triangle_i).\Pi(L, D, C + t).$$

Let A be an adversary of the probabilistic timed transition system **PTS**. Let ${Prob_{fin}}^A : Path_{fin}^A \rightarrow [0, 1]$ be the mapping inductively defined on the length of paths in ${Path_{fin}}^A$ as follows:

1. If $|\omega| = 0$, then ${Prob_{fin}}^A(\omega) = 1$.
2. If $|\omega| \neq 0$, then if $\omega = \omega\prime \stackrel{tick_i, p_i}{\longrightarrow} s$ for some $\omega\prime \in {Path_{fin}}^A$, then we let $Prob_{fin}^A(\omega) = Prob_{fin}^A(\omega\prime) \cdot \mathbf{P}^A(\omega\prime, \omega)$, where let $\mathbf{P}^A(\omega\prime, \omega)$ be $p_i(s_{L \cup D})$.

In general, we can define $Prob_{fin}^A(\omega_n) = \mathbf{P}^A(\omega_0, \omega_1) \cdot \mathbf{P}^A(\omega_1, \omega_2) \cdot \mathbf{P}^A(\omega_2, \omega_3) \cdot \ldots\ldots \cdot \mathbf{P}^A(\omega_{n-1}, \omega_n)$ where $\omega_n = s_0 \stackrel{tick_0, p_0}{\longrightarrow} s_1 \stackrel{tick_1, p_1}{\longrightarrow} s_2 \ldots\ldots \stackrel{tick_{n-1}, p_{n-1}}{\longrightarrow} s_n$.

We verify whether $Prob^A(\{\omega | \omega \in {Path_{ful}}^A(s)$, and, $\omega(i) \models_{\mathcal{A}} q$ for $\forall i \}) \sqsupseteq \lambda$ for all $A \in \mathcal{A}$ are satisfiable or not, where $\omega = s_0 \stackrel{tick_0, p_0}{\longrightarrow} s_1 \stackrel{tick_1, p_1}{\longrightarrow} s_2 \stackrel{tick_2, p_2}{\longrightarrow} s_3 \stackrel{tick_3, p_3}{\longrightarrow} s_4 \ldots\ldots\ldots$.

We must compute the minimal probability of $Prob^A(\{\omega | \omega \in {Path_{ful}}^A(s)$, and, $\omega(i) \models_{\mathcal{A}} q$ for $\forall i \})$ for all $A \in \mathcal{A}$.

Lemma 1. (Minimal probability)
Let **PTS** $= (V, \Theta, prob, \Pi)$ *be a probabilistic timed transition system and an adversary* $A \in \mathcal{A}$. *We can define the minimal probability of* $Prob^A$ *as follows:*

$$p^{min}(\omega) = inf_{A \in \mathcal{A}}\ Prob^A(\{\omega | \omega \in {Path_{ful}}^A, \text{ and, } \omega(i) \models_{\mathcal{A}} q \text{ for } \forall i \}).$$

Then, p^{min} *is the least fixed point of the operator*

$$F : (Path_{ful} \rightarrow [0, 1]) \rightarrow (Path_{ful} \rightarrow [0, 1])$$

that is defined as follows:

$$F(f)(\omega) = min\{\textstyle\sum_{s\prime \in Supp(p(s\prime_{L \cup D})) \wedge \triangle > 0} p(s\prime_{L \cup D}) \cdot f(\omega \stackrel{tick, p}{\longrightarrow} s\prime) \,|\rho_{tick}, p \in \mu(last(\omega))\}$$

where $s_{L \cup D} = last(\omega)$ *and* $C\prime = C + \triangle$.

Here $C\prime$ *denotes the set* C *at* s_i *and* C *denotes the set* C *at* s. ■

Theorem 1. (Minimal probability)
Let **PTS** $= (V, \Theta, prob, \Pi)$ *be a probabilistic timed transition system and an adversary* $A \in \mathcal{A}$. *We can define the minimal probability of* $Prob^A$ *as follows:*

$$p^{min}(s) = inf_{A\in\mathcal{A}}\ Prob^A(\{\omega | \omega \in Path_{ful}{}^A(s),\ and,\ \omega(i) \models_{\mathcal{A}} q\ for\ \forall i\ \}).$$

We can also denote the minimal probability of $Prob^A$ *as follows:*

$$p^{min}(s_{L\cup D}) = inf_{A\in\mathcal{A}}\ Prob^A(\{\omega | \omega \in Path_{ful}{}^A(s_{L\cup D}),\ and,\ \omega(i) \models_{\mathcal{A}} q\ for\ \forall i\ \}).$$

Then, p^{min} *is the least fixed point of the operator*

$$F : (\Sigma_{L\cup D} \rightarrow [0,1]) \rightarrow (\Sigma_{L\cup D} \rightarrow [0,1])$$

that is defined as follows:

$$F(f)(s_{L\cup D}) = min\{\textstyle\sum_{s\prime_{L\cup D}\in\Sigma_{L\cup D}\wedge\Delta>0} p(s\prime_{L\cup D}) \cdot f(s\prime_{L\cup D})\ |\rho_{tick}, p \in \mu(s_{L\cup D})\}.$$

■

Proposition 1. (Computing the minimal probability)
Theorem 1 yields that the value p^{min} *can be approximated with the following iterative method.*

For $s_{L\cup D} \in \Sigma_{L\cup D}$ *and* $n = 0, 1, 2, \ldots\ldots,$

$$p^{min}{}_{n+1}(s_{L\cup D}) = min\{\textstyle\sum_{s\prime_{L\cup D}\in\Sigma_{L\cup D}\wedge\Delta>0} p(s\prime_{L\cup D}) \cdot p^{min}{}_n(s_{L\cup D})\ |\rho_{tick}, p \in \mu(s_{L\cup D})\}.$$

■

Finally, we define verification rule of safety property as follows:

Definition 9. (Verification rule of safety property)
For every adversary A of **PTS** $= (V, \Theta, prob, \Pi)$, *and assertions* φ *and* q, *we define the verification rule as follows:*

1. $\Theta \rightarrow \varphi$
2. $\varphi \rightarrow q$
3. *For every* $\tau \in \mathcal{T}_H$, $\rho_\tau \wedge \varphi \rightarrow \varphi\prime$
4. *For every initial state s, which satisfies* Θ,
   $p^{min}{}_{n+1}(s_{L\cup D}) = min\{\sum_{s\prime_{L\cup D}\in\Sigma_{L\cup D}\wedge\Delta>0} p(s\prime_{L\cup D}) \cdot p^{min}{}_n(s_{L\cup D})\ |\rho_{tick}, p \in \mu(s_{L\cup D})\} \sqsupseteq \lambda$
5. -
6. $[\Box q]_{\sqsupseteq\lambda}$

This rule is a verification rule of safety property. If premises 1,2,3 and 4 are satisfied, $[\Box q]_{\sqsupseteq\lambda}$ *can be verified.* ■

Next, we present the soundness of the rule as follows:

Theorem 2. (The soundness of the rule for verifying the safety property)
If all the premises of the rule are state valid, $[\Box q]_{\sqsupseteq\lambda}$ *is valid.* ■

5 Verifying Liveness Property

In this section, we present methods for verifying liveness property ($[\Box(q \to \Diamond r)]_{\sqsupseteq\lambda}$) of probabilistic timed transition systems. We construct methods for verifying liveness property of probabilistic timed transition systems by extending Z.Manna's and A.Pnueli's verification methods of reactive systems [18] and real-time systems [15].

First, we define the deductive verification rule of liveness property.

The rule uses auxiliary assertions $\varphi_1, \ldots, \varphi_m$ and refers to assertion r also as φ_0. With each assertion φ_i we associate one of the clocks $t_i \in C$, to which we refer as the clock, and a real-valued upper bound b_i. The intention is that while remaining in states satisfying φ_i, the clock t_i is bounded by b_i and never reset. Since time in a computation grows beyond any bound, this will imply that we cannot continually stay at a φ_i for too long. Moreover, for all i, φ_i entails eventually φ_j satisfying $\sqsupseteq \lambda$, where $j \leq i$.

Next, we define the deductive verification rule of liveness property. We can compute the minimal probability of $Prob^A(\{\omega|\omega \in {Path_{ful}}^A(s)$, and, $\omega(i) \models_{\mathcal{A}} q$ and for some $j \geq i$ $\omega(j) \models_{\mathcal{A}} r$ for every i $\}) \sqsupseteq \lambda$.

Lemma 2. (Minimal probability)
Let **PTS** $= (V, \Theta, prob, \Pi)$ *be a probabilistic timed transition system and an adversary* $A \in \mathcal{A}$. *Let* $\omega(k) \in \Sigma_1$, $k = i, i+1, \ldots, j-1$, *and* $\omega(j) \in \Sigma_2$. *We can define the minimal probability of* $Prob^A$ *as follows:*

$p^{min}(\omega) = inf_{A \in \mathcal{A}}\ Prob^A(\{\omega|\omega \in {Path_{ful}}^A$, *and,* $\omega(i) \models_{\mathcal{A}} q$ *and for some* $j \geq i$ $\omega(j) \models_{\mathcal{A}} r$ *for every* i $\})$.

Then, p^{min} *is the least fixed point of the operator*

$$F : (Path_{ful} \to [0,1]) \to (Path_{ful} \to [0,1])$$

that is defined as follows:

If $s \in \Sigma_2$ *then* $F(f)(\omega) = 1$.
If $s \in \Sigma \setminus (\Sigma_1 \cup \Sigma_2)$ *then* $F(f)(\omega) = 0$.
If $s \in \Sigma_1 \setminus \Sigma_2$ *then*

$F(f)(\omega) = min\{\sum_{s\prime \in Supp(p(s\prime_{L \cup D})) \wedge \triangle > 0} p(s\prime_{L \cup D}) \cdot f(\omega \xrightarrow{tick,p} s\prime)\ |\rho_{tick}, p \in \mu(s_{L \cup D})\}$

where $s_{L \cup D} = last(\omega)$ *and* $C\prime = C + \triangle$. *Here* $C\prime$ *denotes* C *at* s_i *and* C *denotes* C *at* s. ∎

Theorem 3. (Minimal probability)
Let **PTS** $= (V, \Theta, prob, \Pi)$ *be a probabilistic timed transition system and an adversary* $A \in \mathcal{A}$. *Let* $\omega(k) \in \Sigma_1$, $k = i, i+1, \ldots, j-1$, *and* $\omega(j) \in \Sigma_2$. *We can define the minimal probability of* $Prob^A$ *as follows:*

$p^{min}(s) = inf_{A \in \mathcal{A}}\ Prob^A(\{\omega|\omega \in {Path_{ful}}^A(s)$, *and,* $\omega(i) \models_{\mathcal{A}} q$ *and for some* $j \geq i$ $\omega(j) \models_{\mathcal{A}} r$ *for every* i $\})$.

We can also denote the minimal probability of $Prob^A$ *as follows:*

$p^{min}(s_{L\cup D}) = inf_{A\in\mathcal{A}}\ Prob^A(\{\omega|\omega \in Path_{ful}{}^A(s),\ and,\ \omega(i) \models_{\mathcal{A}} q\ and\ for\ j \geq i\ \omega(j) \models_{\mathcal{A}} r\ for\ all\ i\ \})$.

Then, p^{min} *is the least fixed point of the operator*

$F : (\Sigma_{L\cup D} \rightarrow [0,1]) \rightarrow (\Sigma_{L\cup D} \rightarrow [0,1])$
that is defined as follows:
If $s \in \Sigma_2$ *then* $F(f)(s_{L\cup D}) = 1$.
If $s \in \Sigma \setminus (\Sigma_1 \cup \Sigma_2)$ *then* $F(f)(s_{L\cup D}) = 0$.
If $s \in \Sigma_1 \setminus \Sigma_2$ *then*

$F(f)(s_{L\cup D}) = min\{\sum_{s\prime\in Supp(p(s\prime_{L\cup D}))\wedge\triangle>0} p(s\prime_{L\cup D}) \cdot f(\omega \stackrel{tick,p}{\longrightarrow} s\prime)\ |\rho_{tick},\ p \in \mu(s_{L\cup D})\}$

where $sL\cup D = last(\omega)$ *and* $C\prime = C+\triangle$. *Here* $C\prime$ *denotes* C *at* s_i *and* C *denotes* C *at* s. ■

Proposition 2. (Computing the minimal probability)
Theorem 1 yields that the value p^{min} *can be approximated with the following iterative method.*

We put $p_n(s_{L\cup D}) = 1.0$ *if* $s \in \Sigma_2$ *and* $p_n(s_{L\cup D}) = 0$ *if* $s \in S \setminus (\Sigma_1 \cup \Sigma_2)$, $n = 0, 1, \ldots$.

For $s \in \Sigma_1 \setminus \Sigma_2$, $n = 0, 1, 2, \ldots\ldots,$

$p^{min}{}_{n+1}(s_{L\cup D}) = min\{\sum_{s\prime_{L\cup D}\in\Sigma_{L\cup D}\wedge\triangle>0} p(s\prime_{L\cup D}) \cdot p^{min}{}_n(s_{L\cup D})\ |\rho_{tick},\ p \in \mu(s_{L\cup D})\}$. ■

Definition 10. (Verification rule of liveness property)
For every Adversary A *of* **PTS** $= (V, \Theta, prob, \Pi)$, *and assertions* q, r, $\varphi_0 = r, \varphi_1, \ldots, \varphi_m$, *clocks* $t_1, \ldots, t_m \in C$, *and real constants* $b_1, \ldots, b_m \in \mathbf{R}$, *we define the verification rule as follows:*

1. $q \rightarrow \bigvee_{j=0}^{m} \varphi_j$
2. *For* $i = 1, \ldots, m$:
   1. *For every* $\tau \in \mathcal{T}$, $\rho_\tau \wedge \varphi_i \rightarrow (\varphi_i\prime \wedge t_i\prime \geq t_i) \vee \bigvee_{j<i} \varphi_j\prime$
   2. *For every* $\tau \in \mathcal{T}$,
      $p^{min}{}_{n+1}(s_{L\cup D}) = min\{\sum_{s\prime_{L\cup D}\in\Sigma_L\wedge\triangle>0} p(s\prime_{L\cup D}) \cdot p^{min}{}_n(s_{L\cup D})\ |\rho_{tick}, p \in \mu(s_{L\cup D})\} \sqsupseteq \lambda$
   3. $\varphi_i \rightarrow t_i \leq b_i$
4. ---------------------------------------
5. $[\Box(q \rightarrow \Diamond r)]_{\sqsupseteq\lambda}$

This rule is a verification rule of liveness property. If premises 1 and 2 are satisfied, $[\Box(q \rightarrow \Diamond r)]_{\sqsupseteq\lambda}$ *can be verified.*

We simply explain the premises as follows:

1. *The premise 1. requires that every q-state satisfies one of* $\varphi_0 = r$, $\varphi_1, \ldots, \varphi_m$.
2. *For* $i = 1, \ldots, m$, *three following premises hold true :*

1. *The premise 2.1. requires that every τ-successor ($\forall\tau \in \mathcal{T}$) of a φ_i-state s is a φ_j-state for some $j \leq i$. In this case that the τ-successor state satisfies φ_i, it is required that the transition does not decrease the value of t_i.*
2. *The premise 2.2. requires that the minimal measure satisfies $\sqsupseteq \lambda$.*
3. *The premise 2.3. requires that assertion φ_i implies that t_i is bounded by the constant b_i.* ■

Next, we present the soundness of the rule as follows:

Theorem 4. (The soundness of the rule)
If all the premises of the rule are state valid, $[\Box(q \to \Diamond r)]_{\sqsupseteq\lambda}$ is valid. ■

6 Verifying Nonzenoness

It is a widely accepted notion that the only interesting real-time systems are those which obey the nonzeno restriction [21]. In the view of the significance of the nonzeno restriction, it is important to be able to verify that an arbitrary given probabilistic timed transition system is nonzeno.

The general strategy we propose for proving that a given probabilistic timed transition system **PTS** is nonzeno in the following rule. We construct the following rule by combing A. Pnueli's verification rule of nonzenoness [15] with M. Kwiatkowska's divergent adversaries [3]. But both A. Pnueli and M. Kwiatkowska have not proposed the proof rule of nonzenoness for probabilistic timed systems. We can compute the minimal probability $Prob^A(\{\omega|\omega \in Path_{ful}{}^A(s)\})$ in the same way as the verification rule of safty property.

Definition 11. (Verification rule of nonzenoness)
For every divergent adversary A_{div} of **PTS** $= (V, \Theta, prob, \Pi)$, *and assertions φ, we define the verification rule as follows:*

1. **PTS** $\|\!= \varphi$
2. **PTS** $\models AG(\varphi \wedge T_a = 0 \to EF(T_a \geq 1))$
3. $\sum_{A\in A_{div}} \{ p^{min}{}_{n+1}(s_{L\cup D}) = min\{\sum_{s\prime_{L\cup D}\ in \Sigma_{L\cup D} \wedge \Delta > 0} p(s\prime_{L\cup D}) \cdot p^{min}{}_n(s_{L\cup D}) \, |\rho_{tick}, p \in \mu(s_{L\cup D})\} \} = 1$
4. ---
5. **PTS** *is nonzeno*

This rule is a verification rule of nonzenoness. If premises 1,2 and 3 are satisfied, **PTS** *is nonzeno can be verified.*

We have already defined the premise 3, but have not defined premises 1 and 2. Now we will define them as follows:

1. *premise 1 :*
   The premise 1 is a rule that establishes the state validity of an assertion φ. We define the rule as follows:
   For every divergent adversary A_{div} of **PTS** $= (V, \Theta, prob, \Pi)$, *and assertions φ and q,*

1. $q \rightarrow \varphi$
2. $\Theta \rightarrow q$
3. *For every* $\tau \in \mathcal{T}$, $\rho_\tau \wedge q \rightarrow q\prime$
4. ------------------------------
5. $\quad$ **PTS** $\| = \varphi$

This rule have been firstly defined by A. Pnueli [15]. This rule follows that φ *holds on every accessible state of* **PTS** *for every divergent adversary* A_{div}, *and therefore, an assertion* φ *is state valid.*

2. *premise 2 :*
The premise 2 belongs to the realm of branching-time temporal logic [15], which is different from the linear-time temporal framework we have been consistently using this paper. We use the branching-time temporal logic CTL [22] for formulating the required property, as in the premise 2. The premise 2 states that, from every φ*-state s, it is possible to trace a path segment in which time increases by at least 1 from its value at s. We use the constant a to represent the global time at s. The proof rule of the premise 2 has been propoesed by A. Pnueli [15]. The proof rule is omitted in this paper because of lack of spaces.* ■

Next, we present the soundness of the rule as follows:

Theorem 5. (The soundness of the rule for verifying nonzenoness)
If all the premises of the rule are state valid, **PTS***'s nonzenoness is valid.* ■

7 Conclusions

In this paper, we have developed probabilistic timed transition systems by generalizing probabilistic timed automata, and verification rules of probabilistic real-time temporal logic. By our proposed methods, we could construct a general computational model and verification method. We have omitted the proofs of completeness of rules because of lack of spaces. We are now planning to apply our proposed methods into real distributed real-time systems. Moreover, we will support deductive verification jobs by mechanical theorem provers. Moreover, we will reduce deductive verification jobs into model-checking by transforming a probabilistic timed transition system into a finite probabilistic timed automaton based on abstract interpretation.

References

1. R. Alur, D.L. Dill. A theory of timed automata. *Theoretical Computer Science*,Vol. 126, pp.183-235, 1994.
2. T. A. Henzinger, X. Nicollin, J. Sifakis, S. Yovine. Symbolic model checking for real-time systems. *Information and Computation*, Vol. 111, pp. 193-244, 1994.
3. M. Kwiatkowska, G. Norman, R. Segala, J. Sproston. Automatic verification of real-time systems with discrete probability distributions. *Theoretical Computer Science 282*, pp 101-150, 2002

4. S. Yamane : Probabilistic Timed Simulation Verification and its application to Stepwise Refinement of Real-Time Systems. *LNCS 2896*, pp.276-290, Springer-Verlag, 2003.
5. S. Hart, M. Sharir, A. Pnueli. Termination of Probabilistic Concurrent Programs. *ACM TOPLAS*, Vol. 5, pp.356-380, 1983. (In 9th ACM POPL , pp.1-6, 1982.)
6. M. Sharir, S. Hart. Probabilistic temporal logics for finite and bounded models. *Proc. of the 16th ACM Symposium on Theory of Computing*, pp. 1-13, 1984.
7. D. Lehmann, S. Shelah. Reasoning about time and chance. *Information and Control*, Vol.53, pp.165-198, 1982.
8. A. Pnueli. On the Extremely Fair Treatment of Probabilistic Algorithms. *Proc. of the 15th ACM Symposium Theory of Computing*, pp. 278-290, 1983.
9. A. Pnueli, L. Zuck. Verification of multiprocess probabilistic protocols. *Distributed Computing*, 1(1), pp.53-72, 1986.
10. H.A. Hansson. Time and Probability in Formal Design of Distributed Systems. *PhD thesis, Uppsala University*, 1991.
11. R. Alur, C. Courcoubetis, D.L. Dill. Verifying automata specifications of probabilistic real-time systems. *LNCS 600*, pp. 28-44, 1991.
12. R. Alur, C. Courcoubetis, D.L. Dill. Model-checking for probabilistic real-time systems. *LNCS 510*, pp. 115-136, 1991.
13. N.A. Lynch, F.W. Vaandrager. Forward and Backward Simulations for Timing-Based Systems. *LNCS 600*, pp.397-446, 1992.
14. R. Segala. Modeling and Verification of Randomized Distributed Real-Time Systems. *PhD thesis*, MIT, 1995.
15. Y. Kesten, Z. Manna, A. Pnueli. Verifying Clocked Transition Systems. *LNCS 1066*, pp. 13-40. Springer-Verlag, 1996.
16. M.Z. Kwiatkowska, G. Norman, J. Sproston. Probabilistic Model Checking of Deadline Properties in the IEEE 1394 FireWire Root Contention Protocol. *Formal Aspects of Computing* 14(3), pp 295-318, 2003.
17. Z. Manna, A. Pnueli. Temporal Verification of Reactive Systems : Safety. *Springer-Verlag*, 1995.
18. Z. Manna, A. Pnueli. Temporal Verification of Reactive Systems: Progress. *Unpublished, Stanford University (http://theory.stanford.edu/ zm/)*, 1996.
19. M.Z. Kwiatkowska. Model Checking for Probability and Time: From Theory to Practice. *Invited talk at LICS'03*, pp.351-360, 2003.
20. M.Y. Vardi. Automatic verification of probabilistic concurrent finite-state systems. *Proc. 26th IEEE Symp. Found. of Comp. Sci.*, pp. 327-338, 1985.
21. M. Abadi, L. Lamport. An Old-Fashioned Recipe for Real Time. *ACM Transactions on Programming Languages and Systems*, Vol.16, no.5, pp.1543-1571, 1994.
22. E.M. Clarke, E.A. Emerson. Synthesis of synchronization skeletons for branching time temporal. *LNCS 131*, 1981.

Specification and Verification Techniques of Embedded Systems Using Probabilistic Linear Hybrid Automata

Yosuke Mutsuda, Takaaki Kato, and Satoshi Yamane

Graduate School of Natural Science & Technology, Kanazawa University,
Kakuma-machi, Kanazawa city, Japan ZIP/CODE 920–1192
Tel: +81.76.234.4856, Fax: +81.76.234.4900
{0163muts, 1118kato, syamane}@is.t.kanazawa-u.ac.jp

Abstract. We can model embedded systems as hybrid systems. Moreover, they are distributed and real-time systems. Therefore, it is important to specify and verify randomness and soft real-time properties. For the purpose of system verification, we formally define probabilistic linear hybrid automaton and its symbolic reachability analysis method. It can describe uncertainties and soft real-time characteristics. Our proposal method is the first attempt to symbolically verify probabilistic linear hybrid automata.

1 Introduction

As ubiquitous computing has progressed, systems are embedded in widespread environments. Then it is important to guarantee their formal correctness, for instance, safety, reliability, dependability, randomization, and soft real-time properties. In this paper, we propose the formal verification of probabilistic hybrid systems. Probabilistic hybrid systems are digital real-time systems that embedded in analog environment and exhibit probabilistic characteristics.

There have been several formal verification methods based on automaton models as follows: 1. Symbolic model-checking procedure and its implementation HyTech for linear hybrid automata have been developed using manipulating and simplifying $(\mathbb{R}, \leq, +)$-formulae [1]. 2. For probabilistic timed automata [5], zone-based symbolic model checking algorithms and tool Prism have been presented [4]. 3. Reachability for probabilistic rectangular automata has been mentioned in [6], but the verification methods for general class of probabilistic hybrid automata have not been developed.

We consider probabilistic linear hybrid automata, an extension of linear hybrid automata [1] with discrete probability distributions or probabilistic timed automata [4] with continuous dynamics. This model contains probabilistic rectangular automata [6], moreover, our reachability analysis method differs from [6] on the point that J. Sproston [6] generates a finite-state reachability graph, but our approach uses symbolic computation of logical formulae without graph construction. To verify probabilistic hybrid systems, we define the polyhedron labeled by probability as the data structure. And we collectively compute state

L.T. Yang et al. (Eds.): ICESS 2005, LNCS 3820, pp. 346–360, 2005.

transitions by the symbolic operations. Probabilistic linear hybrid automata can model uncertain behaviors such as statistical estimates regarding the environment in which a system is embedded. And its verification and performance evaluation allow for soft real-time quantitative properties.

This paper is organized as follows: In section 2, we define probabilistic linear hybrid automata and some preliminary concepts and notations. Section 3 defines the reachability problem of probabilistic linear hybrid automata. The symbolic reachability analysis method and trial examples are presented in section 4, and case study of industrial application is section 5 using prototype tool. Finally, in section 6, we conclude this paper.

2 Probabilistic Linear Hybrid Automata

Probabilistic linear hybrid automata are defined in this section as our model for probabilistic-nondeterministic real-time and hybrid systems. This system description language is an extended linear hybrid automaton [1] by discrete probability distributions.

2.1 Preliminaries

In preparation, we define basic concepts as follows:

Linear Constraints. Let $\boldsymbol{u}$ be a vector of real-valued variables. A *linear term* over $\boldsymbol{u}$ is a linear combination of variables from $\boldsymbol{u}$ with integer coefficients. A *linear inequality* over $\boldsymbol{u}$ is an inequality between linear terms over $\boldsymbol{u}$. A *convex linear formula* over $\boldsymbol{u}$ is a finite conjunction of linear inequalities over $\boldsymbol{u}$. A *linear formula* over $\boldsymbol{u}$ is a finite boolean combination of linear inequalities over $\boldsymbol{u}$. Let $\mathtt{clf}(\boldsymbol{u})$ and $\mathtt{lf}(\boldsymbol{u})$ be the set of convex linear formulae over $\boldsymbol{u}$ and the set of linear formulae over $\boldsymbol{u}$, respectively.

Distributions. A discrete probability *distribution* over a finite set Q is a function $p : Q \to [0,1]$ such that $\sum_{q \in Q} p(q) = 1$. Let $\mathtt{support}(p)$ be the subset of Q such that $\mathtt{support}(p) = \{q \mid p(q) > 0\}$. For a possibly uncountable set Q', let $\mathtt{Dist}(Q')$ be the set of distributions over finite subsets of Q'.

2.2 Syntax

First, we define the syntax of probabilistic linear hybrid automata.

Definition 1. *A* probabilistic linear hybrid automaton $\mathtt{PLHA} = \langle \boldsymbol{x}, L, init, inv, dif, prob, (grd_l)_{l \in L}, E \rangle$ *consists of the following components:*

Data Variables. Let $\boldsymbol{x}$ be the finite vector $(x_1, x_2, \ldots, x_n)$ called real-valued *data variables*. A point $\boldsymbol{s} = (s_1, \ldots, s_n) \in \mathbb{R}^n$ is referred to as a *data state*, or, equivalently, a *valuation* of data variables. The convex linear formula $f \in \mathtt{clf}(\boldsymbol{x})$ defines the convex polyhedron $[\![f]\!] \subseteq \mathbb{R}^n$, where $[\![f]\!] = \{\boldsymbol{s} \mid f[\boldsymbol{x} := \boldsymbol{s}] \textit{ is true.}\}$. A *polyhedron* is a finite union of convex polyhedra. For each data variable x_i, we use the dotted variable $\dot{x_i}$ to denote the *first derivative* of x_i. For data variables

$\boldsymbol{x}$, we use the primed variable $\boldsymbol{x}'$ to denote the *new value* of $\boldsymbol{x}$ after a transition. Let *updated variables* X be the subset of $\boldsymbol{x}$, similarly, $X' \subseteq \boldsymbol{x}'$.

Control Locations. L is a finite set of *control locations*. A *state* $(l, \boldsymbol{s})$ of the automaton PLHA consists of a control location $l \in L$ and a valuation $\boldsymbol{s} \in \mathbb{R}^n$. S_l is the set of data states at location l. A *region* $R = \bigcup_{l \in L}\{(l, S_l)\}$ is a collection of polyhedron $S_l \subseteq \mathbb{R}^n$ with respect to each control location $l \in L$. A *predicate* $\pi = \bigcup_{l \in L}\{(l, f_l)\}$ is a collection of linear formula $f_l \in \mathtt{clf}(\boldsymbol{x})$. The predicate π defines the region $[\![\pi]\!] = \bigcup_{l \in L}\{(l, [\![f_l]\!])\}$.

Initial State. $init = (l_0, \boldsymbol{s}_0)$ is an *initial state* of the probabilistic linear hybrid automaton, $l_0 \in L$ is an initial node, a single point $\boldsymbol{s}_0 \in \mathbb{R}^n$ is an initial value.

Locations Invariants. The function $inv : L \to \mathtt{clf}(\boldsymbol{x})$ assigns *invariant* condition to each location. The control of the automaton PLHA may reside in the location l only as long as the invariant $inv(l)$ is true ($\boldsymbol{s} \in [\![inv(l)]\!]$).

Continuous Flows. $dif : L \to \mathtt{clf}(\dot{\boldsymbol{x}})$ is a labeling function assigning *flows* to locations. The flows constrain the rates at which the values of data variables change: while the automaton control resides in the location l, the values of first derivatives of all data variables stay within the *differential inclusion* $\dot{\boldsymbol{s}} \in [\![dif(l)]\!]$. The probabilistic linear hybrid automaton PLHA is *time-nondeterministic* if there exists a location $l \in L$ such that $[\![dif(l)]\!]$ is not a single point.

Discrete Probability Distributions. The function $prob$: $L \to 2_{fn}^{\mathtt{Dist}(2^{\boldsymbol{x}} \times \mathtt{clf}(\boldsymbol{x} \uplus X') \times L)}$ assigning to each location a finite, non-empty set of *discrete probability distributions* $prob(l) = \{p_l^1, \ldots, p_l^{|prob(l)|}\} \subseteq \mathtt{Dist}(2^{\boldsymbol{x}} \times \mathtt{clf}(\boldsymbol{x} \uplus X') \times L)$.

Enabling Conditions. The family of functions $(grd_l)_{l \in L}$, where for any $l \in L$, $grd_l : prob(l) \to \mathtt{clf}(\boldsymbol{x})$ assigns an *enabling condition* (or *guard*) to each $p_l^i \in prob(l)$ at $l \in L$. It may happen that the intersection of multiple guards is not empty. In such a case, nondeterminism on selecting probability distributions arises, i.e. there are a number of possibilities. We solve this by the adversary. We will explain the concept of the adversary in § 2.3.

Probabilistic Edges. For each $l \in L, p_l^i = p \in prob(l), grd_l(p) = g$, we define the *probabilistic edges* $e = (l, g, p, X, updt, l')$ by discrete probability distributions, where $X \subseteq \boldsymbol{x}, updt \in \mathtt{clf}(\boldsymbol{x} \uplus X'), l' \in L$. Let E be the finite set of probabilistic edges such that $E = \{e \mid p(X, updt, l') > 0\}$. An *update* is a convex linear formula *updt* over the set $\boldsymbol{x} \uplus X'$. The *action* of the update *updt* is the convex linear formula over the set $\boldsymbol{x} \uplus \boldsymbol{x}'$, $act = updt \wedge (\bigwedge_{x_i \in \boldsymbol{x} \setminus X}(x_i' = x_i))$, all data variables that are not updated remain unchanged. In other words, the update *updt* defines a function $act : \mathbb{R}^n \to \mathtt{clf}(\boldsymbol{x}')$ from valuations to convex linear formulae over $\boldsymbol{x}'$. For all valuations $\boldsymbol{s}, \boldsymbol{s}' \in \mathbb{R}^n$, let $\boldsymbol{s}' \in [\![act(\boldsymbol{s})]\!]$ *iff* $act[\boldsymbol{x}, \boldsymbol{x}' := \boldsymbol{s}, \boldsymbol{s}']$ *is true*.

Examples. We will show some simple example as follows:

We consider probabilistic linear hybrid automaton as shown in Figure 1 and its formal description is below. Guard is assigned to the distribution, and both update formula and the probability are assigned to the edge.

$\boldsymbol{x} = \{x, y\}$, $L = \{l_1, l_2\}$, $inv(l_1) = (1 \le y \le 2)$, $inv(l_2) = (y \ge 0)$, $dif(l_1) = (1 \le \dot{x} \le 2 \wedge 1 \le \dot{y} \le 2)$, $dif(l_2) = (\dot{x} = 1 \wedge \dot{y} = 2)$, $prob(l_1) = \{p_{l_1}\}$, $prob(l_2) = \{p_{l_2}\}$, $grd_l(p_{l_1}) = (x \le 3)$, $p_{l_1}(\{x, y\}, x' \ge 1 \wedge y' = x, l_2) = 0.6$, $p_{l_1}(\emptyset, \text{-}, l_1) = 0.4$, $p_{l_2}(\emptyset, \text{-}, l_2) = 1$.

In Figure 1, the initial state *init* is $(l_1, x = 0 \wedge y = 1)$. First, time passes in location 1 or the location changes. If time passes, the values of data variables change at the rate $(1 \le \dot{x} \le 2 \wedge 1 \le \dot{y} \le 2)$. Location might change if the guard $(x \le 3)$ of the distribution is satisfied. If the location changes, the variables are updated according to the action formula of the edge. For example, the transition to location 2 with the probability 0.6 updates the values of data variables according to $(x' \ge 1 \wedge y' = x)$.

We verify whether the automaton reaches the target from the initial state or not by tracing transitions. For example, if the target is $(l_2, 1 \le x \le 2 \wedge 2 \le y \le 3)$, it is possible to reach the target from the initial state $init = (l_1, x = 0 \wedge y = 1)$ with probability 0.6 as follows:

$(l_1, x = 0 \wedge y = 1)$ *passage of one time unit under* $(\dot{x} = 2 \wedge \dot{y} = 2)$
$\rightarrow (l_1, x = 2 \wedge y = 2)$ *transition to* l_2 *under* $(x' = 2 \wedge y' = 2)$ *with probability* 0.6
$\rightarrow (l_2, x = 2 \wedge y = 2)$

We can specify probabilistic hybrid systems, which are reactive systems that intermix discrete and continues components with randomization, using probabilistic linear hybrid automata. Typical examples are digital controllers that interact with continuously changing physical environments, the steam boiler shown in § 5 is the one. Because probabilistic linear hybrid automata can describe the probability, statistical information such as the reliability of the switch can be described, too. Moreover, reset of the values can be described by update formula.

2.3 Semantics

Concurrent Probabilistic Systems. Next, we define concurrent probabilistic systems as a semantic model.

Definition 2. *A* concurrent probabilistic system *is a tuple* $\mathtt{CPS} = \langle Q, \Sigma, Steps \rangle$:

- Q *is a set of* states;
- Σ *is a set of* events;
- $Steps : Q \rightarrow 2^{\Sigma \times \mathtt{Dist}(Q)}$ *is a function which assigns to each state a non-empty set* $Steps(q)$ *of pairs* $(\sigma, \mu) \in \Sigma \times \mathtt{Dist}(Q)$ *comprising an event and a distribution on* Q.

A *probabilistic transition* $q \xrightarrow{\sigma,\mu} q'$ is made from a state q by nondeterministically selecting an event-distribution pair $(\sigma, \mu) \in Steps(q)$, and then making a probabilistic choice of target state q' according to μ, such that $\mu(q') > 0$. An execution of a concurrent probabilistic system is represented by a *path* ω, that is, a non-empty sequence of transitions $\omega = q_0 \xrightarrow{\sigma_0,\mu_0} q_1 \xrightarrow{\sigma_1,\mu_1} q_2 \xrightarrow{\sigma_2,\mu_2} \cdots$. We denote by $\omega(i)$ the ith state of a path ω, $step(\omega, i)$ the ith transition of ω, $|\omega|$ the length of ω and if ω is finite, the last state by $last(\omega)$. We say that a finite path $\omega^{(k)}$ of length k ($\leq |\omega|$) is a *prefix* of ω if $\omega^{(k)}(i) = \omega(i)$ for all $0 \leq i \leq k$, and $step(\omega^{(k)}, i) = step(\omega, i)$ for all $0 \leq i \leq k-1$. $Path_{fin}$ is the set of all finite paths. Event-distribution pair $(\sigma, \mu) \in Steps(q)$, is nondeterministically chosen. According to the general technique [9, 10, 11], we represent concurrency by the nondeterministic choice.

We now introduce adversaries of concurrent probabilistic system as functions which resolve all of the nondeterministic choices of the model.

Definition 3 (Adversaries). *A deterministic* adversary *(or scheduler) of concurrent probabilistic system is a function* $\mathcal{A} : Path_{fin} \to \Sigma \times \mathtt{Dist}(Q)$ *which assigns to each finite path* $\omega \in Path_{fin}$ *an event-distribution pair* (σ, μ) deterministically *such that* $\mathcal{A}(\omega) \in Steps(last(\omega))$.

For an adversary $\mathcal{A}$, we define $Path^{\mathcal{A}}_{fin}$ to be the set of finite paths such that $step(\omega, k) = \mathcal{A}(\omega^{(k)})$ for all $0 \leq k < |\omega|$. $Path^{\mathcal{A}}_{fin}$ means the one (deterministic) computation tree labeled by probabilities. Let *Adv* be the set of adversaries. An adversary decides the nondeterministically selecting performed event-distribution pairs in concurrent probabilistic system. Therefore, given an adversary, the nondeterministic model under the adversary can be described by a deterministic model.

With each adversary, we associate a sequential markov chain, which can be regarded as a set of paths in concurrent probabilistic system. Formally, if $\mathcal{A}$ is an adversary, then $\mathtt{MC}^{\mathcal{A}}$ is a markov chain.

Definition 4 (Markov Chains). *An infinite-state* Markov chain *which corresponds to* $\mathcal{A}$ *is* $\mathtt{MC}^{\mathcal{A}} = \langle Path^{\mathcal{A}}_{fin}, \mathbf{P}^{\mathcal{A}} \rangle$, *where:*

- *A set of states of* $\mathtt{MC}^{\mathcal{A}}$ *is* $Path^{\mathcal{A}}_{fin}$.
- $\mathbf{P}^{\mathcal{A}} : Path^{\mathcal{A}}_{fin} \times Path^{\mathcal{A}}_{fin} \to [0, 1]$ *is a* transition probability matrix, *such that*:

$$\mathbf{P}^{\mathcal{A}}(\omega, \omega') = \begin{cases} \mu(q) & \text{if } \mathcal{A}(\omega) = (\sigma, \mu) \text{ and } \omega' = \omega \xrightarrow{\sigma,\mu} q \\ 0 & \text{otherwise.} \end{cases}$$

Definition 5 (Probabilities over Paths). *Let* $\mathcal{P}^{\mathcal{A}}$ *be the mapping inductively defined on the length of paths in* $Path^{\mathcal{A}}_{fin}$ *as follows. If* $|\omega| = 0$, *then* $\mathcal{P}^{\mathcal{A}}(\omega') = 1$. *If* $|\omega| > 0$ *and* $\omega' = \omega \xrightarrow{\sigma,\mu} q$ *for some* $\omega \in Path^{\mathcal{A}}_{fin}$, *then we let*:

$$\mathcal{P}^{\mathcal{A}}(\omega') = \mathcal{P}^{\mathcal{A}}(\omega) \cdot \mathbf{P}^{\mathcal{A}}(\omega, \omega').$$

Semantics of Probabilistic Linear Hybrid Automata. The following notation ([6]) is used to reason about the next states of the probabilistic edges of PLHA. For the distribution p, if $\mathtt{support}(p) = \{(X^1, updt^1, l'^1), (X^2, updt^2, l'^2), \ldots, (X^m, updt^m, l'^m)\}$, then we let the tuple of actions $\mathtt{extract}(p) = (act^1, act^2, \ldots, act^m)$ and generate the tuple of valuations $\langle v \rangle = (\boldsymbol{v}^1, \boldsymbol{v}^2, \ldots, \boldsymbol{v}^m)$ in the following way: for each $1 \leq j \leq m$, we choose a valuation $\boldsymbol{v}^j \in \mathbb{R}^n$ such that $\boldsymbol{v}^j \in [\![act(\boldsymbol{s})^j]\!]$. Observe that, for any $1 \leq i, j \leq m$ such that $i \neq j$, it may be the case that $[\![act(\boldsymbol{s})^i]\!]$ and $[\![act(\boldsymbol{s})^j]\!]$ have non-empty intersection, and therefore it is possible that $\boldsymbol{v}^i = \boldsymbol{v}^j$, where $\boldsymbol{v}^i \in [\![act(\boldsymbol{s})^i]\!]$ and $\boldsymbol{v}^j \in [\![act(\boldsymbol{s})^j]\!]$. Let $\mathtt{Combinations}(\boldsymbol{s}, \mathtt{extract}(p))$ be the set of all such tuples $\langle v \rangle$ for a given state $(l, \boldsymbol{s})$ and the distribution p.

Definition 6. *The* concurrent probabilistic system $\mathtt{CPS}_{\mathtt{PLHA}} = \langle Q_{\mathtt{PLHA}}, \Sigma_{\mathtt{PLHA}}, Steps_{\mathtt{PLHA}} \rangle$ of probabilistic linear hybrid automaton PLHA *is defined as following infinite-state transition system:*

- $Q_{\mathtt{PLHA}} \subseteq L \times \mathbb{R}^n$ *is the set of states, defined such that* $(l, \boldsymbol{s}) \in Q_{\mathtt{PLHA}}$ *if* $\boldsymbol{s} \in [\![inv(l)]\!]$;
- $\Sigma_{\mathtt{PLHA}} = \mathbb{R}_{\geq 0}$ *is the set of events.* $\mathtt{CPS}_{\mathtt{PLHA}}$ *is not event-driven system using the alphabet but a time-driven system that uses time as a trigger. Therefore, time becomes an event;*
- *For each state* $(l, \boldsymbol{s}) \in Q_{\mathtt{PLHA}}$*, let* $Steps_{\mathtt{PLHA}}((l, \boldsymbol{s})) = Cont(l, \boldsymbol{s}) \cup Disc(l, \boldsymbol{s})$ *be the smallest set of event-distribution pairs such that:*
  - **Time transition** *for each duration* $\delta \in \mathbb{R}_{\geq 0}$*, there exists* $(\delta, \mu_{(l,\boldsymbol{s}')}) \in Cont(l, \boldsymbol{s})$ *such that* $\mu_{(l,\boldsymbol{s}')}(l, \boldsymbol{s}') = 1$ *if and only if either*
    1. $\delta = 0$ *and* $\boldsymbol{s}' = \boldsymbol{s}$*, or*
    2. $\delta > 0$ *and* $\frac{\boldsymbol{s}' - \boldsymbol{s}}{\delta} \in [\![dif(l)]\!]$;
  - **Discrete transition**
    $Disc(l, s) = \bigcup_{p \in prob(l)} Disc(l, \boldsymbol{s}, p)$*, where for each distribution* $p \in prob(l)$*, if* $\boldsymbol{s} \in [\![grd_l(p)]\!]$*, then, for each* $\langle v \rangle \in \mathtt{Combinations}(s, \mathtt{extract}(p))$*, there exists the pair* $(0, \mu_{p,\langle v \rangle}) \in Disc(l, \boldsymbol{s}, p)$ *such that*

$$\mu_{p,\langle v \rangle}(l', \boldsymbol{s}') = \sum_{i \in \{1,\ldots,m=|\mathtt{support}(p)|\} \& l'=l'^j \& \boldsymbol{s}'=\boldsymbol{v}^j} p(X^j, updt^j, l'^j). \quad (1)$$

Expression (1) resolves the case of probabilities summation as the same way [4][6].

An adversary chooses the event-distribution pair $(\sigma, \mu) \in Steps_{\mathtt{PLHA}}((l, \boldsymbol{s})) = Cont(l, \boldsymbol{s}) \cup Disc(l, \boldsymbol{s})$ that can be performed in $\mathtt{CPS}_{\mathtt{PLHA}}$. In other words, it chooses one from various possibilities as follows. At any time, if the system is in a location, then the system can either remain in its current location and let time advance, or make a discrete transition if there exists a distribution. Discrete transitions are instantaneous and consist of the two steps performed in succession: firstly, the system makes a nondeterministic choice between the set of distributions. Secondly, supposing that the distribution is chosen, the system then makes a probabilistic transition according to the distribution. In this nondeterministic choice between the set of event-distribution pairs, if we define an adversary, the nondeterministic model under the adversary can be described by a deterministic model.

3 Reachability Problem

We now formally define our reachability problem.

Definition 7 (Probabilistic Reachability Problem). *Given a probabilistic linear hybrid automaton* $\mathtt{PLHA} = \langle \boldsymbol{x}, L, init, inv, dif, prob, (grd_l)_{l \in L}, E \rangle$*, let* T *be a predicate called the* target*, let* $\sqsupseteq \in \{\geq, >\}$*, and let* $\lambda \in [0, 1]$ *be the* target probability. *Then* probabilistic reachability problem *for* PLHA *can be defined as the tuple* $(\mathrm{T}, \sqsupseteq, \lambda)$*, the answer to this problem is "*YES*, reachable" if and only if there exists an adversary* $\mathcal{A} \in Adv$ *of* $\mathtt{CPS_{PLHA}}$ *(or, equivalently, a series of nondeterministic choices) and a path* $\omega \in Path^{\mathcal{A}}_{fin}$ *starting in an initial state of* PLHA $init = (l_0, \boldsymbol{s}_0)$ *such that* $last(\omega)$ *in* $(l, [\![f_l]\!]) \in [\![\mathrm{T}]\!]$ *with probability (over path)* $\sqsupseteq \lambda$*, and "*NO*" otherwise.*

We now review two subclasses of reachability properties: *time bounded reachability* and *invariance* which are particularly relevant for the verification and the performance evaluation of probabilistic real-time and hybrid systems [5][6]. About the former, PLHA has certain time deadlines. On the other hand, about the latter, PLHA is required that does *not leave* an *invariant* region $[\![\mathcal{I}]\!] \subseteq Q_{\mathtt{PLHA}}$, or, equivalently, *always satisfies* some properties. (*e.g.* $[\![\mathcal{I}]\!]$ as desirable or expected region for safety property).

4 Verification: Symbolic Reachability Analysis

The following extended expression is used to express the probabilities of the transitions of $\mathtt{CPS_{PLHA}}$.

Definition 8 (Polyhedra labeled by Probabilities). *For a linear formula* $f \in \mathtt{lf}(\boldsymbol{x})$ *and a corresponding polyhedron* $[\![f]\!]$*, we define the* probabilistic polyhedron $([\![f]\!], P)$ *to be the pair comprising a polyhedron* $[\![f]\!] \subseteq \mathbb{R}^n$ *and its probability* $P \in (0,1]$*. The function* $\mathtt{plf} : L \to 2^{\mathtt{lf}(\boldsymbol{x}) \times (0,1]}$ *assigning to each location a set of probabilistic linear formulae, where a probabilistic linear formula is the pair of a linear formula* f *and its probability* P *such as* $(f, P) \in \mathtt{lf}(\boldsymbol{x}) \times (0,1]$*. Let* $[\![\mathtt{plf}(l)]\!] \subseteq 2^{\mathbb{R}^n} \times (0,1]$ *be the finite set of probabilistic polyhedra in the location* l *such that* $[\![\mathtt{plf}(l)]\!] = \{([\![f_l]\!], P) \mid$ *for some* $[\![f_l]\!], P > 0\}$*. Note that, for any* $([\![{f_l}^a]\!], P^a), ([\![{f_l}^b]\!], P^b) \in [\![\mathtt{plf}(l)]\!]$ *such that* $[\![{f_l}^a]\!] = [\![{f_l}^b]\!]$*, it is the case that* $P^a \neq P^b$*. In the sequel, we use* $R = \bigcup_{l \in L}\{(l, [\![\mathtt{plf}(l)]\!])\}$ *as a region, and a predicate* π *corresponding to the region* R *is* $\pi = \bigcup_{l \in L}\{(l, \mathtt{plf}(l))\}$*, where* $[\![\pi]\!] = \bigcup_{l \in L}\{(l, [\![\mathtt{plf}(l)]\!])\}$.

We introduce extra edge relations to deal with summing up probabilities with respect to the same next state (*cf.* § 2.3 and expression (1)).

Definition 9 (Extra edge relations). *For a set* E*, let* $\mathcal{E}$ *be the set of* extra probabilistic edges *such that:*

$$\mathcal{E} = \bigcup_{l \in L, p \in prob(l), Act \in 2^{\mathtt{extract}(p)}_{ne}} \{e = (l, g, pr, act, l') \mid \mathtt{condition}\};$$

$$\mathtt{condition} \equiv \forall act^j \in Act \textit{ such that } |Act| \geq 2, l' = l'^j \textit{ and } \Big(\bigcap_{act^j \in Act} [\![act(\boldsymbol{s})^j]\!]\Big) \neq \emptyset,$$

$$\textit{where } pr = \sum_{act^j \in Act} p(X^j, updt^j, l'^j),\ act = \bigwedge_{act^j \in Act} act^j.$$

All the cases of duplication of act or all the nondeterministic combination in addition of probability is treated by $2^{\mathtt{extract}(p)}_{ne}$*, where notation ne means non-empty set.*

We define the following precondition operators to calculate the state transition relation in probabilistic linear hybrid automata symbolically and collectively.

4.1 Precondition Operators

We define the time-precondition operator and the discrete-precondition operator based on the non-probabilistic precedent of [1]. Non-probabilistic hybrid automata case was showed in [1]. So, emphasis is placed on probabilities and the definition of precondition operators follows from probabilistic transition of $\texttt{CPS}_{\texttt{PLHA}}$, we can define the following precondition operators according to Definition 6. Because we use the backward algorithm later, the operations are inverse image computations defined as follows.

Definition 10 (Time Precondition). *We write* $\texttt{tpre}(\texttt{plf}(l))$ *for the probabilistic linear formula such that from any state in the corresponding region* $(l, [\![\texttt{tpre}(\texttt{plf}(l))]\!])$ *a state in* $(l, [\![\texttt{plf}(l)]\!])$ *can be reached in a single time transition.*

$$\texttt{tpre}(\texttt{plf}(l)) = \bigcup_{(f_l,P)\in\texttt{plf}(l)} \{(inv(l) \wedge (\exists\delta \geq 0.\exists \mathbf{c}.(((\delta\cdot dif(l))[\dot{\boldsymbol{x}} := \mathbf{c}] \wedge (f_l \wedge inv(l))[\boldsymbol{x} := \boldsymbol{x} + \mathbf{c}])), P\cdot 1)\}.$$

Definition 11 (Discrete Precondition). *We write* $\texttt{dpre}(l', \texttt{plf}(l'))$ *and* $\texttt{expre}(l', \texttt{plf}(l'))$ *for the predicate, the corresponding region of states from which a state in* $(l', [\![\texttt{plf}(l')]\!])$ *can be reached in a single discrete transition according to probabilistic edges* E *and extra edges* $\mathcal{E}$*, respectively.*

$$\texttt{dpre}(l', \texttt{plf}(l')) = \bigcup_{e=(l,g,p,X,updt,l')\in E} \{(l, \bigcup_{(f_{l'},P)\in\texttt{plf}(l')} \{(inv(l) \wedge \exists \boldsymbol{x}'.(g \wedge act \wedge (f_{l'} \wedge inv(l'))[\boldsymbol{x} := \boldsymbol{x}']), P\cdot p(X, updt, l'))\})\}.$$

$$\texttt{expre}(l', \texttt{plf}(l')) = \bigcup_{e=(l,g,pr,act,l')\in\mathcal{E}} \{(l, \bigcup_{(f_{l'},P)\in\texttt{plf}(l')} \{(inv(l) \wedge \exists \boldsymbol{x}'.(g \wedge act \wedge (f_{l'} \wedge inv(l'))[\boldsymbol{x} := \boldsymbol{x}']), P\cdot pr)\})\}.$$

Definition 11 enables us to calculate the state transitions that follows the same probability distribution symbolically and collectively. By one calculation, the length of path increases by one, (refer to Definition 5). Since calculation of probability is multiplication, we can calculate it reversely.

Finally, we define precondition operator $\texttt{pre}$ consisting of time and discrete precondition operator. For a predicate π, any state in the corresponding region $[\![\texttt{pre}(\pi)]\!]$ can reach to some states in the region $[\![\pi]\!]$ with single probabilistic transitions.

Definition 12 (Precondition Operators).

$\texttt{pre}(\pi) = \texttt{Tpre}(\pi) \cup \texttt{Dpre}(\pi)$, *where*

$$\texttt{Tpre}(\pi) = \bigcup_{l\in L}\{(l, \texttt{tpre}(\texttt{plf}(l)))\},\ \texttt{Dpre}(\pi) = \bigcup_{l'\in L}(\texttt{dpre}(l', \texttt{plf}(l')) \cup \texttt{expre}(l', \texttt{plf}(l'))).$$

It is well known [1, 2, 3] that we can solve the reachability problem by repeating inverse image computations and calculating all the states where it can follow from the target. We use the backward algorithm, because it is said that the backward algorithm is more efficient than the forward algorithm. We can trace all the operation of probabilistic linear hybrid automaton by using precondition operator `pre` previously defined when we perform inverse image computations.

4.2 Symbolic Backward Reachability Analysis Procedure

We propose the symbolic backward reachability analysis procedure as below:

Procedure SRA:
Input: a probabilistic linear hybrid automaton PLHA;
an initial state $init = (l_0, \boldsymbol{s}_0)$;
a target predicate and a probabilistic requirement $(\mathrm{T}, \sqsupseteq, \lambda)$.
Output: YES, *reachable* / NO;
(a region $[\![Q_i]\!]$ which can reach $[\![\mathrm{T}]\!]$.)
$\mathtt{Y} := \mathrm{T}$ /* Q_0 */
$\mathtt{Z} := \mathrm{T}$
repeat
/* computation of a region $[\![Q_i]\!]$ which can reach $[\![\mathrm{T}]\!]$. */
$\mathtt{Z} := \mathtt{pre}(\mathtt{Z}) \setminus \mathtt{Y}$ /* $\mathtt{pre}^i \setminus Q_{i-1}$ */
$\mathtt{Y} := \mathtt{Y} \cup \mathtt{Z}$ /* Q_i */
/* judgment of reachability every time i, z is the form of
$\bigcup_{l \in L}\{(l, \mathtt{plf}(l))\} = \bigcup_{l \in L}\{(l, \bigcup_{(f_l, P) \in \mathtt{plf}(l)}\{(f_l, P)\})\}$. */
for each $\mathtt{z} = (l, \mathtt{plf}(l)) \in \mathtt{Z}$ wrt $l \in L$
if $l == l_0$
for each $(f_l, P) \in \mathtt{plf}(l)$
if $\boldsymbol{s}_0 \in [\![f_l]\!]$
if $P \sqsupseteq \lambda$
return YES, *reachable*.
halt SRA
end if
end if
end for each
end if
end for each
until $\mathtt{Z} == \emptyset$
return NO.

In general, the convergence of the least fixed point, and thus the termination of this reachability analysis procedure is not guaranteed, as already the reachability problem for constant-slope hybrid systems is undecidable [2][1].

Afterwards, we transform predicates into logical formulae with the aim of implementing the above procedure by symbolic computation of logical formulae. Let l_c and P_c be *control variables* that ranges over the set of locations L and

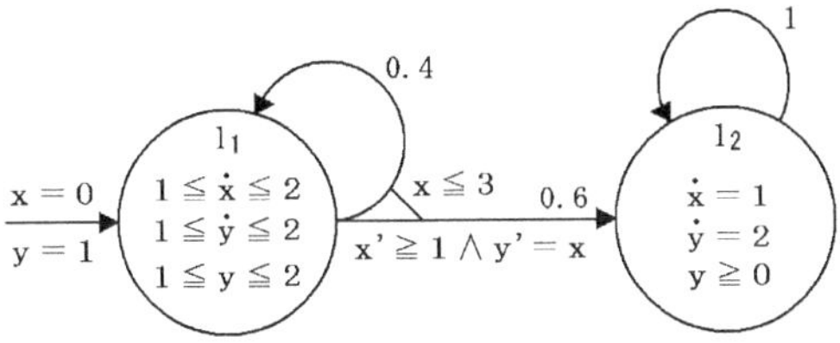

Fig. 1. Probabilistic linear hybrid automaton

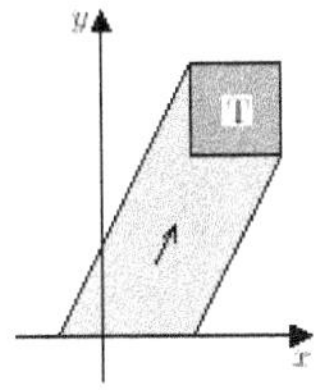

Fig. 2. Time Precondition

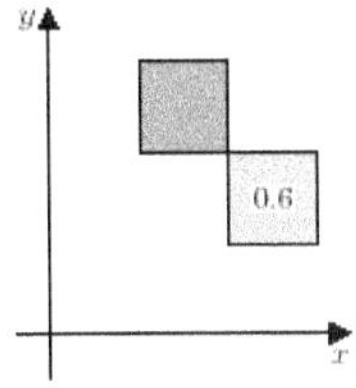

Fig. 3. Discrete Precondition

the set of real numbers $\mathbb{R}$, respectively. The predicate $\pi = \bigcup_{l\in L}\{(l, \mathtt{plf}(l))\} = \bigcup_{l\in L}\{(l, \bigcup_{(f_l,P)\in\mathtt{plf}(l)}\{(f_l, P)\}\}$ defines the logical formula ϕ in the following manner:

$$\phi \equiv \bigvee_{l\in L}(l_c = l \wedge \mathtt{plf}(l)) = \bigvee_{l\in L}(l_c = l \wedge (\bigvee_{(f_l,P)\in\mathtt{plf}(l)}(f_l \wedge P_c = P)))$$

In precondition operators, union operators $\bigcup$ and $\cup$ are replaced by disjunctions $\bigvee$ and $\vee$, respectively.

4.3 Examples

We will show some simple example as follows:

Probabilistic reachability problem $(\mathrm{T}, \geq, 0.35)$.
Probabilistic linear hybrid automaton Figure 1, $init = (l_c = l_1 \wedge x = 0 \wedge y = 1)$, $\mathrm{T} = (l_c = l_2 \wedge 1 \leq x \leq 2 \wedge 2 \leq y \leq 3 \wedge P_c = 1)$.

Predecessor calculation using quantifier elimination [12][1].

$$\begin{aligned}
&\mathtt{tpre}(1 \leq x \leq 2 \wedge 2 \leq y \leq 3 \wedge P_c = 1)\\
&= (y \geq 0 \wedge (\exists\delta \geq 0.\exists c_x, c_y.(c_x = \delta \wedge c_y = 2\cdot\delta \wedge 1 \leq x + c_x \leq 2 \wedge 2 \leq y + c_y \leq 3 \wedge y + c_y \geq 0))\\
&\quad \wedge P_c = 1 \cdot 1)\\
&= (y \geq 0 \wedge (\exists\delta \geq 0.(\ 1 \leq x + \delta \leq 2 \wedge 2 \leq y + 2\delta \leq 3\ )) \wedge\ P_c = 1)\\
&= (x \leq 2 \wedge 0 \leq y \leq 3 \wedge -2 \leq y - 2x \leq 1 \wedge P_c = 1).\ \textit{see Figure 2}\\
&\mathtt{dpre}(l_c = l_2 \wedge 1 \leq x \leq 2 \wedge 2 \leq y \leq 3 \wedge P_c = 1)\\
&= (l_c = l_1 \wedge\\
&\quad (1 \leq y \leq 2 \wedge\ \exists x'.\exists y'.(x \leq 3 \wedge x' > 1 \wedge y' = x \wedge 1 < x' < 2 \wedge 2 < y' < 3 \wedge y' > 0))\\
&\quad \wedge P_c = 1 \cdot 0.6)\\
&= (l_c = l_1 \wedge (1 \leq y \leq 2 \wedge\ \exists x'.(x \leq 3 \wedge 1 \leq x' \leq 2 \wedge 2 \leq x \leq 3)) \wedge\ P_c = 0.6)\\
&= (l_c = l_1 \wedge 2 \leq x \leq 3 \wedge 1 \leq y \leq 2 \wedge P_c = 0.6)\ =\ \phi_1.\ \textit{see Figure 3}
\end{aligned}$$

$$\begin{aligned}
\mathtt{pre}(\mathrm{T})\ &=\ \mathtt{Tpre}(\mathrm{T}) \vee \mathtt{Dpre}(\mathrm{T})\\
&= (l_c = l_2 \wedge x \leq 2 \wedge 0 \leq y \leq 3 \wedge -2 \leq y - 2x \leq 1 \wedge P_c = 1)\ \vee\ \phi_1 \vee \mathrm{T}\\
&= \phi_1 \vee \phi_2 \vee \mathrm{T}.
\end{aligned}$$

Reachability Determination
For $\texttt{pre}^2 = \texttt{pre}(\texttt{pre}(\mathrm{T}) \setminus \mathrm{T}) = \texttt{pre}(\phi_1 \vee \phi_2) = \texttt{pre}(\phi_1) \vee \texttt{pre}(\phi_2)$, $\texttt{cpre}(\phi_1) = (l_c = l_1 \wedge x \leq 3 \wedge 1 \leq y \leq 2 \wedge 2x - y \leq 5 \wedge 2y - x \leq 2 \wedge P_c = 0.6)$ and *init* have a non-empty intersection. Then probabilistic requirement is satisfied ($P_c = 0.6 \geq 0.35$), and therefore we conclude this reachability problem with "YES".

The example of operation shown in § 2.2 is correctly calculated in Figure 2 and 3 that uses the procedure described in § 4.2. This calculation is symbolically performed. We have implemented a prototype of verifier based on MATHEMATICA.

5 Case Study

5.1 Probabilistic Steam Boiler

We now consider the problem of modelling an industrial application [13][14], namely that of a *steam boiler* (Fig. 5), using probabilistic linear hybrid automata. The system consists of a number of physical units, namely a vessel containing an amount of water, a water pump, a series of sensors, and a message transmission system. The vessel is continuously heated in order to produce steam. The constant L denotes the minimal limit level of water, with U denoting the corresponding maximal limit level. When the water level remains within the normal operating interval of $[N_1, N_2]$, the controller need not intervene. However, if the water level falls below N_1, then the pump is switched on, and if the water level rises above N_1, the pump is switched off. There is the possibility of a failure in the water level sensor [15][6]. Given the occurrence of such a failure, the controller uses an approximate guess of the actual water level when deciding whether to switch the pump on or off. Periodically, there is the possibility of the water level sensor being repaired.

5.2 Modelling

Probabilistic linear hybrid automaton to model the steam boiler system described above is given in Figure 4. We ease the graphical notation by enclosing the locations in the dotted boxes, and draw a single edge from each box to the location. The variable w denotes the water level, t and cl are clocks, g_l represents the lower bound on the current guess on the water level, g_u represents the corresponding upper bound.

Location Off and On. When control resides in these two locations, the value of the water level is affected by the steam. We express the rate of change of the steam emission volume as $0 \leq \dot{s} \leq e$ for some positive integer constant e. In the location `On` the pump being on. The pump water the vessel at any rate between 0 and p litres per time units. Both location have the invariant condition $t \leq \Delta$; therefore, control must leave either of these locations if the value of the clock t is equal to Δ.

Location Urgent Off and Urgent On. The purpose of the two locations is to ease the graphical notation of probabilistic linear hybrid automaton. In

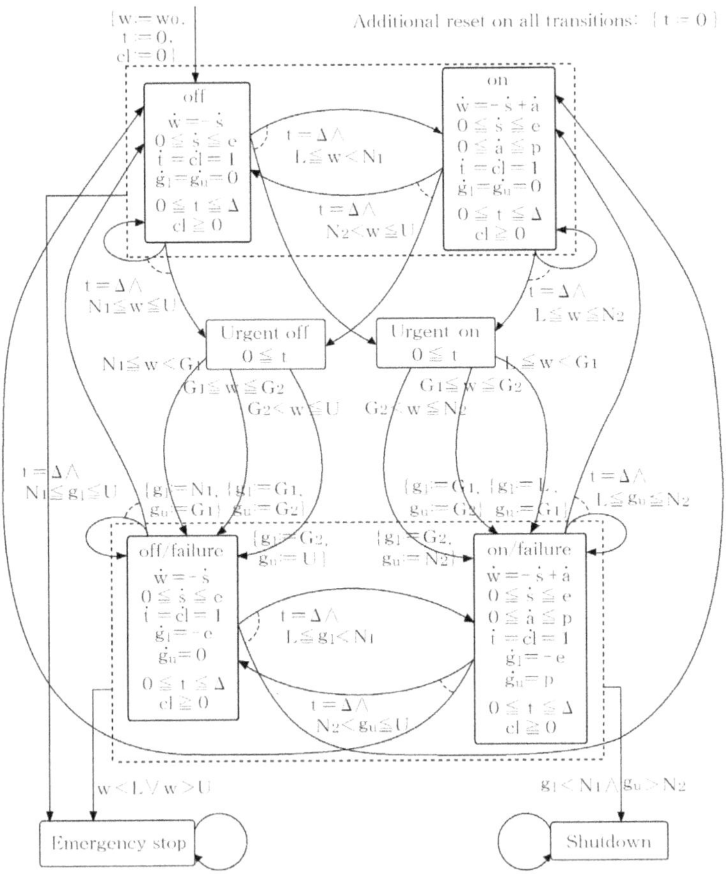

Fig. 4. Probabilistic linear hybrid automaton for probabilistic steam boiler

these locations no time is permitted to elapse. They correspond to the controller making estimates of the water level. All of the distributions available in these locations reset the *guess* variables, g_l and g_u.

Location Off/Failure and On/Failure. Naturally, these two locations correspond to the case in which the water level sensor has failed. As the controller is now maintaining an estimate of the water level, the flow conditions of the variables representing the bounds on the guess of the water level, g_l and g_u, are altered to take into account the fact that the real water level may change as time elapses.

Location Emergency Stop and Shutdown. If the real water level falls below the lower limit L or exceed the upper limit U, then control can pass to the terminal location `Emergency stop`. If the lower bound on the estimate of the water level is below the lower normal water level at the same time as the upper bound on the estimate is above the upper normal level, then control can pass to a terminal location `Shutdown`.

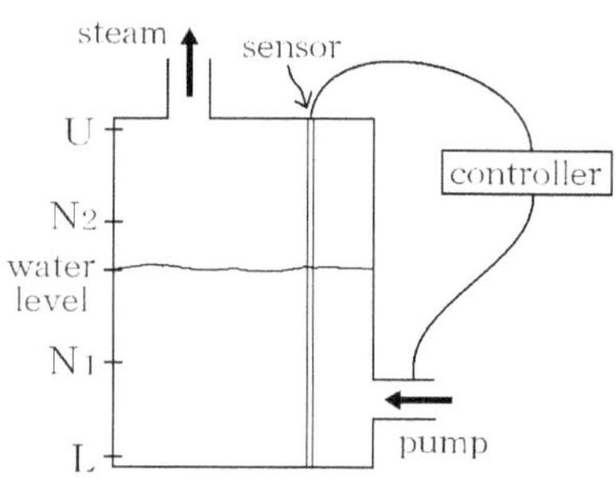

Fig. 5. Steam boiler

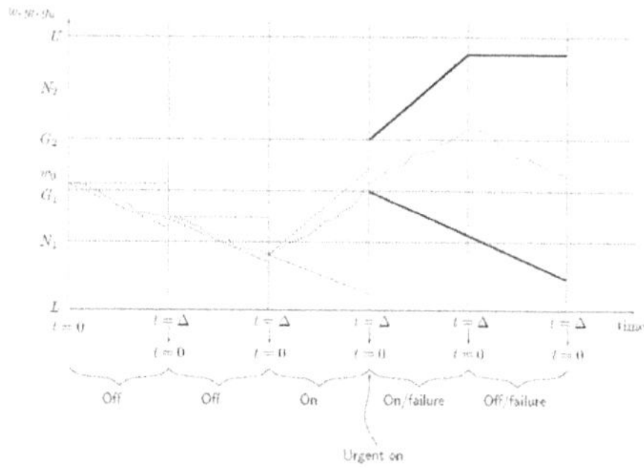

Fig. 6. An example run of the probabilistic steam boiler

An example run of the probabilistic steam boiler control is shown in Figure 6. We assume that the system constants are such that $L < N_1 < G_1 < G_2 < N_2 < U$, and that the initial water level of the boiler, denoted by w_0, is some point in the interval (G_1, G_2). When the system commences operation, the pump is switched off.

5.3 Analysis

Property Description. In this paper, the property that we wish to check is *whether or not the system can reach the terminal location* (`Emergency stop`, `Shutdown`) *in* 10 *time units have elapsed.* However, it is possible to ignore the location `Emergency stop` by doing a little arithmetic as follows; if the amount of the steam emission volume s during Δ time units is not more than N_1 *minus* L at the same time as the amount of water absorption a during Δ time units is not more than U *minus* N_2, then the system never reaches the location `Emergency stop`. Therefore, we consider only the location `Shutdown` the terminal location. We note states T for which it is possible to make a single transition in order to reach `Shutdown`; we omit the actual target states (`Shutdown`) for simplicity. Finally, the probabilistic reachability property that requires that the system reach the location `Shutdown` within 10 time units, with the probability strictly greater than 0, can be expressed as the tuple $(\mathrm{T}, >, 0)$.

Our first task is to specify the probabilities of the discrete transitions of the steam boiler control. For convenience, we select very simple distributions. We decide that the possibility of a failure in the water level sensor is 0.1, otherwise 0.9.

Implementation and Results. The results are as follows. " The system *can reach* the states for which it is possible to make a single transition in order to reach `Shutdown` within 10 time units, with probability 0.1 at 4th transition". This automatic analysis took about 14 minutes and up to 100MB memory. (Intel Pentium 4 CPU 3.00GHz with 2.00GB RAM under MS Windows XP OS on MATHEMATICA 5.0). MATHEMATICA can execute the commands such as *quantifier elimination*,QE [12]. We can transform the formula into another formula that is equivalent to the former, and does not contain $\exists$ by using QE. We use this QE when we compute the `tpre()`, `dpre()`, and `expre()`. This is fully automated in analysis.

Here, we refer to the symbolic run (set of paths) that has reached `Shutdown`, as follows.

$$\begin{aligned}
&(l_c = \texttt{Off} \wedge\ 0 \leq cl < 1 \wedge 0 \leq t \leq 5 \wedge 0 \leq w < 35 - 3t \\
&\ \vee\ 1 \leq cl < 6 \wedge -1 + cl < t \leq 5 \wedge 0 \leq w < 35 - 3t) \\
\rightarrow\ &(l_c = \texttt{Off} \wedge\ 0 \leq w < 20 \wedge 0 \leq cl < 6 \wedge t = 5) \\
\rightarrow\ &(l_c = \texttt{Urgent on} \wedge\ 0 \leq w < 30 \wedge 0 \leq cl < 6 \wedge t = 0) \\
\rightarrow\ &(l_c = \texttt{On/failure} \wedge\ 0 \leq t \leq 5 \wedge \\
&(0 \leq cl \leq 5+t \wedge g_u > 25+5t \wedge g_l < 35-3t \vee 5+t < cl \leq 10 \wedge g_u > 5cl \wedge g_l < 50-3cl)) \\
\rightarrow\ &(l_c = \texttt{On/failure} \wedge\ g_l < N_1 \wedge g_u > N_2 \wedge 0 \leq t \leq \Delta = 5 \wedge 0 \leq cl \leq 10)
\end{aligned}$$

The probability of these paths is 0.1. Note that the first region contains the system commences operation $init = (l_c = \texttt{Off} \wedge\ w = 0 \wedge t = 0 \wedge cl = 0)$, and the last region is contained the target T.

In this paper, we regarded the states for which it is possible to make a single transition in order to reach `Shutdown` as the target region. Generally, it is undesirable that the system can enter `Shutdown`. So, we should remodel the design parameter of the steam boiler control to avoid the above case. Now, we change the parameter (initial water level w_0 and guard G_1) and analyze again. Then the system do not enter the undesirable target within 10 time units in four times transition.

6 Conclusions

In this paper, we have defined the probabilistic linear hybrid automata as system modelling language, and presented its symbolic reachability analysis method. Our proposal method is the first attempt to symbolically verify probabilistic linear hybrid automata. By our method, we will be able to handle many systems such as distributed control systems, timed randomized protocols and so on. We have implemented an experimental verification system using MATHEMATICA, and demonstrated that our method can help the system designer to choose critical system parameters, via case study. We are now working for an abstraction/approximation method of probabilistic linear hybrid automata to handle complicated realistic problems.

References

1. R. Alur, T.A. Henzinger, and P.-H. Ho. Automatic symbolic verification of embedded systems. *IEEE Transactions on Software Engineering*, 22(3):181-201, 1996.
2. R. Alur, C. Coucoubetis, T.A. Henzinger, P.-H. Ho, X. Nicollin, A. Olivero, J. Sifakis, and S. Yovine. The algorithmic analysis of hybrid systems. *Theoretical Computer Science*, 138:3-34, 1995.

3. T.A. Henzinger, X. Nicollin, J. Sifakis, and S. Yovine. Symbolic model checking for real-time systems. *Information and Computation*, 111:193-244, 1994.
4. M. Kwiatkowska, G. Norman, and J. Sproston. Symbolic model checking for probabilistic timed automata. *Technical Report CSR-03-10, School of Computer Science, University of Birmingham*, 2003.
5. M. Kwiatkowska, G. Norman, R. Segala, and J. Sproston. Automatic verification of real-time systems with discrete probability distributions. *Theoretical Computer Science*, 282:101-150, 2002.
6. J. Sproston. Model checking for probabilistic timed and hybrid systems. *PhD thesis, Technical Report CSR-01-04, School of Computer Science, University of Birmingham*, 2001.
7. J. Sproston. Analyzing subclasses of probabilistic hybrid automata. *Technical Report CSR-99-8, School of Computer Science, University of Birmingham*, 1999.
8. J. Sproston. Decidable model checking of probabilistic hybrid automata. *Lecture Notes in Computer Science 1926, pp 31-45, Springer-Verlag*, 2000.
9. S. Hart, M. Sharir, and A. Pnueli. Termination of Probabilistic concurrent program. *ACM Transactions on Programming Languages and Systems (TOPLAS)*, 5(3): 356-380, 1983.
10. E.A. Emerson. Temporal and modal logic. *Handbook of theoretical computer science (vol. B): formal models and semantics, Pages 995-1072, MIT Press*, 1991.
11. C. Courcoubetis and M. Yannakakis. The complexity of probabilistic verification. *Journal of the ACM (JACM)*, 42(4):857-907, 1995.
12. A. Tarski. A decision method for elementary algebra and geometry. *University of California Press, Berkeley and Los Angeles, California*, 2nd ed., 1951.
13. J.R. Abrial, E. Borger, and H. Langmaack, editors. Formal methods for industrial applications: specifying and programming the steam boiler control. *volume 1165 of Lecture Notes in Computer Science. Springer-Verlag*, 1996.
14. T.A. Henzinger and H. Wong-Toi. Using HYTECH to synthesize control parameters for a steam boiler. *in [13]*, pp. 265–282.
15. A. McIver, C. Morgan, and E. Troubitsyna. The probabilistic steam boiler: a case study in probabilistic data refinement. *In Proc. of IRW/FMP'98, Australia*, 1998.
16. E.M. Clarke, O. Grumberg, and D.A. Peled. Model checking. *MIT Press*, 1999.

Formalization of *f*FSM Model and Its Verification

Sachoun Park[1], Gihwon Kwon[1], and Soonhoi Ha[2]

[1] Department of Computer Science, Kyonggi University,
San 94-6, Yiui-Dong, Youngtong-Gu, Suwon-Si, Kyonggi-Do, Korea
{sachem, khkwon}@kyonggi.ac.kr

[2] Department of Computer Engineering, Seoul National University,
Seoul, Korea 151-742
sha@iris.snu.ac.kr

Abstract. PeaCE(Ptolemy extension as a Codesign Environment) was developed for the hardware and software codesign framework which allows us to express both data flow and control flow. The *f*FSM is a model for describing the control flow aspects in PeaCE, but it has difficulties in verifying their specifications due to lack of their formality. Thus we propose the formal semantics of the model based on its execution steps. To verify an *f*FSM model, it is translated into SMV input language with properties to be checked, automatically. As a result, some important bugs such as race condition, ambiguous transition, and circular transition can be formally detected in the model.

Keywords: Finite state machine, Step semantics, Formal verification, Model checking.

1 Introduction

To make narrow the gap between design complexity and productivity of embedded systems, hardware/software codesign has been focused as a new design methodology. Various codesign procedures have been proposed, and formal models of computation for system specification by using "correct by construction" principle make ease design validation. The PeaCE[1] is the codesign environment to support complex embedded systems. The specification uses synchronous dataflow (SDF) model for computation tasks, extended finite state machine (FSM) model for control tasks and task-level specification model for system level coordination of internal models (SDF and FSM). It gives automatic synthesis framework from the proposed specification with good results compared with hand-optimized code, and the automatic SW/HW synthesis from extended FSM model, called *f*FSM(flexible FSM), and automatic SW synthesis from task-model is developed. The synthesis framework generates architecture independent code which can be used for functional simulation, design space exploration, synthesis and verification steps by varying the definitions of APIs.

The *f*FSM is another variant of Harel's Statecharts, which supports concurrency, hierarchy and internal event as Statecharts does. Also it includes global variables as

* This work was supported in part by IT Leading R&D Support Project funded by Ministry of Information and Communication, Republic of Korea.

L.T. Yang et al. (Eds.): ICESS 2005, LNCS 3820, pp. 361 – 372, 2005.

memories in a system. This model is influenced from STATEMATE of i-Logix inc.[2] and the Ptolemy[3] approaches. But the formal semantics for internal models is not defined explicitly. Especially, in the case of *f*FSM(flexible FSM), the absence of formal semantics causes problems such as confidence for simulation, correctness of code generation, and validation of a system specification. Since no formal semantics exit, unexpected behavior may occur after system built and also it dilute original purpose of codesign to produce complex embedded system cost-effectively

In this paper, we define the step semantics for *f*FSM model, which becomes foundation about reliable code generation and formal verification. Step semantics or operational semantics of an *f*FSM defines how the model changes state from one configuration to another on the reception of some events, while it at the same time executes actions consisting of emitting output and internal events and updating of global variables. In this field, many works have proposed, but among these formal semantics, we turned our attention to Erich Mikk's hierarchical automata[4] and Lind-Nielsen's hierarchical state/event model[6].

Hierarchical automata semantics was defined to formally express the STATEMATE semantics of Statecharts described by Harel and Naamad in 1996[5]. After he defined pure hierarchal automata which have no inter-level transition, he described EHA (extended hierarchical automata) to handle the inter-level transition. As the semantics of EHA was presented in the Kripke structure, three rules at EHA were applied to: progress rule, stuttering rule, and composition rule. If any enabled transition is activated, sequential automaton takes progress rule. If an active sequential automaton does not have an enabled transition and the active state is a basic state then the automaton stutters and consumes events. And each automaton delegates its step to its sub-automata with rcspcct to thc composition rulc. But it wasn't dcalt with thc dclta-delay and variables.

HSEM(Hierarchical State/Event Model), the variant of Statecharts in IAR visualSTATE[7], is based on the Unified Modeling Language(UML) state diagram, where again the UML is based on Harel's Statecharts. Although HSEM has its origin in Statecharts, its semantics is distinguishable. The behavior of the model described *N* flat parallel machines, where the *N* is the number of Or-states: serial and history states. Thus a configuration of HSEM consists of exactly one state per each Or-sate, so it may include inactive states. This method is able to perform compositional model checking which one of solution for state explosion problem. However, in the HSEM semantics, there is only use of state reference to express guarding condition, without event occurring.

Firstly, we define the step semantics with concept of the delta-delay, variables and event. And then verifying some system properties, we automatically translate the model to SMV input language with these properties. This translation is based on the proposed step semantics and synchrony hypothesis.

In this paper, the semantics of the *f*FSM model in PeaCE approach is defined by borrowing from EHA and HSEM semantics. In the next section, *N* flat parallel machine of *f*FSM, *p*FSM, is defined with its example. The definition of step semantics of *p*FMS is presented in section 3, our efforts for debugging a model is described at section 4 and then we conclude the paper in section 5.

2 Formal Definition of *p*FSM

2.1 Reflex Game: The Example of *f*FSM Model

This version of reflex game is used for describing formal model of *f*FSM. The set of input events to the system are *coin*, *ready*, *stop*, and *time*. All but the last are user inputs, while the last generated by system simply counts off time. The game scenario is as follows: after a coin is inserted, ready signal becomes on after a randomly distributed latency. When the ready signal is one, the player should put down the stop button as quickly as possible. Then the output is produced to indicate the time duration between the ready signal and the stopping action. To compute the time duration, we use "remain" and "randn" as variable states. The resultant *f*FSM graph is concurrent and hierarchical.

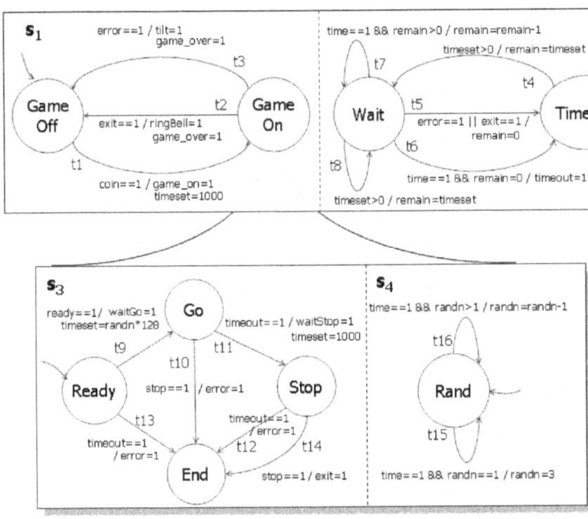

Fig. 1. *f*FSM example of reflex game

Initially, each atomic *f*FSM is triggered by input events and makes a transition when its guard condition is satisfied. If the transition produces internal events, transitions triggered by the internal events are made iteratively until there is no more internal event. After every delta-delay, it clears all existing events and sets newly produced internal events at the previous delta-delay. Briefly, an execution of an atomic *f*FSM consists of a transition triggered by an input event and subsequent transitions triggered by internal events produced by the previous transition. And variable state and output events keep their values to make them persistent.

2.2 Syntax of *p*FSM

In this section, we introduce definitions about *p*FSM which is based on the thesis[8]. To define the step semantics of *f*FSM, we propose *N* flat parallel machine of *f*FSM, *p*FSM. Like an *f*FSM, there exit events, global variables, states, and transition.

I, O, and *IT* are sets of input events, output events, and internal events, respectively. Unlike previous definition of the event of *f*FSM, these sets disjoint each other. Each event e_i in $I \cup O \cup IT = \{e_1, ..., e_n\}$ is composed of its domain D_i and initial value d_i, and $val(e_i)$ denotes current value of the event. *Simple* FSM is defined by 4-tuples (S, s^0, T, scr), where *S* is a set of states, s^0 is the initial state, and *T* is set of transition relations. In the PeaCE approach, dataflow models are controlled by external signals generated by *f*FSM, which can be labeled at a proper state as a set of atomic proposition. We call the labels *scripts*, and *Script* represents the set of all scripts occurring in the *f*FSM. Thus, $scr : S \rightarrow 2^{Script}$ is the label function to map a set of scripts into a state.

*f*FSM has two types of composition like other variants of Harel's Statecharts: concurrent and hierarchical compositions. HSEM used *N* flat parallel machines for describing its operational semantics, because BDD(Binary Decision Diagram) could be easily represented and the compositional model checking applied. In this paper, we refer to HSEM semantics to define the *f*FSM semantics.

Definition 1 (*p*FSM). Now, formal semantics of *f*FSM is defined as *N* flat parallel machines *p*FSM. $pFSM = (I, O, IT, M, \gamma, V)$, where *I, O, IT* are set of events above, *V* is a set of global variables, $v_j \in (D_j, d_j)$, and $M = \{m_1, ..., m_n\}$ is the set of simple FSM. Let $\Sigma = \bigcup_{i=1}^{n} S_i$ be the set of all states in *M*, hierarchical relation γ maps a state to the set of machines which belong to the state: $\gamma : \Sigma \rightarrow 2^M$.

The hierarchical function γ has three properties: there exist a unique root machine, every non-root machine has exactly one ancestor state, and the composition function contains no cycles. Let $sub : \Sigma \rightarrow 2^{\Sigma}$, and $sub(s) = \{s' \mid M_i \in \gamma(s) \wedge s' \in S_i\}$ is another function to relate between a super state and its sub states. sub^+ denotes the transitive closure of *sub* and *sub** denotes the reflexive transitive closure of *sub*.

Definition 2 (*Simple* FSM). $m_i = (S_i, s_i^0, T_i, scr_i)$

i. $S_i = \{s_i^0, s_i^1, ..., s_i^n\}$ is the finite set of states of m_i,
ii. s_i^0 is a initial state,
iii. T_i is the set of transition of m_i, and a transition $t \in T_i = (s, g, A, s')$ is composed of source and target states s, $s' \in S_i$, guarding condition *g* which is Boolean expression, and set of actions *A*,
iv. $scr_i : S_i \rightarrow 2^{Script}$ is a function to map a set of script into a state.

Guards that include variables and events have the following minimal grammar.

$$G ::= true \mid \neg G \mid G_1 \wedge G_2 \mid e < Exp \mid e = Exp \mid v < Exp \mid v = Exp$$
$$Exp ::= n \mid v \mid Exp_1 \bullet Exp_2,$$

where *n* is an integer constant, $v \in V$ is a global variable, $\bullet \in \{+, -, \times, /\}$ represents a set of binary operators. To select some facts of a transition $t = (s, g, A, s')$, following projection functions are useful: *source(t) = s*, *target(t) = s′*, *guard(t) = g*, *action(t) = A*.

Also, in a set of actions A, each action element $a \in A$ consists of variable assignment or event emission:

$$a ::= v{:=}Exp \mid e{:=}Exp.$$

For an action element, following three projection functions are used, because an action set is composed of updating variables, emitting some output events, and producing internal events.

$$update(A) = \{v := Exp \mid \exists v \in V.(v := Exp) \in A\}$$
$$output(A) = \{e := Exp \mid \exists e \in O.(e := Exp) \in A\}$$
$$signal(A) = \{e := Exp \mid \exists e \in IT.(e := Exp) \subset A\}$$

Figure 2 shows *p*FSM corresponding to figure 1, and the below example presents the definition of figure 2.

$I = \{coin, ready, stop, time\}$, $O = \{game\_on, waitGo, waitStop, ringBell, tilt, game\_over\}$
$IT = \{timeset, timeout, error, exit\}$, $V = \{randn, remain\}$
$M = \{m_1, m_2, m_3, m_4\}$, $\gamma(m_1) = \{m_3, m_4\}$, $\gamma(m_2) = \gamma(m_3) = \gamma(m_4) = \varnothing$,
$m_1 = (S_1, s_1^0, T_1, scr_1)$, $S_1 = \{GameOff, GameOn\}$, $s_1^0 = GameOff$,
$T_1 = \{(GameOff, coin = 1, \{game\_on = 1, timeset = 1000\}, GameOn),$
$(GameOn, exit = 1, \{game\_over = 1, ringBell = 1\}, GameOff),$
$(GameOn, error = 1, \{game\_over = 1, tilt = 1\}, GameOff)\}$, $scr_1 = \varnothing$
…

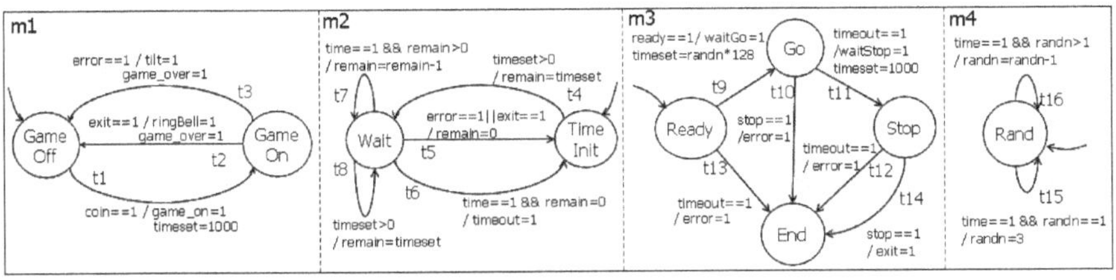

Fig. 2. Flatten machine *p*FSM

3 Semantics of *p*FSM

Step semantics or operational semantics of an *f*FSM defines how the model changes state from one configuration to another on the reception of some events, while it at the same time executes actions consisting of emitting output and internal events and updating of global variables.

Definition 3 (Configuration). Δ represents the whole configurations of *p*FSM model, for each m_i of *p*FSM, its formal definition is $\Delta = \{\{s_1, ..., s_n\} \mid \exists s_i \in S_i, 0 < i \leq n\}$. $\delta_0 \in \Delta$, $\delta_0 = \{s_1^0, \ldots, s_n^0\}$ is an initial configuration.

Erich's definition of a configuration is a set of active states, so the size of the set is not fixed. But the size of a configuration δ is the same of the set of machines M, so we need to define which state is active.

Definition 4 (Active state). It can be defined that a state s is active in configuration δ as follow:

$$\delta \models s \ \textit{iff} \ \forall s' \in \Sigma . s \in sub^*(s') \Rightarrow s' \in \delta .$$

Definition 5 (Satisfiability). To decide which transition is enabled, given the set of events $E \subseteq 2^I \cup 2^{IT}$ and the current configuration δ, configuration δ and events E satisfies a guard g, $\langle \delta, E \rangle \models guard(t)$, is defined inductively.

$$\begin{aligned}
&\langle \delta, E \rangle \models true \quad \textit{iff} \quad true \\
&\langle \delta, E \rangle \models \neg G \quad \textit{iff} \quad not \ \langle \delta, E \rangle \models G \\
&\langle \delta, E \rangle \models G_1 \wedge G_2 \quad \textit{iff} \quad \langle \delta, E \rangle \models G_1 \ and \ \langle \delta, E \rangle \models G_2 \\
&\langle \delta, E \rangle \models e < Exp \quad \textit{iff} \quad e \in E \ and \ val(e) < val(Exp) \\
&\langle \delta, E \rangle \models e = Exp \quad \textit{iff} \quad e \in E \ and \ val(e) = val(Exp) \\
&\langle \delta, E \rangle \models v < Exp \quad \textit{iff} \quad val(v) < val(Exp) \\
&\langle \delta, E \rangle \models v = Exp \quad \textit{iff} \quad val(v) = val(Exp),
\end{aligned}$$

where $val(n) = n$, $val(e)$ denotes the current value of event e, and $val(v)$ denotes the current value of variable v. $val(Exp_1 \bullet Exp_2) = val(Exp_1) \bullet val(Exp_2)$.

Definition 6 (Enabled transition). Through the definitions of active states and satisfiability relation, we define a set of enable transitions for each active state.

$$ET = \{t \mid \forall i \in \{1,...,n\}. t \in T_i \wedge \langle \delta, E \rangle \models guard(t) \wedge \delta \models source(t)\}$$

Definition 7 (Executable transition). The set of executable transitions are non-conflicting set of transitions and every simple FSM must contribute at most one transition. As *f*FSM model has no inter-level transition, the conflict only occurs between two transitions which have different and comparable priorities.

$$\begin{aligned}
&XT = \{t \in ET \mid \neg \exists t' \in ET. source(t) \in sub^+(source(t'))\}, \\
&\forall m_i \in M. \mid XT \cap T_i \mid \leq 1
\end{aligned}$$

Definition 8 (LKS). Step semantics of *p*FSM is defined by *LKS*(Labeled Kripke Structure). $LKS = (Q, q_0, R, L)$ is defined:

$Q = \{q_0, \dots, q_n\}$ is the finite set of states in LKS,

$q_0 = (\delta_0, \varnothing, c_0)$ is an initial state,

$R \subseteq Q \times 2^{Act} \times Q$ is the set of transitions with label as the set of actions,

$L : Q \rightarrow 2^{Script}$ is label function such that $L(q_i) = \bigcup_{\forall s \dashv \delta} scr(s)$.

The step could be explained both micro step and macro step. The micro step stands for one step triggered by input or internal events, and macro step is a finite sequence of micro steps each of which is triggered by one input event or consequent internal events until the produced internal event won't exit any more.

Definition 9 (Micro step). $(\delta, E, c) \xrightarrow{Act} (\delta', E', c')$

Given the current configuration δ and the set of events *E*, the next configuration δ′ is defined as follow:

$$\delta' = \{s' \mid \forall s \in \delta . \exists t \in XT.(s = source(t) \Rightarrow s' = target(t)) \\ \vee (s \in sub^{+}(source(t)) \Rightarrow s' = reset(s)) \\ \vee (s \notin sub^{*}(source(t)) \Rightarrow s' = s)\}$$

where $reset(s) = s_i^0,\ s \in sub(s'') \wedge m_i \in \gamma(s'') \wedge s \in S_i$

$$E' = \bigcup_{\forall t \in XT} signal(action(t)),$$

and $c' = L(q')$,

$$Act = \bigcup_{\forall t \in XT} output(action(t)) \cup \bigcup_{\forall t \in XT} update(action(t))$$

Definition 10 (Macro step). Step semantics of *p*FSM is represented by $q \xrightarrow{Exe} q'$, called *an execution*, which is triggered by input event and produces cascaded input events. Thus one input event and consequent internal events make transitions until any internal event cannot be produced. After each micro step, all previous events are consumed by delta-delay. In the following definition, $k > 1$ is the first k which makes $E_{i,k}$ to ∅, and $Exe_i = \bigcup_{\forall 0<j<k} Act_j$ is a set of all actions during macro step.

$$(\delta_i, E_i, c_i) \xrightarrow{Exe_i} (\delta_{i+1}, \varnothing, c_{i+1}) \ \textit{iff}\ (\delta_{i,1}, E_{i,1}, c_{i,1}) \xrightarrow{Act_1} \cdots \xrightarrow{Act_{k-1}} (\delta_{i,k}, \varnothing, c_{i,k}).$$

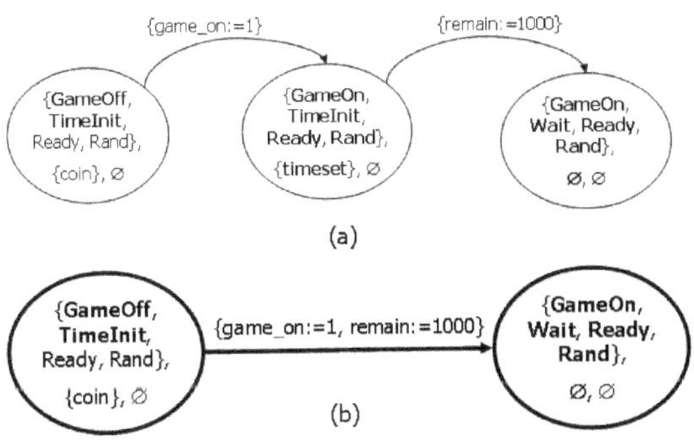

Fig. 3. Example of micro step(a) and macro step(b)

When input event "*coin*" occurs, control of the system is moved from the initial configuration {GameOff, TimeInit, Ready, Rand} to {GameOn, wait, Ready, Rand}. For error detection, we define three kinds of error: Race Condition(There can be multiple writers for an output event or a variable state during an execution of *f*FSM model), Ambiguous transition(Multiple transitions from one state can be enabled simultaneously), and Circular transition(There can be exist circular transitions by cascaded transitions).

For example, if a snapshot of the system contains a configuration {GameOn, Wait, Ready, Rand}, occurring event set is consist of user event "*ready*" and system event "*time*", and variable *remain* is zero, although it is a rare case, it breaks the output constraint that output value must be persistent during one execution, since *remain* have multiple assignments. Table 1 presents it.

Table 1. Violation of Race Condition for a variable "remain"

events	Configuration	Actions
{time, ready}	{GameOn, Wait, Ready, Rand}	{waitGo:=1, remain:=0}
{timeset, timeout}	{GameOn, TimeInit, Go, Rand}	{waitStop:=1, remain:=randn*128}
{timeset}	{GameOn, Wait, Stop, Rand}	{ remain:=1000}
∅	{GameOn, Wait, Stop, Rand}	–

4 Debugging *f*FSM Model

4.1 Stepper: Simulation Tool for *f*FSM Model

To debug a model, simulating a system model is widely used. In the PeaCE approach, integrated simulation is provided. But it could not simulate control model only. Thus, we develop a simulation tool for *f*FSM model with respect to our step semantics. Figure 4 shows the framework of the Stepper.

Stepper receives textual description of *f*FSM model written by design tool in the PeaCE framework. Then, it presents a model like a tree structure and input event generator. Input events generated by a user execute one macro step. The Stepper, then, shows all micro steps during one execution. Also it provides translation from *f*FSM to SMV, with some important properties to be checked automatically. In figure 5, as you can see, after "*time*" and "*ready*" events occur, the variable *remain* is updated in twice 999, 384 at the macro step, STEP[2].

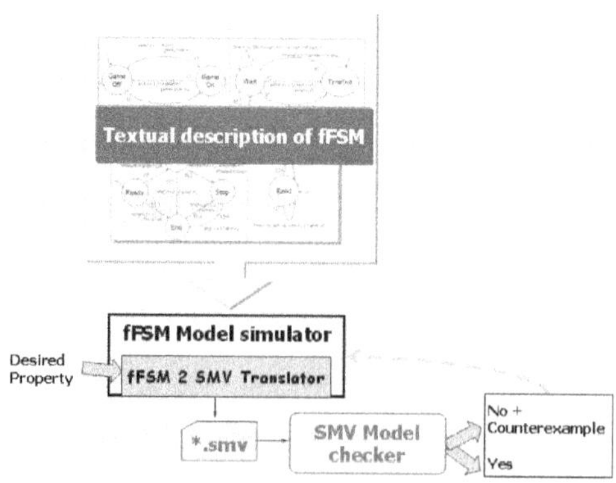

Fig. 4. Framework of the Stepper

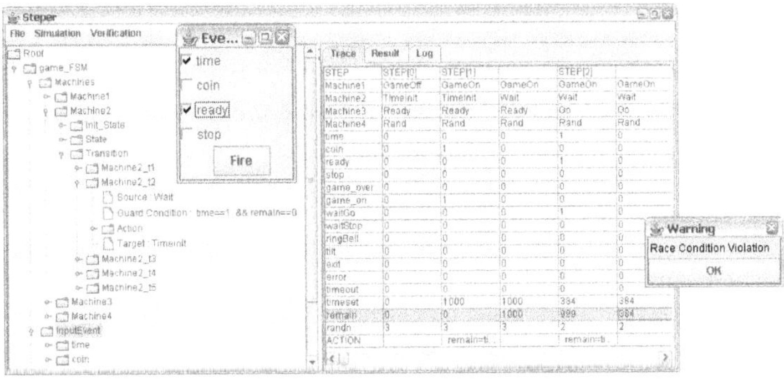

Fig. 5. Detecting a race condition violation via simulation in Stepper

4.2 Model Checking *f*FSM Model

Simulation is very useful tool to present an error in a model, tracing an execution path step by step. But by simulation, it is apt to spend much time or in some cases may be impossible to detect an error. So more efficient debugging, automatic and formal technique is required. Our tool provides formal verification which is implemented by translating *f*FSM into SMV. Figure 6 shows the result of detecting a race condition violation via model checking and the result is the same of simulator's.

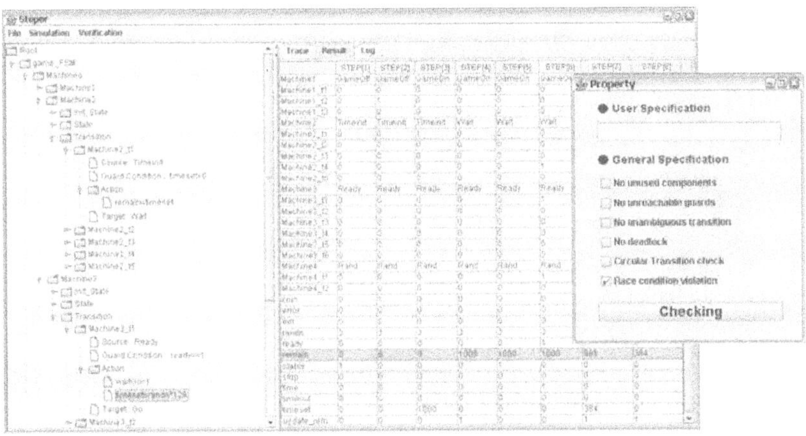

Fig. 6. Detecting a race condition violation via model checking

4.3 Translation *f*FSM Model to SMV

Our translation rules are based on Chan[10] and Clarke[11]. Following translation rules are based on the step semantics defined in the previous section.

Rule 1 (Machine and states). For each machine, $m_i = (S_i, s_i^0, T_i, scr_i)$, machine and its states are encoded as $VAR\ m_i : S_i;\quad ASSIGN\ init(m_i) = s_i^0;$.

Rule 2 (Transitions). Transition relations can be expressed in SMV through the definition 6. For $m_i = (S_i, s_i^0, T_i, scr_i)$ and $t \in T_i$, each transition t in m_i is encoded as $DEFINE\ m_i\_t := up^*(source(t))\ \&\ guard(t);$, where $up(s) = \{s' \mid M_i \in \gamma(s') \wedge s \in S_i\}$ is the function to return a super-state of s and up^* is transitive reflexive closure of up.

```
DEFINE
  Machine1_t1 := Machine1 = GameOn & error=1;
  ⋮
VAR
  Machine1 : {GameOff, GameOn};
ASSIGN
  init(Machine1) := GameOff;
  next(Machine1) :=
       case
         Machine1_t1 : GameOff;
         ⋮
         1 : Machine1;
       esac;
```

Rule 3 (Synchrony hypothesis). To express synchrony hypothesis in SMV, we define a particular variable *stable*, which means that a system stays in stable state where any events does not occur. *stable* is also used in formulating circular transition and race condition. When sets of internal events, input events and variables are respectively $\{internal_1, \ldots, internal_l\}$, $\{input_1, \ldots, input_m\}$ and $\{variable_1, \ldots, variable_n\}$, the translation rule is:

```
VAR
  stable : boolean;
ASSIGN
  init(stable) := 1;
  next(stable) :=
       case
         !(valued1 = next(valued1)) : 0;
              ⋮
         !(valuedn = next(valuedn)) : 0;
         next(input1) | ... | next(inputm) : 0;
         (internal1=0) & ... & (internall=0) : 1;
         1 : 0;
       esac;
```

Rule 4 (Input event). Every input event e whose initial value is d and domain D is $[min, \ldots, max]$ can be translated as follow:

```
VAR
   e : min .. max;
ASSIGN
  init(e) := d;
  next(e) :=
       case
         stable : min .. max;
         1 : 0;
       esac;
```

Rule 5 (Output event and internal event). For a transition $t = (s, g, A, s')$ and each output or internal event *e* whose initial value is *d*, through a set of transitions $\{t_1, \ldots, t_n\}$, a set of expressions $\{exp_1, \ldots, exp_n\}$ and $\{e := Exp \mid \exists e \in O \cup IT.(e := Exp) \in A\}$, the translation rule can be expressed as follow:

```
VAR
  e : min .. max;
ASSIGN
  init(e) := d;
  next(e) :=
     case
       t1 : Exp1;
            ⋮
       tn : Expn;
       1 : 0;
     esac;
```

Rule 6 (Variable). While default value of event *e* is 0 because of delta-delay, each variable *v* stores its previous value. This rule of variable is similar with Rule 5.

```
VAR
  v : min .. max;
ASSIGN
  init(v) := d;
  next(v) :=
     case
       t1 : Exp1;
            ⋮
       tn : Expn;
       1 : v;
     esac;
```

Table 2 shows CTL templates for some important properties which can be automatically generated for user's convenience. The first three are trivial, but the rest are more complex.

Table 2. Built-in properties and its CTL formulae

Properties	CTL formulae
No unused components	$\mathbf{EF}\ component_1 \wedge \ldots \wedge \mathbf{EF}\ component_n$
No unreachable guard	$\mathbf{EF}\ (s_i \wedge \mathbf{EX}\ s_j)$, $source(t) = s_i$ and $target(t) = s_j$
No unambiguous transitions	$\mathbf{AG}\ \neg((t_1 \wedge t_2) \vee (t_2 \wedge t_3) \vee (t_1 \wedge t_3))$, where $\{t_1, t_2, t_3\}$ is a set of outgoing transition from the same state.
No deadlocks	$\neg\mathbf{EF}\ \mathbf{AG}\ Deadlock(fT)$, where $Deadlock(fT) = \neg\bigvee_{t \in fT} t_n$
No divergent behavior	$\mathbf{AG}(\neg stable \Rightarrow \mathbf{A}[\neg\ stable\ \mathbf{U}\ stable])$
Race condition violation	$\mathbf{AG}\ ((update(v) \wedge \neg stable) \Rightarrow \mathbf{AX}\ \mathbf{A}[\neg update(v)\ \mathbf{U}\ stable])$ $\mathbf{AG}\ ((emit(o) \wedge \neg stable) \Rightarrow \mathbf{AX}\ \mathbf{A}[\neg emit(o)\ \mathbf{U}\ stable])$

In below table, components might be all states, events and variables. Checking about a guard is replaced with whether the transition labeled by the guard is enabled or not. Ambiguous transitions must be checked in all states with their possible transitions. In the formula encoding the deadlock, *f*T denotes a set of all transitions of a model. The formula to detect circular transition, "**AG**(¬*stable* ⇒ **A**[¬ *stable* **U** *stable*])", means "whenever the system is in an unstable state, eventually it must reach a stable state." To formulate the race condition, the additional functions *update* and *emit* are introduced. Encoding *update* or *emit* for each output event or variable could be implemented by a new Boolean variable. Thus, user can select some properties or type in CTL properties.

5 Conclusions

*f*FSM is a model for describing the control flow aspects in PeaCE, but due to lack of their formality, it has difficulties in verifying the specification. In this paper, for lifting the reliability for code generation in the codesign framework and enabling formal verification of the control model, we defined the step semantics for the *f*FSM model. And we implemented tool to simulate and verify an *f*FSM model. As a result, some important bugs such as race condition, ambiguous transition, and circular transition can be formally detected in the model. Especially, to obtain the convenience of user to check properties, we constructed some templates for automatic generation of specifications. Now we are developing a specific model checker for *f*FSM and researching an effective abstraction technique to be applied in the new model checker.

References

1. D. Kim, S. Ha, "Static Analysis and Automatic Code Synthesis of flexible FSM Model", ASP-DAC 2005 Jan 18-21, 2005
2. iLogix: http://www.ilogix.com/
3. http://ptolemy.eecs.berkeley.edu/
4. E. Mikk, Y. Lakhnech, M. Siegel, "Hierarchical automata as model for statecharts", LNCS Vol. 1345, Proceedings of the 3rd ACSC, pp. 181-196, 1997.
5. D. Harel, A. Naamad, "The STATEMATE semantics of statecharts", ACM Transactions on Software Engineering Methodology, 5(4), October 1996.
6. J. Lind-Nielsen, H. R. Andersen, H. Hulgaard, G. Behrmann, K. J. Kristoffersen, K. G. Larsen, "Verification of Large State/Event Systems Using Compositionality and Dependency Analysis", FMSD, pp. 5-23, 2001.
7. IAR: http://www.iar.com/products/vs/
8. D. Kim, "System-Level Specification and Cosimulation for Multimedia Embedded Systems," Ph.D. Dissertation, Computer Science Department, Seoul National University, 2004.
9. J. B. Lind-Nielsen, "Verification of Large State/Event Systems," Ph.D. Dissertation, Department of Information Technology, Technical University of Denmark, 2000.
10. W. Chan, "Symbolic Model checking for Large software Specification," Dissertation, Computer Science and Engineering at University of Washington, pp. 13-32, 1999.
11. E. M. Clarke, W. Heinle, "Modular translation of Statecharts to SMV," Technical Report CMU-CS-00-XXX, CMU School of Computer Science, August 2000.

Dynamic Co-allocation of Level One Caches

Lingling Jin[1], Wei Wu[1], Jun Yang[1], Chuanjun Zhang[2], and Youtao Zhang[3,*]

[1] University of California at Riverside, Riverside CA 92521
[2] University of Missouri at Kansas City, Kansas City, MO 64110
[3] University of Texas at Dallas, Richardson, TX 75083

Abstract. The effectiveness of level one (L1) caches is of great importance to the processor performance. We have observed that programs exhibit varying demands in the L1 instruction cache (I-cache) and data cache (D-cache) during execution, and such demands are notably different across programs. We propose to co-allocate the cache ways between the I- and D-cache in responses to the program's need on-the-fly. Resources are re-allocated based on the potential performance benefit. Using this scheme, a 32KB co-allocation L1 can gain 10% performance improvement on average, which is comparable to a 64KB traditional L1.

1 Introduction

Many applications have transitory high or low demands on instructions or data at different running stages [4, 10]. We observed that even if a program has a tendency of favoring one cache over the other, this tendency is drastically different across different programs. Using a "one-size-fits-all" cache for different stages of a program or different programs puts a limit on the attainable performance. Previous reconfigurable cache memories are mostly for one cache [9, 14]. In this paper, we demonstrate an additional source of performance benefits through reconfiguring *between* the I-cache and D-cache in response to the varying needs of programs.

We present a technique for set associative caches where some cache ways can be used in either the I-cache or the D-cache, depending on which setting yields a better performance. Essentially, we treat I-cache and D-cache as a global L1 cache resource and allocate ways to two caches with the goal of maximizing the program performance. We choose to allocate in unit of cache ways instead of subarrays so that the modifications in hardware are trivial. The allocation is performed periodically and hence the I- and D-cache have different set associativities at different time, but the total L1 cache size remains the same. When deciding whether to "move" one way from one cache to the other, we compute the *changes* in the average memory access time in both choices and select the configuration with larger positive impact on performance. Such a criteria proves to be much more accurate than using the cache miss rates alone in traditional performance tuning algorithms.

* Authors are supported in part by NSF grants CCF-0429986 and CCF-0430021.

L.T. Yang et al. (Eds.): ICESS 2005, LNCS 3820, pp. 373–385, 2005.

Using our co-allocation technique, we can utilize moderate-sized L1 caches more efficiently. On a set of 15 SPEC2K benchmarks experimented, the performance improvement can reach as high as 36% with 10% on average. Moreover, our technique can perform equally well with contemporary L1/L2 optimization techniques, demonstrating its effectiveness in achieving better L1 resource utilization.

This remainder of the paper is organized as follows. Section 2 discusses the related work. Section 3 shows the programs' varying requirements on I-cache and D-cache. Section 4 and 5 describes our co-allocation design in details. Experimental results are in Section 6 We conclude this paper in section 7.

2 Related Work

There has been plenty of research on improving cache performance. We will discuss only those that are closely related to ours.

Providing flexibility in utilizing the cache spaces has been investigated previously in several different ways. In a technique developed by Balasubramonian *et al.*, the L1 D-cache and the L2 cache, or the L2 and L3, are combined so that the boundary between them can drift [2]. The variations include set associativities and number of sets which result in variable L1 and L2 sizes. In such a design, it is possible that a cache block is mapped to a wrong position since the number of sets is not always the same among different configurations. Our design exploits the boundary between the *L1* I-cache and D-cache and a mis-map would incur a second access to the cache. Such a situation is not favored in L1 and it could happen quite frequently especially for instruction reads. Therefore, we choose to configure at a larger granularity, i.e. the cache ways, due to the structure symmetry between the I-cache and D-cache and the simplicity in the modifications in the cache circuitry.

Ranganathan *et al.* has proposed to use a portion of cache for another function such as instruction reuse, hardware prefetching, or compiler controlled memory [9]. This design is suitable for multimedia applications where the cache is ineffective for stream data or large working sets with poor locality. We target at the general purpose architectures where a wide range of applications are considered. Therefore, we study the efficiency of L1 space utilization to better capture the program locality rather than refunctioning them for different purposes. Drach *et al.* proposed a technique where one of the L1 caches can be used as a backup for the other [5]. In effect, this design treats I-cache and D-cache as both L1 and L1.5 (accessed after L1 but before L2)*unified* caches, resembling a pseudo-associative unified cache. This design is limited to direct-mapped caches and did not take into account the port contention of instruction and data accesses in L1.5.

Many recent work have been carried for improving the L2 cache performance through compression [1, 13], prefetching [8], and novel indexing [7]. Our co-allocation technique reduces total accesses to the L2 cache, and performs equally well when L2 hit rate is greatly improved by those techniques.

The programs' dynamically changing demands in the L1 cache represent one kind of program characteristic at a finer granularity than the notion of *working set* [4] or *program phases*[10]. In our technique, the change of a cache configuration may comply with a change of a program phase, but may also happen within a single phase. Moreover, since our technique has a specific target, i.e., the L1 caches, our hardware detection mechanism can be implemented in a much lightweight manner. Therefore, we do not need to use the substantial hardware to first detect phases and then change the cache configuration.

3 Program's Varying Demands on L1

To understand the programs' varying demands on the I-cache and D-cache, we performed measurements on the SPEC CPU2K benchmarks with different cache configurations which are statically defined. Without the loss of generality, we used a 4-way set associative L1. The cache sizes were set to 16KB I-cache and 16KB D-cache akin to the PIII [16] or a Celeron processor [17]. The associativity of a cache can vary from 2-way to 6-way, i.e., we leave minimum of 2 cache ways for each, and set 4 ways as configurable between the I-cache and D-cache. The programs were fast forwarded for one billion and executed for another one billion instructions. We collected the IPCs on every ten million instruction interval basis.

We found four main categories of programs: (1) those that favor larger I-cache throughout; (2) those that favor larger D-cache throughout; (3) those that have alternating transitory demands on larger I-cache and D-cache; and (4) those that have huge demands on one (usually data cache) constantly and little demands on the other but giving more resources to the former does not help. For the first type, the programs typically have larger code sizes and using larger I-cache clearly benefits. The second type happens when the data set is relatively large and preserves good locality. Increasing the data portion in the L1 has positive impact. The third type is most interesting: programs have changing preferences to the L1. These programs have changing sizes of working sets and code regions. Lastly, there are some programs that are extremely biased to one type of resource, typically the data cache. Moreover, the working data sets present poor locality, and increasing data caches does no good. For these programs, the

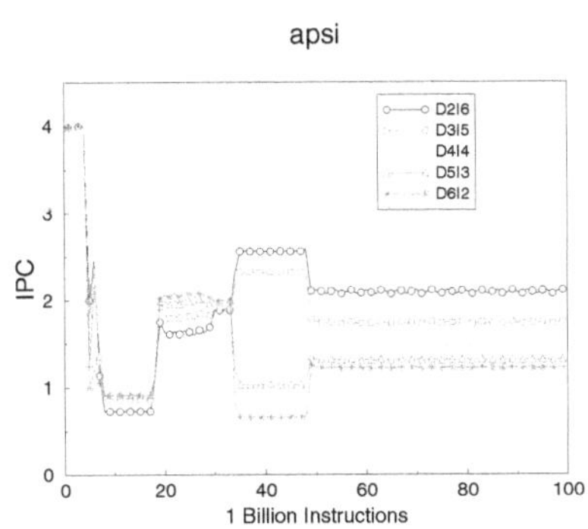

Fig. 1. Varying demands on I-cache and D-cache for program `apsi`

bottlenecks typically lie in other components such as L2. Re-allocation of L1 will work well in joint with other optimization techniques for L2 cache. Fig. 1 shows a sample benchmark `apsi` that belongs to type 3 described above (Due to the space limitation, we do not include graphs for other categories). Legend "`DxIy`" denotes x-way D-cache and y-way I-cache. As we can see that the IPC is improved when the cache configuration adapts to the program's need.

4 Cache Design

4.1 Modifications to the Circuit

The cache circuitry needs to be adjusted so that some of its ways can be used for both instruction and data accesses. This means that these shared ways can take either the instruction address or the data address, and output to either the instruction bus or the data bus, but not both at the same time. Thus, we need to add a multiplexer in front of the cache decoders to select between two addresses. Similarly, the output of the shared ways now can reach both buses depending on the current way configuration. These changes are depicted in Fig. 2 using colored lines.

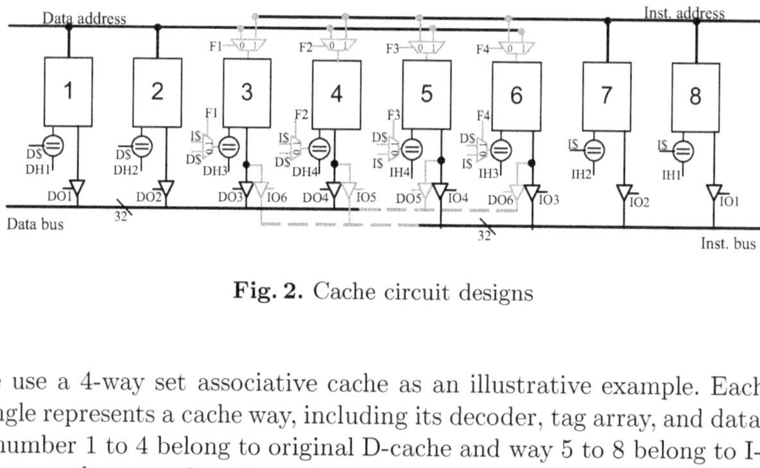

Fig. 2. Cache circuit designs

We use a 4-way set associative cache as an illustrative example. Each large rectangle represents a cache way, including its decoder, tag array, and data array. Way number 1 to 4 belong to original D-cache and way 5 to 8 belong to I-cache. We assume that way 3 to 6 can be used as shared ways. The muxes between the address lines and the cache ways are added as explained above. The output wires are extended to another output bus with a tri-state driver in parallel with the original ones. At any time, only one of them is turned on. The control of the new tri-state drivers are determined by 'IO6', 'IO5', 'DO5', and 'DO6' which are generated by the control flags $F1 \sim F4$. These flags indicate whether the corresponding way has been configured for the other cache, with '1' meaning yes and '0' meaning no. The flags are set by the dynamic cache co-allocation algorithm explained later.

Take way number 3 in Fig. 2 as an example (other ways are similar). When it is accessed as an I-cache way, $F1$ will be '1' so that instruction address (cache set index indeed) will flow through the mux on the top. Next the tag comparison should be carried with the instruction address's tag, as selected by the mux near the comparator controlled by $F1$. Finally, if the selection logic selects the output from way 3 (not shown in the figure), its output wires to the instruction bus should be turned on at the tri-state driver by 'IO6'. The 'IO6' is generated by $F1$ as illustrated in Fig. 3. The 'IO6' should be asserted if both $F1$ and $DH3$ are '1', and that the tri-state buffer is selected by the line offset from the address. Meanwhile, 'DO3' should be low since it is to the data bus. As shown in Fig. 3, 'DO3' is turned off if $F1$ is 1.

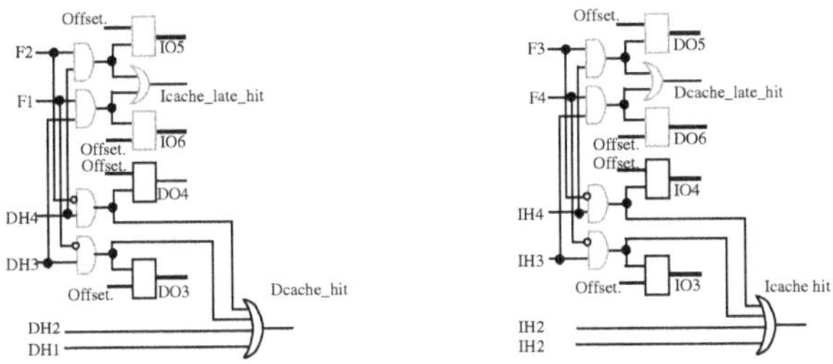

Fig. 3. Circuit of the output control

4.2 Timing Analysis

We have added extra hardware along the critical path of the shared ways from the address input to the data output. The overall overhead amounts to two levels of gate delays plus wire delays from the lengthened buses. The first level of gate delay is from the added mux, and the second level comes from the ANDing of $F1$ and $DH3$ before the OR gate in Fig. 3. The extra gates will increase the cache access time but not necessarily in terms of the number of clock cycles. To verify this claim, we simulated a cache in HSPICE using IBM 0.18μ and 0.13μ technology files from MOSIS. The cache delays, gate delays, and the proper clock frequencies are shown in Fig. 4.

Technology	T_{base}	mux	AND	T_{new}	Frequency	cycles
0.18μ	1.28ns	0.06ns	0.11ns	1.45ns	1GHz	2
0.13μ	1.07ns	0.05ns	0.056ns	1.176ns	2GHz	3

Fig. 4. Timing analysis of the new cache of 16K-byte using HSPICE

Take the 0.13μ technology as an example. The absolute access time to this 16KB cache is 1.07ns while the number of clock cycles allocated to this cache is 3 (since 2 would not be enough at 2GHz clock frequency). We illustrate the time distribution of a cache access in each clock cycle in Fig. 5. The activities and their required time are indicated in shaded slots. As we can see, every cycle has some slack in the end. When we insert extra timing due to mux and the AND

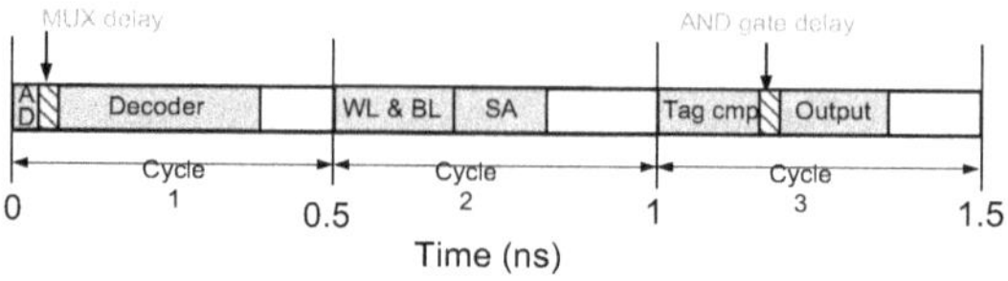

Fig. 5. Cache access time breakdown (0.13μ). The extra time are pointed by arrows.

gate before the address decoding (`AD`) and before the output driving (`output`), the overall time requirements still fit in each clock cycle. The same observation is made for the 0.18μ technology as well. Therefore, we conclude that even though the cache access time is increased, the number of cycles needed by this cache remains the same.

Let us still assume that way 3 is configured to the I-cache. If 'IO6' is '1', meaning that this is an I-cache hit, we generate an "Icache_late_hit" signal. This hit comes a little bit later than those hits from way 5 to 8 since the instructions sent on the bus need to be sent over a longer wire. The wire delay will become a major concern in future smaller technology size. And thus, we conservatively charge several clock cycles due to the wire delay. In the evaluation section, we will vary the number of cycles on the wires and show its impact on the performance.

Other design issues. Our design will be easy to implement if the I-cache and D-cache are of a *symmetric* structure, e.g, same size and associativity such as the AMD Opteron 64-bit core [15]. For different sized caches, especially different sized ways of I- and D-cache, extra handling to the cache indexing must be present, similar to that in [2]. Our technique does not favor specialized caches, e.g., trace caches since the architecture of a trace cache and a conventional D-cache are significantly different. Adding complex control for reconfigurability may be an overkill. We do not consider the case where I-cache and D-cache have different number of ports. This is because additional control logic must be added and the cache access time will be prolonged. On the other hand, some processors provide virtually different number of ports for I-cache and D-cache. Internally, an interleaved banking technique is used and the physical ports per cache way is the same between I-cache and D-cache [15]. In those cases, our technique can still be applied.

5 Dynamic Co-allocation Algorithm

In this section, we explain our dynamic cache way co-allocation algorithm in details. We keep track of several statistics counters in the cache hardware. Periodically, we examine those counters and judge whether the current cache configuration should be changed. If there could be an increase in performance, we set proper flag bits $F1 \sim F4$ in Fig. 2. Otherwise, the cache configuration stays the same. The statistics counters are then reset to reflect new cache performance in the next time interval.

When it is decided that an I-cache way should be moved to D-cache, the invalid bits of that array are all reset so that the D-cache can use it as a clean way. Reversely, when a D-cache way is moved to the I-cache, the dirty entries in that way should be written back to the L2 first. We modeled this overhead by stalling the CPU while flushing all dirty lines. Since our monitoring period is quite long (10 million instruction), the overhead due to dirty write backs are not noticeable. Both caches' MSHRs may be non-empty when the reconfiguration takes place. This is not of much a concern since we simply block the updating of the new line to the reallocated ways. The new instruction/data can still be forwarded to the CPU.

5.1 Analyzing the Changes in Performance

The most important part in the dynamic co-allocation algorithm is to calculate whether there is a gain or a loss in the performance by adding or removing a way from a cache. Since this is a *co*-allocation scheme, adding a way to a cache means removing it from another. Therefore, the net change in the memory performance is the gain by adding a way to one minus the loss by removing a way from the other. We calculate the net change for I-cache, denoted as ΔI, and the net change for D-cache, denoted as ΔD. If $\Delta I > \Delta D > \epsilon$, one cache way is moved from the D-cache to the I-cache. We require that they be greater than a small positive value since both Δ's can be negative which means moving one way from another cache over will hurt performance. Similarly, one way is moved from I-cache to D-cache if $\Delta D > \Delta I > \epsilon$.

Take the I-cache as an example. To obtain ΔI, we must calculate the performance gain, G_I, when a new way is added, and the performance loss, L_D, when this way is removed from the D-cache. That is, $\Delta I = G_I - L_D$. Assume components other than the L1 caches are not affected by the reconfiguration, and so the performance change from them is not considered. Therefore, G_I is the reduction in the *memory access time* contributed by the I-cache. This reduction is due to the additional I-cache hits brought in by the new way. Ignoring the cold start of this new way, the increase in the I-cache hits is the difference between the hits of an $n+1$ way cache ($Ihit_{n+1}$) and an n way cache ($Ihit_n$) where n is the current set associativity of I-cache. Let $Ihit \uparrow = Ihit_{n+1} - Ihit_n$. Therefore,

$$\begin{aligned} G_I &= [Ihit_n \times T_{I\$} + (1 - Ihit_n) \times \underbrace{(T_{L2} + M_{L2} \times T_M)}_{A}] \\ &\quad -[Ihit_{n+1} \times T_{I\$} + (1 - Ihit_{n+1}) \times A] \\ &= Ihit \uparrow \times (A - T_{I-\$}) = Ihit \uparrow \times (T_{L2} + M_{L2} \times T_M - T_{I\$}) \end{aligned} \quad (1)$$

where $T_{I\$/L2/M}$ stands for I-cache/L2/memory access time, and M_{L2} means L2 miss rates. By replacing the I with D above and considering the D-cache is now reduced by one way, we can obtain L_D as follows:

$$\begin{aligned} L_D &= [Dhit_{n-1} \times T_{D\$} + (1 - Dhit_{n-1}) \times A] - [Dhit_n \times T_{D\$} + (1 - Dhit_n) \times A] \\ &= Dhit \downarrow \times (T_{L2} + M_{L2} \times T_M - T_{D\$}) \end{aligned} \quad (2)$$

where $Dhit \downarrow = Dhit_n - Dhit_{n-1}$. Combining the G_I and L_D into ΔI and assume $T_{I\$} = T_{D\$} = T_{L1}$ we obtain

$$\Delta I = G_I - L_D = (Ihit \uparrow - Dhit \downarrow) \times (T_{L2} + M_{L2} \times T_M - T_{L1}) \tag{3}$$

Using the same derivation, we can obtain ΔD as:

$$\Delta D = G_D - L_I = (Dhit \uparrow - Ihit \downarrow) \times (T_{L2} + M_{L2} \times T_M - T_{L1}) \tag{4}$$

The most naive way of making a reconfiguration decision seems to be using the cache miss rates for two caches and comparing them to predefined thresholds. From equation (3), we can see that there are three variables that determine the value of ΔI: $Ihit \uparrow = Ihit_{n+1} - Ihit_n = IMiss_n - IMiss_{n+1}$, $Dhit \downarrow = Dhit_n - Dhit_{n-1} = DMiss_{n-1} - DMiss_n$, and *L2 miss rates*. Clearly, using $IMiss_n$ and $DMiss_n$ instead of ΔI is overly rough since other three terms are neglected even though they contribute equally to the performance. In fact, we experienced that dropping terms in $(Ihit \uparrow - Dhit \downarrow)$ results in inferior performance and using $IMiss_n$ and $DMiss_n$ in place of ΔI sometimes gives mis-configured L1 that could hurt the performance. The $Ihit \uparrow$ and $Dhit \downarrow$ can be found in a similar way as in previous techniques [12, 1]. The cost of finding them is an extra tag array for both caches. We will show the effect of narrowing such tags to reduce the area overhead in the experiment section.

Note that we have been using the *memory access latency* in our analysis as the indication to the performance. In out-of-order execution processors, some of the memory latency are overlapped with the CPU execution, and therefore do not contribute to the overall performance. We do not account for the overlapping part for the following two reasons. First, measuring it at runtime is complex and may not be very beneficial since it is a secondary factor to the performance as analyzed by Karkhanis *et. al.* [6]. Second, reducing the total memory access latency means the memory hierarchy can respond more quickly to the CPU making it proceed to the dependent instructions sooner. Consequently, more overlapping between the CPU and the memory time is likely, further reducing the non-overlapping portion and improving the performance.

5.2 Overhead

The overhead of calculating ΔI and ΔD is merely four multiplications and four additions ($T_{L2} - T_{L1}$ can be pre-computed). We need four counters for the hits, which will be explained next, and a couple of temporary registers. Since we perform such an analysis on every 10 million executed instructions, such an overhead is negligible. Nevertheless, we still conservatively charge 200 clock cycles for this overhead.

Our algorithm currently considers of moving only one cache way at a time. It is not necessary to have this restriction. In fact, we can find a best configuration by attempting to add more ways. That is, we can iterate our algorithm several times to find the best number of ways that should be moved at once, forming a *greedy* algorithm. Of course, the time spent on such an algorithm will increase and the hardware counters required also increase since now we need to consider beyond the second least recently used access numbers. If the maximum number of cache ways allowable to move is N, $N \leq$ cache associativity. The maximum number of iterations is N, and the maximum number of hardware counters is $N \times 2$. We will compare the performance differences between a single-step algorithm and the greedy algorithm in our experiments.

6 Evaluations

We performed experiments using the SimpleScalar Tool Set [3]. The benchmarks we used are 15 programs from SPEC CPU2K compiled into Alpha binaries. All the programs were fast forwarded for one billion and executed for one billion instructions. The processor configurations are shown in Fig. 6.

Parameter	Value	Parameter	Value	Parameter	Value
Fetch queue entry	8	Branch miss penalty	3	RUU size	128
Issue width	8	L1 I/D-cache	16KB 4way	L2 latency	15 cycles
Integer ALU/Multiplier	4/4	L1 latency	2 cycles	LSQ entry	32
FP ALU/Multiplier	4/4	L2	512K	Memory latency	100 cycles

Fig. 6. Architectural parameters

6.1 Performance Improvements

In this section, we show the performance improvements four aforementioned algorithms: 1) *Single-step.* This refers to our basic co-allocation scheme which moves only one cache way at a time; 2) *Greedy.* This refers to the greedy algorithm which intends to find the configuration that can maximize the performance by iterating the Single-step algorithm multiple times; 3) *Reduced-tag.* This refers to the Single-step algorithm but with a narrower width for the extra tags that we maintain for both I-cache and D-cache. We used only a 4-bit array recording only the least significant portion of a regular tag; 4) *Using the miss rates.* This refers to the Single-step algorithm that does not use $Ihit \uparrow - Dhit \downarrow$, and $Dhit \uparrow - Ihit \downarrow$ in equation (3) and (4) respectively. Instead, the I-cache and D-cache miss counts during current monitoring interval were used as discussed in Section 5.1.

The percentages of IPC improvements are plotted in Fig. 7. We can see that the Single-step scheme achieves significant speedups — up to 36% for `crafty` and 10% on average. The greedy algorithm generally equals Single-step or does slightly better but the differences are very small. Only in one benchmark `twolf` did the greedy algorithm perform worse than the Single-step. This is because our co-allocation decision is based on the performance in the last monitoring interval. This is beneficial when the program does not have dramatic changes from interval to interval. Otherwise, a wrong decision, as in case of `twolf`, might be made. Here we can see the advantage of the Single-step algorithm: it makes

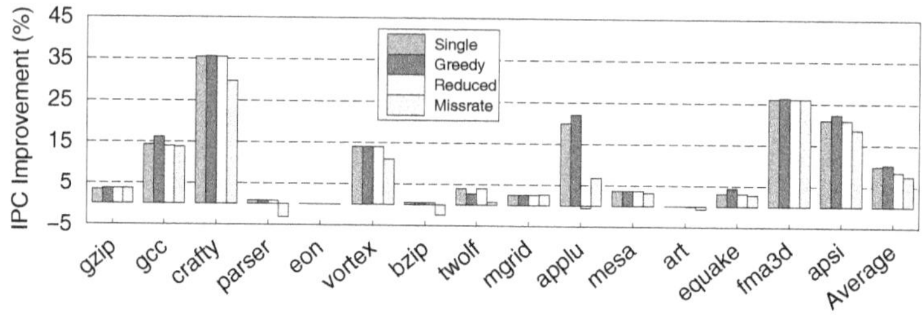

Fig. 7. Speedups for single-threaded workloads

only "one step" away from the current configuration. If it was wrong, it is not too late to correct it back in the next interval. Whereas in the greedy algorithm, it tries to make "multiple steps" aggressively. This is good if the decision is correct, but damaging otherwise.

Using a narrower tag array ('Reduced' bar in the chart) achieves very good approximation to using a full-width tag array. A narrow tag array may generate some false positive hits, i.e., the 4 bits match with the address but it is not a hit. Such a situation affects only one benchmark `applu` where we observed 20% of hits are false positive in the extra tag array for the D-cache. This resulted in a very high hit count that increases the ΔD which then generates more configurations favoring the D-cache. The last algorithm uses the miss rates in equation (3) and (4). The only advantage is to remove the extra tag that helps in collecting the cache hit changes. However, using the miss information greatly degrades our performance gains, and sometimes even slows down the programs (`parser`, `bzip` and `art`). This is due to the inaccuracy of using miss rates only to characterize program performances.

6.2 Sensitivity to L2 and L1 Optimizations

There has been abundant research on improving the L2 cache performance. Examples are content compression, prefetching, using novel indexing schemes, etc. We would like to see the potential of our L1 cache co-allocation scheme with the presence of those L2-based techniques in this section. Since most of those techniques aim at reducing the L2 miss rates, we increased the L2 size (effectively decreasing its miss rates) to mimic those techniques in a uniform way. The results are presented in Fig. 8.

On average, our L1 co-allocation scheme performs even better than before. This is mainly because when a major bottleneck in L2 has been removed, the next important component is likely to be the L1 caches. Hence, any improvement in the L1 will be very sensitive to the overall performance. Of course, a slight decision mistake may introduce negative impact on the performance as in `parser`. Nevertheless, this experiment also demonstrates that our L1 co-allocation scheme is not only not diminished by, but also additive to existing L2-based optimization schemes.

It is also of great interest to see similar effects to existing L1 optimization techniques. The well known L1 cache performance improvements include line

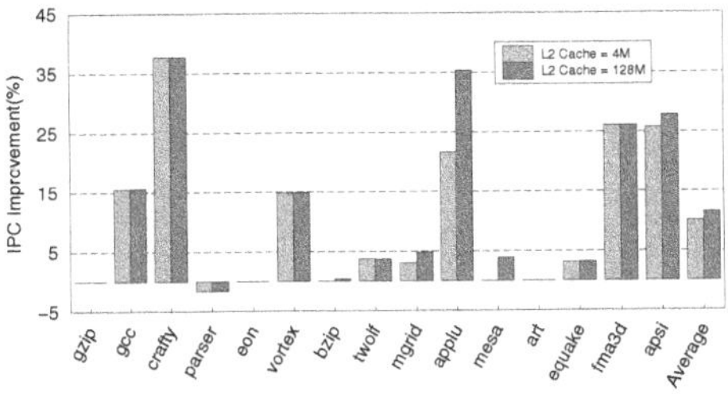

Fig. 8. With a near-ideal L2 cache

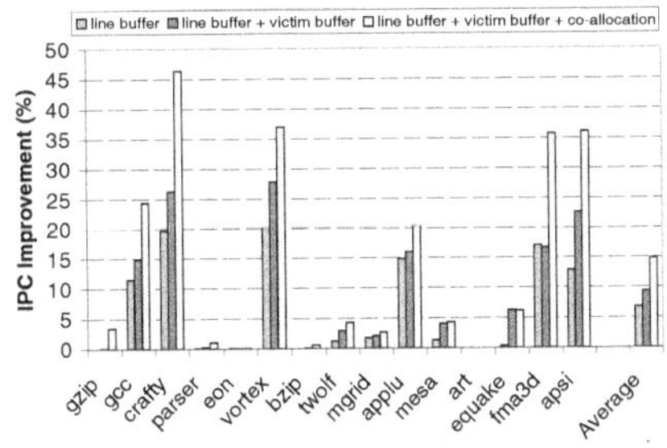

Fig. 9. Comparison among line buffer, victim buffer, and co-allocation scheme

buffer for I-cache, victim buffer for D-cache, prefetching for D-cache, pseudo-set associative I- or D-cache etc. We will compare the former two since prefetching into L1 has the risk of polluting the cache and is thus more suitable for L2, and pseudo-set associative L1 cache is more applicable to direct-mapped caches.

In Fig. 9, we show the results of the following three techniques: 1) add a single-entry line buffer to the I-cache; 2) on top of 1), add an 8-entry victim buffer to D-cache; and 3) on top of 2), add our co-allocation technique. The purpose of this experiment is to see if the performance gain we showed earlier cannot be achieved by simply a line buffer, a victim buffer or both. The conclusion is quite clear from the results. For programs such as `appsi`, `crafty`, `fma3d` etc, the IPC increase from case 2) to case 3) is 14%, 20%, and 19% respectively. On average, a single line buffer improves IPC by 6.7%. With victim buffer, the IPC is further improved by 3%. Finally, with our co-allocation technique, the IPC is increased further by 5.3%. The reason the co-allocation technique being constantly effective is that it exploits a dynamic program execution demand that is distinct from those phenomena exploited by line buffer or a victim buffer.

6.3 Using a Larger L1

Another interesting result we want to show is that using 32KB L1 cache (16KB each) with our cache co-allocation scheme can achieve comparable performance to a 64KB baseline L1 (32KB each). This is shown in Fig. 10. As we can see that except for a few programs, e.g. `crafty` and `apsi`, our claim is true for most other programs. Thus, we can reduce the area cost of L1 yet still achieve the performance of a larger L1. This is a beneficial feature to embedded type of processors where area is of a big concern.

6.4 Sensitivity to Wire Delays

With the trend in technology size shrinking, wire delays will become evident in future processors. To accommodate locations of I-cache and D-cache in different floorplans of different processor models, we vary the number of cycles that might be taken when data/instruction comes from the opposite cache ways. However, when significant wire delays are taken into account, our analytical models for

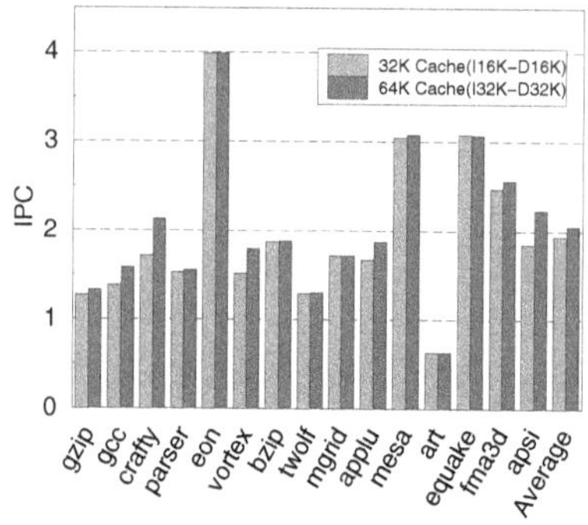

Fig. 10. Comparing our 32KB L1 and a normal 64KB L1

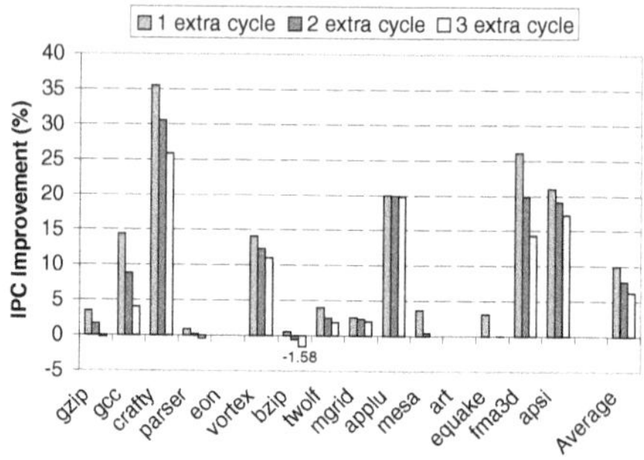

Fig. 11. Performance sensitivity to wire delays

performance gain and loss in section 5.1 should be revised to accommodate the delays. We measured IPC increases when 1, 2, or 3 additional cycles are added to the wires in Fig. 11.

We can see that our scheme is quite resistant to the impact from wire delays. This is because when co-allocation algorithm calculates that moving ways does not yield benefit, it simply keeps the original configuration. We observed that the worst case happens only in `bzip` when 3 extra cycles are added to the wires. The slowdown is 1.58%. On average, there are still 7.8% (6.3%) IPC improvements when 2 (3) extra cycles are added on the wires.

7 Conclusion

We have presented a simple and accurate technique of dynamically co-allocating cache ways between L1 I-cache and D-cache according to the programs' varying demands. Our cache co-allocation algorithm can accurately capture the changing demands on L1 caches. It works even better when combined with other L1 or L2-cache optimization techniques. For many programs we tested, a 16KB I-cache and a 16KB D-cache can achieve the same or better performances of L1 caches doubling the size. On average, our cache co-allocation scheme can yield 10% speedup for the benchmarks we tested.

References

1. A. Alameldeen, D. Wood, "Adaptive cache compression for high-performance processors," *ISCA*, pp. 212-223, 2004.
2. R. Balasubramonian, D. Albonesi, A. Buyuktosunoglu, S. Dwarkadas, "Memory Hierarchy Reconfiguration for Energy and Performance in General-Purpose Processor Architectures," *Micro*, pp. 245-257, 2000.
3. D. Burger and T. Austin, "The SimpleScalar Tool Set, Version 2.0," *Technical Report 1342, Univ. of Wisconsin-Madison, Comp. Sci. Dept.*, 1997.
4. P. Denning, "The working set model for program behavior," *Communications of the ACM*, Vol. 11, Iss. 5, pp. 323-333, 1968.

5. N. Drach, A. Seznec, "semi-unified caches," *ICPP,* pp. 25-28, 1993.
6. T. Karkhanis, J. Smith, "A first-order superscalar processor model," *ISCA,* pp. 338-349, 2004.
7. M. Kharbutli, K. Irwin, Y. Solihin, J. Lee, "Using prime numbers for cache indexing to eliminate conflict misses," *HPCA,* pp. 288-299, 2004.
8. K. J. Nesbit, J. E. Smith, "Data cache prefetching using a global history buffer," *HPCA,* pp. 96-105, 2004.
9. P. Ranganathan, S. Adve, N. Jouppi, "Reconfigurable caches and their application to media processing," *ISCA,* pp. 214-224, 2000.
10. T. Sherwood, E. Perelman, G. Hamerly, B. Calder, "Automatically Characterizing Large Scale Program Behavior," *ASPLOS,* pp. 45-57, 2002.
11. P. Shivakumar, N. P. Jouppi, "CACTI 3.0 An Integrated Cache Timing, Power, and Area Model," *WRL Research Report,* 2001/2.
12. G. E. Suh, S. Devadas, L. Rudolph, "A new memory monitoring scheme for memory-aware scheduling and partitioning," *HPCA,* pp. 117-128, 2002.
13. J. Yang, Y. Zhang, R. Gupta, "Frequent value compression in data caches," *MICRO,* pp. 258-265, 2000.
14. C. Zhang, F. Vahid, W. Najjar, "A highly configurable cache architecture for embedded systems," *ISCA,* pp. 136-146, 2003.
15. "Understanding the detailed architecture of the AMD's 64 bit core," *http://www.chip-architect.com/news/2003_09_21_Detailed_Architecture_of_AMDs_64bit_Core.html#3*
16. Intel, "Intel Pentium III Processor for the SC242 at 450 MHz to 1.0 GHz Datasheet," *http://www.intel.com/design/pentiumiii/datashts/244452.htm*
17. CPU Comparison *http://www.pantherproducts.co.uk/Articles/CPU/CPU %20Comparison.shtml*

Jaguar: A Compiler Infrastructure for Java Reconfigurable Computing*

Youngsun Han, Seon Wook Kim, and Chulwoo Kim

Department of Electronics and Computer Engineering,
Korea University, Seoul, Korea 136-701
Tel.: +82-2-3290-3252
ckim@korea.ac.kr

Abstract. In this paper, we present our compiler infrastructure, called Jaguar for Java reconfigurable computing. The Jaguar compiler translates compiled Java methods, i.e. sequence of bytecodes into Verilog synthesizable code modules with exploiting the maximum operational parallelism within applications. Our compiler infrastructure consists of two major components. One is a compiler to generate synthesizable Verilog codes from Java applications, which performs full compilation passes, such as bytecode parsing, intermediate representation (IR) construction, program analysis, optimization, and code emission. The other component is the Java Virtual Machine (JVM) which provides Java execution environment to the generated Verilog modules. The JVM closely interacts with hardware during the execution through an interrupt method. We discuss the performance issues and code transformation techniques to reduce the interaction overhead in our Java reconfigurable computing environment.

Keywords: Reconfigurable computing, compiler, Java, Verilog, FPGA.

1 Introduction

The applications written in Java can be compiled into location-independent codes moving on the Internet and running on every platform. Java's portability is achieved by compiling its classes into a distribution format, called a class file. The class file contains information about class fields and methods, and each method is represented as architecturally-neutral representation, i.e., a sequence of bytecodes. The class files are interpreted and executed on any computer supporting the Java Virtual Machine (JVM). Java's code portability, therefore, depends on both platform-independent class files and the implicit assumption that the full featured JVM is supported on every client machine. However, despite of the distinguished advantages over other programming languages, performance limitation due to interpretation in software-manner is a serious shortcoming to prevent from using Java on small devices like mobile phones and PDAs.

* This work was supported by grant No. R01-2005-000-10124-0 from Korea Science and Engineering Foundation in Ministry of Science & Technology.

L.T. Yang et al. (Eds.): ICESS 2005, LNCS 3820, pp. 386–397, 2005.

Nowadays according to fast development of semiconductor technologies, the speed of FPGAs (Field Programmable Gate Arrays) has been dramatically improved as much as that of microprocessors. Several approaches to accelerate execution of Java applications using a reconfigurable hardware have been proposed. There are three closely related works in area of reconfigurable hardware generation using high-level languages such as C/C++ and Java.

NENYA [1] compiler was developed to generate VHDL hierarchical RTL descriptions from user-specified regions of a Java program. The intermediate representations of NENYA is best-tailored to performance-driven hardware synthesis described in terms of interconnections between macro-cells in hardware libraries. And a C to HDL compiler [2] is designed to generate high speed pipeline circuits for loop and recursive parts written in C language, which consumes the most execution time of many applications. The compiler aims at extracting the most exhaustive parts of a C program, such as loop and recursive function, that can be accelerated by FPGAs and achieving the co-computation by microprocessor and FPGAs. But, full functions are not supported by the compiler yet. Finally, the Streams-C compiler [3] synthesizes hardware circuits for reconfigurable FPGA-based computers from parallel programs written in Streams-C language, including a small number of native libraries added to a synthesizable subset of C, and supporting a communicating process programming model. The Streams-C language and compiler make it easy to develop reconfigurable computing applications with high level expressibility.

In contrast of JOP [4] (full-featured hardware JVM), these researches are commonly based on a concept for reconfigurable computing which is supported by automatic code translation from high level languages such as C and Java into synthesizable hardware descriptions. There are large number of related work to reconfigurable computing, such as hardware/software co-design [5], software compilation [6], and high-level synthesis (HLS) [7].

In this paper we present code translation and optimization techniques for Java reconfigurable computing. For this purpose, we have developed a compiler infrastructure, called *the Jaguar compiler* which translates compiled Java methods, i.e. sequence of bytecodes into Verilog synthesizable code modules with exploiting the maximum operational parallelism within applications. Our compiler infrastructure consists of two major components. One is a compiler to generate synthesizable Verilog codes from Java applications. The compiler performs full compilation passes, such as bytecode parsing, intermediate representation (IR) construction, program analysis, optimization, and code emission. The compiler emits Verilog codes by using macro-cell libraries, which is a set of Verilog codes to represent semantics of a bytecode. The other component is Java Virtual Machine (JVM) which provides Java execution environment to the generated Verilog modules. The JVM closely interacts with hardware during execution through an interrupt method. We discuss the performance issues and code transformation techniques to reduce the interaction overhead in our Java reconfigurable computing environment. Differently from [1, 2] our infrastructure is a *complete* compiler solution for Java reconfigurable computing, i.e. there is no limitation in use to generate synthesizable Verilog codes from Java bytecodes.

The paper is organized as follows: In Section 2 we present the execution model for our Java reconfigurable computing and the structure of our Jaguar compiler infrastructure, and in Section 3 we analyze the performance of our execution platform using SciMark 2.0 benchmark [8]. Finally in Section 4 the conclusion is made.

2 Jaguar Compiler Infrastructure

2.1 Execution Model

Figure 1 shows an architecture of the Jaguar system for Java reconfigurable computing. The Jaguar execution consists of software-only and hardware-only execution, and their interactions. The software execution is done by Java Virtual Machine (JVM) running on the ARM processor, and the hardware execution is done by a set of synthesizable Verilog method blocks (MBs), i.e. Jaguar Hardware (Java Hardware), called J-Hardware on FPGA. The J-Hardware is connected to ARM through the AMBA protocol as a passive slave. We use the Altera Excalibur FPGA to support our execution model. We need an interaction between JVM and J-Hardware to control hardware-implemented method blocks on the FPGA, and to maintain program and data consistency. For this purpose, we use an interrupt method, and the JVM has been modified to handle interrupt requests from J-Hardware.

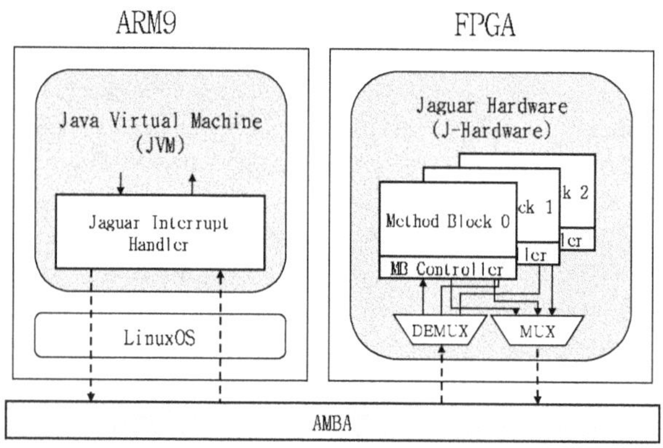

Fig. 1. Jaguar execution model for Java reconfigurable computing

Figure 2 shows the Jaguar execution flow, which is very similar to Just-In-Time (JIT) compiler execution. When JVM interprets bytecodes for a method invocation, the JVM checks whether the invoked method block is available in J-Hardware or not. If the desired method block exists in hardware, the JVM enables the J-Hardware to execute. Otherwise, the JVM executes bytecodes in software manner. After enabling J-Hardware, the JVM waits for interrupt signals from the J-Hardware. The J-Hardware interacts with the JVM when the J-Hardware needs 1) to access heaps inside the JVM, 2) to determine a method invocation at runtime, and 3) to handle exception handling. The J-Hardware is waiting in a *wait* state, while the JVM services the interrupt requests except for *return*, i.e. a termination state. The JVM also contains other components in order to execute Java applications, such as a class loader, an execution engine, a memory manager, and so on, which are the basic functionalities of the Java virtual machine.

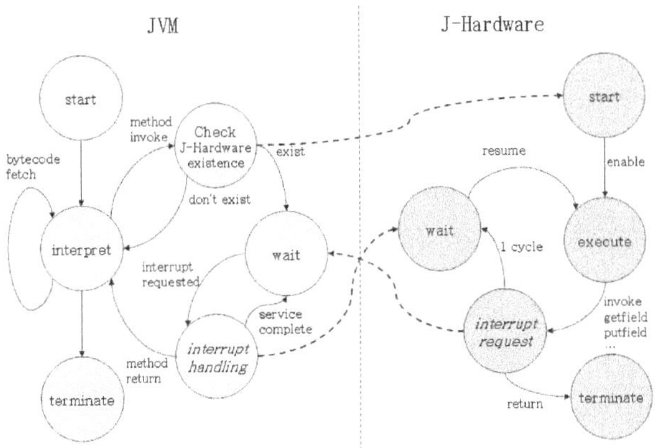

Fig. 2. Jaguar execution flow diagram

2.2 Compiler Structure

The Jaguar compiler is designed to translate the most time consuming and arithmetic intensive Java methods into Verilog synthesizable modules with exploiting the maximum operational parallelism. The whole compilation flow of our Jaguar compiler appears in Figure 3.

First, the Java decoder decodes a class file, and the Java analyzer analyzes bytecode sequences of an application and builds the application's intermediate representation, called Java IR. The Java IR includes basic information for code analysis and generation, such as a control flow and a data flow. The control dependence between basic blocks is resolved by *control* bytecodes, such as 1) general control jump bytecodes, 2) switch-type bytecodes that select one of multiple outgoing edges based on an operand value, and 3) exception handling bytecodes such as *athrow, jsr* and *ret.* The data dependence between bytecodes inside a basic block, except for bytecodes to need to interact with JVM such as *getfield, invokevirtual* and so on, is resolved by simulating Java operand stacks and local variable arrays. Additionally, we have integrated our compiler with the Jikes compiler [9] to get dependence information between bytecodes accessing

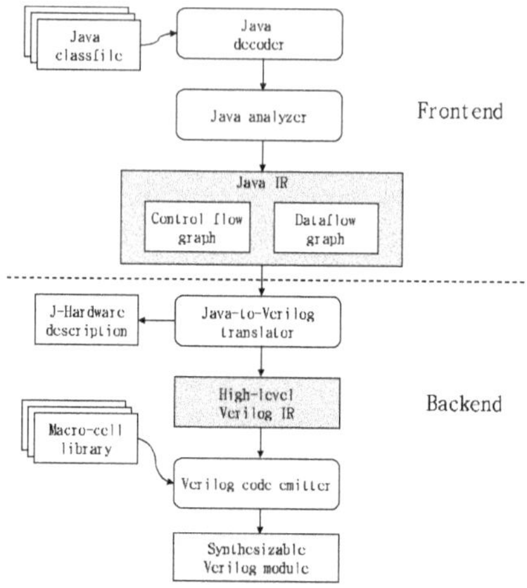

Fig. 3. Jaguar compilation flow for Java reconfigurable computing

the heap inside JVM. The Java IR for a basic block is scheduled and optimized to exploit maximum operational parallelism by using dependence information.

The Java-to-Verilog IR translator translates Java IR into High-Level Verilog IR. And the translator generates J-Hardware description to contain hardware-implemented method block information, such as a list of method names and interactions. The JVM reads the J-Hardware description when starting JVM execution. When the JVM interprets bytecodes for a method invocation, the JVM uses the J-Hardware description to know which method blocks are available into J-Hardware. And each entry for an interaction list has three fields: an interrupt index, a bytecode number and a program counter (PC). During execution, the entry is hashed by the interrupt index as a hash key and a value of the entry consists of a pair of the bytecode number and the PC. The interrupt information is used to know what kind of interrupts are requested and how they should be handled by the JVM.

The Java-to-Verilog IR translation generates three hardware components for a method block module, such as a basic block, and connection between basic blocks, and a method block controller to handle interrupts from basic block modules. Figure 4 shows an architectural organization for a method block module. Two interrupt masks are used to check interrupts from basic block modules and to support control speculation between basic block modules for future research. But the current version is to use only one interrupt mask at one time. When an interrupt mask is set by interrupts, an interrupt checker enables an operand fetcher to get operands from an operand table. The operand table includes a start index of operands for each interrupt. The operand fetcher enqueues the fetched operands into an operand queue, which is dequeued by JVM for an interrupt service.

Each basic block in the Java IR is translated into Verilog as shown in Figure 5. The Verilog code for a basic block consists of a basic block controller to

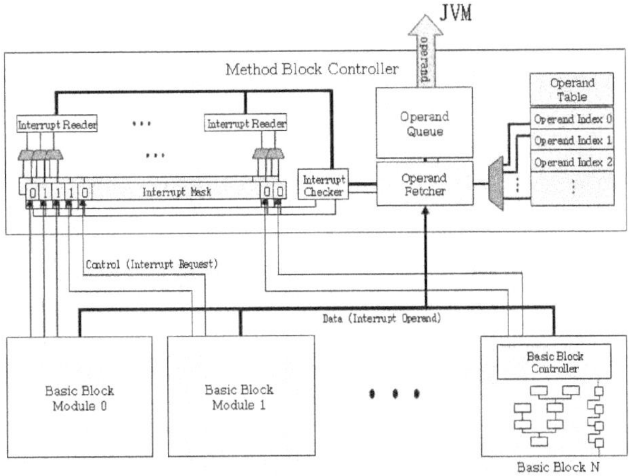

Fig. 4. Architectural organization of a method block

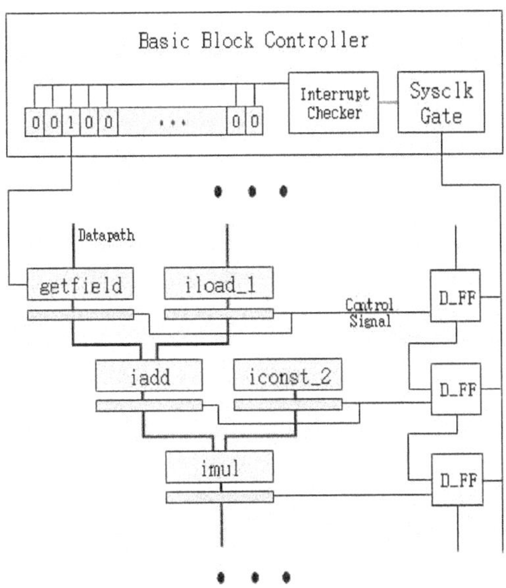

Fig. 5. Architectural organization of a basic block

handle a system clock for itself and a set of bytecode modules. If an interrupt is generated by *getfield* bytecode module, the interrupt checker inside a basic block disables the system clock. When an acknowledge signal from the method block controller is received, the system clock is enabled again. And the bytecode modules are connected to each other by using data flow information, and scheduled synchronously by using D FFs.

We connect basic blocks by considering control and data flow information. The control flow is represented as an *enable* signal to start execution of successor basic blocks. Similarly data flow is represented as wires and tri-state buffers controlled by the enable signal.

Finally, High-Level Verilog IR is emitted and linked with macro-cell libraries to generate synthesizable Verilog codes. Figure 6 shows *iadd* macro-cell written in Verilog as an example.

```
module Bc_iadd(data_out, data_op1, data_op2);
     parameter WIDTH = 32;
     output [WIDTH-1:0] data_out;
     input [WIDTH-1:0] data_op1, data_op2;

     assign data_out = data_op1 + data_op2;
endmodule
```

Fig. 6. Example of a macro-cell for *iadd* bytecode

2.3 Interaction Between JVM and J-Hardware

For interaction between JVM and J-Hardware, Figure 7 shows an interrupt sequence diagram, whose mechanism consists of the following three steps: (i) When J-Hardware needs an interaction with JVM for a heap access, a method invocation, and an exception handling, it sends an *interrupt request* signal to JVM. When J-Hardware receives an *acknowledgment* (ACK) signal from the JVM, J-Hardware inactivates itself and waits for completion of the interrupt service. (ii) In order that JVM provides an interrupt service, the JVM needs operands from J-Hardware. The JVM reads all 32 bit operands which are generated by simultaneously occurring interrupts. The operands are provided by the operand queue in Figure 4 from the J-Hardware (*read an operand*). (iii) In the last step, the

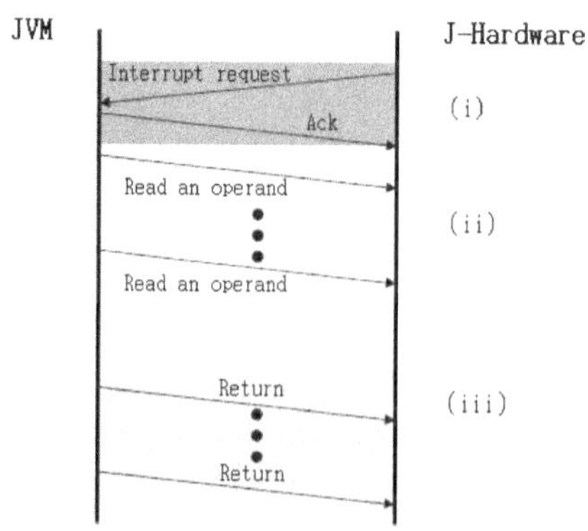

Fig. 7. An interrupt sequence diagram

JVM executes an interrupt handling routine and returns a service completion signal to J-Hardware one by one.

2.4 Code Optimization

In performance evaluation of our infrastructure, we have found that the performance of the Jaguar system highly depends on the number of interactions between JVM and J-Hardware through an interrupt mechanism. The interaction is required for heap accesses, method invocations, and exception handling. In this subsection, we discuss code optimization issues in heap accesses, since interactions due to method invocations can be reduced only by control speculation and aggressive inlining. In order to alleviate the overhead, we applied the following three code optimization techniques as shown in Figures 8 and 9: an interrupt scheduling, a common subexpression elimination (CSE) and a loop unrolling.

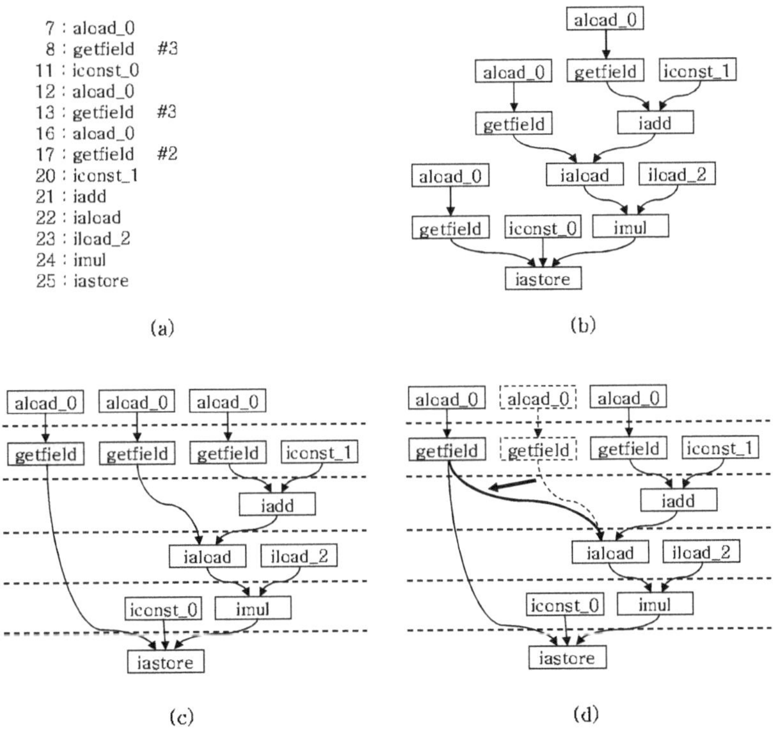

Fig. 8. Jaguar code optimization. The shaded nodes in DFG are the target of each optimization. (a) Bytecode sequence. (b) DFG. (c) DFG after interrupt scheduling. (d) DFG after CSE.

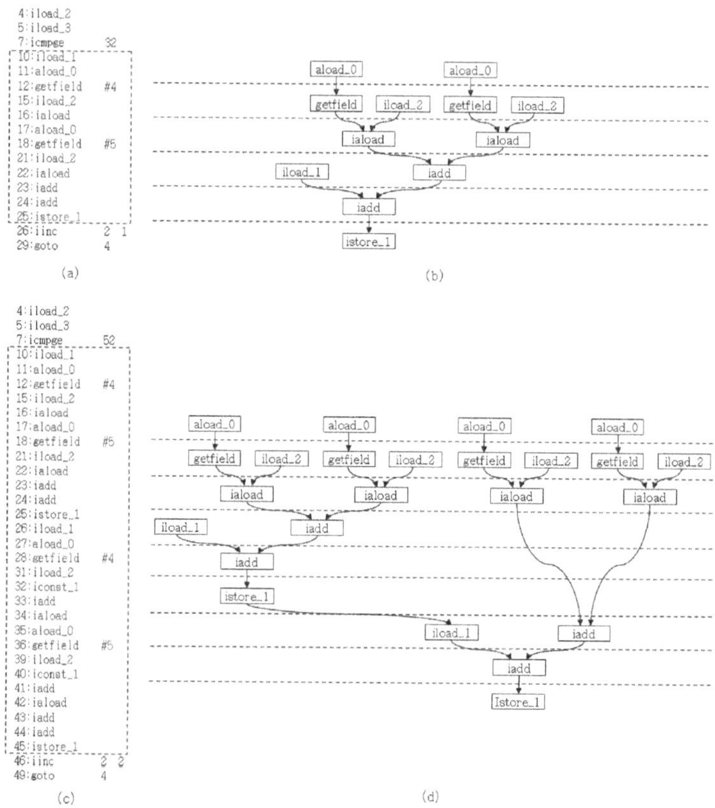

Fig. 9. Loop unrolling optimization in Jaguar. The shaded nodes in DFG are the target of each optimization. (a) Bytecode sequence. (b) DFG. (c) Bytecode sequence after loop unrolling. (d) DFG after loop unrolling.

Interrupt Scheduling. Some interrupt requests from J-Hardware can be generated at the same time. For example, if there is no data dependence between heap accesses, the related bytecodes can be scheduled to ask interrupt services simultaneously to JVM, as shown in Figure 8 (c). The method block controller in Figure 4 is designed to manipulate several interrupts at the same time. The interrupt scheduling technique reduces the overhead (i) described in Section 2.3.

Common Subexpression Elimination (CSE). If there exists only input dependence, we can apply a common subexpression elimination technique to heap access bytecodes. This technique reduces overhead (ii) and (iii) described in Section 2.3. If the heap access bytecodes access the same data space, we can remove all the bytecodes except for an input dependence source. The example is shown in Figure 8 (d).

Loop Unrolling. For more aggressive interrupt schedule, we apply a loop unrolling if there is no cross-iteration dependence. In the applications which include loop intensive codes like SparseMM, our Jaguar compiler can reduce interaction occurrences significantly. The example is shown in Figure 9. The bytecode sequence in Figure 9 (a) is unrolled by two, and heap accesses in loop unrolled two iterations (Figure 9 (d)) can ask an interrupt service at the same time.

3 Performance Analysis

The performance of the Jaguar compiler has been tested using three Java SciMark 2.0 benchmarks, FFT, SOR and SparseMM [8] on Altera Excalibur Device [10]. The JVM runs on the 50 MHz ARM processor and Embedded

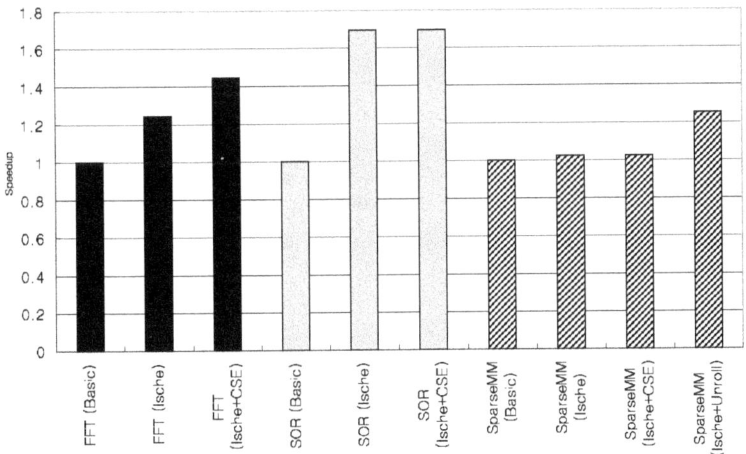

Fig. 10. Speedup of code optimizations. Ische: Interrupt scheduling. CSE: Common expression elimination. Unroll: Loop unrolling by 4.

Table 1. Reduction of interrupt occurrences by code optimization. Ische: Interrupt scheduling. CSE: Common expression elimination.

Benchmark	Optimization	No. of interrupt occurrences	No. of interrupts in codes	Reduction (%)
FFT	Basic	122936	204900	40.0
	Ische	61496	204900	70.0
	Ische + CSE	61496	163940	62.5
SOR	Basic	38615	57922	33.3
	Ische	19407	57922	66.5
	Ische + CSE	19407	57922	66.5
SparseMM	Basic	22992	32987	30.3
	Ische	21992	32987	33.3
	Ische + CSE	21922	32987	33.3
	Ische + Loop unrolling by 4	8799	32987	73.3

Linux. And J-Hardware executes at 25 MHz, being connected to AMBA as a slave. There is difference in clock speeds between the JVM and the J-Hardware due to the Excalibur chip. The Excalibur enables the PLD circuits like J-Hardware to be connected only to the secondary bridge as a slave of the main bridge.

Figure 10 shows the speedup with respect to execution without any code optimization. The performance gain comes from reducing the number of interactions between JVM and J-Hardware, and it is shown in Table 1.

Table 1 shows that our code optimization schemes reduce the interrupt occurrences by up to 73%, and all schemes are very effective.

4 Conclusion

Several approaches to facilitate the hardware development have been studied. Especially, demands for researches on the hardware description using high-level languages like C and Java is dramatically increasing as the size of hardware system is getting larger and hardware complexity becomes larger.

In this paper, we presented the Jaguar compiler infrastructure which translates compiled Java applications to hardware, written in synthesizable VerilogHDL, without any modification of source bytecodes. Also we evaluated the performance on Excalibur device, where JVM executes on the ARM processor and our hardware executes on the FPGA. The heap accesses and method invocations from Java hardware need to interact with JVM through interrupts. The interactions incur huge overhead in time, so we applied three compiler optimization techniques to code generation.

For our ongoing research, we have integrated our Jaguar infrastructure with a hardware-based Java processor. On this architecture, the interaction overhead can be significantly reduced because the reconfigurable Java hardware can directly accesses the heap area.

References

1. J. M. P. Cardoso and H. C. Neto. Macro-based hardware compilation of java bytecodes into a dynamic reconfigurable computing system. In K. L. Pocek and J. M. Arnold, editors, *Proceedings of the IEEE Workshop on FPGAs for Custom Computing Machines*, pages 2–11, Napa, CA, 1999. IEEE.
2. Tsutomu Maruyama and Tsutomu Hoshino. A C to HDL compiler for pipeline processing on FPGAs. In *IEEE Symposium on Field-Programmable Custom Computing Machines*, pages 101–110, April 2000.
3. Jan Frigo, Maya Gokhale, and Dominique Lavenier. Evaluation of the streams-C C-to-FPGA compiler: An applications perspective. In *International Symposium on Field Programmable Gate Arrays*, pages 134–140, Monterey, CA, 2001.
4. JOP - Java Optimized Processor. http://www.jopdesign.com/.
5. G. De Micheli and R. Gupta. Hardware/software co-design. *Proceedings of the IEEE*, 85(3):349–365, March 1997.

6. S. S. Muchnick. *Advanced Compiler Design and Implementation.* Morgan Kaufmann Publishers, Inc., 1997.
7. G. De Micheli. *Synthesis and Optimization of Digital Circuits.* McGraw Hill, 1994.
8. SciMark 2.0. http://math.nist.gov/scimark2/.
9. David Bacon, Stephen Fink, and David Grove. Space and time efficient implementation of the Java object model. In *European Conference on Object-Oriented Programming (ECOOP2002)*, pages 10–14, Malaga, Spain, June 2002.
10. Excalibur devices. http://www.arm.com/.

CCD Camera-Based Range Sensing with FPGA for Real-Time Processing

Chun-Shin Lin[1] and Hyongsuk Kim[2]

[1] Electrical and Computer Engineering, University of Missouri-Columbia, Columbia, MO 65211 USA
LinC@missouri.edu

[2] Electronics and Information Engineering, Chonbuk National University, Republic of Korea
hskim@chonbuk.ac.kr

Abstract. A depth measurement system that consists of a single camera, a laser light source and a rotating mirror is investigated. The camera and the light source are fixed at position and face a rotating mirror. The laser light is reflected by the mirror and projected to the scene for depth measurement. The camera detects the laser light location on object surfaces through the same mirror. The scan over the measured area is done by mirror rotation. FPGA is used to quickly process the collected images to generate a range image. A 136 × 240 range image can be generated in 2.3 seconds. This speed is 4 times faster than that of a PC with a 2.8GHz clock. If the frame rate can be increased to 300 per second, the speed improvement will be about 15 times. The technology, on the other hand, offers a solution for embedded implementation.

1 Introduction

Depth images have applications in environment modeling and understanding, and robot navigation. An efficient method for depth measurement is the active lighting with structured patterns [1][2]. The active lighting-based technique has one camera of a stereo vision system replaced by a light source [3-5]. Projecting multiple striped [6][7] or rectangular grid patterns of lights [9] on objects makes depth measurement easier and results more reliable. However, potential ambiguities in matching stripe segments resulting from object surfaces at different *depths* remain [10]. Though such ambiguity can be avoided by employing the encoded striped lighting technique [3][8] or color lighting [1][5], their spatial resolution is relatively low. One alternative to achieve a higher resolution is to use a single light stripe and have it swept over the scene [11][12] by rotating the light projector. One drawback of this method is that the image of projected light gets blurred easily due to the movement of the projected light during each frame of acquisition period.

In this study, a CCD camera based depth image system is investigated. The system is composed of a single camera, a laser light projector and a rotating mirror. The striped laser light is projected toward the rotational axis of the mirror, and reflected to the surface to be measured. The camera detects the striped light on object surfaces through the same mirror. One special characteristic of this new system is that the light projected to any point (at any direction) at the same horizontal level with the

L.T. Yang et al. (Eds.): ICESS 2005, LNCS 3820, pp. 398 – 407, 2005.

same distance to the mirror axis always forms an image at the same pixel on the camera. Consequently, there exists a unique association of pixel location to object depth. This association can be stored in a lookup table for direct pixel to depth mapping. From each video frame, only the depth on the laser light projection plane is collected. With the light scanning over an area, a sequence of depth data can be collected from a sequence of images. For real-time response, FPGA is used for processing. The WildCard-II from Annapolis Micro Systems Inc. has an embedded analog to digital converter, which can be used to convert analog video signal into digital values. A logic system that detects synchronization signals, captures frames, detects the laser light on each line, converts the light locations into depth data, and transfers the range image back to the host has been designed. The real-time processing finishes 136 frames in 2.3 seconds to derive a range image.

In this paper, the new system is presented in Section 2. Equations for depth calculation are derived. The calibration procedure for two system parameters is introduced in Section 3. In Section 4, realization of the real-time processing using FPGA is introduced with experimental results provided. Conclusions are given in Section 5.

2 The New Depth Measurement System with Striped Lighting

The new depth measurement system has the single vertical laser light stripe projected to the rotating mirror, and reflected to the scene. The image formed by the same mirror is acquired by the CCD camera. Fig. 1 shows the picture of the developed measurement device and the triangulation geometry for the single point projection. Without losing the generality, we focus on the image formation of a single light point. Fig. 1(b) shows that the light is reflected by the mirror and projected to an object surface. Note that the mirror can be rotated.

Let the angle between the vertical line and the light source be ζ, and the angle of the mirror from the horizontal axis be θ. Also, let the distance between the camera

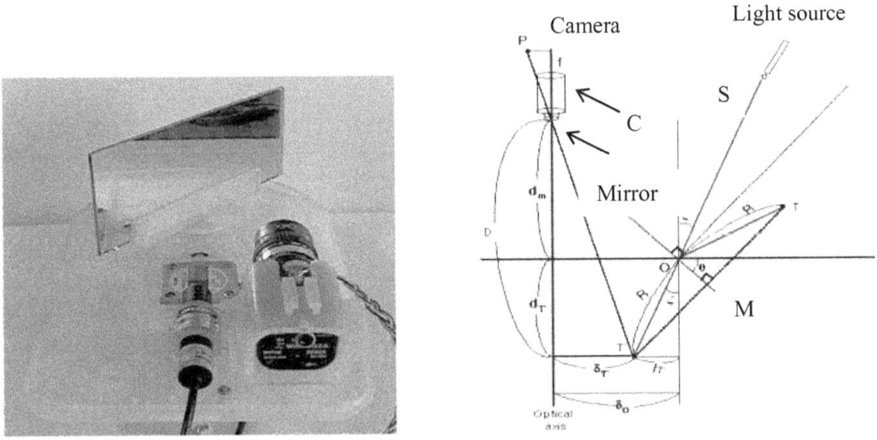

Fig. 1. Depth measurement with light projection and mirror reflection. (a) The measurement device. (b) Triangulation geometry for a single point projection.

axis and the rotating axis of the mirror be δ_o, the distance between the focal point of the camera and the horizontal axis be d_m, and the focal distance of the camera be f.

The laser light is reflected onto the object at point T with the mirrored image at T'. When the mirror angle is θ, $\angle$SOT, which is the angle between the projected light and the reflected light, equals $2(\theta-\zeta)$ and the angle $\angle$TOM equals $(90^o-\theta+\zeta)$. Since T' is the mirrored image of T, we have $\angle$T'OM $= \angle$TOM $= 90^o-\theta+\zeta$. Consequently, $\angle$SOT' $= 2(\theta-\zeta) + (90^o-\theta+\zeta) + (90^o-\theta+\zeta) = 180^o$. This shows that T' will always be on the line along the laser beam, at a distance R from the point O. This characteristic makes it possible to use a lookup table for converting the light position to depth.

To derive equations for projection in 3-dimensional space, let's use the cylindrical coordinate system with the mirror axis as the Z-axis. Assume that the light point T with coordinates (R, ϕ, Z) has its image on the CCD sensor at $p = (p_x, p_z)$ in the coordinates of image plan. Fig. 1(b) shows the projection of a point on x-y plane. In this figure, p_x is the distance from P to the camera optical axis. Using the property of similar triangles, one obtains

$$p_x : f = \delta_{T'} : D, \qquad \text{where } D = d_m + d_{T'} \tag{1}$$

or

$$p_x(d_m + d_{T'}) = f\delta_{T'}. \tag{2}$$

Note that $d_{T'} = R\cos\zeta$, $\delta_{T'} = \delta_O - l_{T'}$ and $l_{T'} = R\sin\zeta$. Thus

$$p_x(d_m + R\cos\zeta) = f(\delta_O - R\sin\zeta). \tag{3}$$

Solving the above equation for R gives

$$R = \frac{f\delta_O - p_x d_m}{f\sin\zeta + p_x\cos\zeta}. \tag{4}$$

The angle for the observed point T is ϕ, which is defined as the angle measured clockwise from the vertical axis to the line OT. This angle is determined by the laser light direction and the mirror angle as

$$\phi = 2(\theta-\zeta) + \zeta = 2\theta - \zeta. \tag{5}$$

For the value Z, the triangular similarity will give

$$p_z : f = Z : D, \text{ or} \tag{6}$$

$$p_z(d_m + d_{T'}) = fZ. \tag{7}$$

Dividing (7) by (2), one obtains

$$p_z / p_x = Z / \delta_{T'} = Z / (\delta_0 - R\sin\zeta). \tag{8}$$

Solving the above equation for Z gives

$$Z = \frac{p_z(\delta_0 - R\sin\zeta)}{p_x}. \tag{9}$$

As a summary, R, ϕ, and Z can be computed by

$$R = \frac{f\delta_O - p_x d_m}{f\sin\zeta + p_x\cos\zeta} \tag{4}$$

$$\phi = 2\theta - \zeta, \text{ and} \tag{5}$$

$$Z = \frac{p_z(\delta_0 - R\sin\zeta)}{p_x}. \tag{9}$$

Note that the mirror angle is not involved in equation (4) for depth computation. Only the fixed angle ζ is included and needs to be carefully calibrated. Conceptually, one can consider the 3-D measurement problem as one to determine the position of T', which is the intersection of lines SO and PC (see Fig. 1(b)); an error arises when either of those two lines is inaccurately determined. In this setup, the error from inaccurate SO can be minimized by calibrating the angle ζ. Note that for a setup with its laser projector rotated, a measurement error of the projection angle is harder to prevent; so is the depth error. The error from inaccurate PC is caused by inaccurate position of P. Since P is the pixel position of the light point, a sharper image tends to provide a more precise and reliable result. The characteristic of sharp image illustrated in Fig. 2 helps minimize the error from this factor.

Although equations for R, ϕ, and Z have been provided, in this study, we are more interested in the depth R, which will be the focus in the following sections.

3 Calibration and Depth Computation

To use equations (4) to determine the range R, system parameters must be either measured or calibrated. In our experiments, δ_0 and d_m are measured and known parameters. Other parameters needed include f, inter-cell distance δ_{cell} on the CCD sensor and the angle ζ. Since the measurement precision is very sensitive to the error of ζ, it is impractical to measure ζ directly. This parameter must be determined through careful calibration. Precise values of internal parameters of camera such as the inter-cell distance on the CCD plane and the focal length f may not be available and need to be obtained through calibration too.

It is noted that equation (4) can be rewritten such that only the ratio $k=f/\delta_{cell}$ needs to be calibrated. Let the integer n_x be the pixel number corresponding to p_x, which is the distance from the center of image plane to P. Then p_x can be expressed as

$$p_x = \delta_{cell}\, n_x \tag{10}$$

Plugging (10) into (4) gives

$$R = \frac{f\delta_0 - \delta_{cell} n_x d_m}{f\sin\zeta + \delta_{cell} n_x \cos\zeta} = \frac{\frac{f}{\delta_{cell}}\delta_0 - n_x d_m}{\frac{f}{\delta_{cell}}\sin\zeta + n_x \cos\zeta} \tag{11}$$

Replacing $\frac{f}{\delta_{cell}}$ by k in (11) results in

$$R = \frac{k\delta_0 - n_x d_m}{k\sin\zeta + n_x\cos\zeta} \tag{12}$$

3.1 Calibration of the Internal Parameter $k = \dfrac{f}{\delta_{cell}}$

The camera and the projector can be set up in parallel, *i.e.*, with $\zeta = 0$. This is achieved by adjusting the laser light source orientation so that the distance between the laser beam and the camera optical axis at a long distance (*e.g.*, longer than 5 meters) equals δ_0. Upon having ζ set to 0, experiments can be performed to obtain n_x's for different known ranges of R. The collected pairs of R and n_x can be plugged into (12) to obtain the estimated values of parameter k; the average of these estimated values is used. This parameter needs to be calibrated only once.

3.2 Calibration of the External Parameter ζ

For a system with unknown ζ, equation (12) can be used for calibration. One can set up the system to measure a known distance R. The value n_x can be obtained from image. Values of δo and d_m are known and k has been calibrated. As a result, the only unknown in (12) is ζ, which can be solved. Since the value of depth is sensitive to the error of angle ζ, recalibration is recommended if the angle is possibly changed.

3.3 Experimental Results on Depth Measurement

Performance was evaluated for objects at different distances. Fig. 2 shows the results for calculations with $\zeta = 3.869°$ and $\zeta = 4°$. The result for $\zeta = 4°$ is provided to show the sensitivity of the precision to ζ and the importance of good calibration. The mirror angle for this experiment was set to 40°.

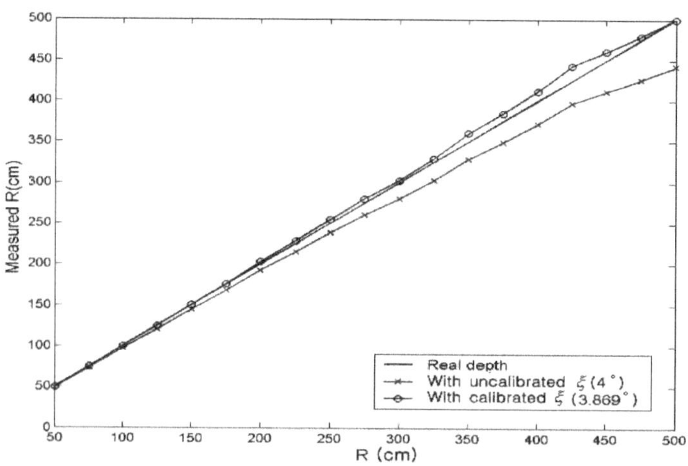

Fig. 2. Results with and without having ζ calibrated

4 FPGA Realization of the Design

For real-time processing, FPGA is used for the implementation. The WildCard-II from Annapolis Micro Systems Inc. was selected for the experiment. This device has an embedded analog to digital converter that samples analog signal at a rate of 64MHz. In our design, one out of five sampled data is used. Fig. 3 shows an example of captured signal. The signal near the sample numbers 7000-9800 is the vertical synchronization signal. At two ends, there are segments of signals for about 9 horizontal lines.

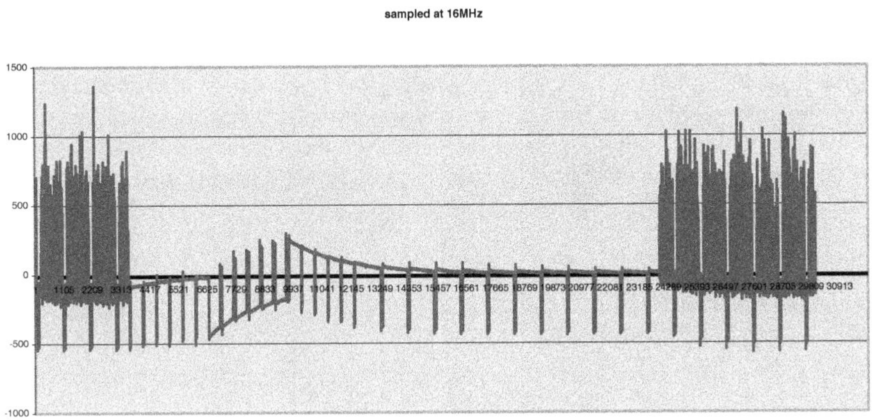

Fig. 3. Video signal from our camera (consisting of a vertical synchronization pulse)

The A/D converter converts the analog video signal into digital values. Our signal analyzer implemented on FPGA chip at first finds the vertical synchronization and then starts to process the video signal line by line. It finds the brightest point in each line and converts the pixel position into a range value. Each frame consists of 240 horizontal lines. The 240 locations for the 240 lines from the nth frame give the depth information for the nth column of the range image. In our experiments, 136 frames were collected in nearly 2.3 seconds (60 frames per second). With the FPGA for real-time processing, a range image of 136 × 240 pixels can be generated in 2.3 seconds. Due to the use of brightest points, one restriction is that the surrounding light must be dimmed and controlled in order to clearly see the laser light and obtain a good range image.

The state machine (SM) chart for the major process to locate the brightest pixel is given in Fig. 4. The SM chart, which is a different form of the state transition diagram, gives details for developing VHDL models. The three different shapes - rectangle, diamond and oval - represent the state, decision box, and list of conditional outputs, respectively. Notation for the control actions and conditions in the SM chart is described below:

Actions/Control Signals of the State Machine:

- global_reset: reset all values to default. State <= "11", most other variables set to zero
- found_pul: signal that a pulse has been located.
- clr_line_no: set the line number to zero (at the beginning of each frame)
- clr_line_loc: set the current line location to zero (at the beginning of each line).
- clr_max: clear the max A/D reading value and clear the location of the max value (same time as clr_line_loc)
- clr_pw: set the pulse width to zero (reset for the next time we need to count).
- inc_line_no: increment the line number to keep track of the position within the frame.
- inc_pw: increment the count for the duration of the current pulse.
- save_max: record the current (max) reading and line location of said reading.
- write_line: signal that we have reached the end of the line and may record the data if desired. This signal is only part of the global write_enable signal. Another condition is that the line number must be within a specified range.

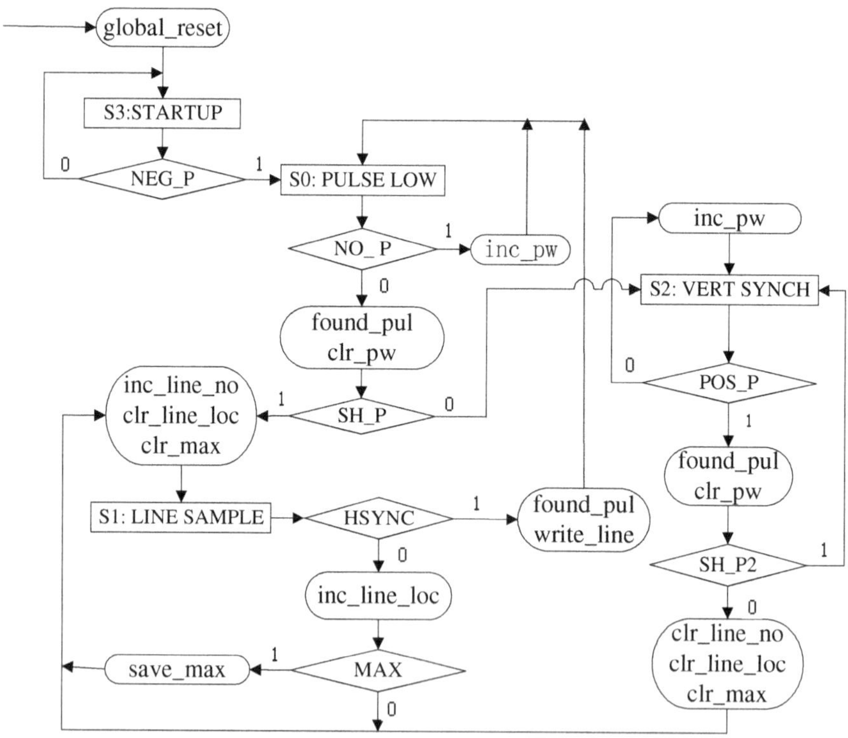

Fig. 4. SM Chart for the process that detects lines and locates the brightest pixel in each line

Conditions:

- NEG_P: a negative pulse has been located (large negative derivative).
- POS_P: a positive pulse has been located (large positive derivative).
- NO_P: the opposite of POS_P.
- SH_P: the pulse width is shorter than the width of a vertical synch pulse.
- SH_P2: the pulse width is shorter than the width of a line.
- HSYNC: the line location is close to its end and a negative pulse is detected.
- MAX: the current reading is larger than the saved maximum reading.

Fig. 5 gives two range images generated by our design. The scene for Fig. 5(a) includes part of a monitor at the right with an electrical cable (0.6m away) and three boxes stacked together on a 4-leg stool (1.5m away). A shelf on the back is about 5-7 meters away. The scene for Fig. 5(b) includes the back of a chair (with a hollow portion on it) at the right (1 meter away), A small corner of a table can be seen to its right. A tripod at a distance of 2.5 meters is to the left of the chair with a bookshelf behind it. Another chair is at the left. A tiny part of a third chair appears at the left (dark stripe). All the pixel positions outside of the reasonable range are set to infinity (white). The white shadow in Fig. 5(a) illustrates the portion where the camera cannot see the projected light because the displacement between the camera and projector. Shadow is larger when object is at a closer distance.

(a) Range image 1

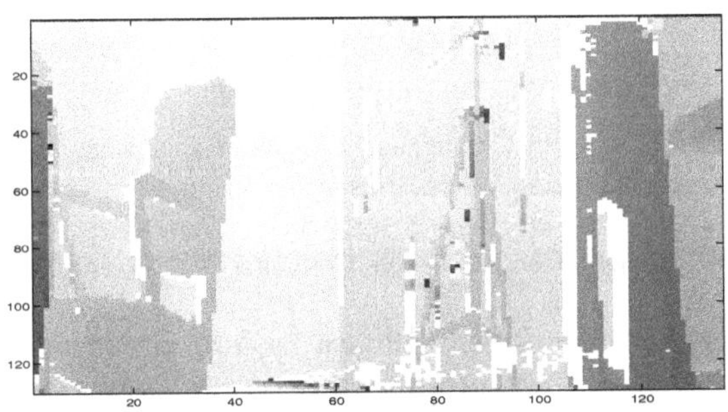

(b) Range image 2

Fig. 5. Two range image examples

A C++ program for finding the light stripe in the same way used by the FPGA has been tested on a PC with a CPU clock of 2.8GHz. The processing time for the same size of image (189696 pixels) is 51 ms. The major runtimes will then be 51 ms + t_{FC}, where t_{FC} is the time for frame capture. If t_{FC} is 16.67ms, it will take at least 9.2 seconds (from 136*(51ms+16.67ms)) to generate a range image and the technique using the FPGA will take only 2.3 seconds (a speedup of 4 times). It is noted that with the use of FPGA, the actual processing time is much shorter than that for typical frame capture. If the design uses the full speed of the A/D converter, the frame rate that can be handled will be 300 frames/second. At this frame rate, t_{FC} will be 3.33ms and the processing time to generate a range image using FPGA will be reduced to 460 ms (2.3s/5) while the time for PC will be 7.4 seconds (from 136*(51ms+3.33ms)).

5 Conclusions

A new depth measurement system that consists of a single camera, a laser light stripe projector and a rotating mirror has been investigated. Error analysis provides an idea on the magnitude of expected measurement error. For the distance 400-500cm, a 20cm depth error is expected to be from one-pixel error. Experimental results show a similar magnitude. This arrangement makes it possible to use a lookup table to determine the depth directly from pixel location. Real-time processing is implemented on an FPGA card with an A/D converter. It is capable of processing 136 frames in 2.3 seconds to obtain a 136 x 240 range image. Compared to the use of a PC with a clock rate of 2.8GHz, the speed of the design is 4 times faster and could be 15 times faster if the frame capture rate is increased to the limit of the A/D converter (64MHz).

Acknowledgement

The research was partially supported by an International Research Collaboration Project sponsored by IITA, Republic of Korea. Mr. Ryan Duren helped develop the VHDL codes for FPGA implementation.

References

1. C. S. Chen, Y. P. Hung, C. C. Chiang, and J. L. Wu: Range Data Acquisition Using Color Structured Lighting and Stereo Vision. Image and Vision Computing 15 (1997) 445-456.
2. D. Scharstein and R. Szeliski, High-accuracy Stereo Depth Maps Using Structured Light. IEEE Computer Society Conference on Computer Vision and Pattern Recognition 1 (2003) I-195-202.
3. J. Batlle, E. Mouaddib and J. Salvi: Recent Progress in Coded Structured Light as a Technique to Solve the Correspondence Problem: A Survey. Pattern Recognition 31 (1998) 963-982.
4. R. A. Jarvis: A Perspective on Range Finding Techniques for Computer Vision. IEEE Trans. on Pattern Analysis and Machine Intelligence 5 (1983) 122-139.

5. K. L. Boyer and AC. Kak: Color-encoded Structured Light for Rapid Active Ranging. IEEE Trans. on Pattern Analysis and Machine Intelligence 9 (1987) 14-28.
6. V. Srinivasan and R. Lumia: A Pseudo-interferometric Laser Range Finder for Robot Applications. IEEE Trans. on Robotics and Automation 5 (1989) 98-105.
7. M. Baba and T. Konishi: Range Imaging System with Multiplexed Structured Light by Direct Space Encoding. IEEE Instrumentation and Measurement Technology Conference (1999) 1437-1442.
8. R. J. Valkenburg and A. M. McIvor: Accurate 3D Measurement Using a Structured Light System. Image and Vision Computing 16 (1998) 99-110.
9. P. M. Will and K. S. Pennington: Grid Coding: A Preprocessing Technique for Robot and Machine Vision. Artificial Intelligence 2 (1971) 319-329.
10. R. Jain, R. Kasturi, and B. G. Schunck: Machine Vision. McGraw-Hill Inc. (1995).
11. Y. Shirai and M. Suwa: Recognition of Polyhedrons with a Rangefinder. International Joint Conference on Artificial Intelligence (1971) 80-87.
12. T. C. Strand: Optical Three-dimensional Sensing for Machine Vision. Optical Engineering 24 (1985) 33-40.

Best Web Service Selection Based on the Decision Making Between QoS Criteria of Service

Young-Jun Seo[1], Hwa-Young Jeong[2], and Young-Jae Song[1]

[1] Dept. of Computer Engineering, Kyunghee University,
1, Seocheon-ri, Giheung-eup, Yongin-si, Gyeonggi-do 449-701, Republic of Korea
{yjseo, yjsong}@khu.ac.kr

[2] Faculty of General Education, Kyunghee University,
1, Hoegi-dong, Dongdaemun-gu, Seoul 130-701, Republic of Korea
hyjeong@khu.ac.kr

Abstract. Recently, extensive studies have been carried out on web service standards because of the necessity of developing large-scale applications in open environments. In particular, they enable services to be dynamically bound. However, current techniques fail to address the critical problem of selecting the right service instances. Service selection should be determined based on customer preferences and service level. We propose a best web service selection method which helps to find a service provider providing the optimal quality. Web service selection process was described with multi-criteria decision making approach(e.g. PROMETHEE) on the basis of evaluated values of qualities and the defined service level. The PROMETHEE method has advantages in comparison with the others(e.g. MAUT, AHP) as follows. First, the PROMETHEE method classifies alternatives which is difficult to be compared because of a trade-off relation of evaluation standards as non-comparable alternatives. Second, the PROMETHEE method is different from the AHP method in that there's no need to perform a pair-wise comparison again when comparative alternatives are added or deleted. Therefore, this method is a suitable approach in the web service selection problem. Because the problem has a lot of quality parameters which are measured and evaluated at the same time and frequently induces a drop of another quality parameter by the improvement of one quality attribute. Consequently, our approach enables applications to be dynamically configured at runtime in a manner that continually adapts to the preferences of the customers. We verify our approach through case study.

1 Introduction

Recently, there has been increasing interest in web service because of the following advantages: platform independent, interoperability and service availability. IDC estimated that the amount of sales of software related to web service is about 3 billion dollars in the year 2004 which are just 1.6% of 188 billion dollars,

L.T. Yang et al. (Eds.): ICESS 2005, LNCS 3820, pp. 408–419, 2005.

the whole software market. But it is expected to grow by 58% per year for next 5 years and will be 11 billion dollars in the year 2008[1].

Web service is a component-based distributed computing service independent of a platform and an implementation language in the wired/wireless web and consists of three operations, i.e. publish-find-bind. Each operation means a service provider which develops a web service and publishes in UDDI registry, the UDDI registry which helps service consumers to find the web service they need and a service consumer which binds to the web service and uses the function of the web service actually.

In a current web service model, the UDDI registry includes not an evaluation for the web service but an explanation and has defects that 48% of the UDDI registry have a link which contains information that are lost or broken or incorrect[2]. When a service consumer chooses one among a lot of similar web services, he generally gets to need information about the service quality(QoS) of the web service. Although UDDI was not designed to provide service quality information, UDDI registries tend to include this information to give convenience to service consumers.

This paper suggests the best web service selection method which helps to find a service provider providing the optimum quality that the consumer needs in a position of service consumer. In this paper, we considered the multi-criteria of QoS(Quality of Service) and CoS(Cost of Service) in the evaluation process to solve the problem of existing researches[3,4] related to the web service selection and used PROMETHEE as an evaluation method which is most suitable for the web service selection among MCDM approaches. The PROMETHEE method has advantages in comparison with the others(e.g. MAUT, AHP) as follows[5]. First, the PROMETHEE method classifies alternatives which is difficult to be compared because of a trade-off relation of evaluation standards as non-comparable alternatives. Second, the PROMETHEE method is different from the AHP method in that there's no need to perform a pair-wise comparison again when comparative alternatives are added or deleted. Therefore, this method is a suitable approach in the web service selection problem. Because the problem has a lot of quality parameters which are measured and evaluated at the same time and frequently induces a drop of another quality parameter by the improvement of one quality attribute[6].

This paper was organized as follows. We introduced the research trend about the web service selection and the theoretical background about the multi-criteria decision making approach in chapter 2 and suggested the quality evaluation criteria and the selection method used in the best web service selection process in chapter 3. In chapter 4, the selection method was verified through a case study and lastly conclusions and future works were described in chapter 5.

2 Related Work

In this chapter, we reviewed existing researches related to the web service selection and representative approaches about the multi-criteria decision making.

2.1 Research Trends of Web Service Selection

Patrick's[3] research proposed the combination that could increase the whole value between two issues(QoS and CoS) by trading more preferred issue for less preferred issue between two parties. In this model, QoS is related to the performance-oriented capability(distance and time), CoS is related to resources (ca-pital, hardware, software, network bandwidth) which are required to ensure QoS and a token-based approach was suggested to quantify the two-issue. In the proposed token-based approach, Resource is measured by the unit of QoS-token and Dollar is measured by the unit of CoS-token. If QoS and CoS are measured by token, the token trading between two parties is possible. As a result, the efficient allocation of resources can be caused. But, since this model considered just two issue groups except the other sub-issues included in QoS and CoS, there are defects that it can not handle a multi-issue and a multi-party.

Julian[4]'s research adopted a semantic model based on RDF and OWL to model the interaction between the client and the web service and proposed a reasoning engine constructed with JESS(Java Expert Systems Shell) to allow the client to reason what can provide the best web service among many web services that have the same sentences. This proposed research adopted the client-side augmentation approach to gain the experience information that is shared. The experience related to the generic QoS parameter is availability, reliability and execution time and is stored in the QoS forum that can be accessed in common. The QoS forum returns vectors of semantic models and the reasoning engine extracts the experience information from them. Through the evaluation equation that is the set of extracted experience information and weights, the service with the highest weighted sum is selected as the best one. But, in Julian's research, the web service selection problem was handled only as the past-experience standpoint and, since the cost was not considered, the negotiation strategies were not used.

2.2 Multi-criteria Decision Making Approach

MAUT(Multi-Attribute Utility Theory)[7] is a commonly used method to provide analytical support to the decision-making process. Utility theory allows decision makers to give formalized preference to a space defined by the alternatives and criteria. For example, in one method, each alternative/criteria pair is given a score reflecting how well the alternative meets the criteria. The scores for each alternative are combined with measures of each criterion's importance (i.e. weight) to give a total utility for the alternative. Utility is a measure of preference for one alternative relative to another.

AHP(Analytic Hierarchy Process)[8] proposed by Thomas Saaty is the approach on the basis of following three main principles: the principle of constructing hierarchies, the principle of establishing priorities, and the principle of logical consistency. The use of hierarchies helps to itemize the alternatives and attributes. Establishing priorities is based on pair-wise comparisons between the alternatives, one criterion at a time. Thus a problem with 5 alternatives and 4 criteria requires 40 comparisons. He then reduces this data using a weighted

Table 1. MCDM approaches[10]

	MAUT	AHP	PROMETHEE
Foundation	Classical MCDM Approach	Saaty's Eigenvector Approach	Outranking Approach
Basis	Utility Function additive model	Pair-wise Comparison matrix by means of 9 point scale	Pair-wise Comparison by means of Preference Function
Approaches to determine criteria weights	Trade-off Swing Direct-ratio Eigenvector approach	Saaty's Eigenvector approach	No
Result	Relative preference order	Relative preference order	Partial and complete ranking order

average to find the ranking of the alternatives. The method allows for checking consistency, the third principal.

PROMETHEE(Preference Ranking Organization METHod for Enrichment Evaluations)[9] have been proposed for the outranking analysis. PROMETHEE is based on the positive(out-) and negative(in-) preference flows for each alternative in the valued outranking relation to derive the ranking. The positive flow is expressing how much an alternative is dominating the other ones. And the negative flow how much it is dominated by the other ones. Based on the preference flows, PROMETHEE I provides a partial preorder. PROMETHEE II is also introduced to obtain a complete preorder by using a net flow, though, it loses much information of preference relations.

Table 1 gives an overview on the basic characteristics of the mentioned MCDM approaches[10].

3 Web Service Selection Method Using PROMETHEE Approach

3.1 Selection Process

Web service selection process consists of QoS Identification, QoS Selection, QoS Evaluation, Decision Making and Service Selection steps as illustrated in Figure 1[11]. QoS Identification step finds all quality characteristics related to the web service. QoS Selection step chooses the characteristics which can be measured among all quality characteristics that are found in previous step. In QoS Evaluation step, the service level[12] for selected quality characteristics should be defined by service provider or consumer and according to the measurement criteria, measured values are calculated. Decision Making step calculates the outranking relation of web services provided by service providers by applying PROMETHEE approach on the basis of measured result values. Finally, Service Selection step compares net flows of web service providers on the priority(partial

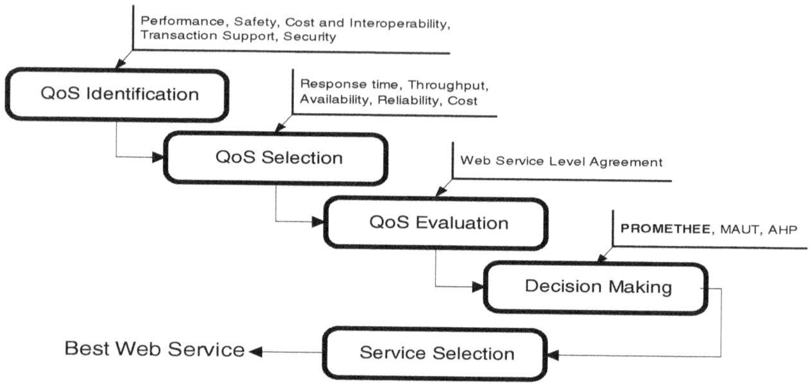

Fig. 1. Web Service Selection Process

ranking) and decides the web service having the largest net flow as the best web service.

3.2 Quality Evaluation Criteria

Since there is no the international web service quality standards model, in this paper, we classified qualities from five different views roughly[13,14]. Performance and safety quality mean that the provided web service is how performance is outstanding and provides services stably. Transaction support quality means the quality that can ensure the integrity when one web service transaction interacts with another web service transaction. Cost and Interoperability quality mean the service cost and the quality level that can be operated with several web services just like one system. Security quality means the web service quality that provides confidentiality and non-repudiation by providing authentication, message encryption and authorization of parties concerned in the web service.

From the web service characteristics, since the quality at the point of time when a customer use the web service acts as an important decision factor, we considered just performance and safety quality and cost in this paper. Table 3 shows the list of qualities except for unmeasurable cases among selected qualities and each quality is measured by given measurement method through web service stress tool periodically. At present, there are two type servers providing web services and these are divided into QoS server and legacy server according to supporting QoS or not[15].

In case of QoS server, service provider can provide the web service according to various service level like gold, silver and bronze and each service level are differentiated by each different quality parameter[12]. But at present most web service provider is a legacy server without the service quality level concept. Therefore, in this paper subjected to the legacy server, we considered the service level in Table 3 according to the level criteria of qualities requested by service consumers.

Table 2. Web Service QoS Criteria

Characteristic	Subcharacteristic	Definition
Performance	Response time	Time form sending Request to receiving response
	Throughput	Ratio of service request completed in unit time
Safety	Availability	Whether a service exists and is available instantly
	Reliability	Reliability degree for service
Cost and Interoperability	Cost	The cost involved in requesting the service
	Standardization	Service compliance with standard
	Compatibility	Compatibility with another web services
Transaction Support	Integrity	Guarantee of integrity when the web service transaction interacts with another web service transaction
Security	Authentication	Authentication of principals for the accessibility to service and data
	Authorization	Authorization allowance for only parties concerned to accessing the protected services
	Confidentiality	Only authorized principals can access data or treat data to modify
	Data encryption	Method that the service encrypt data
	Non-Repudiation	A principal cannot deny requesting a service or data after the fact

Table 3. Selected Web Service QoS Criteria to be measured

Characteristic	Unit	Measurement Method	Service Level		
			gold	silver	bronze
Response time	ms	The time taken to deliver services between service requestors and providers	≤0.3	≤0.7	≤0.9
Throughput	requests/s	Number of service invocation in a given period	200≥	150≥	100≥
Availability	probability	P(Number of Successful executions/Total number of invocations)	1≥	0.6≥	0.3≥
Reliability	probability	$1-P_{Availability}$	0≤	0.4≤	0.7≤
Cost	€	Cost(enactment)+Cost(licensing)	0.05	0.03	0.01

3.3 Web Service Selection Method

In order to select the best web service with result values calculated by 5 quality criteria, this paper adopted PROMETHEE approach and five steps are necessary[5]. The algorithm can be summarized as follows:

Step 1: Define criteria

PROMETHEE is built on the basic notation, with as set A of N alternatives that must be ranked, and K criteria that must be optimised:

$A := a_1, ..., a_N$: Set of discrete alternatives a_t(t=1...N)
$F := f_1, ..., a_K$: Set of criteria relevant for the decision f_k(k=1...K)

First step requires the definition of attributes concerning criteria. Relevant aspects of this input procedure are shown next.

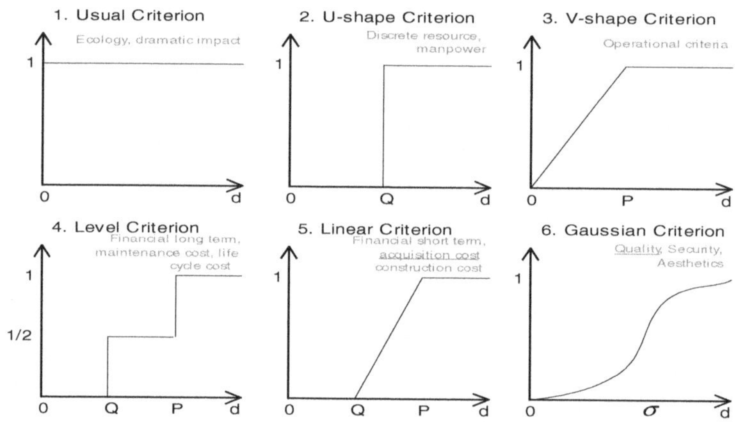

Fig. 2. The ranking obtained using the PROMETHEE method

In Min/Max, Max means an index which gives more positive influence to the relevant web service selection as the evaluation criteria value increases and Min means an opposite case. Weight is decided by experiences of the past and opinions of service consumers. Preference function is defined with 6 kinds as illustrated in Figure 2 and each function is selected by the type of criteria. Here, P and Q and σ mean preference, indifferent and Gaussian threshold that are needed to decide the concrete form of the preference function per evaluation criteria.

In this paper, we considered multi-party and multi-issue negotiation which contains service requester, several service providers and attributes, and focused on the method which finds the optimal compromise suggestion between both sides and decides the service provider offering the maximum gains.

Step 2: Define a vector containing the weigths

Define a vector containing the weights, which are a measure for the relative importance of each criterion, $w^N = [w_1, ..., w_K]$. If all the criteria are of the same importance in the opinion of the decision maker, all weights can be taken as being equal.

Step 3: Define for all the alternatives $WSP_i, WSP_j \in$ WSP the Outranking-Relation Π:

First, the preference function value per quality criteria should be calculated and the preference function value $p_k(WSP_i, WSP_j)$ of the basis k means $p_k(f_k(WSP_i), f_k(WSP_j))$ which is the difference between WSP_i and WSP_j. The preference index $\Pi(WSP_i, WSP_j)$ is a measure for the intensity of the service consumer's preference for an alternative WSP_i in comparison with an alternative WSP_j for the simultaneous consideration of all quality criteria. It is basically a weighted average of the preference functions $p_k(WSP_i, WSP_j)$.

$$\Pi(WSP_i, WSPj) = \sum_{k=1}^{K} W_k \cdot p_k(WSP_i, WSP_j) \tag{1}$$

Step 4: As a measure for the strength(weakness) of the alternatives $WSP_i \in$ WSP, the outranking flow is calculated:

The outranking relation of alternatives is calculated by figuring out leaving flow(ϕ^+), entering flow(ϕ^-) and net flow(ϕ) like equation 2 with preference index $\Pi(WSP_i, WSPj)$.

$$\phi^+(WSP_i) = \frac{1}{N} \sum_{\substack{n=1 \\ n \neq i}}^{N} \Pi(WSP_i, WSP_n) \tag{2}$$

$$\phi^-(WSP_i) = \frac{1}{N} \sum_{\substack{n=1 \\ n \neq i}}^{N} \Pi(WSP_i, WSP_n)$$

$$\phi^{net}(WSP_i) = \phi^+(WSP_i) - \phi^-(WSP_i)$$

Step 5: Graphical evaluation of the outranking relation:

The higher the leaving flow and the lower the entering flow, the better the alternative. In case a complete pre-order is requested, PROMETHEE II yields the so-called net flows. As the net flow $\phi^{net}(WSP)$ of preference is higher, the relevant WSP means the more superior alternative.

4 Case Study

In order to exemplify concretely the application process of PROMETHEE in this chapter, we evaluated web services provided by five different web service providers and selected the most suitable web service considering QoS among them.

4.1 Decision of Weight, Preference Function and Threshold by Evaluation Criteria

Table 5 gives the QoS parameters for the five criteria considered to have the same importance for the web service consumer, therefore all the weights are equal to 0.2. The Response time can become lower in case of failure than in case of accessing the reliable service. On this account, the default weight of the response time tends to be lower than that of the availability or the reliability[4]. But, for the convenience of analysis, we endowed the same weight as another criteria.

Table 5. Decision Table for the Criteria

	RESP	THRO	AVAI	RELI	COST
Min/Max	Min	Max	Max	Min	Min
Weight	0.2	0.2	0.2	0.2	0.2
Preference Function	Gaussi an	Gaussi an	Gaussi an	Gaussi an	Linear
Indifference Threshold	–	–	–	–	0.01
Preference Threshold	–	–	–	–	0.03
Gaussian Threshold	0.2	25	0.15	0.15	–
Unit	Ms	reques ts/s	proba bility	proba bility	€
WSP_1	0.2	100	0.9	0.1	0.04
WSP_2	0.8	160	0.4	0.6	0.02
WSP_3	0.6	130	0.8	0.2	0.05
WSP_4	0.5	180	0.5	0.5	0.04
WSP_5	0.1	140	0.7	0.3	0.03

As illustrated in Figure 2, the preference function of COST criterion was established as a linear type. The others were established as a Gaussian type. Web service consumer must endow a threshold to decide the concrete form of the preference function per evaluation criteria and for this we referred to service level of previous Table 3 in this paper. This paper supposed that the web service consumer require bronze level as COST criterion and more than silver level as other criteria. If the web service consumer is indifferent from 0.01 to 0.02(indifference threshold=0.01) and increases the preference from 0.02 to 0.04(preference threshold=0.03), the consumer definitely chooses the cheapest web service. Gaussian thresholds of other criteria were fixed at the middle value between the lowest limit of the gold level in which the preference increases and the lowest limit of the silver level which was set up as a default.

4.2 Calculation for Leaving Flow, Entering Flow and Net Flow of Preference

Table 6 shows the calculation result for the preference function value per the evaluation criteria. For example in Table 6, by the preference function between WSP_i and WSP_2 in case of the response time(RESP), each preference function value($p_j(WSP_1, WSP_2)$=0.9889, $p_j(WSP_2, WSP_1)$=0.0000) is calculated

Table 6. Preference Function Value per Evaluation Criteria

	RESP	THRO	AVAI	RELI	COST
p_j(WSP1,WSP2)	0.9889	0.0000	0.9961	0.9961	0.0000
p_j(WSP1,WSP3)	0.8647	0.0000	0.1993	0.1993	0.0000
p_j(WSP1,WSP4)	0.6753	0.0000	0.9714	0.9714	0.0000
p_j(WSP1,WSP5)	0.0000	0.0000	0.5889	0.5889	0.0000
p_j(WSP2,WSP1)	0.0000	0.9439	0.0000	0.0000	0.5000
p_j(WSP2,WSP3)	0.0000	0.5132	0.0000	0.0000	1.0000
p_j(WSP2,WSP4)	0.0000	0.0000	0.0000	0.0000	0.5000
p_j(WSP2,WSP5)	0.0000	0.2739	0.0000	0.0000	0.0000
p_j(WSP3,WSP1)	0.0000	0.5132	0.0000	0.0000	0.0000
p_j(WSP3,WSP2)	0.3935	0.0000	0.9714	0.9714	0.0000
p_j(WSP3,WSP4)	0.0000	0.0000	0.8647	0.8647	0.0000
p_j(WSP3,WSP5)	0.0000	0.0000	0.1993	0.1993	0.0000
p_j(WSP4,WSP1)	0.0000	0.9940	0.0000	0.0000	0.0000
p_j(WSP4,WSP2)	0.6753	0.2739	0.1993	0.1993	0.0000
p_j(WSP4,WSP3)	0.1175	0.8047	0.0000	0.0000	0.0000
p_j(WSP4,WSP5)	0.0000	0.7220	0.0000	0.0000	0.0000
p_j(WSP5,WSP1)	0.1175	0.7220	0.0000	0.0000	0.0000
p_j(WSP5,WSP2)	0.9978	0.0000	0.8647	0.8647	0.0000
p_j(WSP5,WSP3)	0.9561	0.0769	0.0000	0.0000	0.5000
p_j(WSP5,WSP4)	0.8647	0.0000	0.5889	0.5889	0.0000

Table 7. Preference index per evaluation criteria and leaving, entering and net flow

	WSP_1	WSP_2	WSP_3	WSP_4	WSP_5	ϕ^+	$\phi = \phi^+ - \phi^-$
WSP_1		0.5962	0.2527	0.5236	0.2356	0.4020	0.2125
WSP_2	0.2888		0.3026	0.1000	0.0548	0.1865	-0.2831
WSP_3	0.1026	0.4673		0.3459	0.0797	0.2489	-0.0157
WSP_4	0.1988	0.2696	0.1964		0.1444	0.2023	-0.1422
WSP_5	0.1679	0.5454	0.3066	0.4085		0.3571	0.2285
ϕ^-	0.1895	0.4696	0.2646	0.3445	0.1286		

like followings. Since RESP criterion has a more positive effect on the web service selection as it is smaller, in case that x, the difference of evaluation scores between two WSP, is negative, we calculated the selected preference function, Gaussian type func-tion, by substituting ($x = 0.8 - 0.2$) for the difference of evaluation scores and ($\sigma = 0.2$) for Gaussian threshold. Reversely, in case that x is positive, it was calculated at 0.0000 since it is not preferred. The preference index can be calculated by summing up preference function values per evaluation criteria and then by multiplying them by the weight. For example, the preference index between WSP_1 and WSP_2 can be calculated by summing up preference function values per evaluation criteria shown at each row of Table 6 and then by multiplying them by weight(0.2) like equation (3).

$$\Pi(WSP_1, WSP_2) = \frac{1}{5}(0.9889 + 0 + 0.9961 + 0.9961 + 0) = 0.5962 \quad (3)$$

$$\Pi(WSP_2, WSP_1) = \frac{1}{5}(0 + 0.9439 + 0 + 0 + 0.5) = 0.2888$$

Table 7 represents calculation results for the preference index per evaluation criteria, the leaving flow, the entering flow and net flow by applying above calculation procedures to all pairs of (WSP_i, WSP_j). The leaving flow and the entering flow of each WSP_i are the average values for the summation of all preference indexes in each ith row and column in table 7 and the net flow is the difference between them.

4.3 Graphical Evaluation of the Outranking Relation

Figure 3 presents the graphical ranking of the investigated alternatives for best web service selection resulting from the outranking method PROMETHEE. According to this evaluation, the web service provided by 5th Web Service Provider (WSP5) is the best choice, followed by the 1st Web Service Provider(WSP1), while the use of 2nd Web Service Provider(WSP2) comes offer as the worst alternative. Since no incomparibilities occur, both PROMETHEE I and the complete ranking in PROMETHEE II give the same order of investigated alternatives.

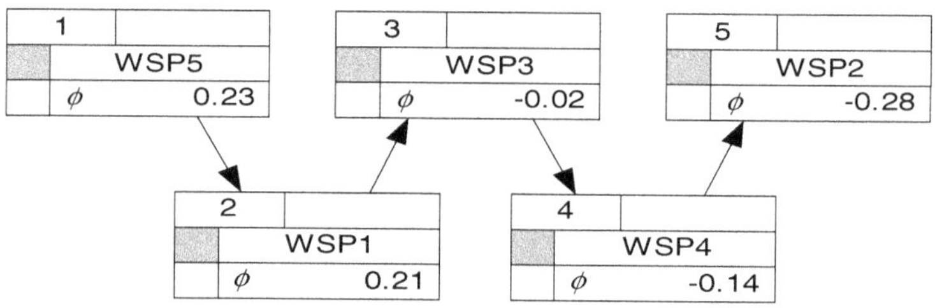

Fig. 3. The ranking obtained using the PROMETHEE II method

5 Conclusion

In this paper, we have presented the web service selection method that can help service consumers to find the service provider who provides the most optimal quality. Our approach allows the dynamic selection of Web services depending on various QoS values and defined service level. The results show that the proposed approach effectively selects high quality web service (i.e., web service which have higher overall QoS). From what has been discussed above, we can conclude that the proposed web service selection approach can be used as a solution for the complexity and reliability problem.

In future work, we will include the support for exception handling during service binding. For example, after a best web service has been decided and while it is being bounden, an exception may occur (e.g., unavailability of a web service). Another interesting issue is to extend our framework with support for mobile clients.

References

1. Sandra Rogers, "Web Services Software 2004-2008 Forecast", IDC, April, (2004)
2. Mike Clark, "UDDI weather report", Nov, (2001), Available online: http://www.webservicesarchitect.com/content/articles/clark04.asp

3. Hung, P.C.K, "Web Services Discovery Based on the Trade-off between Quality and Cost of Service: A Token-based Approach", in the ACM SIGecom Exchanges, Vol. 4.2, Sept, (2003), 20-26
4. Julian Day, Ralph Deters, "Selecting the Best Web Service", In Proceedings of the 14th Annual IBM Centers for Advanced Studies Conference (CASCON), Oct, (2004), 293-307
5. Jae Hyung Min, Young Min Song, "A Comparison of MAUT, AHP and PROMETHEE for Multicriteria Decisions", Proceedings of the Korean Operations and Management Science Society Conference, (2003), 229-232
6. K.H.Bennett, and others, "A Broker Architecture for Integrating Data Using a Web Services Environment", ICSOC, Vol.2910, (2003) 409-422
7. David G. Ullman, "The Ideal Engineering Decision Support System", Technical paper, Robust Decisions Inc., (2004)
8. Thomas Saaty, "Decision Making for Leaders", RWS Publications, (1995)
9. Brans, J. and P. Vincke, "A Preference Ranking Organization method(The PROMETHEE Method for Multiple Criteria Decision-Making)", Management Science, Vol. 31, No. 6, (1985), 647-656
10. Jutta Geldermann, Otto Rentz, "Multi-criteria analysis for the assessment of environmen-tally relevant installations", Journal of Industrial Ecology, (2004)
11. Torsten Bissel, Manfred Bogen, Christian Bonkowski, Volker Hadamschek, "Service Level Management with Agent Technology", Proceedings of the TARENA Networking Confer-ence, (2000), 831-841
12. Asit Dan, Heiko Ludwig, Giovanni Pacifici, "Web Services Differentiation with Service Level Agreements", White Paper, IBM Corporation, May, (2003)
13. Shuping Ran, "A Model for Web Services Discovery With QoS", ACM SIGecom Ex-changes, Vol.4, Issue.1, (2003), 1-10
14. NCA, "A Study on Technical Trends and Deployment Strategies of Web Service Quality Management", National Computerization Agency Research Report, Dec, (2003), Available online: http://www.nca.or.kr/eindex.htm
15. Yu, T., Lin, K.-J., "The Design of QoS Broker Algorithms for QoS-Capable Web Services", Proceedings of the e-Technology, e-Commerce and e-Service Conference, (2004), 17-24

Data Storage in Sensor Networks for Multi-dimensional Range Queries

Ji Yeon Lee[1], Yong Hun Lim[2], Yon Dohn Chung[3,*], and Myoung Ho Kim[4]

[1] E-Government Team, National Computerization Agency, Seoul, Korea
jylee@nca.or.kr
[2] Home Platform Group, Samsung Electronics, Seoul, Korea
yonghun.lim@samsung.com
[3] Department of Computer Engineering, Dongguk University, Seoul, Korea
ydchung@dgu.edu
[4] Department of Computer Science, KAIST, Daejon, Korea
mhkim@dbserver.kaist.ac.kr

Abstract. In data-centric sensor networks, various data items, such as temperature, humidity, pressure and so on, are sensed and stored in sensor nodes. As these attributes are mostly scalar values and inter-related, multi-dimensional range queries are very useful. However, the previous work on range query processing in sensor networks did not consider overall network lifetime. To prolong network lifetime and support multi-dimensional range queries, we propose a dynamic data placement method for multi-dimensional data, where data space is divided into equal-sized regions and placed over sensor nodes in a dynamic way. Through experiments, we show the efficiency of the proposed method compared with the previous work.

Keywords: Sensor network, data-centric storage, multi-dimensional range queries, data placement and distribution.

1 Introduction

A sensor network consists of widely distributed sensors, where each sensor node is a small device with some limited computing, storage and wireless communication capacity [1, 2, 4, 5, 8]. The applications of sensor networks have been widely expanded into areas of military, environment, health, and so on. For example, in an environmental monitoring application, sensor nodes which are widely and randomly deployed over deserts or volcanic areas periodically sense environmental parameters such as the temperature, humidity, and air pressure. The sensor data can be stored locally into sensor nodes or delivered to other sensor nodes/outer gateways. The sensor network where measured data are stored within sensor nodes is called *data-centric*, which is the target environment of this paper. The stored data are analyzed or processed through various queries including point queries, range queries, aggregation queries, and so on.

* Corresponding author.

L.T. Yang et al. (Eds.): ICESS 2005, LNCS 3820, pp. 420–429, 2005.

Sensor network has some unique properties compared with the conventional wireless network [2, 4, 5, 7, 8]. First, the capacity or resource of a sensor such as computing power, storage, and energy is very restricted. Especially, since sensor nodes use batteries for their energy source and the batteries cannot be re-charged or replaced, efficient control of energy consumption in sensor nodes is very important. Second, sensor nodes are randomly (i.e., not-controlled) deployed over a target area, and hence they are not informed of the overall network configuration. (That is, a sensor node is aware of only its neighbor nodes within its radio scope.) Third, the sensor node is not gathered and reused, so it is important to fully use the deployed sensors by prolonging their lifetimes. Since the lifetime of a sensor network is determined by that of the shortest-life sensor node, we have to elaborate on the energy consumption of sensor network not to be concentrated on some hot-spot nodes.

In data-centric sensor networks [5, 7, 8], data are stored in sensor nodes based on their values, not stored in the collector node or delivered to external storage (or a predefined processor). In this approach, each sensor node has a predefined region of data domain it will store. This prevents the cases that the sensor nodes which are located near to external storage or collect more data than the others become hot-spot (i.e., consuming much more energy than the others). In this paper, in order to balance the energy-consumption of sensor nodes, we propose a dynamic data placement method, where we initially assign each sensor node a range of data domain, and dynamically adjust the ranges of sensor nodes based on their workload. For region assignment, we linearize the multi-dimensional data space by using Hilbert space-filling curves, and make a linear address space by zigzag traversing of sensor nodes.

The rest of the paper is organized as follows. In Chapter 2, we describe some related work on data-centric sensor networks. In Chapter 3, we propose a dynamic data placement method for multi-dimensional queries on sensor networks. In Chapter 4, we show the performance of the proposed method through experimental results. In Chapter 5, we conclude the paper with some remarks on future work.

2 Related Work

In data-centric sensor networks, addressing scheme which determines sensor node to store data is needed. The address (also called the '*index*') denotes the logical position of data storage, which is used for routing data or queries to target sensors. A popular addressing scheme in the conventional data-centric sensor networks is GHT (Geographic Hash Table) [8]. In the GHT method, data are stored sensor nodes which are determined based on their geographic locations. Although this method is so effective for exact-match queries and prefix queries, it is not efficient for range queries. It is because data objects of similar values are stored into geographically dispersed sensor nodes, and hence partial queries should be transmitted over many sensor nodes in the network for range-query processing.

In the DIM (Distributed Index for Multi-dimensional data) approach [5], the geographic area of sensor networks are iteratively divided by X-dimension and Y-dimension in an alternative way until there remains one sensor node for a region. Then, the data space is partitioned and assigned into the geographic regions of sensor nodes. Differently from GHT, DIM assigns data objects of similar values into geographically near sensor nodes. This improves energy-efficiency for range-query processing because the number of communications between sensor nodes is reduced compared with GHT. However, since the sensor nodes are deployed in a *not-controlled* manner, the data region assignments of sensor nodes cannot be guaranteed to be *balanced*. (In Figure 1(b), you can observe that the data allocation for each sensor node is not equal.) Because the energy-consumption of sensor nodes for query processing is in proportion to the amount of data it stores, non-uniform data assignment to sensor nodes will cause non-uniform energy-consumption between sensor nodes, which results in shortening the lifetime of the sensor networks.

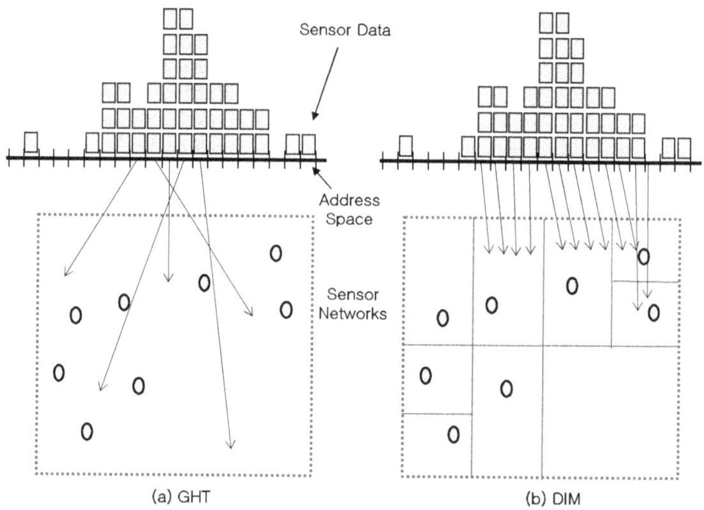

Fig. 1. Data Distribution in GHT and DIM Methods

3 The Proposed Method

Our solution for dynamic distribution of sensor data consists of the following steps: **(1)** We construct a single dimensional address space of sensor nodes (i.e., linearization of sensor nodes) through a zigzag traversing such that geographically near nodes are located near in the linear address space. **(2)** We transform the multi-dimensional data space into a single dimensional data space (i.e., linearization of data space) using Hilbert space-filling curves. **(3)** Initially, the data regions on the one dimensional data space are uniformly assigned into one dimensional address space of sensor nodes. Then, during the lifetime of the sensor networks, parts of data regions initially allocated to sensor nodes are dynamically migrated to near sensor nodes based on the workload of sensor nodes.

3.1 Construction of One Dimensional Address Space of Sensor Nodes

If we assign data regions into sensor nodes based on geographic positions as in DIM, the amount of data allocated to sensor nodes may be unbalanced. This causes the energy-consumption of some nodes that covers relatively large data regions to be more than the others, which leads to shortening the lifetime of entire sensor networks.

For addressing sensor nodes without geographic position information, we construct a linear address space of sensor nodes through *zigzag* traversing. The zigzag traversing allows sensor nodes which are deployed geographically near to be assigned near addresses in the linear address space.

The procedure for zigzag traversing is shown in Figure 2. All nodes are initially assigned level numbers through constructing a spanning tree via flooding (See Figure 3(a)). A level number denotes the number of hops needed for reaching the node from an outer point. After complete level numbering, we traverse the sensor nodes in a zigzag way. The sequence of traverse becomes the one dimensional address space of sensor nodes, where the start node is numbered as '1'. Figure 3(b) shows an example of zigzag traversing. In the figure, sensor node 'a' has three same-level neighbors (node 'b', 'c' and 'd'). According to Step 1.A of Figure 2, node 'b' is selected.

```
1. Choose a sensor node in the lowest level among ne
ighboring sensor nodes.

    A. When there are multiple candidates (i.e., the
     same level), choose a sensor the number of neig
    hbors of which is minimal. (This is a heuristic
    for selecting outlier nodes first.)

        i. When there are still multiple candidates
        (i.e., the same level and the same number of
         neighbors), choose the nearest one

2. When no more neighbor node exists, we backtrack o
n the traversed path and checked if there are still
not-chosen neighboring sensor nodes. If any, we proc
eed to the above Step1 from that node.

3. When we backtrack to the start node (i.e., number
 '1' node), the traversal is terminated.
```

Fig. 2. The Algorithm of Zigzag Traversing

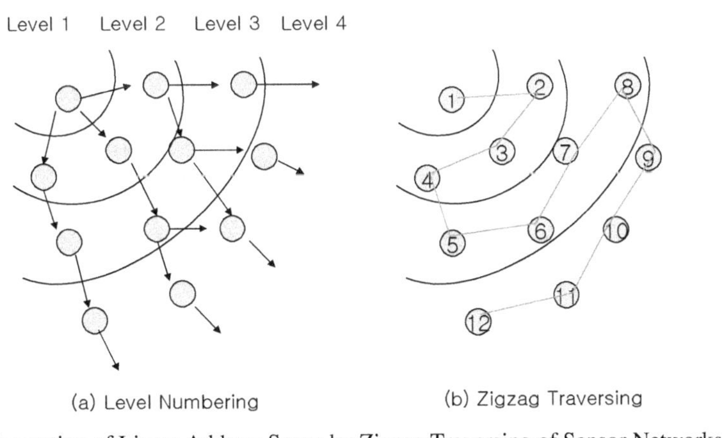

Fig. 3. Generation of Linear Address Space by Zigzag Traversing of Sensor Networks

3.2 Transforming Multi-dimensional Data Space into One Dimensional Data Space

In this paper, we consider multi-attribute sensor data (e.g., temperature, humidity, air pressure, lightness and so on) on which multi-dimensional range queries are processed. In order to store multi-dimensional data into sensor nodes, we transform the multi-dimensional data space into one dimensional one. For this purpose, we use a popular space-filling curve, called the *Hilbert curve*. It is known that the *Hilbert curve* has the best locality-preserving characteristic among many space-filling curves such as *Z-ordering*, *Peano curve*, etc [3, 6].

Since the Hilbert curve method assumes a normalized data space, we have to normalize the sensor data. In this paper we assume that sensor nodes are aware of all domains of sensor data space, and compute the normalized values as $a_N = (a - a_{MIN}) / (a_{MAX} - a_{MIN})$, where a is the measured data , a_N is normalized data value of a, a_{MIN} is the minimum value of the attribute, and a_{MAX} is the maximum value.

3.3 Data Allocation and Dynamic Adjustment

After generating linear address space of sensor nodes via zigzag traversing and linear data space via Hilbert curve, we map the data regions evenly into sensor nodes as in Figure 4. Since both the zigzag traversing and Hilbert space-filling curve tend to preserve the locality property, this data placement on sensor nodes also has good clustering effects on range queries. For example, in Figure 4, data regions 31~34 which are adjacent with each other in the original multi-dimensional data space are actually allocated in neighboring sensor nodes 4 and 5. This entails low cost when a range query includes data regions 31~34 is processed, since partial queries need not be delivered to other far-away nodes.

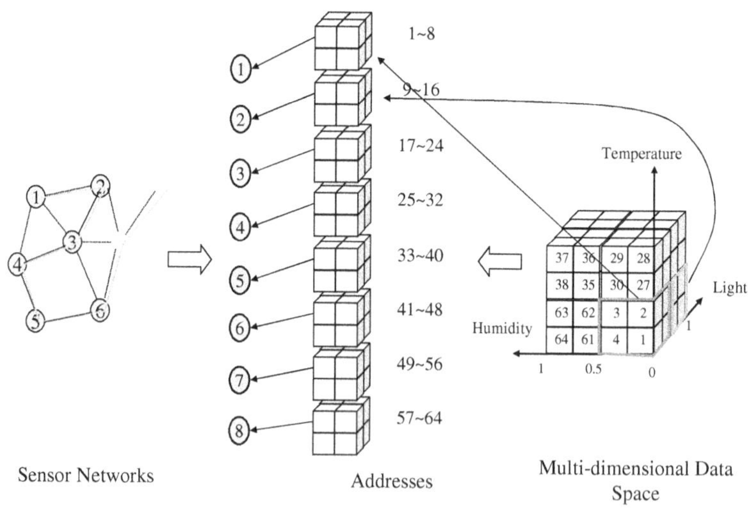

Fig. 4. Allocation of Data Regions to Sensor Nodes

The above allocation of data is fair when the workload on every data regions is uniform, since the amount of data space allocated to each sensor node is equal. However, according to specific characteristics of attributes, some data regions will be highly accessed than other regions. Query patterns are also dynamically changed during the lifetime of sensor networks. If the workload of sensor nodes is not uniform, the energy-consumption could be skewed. For the purpose of balancing the workload of sensor nodes, which is the goal of our proposed method, we dynamically adjust the data regions allocated to sensor nodes based on the *current* workload of sensor nodes.

Region Adjustment for Overloaded Sensor Nodes

For balancing the workload, we have to measure the amount of load of a sensor node in a quantitative way. Based on the assumption that the amount of energy consumption of a sensor node primarily depends on the amount of data it has stored and the frequency of queries it has processed, we define the load of a sensor node as follows:

Definition 1. The load(L_i) of sensor node i is defined as $L_i = \sum_j e_j q_j$, where j are the data regions allocated to sensor node i, e_j is the amount of data region j, and q_j is the frequency of queries for j. □

In the paper, we use the following two terms, '*neighboring sensor*' and '*adjacent sensor*'. The *neighboring sensor* denotes the sensor which is connected directly i.e., located in a single hop communication range. The *adjacent node* denotes the sensor node whose data region is adjacent. Usually, the adjacent node of a sensor node is chosen among its neighboring nodes. When a node is overloaded, its two adjacent nodes will take parts of data of the overloaded node for load balancing.

The state of '*overloaded*' means the sensor has been consuming relatively more energy than the other sensors. In the proposed method, dynamic adjustment of data regions between sensor nodes is activated by detection of any overloaded sensor nodes. In this paper, we define the criteria of being *overloaded* as follows: "Compared with the initial amount of energy in the battery and the amount of storage space, when the amount of currently remained energy or the amount of currently available free storage space are below the half of initial ones, we call those sensor nodes are *overloaded*." (The criteria can be modified according to target environments and applications.)

When adjusting data regions of sensor nodes, parts of data regions of overloaded sensor nodes are distributed into their adjacent nodes. Here, the amount of data for migration is determined according to the relative loads of overloaded node and its adjacent nodes.

Definition 2. The amount of data space (Δ_{pq}) to be transferred from sensor node p to sensor node q is as follows: (Here, p_{max} and p_{min} are the max/min addresses (on the 1-dimensional address space) for sensor node p, L_p and L_q are the amount of load of sensor nodes p and q, respectively.

$$\Delta_{pq} = \frac{p_{\max} - p_{\min}}{2} \times \frac{L_p - L_q}{L_p}$$ □

When data transfer is performed on two (i.e., left and right) adjacent nodes, these nodes might be overloaded due to the transferred data. Then, those nodes can also transfer parts of their data to their adjacent nodes progressively. For example, in Figure 5, some data are transferred from n_3 (initially overloaded sensor node) to node n_2 and n_4, then n_2 and n_4 can send parts of their data to n_1 and n_5, respectively.

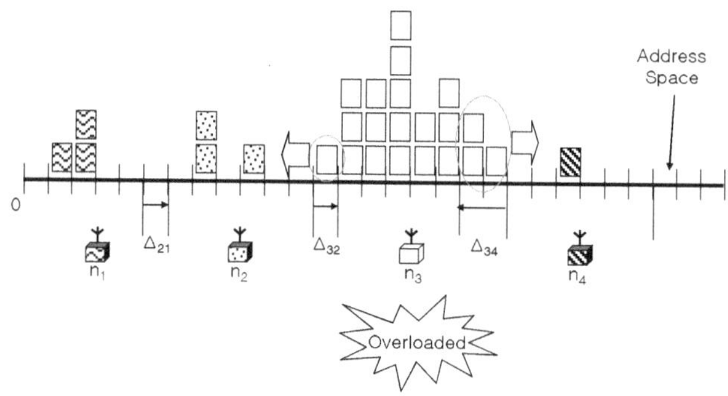

Fig. 5. Data Transfer for Overloaded Sensor Nodes

4 Performance Experiments

We have conducted simulation experiments for evaluating the performance of our approach compared with the previous one. We set the size of area for deploying 300 sensor nodes as 800m x 800m, where a sensor node has 14 neighbor nodes (in average) within its radio coverage 100m. A data record in a sensor consists of 5 attributes, and a sensor node contains 100 data records at the beginning. We have conducted the experiment until a failure of sensor node is occurred. We have generated multi-dimensional range queries which cover 5%, 10% and 20% of data space in a normalized way and in randomly chosen sensor nodes. The amount of energy consumption is determined by the number of message hops multiplied by the number of bytes for each message. In this experiment, the energy consumption for data storage is ignored for convenience.

Energy Consumption

In DIM, when two sensor nodes are located very closely, one sensor is assigned a very big region of data space while the other is assigned a small one. Observed through experiments, the size of maximum region assignment is 5 times bigger than that of the average one. This unbalanced region assignment leads to the increase of differences of energy consumption between sensor nodes, which results in shortening the lifetime of overall networks.

Figure 6 shows the comparison result of energy consumption of our method and the DIM, where the data records are uniformly generated over the entire data space, and range queries access the data space uniformly. The results indicate energy consumption ratios of sensor nodes at the time when a sensor node has failed due to exhaustion of its energy. The DIM method has many highly consumed nodes compared with our method.

We have tested a non-uniform setting, where data generation follows a normal distribution with the mean value of 0.5 and the standard deviation of 0.1, and also the query generation is based on the normal distribution of 0 and 0.1. Figure 7 shows the result of experiment, where we have measured the energy consumption ratios of sensor nodes at the time when 10% of the sensor nodes in our method are failed. (Here, we sort the id's of sensor nodes for readers convenience.) In the result we can see that more than half of the sensor nodes in DIM have consumed most of their energy at the time of 10% node failure whereas our sensor nodes consume relatively little energy.

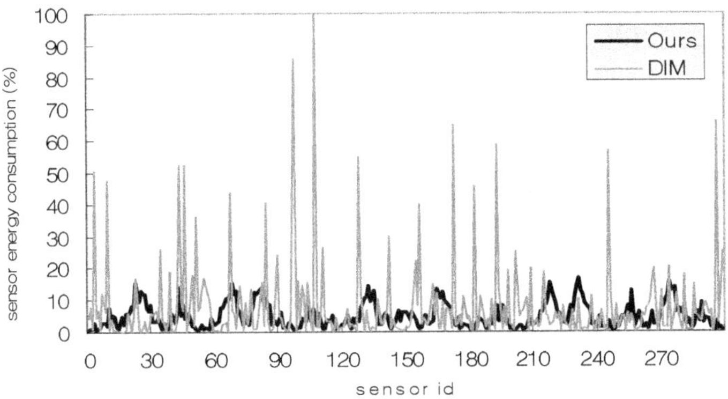

Fig. 6. Energy Consumption Ratios under Uniform Data and Queries

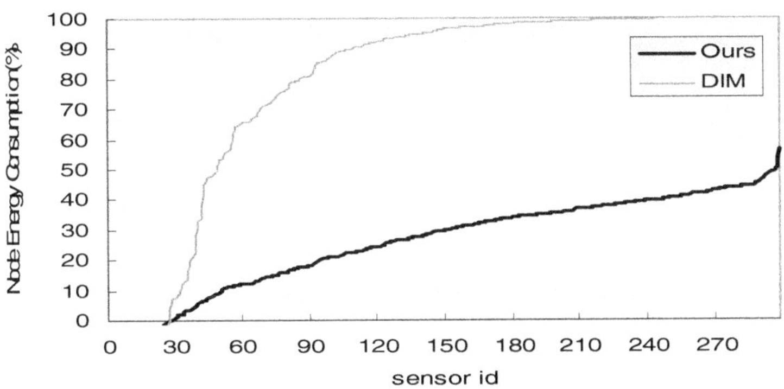

Fig. 7. Energy Consumption Ratios under Non-uniform Data and Queries

Network Lifetime

Figure 8 shows the network lifetime (in terms of unit time) comparison result of our method and DIM. As you can see in the figure, the lifetime until one node failure of DIM is very short compared with ours. This indicates that DIM is not appropriate for mission-critical applications where a single node failure would not be admitted. By the time of 15% node failure, our method survives longer (about 150%) than DIM.

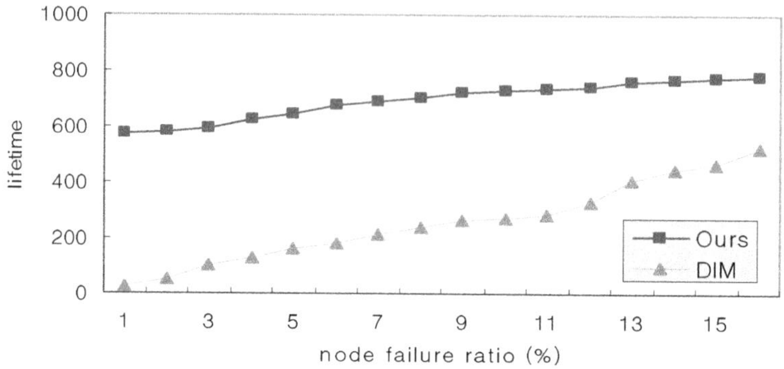

Fig. 8. Network Lifetime according to Node Failure Ratios

5 Conclusion

In data-centric sensor networks, the lifetime significantly depends on data placement (or distribution). The use of hash functions is effective for load balancing since it distributes (i.e., de-cluster) data over the entire network. However, it is inefficient for range queries since many sensor nodes must be involved for the query processing. In other aspects, the previous approach DIM for range query processing did not consider load balancing on sensor nodes, which results in differences of energy consumption between sensor nodes and thus short network lifetime.

In this paper we have proposed a new data storage method which balances workloads of sensor nodes, and thus improves overall network life time. We have constructed the address space of sensor nodes by using zigzag traversing, and assigned the linearly transformed (via Hilbert curves) data space on it. Since this approach assigns adjacent addresses onto neighboring sensor nodes, (multi-dimensional) range queries can be efficiently processed. In addition, the dynamic and progressive update of address assignments effectively copes with the changes of workloads and balances energy consumption ratios of sensor nodes. Through simulation experiments, we have shown that the proposed approach efficiently balances the energy-consumption of sensor nodes and improve the lifetime of sensor networks.

We in the paper considered that the data are stored on sensor nodes in a non-replicated way. For future work, we will investigate on data replication in sensor networks and query processing over replicated data. If some replication of data between sensor nodes is allowable, the performance of query processing and the availability of sensor database will be significantly improved.

Acknowledgement

This work was done as a part of Information & Communication Fundamental Technology Research Program, supported by Ministry of Information & Communication in Republic of Korea.

References

[1] Bhardwaj, M.. and Chandrakasan, A. P. *Bounding the Lifetime of Sensor Networks Via Optimal Role Assignments*, IEEE INFOCOM 2002.

[2] Greenstein, B. et. al. *DIFS: A Distributed Index for Features in Sensor Networks*, Elsevier Journal of Ad Hoc Networks, 2003.

[3] Jagadish, H. V., *Linear clustering of objects with multiple attributes*, International Conference on Management of Data, Proceedings of the ACM SIGMOD 1990.

[4] Karp, B. and Kung, H. *Greedy Perimeter Stateless Routing* In Proceedings of the Sixth Annual ACM/IEEE International Conference on Mobile Computing, pp. 243~254, 2000.

[5] Li, X. et. al. *Multi-dimensional Range Queries in Sensor Networks*, Proceedings of the 1st international conference on Embedded networked sensor systems, pp. 63~75, 2003.

[6] Moon, B. et. al. *Analysis of the clustering properties of Hilbert space-filling curve*. IEEE Trans. on Knowledge and Data Engineering, pp 124~141, 1996.

[7] Newsome, J. and Song, D. *GEM: Graph EMbedding for Routing and Data-Centric Storage in Sensor Networks without Geographic Information*. SenSys 2003.

[8] Ratnasamy, S. et. al. *Data-Centric Storage in Sensornets with GHT, a Geographic Hash Table*, Mobile Networks and Applications, 8, pp. 427-442, 2003.

An OSEK COM Compliant Communication Model for Smart Vehicle Environment

Guoqing Yang, Minde Zhao, Lei Wang, and Zhaohui Wu

College of Computer Science, Zhejiang University,
Hangzhou, Zhejiang, China 310027
{ygq78, zmdd48, alwaysbeing, wzh}@zju.edu.cn

Abstract. Smart Vehicle Environment (SVE) is an important application of the idea of smart spaces. This paper presents Smart Vehicle Multi-Agent System (SVMAS) to achieve the goal of SVE and put forwards a commutation model for SVMAS based on SmartOSEK COM [1] to support data exchange. The paper also presents an approach to encapsulate the message to transport by CAN bus, and bring forward a simulator model for SVMAS. Finally the paper gives an example of the communication model which implements a dialogue between two agents and analyzes the performance. The contribution of our work is three-fold. First, we adopt Knowledge Query and Manipulation Language (KQML) to describe the communication in vehicles. Second, we develop SmartOSEK COM to implement communication in vehicles. Third, we define the ACLcan protocol to transform the message from SmartOSEK COM to CAN frame.

1 Introduction

Weiser introduced the field of Ubiquitous Computing [2] and presented a vision of people and environments augmented with computational resources that provide information and services when and where desired [3]. Smart spaces adopt the concept of ubiquitous computing, and embed computation resource and perceptive equipment into our daily life and working spaces [4]. Smart spaces offer active services by inter-connected embedded devices.

Smart Vehicle Environment (SVE) [5] is an important application of the idea of Smart spaces, and it turns the vehicle into a smart human-vehicle environment by advanced technology and equipments to gather, transmit and process the environment information. Therefore, Smart Vehicle Environment needs the cooperation of many disparate embedded devices in vehicles.

Smart Vehicle Multi-agent System (SVMAS) is a multi-agent system for SVE, which we develop to achieve the goal of SVE. In SVMAS, the function modules in SVE can cooperate with each other in form of agents. In order to implement SVMAS, we develop kinds of Electronic Control Units (ECUs) to accomplish the lamp control, window control, and door control in the vehicle. The ECUs are connected by Controller Area Networks (CAN) [6]. We develop the SmartOSEK COM to provide communication support for the agents run in ECUs, and define ACLcan protocol to fill the gap between SmartOSEK COM and CAN.

L.T. Yang et al. (Eds.): ICESS 2005, LNCS 3820, pp. 430–440, 2005.

The remainder of this paper is organized as follows. Section 2 introduces the related work of the field. Section 3 puts forward a framework of multi-agent system in smart vehicle (SVMAS). Section 4 provides a communication model for SVMAS. Section 5 presents an implementation for the communication model. Section 6 gives an example of the communication model for SVMAS which implements a dialogue between two agents. Finally, we conclude our paper in section 7.

2 Related Work

CAN (Controller Area Network) is a serial bus system, which was originally developed for automotive applications in the early 1980's. The CAN protocol was internationally standardized in 1993 as ISO 11898-1. CAN provides the basic services of the communication for automotive electronics, but users prefer to CAN application protocols to communicate easily. SAE's J1939 [7] standards family is the preferred controller area network (CAN) for equipment used in industries ranging from agriculture, construction, and fire/rescue to forestry, materials handling, and on- and off-highway. Although J1939 is a mature protocol for CAN application layer, it does support multi-agent system for the lacking of the ability of knowledge description.

OSEK/VDX is a joint project of the automotive industry. It aims at an industry standard for an open-ended architecture for distributed control units in vehicles [8] and put forward OSEK COM specification to increase the portability of application software modules by defining common software communication interfaces and behaviors for internal communication (communication within an electronic control unit) and external communication (communication between networked vehicle nodes), which is independent of the communication protocol used [9].

OSEK COM offers services to exchange data between tasks and/or interrupt service routines. Different tasks may reside in the same ECU (internal communication) or in different ECUs (external communication). The aim of the OSEK COM specification is to support the portability, reusability and interoperability of application software. The Application Program Interface (API) hides the differences between internal and external communication as well as different communication protocols, bus systems and networks. An OSEK COM implementation can run on many hardware platforms. The implementation shall require only a minimum of hardware resources, therefore different levels of functionality (conformance classes) are provided [9].

As OSEK COM specification is brought forward, we can achieve communication in vehicles easily, and we can integrate Knowledge Query and Manipulation Language (KQML) [10] together with OSEK COM into a communication platform to achieve communication between agents.

Some platforms compliant with OSEK COM specification have been developed such as OSEKTurbo, OSEKWorks and OSCan, etc, but none of them have been applied into multi-agent system.

In this paper, we put forward SVMAS by which we apply the multi-agent system into the field of automotive electronics to achieve the goal of SVE, and describe the information in smart vehicle environment by agent communication language (ACL) [11], and we develop a communication software platform according to OSEK COM to fulfill the communication requirement in automotive electronics.

3 The Agent Framework of SVMAS

The paper puts forward SVMAS to assist the driver to finish complex operations. Using SVMAS, all ECUs in the car can share the information, cooperate with each other, and can accomplish complex tasks as a whole.

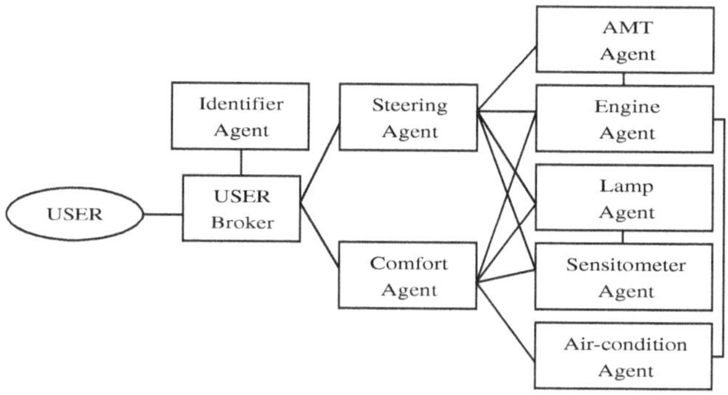

Fig. 1. Agent framework of SVMAS

As there are differences in processing ability and function among ECUs in SVE, the abilities of agent in every ECU are different too. We classify agents of SVMAS into different hierarchies: task agent and function agent. Task agent is used to accomplish grand tasks that require the collaborative work of many function units. Function agent undertakes small tasks that can be done by smaller ECU individually.

Each ECU has a function agent. Tasks agent partition the task into smaller ones and then hand them over to different function agents. At the mean time task agents are in charge of the coordination of different function agents. The coordinator of function agents is dynamic. The goal of coordination is achieved by passing messages and negotiations.

The agent framework of SVMAS is shown in Fig. 1. There are different types of agents in the framework. They are interrelated with each other. When a driver enters SVE, agents are started, and services are provided initiatively. Firstly an USER Broker is assigned to the user, and then the USER Broker would contact with SVMAS instead of the user. Identifier Agent would identify the user. If the user has the legal identity, he can obtain kinds of services provided by SVMAS, such as starting the car, starting the air conditioner, etc. The service of starting the car is provided by Steering Agent, which is a task agent. Steering Agent divides the function of starting car into opening the engine, modulating the state of AMT, and operating the car lamp etc. Opening the engine is finished by Engine Agent, and operating the car lamp is finished by Lamp Agent. When the function agent accomplishes the given function, it needs to communicate with other function agents. For example, Lamp Agent needs the information of lightness when it accomplishes the lamp operating, and it needs to communicate with Sensitometer Agent to obtain the information of lightness. For the method of agent communication, we will give an example of the dialogue between two agents in section 6.

4 The Communication Model for SVMAS

The communication model for SVMAS is shown in Fig. 2. Communication is the key for agents to share the information they collected, and to coordinate their actions. In the communication model for SVMAS, four layers are brought forward as follows: agent layer, SmartOSEK COM layer, ACLcan layer, and underlying networks layer. In agent layer, the communication form of SVMAS is dialogue; in SmartOSEK COM layer, the communication form of SVMAS is message; in ACLcan layer, the communication form of SVMAS is CAN frame defined by ACLcan; and in underlying networks layer, the communication form of SVMAS is electric signal.

The communication between agents is described in KQML, a well known ACL, and it is in dialogue form. The dialogue could be transformed into messages in SmartOSEK COM. ACLcan protocol processes the messages from SmartOSEK COM, and transforms them into the CAN frame form, and then sends them out by CAN Bus.

In SVMAS, we describe dialogues between agents in KQML to improve the compatibility of the communication model, so each agent should have a parser of KQML. The parser interprets the performative of KQML, by which the agents can understand each other.

For SVMAS, we adopt CAN bus as the underlying communication protocol because CAN is developed specially as a communication bus to in-vehicle networks and has high performance. Thus, the innovation of our SmartOSEK COM is to integrate OSEK to CAN bus, and to provide an approach to set the frame ID of CAN. We develop ACLcan protocol as the interface between SmartOSEK COM and CAN bus. In ACLcan, the frame ID of CAN is set according to the ECUs' addresses of sender and receiver and the agent identifiers of sender and receiver. Moreover, the performative of ACL is also considered in the frame ID of CAN.

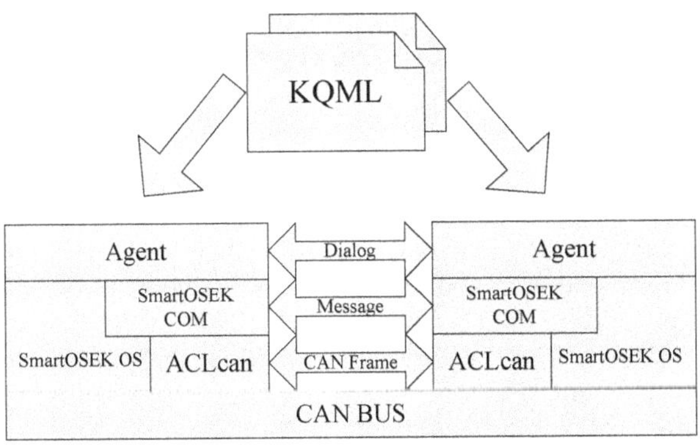

Fig. 2. The communication model for SVMAS

5 The Implementation of the Communication Model for SVMAS

To implement the communication model for SVMAS, we develop SmartOSEK COM which is a specialized communication platform for automobile electronics, and develop ACLcan which is a protocol to convert a message from SmartOSEK COM to CAN bus frame.

5.1 KQML: The Agent Communication Language for SVMAS

In the multi-agent system field, the exchange of knowledge among disparate computer systems is the most important. Knowledge Interchange Format (KIF) [12] is a language designed for the exchange of knowledge among disparate computer systems. It has declarative semantics; it is logically comprehensive; it provides for the representation of knowledge about the representation of knowledge, and provides for the definition of objects, functions, and relations. Recently, research on multi-agent system makes great progress. Agents contact with each other by Agent Communication Language (ACL). KQML, a well known ACL, is a part of the ARPA Knowledge Sharing Effort and is developed as an agent communication language and protocol for exchanging information and knowledge. Agents can use KQML to communicate attitudes about information, such as querying, stating, believing, requiring and subscribing.

As the research of multi-agent system in vehicles is deficient and few works have been done to apply KQML into automotive electronics field, we adopt KQML to describe the information to interchange between agents in vehicles, and the description in KQML can be parsed by agent itself and others.

5.2 SmartOSEK COM: The Foundation of Communication for SVMAS

According to OSEK/VDX specifications, we develop the SmartOSEK system. SmartOSEK system includes SmartOSEK OS compliant with the OSEK/VDX Operating System specification [13] and SmartOSEK COM (compliant with the OSEK/VDX Communication specification).

SmartOSEK COM is based on messages. A message contains application-specific data. Messages and message properties are configured statically in the OSEK Implementation Language (OIL) [14]. The content and usage of messages is not relevant to SmartOSEK COM.

SmartOSEK COM supports two kinds of communications, internal communication and external communication. Interaction Layer (IL), an important part of SmartOSEK, provides users with the OSEK COM API which contains services for the transfer (send and receive operations) of messages. In the case of internal communication, the IL makes the message data immediately available to the receiver. In the case of external communication the IL packs one or more messages into assigned Interaction Layer Protocol Data Units (I-PDU) and passes them to the underlying layer.

Administration of messages is done in the IL based on message objects. Message objects exist on the sending side (sending message object) and on the receiving side (receiving message object). The data communicated between the IL and the underlying layer is organized into I-PDUs which contain one or more messages. The IL offers an API to handle messages. The API provides services for initialization, data transfer and communication management. Services transmitting messages over network are non-blocking. SmartOSEK COM provides notification mechanisms for an application to determine the status of a transmission or reception [9].

5.3 ACLcan: The Interface Between SmartOSEK COM and CAN Bus

In SVMAS, agents communicate with each other under the message mechanism. The communication mechanism based on message is provided by SmartOSEK COM. We transform the message in KQML to message into the message in SmartOSEK COM. The message in SmartOSEK COM is defined in OIL [15]. Each message in SmartOSEK COM is described by a set of attributes and references, and in SVMAS, each performative in KQML has a corresponding kind of message.

	7	6	5	4	3	2	1	0
Byte1	Frame Format	RTR	X	X	DLC			
Byte2	ID.28-ID.21(sender's node address)							
Byte3	ID.20-ID.13(receiver's node address)							
Byte4	ID.12-ID.7(performative)						ID.6-ID.5(sender)	
Byte5	ID.4(sender)	ID.3-ID.1(receiver)			ID0(Type)	X	X	X
Byte6	Index of Message Content							
Byte7 .. Byte13	Message Content							

Fig. 3. CAN frame format in ACLcan protocol

ACLcan is the interface between SmartOSEK and CAN Bus. Since we choose CAN as the network communication bus for SVMAS, the transmission of the message between agents in SVMAS will use the CAN BUS. The ID of each CAN frame is defined in message and each message has a unique CAN ID. We develop ACLcan to configure the CAN frame's ID. The configuration mechanism of CAN ID in the message is shown in Fig. 3. In SVMAS, every transmission of message uses extended frame. The frame header of the extended frame has 29 bits (ID.28-ID.0) to show the ID of the CAN extended frame. ID.28-ID.21 is the sender's node address. We give each ECU in SVMAS a unique node address. In CAN ID, we use 8 bits to denote the node address, thus 256 nodes are admitted at most in SVMAS. ID.20-ID.13 is the receiver's node address. ID.12-ID.7 is the identifier of KQML performative. Each performative is accorded with a unique ID. ID.6-ID.4 is the agent identifier of sender. We identify the agents of each ECU, and agents in different ECU can use the same agent identifier. ID.3-ID.1 is the agent identifier of receiver. ID.0 shows whether the message is simple frame or multiple frames. If ID.0 is 1, then the message is multiple frames. In CAN frame format, the content of Byte6 shows the index of the frame in the message, or else it shows the content of message.

5.4 Simulation of the SVMAS

We develop Smart Simulator to provide the ability of simulation to evaluate the performance of communication of the multi-agent system by the included sub-simulators.

The architecture of Smart Simulator is shown in Fig. 4. The simulator provides Smart OSEK COM Simulator to simulate the communication compliant with OSEK/VDX, and SmartOSEK OS Simulator to simulate the scheduling of the tasks. For external communication between ECUs, the simulator provides CAN Simulator to simulate the in-vehicle networks. As a real system has inputs and outputs, the simulator also provides Interrupt Simulator and Actuator Simulator to simulate the signal inputs and outputs.

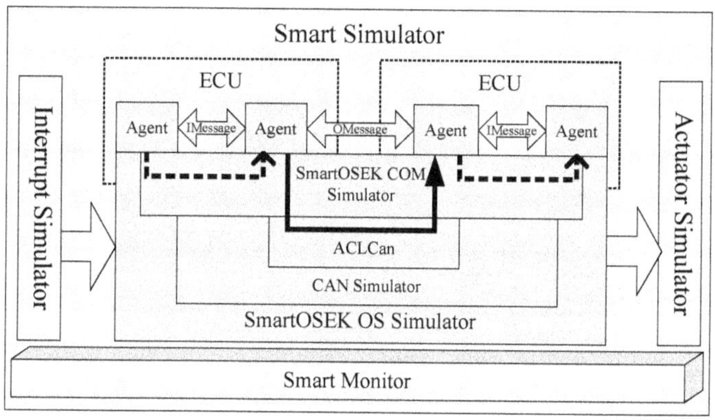

Fig. 4. The Architecture of Smart Simulator

In the simulator, the messages are classified into two types, one is internal message denoted by *IMessage* and the other is external message denoted by *OMessage*. The agents communicate in the same ECU by *IMessage*, and the communication process is simulated by SmartOSEK COM Simulator. When an agent communicates with an agent in other ECUs by *OMessage* through CAN bus, CAN Simulator would firstly encapsulate the message into CAN frame and decapsulate it after a delay according to the baud rate of CAN bus. ACLcan Simulator would encapsulate and decapsulate the *OMessage* by the ACLcan protocol. The simulation results are displayed by Smart Monitor and saved into files which the developers can refer to modify the network configuration. Smart Simulator simulates the running process of the system, and the temporal behavior of the system.

6 A Case Study of the Communication Model for SVMAS

In this section, we give an example of communication model for SVMAS. Suppose there are two agents, one is named Lamp and the other one is Sensitometer, as shown in Fig. 5. The scenario we assume is that when it becomes dark, the Lamp Agent needs the information of the lighteness to decide whether it should open the lamp or not, thus it needs to communicate with Sensitometer Agent to obtain the information of lightness.

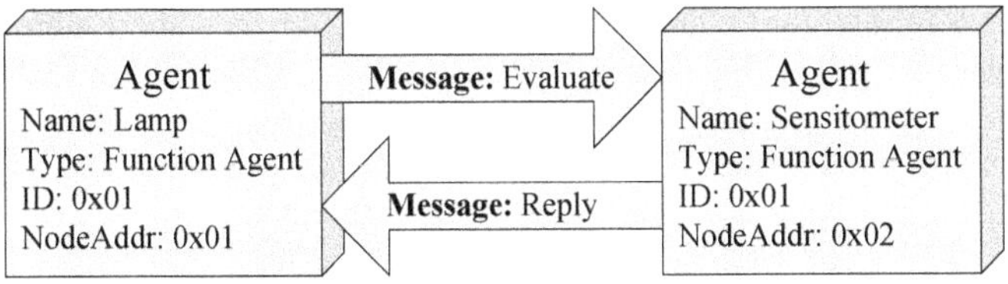

Fig. 5. Communication example of SVMAS

```
Dialogue ( Example )
(evaluate
  :sender           Lamp
:receiver           Sensitometer
  :language  KIF
:ontology   LampControl
  :reply-with       q1
:content            ( val  ( luminance L1 ) )
)
(reply
  :sender           Sensitometer
:receiver           Lamp
  :language  KIF
:ontology   LampControl
  :reply-with       q1
:content            ( =  (luminance L1 ) (scalar 880 lumen) )
)
```

Fig. 6. Dialogue Example in KQML

```
MESSAGE evaluate {
TYPE = EXTERNAL;
  LENGTH=5;
  QUEUED = False;
  TRANSMISSION = DIRECT;
IPDU = lamp_control;
NOTIFICATION = FLAG {
FLAGNAME = "require_luminance";
};
  CANID = Get_Can_ID (evaluate, Lamp, Sensitometer)
};
MESSAGE reply {
TYPE = EXTERNAL;
  LENGTH=5;
  QUEUED = False;
  TRANSMISSION = DIRECT;
IPDU = lamp_control;
NOTIFICATION = FLAG {
FLAGNAME = "respond_luminance";
};
  CANAID = Get_Can_ID (reply, Sensitometer, Lamp)
};
```

Fig. 7. Messages defined in OIL

Lamp agent and Sensitometer agent process a dialogue for the lighteness of the current environment, and we use KQML to describe this dialogue as shown in Fig. 6 [16]. Firstly, lamp sends a message to request for the lightness. The format of the message uses KIF, and the request is defined as ql. The message is sent by SmartOSEK COM via CAN Bus. The ontology of the dialogue is defined as "LampControl". After receiving the message, Sensitometer sends the request result to lamp via another message. Definitions of these two messages for the dialogue are shown in Fig. 7.

The first message is "evaluate", and it is an external message which can provide communication between ECUs. The CAN ID of "evaluate" defines the ID of CAN frame. When the message is sent, a flag named "require_luminance" would be set.

The agent Lamp could tell agent Sensitometer about its requirement by calling a SmartOSEK API *SendMessage*. Then the requirement of Agent Lamp would be transformed into message in predefined format. Subsequently, messages would be split into CAN frames in order to be transmitted on CAN bus, and ACLcan protocol would participate in setting the CAN frame's ID. When the agent Sensitometer receives the requirement of Lamp, it would decode the CAN frame, and find the requirement of the agent Lamp.

In the example, the "evaluate" has a CAN ID as "0x01020490". In the same way the "reply" has a CAN ID as "0x02010590" by ACLcan.

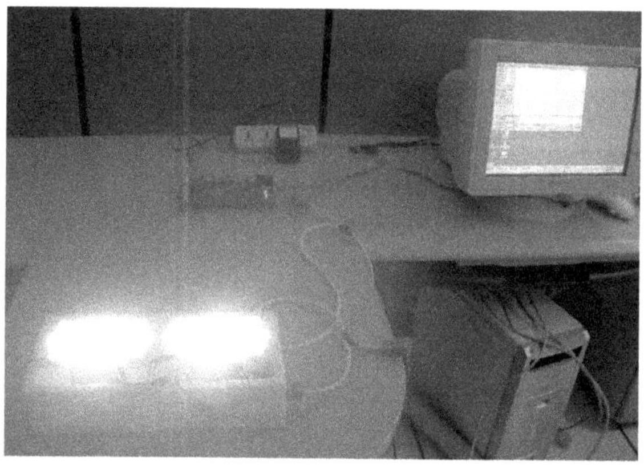

Fig. 8. Scenario of the Communication Model for SVMAS

To evaluate the performance of the communication model for SVMAS, we measure the time of the process on CPUs by Smart Simulator. In the simulator, we set the CAN bus baud rate at 125kbps and configure the CPU as MPC555. Fig. 9 shows the simulation results. To test the real performance of the model on CAN bus, we experiment the example by the hardware platform MPC555. As shown in Fig.8, in the experimentation, the sensitometer gets the lighteness of the environment, and sends the information to the lamp by the communication model we present. When the room becomes dark, the lamp would be lighted. We set the CAN bus baud rate as the same with the simulator, and measure three parameters, the encapsulation time and the decapsulation time by the logic analysis device LA5540 at 50MHz. For each parameter, we have measured ten times and the minimum time, maximum time and average time are shown in Fig. 9.

As shown in Fig. 9, we find the average time of decapsulation is 53.46us and it is a little faster than the average time of encapsulation, which is 56.38us because of adopting speculative arithmetic. As the average times of decapsulation and encapsulation are about only 8 times than the task switch time in SmartOSEK OS which is 7.6us, we can draw the conclusion that the communication model for SVMAS we present is applicative and has high performance, and is suitable to develop automotive electronics software.

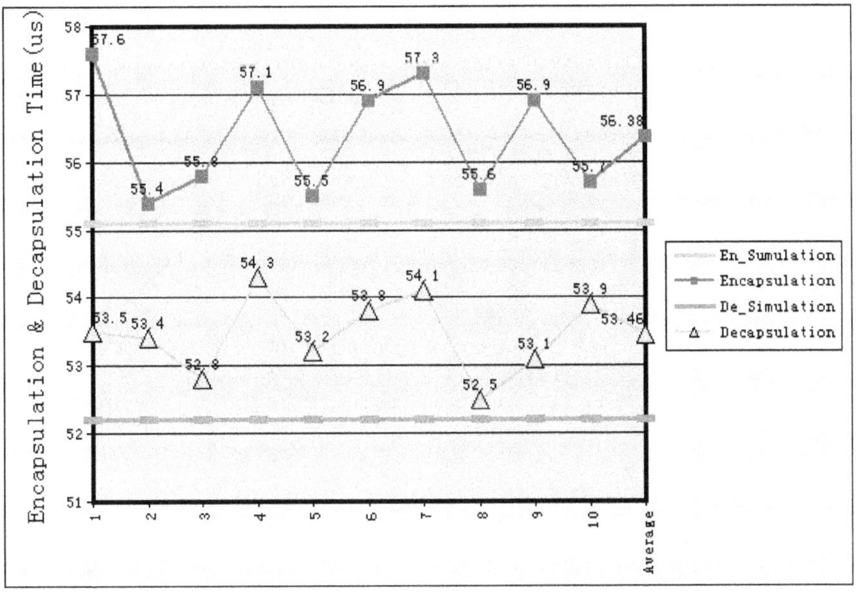

Fig. 9. Simulation and experiment results of the communication model for SVMAS

7 Conclusion

In this paper we make a valiant try in smart spaces field, and put forward a communication model for SVMAS. The innovation is applying agent communication language-KQML to SVMAS and adopting CAN bus as the underlying networks for agent communication. Moreover, we develop ACLcan protocol to provide good support for the CAN based communication of agents. In the example of the communication model for SVMAS, we accomplish a dialogue between two agents and get good results in our simulation and experimentation, thus the cooperation of multiple agents could be achieved easily by dialogues among agents. The communication platform we present works well, and is suitable to develop automotive electronics devices.

Acknowledgement

This work is supported by 863 National High Technology Program under Grant No. 2003AA1Z2140 and No. 2004AA1Z2180.

References

1. Minde Zhao, Zhaohui Wu, Guoqing Yang, Lei Wang, Wei Chen: SmartOSEK: A Dependable Platform for Automobile Electronics. The First International Conference on Embedded Software and System. (2004), vol. Springer-Verlag GmbH ISSN: 0302-9743, pp. 437.
2. Mark Weiser: The Computer for the 21st Century. Scientific American. (1991) pp. 94-100.
3. Gregory D.Abowd, Elizabeth D. Mynatt: Charting Past, Present, and Future Research in Ubiquitous Computing. ACM Transactions on Computer-Human Interaction. (2000), vol. 7, No. 1.
4. Michael Coen: Design Principles for Intelligent Environments. Proceedings of The Fifteenth National Conference on Artificial Intelligence. (Madison Wisconsin, 1998).
5. Guoqing Yang, Zhaohui Wu, Xiumei Li, Wei Chen: SVE: Embedded Agent Based Smart Vehicle Environment. The 2003 IEEE International Conference on Intelligent Transportation Systems. (2003).
6. Cia: CAN. http://www.can-cia.de/can/.
7. Sae: J1939. http://www.sae.org/standardsdev/groundvehicle/j1939.htm.
8. Osek/Vdx: OSEK/VDX Binding Specification Version 1.4.1. (2003). http://www.osek-vdx.
9. Osek/Vdx: OSEK/VDX Communication Specification Version 3.0.3. (2004). http://www.osek-vdx.org.
10. T.Finin, J.Weber, G.Wiederhold, M.Genesereth: Specification of the KQML agent communication language. DARPA knowledge sharing initiative external interfaces working group. (Enterprise Integration Technologies, University of Toronto, 1994).
11. Munindar P.Singh: Agent Communication Languages: Rethinking the Principles. IEEE Computer. (1998), vol. 31, pp. 40--47.
12. Matt Ginsberg: Knowledge interchange format: The KIF of death. AI Magazine. (1991). http://logic.stanford.edu/kif/dpans.html.
13. Osek/Vdx: OSEK/VDX Operating System Specification Version 2.2.2. (2004). http://www.osek-vdx.org.
14. Osek/Vdx: OSEK/VDX OSEK Implementation Language Specification Version 2.4.1. (2003). http://www.osek-vdx.org.
15. Joseph Lemieux: Programming in the OSEK/VDX Environment. (CMP Books, 2001).
16. Michael Wooldridge: An Introduction to Multiagent systems. (John Wiley&Son, Inc, 2002).

Resource Allocation Based on Traffic Load over Relayed Wireless Access Networks*

Sung Won Kim[1] and Byung-Seo Kim[2]

[1] School of Electrical Engineering and Computer Science, Yeungnam University, Gyeongsangbuk-do, 712-749, Korea
ksw@ieee.org

[2] Motorola Inc., 1301 Algonquin Rd. Schaumburg, IL, 60196 USA
Byungseo.Kim@motorola.com

Abstract. In this paper, we develop a traffic load-based resource allocation scheme, called LOAD, to enhance the capacity of relayed wireless access networks for asymmetric traffic load such as transmission control protocol (TCP). In order to estimate the current traffic load status in relayed wireless access networks, we propose a load estimation method. A relay gateway estimates the current traffic load status by keeping track of the sizes of the frames it encounters, and computes accordingly the current traffic load of the uplink and the downlink. The results are then used to allocate the system resource between the uplink and the downlink. The proposed method can be implemented without the modification of the deployed IEEE 802.11 nodes.

We analyze the throughput ratio between the uplink and the downlink, and validate the analysis result with a comprehensive simulation study. The simulation results indicate that the utilization of the proposed method is better than that of IEEE 802.11 Distributed Coordination Function (DCF).

1 Introduction

Wireless local area networks (WLANs) based on the IEEE 802.11 standard [1] are becoming increasingly prevalent for offices, public places, and homes. The focus is now turning to deploying these networks over relayed wireless access networks (RWANs) [2]–[4]. A RWAN is a network where each node has connection with a relay gateway (RG) in its radio coverage and the RG has connections with other RGs. Thus, each node can access wired networks through one or more wireless hops managed by RGs. One form of RWAN is the complementary use of so-called hotspots [5]–[7] such as airports, hotels, cafes, and other areas in which people can have untethered public accesses to the Internet. Low cost and high speed WLANs can be integrated within the cellular coverage to provide hotspot coverage for high speed data services. WLAN offers an interesting possibility for cellular operators to offer additional capacity and higher bandwidth for end

* This work was supported by the 2005 research grants of the Institute of Information and Communication at Yeungnam University.

L.T. Yang et al. (Eds.): ICESS 2005, LNCS 3820, pp. 441–451, 2005.

users without sacrificing the capacity of cellular users, since WLANs operate on unlicensed frequency bands.

Medium Access Control (MAC) protocol in the IEEE 802.11 standard consists of two coordination functions: mandatory Distributed Coordination Function (DCF) and optional Point Coordination Function (PCF). In the DCF, a set of wireless nodes communicates with each other using a contention-based channel access method, namely Carrier Sense Multiple Access with Collision Avoidance (CSMA/CA). CSMA/CA is known for its inherent fairness between nodes and robustness. It is quite effective in supporting symmetric traffic loads in ad hoc networks where the traffic loads between nodes are similar. However, this form of random access protocol is not recommended for asymmetric traffic loads where most of the traffic loads converge into RGs. For example, Internet access or mobile computing uses transmission control protocol (TCP) or user datagram protocol (UDP) in which the offered traffic load is strongly biased toward the downlink (from RG to nodes) against the uplink (from nodes to RG) or the direct link (from nodes to nodes). Thus, these traffic flows for the downlink are completely blocked due to the CSMA/CA MAC protocol in distributed environments. We propose an enhanced MAC protocol to overcome such problems. The proposed algorithm can be implemented without the modification of the IEEE 802.11 standard for nodes.

The remainder of this paper is organized as follows. The next section presents related works. Section 3 describes the proposed method. In Section 4, we investigate the enhancement of the proposed method with some numerical results. Finally, the paper is concluded in Section 5.

2 Preliminaries

2.1 Operations of IEEE 802.11

The DCF achieves automatic medium sharing between compatible nodes through the use of CSMA/CA. Before initiating a transmission, a node senses the channel to determine whether or not another node is transmitting. If the medium is sensed idle for a specified time interval, called the distributed interframe space (DIFS), the node is allowed to transmit. If the medium is sensed busy, the transmission is deferred until the ongoing transmission terminates.

If two or more nodes find that the channel is idle at the same time, a collision occurs. In order to reduce the probability of such collisions, a node has to perform a backoff procedure before starting a transmission. The duration of this backoff is determined by the Contention Window (CW) size which is initially set to CW_{min}. The CW value is used to randomly choose the number of slot times in the range of $[0, CW - 1]$, which is used for backoff duration. In case of an unsuccessful transmission, the CW value is updated to $CW \times 2$ while it does not exceed CW_{max}. This will guarantee that in case of a collision, the probability of another collision at the time of next transmission attempt is further decreased.

A transmitter and receiver pair exchanges short RTS (Request-To-Send) and CTS (Clear-To-Send) control frames prior to the actual data transmission to avoid the collision of data frames. An acknowledgement (ACK) frame will be sent by the receiver upon successful reception of a data frame. It is only after receiving an ACK frame correctly that the transmitter assumes successful delivery of the corresponding data frame. Short InterFrame Space (SIFS), which is smaller than DIFS, is a time interval between RTS, CTS, data frame, and ACK frame. Using this small gap between transmissions within the frame exchange sequence prevents other nodes from attempting to use the medium. As a consequence, it gives priority to completion of the ongoing frame exchange sequence.

2.2 Related Works

The authors in [8]–[10] propose to scale the contention window, vary the inter-frame spacings, and change the backoff period according to the priority level of the traffic flow. Kim and Hou [11] propose a frame scheduling method based on the IEEE 802.11 fluid model to improve the capacity for UDP/TCP traffic. The proposed model assumes that the frame size and the transmission rate are constant. Because all these studies are focused on the fairness or priority among nodes in a WLAN, the unfair sharing of bandwidth between the uplink and the downlink still remains.

The works for resource allocation between the uplink and the downlink are proposed in [12]–[14]. In [12], the authors observe a significant unfairness between the uplink and the downlink flows when the DCF is employed in a WLAN. Since the DCF protocol allows equal access to the media for all hosts, the RG and the nodes have equal utilization to the medium. Thus, when the downlink has much more offered traffic load than that of the uplink, the downlink becomes bottleneck of the system capacity and much more RGs should be deployed to accommodate such nodes. The TCP fairness issues between the uplink and the downlink in WLANs has been studied in [13]. The authors are interested in a solution that results in uplink and downlink TCP flows having an equal share of the wireless bandwidth (utilization ratio of one). Because this solution operates on the TCP layer, it is not effective when there exist traffic flows other than TCP. The resource allocation method between the uplink and the downlink is proposed in [14]. The number of nodes is taken into consideration to decide the required utilization ratio between the uplink and the downlink. The proposed method assumes a constant transmission rate and a constant frame length for the uplink and the downlink traffics. These assumptions are not efficient when the transmission rates are changed according to the channel fading or the frame lengths are different between the uplink and the downlink traffics.

3 Proposed Resource Allocation Method

3.1 System Model

In RWAN, each node can communicate with a RG (uplink or downlink) or with other nodes (direct link). Since we focus on the resource allocation between uplink and downlink, we do not consider the direct link throughput in this paper although it is noted that the throughput sharing between uplink and direct link is proportional to the ratio of the number of active nodes for the uplink and that for the direct link.

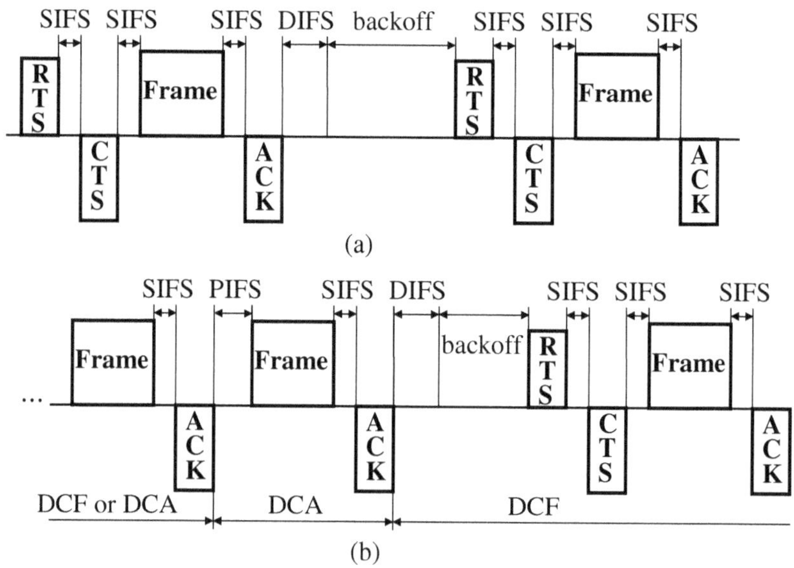

Fig. 1. Timing structure of DCF and DCA. (a) DCF (b) DCA followed by DCF.

Nodes and RG use the DCF mechanism with RTS/CTS handshaking as shown in Fig. 1(a), where the next channel access should wait for DIFS and backoff window time after previous ACK frame. A two-way handshaking technique without RTS/CTS handshaking called basic access mechanism is not considered in this paper although our proposed method can be easily extended to the basic access mechanism.

The number of data bits that are transmitted successfully through the uplink (downlink) is called the *uplink (downlink) throughput*. The system throughput is the sum of the downlink throughput and the uplink throughput. We define the throughput ratio γ such that

$$\gamma = \frac{\text{downlink throughput}}{\text{uplink throughput}}. \tag{1}$$

In DCF, the allocated downlink throughput decreases as the number of nodes increases because the system throughput is shared equally between nodes. Let N be the number of active nodes except RG. Then, the throughput ratio γ for DCF is given as

$$\gamma_{\mathrm{DCF}} = \frac{1}{N}, \tag{2}$$

where the frame sizes of uplink and downlink are the same. When the frame sizes of uplink and downlink are different, the throughput ratio for DCF is given as

$$\gamma_{\text{DCF}} = \frac{P_d}{NP_u}, \tag{3}$$

where P_u and P_d are the frame sizes of uplink and downlink, respectively. The γ_{DCF} in (2) is a special case of (3). Hereafter, the subscripts u and d in the notation denote the uplink and the downlink, respectively.

In FAIR [14], system resource is allocated by the number of active connections and the resulting throughput ratio is given as

$$\gamma_{\text{FAIR}} = \frac{N}{N} = 1, \tag{4}$$

where each active node has a connection with RG.

These methods are not efficient when the traffic load is asymmetric between the uplink and the downlink such as TCP and UDP. Assume that there are N TCP connections between RG and each nodes. Note that the offered load to the downlink and the uplink are $\alpha_d N_d P_d$ and $\alpha_u N_u P_u$, respectively, where α is a frame arrival rate. Then, a *required throughput ratio* Γ based on the offered load should be

$$\Gamma = \frac{\alpha_d N_d P_d}{\alpha_u N_u P_u} = \frac{P_d}{P_u}, \tag{5}$$

because $\alpha_u = \alpha_d$ and $N_u = N_d$ for TCP traffics. For TCP traffics, P_d is larger than P_u and Γ in (5) is larger than one. However, γ in (3) is smaller than one and γ in (4) is equal to one which result in reduced throughput and increased delay for the downlink. Even in the case of symmetric traffic load where Γ is one, the downlink traffics in DCF get less throughput than that of the uplink and this causes the increased delay of the downlink traffics.

3.2 Resource Allocation Algorithm

In order to provide the downlink traffic with an appropriate throughput, we propose a new resource allocation algorithm based on the IEEE 802.11 WLAN standard. The design goal of the proposed algorithm is to keep the resource allocation ratio γ to be equal to Γ. However, the required value Γ is changed by the traffic load conditions and the traffic load is changed dynamically during the system operation. Thus, to achieve the design goal, RG has to estimate the values of γ and Γ dynamically. These estimated values of γ and Γ are denoted by $\hat{\gamma}$ and $\hat{\Gamma}$, respectively. The estimation method is explained in the next subsection.

When $\hat{\gamma}$ becomes less than $\hat{\Gamma}$, there should be some compromise between the uplink and the downlink throughput. In this case, the RG can transmit data frames using point interframe space (PIFS) following the previous ACK frame until it becomes $\hat{\gamma} \geq \hat{\Gamma}$ as shown in Fig. 1(b). During this mechanism called downlink compensation access (DCA), the handshake mechanism of RTS and CTS is not necessary and the RG can transmit multiple data frames while $\hat{\gamma} < \hat{\Gamma}$. Note that the RG accesses the wireless channel without collision during the DCA because it transmits data frame using PIFS which is shorter than DIFS. Also note that the RG accesses the wireless channel with the DCF when $\hat{\gamma} \geq \hat{\Gamma}$. In this way, the system throughput ratio is maintained equal to the value of $\hat{\Gamma}$.

In DCF, each node uses random backoff time to transmit frames. Thus, the frame collision happens when more than two nodes use the same backoff time. This collision degrades the system throughput. On the contrary, in DCA, RG accesses the channel without collision and the throughput increases compared with the DCF. Thus, the system that uses the DCA when $\hat{\gamma} < \hat{\Gamma}$ can enjoy the benefit of increased throughput due to the reduced probability of collision. As the value of $\hat{\Gamma}$ increases, more gain in the system throughput is expected.

3.3 Throughput Estimation Algorithm

To keep up with the dynamic changes of traffic load conditions, $\hat{\Gamma}$ and $\hat{\gamma}$ should be estimated adaptively. We propose an estimation method for $\hat{\Gamma}$ and $\hat{\gamma}$ as follows.

Let ρ_u and ρ_d denote the time-average of the accumulated offered load on the uplink and the downlink, respectively. To allocate the network resource according to the offered load, the value of $\hat{\Gamma}$ should be proportional to the offered load, i.e.,

$$\hat{\Gamma} = \frac{\rho_d}{\rho_u}. \tag{6}$$

Under real situations, ρ_u and ρ_d can be a long-term average value, measured for a predefined duration. For example, the duration can be a daytime, a working hour, or a busy hour, according to the network design criteria. Based on these measurements, the RG may calculate the value of $\hat{\Gamma}$ or network operator may send the value of $\hat{\Gamma}$ to the RG through the control channel. The RG can accurately measure ρ_d since the RG transmits the downlink traffic. On the contrary, each node has to transmit the load status to the RG through the control frames for the RG to estimate ρ_u. To reduce the overhead caused by these control frames, we propose a simple update method for $\hat{\Gamma}$.

Let $\phi_u(t)$ and $\phi_d(t)$ be the length of the data frame that has been successfully transmitted through the uplink and the downlink at time t, respectively. The RG manages an internal memory that records the $\phi_u(t)$ and $\phi_d(t)$ during a sliding time window W. Let $\Phi_u(t)$ and $\Phi_d(t)$ denote the sum of $\phi_u(t)$ and $\phi_d(t)$ during W respectively, i.e., $\Phi_u(t) = \sum_{i=t-W}^{t} \phi_u(i)$ and $\Phi_d(t) = \sum_{i=t-W}^{t} \phi_d(i)$. The required throughput ratio at time t is updated by

$$\hat{\Gamma}(t) = \frac{\Phi_d(t)}{\Phi_u(t)} = \frac{\sum_{i=t-W}^{t} \phi_d(i)}{\sum_{i=t-W}^{t} \phi_u(i)}, \tag{7}$$

where $\Phi_u(t)$ and $\Phi_d(t)$ are the estimated offered load in the uplink and the downlink from $t - W$ to t, respectively.

Although this estimation does not exactly reflect the offered load, it is easy to be implemented in the RG and does not require a feedback information from nodes. Moreover, the proposed method does not require the modification of the standard for nodes, which makes it compatible with the deployed nodes.

Instead of estimating $\hat{\gamma}$, we propose a system parameter $\omega(t)$ that is used for a decision criterion at time t. The initial value of $\omega(t)$ is set to zero, i.e. $\omega(0) = 0$. The value of $\omega(t)$ is updated at every successful frame transmission. Let t_n be the time instant of the nth successful frame transmission. Then $\omega(t)$ is update at every time instants of the successful frame transmission by

$$\omega(t_n) = \omega(t_{n-1}) + \phi_d(t_n) - \hat{\Gamma}(t_{n-1})\phi_u(t_n). \tag{8}$$

Note that $\omega(t)$ is a normalized surplus of the downlink throughput and we use $\omega(t)$ as an estimation for $\hat{\gamma}(t) - \hat{\Gamma}(t)$. Thus, the case of $\omega(t) = 0$ corresponds to $\hat{\gamma}(t) = \hat{\Gamma}(t)$. The case of $\omega(t) < 0$ is the state that requires the DCA. We propose that the RG adopts $\omega(t)$ to decide the access method. When $\omega(t) < 0$ and there is an ACK frame transmitted on the channel, the RG uses the DCA whenever it has pending frames. Otherwise, the RG uses the DCF. Other nodes use the DCF for the channel access.

4 Numerical Results

We evaluate the performance of the proposed method by computer simulations. The IEEE 802.11 DCF and FAIR in [14] are compared with the proposed method, called LOAD, which allocates the system resource based on the offered traffic load.

Table 1. Parameter values

Parameter	Value
$CWmin$	32
$CWmax$	1024
SIFS time	10 μs
PIFS time	30 μs
DIFS time	50 μs
slot time	20 μs
MAC header	272 bits
PHY header	48 bits
Preamble	144 μs
ACK time	304 μs
RTS time	352 μs
CTS time	304 μs
W	30 sec

The parameter values used to obtain numerical results for the simulation runs are summarized in Table 1. The values of these parameters are based on the IEEE 802.11b direct sequence spread spectrum (DSSS) standard [15].

To reflect the fact that the surrounding environmental clutter may be significantly different for each pair of communication nodes with the same distance separation, we use the log-normal shadowing channel model [16]. The path loss PL in dB at distance d is given as

$$PL(d) = PL(d_0) + 10n\log(d/d_0) + X_\sigma, \tag{9}$$

where d_0 is the close-in reference distance, n is the path loss exponent, and X_σ is a zero-mean Gaussian distributed random variable with standard deviation σ. We set n to 2.56 and σ to 7.67 according to the result of measurements for a wideband microcell model [16]. To estimate $PL(d_0)$, we use the Friis free space equation

$$P_r(d_0) = \frac{P_t G_t G_r \lambda^2}{(4\pi)^2 d_0^2 L}, \tag{10}$$

where P_t and P_r are the transmit and receive power, G_t and G_r are the antenna gains of the transmitter and receiver, λ is the carrier wavelength, and L is the system loss factor which is set to 1 in our simulation. Most of the simulation parameters are drawn from the data sheet of Cisco 350 client adapter. The received power is

$$P_r(d) = P_t - PL(d). \tag{11}$$

The minimum received power level for the carrier sensing is set to -95 dBm, which is the noise power level. The long-term signal-to-noise ratio (SNR) is

$$SNR_L = P_t - PL(d) - n + PG, \tag{12}$$

where n is the noise power set to -95 dBm and PG is the spread spectrum processing gain given by

$$PG = 10\log_{10}\frac{C}{S}, \tag{13}$$

where C is the chip rate and S is the symbol rate. Since each symbol is chipped with an 11-chip pseudonoise code sequence in the IEEE 802.11 standard, PG is 10.4 dB. The received SNR is varied by the Ricean fading gain δ. Under this model, the SNR of the received signal is

$$SNR = 20\log_{10}\delta + SNR_L. \tag{14}$$

For the data rate in the physical layer for each communication link, we assume that the system adapts the data rate by properly choosing one from a set of modulation scheme according to the channel condition. The set of modulation schemes used in our simulation studies are BPSK, QPSK, 16QAM, 64QAM, and 256QAM. For simplicity, we ignore other common physical layer components such as error correction coding. With 1 MHz symbol rate and the above modulation schemes, the achieved data rates are 1, 2, 4, 6, and 8 Mbps, respectively.

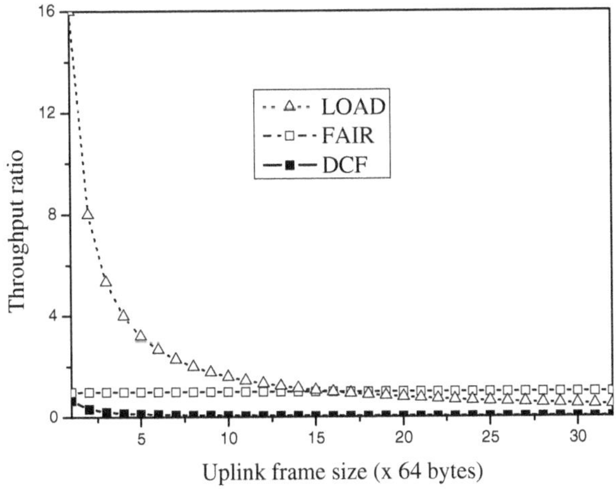

Fig. 2. Throughput ratio versus uplink frame size

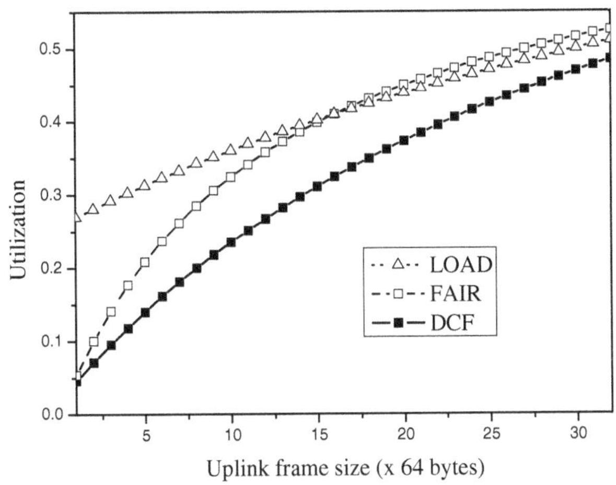

Fig. 3. System utilization versus uplink frame size

We assume that all nodes except the RG are uniformly distributed in the circle area with diameter 150 meters. The RG is located at the center of the area. In each nodes, frames arrive with the exponential distribution where the arrival rate is set to 2.5 frames/sec and the destination addresses of the frames are the RG. In the RG, there are N connections, each for one node, and frames are generated for each connections with the same exponential distribution as those in each nodes. The size of the downlink frame is 1024 bytes and $N = 25$.

The throughput ratio of the proposed method LOAD is compared with DCF and FAIR in Fig. 2. The simulation results match with the theoretic throughput ratios of DCF, FAIR, and LOAD given by (3), (4), and (5), respectively. In TCP traffics, the uplink frame size is smaller than the downlink frame size and LOAD provides larger throughput to the downlink traffics.

Fig. 3 shows the system utilization for LOAD, FAIR, and DCF. In this figure, the utilization is the normalized time that is used for the successful frame transmission. The overall utilization increases as the uplink frame size increases. This increase of the utilization comes from the reduced overhead that is used for each frame transmission. In other words, for the same size of the overhead, the size of the data frame transmission increases as the uplink frame size increases. When the uplink frame size is small, the utilization of LOAD is larger than those of other methods. This is because LOAD uses DCA more frequently compared with other methods and DCA reduces the probability of frame collisions. Thus, LOAD is an efficient method for an asymmetric traffic load such as TCP or UDP which has small uplink frame size.

5 Conclusion

We have proposed an easy implementation method to control the throughput ratio of uplink and downlink and to enhance the system utilization of the IEEE 802.11 DCF. The proposed method can be implemented without the modification of the IEEE 802.11 standard for nodes that are widely deployed. The throughput sharing between the uplink and the downlink can be controlled by the network operator or by the offered traffic load.

The efficiency of the proposed system has been demonstrated by computer simulation. The results show that the proposed method enhances the system utilization used for the successful data frame transmission for asymmetric traffic load. The proposed method distributes the throughput between the uplink and the downlink according to the offered load. This, in turn, drastically reduces the blocking probability of multimedia data frames in the proposed systems compared with that in the IEEE 802.11 DCF where most of bandwidth is occupied by the uplink. Thus, the proposed system can be a good candidate for relayed wireless access networks, which aim for Internet services.

References

1. ANSI/IEEE Std 802.11: 1999(E): Wireless LAN Medium Access Control (MAC) and Physical Layer (PHY) Specifications. (1999)
2. Zhao, D., Todd, T.D.: Real-time traffic support in relayed wireless access networks using IEEE 802.11. IEEE Trans. Wireless Commun. (2004) 32–39
3. Wei, H.Y., Gitlin, R.D.: Two-hop-relay architecture for next-generation WWAN/WLAN integration. IEEE Trans. Wireless Commun. (2004) 24–30
4. Fitzek, F.H.P., Angelini, D., Mazzini, G., Zorzi, M.: Design and performance of an enhanced IEEE 802.11 MAC protocol for multihop coverage extension. IEEE Trans. Wireless Commun. (2003) 30–39
5. Honkasalo, H., Pehkonen, K., Niemi, M.T., Leino, A.T.: WCDMA and WLAN for 3G and beyond. IEEE Wireless Commun. Mag. (2002) 14–18

6. Doufexi, A., Tameh, E., Nix, A., Armour, S.: Hotspot wireless LAN to enhance the performance of 3G and beyond cellular networks. IEEE Commun. Mag. (2003) 58–65
7. Kishore, S., Greenstein, L.J., Poor, H.V., Schwartz, S.C.: Uplink user capacity in a CDMA macrocell with a hotspot microcell: Exact and approximate analyses. IEEE Trans. Wireless Commun. **2** (2003) 364–374
8. Deng, D.J., Chang, R.S.: A priority scheme for IEEE 802.11 DCF access method. IEICE Trans. Commu. **E82-B** (1999) 96–102
9. Barry, M., Campbell, A.T., Veres, A.: Distributed control algorithms for service differentiation in wireless packet networks. In: Proc. IEEE Infocom'01, Anchorage, AK, USA (2001)
10. Aad, I., Castelluccia, C.: Differentiation mechanisms for IEEE 802.11. In: Proc. IEEE Infocom'01, Anchorage, AK, USA (2001)
11. Kim, H., Hou, J.C.: Improving protocol capacity for UDP/TCP traffic with model-based frame scheduling in IEEE 802.11-operated WLANs. IEEE J. Select. Areas Commun. **22** (2004) 1987–2003
12. Grilo, A., Nunes, M.: Performance evaluation of IEEE 802.11e. In: Proc. IEEE PIMRC'02, Lisboa, Portugal (2002)
13. Pilosof, S., Ramjee, R., Raz, D., Shavitt, Y., Sinha, P.: Understanding TCP fairness over wireless LAN. In: Proc. IEEE Infocom'03, San Francisco, CA, USA (2003)
14. Kim, S.W., Kim, B., Fang, Y.: Downlink and uplink resource allocation in IEEE 802.11 wireless LANs. IEEE Trans. Veh. Technol. **54** (2005) 320–327
15. IEEE Std 802.11b-1999: Wireless LAN Medium Access Control (MAC) and Physical Layer (PHY) Specifications: Higher-Speed Physical Layer Extension in the 2.4 GHz Band. (1999)
16. T. S. Rappaport: Wireless communications: principles and practices. Prentice Hall (1996)

An Adaptive Cross Layer Unequal Protection Method for Video Transmission over Wireless Communication Channels*

Jinbo Qiu[1], Guangxi Zhu[1], and Tao Jiang[2]

[1] Department of Electronics and Information Engineering,
Huazhong University of Science and Technology,
Wuhan, China 430074
jbqiu@263.net, gxzhu@mail.hust.edu.cn

[2] Electronic and Computer Engineering, School of Engineering and Design,
Brunel University,
Uxbridge, UB8 3PH, U.K.
Unique_jt@yahoo.co.uk

Abstract. In this paper, a new scheme, called Adaptive Cross Layer Unequal Protection (ACLUEP), has been proposed for video transmission over wireless channels. The proposed scheme performs joint optimization across application layer, link layer and physical layer to provide unequal protection ability for video bit-streams with different priority levels. Analysis and simulation results show an extraordinary improvement in Peak Signal-to-Noise Ratio (PSNR) of the proposed method over a variety of channel conditions.

1 Introduction

With increasing demands for supporting real-time multimedia services over wireless communication channels in the next generation of wireless networks, the traditional layered approaches come with static and layer independent protocol stacks, which have not adapted to cope with the addition challenges presented by mobile radio channel, for example time-varying channel conditions. So the layered strategy suffers from performance degradation and does not always result in an optimal overall performance in the wireless environment. Therefore a protocol architecture that considers cross layer interaction is required to optimize the operation of different layers. A cross layer scheme can provide higher spectral and power efficiency and satisfy Quality of Service (QoS) requirements for different applications.

High quality video delivery over wireless communication channels is very challenging. Each network layer addressed these challenges by providing its own optimized adaptation and protection mechanisms, respectively. Joint Source and Channel Coding (JSCC), which regards the channel as a "black box", performs joint rate control for source coding and channel coding at the application layer in the

* This work is supported by the National Science Foundation of China under Grant No. 60496315.

L.T. Yang et al. (Eds.): ICESS 2005, LNCS 3820, pp. 452 – 461, 2005.

presence of a time-varying wireless channel [1]. In order to obtain maximum spectral efficiency and to satisfy stringent QoS demand, a cross layer design combined adaptive modulation and coding at the physical layer with a truncated Automatic Repeat reQuest (ARQ) protocol at the data link layer has been proposed in [2]. A cross layer protection scheme has also been proposed, which combines Media Access Control (MAC) retransmission strategy, application-layer forward error correction, and bandwidth-adaptive compression using scalable coding and adaptive packetization strategies, to provide robust and efficient transmission of video over WLANs [3]. A cross layer ARQ method has been proposed, which combined the application level information about the perceptual and temporal importance of each packet drives packet selection at each retransmission opportunity, and provide unequal protection for packets having different priority [4].

In this paper, a new cross-layer scheme, named Adaptive Cross Layer Unequal Protection (ACLUEP), has been proposed to provide high quality video transmission over wireless communication channels. ACLUEP combines the physical layer, the link layer and the application layer with a joint optimization to achieve the best video transmission quality. The analysis and simulations have also proven that it can offer good performance in terms of PSNR for adaptive OFDM systems.

The rest of this paper is organized as follows. In Section II, we introduce the system model, and analyze the distortion model for Fine Granular Scalability (FGS) video coding and the transmission performance. In Section III, the procedure of new cross layer scheme, namely ACLUEP, is proposed and analyzed. In Section IV, the performance of ACLUEP is studied through computer simulations, followed by the conclusions in Section V.

2 System Model and ACLUEP Scheme

Due to the heterogeneity of radio access network, the traditional layered network protocol cannot satisfy the QoS requirements of video transmission over time-varying wireless channels. Here we develop an adaptive cross layer unequal protection method for video transmission. The system model is shown in Fig. 1.

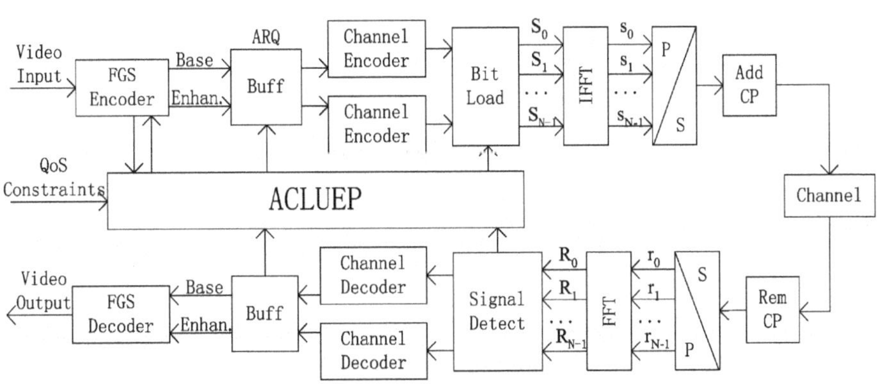

Fig. 1. System Model

The FGS video encoder at the application layer generates scalable bit-streams to suit the variation of the wireless channel. It does making use of the different combinations of the bit-rate for the base layer and the enhancement layer and so provide different error resilient abilities. At the link layer, a selective repeat ARQ protocol is implemented. With retransmission of the error packet, the packet loss rate for the application layer will be decreased at a cost in throughput and delay. Adaptive OFDM (AOFDM) chooses an appropriate modulation mode for each sub-carrier at the physical layer and can provide higher spectrum efficiency. The flexibility of AOFDM can satisfy various performances by different constraints.

It is clear that the overall quality of the transmitted video depends on the parameters of each layer. It is very important to improve the quality by jointly optimizing the parameters across these layers. In this paper, we propose a new cross layer design scheme, which named ACLUEP, to improve the quality of video transmission. With the variation of the wireless channel, an optimized parameter combination at different layers can be chosen by ACLUEP to provide unequal protection for different parts of FGS video stream having different priority.

At first, ACLUEP collects the information for each layer, including the channel state information, the allocation of sub-carriers in the AOFDM system, the packet loss rate at the link layer, the priority for different video streams, etc. Then, ACLUEP choose the optimal parameter combination for each layer to maximize the estimated quality for decoded video according to the FGS Rate Distortion (R-D) model and the QoS constraints. These parameters include the allocation of sub-carrier at the physical layer in AOFDM system, the retransmission strategy for different packets with different priority level at the link layer and the bit-rate allocation for the base layer and the enhancement layer at the application level.

2.1 Analysis of R-D Model for FGS

FGS is a part of MPEG-4 video coding standard, and it has the structure shown in Fig.2.

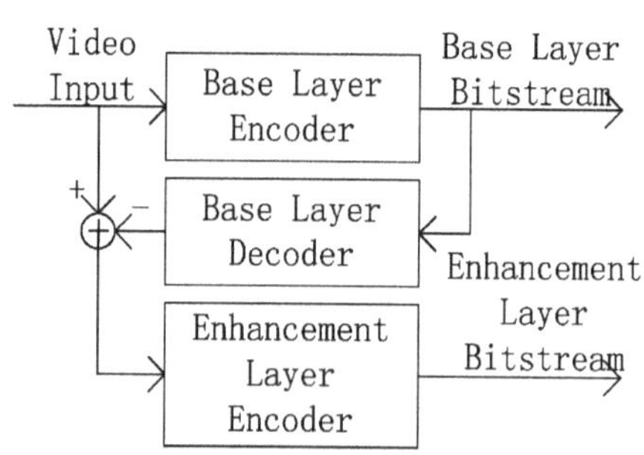

Fig. 2. Structure of FGS

Base layer encoder of FGS is the same as that performed by a traditional motion compensated video encoder. It compresses the input video signal into the base layer bit-stream, which has a bit-rate is close to the minimum channel capacity. The base layer bit-stream contains the most important and lower quality video information. The enhancement layer encoder compresses the difference between the original video and the reconstructed video at the base layer to obtain an embedded enhancement layer bit-stream, which can be truncated at arbitrary position.

The scalability of the enhancement layer bit-stream can be adjusted to suit the variation of the wireless channel. The refinement of the enhancement layer bit-stream depends on the decoded base layer video, which makes the base layer bitstream a higher priority than the enhancement layer bit-stream.

FGS is especially suitable for video transmission over wireless channels. Firstly, FGS provide an easy mechanism for adaptation to bandwidth variations. Secondly, FGS can improve the resilience to errors because the enhancement layer bitstream does not depend on last frame that has been decoded. The loss of enhancement packets does not give noise to error propagation in the next frame. Lastly, the layered bit-stream has different priority level, so we can utilize this characteristic to employ unequal protection during video transmission.

There is no motion estimation and compensation in the enhancement layer encoder, so we can make use of a linear model to describe the relationship between the quality of reconstructed video and the bit-rate

$$Q = \theta(R - R_b) + Q_b = \theta R_e + Q_b \tag{1}$$

Where Q is the total PSNR, Q_b is the PSNR of base layer, R is the total bit-rate, R_b is the base layer bit-rate, R_e is the enhancement layer bit-rate and θ is the rate distortion parameter that depends upon the characteristics of the video sequence. Fig.3 shows that the R-D line model is very accurate for various video sequences.

The rate distortion analysis of base layer can be found in [1]. One single packet loss within the enhancement layer can render the remainder packets associated with that

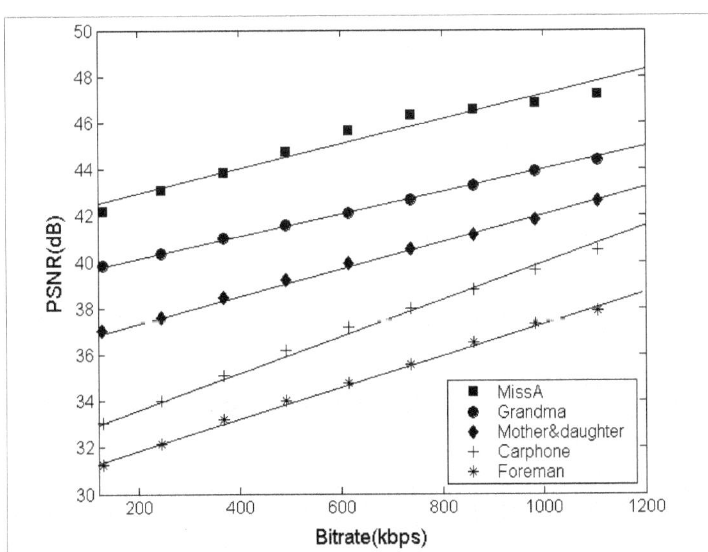

Fig. 3. Rate-Distortion for FGS video encoder

frame useless. Denoting the packet length for the enhancement layer bit-stream L, the number of packets N, and the frame rate of the video sequence f, the bit-rate of the enhancement layer at the encoder is $R_e = L{\cdot}N{\cdot}F$. The effective bit-rate $R_e^{'}$ of the enhancement layer at the decoder can be defined as following

$$R_e^{'} = [\sum_{n=1}^{N-1} n(1-p_e)^n p_e + N(1-p_e)^N] \cdot L \cdot f \quad (2)$$

where p_e denotes the packet loss rate. Combined (1), (2), and the rate distortion model of the base layer, we can estimate the quality of FGS video coding after transmission.

2.2 Analysis of Re-transmission at the Link Layer

At the link layer, a truncated ARQ is implemented to maintain the delay constraint of video transmission. A packet will be dropped when it is received incorrectly with a maximum number of N_{max} retransmissions. Suppose that the packet loss rate is p, the average number of transmissions per packet can be defined

$$\begin{aligned}\overline{N}(p, N_{\max}) &= [(1-p) + 2p(1-p) + \cdots \\ &\quad + (N_{\max}+1)p^{N_{\max}}(1-p)] + (N_{\max}+1)p^{N_{\max}+1} \\ &= 1 + p + p^2 + \cdots + p^{N_{\max}} = \frac{1-p^{N_{\max}+1}}{1-p}\end{aligned} \quad (3)$$

According to the retransmission rule, each packet is equivalently transmitted $\overline{N}(p, N_{\max})$ times. Hence the overall average bit-rate for the application layer can be considered as the function $R / \overline{N}(p, N_{\max})$, supposing that the throughput of physical layer is R.

2.3 Performance of AOFDM

Each OFDM sub-carrier signal has a different channel state owing to the presence of frequency selective fading. The AOFDM system can choose an appropriate modulation and transmit power for each sub-carrier in order to improve the overall performance or capacity of the system [5]. AOFDM can be classed into one of two types: one is known as the Constant Throughput AOFDM system (CT-AOFDM), and the other is known as the Variable Throughput AOFDM system (VT-AOFDM). The target of CT-AOFDM is to maintain a minimum BER or transmit power with a limited throughput. But the target of VT-AOFDM is to get maximum spectrum efficiency with a certain average transmit power or BER constraint. In order to keep the system low complexity, the modulation is not varied on a sub-carrier by sub-carrier basis, but instead the total OFDM bandwidth is split into blocks of adjacent sub-carriers, referred to as sub-bands, and the same modulation mode is employed for all sub-carriers in the same sub-band.

In the proposed scheme, we choose the CT-AOFDM at the physical layer. Denote n the subcarrier index, s=1~5 represents the modulation index "no transmission", BPSK, 4QAM, 16QAM and 64QAM respectively, $e_{n,s}$ the number of bit errors and $b_{n,s}$ the number of bits can be transmitted by one symbol when s is chosen for subcarrier n. The index s of each sub-carrier is initialized to the lowest order. So the set of cost values $c_{n,s}$ can be calculated for each sub-carrier according to

$$c_{n,s} = \frac{e_{n,s+1} - e_{n,s}}{b_{n,s+1} - b_{n,s}} \tag{4}$$

Then CT-AOFDM searches for the sub-carrier with the lowest $c_{n,s}$, and increases its index from s to $s+1$ repeatedly until the total number of bits in the OFDM symbol reaches the target number of bits. We calculate current Bit Error Ratio (BER) according to [6]

$$BER = 0.2\exp(-g\gamma) \tag{5}$$

where γ is channel Signal to Noise Ratio (SNR), and g=6/(5M-4) for BPSK, but for M-QAM g=1.5/(M-1).

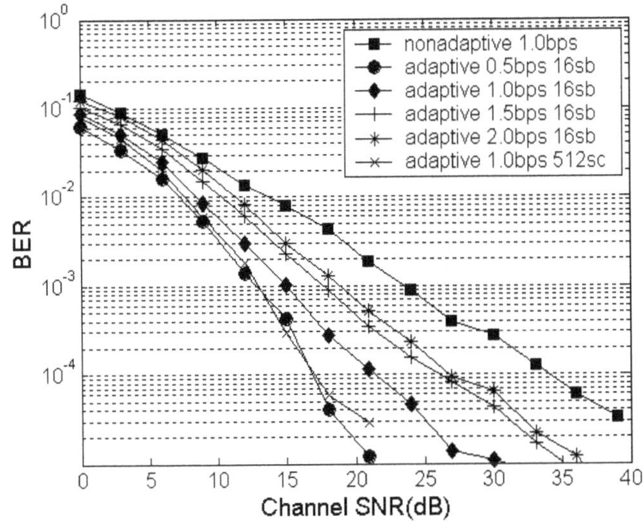

Fig. 4. Performance comparison of CT-AOFDM and non-adaptive OFDM

We simulate CT-AOFDM under conditions of various average channel SNR values. The simulation results are shown in Fig.4. It can be seen that the sub-carrier based AOFDM has a gain of 5~10 dB compared with the non-adaptive OFDM. The performance penalty of sub-band based AOFDM is related to the coherence bandwidth. If the bandwidth of a sub-band is less than the coherence bandwidth, the performance of subband based AOFDM is similar to sub-carrier based AOFDM.

3 ACLUEP Procedures

The notation used at the various layers is summarized in Table 1.

Table 1. Parameters at different layers

Layer	Parameters	Symbol
PHY	Throughput	R
PHY	Packet loss rate	p
LNK	Max retrans. number for base layer	N_{maxb}
LNK	Max retrans. number for enhan. layer	N_{maxe}
LNK	Avg. retrans. number for base layer	$\overline{N}_b$
LNK	Avg. retrans. number for enhan. layer	$\overline{N}_e$
APP	Packet loss rate for base layer	p_b
APP	Packet loss rate for enhan. layer	p_e
APP	Bitrate for base layer	R_b
APP	Bitrate for enhan. layer	R_e

The steps for implementing the ACLUEP method are as following

- Step 1) Based on current channel state and throughput constraint R at the physical layer, AOFDM choose appropriate modulation mode for each sub-band via (4), and estimate the corresponding packet lost rate p;
- Step 2) For the estimated p and current N_{maxb}, N_{maxe} calculate p_b, p_e, and $p_b = p^{N_{\max b}+1}$, $p_e = p^{N_{\max e}+1}$;
- Step 3) Calculate $\overline{N}_b$ and $\overline{N}_e$ via (3);
- Step 4) For the calculated p_b, p_e, determine an optimized R_b and R_e which maximize (1) to get a best video quality and satisfy the constraint $R \geq R_b \cdot \overline{N}_b + R_e \cdot \overline{N}_e$;
- Step 5) For the R_b and R_e obtained in step 4), FGS video encoder generates the bit-stream to be transmitted;

- Step 6) Based on current occupancy of the link layer buffer, adjust the N_{maxb} and N_{maxe} to avoid buffer overflow or underflow.

The analysis performed in the previous section let it choosing appropriate values for the various parameters.

4 Simulations and Results

The overall delay for end-to-end video transmission has three component parts: codec delay, packetization delay and transmission delay. The former two parts are fixed and the delay jitter is induced by transmission. As an example, consider 3GPP with an MPEG-4 video payload. In this case, the quality of service requires an end-to-end delay of between 150 and 400ms. If the average round trip delay is 100 ms, the maximum number of retransmissions should be at most 4. Considering the fixed delay by codec and packetization we limit the number of retransmissions to 2. Consequently ACLUEP determines an appropriate number of retransmission in the range from 0 to 2. To simplify the implementation, we use sub-band based CT-AOFDM. In this case, the whole available bandwidth is split to 16 sub-bands, and each subband has 32 sub-carriers. The video sequence is “carphone”. Perfect channel estimation is assumed. The channel is modeled by its time-variant impulse response and additive white Gaussian noise (AWGN). The impulse response for the experiments was generated on the basis of the symbol-spaced impulse response shown in Fig.5 by fading each of the impulses obeying a Rayleigh distribution of a normalized maximal Doppler frequency of $f_d'=1.235 \cdot 10^{-5}$, where the normalization time duration was the length of the OFDM symbol.

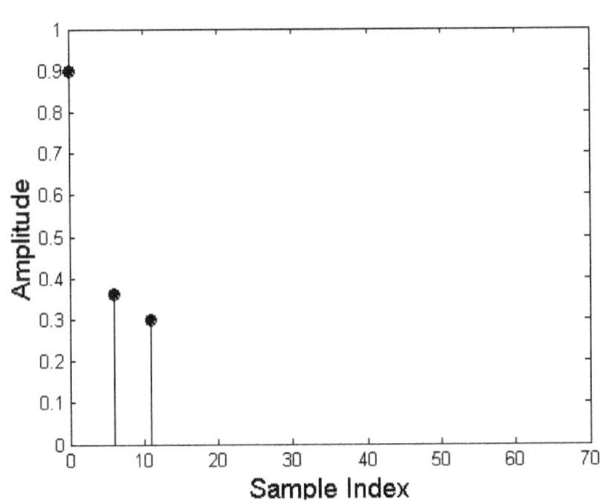

Fig. 5. Unfaded symbol spaced impulse response

We implemented the proposed ACLUEP method and compare it to four other transmission methods. These methods are summarized in Table 2.

Table 2. Transmission methods list

	Physical Layer	Link layer	Application layer
Method 1	Fixed OFDM	No ARQ	CBR, No FGS
Method 2	CT-AOFDM	No ARQ	CBR, No FGS
Method 3	CT-AOFDM	No ARQ	CBR, FGS
Method 4	CT-AOFDM	$N_{maxb}=N_{maxe}=1$	VBR, FGS
ACLUEP	CT-AOFDM Adaptive bit load	$N_{maxb}=0, 1, 2$ $N_{maxe}=0, 1$	VBR, FGS

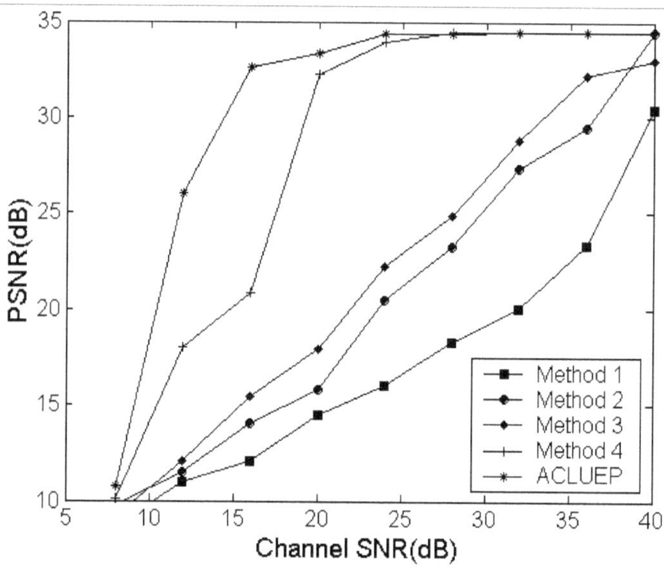

Fig. 6. PSNR versus Channel SNR

Fig.6 shows the average decoded PSNR of the video sequence at the receiver under various channel SNR. Method 1 has no adaptation and its PSNR performance is the worst. Method 2 employs CT-AOFDM at the physical layer. CTAOFDM tracks the variation of the channel and improves the PSNR by 1~7 dB over that of method 2. Method 3 uses FGS video at the application layer. FGS increase the error resilience ability of the video bit-stream at the cost of compress efficiency. Under most of the channel conditions, method 3 is about 1 dB better than method 2. However, for high SNR values, the PSNR performance of method 3 is degraded rightly owing to the compression efficiency penalty. Method 4 employs retransmission at the link layer, which sacrifices the throughput and delay performance to decrease the packet loss rate. Method 4 improves the PSNR for 5~10 dB over that of method 3. Finally, it can be seen from the simulation results that the proposed ACLUEP method is the best in terms of PSNR performance. At low SNR values, the ACLUEP method is 7~10 dB better than method 4. Moreover, ACLUEP can adjust retransmission strategy and satisfy the delay constraint for video transmission. This is a significantly improvement for video transmission over wireless channels.

As we assume perfect channel estimation in simulations. If the assumption is not true, system stability may be affected by the delay and errors of estimation of the channel status in practical systems. Due to the delay and errors of channel status information, AOFDM at the physical layer can not chose the most appropriate modulation and coding mode and result in some degradation of spectrum efficiency. But this degradation will not affect the adaptation at the application and link layer. The ACLUEP method still works well than traditional layered approaches.

5 Conclusions

In this paper, an adaptive cross layer unequal protection method (ACLUEP) is proposed. This method handles the variation of the wireless channel by selecting optimized parameters combination at various layers and provides unequal protection for different parts of FGS video stream having different priority levels. Experimental results show a marked improvement in PSNR performance of the proposed ACLUEP method over various other fixed and adapting schemes over a range of channel SNRs.

Acknowledgment

The authors are grateful to Dr. Laurence T. Yang, Dr. Dapeng Oliver Wu and Dr. I.J. Wassell, for their valuable comments and suggestions, which helped to improve the presentation of the paper.

References

1. Z. He, J. Cai, and C. Chen, "Joint source channel rate-distortion analysis for adaptive mode selection and rate control in wireless video coding," IEEE Transactions Circuits and Systems for Video Technology, vol. 12, pp. 511–523, June 2002.
2. Q. Liu, S. Zhou, and G. B. Giannakis, "Cross-layer combining of adaptive modulation and coding with truncated arq over wireless links," IEEE Transactions on Wireless Communications, vol. 3, pp. 1746–1755, sept. 2004.
3. M. van der Schaar, S. Krishnamachari, S. Choi, and X. Xu, "Adaptive cross-layer protection strategies for robust scalable video transmission over 802.11 wlans," IEEE Journal on Selected Areas in Communication, vol. 21, pp. 1752–1763, Dec. 2003.
4. P.Bucciol, G. Davini, E. Masala, E. Filippi, and J. D. Martin, "Cross-layer perceptual arq for h.264 video streaming over 802.11 wireless networks," in Proceeding of the IEEE GLOBECOM'04, pp. 3027–3031, Nov. 2004.
5. T. Keller and L. Hanzo, "Adaptive multicarrier modulation: A convenient framework for time-frequency processing in wireless communications," Proceedings of the IEEE, vol. 88, pp. 611–642, May 2000.
6. S. Zhou and G. B. Giannakis, "Adaptive modulation for multiantenna transmissions with channel mean feedback," IEEE Transactions on Wireless Communications, vol. 3, pp. 1626–1636, Sept. 2004.

Power-Efficient Packet Scheduling Method for IEEE 802.15.3 WPAN*

Sung Won Kim[1] and Byung-Seo Kim[2]

[1] School of Electrical Engineering and Computer Science, Yeungnam University, Gyeongsangbuk-do, 712-749, Korea
ksw@ieee.org

[2] Motorola Inc., 1301 Algonquin Rd. Schaumburg, IL, 60196 USA
Byungseo.Kim@motorola.com

Abstract. Power efficiency is the key issue for mobile devices, which mainly rely on limited battery power. The IEEE 802.15.3 wireless personal area network (WPAN) standard adopts a time division multiple access (TDMA) protocol controlled by a central device to support isochronous traffics. In the TDMA-based wireless packet networks, the packet scheduling algorithm plays a key role in power efficiency. However, the standard suffers from long access delay and association delay which increase the power consumption. In this paper, we propose a packet scheduling method to improve the power efficiency. Performance evaluations are carried out through simulations and significant performance enhancements are observed. Furthermore, the performance of the proposed scheme remains stable regardless of the variable system parameters such as the number of devices and superframe size.

1 Introduction

The IEEE 802.15.3 task group (TG) has been chartered to create a high-rate WPAN (HR-WPAN) standard and has published a final standard [1]. The IEEE 802.15.3 provides short range wireless connectivities among consumer electronics and portable devices. HR-WPAN adopts a time division multiple access (TDMA)-based medium access control (MAC) protocol. In HR-WPAN, a pair of devices (DEVs) can communicate through peer-to-peer connectivity without contention during an allocated time slot called *channel time*. The data packet can be transmitted during the channel time and the allocation of channel time for each DEVs is controlled by a scheduler in a piconet coordinator (PNC). Thus, the packet scheduling algorithm in the IEEE 802.15.3 standard is expected to play an essential role in the system performance. However, the standard does not define how to assign the channel time and leaves this for vendors.

Some efforts to define the packet scheduling method for the HR-WPAN have been made since the standard is published. Performance enhancement achieved by informing queue-status to a PNC using MAC header of every packet is proposed in [2]. This scheme adopts a flexible superframe size to handle variable bit

* This research was supported by the Yeungnam University research grants in 2005.

L.T. Yang et al. (Eds.): ICESS 2005, LNCS 3820, pp. 462–472, 2005.

rate (VBR) traffics. The piggybacked information may be useful when there is a burst transmission. However, the channel time allocation algorithm for different traffic types is not considered. An algorithm proposed in [3] focuses on utilizing wasted or remained channel times. The authors in [4] propose a channel time allocation scheme for a specific application, MPEG 4 traffic. Since packets generated from an MPEG 4 encoder are classified into three types and are arranged by a periodic pattern, a central device can allocate channel time for transmissions of MPEG 4 packets according to the packet pattern. A packet transmission method without a preamble is introduced in [5] to reduce the preamble overhead in a high transmission rate. A scheduling method based on the queueing model is proposed in [6] to reduce the average waiting time.

Power management is an important issue for the battery-powered portable DEVs and its objective is to assist the DEVs to sleep and reduce the wakeup time as much as possible. There has been several work on the MAC design for power management in wireless system. However, most of them are based on the MAC of IEEE 802.11 WLAN [7]–[9] or IEEE 802.15.4 low-rate WPAN [10][11]. There is little work to address the power efficiency in HR-WPAN [12][13]. In [12], a power management method for intra-superframe is proposed for HR-WPAN. The proposed algorithm finds the suboptimal order to reduce the wakeup time by using graph theory. However, the inter-superframe power management problem and the VBR traffics are not considered in [12]. The authors in [13] utilize the network topology and UWB physical layer information to minimize the energy consumption per bit. This method increases the overhead since it requires power information, position information, and relay DEVs for its operation.

As far as we know, there is no work to minimize the power consumption in HR-WPAN combined with the packet scheduling method supporting constant bit rate (CBR) and VBR traffics. In this paper, we propose a packet scheduling method for HR-WPAN to efficiently reduce the power consumption. The proposed scheduling concepts apply to wireless packet systems in general. In the next section, MAC protocol in the IEEE 802.15.3 standard is briefly described. The proposed scheduling method for HR-WPAN is introduced in Section 3. Section 4 describes the simulation environment and evaluates the simulation results. Finally, the paper is concluded in Section 5.

2 IEEE 802.15.3 (HIGH-RATE WPAN)

2.1 MAC Protocol

In the HR-WPAN standard specifications, DEVs are communicating on a centralized and connection-oriented ad-hoc network called piconet. One of the participating DEVs must be designated as a piconet coordinator (PNC). The PNC provides basic timing information for the operation of the piconet and manages the QoS for delay sensitive applications.

The MAC layer in the IEEE 802.15.3 standard employs a time-slotted superframe structure. Fig. 1 illustrates the superframe structure in the HR-WPAN standard. The superframe consists of three major parts: a beacon, an optional

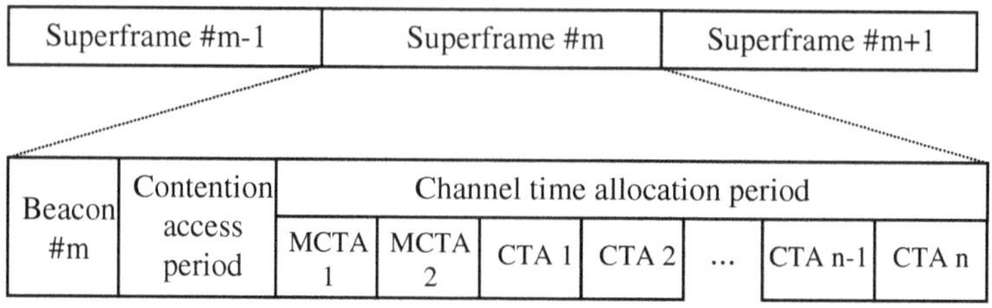

Fig. 1. Superframe structure of IEEE 802.15.3

contention access period (CAP) and a channel time allocation period (CTAP). The beacon packet is transmitted by the PNC at the beginning of each superframe. It allows all DEVs in a piconet to know about the specific information for controlling a piconet. The CAP is used for transmissions of short and non-QoS data packets and command/response packets. The remained period in the superframe is the CTAP. The CTAP is composed of management channel time allocation (MCTA) and channel time allocation (CTA) periods. The MCTA is used for sending command packets like CAP using the slotted ALOHA mechanism.

When a DEV needs a CTA on a regular basis, it sends a *channel time request* (CTRq) command to the PNC during the CAP or MCTA. Thus the PNC decides the durations of the superframe, CAP, and CTAP based on the DEVs requests. During a CTA period, a DEV can transmit several packets to a target DEV without collision. Each packet transmission may be followed by an acknowledgement (ACK) packet. The specification for the MAC protocol defines three acknowledgement types: no-acknowledgement (No-ACK), immediate-acknowledgement (Imm-ACK), and delayed-acknowledgement (Dly-ACK). For Imm-ACK, the receiver issues an ACK packet to the transmitter on every received packet. No-ACK means no ACK packet is issued. In Dly-ACK, which is a tradeoff between these two methods, the receiver issues an ACK packet for multiple received packets.

2.2 Association Process

In order to participate in a piconet, a DEV needs to join the piconet using the association process. Associating with the piconet provides the DEV with a unique identifier, the DEVID, for that piconet. When a DEV wants to leave the piconet or if the PNC wants to remove a DEV from the piconet, the disassociation process is used.

Before a DEV has completed the association process, all frames sent to the PNC by the DEV shall be exchanged either in the CAP of the superframe or in an association MCTA. An unassociated DEV initiates the association process by sending an Association Request command to the PNC. When the PNC receives an Association Request command, it shall send an Association Response command, indicating that the DEV has been associated. The PNC starts the association timeout period (ATP) timer once it has sent the Association Response command for the new DEV. The associating DEV needs to send the

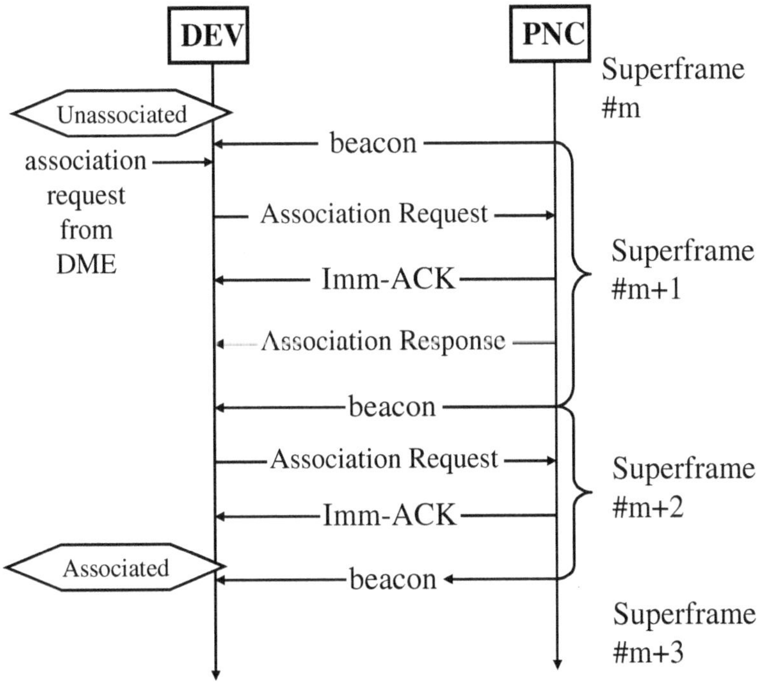

Fig. 2. An example of association delay

second Association Request command before the ATP timer expires. If the PNC receives the second association request command after the ATP timer expires, the PNC shall send the Disassociation Request command to the DEV requesting association to indicate that it has failed the association process. Fig. 2 illustrates the message flow for a successful association process. The association process is initiated by a device management entity (DME). Note that the completion of the association process may be delayed for more than two superframes when the CAP or the MCTA is not available at appropriate time instant in superframes $m+1$ and $m+2$.

2.3 Power Management

An important goal of the 802.15.3 standard is to enable long operation time for battery-powered DEVs. The best method for extending the battery life is to enable DEVs to turn off completely or reduce power for long periods of time. This standard provides three techniques to enable DEVs to turn off for one or more superframes: device synchronized power save (DSPS) mode, piconet-synchronized power save (PSPS) mode, and asynchronous power save (APS) mode. In any given power management mode, a DEV may be in one of two power states, either AWAKE or SLEEP states. AWAKE state is defined as the state of the DEV where it is either transmitting or receiving. SLEEP state is defined as the state in which the DEV is neither transmitting nor receiving.

PSPS mode allows DEVs to sleep at intervals defined by the PNC. A DEV in PSPS mode shall listen to all system wake beacon, as announced by PNC and is required to be in the AWAKE state during system wake superframes. DSPS mode is designed to enable groups of DEVs to sleep for multiple superframes. DEVs synchronize their sleep patterns by joining a DSPS set which specifies the interval between wake periods for the DEVs and the next time the DEVs will be awake.

The problem of PSPS and DSPS modes is that they are not efficient for multimedia traffics which have non-periodic inter-arrival time. APS mode is appropriate for these non-periodic traffics. The only responsibility of a DEV in APS mode is to communicate with the PNC before the end of its ATP in order to preserve its membership in the piconet. However, when the required sleep time is much longer than ATP, this method increases the overhead to maintain the membership and results in increased power consumption. Besides power consumption, the use of power management in the standard makes it difficult for the PNC to determine the interval for sleep period because of burst traffic arrivals.

3 Proposed Packet Scheduling Method

3.1 Motivation

Due to the TDMA property of IEEE 802.15.3 MAC, one of the key issues for power consumption is to schedule the order of the multiple CTAs among multiple DEVs to minimize the total wakeup times. The time duration from the packet arrival at the MAC layer to the transmission of the packet is called *access delay*. Fig. 3 shows an example of access delay caused by the lack of information about the actual packet arrival instant. Since the information given by a CTRq command does not inform the optimal time instant of a CTA, the packet arrival and

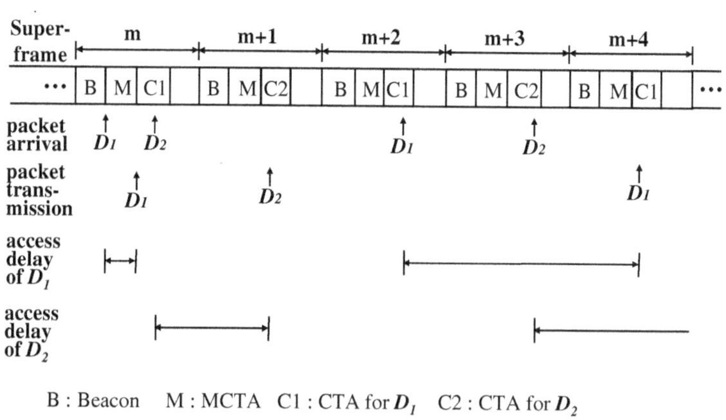

Fig. 3. An example of access delay

the CTA are not synchronized. The information delivered by a CTRq command is insufficient for the PNC to decide the duration and the location of a CTA for the requesting DEV. Thus, the average access delay increases as the packet inter-arrival time increases and may maintain until the end of the flow. Furthermore, it can be longer in heavy load cases since several CTAs overlap. Nevertheless, the packet scheduling method that considers the power consumption is not proposed in the standard and previous literatures.

The power management methods presented in the standard can not cope with the fast traffic changes and may cause incorrect system parameters which leads to the performance degradation. Moreover, these power management methods are futile for traffics which have long packet inter arrival time. The IEEE 802.15.3 TG considers the scenario that DEVs frequently join and leave a piconet as mentioned in [14]. In this scenario, many system parameters such as a superframe length and the number of flows change dynamically. Thus, instead of using the power management method of the standard, we propose that a DEV leaves a piconet when it is neither transmitting nor receiving. This method is easy to be implemented and can reduce the overhead caused by the power management. In addition, we propose the packet scheduling method to reduce the wakeup time caused by the access delay and the association delay.

3.2 Packet Scheduling Method

A timer τ, which indicates the remained time until the CTA allocation, is used for the packet scheduling. The PNC selects DEVs whose values of τ are less than the time duration of a superframe, D_s. The selected DEVs are called a *candidate set*. DEV n in the candidate set is allocated Φ_n CTAs in the current superframe and Φ_n is given as

$$\Phi_n = \left\lceil \frac{D_s - \tau_n}{\alpha_n} \right\rceil, \tag{1}$$

where $\lceil x \rceil$ is the smallest integer value not less than x, α is an average packet inter-arrival time, and the subscript n in the notation denotes the nth DEV. For the candidate set, the time duration from the beginning of current superframe to the beginning of the cth CTA is given as

$$T_n^c = \tau_n + (c-1) \times \alpha_n, \quad \text{for} \quad 1 \le c \le \Phi_n. \tag{2}$$

During the MCTA, a DEV sends the status information to the PNC by using a *status report command* packet. We denote the values of queue size, access delay, and transmission rate in the status report command packet as F_n^Q, F_n^D, and F_n^R, respectively. Then the packet transmission time γ is given as

$$\gamma_n = \left(\frac{P_n}{F_n^R} + D_{\text{overhead}} \right) F_n^Q + D_{\text{guard}}, \tag{3}$$

where P is the packet size and D_{overhead} and D_{guard} are the time durations for the overhead and guard time, respectively. Thus, the scheduler assigns a CTA at T_n^c with γ_n duration for DEV n. When two or more scheduled CTAs overlap with each other, the CTA with lower value of T_n^c is allocated in advance.

The MCTA allocation method is proposed as follows. If there is time duration remained between two consecutive CTAs, this duration becomes MCTA for transmitting command packets. However, if the remained duration is less than the threshold, it is merged to previous or next CTA. The threshold is a sum of the slot time and the time duration of a CTRq packet. This threshold ensures that at least one command packet can be transmitted in an MCTA. The sum of CTAs and MCTAs durations allocated in a superframe should be less than D_s. If the duration sum is more than D_s, the CTAs at the tail will be removed until it becomes less than D_s.

Note that T_n^c and Φ_n are required (ideal) values for CTA allocations. Because of the aforementioned reasons of CTA overlap and dynamic traffic pattern, it may happen that the packet scheduler uses smaller values than T_n^c and Φ_n. In this case, the selected (real) values instead of T_n^c and Φ_n are denoted by t_n^c and ϕ_n, respectively.

At the start of a new superframe, τ_n is updated to a new value by

$$\tau_n \Leftarrow \begin{cases} \max\{0, \tau_n - D_s - F_n^D\} & , \text{ for } \tau_n \geq D_s, \Phi_n = 0 \\ \max\{0, \alpha_n - (D_s - t_n^{\Phi_n}) - F_n^D\}, & \text{ for } \tau_n < D_s, \Phi_n = \phi_n > 0 \\ 0 & , \text{ otherwise.} \end{cases} \tag{4}$$

The first equation represents a DEV whose CTA is not allocated in the current superframe and the corresponding τ_n is subtracted by D_s and F_n^D in the next superframe. The F_n^D is an adjusting factor used to synchronize time instants between the CTA and the packet arrival. The second equation shows a DEV who belongs to the candidate set and transmits packets as required. In the third equation, when a DEV in the candidate set does not transmit packets as required, it gains higher priority in the next superframe.

In our proposed scheme, the transmission of status report commands plays an important role in allocating CTAs in a superframe. However, the PNC may form a superframe without any MCTA due to a heavy traffic load or an insufficient superframe size. To ensure that at least one status report command can be transmitted in a superframe, the PNC allocates at least one MCTA with the minimum MCTA time duration. Moreover, the last channel time in a superframe must be an MCTA, called essential MCTA (E-MCTA). This allows the latest status information of each DEV to be delivered to the PNC and to be reflected in the next superframe. The beacon packet in a superframe has information fields for the locations and durations of all CTAs as described in the IEEE 802.15.3 standard. Thus, the proposed scheme can be implemented with the operational compatibility to the standard.

The association delay is also expected to be reduced by using the proposed method. In the HR-WPAN standard, the DEV whose association request arrives during the CTA period should wait until the MCTA of the next superframe. On the contrary, in the proposed method, there are multiple MCTAs and E-MCTA in a superframe and the DEVs can send the association request packet at the next available MCTA in the same superframe. The disassociation request packet should also be transmitted during the MCTA and the proposed method may have less disassociation delay than that for the HR-WPAN standard. Because the DEV turns off the power after the completion of the disassociation process, the proposed method can reduce more power consumption.

4 Numerical Results

4.1 Simulation Environment

We assume that all DEVs except the PNC are uniformly distributed in the coverage area of a piconet with diameter 20 meters. The PNC is located at the center of the area. We consider one piconet in this simulation. The parameters used in this simulation are based on the IEEE 802.15.3 standards [1].

We study two real-time traffic types, CBR and VBR in the simulation. The CBR traffic flow is generated at 912 kbps [15]. For the VBR traffic model, actual MPRG-4 video streams of "Silence of the Lambs" with a mean bit rate of 580 Kbps and a peak rate of 4.4 Mbps, are used [16]. The packet sizes for both traffics are 2048 octets defined in the IEEE 802.15.3 standard. For the simulation of the association process, the intervals of the association and the disassociation requests are exponentially distributed with mean value of two seconds. In this simulation, CAP allocation is not considered since it is optional in the standard [1].

The scheme proposed in this paper, namely enhanced WPAN (EWPAN), is compared with the WPAN proposed in [2]. Each scenario is simulated for 10 minutes. We use the log-normal shadowing channel model [17]. We set the path loss exponent to 3.3 according to the SG3a alternate PHY selection criteria in [18] and the standard deviation to 7.67 [17]. The transmit power and antenna gain are set to 0 dBm and 0 dBi, respectively [18]. The received SNR is varied by the Ricean fading gain, which is generated according to the modified Clarke and Gans fading model [19]. For the data rate of the physical layer of each communication link, we assume that the system adapts the data rate by properly choosing one from a set of modulation schemes according to the channel condition as described in [20].

4.2 Simulation Results

The simulation results of the power efficiency, i.e. the number of transmitted packets divided by wakeup time are shown in Fig. 4 where the superframe durations (SF) are set to 65 ms, 45 ms, and 25 ms. The power efficiency of the proposed method (EWPAN) is better than that of the WPAN standard. This is because the access delay and the association delay of the proposed method is less than those of the WPAN standard. Note that the system parameters such as the duration of the superframe and the number of nodes have less effect on the performance of the proposed method compared with the WPAN standard. When the number of devices is 22, the power efficiency of the WPAN for the 25ms superframe duration is much lower than other cases because there is not enough MCTAs in a superframe.

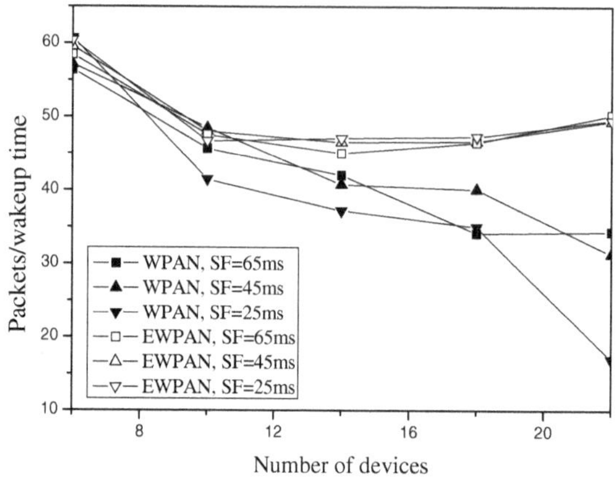

Fig. 4. Power efficiency for WPAN and EWPAN

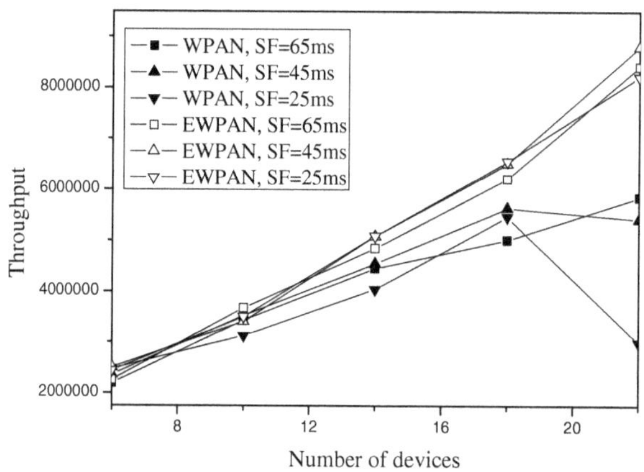

Fig. 5. Throughput for WPAN and EWPAN

The simulation results of the throughput are shown in Fig. 5. The proposed method has consistent performance while the WPAN has different performance depending on the system parameters such as the number of devices and the superframe duration. In WPAN, when the number of DEVs increases or the superframe duration decreases, the throughput decreases because the access delay and the association delay increases. The more important thing is that the proposed method shows better throughput than that of WPAN.

5 Conclusion

The access delay and the association delay of the HR-WPAN standard depend on the superframe duration or the packet inter-arrival time. Thus, the power consumption is restricted by the system parameters. In this paper, we propose an enhanced packet scheduling algorithm for the HR-WPAN to alleviate these design restrictions. The proposed scheme targets on battery-powered portable DEVs in HR-WPAN. The proposed algorithm synchronizes CTA to the packet arrival time and allocates sufficient time duration for the transmissions of pending packets.

We verify the performance enhancement by the simulation. From the simulations, we have shown that the proposed scheme gives significant performance improvements. We note that the performance of the proposed scheme is less influenced by the variable factors such as the superframe size and the number of flows. As a result, the proposed method shows less power consumption and more throughput than those of the HR-WPAN standard.

References

1. IEEE: Wireless medium access control (MAC) and physical layer (PHY) specifications for high rate wireless personal area networks (WPANs). (2003)
2. Mangharam, R., Demirhan, M.: Performance and simulation analysis of 802.15.3 QoS. IEEE 802.15-02/297r1 (2002)
3. Torok, A., Vajda, L., Youn, K.J., June, S.D.: Superframe formation algorithms in 802.15.3 networks. In: Proc. IEEE WCNC'04, Atlanta, Georgia (2004) 1008–1013
4. Rhee, S.H., Kim, C.Y., Yoon, W., Chang, K.S.: An applicatoin-aware MAC scheme for IEEE 802.15.3 high-rate WPAN. In: Proc. IEEE WCNC'04, Atlanta, Georgia (2004) 1018–1023
5. Brabenac, C.: MAC performance enhancements for Alt-PHY. IEEE 802.15-02/472r0 (2002)
6. Zeng, R., Kuo, G.S.: A novel scheduling scheme and MAC enhancements for IEEE 802.15.3 high-rate WPAN. In: Proc. IEEE WCNC'05, New Orleans, LA (2005) 2478–2483
7. Chen, J., Sivalingam, K., Agrawal, P., Kishore, S.: A comparison of MAC protocol for wireless local networks based on battery power consumption. In: Proc. IEEE Infocom'98. Volume 1. (1998) 150–157
8. Woesner, H., Ebert, J., Schlager, M., Wolisz, A.: Power-saving mechanism in emerging standards for wireless LANs: the MAC level perspective. IEEE Personal Commun. Mag. **5** (1998) 40–48
9. Stine, J., Vecianna, G.: Improving energy efficiency of centrally controlled wireless data networks. Wireless Networks **8** (2002) 681–700
10. Liang, Q.: A design methodology for wireless personal area networks with power efficiency. In: Proc. IEEE WCNC'03, New Orleans, Louisiana (2003) 1475–1480
11. Sikora, A.: Design challenges for short-range wireless networks. IEE Proc.-Commun. **151** (2004) 473–479
12. Guo, Z., Yao, R., Zhu, W., Wang, X., Ren, Y.: Intra-superframe power management for IEEE 802.15.3 WPAN. IEEE Commun. Lett. **9** (2005) 228–230
13. Wang, X., Ren, Y., Zhao, J., Guo, Z., Yao, R.: Energy efficient transmission protocol for UWB WPAN. In: Proc. IEEE VTC2004-Fall, Los Angeles, CA (2004) 5292–5296
14. Gandolfo, P., Allen, J.: 802.15.3 Overview/Update. The WiMEDIA Alliance (2002)
15. http://www.disctronics.co.uk/technology/dvdvideo/dvdid_audenc.htm: (DVD-video audio coding)

16. http://www-tkn.ee.tu berlin.de/research/trace/trace.html: (MPEG-4 and H.263 video traces for network performance evaluation)
17. Rappaport, T.S.: Wireless communications: principles and practices. Prentice Hall (1996)
18. Siwiak, K., Ellis, J.: SG3a alternate PHY selection criteria. IEEE 802.15-02/105r20 (2002)
19. Punnoose, R.J., Nikitin, P.V., Stancil, D.D.: Efficient simulation of ricean fading within a packet simulator. In: Proc. IEEE VTC-Fall'00. Volume 2., Boston, USA (2000) 764–767
20. Kim, B., Fang, Y., Wong, T.F.: Rate-adaptive MAC protocol in high-rate personal area networks. In: Proc. IEEE WCNC'04, Atlanta, Georgia (2004)

Two Energy-Efficient, Timesaving Improvement Mechanisms of Network Reprogramming in Wireless Sensor Network

Bibo Wang[1], Yu Chen[2], Hongliang Gu[2], Jian Yang[1], and Tan Zhao[1]

[1] School of Software, Tsinghua University, Beijing, China
wangbibo@tsinghua.org.cn,
{yang-jian03, zhaot03}@mails.tsinghua.edu.cn
[2] Department of Computer Science and Technology, Tsinghua University, Beijing, China
yuchen@mail.tsinghua.edu.cn, ghl02@mails.tsinghua.edu.cn

Abstract. Loading program code to sensor nodes is a basic function of wireless sensor network. However, it is infeasible to gather all sensor nodes once they are deployed. Thus, network reprogramming is greatly required. In this paper, we present two improvement mechanisms to current network reprogramming approaches: the resident mechanism to reduce the size of binary code to be disseminated and stored, and the hierarchical full indexing with sliding window mechanism to record lost code capsules. Both mechanisms can reduce radio transmission and storage access, which are main consumers of energy and time. Accordingly, our mechanisms are energy-efficient and timesaving.

1 Introduction

Wireless sensor network (WSN) combines computation, communication with sensing. Owing to its low cost and sufficient function, WSN has been used in many application scenes, such as environment monitoring, health application, etc.

Loading program code to sensor nodes is one of the most basic functions of WSN. Traditionally, program code is developed in a host machine and then loaded to sensor nodes through directly connected parallel or serial cables one at a time. This is called In-System-Programming (ISP). After programmed, sensor nodes are usually deployed to different locations of the environment and become hard to gather. If bugs are found or new functions are added to the program, new program code needs to be loaded to all sensor nodes. Requiring physical connection, ISP becomes costly and infeasible.

Network reprogramming is a more flexible approach. In network reprogramming, program code is loaded to many sensor nodes by radio at one time, without wiring the host machine. Network reprogramming is also called In-Network-Programming (INP). TinyOS [1], an operating system designed specifically for WSN, has provided a simple INP module, Crossbow Network Programming (XNP) [2], for some kinds of sensor nodes (such as mica2 [3]). Later, many works are presented to improve XNP to support multi-hop and incremental upgrade. However, these approaches involve two main drawbacks: enormous energy consumption and lengthy loading time.

In WSN, the most energy-intensive operations are radio usage and static storage access [4, 5]. Moreover, transmitting some bytes by radio consumes about eight times

L.T. Yang et al. (Eds.): ICESS 2005, LNCS 3820, pp. 473–483, 2005.

the amount of energy required for writing the same bytes to storage, and at least eighty times the amount of energy required for reading these bytes from storage [6]. Radio transmission and storage access are more time-consuming than computation, too. Thus, our mechanisms primarily aim to reduce radio usage and storage access.

Two mechanisms are presented in this paper. First, instead of transmitting both the user application and the INP module, resident mechanism is adopted: only binary code of the user application is disseminated by radio, while the INP application is resident in sensor nodes. Second, hierarchical full indexing with sliding window mechanism is used to record serial numbers of packets which are lost during radio transmission. Both mechanisms reduce radio transmission and storage access, which makes them to be energy-efficient and expeditious. Our mechanisms are versatile amendments and can be easily incorporated with many other INP approaches.

The remainder of this paper is organized as follows. In Section 2 of this paper, related works are reviewed. In Section 3 the implementation of XNP and its flaws are discussed in detail. Our mechanisms are described and evaluated in Section 4 and Section 5. Finally, the conclusion and future work are given in Section 6.

2 Related Works

2.1 Crossbow Network Reprogramming

Crossbow Network Reprogramming (XNP) [2] is the INP module in TinyOS 1.1 release version. It only implements basic network reprogramming functions. The implementation and drawbacks of XNP will be discussed in Section 3 in detail.

2.2 Multi-hop Network Reprogramming

These approaches implement multi-hop network reprogramming functions, which can load program code to all nodes in WSN with the help of multi-hop routing.

A representative multi-hop approach is called Multihop Over-the-Air Programming (MOAP) [6]. MOAP can disseminate the program code to a selective number of nodes without flooding the network. And the receivers are responsible to recording missed packets and requesting these packets.

Deluge in [7] mainly focus on multi-hop data dissemination protocol for network programming. It disseminates the program code in an epidemic fashion while regulating the excess traffic. Unlike MOAP, Deluge represents the data as a set of fixed-sized pages, which can support spatial multiplexing and incremental upgrades.

Another approach named MNP [8] proposes a sender selection mechanism to reduce message collision and address the hidden terminal problem. Source nodes compete with each other based on the number of distinct requests they have received. Also, pipelining is used to enable fast data propagation.

2.3 Incremental Network Reprogramming

These approaches implement incremental upgrade. They only disseminate the differences between the new program code and the old one.

In the incremental algorithm in [9], the host machine generates an edit script of commands to describe the differences between the two versions of program codes and disseminates the edit script by radio. Sensor nodes then can build the new program code by interpreting the received edit script.

Another incremental approach in [10] does not generate any extra script. For each block of program code, it is compared with the corresponding block of the previous version. If they are the same, sensor nodes are told to copy this block from the previous code. Otherwise, the new block is transmitted and sensor nodes insert this block to the current code.

2.4 Other Important Works

Maté [11] is different with other INP approaches in many aspects. First, all above approaches disseminate the program code in binary code, while Maté distributes code in virtual machine instructions. Second, above approaches transmit both INP module and the user application, while Maté only transmits the user application. Because Maté runs only in virtual machine instructions, user application needs to be converted to virtual machine instructions. Trickle [12] improves Maté by using an epidemic algorithm to propagate the program code only to nodes that need to be modified.

3 Crossbow Network Reprogramming

XNP [2] is a basic INP implementation. Instead of loading program code to the program memory directly, XNP first downloads the binary code to the external storage, and then tells the boot loader to copy the code to program memory (Fig. 1).

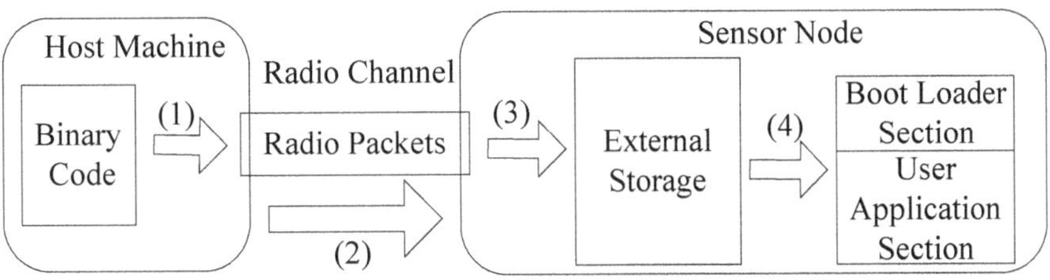

Fig. 1. Process of XNP. (1) Host machine divides the binary code to multiple radio packets (2) Host machine broadcasts code capsules one by one (3) Each sensor node stores received binary code in the external storage (4) Boot loader copies binary code to program memory.

In the first step, the host machine divides the binary program code as radio packets and broadcasts these code capsules via a base station. Sensor nodes within single-hop bidirectional communication range of the base station receive radio packets and store the binary code in external storages. During the code delivery, some code capsules may be lost. Sensor nodes request any lost capsules until entire binary code is stored.

In the second step, the XNP module of each node calls the boot loader, a program resident in the high program memory area. The boot loader is responsible for copying the program code from the external storage to the program memory. Once entire program code is copied, the boot loader restarts the sensor node with new code.

Four main drawbacks of XNP are listed as follows:

First, XNP does not support multihop mechanism. Only sensor nodes within direct bidirectional communication range of the base station can be reprogrammed at one time. MOAP [6], Deluge [7] and MNP [8] have effectively addressed this problem.

Second, loading program code by XNP is much slower than by ISP. Incremental upgrade mechanisms have been proposed in [9] and [10] to reduce loading time. Our mechanisms address this problem in different ways.

Third, the huge XNP module occupies nearly one quarter of the overall capacity of program memory. Our resident mechanism will solve this problem.

Fourth, the huge blocks to be transmitted by radio and vast storage access in XNP process consume too much energy. Our mechanisms effectively reduce the radio transmission and storage access, and thus are much more energy-efficient.

4 Resident Mechanism

4.1 Basic Conception

In XNP process, the binary code to be disseminated contains both the user application and XNP module. Take the TinyOS application *Blink* for example. To support INP, *Blink* has to wire the XNP module to form a combined application *XnpBlink*. The size of binary code and the quantity of code capsules of *XnpBlink* are almost 12 times larger than those of *Blink* for mica2 platform (as Table 1 shows).

Table 1. Binary code size and quantity of code capsules of *Blink* and *XnpBlink* for mica2

Application	Blink	XnpBlink
Size of Binary Code	3,974 Byte	48,062 Byte
Quantity of Code Capsules	91	1092

The huge INP module greatly decelerates the reprogramming process, consumes too much energy, and occupies nearly one quarter of the overall capacity of program memory. In fact, the XNP module remains same for most time.

Our resident mechanism solves these problems. In our mechanism, only the user application is transmitted by radio, an independent resident network reprogramming (ab. RNP) application is resident in sensor nodes since the first-time programming.

Our approach is similar to Maté [11] in that only the user application needs to be transmitted. However, binary code is disseminated directly in our resident mechanism without being converted to virtual machine instructions.

4.2 Memory Layout

External storage, which is many times larger than program memory, is used to store the RNP application in our mechanism. The memory layout of our RNP mechanism is depicted in Fig. 2. The external storage is divided into four continuous sections. The first section stores new program code. The next section stores old program code to support incremental mechanism in [10]. The third section is used to store RNP application and the fourth is reserved for other purpose. The program memory is composed of two sections. The highest section is boot loader section as in XNP. While the other section stores user application in application running process, and stores RNP application in reprogramming process.

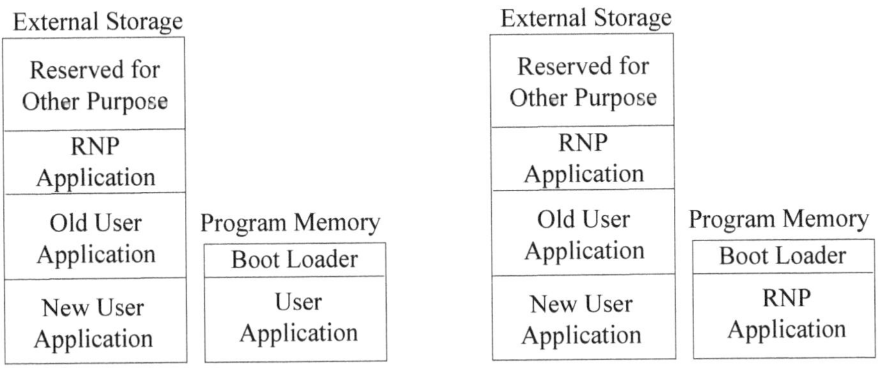

(a) User application running process (b) network reprogramming process

Fig. 2. Memory Layout of resident mechanism in different processes

Because user application and RNP application do not coexist in the program memory, more space in the program memory is available for user application.

4.3 Design and Usage

To make a sensor node be able to perform resident network reprogramming, some works should be done in advance. First, the RNP application should be loaded to the external storage in the first-time programming, which is responsible for downloading and storing code capsules in the external storage. Second, application that includes functions of receiving radio messages and calling boot loader is loaded to program memory. Third, the boot loader should be loaded to the boot loader section of program memory. Then, resident network reprogramming can start anytime.

Our resident mechanism works in the following steps: at the beginning, the user application is modified to receive radio messages and call boot loader. Then, the host machine broadcasts a command indicating the start of reprogramming. In response, boot loader in each node loads RNP application to program memory. After loading is finished, sensor nodes start to wait for the code capsules. Then, the host machine broadcasts code capsules one by one. Sensor nodes store obtained code capsules in their external storages and maintain indexes to record lost code capsules (using one bit to record one code capsule). Lost capsules are requested to retransmit in a separate query phase. Once a sensor node stores the entire binary code, boot loader is called to copy the binary code to program memory and restart the node.

After the RNP application starts running, if no code capsule is received for a long time, this application considers itself to be a new version of RNP application, and calls the boot loader to copy this application to RNP application section of the external storage. This function is used to upgrade the RNP application itself.

4.4 Evaluation

Our resident mechanism is compared with XNP using standard TinyOS application *Blink* in Mica2 nodes. Because radio module should be added to *Blink*, the combined application *RnpBlink* is larger than *Blink*, but it is much smaller than the combined XNP application *XnpBlink* (Table 2). Accordingly, code capsules are much less.

Table 2. Comparison of *Blink*, *RnpBlink* and *XnpBlink*. Our implementation adds only a few codes to receive message, its size is much smaller

Application	Blink	RnpBlink	XnpBlink
Size of Binary Code	3,974 Byte	28,158 Byte	48,062 Byte
Quantity of Code Capsules	91	640	1092

Table 3. Network programming time of XNP and RNP

Timing (sec)	Case 1		Case 2		Case 3	
	RNP	XNP	RNP	XNP	RNP	XNP
Download	141.3	240.1	141.4	239.4	141.4	240.2
Query	13.0	19.4	15.4	22.4	17.7	25.2
Reprogram	1.7	1.7	1.7	1.7	1.7	1.7
Total	156.0	261.2	158.5	263.7	160.8	267.1

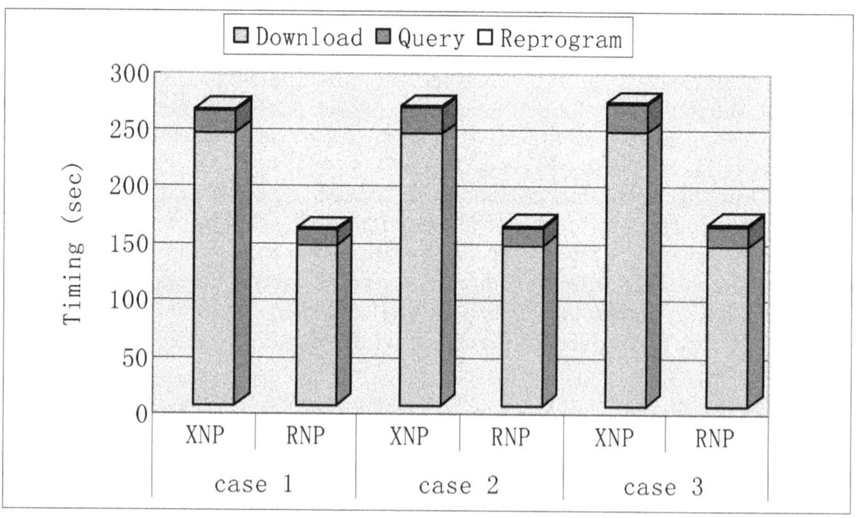

Fig. 3. Network programming time of XNP and RNP

The time and energy consumptions of reprogramming are in direct ratio to the size of binary code and the quantity of code capsules. Thus, our resident mechanism is more energy-efficient and timesaving. Also, without spatial occupation of INP module, more space is available in program memory for user application.

We run experiments using real Mica2 nodes to test the programming time of the same application *Blink* in XNP and RNP mechanism. Three cases using different number of nodes are performed. For case 1, only one node is reprogrammed by network; for case 2, two nodes are reprogrammed; and for case 3, four nodes are reprogrammed. For all cases, we run three times and count the average time.

We timed the INP process for the major three steps: download, query and reprogram. Table 3 and Fig. 3 show the results. The reprogram step takes almost same time for all cases either with XNP or our resident mechanism. However, our resident mechanism is much more timesaving in download and query stages.

5 Hierarchical Full Indexing with Sliding Window Mechanism

5.1 Basic Mechanism

During the code delivery, a mechanism is needed to record whether some capsules are lost and which they are. However, no such mechanism is used in XNP. Full indexing, which uses one bit to record one code capsule, is a simple and useful approach. However, it leads to excessive RAM usage, while RAM is also scarce besides in RNP. A sliding window mechanism is presented in [6]. Only code capsules within the sliding window are accepted, others are all discarded. It requires less storage access and occupies less RAM space, but greatly impairs the effect of radio receiving.

Our mechanism is mainly ground on hierarchical full indexing. Hierarchical full indexing is similar to full indexing, but indexes are stored in two levels, using both RAM and static storage (usually internal EEPROM). The bottom level is kept in static storage. It uses full indexing for a subset of the binary code, which we call a snippet. The index of entire program is kept in the top level in RAM, using one bit to represent a snippet. Since a snippet can be relatively large, the RAM usage is small. When a code capsule is received, if the relevant bit in top-level index indicates an incomplete snippet, hierarchical full indexing has to read the storage to determine if the capsule is a duplicate. If the segment has not been stored, both the bottom-level index and this code capsule need to be written - write storage twice. This is a waste of energy.

To reduce storage access without impairing radio performance, we present hierarchical full indexing with sliding window mechanism. The sliding window works as a temporary cache for the bottom level indexes, and helps to reduce the update operation of bottom level indexes in the static storage. To facilitate discussions below, we define $f(x)$ to be the least positive integer that is larger than or equal to x.

Providing the size of a snippet is k bits, one bit in the top level indicates whether k capsules are received. If k capsules are all obtained, the corresponding bit in the top level index is updated to 1 and other capsules whose indexes are within this snippet are discarded without any storage access. The sliding window is n times of k in size (where n is a positive integer), and slides in step of k. The sliding window temporarily acts as bottom-level indexes of n bits in the top level (Fig. 4).

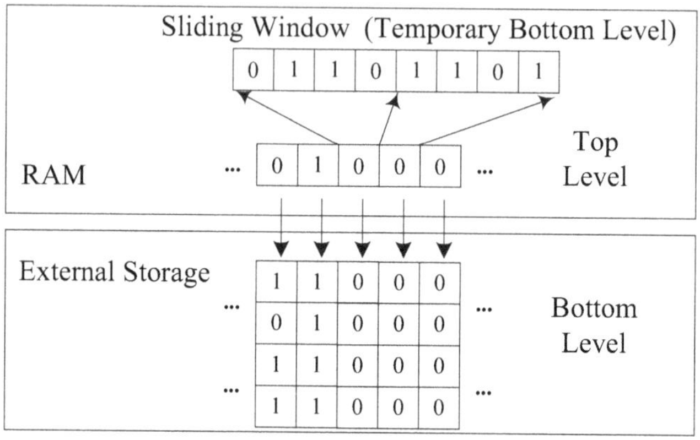

Fig. 4. Hierarchical full indexing with sliding window if n=2, k=4. The sliding windowing acts as temporary bottom-level indexes and updates actual bottom level only when it slides

Assuming the current location of sliding window is from *mk+1* to *mk+nk*, code capsules within the sliding window are written to the storage directly and the sliding window in RAM is updated. Instead of reading storage once and writing twice, only one necessary *Write* operation is performed. If coming code capsule *C* is larger than *mk+nk*, then the program checks whether all the lowest *k* bits of the sliding window are 1. If so, the window slides to contain this capsule; if some of the *k* bits are equal to 0, these *k* bits are written to actual bottom-level index in storage and the window slides. Only if the received code capsule *C* is smaller than *mk+1* and the $f(C/k)_{th}$ bit in the top-level index equals 0, one *Read* and two *Write* operations are needed.

5.2 Snippet Size and Sliding Window Size

Here, we discuss how to choose a reasonable size of a snippet and the sliding window to minimize RAM usage.

Table 4. The minimum RAM cost to record lost packets when *n* select from 1 to 4. *k* is the closest positive integer of the extraction of *8000/n*

n (bit)	k (bit)	Minimum RAM Cost(bit)
1	89 or 90	179
2	63 or 64	253
3	51 or 52	310
4	44 or 45	358

In Mica2 node, the capacity of program memory is 128KB. If each code capsule contains 16 byte, the maximum quantity of code capsules is 8000. If size of each snippet is *k* bits, *f(8000/k)* bits are needed in RAM for the top-level index. Providing the size of the sliding window is *n* times of *k*, the total RAM cost (S_{RAM}) in bit is:

$$S_{RAM} = f(8000/k) + n \times k \approx 8000/k + n \times k \geq 2\sqrt{(8000/k)(n \times k)} = 2\sqrt{8000 \times n} \quad (1)$$

If n is given, S_{RAM} can reach the minimum only when $8000/k$ equals $n \times k$, or

$$k = \sqrt{8000/n} \quad (2)$$

The minimum RAM cost to record lost packets with different n is listed in Table 4.

The smaller n is, if proper k is chosen, the less RAM is used. However, small n means short sliding window, and thus received code capsules are more likely to be out of the window, which may lead to an increase in storage access.

5.3 Evaluation

The storage operations needed to record packets loss in single-hop INP are different from in multi-hop INP. So they are discussed respectively. For convenience, R is used to represent reading storage once and W is used to represent writing storage once.

In single-hop INP, code capsules are transmitted one by one with consecutive serial number and are received by sensor nodes in the same order as the sequence transmitted. The capsule $C+1$ can never reach sensor nodes earlier than capsule C. Code capsules are written to external storage directly without any *Read* operation. Only when sliding window is full and some of the lowest k bits are equals to 0, one snippet needs to be written to storage. Thus, only $f(N/k)$ *Write* operations are needed even in the worst case, where N is the actual quantity of code capsules transmitted.

In multi-hop INP, the problem is more complicated. First, code capsules may reach at any sequence; second, each capsule may reach a sensor node many times. We first count the storage operations needed to manage all the new capsules (which have not been received before), then count the operations needed to manage all duplicate capsules (which are same as capsules that have been stored in the external storage).

Assume all code capsules can be obtained at last, and the time that capsule i is received for the first time is t_i. All the new capsules can be reordered by their reaching time, for example t_1, t_5, t_7, t_2... Define L_i to be the amount of capsules that (1)are new capsules; (2)are received between t_i and time of next capsule whose serial number is larger than i; (3)are smaller than $f(i/k) \times k - n \times k$ in serial number, where $f(i/k) \times k$ is the ceiling of sliding window and $n \times k$ is the size of sliding window. For these capsules, they missed sliding window and thus the program need to read static storage once and write twice. The storage operation for these capsules is $\sum_{i=1}^{N} L_i(R+2W)$. If the serial number of the new capsule is within the sliding window, only one necessary *Write* operation is needed. Thus, the overall storage operations needed to manage all new capsules RX_{new} meet the following condition:

$$RX_{new} = \sum_{i=1}^{N} L_i(R+2W) + (N - \sum_{i=1}^{N} L_i)W = N(R+2W) - (N - \sum_{i=1}^{N} L_i)(R+W) \quad (3)$$

Where $N(R+2W)$ is equal to the storage operations needed to manage all the new capsules in traditional hierarchical full indexing. In most cases, $N >> \sum_{i=1}^{N} L_i$, and thus RX_{new} is only a little larger than NW. Even in the worst case, $\sum_{i=1}^{N} L_i \approx N - n \times k$, our approach is still slightly better than traditional hierarchical full indexing.

For duplicate capsules, define D_i to be the quantity of code capsules (1) that are duplicates of capsule i; (2) that miss the sliding window; (3) whose relevant bits in the top-level index are equal to 0. For these capsules, the program has to read static storage to check whether they are duplicates. The overall storage operations needed to manage all duplicate capsules RX_{dup} meet the following condition:

$$RX_{dup} = \sum_{i=1}^{N} D_i R \tag{4}$$

In most cases, $\sum_{i=1}^{N} D_i$ is much less than the overall received duplicate capsules.

The storage operations needed to receive all the new capsules and all the duplicate capsules and the RAM occupation of different approaches are compared in Table 5. It seems as if sliding window in [2] excels for all these attributes. However, sliding window reduces storage access at the cost of discarding all capsules outer the window. For instance, if the first capsule reaches very late or is missed, all capsules whose serial numbers are larger than the ceiling of sliding window are discarded.

Table 5. Static storage operations needed to receive all the new capsules and duplicate capsules and overall RAM occupation in multi-hop INP. Where R represents reading storage once and W represents writing storage once. Providing N_{max} to be the maximum amount of capsules, N to be the actual amount of capsules, dN to be the amount of duplicate capsules.

Approach	RXnew	RXdup	RAM (bit)
No indexing	$N(R+W)$	$dN(R+W)$	0
Full indexing	NW	0	N_{max}
Hierarchical full indexing (bottom-level is k bits in size)	$N(R+2W)$	$dN \times R$	N_{max}/k
Sliding window [2]	NW	0	window size
Hierarchical full indexing with sliding window (bottom -level index is k bits in size)	$N(R+2W)$- $(N-\sum_{i=1}^{N} L_i)(R+W)$	$\sum_{i=1}^{N} D_i R$	N_{max}/k+ window size

6 Conclusion and Future Work

By loading binary code to many sensor nodes by radio at one time, INP saves great efforts. Among all the attributes of INP, energy and time are of the most importance.

Our resident mechanism reduces the size of binary code to be disseminated and stored. Hierarchical full indexing with sliding window mechanism to record lost capsules reduces storage access without enlarging RAM consumption. Thus, they are energy-efficient and timesaving. Moreover, the resident mechanism avoids spatial occupation of INP module in program memory. Our mechanisms are based on XNP but can easily be incorporated with many other mechanisms.

Large amount of data are disseminated in network with unpredictable topology in INP, and all capsules should be obtained by all sensor nodes. Thus, high reliability and good scalability are greatly required in the data dissemination. So we will try to adopt the hybrid data dissemination framework [13] to satisfy these requirements.

References

1. Jason Hill, Robert Szewczyk, Alec Woo, Seth Hollar, David Culler, and Kristofer Pister. System Architecture Directions for Networked Sensors. In the 9th International Conference on Architectural Support for Programming Languages and Operating Systems, Nov. 2000
2. Jaein Jeong, Sukun Kim and Alan Broad. Network Reprogramming. Available in: http://webs.cs.berkeley.edu/tos/tinyos-1.x/doc/NetworkReprogramming.pdf
3. Crossbow Technology. Mica2: Wireless Measurement System. Mica2 Datasheet. Available in: http://www.xbow.com/products/Product_pdf_files/Wireless_pdf/MICA2_Datasheet.pdf
4. Mark Hempstead, Nikhil Tripathi, Patrick Mauro, Gu-Yeon Wei, David Brooks. An Ultra Low Power System Architecture for Sensor Network Applications. Proceedings of 32nd International Symposium on Computer Architecture, Jun. 2005
5. Alan Mainwaring, Joseph Polastre, Robert Szewczyk, David Culler, John Anderson. Wireless Sensor Networks for Habitat Monitoring. First ACM International Workshop on Wireless Sensor Networks and Applications, Sep. 2002
6. T. Stathopoulos, J. Heidemann, and D. Estrin. A remote code update mechanism for wireless sensor networks. Technical report CENS-TR-30, UCLA, Nov. 2003
7. Adam Chlipala, Jonathan Hui and Gilman Toll. Deluge: Data Dissemination in Multi-Hop Sensor Networks. Project Report CS294-1, UC Berkeley, Dec. 2003
8. Sandeep S. Kulkarni, Limin Wang. MNP: Multihop Network Reprogramming Service for Sensor Networks. Proceedings of the 25th IEEE International Conference on Distributed Computing Systems, Jun. 2005
9. N. Reijers and K. Langendoen. Effcient code distribution in wireless sensor networks. In Proceedings of the 2nd ACM international conference on Wireless sensor networks and applications, Sep. 2003
10. Jeong Jaein, Culler David. Incremental network programming for wireless sensors. First Annual IEEE Communications Society Conference on Sensor and Ad Hoc Communications and Networks, Oct. 2004
11. Philip Levis and David Culler. Maté: A Tiny Virtual Machine for Sensor Networks. In the 10th International Conference on Architectural Support for Programming Languages and Operating Systems, Oct. 2002
12. Philip Levis, Neil Patel, Scott Shenker, and David Culler. Trickle: A Self-Regulating Algorithm for Code Propagation and Maintenance in Wireless Sensor Networks. In Proceedings of the First USENIX/ACM Symposium on Networked Systems Design and Implementation, Mar. 2004
13. Wei Liu, Yanchao Zhang, Wenjing Lou, Yuguang Fang, and Tan Wong, Scalable and robust data dissemination in wireless sensor networks. IEEE Global Telecommunications Conference, Nov. /Dec. 2004

On Location-Free Node Scheduling Scheme for Random Wireless Sensor Networks

Jie Jiang[1], Chong Liu[2], Guofu Wu[1], and Wenhua Dou[1]

[1] School of Computer, National University of Defense Technology, China
jiangjie@nudt.edu.cn
[2] Dept. of Computer Science, University of Victoria, Canada
chongliu@cs.uvic.ca

Abstract. In this paper, we have done thorough mathematical analysis and extensive simulations on the distributed, lightweight and location-free node scheduling scheme proposed in [11]. The basic idea of this scheduling scheme is to organize sensor nodes into disjoint node sets, which work alternately to extend network lifetime effectively. Distinguished from the work in [11], we reevaluate the performance of this scheduling scheme under different assumption that sensor nodes are deployed randomly in the target region according to a Poisson point process, which is a more realistic deployment model in large scale randomly deployed sensor networks. We also analyze the performance in terms of average event detection latency, which is another straightforward coverage quality measure. Our analysis results reveal the relationship among coverage quality, expected network lifetime and node deployment intensity. Impact of normally distributed time asynchrony on network coverage quality is also investigated.

1 Introduction

Due to advances in micro-sensors, wireless networking and embedded processing, wireless sensor networks (WSNs), which consists of a large number of tiny sensor nodes with limited computation, communication capabilities and constrained energy resource, are becoming increasingly applicable to civilian and military applications, such as environmental monitoring, chemical attack detection, and battlefield surveillance, etc [1, 2].

The lifetime of each individual sensor node is short and limited due to the following two factors. First, sensor nodes are usually supported by batteries with limited capacity due to low cost and extremely small dimensions. Second, it is usually hard to replace or recharge the batteries after deployment, either because the number of sensor nodes is very large or the deployment environment is hostile and dangerous (e.g. remote desert or battlefield). But on the other hand, the sensor networks are usually expected to operate several months or years once deployed. Therefore reducing energy consumption and extending network lifetime is one of the most critical challenges in the design of wireless sensor networks.

L.T. Yang et al. (Eds.): ICESS 2005, LNCS 3820, pp. 484–493, 2005.

Most of existing work [3, 4, 5, 6, 7, 8, 9, 10] on energy efficiency in WSNs relies on exact location information, which is expensive and difficult to obtain in large scale wireless sensor networks. Liu [11] proposed a distributed, lightweight and location-free node scheduling scheme to extend network lifetime.

In this paper, we do thorough mathematical analysis and extensive simulation on scheme proposed in [11]. Distinguished from the work in [11], we reevaluate the performance of this scheduling scheme under different assumption that sensor nodes are deployed randomly in the target region according to a Poisson point process. This is a more realistic deployment model compared to the network-wide uniformly random deployment model in [11]. We also analyze the performance in terms of average event detection latency, which is another straightforward coverage quality measure. Impacts of normally distributed time asynchrony on network coverage quality is also investigated.

2 Location-Free Node Scheduling Scheme

The basic idea of the scheme in [11] is simple. Given the parameter k, in the initial phase each sensor node randomly selects a number between 0 and $k-1$ with equal probability of $1/k$, and all nodes choosing number i form the i'th node set. In the following working phase, these k node sets work in a round-robin manner and there is only one node set working at any time instance.

2.1 Performance Analysis

A. System Model

We consider static sensor networks in a two-dimensional region. And we use binary sensing model to model sensor node's sensing capability. In binary sensing model, sensor can reliably detect events within the circle centered at the sensor node with radius R_s. We assume that the sensor network is homogenous, i.e., all sensor nodes have the same sensing radius.

We consider the random sensor network where sensor nodes are randomly deployed (e.g., dropped form airplane) according to Poisson point process [13]. In Poisson point process, the probability that an region A contains m sensor nodes is given by

$$\Pr\{N(A) = m\} = \frac{(\lambda \|A\|)^m e^{-\lambda\|A\|}}{m!} \tag{1}$$

where $\|A\|$ denotes the area of A, $N(A)$ denotes the number of nodes in region A, and λ is the intensity of Poisson point process.

B. Performance Analysis

Definition 1. ***Coverage Intensity for a Specific Point*** *[11]*
For a given point p in the deployed region, the coverage intensity for this point is $C_p = T_c/T$, where T is any given long time period and T_c is the total time during T when point p is covered by at least one active sensor node.

Definition 2. ***Network Coverage Intensity*** *[11]*
The network coverage intensity, C_n, is defined to be the expectation of C_p: $C_n = E(C_p)$.

Theorem 1. *With the proposed scheduling scheme,*

$$C_n = 1 - \exp\left(-\frac{\|\lambda A\|}{k}\right) \tag{2}$$

where k is the given network lifetime requirement, λ is the intensity of the Poisson point process, and $\|A\| = \pi {R_s}^2$ is the area of sensor node's sensing disk.

Proof. For any given point p in the deployment region, suppose there are totally N_p sensor nodes that cover point p . Let S_p denote the set of these N_p sensor nodes. Using the proposed scheduling scheme, each node in S_p assigns itself to one of the k node sets with equal probability $1/k$. Let A_i denote the event that the $i\,(0 \le i \le k-1)$'th node set NS_i does not include any node in S_p, then $Pr\left\{A_i\right\} = \left(1-\frac{1}{k}\right)^{N_p}$, and $Pr\left\{\overline{A_i}\right\} = 1 - \left(1-\frac{1}{k}\right)^{N_p}$.

Let's define an indicator function as follows:

$$I_i = \begin{cases} 1 & \text{if } A_i \text{ not holds} \\ 0 & \text{otherwise} \end{cases}$$

Then $I = \sum\limits_{j=0}^{k-1} I_j$ is the total number of the node set that can cover point p. As $E[I] = E\left[\sum\limits_{j=0}^{k-1} I_j\right] = \sum\limits_{j=0}^{k-1} E[I_j]$ and $E[I_j] = 1 - \left(1-\frac{1}{k}\right)^{N_p}$, we have $E[I] = k \times \left[1 - \left(1-\frac{1}{k}\right)^{N_p}\right]$. Therefore $C_p = \frac{E[I] \times T}{k \times T} = 1 - \left(1-\frac{1}{k}\right)^{N_p}$. According to the binary sensing model and the definition of Poisson point process,

$$C_n = E[C_p] = 1 - E\left[\left(1-\frac{1}{k}\right)^{N_p}\right] = 1 - \sum_{N_p=0}^{\infty}\left(1-\frac{1}{k}\right)^{N_p} \times \frac{(\lambda\|A\|)^{N_p} e^{-\lambda\|A\|}}{N_p!}$$
$$= 1 - \exp\left(-\frac{\lambda\|A\|}{k}\right)$$

where $||A|| = \pi R_s^2$. ■

Corollary 1. *For a given λ, the possible maximal number k of disjoint node sets while the network coverage intensity is at least α is given by $\frac{\lambda\|A\|}{-\ln(1-\alpha)}$.*

Corollary 2. *For a given k and a required network coverage intensity α, the lower bound of the intensity of the Poisson point process, λ, is given by $\frac{-k\ln(1-\alpha)}{\|A\|}$.*

These two corollaries, which point out the internal relationship among the network coverage intensity, the expected network lifetime, and the intensity of the Poisson point process, can be easily proved by using $C_n \ge \alpha$.

3 Analysis on Average Detection Delay

For some event-detection applications in wireless sensor networks, the quick detection of persistent event is desired. Therefore, average detection delay is an important application layer performance metric and is defined as the average time elapsed between a persistent event occurrence at a point and its detection by a nearby sensor node [12]. It evaluates how responsive the network will be in reacting to the events of interests. Note that average detection delay is a point-specific metric. Different point has different detection delay due to different number of sensor nodes covering it and different working schedules of these nodes. Given a specific point in the monitored field, which is not covered 100 percent of time by its nearby sensor nodes, the event detection delay depends on event occurrence time, hence is a random variable. That is why we use average detection delay to measure it statistically.

Because in this paper, we assume sensor nodes are deployed randomly into the field, it is possible that there are some points in the field, which are not within the sensing range of any sensor node, hence can not be covered by any sensor node. For these blind points, the event detection delay is infinite. The number of these points can be dramatically decreased and approximate to 0 by deploying more sensor nodes (i.e., increasing the intensity of Poisson point process).

For any specific point, which is within the sensor range of $s(s > 0)$ sensor nodes, we can calculate the average detection delay for the events occurring at that point after utilizing the proposed scheduling scheme. The only assumption of our analysis is that events arrive uniformly at random in time domain and last for a duration larger than a scheduling cycle kT. The analysis result is presented as below.

Theorem 2. *With the proposed scheduling scheme, when all sensor nodes are precisely synchronized with the standard time, the average detection delay d_p for an event occurring at point p, which is covered by $s(s > 0)$ sensor nodes, is equal to*

$$d_p = \frac{T}{2}\left[\left(\frac{k-1}{k}\right)^s + 2\sum_{i=2}^{k-1}\left(\frac{k-i}{k}\right)^s\right] \tag{3}$$

Proof. Suppose an event occurs at time instance t. Not loosing any generality, we number the time slot which contains t as time slot 0. It is followed by time slot $1, 2, \ldots, k-1$. Each time slot i is associated with the working shift of subset i. Therefore, time slots 0 to $k-1$ consist of a scheduling cycle. We let H_i denote the event that subset i doesn't contain any sensor nodes that can cover point p and $\overline{H_i}$ denote the event that subset i contains at least one sensor node that can cover point p. As all sensor nodes are well synchronized with the standard time, if $\overline{H_0}$ holds, the average detection delay, d_p, is 0. Therefore, the average detection delay of an event occurring at point p can be calculated as

$$
\begin{aligned}
d_p &= \sum_{i=1}^{k-1} \int_0^T \frac{1}{T} \times \Pr\left(H_0 \cap H_1 \cap \ldots \overline{H_i}\right) \times (i \times T - t)\, dt \\
&= \sum_{i=1}^{k-1} \int_0^T \frac{1}{T} \times \left[\left(\frac{k-i}{k}\right)^s - \left(\frac{k-i-1}{k}\right)^s\right] \times (i \times T - t)\, dt \\
&= \sum_{i=1}^{k-1} \frac{(2i-1)\,T}{2} \left[\left(\frac{k-i}{k}\right)^s - \left(\frac{k-i-1}{k}\right)^s\right] \\
&= \frac{T}{2}\left[\left(\frac{k-1}{k}\right)^s + 2\sum_{i=2}^{k-1}\left(\frac{k-i}{k}\right)^s\right]
\end{aligned}
$$

■

From the expression of the d_p given above, we can see that the average event detection delay for a specific point p is influenced by three factors.

(1) T: the working time duration for each subset in one round. d_p increases with the increase of T. This is because a larger T will lead to a lager waiting time for the event to be detected by the active sensor nodes of next working subset, if the event can not be detected instantly by current working subset.
(2) k: the number of total disjoint subsets. d_p increases with the increase of k. This is because increasing k will potentially increase the probability that a node subset doesn't include any sensor node that can cover point p, hence prolong the event detection delay
(3) s: the number of sensor nodes that can cover point p. d_p decreases with the increase of s. This is because a larger s decreases the probability that a node subset doesn't include any sensor node that can cover point p, and the detection delay is decreased consequently.

4 Network Coverage Intensity with Clock Asynchrony

In this section, we analyze the impact of clock asynchrony on the performance of the proposed scheduling scheme.

Consider any point p in the deployment region. Assume there are totally N_p sensor nodes that can cover point p initially and ${N_p}^i$ sensor nodes are assigned to node set NS_i. Point p will not be covered during the working shift of node set NS_i only in three situations. First, all ${N_p}^i$ sensor nodes start working ahead of the starting time of NS_i. Then there will be a time interval at the end of the working shift of NS_i when all the ${N_p}^i$ sensor nodes have stopped and p will not be covered. Second, all ${N_p}^i$ sensor nodes start working behind the starting time of NS_i. In this situation, there will be a time interval at the beginning of the working shift of NS_i when all the ${N_p}^i$ sensor nodes haven't waken up and therefore p will not be covered. Third, and finally, a part of ${N_p}^i$ sensor nodes starts working ahead of the starting time of NS_i while the remains are behind the time, and there is a gap period between them. Therefore in this gap period p is not covered by any sensor nodes.

We make the following assumptions in our following analysis.

(1) The starting time of each sensor node may not be synchronized precisely with the standard time, but the internal time ticking frequency is accurate. So there will be no accumulation of time drift.
(2) Let T denote the working duration of each node set in one round. We assume that the difference between the starting time of each sensor node and the standard time, Δt, is less than $T/2$. We assume that $\Delta t \geq T/2$ is an extremely rare case and could be ignored. This assumption eliminates the possibility of the third case described above and reduces the complexity of analysis.
(3) The time difference, Δt, is a random variable which is normally distributed with parameters 0 and σ, i.e, $\Delta t \sim N(0, \sigma)$.

We are interested in the expectation of the length of time when point p is not covered by any of these ${N_p}^i$ sensor nodes during the working shift of node set NS_i. Let ${E_{uc}}^i$ denote this expectation. Obviously, $E_{uc}^i = T$ if ${N_p}^i = 0$. When ${N_p}^i > 0$,

$$E_{uc}^i = \int_0^{\infty} x f_1(x) dx + \int_{-\infty}^{0} -y f_2(y) dy \tag{4}$$

where $x = \min\left\{\Delta t_j, 0 \leq j \leq N_p^i - 1\right\}$, $y = \max\left\{\Delta t_j, 0 \leq j \leq N_p^i - 1\right\}$ and Δt_j denotes the difference between node j's starting time and the standard time, $f_1(x)$ and $f_2(y)$ are the $p.d.f$ of x and y respectively. The first and the second item in equation (4) correspond respectively with the time interval when point p is not covered due to the first and the second reasons described previously. Since $\Delta t_1, \Delta t_2, \ldots, \Delta t_j$ are independently random variables normally distributed with parameters 0 and σ, we can get [11]

$$\begin{aligned} E_{uc}^i &= 2\int_0^{\infty} x f_1(x) dx = 2\int_0^{\infty} N_p^i x \phi(x) \left[1 - \Phi(x)\right]^{N_p^i - 1} dx \\ &\leq 2\int_0^{\infty} N_p^i x \phi(x) \left(\frac{1}{2}\right)^{N_p^i - 1} dx = N_p^i \left(\frac{1}{2}\right)^{N_p^i - 2} \frac{\sigma}{\sqrt{2\pi}} \end{aligned}$$

Note that the number of sensor nodes that can cover point p in set NS_i, N_p^i, is a random variable varying from 0 to N_p. And with our proposed scheduling scheme,

$$\Pr\left\{N_p^i = j\right\} = \binom{N_p}{j} \left(\frac{1}{k}\right)^j \left(1 - \frac{1}{k}\right)^{N_p - j}$$

Therefore we can further calculate the expectation of E_{uc}^{i}:

$$
\begin{aligned}
E_{uc} &= \sum_{j=0}^{N_p} E_{uc}^{i} \times \Pr\left\{N_p^i = j\right\} \\
&= T \times \left(1-\frac{1}{k}\right)^{N_p} + \sum_{j=1}^{N_p} E_{uc}^{i} \times \Pr\left\{N_p^i = j\right\} \\
&\leq T \times \left(1-\frac{1}{k}\right)^{N_p} + \sum_{j=1}^{N_p} j \left(\frac{1}{2}\right)^{j-2} \frac{\sigma}{\sqrt{2\pi}} \binom{N_p}{j} \left(\frac{1}{k}\right)^{j} \left(1-\frac{1}{k}\right)^{N_p-j} \\
&= T \times \left(1-\frac{1}{k}\right)^{N_p} + \frac{2\sigma N_p}{k\sqrt{2\pi}} \left(1-\frac{1}{2k}\right)^{N_p-1}
\end{aligned}
$$

Note that the second item in the above equation given in [11] is wrong and should be corrected as given here.

By now, for any point p which is initially covered by N_p sensor nodes, we can calculate the expectation of the time interval when p is covered during the working shift of any node set,

$$
E_c = T - E_{uc} \geq T - T \times \left(1-\frac{1}{k}\right)^{N_p} - \frac{2\sigma N_p}{k\sqrt{2\pi}} \left(1-\frac{1}{2k}\right)^{N_p-1}
$$

According to the Poisson point process, point p is covered by N_p sensor nodes is equal to that there are N_p sensor nodes in the circle centered at point p with radius R_s.

Therefore, the expectation of E_c, which is the expected time interval that p is covered in the working shift of any node set, is given by:

$$
\begin{aligned}
E\left(E_c\right) \geq T &- \sum_{N_p=0}^{\infty} T \times \left(1-\frac{1}{k}\right)^{N_p} \times \frac{e^{-\lambda\|A\|} \times (\lambda\|A\|)^{N_p}}{N_p!} \\
&- \sum_{N_p=0}^{\infty} \frac{2\sigma N_p}{k\sqrt{2\pi}} \left(1-\frac{1}{2k}\right)^{N_p-1} \times \frac{e^{-\lambda\|A\|} \times (\lambda\|A\|)^{N_p}}{N_p!} \\
&= T - T \times \exp\left(-\lambda\|A\|\right) \times \exp\left(\lambda\|A\| \times \left(1-\frac{1}{k}\right)\right) \\
&- \frac{2\sigma\lambda\|A\|}{k\sqrt{2\pi}} \times \exp\left(-\lambda\|A\|\right) \times \exp\left(\lambda\|A\| \times \left(1-\frac{1}{2k}\right)\right) \\
&= T - T \times \exp\left(-\frac{\lambda\|A\|}{k}\right) - \frac{2\sigma\lambda\|A\|}{k\sqrt{2\pi}} \exp\left(-\frac{\lambda\|A\|}{2k}\right)
\end{aligned}
$$

For any point p, by symmetry, each node set NS_i has the same value $E\left(E_c\right)$, so the network coverage intensity $C_n{}'$ with normally distributed time asynchrony can be calculated as

$$\begin{aligned} C_n{}' &= \frac{k \times E(E_c)}{k \times T} \\ &\geq \frac{T - T \times \exp\left(-\frac{\lambda\|A\|}{k}\right) - \frac{2\sigma\lambda\|A\|}{k\sqrt{2\pi}} \exp\left(-\frac{\lambda\|A\|}{2k}\right)}{T} \\ &= 1 - \exp\left(-\frac{\lambda\|A\|}{k}\right) - \frac{2\sigma\lambda\|A\|}{kT\sqrt{2\pi}} \exp\left(-\frac{\lambda\|A\|}{2k}\right) \end{aligned}$$

Compared to equation (2), we have

$$C_n{}' \geq C_n - \Delta \tag{5}$$

where $\Delta = \dfrac{2\sigma\lambda\|A\|}{kT\sqrt{2\pi}} \exp\left(-\frac{\lambda\|A\|}{2k}\right)$.

Note C_n is the network coverage intensity when all sensor nodes are precisely synchronized. The above equation gives the lower bound of the network coverage intensity with normally distributed time asynchrony. The item Δ approximately indicates the impact of the time asynchrony on the network coverage intensity.

5 Simulation

5.1 Simulation Setup

In our simulation, we use the binary sensing model describe in section 2. Based on the information from [14], we set the sensing radius to be 6. This is consistent with other current sensor types, such as Smart Dust (U.C.Berkeley) and WINS (Rockwell) [15]. And the target region is a square of 50×50. Sensor nodes are randomly distributed in the target region according to the Poisson point process with intensity λ. All simulations are conducted using MATLAB. For each simulation scenario, ten runs with different random node distributions are conducted and only the average is presented.

5.2 Simulation Results

Fig.1 shows how the network coverage intensity varies with the intensity of Poisson point process when the value of k equals to 3, 6, 9, and 12 respectively. From this figure, we see that the simulation results are very close to the theoretical results. We observe that the network coverage intensity increases with the increase of the intensity of Poisson point process when given a fixed k. Larger deployment intensity will deploy more sensor nodes in the network and each node set will include more sensor nodes when k is fixed. Therefore the network coverage intensity of each node set is improved. But the network coverage intensity becomes saturated at some node intensity. For example, the network coverage intensity is larger than 99.9% when $\lambda = 0.5$ and $k = 6$. This means that larger node intensity will not benefit the network coverage intensity remarkably, but increase the deployment cost hugely. We also observe that when λ is fixed, smaller k will lead to better network coverage intensity. This is because when the node number is fixed, smaller k means fewer node sets and each node will include more sensor nodes.

Fig.2 shows how the network coverage intensity varies with the intensity of Poisson point process when sensor nodes are not precisely synchronized and the time difference is normally distributed. In this simulation, we set $\sigma = T/6$. According to the "3σ" rule of normal distribution, the probability of $\Delta t \geq T/2$ is smaller than 0.01, thus can be ignored. The simulation values are always larger than the values of $C_n - \Delta$, which demonstrate the correctness of our analysis. And we note that even when $k = 12$ and $\sigma = T/6$, the network coverage intensity is still above 0.9 when $\lambda = 0.3$. And Fig.3 shows the value of Δ/C_n when k and λ varies. Even when $k = 12$ and $\lambda = 0.2$, the value of Δ/C_n is less than 0.06.

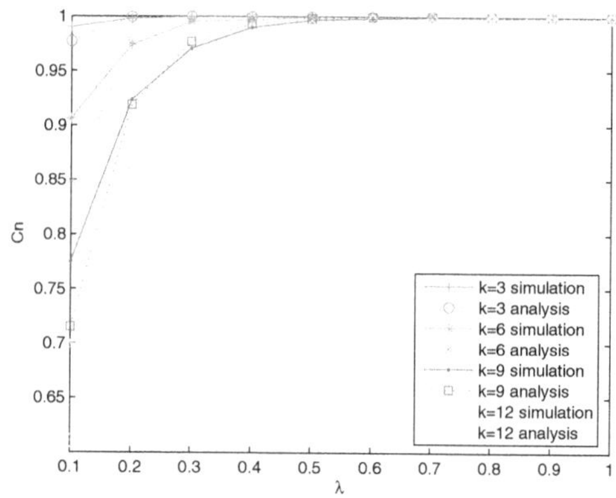

Fig. 1. C_n vs. λ

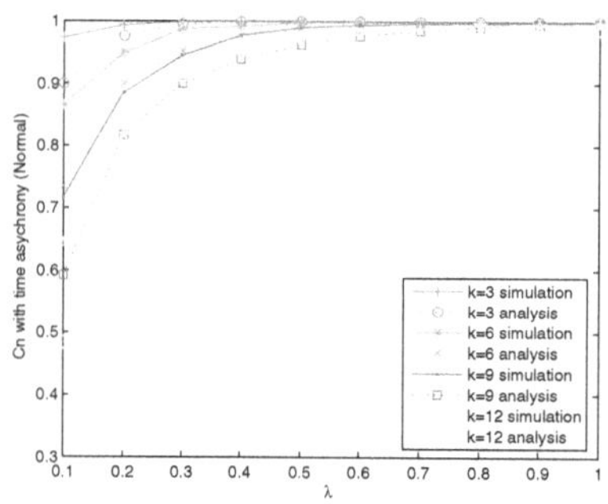

Fig. 2. $C_n{}'$ vs. λ

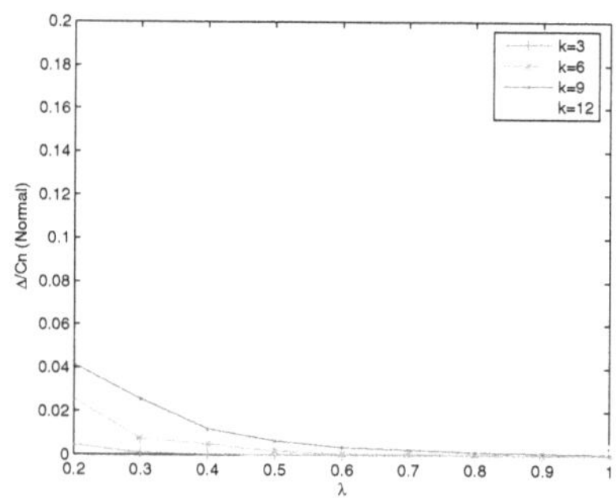

Fig. 3. Δ/C_n vs. λ

6 Conclusions

In this paper, we have done thorough mathematical analysis and extensive simulation on the distributed, lightweight and location-free node scheduling scheme proposed in [11]. Distinguished from the work in [11], we reevaluate the performance of this scheduling scheme under different assumption that sensor nodes are deployed randomly in the target region according to a Poisson point process. We also analyze the performance in terms of average event detection latency, which is another straightforward coverage quality measure. Impact of normally distributed time asynchrony is also investigated.

References

1. I. F. Akyildiz, W. Su, Y. Sankarasubramaniam, and E. Cayirci. Wireless Sensor Networks: A Survey. Computer Networks (Elsevier) Journal,pp.393-422, 2004.
2. J. Elson and D. Estrin. Sensor Networks: A Bridge to the Physical World. Wireless Sensor Networks, Kluwer, 2004.
3. S. Slijepcevic and M. Potkonjak. Power Efficient Organization of Wireless Sensor Networks. In Proc. of IEEE ICC'01, Helsinki, Finland, 2001.
4. Z. Abrams, A. Goel, and S. Plotkin. Set K-Cover Algorithms for Energy Efficient Monitoring in Wireless Sensor Networks. in Proc. of IPSN'04, Berkeley, California, USA, 2004.
5. D.Tian and N.D.Georganas. A Coverage-Preserving Node Scheduling Scheme for Large Wireless Sensor Networt. In Proc. of WSNA'02, Atlanta, Geogia, USA, 2002.
6. H. Chen, H. Wu, and N. Tzeng. Grid-Based Approach for Working Node Selection in Wireless Sensor Networks. In Proc. of IEEE ICC'04, Paris, France, 2004.
7. B. Carbunar, A. Grama, J. Vitek, and O. Carbunar. Coverage Preserving Redundancy Elimination in Sensor Networks. In Proc. of SECON'04, Santa Clara, CA, USA, 2004.
8. T. Yan, T. He, and J. Stankovic. Differentiated Surveillance Service for Sensor Networks. In Proc. of SenSys'03, Los Angels, CA, USA, 2003.
9. X. Wang, G. Xing et al. Integrated Coverage and Connectivity Configuration in Wireless Sensor Networks. In Proc. of SenSys'03, Los Angeles, CA, 2003.
10. H. Gupta, S. R. Das, and Q. Gu. Connected Sensor Cover: Self-Organization of Sensor Networks for Efficient Query Execution. In Proc. of MobiHoc'03, Annapolis, Maryland, USA, 2003.
11. C. Liu, K. Wu, and V. King. Randomized Coverage-Preserving Scheduling Schemes for Wireless Sensor Networks. in Proc. of IFIP Networking 2005, Waterloo Ontario, Canada, 2005.
12. Q. Cao, T. Abdelzaher, T. He, and J. Stankovic. Towards Optimal Sleep Scheduling in Sensor Networks for Rare Event Detection. in Proc. of IPSN'05,Los Angeles, 2005.
13. A. Okabe, B. Boots, K. Sugihara, and S. N. Chiu. Spatial Tessellations: Concepts and Applications of Voronoi Diagram. John Wiley & Sons, New York, 1999.
14. http://www-bsac.eecs.berkeley.edu/shollar
15. http://wins.rsc.rockwell.com

Leading Causes of TCP Performance Degradation over Wireless Links

Chunlei Liu

Department of Mathematics and Computer Science,
Valdosta State University, Valdosta, GA 31698, USA
cliu@valdosta.edu

Abstract. TCP is known to have performance degradation over wireless links but causes of the performance degradation have not been well studied. In order to understand the causes and to gain insight for future enhancements, we design a series of simulations to collect performance data and use stepwise multiple regression to find the leading causes. Our analysis indicates that timeout is the dominant cause of wireless TCP performance degradation. Simulations show current enhancements fail to improve the timeout behavior and thus have limited improvement. Based on these findings, we propose a new enhancement that uses ECN to deliver congestion signals and utilizes the coherence among congestion signals to distinguish wireless losses from congestion losses. Simulation results demonstrate that this enhancement thoroughly changes TCP's timeout behavior and improves the overall performance to a new level.

Keywords: TCP, wireless networks, performance analysis, explicit congestion notification, congestion coherence.

1 Introduction

Transmission Control Protocol (TCP) was designed mainly for wired networks, where transmission errors are rare and the majority of packet losses are caused by congestion. An underlying assumption of TCP algorithm is that packet losses and the resulting timeout at the source are indications of network congestion and the source should reduce its transmission upon timeout [12]. When TCP is deployed over wireless networks, packet losses due to transmission errors may be regarded as congestion signals and thus lead to severe performance degradation.

Many enhancements have been proposed to enhance TCP over wireless links. These enhancements can be classified into four categories.

1. **Local link layer retransmissions** use Forward Error Correction and Automatic Retransmission Request to build a reliable link layer so that upper layers are less affected by the lossy characteristic of the wireless link. Example enhancements are [23, 8, 11, 13, 15, 14]. In reality, retransmission mechanisms in multiple layers may respond to the same loss event and cause undesirable interaction. Although some studies show that a reliable link layer through retransmissions can achieve good TCP performance, they also pointed out that these enhancements are designed for

L.T. Yang et al. (Eds.): ICESS 2005, LNCS 3820, pp. 494–505, 2005.

the characteristics of specific TCP connections and transmission error conditions. When error condition and connection characteristics change, undesirable interactions and performance degradation may happen.
2. **Split connection enhancements** divide the entire transmission path into two connections (a wired one and a wireless one) and run TCP separately on both connections. I-TCP [4] is a representative of this category. These enhancements violate TCP's end-to-end semantic and may result in unrecoverable data loss. Thus they are a deviation from the original purpose of TCP as a reliable transport protocol.
3. **Sender-side enhancements** modify TCP code at the sender to estimate the available bandwidth, experienced delay or other congestion signal and change the congestion control accordingly. Examples include Wireless TCP [18], TCP Santa Cruz [16], TCP Peach [1], TCP Peach+ [2], TCP Westwood [10] and TCP Jersey [22]. Their major problem is the location of needed changes. Instead of making changes local to the wireless link and host, they require changing computers that the wireless host communicates with. In a typical scenario where a wireless user browses the Internet, these enhancements would require virtually all the computers on the Internet to change their TCP code. Obviously, these are not practical solutions.
4. **Wireless-side enhancements** modify the behavior of base station or mobile host. Examples are the Snoop protocol [5, 6] and the Delayed Duplicate Acknowledgments (DDA) [21]. Since the changes are local to the wireless hosts and links, these enhancements are considered to be more practical.

Some enhancements, such as Multiple Acknowledgments [9] and Control Connection [7], require changes at multiple locations. They may fall into multiple categories and are less desirable.

Although many enhancements have been proposed, not much research work has been done to analyze the causes of the performance degradation. In order to understand the nature of the performance degradation, we design a series of simulations to collect TCP performance data under different loss scenarios, and use stepwise multiple regression to analyze the leading causes of TCP performance degradation. Our purpose is not to find an exact formula for calculating degradation in general cases, nor to analyze the degradation in all configurations, but instead, is to gain insight for future enhancements. Based on the conclusion of this study, we propose a new enhancement that thoroughly changes TCP's timeout behavior and improves the overall performance to a new level.

2 Causes of TCP Performance Degradation

Our analysis of TCP's congestion control mechanisms [3] indicates that TCP performance can be affected by three causes: end-to-end retransmission, unnecessary slowdown and timeout.

End-to-end retransmission happens in three occasions: when a packet is lost because of congestion, when a packet is lost due to wireless transmission error but not locally retransmitted, or when timeout occurs.

The unnecessary slowdown is a direct result of TCP's false assumption about packet losses. When a packet is lost because of wireless transmission error, TCP treats the packet loss as an indication of congestion and slows down the transmission. Such slowdown is unnecessary and causes big performance degradation, because every unnecessary slowdown reduces the effective transmission rate to half. If wireless transmission errors happen frequently, the wireless connection can become a trickle.

Timeout can also degrade TCP performance dramatically. TCP Tahoe and TCP Reno can recover only one packet loss in a window using fast retransmit. Two or more packet losses (congestion or wireless) in the same window usually result in timeout. When timeout occurs, it takes many round trip times to bring the transmission rate to the previous level. On wireless networks, the combination of wireless losses with congestion losses dramatically increases the chance of timeout.

3 Simulation Design and Data Collection

To collect performance data, we design a series of simulations using the *ns* simulator [20]. We choose a simple network model as shown in Figure 1, where s_1, s_2 are the sources and d_1, d_2 are the destinations. The purpose of choosing this simplest network model is to show the failure of existing enhancements even in such a simple model. The numbers beside each link represent its rate and delay. The link between intermediate routers r_1 and r_2 is the bottleneck link. The link between r_2 and d_1 is a wireless link.

The experiment traffic is an FTP session from s_1 to d_1 using TCP Reno as the transport protocol. The background traffic is a UDP flow from s_2 to d_2 generated by an exponential on-off model. The mean burst period and the mean silence period are both 100 ms. The burst data rate is 500 kbps. Both TCP and UDP packet sizes are 1000 bytes, and TCP acknowledgments are 40 bytes long.

Link layer retransmission is implemented on the wireless link. Packets sent but not acknowledged at the link level within 40 ms are resent. Retransmitted packets are also subject to wireless errors at the same rate. The packet error rate of the wireless link is varied to test the performance of various enhancements under different loss scenarios.

The simulations are 500 seconds long to smooth out random fluctuations. In each simulation, we collect the following measurements.

RETRANS: the number of end-to-end retransmissions, including congestion losses, wireless losses that are retransmitted end-to-end, and packets retransmitted during timeout periods.

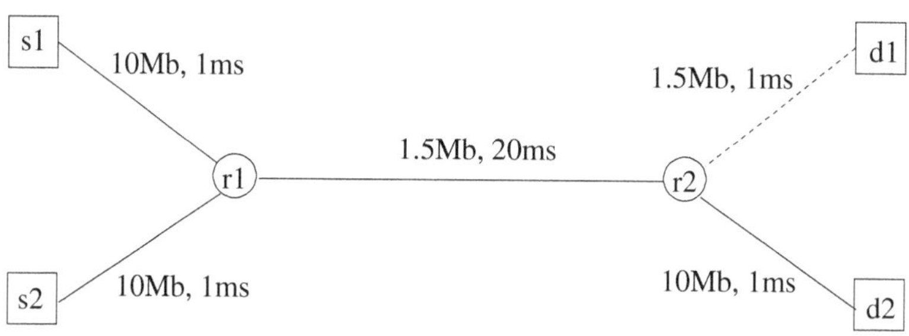

Fig. 1. Simulation model

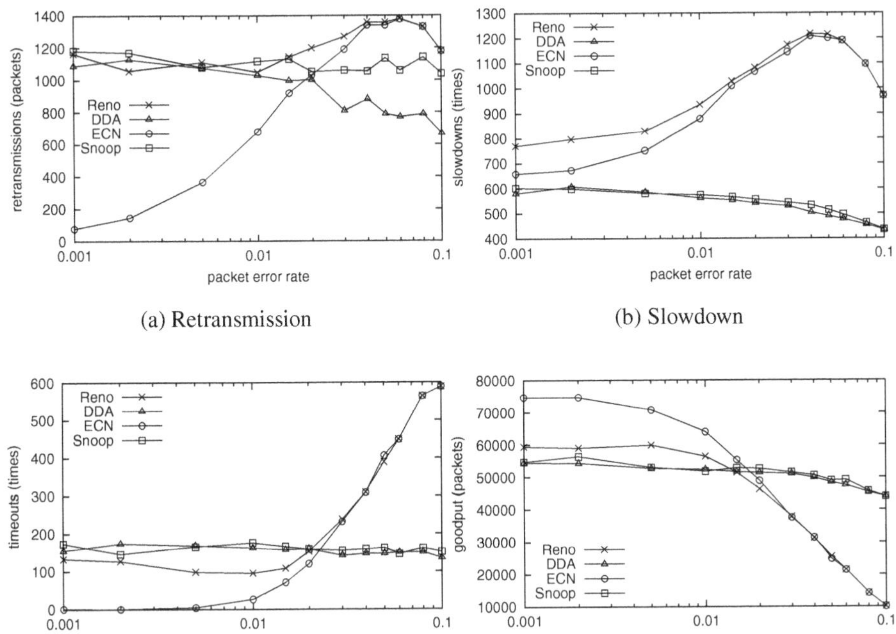

(a) Retransmission (b) Slowdown

(c) Timeout (d) Goodput

Fig. 2. Collected data for TCP Reno, ECN, DDA and Snoop

SLOWDOWN: the number of slowdown actions taken at the source. The slowdown actions can be triggered by duplicate acknowledgments or by ECN-Echo's when ECN is used.
TIMEOUT: the number of timeout actions at the source.
GOODPUT: the number of packets successfully received and acknowledged.

The methods we simulate include TCP Reno, Snoop, DDA and Explicit Congestion Notification (ECN). ECN is not an enhancement for wireless network, but it improves TCP performance in certain cases by avoiding congestion losses. We have not simulated pure local link layer retransmission enhancements, I-TCP, Multiple Acknowledgements, Control Connection and other sender-side enhancements because of their practicality problems. For each method, we collect performance data for 51 packet error rates equally spaced on the log scale from 0.001 to 0.1. The collected data are summarized in Figure 2.

4 Regression Methodology and Analysis Results

The goal of our regression analysis is to find a set of variables $\{X_1, X_2, \ldots, X_m\}$ from RETRANS, SLOWDOWN and TIMEOUT to form a good regression for goodput:

$$goodput = b_0 + b_1 X_1 + b_2 X_2 + \cdots + b_n X_m. \quad (1)$$

By studying the regression model, we hope to find the leading causes of TCP performance degradation.

The difficulty in this regression comes from the intercorrelation among variables. The three variables — RETRANS, SLOWDOWN and TIMEOUT — affect each other. Adding or removing a variable from the model can significantly affect the coefficients. Stepwise variable selection is a frequently used procedure to select the minimal set of variables to constitute a satisfactory regression, especially when the candidate variables have strong correlations among them [19].

In each step of the stepwise selection, a variable is added to or removed from the regression model (1). The first variable entered at step 1 is the one with the strongest positive (or negative) simple correlation with GOODPUT. At step 2 (and at each subsequent step), the variable with the strongest partial correlation is entered. At each step, the hypothesis that the coefficient of the entered variable is 0 is tested using its F statistic. Stepping stops when an established criterion for the F no longer holds.

The entire selection procedure is carried out using the SPSS software. The results are presented in Tables 1 through 6.

Table 1 characterizes the mean, standard deviation of the variables, which are defined respectively as

$$\bar{x} = \frac{1}{n}\sum_{i=1}^{n} x_i \quad \text{and} \quad s_x = \sqrt{\frac{\sum_{i=1}^{n}(x_i - \bar{x})^2}{n-1}}. \tag{2}$$

Here $n = 204$ and x_i is the observed value in the i-th data entry.

Table 1. Descriptive Statistics

	Mean	Std. Deviation	N
GOODPUT	51340.19	13820.967	204
RETRANS	996.39	316.490	204
SLOWDOWN	744.35	234.828	204
TIMEOUT	167.57	127.428	204

The correlation between two variables x and y is defined as

$$r_{xy} = \frac{\sum_{i=1}^{n}(x_i - \bar{x})(y_i - \bar{y})}{(n-1)s_x s_y}. \tag{3}$$

The correlation among the collected variables is listed in Table 2. This table reveals that TIMEOUT has the strongest correlation with GOODPUT, and the correlation level among these variables is pretty high.

In the stepwise selection, the criterion to enter a variable is that the probability of F statistic is smaller or equal to 0.05; the criterion to remove a variable from the model is that the probability of F statistic is greater than or equal to 0.10. Table 3 records the order that the variables are entered into or removed from the model.

Table 4 summarizes the goodness of each regression model fitting the observed data. R, the coefficient of multiple regression, is the correlation between the observed and

Table 2. Correlation

	GOODPUT	RETRANS	SLOWDOWN	TIMEOUT
GOODPUT	1.000	-.710	-.504	-.952
RETRANS	-.710	1.000	.317	.680
SLOWDOWN	-.504	.317	1.000	.469
TIMEOUT	-.952	.680	.469	1.000

Table 3. Variable Entered/Removed

Model	**Variables Entered**	**Variables Removed**
1	TIMEOUT	—
2	RETRANS	—
3	SLOWDOWN	—

predicted values of the dependent variable. R^2 is often interpreted as the proportion of the total variation in the dependent variable accounted for by the regression model (1). R^2 ranges from 0 to 1. If there is no linear relation between the dependent and independent variables, R^2 is 0 or very small. If all the observations fall on the regression line, R^2 is 1. This measure of the goodness of fit of a linear model is also called the *coefficient of determination*. R_a^2, the adjusted R^2, is designed to compensate for the optimistic bias of R^2. It is a function of R^2 adjusted by the number of variables in the model and the sample size.

$$R_a^2 = R^2 - \frac{p(1 - R^2)}{N - p - 1}, \tag{4}$$

where p is the number of independent variables in the equation. The last column in Table 4, standard error of the estimate, is the square root of the residual mean square in the ANOVA table below. It measures the spread of the residuals (or errors) about the fitted line using the regression model (1).

A noticeable point in Table 4 is that R^2, the goodness of fitting, has a very high value starting from the first model. It indicates that 90% of the variation of goodput can be explained solely by timeout. Adding SLOWDOWN and RETRANS into the model increases the coefficient of determination, but the increase is small.

Table 5 is the analysis of variance or ANOVA table. Denote y_i as the i-th observed value of the dependent variable, $\bar{y}$ as their mean, and $\hat{y}_i$ as the i-th predicted value. The sums of squares for regression, for residual and for total are defined as

Table 4. Model Summary

Model	**Predictors**	R	R^2	R_a^2	**Std Error of the Estimate**
1	(Constant), TIMEOUT	.952	.907	.906	4235.416
2	(Constant), TIMEOUT, RETRANS	.956	.914	.913	4077.532
3	(Constant), TIMEOUT, RETRANS, SLOWDOWN	.958	.918	.917	3985.823

$$SS\ Reg. = \sum_{i=1}^{n}(\hat{y}_i - \bar{y})^2, \quad SS\ Res. = \sum_{i=1}^{n}(y_i - \hat{y}_i)^2, \quad SS\ Total = \sum_{i=1}^{n}(y_i^2 - \bar{y})^2. \quad (5)$$

The degrees of freedom are listed in the third column. Mean squares are the sums of squares divided by their respective degree of freedom. The F statistic is the ratio of mean square of regression to the mean square of residual. It is used to test the hypothesis that all regression coefficients are zero:

$$b_1 = b_2 = \cdots = b_n = 0, \quad (6)$$

i.e., no linear relation exists between the dependent variable and the independent variables. F is large when the independent variables help to explain the variation in the dependent variable. Here the linear relation is highly significant (in all three models, the p value for the F is less than 0.0005).

Table 5. ANOVA

Model		Sum of Squares	df	Mean Square	F	Sig.
1	Regression	35153253390.678	1	35153253390.678	1959.627	.000
	Residual	3623627402.866	202	17938749.519		
	Total	38776880793.544	203			
2	Regression	35435001755.524	2	17717500877.762	1065.633	.000
	Residual	3341879038.020	201	16626263.871		
	Total	38776880793.544	203			
3	Regression	35599524396.335	3	11866508132.112	746.942	.000
	Residual	3177356397.209	200	15886781.986		
	Total	38776880793.544	203			

The second column of Table 6 lists the estimate of coefficients in the regression model (1) to compute the predicted values for the dependent variable. The standard error of the coefficients is listed in the third column. When all variables are transformed into z-score,

$$U = \frac{Y - \bar{Y}}{s_Y}, \quad Z_i = \frac{X_i - \bar{X}_i}{s_{X_i}}, \quad (7)$$

model (1) can be written as

$$U = \beta_1 Z_1 + \beta_2 Z_2 + \cdots + \beta_n Z_n, \quad (8)$$

with

$$\beta_i = \frac{S_{X_i}}{S_Y} b_i, \quad i = 1, \ldots, n. \quad (9)$$

where S_{X_i} and S_Y are the standard deviation of X_i and Y. The β's are called standardized coefficients. They are an attempt to make the regression coefficients more comparable. The t statistic in the next column provides some clue regarding the relative importance of each variable in the model. They are obtained by dividing the coefficients by their standard error. Clearly TIMEOUT is much more important than RETRANS and

Table 6. Coefficients

Model		Unstandardized Coefficients		Standardized Coefficients		
		B	Std Error	Beta	t	Sig.
1	(Constant)	68645.314	1490.666		139.902	.000
	TIMEOUT	-103.269	2.333	-.952	-44.268	.000
2	(Constant)	72267.513	998.691		72.362	.000
	TIMEOUT	-94.690	3.064	-.873	-30.906	.000
	RETRANS	-5.078	1.234	-.116	-4.117	.000
3	(Constant)	74879.746	1269.624		58.978	.000
	TIMEOUT	-90.912	3.217	-.838	-28.262	.000
	RETRANS	-5.092	1.206	-.117	-4.223	.000
	SLOWDOWN	-4.341	1.349	-.074	-3.218	.002

SLOWDOWN. The last column is the significance level calculated from the percentile of the t distribution.

Based on the model consisting of all three variables, performance degradation of each method is broken down according to the three causes. Figure 3 shows the relative size of the degradation by the three causes. The projected total degradation and the actual degradation are also shown. The actual degradation is computed from a hypo-

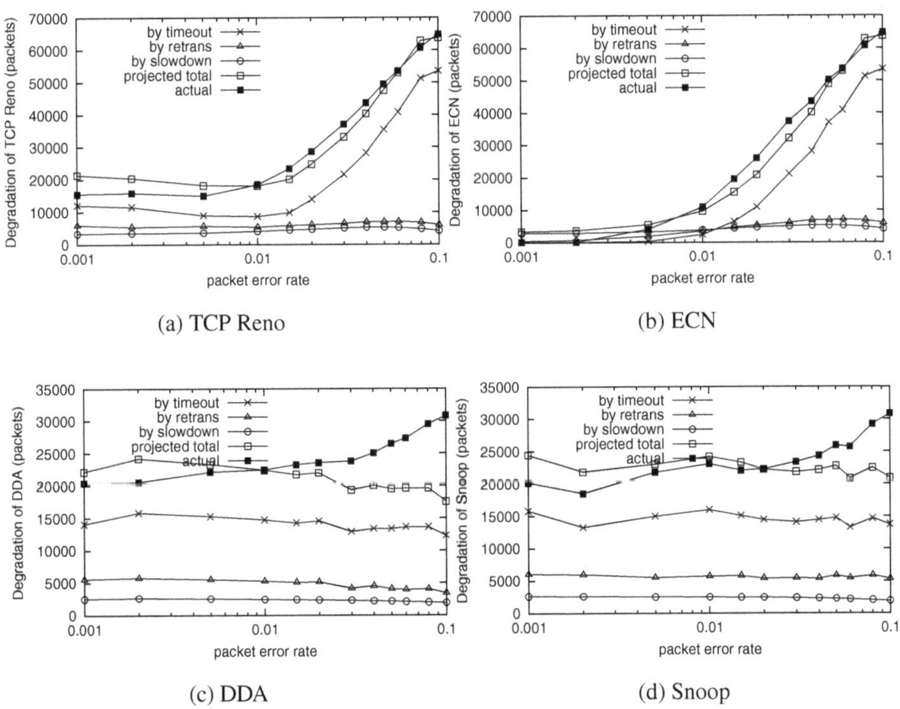

Fig. 3. Breakdown of performance degradation

thetical goodput based on the projection with no retransmission, no slowdown and no timeout. Obviously timeout makes up the main part of the degradation. Retransmission is the second leading cause. Slowdown contributes the least to the degradation.

From Figure 2(c)(d) and Figure 3(c)(d), we can clearly see that Snoop and DDA have poorer performance than TCP Reno when the packet error rate is not very high, mainly due to their failure to improve TCP's timeout behavior.

5 A New Enhancement: Congestion Coherence

Analysis results in the previous section suggest that a thorough enhancement must change TCP's timeout behavior. We can achieve this by stopping using packet losses as the mechanism for delivering congestion signals. Based on these findings, we propose an enhancement called *Congestion Coherence*. We assume that TCP connections use ECN [17] to deliver congestion signals, and the wireless link performs local link layer retransmission for corrupted packets.

- The TCP destination follows existing algorithm for sending new acknowledgments, first and second duplicate acknowledgments.
- When the third duplicate acknowledgment is to be sent, TCP destination checks whether the coherence context is marked. If yes, the acknowledgment is sent right away. Otherwise, it is deferred for w ms, which is predetermined according to the time to complete a local link layer retransmission. A timer of w ms is started.
- If the expected packet arrives during the w ms, a new acknowledgment is generated and the timer is cleared.
- If the timer expires, all deferred duplicate acknowledgments are released.

Fig. 4. Congestion Coherence Destination Algorithm

- The TCP source follows existing algorithm for sending packets and updating the congestion window upon receiving new acknowledgments, and first and second duplicate acknowledgments.
- When the third duplicate acknowledgment arrives, the source checks whether any acknowledgment in the coherence context is an ECN-Echo. If yes, the packet corresponding to the duplicate acknowledgments is sent right away and the congestion window is reduced to half if a reduction has not been done in the previous RTT. Otherwise, the source ignores the duplicate acknowledgment and a timer of w ms is started.
- If a new acknowledgment arrives during the w ms, the timer is cleared and new packets are sent as if the duplicate acknowledgments did not happen.
- If the timer expires, the packet corresponding to the duplicate acknowledgments is sent and the congestion window is reduced to half if a reduction has not been done in the previous RTT.

Fig. 5. Congestion Coherence Source Algorithm

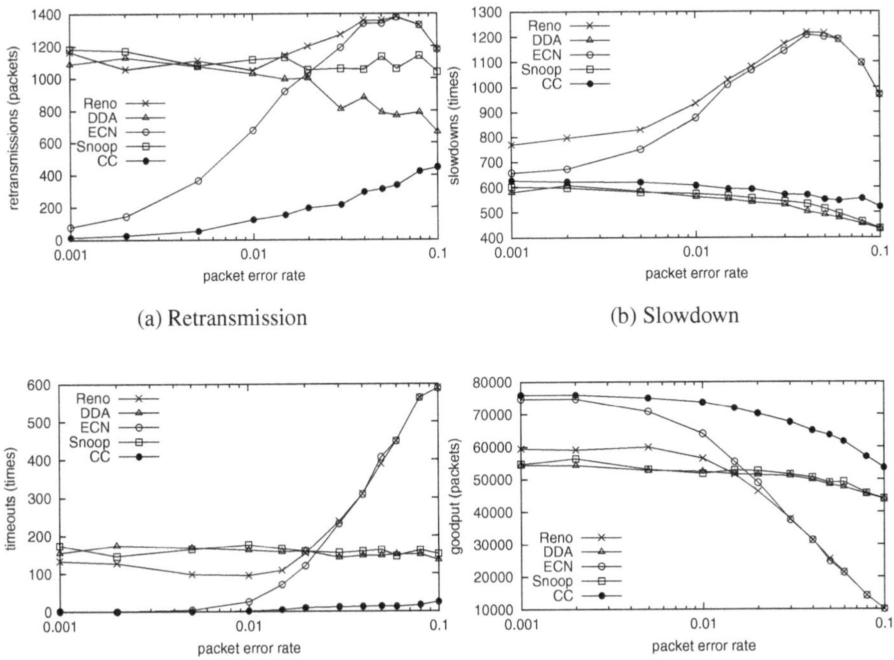

(a) Retransmission (b) Slowdown

(c) Timeout (d) Goodput

Fig. 6. Performance of Congestion Coherence compared with current enhancements

The scheme to determine the cause of packet losses is based on the observation that congestion neither happens nor disappears suddenly. Before congestion becomes so severe that a packet has to be dropped, some packets must be marked as "Congestion Experienced" by ECN. Similarly, after a packet is dropped, congestion does not disappear immediately. The queue size falls gradually and some packets are marked. As a result, congestion losses are normally preceded and followed by marked packets. We call this phenomenon the **congestion coherence** of ECN marking.

In contrast to the congestion loss situation, if none of the neighbors of a lost packet is marked, the lost packet is most likely lost due to a wireless error. In such cases, the wireless host holds the duplicate acknowledgments until the packet is successfully received through retransmissions on the local link layer. There are cases where a wireless loss happens during congestion and the Congestion Coherence algorithm may make a mistake in determining the cause of packet loss. But the congestion control actions are needed because of the on-going congestion.

Figures 4 and 5 show the modified destination and source algorithms. It should be noticed that the modifications to the receiving and sending algorithms are made on the same end. The Congestion Coherence algorithm at the wireless end hides the lossy characteristic from the other end. So no change is needed in the fixed end, intermediate routers or the base station.

The performance of Congestion Coherence and its comparison with other methods are summarized in Figure 6. Clearly the timeout and retransmission behaviors have been thoroughly improved and the overall performance of Congestion Coherence is much better than Snoop, DDA and other methods.

6 Conclusion

Through simulation results, stepwise multiple regression and breakdown of performance degradation, we have demonstrated that timeout is the dominant cause of TCP's performance degradation over wireless links. Future wireless TCP enhancements must change TCP's timeout behavior. Simulations indicate that our new enhancement thoroughly changes TCP's timeout behavior and has much better improvement than existing enhancements.

References

[1] I. F. Akyildiz, G. Morabito and S. Palazzo, TCP-Peach: A new congestion control scheme for satellite IP networks, *IEEE/ACM Trans. Networking*, vol. 9, pp. 307–321, June 2001.

[2] I. F. Akyildiz, X. Zhang and J. Fang, TCP-Peach+: Enhancement of TCP-Peach for satellite IP networks, *IEEE Commun. Lett.*, vol. 6, pp. 303–305, July 2002.

[3] M. Allman, V. Paxson and W. Stevens, TCP congestion control, RFC 2581, April 1999.

[4] A. Bakre, B. R. Badrinath, I-TCP: indirect TCP for mobile hosts, *Proceedings - International Conference on Distributed Computing Systems*, Vancouver, Canada, pp. 136–146, 1995.

[5] H. Balakrishnan, S. Seshan and R. H. Katz; Improving reliable transport and handoff performance in cellular wireless networks; *Wireless Networks*, 1, 4, pp. 469 – 481, February 1995.

[6] H. Balakrishnan and R. H. Katz; Explicit loss notification and wireless web performance, in *Proceedings of IEEE Globecom 1998*, Sydney, Australia, November, 1998.

[7] S. Banerjee and J. Goteti, Extending TCP for wireless networks, University of Maryland, College Park, www.cs.umd.edu/users/suman/docs/711s97/ 711s97.html.

[8] P. Bhagwat, P. Bhattacharya, A. Krishna, S. K. Tripathi, Using channel state dependent packet scheduling to improve TCP throughput over wireless LANs, *ACM/Baltzer Wireless Networks Journal*, Vol. 3, No. 1, January 1997.

[9] S. Biaz, N. Vaidya et al, TCP over wireless networks using multiple acknowledgment, *Texas A&M University, Technical Report 97-001*, www.cs.tamu.edu/faculty/vaidya/papers/mobile-computing/97-001.ps, January 1997.

[10] C. Casetti, M. Gerla, S. Mascolo, M. Y. Sanadidi and R. Wang, TCP Westwood: Bandwidth estimation for enhanced transport over wireless links, *ACM Mobicom*, pp. 287–297, July 2001.

[11] D. A. Eckhardt, P. Steenkiste, Improving wireless LAN performance via adaptive local error control, *Proceedings of IEEE ICNP 98*, 1998.

[12] R. Jain, A timeout-based congestion control scheme for window flow-controlled networks, *IEEE Journal on Selected Areas in Communications*, Vol. SAC-4, No. 7, pp. 1162-1167, October 1986.

[13] R. Ludwig, A. Konrad, A. D. Joseph, Optimizing the end-to-end performance of reliable flows over wireless links, pp. 113-119, *Proceedings of ACM/ IEEE MOBICOM 99*.

[14] R. Ludwig, R. H. Katz, The Eifel algorithm: making TCP robust against spurious retransmissions, *ACM Computer Communication Review*, Vol. 30, No. 1, January 2000.

[15] M. Meyer, TCP Performance over GPRS, *Proceedings of IEEE WCNC 99.*

[16] C. Parsa and J.J.Garcia-Luna-Aceves, Improving TCP congestion control over internets with heterogeneous transmission media, in *Proc. of the Seventh Annual International Conference on Network Protocols*, Toronto, Canada, Nov. 1999.

[17] K. Ramakrishnan and S. Floyd, A proposal to add explicit congestion notification (ECN) to IP, *RFC 2481*, January 1999.

[18] P. Sinha, N. Venkitaraman, R. Sivakumar and V. Bharghavan, WTCP: A Reliable Transport Protocol for Wireless Wide-Area Networks, in *ACM Mobicom 99*, Seattle, Washington, Aug. 1999.

[19] SPSS: SPSS Basc 11.0 User's Guide, SPSS Inc, Chicago, IL, 2001.

[20] UCB/LBNL/VINT Network Simulator - ns, http://www-mash.CS.Berkeley.EDU/ns/.

[21] N. H. Vaidya, M. Mehta, C. Perkins, G. Montenegro, Delayed duplicate acknowledgments: a TCP-unaware approach to improve performance of TCP over wireless, *Technical Report 99-003*, Computer Science Dept., Texas A&M University, February 1999.

[22] K. Xu, Y. Tian and N. Ansari, TCP-Jersey for Wireless IP Communications, *IEEE Journal on Selected Area in Comm*, vol. 22, no. 4, May 2004.

[23] G. Xylomenos, Multi Service Link Layers: An approach to enhancing Internet performance over wireless links, *PhD dissertation at University of California, San Diego*, 1999.

The Study and Implementation of Wireless Network Router NPU-1

Yi'an Zhu

School of Computer, Northwestern Polytechnical University,
Xi'an, China 710072
zhuya@nwpu.edu.cn

Abstract. Wireless network has been used widely because its convenience, agility and no cable. But we can find the critical problems for wireless LAN are communication bandwidth, reliability and security. This paper will introduce our wireless network router NPU-1. It has not only generic route functions, but it also has some special functions for wireless network such as access point, wireless bonding, PPPoW etc. Specially, in order to solve the wireless network problems of bandwidth limit and unstableness, we have put forward a self-adaptive bonding method which can solve above problems well. The key issues for this technology are bundling multiple wireless connection to improve the bandwidth and selecting better channel automatically based on monitoring the signal strength and communication quality to improve the bandwidth and stableness. This router can support wireless connection automatic recovery, automatic fail-over and it can support to connect wireless and wired LAN easily and seamlessly.

1 Introduction

If you are integrating a network which combines wireless and wired LAN, You will find although wireless LAN has been used widely and its technology develops quickly[1, 3], it still has some critical problems such as communication bandwidth, reliability and security[1-7]. Supposing you want to connect two or more buildings or parts or sub-campus of a university or a company, you can not use wired network because some results. It is evident that using wireless LAN is the best solution. You know, for wired Ethernet, its speed is usual 100Mbps or 1000Mbps. By now, wireless Ethernet can only achieve the speed of 11Mbps or 54Mbps. Moreover these speeds are only ideal value. In real application, it can only get about 60%-70% of their ideal values. So, this is too slow comparing with wired LAN. If we can not find the way to improve the wireless bandwidth, this will be a bottleneck of communication in this kind of applications. Second, because the air interfering, the communication quality for each channel is variable. Some time it is good and some time it becomes bad. So we need to monitor the performance of communication, to select better channel to use. This paper will introduce our wireless router NPU-1 which can effectively solve these problems and it can also support wireless and wired LAN connection easily and seamlessly.

L.T. Yang et al. (Eds.): ICESS 2005, LNCS 3820, pp. 506–511, 2005.

2 Hardware Architecture

Figure 1 shows the system hardware Architecture of NPU-1. It consists of an AMD ELAN SCS520 CPU, 64 M bytes memory, two 100 base TX Ethernet devices, two PC card slots which are used to put wireless cards in, two serial ports which are for connecting modem or serial console. In this system, it also has a 64M bytes flash memory which is for storing embedded operating system kernel and all applications. We use two Z-COM wireless cards whose speeds are 11Mbps (802.11b). Of course, 54Mbps D-link wireless card is also supported by this system. This is only version 1.0. Now it can only support two wireless cards. Version2.0 will support 4 wireless Ethernet devices. We use PC card is because it can support plug and play and we can control its power on/off easily. We find some time power off and then power on is very effective for recovering wireless Ethernet device. Otherwise we find lots of applications are located in remote and rural areas and there is no high speed internet service. Besides to select wireless connection, users can use modem to get internet or intranet service. If one modem's bandwidth is not enough, we can use two or more modems' bonding to provide higher speed connection. Also you can select wireless connection as primary connection and modem connection as backup connection. NPU-1 has two power supplies. One is AC power. Another one is a DC power. Normally AC power will work. When AC power supply has some problem, the system will switch to DC power supply automatically and will inform system administrator at same time.

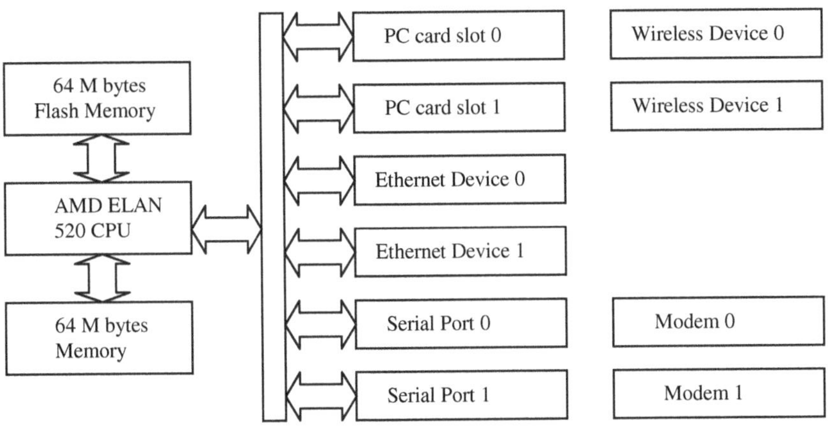

Fig. 1. Hardware Architecture

3 Software Architecture

For this system, its software architecture has four layers. The bottom is all device drivers such as wireless Ethernet device driver, Ethernet device driver, modem device driver, serial port driver and so on. The next layer is embedded operating system kernel which provides process management, file system management, network management and I/O management. Third layer from the bottom consists of all applications. NPU-1 has very abundant applications. Here we only list small part. The top layer is user interface which we call it as command line. Users can easy configure this system through using the command line. By the way, we call whole software system as NPUOS. This is a convergence gateway operating system designed specifically for internet or intranet applications. Figure 2 shows the system software architecture.

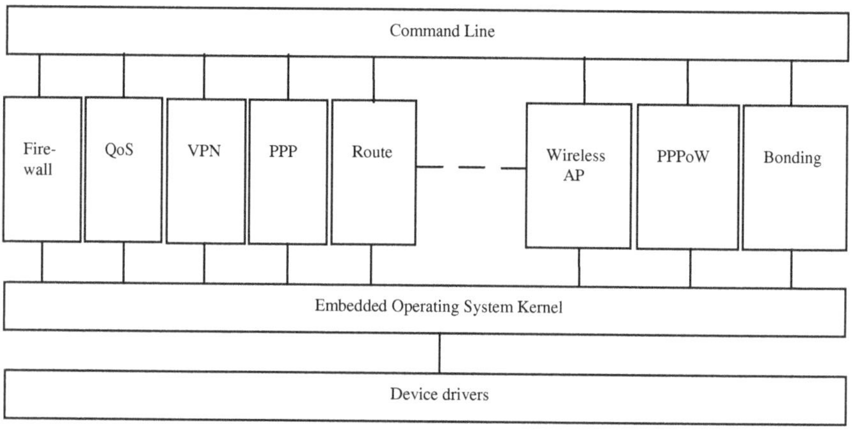

Fig. 2. Software Architecture

NPUOS's feature set includes:

- Routing Engine - This system supports generic route functions such as RIP, BGP and OSPF etc.
- Firewall - This system supports two level firewalls.
- SVPN – This system supports PPTP, L2TP and IPSEC.
- Quality-of-Service
- Wireless IP
- PPPoW
- Accounting, Management, and Authentication.
- Bonding
- VLAN
- Security tunnel

Using PPPoW (Point to Point Protocol over Wireless) in wireless is one of characteristic of our system. PPPoW comes from PPPoE. PPPoE is the short for Point to Point Protocol over Ethernet. PPPoE is mainly used at ADSL networks. Through analyzing, we find ADSL is actually a large public network where the ADSL concentrator acts like a regular Hub; the possibilities for abuse are there. For example one might hook up an ADSL modem and just use any IP address within the valid range he wants. In fact, for a wireless network, it is as same as ADSL in this point. Wireless networks are actually bridged networks where every node or client is attached to each other, the possibility of abuse are also present. By using PPPoE we can maintain and keep the wireless network safer. Briefly say the benefit of using PPPoE in wireless LAN includes:

- Using user authentication by user name and password, we can avoid some interlopers come in.
- Using Radius as auth server, we can manage all users centrally. This will be good for wireless network security and this will make system management easily and effectively also.

Besides this, we have added some new functions such as automatic recovery and automatic change channel etc. based on the problems of wireless network. We call this new composite function (PPPoE plus some Add-ons functions) as PPPoW.

4 Self-adaptive Bonding Method

Bonding [3, 6] is kind of technology which can combine two or more communication links into one virtual link which has more bandwidth. Ideally this bandwidth will equal the sum of all real links' bandwidth. During application, it will split all TCP/IP sessions and distribute their data packets over separate links at same time, across multiple connections, and then recombines them in the correct sequence at the service provider for delivery on to the internet or intranet. Each and every TCP/IP session will gain the combined throughput of all the multiple internet connections. This is transparent to users and applications. Besides, this service will decrease your downtime by utilizing multiple connections and will enhance system reliability by redundant links.

For our bonding, it has following features:

- High Availability

The combination of multiple Connections will ensure that your network communication will not be subject to any connection related access failure. This method can reduce downtime.

- Connection Redundancy

Automatically detects downed Connections and fails-over to the remaining connection(s).

- Automatic Recovery

Automatically detect the recovery of the connection and immediately re-combines the connection back into the bonding session. Instantaneously it gains back the bandwidth throughput of that connection.

- Automatic Fail-Over

Automatically fails down to any available Connections. This means that in the event of a catastrophic service failure, the customer network will fail-over back to regular Internet access.

- Automatic Select Channel

Automatically select channel when the signal strength and communication quality is not good for the channel being used.

- Automatic Reset Wireless Ethernet Device

Automatically reset wireless Ethernet device when the system finds this device can not come back within a given time. This is implemented by power off and power on this wireless device.

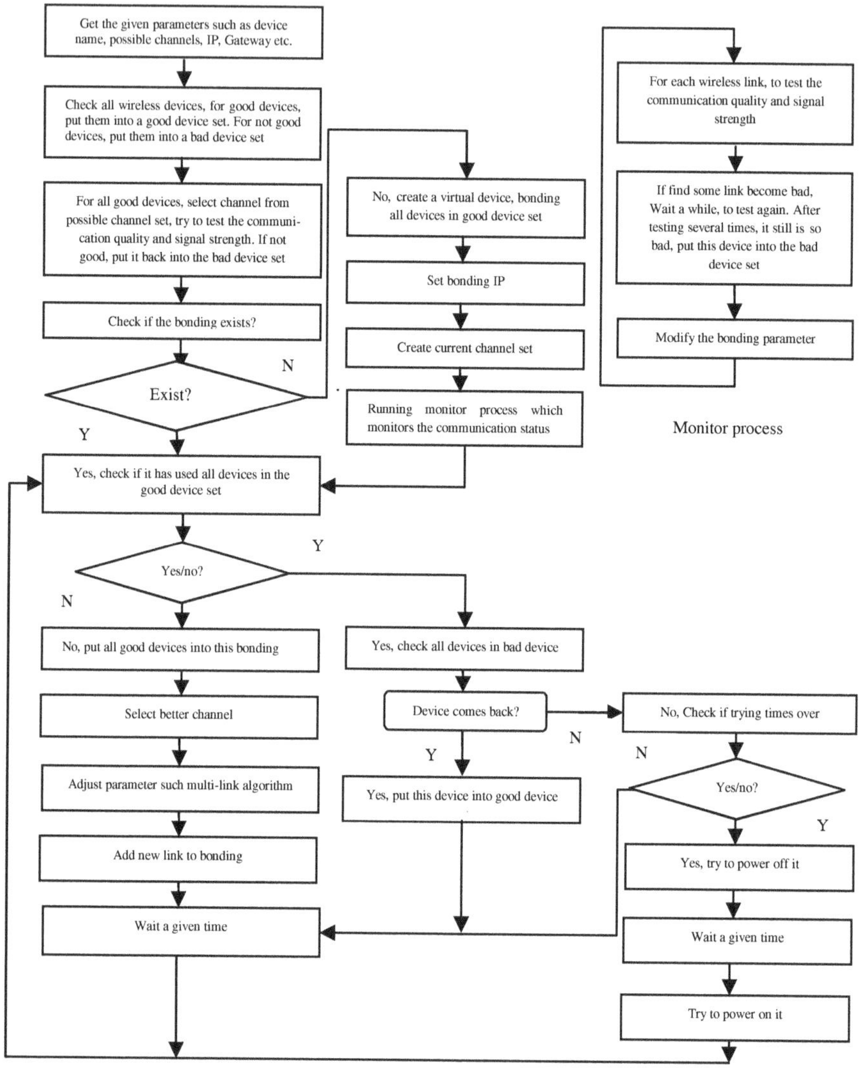

Fig. 3. Bonding process flow chart

- Self-adaptive Feature

The system can adjust itself automatically based on application environment. Figure 3 shows this bonding process flow chart.

This system has two ways to select the new channel. One is negotiating through a good connection. This needs a no wireless backup link or there is one good wireless connection. Another way is using the double wheel algorithm. For the double wheel algorithm, both sides have same possible channel set, one side uses each channel in the possible channel set to try communication with its peer in an increase sequence and another side will use the decrease sequence to do same thing. But the intervals between changing the test channel are different. One side is fast and another side is slow. This interval depends on the channel number in the possible channel set. This algorithm is just like there are two wheels. Each side has one. One wheel rotates clockwise. Another wheel rotates anti-clockwise. One is fast and one is slow. The difference of two speeds equals the channel number in the possible channel set. It is evident we can select a better channel through monitoring the signal strength and communication quality. Using two different speeds is for avoiding two sides can not synchronize. For the bonding, it has two algorithms to transmit data. One is round-robin. Another one is trying best algorithm. Based on our test, the bonding bandwidth of two wireless connections can achieve to the 1.95 times of the bandwidth of one.

5 Conclusion and Future Work

This paper presented a simple, useful, effective wireless network router. It not only has generic route functions, but also has some special functions for wireless network. In order to improve wireless network bandwidth and reliability, we have put forward a self-adaptive bonding technology. In order to improve the wireless network security, we have provided many methods to solve this problem such as PPPoW, VPN, security tunnel and so on. We can summarize the strongpoint of this system here.

- Specially designed for wireless network applications
- Support wireless and wired LAN connection seamlessly
- Increased bandwidth and decreased downtime
- Reduced costs and high availability
- Automatic fail-over and connection redundancy
- Managed solution
- Support VPN, PPPoE, VLAN
- Firewall , IP-QoS

Next step, we will add some new functions based on mobile computing demand [2, 3, 5], and make it to support Ad Hoc network and so on.

References

1. MattBishop: Introduction to Computer Security, 2005, printed by Addison-Wesley
2. Charles E. Perkins: Mobile Networking Through mobile IP, IEEE Internet Computing, (January. February 1998) 58-69
3. Paolo Bellvista, Antonio Corradi and Rebecca Montanari: Dynamic Binding in Mobile Applications, IEEE Internet Computing, (March • April 2003) 34-42
4. Kris Read and Frank Maurer: Developing Mobile Wireless Application, IEEE Internet Computing, (January • February 2003) 81-86
5. Taejoon Park and Kang G. Shin: Optimal Tradeoffs for Location-Based Routing in Large-Scale Ad Hoc Networks, IEEE/ACM Transactions on Networking, Vol. 13, No. 2, (April 2005)398-411
6. Gregor Gaertner and Vinny Cahill: Understanding Link Quality in 802.11 Mobile Ad Hoc Networks, IEEE Internet Computing, (January • February 2004) 56-60
7. Prithwirh Basu and Jason Redi: Movement Control Algorithms for Realization of Fault-Tolerant Ad Hoc Robot Networks, IEEE Network, (July. August 2004) 36-44 9

Performance Evaluation of Air Indexing Schemes for Multi-attribute Data Broadcast*

Qing Gao[1,2], Shanping Li[1], and Jianliang Xu[2]

[1] College of Computer Science, Zhejiang University, Hangzhou, China
[2] Hong Kong Baptist University, Kowloon Tong, Hong Kong
shan@cs.zju.edu.cn
{qgao, xujl}@comp.hkbu.edu.hk

Abstract. In this paper, we study power conservation techniques for multi-attribute queries in a wireless data broadcast environment. Most existing indexing techniques are based on a centralized tree structure and thus are inefficient for sequential-access wireless broadcast media. To conserve energy for mobile devices while maintaining acceptable data access latency, we extend the *exponential index* for single-attribute queries to multi-attribute queries. By maintaining a distributed structure and making full use of indexing space, the exponential index can reduce the energy consumption considerably. We conduct experiments to evaluate the performance of the extended exponential index against the well-known distributed tree index. The results show that the exponential index achieves a better performance than the index tree method.

1 Introduction

Recent advances in wireless networks and mobile computing have attracted an increasing interest in wireless devices among both industrial and academic communities. *Point-to-point* and periodic broadcast are two fundamental delivery methods for wireless data services [7]. Compared with point-to-point data access, wireless data broadcast is an attractive and important service for data dissemination in mobile environments [1][10]. It allows simultaneous access by an arbitrary number of mobile clients, and thus makes use of the limited wireless bandwidth efficiently. Moreover, by monitoring the broadcast channels mobile clients need not send requests to the server, which can conserve battery power. Many studies have been carried out to develop data dissemination schemes [1][2][3][14].

In the literature, *access latency* and *tuning time* are two main performance metrics that are used to measure access efficiency and power conservation, respectively [8][11]:

* Shanping Li's work was supported by National Nature Science Foundation of China (No. 60473052). Jianliang Xu's work was partially supported by grants from the Research Grants Council of the Hong Kong SAR, China (Project Nos. HKBU 2115/05E, HKBU FRG/04-05/I-17, and HKBU FRG/04-05/II-26).

L.T. Yang et al. (Eds.): ICESS 2005, LNCS 3820, pp. 512–521, 2005.

- Access Latency: The time elapsed from the moment a query is issued to the moment the requested data is responded.
- Tuning time: The amount of time a mobile client stays active to obtain the requested data.

To facilitate power conservation, a mobile client needs to support switching between the active mode and the doze mode. For instance, a typical wireless PC card, ORINOCO, consumes 60 mW during the doze mode and 805-1,400 mW during the active mode [15]. Mobile client switches to the active mode to retrieve the indexing information, predicts the arrival of desired data. It then stays in the doze mode until when the desired data arrives. Different indexing techniques achieve different trade-offs between access latency and tuning time. A distributed tree indexing scheme was proposed in [10]. And in [16], Xu *et al.* studied a tunable distributed indexing scheme namely exponential index.

Most existing studies focus on indexing techniques for queries with single attributes. However, the application data items usually contain multiple attributes. Thus, it's important to develop power conserving indexing techniques for multi-attribute queries. In this paper, we extend the previously proposed exponential index to multi-attribute queries. For data items with multiple attributes, we make one attribute clustered and other attributes non-clustered. In the exponential method, we construct the index for each attribute separately. For the clustered major attribute, the exponential index will index the whole broadcast cycle. For a non-clustered attribute, the exponential method will index index data space up to a proper data item within the next meta-segment. We compare the exponential index with existing distributed tree index for multi-attribute data queries. A performance analysis of both techniques in terms of the access latency and initial probing time are provided. Experiment results show that the exponential index gives superior performance to the tree index.

The rest of the paper is organized as follows. Section 2 gives the background for indexing data and reviews related work. In Section 3, we introduce the proposed exponential index and access methods for multi-attribute data access. Section 4 evaluates the indexing techniques and analyzes the evaluation results. Finally, we conclude the paper in Section 5.

2 Background

2.1 Preliminaries

Consider a data dissemination system that periodically broadcasts a collection of data items with multiple attributes (e.g. stock quotes) to mobile clients through the broadcast channel. Each data item is a tuple of attribute values, and can be identified by a set of key values. Similar to [8][11], the logic unit of information broadcast on the air is referred to as a *bucket*, which physically consists of a fixed number of packets which are the physical unit of broadcast. The buckets that hold the index and possibly some data are called *index buckets*, and the buckets that hold only the data are called *data buckets*. A complete broadcast of index buckets and data buckets is called a broadcast cycle.

Broadcast can be classified as *flat broadcast* and *skew broadcast* [1][2]. Flat broadcast broadcasts each bucket once in a broadcast cycle. And a bucket may appear more than once in skew broadcast schedule, called broadcast disk. Broadcast disk is useful for reducing the average access latency for non-uniform data access. However, it increases the length of broadcast cycle and the tuning time of the clients. For multi-attribute data items, a cycle can be organized in broadcast disk based on one of the attributes [8][9]. Thus broadcast disks are not suitable for data items with multiple attributes. In contrast, flat broadcast is simple and achieves a good performance for queries requesting multiple items [13]. Therefore, in this paper, we assume that flat broadcast is used.

Clustered broadcast and *non-clustered* broadcast are two basic data organizations with respect to an attribute within a broadcast cycle. For the clustered data organization, clients can retrieve all data items with the same value of the desired attribute value consecutively; otherwise, they are non-clustered. A broadcast cycle can only be clustered based on one attribute. For data items with multiple attributes, we can make one attribute clustered and the other attributes non-clustered. For non-clustered attributes broadcast cycle can be partitioned into a number of segments called meta-segment, each of which holds a sequence of items with non-descending (or non-ascending) values of the attribute [8][10]. Thus, when we look at each individual meta-segment, the data items are clustered on that attribute and the indexing techniques developed for clustered broadcast can still be applied to a meta-segment. To facilitate our study, the scatter factor of an attribute is defined as the number of meta-segments for the attribute in the broadcast cycle. Thus we assume that the data items within a broadcast cycle are partitioned into meta-segments based on the multiple attributes in turn.

2.2 Related Work

Several indexing techniques have been proposed to solve air indexing. Imielinski *et al.* applied the B^+ index tree [10]. The distributed indexing technique was proposed to efficiently replicate and distribute the index tree in a broadcast cycle. Chen *et al.* proposed unbalanced tree structures to minimize the average search cost to conserve the energy for non-uniform data access [5]. Xu *et al.* proposed exponential index [16] enhances the flexible index in at least three aspects: 1) exponential index allows indexing spaces to be partitioned at any base value; 2) intelligently exploits the available bucket space for indexing; 3) allows the current broadcast cycle to index into the next cycle to complete an efficient search.

Hu *et al.* investigated the index tree and signature index for multiple attributes queries for consideration of power conservation [8][9]. Moreover, they developed a hybrid indexing scheme that takes the advances of both the tree index and signature index. Other related work include: Data scheduling in the papers [6][13][14], which focus on efficient data disseminations. Broadcast of location-dependant data [17], which studies different aspects of broadcast. They try to improve the reliability of data transmission.

3 Exponential Index for Multiple Attributes

In this section, we investigate the application of the exponential index technique to broadcast data with multiple attributes. The comparisons between the exponential index and the tree index in terms of access time and probing time are presented in the next section.

We first describe the system parameters used in our study before we discuss the multi-attribute exponential indexing technique. We assume that there are n common attributes in each data item. We sort the attributes based on their access frequency. Let the ordered attributes be $a_1, a_2, \ldots, a_m$, and their corresponding query probabilities be $p_1, p_2, \ldots, p_m$, where $p_i > p_{i+1}$ $(1 \leq i < m)$. a_1 called the major attribute, is the most frequently accessed attribute and all other attributes are called minor attributes. Table 1 summarizes the parameters that we used.

Table 1. Summary of Parameters

Notation	Description
N	Number of data items
M	Attribute number in a data item
Q	Attribute number in a query $(1 \leq q \leq m)$
S_i	Percentage of data items with required attribute

A multi-attribute query generally contains more than one attribute and consists of many combinations of Boolean operators, such as conjunction $(\wedge)$ and disjunction $(\vee)$. For simplicity, we only consider the query with either all conjunction or all disjunction operators.

We use $Q\{a_1 \wedge \ldots \wedge a_m\}$ to denote a q-attribute conjunction query, and $Q\{a_1 \vee \ldots \vee a_m\}$ to denote a q-attribute disjunction query.

For a multi-attribute data set, we can construct exponential index for each attribute separately. The selectivity and access probability are two main factors that influence the index efficiency. We have to determine the order of attribute to be indexed, thus to get a trade-off between the access probability and the attribute selectivity. Based on research result in [10], data access is more efficient for clustered attribute than for non-clustered attribute. Since data items can be clustered on one attribute, we cluster data items based on the major attribute (i.e., a_1). Therefore, other attributes are non-clustered. The broadcast cycle is partitioned separately by m attributes of the data items, and we can denote the scattering factor as M_i . M_i increases with the footnote i. The value of M_j depends on S_i and inter-relation between a_i and a_j, where $i < j$. For simplicity, we assume that the attributes are random and independent. Based on this assumption, we can get a simple estimation on M_i:

$$M_i = \frac{1}{\prod_{j=1}^{i-1} S_j} \tag{1}$$

$M_1 = 1$.

We also assume that, each attribute has a pointer, which point to the subsequential data item with the same attribute value. Based on this assumption, we can retrieve all the data items with the desired attribute once we find just one.

3.1 A Simple Example

Assume a server broadcasts stock information with three attributes periodically (e.g., stock ticks, prices, trading volumes, etc). Suppose the server maintains 16 stock items that are arranged in a broadcast cycle in ascending order based on their identifiers. The other two attributes are also clustered separately within the meta-segment partitioned by the former attributes.

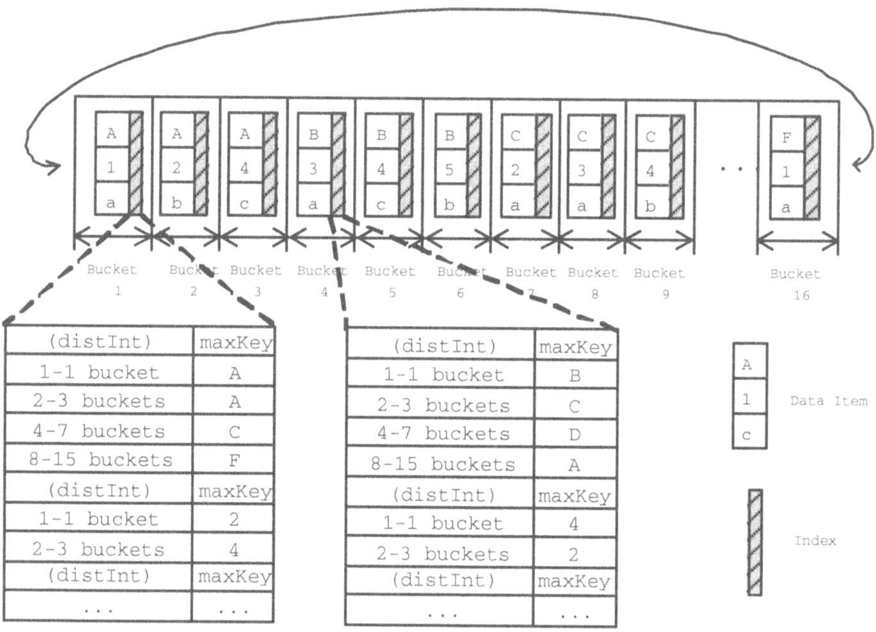

Fig. 1. A Simple Exponential Index for Multi-attribute Index

For simplicity, each bucket holds only one data item and the index information. As shown in Figure 1, each bucket contains a data part and three index tables. The index table for the major attribute identifier consists of four entries. Each entry indexes a segment of buckets in the form of a tuple $\{$*distInt, maxKey*$\}$, where *distInt* specifies the distance range of the bucket from the current bucket (measured in the unit of *buckets*), and *maxKey* is the maximum identifier value of these buckets. The sizes of the indexed space grow exponentially. The first entry describes a single bucket segment (i.e., the next bucket), and for each $i > 1$, the *ith* entry indexes the segment of buckets that are 2^{i-1} to $2^i - 1$ away (i.e., 2^{i-1} buckets). The index table for the second attribute consists of two entries. Each entry indexes a segment of buckets within the meta-segment. However, instead of indexing a whole broadcast cycle, the index table for the second attribute describes the buckets up to the farthest one in the next meta-segment whose second attribute value is less than that of the current bucket. In the case that there is no bucket whose second attribute is less than the current bucket's, the index table will index up to the last bucket in the current meta-segment. As shown in Figure 1, the index table for second attribute in *bucket 1* indexes up to *bucket 3*, since in the next meta-segment there is no bucket whose second attribute is less than that of *bucket 1*. And the index table in *bucket 4* indexes up to *bucket 8*, because *bucket 8* is the farthest one whose second attribute is less than that of *bucket 4* in the next meta-segment. The index table for the third attribute indexes the buckets within the meta-segment partitioned by the major attribute and the second attribute.

Suppose that a client issues a query $Q\{B, 5, b\}$ right before *bucket 1* is broadcast. The client tunes into the broadcast channel and retrieves the index table in *bucket 1*. Since "B" falls between the second index entry and the third index entry, the target item must lie in the buckets that are 2 to 3 slots away. The client stays in the doze mode until *bucket 3* is broadcast and then checks the index table. Since "B" matches the first index key, the target item must be located in the following buckets. Once the *bucket 4* is broadcast, the client checks the major attribute, and it matches. Moreover, the client checks the index table for the second attribute, the client then finds that target item must lie in the buckets that are 2 to 3 slots away. Switches to doze mode, and tunes into the broadcast channel when *bucket 5* is broadcast. It then retrieves the desired item in next bucket. The worst tuning time is bounded by $\sum_{i=1}^{3} O(M_i log_2 N)$.

3.2 Implementation

Table 2 summarizes the notations used in the following descriptions. Let B denote the number of data items that a bucket without an index can hold. Let B' denote the number of data items with an index. The value of B' is a function of the parameters of I and r. The value of r is difficult to determine because the

Table 2. Summary of Notations

Notation	Description
N	Number of data items
B	capacity of a data bucket without an index
B'	capacity of a data bucket with an index
s_o	size of a data item
s_e	size of a index entry
I	Chunk size
r	Index base
C	Number of chunks in a broadcast cycle

bucket number in a meta-segment varies greatly. To simplify our experiment, we set the value of r as 2 and the value of I as 1. Based on the analysis in [9], we can get the chunks number of ith attribute in a broadcast cycle:

$$C_i \leq 2^{n_{c_i}} \tag{2}$$

where $C_i = N/M_i$

We get the formula which shows how many data items a bucket can hold:

$$B' \leq B - \frac{s_e \times \sum_{i=1}^{m} n_{c_i}}{s_o} \tag{3}$$

Therefore, the maximum value of B' can be obtained by numerically solving the following inequality:

$$B' \leq B - \frac{s_e \times \sum_{i=1}^{m} log_2 \frac{N}{M_i}}{s_o} \tag{4}$$

The general access method for $Q\{a_1 \wedge \ldots \wedge a_m\}$ is:

Algorithm 1. Multi-attribute Index Search for the Exponential Index
1: wait until the first bucket of next chunk is broadcast
2: **for** each data item in the bucket **do**
3:    **if** it is the requested data item **then**
4:       stop the search and retrieve the desired items
5:    **end if**
6: **end for**
7: initial probe the exponential index built on a_i within the segment qualified for a_{i-1}
8: search the exponential index based on a_i , follows a list of pointers to find out the arrival time of the desired data item

The general access method for $Q\{a_1 \vee \ldots \vee a_m\}$ is:

Algorithm 2. Multi-attribute Index Search for the Exponential Index
1: wait until the first bucket of next chunk is broadcast
2: **for** each data item in the bucket **do**
3:    **if** it is the requested data item **then**
4:       stop the search and retrieve the desired items
5:    **end if**
6: **end for**
7: client search for any exponential index built on $a_1, \ldots, a_q$, simultaneously, determines when the next item with index are broadcast
8: search the exponential index built on $a_1, \ldots, a_q$, follows a list of pointers to find out the arrival time of the desired data item

4 Performance Evaluation

This section evaluates the performance of the proposed multi-attribute exponential index. We develop a simulator based on ns-2 to simulate the GPRS wireless network with reliability classes 2 and 3 [4][12]. We compare our proposed exponential index with the multi-attribute tree index proposed in [8][9]. The study addresses two kinds of Boolean query expressions: conjunction and disjunction.

Table 3. Parameters Settings

Parameter	Setting	Parameter	Setting
N	10000-1000000	B	3
s_o	400 bytes	s_e	8 bytes
S	0.01	m	3

Table 3 lists the parameters settings used in the comparisons. We assume that a data item contains three attributes. Flat broadcast is used for data broadcast. To simplify the evaluation, the selectivity of all the attributes is set to the same value (i.e., 0.01). A bucket consists of three data items and a data item contains 400 bytes. The index entry size is 8 bytes. We compare the indexing schemes in terms of the tuning time and access latency, both of which are measured in the unit of bucket. And we normalize the experiment results by the latency of a non-index scheme, i.e., $\lceil \frac{N}{2B} \rceil$.

4.1 Comparison of Conjunction Queries

In this set of experiments, we use the queries with three attributes a_1, a_2, and a_3. Figures 2 and 3 illustrate the access latency and the tuning time for $Q\{a_1 \wedge a_2 \wedge a_3\}$ when the broadcast cycle is varied. As Figure 2 shows, the access latency of the index tree is longer than that of the exponential index, because the tree index needs to use a whole bucket to hold the index tables and to replicate some of the buckets. This makes the overhead of the index tree too large, thus the access latency is worse than that of the exponential index. As expected, the tuning time performance of the exponential tree is better than that of the tree index. The exponential index has a linear yet distributed structure. Hence it enables an index search from the next bucket immediately, there by saving the access latency.

4.2 Comparison of Disjunction Queries

This section compares the access latency and tuning time performance of disjunction queries. In Figures 4 and Figures 5, the experiment results for $Q\{a_1 \vee a_2 \vee a_3\}$ are shown. The performance of the exponential index is much better than that of the index tree method. The disjunction queries tuning time of index tree increases rapidly with the increasing database size. This is due to the increasing number of buckets that hold the index table in each meta-segment. For the exponential index, the searching space can be extended to the next meta-segment, which uses the index resource more efficiently.

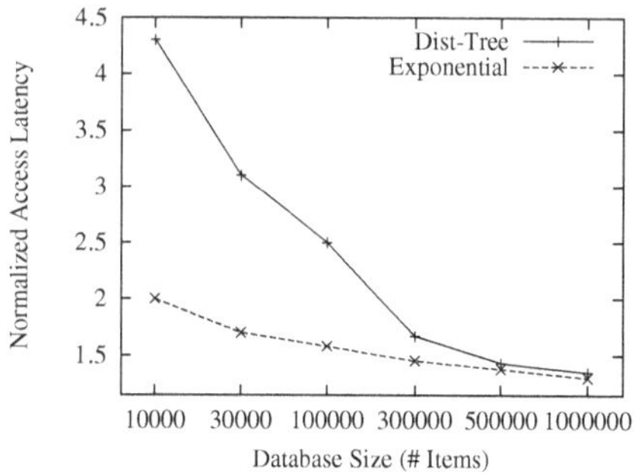

Fig. 2. Access Latency for Conjunction

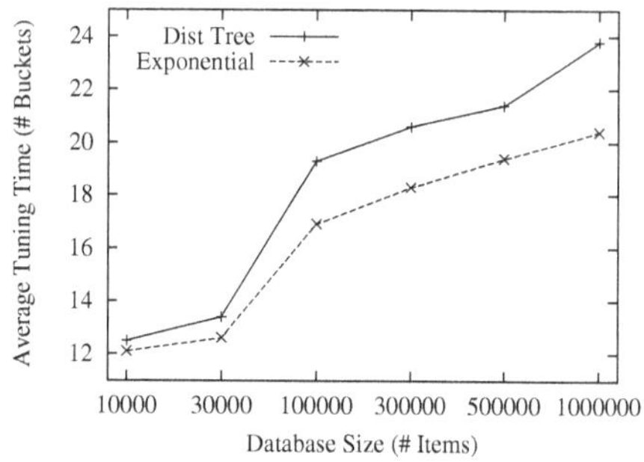

Fig. 3. Tuning Time for Conjunction

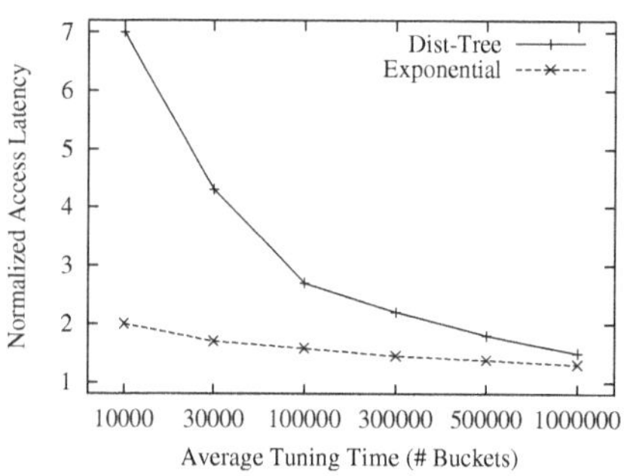

Fig. 4. Access Latency for Disjunction

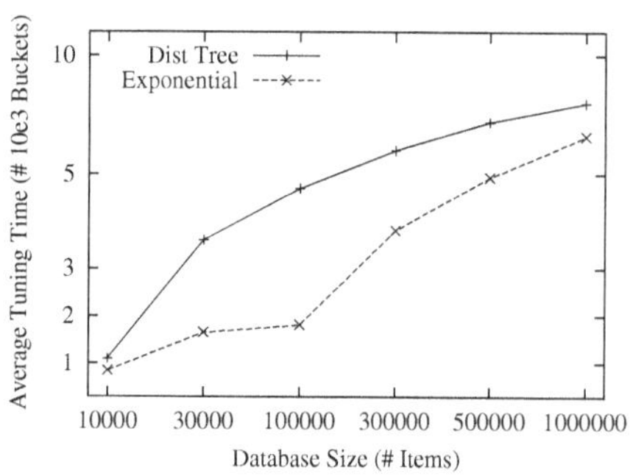

Fig. 5. Tuning Time for Disjunction

5 Conclusion and Future Work

In this paper, we have extended the exponential index to answer multi-attribute queries. Simulation experiments have been conducted to evaluate the performance of the extended exponential index against the existing distributed tree index. The results show that the exponential index outperforms the tree index in terms of access latency and tuning time. This is because the exponential index can exploit the available space and naturally facilitate the index replication by sharing link in different trees, thus minimizing the storage overhead and conserving the client energy.

In this paper, we only compared two indexing schemes with simple query conditions (i.e., conjunction, disjunction). In the future, we will investigate more complicated queries and develop corresponding cost models to estimate the performance of multi-attribute indexing techniques.

References

1. S. Acharya, R. Alonso, M. Franklin, and S. Zdonik. Broadcast disks: Data management for asymmetric communications environments. In *Proceedings of ACM SIGMOD Conference on Management of Data*, pages 199-210, San Jose, CA, May 1995.

2. S. Acharya and S. Muthukrishnan. Scheduling on-demand broadcast: New metrics and algorithms. In *Proceedings of the Fourth Annual ACM/IEEE International Conference on Mobile Computing and Networking (MobiCom'98)*, pages 43-54, Dallas, TX, October 1998.
3. D. Aksoy and M. Franklin. Scheduling for large-scale on-demand data broadcasting. In *Proceedings of IEEE INFOCOM'98*, pages 651–659, San Francisco, CA, March 1998.
4. C. Bettstetter, H.J. Vogel, and J. Eberspacher. GSM phase 2+ general packet radio service GPRS: Architecture, protocols, and air interface. *IEEE Communications Surveys*, 2(3), 1999.
5. M.-S. Chen, K.-L. Wu, and P. S. Yu. Optimizing index allocation for sequential data broadcasting in wireless mobile computing. *IEEE Transactions on Knowledge and Data Engineering (TKDE)*, 15(1):161-173, January/February 2003.
6. C.-L. Hu and M.-S. Chen. Dynamic data broadcasting with traffic awareness. In *Proceedings of IEEE International Conference on Distributed Computing Systems (ICDCS'02)*, pages 112-119, Vienna, Austria, July 2002.
7. Q. L. Hu, D. L. Lee, and W.-C. Lee. Performance evaluation of a wireless hierarchical data dissemination system. In *Proceedings of the 5th Annual ACM International Conference on Mobile Computing and Networking (MobiCom'99)*, pages 163-173, Seattle, WA, August 1999.
8. Q. L. Hu, W.C. Lee, and D. L. Lee. Power conservative multi-attribute queries on data broadcast. In *Proceedings of the 16th International Conference on Data Engineering (ICDE'00)*, pages 157-166, San Diego, CA, February 2000.
9. Q. L. Hu, W.C. Lee, and D. L. Lee. A hybrid index technique for power efficient data broadcast. *Distributed and Parallel Databases (DPDB)*, 9(2): 151-177, March 2001.
10. T. Imielinski, S. Viswanathan, and B. R. Badrinath. Data on air - Organization and access. *IEEE Transactions on Knowledge and Data Engineering (TKDE)*, 9(3): 353-372, May/June 1997.
11. T. Imielinski, S. Viswanathan, and B. R. Badrinath. Power efficient filtering of data on air. In *Proceedings of the 4th International Conference on Extending Database Technology (EDBT'94)*, pages 245-258, Cambridge, UK, March 1994.
12. R. Jain. GPRS simulations using ns - network simulator. Mater Thesis, Dept. of Electrical Engineering, India Institute of Technology - Bombay, June 2001. Source code available at *http://www.isi.edu/nsnam/ns/ns-contributed.html*
13. V. Liberatore. Multicast scheduling for list requests. In *Proceedings of IEEE INFOCOM'02*, pages 1129-1137, New York, NY, June 2002.
14. C. Su and L. Tassiulas. Broadcast scheduling for information distribution. In *Proceedings of IEEE INFOCOM'97*, Kobe, Japan, April 1997.
15. M. A. Viredaz, L. S. Brakmo, and W. R. Hamburgen. Energy management on handheld devices. *ACM Queue*, 1(7):44-52, October 2003.
16. J. Xu, W.C. Lee, and X. Tang. Exponential Index: A Parameterized Distributed Indexing Scheme for Data on Air. *In Proceedings of the 2nd ACM/USENIX International Conference on Mobile Systems, Applications, and Services (MobiSys '04)*, pages 153 - 164, Boston, MA, June 2004.
17. J. Xu, B. Zheng, W.-C. Lee, and D. L. Lee. Energy efficient index for querying location- dependent data in mobile broadcast environments. In *Proceedings of the 19th IEEE International Conference on Data Engineering (ICDE'03)*, pages 239-250, Bangalore, India, March 2003.

Hierarchical Route Optimization in Mobile Network and Performance Evaluation*

Keecheon Kim[1,**], Dongkeun Lee[1], Jae Young Ahn[2], and Hyeong Ho Lee[2]

[1] Department of Computer Science & Engineering, Konkuk University, Seoul, Korea
{kckim, dklee}@konkuk.ac.kr
[2] ETRI PEC, 161 Gajeong-Dong, Yuseong-gu, Daejeon 305-700, Korea
{ahnjy, holee}@etri.re.kr

Abstract. With a current basic Network Mobility (NEMO) Support, all the communications to and from a node in a mobile network must be able to go through the bi-directional tunnel established between the Mobile Router and its Home Agent when the mobile network is away from the home. One of the issues in designing mobile network with MR-HA bi-directional tunnel is to solve the route optimization problem in the nested mobile networks. Since the aggregated hierarchy of mobile networks becomes a single nested mobile network, in order to forward packets to the nested mobile network nodes, multiple levels of bi-directional nested tunnels are required. We propose a hierarchical mechanism that allows direct packet tunneling between HA and MR and allows localized mobility management for MR.

1 Introduction

A mobile network is an entire network, moving as a unit, which dynamically changes its point of attachment to the Internet and its reachability in the topology[1]. A mobile network is connected to the global Internet via one or more Mobile Routers (MRs). With a current basic Network Mobility (NEMO) Support[3], all the communications to and from a node in a mobile network must go through the bi-directional tunnel established between the Mobile Router and its Home Agent(HA) when the mobile network is away from the home. Basic support protocol for mobile network is based on mobile IPv6[4]. When the MR moves away from the home link and attaches to a new access router, it acquires a CoA(Care-of Address) and immediately sends a Binding Update(BU) to its HA as described in [3]. And the MR may also include

* This research was supported by the ETRI, Korea, under the research support program. This research was also partially supported by Konkuk University under the sabbatical year research support program and the MIC(Ministry of Information and Communication), Korea, under the ITRC(Information Technology Research Center) support program supervised by the IITA(Institute of Information Technology Assessment).

** Corresponding author.

L.T. Yang et al. (Eds.): ICESS 2005, LNCS 3820, pp. 522 – 532, 2005.

information about the mobile network prefix in BU, so that the HA can forward the packets destined for nodes in the mobile network to MR.

When a packet is sent by a correspondent node(CN) to a node in the mobile network, it gets routed to the HA of the MR. And the HA tunnels the packet to the MR. The MR decapsulates the packet and forwards it to the node. On the other hand, if the node in the mobile network sends a packet to the CN, the MR tunnels the packet to the HA. In this way, mobile network nodes don't change their own points of attachment as a result of the movement of mobile network.

However, a mobile network may be nested. Using the proposed protocol by [3] on the nested mobile network, it builds a tunnel within a tunnel overhead limit. In order to avoid this overhead, it is required to optimize the routing path from the MR in the nested mobile network to the HA of the MR.

In this paper, we propose the route optimization based on the hierarchical algorithm for nested mobile network, it can reduce the amount of signaling between MR and HA. Nested mobile network has an aggregated hierarchy of mobile networks, so the hierarchical mobility management is well applicable. Our proposal can give localized mobility management functions as well as route optimization for the nested mobile networks.

This paper is organized as follows. Section 2 shows the routing problems in a nested mobile network. In section 3, we explain the other proposals as related works. In section 4, we present how our solution operates. Performance evaluation of the proposed solution is followed in section 5. Finally, in section 6, we present some concluding remarks.

2 Routing Problem of Nested Mobile Network

Nested mobile network is considered[2] since it is one of the requirements of mobile network. By allowing other mobile nodes to join a mobile network, it is possible to form an arbitrary level of nested mobile networks. Fig. 1 represents an example of nested mobile network. using NEMO Basic Support, the flow of packets between a Local Fixed Node, LFN, and a Correspondent Node, CN, would need to go through three separate tunnels, illustrated in Figure 2.
With such nesting, this leads to the following problems[10]:

- Sub-optimal routing : Both inbound and outbound packets will flow via the HAs of all the MRs on their paths within the mobile network, with an increased latency, less resilience and more bandwidth usage.
- Increased Packet Size : An extra IPv6 header is added per level of nesting to all the packets.

In particular, with NEMO basic support, each Mobile Router is attached to another Mobile Network by a single interface, and if loops are avoided, the graph will be a tree[3].

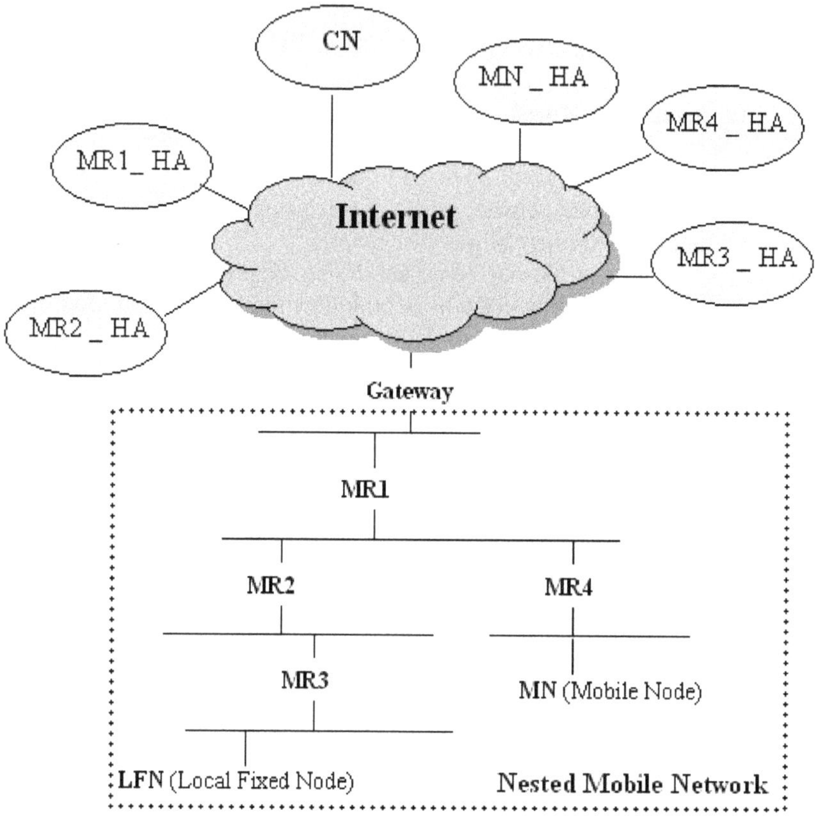

Fig. 1. An example of nested Mobile Network

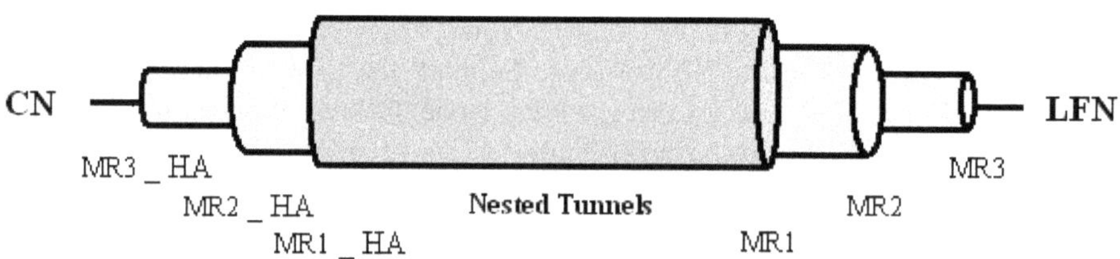

Fig. 2. Nesting of bi-directional tunnels

3 Related Work

Route optimization with RRH(Reverse Routing Header)[5] allows the building of a nested mobile network avoiding the nested tunnel overhead. It uses a new routing header, called the RRH, to provide an optimized path for the single tunnel. RRH records the route out of the nested mobile network and can be converted into a routing header for packets destined to the mobile network. In Fig. 1, when LFN(Local Fixed node) sends a packet to CN, the first MR on the path(MR3), tunnels the packet to its HA(MR3_HA), adding RRH with N = 3 in pre-allocated slots. The second router on the path, MR2, overwrites the source address of the packet with its own CoA, putting the old source address in the first free slot of RRH. The process followed by the second router is repeated by all the routers on the path, including the top level MR. When the packet leaves MR1, the source address is MR1's CoA and the RRH is MR2_CoA | MR3_CoA | MR3_HAddr(Home Address). When the MR3_HA receives the packet, it looks at the bottom entry, MR3_HAddr. This entry is used as an index into the binding cache. MR3_HA stores two items in the bind cache entry associated with MR3. One is the address entry from RRH, to be used to build the extended type 2 routing header. And the other is a packet source address MR1_CoA, to be used as the first hop. The routing header is built out of the previous RRH.

In [5], type 2 routing header(RH2) that is defined in [4] is extended to contain more than one address. Processing the extended RH2 inherits from the RH type 0 described in [6]. The last address of extended RH 2 must be the home address of the MR. Using RH2, the path from CN to LFN is *CN -> MR3_HA -> MR1 -> MR2 -> MR3 -> LFN.*

Binding updates are still used for home registration and de-registration, but only when the MR registers for the first time with HA. The full path to the MR is contained in every packet from MR to HA, and HA must maintain the list of reverse routing headers for each mobile router. This is more expensive to maintain than binding cache. The extended RH2 is also introduced in [9], but it is not standard. Thus extended RH2 must be used more carefully.

4 Hierarchical Route Optimiation in Nested Mobile Network

In fig.1, if a CN sends a packet to MN using the proposed solution in this paper, the path from CN to LFN will be: *CN-->MR3_ HA -->MR1-->MR2-->MR3-->LFN.*

Our solution extends HMIPv6[7] slightly to support the nested mobile network. In our solution, MAP(Mobility Anchor Point), which is newly introduced in HMIPv6, can be pre-located in a gateway to the Internet. A root-MR can act as a MAP as well.

4.1 Binding Updates

In fig. 1, MR1(root-MR) becomes a MAP and entire nested mobile network becomes a local MAP domain. All MRs and MNs in the nested mobile network (i.e. MR2, MR3, MR4 and MN) configure RCoA(Regional CoA) based on the mobile network prefix of the root-MR(MR1) and configure LCoA(On-link CoA) based on the mobile network prefix of its access router(MR or fixed router) as described in [7]. For example, MR3 configures LCoA based on the prefix of MR2. Thus, MR2's LCoA is identical with its RCoA.

The MR1's MAP option must be included in router advertisements(RAs) of all routers in the nested mobile network. In addition to the basic MAP option of HMIPv6, current CoA of MAP(MR1) is included in RA. The MAP's CoA must also be included in RAs of all routers in the nested mobile network as the MAP option.

In order to simply explain our solution, we focus on MR3 in fig. 1. When MR3 moves into MAP-MR1 domain, it receives RA with the MAP option containing MR1's home address and MR1's current CoA. After forming the RCoA and LCoA, MR3 sends a BU to MR1 as described in [7]. However this BU message contains mobile network prefix option[3] in order to inform the MAP(MR1) of the prefix information for the mobile network. The mobile network prefix is used for route optimization. When MN sends a local BU to MR1, it just operates as described in [7]. Table 1 represents a subset of binding cache table stored in MR1 as a result of local BUs of all sub-MRs and MN.

Table 1. Subset of MR1's binding cache

Node	RCoA	LCoA	Network Prefix
MR2	MR2_RCoA	MR2_LCoA	Mobile Network Prefix of MR2
MR3	MR3_RCoA	MR3_LCoA	Mobile Network Prefix of MR3
MR4	MR4_RCoA	MR4_LCoA	Mobile Network Prefix of MR4
MN	MN_RCoA	MN_LCoA	-

After receiving a binding acknowledgement from the MAP(MR1), MR3 sends BU to MR3_HA as described in [3]. Thus, the RCoA of MR3 is used as the CoA of MR3. And this BU message contains a new option to inform the MR3_HA of the MR1(MAP)'s current CoA. MR3_HA records this CoA together with the binding update entry in its binding cache. And this MR1's CoA will be used as the destination address of all packets being forwarded to MR3.

4.2 Hierarchical Route Optimiation

Every MR(including root-MR) in the nested mobile network must not encapsulate the packet, if the source or the destination address of packet is RCoA. Instead, the MR forwards the packet to its egress interface. Now, consider the case where a LFN sends a packet to CN. When LFN sends a packet to CN, MR3 will encapsulate the packet to be sent through the reverse tunnel with its HA(MR3_HA). When MR3 encapsulate the packet, it must use its RCoA as a source address of tunneled packet and forward it to MR2. Because MR2 knows the prefix of MR1's home address, it will know that the source address of the packet is RCoA of one of nodes which belongs to the same MAP domain of MR2. And MR2 forwards the packet to MR1 without encapsulation. Receiving an outbound packet, MAP-MR1 must check if the source address of the packet is stored in its binding cache. If so, MR1 sends the packet to the destination directly. Otherwise, the packet is tunneled to MR1_HA. Thus, the path from LFN to CN is *LFN->MR3->MR2->MR1->MR3_HA->CN.*

When CN sends a packet to LFN, MR3_HA intercepts and encapsulates the packet. The encapsulated packet will have the source address set to the address of MR3_HA, and the destination address set to the address of MAP(MR1)'s CoA stored in the binding cache entry, and an type 0 routing header with one address entries, care-of address of MR3. According to the destination address, the packet will be transferred to MR1. In order to send the packet to MR3 correctly, MR1 tunnels the packet to MR3's LCoA using type 0 routing header.

If MR1 receives a packet, it acts as a MAP encapsulation point and sends the packet to the final destination. First of all, MR1 processes the routing header and checks whether it has a binding cache entry of the new destination address. If so, MR1 encapsulates the packet and forwards it to the new destination. In order to send the packet to the destination, MR1 uses type 0 routing header(RH 0). If MR1 has no binding cache entry, it uses normal routing process. In order to construct a routing header of the outer packet, MR1 uses the pseudo algorithm depicted below.

```
empty a stack;
set finished = false;
find an entry in binding cache with RCoA field == des-
tination address of original packet(i.e. destination
MR's RcoA)

if (no binding cache entry is found) {
    use normal routing process;
} else {
    If (RCoA of entry is identical with its LCoA) {
         use normal routing process;
    }
    while (not finished) {
          push LCoA of entry to stack;
          get prefix of LCoA;
          find an entry in binding cache with
          prefix field == prefix of LCoA;
          if (no binding cache entry is found) {
              finished = true;
          }
    }
    set source address field = HAddr of root-MR(MR1);
    pop top of stack to destination address field;
    prepare a type 0 routing header(RH 0);
    set Hdr Ext Len field of RH = (size of stack-1)x 2;
    set Segment Left filed of RH = size of stack -1;
    for i=1 to Segment Left filed of RH 0{
         pop top of stack to Address[i] of RH 0;
    }
    prepare a type 2 routing header (RH 2);
    set Address of RH 2 = RCoA of destination MR(MR3)
}
```

According to the above algorithm, MR1 find an entry in a binding cache with RCoA of MR3. And then, MR1 gets prefix of MR3's LCoA. Has been configured MR3's LCoA based on the network prefix of MR2, MR1 can find an entry of MR2.

When each sub-MR receives a packet, it processes the routing header and forwards it to the new destination. Using the proposed route optimization, the path from CN to LFN is *CN -> MR3_HA -> MR1 -> MR2 -> MR3 -> LFN.*

Fig.3 represents the packet encapsulation and processing of the message delivered from MR3_HA to MR3.

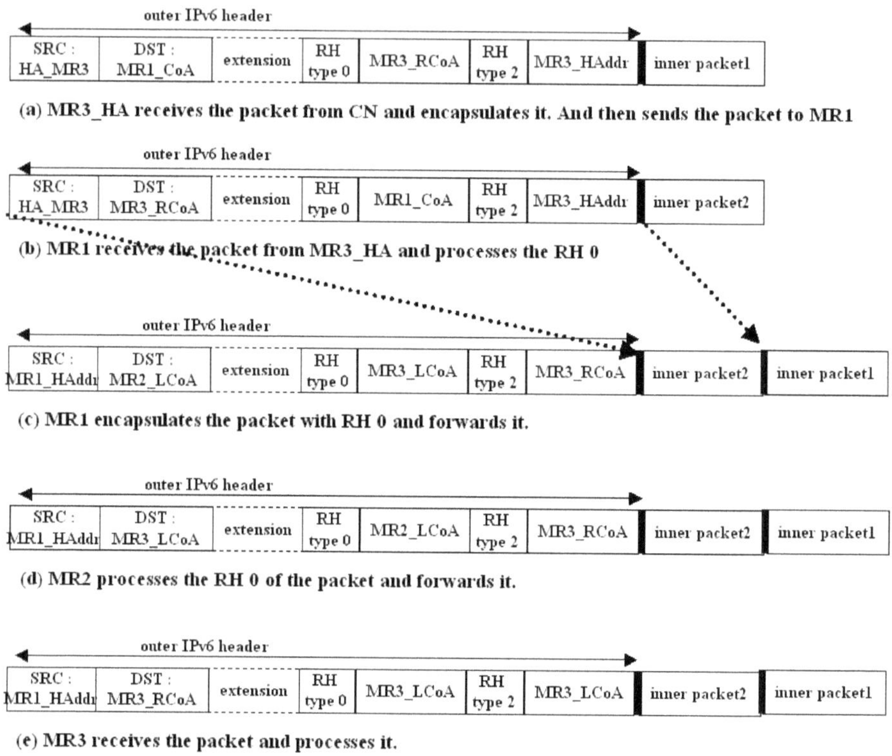

Fig. 3. Packet encapsulation

If we assume that MR3 is a Mobile Node, it is obvious that our route optimization mechanism is applicable to a Mobile IPv6 Node.

4.3 Localied Mobility Management

Our solution allows local mobility. Considering the case where MR2 moves into MR4 with its sub-network (fig.4), the only thing MR2 has to do is sending a BU to MR1.

If MR1 receives a BU from MR2, it modifies the entry of MR2 in the binding cache. There is no need to send BU to MR2_HA. The RCoA and the LCoA of MR(MR3) are not affected by the movement of its upper MR(MR2). Thus, as a result of local BU of MR2, the reachability of nodes behind MR2 is preserved. In this way, any change in the nested network topology is immediately reflected by a local BU. On the other hand, if MR2 moves alone into another MR's link without sub-NEMO, MR3 will receive a new router advertisement from MR1(or other MRs) and it will perform local BU to MR1 as it moves into another MR's link.

When MR moves into other nested mobile network, in other words, the MR receives RA containing a new MAP option, it must configure a new RCoA and a new

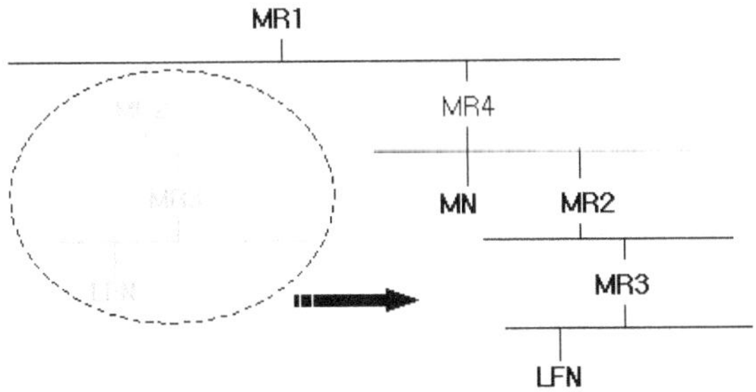

Fig. 4. Movement of MR in the nested mobile network

LCoA. And then the MR must update the bindings with the new MAP and the HA. If the MR does not change its point of attachment and receives a new MAP option, it is not necessary to configure a new LCoA.

5 Performance Evaluation

In this section we analyze the performance of our proposal. Among several mobility factors, three are particularly important[8]: the scalability property, the routing performance and the transition performance.

5.1 Routing and Transition Performance

In our proposal, there is only one MR-HA bi-directional tunnel regardless of the number of MRs. Thus, we can avoid the tunnel within a tunnel overhead of the basic NEMO support protocol. And our proposal support localized mobility management, thus local handoffs are managed within the MAP domain. If we ignore the processing delays of each MR and HA, the binding update delay of moving MR is defined as:

$$BU_{delay} = 2 \times (H_M + q \times H_R) \times d \tag{1}$$

H_M: hop count between MR and root-MR
H_R: hop count between HA_MR and root-MR
q: the probability of the non-local mobility
d: one way transmission delay of one hope

Thus, as the probability of the local mobility becomes greater, the gain of our proposal from binding update delay is more increased. The average gain of our approach over basic NEMO approach is defined as equation(2). Fig. 5 shows the results.

$$G_{AVG} = \alpha \times G_{\text{int}\,ra} + \beta \times G_{\text{int}\,er} = \alpha \times G_{\text{int}\,ra} = (N-1)/N \times (b/a) \tag{2}$$

$$G_{\text{int}\,er} = 0;\; G_{\text{int}\,ra} = \{\,(a+b) - a\,\}/a = b/a;\; \alpha = (N-1)/N;\quad \beta = 1/N$$

N: the average number of different points of attachment of a MR within a nested NEMO.

G_{intra}: the gain when the MR is moving within a nested NEMO

G_{inter}: the gain when the MR is moving from one nested NEMO to another.
a: the delay from MR to root-MR
b: the delay from root-MR to HA_MR

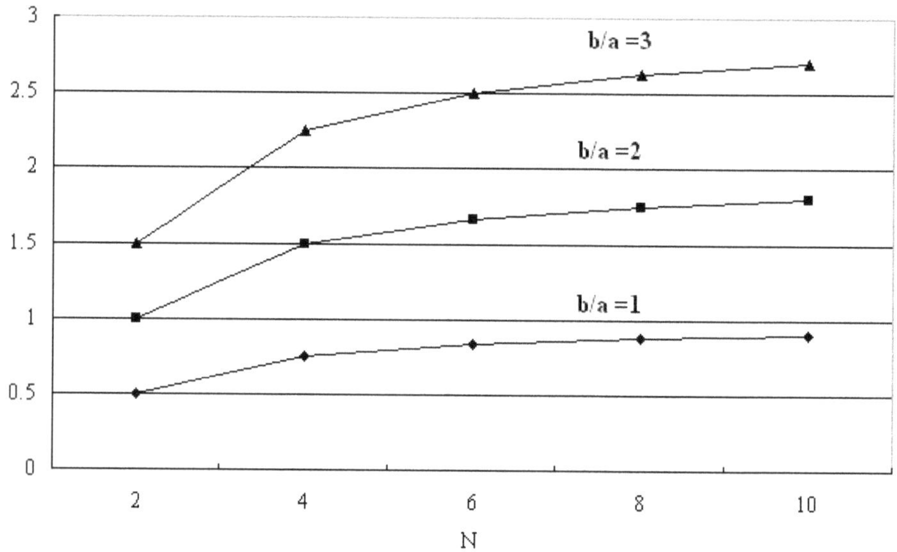

Fig. 5. The gain over basic NEMO from binding update delay

In RRH approach[5], binding updates are used only when the MR registers for the first time with the HA. When the MR becomes aware of a topology change in the nested network or in the absence of traffic(detected by a timeout) to the HA, it must send a RRH Heartbeat to the HA. Thus, from the localized mobility prospect, our proposal is more efficient than RRH approach.

5.2 Scalability Performance

In this section, we compare the transmission load introduced by basic NEMO approach and our approach. The transmission load, T, is defined as:

$$T = packet\_size \times hop\_count \tag{3}$$

packet_size and hop_count are functions of N (N : level of nested NEMO)

In our proposal, MR do not use routing header when it forwards a packet to the HA. However, our proposal uses additional tunnel in nested mobile network. In order to calculate the both directional transmission load between MR and MR_HA, T_{Basic} for basic approach and T_{Hier} for our proposal are defined as follows.

$$T_{Basic} = \sum_{i=1}^{n}(i \times H_{size}) + \sum_{i=1}^{n-1}(i \times H_{size}) \ . \tag{4}$$

$$T_{Hier} = (H_{size} + A_{size}) + (n-1) \times \{2 \times H_{size} + (n-1) \times A_{size}\} \tag{5}$$

Hsize : IPv6 header size + MIPv6 RH2 size; Asize : IPv6 RH 0 size
n : level of nested NEMO

We assume that there is no IPv6 extension header except routing header and we do not consider a payload(i.e. original packet). According to equation (4) and (5), we evaluated the gain achieved by our proposal. We note G_{Basic} the gain over basic approach.

$$G_{Basic} = (T_{Basic} - T_{Hier}) / T_{Hier} \tag{6}$$

Fig. 6 shows the gain over basic NEMO from transmission load. As the level of nested NEMO is more increased, the gain of our proposal is more increased. RRH and our proposal allow only one HA-MR bi-directional tunnel. In addition, they use routing header to forward packet. In our proposal, MR do not use routing header when it forwards a packet to the HA. Thus the packet size of our proposal is less than the packet size of RRH and, comparing with RRH, our proposal can acquire more benefit.

Our proposal does not propagate the local routing information of nested mobile network to the external domains, so it is more secure.

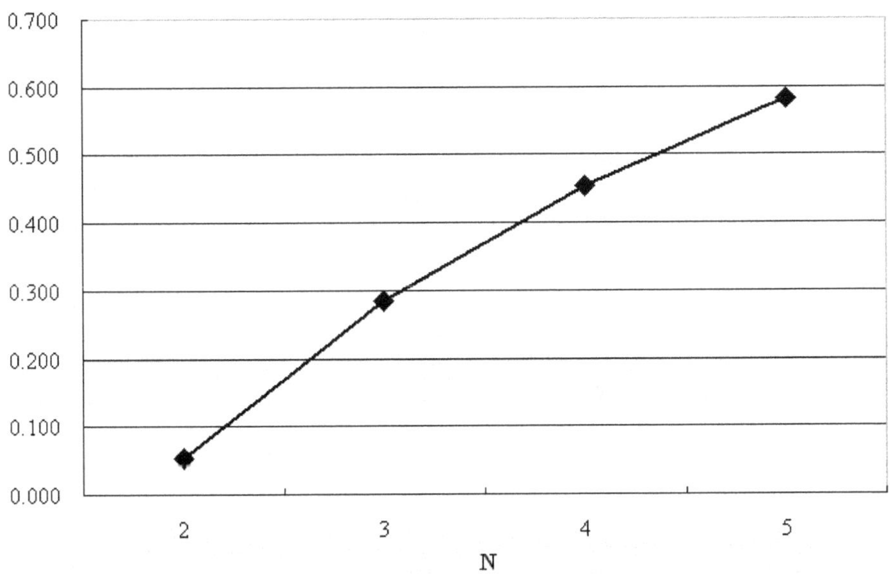

Fig. 6. The gain over basic NEMO from transmission load

6 Conclusion

In this paper, we described route optimization based on a hierarchical algorithm. Our proposal is more secure in terms of security. It does not propagate the local routing information of nested mobile network to the external domains. Adapting our solution to nested mobile networks, we may expect better throughput and more efficient network bandwidth usage.

In an aircraft, a ship, or a train, root MR of the nested mobile networks may get connected to the Internet through a geostationary satellite. In this scenario, handoffs of root MR do not occur very often. On the contrary, local handoffs of sub-MRs will occur frequently. For that reasons, hierarchical mobility management in the nested mobile networks is required for fast handoff. Our proposal can give hierarchical mobility management functions as well as route optimization for the nested mobile networks.

However, smooth handoff in nested mobile network will be the subject of the future research. In mobile networks, movement of MR means many packets must be retransmitted to a new address of the destination node. For a very fast moving mobile network, this remains as a future research.

References

1. T. Ernst, and H. Lach : Network Mobility Support Terminology, IETF internet draft, draft-ietf-nemo-terminology-03.txt (work in progress), Feb. 2005.
2. T. Ernst : Network Mobility Support Goals and Requirements, IETF internet draft , draft-ietf-nemo-requirements-04.txt (work in progress), Feb. 2005.
3. V. Devarapalli, R. Wakikawa, A. Petrescu, and P. Thubert : Network Mobility (NEMO) Basic Support Protocol, IETF RFC 3963, Jan. 2005.
4. C. Perkins, D. Johnson, and J. Arkko : Mobility Support in IPv6, IETF RFC 3775, June 2004.
5. P. Thubert, and M. Molteni : IPv6 Reverse Routing Header and its application to Mobile Networks, IETF internet draft, draft-thubert-nemo-reverse-routing-header-05 (work in progress), June 2004
6. S. Deering, and R. Hinden : Internet Protocol, Version 6 (IPv6) Specification, RFC 2460, IETF, December 1998.
7. H. Soliman, C. Castelluccia, K. El-Malki, and L. Bellier : Hierarchical Mobile IPv6 Mobility Management (HMIPv6), IETF internet draft, draft-ietf-mipshop-hmipv6-04.txt (work in progress), Dec. 2004.
8. A. Myles and D. Skellen : Comparing Four IP Based Mobile node Protocols, In proceedings of the 4th joint European Networking Conference, 1993, pp.191-196
9. C. W. Ng and T. Tanaka : Securing Nested Tunnels Optimization with Access Router Option, IETF internet draft, draft-ng-nemo-access-router-option-01.txt , July 2004.
10. C. Ng, P. Thubert, M. Watari and F. Zhao: Network Mobility Route Optimization Problem Statement, IETF internet draft, draft-ietf-nemo-ro-problem-statement-00(work in progress), July 2005

Swarm Based Sensor Deployment Optimization in Ad Hoc Sensor Networks

Wu Xiaoling, Shu Lei, Yang Jie, Xu Hui, Jinsung Cho, and Sungyoung Lee*

Department of Computer Engineering, Kyung Hee University, Korea
{xiaoling, sl8132, yangjie, xuhui, sylee}@oslab.khu.ac.kr
chojs@khu.ac.kr

Abstract. In ad hoc sensor networks, sensor nodes have very limited energy resources, thus energy consuming operations such as data collection, transmission and reception must be kept at a minimum. This paper applies particle swarm optimization (PSO) approach to optimize the coverage in ad hoc sensor networks deployment and to reduce cost by clustering method based on a well-known energy model. Sensor nodes are assumed to be mobile, and during the coverage optimization process, they move to form a uniformly distributed topology according to the execution of algorithm at base station. The simulation results show that PSO algorithm has faster convergence rate than genetic algorithm based method while demonstrating good performance.

1 Introduction

Recent military operations have limitations of surveillance missions performed by high-altitude platforms (UAV, U2, satellite) even when equipped with state of the art sensors. Most of the limitations are inherent to long-distance surveillance and cannot be resolved by any improvement in the onboard-sensor technology [1].

In order to get a clear understanding of the situation on the ground, it is important to observe from close range, using remote sensing device placed in the region of interest (ROI) to form a sensor network. Ad hoc sensor networks that employ ad hoc networking have become an area of intense research activity. In most cases, a large number of wireless sensor devices can be deployed in hostile areas without human involved, e.g. by air-dropping from an aircraft for remote monitoring and surveillance purposes. Such airdropped networks are called *ad hoc* sensor networks to distinguish them from other types of sensor networks where nodes are laid out in some fixed predetermined pattern. Due to their attractive characteristics, ad hoc sensor networks have been applied to many military and civil applications such as target tracking, surveillance, and environmental control. Usually, once the sensors are deployed on the ground, their data are transmitted back to the base station to provide the necessary situational information.

The limited energy storage and memory of the deployed sensors prevent them from relaying data directly to the base station. It is therefore necessary to form a cluster based topology, and the cluster heads (CHs) provide the transmission relay to base station such as a satellite. And the aircraft carrying the sensors has a limited payload,

* Corresponding author.

L.T. Yang et al. (Eds.): ICESS 2005, LNCS 3820, pp. 533 – 541, 2005.

so it is impossible to randomly drop thousands of sensors over the ROI, hoping the communication connectivity would arise by chance; thus, the mission must be performed with a fixed maximum number of sensors. In addition, the airdrop deployment may introduce uncertainty in the final sensor positions. Though many scenarios adopt random deployment for practical reasons such as deployment cost and time, random deployment may not provide a uniform sensor distribution over the ROI, which is considered to be a desirable distribution in sensor networks. These limitations motivate the establishment of a planning system that optimizes the sensor reorganization process after initial random airdrop deployment assuming sensor node mobility, which results in the maximum possible utilization of the available sensors.

There exist a lot of research work [2], [3], [4] related to the placement of sensor nodes in network topology design. Most of them focused on optimizing the location of the sensors in order to maximize their collective coverage. However only a single objective was considered in most of the research papers, other considerations such as energy consumption minimization are also of vital practical importance in the choice of the network deployment. Self-deployment methods using mobile nodes [4□9] have been proposed to enhance network coverage and to extend the system lifetime via configuration of uniformly distributed node topologies from random node distributions. In [4], the authors present the virtual force algorithm (VFA) as a new approach for sensor deployment to improve the sensor field coverage after an initial random placement of sensor nodes. The cluster head executes the VFA algorithm to find new locations for sensors to enhance the overall coverage. They also considered unavoidable uncertainty existing in the precomputed sensor node locations. This uncertainty-aware deployment algorithm provides high coverage with a minimum number of sensor nodes. However they assumed that global information regarding other nodes is available. In [1], the authors examined the optimization of wireless sensor network layouts using a multi-objective genetic algorithm (GA) in which two competing objectives are considered, total sensor coverage and the lifetime of the network. However the computation of this method is not inexpensive.

In this paper, we attempt to solve the coverage problem while considering energy efficiency using particle swarm optimization (PSO) algorithm, which can lead to computational faster convergence than genetic algorithm used to solve the deployment optimization problem in [1]. Sensor nodes are assumed to have mobility, and during the coverage optimization process, they move to form a uniformly distributed topology according to the execution of algorithm at the base station. To the best of our knowledge, this is the first paper to solve deployment optimization problem by PSO algorithm.

In the next section, the PSO algorithm is introduced and compared with GA. Modeling of sensor network and the deployment algorithm is presented in section 3, followed by simulation results in section 4. Some concluding remarks and future work are provided in section 5.

2 Particle Swarm Optimiation

PSO, originally proposed by Eberhart and Kennedy [5] in 1995, and inspired by social behavior of bird flocking, has come to be widely used as a problem solving method in engineering and computer science.

The individuals, called, particles, are flown through the multidimensional search space with each particle representing a possible solution to the multidimensional problem. All of particles have fitness values, which are evaluated by the fitness function to be optimized, and have velocities, which direct the flying of the particles. PSO is initialized with a group of random solutions and then searches for optima by updating generations. In every iteration, each particle is updated by following two "best" factors. The first one, called *pbest*, is the best fitness it has achieved so far and it is also stored in memory. Another "best" value obtained so far by any particle in the population, is a global best and called *gbest*. When a particle takes part of the population as its topological neighbors, the best value is a local best and is called *lbest*. After each iteration, the *pbest* and *gbest* (or *lbest*) are updated if a more dominating solution is found by the particle and population, respectively.

The PSO formulae define each particle in the D-dimensional space as $X_i = (x_{i1}, x_{i2}, x_{i3}, \ldots\ldots, x_{iD})$ where *i* represents the particle number, and *d* is the dimension. The memory of the previous best position is represented as $P_i = (p_{i1}, p_{i2}, p_{i3} \ldots\ldots p_{iD})$, and a velocity along each dimension as $V_i = (v_{i1}, v_{i2}, v_{i3} \ldots\ldots v_{iD})$. The updating equation [6] is as follows,

$$v_{id} = \varpi \times v_{id} + c_1 \times rand() \times (p_{id} - x_{id}) + c_2 \times rand() \times (p_{gd} - x_{id}) \tag{1}$$

$$x_{id} = x_{id} + v_{id} \tag{2}$$

where ϖ is the inertia weight, and c_1 and c_2 are acceleration coefficients.

The role of the inertia weight ϖ is considered to be crucial for the PSO' s convergence. The inertia weight is employed to control the impact of the previous history of velocities on the current velocity of each particle. Thus, the parameter ϖ regulates the trade-off between global and local exploration ability of the swarm. A large inertia weight facilitates global exploration, while a small one tends to facilitate local exploration, i.e. fine-tuning the current search area. A suitable value for the inertia weight ϖ balances the global and local exploration ability and, consequently, reduces the number of iterations required to locate the optimum solution. Generally, it is better to initially set the inertia to a large value, in order to make better global exploration of the search space, and gradually decrease it to get more refined solutions. Thus, a time-decreasing inertia weight value is used. The initial swarm can be generated randomly [7].

PSO shares many similarities with GA. Both algorithms start with a group of a randomly generated population, have fitness values to evaluate the population, update the population and search for the optimum with random techniques. However, PSO does not have genetic operators like crossover and mutation. Particles update themselves with the internal velocity. They also have memory, which is important to the algorithm [8].

Compared with GA, PSO is easy to implement, has few parameters to adjust, and requires only primitive mathematical operators, computationally inexpensive in terms of both memory requirements and speed while comprehensible. It usually results in faster convergence rates than GA. This feature suggests that PSO is a potential algorithm to optimize deployment in a sensor network.

3 The Proposed Algorithm

First of all, we present the model of wireless sensor network. We assume that each node knows its position in the problem space, all sensor members in a cluster are homogeneous and cluster heads are more powerful than sensor members. Sensing coverage and communication coverage of each node are assumed to have a circular shape without any irregularity. The design variables are 2D coordinates of the sensor nodes, $\{(x_1, y_1), (x_2, y_2), \ldots\ldots\}$. And the sensor nodes are assumed to be mobile. Many research efforts into the sensor deployment problem in wireless sensor network [4, 9] make this sensor mobility assumption reasonable.

3.1 Optimiation of Coverage

We consider coverage as the first optimization objective. It is one of the measurement criteria of QOS of a sensor network.

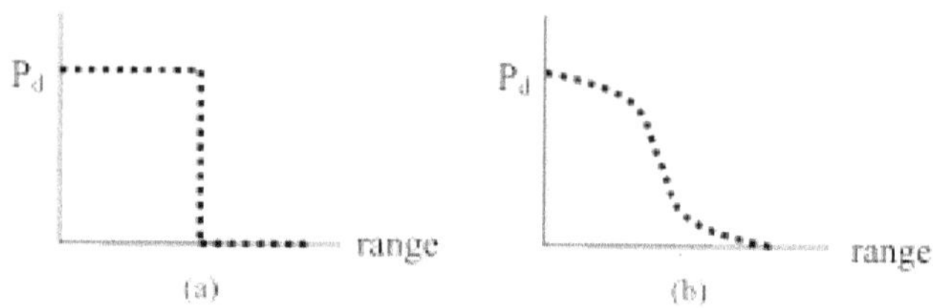

Fig. 1. Sensor coverage models (a) Binary sensor and (b) stochastic sensor models

The coverage of each sensor can be defined either by a binary sensor model or a stochastic sensor model as shown in Fig. 1 [9]. In the binary sensor model, the detection probability of the event of interest is 1 within the sensing range, otherwise, the probability is 0. In the stochastic sensor model, the probability of detection of the event of interest follows a decaying function of distance from the sensor. In this paper, the binary sensor model is employed and coverage is defined as the ratio of the union of areas covered by each node and the area of the entire ROI, as shown in Eq (3). Here, the covered area of each node is defined as the circular area within its sensing radius [9].

$$C = \frac{\bigcup_{i=1,\ldots,N} A_i}{A} \tag{3}$$

where

A_i is the area covered by the ith node;
N is the total number of nodes;
A stands for the area of the ROI.

In order to prevent recalculating the overlapped area, the coverage here is calculated using Monte Carlo method by meshing the network space, i.e., by creating a uniform grid in the ROI. All the grid points being located in the sensing area are labeled 1 otherwise 0, depending on whether the Euclidean distance between each grid point and the sensor node is longer or shorter than sensing radius, as shown in Fig 2. Then the coverage can be approximated by the ratio of the summation of ones to the total number of the grid points.

If a node is located well inside the ROI, its complete coverage area will lie within the ROI. In this case, the full area of that circle is included in the covered region. If a node is located near the boundary of the ROI, then only the part of the ROI covered by that node is included in the computation.

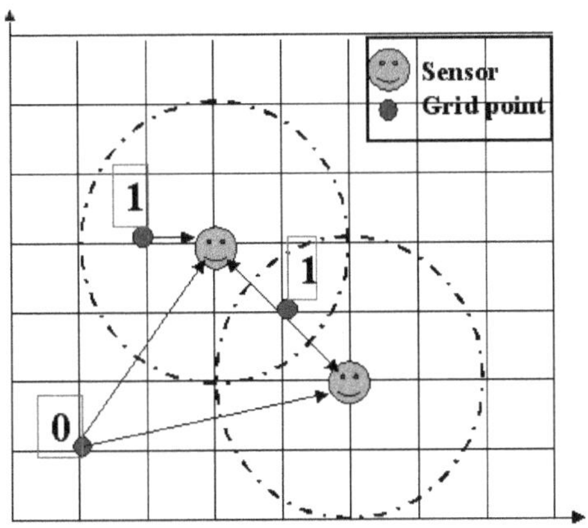

Fig. 2. Sensing coverage calculation (dashed circle indicating the sensing area boundary)

3.2 Optimiation of Energy Consumption

After optimization of coverage, all the deployed sensor nodes move to their own positions. Now we can disregard the assumption of sensor mobility since our goal is to minimize energy usage in a cluster based sensor network topology by finding the optimal cluster head (CH) positions. For this purpose, we assume a power consumption model [10] for the radio hardware energy dissipation where the transmitter dissipates energy to run the radio electronics and the power amplifier, and the receiver dissipates energy to run the radio electronics. This is one of the most widely used models in sensor network simulation analysis. For our approach, both the free space (*distance*^{2} power loss) and the multi-path fading (*distance*^{4} power loss) channel models were used. Assume that the sensor nodes inside a cluster have short distance *dis* to cluster head but each cluster head has long distance *Dis* to the base station. Thus for each sensor node inside a cluster, to transmit an *l*-bit message a distance *dis* to cluster head, the radio expends

$$E_{TS}(l,dis) = lE_{elec} + l\varepsilon_{fs}dis^2 \tag{4}$$

For cluster head, however, to transmit an *l*-bit message a distance *Dis* to base station, the radio expends

$$E_{TH}(l, Dis) = lE_{elec} + l\varepsilon_{mp}Dis^4 \tag{5}$$

In both cases, to receive the message, the radio expends:

$$E_R(l) = lE_{elec} \tag{6}$$

The electronics energy, E_{elec}, depends on factors such as the digital coding, modulation, filtering, and spreading of the signal, here we set as E_{elec}=50*nJ/bit*, whereas the amplifier constant, is taken as ε_{fs} =10*pJ/bit/m*^{2}, ε_{mp} = 0.0013*pJ/bit/m*^{2}.

So the energy loss of a sensor member in a cluster is

$$E_s(l, dis) = l(100 + 0.01dis^2) \tag{7}$$

The energy loss of a CH is

$$E_{CH}(l, Dis) = l(100 + 1.3\times10^{-6}\times Dis^4) \tag{8}$$

Since the energy consumption for computation is much less than that for communication, we neglect computation energy consumption here.

Assume m clusters with n_j sensor members in the jth cluster C_j. The total energy loss E_{total} is the summation of the energy used by all sensor members and all the m cluster heads:

$$E_{total} = l\sum_{j=1}^{m}\sum_{i=1}^{n_j}(100 + 0.01dis_{ij}^2 + \frac{100}{n_j} + \frac{1.3\times10^{-6}Dis_j^4}{n_j}) \tag{9}$$

Because only 2 terms are related to distance, we can just set the fitness function as:

$$f = \sum_{j=1}^{m}\sum_{i=1}^{n_j}(0.01dis_{ij}^2 + \frac{1.3\times10^{-6}Dis_j^4}{n_j}) \tag{10}$$

4 Performance Evaluation

The PSO starts with a "swarm" of sensors randomly generated. As shown in Fig. 3 is a randomly deployed sensor network with coverage value 0.4484 calculated using Eq. (3). A linear decreasing inertia weight value from 0.95 to 0.4 is used, decided according to [6]. Acceleration coefficients c_1 and c_2 both are set to 2 as proposed in [6]. For optimizing coverage, we have used 20 particles, which are denoted by all sensor nodes coordinates, for our experiment in a 50×50 square sensor network, and the maximum number of generations we are running is 500. The maximum velocity of the particle is set to be 50. The sensing range of each sensor is set to be 5 units. An upper bound on the coverage is given by the ratio of the sum of the circle areas (corresponding to sensors) to the total area of the sensor field. In this simulation, the upper bound evaluates to be 0.628, which is calculated from the perfect uniform distribution case without any overlapped area. The coverage is calculated as a fitness value in each generation.

After optimizing the coverage, all sensors move to their final locations. Now the coordinates of potential cluster heads are set as particles in this static sensor network. The communication range of each sensor node is 15 units with a fixed remote base station at (25, 80). We start with a minimum number of clusters acceptable in the problem space to be 4. The node, which will become a cluster head will not have any restriction on the transmission range. The nodes are organized into clusters by the base station. Each particle will have a fitness value, which will be evaluated by the fitness function (10) in each generation. Our purpose is to find the optimal location of cluster heads. Once the position of the cluster head is identified, if there is no node in that position then a potential cluster head nearest to the cluster head location will become a cluster head.

We also optimized the placement of cluster head in the 2-D space using GA. We used a simple GA algorithm with single-point crossover and selection based on a roulette-wheel process. The coordinates of the cluster head are the chromosomes in the population. For our experiment we are using 10 chromosomes in the population. The maximum number of generations allowed is 500. In each evolution we update the

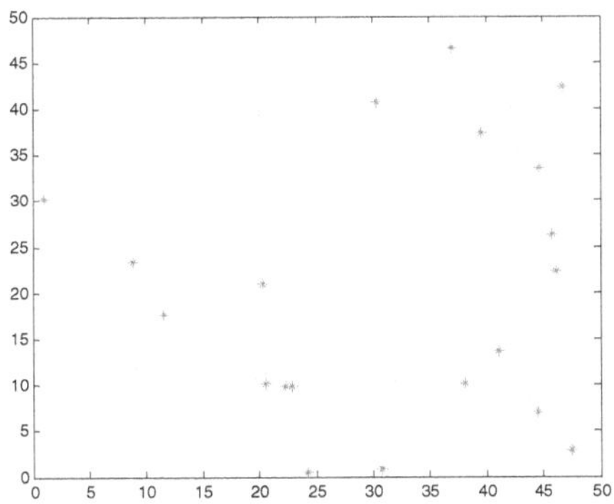

Fig. 3. Randomly deployed sensor network (Coverage value=0.4484)

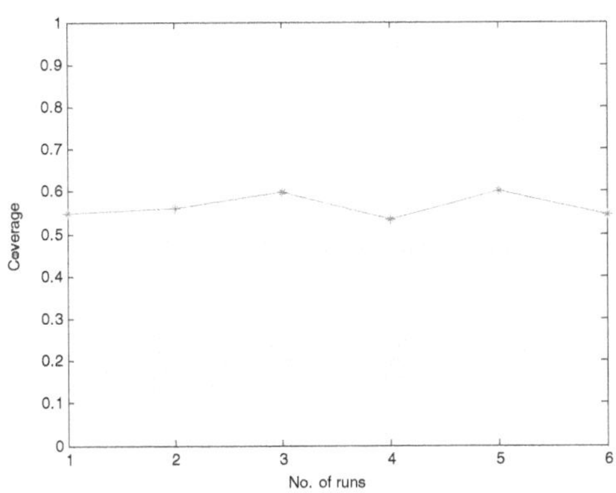

Fig. 4. Optimal coverage results for 6 runs

number of nodes included in the clusters. The criterion to find the best solution is that the total fitness value should be minimal.

Fig. 4 is the coverage optimization results after 6 runs. Compared with the upper bound 0.628, the difference between them is small. Fig. 5 shows the convergence rate of PSO and GA. We ran the algorithm for both approaches several times and in every run PSO converges faster than GA, which was used in [1] for coverage and lifetime optimization. The main reason for the fast convergence of PSO is due to the velocity factor of the particle.

Fig. 6 shows the final cluster topology in the sensor network space after coverage and energy consumption optimization when the number of clusters in the sensor space is 4. We can see from the figure that nodes are uniformly distributed among the clusters compared with the random deployment as shown in Fig 3. The four stars denote cluster heads, the small circles are sensor members, and the dashed circles are communication range of sensor nodes. The energy saved is the difference between the initial fitness value and the final minimized fitness value. In this experiment, it is approximately 16.

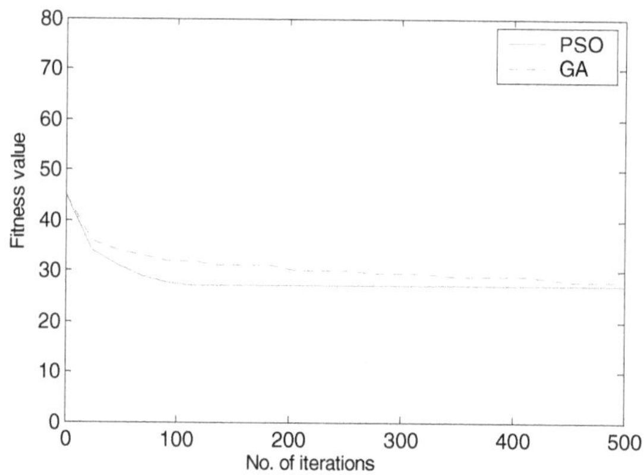

Fig. 5. Comparison of convergence rate between PSO and GA based on Eq. (10)

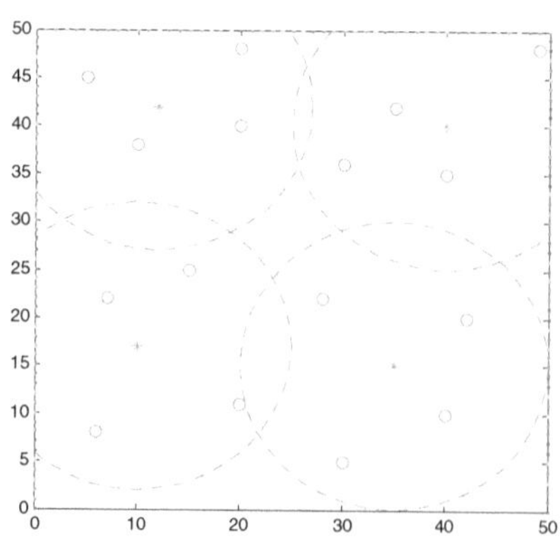

Fig. 6. Energy efficient cluster formation using PSO

5 Conclusions and Future Work

The application of PSO algorithm to optimize the coverage in ad hoc sensor network deployment and energy consumption in cluster-based topology is discussed. We have used coverage as the first optimization objective to place the sensors with mobility, and a distance based energy model to reduce cost based on clustering method. The simulation results show that PSO algorithm has faster convergence rate than GA based layout optimization method while demonstrating good performance.

In the future work, we will take the uncertainty in the position of the sensors due to the initial random deployment into account. Moreover, other objectives, such as time and distance for sensor moving will be further studied.

Acknowledgement

This work was supported by grant No. R01-2005-000-10267-0 from Korea Science and Engineering Foundation in Ministry of Science and Technology.

References

1. Damien B. Jourdan, Olivier L. de Weck: Layout optimization for a wireless sensor network using a multi-objective genetic algorithm. IEEE 59th Vehicular Technology Conference (VTC 2004-Spring), Vol.5 (2004) 2466-2470
2. K. Chakrabarty, S. S. Iyengar, H. Qi and E. Cho: Grid coverage for surveillance and target location in distributed sensor networks. IEEE transactions on computers, Vol.51 (2002) 1448-1453
3. A. Howard, M.J. Mataric and G. S. Sukhatme: Mobile sensor network deployment using potential fields: a distributed, scalable solution to the area coverage problem. Proc. Int. Conf. on distributed Autonomous Robotic Systems (2002) 299-308
4. Y. Zou and K. Chakrabarty: Sensor deployment and target localization based on virtual forces. Proc. IEEE Infocom Conference, Vol. 2 (2003) 1293-1303
5. Kennedy and R. C. Eberhart: Particle Swarm Optimization. Proceedings of IEEE International Conference on Neural Networks, Perth, Australia (1995) 1942-1948
6. Yuhui Shi, Russell C. Eberhart: Empirical study of Particle Swarm Optimization. Proceedings of the 1999 Congress on Evolutionary Computation, Vol. 3 (1999) 1948-1950
7. K.E. Parsopoulos, M.N. Vrahatis. Particle Swarm Optimization Method in Multiobjective Problems. Proceedings of the 2002 ACM symposium on Applied computing, Madrid, Spain (2002): 603- 607
8. http://www.swarmintelligence.org/tutorials.php
9. Nojeong Heo and Pramod K. Varshney: Energy-Efficient Deployment of Intelligent Mobile Sensor Networks. IEEE Transactions on Systems, Man, and Cybernetics—Part A: Systems And Humans, Vol. 35, No. 1 (2005): 78 - 92
10. Wendi B. Heinzelman, Anantha P. Chandrakasan, and Hari Balakrishnan: An Application-Specific Protocol Architecture for Wireless Microsensor Networks. IEEE Transactions on Wireless Communications, Vol. 1, No. 4 (2002): 660 - 670

Weighted Localized Clustering: A Coverage-Aware Reader Collision Arbitration Protocol in RFID Networks*

Joongheon Kim[1], Wonjun Lee[1,**], Jaewon Jung[1], Jihoon Choi[1], Eunkyo Kim[2], and Joonmo Kim[3]

[1] Department of Computer Science and Engineering, Korea University, Seoul, Korea
wlee@korea.ac.kr
[2] LG Electronics Institute of Technology, LG Electronics Co., Seoul, Korea
[3] School of Electrical, Electronics, and Computer Engineering, Dankook University, Seoul, Korea

Abstract. This paper addresses a weighted localized scheme and its application to the hierarchical clustering architecture, which results in reduced overlapping areas of clusters. Our previous proposed scheme, *Low-Energy Localized Clustering (LLC)*, dynamically regulates the radius of each cluster for minimizing energy consumption of cluster heads (CHs) while the entire network field is still being covered by each cluster in sensor networks. We present *weighted Low-Energy Localized Clustering (*w-*LLC)*, which has better efficiency than LLC by assigning weight functions to each CH. Drew on the *w*-LLC scheme, *weighted Localized Clustering for RFID networks (*w-*LCR)* addresses a coverage-aware reader collision arbitration protocol as an application. *w*-LCR is a protocol that minimizes collisions by minimizing overlapping areas of clusters.

Keywords: RFID networks, reader collision arbitration, clustering.

1 Introduction

In wireless networking environment, because the mobile devices are generally energy-constraint, the power management of mobile devices is an important issue. Due to the limited power source of mobile devices, energy consumption has been considered as the most critical factor in designing network protocols. Facing these challenges, several approaches to prolong network lifetime, including clustering schemes and structured schemes with a two-tiered hierarchy, have been investigated [1–4]. The clustering technology facilitates the distribution of control over the network and enables locality of communications [2]. The two-tiered hierarchical structuring method is an energy-efficient scheme for wireless networking [5]. It consists of the upper tier for communicating among cluster heads

* This work was in part funded by SK Telecom under Contract Number KU-R0405721 to Korea University and by KOSEF (Grant No. R01-2005-000-10267-0).
** Corresponding author.

L.T. Yang et al. (Eds.): ICESS 2005, LNCS 3820, pp. 542–553, 2005.

(CHs) and the lower tier for acquired events and transmitting them to CHs. However, in clustering scheme and two-tiered hierarchical structuring scheme, if the cluster range is larger than optimal one, a CH consumes more energy than required. On the other hand, a smaller-than-necessary range results in the shortage of covering the entire network field. Based on these reasons, we proposed a novel clustering-based algorithm which aims to minimize the energy consumption of CHs under the hierarchical structure [6]. Our proposed clustering scheme, *Low-Energy Localized Clustering (LLC)*, is able to regulate the cluster radius by communicating with CHs for energy savings. We extend our basic scheme to *weighted Low-Energy Localized Clustering (w-LLC)* to cope with the case that events occur more frequently in a certain area of the sensor network field. Also when the CHs have different computing power each other, we need to assign weight factors to each CH. In these cases, w-LLC, therefore, is better than LLC in practical environment to apply the algorithm. The major application areas of w-LLC are 'wireless sensor networks (WSN)' and 'RFID networks'. In WSN, sensors are deployed over the network sensing fields, and perform the specific tasks with the processing, sensing, and communicating capacities [7] [8]. Because of the limited power source of sensors, energy consumption has been concerned as the most critical factor in designing WSN protocols. To achieve energy-efficiency, the clustering schemes and hierarchically structured schemes are proposed [1–5]. RFID networks, also, has two-tiered hierarchical structure. In the upper tier, there are RFID readers to receive the signals from the RFID tags. In the lower tier, there are RFID tags. In the hierarchical clustering-based two-tiered network architecture, the larger overlapping areas of clusters that RFID readers form, the higher collision probability among the readers. We propose *weighted localized clustering for RFID networks (w-LCR)* as an application area of w-LLC that minimizes the overlapping areas among clusters by regulating a RFID reader's cluster radius dynamically to minimize the RFID reader collisions. The remainder of this paper is organized as follows. In Section 2, we investigate previous work in WSN and RFID networks. Section 3 propose w-LLC, a weighted dynamic localized scheme. We evaluate the effectiveness of w-LLC with simulations in Section 4. In Section 5, we apply w-LLC to RFID reader collision arbitration algorithm and, in Section 6, show the performance evaluation. Section 7 concludes this paper and presents future work.

2 Related Work

Numerous clustering schemes and hierarchical schemes are developed in WSN. LEACH (Low Energy Adaptive Clustering Hierarchy) [3], a protocol architecture for WSN that combines the ideas of energy-efficient cluster-based routing with application-specific data aggregation to achieve a good performance. It preserves limited amount of energy by selecting a CH at random among sensors. By doing this way, LEACH must have the energy constraint in each CH, whereas w-LLC has less energy constraint than LEACH. In [4], Gupta et al. proposed a two-tiered hierarchical clustering scheme in which a CH with less energy constraint is selected among sensors. However, a CH is selected among the sensors under restricted assumptions as assumed in [3]. Similar to LEACH, the CH of proposed scheme in [4] has more energy constraint than the CH of w-LLC, because the CH in [4] is a sensor with low energy and computing power while the CH of w-LLC has more computing power than regular sensors. The clustering-based topology control scheme [5] consists of two tiers; (1) upper tier for communicating between CHs and (2) lower tier for sensing, processing, and transmitting by sensors. It has similarity on hierarchical structuring concept like w-LLC. However, the performance depends on the radius of each cluster; as a cluster is increased covering the whole WSN, the energy consumption can be increased. On the other hand, w-LLC can regulate the radius of each cluster to minimize the energy consumption of each CH and consider the local properties of the region by assigning weight functions to each CH. As for another example, RFID network also has the two-tiered clustering-based hierarchical architecture. RFID systems consist of RFID readers as an upper layer and RFID tags as a lower layer in a clustering-based logical hierarchical model. After clustering tags in the lower layer, RFID readers recognize RFID tags in the cluster of RFID reader and send the information stored or delivered in RFID tags to a server. RFID tags have one-hop communication with RFID readers, which allows us to exploit general clustering schemes. Therefore the RFID system has the similar architecture to the hierarchical clustering-based two-tiered WSN architecture proposed in [5].

3 w-LLC: Weighted Low-Energy Localized Clustering

w-LLC aims to minimize overlapping areas of clusters by regulating the cluster range of each cluster. If the cluster range is larger than optimal one, a CH consumes more energy than required. On the other hand, a smaller cluster range than optimal one results in the entire wireless network field of lower tier not being covered. In w-LLC, the whole wireless network area of low tier is totally being covered by CHs and the CHs in network field of upper tier consider their weights assigned by *'weight functions'*. For achieving more energy efficiency, a server computes equations presented below. Energy-efficient radii for each cluster are calculated based on the objective functions given by w-LLC. w-LLC consists of two phases and one policy. Followings are what we assume in w-LLC.

- The proposed architecture has two-tiered hierarchical structure.
- A server knows the position of each CH.

3.1 Initial Phase

In initial phase, the CHs deployed at random construct a triangle to determine a *Cluster Radius Decision Point (CRDP)* that is able to minimize overlapping areas of clusters. The distance between CRDP and each point can be estimated as the radius of each cluster. *Delaunay* triangulation [9] [10], which guarantees the construction of an approximate equilateral triangle, is used for constructing a triangle. The construction of equilateral triangles leads to load-balanced energy consumption of each CH. By the concept of load-balancing, the prolonging of network lifetime can be achieved [11].

3.2 Weighted Localized Clustering Phase

The cluster radius of three points including the construction of a triangle can be dynamically controlled by using a CRDP as a pivot. In LLC, our previous work [6], the goal is to determine the CDRPs which minimize the overlapping areas of clusters by finding optimal cluster radii. However, in some cases where a subset of CHs are assigned to specific tasks or in some cases of the computing power of each CH are not same each other, they need to assign weight factors to each CH. Therefore, we suggest an extended algorithm of LLC, *w-LLC*, by assigning priorities to the CHs using weight functions.

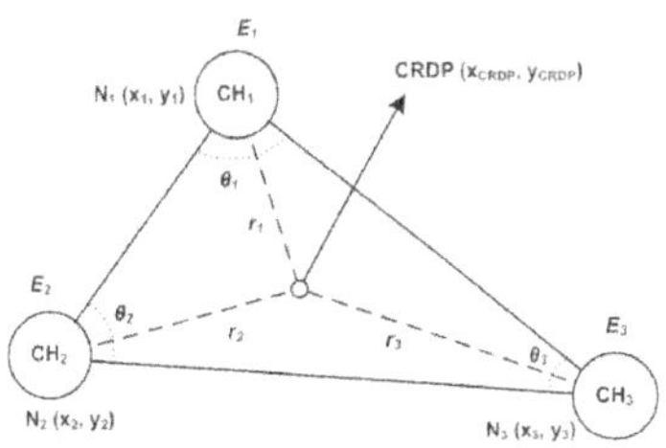

Fig. 1. Notations for NLP-based approach for *w*-LLC

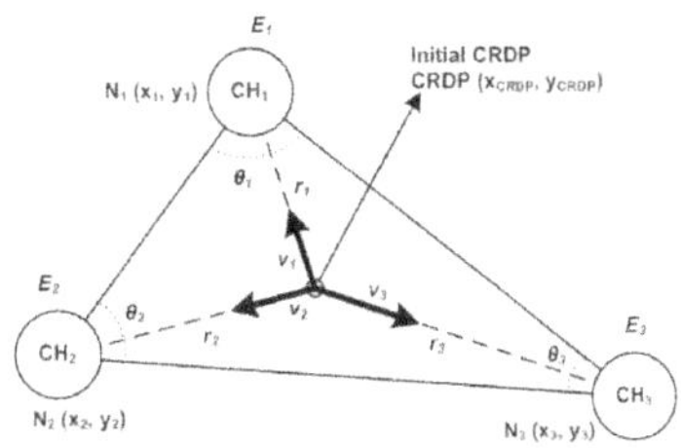

Fig. 2. Notations for VC-based approach for *w*-LLC

NLP-Based Approach for *w*-LLC. In LLC, by using NLP-based approach, a CRDP is determined by an energy-constrained objective function as the Eq. (1).

minimize: $f(r_1, r_2, r_3, \theta_1, \theta_2, \theta_3, E_1, E_2, E_3)$

$$= \frac{1}{2}\sum_{k=1}^{3} \theta_k \cdot r_k^2 \cdot \frac{E_k}{\frac{1}{3}\sum_{j=1}^{3} E_j} - S_{triangle} \tag{1}$$

$$\text{s.t. } r_i^2 = (x_{CRDP} - x_i)^2 + (y_{CRDP} - y_i)^2$$

In Eq. (1), θ_k denotes the angle value of CH_k, r_k means the distance between $CRDP$ and CH_k, and E_k denotes the energy state of CH_k. Also $S_{triangle}$ is the triangle area by *Delaunay* triangulation. Fig. 1 shows the conceptual diagram for Eq. (1). The purpose of Eq. (1) is to minimize the overlapped cluster coverage by considering the residual energy of each CH. If the overlapping area is getting to be larger, CHs may consume their energy more and more. Therefore, maintaining the minimized overlapping area can save the energy of each CH a lot. To compute the position of a CRDP which can minimize the overlapping areas, we obtain the areas of three sectors which have the angles of CHs and the area of $S_{triangle}$. For the purpose of computing the area of $S_{triangle}$, 'Heron's formula' is used. A server calculates the area of $S_{trinagle}$ using this formula. As for an NLP method to solve Eq. (1), we use a *'L-BFGS method'* [12, 13], one of the most efficient NLP methods for solving unconstraint optimization problem. In [12], the theoretical concept of non-linear programming is presented. In [13], the L-BFGS algorithm is presented. The other values except the angular values can be transmitted to the server; however, all the CHs should be aware of these values. Taking communication overheads into account, it is desirable to compute these at the server rather than CHs since a server is less energy constrained than CHs or mobile devices. The server eventually obtains the energy state and the positions of each CH. Each angular value is computed by the second law of cosine in the server. As shown in the Eq. (1), the CH of NLP-based approach has the same priorities. However in certain cases, we need to assign a different weight to each CH. If the CH in certain area is more important than the other CHs, we need to assign higher priority to the CH. Also if events occur in some endemic specific area, the CH in that area must be assigned with a higher priority. By these necessaries, the consideration of weight functions is necessary. Finally, in the case of the CHs have different computing power each other, the different weight factors must be considered. If one CH has more computing power than the other CHs, the CH needs to enlarge its cluster range to preserve the energy of the neighbor CHs to achieve load-balancing effect. Therefore we also need to assign the weight functions to each CH in the aspect of computing power of each CH. We can consider *'penalty functions'* and *'reward functions'* for the weight functions. If the penalty function of a CH has a large value, the CH must reduce its cluster radius. If the reward function of a CH has a large value, the CH must enlarge its cluster radius. In other word, a smaller penalty function value means a higher priority for a CH, while a smaller reward function value indicates a lower priority. Eq. (2) shows the objective function of NLP-based approach for w-LLC.

$$\textbf{minimize: } f(r_1, r_2, r_3, \theta_1, \theta_2, \theta_3, \phi_{1,1}(\overrightarrow{x}), \ldots, \phi_{m,3}(\overrightarrow{x}), \psi_{1,1}(\overrightarrow{x}), \ldots, \psi_{n,3}(\overrightarrow{x}))$$

$$= \frac{1}{2}\sum_{k=1}^{3} \theta_k \cdot r_k^2 \cdot \prod_{l=1}^{m} \frac{\phi_{l,k}(\overrightarrow{x})}{\frac{1}{3}\sum_{i=1}^{3} \phi_{l,i}(\overrightarrow{x})} \cdot \prod_{g=1}^{n} \frac{\frac{1}{\psi_{g,k}(\overrightarrow{x})}}{\frac{1}{3}\sum_{i=1}^{3} \frac{1}{\psi_{g,i}(\overrightarrow{x})}} - S_{triangle} \qquad (2)$$

$$\text{s.t. } r_i^2 = (x_{CRDP} - x_i)^2 + (y_{CRDP} - y_i)^2$$

The notations of Eq. (2) are the same as the notations of Fig. 1 and Eq. (1). In Eq. (2), w-LLC assigns a weight function to each CH where $\phi_{l,k}(\overrightarrow{x})$ and $\psi_{l,k}(\overrightarrow{x})$ represents a penalty function and a reward function, respectively. This objective function, Eq. (2), has m penalty functions and n reward functions. The example of penalty function and reward function is 'residual energy' and 'priority', respectively. If residual energy is quite small in a CH, the CH must preserve its residual energy. In this case, the CH becomes more important than the other CHs in the aspect of energy conservation. The CH needs to reduce its cluster radius for preserving its energy for load-balancing. Therefore, the smaller residual energy of a CH, the higher weight of the CH. Therefore the 'residual energy' is considered as the example of 'penalty function'. If the priority of a CH is higher, the importance of CH also becomes higher. Therefore, the priorities can be an example of reward functions.

VC-Based Approach for w-LLC. In NLP-based approach, it may generate computation overheads due to an iterative NLP method. We thus consider another method to reduce the computation overheads. The notations of VC-based approach is depicted in Fig. 2. It initially executes an NLP computation at first. Any weight factors do not need to be considered in the initial NLP-computation. The basic notations and the objective function for obtaining minimized energy consumption in VC-based method are the same as those in NLP-based method, except that the former does not considers any energy constraints and weight factors. The equation to obtain the initial position of a CDRP is described as Eq. (3)

$$\textbf{minimize: } f(r_1, r_2, r_3, \theta_1, \theta_2, \theta_3) = \frac{1}{2}\sum_{k=1}^{3} \theta_k \cdot r_k^2 - S_{triangle} \tag{3}$$

$$\text{s.t. } r_i^2 = (x_{CRDP} - x_i)^2 + (y_{CRDP} - y_i)^2$$

As time goes, however, the objective function may move a CRDP towards the CH that has consumed the most amount of energy. In the objective function of VC-based approach, we do not consider the energy factor. In the iterative procedure, we need to consider the energy factor. Therefore, the next position of CRDP is determined by Eq. (4) under the iteration policy.

$$CRDP_{i+1} = CRDP_i - \sum_{k=1}^{3} \frac{E_k}{\frac{1}{3}\sum_{j=1}^{3} E_j} \cdot \frac{v_k}{\|v_k\|} \tag{4}$$

$$\text{s.t. } CRDP_k = (x_{CRDP_k}, y_{CRDP_k})$$

Eq. (3), the objective function of 'VC-based approach', does not consider the energy state of each CH when it determines the position of CRDP. Therefore by using Eq. (4), we can consider the energy state of each CH. By Eq. (4), the CH which has more energy consumption is assigned with higher priority whereas the CH which has less energy consumption is assigned lower priority. By this operation, we can obtain load-balanced energy consumption and optimal position of a CRDP. Using this VC-based approach, we can preserve the energy of CHs as much as the NLP-based approach so that we can reduce computation overheads. In VC-based approach, we have to update the coordination of CRDP given in previous step. In NLP-based approach, however, re-computation to find the optimal solution to the objective function using NLP method can be overburden. Therefore, the repeated vector computation is much simpler than the NLP-based computation in the aspect of algorithm complexity. To apply the concept of assigning the weight factors in CHs, we can update Eq. (4) as

$$CRDP_{i+1} = CRDP_i - \sum_{k=1}^{3}\prod_{l=1}^{m} \frac{\phi_{l,k}(\overrightarrow{x})}{\frac{1}{3}\sum_{l=1}^{3} \phi_{l,i}(\overrightarrow{x})} \prod_{g=1}^{n} \frac{\frac{1}{\psi_{g,k}(\overrightarrow{x})}}{\frac{1}{3}\sum_{i=1}^{3} \frac{1}{\psi_{g,i}(\overrightarrow{x})}} \cdot \frac{v_k}{\|v_k\|} \tag{5}$$

$$\text{s.t. } CRDP_k = (x_{CRDP_k}, y_{CRDP_k})$$

by assigning weight functions. The notations of Eq. (5) are the same as Eq. (2) and Eq. (4). By re-modeling Eq. (4) as Eq. (5), we can consider the many weight factors. As shown in Eq. (5), we can consider m penalty functions and n reward functions for the purpose of finding the coordination of CRDP. The coordination of CRDP can provide minimized energy consumption in each CH.

3.3 Iterative Policy

When events occur most frequently in some specific areas where a certain CH consumes its energy a lot. In this situation, the CHs in the target region will consume more energy and the operation will be relatively more important than the other CHs in the other area of the network of lower tier. Then a server has to change the radius of clusters to balance energy consumption of each CH and to preserve the energy of the CH which has higher priority than the other CH. Moreover, since the server has an iteration timer, if no events occur until the timer is expired, the server requests energy information to all the CHs and starts the w-LLC algorithm. The server collects data including energy information of CHs and executes w-LLC periodically.

4 Effectiveness of w-LLC

In this section, we evaluate and analyze the performance of w-LLC through simulation-based performance evaluation. As a simulation environment, we consider the WSN environment. To consider the WSN environment with the network architecture proposed in this paper, the wireless network system consists of the upper tier for communicating among CHs and the lower tier for sensing events and transmitting them to CHs. There are 'clustering scheme with fixed radius (FR)' and LLC for the comparison studies with w-LLC. Fig. 3 presents the average lifetime and variance of the five CHs evaluated by FR, LLC, and w-LLC. We generate the events in some specific areas, and assign weight functions to the CH. In the case of FR where cluster radii are fixed, the variance is constant. w-LLC shows less variance than LLC, which denotes the fairness of energy consumption. As shown in Fig. 4, FR shows the worst performance among others in terms of the average lifetime of five CHs. When events occur in certain specific areas more frequently, w-LLC shows better performance than LLC. We also consider two different scenarios, (1) sensing events occur around in

Evaluation	Schemes	Round 1	Round 2	Round 3	Round 4	Round 5
var.	FR	0.9151	0.9151	0.9151	0.9151	0.9151
	LLC	9.1334	3.7465	1.6010	0.6715	3.8771
	w-LLC	**6.6106**	**1.3900**	**1.6251**	**0.3749**	**0.7259**
avg.	FR	13.9311	13.9311	13.9311	13.9311	13.9311
	LLC	34.2577	34.0341	33.5493	33.8866	33.9239
	w-LLC	**35.5435**	**35.0131**	**35.2474**	**34.6837**	**35.1925**

Standard unit: a minute

Fig. 3. Comparison of FR, LLC, and w-LLC

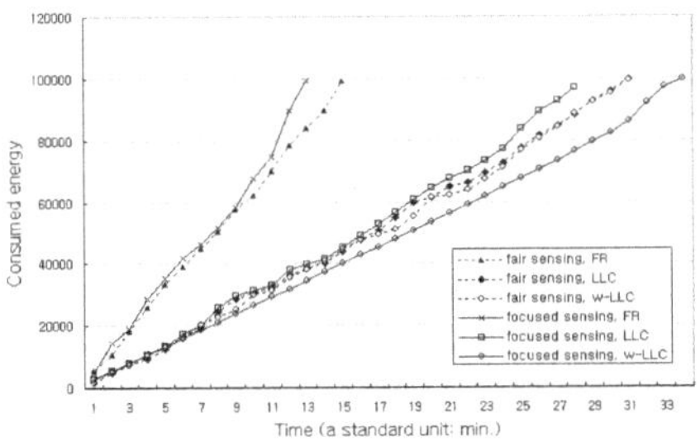

Fig. 4. Comparison of the residual energy

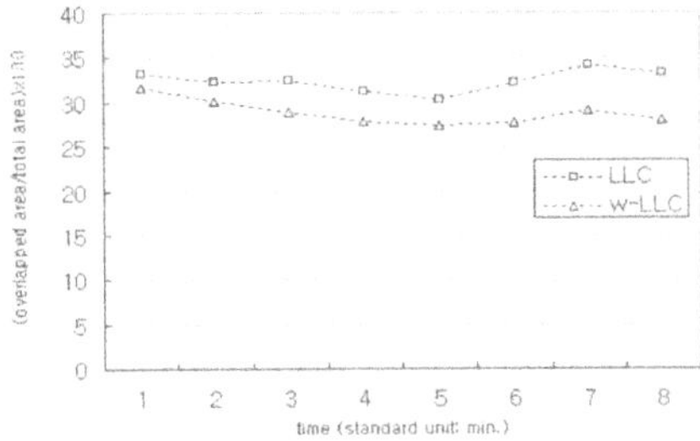

Fig. 5. Percentage of overlapped area (events intensively occur in certain area)

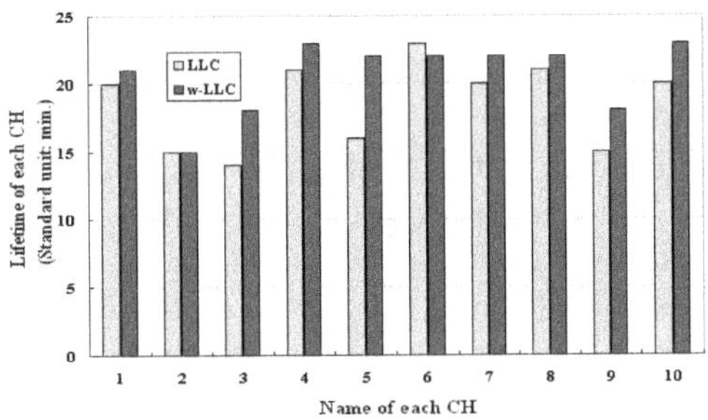

Fig. 6. Comparison of LLC and w-LLC in the aspect of load-balancing on CHs

certain hot spots, named focused sensing; and (2) events occur evenly across the sensor network, named fair sensing. As shown in Fig. 4, residual energies in FR are further quickly consumed than LLC and w-LLC. FR shows a longer lifetime in fair sensing than focused sensing. The CHs in the hot spots of focused sensing exhaust their own energies rapidly. In focused sensing, w-LLC is the most energy efficient, since it uses weight functions that reflect territorial characteristics. We evaluate the performance of a scenario that sensing events intensively occur in a certain area. In the environment, the weight factors of w-LLC can deal with the situation very well. As shown in Fig. 5, w-LLC outperforms the earlier version, LLC. The range of overlapping area per total area of LLC is between 0.30 and 0.34. However the range of overlapping area per total area of w-LLC is between 0.26 and 0.31. Therefore w-LLC is more energy efficient than LLC.

If the CHs in the system achieve load-balancing, the system lifetime can increase [11]. As shown in Fig. 6, the standard deviation of CHs in LLC is 3.171049598 and the average lifetime of CHs in LLC is 18.5 minutes. The other side, the standard deviation of CHs in w-LLC is 2.67498702 and the average lifetime of CHs in w-LLC is 20.6 minutes. By the result of this simulation, we shows that w-LLC is more energy-efficient than LLC in the aspect of lifetime of CHs.

5 Adaptability for RFID Reader Collision Arbitration

Radio Frequency IDentification (RFID) is the next generation wireless communication technology applicable to various fields such as distribution, circulation, transportation, etc. RFID is a non-contact technology that identifies objects attached with tags. Tags consist of a microchip and antenna. RFID readers obtain the information of objects and surroundings through communication with tag antennas [14]. Minimizing collisions among RFID reader and tag signals has a substantial effect on performance because tag recognition rate effectively determines RFID system performance. However, the RFID reader and tag collision problem has not received much attention. Therefore, as one of the promising application areas of w-LLC, RFID networks can be considered to develop an RFID reader collision arbitration protocol. RFID systems consist of RFID readers which are fixed a priori, as an upper layer and RFID tags as a lower layer in a two-tiered logical hierarchical model. After clustering tags in the lower layer, RFID readers recognize tags in the cluster and send information stored in tags to a server by using multi-hop routing among RFID readers. RFID tags have one-hop communication with RFID readers, which allows us to exploit general clustering schemes. In other words, this RFID system has the similar architecture to the w-LLC. Based on the w-LLC like system architecture, we can reduce overlapping area of RFID reader clusters. By reducing the overlapping area, we can reduce the collision of signals from RFID readers.

5.1 Classification on RFID Reader Collision Arbitration

Research efforts for the RFID collision arbitration problem [14] can be classified into two groups: RFID reader collision arbitration protocols [15] and RFID tag collision arbitration protocols [16]. The main focus of this paper will be behind a motivation to develop a RFID reader collision arbitration protocol based on w-LLC. The approaches to RFID reader collision arbitration protocols are further divided into scheduling-based approach which prevents RFID readers from simultaneously transmitting signal to a RFID tag, and coverage-based approach. A widely known scheduling-based protocol is the *Colorwave* proposed in [15]. The *Colorwave* performs scheduling instructed by RFID readers using Distributed Color Selection (DCS) or enhanced DCS, Variable-Maximum Distributed Color Selection (VDCS), after it divides medium into time slot. The other reader collision arbitration approach is the coverage-based approach, which minimizes collision possibility by optimizing the overlapping areas of clusters which RFID readers have to cover up. Under the concept of a coverage-aware RFID reader collision arbitration mechanism to minimize the overlapping area of the cluster, we can apply w-LLC, to overcome reader collision problems occurring among RFID readers which have different computing power.

5.2 Coverage-Aware RFID Reader Collision Arbitration: w-LCR

In the hierarchical clustering-based two-tiered network architecture, the larger overlapping the areas of clusters that RFID readers form, the higher the collision probability among the readers. We propose an algorithm that minimizes the overlapping areas among clusters by regulating RFID readers cluster radii dynamically to minimize the reader collisions. Our initial version of the dynamic cluster coverage algorithm, named as LLC, is presented in [6]. Also, each RFID reader in the RFID networks has different computing power. Therefore it is hard to apply LLC to the RFID networks directly. By this constraint, we can use w-LLC for considering the different computing power of each RFID reader. The w-LLC is to minimize the energy consumption of each CH by dynamically adjusting cluster radius. Based on it, this paper proposes *weighted localized clustering for RFID networks (w-LCR)* scheme to minimize the overlapping areas and then minimizes RFID reader collisions.

6 Performance Evaluation of w-LCR

A simulation study is conducted to evaluate the performance of w-LCR. RFID tags were randomly deployed and RFID reader was placed according to each simulation metric. Our simulations were designed to evaluate the effect of (1) probability of RFID reader collision and (2) energy consumption. We compare w-LCR against the method that has a fixed cluster radius.

6.1 Possibility of RFID Reader Collision

Fig. 7 shows the possibility of collision in FR and w-LCR in RFID networks. w-LCR have much lower possibility of collision than FR method because w-LCR algorithm regulates cluster radius dynamically and minimizes the overlapping areas. As shown in Fig. 7, the possibility of collision of w-LCR is between 0.09 and 0.11. However the possibility of collision of FR is between 0.25 and 0.35. Therefore w-LCR has better performance than FR almost three times. Furthermore, as shown the shape of graph, the FR has more variance than the w-LCR. The variance of FR is 0.1 and the one of w-LCR is 0.02. FR has more variance than w-LCR almost five times. The load-balancing concept based on the weight functions of w-LCR can make the variance smaller than FR as shown

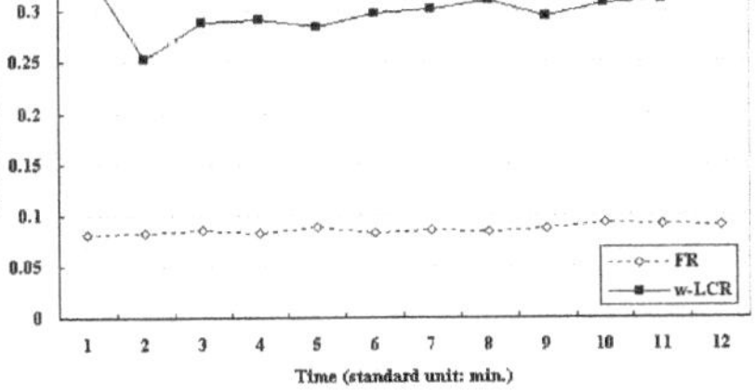

Fig. 7. Possibility of collision in RFID networks

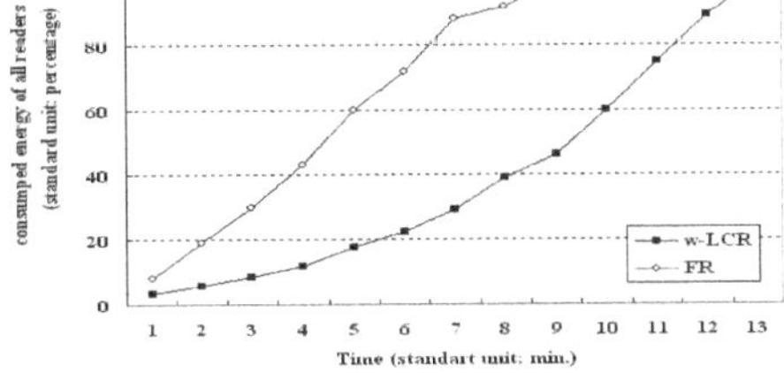

Fig. 8. Energy consumption in RFID networks

the Fig. 7. Also, as shown the shape of FR graph, the possibility of collision is continuously increasing. On the other side, the *w*-LCR is not continuously increasing. This situation occurred on the effect of load-balancing concept of weight functions.

6.2 Energy Consumption

w-LCR consider the residual energy state of RFID readers as another important metric. We compare the performance of proposed schemes in terms of energy consumption in RFID networks. Fig. 8 shows the results of simulation. As shown in Fig. 8, the *w*-LCR can achieve more energy-efficiency than FR. Under the FR consumes entire energy of all RFID readers at 8.7 minutes. However the *w*-LCR consumes entire energy of all RFID readers at 12.6 minutes. Therefore the *w*-LCR has more energy efficient than FR 1.45 times. Furthermore, Under the FR consumes half energy of all RFID readers at 4.1 minutes. However the *w*-LCR consumes half energy of all RFID readers at 9.4 minutes. Therefore the *w*-LCR has more energy efficient than FR based algorithm 2.29 times. As shown until now, at the beginning of the operating the protocol, *w*-LCR has more energy efficient that the terminal stage. As shown in the shape of *w*-LCR graph, the increment of the beginning is smaller. However the time has gone, the increment of the graph is higher. As time has gone, some RFID readers are consumes all energy and becomes 'battery-drained RFID reader' until recharge. Then the neighbor RFID readers must cover the area controlled by the 'battery-drained RFID reader'. Therefore time has gone, the increment become higher. In FR, FR does not control its cluster radius. Therefore RFID reader, which uses the FR, consumes fixed amount of energy. Hence the shape of FR has linear form.

7 Conclusions and Future Work

We extended our previous research, LLC, [6] to *weighted Low-Energy Localized Clustering (w-LLC)*. For improving our previous work, we apply the concept of weight functions to the LLC. Based on the simulation based performance evaluation, we observed that *w*-LLC achieves better throughput than LLC. As an application area, we consider the RFID networks to solve RFID reader collision problem. We developed *weighted Localized Clustering for RFID networks (w-LCR)* scheme based on the concept of *w*-LLC. By reducing the overlapping areas of clusters, we can reduce the possibility of collision of signals. The proposed RFID reader collision arbitration protocol in this paper is a coverage-aware reader collision arbitration protocol. As a future research direction, we will design more efficient RFID reader collision arbitration with the concept of 'hybrid RFID reader anti-collision algorithm' which has the concept of scheduling-based RFID reader anti-collision algorithm used by the *Colorwave*, based on *w*-LCR.

References

1. V. Mhatre and C. Rosenberg, "Design Guidelines for Wireless Sensor Networks: Communication, Clustering and Aggregation," Elsevier Ad Hoc Networks, 2(1):45-63, 2004.
2. O. Younis and S. Fahmy, "HEED: A Hybrid, Energy-Efficient, Distributed Clustering Approach for Ad Hoc Sensor Networks," IEEE Trans. on Mobile Computing, 3(1):366-379, 2004.
3. W. B. Heinzelman, A. P. Chandrakasan, and H. Balakrishnan, "An Application-Specific Protocol Architecture for Wireless Microsensor Networks," IEEE Trans. on Wireless Comm., 1(4):660-670, 2002.
4. G. Gupta and M. Younis, "Load-Balanced Clustering for Wireless Sensor Networks," in Proc.of IEEE ICC, AK, USA, May 2003.
5. J. Pan, Y. T. Hou, L. Cai, Y. Shi, and S. X. Shen, "Topology Control for Wireless Sensor Networks," in Proc. of ACM MobiCom, CA, USA, Sep. 2003.
6. J. Kim, E. Kim, S. Kim, D. Kim, and W. Lee, "Low-Energy Localized Clustering: An Adaptive Cluster Radius Configuration Scheme for Topology Control in Wireless Sensor Networks," in Proc. of IEEE VTC, Stockholm, Sweden, May 2005.
7. I. F. Akyildiz, W. L. Su, Y. Sankarasubramaniam, and E. Cayirci, "Wireless Sensor Networks: A Survey", Elsevier Computer Networks, 38(4):393-422, Mar. 2002.
8. D. Estrin, R. Govindan, J. Heidemann, and S. Kumar, "Next Century Challenges: Scalable Coordination in Sensor Networks," in Proc. of ACM MobiCom, WA, USA, Aug. 1999.
9. M. de Berg, M. van Kreveld, M. Overmars, and O. Schwarzkopf, Computational Geometry: Algorithms and Applications, 2nd Ed., Springer-Verlag, 2000.
10. F. Aurenhammer, "Voronoi Diagrams - A Survey of a Fundamental Geometric Data Structure," ACM Computing Surveys, 23(3):345-405, Sep. 1991.
11. S. Yin and X. Lin, "Adaptive Load Balancing in Mobile Ad Hoc Networks," in Proc. of IEEE WCNC, Mar. 2005.
12. M. S. Bazaraa, H. D. Sherali, and C. M. Shetty, Nonlinear Programming: Theory and Algorithms, 2nd Ed., Wiley, 1993.
13. D. C. Liu and J. Nocedal, "On the Limited Memory BFGS Method for Large Scale Optimization," ACM Mathematical Programming, Dec. 1989.
14. F. Zhou. C. Chen, D. Jin, C. Huang, and H. Min, "Evaluating and Optimizing Power Consumption of Anti-Collision Protocols for Applications in RFID Systems," in Proc. of ACM ISLPED, 2004.
15. J. Waldrop, D. W. Engels, and S. E. Sarma, "Colorwave: An Anticollision Algorithm for the Reader Collision Problem," in Proc. of IEEE ICC, AK, USA, May 2003.
16. C. Law, K. Lee, and K.-Y. Siu, "Efficient Memoryless Protocol for Tag Identification," in Proc. of ACM DIALM, 2000.

A Kind of Context-Aware Approach Based on Fuzzy-Neural for Proactive Service of Pervasive Computing

Degan Zhang, Guangping Zeng, Xiaojuan Ban, and Yixin Yin

School of Information Engineering,
University of Science and Technology Beijing, Beijing 100083, P.R. China
gandegande@sohu.com, zhangdegan@tsinghua.org.cn

Abstract. The task-oriented proactive seamless migration is one of difficult problems to be solved in pervasive computing paradigm. Apparently, this function of seamless mobility is suitable for mobile services, such as mobile Web-based learning. But when seamless migration for computing task of learning is realized among PC, laptop, or PDA, there are several difficult problems to be solved, such as how to supply the proactive/attentive service with uncertainty for aware context. In order to realize E-learning based on proactive seamless migration, we design and improve relative fuzzy-neural approach (of course, besides it, there are other approaches). Generally, the network can be classified into two. One is that fuzzy logic reasoning is completed by fuzzy weight in neural system. The other is that the input data must be fuzzified in the first or second level, but not weight. We discuss and study the second in this paper. For proactive decision, fusion method based on fuzzy-neural can make Web-based learning system keep advantage of fuzzy logic system and remain adaptive optimum in proactive/attentive service. The correctness and validity of our new approach have been tested.

1 Introduction

With the development of mobile communication and Internet, the next great information process paradigm shift, to pervasive computing, is already well under way and will have no less of an impact on industry, government, and daily life than the personal computing revolution. The proactive/attentive service is fused the technologies of computing, communication and digital multimedia, which integrates information space and physical space of human being's life. This paradigm meets the requirements of human being in "5A" that is anybody maybe obtain anything with any device anywhere and at anytime. There are a bunch of branch research fields under the banner of it, such as human-centric universal access, instead of traditional machine-centric. Consequently, technologies that allow the integration of existing and foreseen heterogeneous and homogenous networks into a single platform will be of major importance [1-3]. Nowadays, many ambitious projects have been proposed and carried on to welcome the advent of pervasive computing, such as Seamless mobility. For seamless mobility, the history and context of computing task will be migrated

L.T. Yang et al. (Eds.): ICESS 2005, LNCS 3820, pp. 554 – 563, 2005.

with person's mobility, and the computing device and software resource around this task will make adaptive change. The chief function requirement of seamless mobility is on the continuity and adaptability of computing task [4-6]. we are entering a new age of computing, namely, the era of pervasive computing era, which is studied only recently computing mode.

Apparently, this function of seamless mobility is suitable for mobile services, such as mobile Web-based learning. For learner, it is necessary and accessible when he/she can not complete his/her learning task/courseware, such as video, audio, text, picture, etc., in one specified scene, he/she can go on learning the uncompleted task/courseware in other spots by seamless mobility based on the Web. But when seamless migration for computing task of learning is realized among PC, laptop, or PDA, there are several difficult problems to be solved, such as how to supply the proactive/attentive service with uncertainty for aware context [7-10] because it should fuse relative multi-source information with identity, location and time among different computing nodes [9]. As we know, based on fuzzy-neural network, we can reason and make decisions (of course, besides it, there are other approaches) [11-14], so it can be used for deciding when supply the proactive/attentive service. In order to realize proactive service of pervasive computing, we will design and improve relative fuzzy-neural approaches.

The rest of this paper is arranged as follows: Section 2 introduces fuzzy-neural structure and learning algorithm for context-aware. Section 3 is context-aware computing method based on fuzzy-neural network. Section 4 explains Implemented platform for proactive service. Section 5 shows the test & comparison. Section 6 draws the conclusion.

2 Fuzzy-Neural Learning Algorithm for Context-Aware

2.1 Fuzzy-Neural Structure

The proposed fuzzy-neural structure is divided into four layers: input layer, fuzzification layer, reasoning layer, non-fuzzification layer. Suppose M inputs one output, N rules, that is to say, there will be M input nerve cells in input layer, MN nerve cells in fuzzification layer, N nerve cells in reasoning layer, only one nerve cell in non-fuzzification. So, once the M and N are determined, the fuzzy-neural structure will be decided. Now, the key problem is to determine the N. We can estimate the value of N by defined fuzzy curve. In order to introduce conveniently fuzzy-neural model, we first define the basic nerve cell node model. Classic neural network consists of these nerve cell nodes. The input of nerve cell is obtained by action of former relative nerve cell output and weight. The input of basic nerve cell is a sum function $f(\bullet)$, this function can combine and stimulate information from other nerve cells. The pure input of this nerve cell can be expressed as $f(\mu_1, \mu_2, \ldots, \mu_p, w_1, w_2, \ldots, w_p)$, the output as $a(f(\bullet))$, $a(\bullet)$ is stimulating function. Now, we introduce each layer of the proposed structure.

The first layer: the nerve cell in this layer only transfers input data into the second layer, then,

$$f(x_i)=x_i \text{ and } a(\bullet)=f(\bullet),$$

The weight is unit 1.

The second layer: the fuzzy membership function will form simply in this layer, fuzzification layer. In this paper, we select

$$f(\bullet)=(w_{ij1}x_i+ w_{ij0})^{2Lij},$$

w_{ij0} is weight, the threshold is

$$\mu_{ij} = a(\bullet)=\exp(-f(\bullet)),$$

Which is Gaussian-like function. The third layer: reasoning layer, by multiple multiply reasoning, namely,

$$f(\bullet)=\mu_{ij}\ ,\ a(\bullet)=\prod_{i=1}^{M} f(\bullet)=\prod_{i=1}^{M}\mu_{ij}\ .$$

The last layer:

$$f(\bullet)=\sum_{j=1}^{N}\mu_j v_j \quad a(\bullet)=1/(1+\exp(-f(\bullet)))\,.$$

In this layer, It is important that $a(\bullet)$ keeps Sigmoid function because it can ensure the system convergence which is better than reference [4]. After setting up fuzzy-neural network, each fuzzy rule rl_j can be defined according to the condition sentence as follows:

IF x_1 isμ_{1j} and x_2 isμ_{2j} and … and x_M isμ_{Mj} THEN Y is v_j .

Noticeable, neural weight $V\{v_j\}$ and $\{\ w_{ij1}\ ,w_{ij0}\ \}$ decide fuzzy rule basically. Lastly, the output by non-fuzzifying is:

$$o(x_1, x_2,..., x_M)=f(\bullet) \quad f(\bullet)=1(1+\exp(-\sum_{j=1}^{N}\mu_j v_j))$$

In this model, the number of fuzzy rule only be determined by data itself.

2.2 Fuzzy-Neural Learning Algorithm for Context-Aware

After the number of fuzzy rule N is determined, the fuzzy-neural structure will be done. The network will go to the second step. The fuzzy membership function and tuned weight will be obtained by learning optimum. Based on the traditional BP learning algorithm, the steepest grads go-down, we can obtain the learning algorithm of this fuzzy-neural network. The purpose of learning is to make E smallest.

$$E=\frac{1}{2}\sum_{k=1}^{m}(o^{(k)}-so^{(k)})^2$$

$so^{(k)}$ is ideal output of the k-th sample, $o^{(k)}$ is current output of the k-th sample during learning. In order to make E come smallest, a high-speed BP learning algorithm will be improved to train the fuzzy-neural network and tune the variables v_j, w_{ij0}, w_{ij1} *and* l_{ij} , Under the condition of convergence, we select a small positive number (close to 0) c>0 or a biggest iterative number H uses as learning end condition. Until E<c or up to H, learning can be ended. The following equations are for learning variables, in order to speed the learning process, a moment item has been added in each equation.

$$v_j(n+1)=v_j(n)+c_1(-\partial E/\partial v_j)+tt1(v_j(n)-v_j(n-1)) \qquad (1)$$

$$l_{ij}(n+1) = l_{ij}(n) + c_2(-\partial E / \partial l_{ij}) + tt2(l_{ij}(n) - l_{ij}(n-1)) \tag{2}$$

$$w_{ij0}(n+1) = w_{ij0}(n) + c_3(-\partial E / \partial w_{ij0}) + tt3(w_{ij0}(n) - w_{ij0}(n-1)) \tag{3}$$

$$w_{ij1}(n+1) = w_{ij1}(n) + c_4(-\partial E / \partial w_{ij1}) + tt4(w_{ij1}(n) - w_{ij1}(n-1)) \tag{4}$$

$$-\partial E / \partial v_j = -\sum_{k=1}^{m}(o^{(k)} - so^{(k)})\mu_j^{(k)} \tag{5}$$

$$\begin{aligned} -\partial E / \partial l_{ij} &= -(\partial E / \partial o^{(k)}) \times (\partial o^{(k)} / \partial \mu_j^{(k)}) \times (\partial \mu_j^{(k)} / \partial \mu_{ij}^{(k)}) \times (\partial \mu_{ij}^{(k)} / \partial l_{ij}) \\ &= \sum_{k=1}^{m}(o^{(k)} - so^{(k)})v_j \prod_{h \neq i} \mu_{hj}^{(k)} \exp(-(w_{ij1}x_i^{(k)} + w_{ij0})^{2l_{ij}}) \times (w_{ij1}x_i^{(k)} + w_{ij0})^{2l_{ij}+2.0} \end{aligned} \tag{6}$$

$$\begin{aligned} -\partial E / \partial w_{ij0} &= -(\partial E / \partial o^{(k)}) \times (\partial o^{(k)} / \partial \mu_j^{(k)}) \times (\partial \mu_j^{(k)} / \partial \mu_{ij}^{(k)}) \times (\partial \mu_{ij}^{(k)} / \partial w_{ij0}) \\ &= \sum_{k=1}^{m}(o^{(k)} - so^{(k)})v_j \prod_{h \neq i} \mu_{hj}^{(k)} \exp(-(w_{ij1}x_i^{(k)} + w_{ij0})^{2l_{ij}}) \times 2.0 l_{ij}(x_i^{(k)} + w_{ij0})^{2l_{ij}-1.0} x_i^{(k)} \end{aligned} \tag{7}$$

$$\begin{aligned} -\partial E / \partial w_{ij1} &= -(\partial E / \partial o^{(k)}) \times (\partial o^{(k)} / \partial \mu_j^{(k)}) \times (\partial \mu_j^{(k)} / \partial \mu_{ij}^{(k)}) \times (\partial \mu_{ij}^{(k)} / \partial w_{ij1}) \\ &= \sum_{k=1}^{m}(o^{(k)} - so^{(k)})v_j \prod_{h \neq i} \mu_{hj}^{(k)} \exp(-(w_{ij1}x_i^{(k)} + w_{ij0})^{2l_{ij}}) \times 2.0 l_{ij}(x_i^{(k)} + w_{ij0})^{2l_{ij}-1.0} x_i^{(k)} \end{aligned} \tag{8}$$

Eq.(1)~(8) is improved high-speed BP learning algorithm for fuzzy-neural network, according to initial method of reference [5], by input and output data, the optimal network model can be obtained. For example, after training, if the performance is not ideal, you can add the number of fuzzy rule, on the contrary, if the performance is very good, in order to decrease model complexity, you can reduce the rule number. During learning, if the fuzzy membership function is always close to a certain value in whole discussed range, you can cut off the rule and no necessary nerve cells or stop training and learning. Generally, based on the fuzzy data curve , the network structure is close to optimum.

2.3 Fuzzy Data Curve for Network Structure

In order to express conveniently, we consider a multi-input and multi-output system with input and output data. Two things can be done on fuzzy data curve: I) evaluate the influence to output by input variable. II) determine the rule number N primarily. x_i (i=1,2,…,n) expresses input variable data, and o expresses output. Suppose m training sample points, x_{ik} (i=1,2,…,n,k=1,2,…,m) is sample point of the k-th sample connecting the i-th input variable. For each input variable x_i, the define of variable fuzzy membership degree function is:

$$y_{ik}(x_i) = 1.0 - \exp(-(a/(x_{ik} - x_i))^{4.0}) \quad (k = 1,2,\ldots,m) \tag{9}$$

Where y_{ik} is membership degree function of input x_i to sample point k. a is about 5% of least gap of x_i. Each pair (y_{ik} ,$o^{(k)}$) has the relative fuzzy rule for x_i, that is to say, IF x_i is y_{ik} (x_i), THEN o is $o^{(k)}$. For each input variable x_i, with the following equation, we can obtain a fuzzy data curve r_i:

$$r_i(x_i) = \frac{\sum_{k=1}^{m} y_{ik}(x_i) o^{(k)}}{\sum_{k=1}^{m} y_{ik}(x_i)} \tag{10}$$

3 Method of Context-Aware Computing Based on Fuzzy-Neural

The proposed fusion architecture based on fuzzy-neural is as follow. Firstly, through a data assignment network, the input data from each sensor are allotted to every fusion sub-node, the sub-node will preprocess, filter according to fusion proposition, after selecting, sub-node can do data fusion. Each sub-node is fuzzy-neural network.

The three steps can be completed data fusion [15-17] by fuzzy-neural network. At first, the fuzzy rule must be initialized from experience information. Then, the fuzzy-neural network must be trained according to classic prior obtained data so that it can fit sample data. At last, It can fuse input data based on trained fuzzy-neural network and it can tune slightly under the fusion belief degree.

In order to apply to different environment better, the fuzzy-neural network must be adaptive. Because the change speed of environment and input signal data is slow, slight tune can be do with online training in fuzzy-neural network. As we know, the change speed of fusion result is faster and more than the input signal variable or data, so according to the change of input data as input can be designed a function, a expectation can be got by fusion result and this function, and the expectation can be used as training sample to do online slight tuning. Suppose the belief degree of input data is $\mu_1, \mu_2, ..., \mu_n$, the constructed function may select as follow:

$$f(\mu_1, \mu_2, ..., \mu_n) = \begin{cases} +0.01, & \sum_{i=1}^{n} \mu_i(k) - \sum_{i=1}^{n} \mu_i(k-1) \succ 0 \\ -0.01, & \sum_{i=1}^{n} \mu_i(k) - \sum_{i=1}^{n} \mu_i(k-1) \leq 0 \end{cases} \tag{11}$$

Where $\mu_i(k)$, $\mu_i(k-1)$ is the k-th and the (k-1)-th belief degree of i-th input signal data, respectively. The expectation value of slight tuning is *y+f* during each fusion, *y* is fusion result.

4 Implemented Platform for Proactive Service

In the implemented platform, our key idea is adopted fuzzy-neural network theory to make decision for proactive seamless transfer. The function of fuzzy-neural network is encapsulated based on agent during proactive seamless migration. Our implemented platform can work in Client/Server, Browse/Server and Peer-to-Peer paradigm.

Fig.1 is supported structure of the platform for proactive service. This is a kind of structure with multi-agent. The structure can be divided into multiple levels. Multiple agents are collaborated for proactive seamless services, such as Web-based learning. Each agent has its special function. Fig.2 is the structure of seamless migration embedded in this implemented platform, which includes four layers: SM-link layer,

SM-path layer, SM-connection layer and SM-session layer. In Fig.2, "T" stands for "Task", "A" stands for "Agent", "MA" stands for "Mobile Agent" and "C" stands for "Container", which is a daemon threads component installed in each relative mobile devices. Their working principle has mentioned above.

This fusion agent is the most important computing agent with fuzzy-neural network. The dataset from database is processed in fuzzy technology, such as clustering. The sensors of neural network may modify the weight of training. The *mass* belief function has timely tracked dynamic process of learner. The membership function has measured correlative degree of evidences based on their correlative degrees.

Because the migrating mode based on agent for learning task is distributed, peer-to-peer / end-to-end, we have designed several relative communication primaries and class for migrating, such as,

```
BeginToListen(UINT nPort,ACCEPT_CALLBACK callback);
      Void (CAgent::* ACCEPT_CALLBACK) (UINT& Connection_ID)
BeginToRequest(UINT &nConnection_ID, CString IP,UINT nPort);
Migrate (UINT nConnection_ID, CString strMsg, CDate time_stamp)
PrepareForRecv(UINT nConnection_ID, RECEIVE_CALLBACK callback);
      Void (CAgent::* RECEIVE_CALLBACK) (CString &strMsg, UINT&
      ConnectionID), ...
class CAgent {
public:
          CAgent();
          virtual ~CAgent();
          BOOL Register();
          BOOL Quit();
          BOOL Subscribe(CString strGrpName, NOTIFY_CALLBACK callback,
                      CString strTemplate="");
          UINT GetSharedFile(LPCTSTR url,LPCTSTR lpszTagInfo=NULL);
          virtual void OnConnect();
          virtual void OnDisconnect(); ...};
class Ccontainer {public:
   CContainer();
   virtual ~CContainer();
   BOOL LaunchAgentByName(CString strAgtName);
   BOOL LaunchAgentByPath(CString strPath);
   void ProcessDSCmd(CDSMsg & msg);
   typedef struct _MINIHTTP_REQUEST {
          SOCKET        socket;
          char*         http_data;
          unsigned long     http_data_size;
          MINIHTTP_FIRST_LINE*  first_line;
   } MINIHTTP_REQUEST;
   typedef struct _MINIHTTP_RESPONSE {
          unsigned int      range_begin;
```

```
    unsigned int        range_end;
    unsigned long       http_data_size;
    int                 http_response_code;
} MINIHTTP_RESPONSE; ... }
```

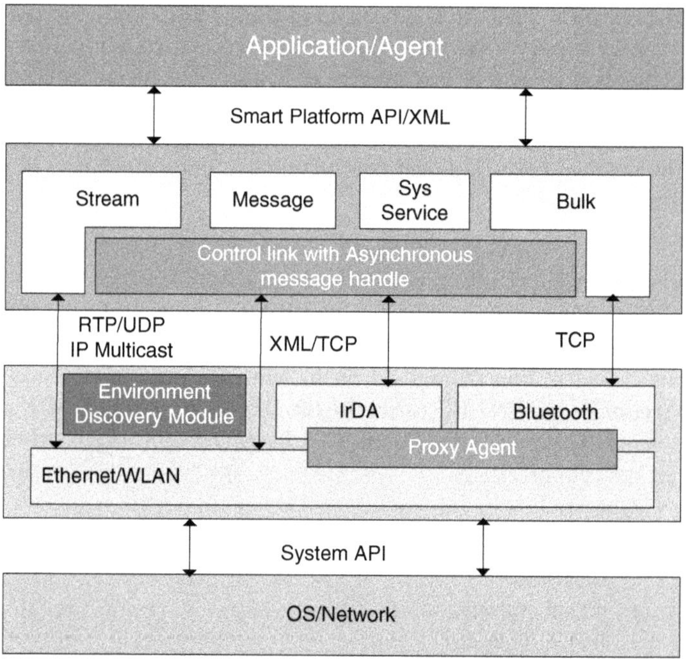

Fig. 1. Supported structure for proactive service on the platform

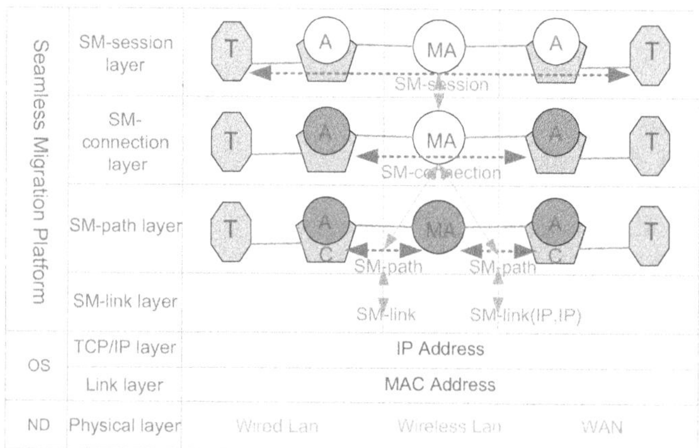

Fig. 2. Structure of seamless migration embedded in the platform

5 Test and Comparison

In our test of mobile services based on context-aware approaches of fuzzy-neural network mentioned above during proactive seamless migration, we have adopted the following dataset [7-10] and gotten the following results.

Table 1. One part of dataset for test

No	Number of learning task	Number of joined persons	Hit rate of specified learner	Output of fuzzy-neural network	Output of Classic model
1	15	57	47	53.1	62
2	16	67	53	62.9	73.5
3	15	75	62	71.5	79.8
4	24	78	72	76.5	80.1
5	25	73	68	76.9	78.2
6	25	62	56	65.5	73.1
7	26	77	67	74.6	72.9
8	26	78	57	80.6	74.4
...	...	...	...	...	...

The average error is as follows:

$$M_z = \frac{1}{10} \times \sum_{i=1}^{10} \left| Y_i - Z_i \right| = \frac{28.5}{10} = 2.85$$

The comparison error is as follows:

$$(1 - \frac{M_z}{\frac{1}{10} \times \sum_{i=1}^{10} Y_i}) \times 100\% = 1 - \frac{2.85}{72.5} \times 100\% = 3.93\%$$

The result comparison between FNF and NNF [18-19] is as Table 2 and Table 3.

Table 2. Result comparison between FNF and NNF

Name	Number of task	Sample dataset	Number of joined learners	Cluster	Trained number	Belief degree (%)
NNF	30	2000KB	200	–	4500	85.1
FNF	30	2000KB	200	14	4500	91.8

Table 3. Comparison of used memory, time and belief degree between FNF and NNF

Name	Number of task	Sample dataset	Number of joined learners	Cluster	Trained number	Used space	time	Belief degree
NNF	30	2000KB	200	–	4500	93KB	132s	85.1
FNF	30	2000KB	200	14	4500	95KB	120s	91.8

After finishing the steps of learning (training), forecasting, analyzing, we can judge where the fault forecast result is consistent with the field practice or not. If it is, that is to say, the fusion belief degree is high, close to 1. According to the introduced method, the relative comparisons' result shows the change of belief degree with fusion result. By online slight tuning, the time of fusion process is shorten, and the belief degree of fusion result is improved. The curve figures of comparison are dismissed.

6 Conclusion

In order to solve the task-oriented seamless proactive migration for Web-based learning under the banner of pervasive computing, we have designed and improved relative fuzzy-neural approaches. In this paper, we have improved the method of fuzzy-neural network modeling and have proposed a kind of fusion architecture of fuzzy-neural network based on input and output signal data or variable. From the input data, we can obtain fuzzy data curve, through the curve, the fuzzy rule number of the network may be known, and the influence to system is evaluated. A proposed high-speed learning algorithm is used to initialize the net weight and train the network. From the fuzzy membership function, the net structure can be optimized. The proposed fusion architecture base on fuzzy-neural network can make the input signal data or variable to fuse better, by online slight tuning, the fusion processing can be sped, and the fusion belief degree can be improved. The validity of our approach for proactive/attentive service with uncertainty, such as web-based mobile learning, has been tested and evaluated by the implemented demo.

References

1. Garlan D, Siewiorek D P. Project aura: toward distraction-free pervasive computing [M]. IEEE Pervasive Computing, 2002, vol1, April–June: 22-31.
2. R. Bagrodia, W. Chu, L. Kleinrock and G. Popek, Vision, Issues, and Architecture for Nomadic Computing, in *IEEE Personal Communications*, Pages 14-27, December 1995.
3. Satyanarayanan M. Pervasive computing: vision and challenge. IEEE Personal Communications, 2001, vol. 8, August: 10-17.
4. Paul C. Managing context data for smart spaces [J]. IEEE Personal Communications, 2000, 10: 44-46.
5. Xu Guangyou, Shi Yuanchun, Xie Weikai. Pervasive computing [J]. Chinese Journal of Computer, 2003,26(9): 1042-1050(in Chinese)
6. Yuanchun Shi, Weikai Xie, Guangyou Xu. Smart Classroom: Merging Technologies for Seamless Teleducation, IEEE Pervasive Computing Magazine, April-June 2003,2, No. 2.
7. Degan Zhang, Guangyou Xu, Yuanchun Shi. Moblie agents with intrusion detection during sealess transfer[C]. The 2nd Internation Conference of Pervasive Computing, April 18,2004.
8. Degan Zhang, Yuanchun Shi, Guangyou Xu. A Kind of Smart Space for Remote Interactive Access Based on Pervasive Computing [C]. The 2nd International Conference on Web-based Learning (ICWL 2003). Springer-Verlag, LNCS, Sydney, Australia, 2004.
9. Degan Zhang, Yuanchun Shi, Guangyou Xu. Learning by Seamless Migration---A Kind of Mobile Working Paradigm. In Proceedings of the 3nd International Conference on Web-based Learning (ICWL2004), Springer-Verlag, LNCS, Beijing, China, 2004.

10. Degan Zhang, Yuanchun Shi, Guangyou Xu. Context-aware Computing during Seamless Transfer Based on Random Set Theory for Active Space, The 2004 Internation Comference on Eembedded and Ubiquitous Computing (EUC2004), Springer-Verlag, LNCS, Aizu, Japan, 2004.
11. Kang Yao-hong. Data Fusion Theory and Applicaiton. Xi'an Electrical Technology University Press, 1998.
12. Harney RC. Practical Issues Multisensors Target Recongnition. SPIE,Sensor Fusion, 1990,1306.
13. Xu Ling-yu, Zhao Hai, Applicaion of Neural Fusion to Accident Forecast in Hydropower station, Proceedings of The Second International Conference on Information Fusion, Vol 2, 1999.
14. Du Qing-dong, Zhao Hai, D-S Evidence Theory Applied to Fault Diagnosis of Generator Based on Embedded Sensors, Proceedings of The Third International Conference on Information Fusion, Vol 1,2000.
15. Tan Zhu-xun. Usual Process of Information Fusion and Application in Fault Diagnosis. Detection Technology, 1995,(3):15-17.
16. Zhang Yan-duo, Jiang Xingwei. Multisensor Information Fusion and Application in Intelligent Fault Diagnosis. Sensor Technology. 1999,18(2),18-22.
17. Hall D. Mathmatical Techniques in Multisensor Data Fusion. Artech House Inc, 1992
18. Ishibuchi H, Tanaka H. Fuzzy neural networks with fuzzy weights and fuzzy bias .in Proc ICNN'93,1993, 1650-1655.
19. Lin Y H, George A. A new approach to fuzzy-neural system modeling. IEEE Trans. Fuzzy System, 1995,3(2): 190-197.

A Novel Block-Based Motion Estimation Algorithm and VLSI Architecture Based on Cluster Parallelism

Tie-jun Li and Si-kun Li

Office 621, School of Computer Science, National University of Defense Technology, 410073 ChangSha, China
tj_li@sohu.com

Abstract. This paper proposes a novel block-based motion estimation algorithm and the corresponding architecture based on cluster parallelism. In this algorithm, up to 18 predictors are employed to improve the encoding quality while the computation time is not increased compared with PMVFAST. Experiment results verify the superiority of the proposed algorithm and architecture. The PSNR improvement effect on PMVFAST is 8.14 times higher than that of existing enhanced algorithm EPZS. In particular, they greatly improve the encoding quality of video sequence with large or irregular motion. Designed and synthesized on SMIC 0.18um technology, the architecture works on the frequency of 200MHz. Its throughput is about 15 times higher than the well-known FS architecture with 16 PEs while it consumes only 9.1% memory bandwidth of the FS architecture.

1 Introduction

BMA (Block Matching Algorithm) is regarded as an efficient method to get high compression ratio by reducing the redundancy among video sequences. BMA is an essential part of several video-coding standards, such as MPEG-1/2/4 and ITU H.261/263/264. Full Search (FS) is a brute force algorithm and its computation complexity is so high that it is usually regarded as the test benchmark. Because of its regular structure and simple control, FS is suitable for algorithm-specific architectures [1][2][3]. However, the inherently high computation complexity of FS limits the real time performance and leads to high power dissipation of its architectures.

Many fast BMAs, such as the Three-Step Search (TSS) [4], 2-D log Search [5] and Diamond Search (DS) [6], reduce the computation complexity at the cost of a significant loss of visual quality. Several new algorithms, such as PMVFAST (Predictive Motion Vector Field Adaptive Search Technique)[7] and EPZS (Enhanced Predictive Zonal Search)[10], have been developed to explore the spatial and temporal correlation among video sequences. PMVFAST and EPZS improve the performance and encoding quality greatly and have been adopted by MPEG-4 [8] and applied to H.264/AVC [9]. To further accelerate PMVFAST and EPZS, we have proposed an efficient VLSI architecture in previous work [11].

Although PMVFAST and EPZS have developed some MV (Motion Vector) predictors successfully, their accuracy to the video sequences with large or irregular motion is not sufficient. Besides, the serial evaluations of MV predictors limit

L.T. Yang et al. (Eds.): ICESS 2005, LNCS 3820, pp. 564 – 575, 2005.

computation performance and the number of predictors. Based on the analysis of PMVFAST and hardware/software co-design method, this paper proposes a parallel algorithm to evaluate predictors and a VLSI architecture to support this algorithm. Because of the parallel algorithm, although the number of MV predictors is increased from 6 in PMVFAST to 18, the encoding quality is improved and the computation time decreases. Compared with existing PMVFAST architecture [11], the new architecture employs more configurable VDUs(Variable Delay Units) and two more PEs (Processing Elements). It can support much more flexible cluster to compute in parallel while consuming a little more VLSI area and memory bandwidth.

The paper is organized as follows: PMVFAST algorithm is introduced and analyzed in Sec. 2. Sec. 3 shows the efficiency to improve encoding quality by multi-predictors. To overcome the disadvantage of multi-predictors, Sec. 4 introduces the definition of cluster and discusses the utilization of it to reuse data. The new VLSI parallel array architecture is proposed in Sec. 5 to support cluster parallelism. Sec. 6 proposes the new BMA based on cluster parallelism. Sec.7 implements the new algorithm and architecture and compares them with the existing ones. Finally, a conclusion is given in Sec. 8.

2 Analysis of PMVFAST

PMVFAST mainly utilizes spatial and temporal correlation to improve the performance and encoding quality of BMA[7]. Their efficiency comes from three aspects: MV (Motion Vector) predicting, adaptive early termination and prediction refinement. MV predicting checks a set of potentially similar predictors, such as the MVs of spatial adjacent and temporal correlative MBs (Macro Blocks), and then selects the best one. The adaptive early termination allows terminating the search at given stages of the estimation if some rules are satisfied. The prediction refinement employs a search pattern around the best predictor to essentially improve the final prediction.

According to [7], PMVFAST is roughly 4.5, 4.8, and 4 times faster whereas its PSNR (Peak Signal to Noise Ratio) is approximately 0.87dB, 0.81dB, and 0.73dB higher than TSS, NTSS, and DS, respectively. PMVFAST is about 654 times for SA 32 while having an average PSNR loss of only 0.06dB versus FS. EPZS [8] improves PMVFAST by increasing the number of MV predictors from 6 to 11 and a new predicting method of SAD(Sum of Absolute Differences). Although it improves encoding quality by about 0.01 dB on average, EPZS consumes about 8 % more computation time than PMVFAST.

With the algorithm PMVFAST, six typical video sequences (CIF format, 300 frames) are encoded: Foreman, Stefan, Coast, Flowers, News, and Mobile. There is much large or irregular motion in Foreman and Stefan, while the motion in News and Mobile is small and regular. Other experiment condition includes: half pixel search, N_{MB}=16, the search area of FS is 16.

Shown in Fig. 1, the encoding quality on the video sequences with large or irregular motion is not yet sufficient. For example, compared with FS, the PSNRs on 'Foreman' and 'Stefan' decrease by 0.2195dB and 0.1805dB respectively, which are much larger than other video sequences with small motion. Besides, the probabilities to terminate early on these two sequences are much smaller than those on other sequences. The fact implies that the accuracy of MV prediction on these sequences decreases.

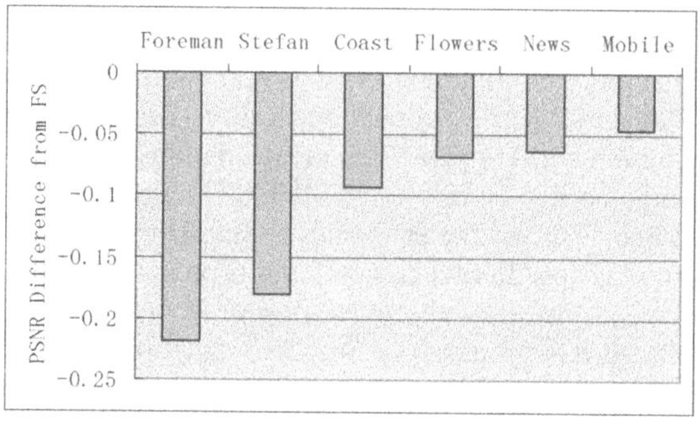

Fig. 1. Comparison of encoding qualities on different video sequences

In PMVFAST and EPZS, all predictors are evaluated one by one to select the best one. The computation time increases linearly with the number of predictors. To reduce the computation time, the predictors could be evaluated in parallel.

Above all, this paper proposes the idea of increasing the number of predictors to improve encoding quality, a parallel algorithm to evaluate predictors cluster and a new VLSI architecture to support this algorithm.

3 Multi-predictors ME

3.1 Acceleration Prediction

In order to achieve more accurate prediction, EPZS [10] suggests the accelerator motion vector ($TACCMV_{x,y}$), which takes into account both the motion vector of the corresponding reference frame MB and its acceleration. The computation formula is as follows:

$$TACC_{x,y}^{t-1}=(MV_{x,y}^{t-1}-MV_{x,y}^{t-2})$$
$$TACCMV_{x,y}=MV_{x,y}^{t-1}+TACC_{x,y}^{t-1}$$

where $TACC_{x,y}^{t-1}$ is the acceleration of the MB positioned at (x,y), computed according to motion information of the t-1frame (the reference frame) and the t-2 frame. As to the video sequences with irregular motion, e.g. Forman, the acceleration of video objects varies acutely. The prediction will not be accurate if producing the prediction velocity using the reference frame's acceleration.

Much information of the video objects has spatial correlation, including the motion vector, the adjacent info, the acceleration, etc. Among them, the spatial correlation of the motion vector has been widely used in motion vector prediction, whereas this paper utilizes the spatial correlation of the acceleration to perform acceleration prediction, likewise leading to good results.

The acceleration prediction predicts the current block's acceleration using the computed accelerations of the adjacent blocks. For instance, it can compute the linear or nonlinear combination of the three spatial adjacent MBs' acceleration as the acceleration of the current block. This paper considers the median value as the prediction acceleration, as follows:

$$SACC_{x,y}^{t}=Median(ACC_{x-1,y}^{t}, ACC_{x,y-1}^{t}, ACC_{x+1,y-1}^{t})$$

where $ACC_{x-1,y}^{t}$, $ACC_{x,y-1}^{t}$ and $ACC_{x+1,y-1}^{t}$ is the three available spatial adjacent MB's acceleration of the current frame respectively. Then the current block's prediction MV $STACCMV_{x,y}$ is computed according to the prediction acceleration and the velocity of the reference frame's interrelated block, using the following formula:

$$STACCMV_{x,y}=MV_{x,y}^{t-1} + SACC_{x,y}^{t}$$

3.2 Multi-predictor ME

Valid predictors are added to improve the prediction accuracy, so as to obtain better encoding performance. In this way, the process of checking the predictors is to verify which point has the least difference with the current MB, in which the metric is generally the SAD (Sum of Absolute Differences).

Some predictors of the temporal and spatial correlation are depicted in Fig. 2, where the motion information of the MBs with the white color filled is known and not for the gray filled MBs. The position indicated by the grid is that of the current MB for motion estimation. The dots in the figure denote that the motion vectors are known, which can be used in the prediction thanks to the strong correlation with the current MB temporally and spatially.

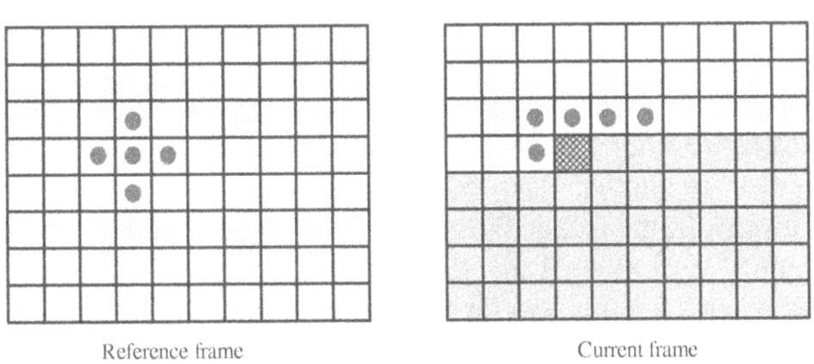

Fig. 2. Spatial and temporal correlative predictors of current MB

Besides that listed in Fig. 2, the predictors used in this paper also include (0,0), MedianMV, TACCMV, STACCMV and the accelerator motion vectors of the four adjacent MBs in the reference frame($TACCMV_{x-1,y}$, $TACCMV_{x,y-1}$, $TACCMV_{x+1,y}$, and $TACCMV_{x,y+1}$), totally eighteen. In order to analyze how the predictors affect the encoding quality, we verify the change trend of the encoding quality by adding the predictor gradually with Foreman, Stefan, Coast (CIF format, 300 frames) as the test sequences. Fig. 3 gives the experiment result, from which we can see that the encoding quality of the Stefan with large motion and the Foreman with irregular motion is enhanced by the addition of predictors. Note that, it can be observed from the figure that the improvement curve tends to mildness when the number of the predictors is added to eighteen, which means it is hard to increase the encoding quality by adding more predictors.

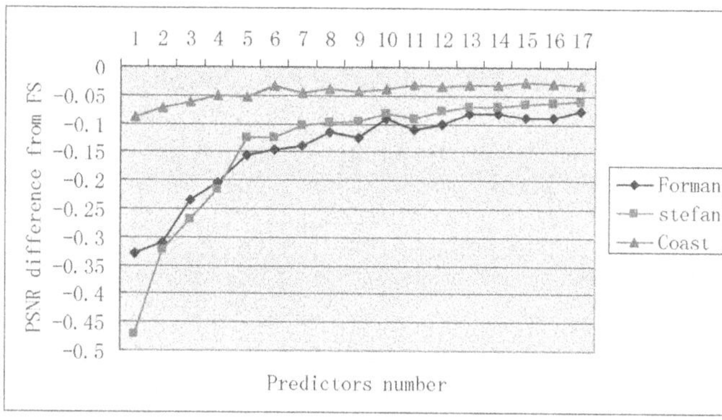

Fig. 3. Change of encoding quality as the number of predictors is increasing

4 Predictors Cluster

Although more predictors are added to improve encoding quality, the computation time increases linearly with their number. To solve this contradiction, the predictors should be calculated in parallel. Parallelism is limited by memory bandwidth in hardwarc implcmcntation, so it is rcquircd that thc loadcd data bc rcuscd in maximum extent. To reuse data and to compute in parallel, some concepts are introduced in this section firstly.

1) Scan: Loading of the pixel data in current frames or reference frames.
2) RD(i,j) (Reference frame scan Distance): The time interval to scan from one checked point ‘i’ to another ’j’ in reference frame.
3) CD(i,j) (Current frame scan Distance): The time interval to scan from one checked point ‘i’ to another ’j’ in current frame.
4) CLUSTER: A set of predictors in reference frame which can reuse loaded data well.
5) NUM(CLUSTER): The number of predictors in CLUSTER.

To reuse data and compute the predictors in parallel, CLUSTER must satisfy the following constraint.

Constraint 1: N_{PE}(cluster dimension constraint). The number of predictors in CLUSTER to be computed in parallel is limited by N_{PE} (the number of processing elements in hardware).

$$NUM(CLUSTER) \le N_{PE}$$

Constraint 2: RDC (Reference frame scan Distance Constraint). To reuse scanned data in reference frame, the checked points in a cluster should distribute in a small area and the reference frame scan distance should be limited by a distance constraint.

$$RD(i,i+1) \leq RDC$$

Constraint 3: CDC (Current frame scan Distance Constraint). When computing a predictor, the pixel data of current frame and reference frame must reach the corresponding PE(Processing Element) at the same time. To reuse data, the loaded data of current frame for the previous PE should be buffered until it can be used for the next PE. CDC is determined by the depth of buffers between PEs in the hardware implementation.

$$CD(i,i+1) \leq CDC$$

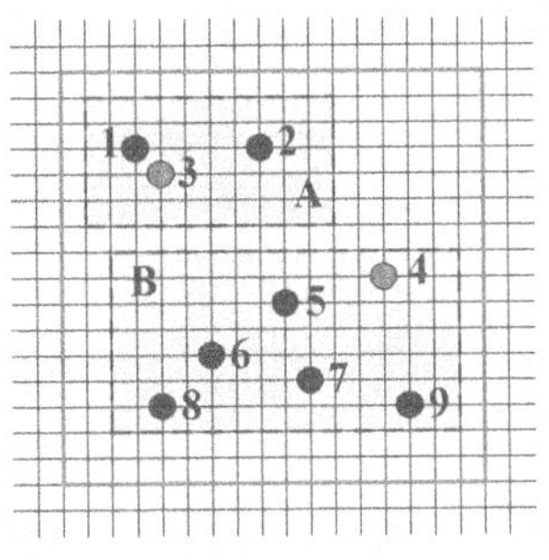

Fig. 4. Clusters

From the condition: N_{MB} is 16, the max buffer depth is 30 and the number of PEs is 11, we can deduce the following cluster constraints : N_{PE} 11, RDC=256, and CDC=30. Fig. 4 gives an example of clusters based on above constraints. All the predictors in Fig. 4 satisfy RDC. However, they cannot be included in a single cluster because that CD(3,4)=90, which is against CDC. Thus, all the predictors are divided into two different clusters: A and B. For cluster A as an example, it satisfies N_{PE} that the number of predictors is 5. In addition, the current frame scan distance between 5 and 6 is the max among all adjacent predictors and their CD(5,6) is 29, which satisfies CDC.

Note that small diamond, large diamond and square search patterns all satisfy above constraints, and they are the specific examples of cluster.

5 Motion Estimation Architecture for Cluster Parallelism

5.1 Top Level Architecture

Fig.5 depicts the top level of the motion estimation architecture for cluster parallel computation. This architecture is a hardware/software co-design structure including two parts: CPU and CPAME (Configurable Parallel Array Motion estimation Engine). CPU is responsible for the tasks with complicated controls, such as loading and selecting predictors, partitioning and mapping clusters, and determining early termination. CPAME is the core engine of the architecture. It contains a datapath with 11 PEs, AGU

(Address Generator Unit), FSM (Finite State Machine) and several configurable registers. CPAME is responsible for the tasks with density data, search patterns refinement and cluster computation. Since each part except the datapath in CPAME is similar to PMVFAST engine [11], this paper only describes the design of the datapath.

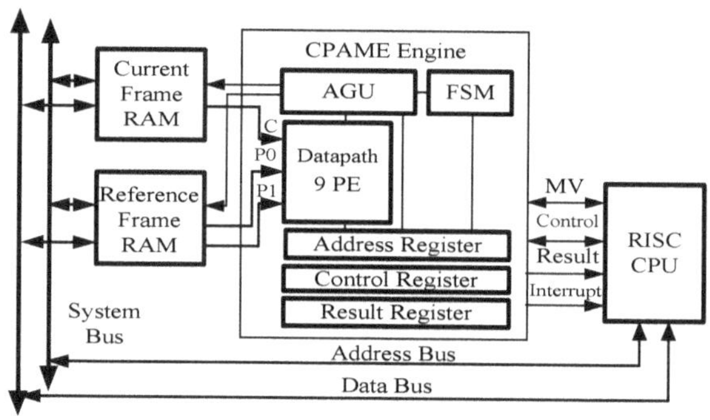

Fig. 5. Top level architecture of motion estimation

5.2 CPAME Architecture

Fig. 6 shows the parallel PEs array architecture of CPAME. The 'PE' is responsible for the computation of a search point SAD (Sum of Absolute Differences). 'D' denotes VDU (Variable Delay Unit). 'C' is the data port of the current frame. 'P0' and 'P1' are the data ports of the reference frame. The data of the current frame is transmitted to every PE one by one through the VDUs and the data of the reference frame is broadcasted to every PE. In CPAME, the data of the current frame and the reference frame is loaded only once through the above mechanism. The parallelism is maximized and the memory access bandwidth is minimized. The SAD results of PEs are compared by 'MIN' in different cycles and the minimal SAD is achieved at the end of computation.

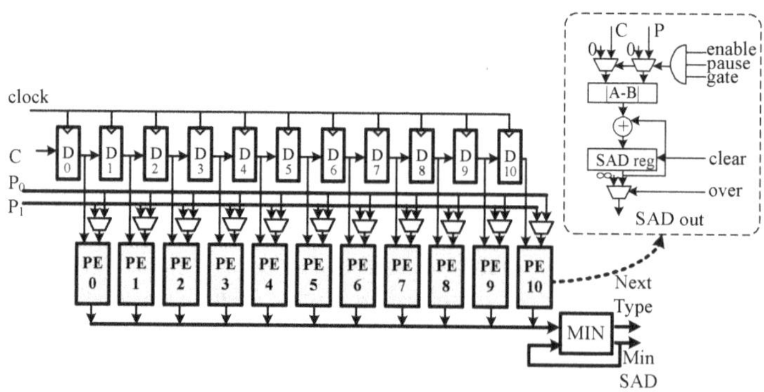

Fig. 6. Architecture of CPAME

There are two important differences between CPAME engine and PMVFAST engine [11]:

1) PMVFAST engine employs three types of VDUs and supports only three types of search patterns. A single type of VDU is used in CPAME, and it can be configured to arbitrary delay from 1 to 15. This change enables that the checked points can distribute more freely. Setting N_{MB}=16, we can deduce the constraints: CDC = 15, RDC = 256.
2) PMVFAST engine employs 9 PEs, which are corresponding to the 9 checked points in diamond search pattern or square search pattern. Here, the number of PEs in CPAME becomes 11. There are two reasons for this improvement. The first is that 11 PEs can fit most clusters nicely. Since many of the 18 predictors introduced in Sec. 3.2 are the same, there are only 8.7 different predictors on average in every ME search. 11 PEs are enough for most cluster computation. Secondly, there should be some additional PEs to relax scan distance constraint. When CD is greater than 15, two additional VDUs could be merged to support the delay from 1 to 30 and then CDC constraint could be relaxed to 30. The PE between merged VDUs would not be used any longer, so the N_{PE} become 10. We can further relax CDC constraint if more adjacent VDUs are merged.

CPAME can be configured to support diamond pattern and square pattern, so PMVFAST and EPZS are also supported by this engine.

6 Fast BMA Based on Cluster Parallelism

6.1 Cluster Parallel Algorithm

To increase predictors without increasing computing time, we propose a cluster parallel algorithm. The idea of cluster parallel algorithm is that: first we divide the predictors into clusters; then each predictor and scan distance in the cluster are mapped to corresponding PE and VDU in CPAME engine; at last the evaluating computation of the predictors is completed in parallel by different PEs. The algorithm consists of two main steps: cluster partition and cluster mapping.

6.1.1 Cluster Partition

The goal of cluster partition is to find the cluster with the largest number of predictors. Considering all the predictors introduced in Sec.3.2, since their total number is small, we can use a window(N_{MB}×N_{MB} square) to glide along with the predictors and count the predictors under cluster constraints in the window. If the number of predictors is less than N_{PE}, the relaxed constraint discussed in Sec. 3.2 would be used to increase the number of predictors in the cluster. A partition by the above method will not complete until the largest cluster is found. The process of cluster partition will be continued for the remained predictors until all the predictors have been partitioned into clusters. The algorithm of cluster partition is as follows.

Problem: Given predictors: AllPoints={(x_i, y_i) | i=0,1,..,N} and the cluster constraints: N_{MB}(corresponding to RDC), CDC and N_{PE}, find the cluster with the max number of predictors.

Algorithm:

Step1: Sort the predictors in AllPoints by ascend along with vertical direction firstly and then with horizontal direction.

Step2: For each predictor (a, b)∈AllPoints, draw two lines: x=a and y=b. Supposed all these lines intersect on M points, name them as CrossPoints={(x_j,y_j)|j=0,1,..,M}.

Step3: For each point (x_j,y_j)∈CrossPoints, j=0,1,..,M, get the dimension of cluster starting from the point. Count all predictors which satisfy cluster constraints or relaxed cluster constraints discussed in Sec. 5.2, and name N_j as its number.

Step4: Find max predictors number: max(N_j), j=0,1,..,M, and return the cluster with max(N_j).

Fig. 7. Cluster partition algorithm

6.1.2 Cluster Mapping

Cluster mapping consists of two parts: mapping the predictors in cluster to PEs, and mapping the scan distance CDs of current frame to VDUs. If a CD is greater than 15, we must merge two VDUs together as the delay of this CD, since VDU can only support 15 cycles delay. We can turn off the invalid PE between the merged VDUs to save energy.

Table 1 and Table 2 show the cluster mapping from cluster B in Fig. 4 to CPAME engine in Fig. 5. We can see that both CD(5,6) and CD(6,7) are larger than 15, so as shown in Table 1, we merge D2 with D3 and D4 with D5 to support these two scan distance delays. As shown in Table 2, PE2 and PE4 between the merged VDUs can't participate in computation at this configuration, so we turn them off to save energy.

Table 1. Mapping from CDs to VDUs

VDUs	D_0	D_1	D_2	D_3	D_4	D_5	D_6	D_7	D_7~D_{10}
Configurations	9	12	15	14	15	5	10	10	close
Scan Distances	9	12	29		20		10	10	NA

Table 2. Mapping from predictors to PEs

PEs	PE_0	PE_1	PE_2	PE_3	PE_4	PE_5	PE_6	PE_7	PE_8~PE_{10}
Predictors	4	5	close	6	close	7	8	9	close

6.2 Fast BMA Based on Cluster Parallelism

Based on the above discussions, Fig. 8 gives the flow of PCMEFast(Parellel Cluster Motion Estimation Fast algorithm). The algorithm inherits some ideas of PMVFAST[7] and takes the new idea of increasing predictors to improve the accuracy of ME and cluster parallel computation. In addition, the algorithm abandons large diamond and small diamond search patterns and uses only square search pattern to refine prediction. The parameters' definitions in the algorithm are the same as Cluster Partition.

Step1: Partition the predictors into clusters.

Step2: Set T1 =256, and map the max cluster to PAME. If the computation result of PAME is less than T1, go to Step5, otherwise go to next step;

Step3: Set $T_2 = \min(SAD_{x-1,y}^{t}, SAD_{x,y-1}^{t}, SAD_{x-1,y-1}^{t}, SAD_{x,y}^{t-1}) \times 1.2 + 64$, and map the other clusters to PAME. If any computation result of PAME is less than T2, go to Step5, otherwise go to next step;

Step4: Set the result position of preceding steps as the start point and start square pattern search. Continue the search until the point with minimum SAD is at the center of the square;

Step5: Process to terminate the algorithm.

Fig. 8. PCMEFast algorithm

7 Implementation and Comparison

PCMEFast algorithm is simulated and compared with PMVFAST[7] and EPZS[10]. The video sequence and the settings of parameters are same as that of Sec. 2. Fig. 9 shows the result of simulation and comparison. The result shows that the PSNR of PCMEFast is approximately 0.0697dB higher than PMVFAST, while EPZS's PSNR is only about 0.00763dB higher than PMVFAST. Apparently, the improvement effect of PCMEFast is 8.14 times higher than that of EPZS. The improvement is obvious in the video sequence with irregular and large motion. For example, its PSNR improves 0.1433dB in Forman with irregular motion and 0.1193dB in Stefan with large motion. Above all, PCMEFast improves encoding quality efficiently and makes it close to that of FS.

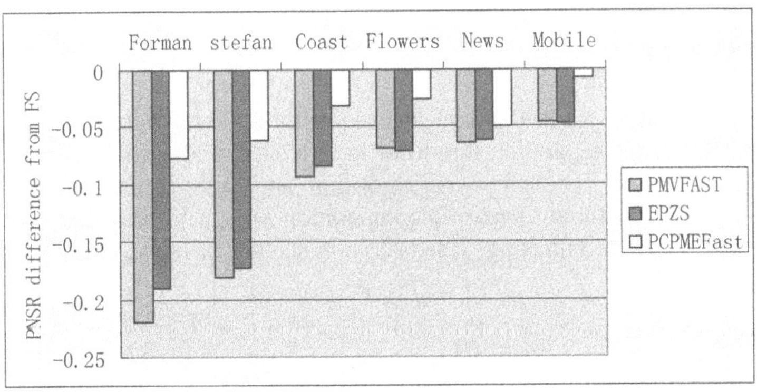

Fig. 9. Comparison of three algorithms

The proposed architecture CPAME is designed and simulated in Verilog HDL. The logic is synthesized by Synopsys' DC with SIMIC 0.18um 1P5M process. Table 3 lists the result of implementation and comparison with two existing ones.

Table 3. Comparison of three ME architectures

Architectures	FS[-16,15]	PMVFAST		PAME
Number of PEs	16	9		11
Process(*um*)	0.25	0.18		0.18
Area(K gates)	22.3	17.5		20.48
Processing Power	100MHz	200MHz		200MHz
Algorithm	FS	PMVFAST	EPZS	PCMEFast
Clock Cycles/MB	16,399	1,042	1,122	1,021
Bandwidth(Bytes)	31,744	2,674	3,314	2,886
Reference	[2]	[11]		This paper

The result of simulation shows that it takes 1,021 clock cycles and 2,986 bytes memory bandwidth to run PCMEFast once on CPAME. Although the predictors of PCMEFast are 12 more than that of PMVFAST(6 predictors), PCMEFast takes 2% execution cycles less than that of PMVFAST because of cluster parallelism. Besides, PCMEFast on CPAME works 9% faster and consumes 12.9% less bandwidth than EPZS does. Note that the results of PMVFAST and EPZS are all got from the experiments accelerated by PMVFAST hardware engine.

The results of synthesis with Design Compiler show that CPAME engine consumes 2,980 gates more than PMVFAST engine, which are consumed on the added PEs and VDUs. We can see also that the throughput of CPAME engine is about 16 times more than that of the FS ME engine with 16 PEs. The CPAME engine takes only 9.1% memory bandwidth of that of FS engine and 91.8% logical area of that of FS engine.

8 Conclusion

Based on the analysis of PMVFAST and the method of hardware/software co-design, this paper proposes a parallel algorithm to evaluate predictors cluster and a VLSI parallel architecture. The proposed algorithm and architecture improve encoding quality efficiently without increasing computation time. They can find applications in video fields, e. g. video meeting, video surveillance and wireless video transmission.

References

1. Yen-Kuang Chen, S. Y. Kung, A Systolic Design Methodology with Application to Full-Search Block-Matching Architectures, [J]. Journal of VLSI Signal Processing Systems, May 1998, 19(1): 51-77
2. P. Kuhn, Algorithms Complexity Analysis and VLSI Architectures for MPEG-4 Motion Estimation. Boston: Kluwer Academic Publishers, 1999
3. Hao-Chieh Chang. Architecture Design for MPEG-4 Video Coding System. [Ph D dissertation]. Taipei, Depart. of Electrical Engineering at National Taiwan University, 2001

4. T. Koga, K. Iinuma, A. Hirano, Y. Iijima, and T. Ishiguro. Motion compensated interframe coding for video conferencing. Nat. Telecommun. Conf. New Orleans, LA, 1981
5. J.R. Jain and A.K. Jain. Displacement measurement and its application in interframe image coding. [J]. IEEE Trans. on Communications,1981,COM-29(12): 1799-1808
6. Zhu S, Ma KK, A new diamond search algorithm for fast block matching motion estimation [J]. IEEE Trans. on Image Processing, 2000, 9(2): 287-290
7. Alexis. M. Tourapis, O. C. Au, and M. L. Liou. Predictive Motion Vector Field Adaptive Search Technique (PMVFAST) - Enhancing Block Based Motion Estimation. In: proceedings of Visual Communications and Image Processing 2001 (VCIP-2001). San Jose, CA, January 2001
8. "Optimization Model Version 1.0", ISO/IEC JTC1/SC29/WG11 MPEG2000/N3324, Noordwijkerhout, Netherlands, March 2000.
9. Hye-Yeon Cheong Tourapis, Alexis Michael Tourapis, FAST MOTION ESTIMATION WITHIN THE H.264 CODEC, ICME2003, Baltimore, Maryland, 9 July 2003
10. A. M. Tourapis, "Enhanced Predictive Zonal Search for Single and Multiple Frame Motion Estimation" in proceedings of Visual Communications and Image Processing 2002 (VCIP-2002), San Jose, CA, January 2002.
11. Tiejun Li, Chengdong shen, Sikun Li. A VLSI Architecture for PMVFAST Block-based Motion Estimation Algorithm. Journal of Computer Research and Development, 2005, 5

Software-Based Video Codec for Mobile Devices

Jiajun Bu, Yuanliang Duan, Chun Chen, and Zhi Yang*

College of Computer Science, Zhejiang University,
310027 Hangzhou, P.R. China
{bjj, duanyuanliang, chenc, yangzh}@zju.edu.cn

Abstract. With the rapid development of wireless networks and consumer electronics, various mobile applications have emerged. However, due to some constraints such as weak computational power, limited memory and small display screen, traditional video coding applications can not work well on mobile devices. In this paper, we proposed a software-based video codec framework and its implementation which is suitable for real-time video coding applications on mobile devices. Some key optimizing techniques, such as fast predictive motion estimation (ME), zero-coefficients prejudgment and multiplierless integer discrete cosine transform (DCT), are used in our codec. Experimental results demonstrate the flexibility of our framework and the good speedup we achieved while video quality degradation is negligible. The codec is suitable for scenarios where low-complexity computing is required.

1 Introduction

In recent years, with the rapid development of hardware capability, mobile devices such as mobile phones and pocket PCs become popular in our daily lives. More and more users are seeking real-time mobile video communication services. However, because of some constraints such as weak computational power and limited memory size, many highly efficient but complex algorithms cannot be used directly for real-time video coding on mobile devices. How to reduce the computational requirements as much as possible while achieving good coding performance becomes a key research issue for video codec [1].

Many efforts have been done in this area. In [2], a practical real-time video codec is presented for mobile devices. It proposed a codec based on the reference software of H.263 and did some optimization works on ME and DCT. Experimental results on pocket PC showed its feasibility. However, the codec is based on H.263 standard only and does not consider the flexibility. An optimized MPEG-4 video codec is proposed in [3], it presented an optimized encoder focused on ARM chips. Besides algorithmic optimization, architecture level optimization is also adopted and showed its great advantage; whereas, the optimization schemes

* The work was supported by National Natural Science Foundation of China (60203013), 863 Program (2004AA1Z2390) and Key Technologies R&D Program of Zhejiang Province (2005C23047 & 2004C11052).

L.T. Yang et al. (Eds.): ICESS 2005, LNCS 3820, pp. 576–585, 2005.

aim at ARM cores without a view to the universality and scalability. Other optimization schemes [4][5] only consider some specific algorithms in video codec.

In this paper, we proposed a software-based video codec for mobile devices. Considering both of the flexibility and scalability, our codec is designed on a base of component framework. The convenience of the proposed framework will be shown in the following section. Besides, some key optimizing techniques such as fast predictive motion estimation, zero-coefficients prejudgment and multiplierless integer DCT, etc, are used in our codec to reduce the computational complexity. Experimental results show that our codec can achieve a good speedup with negligible video quality degradation. Our codec performs well on HP Pocket PC iPAQ, e.g. for some QCIF sequences (176*144), the encoding speed can reach 20 frames per second (fps). Moreover, the flexible framework of our codec is independent of video coding standards, such as H.263, MPEG-4, etc.

The paper is organized as follows. In Section 2, we present our flexible framework of video codec design. The key optimizing techniques are proposed in Section 3. In Section 4, we show the experimental results and comparative analysis. The last section gives the conclusions and future works.

2 Flexible Codec Framework for Mobile Devices

Fig.1 shows the flowchart of conventional hybrid DPCM/DCT video encoder model. Traditional software implementation of the codec is the workflow of the diagram. Almost all the existed reference software modules are such kind of implementation. However, in our proposed software codec framework, we classify the different modules into three layers. Fig.2 shows the architecture of the proposed framework. Layer one is basic algorithm layer; it includes the common-used algorithms such as DCT, Quantization, Colorspace Conversion, Motion Estimation and Compensation, etc, which are also the kernel algorithm modules of the conventional codec. Common Interface layer is the second layer, which is special for the convenience. Developers need not care for the implementation and detail of the algorithms but the interfaces. Specification related layer, which includes

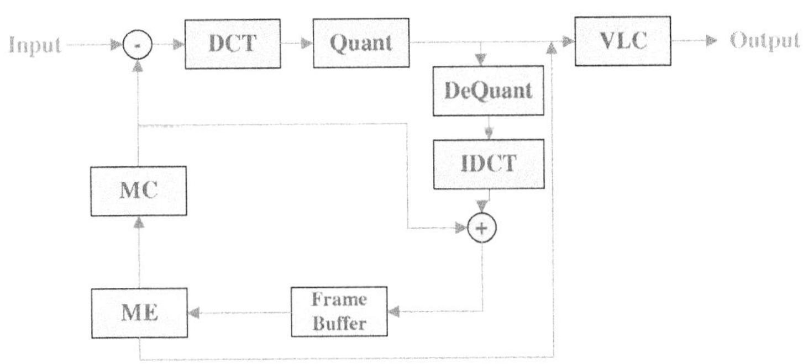

Fig. 1. The flowchart of the encoder

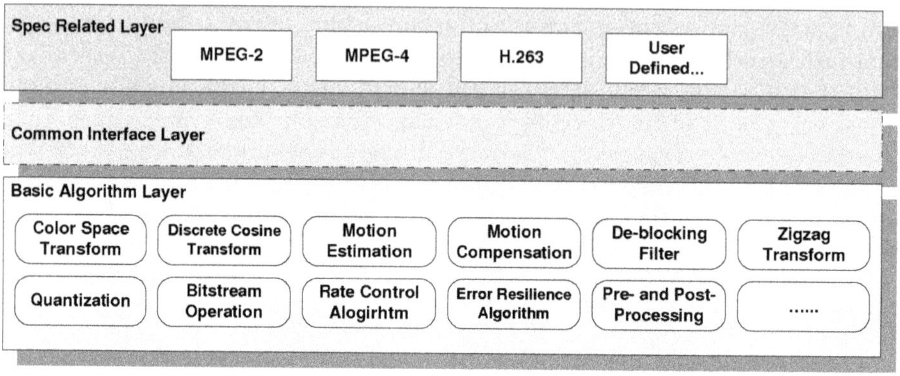

Fig. 2. Framework of video codec for mobile devices

the specific encoder and decoder, is classified as the third layer. This layer is standard related, i.e., we introduce bitstream syntax here.

The main advantage of this framework is the flexibility. All the modules in basic algorithm layer have fixed interfaces, which are presented in the common interface layer. A new DCT algorithm is invented, for example, we only need to replace the new component with the old one, which doesn't influence up-layers. We can also add some complex modules into basic algorithm layer as optional components, such as rate control module and error resilience module, etc.

Another merit of this framework is that we can set up our codec software to match MPEG-x or H.26x standard on demand, because all the basic algorithms are similar, what's the difference is the bitstream syntax according to the different standards.

3 Proposed Optimizing Techniques

We implemented the codec software according to the component framework proposed above. In order to get the distribution of computing time, full search motion estimation and floating DCT/IDCT are used in our testing. It can be seen from Fig.3, motion estimation, DCT/IDCT and quantization are three critical modules which consumes the majority of computing time. Obviously, our main target is optimization of the three time-consuming modules. Next four sub-sections will give the proposed optimizing techniques which can significantly reduce the complexity.

3.1 Fast Predictive Motion Estimation

Motion estimation (ME) is efficient in eliminating temporal redundancy between adjacent frames. At the same time, motion estimation is considered the most time-consuming part. There are significant advances in fast motion estimation techniques in recent years for alleviating the heavy computation load, e.g. the diamond search (DS) [4], the efficient fast ME prediction and early termination strategy [5].

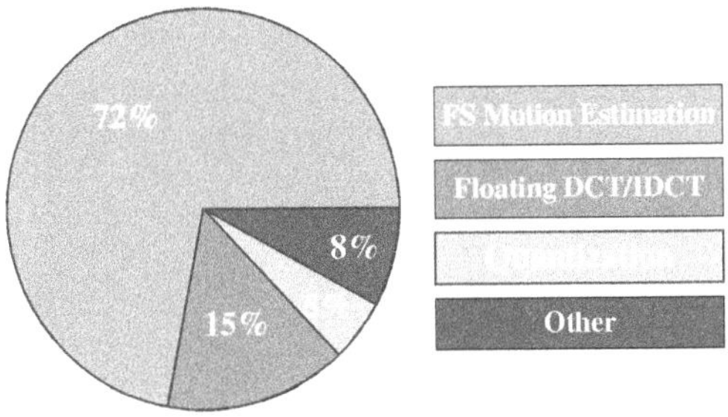

Fig. 3. Test result of foreman sequence at QCIF format, QP = 4

In [5], four prediction methods are proposed, includes median prediction (MP), uplayer prediction (UP), last frame prediction (LFP) and last reference frame prediction(LRFP). We introduce two simple prediction methods here. MP is defined by

$$MV_{pred\_MP} = median\{MV_A, MV_B, MV_C\} \tag{1}$$

Where $MV_A/MV_B/MV_C$, is the motion vector (MV) of A/B/C block in Fig.4(a) respectively. Note that A/B/C may not be in same modes. LFP is defined by

$$MV_{x,y,n} = mv_{x,y,n-1} \tag{2}$$

Where $mv_{x,y,n-1}$ is the corresponding MV of the previous frame, Fig.4(b).

In our proposed codec, considering the trade-off between coding efficiency and computation complexity, we choose MP as the prediction method. After the MV prediction, a diamond search process (Fig.5) is used in ME.

We compared the fast predictive ME algorithm with the full search ME and the following *Table 1* shows the results. More than 20 speedup on motion estimation is achieved while PSNR degradation is negligible.

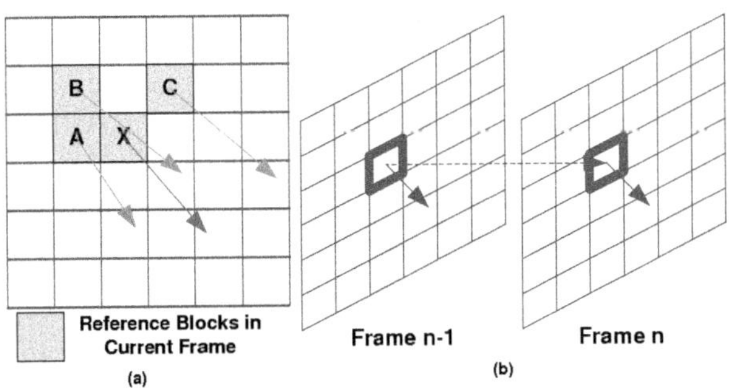

Fig. 4. Prediction pattern: (a) Median prediction; (b) Last frame prediction

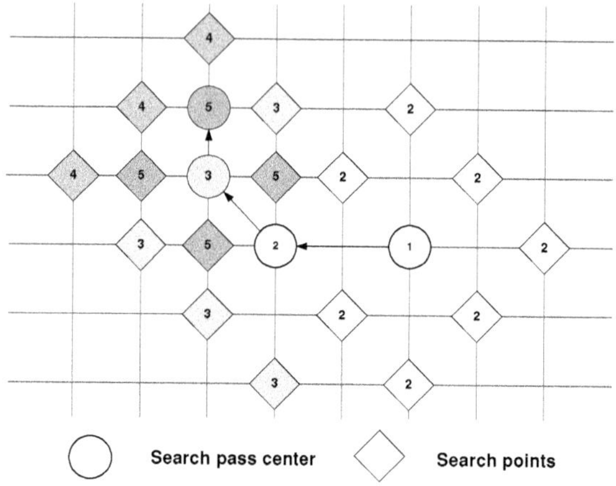

Fig. 5. Diamond search (DS) process

Table 1. Average PSNR degradation and speedup of the ME module comparing to full search with a search range of 32 pixels, QP=4, QCIF format sequence

Sequence	PSNR Loss	Speedup
Akiyo	0.05	25.48
Coastguard	0.11	23.43
Foreman	0.16	19.12

3.2 Zero-Coefficient Prejudgment

Discrete cosine transform (DCT) is applied to compress motion compensation data in the spatial domain, and a special case for the encoder occurs when all the coefficients from the DCT are quantized to zero. In this situation, instead of sending multiple zeros to the decoder, the encoder sends a special signal indicating the 'skip' state.

The traditional method to detect whether one block is 'skipped' or not is rather complex, because it needs the computation of DCT and quantization, then followed by a check to see if all the coefficients are zero or not. For some special application, such as video conference or video phone, there are many stationary blocks, so zero-coefficient prejudgment could significantly reduce the amount of computation.

In [6], a good zero coefficient prejudgment method is proposed and in [7], an improved method is presented to enhance the judgment efficiency.

The discrete cosine transform of a discrete function $f(x, y)$ $x, y = 0, 1, .., N-1$, is defined as

$$F(u, v) = \left(\frac{2}{N}\right) k_u k_v \sum\sum f(x, y) \cos\left(\frac{(2x+1)u\pi}{2N}\right) \cos\left(\frac{(2y+1)v\pi}{2N}\right) \quad (3)$$

$$u, v = 0, 1, .., N-1 \quad where\ k_u, k_v = \begin{cases} \frac{1}{\sqrt{2}} & for\ u, v = 0 \\ 1 & for\ u, v = 1, 2, ..N-1 \end{cases}$$

In our proposed codec, N = 8, so *formula 3* gives

$$|F(u,v)| = \frac{1}{4}\sum_{x=0}^{7}\sum_{y=0}^{7} abs(f(x,y)) \tag{4}$$

The condition for all-zero DCT coefficients is

$$|F(u,v)| < 2Q \tag{5}$$

Where $u, v = 0, 1, .., 7$, and Q denotes the quantization level. Thus

$$\sum_{x=0}^{7}\sum_{y=0}^{7} abs(f(x,y)) < 8Q \tag{6}$$

The *formula 6* gives the condition under which the DCT has all-zero coefficients. The left part of *formula 4* is the SAD of the motion compensation block, which can be obtained during the motion estimation. Therefore no additional computation is needed. The threshold $8Q$ can be increased or decreased, according to practical requirement. We adopt this algorithm to our codec and experimental results show that large parts of zero blocks are prejudged as all-zero. *Table 2* presents the results.

Table 2. Zero-coefficient prejudgment and speedup for the encoder, QCIF format sequence

Sequence	QP	All-zero blocks ration in total	Blocks correctly judged as all-zero	Speedup
Akiyo	4	75.1%	55.1%	1.13
	8	84.4%	71.5%	
Coastguard	4	47.9%	31.2%	1.10
	8	65.1%	43.5%	
Foreman	4	40.6%	29.2%	1.08
	8	58.3%	50.8%	

3.3 Mutiplierless Integer DCT

The DCT is widely used in DPCM/DCT video coding. However, the conventional floating-point DCT (FloatDCT) contains floating-pointing operations, especially the multiplications. An integer DCT (IntDCT)[8] method can get great improvement. One implementation of IntDCT for an 8*8 block needs only 45 additions and 18 shifting operations. There are no multiplications which require heavy computational power in mobile devices. Therefore, IntDCT is adopted in our proposed codec. Although there is a little PSNR degradation, it does not influence the visual quality, especially on mobile devices.

In the experiment, the forward IntDCT is used in the encoder followed by the inverse IntDCT in the decoder. The following *Table 3* shows the degradation of the PSNR and the speedup of DCT/IDCT module.

Table 3. Average PSNR degradation and speedup of DCT/IDCT module, QP=4, QCIF format sequence

Sequence	PSNR Loss	Speedup
Akiyo	0.20	3.03
Coastguard	0.24	2.62
Foreman	0.32	2.18

3.4 Other Optimization Techniques

Using Reversible 16-bit-color Transform. One speciality of mobile devices is the display format and most of them adopt 16-bit-color (RGB555 or RGB565). Those color systems are actually ubiquitous nowadays as a result of the popularity of hand-on devices from mobile phones to Personal Digital Assistants (PDA).

Traditional color transform method from RGB to YUV is the most widely used one in digital image and video coding. The linear transform from R'G'B' to Y'CrCb in Rec.601-1 [1] is

$$\begin{bmatrix} Y' \\ Cb \\ Cr \end{bmatrix} = \begin{bmatrix} 16 \\ 128 \\ 128 \end{bmatrix} + \frac{1}{256} \begin{bmatrix} 65.738 & 129.057 & 25.064 \\ -37.945 & -74.494 & 112.439 \\ 112.439 & -94.154 & -18.252 \end{bmatrix} \bullet \begin{bmatrix} R' \\ G' \\ B' \end{bmatrix} \tag{7}$$

Obviously, there are multiplier operations during the procedure, which require much CPU cycles. In our previous work [9], a new color transform method is proposed special for 16-bit RGB565 (RGB555 can be handled as a special case where the right most bit of G is zero). The forward transform matrix is defined as

$$\begin{aligned} Y_r &= R' + G' + B' \\ Cb_r &= 4B' - Y_r = -R' - G' + 3B' \\ Cr_r &= 4R' - Y_r = 3B' - G' - B' \end{aligned} \tag{8}$$

And the inverse transform is

$$\begin{aligned} G' &= (2Y_r - Cb_r - Cr_r)//4 \\ R' &= (Y_r + Cr_r)//4 \\ B' &= (Y_r + Cb_r)//4 \end{aligned} \tag{9}$$

where // denotes rounding to the nearest integer, R', G', B' is of 5, 6, 5 bits respectively. Compared to *formula 7*, the new transform method is multiplierless. It saves a lot of pre-encoding time. We adopt the new proposed transform method and experimental results show the encoding speedup with tiny PSNR loss.

Table 4. Average PSNR degradation and speedup of colorspace conversion module, QP=4, QCIF format sequence

Sequence	PSNR Loss	Speedup
Akiyo	0.02	1.21
Coastguard	0.04	1.18
Foreman	0.05	1.17

Optimization of ABS Function. $ABS()$ function is used frequently in the encoder, especially SAD calculating module. The $ABS(x)$ macro is always defined by

```
#define ABS(X)   (((X)>0)?(X):-(X))
```

In this definition, one comp operation and one branch judge operation is needed at least. We proposed a lookup table to replace the function. For the max value of the difference between two pixel is 512, we set up a table costs 512*2 bytes = 1k bytes. The initialization of the table is defined by

```
for(int i=-256; i<256; i++)
    table[i] = (i<0) ? -i : i;
```

All the $ABS()$ function can be replaced by a simple lookup operation. Experimental results show the advantage of the optimization.

Table 5. Speedup after using the lookup table to replace the $ABS()$ function for encoder. No PSNR degradation. QP=4, QCIF format sequence.

Sequence	Speedup
Akiyo	1.29
Coastguard	1.21
Foreman	1.17

4 Experimental Results

We have implemented an optimized version of our proposed software-based codec. Based on the codec, we examined the effectiveness of the proposed algorithms on computation time and video quality. The test sequences adopted includes Akiyo, Coastguard and Foreman with QCIF format. It can be seen

Table 6. PSNR degradation and speedup in our codec, QP=4, QCIF format sequence

Sequence	PSNR-Y(loss)	PSNR-U(loss)	PSNR-V(loss)	Speedup
Akiyo	0.36	0.24	0.30	12.85
Coastguard	0.42	0.32	0.31	10.24
Foreman	0.49	0.42	0.40	9.78

Table 7. Average encoding frame rates (fps) on HP iPAQ PPC, QP=4, QCIF format sequence

Sequence	Unoptimized Encoder	Proposed Encoder
Akiyo	2.42	22.62
Coastguard	2.26	19.36
Foreman	2.05	18.21

that: for 'Akiyo' sequence with motion limited in the center region, our proposed codec achieves more than 10 speedup compared to unoptimized one; for 'Coastguard' sequence with global motion and for 'Foreman' sequence with disordered motion, we achieves about 10 speedup. The experimental result was listed in the following *Table 6*.

We also did experiment on HP Pocket PC iPAQ, which possesses a 400MHz StrongARM processor and 128MB RAM. We can draw the conclusion from the results in *Table 7* that our proposed software-based codec improves the frame rate significantly.

5 Conclusions and Future Works

In this paper, we propose a flexible framework of video codec design for mobile devices, which is composed of three layers: basic algorithm layer, common interface layer and specification related layer. Based on the framework we can easily construct a special codec through the common interfaces rather than considering the detailed algorithms.

Meanwhile, we gave some advanced optimization methods in detail. To alleviate the constraints of mobile devices, we must take great effort to reduce the computational load and memory requirement in the proposed solution. Therefore, we introduced some key optimization techniques, such as fast predictive ME, zero-coefficient prejudgment and multiplierless integer DCT, etc.

Experimental results show that our proposed framework and software-based codec achieve significant efficiency and are very suitable for mobile devices.

Future directions include offering adaptive rate control and error resilience for wireless transportation.

Acknowledgement

The authors thank Linjian Mo, Yongbao Tan and Xu Li for giving some useful suggestions about the paper.

References

1. Richardson, I.E.G.: Video Codec Design, John Wiley & Sons Ltd, (2002)
2. Yu, K.M., Lv, J.B., Li, J., Li, S.P.: Practical Real-time Video Codec For Mobile Devices, Multimedia and Expo, ICME, vol.3, (2003), 509-512

3. Prasad, R.S.V., Ramkishor, K.: Efficient Implementation Of MPEG-4 Video Encoder On Risc Core, ICCE, Digest of Technical Papers, (2002), 278 - 279
4. Zhu, S., Ma, K.K.: A New Diamond Search Algorithm for Fast Block-Matching Motion Estimation, IEEE Transactions on Image Processing, Vol. 9, (2000),break 287–290
5. Xu, J.F., Chen, Z.B., He, Y.: Efficient Fast ME Prediction and Early-termination Strategy Based on H.264 Statistical Characters, ICICS-PCM, vol.1, (2003), 218 - 222
6. Zhou, X., Yu, Z.H., Yu, S.Y.: Method for detecting all-zero DCT coefficients ahead of discrete cosine transformation and quantization, Electronics Letters, Volume 34, (1998), 1839 - 1840
7. Jun, S., Yu, S.Y.: Efficient method for early detection of all-zero DCT coefficients, Electronics Letters, Volume 37, (2001), 160 - 161
8. Chen, Y.J., Oraintara, S., Nguyen, T.: Integer Discrete Cosine Transform (IntDCT), IEEE Trans. Signal Processing, (1999)
9. Li, N., Bu, J.J., Chen, C.: A Reversible Color Transform for 16-bit-color Picture Coding, ACM Multimedia, (2004)

Real-Time Expression Mapping with Ratio Image*

Weili Liu, Cheng Jin, Jiajun Bu, and Chun Chen

College of Computer Science, Zhejiang University,
Hangzhou, China, 310027
liuweili@21cn.com
{chengjin, bjj, chenc}@zju.edu.cn

Abstract. Video Conference under low bandwidth condition, such as conference among hand-held sets (PDAs), requires transmission algorithm to be robust and effective. The real-time issue is always the focus of research. We propose in this paper a fast algorithm in mapping one's facial expression onto another's face. The algorithm divides workload into online and offline part and hence speeds up the performance. By using this, it is possible to transmit small data of facial features to end users of conference participants. Expressions can be then synthesized at end user side to produce pseudo-video-sequence of the participants. Thus, real-time transmission can be achieved.

Keywords: ERI, Real-Time Video Conference, Embedded System.

1 Introduction

Photorealistic facial expression synthesis is applied widely in video, games and filmmaking industry.

One class of expression synthesis methods is 3D-model-based techniques [1] and [2]. These methods generate perfect geometry details. With some tracking techniques [3, 4], they transfer facial expression in video. However, one problem of these methods is that they are computationally expensive, which makes it impossible to be used in real-time face synthesis. The other problem is that they require special device to obtain 3D data of human faces.

Another class of approaches is image-based techniques. They either use image-morphing techniques [5] to morph one expression to another, or use expression mapping techniques [6, 7] to warp an input face to given expressions. The image-morphing method may suffer from the common ghost-effect and is only applicable providing the sample expressions of the person. The latter one cannot generate expression details, as we will discuss later.

In this paper, we will discuss a practical real-time facial expression synthesis method. Our method is based on Expression Ratio Image (ERI), which records

* This paper is supported by National Natural Science Foundation of China (60203013), Key Technologies R&D Program of Zhejiang Province (2005C23047 & 2004C11052) and HP Labs.

L.T. Yang et al. (Eds.): ICESS 2005, LNCS 3820, pp. 586–595, 2005.

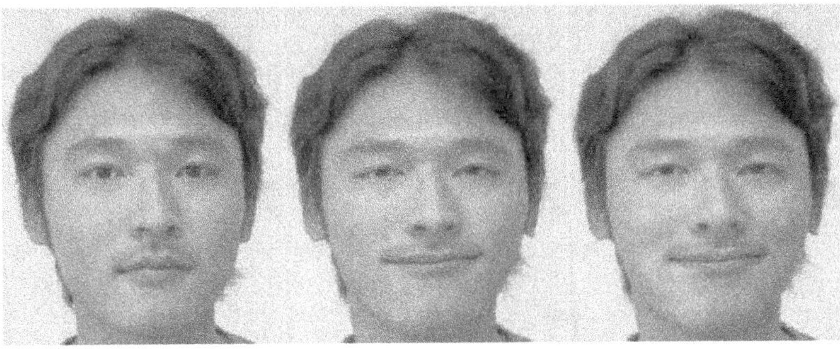

Fig. 1. Expression mapping of a "big smile" with details. Left: the neutral face. Middle: result from geometry warping. Right: result from our method.

illumination changes due to expression change. By recording expressional change between a neutral face and a face with expression, we could map the expression to a new face in real time. This mapping can be applied to any person. It is also possible to implement our method on PDA or some real-time systems. In addition, our method can handle unexpected noise in labeled sample images. ERI Computing and filtering are fully automatic. Users only need to provide labeled images.

The rest of the paper is organized as follows. Three most important facial synthesis methods are discussed in the next section. Necessary background knowledge of expression ratio image are introduced in section 3. In section 4, we discuss the automatic filtering process in detail. Some results are shown in section 5. Section 6 gives a discussion on the limitations of our method, a potential usage of our method and a future research direction.

2 Related Works

Performance-driven facial synthesis technique, proposed by L. Williams et. al.[6], is an early research on facial expression synthesis. It can be used to animate 2D images and textured or non-textured 3D face models. Given an image with a person's neutral face and an image of the same person with expression, both of which have feature points located through manual or automatic methods [8, 9], the feature points of the new face is set according to the difference vector between the neutral face and the expression face. Then the new expression is generated through geometry controlled image warping [5, 7]. One disadvantage of this approach is that it only synthesizes the geometry change but completely ignoring the detailed expression features such as wrinkles.

Z. Liu et. al.[10] proposed a technique, called Expression Ration Image (ERI), to record and map one person's expression to another person's face. To create a new ERI of an expression, it needs a neutral face (reference image) and an image with the expression of the actor. In other words, it needs a sample for each expression. It is only possible to map the already recorded expression to a new face. Although recording each expression (offline process) is difficult and time consuming, mapping an expression (online process) is fast and the result is photorealistic with creases and wrinkles well preserved as the original expression.

Q. Zhang et al.[11] used a geometry-driven facial expression synthesis method, which generates photorealistic expressions with arbitrary feature points. This method calculates each sub-region on the face and then blends all sub-regions together. Computing a sub-region is time consuming because it needs to combine the same sub-regions in all sample faces to generate the new sub-region. Number of samples is 30-40 for each person in [11]. The author achieved 2-4 frames per second on a 2GHz PC for 600x800 images.

3 Expression Ratio Image

As described in [10], Expression Ratio Image (ERI) retains the illumination changes due to expression change. Such changes are vital to an expression that a human would conceive as "real". A similar technique [12] used the color difference between one reference image and the other with something changed. Under the Lambertian model, let the initial intensity at point p be I and the intensity after surface deformation be I'. The relationship between illumination change of I and I' at point p is

$$\Re = \frac{I'}{I} \ or \ I' = I\Re \tag{1}$$

Equation (1) shows it possible to form the illumination after deformation by simply multiplying the illumination before deformation with $\Re$, regardless of the reflectance coefficient of the surface.

When mapping an expression to a neutral face, let the two faces be A and B, A is the neutral face of A, A' is the face of A with expression, B is the neural face of B and B' is the synthesized face with A's expression.

We suppose all features of a face are aligned correctly in the above discussion. In real cases, the features are usually not aligned correctly. We must align corresponding feature points in different image. To reduce computational expense, we divide the algorithm into offline process (record changes between a neutral face and a face with expression) and online process (mapping an expression to a new face). Alignment is done through warping in both offline and online process.

Because the ERI records the illumination changes(equation 1), it is desirable to compute only the ratio of illumination component of a pixel. However, our input image are of RGB color. We alter the RGB color space to YUV color space of input images before both online and offline process and change it back to RGB color space after each process. In YUV color space, the Y component represents the luminance [13]. Therefore, only the ratio of the Y component of the input images is computed.

3.1 Offline Process

Let $\tilde{A}$ be the raw neutral face of A and A' be A's raw expressional face. The above images are not aligned properly. We must align them before computing ERI. The aligning process goes with the warping process.

Step 1: Find face features of $\tilde{A}$ and A'(manually or using some automatic methods).
Step 2: Move the features of $\tilde{A}$ to A', and warp accordingly. The warped image is A.
Step 3: Compute the difference vector between A' and A. The result is processed to reflect relative position change.
Step 4: Compute the ratio image $\Re(x,y) = \frac{A'}{A}$
Step 5: Filter $\Re$. Then store the difference vector, feature positions of A' and $\Re$ to an expression file.

3.2 Online Process

After we compute an expression file, we can map this expression to any face. Let $\tilde{B}$ be the labeled new face.

Step 1: Load the difference vector, feature positions and $\Re$ of the expression.
Step 2: Move the features of according to the difference vector, and warp $\tilde{B}$ accordingly. The warped image is $\tilde{B}'$.
Step 3: Move the feature of $\Re$ to $\tilde{B}'$, and warp accordingly. The warped ERI is $\Re'$
Step 4: Set $B' = \tilde{B}'\Re$ for every pixel.

4 Automatic Filtering

The directly computed ERI is very noisy. The noise comes from various sources: change of camera aperture and shutter; slight change in the person's face direction and pose; misalignment in the warping process. In Figure 2, only the creases between the eyebrows are our required facial expression details. The noises will create undesirable artifacts in the eyes, eyebrows and lips(Figure 2(d)).

4.1 Normalized Auto-correlation Method

Z. Liu et al. [10] proposed to use an adaptive Gaussian filter with different window size. For each pixel, they computed a normalized cross-correlation c between the neutral face and the expressional face. An adaptive Gaussian filter is then applied to the ERI. The smaller c is, the larger the window of the filter is.

However, the method in [10] does not fit for our applications for its inherent defects. Firstly, normalized cross-correlation is very time consuming. For an $M \times N$ image, the computational complexity is $O(M \times N \times S^2)$(S is the size of the correlation block). The complexity is still high ($O(M \times N \times SlogS)$) even if we use Fast Fourier Transformation and convolution theorem[13].

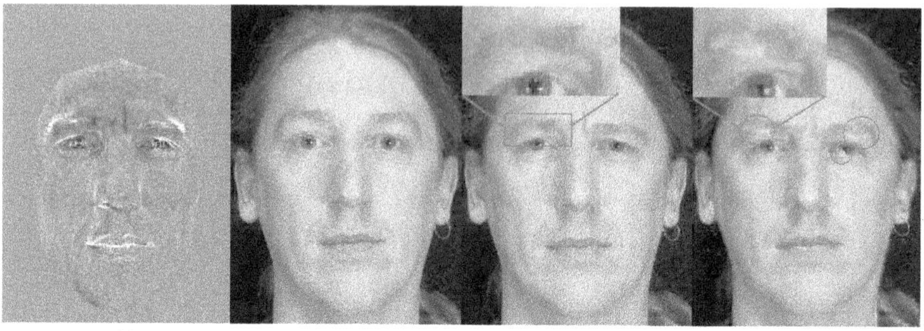

(a) (b) (c) (d)

Fig. 2. The ERI compute from two images. (a) the ERI. We visualize the ratio for display purpose. White means large ratio and black means small ratio. (b) the neutral face. (c) the expression face. (d) mapping (a) to (b). Red circles point out some artifacts.

Second, an adaptive Gaussian filter alone is insufficient for filtering. Gaussian filters only smooth the image. However, the noise in ERI often gathers at certain parts of the face, such as eyebrows, eyes and the edges(Figure 2(a)). In such areas, Gaussian filters merely smooth the noise. Without other filters, the filtered ERI is still noisy and it will cause artifacts in the mapping process.

Third, the algorithm ideally considers the area with low texture complexity the area where facial expression details located. Due to noises, a small c may also mean a noisy area.

4.2 Our Method

After studying what human consider important expression details in different expressions, we conclude that humans are more likely to sense slight brightness change in the "smooth" areas (cheek, forehead, jaw and area between eyes and eyebrows). We call the map that tells the smoothness of each pixel the *smoothness map*. The more complex the area is, the less important the detail change of it is. The darken areas in Figure 4(right) are the areas that contain important expression details.

For this reason, we need to compute the smoothness map for a given face. A direct approach is to mark the "smooth" areas manually on the face. However, it is inefficient and cannot adapt to new faces. Another choice is to compute auto-correlation between an area and its neighborhood areas. A large c means a smooth area and small means the opposite. Nevertheless, it is computationally expensive. After experiment and comparison between several methods, we propose to use a statistical method by computing the standard deviation σ of an $T \times T$ area S_{xy} centered at (x, y), where T is chosen according to the size of the face. Figure 4(middle) is the result of our method.

$$E = \frac{1}{T^2} \sum_{P(x,y) \in S_{xy}} P(x,y) \tag{2}$$

$$\sigma(x,y) = \frac{1}{T}\sqrt{\sum_{P(x,y)\in S_{xy}} (P(x,y) - E)^2} \tag{3}$$

By applying (2) and (3) to each area S_{xy} centered at point $P(x,y)$, we get the smoothness map $R(x,y) = \sigma(x,y)$ for each point. A small $R(x,y)$ means a smooth area and a large one means the opposite.

After R is obtained, we apply an improved Gaussian filter to it, which we call *Weaken-Gaussian Filter (WGF)*. From equation 1, we know that a ratio of 1 means no illumination change in that pixel. In the non-smooth areas, it is desirable to attenuate or eliminate the ratio variations that we consider noises. Therefore, we want to make $\Re(x,y)$ closer to 1 if $R(x,y)$ is large. For each pixel $\Re(x,y)$, let $\Re'(x,y)$ be the filtered ERI, $G(x,y)$ be the weakened ratio, R_{min} and R_{max}be the minimum and maximum value of R

$$\Re'(x,y) = 1 + \sum_{m=0}^{T}\sum_{n=0}^{T}(\Re(x+m,y+n) - 1)F(m,n)G(x+m,y+n) \tag{4}$$

$$G(x,y) = \frac{R_{max} - R(x,y)}{R_{max} - R_{min}} \tag{5}$$

where $R_{min} = argmin[P|P \in R], R_{max} = argmax[P|P \in R]$ and F is a adaptive Gaussian filter with window size of $T \times T$ and σ of F is decided by $R(x,y)$. The larger $R(x,y)$ is, the larger the σ of F will be.

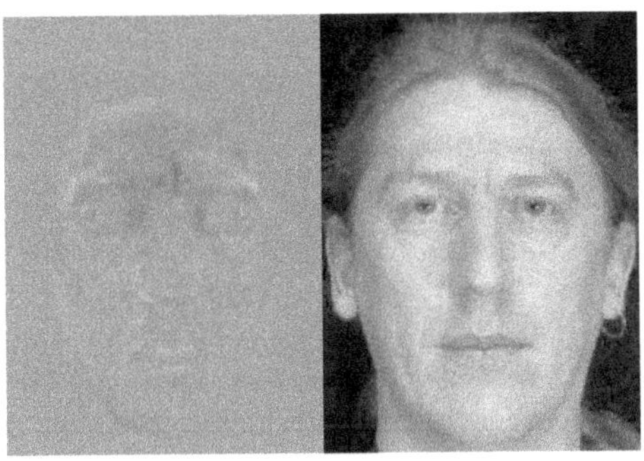

Fig. 3. Left: result of filtering Figure 2(a) with our method. Right: Mapping the left ERI to Figure 2(b).

WGF is better than traditional Gaussian filters. It adaptively uses different Gaussian kernels with different σ according to the smoothness map, which helps to smooth the noise. It also attenuates the noise by making $\Re(x,y)$ closer to 1. And the the weaken ratio $G(x,y)$ is also related to the smoothness map. We can see the result of our method is good. From Figure 3(left), it is obvious that filtering Figure 2(a) with our method can greatly reduce the noise. In consequence, the result of mapping the filtered ERI to the neutral face(Figure 3(right)) is more close to the ground truth(Figure 2(c)).

4.3 Comparison of the Methods

Compared with the normalized auto-correlation method, our method has several advantages.

First, it is fast. We experiment the two methods on a machine with Pentium-M 1.4G processor and 512MB memory. We test the same input for several times and calculate the average time. It takes 6.2 seconds to compute a 205×275 smoothness map using the normalized auto-correlation method. For the same input, our method takes only 0.12 seconds.

Second, it is comparatively accurate in computing the smoothness map. From Figure 4, we find that our method tends to classify some "smooth" areas as non-smooth areas. For example, due to the gradual illumination change on the "slope" areas, statistical method will classify such areas as not-so-smooth area. However, the correlation tends to do the opposite. It classifies the eyebrows as smooth areas. Overall, result of our method better matches the idea smooth area(Figure 4(right)) than the correlation method.

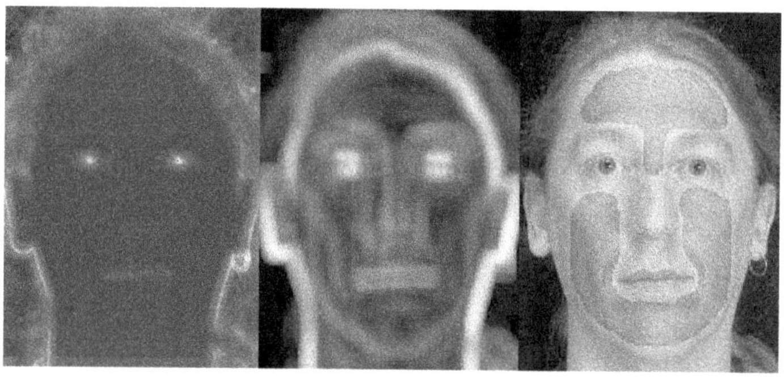

Fig. 4. Left: applying normalized auto-correlation on Figure 2(b). Middle: applying our statistical method to the same image. Right: areas that contain important expression details. For each pixel, smoothness is proportional to darkness.

Last but not least, it attenuates the noise while retaining the necessary details. Comparison between Figure 2(a) and Figure 3(left) shows that the noise in areas such as eyes, eyebrows, lip, nose and the edge of the face has been reduced or eliminated. In the meantime, the important detail(wrinkle between the eyebrows) is well preserved.

Overall, our filtering method is fast and overcomes the shortcomings of the method in [10]. It is an automatic filtering method that can be transplant to embedded systems with excellent performance.

5 Experiments and Results

We implemented our method both on PC and hand-held sets (PDAs). We manually labelled the mark points for each input image. The warping process was implemented in software by applying Delaunay triangulation to the mark points. To test our method, we find several expressions from different sources and map them to different people.

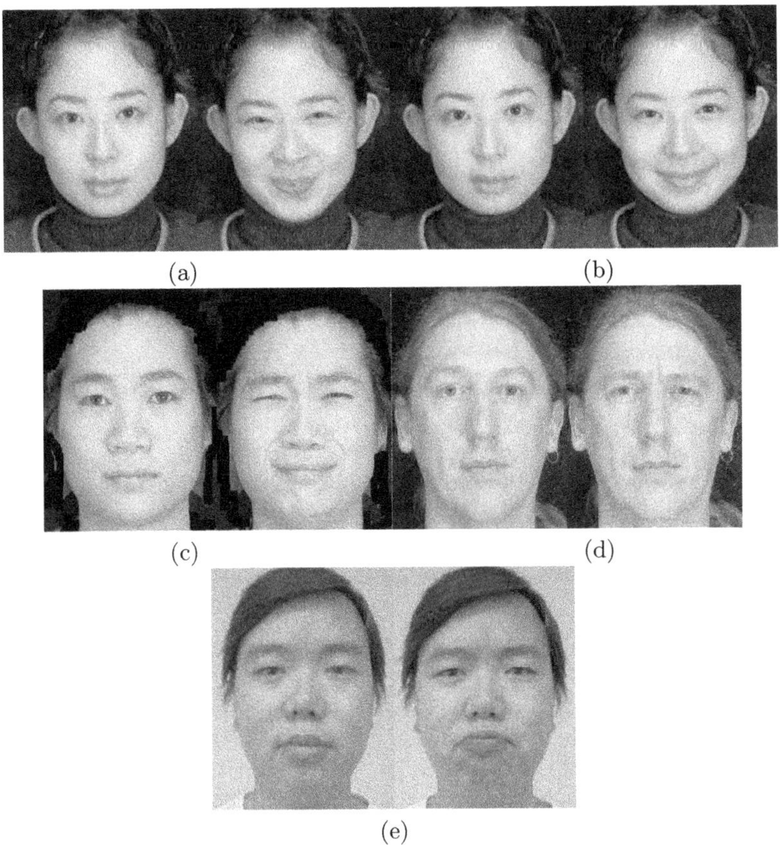

Fig. 5. The sample expressions. For each pair, left column is the neutral face and right column is the expression. (a) smile; (b) big smile; (c)sad; (d) thinking; (e) "special" expression.

In Figure 5, we give five sample expressions. The left column is the neutral face and the right column is the face with certain expression. The expressions are smile, big smile, sad, thinking and a special expression.

Our first results are mapping the expressions back to the neutral faces of the person where each expression comes from.

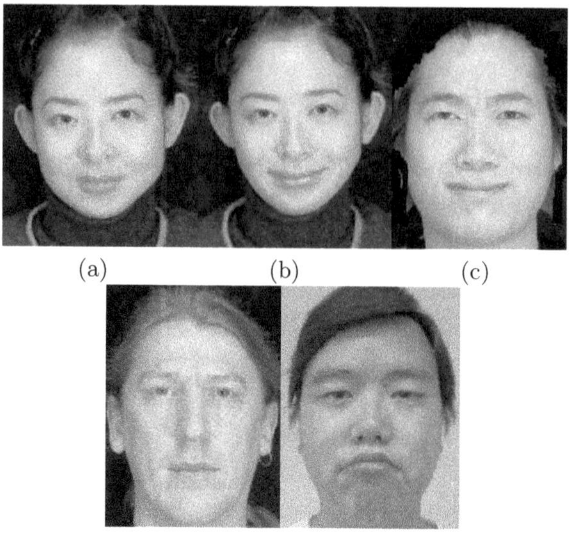

Fig. 6. Mapping the expression back. (a)smile; (b) big smile; (c) sad;(d) thinking; (e) "special" expression.

6 Conclusion and Future Works

We have shown that our method is a fast automatic facial expression synthesis technique. The method in [10] first gave a way of expression synthesis by ERI, but it didn't consider the characteristics of the face image. Therefore, we presented in this paper a faster and better filtering method and finally form our solution. Our filtering method can process an image in 0.12 second.

We also transplanted our algorithm to embedded systems. In our test, the offline process takes 0.15 seconds for a 205×275 image on a machine with Pentium-M 1.4G processor and 512MB memory. The online process takes 0.014 for the same image on the same machine. In an HP 5550 PDA (400MHz), it takes 0.4 seconds and 0.02 seconds respectively. The most time consuming process is the filtering process. If it is implement in hardware, the speed could be greatly increased. We avoid using non-standard libraries for there may not be such libraries in embedded systems. We use shifted integers instead of floats because most embedded systems have better performance for integers than floats. We also optimize the code so that they can run at real-time.

The synthesized expression looks real with expressive details. However, since the warping algorithm is quite simple, the mapping result is distorted in some complex expressions. It could be improved by adopting advanced warping algorithm and carefully selecting the feature points.

In our implementation, we find the facial features manually. A further improvement could add some automatic feature-locating algorithm [8, 9]. Although our current research is based on static images, we could extend our research to facial mapping on video. By using some tracking algorithms such as AAM (Active Appearance Model)[3] or KLT (Kanade-Lucas-Tomasi)[4], it is possible to animate an expression on a given person. Combined with the automatic feature-locating algorithm and video compression techniques, a low-bandwidth real-time video meeting system can be established.

References

1. Daniel Vlasic, Matthew Brand, H.P., Popovic, J.: Face transfer with multilinear models. Computer Graphics (2005)
2. Jin-xiang Chai, Jing Xiao, J.H.: Vision-based control of 3d facial animation. Eurographics/SIGGRAPH Symposium on Computer Animation (2003) 193–206
3. Cootes, T.F., Edwards, G.J., Taylor, C.J.: Active appearance models. Lecture Notes in Computer Science **1407** (1998) 484–??
4. Tomasi, C., Kanade, T.: Detection and tracking of point features. Technical Report CMU-CS-91-132, Carnegie Mellon University (1991)
5. Beier, T., Neely, S.: Feature-based image metamorphosis. Computer Graphics (1992) 35–42
6. Williams, L.: Performace-driven facial animation. Computer Graphics (1990) 235–242
7. Litwinowicz, P., Williams, L.: Animating images with drawings. Computer Graphics (1990) 235–242
8. Hua Gu, Guangda Su, C.D.: Feature points extraction from faces. Image and Vision Computing New Zealand (2003)
9. Debevec, P.: Hierarchical wavelet networks for facial feature localization. Proceedings of the Fifth IEEE International Conference on Automatic Face and Gesture Recognition (2002) 118–123
10. Zicheng Liu, Y.S., Zhang, Z.: Expressive expression mapping with ratio images. Computer Graphics, Annual Conference Series (2001) 271–276
11. Qingshan Zhang, Zicheng Liu, B.G., Shum, H.: Geometry-driven photorealistic facial expression synthesis. Eurographics/SIGGRAPH Symposium on Computer Animation (2003)
12. Debevec, P.: Rendering synthetic objects into real scenes: Bridging traditional and image-based graphics with global illumination and high dynamic range photography. Computer Graphics, Annual Conference Series (1998) 189–198
13. Rafael C. Gonzalez, R.E.W.: Digital Image Processing (2nd Edition). Prentice Hall (2002)

Power Consumption Analysis of Embedded Multimedia Application*

Juan Chen, Yong Dong, Huizhan Yi, and Xuejun Yang

School of Computer, National University of Defense Technology,
Changsha 410073, P.R. China
juanchen@nudt.edu.cn, luckpeople@163.com, huizhanyi@nudt.edu.cn

Abstract. In the past few years, the ubiquity of embedded mobile computing brings about a new challenge for multimedia application. Not only the performance but also the power consumption is vital to the multimedia application because mobile clients are powered by battery. In this paper, we make the detailed power consumption analysis of multimedia applications with two power reduction techniques—ideal clock gating and ideal power gating. Experimental results show the power consumptions can be reduced to 35.22% and 15.68% by ideal clock gating and ideal power gating, respectively. Our primary contributions lie in evaluating the power characteristics of multimedia applications using MediaBench benchmark suite, and evaluating the impact of unideal power reduction techniques on the performance. Such an analysis can help the multimedia applications developers determine the efficient power optimization policy besides the performance optimization. Low-power embedded multimedia applications are promising in the future.

1 Introduction

Power consumption is a vital resource for battery-operated mobile systems or embedded systems. However, the advances in battery technology and low-power circuit design cannot keep up with the energy demands of the future embedded mobile computing. Some energy-efficient methods for the embedded applications have been proposed [11]. But a main limiting factor is the lack of effective power analysis for the embedded multimedia applications. The detailed and the effective power analysis can help mobile computing designers determine power saving policy. Our article provides the detailed power analysis for the embedded multimedia application by running MediaBench under PowerImpact [2] simulator environment.

The performance issue is an important issue for the multimedia applications since the computation needs to be completed in time. Therefore, in our article we also obtain the impact of unideal power reduction technique on the performance by changing wake-up time.

Our article refers to three different kinds of power consumption: dynamic power, short-circuit power and leakage power. The Short-circuit power is the least important

* This work was supported by the National High Technology Development 863 Program of China under Grant No. 2002AA1Z2101 and No. 2004AA1Z2210.

L.T. Yang et al. (Eds.): ICESS 2005, LNCS 3820, pp. 596 – 607, 2005.

since it is only introduced for a short period of time. Dynamic power generally dominates the total power consumption. The leakage power is becoming an increasingly important concern [3]. It has been pointed out that the leakage power can be up to 40% of the total power for high-performance VLIW processors [4]. In 2002, Intel's Grove ever said chips constructed of increasing numbers of transistors could suffer power leakage of up to 40% [8]. Facts approve the power is largely dissipated as heat causing the cooling problems for the powerful chips. The power simulator we use in this paper is PowerImpact, which explores leakage power dissipation.

Our article refers to three power models: power without gating, power with ideal clock gating, and power with ideal power gating, whose definitions are given in Section 3. From simulation results, we find two power reduction techniques (ideal clock gating and ideal power gating) is effective, whose power consumption can be reduced to 35.22% and 15.68%, respectively. We also identify which component is the most responsible for power consumption.

In summary, the primary contributions of this paper are the following:

- We present a detailed power consumption analysis for the MediaBench benchmark suite.
- We identify the component, which is the most responsible for power consumption.
- We analyze the impact of unideal power reduction technique on the performance by adjusting wake-up time.

The rest of this paper is organized as follows. Section 2 reviews the previous work. Section 3 introduces three power models. Section 4 introduces the simulation methodology and the benchmark. Section 5 gives the experimental results. Section 6 concludes the paper and discusses some future work.

2 Related Work

In this section we review the previous work in mobile multimedia application. Along with the ubiquity of the Internet and the advent of wireless communication and mobile computing, the research on mobile multimedia communications for wireless Internet is more and more comprehensive. MediaBench [9] is a representative of multimedia and communications applications.

Chunho Lee et al. [6] tested the performance characteristics of MediaBench. Their work is valuable because at that time the vast majority of ILP research focused on general-purpose computing (popular benchmark is the integer SPEC benchmark [10]), and the essential elements of embedded multimedia and communications applications were not captured well. They tested MediaBench suite performance characteristics based on some set of metrics using IMPACT tool suite [12]. Their experimental results shows the obvious performance difference occurs in the following four areas: achieved instructions-per-clock, instruction cache hit rate, data cache read hit rate, and memory bus utilization.

Benjamin Bishop et al. [5] presented a detailed analysis of the MediaBench benchmark suite. They examined MediaBench performance characteristics by running MediaBench under the SimpleScalar simulation environment [13]. Characteristics such as instruction mix, branch prediction accuracy, and cache hit rates, memory usage, and integer bit utilization were considered. Our work is different from theirs because we are concerned about power characteristics besides performance characteristics.

In order to test power characteristics of MediaBench, we choose PowerImpact simulator, which includes leakage power models, while other power simulators, such as Wattch [7], don't consider the leakage power consumption. More and more researchers are concerned about the research on leakage power modeling. Weiping Liao et al. [4] studied the leakage power reduction using power gating in the forms of the Virtual power/ground Rails Clamp (*VRC*) and Multi-threshold CMOS (*MTCMOS*) techniques. Their experimental results show the leakage power can be over 40% of the total power consumption for VLIW processors. They also proposed a time-out scheduling of VRC to reduce power up to 85.65% for L2 cache. Their experimental benchmarks are partly drawn out from SPECint and SPECfloat. We use MediaBench as our benchmark and power consumption characteristic of MediaBench are quite differently from that of SPEC2000. One of our contributions is that we consider the impact of unideal power reduction technique on the performance. Weiping et al. only considered ideal clock gating and ideal power gating effectiveness on power reduction.

3 Power Models

In this paper, three kinds of power models are examined: one is the total power without gating; another is the total power with ideal clock gating; the third one is the total power with power gating. In this section, we will describe clock gating technique and power gating technique in detail.

3.1 Clock Gating and Clock Ramping

Clock gating is effective to reduce the dynamic power consumption of the functional units, but turning on/off a functional unit in a short time will lead to a large surge current. To reduce the surge current by these clock gating technologies, M. Pant et al. [14] first proposed to insert wake up and go to sleep time between the on and off states to extend the switch on/off time. Since the clock gating need to take several cycles, Weiping [1] called this case clock ramping to be different from the conventional clock gating approach. He proposed two kinds of techniques, one is clock ramping with hardware prescan (*CRHP*), and the other is clock ramping with compiler-based prediction (*CRCP*). This improved *CRHP* technique for VLIW architecture has a finer clock ramping granularity, which can achieve more power reduction compared to superscalar architecture. *CRCP* is a new compiler optimization technology, which automatically inserts ramp-up instructions (RUI) based on hyperblock scheduling to instruct the in-time ramping up of functional units. Therefore, no extra fetch and decode logic used in the hardware prescan is needed. The detailed explanation sees to [1]. In our simulation, we use PowerImapct, which implemented *CRHP* and *CRCP* techniques. In the section 5, the effectiveness of clock gating is shown.

3.2 Power Gating

There are three different kinds of power consumption: dynamic power, short-circuit power and leakage power. Short-circuit power is the least important since short-circuit current is only introduced for a short period of time. Dynamic power generally dominates the total power consumption. However, the leakage power is becoming an increasingly important concern [3]. In 2002, Intel company chairman Andy Grove told an audience at the international Electron Devices Meeting in San Francisco: one of the major technical headaches facing chipmaker Intel is the leaking current from the inactive processors. He said the problem of leakage threatens the future validity of Moores Law. As chips become more powerful and consume more power consumption, leakage tends to increase. The industry is used to power leakage rates of up to fifteen percent, but chips constructed of the increasing numbers of the transistors can suffer power leakage of up to 40 percent [8].

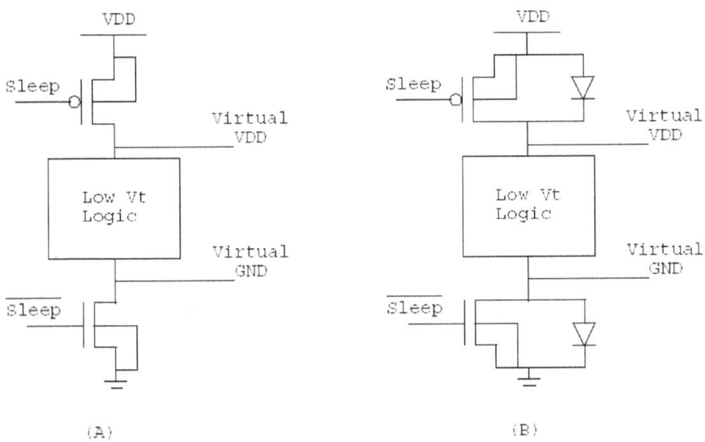

Fig. 1. Two kinds of power gating technique: (A) MTCMOS (B) VRC. (source figure is from [4]).

The simulator we use have implemented two power gating techniques: *MTCMOS* (Multi-threshold CMOS) and *VRC* (Virtual power/ground Rails Clamp) which both reduce the leakage power. The use of power gating exhibits three operating modes: active mode, standby mode and inactive mode. In active mode, a circuit performs an operation and dissipates both the dynamic and the static power. In standby mode, it is active but idle and waiting to execute an operation, which dissipates only the static leakage power. However in inactive mode, a circuit is deactivated by power gating, which dissipates a reduced static leakage power.

[4] described *MTCMOS* and *VRC* and how they implement power gating to reduce the leakage power. In this section, we do a summary about them. First, we introduce *MTCMOS*: from Figure 1(A), we can see high-V_t sleep transistors are connected to VDD and GND, among which the logic are implemented by low-V_t transistors. In the active and standby modes, for which the sleep transistors are turned on, the virtual

VDD and GND rails function as the actual rails. In inactive mode, the large leakage current of the low-V_t logic is greatly reduced by the gating of the power supplies. *VRC* places diodes across the sleep transistors for VDD and GND, so it solves the problem of data retention (Figure 1(B)). In the active and standby modes, virtually all current flows through the sleep transistors, which are turned on. At the switch to inactive mode, these transistors are turned off; a small current flows through the diodes, the virtual VDD level decays from VDD, and the virtual GND level rises from GND.

MTCMOS and *VRC* are applied to two circuit types: datapath componets and memory-based units respectively. *MTCMOS* scheduling is mainly for float and integer functional units because either compiler or runtime hardware can predict the behavior of integer and floating-point units. Our experimental results for MediaBench benchmark show power reduction up to 94.01% for *FPUs* at worst. On the other hand, *VRC* Scheduling here is mainly for L2 cache because L2 cache consumes much more power than L1 cache, and L2 cache exposes more chances for throttling. Our experimental results show that *cjpeg* power reduction is up to 98.28% for L2 cache.

4 Simulation Methodology and Benchmark

4.1 PowerImpact and System Configuration

In this section, we give some information about our simulation environment. In this work, in order to obtain power values of each component, we use PowerImapct [2], an architecture-level, cycle-accurate energy simulator. PowerImpact is an execution-driven power estimation tool. It is based on the IMPACT [12] toolset. Figure 2 illustrates the overall structure of PowerImpact [1].

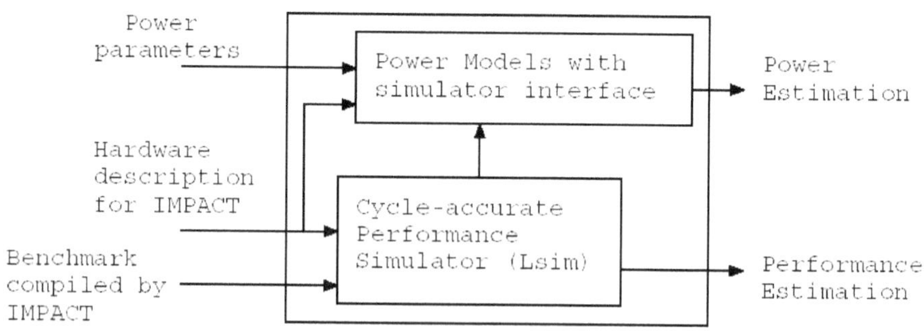

Fig. 2. Structure of PowerImpact (source figure is from [1])

PowerImpact includes two kinds of components: memory-based components and memory-less components. Memory-based components include BTB, L1 instruction cache, L1 data cache, L2 cache, and register file. Memory-less components include decoder, integer components, and floating-point components. *VRC* technique is applied to the memory-based components and *MTCMOS* technique is applied to memory-less components. For each component, there are three energy stages: active (P_a), standby (P_s), and inactive (P_i). The power consumption of one component is calculated by

$$E = P_a \times C_a + P_s \times C_s + P_i \times C_i + E_{overhead} \quad (1)$$

where C_a, C_s and C_i represent active cycles, standby cycles, and inactive cycles, respectively. These values are counted by the PowerImpact. $E_{overhead}$ represents the total transition energy when turning on/off components.

We summarize the system configuration used in our experiment in Table 1.

Table 1. System configuration for experiments

Component	Configuration
Decode	8-issue width
BTB	1024 entries 2-way assoc, two-level predictor, automaton_A3 counter type
Reg	64 integer and 64 floating-point registers with 32-bit data width
Memory	Page size 4096 bytes, latency 30 cycles
Memory Bus	8 bytes/cycle

Cache	Size	Block size	Associativity	Policy
L1 I-cache	128 KB	64 bytes	2	LRU
L1 D-cache	128 KB	64 bytes	4	LRU
L2 cache	1024 KB	256 bytes	1	LRU

Table 2. Power-related parameters. The percentage value in the column of P_a is the percentage of each components contribution to total processor power. We assume a 2 GHz clock frequency and 0.10um technology.

Component	P_a (mW)	P_s (mW)	P_i (mW)
Decode	187.61 (10.58%)	5.87	0.04
BTB	11.72 (0.66%)	1.97	0.01
Integer ALU	281.42 (15.87%)	8.80	0.06
FPU	562.84 (31.74%)	17.60	0.12
I-L1 Cache	86.63 (4.89%)	21.32	0.02
D-L1 Cache	87.10 (4.91%)	21.39	0.02
L2 Cache	554.19 (31.25%)	319.10	0.20
Registers	1.77 (0.001%)	0.13	0.001

The system power distribution is given in Table 2. We assume that the clock frequency is 2 GHz and $0.10\mu m$ technology.

4.2 Benchmark

MediaBench has been proposed as a benchmark set representative of multimedia and communications applications. The MediaBench argues that many existing benchmarks, SPEC2000, DSPstone for example, are not representative of multimedia and communications applications. One of this article works is to evaluate the power consumption characteristics of MediaBench.

Table 3 gives a brief description of the benchmark simulated.

Table 3. Description of benchmarks

Benchmark	Descriptions
JPEG	Lossy compression for still images. Two applications are derived from the JPEG source code: cjpeg does image compression and djpeg, which does decompression.
MPEG	Lossy compression for video. Two applications are derived from the MPEG source code: mpeg2enc and mpeg2dec for encoding and decoding respectively.
GSM	European standard for speech transcoding. (Encode/Decode)
G721	CCITT voice compression. (Encode/Decode)
PGP	IDEA/RSA public-key encryption algorithm. (Encrypt/Decrypt)
PEGWIT	a program for public key encryption and authentication.
Ghostscript	Postscript interpreter.
Mesa	a 3-D graphics library clone of OpenGL. Three applications are Mipmap, Osdemo, Texgen.
RASTA	Speech recognition that supports the following three techniques: PLP, RASTA, and Jah-RASTA.
EPIC	Experimental image compression utility. (Encode/Decode)
ADPCM	Adaptive differential pulse code modulation audio coding. (Encode/Decode)

5 Experimental Results

5.1 MediaBench Power Consumption Characteristics

In this section, we present the experimental results using the simulation methodology described above.

For the ideal power gating, it is assumed that we can schedule a power gating event in time for any idle period longer than the minimum idle time to maximize power reduction, and a component can be woken up in time to avoid performance loss. Since the ideal scheduling assumes the unit can be turned on in time when it is required, cache behavior is not changed. We assume we can schedule a clock gating event in time for any idle period shorter than the minimum idle time. That means ideal power gating combines both clock and power gating. We can calculate the power reductions of ideal power gating by analyzing the trace of usages of each component, providing a theoretical upper bound of the leakage power reduction without performance loss [4].

In Table 4, we combine the power of different components and compare the total power of the entire processor. Compared to no power gating, the total power can be reduced to 35.22% and 15.68% by using ideal clock gating and ideal power gating, respectively. However, unideal clock gating can cause performance loss than ideal clock gating because a clock gating probably cannot be scheduled in time in actual situation. In section 5.2, we will discuss this performance loss.

Table 4. Three kinds of the total power comparison

	No gating	Clock gating	Power gating
cjpeg	100%	36.81%	16.83%
djpeg	100%	33.79%	14.55%
mpeg2dec	100%	35.42%	15.33%
unepic	100%	34.85%	16.01%

In order to identify the component most responsible for each power modeling, we give the power consumption proportion of each functional unit in Figure 3. Three horizontal columns represent the power without gating, power with clock gating and power with power gating from bottom to top, respectively.

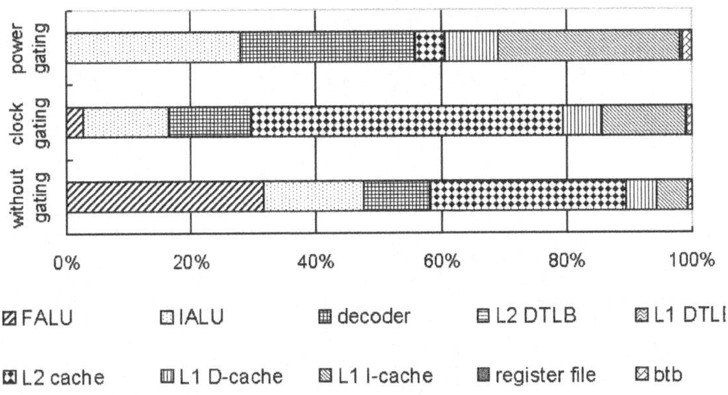

Fig. 3. The total power consumption partitioned by all FUs

In Figure 3, each column takes the total power consumption value as base case (100%), and power consumption proportion of each unit compared the total power consumption is given. Here each power percentage is the arithmetic mean of all MediaBench benchmarks. Due to Figure 3, we can see the power consumption proportion of each unit is quite different from each other. For example, the power consumption proportion of FALU is greatly reduced by clock gating or power gating compared to power without gating. And the power consumption proportion of L2 cache is also greatly reduced by power gating. In addition, clock gating and power gating can obtain great power reduction in average (power consumption can be reduced to 35.22%, 15.68%, respectively).

For the space limits, we only show four benchmarks in Figure 4. Fortunately, they can represent power consumption characteristics of MediaBench. Figure 4 compares the power consumption of each unit for (1) without gating; (2) clock gating and (3) power gating. For each component, the total power without gating is the base case (100%), and the other two cases are normalized to this base case.

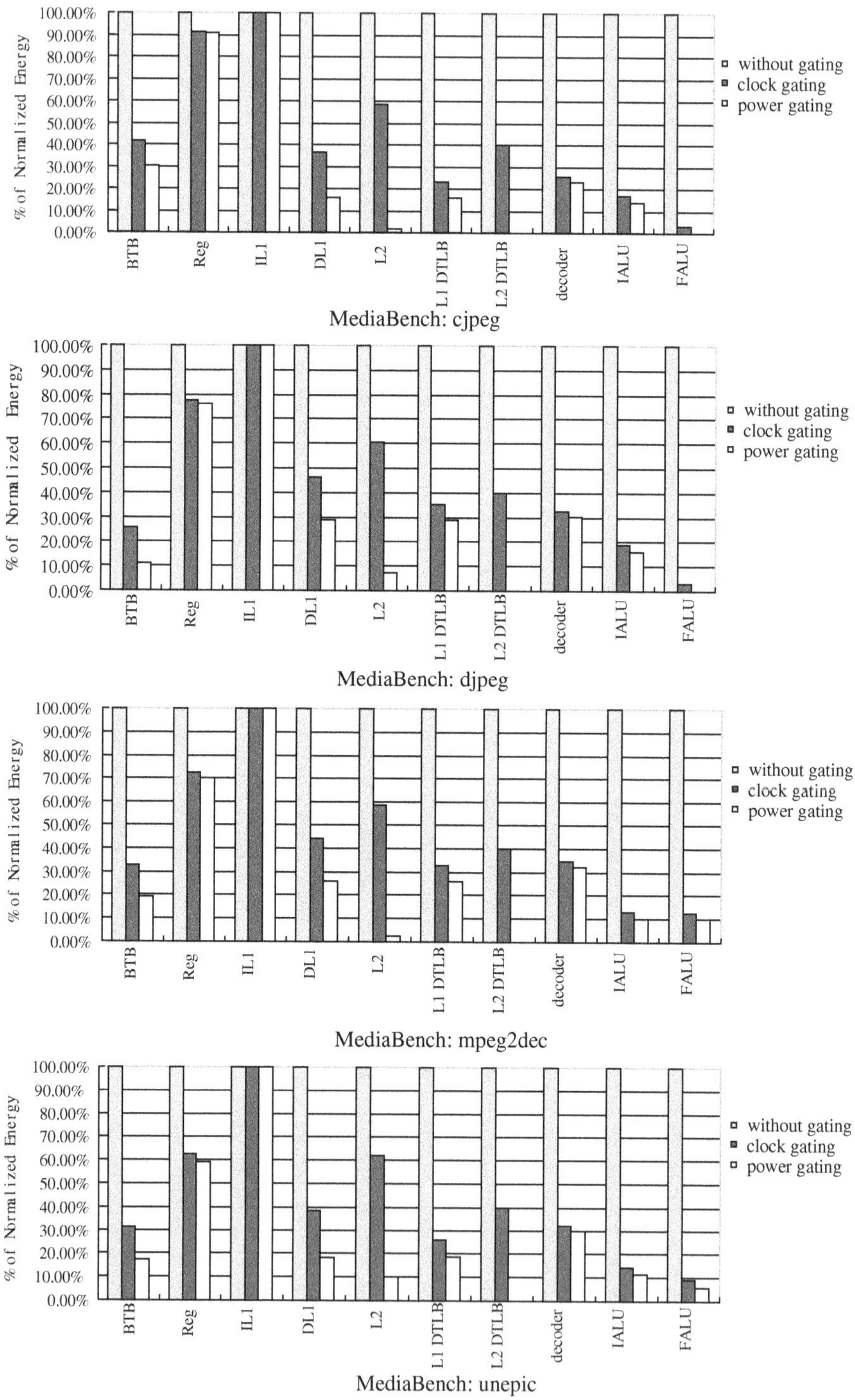

Fig. 4. Power consumption reduction under clock gating and power gating

Let us start with the power reduction effects of clock gating. From Figure 4, it is easy to see that clock gating is effective to reduce power for the BTB, L1 D-cache, L1 DTLB, L2 DTLB, decoder, IALU and FALU. Compared to the no-gating case, above seven components' total power consumption can all be reduced to below 50%, among which FALU obtains the largest power reduction, at the same time L1 D-cache obtains more power reduction than L2 cache. For memory-less components (decoder, IALU and FALU), effects of power consumption reduction are all obvious, among which FALU obtains the largest power reduction.

It is also easy to see that power gating is effective to reduce power for BTB, DL1, L2, L1 DTLB, L2 DTLB, IALU and FALU. Compared to the no-gating case, above seven components' total power consumption can all be reduced to below 30%. L2 DTLB obtains the largest power reduction. Among memory-based components, L2 cache obtains the largest power reduction, which is different from the clock gating case. Compared to clock gating, power gating is more effective in reducing L2 DTLB and L2 cache. This in fact validates the impact of *VRC* scheduling on L2 cache. Also, we can see L1 I-cache can hardly obtain power reduction from either clock gating or power gating.

Combining Figure3 and Figure 4, we can conclude that:

- Clock gating and power gating hardly can reduce L1 I-cache power consumption, so I-cache power consumption proportion to the total power consumption is increasing by clock gating and power gating;
- Power gating is more effective than clock gating on L2 cache power consumption reduction;
- Clock gating and power gating are both effective on IALU and FALU power consumption reduction.

5.2 The Impact of the Unideal Power Reduction on Performance

In multimedia applications the requirements are often on time for complete a computation, so we cannot ignore the performance issue. In this section, we will discuss the impact of power optimization techniques on performance. Since we refer to the ideal clock gating and the ideal power gating in the above, and we assume no performance loss under ideal clock gating and ideal power gating. The difference between the ideal power reduction and the unideal power reduction depends on the overhead especially the wake-up time.

In the ideal power gating, it is assumed that we can wake up a component in time to avoid performance loss. In order to observe the impact of the longer wake up on performance, we adjust wake-up time from 1 cycle to 2 cycles and 4 cycles, respectively. Performance loss of each memory-less component (BTB, Reg, decoder, IALU, and FALU) is obtained in Figure 5. In Figure 5, we use 1-cycle wake-up time as our base case, and we obtain the normalized performance loss caused by 2-cycle and 4-cycle wake-up time. According to Figure 5, we can see the Register file obtains the most performance loss (up to 10.2%). Here the performance refers to the execution time consumed on that component.

Besides, we also can change memory-based components correlative settings from ideal power gating to unideal power gating. This is one of our works in future.

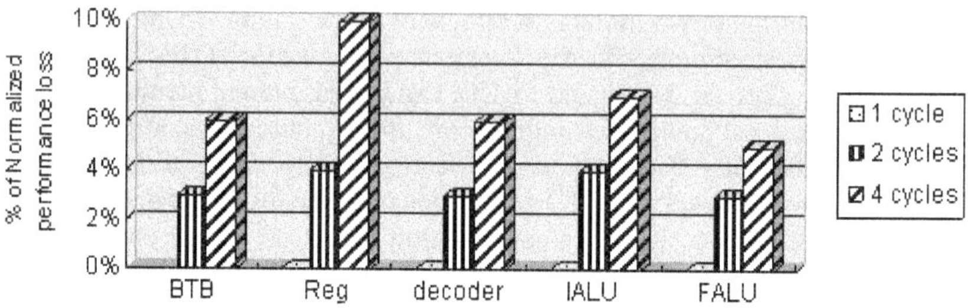

Fig. 5. The impact unideal power gating on performance

6 Conclusions and Future Works

Power consumption is a key limiting factor for mobile multimedia application. How to save more power consumption has been becoming important issue considered by many mobile computing researchers. However the research about evaluating power characteristics of embedded multimedia applications is scarce. Detailed and effective power analysis can help embedded mobile computing designer and application developments determine the power reduction policy. Our article provides the detailed power analysis for embedded multimedia application by running MediaBench under PowerImpact [2] simulator environment. According to detailed power analysis, each component's power consumption proportion is obtained, and the component most responsible for power consumption is identified. For example, the total power consumption can be reduced to 35.22% and 15.68% by using ideal clock gating and ideal power gating, respectively. FALU can obtain the largest power consumption reduction from clock gating, and L2 DTLB can obtain the largest power reduction from the power gating.

Since we refer to two ideal power reduction techniques (ideal clock gating and ideal power gating), memory-less components performance loss are avoided and cache behavior is unchangeable. However, performance issue is an important issue for multimedia applications since the real time demand. In simulation, we obtain the impact of unideal power gating on the performance by changing wake-up time.

Our next works include that analyzing the impact of the unideal clock gating and unideal power gating on power reduction in real applications, not just ideal clock gating and ideal power gating techniques, and exploring more power reduction opportunities. Low-power mobile multimedia applications are promising in the future embedded mobile computing.

Acknowledgements. The authors would like to thank Mr. Weiping Liao at UCLA for helpful discussions.

References

1. W. Liao and L. He. Power Modeling and Reduction of VLIW Processors. In the Proceedings of Workshop on Compilers and Operating Systems for Low Power, in conjunction with International Conference on Parallel Architectures and Compilation Techniques, 2001.

2. http://eda.ee.ucla.edu/PowerImpact/.
3. Hongbo Yang. Ph D. dissertation. Power-Aware Compilation Techniques for High Performance Processors. The Department of Computer Engineering, the University of Delware, USA, winter 2004.
4. W. Liao, J. Basile and L. He. Leakage Power Modeling and Reduction with Data Retention. In the Proceedings of International Conference on Computer Aided Design, 2002.
5. Benjamin Bishop, Thomas P. Kelliher, Mary Jane Irwin. A Detailed Analysis of MediaBench. In the Proceedings of Workshop on Signal Processing Systems, pp. 448-455, Taipei, Taiwan, Oct. 1999.
6. Chunho Lee, Miodrag Potkonjak and William H. Mangione-Smith. MediaBench: A Tool for Evaluating and Synthesizing Multimedia and Communications Systems. In the Proceedings of 30th Annual International Symposium on Microarchitecture (Micro 97) December 01-03, 1997 Research Triangle Park, NC. pp.330.
7. D. Brooks, V. Tiwari and M. Martsoni. Wattch: A Framework for Architectural-Level Power Analysis and Optimizations. In the Proceedings of 27th International Symposium on Computer Architecture, Jun 2000 (ISCA-00).
8. Interl's Grove warns of the end of Moore's Law. http://www.theinquirer.net/?article=6677
9. http://www.trimaran.org/ftp/MEDIA.tgz.
10. http://www.trimaran.org/ftp/SPECint00.tgz.
11. Jason Flinn and M. Satyanarayanan. Energy-Aware Adaptation for Mobile Applications. In the Proceedings of the 17th ACM Symposium on Operating Systems Principles (SOSP 99), Kiawah Island Resort, SC, December 1999. pp: 48-63.
12. P. P. Chang, S. A. Mahlke, W. Y. Chen, N. J. Warter, and W. Hwu. IMPACT: An Architectural Framework for Multiple-Instruction-Issue Processors. In the Proceedings of International Symposium on Computer Architecture, May 1991.
13. Doug Burger, Todd M. Austin, Steve Bennett. Evaluating Future Microprocessors: The SimpleScalar Tool Set. University of Wisconsin-Madison, Technical Report: CS-TR-96-1308, July 1996.
14. M. Pant, P. Pant, D. Wills, and V. Tiwari. An Architectural Solution for the Inductive Noise Problem due to Clock-gating. In the Proceedings of International Symposium on Low Power Electronics and Design. pp. 255-257, 1999.

A Dynamic Threshold and Subsection Control TCP Slow-Start Algorithm

ShiNing Li[1,2], JiPing Fang[3], Zheng Qin[1], and XingShe Zhou[2]

[1] E-commerce Research Laboratory Xi'an Jiaotong University, Postcode 710049, Xi'an Shaanxi, China
dtlsn@yahoo.com.cn

[2] Northwestern Polytechnic University, Xi'an Shaanxi, China 710072

[3] Datang Telecom Technology Co., Ltd. Xi'an Shaanxi, China 710075

Abstract. DSSC, a Dynamic Slow-start threshold and Subsection Control TCP Slow-start algorithm, is proposed. The key technologies of Vegas and TCP Westwood are applied to the first slow start process in DSSC, which dynamically configures TCP Slow-Start threshold and adaptively adjusts the increasing rate of TCP transmitting windows. DSSC can reach the steady state rapidly because its configuration of slow-start threshold is based on the bandwidth estimation, thus the lost packages will be limited and the entrance of congestion avoidance stage will not be too early. An important phenomenon, the TCP congestion bottleneck buffer response, is discovered, and the reason of this phenomenon is given. The result of simulation proves that this algorithm can avoid data packets loss, get to steady state quickly, and improve TCP throughput on complex network. This algorithm is robust to bottleneck buffer, adapts to WEB service, and is compatible with the present TCP protocol. Finally It is simple and practical in that it only modifies the sender of TCP.

1 Introduction

The TCP first slow-start algorithm gets involved with a lot of disadvantages. At the period of the first slow-start, because the TCP sets the SSTH to a big default value improperly due to lack of the information about network bandwidth, a great many successive packets are lost. Meanwhile, the exponential rate increasing mechanism is lack of robustness to the bottleneck buffer size[2]. When the size is set too small, the slow-start phenomenon will happen again and again and severely damage the performance of the TCP. Many kinds of modified algorithms were proposed, and could be classified according to their purposes to the 3 following classes:

A: increasing the initial window [3]. Web applications are the main kind of applications that are built on the TCP protocol recently. When the initial size of window is set to 4, the performance of the TCP is enhanced dramatically. However, since the increasing size of the initial window, lots of the packets will be lost and the utilization ratio will be damaged when the TCP protocol is used in the applications which run in the conditions with small bottleneck buffer, narrow bandwidth and short delayed link circuit.

L.T. Yang et al. (Eds.): ICESS 2005, LNCS 3820, pp. 608 – 617, 2005.

B: setting the proper SSTH [1] [4]. Sending end will avoid the congestion before the loss of the packets by setting the SSTH accurately. Article 4 proposed to set the SSTH to an accurate value in the period of the first slow-start and suggested the value should be the BDP of link circuit. Article 1 introduces the concept of "equivalent bandwidth", and insists on setting the SSTH to the product of equivalent bandwidth and RTT. Because of the ABCD errors[5], the estimated result will have the biggest error without a good filter mechanism to filter the sampling results. The bandwidth estimating algorithm should take the phenomenon of the random packets loss in the wireless circumstance into account.

C: changing the window increasing granularity dynamically [6]. Article 6 proposed a linear window increasing mechanism. The experiments show this new algorithm will decrease the time of the slow-start in the condition of no overload. And its linear window increasing mechanism is robust to the bottleneck buffer. Unfortunately the setting of the Wth is lack of the apriority.

2 A New Slow-Start Algorithm (DSSC)

Base on analysis, we could propose the principles that should be considered when designing the first slow-start algorithm.

1) the algorithm should be robust to the buffer size B, the bottleneck buffer size is the key factor that affects the performance of the slow-start, and although decreasing the B could decrease the number of the lost packets, too small B would probably result in the buffer overflow too early and hurt its performance.
2) Manage the window increasing granularity K properly to increase the average throughput and network utilization ratio at SS time. Increasing K could enhance average throughput at SS time, but big K will probably result in the buffer overflow too early. The K should be set carefully to meet the requirement on the equilibrium of the two sides.
3) A proper SSTH should be set to decrease the number of the lost packets. Lots of the packets will be lost at the end of the slow-start, this will hurt the performance of TCP. Decreasing B and setting a proper SSTH will decrease the lost packets number.
4) Feasibility in the real network; No modification at the receiving end; Compatibility to the existed network protocol.

Based on the thoughts of estimating the bandwidth available and the mechanism of judging the state of the intermediate routers packets queues in Vegas[7], and considering that the TCP Westwood (TCPW)[8] estimating algorithm takes the random loss in wireless environment into account and could be used in the field of the wireless relay link circuit, a new first slow-start DSSC (Dynamic Ssth and Subsection Control) using the bandwidth estimating algorithm in TCPW is proposed. Since it is supposed that the packets loss is caused by the congestion in the traditional TCP protocol, the phenomenon of link random data exists broadly as the development of the wireless communication technology. If the random loss is neglected in the algorithm, the performance of the algorithm will be hurt badly. The detail about the algorithm is as follow:

With the help of the DIFF*BaseRTT in Vegas and the mechanism of developed bandwidth estimation filtering mBE, the window increasing granularity is controlled in different phases. The time is divided into four control phases called A phase, B phase, C phase and D phase.

A Phase: When DIFF*BaseRTT is smaller than 1; the router buffers in the network are almost empty, and the window could be increased. If the sending window is smaller than the size of the window that could be permitted by the network bandwidth available, it means that the bandwidth is not made full use of, and the increasing granularity should be set to 2(faster than Reno, 1 in Reno). On the contrary, if the window size is bigger than the permission value, the increasing granularity should be set to 1. Because of the almost empty buffer at this time, the buffer will not overflow.

B Phase: When DIFF*BaseRTT is between 1 and 2, there are a few data packets in the bottleneck routers buffer queue in the network and the biggest increasing granularity could not make the buffer overflow quickly. So if the sending window is smaller than the window size that the bandwidth available (estimated) allows, the increasing granularity is set to 1, or it should be 0.5.

C Phase: When DIFF*BaseRTT is between 2 and 3, there are certain number of the packets stay in the buffer. Too big increasing granularity could result in the quick overflow in the buffer easily. At this time, if the bandwidth available (estimated again) is made full use of, the biggest increasing granularity makes no sense and it should be set to 1/cwnd. On the contrary, if the bandwidth available is not made full use of, the increasing granularity should be 0.1 in order to enhance the bandwidth utilization ratio quickly meanwhile prevent the buffer from overflowing quickly.

D Phase: While DIFF*BaseRTT is bigger than 4, there are lots of packets in buffer and the buffer is close to the overflow state, so the increasing granularity should be decreased whether the link bandwidth is made full use of or not, otherwise it will cause the packets loss. The increasing granularity should be set to 1/cwnd.

3 The Performance Analysis Based on Simulation

Here NS2 is what we use to accomplish simulating. The topology structure of the network is shown in Figure 1, including 6 hosts and 4 routers. The Host S1, S2, S3 and the router Ra are connected by the 100Mbps Ethernet as same as the host D1, D2, D3 and the router Rb. The router Ra and R1 are connected by the 10Mbps link as same as Rb and R2, and the time delay is 25ms; the router R1 and R2 are connected by the 3Mbps link, and the time delay is 60ms.

In the simulation, the network parameters relevant to the TCP are the data packet size that is 800byte, and the receiving announced window size that is 450(packets). Now, we will try to prove that DSSC will enhance the performance efficiently in the slow-start phase by comparing the TCPW adopting DSSC (DSSC+TCPW), TCPW without DSSC and Reno without DSSC.

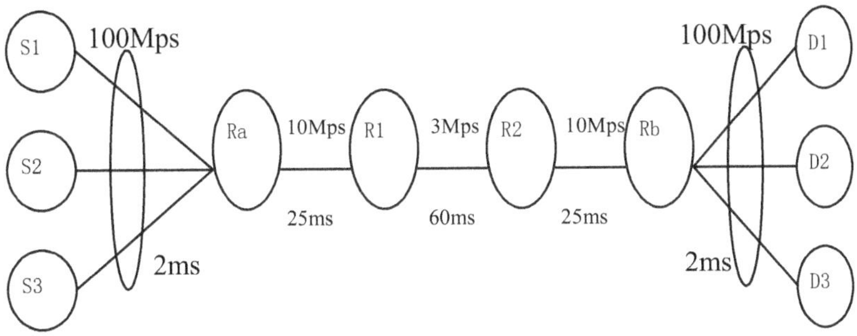

Fig. 1. The topology structure of the network

3.1 The DSSC Robustness Effectiveness Simulation to Bottleneck Buffer and the Segmentation Control Effectiveness Simulation

At first, we run the DSSC robustness to bottleneck buffer effectiveness simulation, the NBS (normalized buffer size) is equal to the ratio of BBS(bottleneck buffer size) and BDP(bandwidth-delay product). This means NBS=BBS/BDP. BDP means maximal packet (excluding the packets in queue of router buffer) size in the pipe that connects the sending end and the receiving end on the condition of no congestion. And the essential of NBS is the ratio of maximal number of the packets in queue of the bottleneck buffer and the maximal packet size in pipe.

DSSC+TCPW is built between the host S1 and D1 to transfer CBR flow. While the bottleneck buffer size is changed from 0.1s to 120s, we review the performance of DSSC+TCPW when NBS is 1, 0.75, 0.5 and 0.25 respectively, then change the connection type to TCPW and Reno meanwhile keeping the other conditions constant. Figure 2 includes sub-figure (a), (b), (c), and (d).which represent respectively the TCP throughput when NBS is 1, 0.75, 0.5 and 0.25. Table 1 represents the time to stable state of DSSC+TCPW, TCPW and Reno, the total packet lost number and the average throughput when getting to stable state.

We can tell that the throughput is equal in DSSC+TCPW, TCPW and Reno when they reach the stable state, whatever the value of NBS is, from the Figure 2. However, they differ in the time of reaching stable.

First, based on the sub-Figure 2a, here NBS=1, two items could be identified.

- DSSC+TCPW could get to stable state quickly, however, the Reno and the TCPW could not.
- Comparing the Reno and the TCPW, we could find that the TCPW needs more time to reach stable than the Reno.

It could be concluded that the main reason is that Reno and the TCPW know nothing about the link bandwidth available, and increase the congestion buffer exponentially until lots of packets are lost and slow- start is over. Restoring the lost packets expands (prolongs) the time to reach stable state. And that could be very different from the DSSC+TCPW. DSSC+TCPW could set SSTH by estimating the link bandwidth available at the time of

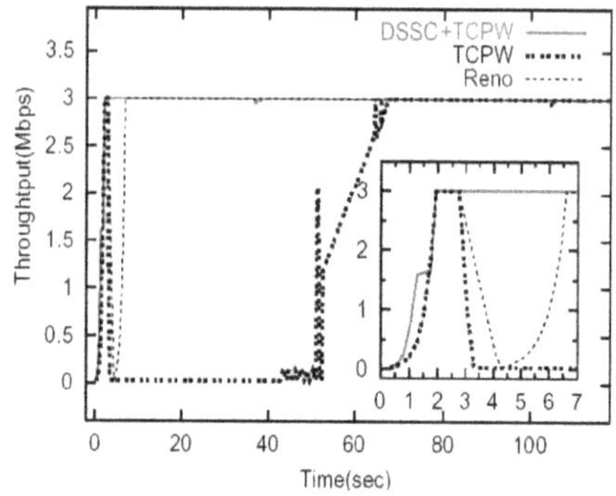

2a When NBS=1

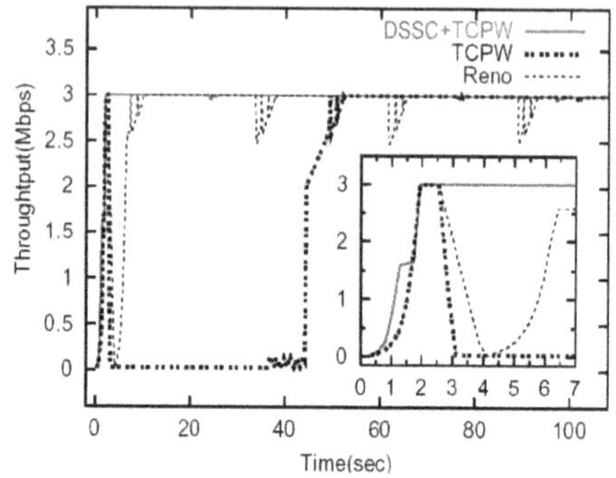

2b When NBS=0.75

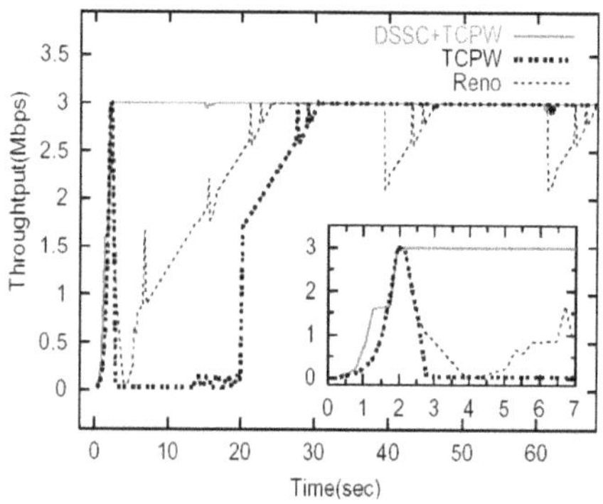

2c When NBS=0.5

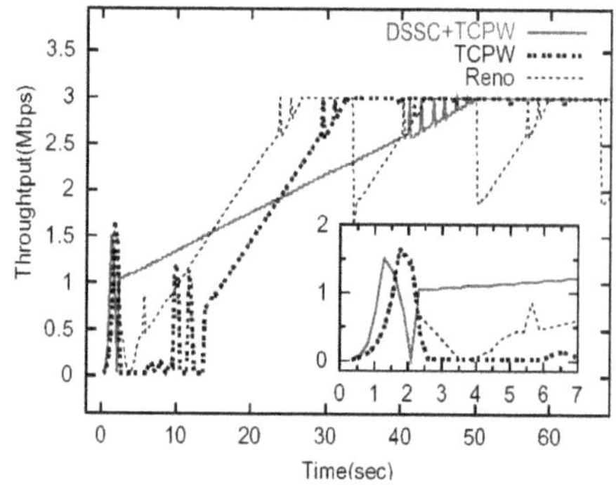

2d When NBS=0.25

Fig. 2. TCP' throughput in four kinds of NBS environments

Table 1. TCP' performance parameter comparison at the slow start-up stage

TCP / parameter	b=1			b=0.75		
	DSSC+TCPW	TCPW	Reno	DSSC+TCPW	TCPW	Reno
time to stable state	1.96s	67s	6.6s	1.96s	52s	10.1s
packet lost number	1	208	410	1	179	353
average throughput	1.08(Mbps)	0.57(Mbps)	0.94(Mbps)	1.05(Mbps)	0.49(Mbp	1.56(Mbps)

(a) When NBS=1, 0.75

TCP / parameter	b=0.5			b=0.25		
	DSSC+TCPW	TCPW	Reno	DSSC+TCPW	TCPW	Reno
time to stable state	1.97s	30s	24.1s	47s	30s	26s
packet lost number	1	76	180	3	33	82
average throughput	1.04(Mbps)	0.9(Mbps)	1.59(Mbps)	1.9(Mbps)	1.2(Mbps)	1.43(Mbps)

(b) When NBS=0.5, 0.2

slow-start, make sure to prevent losing many packets and getting involved in the congestion-avoiding period. Therefore, DSSC+TCPW could come to be stable quickly.

Comparing the Reno and the TCPW, the same mechanism (window increasing exponentially) is adopted in both of them, but at the time of restoring the many lost packets when the slow-start is over, they use different retransmission strategies. The TCPW uses the single packet retransmission mechanism adopted in the New Reno. Although the window just decreases once (keeping in a relative big value), a single lost packet is retransmitted at a RTT time. When lots of lost packets exist, the retransmission time is prolonged dramatically.We call this IR (Inefficient Retransmission). Considering the Reno, the loss of lots packets triggers the slow-start mechanism, the window shorten the retransmission time by increasing exponentially, so the time to reach stable state in the Reno is shorter than in the TCPW. But since the SSTH is set too small after detecting the loss of many packets and the Reno gets into the congestion-avoiding period too early.

Secondly, when NBS decreased continually from 1 to 0.25 with a step of 0.25, comparing the sub-Figure 2a, 2b, 2c and 2d, we could find that the same TCP mechanism with different B could perform very differently at the stable state reaching time. The main reason is that the robustness of DSSC+TCPW, TCPW and Reno to buffer B varies.

When B decreased gradually and NBS decreased from 1 to 0.25 with a step 0.25, the time to reaching stable state expands gradually from 6.6s to 26s (6.6s->10.1s->24.1s->26s). It is obvious that the value of B influences the performance of the Reno directly, and the robustness of the Reno to B is not satisfactory. And this is mainly caused by that while B is decreased, the exponential increasing of window makes the buffer to overflow too early. Reno needs several slow-start procedures to investigate the bandwidth, and this prolongs the time to stable state accordingly. Contrary to the Reno, when B decreased gradually, TCPW needs less and less time to reach the stable state (67s-52s-30s-30s), and the main reason is that TCPW adopts the single packet retransmission mechanism in New Reno, when B is decreasing, the packets loss less and less, so TCPW needs less time to retransmit after the first slow-start is over and shortens the time to the stable state.

As B decreases, NBS drops down from 1 to 0.5 with a step of 0.25, the time to the stable state almost keeps constant in DSSC+TCPW (1.96s-1.96s-1.97s), and its performance could not be influenced by the changing of B, so we could figure out that when B is in this range, DSSC+TCPW is very robust to the B. this is due to the (vary) rate window increasing mechanism in the DSSC+TCPW, this mechanism could adjust the window increasing granularity according to the state of the queue in buffer. But when NBS=0.25, the time to the stable state rockets to 47s in TCPW, so, we could see that DSSC+TCPW could not eradicate the bad effect to the performance caused by the too big B. from Figure 2, we could find that although the time to the stable state is longest in DSSC+TCPW, it keeps a high throughput with 2, in addition, considering the number of lost packets, the DSSC+TCPW does the best job. So it is found that the new mechanism could not aggravate the performance of original TCP on the condition of the very small B. Compared with the TCPW and the Reno, the DSSC+TCPW is better.

All in all, we identify an important phenomenon that the time to the stable state in different TCP congestion control mechanism reacts differently to the changes of transmission link bottleneck buffer B. and we define it as "TCP congestion control bottleneck buffer reaction".

3.2 The Simulation Analysis of Transmission Capability in the DSSC

The network topology shown in Figure 1 is still adopted, a DSSC+TCPW is built between the host S2 and D2 to support FTP flow, NBS=1, we change the FTP file size, observe the transmission time in DSSC+TCPW, then change the connection type to the TCPW and the Reno respectively while keeping the other condition unchanged. Table 2 shows the time of transmitting the different size files and the average throughput in the DSSC+TCPW, the TCPW and the Reno.

As shown in Table 2, the ratio of average throughput in DSSC+TCPW and in TCPW or Reno changes 3 times along with the change of transmitted file size. When file size increases from 16K to 1Mbit, the ratio of the throughput decreases gradually; when the file size enhances from 1Mbit to 5Mbit, the ratio rockets dramatically, then deceases to 0 along with the augment of the file size. In the following section, we will analyze the whys.

Table 2. The time of transmitting the different size files and the average throughput

TCP / File size	Transmission time(s)/ Average throughput (Kbps)			Improvement of Ratio of average throughput	
	DSSC+TCPW	TCPW	Reno	DSSC+TCPW for TCPW	DSSC+TCP for Reno
16Kbit	0.329 / 48.5	0.525 / 30.5	0.525 / 30.5	59%	59%
32Kbit	0.542 / 58.9	0.741 / 43.2	0.741 / 43.2	36%	36%
100Kbit	0.737 / 135.7	0.935 / 107.0	0.935 / 107.0	27%	27%
1Mbit	1.506 / 665.6	1.787 / 559.6	1.787 / 559.6	19%	19%
5Mbit	3.02 / 1656	38.9 / 628.6	7.71 / 664.6	163%	149%
50Mbit	18.2 / 2771	66.9 / 1750.2	38.1 / 1324	58%	109%
100Mbit	35 / 2883	79.1 / 2282	55 / 1828	26%	57.6%
800Mbit	275 / 2912	282 / 2834	291 / 2729	2.7%	6.7%

At the beginning of the TCP link, because of the empty link, the DSSC+TCPW window-increasing granularity is 2, twice of that in the TCPW and the Reno, the average throughput increased dramatically, and this feature is benefit for the small Web flow applications. When the file size becomes big and big, the transmission time expands, and the window size increases meanwhile the window increasing granularity decreases gradually. When the sending rate is equal to the bandwidth available, the increasing granularity is 1/cwnd, so the throughput increasing scope decreased gradually. But when the file size is 5Mbit, the ratio of the average throughput in the DSSC+TCPW and the TCPW or the Reno rockets dramatically, and the main reason is that the rapid increasing of the window in the TCPW and the Reno results in the plenty of packets being lost. Transmitting the 5Mbit file makes the TCPW and the Reno get involved in the restoring time between losing of lots of packets and the stable state. We called this phenomenon as "delay restoring". after that, along with the increasing of the file size, both of the TCPW and the Reno are in the stable state, meanwhile the performance of the DSSC+TCPW, the TCPW and the Reno are equal. The effect of TCP caused by the performance distinction in the TCP slow-start time is diluted, so the throughput of the DSSC+TCPW increasing rate is decreased. By this simulation we could see clearly that the throughput of DSSC+TCPW algorithm is nearly equal to it of the TCPW and the Reno after entering the congestion-avoiding stage, and TCP congestion control algorithm works at congestion-avoiding stage in most of the time. The aim of DSSC+TCPW algorithm is trying to reduce the packet loss number at the slow start stage, and make the slow startup to stable state as soon as possible. At the same time, it adopts subsection control principle to improve the throughput of the slow stage with the premise of reducing the packet lost number. This is mainly to improve the efficiency of WEB business, because small Web flow applications finish at the slow start stage generally So this simulation incarnates the improvement of efficiency for small Web flow applications by DSSC+TCPW algorithm.

3.3 The DSSC Simulation Validity in the Condition of the Different Flux in Multi-connections

In order to study the adaptability of the DSSC, we run the DSSC+TCPW with different flows in multi-connection, and compare it with the TCPW and the Reno.

The network topology shown in Figure 1 is adopted again. A UDP connection and a Reno TCP connection are built between S1 and D1, meanwhile a Reno TCP connection and a TCPW TCP connection are built between S2 and D2. The CBR flow is loaded on the two connections mentioned above. On this condition, DSSC+TCPW, TCPW and Reno are built respectively between S3 and D3 to run FTP flow. FTP starts at 30s and CBR starts at 2s. The DSSC+TCPW performances on different background flows are simulated through our controlling the magnitude of the CBR flow. Sub-figure (a), (b) and (c), composing the Figure 3, represent the TCP throughput with 300kb background flow (light network load), 1500kb (middle network load) and 3300kb (network congestion). Figure 2 records the time to stable state of TCP and the number of lost packets.

From Figure 3, we could figure out that when network is on the state of light load (shown in sub-Figure 3a) and middle load (3b), the performance of the DSSC+TCPW is better obviously, and time to stable state is much less than TCPW and Reno (shown in Figure 2). The main reason is that lots of packets is lost during the slow-start time in TCPW and Reno, on the contrary, the DSSC+TCPW is efficient to prevent a great number of packets from being lost, and it is shown in Figure 2. When network is in congestion, compared with the TCPW, the performance advantage is not obvious, just little better. And the main reason is that the buffer available for new TCP decreases when the network load is more and more heavy. In the view of new TCPW connections, that is equal to the decreasing of link B. The number of lost packets is less and the time to stable state is less at slow-start time in TCPW, so the distinction between TCPW and

DSSC+TCPW is reduced. Also from Figure 3, we could see that DSSC+TCPW has a good compatibility to UDP and other types of TCP. Since DSSC+TCPW just modifies the first slow-start time algorithm meanwhile adopts the original mechanisms at other TCP periods, it has the same property and a good compatibility compared with TCP Reno and TCPW when it is stable.

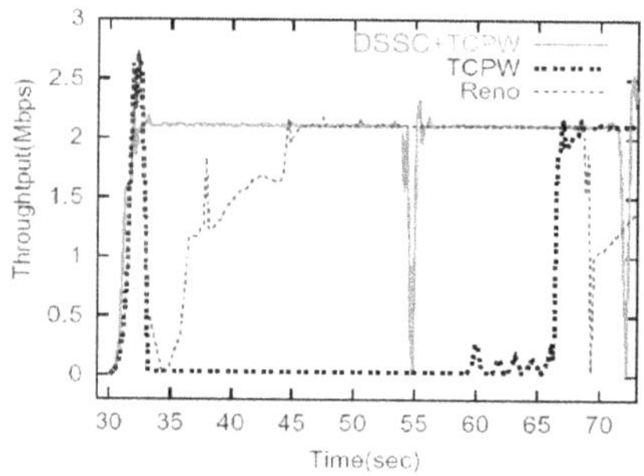

(3a) Background flow with 300Kbps

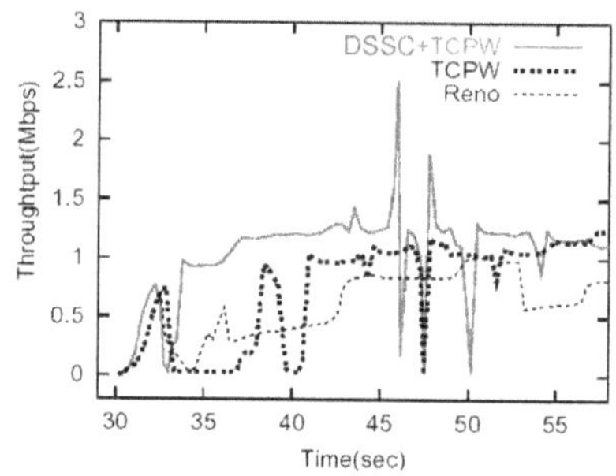

(3b) Background flow with 1500Kbps

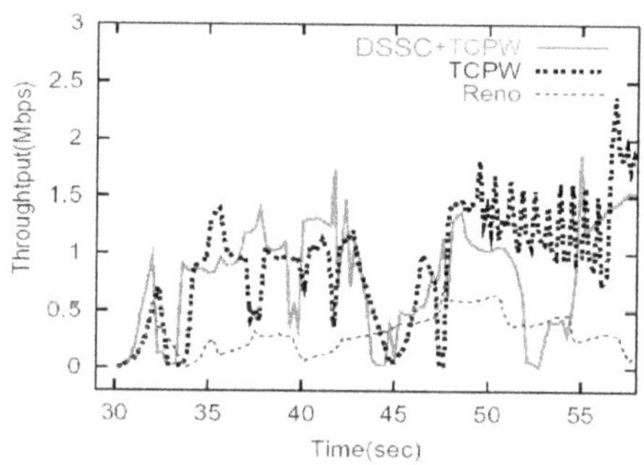

(3c) Background flow with 3300Kbps

Fig. 3. TCP' throughputs under the three kinds of background flow

Table 3. TCP' performance under the different background flow

TCP / background flow	Stable time(s)/ packet lost number(Packet)		
	DSSC+TCPW	TCPW	Reno
300Kb	32.7 / 3	67.7 / 143	44.1 / 342
1500Kb	36.7 / 4	46.2 / 22	45.1 / 75
3300Kb	37.1 / 6	38 / 7	46.1 / 23

4 Conclusion

Based on the theoretic academic analysis, this article proposes the principles of the TCP slow-start mechanism. Combining the network bandwidth available estimating, link buffer estimating and bandwidth estimating filter mechanism, adopting the design principles of dynamic setting slow-start threshold and controlling the window increasing granularity at different phases, this article proposes a new TCP slow-start algorithm named DSSC used in heterogeneous network. In order to validate the efficiency of the DSSC, the detailed simulation is run, the result is analyzed, a phenomenon called "TCP congestion control bottleneck buffer reaction" is found, and the substance of this phenomenon is analyzed. DSSC algorithm could be adopted in different networks to protect the great many packets from being lost at the slow-start time, to help the network reaching the stable state quickly, and to enhance the throughput at the slow-start time. In addition, this algorithm has a good robustness to link bottleneck buffer and a good adaptability to WEB services. DSSC needs simple protocol upgrading at the sending end, and is compatible to the existed TCP protocol.

References

1. Liyun, Chenqianbin, Longkeping, Wushiqi. A TCP Slow-Start Algorithm Based on Link Band-Width Estimation. Computer science. 2003. 26(6) : 693–700.
2. Chadi Barakat, Eitan Altman. Analysis of the phenomenon of several slow start phases in TCP. The ACM SIGMETRICS international conference on Measurement and modeling of computer, California,2000.
3. Mark Allman. Improving TCP performance over satellite channels. Master of Science Degree dissertation, Ohio University, 1997.
4. Hoe J C. Improving the Start-up Behavior of a Congestion Control Scheme for TCP. The ACM SIGCOMM, Stanford, CA,1996.
5. Kevin Lai, Mary Bake . Nettimer:A Tool for Measuring Bottleneck Link Bandwidth. The USENIX Symposium on Internet Technologies and Systems, California, 2001.
6. Chadi Barakat, Eitan Altman. Performance of short tcp transfers. In Proceedings of NETWORKING 2000, Paris, France, 2000.
7. Lawrence Brakmo, Sean O'Malley, and Larry Peterson. TCP Vegas: New Techniques for Congestion Detection and Avoidance. In ACM SIGCOMM [C]. August 1994, 24-35.
8. M. Gerla, M. Sanadidi, R. Wang, A. Zanella, C. Casetti, S. Mascolo. TCP Westwood: Window Control Using Bandwidth Estimation [R]. IEEE Globecom 2001, Texas,, 2001.

An Improved DRR Packet Scheduling Algorithm Based on Even Service Sequence

Fan Zhang, Shoumeng Yan, Xingshe Zhou, and Yaping Wang

School of Computer, NorthWestern Polytechnical University,
Xi'an, Shaanxi 710072, China
Zhangfan@nwpu.edu.cn

Abstract. With the emerging of many new kinds of network services, it is critical for the network to give service differentiation and QoS guarantee. One of the most important components in existing QoS frameworks is packet scheduler. A good scheduler should provide QoS guarantee and, at the same time, show low complexity. However, existing algorithms often fail to provide the two features at the same time. This paper proposes an improved DRR-like packet scheduling algorithm based on even service sequence, which combining advantages of DRR and WF^2Q. Our simulation experiments show that this algorithm can provide good fairness, low scheduling delay and low complexity.

1 Introduction

With development of networking technology, the functions of router have transferred from forwarding packets with best effort to supporting QoS (quality of service). Packet loss rate, deadline, delay variance, which are the most important QoS properties, should be maintained without compromising the processing speed of incoming data streams.

One of the most important components in existing QoS frameworks is packet scheduler, which is deployed in router to offer different service for input packets which has different priority. How to schedule the input packets so the packets from different flows can get processed in proper order and some packets can be dropped to save computational power or bandwidth for more urgent packets, many scheduling algorithms have been proposed to solve this problem.

In this paper, we present the even service sequence structure to improve the DRR packet scheduling algorithm. This structure is shown to be able to combine advantages of DRR [1] and WF^2Q [2]. The algorithm can provides good fairness, low scheduling delay, low complexity and ease to implement.

The rest of the paper is organized as follows. Section 2 describe the relevant previous works, section 3 presents the Improved DRR Packet Scheduling Algorithm Based on Even Service Sequence, section 4 reports the results of the simulation study of the algorithm. Finally, Section 5 concludes the paper.

2 Related Work

Schedule problem was first studied in General Processor Sharing (GPS) [4] system, but it's an unrealistic algorithm for achieving perfect fairness and isolation among all

L.T. Yang et al. (Eds.): ICESS 2005, LNCS 3820, pp. 618 – 628, 2005.

flows. GPS algorithm forms a basis for most packet schedulers. Weighted Fair Queuing (WFQ) [7] and Worst-case Fair Weighted Fair Queuing (WF^2Q) [2], closely approximate the GPS. These schedulers compute a timestamp for each packet by emulating the progress of a reference GPS server and transmit packets in the increasing order of their timestamps. Both WFQ and WF^2Q have an O(1) GPS-relative delay. These scheduling algorithms require complex data structures and are not suitable for hardware implementation.

Another type of scheduling algorithms is based on round-robin scheme [1, 5, 6, 9, 10]. Round-Robin schedulers serve backlogged flows in some kind of round-robin fashion and have an O(1) per packet processing complexity. The Deficit Round Robin (DRR) algorithm is the base for many recent improvements. SRR [9] and Aliquem [10] improve the average packet delay over DRR, but the worst-case single packet delay bound is proportional to the number of flows in the system. By using a deadline based scheduling scheme, the single packet delay bound of the Stratified Round Robin [5] algorithm is related to the guaranteed rate of the flow and is independent of the number of flows in the system.

GPS based algorithms have good bounded delay and fairness properties, but have high complexity, O(log N). It's difficult to implement GPS based algorithms in high speed networks. Round-robin based algorithm takes O(1) processing work per packet and ease for implementation, but it can only provide long term fairness in bandwidth allocation, do not provide good bounded delay and short term fairness properties.

In this paper, we present an improved DRR packet scheduling algorithm based on even service sequence which combines the advantage of WF^2Q and DRR. We want to achieve good fairness, low scheduling delay, low complexity and ease to implement.

3 ESSDRR Algorithm

Since the ESSDRR algorithm is based on DRR, we will briefly describe DRR. DRR works in round. Within each round, each backlogged flow has an opportunity to send packets. Each flow f_i is associated with a quantity $quantum_i$ and a variable $deficitcounter_i$. The quantity $quantum_i$, which indicates the share given to flow i, is assigned based on the guaranteed rate for f_i and specifies the target amount of data that f_i should send in a round. The variable $deficitcounter_i$ is introduced to record the quantum that is not used in a round so the unused quantum can be passed to the next round. To ensure that each flow can send at least one packet per round, in this paper, we will assume that $quantum_i$ is larger than the maximum packet size, That is,

$quantum_i \geq L_{\max}$. According to [1], the $Quantum_i$ is in direct ratio with the rate of flow i ,that is, $\frac{Quantum_i}{Quantum_j} = \frac{r_i}{r_j}$, and the rate of flow i is in direct radio with the weight of the flow i, thus we get $\frac{w_i}{w_j} = \frac{r_i}{r_j}$, which w_i denotes the weight of the flow i and $w_i \geq 1$. From above, we get $\frac{Quantum_i}{Quantum_j} = \frac{w_i}{w_j}$ and $Quantum_i = w_i \times L_{\max}$ .More details can be found in [1].

DRR is an excellent scheduler when the weights of flows are similar. The problem with DRR is that, for flow i , DRR try to send packets no more than $DeficitCounter_i + Quantum_i$ bits in one time a round, when the weights of the flows differ significantly, flows with large weights can be significantly affected by the flows with small weights both in terms of packet delay and short term bandwidth allocation [3].

ESSDRR, our proposed scheduler, extends DRR QoS properties for any weight distribution, while maintaining an O (1) complexity. The basic idea of ESSDRR is as follows. For flow i, DRR algorithm send the max of $Quantum_i = w_i \times L_{\max}$ bits of packet one time in a round, w_i is the weight of the flow i. From another side, we can think that the DRR scheduler serve flow i w_i times continuously, each time the scheduler send the max of $L_{\max}$ bits of data. In ESSDRR, we want to spread the services of flow i , which is amount to w_i times, distribute evenly in $\sum_{i=0}^{i=N-1} w_i$ times of services which is the sum of all flows' weight. Thus, the challenge of ESSDRR is how to build a service sequence which length is $\sum_{i=0}^{i=N-1} w_i$, and flow i occupies w_i nodes among them. The construction of service sequence is the key of ESSDRR, and we call this service sequence is ESS (Even Service Sequence). After the construction of sequence, a round is one round-robin iteration over the even service sequence, and scheduler just choose node in sequence in order, and transmit packets no more than $L_{\max}$ bits, which of the flow defined by the node been choose.

Bennett [2] shows that the WF^{2}Q can provides almost identical service to GPS differing by no more than one maximum size packet and shares both the bounded-delay and worst-case fairness properties of GPS. Thus, we use WF^{2}Q to build the ESS. Assume we have N active flows of which packet size in the flow is $L_{\max}$, we use WF^{2}Q discipline to serve all the flow $\sum_{i=0}^{i=N-1} w_i$ times a round, and then record the sequence of service to each flow into a service list, and this service list is the ESS. From another point of view, we use WF^{2}Q to allocate the $\sum_{i=0}^{i=N-1} w_i$ nodes to N flows, and each node represents one time service to the flow which we allocate to this node.

Now consider the procedure of $\sum_{i=0}^{i=N-1} w_i$ nodes allocation with WF^{2}Q algorithm. Let us denote $TermCount_i$ the total number of nodes which have been allocated to flow i, we define the virtual start time and finish time of packets in flow i as:

$$S_i^{TermCount_i} = S_i^0 + TermCount_i \times L_{\max} / r_i$$

$$F_i^{TermCount_i} = S_i^{TermCount_i} + L_{\max} / r_i = S_i^0 + (TermCount_i + 1) \times L_{\max} / r_i$$

Without losing generality, let $S_i^0 = 0$, so we have

$$S_i^{TermCount_i} = TermCount_i \times L_{\max} / r_i$$

$$F_i^{TermCount_i} = (TermCount_i + 1) \times L_{\max} / r_i$$

When allocate the j th node, while $j = \left\{0,1,2,..., \sum_{i=}^{i=N-1} w_i - 1\right\}$, and we let t be the time at which the j th service begin. According the WF^{2}Q, the procedure of ESS construction as follows:

1. Construct a flow set E of which elements meets the condition "the start time is early than time t", $S_i^{TermCount_i} \le t$;
2. Choose within E a flow k which meets the condition "flow k have a minimal finishing time", $F_k^{TermCount_k} = \min_{i \in E}\{F_i^{TermCount_i}\}$, and allocate the node j to flow k, and update the $TermCount_k = TermCount_k + 1$;
3. Repeat the upper process until all $\sum_{i=0}^{i=N-1} w_i$ nodes are allocate to N N flows.

Since $L_{\max} / r_i$ occur in every formula above, and $\frac{w_i}{w_j} = \frac{r_i}{r_j}$ and the allocation process only uses compare operation, so we simplify $S_i^{TermCount_i}, F_i^{TermCount_i}, \tau$ as follows:

$$S_i^{'TermCount_i} = TermCount_i / w_i$$
$$F_i^{'TermCount_i} = (TermCount_i + 1) / w_i$$
$$t' = j / \sum_{i=0}^{i=N-1} w_i$$

With $S^{'}, F^{'}, t^{'}$, The ESS is computed using algorithm shown in Fig 1.

calc_servlist(listID)

{

local variable: $TermCount_i$ =0;

for(j=0;j< $\sum_{i=0}^{i=N-1} w_i$;j++)

{

Construct a flow set E of which elements meets $TermCount_i / w_i \le j / \sum_{i=0}^{i=N-1} w_i$;

Choose within E a flow k which meets $(TermCount_k + 1) / w_k = \min_{i \in E}\{(TermCount_i + 1) / w_i\}$;

Fig. 1. The algorithm for computing ESS

```
        TermCount_k = TermCount_k + 1;

        pTerm =Make_Node(k, TermCount_k ) //record flow id k and
current TermCount_k in a Term of servlist;

        Append(servlist[listID], pTerm);
    }
}
```

Fig. 1. *(Continued)*

Let us now examine the algorithm in Figure 1. servlist is a global variables used to record the ESS, Make_Node function are used to generate a ESS node to record the flow id, Append function are used to append a new node at the tail of the servlist. After the construction of ESS, the ESSDRR algorithm becomes simple. The major variables used in ESSDRR are summarized in Table 1.

Table 1. Major variables used in the essdrr algorithm

Variable	Explanation
listID	The ID of servlist, used to differentiate the servlist
servlist	A list used to record the ESS node.
P	A pointer point to current node in servlist.
$deficit_f$	Used to record the unused quantum of flow f after this time's service.
L_{max}	The maximum packet size that can transmit in one time.
$queue_f$	A FIFO queue which formed by the packets of flow f
P_f	The packet at the head of the queue of flow f
L_f	The length of P_f which sized in Bytes
w_f	The weight of flow f

ESSDRR scheduler is composed by three asynchronous actions, Schedule, AddFlow and DelFlow. Schedule is the main component of the scheduler and the pseudo-code for schedule function is shown in figure 2. AddFlow is used when the new flow is added to the system, and the DelFlow is used when the flow is deleted from the system.

```
Schedule()
{
        local variable: f; //f denote ID of current flow
        listID = 0;
        P = servlist[listID];//initialize P as the head of servlist
        while(in backlogged-period)
        {
              f = P->fid;

              defict_f = defict_f + L_max ;

              if(P->next!=NULL)          //check if we have got tail of servlist
              P = P->next;               //not tail, go to next node
              else P = servlist;         //when we got tail, just go back to list head

              while( defict_f >0)    //service current flow until defict_f is consumed

              {

                   if( L_f > defict_f ) break;

                   else{

                              dequeue( P_f ); send( P_f );

                              defict_f = defict_f - L_f ;

                              if( queue_f is empty)

                              {
                                    DelFlow(f); break;
                              }

                   }

              }//while( defict_f >0)

        } //while(in busy-period)
}// Schedule
```

Fig. 2. Pseudo-Code of Schedule function for ESSDRR

ESSDRR maintain two servlist, and backup for each other. One used to schedule and another used to update the ESS structure. In the running of the algorithm , ESSDRR serve all the flows in system according to the current servlist, and when flow changed (add or delete), Schedule use WF^2Q compute a new ESS list, and save the list result to the backup servlist, and then switch the current servlist with backup servlist.

4 Simulation Experiment

We design some experiments to investigate ESSDRR properties and to compare ESSDRR with other scheduling disciplines, including WF^2Q, SRR, FRR and DRR. All experiments are performed using ns-2[8]. We will only report the results of two representative experiments, one for end-to-end delay and the other one for throughput-time distribution characteristic. The network-topology and experiments in our simulation experiments are the same with which used in FRR. Figure 3 shows the network-topology and all the links have a bandwidth of 2Mbps and a propagation delay of 1ms.

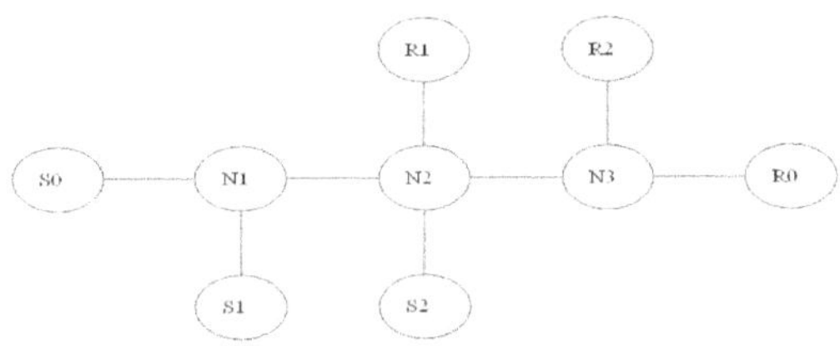

Fig. 3. Simulated network topology

4.1 End-to-End Delay Experiment

In the experiment, there are 10 CRB flows between S0 and R1 with average rates of 10Kbps, 20 Kbps, 40 Kbps, 60 Kbps, 80 Kbps, 100 Kbps, 120 Kbps, 160 Kbps, 200 Kbps and 260 Kbps. The packet delay of these 10 CBR flows is measured. In addition to the 10 observed flows, there are 5 exponential on/off flows from S1 to R1 with rates 10Kbps, 40 Kbps, 80 Kbps, 120 Kbps and 240 Kbps. The on-time and the off time are 500ms. There are five Pareto on/off flows from S2 to R2 with rates 10Kbps, 40 Kbps, 80 Kbps, 120 Kbps and 240 Kbps. The on-time and off-time are 500ms and the parameter shape of the Pareto flows is 1.5. Two 7.8Kbps FTP flows with infinite traffic are also in the system, one from S1 to R1 and the other one from S2 to R2. CBR flows have a fixed packet size of 210 bytes, and all other flows have a fixed packet size uniformly chosen between 128 bytes and 1024 bytes.

Figure 4 and Figure 5 show the average end-to-end delay and maximal end-to-end delay for the ten CBR flows. We can see that WF^2Q algorithm has the best characteristics on both average end-to-end delay and maximal end-to-end delay while

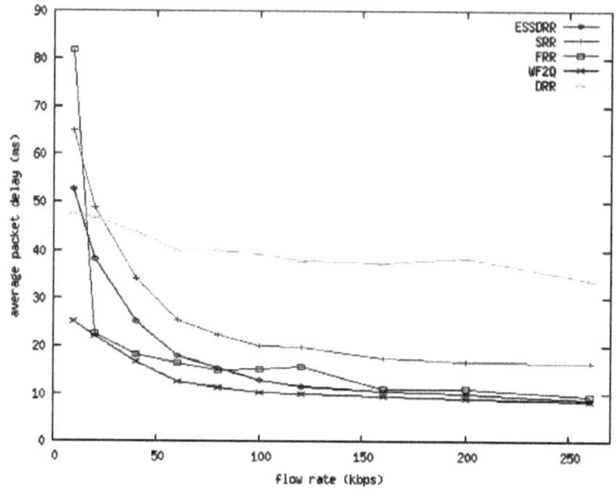

Fig. 4. Average end-to-end delay

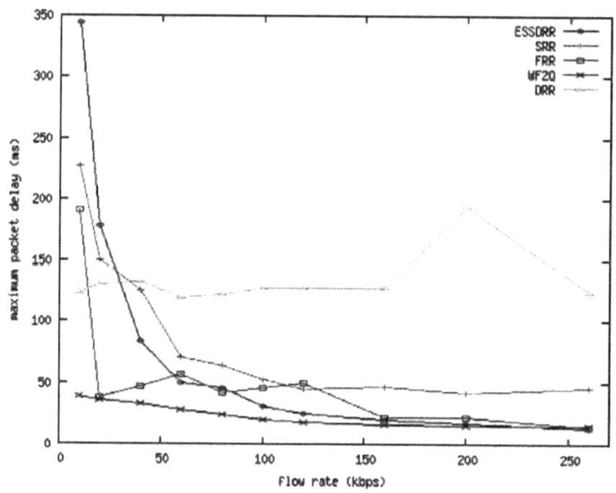

Fig. 5. Maximal end-to-end delay

DRR algorithm has the worst by contrast. The average and maximal end-to-end delay characteristics changed less with different rates. Other algorithms' delay curves tend towards similar: dropping rapidly when flow's rate is increasing.

Now we observe three improved algorithms of DRR (ESSDRR, SRR and FRR). There is a certain distance between the SRR and WF^2Q. It indicates that the delay characteristic of SRR is the worst in these three algorithms. It has the largest average delay and maximal delay. The time delay of ESSDRR and FRR are very closer to WF^2Q algorithm and the delay of ESSDRR is appreciably under FRR. A very interesting fact is that ESSDRR is very smooth while FRR has a certain fluctuation by contrast. This indicates that ESSDRR could strictly guarantee the packet delay which is proportional to flow rates.

4.2 Throughput-Time Distribution Characteristic Experiment

This experiment is designed to demonstrate that the ESSDRR algorithm has a good short-term fairness property. If the flow's throughput is not far away from the pre-assigned value in a short-time period, it means the algorithm has a good short-term fairness property, and it will not cause flow burst. The previous simulation network topology is used here. There are 52 CBR flows between S0 and R0, two of them have the transmit rates of 300Kbps and 600bps and the others 10Kbps. The background flows are the same as the previous experiments.

Figure 6 shows the short-term throughput of the 300kbps flow with different scheduling schemes. Each point in the figure represents the throughput in an interval of 100ms. As the figure shows, the short term throughputs for DRR exhibit heavy fluctuations. It is because the one time service quantum of DRR, which is $w_i \times L_{max}$. Surprisingly, the short-term throughput of SRR exhibits heavy fluctuation too. We consider that it is because we have too many flows in this experiment and the rate difference between these flows is too large. This makes the higher rank of WSS in SRR, and the short-term fairness of SRR has great relationship with the rank. On the other hand, ESSDRR, FRR, and WF^2Q exhibits stable throughput, the throughputs are always close to the ideal rate. This shows that ESSDRR has good short term fairness property while simpler than WF^2Q and FRR.

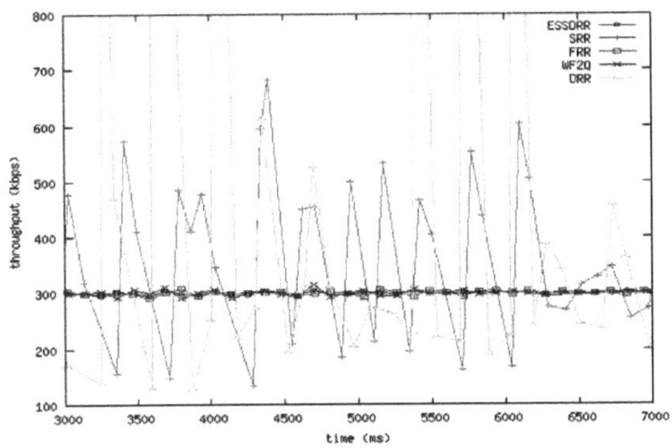

Fig. 6. Short-term throughput

5 Conclusion

In this paper we have proposed ESSDRR, an improved DRR packet scheduling algorithm based on even service sequence, which combining advantages of DRR and

WF^2Q. Our simulation experiments show that this algorithm can provide good fairness, low scheduling delay and low complexity.

Acknowledgements

This work is supported by the 863 project of China (No. 2003AA1Z2100) and the Scientific and Technological Innovation Foundation for Youth teachers of NPU (No. M016213). We gratefully acknowledge the financial and technical support from the committee of the 863 project. We also wish to thank the anonymous reviewers for their constructive comments.

References

1. M. Shreedhar, George Varghese. Efficient fair queuing using deficit round-robin. IEEE/ACM Transactions on Networking, 4(3): 375-385, 1996
2. J. BENNET, H. Zhang. WF2Q: worst case fair weighted fair queuing. In Proceedings of INFOCOM'96, 1996
3. X. Yuan and Z. Duan. "FRR: a Proportional and Worst-Case Fair Round Robin Scheduler " IEEE INFOCOM, 2005
4. A. K. Parekh and R. G.. Gallager, A generalized processor sharing approach for flow control – the single node case. In Proceedings of INFOCOM'92, vol. 2, pp. 915-924, May 1992
5. S. Ramabhadran and J. Pasquale, Stratified Round Robin: A Low Complexity Packet Scheduler with Bandwidth Fairness and Bounded Delay," in ACM SIGCOMM'03 (2003), pages 239-249.
6. S.Cheung and C. Pencea, BSFQ: Bin Sort Fair Queuing," in IEEE INFOCOM'02 (2002).
7. A. Demers, S. Keshav, and S. Shenker, Analysis and Simulation of a Fair Queuing Algorithm," in ACM SIGCOMM'89 (1989).
8. The Network Simulator - ns-2, http://www.isi.edu/nsnam/ns
9. C. Guo, SRR, an O(1) Time Complexity Packet Scheduler for Flows in Multi-Service Packet Networks," in ACM SIGCOMM'01 (2001).
10. L Lenzini, E. Mingozzi, and G. Stea, Aliquem: a Novel DRR Implementation to Achieve Better Latency and Fairness at O(1) Complexity," in IWQoS'02 (2002).

An Improvement on Strong-Password Authentication Protocols

Ya-Fen Chang[2] and Chin-Chen Chang[1, 2]

[1] Department of Information Engineering and Computer Science,
Feng Chia University, Taichung, Taiwan 40724, R.O.C.
ccc@cs.ccu.edu.tw

[2] Department of Computer Science and Information Engineering,
National Chung Cheng University, Chiayi, Taiwan 621, R.O.C.
cyf@cs.ccu.edu.tw

Abstract. Password authentication schemes can be divided into two types. One requires the easy-to-remember password, and the other requires the strong password. In 2000, Sandirigama et al. proposed a simple and secure password authentication protocol (SAS). Then, Lin et al. showed that SAS suffers from two weaknesses and proposed an improvement (OSPA) in 2001. However, Chen and Ku pointed out that both SAS and OSPA are vulnerable to the stolen-verifier attack. We also find that these two protocols lack the property of mutual authentication. Hence, we propose an improvement of SAS and OSPA to defend against the stolen-verifier attack and provide mutual authentication in this paper.

1 Introduction

Password authentication is considered as the most common and simplest authentication mechanisms [1, 2, 6, 8, 12]. Existing password authentication schemes can be divided into two types. One only requires the memorable password and usually results in heavy computation load to the whole system. The other uses the strong password and needs a temper-resistant storage token, e.g. a smart card, to store the strong password. The strong-password authentication scheme needs lighter computation load than the former type; moreover, its design and implementation is simpler.

Recently, Sandirigama et al. proposed a simple strong-password authentication protocol (SAS) [13]. SAS is superior to several well-known protocols [5, 10, 14, 15] by utilizing storage and reducing the processing time and transmission overhead. However, Lin et al. presented that SAS is vulnerable to two weaknesses and proposed an improvement (OSPA) [11].

In most password schemes [3, 6-11, 13-17], the verifiers of the user's passwords are stored by the server to prevent the user's password from being compromised. In [2, 4, 11], the stolen-verifier attack is an attack that the adversary can impersonate the user after stealing the verifier of the user's password. It is obvious that the stolen-verifier attack can be achieved by employing the dictionary attack if weak passwords are used. In [4], it was mentioned that the approach of employing strong passwords does not guarantee the resistance to the stolen-verifier attack even though the dictionary attack can be prevented. Hence, Chen and Ku [4] pointed out that both SAS and

L.T. Yang et al. (Eds.): ICESS 2005, LNCS 3820, pp. 629 – 637, 2005.

OSPA suffer from the stolen-verifier attack. With a deep insight into both of the protocols, we also find that these two protocols do not preserve the property of mutual authentication such that any malicious user can impersonate the server. As a result, we propose an improvement of SAS and OSPA to defend against the stolen-verifier attack and provide mutual authentication in this paper.

The paper is organized as follows. In Section 2, we review SAS and OSPA. Then, we show the ways to mount the stolen-verifier attacks on the SAS and OPSA and how malicious user impersonates the server in Section 3. In Section 4, we present the proposed strong-password authentication protocol. Then, some discussions on our proposed protocol are shown in Section 5. Finally, we draw some conclusions in Section 6.

2 Reviews of SAS and OSPA

First, we describe the notations used throughout this paper in Subsection 2.1. Then, we review SAS and OPSA in Subsections 2.2 and 2.3, respectively.

2.1 Notations

In this subsection, the notations used throughout this paper are introduced as follows.

A: the user
S: the server.
E: the adversary
ID_A/ID_S: the identity of A/S
P_A: the strong password of A
T: a positive integer indicating the number of times the authentication is being executed
N_n: a random number used for the n-th authentication
$\oplus$: the bitwise XOR operation
||: the concatenation symbol
h: a one-way hash function, where $h^2(m)$ denotes m is hashed twice

2.2 A Review of SAS

In this subsection, we are going to show SAS. SAS is divided into two phases: the registration phase and the authentication phase.

2.2.1 Registration Phase

The registration phase is invoked only once when the user joins the system.

Step 1. A calculates $h^2(P_A||N_1)$, where N_1 is an initial random number chosen by A.
Step 2. A sends (ID_A, $h^2(P_A|| N_1)$, N_1) via a secure channel to S.
Step 3. S stores (ID_A, $h^2(P_A|| N_1)$, N_1).

2.2.2 Authentication Phase

The authentication phase is invoked whenever the user wants to access the server. Note that the delivered information is transmitted via a common channel.

For A's n-th login:

Step 1. A sends ID_A and service request to S.

Step 2. S sends N_n to A.

Step 3. A sends (c_1, c_2, c_3) to S, where $c_1=h(P_A \| N_n) \oplus h^2(P_A \| N_n)$, $c_2=h^2(P_A \| N_{n+1}) \oplus h^2(P_A \| N_n)$, and $c_3=N_{n+1}$.

Step 4. S uses the stored verifier $h^2(P_A \| N_n)$ to compute $y_1 = c_1 \oplus h^2(P_A \| N_n)$ and $y_2 = c_2 \oplus h^2(P_A \| N_n)$. If $h(y_1) = h^2(P_A \| N_n)$ holds, S replaces $(ID_A, h^2(P_A \| N_n), N_n)$ with (ID_A, y_2, N_{n+1}) for A's (n+1)-th authentication and grants A his/her service request.

2.3 A Review of OSPA

In this subsection, the detail of OSPA is shown as follows. As SAS, OSPA is also divided into two phases: the registration phase and the authentication phase.

2.3.1 Registration Phase

The registration phase is invoked only once when the user joins the system.

Step 1. A calculates $h^2(P_A \oplus 1)$.

Step 2. A sends $(ID_A, h^2(P_A \oplus 1))$ via a secure channel to S.

Step 3. S stores $(ID_A, h^2(P_A \oplus 1), T=1)$.

2.3.2 Authentication Phase

The authentication phase is invoked whenever the user wants to access the server. Note that the delivered information is transmitted via a common channel.

For A's n-th login:

Step 1. A sends ID_A and service request to S.

Step 2. S sends n to A.

Step 3. A sends (c_1, c_2, c_3) to S, where $c_1=h(P_A \oplus n) \oplus h^2(P_A \oplus n)$, $c_2=h^2(P_A \oplus (n+1)) \oplus h(P_A \oplus n)$, and $c_3=h^3(P_A \oplus (n+1))$.

Step 4. S first checks whether $c_1 \neq c_2$ holds or not. If it holds, S computes $y_1 = c_1 \oplus h^2(P_A \oplus n)$ and $y_2 = c_2 \oplus y_1$, where $h^2(P_A \oplus n)$ is the stored verifier. Then, S checks if $h(y_1) = h^2(P_A \oplus n)$ and $c_3 = h(y_2)$. If they hold, S uses y_2 to be the new verifier for the (n+1)-th authentication and grants A his/her service request.

3 The Weakness of SAS and OSPA

In this section, we are going to show the ways to mount the stolen-verifier attacks on SAS and OPSA and how malicious user impersonates the server in Subsections 3.1 and 3.2, respectively.

3.1 The Stolen-Verifier Attacks

In this subsection, we present the ways, mentioned in [4], to mount the stolen-verifier attacks on the SAS and OPSA. Although the legal user may discover the attack when he/she tries to login next time, E can obtain the needed resource before being detected.

3.1.1 Attack Scenario of SAS

Suppose E has stolen A's verifier $h^2(P_A\|N_n)$ after A's (n-1)-th login.
For A's n-th login:

Step 1. A sends ID_A and service request to S.

Step 2. S sends N_n to A.

Step 3. A sends (c_1, c_2, c_3) to S, where $c_1=h(P_A\|N_n) \oplus h^2(P_A\|N_n)$, $c_2=h^2(P_A\|N_{n+1}) \oplus h^2(P_A\|N_n)$, and $c_3=N_{n+1}$. E intercepts the transmitted data (c_1, c_2, c_3) and computes $c_2'=h^2(P_A'\|N'_{n+1}) \oplus h^2(P_A\|N_n)$, and $c_3'=N'_{n+1}$, where P_A' and N'_{n+1} are selected by E. Then, E sends (c_1, c_2', c_3') to S.

Step 4. S uses the stored verifier $h^2(P_A\|N_n)$ to compute $y_1 = c_1 \oplus h^2(P_A\|N_n)$ and $h^2(P_A'\|N'_{n+1}) = c_2' \oplus h^2(P_A\|N_n)$. $h(y_1) = h^2(P_A\|N_n)$ must hold because c_1 is calculated by A himself/herself. Hence, S will replace $(ID_A, h^2(P_A\|N_n), N_n)$ with $(ID_A, h^2(P_A'\|N'_{n+1}), N'_{n+1})$ for A's (n+1)-th authentication. Because P_A' is chosen by E, E can use P_A' to access the server as A until the attack is found.

3.1.2 Attack Scenario of OSPA

Suppose E has stolen A's verifier $h^2(P_A \oplus n)$ after A's (n-1)-th login.
For A's n-th login:

Step 1. A sends ID_A and service request to S.

Step 2. S sends n to A.

Step 3. A sends (c_1, c_2, c_3) to S, where $c_1=h(P_A\oplus n) \oplus h^2(P_A\oplus n)$, $c_2=h^2(P_A\oplus(n+1)) \oplus h(P_A\oplus n)$, and $c_3=h^3(P_A\oplus(n+1))$. E intercepts the transmitted data (c_1, c_2, c_3) and computes $c_2'=h^2(P_A'\oplus(n+1)) \oplus (c_1 \oplus h^2(P_A\oplus n))$, and $c_3'=h(h^2(P_A'\oplus(n+1)))$, where P_A' is selected by E. Then, E sends (c_1, c_2', c_3') to S.

Step 4. S first checks whether $c_1\neq c_2'$ holds or not. If it holds, S computes $y_1 =c_1 \oplus h^2(P_A\oplus n)$ and $h^2(P_A'\oplus(n+1)) = c_2'\oplus y_1$, where $h^2(P_A\oplus n)$ is the stored verifier. Then, S checks if $h(y_1) = h^2(P_A\oplus n)$ and $c_3' = h(h^2(P_A'\oplus(n+1)))$. It is obvious that they must hold. As a result, S uses $h^2(P_A'\oplus(n+1))$ to be the new verifier for the (n+1)-th authentication and grants E his/her service request. Because P_A' is chosen by E, E can use P_A' to access the server as A until the attack is found.

3.2 Impersonation Attacks

In this subsection, we show how malicious user can impersonate the server S when the legal user A wants to access the server.

3.2.1 Attack Scenario of SAS

Suppose E wants to impersonate S during A's n-th login.
For A's n-th login:

Step 1. A sends ID_A and the service request to S.

Step 2. E intercepts the data sent by A and sends N'_n to A. Note that N'_n is not needed to be equal to N_n since A does not record N_n locally.

Step 3. A sends (c_1, c_2, c_3) to S, where c_1=h(P_A|| N'_n) ⊕ h^2(P_A|| N'_n), c_2=h^2(P_A|| N_{n+1}) ⊕ h^2(P_A|| N'_n), and c_3=N_{n+1}. E just intercepts the transmitted data (c_1, c_2, c_3) and grants A his/her service request. A cannot authenticate S in SAS such that E is considered to be S.

In this case, it is probably that A will reveal more personal secrecy since A will use the resource provided by E.

3.2.2 Attack Scenario of OSPA

Suppose E wants to impersonate S during A's n-th login.

For A's n-th login:

Step 1. A sends ID_A and service request to S.

Step 2. E intercepts the data sent by A and sends n′ to A. Note that n′ is not needed to be equal to n since A does not record n locally.

Step 3. A sends (c_1, c_2, c_3) to S, where c_1=h(P_A⊕n′) ⊕ h^2(P_A⊕n′), c_2=h^2(P_A⊕(n′+1)) ⊕ h(P_A⊕n′), and c_3=h^3(P_A⊕(n′+1)). E intercepts the transmitted data (c_1, c_2, c_3) and grants A his/her service request. As in SAS, A cannot authenticate S in OPSA such that E is considered to be S.

As mentioned in the previous subsection, it is probably that A will reveal more personal secrecy since A will use the resource provided by E. Moreover, E can also use (c_1, c_2, c_3) to impersonate A to access S for A's n′-th login if n′>n. In this case, A reveals important and useful information to E because A cannot authenticate S.

4 The Proposed Strong-Password Authentication Protocol

In this section, we are going to introduce our proposed strong-password authentication protocol, which can defend against the stolen-verifier attack and provides mutual authentication to prevent malicious users from impersonating S. As SAS and OSPA, the proposed strong-password authentication is divided into two phases: the registration phase and the authentication phase. Unlike SAS and OSPA, S has a unique seed value SEED for the system users in our proposed protocol. As mentioned in Section 1, the user needs a temper-resistant storage token, e.g. a smart card, to store the strong password. SEED can be also stored in the smart card while the user joins the system. Moreover, the unique seed value SEED enables the user to set a single secret on several servers since the user only needs a strong password. Our proposed protocol is presented as follows.

4.1 Registration Phase

The registration phase is invoked only once when the user joins the system. Note that the delivered data is transmitted through a secure channel.

Step 1. A calculates h^2(P_A||N_1), where N_1 is an initial random number chosen by A.

Step 2. A sends (ID_A, h^2(P_A|| N_1), N_1) to S.

Step 3. S stores (ID_A, h^2(P_A|| N_1)⊕h(SEED), N_1) for A's first authentication and stores (ID_S, SEED) in A's smart card.

4.2 Authentication Phase

The authentication phase is invoked whenever the user wants to access the server. Note that the delivered information is transmitted via a common channel.

For A's n-th login:

Step 1. A inserts his/her smart card into the card reader and sends ID_A and service request to S.

Step 2. S randomly chooses numbers D and N_{n+1}, which are not used before, and sends N_n, N_{n+1}, ID_S, SEED $\oplus$ D, $h(D) \oplus h(N_n)$, $h(D) \oplus h(N_{n+1})$ to A.

Step 3. A computes r_1= (SEED $\oplus$ D) $\oplus$ SEED and checks whether $h(N_n)= (h(D) \oplus h(N_n)) \oplus h(r_1)$ and $h(N_{n+1})= (h(D) \oplus h(N_{n+1})) \oplus h(r_1)$. If they hold, A sends (c_1, c_2, c_3) to S, where $c_1=h(P_A|| N_n) \oplus h(h^2(P_A|| N_n) ||D)$, $c_2=h^2(P_A|| N_{n+1}) \oplus h(h(P_A|| N_n)||D)$, and $c_3=h(h^2(P_A|| N_{n+1})||D)$ to S.

Step 4. S uses the stored verifier $h^2(P_A|| N_n)= (h^2(P_A|| N_n)\oplus h(SEED)) \oplus h(SEED)$ to compute $y_1 = c_1 \oplus h(h^2(P_A|| N_n) ||D)$ and $y_2 = c_2\oplus h(y_1||D)$. If $h(y_1) = h^2(P_A|| N_n)$ and $c_3=h(y_2||D)$ hold, S replaces (ID_A, $h^2(P_A|| N_n) \oplus h(SEED)$, N_n) with (ID_A, $y_2\oplus h(SEED)$, N_{n+1}) for A's (n+1)-th authentication and grants A his/her service request.

5 Discussions

In the following, we will show the properties that the proposed protocol achieves to demonstrate that it is secure, efficient and practical.

***Property 1*: The protocol provides mutual authentication**

As mentioned in Subsection 4.1, the user gets the unique seed value SEED after joining the system. In the authentication phase, S sends N_n, N_{n+1}, ID_S, SEED $\oplus$ D, $h(D) \oplus h(N_n)$, and $h(D) \oplus h(N_{n+1})$ to the user A in Step 2. Then, A can determine whether N_n and N_{n+1} are sent by S by checking if $h(N_n)$ = h(SEED $\oplus$ (SEED $\oplus$ D)) $\oplus$ $(h(D) \oplus h(N_n))$ and $h(N_{n+1})$ = h(SEED $\oplus$ (SEED $\oplus$ D)) $\oplus$ $(h(D) \oplus h(N_{n+1}))$ hold or not. Since SEED is stored in the smart card and all computing operations are done by the smart card [18], no malicious user can get SEED to cheat the innocent users by impersonating S.

In Step 3 in the authentication phase, A sends (c_1, c_2, c_3) to S, where $c_1=h(P_A|| N_n) \oplus h(h^2(P_A|| N_n)||D)$, $c_2=h^2(P_A|| N_{n+1}) \oplus h(h(P_A|| N_n)||D)$, and $c_3=h(h^2(P_A|| N_{n+1})||D)$ to S. Then, S uses the stored verifier $h^2(P_A|| N_n)$ to compute $y_1 = c_1 \oplus h(h^2(P_A|| N_n)||D)$ and $y_2 = c_2\oplus h(y_1||D)$. If $h(y_1) = h^2(P_A|| N_n)$ and $c_3=h(y_2||D)$ hold, it denotes that the requesting user must be A since A owns not only the strong password P_A but also SEED in his/her smart card. According to the above analyses, this property is confirmed.

***Property 2*: The proposed scheme can defend against the stolen-verifier attack**

Suppose the scenario that E has stolen A's verifier $h^2(P_A || N_n) \oplus h(SEED)$ after A's (n-1)-th login. First of all, since SEED is unknown to E, E cannot retrieve $h^2(P_A || N_n)$. That is, A can get neither $h^2(P_A || N_n)$ nor A's password.

For A's n-th login:

Step 1. A inserts his/her smart card into the card reader and sends ID_A and service request to S.

Step 2. S sends N_n, N_{n+1}, ID_S, SEED ⊕ D, h(D) ⊕ $h(N_n)$, h(D) ⊕ $h(N_{n+1})$ to A, where D and N_{n+1} are random numbers chosen by S. E eavesdrops the data sent by S.

Step 3. A computes r_1= (SEED ⊕ D) ⊕ SEED and checks whether $h(N_n)$= (h(D) ⊕ $h(N_n)$) ⊕ $h(r_1)$ and $h(N_{n+1})$= (h(D) ⊕ $h(N_{n+1})$) ⊕ $h(r_1)$. If they hold, A sends (c_1, c_2, c_3) to S, where c_1=$h(P_A|| N_n)$ ⊕ $h(h^2(P_A|| N_n)||D)$, c_2=$h^2(P_A|| N_{n+1})$ ⊕ $h(h(P_A|| N_n)||D)$, and c_3=$h(h^2(P_A|| N_{n+1})||D)$ to S. E intercepts the transmitted data (c_1, c_2, c_3); however, E does not know SEED to get D to reveal $h(P_A|| N_n)$ and $h^2(P_A || N_n)$ for computing $c_2'$and c_3' as shown in Subsection 3.1.

It is obvious that E cannot mount the stolen-verifier attack on our proposed protocol successfully even the user's verifier is stolen.

***Property 3*: The proposed protocol is secure**

As mentioned in Property 1, our proposed protocol confirms mutual authentication between the user and the server. Hence, it is sure that the proposed protocol is resistant to server spoofing attack and impersonation attack. Because S generates random numbers D and N_{n+1} during the user's n-th login, S can easily check whether the data sent by the user in Step 3 in the authentication phase is received before. As a result, replay attack cannot succeed in our proposed protocol. In Property 2, we have shown that the proposed protocol can defend against the stolen-verifier attack. As shown in Step 4 of authentication phase, S uses the stored verifier $h^2(P_A|| N_n)$= ($h^2(P_A|| N_n)$⊕h(SEED)) ⊕h(SEED) to compute y_1 = c_1 ⊕ $h(h^2(P_A|| N_n) ||D)$ and y_2 = c_2⊕ $h(y_1||D)$. If $h(y_1)$ = $h^2(P_A|| N_n)$ and c_3=$h(y_2||D)$ hold, S replaces (ID_A, $h^2(P_A|| N_n)$ ⊕ h(SEED), N_n) with (ID_A, y_2 ⊕ h(SEED), N_{n+1}) for A's (n+1)-th authentication and grants A his/her service request. The above approaches ensure both the legality of the user and the validity of the new verifier. That is, the denial-of-service attack cannot work in our proposed scheme. As far as the password guessing attacks are concerned, it is obvious that our proposed method can defend against them. It is because all parameters transmitted are all concealed with the secret number D, which is used only once. According to the above analyses, we can sum up that our proposed protocol is secure.

***Property 4*: The proposed protocol is efficient and practical**

As mentioned in Section 4, either S or A only computes hash operations. No time-consuming operation, e.g. exponentiation, asymmetric en/decryption, or symmetric en/decryption, is needed. Moreover, the unique seed value SEED enables the user to set a single secret on several servers. The user only needs a smart card to store the strong password and the unique seed values issued by different servers. According to the above characteristics, it is sure that our proposed protocol is not only efficient but also practical.

6 Conclusions

Chen and Ku pointed out that both SAS and OSPA are vulnerable to the stolen-verifier attack. Moreover, we find that mutual authentication is not confirmed in these two protocols. As a result, we propose an improvement of SAS and OSPA to defend against the stolen-verifier attack and provide mutual authentication. As mentioned in the previous section, it is obvious that the proposed protocol is secure, practical, and efficient.

References

1. Bellovin, S. and Merritt, M., "Encrypted Key Exchange: Password-based Protocols Secure against Dictionary Attacks," Proceedings of IEEE Symposium on Research in Security and Privacy, Oakland, California, May 1992, pp. 72-84.
2. Bellovin, S. and Merritt, M., "Augmented Encrypted Key Exchange: A Password-based Protocol Secure against Dictionary Attacks and Password-file Compromise," Proceedings of 1st ACM Conference on Computer and Communications Security, Fairfax, Virginia, November 1993, pp. 244-250.
3. Boyko, V., MacKenzie, P., and Patel S., "Provably Secure Password Authentication Key Exchange Using Diffie-Hellman," Proceedings of EuroCrypt 2000, May 2000, pp. 156-171.
4. Chen, C.M. and Ku, W.C., "Stolen-verifier Attack on Two New Strong-password Authentication Protocol," IEICE Transactions on Communications, Vol. E85-B, No. 11, November 2002, pp. 2519-2521.
5. Haller, N., "The S/KEY One-time Password System," Proceedings of Internet Society Symposium on Network and Distributed System Security, San Diego, California, February 1994, pp. 151-158.
6. Jablon, D., "Strong Password-only Authenticated Key Exchange," ACM Computer Communication Review, Vol. 26, No. 5, September 1996, pp. 5-26.
7. Jablon, D., "B-SPEKE," Integrity Science White Paper, September 1999.
8. Kwon, T., "Ultimate Solution to Authentication via Memorable Password," A Proposal for IEEE P13631: Password-based Authentication, May 2000.
9. Kwon, T., "Authentication and Key Agreement via Memorable Password," Proceedings on NDSS 2001 Symposium Conference, San Diego, California, February 2001.
10. Lamport, L., "Password Authentication with Insecure Communication," Communications of ACM, Vol. 24, No. 11, November 1981, pp. 770-772.
11. Lin, C.L., Sun, H.M., Steiner, M., and Hwang, T., "Attacks and Solutions on Strong-password Authentication," IEICE Transactions on Communications, Vol. E84-B, No. 9, September 2001, pp. 2622-2627.
12. Lomas, M., Gong, L., Saltzer, J., and Needham, R., "Reducing Risks from Poorly Chosen Key," Proceedings of the 12th ACM Symposium on Operating Systems Principles, Litchfield Park, Arizona, December 1989, pp. 14-18.
13. Sandirigama, M., Shimizu, A., and Noda, M.T., "Simple and Secure Password Authentication Protocol (SAS)," IEICE Transactions on Communications, Vol. E83-B, No. 6, June 2000, pp. 1363-1365.
14. Shimizu, A., "A Dynamic Password Authentication Method by One-way Function," IEICE Transactions on Information and Systems, Vol. J73-D-I, No. 7, July 1990, pp. 630-636.

15. Shimizu, A., "A Dynamic Password Authentication Method by One-way Function," System and Computers in Japan, Vol. 22, No. 7, 1991.
16. Shimizu, A., Horioka, T., and Inagaki, H., "A Password Authentication Method for Contents Communication on the Internet," IEICE Transactions on Communications, Vol. E81-B, No. 8, August 1998, pp. 1666-1763.
17. Wu, T., "The Secure Remote Password Protocol," Proceedings of Internet Society Symposium on Network and Distributed System Security, San Diego, California, March 1999, pp. 97-111.
18. Yi, X., Tan, C.H., Siew, C.K. and Syed, M.R., "ID-based Key Agreement for Multimedia Encryption," IEEE Transactions on Consumer Electronics, Vol. 48, No. 2, May 2002, pp. 298-303.

Two-Step Hierarchical Protocols for Establishing Session Keys in Wireless Sensor Networks

Kyungsan Cho[1], Soo-Young Lee[2], and JongEun Kim[1]

[1] Division of Information and Computer Science,
Dankook University, Seoul, Korea
{kscho, semico}@dankook.ac.kr
[2] Department of Electrical and Computer Engineering,
Auburn University, Auburn, AL 36849, U.S.A.
leesooy@eng.auburn.edu

Abstract. Secure communication between sensor nodes is required in most of sensor networks, especially those deployed in a hostile environment. Due to the limited energy and computational capability on each sensor node, a public key cryptosystem is not a viable option for a wireless sensor network. Hence, the idea of key pre-distribution has been widely adopted in most of the session key establishment protocols proposed so far. In this paper, 1) several typical session key establishment protocols are analyzed and compared in terms of common criteria, 2) the requirements for improving upon the existing protocols are derived, and 3) two advanced protocols which take a two-step hierarchical approach to satisfying the requirements are proposed. Through the performance analysis, it has been shown that the proposed protocols improve the connectivity of a sensor network, uniqueness of session keys and security over the existing protocols.

1 Introduction

Sensor networks are expected to provide cost-effective solutions in various applications. A sensor network consists of a large number of sensor nodes deployed in a certain area and few base nodes. Each sensor node is equipped with a small size of memory and limited computational capability, and is battery-powered. Therefore, energy and storage-efficient operation of sensor nodes is essential in practical sensor networks.

In many applications, it is required to achieve a certain level of security in exchanging information between sensor nodes, especially when a sensor network is deployed in a hostile environment as in military applications. Thus, one of the important issues that need to be addressed in designing a sensor network is its security [1]-[4].

A sensor node may communicate with other sensor nodes and also base nodes. Security of communication channel between a sensor node and a base node can be provided by a public key based protocol since base nodes have sufficient energy and hardware required for executing such a protocol [2][3]. Alternatively,

L.T. Yang et al. (Eds.): ICESS 2005, LNCS 3820, pp. 638–649, 2005.

a secret key may be assigned to each sensor node before deployment, which is to be shared with the base node. Communication between sensor nodes can be realized indirectly via a base node in order to utilize the secure channels between sensor nodes and the base node. While this approach guarantees full connectivity of sensor nodes, it incurs a longer communication latency and leads to a poor fault tolerance. Also, the base node becomes a bottleneck which can cause traffic congestion. Therefore, direct communication is preferred between sensor nodes.

However, the limited resources available on sensor nodes do not allow a public key cryptosystem to be employed for direct communication between sensor nodes. As a result, various schemes where information for establishing session keys to be shared between communicating sensor nodes is distributed before their deployment have been proposed [5]-[10]. While each of the protocols achieves a certain degree of security, there exists significant room for improvement in terms of security, connectivity, overhead, etc. In this paper, several existing protocols for establishing session keys between sensor nodes are analyzed and compared in terms of a set of important security and performance metrics. From the analysis results, we derive a set of requirements desirable for advanced protocols improved upon the existing protocols. Then, we propose a couple of two-step hierarchical protocols satisfying the requirements. Our main objective is to improve the connectivity of a sensor network, uniqueness of sensor keys and security over the existing protocols by taking the hierarchical approach.

In Section 2, various typical key management protocols are analyzed and compared. In Section 3, the requirements for improving the existing protocols are discussed and two new advanced protocols satisfying the requirements are proposed. In Section 4, the performance of the proposed protocols is analyzed. In Section 5, a summary is provided.

2 Analysis of Existing Protocols

2.1 BROSK (BROadcast Session Key Negotiation Protocol)

In order to enhance security of the single session-key protocol, the BROSK protocol employs a common master key which is used by all sensor nodes during the session key negotiation phase [5]. Each sensor node first broadcasts an introduction message of its ID, nonce and MAC (Message Authentication Code). Once a sensor node receives the introduction messages broadcasted by its neighbors, it can generate a session key for each neighbor through the MAC of two nonces.

This protocol requires lower communication overhead and generates a unique session key for each pair of sensor nodes. However, if the master key is exposed to a third party, all session keys of a sensor network may be compromised.

2.2 Random Key Pre-distribution

Eschenhaur and Gligor proposed a random key pre-distribution protocol which saves the storage space required on each sensor node without sacrificing the sensor network security significantly [6]. It consists of pre-distribution of random keys before deployment and discovery of a common key afterward. A large pool, P, of keys is defined within the domain of all possible keys that can be used as session keys. A set of m keys (referred to as *key ring*) randomly selected from P and their respective IDs are assigned to each sensor node prior to its deployment. Once the sensor network is deployed, each sensor node recognizes its neighbors through broadcasting of node IDs, and then communicates with each of its neighbors, looking for a common key in their key rings. This key agreement process can be carried out by exchanging the key IDs or encrypted messages. In the case of exchanging the key IDs, each sensor node broadcasts the IDs of keys in its key ring as plain-text. If there is a common ID between two sensor nodes, the corresponding key becomes the session key for them. In the case of exchanging the encrypted messages, each sensor node encrypts the challenge α with a key (k_i where i is the key index) in its key ring, and broadcasts the challenge (α) and encrypted challenge ($Ek_i(\alpha)$). If the intended neighbor can decrypt $Ek_i(\alpha)$ by one of its keys, which must be identical with k_i, and reveal the challenge, k_i is used as the session key between them.

One of the drawbacks in this approach is that the secure channel between two sensor nodes can be established only when there is a common key between them. Also, uniqueness of each session key is not guaranteed, and there is no explicit session key verification process. In addition, a third party may eavesdrop the plain-text messages of IDs or launch the DoS attack when the encryption is used for key agreement.

2.3 OKS (Overlap Key Sharing)

The OKS protocol uses a long bit sequence, instead of a large pool of keys, for deriving session keys [5]. Before deployment, a random segment of the bit sequence is stored in each sensor node. After deployment, each sensor node broadcasts its bit segment, and checks if there is any overlap between its bit segment and the one received from each of its neighbors. When there is an overlap, the overlapping portion of the bit segment is used to generate a session key of certain length through hashing for the two sensor nodes.

While, compared to the random key pre-distribution method, the storage and communication requirements can be reduced, the network connectivity is lower.

2.4 Q-Composite Key

The q-composite key protocol improves security of a sensor network, over the random key pre-distribution protocol, by enhancing uniqueness of each session key [7]. Its key pre-distribution step is the same as that of the random key pre-distribution protocol. In the session key agreement step, each sensor node makes a puzzle for each of the keys in its key ring and broadcasts the puzzles. When a sensor node receives a puzzle, it finds a key in its key ring, which gives the correct answer to the puzzle, if there is one. The answer is then sent to the neighboring sensor node from which the puzzle was received. If the number of such common keys is at least q between two sensor nodes, a session key for the nodes is generated from the common keys through hashing. This protocol lowers the probability that two or more pairs of sensor nodes use the same session key, and is less vulnerable to eavesdropping attacks since the puzzles (instead of the key IDs) are broadcast. However, the puzzles are to be broadcast individually, which increases the energy consumption. In addition, the network connectivity becomes lower.

2.5 Node ID Based Keys

A protocol that is similar to the ABK protocol [11] developed for mobile networks was proposed, and it uses node IDs to reduce communication overhead [8]. Before deployment, each sensor node is assigned with a set of keys whose IDs are generated from its node ID through a random mapping function. The mapping function is known to all sensor nodes. Therefore, any sensor node can compute the IDs of all the keys stored in each of its neighbors once it finds out the node ID of the neighbor.

The advantages of this protocol are the lower communication overhead required and the improved security of session keys generated. However, a drawback is that every sensor node can find out the IDs of keys shared between any two nodes.

2.6 Blom's Protocol

The Blom's protocol exploits a symmetric matrix for generation of session keys, which guarantees security of a sensor network as long as no more than λ nodes are compromised [12]. Let N denote the number of nodes in a sensor network. A $(\lambda + 1) \times N$ matrix G is constructed and is kept public. Also, a random $(\lambda + 1) \times (\lambda + 1)$ symmetric matrix D is generated and kept secret. Let's define matrix A to be $(D \cdot G)^t$. Then, it is easy to see that $K = A \cdot G = (A \cdot G)^t$. That is, K is symmetric, i.e., $K_{ij} = K_{ji}$ where K_{ij} is the element in K in the ith row and the jth column.

Now, before deployment, the ith row of matrix A and the ith column of matrix G are stored in sensor node i. Note that the ith row of matrix A is known to sensor node i only. Any two nodes exchange their columns of matrix G, and then each of them computes the dot product between its row of matrix A and the column of matrix G received from the other node. The dot product K_{ij} computed by node i is the same as K_{ji} obtained by node j, which is used as their session key. Full connectivity of a sensor network is achieved by this protocol.

Du et. al. proposed a modified version of the Blom's protocol in order to improve security of a sensor network and lower the storage requirement by employing multiple key spaces (a key space is a pair of matrices G and D), at the expense of sacrificed network connectivity [13].

2.7 Comparison of Existing Protocols

In Table 1, the existing protocols reviewed in this section are compared in terms of several metrics. It is assumed that two neighboring sensor nodes can directly communicate with each other. In the table, communication overhead includes all the transmissions for establishing a session key between two sensor nodes, and computation overhead is per a pair of sensor nodes. As shown in the table, all the existing protocols reviewed have one or more limitations. The existing protocols with the pre-distributed key information (refer to Sections 2.2, 2.4, 2.3, and 2.5) show weakness in the connectivity, key uniqueness and security. The other protocols have vulnerability to various attacks.

Table 1. Comparison of the existing protocols where m is the size of key ring

	BROSK	Random (Encrypt)	OKS	q-composite	Node ID	Blom
Pre-distributed information	master key	$m\times$ (key, ID)	bit seq.	$m\times$ (key, ID)	mapping func.	row/ column
session key generation	random	single shared	overlapping bit seq.	composite shared	composite shared	single shared
Connectivity	○	△	△	△	△	○
key uniqueness	○	×	△	△	△	○
key verification	×	×	×	×	○	×
communication (1)	2	$2\times m$	2	$2\times m$	2	2
communication (2)	2	2	2	2	2	2
computation (3)	MAC 6	encrypt/decr 2m/$2m^2$	comp/hash 2/2	puzzle/sol/hash 2m/2m/2	keygen/comp 2/$2m^2$	product $2(\lambda+1)$
DoS attack	×	×	△	×	△	○
Eavesdropping	○	○	×	○	△	△
Node attack	×/○	×	○	△	×	△

○: good, △: fair, ×: poor, (1) number of transmissions for setting up session keys ; (2) number of transmissions for exchanging session keys and verification(we add two transmissions to the protocols without verification process) ; (3) computation for setting up session keys only(operations and times).

3 Proposed Protocols with Two Step Hierarchy

3.1 Requirements for Advanced Protocols

To improve the existing protocols analyzed in Section 2, the desirable characteristics for a session key generation protocol are defined on connectivity, uniqueness of the session key, communication overhead and non-vulnerability to various attacks.

- Connectivity: For the direct communication between neighboring sensor nodes, higher connectivity is required. The protocols using the pre-distributed key information have a limited connectivity. One way to increase connectivity of a sensor network is to reduce the size of key pool and/or increase that of key ring. However, this makes it more likely that a third party

may find out most session keys in a sensor network by attacking fewer sensor nodes. Hence, a protocol is to enhance connectivity of a sensor network without jeopardizing its security.
- Uniqueness of Session Key: In order to minimize the probability that compromising some sensor nodes exposes session keys of other nodes, as many session keys as possible are to be unique. However, session keys generated by the pre-distributed key information could be duplicated. Thus, uniqueness should be supported for the pre-distributed key approaches.
- Communication Overhead: Transmission is the most energy consuming process. In sensor networks, exchanging node IDs of neighboring sensor nodes and agreement of sensor key between two sensor nodes (transferring session keys and verifying them) are inevitable. Thus, four transmissions are unavoidable. Encrypting messages or employing puzzles for a higher level of network security causes additional transmissions. A protocol needs to minimize the communication overhead while achieving a required level of security.
- Non-vulnerability to Attacks: Any information transferred in the plain text is vulnerable to the eavesdropping attacks. A third party may launch the DoS attack on certain sensor nodes by sending a large number of encrypted messages or puzzles to them. For enhancing security of a sensor network, it is desirable to limit the amount or effective period of information that may be made public, and to make it impossible to derive session keys from such information.

3.2 Proposed Protocols

In this section, we propose two hierarchical protocols for session key establishment to satisfy the above requirements. They are referred to as Protocol I and Protocol II. The common feature of the proposed protocols is that they all take a two-step approach to establishing session keys after deployment of sensor nodes. In the first step, a secret initial key is generated by each pair of neighboring nodes, which is used for the agreement of a session key in the second step and then discarded. The second step allows two neighboring sensor nodes to decide on their session key through random generation, which makes session keys unique and, thus, a high level of network security is achieved.

This two-step approach has the following advantages. Since the initial key generated in the first step is used only once, its required security level doesn't have to be as high as that for a session key, which enhances connectivity of the sensor network. Each sensor node can filter out those encrypted session keys, which do not need to be decrypted, by examining the IDs of senders. Hence, both of the proposed protocols are not vulnerable to DoS attacks.

3.3 Protocol I

In the first step, the node ID based approach is employed in generation of the initial keys, followed by session key establishment in the second step. The random key pre-distribution of the node ID based protocol is carried out before sensor node deployment. The overall operation of Protocol I may be described as follows:

1. Each sensor node broadcasts its node ID.
2. Each sensor node computes the IDs of keys stored in each of the neighboring nodes. If the sensor node finds one or more key IDs common to its and neighbor's key rings, it generates an initial key by hashing the common keys in its key ring.
3. Each pair of neighboring sensor nodes generates a session key for their secure communication. One of the two nodes (sender), which may be determined by their node IDs, e.g., whichever node with a smaller ID when the sum of the two IDs is odd, creates a random key to be used as their session key and encrypts it with the initial key. The encrypted session key is sent to the other node (receiver).
4. The receiver node extracts the session key from the encrypted session key through decrypting and, for verification purpose, sends the session key encrypted by the session key back to the sender.

Protocol I has the following characteristics:

- The size of key ring on each sensor node and the size of key pool can be selected to enhance the network connectivity without affecting security of session keys negatively since session keys are independent of initial keys.
- Session keys are guaranteed to be unique.
- Communication overhead is minimal (four transmissions) since only the node IDs and the encrypted session keys are exchanged between sensor nodes.

3.4 Protocol II

One way to achieve full connectivity of a sensor network is to employ the Blom's approach in the first step. That is, the first step of Protocol II generates initial keys by the Blom's protocol, and the second step creates session keys using the initial keys as in Protocol I.

The characteristics of Protocol II are:

- Connectivity between any two sensor nodes is guaranteed by the Blom's protocol.
- A third party cannot derive the initial keys by eavesdropping alone since the rows of matrix A are not exchanged between sensor nodes.
- Communication overhead is low (four transmissions) since only the node IDs, columns of matrix G, and (encryted) session keys are exchanged between sensor nodes.
- By having the columns of matrix G independent of each other, the initial keys generated in the first step can be made unique, which prevents other initial keys (and accordingly session keys) from being compromised due to a node capture.

4 Performance Analysis

In this section, the performance of the two proposed protocols is analyzed in terms of network connectivity, uniqueness of session key, communication and computation overheads, and storage requirements. We define *connectivity* to be the probability that any two sensor nodes share a sufficient number (q) of keys in their key rings from which a session key can be derived for a secure connection. Also, *interdependency* of session keys is defined to be the probability that a session key between two un-compromised sensor nodes is exposed when some other nodes are captured by the attacker.

Since connectivity in the existing protocols with the pre-distributed key information is determined probabilistically, there is always the chance that neighboring sensors may not be connected. One way to enhance the network connectivity is to reduce the size of key pool (P) and/or to increase the size of key ring (m). However, it substantially sacrifices the uniqueness of session keys and thus the network security. In addition, as the size of the key ring, m, is increased for high connectivity, the computational overhead and storage requirement in each sensor node also increase. However, the first step in the proposed protocols enhances the connectivity of sensor network greatly and the uniqueness of session keys is guaranteed by the second step.

4.1 Protocol I

Network Connectivity and Uniqueness of Session Key. In Protocol I, the initial keys generated in the first step are used only once and, therefore, it can increase connectivity between neighboring sensor nodes. In the second step of Protocol I each pair of neighboring sensor nodes derives a session key through random generation, which guarantees uniqueness of each session key and hence improves security of a sensor network greatly.

In Figure 1, the network connectivity that can be achieved by Protocol I is shown with P in the range of 2000 to 10000 and m not greater than 200. As shown in the figure, one can achieve high connectivity over 0.99, and low computational and memory requirements, by properly selecting small m and P. Note that such small m and P would not affect the interdependency of session keys since the session keys are independent of m and P in the proposed protocols.

Communication Overhead. There are 4 transmissions required between two neighboring sensor nodes. Each sensor node broadcasts its node ID (n bits where the number of nodes, N, is not greater than 2^n) in the first step. In the second step, one of them sends the encrypted session key to the other which in turn sends back the encrypted initial key for session key verification (B bits). Thus, the communication overhead is minimized.

Computation Overhead. In the first step, each sensor node computes the IDs of m keys in each of its neighbors, and generates an initial key through hashing. In the second step, a session key is created, which is encrypted and subsequently

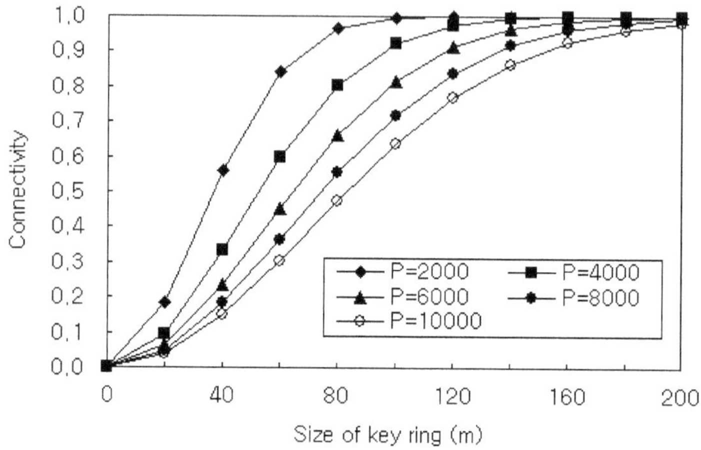

Fig. 1. Connectivity achieved by Protocol I (equivalent to q=1)

decrypted, and for verification of the session key the initial key is also encrypted and decrypted later.

Storage Requirement. Each sensor node needs to store its node ID (n bits) and key ring (m keys: $m \times B$ bits, and m key IDs: $m \times n$ bits).

The characteristics of Protocol I analyzed above are summarized in Table 2.

Table 2. Characteristics of Protocol I

pre-distribution info.	session key				communication		computation		DoS	eaves-drop	node attack
	key gen.	uni-queness	connec-tivity	verifi-cation	key gen.	key exch.	key gen.	key exch.			
mapping function	random gen.	○	○	○	2× node ID	session key veri. info.	†	2×encrypt 2×decrypt	△	○	○

† : $2m\times$ key ID calculations, $2m^2$ key ID comparisons, 2× initial key generations, and a session key generation.

4.2 Protocol II

Network Connectivity and Uniqueness of Session Key. The Blom's protocol employed in the first step guarantees full connectivity of a sensor network, i.e., any two sensor nodes are connected. As in Protocol I, every session key is unique.

Communication Overhead. In the first step, each sensor node broadcasts its node ID and one column ($(\lambda + 1) \times 1$) of matrix G ($B(\lambda + 1)$ bits) in one transmission. In the second step, the encrypted session key (B bits) and verification message (B bits) are transmitted between two neighboring sensor nodes. That is, the total number of transmissions between the two sensor nodes is 4.

Computation Overhead. In the first step, each sensor node computes the dot product with a row of matrix A and a column of matrix G, each with $\lambda + 1$ elements. In the second step, each pair of neighboring sensor nodes generates a session key, encrypts the session key and verification information, and decrypts them.

Storage Requirement. Each sensor node is to store its node ID (n bits), a column of matrix G ($B(\lambda + 1)$ bits) and a row of matrix A ($B(\lambda + 1)$ bits).

Table 3 summarizes the characteristics of Protocol II.

Table 3. Characteristics of Protocol II

pre-distribution info.	session key				communication		computation		DoS	eaves-drop	node attack
	key gen.	uniqueness	connectivity	verification	key gen.	key exch.	key gen.	key exch.			
matrix row column	random gen.	○	○	○	2× (node ID, column)	session key veri. info.	†	2×encryp 2×decryp	△	○	○

† : 2× initial key generation ($\lambda + 1$ multiplications) and session key generation.

4.3 Comparison of Communication Overhead

It has been shown that the proposed protocols improve the connectivity of a sensor network and uniqueness of session keys over the existing protocols. The existing protocols and the proposed protocols are compared in Table 4, in terms of transmission overhead. Note that transmission is the most energy-consuming process. As shown in the table, there must be at least 4 transmissions required for generating and verifying a session key. Protocol I incurs the minimum communication overhead, and the added communication overhead for Protocol II is negligible for a small value of λ. Thus, the proposed protocols achieve high/full connectivity and enhance the security greatly without increasing the communication overhead.

5 Summary

A sensor network usually consists of a large number of sensor nodes and they communicate with each other through radio transmission. This makes sensor networks vulnerable to various attacks by the adversary. In the applications where a certain level of security is required, it is necessary for each sensor node to authenticate its neighbor nodes and use session keys for secure communication. However, since the communication and computation capabilities and the storage capacity of sensor nodes are very limited, the conventional public key cryptogram cannot be employed. Various protocols for establishing session keys have been proposed taking these characteristics into account.

In this paper, several existing protocols for session key derivation are analyzed and compared in terms of common criteria. We found that the protocols which

Table 4. Comparison of communication overhead

	BROSK	Random (Encrypt)	*q-composite*	Node ID	Blom	Protocol I	Protocol II
number of transmission	4	$2 \times m + 2$	$2 \times m + 2$	4	4	4	4
contents of transmissions†	(ID, Nonce, MAC) $\times 2$	(ID, a, E(a)) $\times m \times 2$	(ID, puzzle) $\times m$ (ID, sol.) $\times m$	ID $\times 2$	(ID, col.) $\times 2$	ID $\times 2$	(ID, col.) $\times 2$
bits transferred†	(16+64+64) $\times 2$	(16+64+64) $\times m \times 2$	(16+64+64) $\times m \times 2$	16 $\times 2$	(16+ $64(\lambda + 1)$) $\times 2$	16 $\times 2$	(16+ $64(\lambda + 1)$) $\times 2$

†: the contents and bits transferred, which are required in the last two transmissions in all protocols, are excluded.

derive session keys from the pre-distributed key information have disadvantages in network connectivity, session key uniqueness, and network security. Based on the analysis results, some requirements for the advanced protocols are presented.

In addition, we propose new advanced two-step hierarchical protocols to satisfy the requirements. In the first step of our protocols, the initial keys which are used only once are derived from the pre-distributed information. In the second step, session keys are randomly generated and verified using the initial keys. Thus, the proposed protocols enhance the connectivity of the sensor network while providing the guaranteed uniqueness of session keys. Protocol I achieves more than 99 % of connectivity and Protocol II guarantees full connectivity of a sensor network. In addition, they reduce the energy consumption by minimizing the number of transmissions in the both protocols and the size of messages transmitted in Protocol I. As an extension, the proposed protocols may be applicable to mobile sensor networks. Each sensor node which moves to a new location can follow the same two-step procedure in Section 3 to derive session keys with the new neighbors.

References

1. A. Perrig, J. Stankovic and D. Wagner, "Security in Wireless Sensor Networks," *Communications of the ACM*, Vol. 47, No. 6, pp53 -57, 2004.
2. N. H, R. Smith, and P. Bradford, "Security for Fixed Sensor Networks," *Proc. of ACMSE'04*, pp 212-213, 2004.
3. Y. Wang, "Robust Key Establishment in Sensor Networks," *SIGMOD Record*, Vol. 33, No. 1, pp 14-19, 2004.
4. A. Perrig, etc., "SPINS: Security Protocols for Sensor Networks," *Journal of Wireless Nets.*, Vol 8, No.5, pp 521-534, 2002.
5. B. Lai, etc., "Reducing Radio Energy Consumption of Key Management Protocols for Wireless Sensor networks," *Poc. of ISLPED'04*, pp 351-356, 2004.
6. L. Eschenhaur and V. Gligor, "A Key-Management Scheme for Distributed Sensor Networks," *Proc. of CCS'02*, pp 41-47, 2002.

7. H. Chan, A. Perrig and D. Song, "Random Key Predistribution Schemes for Sensor Networks, *Proc. of 2003 IEEE Symposium on Security and Privacy(SP'03)*, pp 197-213, 2003.
8. R. Pietro, L. Mancini and A. Mei, "Random Key-Assignment for Secure Wireless Sensor Networks," *Proc. of 1st Workshop Security of Ad Hoc and Sensor Networks*, pp 62-71, 2003.
9. D. Liu and P. Ning, "Location-based Pairwise Key Establishments for Static Sensor Networks," *Proc. of 1st Workshop Security of Ad Hoc and Sensor Networks*, pp 72-82, 2003.
10. W. Du, etc., "A Key Management Scheme for Wireless Sensor Networks Using Deployment Knowledge," *Proc. of the IEEE INFOCOM'04*, pp 586-597, 2004.
11. S. Okazaki, A. Desai, C. Gentry and et.el., "Securing MIPv6 Binding Updates Using Address Based Keys (ABKs)," IETF, draft-okazaki-mobileip-abk-01.txt, Oct. 2002. Work in progress.
12. R. Blom, "An Optimal class of symmetric key generation systems," *Proc. of EUROCRYPT84, Lecture Notes in Computer Science*, Springer-Verlag 209, pp 335-338, 1984.
13. W. Du, etc.,"A Pairwise Key Pre-Distribution Scheme for Wireless," *Proc. of CCS'03*, pp 27-31, 2003.

A Revenue-Aware Bandwidth Allocation Model and Algorithm in IP Networks

Meng Ji[1,2] and Shao-hua Yu[1,2]

[1] School of Computer Science, Huazhong University of Science and Technology
[2] Wuhan Fiberhome Networks Co. Ltd.,
Wuhan, Hubei Province 430074, P.R. China
{jupiter, shuyu}@fhn.com.cn

Abstract. This paper proposes a generic revenue-aware bandwidth allocation (RBA) model. This model satisfies diverse QoS requirements of different IP services with revenue as the optimization criterion. Based on this generic model, this paper provides Enhanced Greedy Algorithm (EGA) to solve RBA problems. Unlike other algorithms, the proposed algorithm is deterministic and can be calculated in polynomial time. The experiments on a switched router show that EGA is efficient and applicable for embedded systems.

Keywords: Revenue-aware Bandwidth Allocation, Generic RBA model, Knapsack problem.

1 Introduction

The future IP networks must carry a wide range of different service types being still able to provide performance guarantees to real-time sessions such as Voice over IP (VoIP), Video-on-Demand (VoD), or Interactive game. For the future multi-service Internet, users will have to pay the network operators based on pricing strategies agreed in their SLA (Service-Level-Agreements). The pricing strategy will specify the relationship between the price paid by each class of users and the QoS (e.g., delay, bandwidth) provided by the network operators, which normally states that the network provider will get a revenue when the offered QoS meets the defined performance requirement. Thus, the diverse service requirements of emerging Internet services foster the need for flexible and scalable revenue-aware bandwidth allocation (RBA) schemes.

In current networks, bandwidth assignment is based on three major service models: best-effort, integrated services (IntServ [1]) and differentiated services (DiffServ [2]). In best-effort model, applications could send arbitrary packets in arbitrary time without previous grant. Intermediate routers treat all the packets equally and queue them by a simple First-In-First-Out way. Best-effort mechanism is designed for time-extensive applications like E-mail and HTTP. It does not satisfy the strict QoS requirements from time-intensive value-added services (Multi-media, etc.). IntServ, based on RSVP signaling, requires the whole IP networks to reserve an end-to-end bandwidth path for each flow. IntServ places a heavy processing load on routers in the core of the network; and does not scale well in large networks with numerous IntServ

L.T. Yang et al. (Eds.): ICESS 2005, LNCS 3820, pp. 650 – 658, 2005.

flows. To eliminate the drawbacks of IntServ, Diffserv was proposed by IETF in 1998. Adopting a two-level service model, Diffserv achieves scalability by implementing complex classification and conditioning functions at network boundary nodes, while the core nodes only need to fulfill simple Per-Hop Behaviors (PHBs). Because of its scalability, many present researches, as in [3], [4], [5], focus on how to fairly allocate bandwidth in DiffServ domains.

With the introducing of new technologies (EPON [6], RPR [7], etc.), bandwidth allocation needs to be implemented in link layer and/or even physical layer, as in [8], [9]. Recent proposals in IETF, as in [10], [11], outline that MPLS layer2 encapsulation technologies are used to emulate TDM, Frame Relay and ATM services. To support such pseudo-wire services, it is necessary to allocate bandwidth effectively in data-link layer. Moreover, ITU-T [12] mentions one research goal in NGN is how to ensure high-layer QoS via low-layer mechanism.

From the discussion above, we can find present BA approaches have several limitations: (1) Present schemes are not revenue-oriented and not sufficient to satisfy carriers' requirements for maximal revenue. (2) Though DiffServ is proved to be an effective QoS model in IP layer, it could not resolve the BA problem in data-link and physical layers.

This paper proposes a generic revenue-aware bandwidth allocation model, which has several unique characteristics. First, the proposed model is a generic one, which is logically independent from any embodied equipments and underlying technologies. It can be not only used in layer 3 and above IP applications, but also used in link-layer applications (Circuit Emulation, etc.) and/or even physical-layer devices (Passive Optical Network). Second, it is designed for meeting the profit requirements of carriers. It allocates the bandwidth based on maximal revenue goal. According to this model, we classify RBA problems into SRBA (Strict RBA) and FRBA (Flexible RBA) problems. We prove that RBA problem is theoretically equal to Knapsack problem and provide an efficient algorithm to calculate it. This algorithm is fair and can be calculated in polynomial time. The remainder of this paper is organized in the following way: Section II illustrates the generic revenue-based bandwidth allocation model. Section III presents the algorithms for RBA problem. Section IV introduces our experiments on a 128Gbps switched router and analyzes the while Section V concludes the paper and proposes some future works.

2 Generic Bandwidth Allocation Model

In IP networks, the entities performing bandwidth allocation are versatile. They could be routers, switches, Broadband Remote Access Server (BRAS), Optical Line Terminal (OLT) or RPR equipments. And the accessing methods could be xDSL, cable, Ethernet, Fiber or Circuit Emulation. Thus, a generic model for revenue-aware bandwidth allocation should meet the following requirements: It should be logically independent from specific devices and underlying technologies. It could be applied into different application environments.

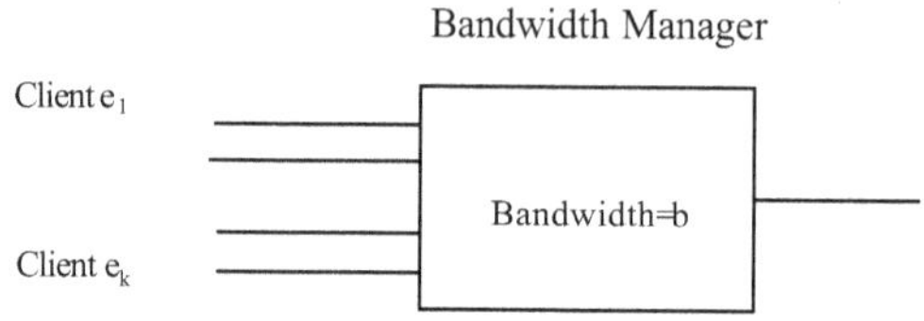

Fig. 1. Generic RBA model

Fig. 1 shows a generic RBA model proposed in this paper. In this model, we are given a set $E=\{e_i\}$ of k clients and a bandwidth of link capacity b. Each client represents the minimal bandwidth-requesting element with three service parameters: bandwidth request value b_i, class of service (CoS) c_i and generating revenue $r_i(i)$, in which CoS is proportional to the revenue density (In this paper, the revenue density is defined as the revenue to bandwidth ratio- r_i / b_i.) It should be noted that a concrete user might issue several clients with different CoS simultaneously, because one user may have different service (TDM, Voice and video, etc.) requests at the same time.

Therefore, RBA problem can be described as follows: Given that clients $\{e_1, e_2 ... e_k\}$ of CoS $\{c_1, c_2 ... c_k\}$, bandwidth request $\{b_1, b_2 .. b_k\}$ and revenue $\{r_1, r_2 .. r_k\}$ are offered to a link of bandwidth b, can the Bandwidth Manager (BM) select enough clients to utilize the available bandwidth and generate the maximum possible revenue while the bandwidth requirements are satisfied for the selected clients? When the BM must strictly satisfy the bandwidth request of each client, the RBA problem is classified as Strict RBA or SRBA problem. When the BM can partially satisfy the bandwidth request of clients, the RBA problem is classified as Flexible RBA or FRBA problem.

BM obtains the service parameters of each client via platform-dependent UNI (User Network Interface) or authentication protocols (Radius, etc). Since that our research focuses on the BA model and algorithm, the fetching of service parameters are out of the scope of this paper. Obviously, the model satisfies the above requirements. It is a single node model and has no relationship with physical embodiments. In this scheme, there is no need to analyze the content of packet (e.g., DSCP in DiffServ). As a result, it could be used in data-link and even physical layer applications.

3 Algorithms for RBA Problems

3.1 RBA Problem Is Equivalent to Knapsack Problem

We initially redefine the RBA problem stated above more precisely.

Problem Instance: Clients $\{e_1, e_2, ... e_k\}$ of CoS $\{c_1, c_2, ... c_k\}$, bandwidth request $\{b_1, b_2, ... b_k\}$ and revenue $\{r_1, r_2, ... r_k\}$, link capacity B and a revenue goal R.

Question: Can the bandwidth manager select enough clients with generation revenue $\geq R$ and total bandwidth requirements $\leq B$?

It is easy to see that SRBA$\in$ NP since a non-deterministic algorithm designed to solve the problem has to guess a collection of client requests and verify the following in polynomial time:

1) Check whether the selected clients fit with in the available bandwidth.
2) Check whether the generated revenue is more than *R*.
3) Check whether the bandwidth request is fully satisfied.

We will give the proof that SBA problem is NP-hard and has no deterministic algorithm to solve it.

Theorem 1: *SRBA problem is NP-hard.*

Proof: There is a known Theorem: if Q is a NP-complete problem and Q could be restricted to L in polynomial time. And then L is NP-hard.

Therefore, in order to prove SRBA is NP-hard, we only need to find one well-known NP-complete problem which could be restricted to SRBA in polynomial time. From the description of SBA problem, we find that it is very similar to Binary Knapsack Problem (BKP) in [13]. The BKP can be described as follows:

Problem Instance: A finite set of objects U, a weight $w(u)$ for each $u \in U$, a profit $p(u)$ for each $u \in U$ and positive integers W (Knapsack Capacity) and P (Desired Profit).

Question: is there a subset $U^{'} \in U$ of such that the sum of the profits of the elements in the subset exceeds the profit goal P without violating knapsack capacity W?

Now we can show BKP is a special case of SRBA problem. The finite set U defined in Knapsack is the set of clients, $w(u)$ is b_i, $p(u)$ is r_i, Knapsack size W is b, profit goal P is R. This above restriction can be carried out in $O(1)$ time. Theorem 1 is proven.

Since the SRBA is proven to be NP-hard, there can be no polynomial time deterministic algorithm that solves the problem optimally.

The definition of FRBA is very similar to the one of SRBA. The only distinction is to change the strict satisfaction to partial satisfaction. So we can deduce that FRBA is equivalent to continuous Knapsack problem, which is a P problem.

Theorem 2: *FRBA problem is a P problem and there can be deterministic algorithms that solve it optimally in polynomial time.*

3.2 Solution to SRBA Problem

BKP is among the widely studied problems of discrete optimization. A number of computational algorithms, as in [14], [15], have been proposed based on branch and bound, dynamic programming or heuristics. However, they still require a lot of execution time and memory space in case that n is a large number, and are not applicable to the embedded system, which has limited system resources. Therefore, considering practicability and scalability, we attempt to find approximation algorithms that may be close to the optimal solution.

The Greedy Algorithm (GA) is an obvious approximation algorithm for BKP. The idea behind GA is to consider the items one-by-one in the order decreasing revenue or revenue to bandwidth ratio. Each item is inserted into the knapsack if adding it does not cause the set of current items to exceed the knapsack capacity. Although GA can be calculated in deterministic time, the simple GA could not do well in the worst case if we execute the GA only based on revenue or revenue density. For example, consider the case where there are only two clients: the first item has bandwidth request 1 and payoff 3, while the second has bandwidth request B and payoff B. The execution result of revenue density based GA is the first one, while the optimal solution should be the second one.

Thus, we propose an Enhanced Greedy Algorithm (EGA) to solve the SRBA problem. EGA-SRBA picks the better of the solutions provided by revenue density based GA and the best solution obtained by selecting the client with the largest revenue into the set. The detailed algorithm is described in the following Fig. 2.

Algorithm EGA -SRBA:

INPUT: link bandwidth b, the item bandwidth request $\{b_1, b_2 .. b_k\}$, CoS $\{c_1, c_2 .. c_k\}$ and revenue $\{r_1, r_2 .. r_k\}$

OUTPUT: Subset of the items at most revenue

1. Sort the items in non-increasing order of their revenue densities or CoS (r_i / b_i or c_i).
2. $U' \leftarrow \Omega$
3. for $i = 1$ to k do begin

    if $\sum_{j \in U'} b_j + b_i \le b$, then $U' \leftarrow U' + i$

4. $U'' \leftarrow \Omega$
5. Find the client e_m with largest revenue
6. if $m \in U'$ then output U'; return;

    else $U'' \leftarrow U'' + m$

7. for $i = 1$ to k, $i \ne m$ do begin

    if $\sum_{j \in U''} b_j + b_i \le b$, then $U'' \leftarrow U'' + i$

8. Compare the generated revenue from U' and U'', output the one with larger revenue

END

Fig. 2. Enhanced Greedy Algorithm for SRBA

The first step of EGA-SRBA can be implemented by a standard sorting routine and the best possible complexity of it is $O(N \log N)$. In the following way, both the revenue density based GA and client selection can be implemented with linear complexity $O(N)$. Thus, the time complexity of EGA-SRBA is $O(N \log N)$. The maximal storage space is two arrays with the length of K and then the space complexity of EGA-SRBA is $O(N)$.

3.3 Solution to FRBA Problem

From Theorem 2, we notice that FRBA problem is equal to continuous knapsack problem and could be solved in polynomial time by revenue density based GA. Considering fairness for clients with lower CoS, we propose another EGA for FRBA problems. The EGA-FRBA is implemented in a two-step way:

1) BM assigns minimum bandwidth to all clients for transmission. Configured guaranteed bandwidth is first supplied per client in Weighted Round Robin (WRR) manner.
2) The remaining bandwidth is distributed to clients by revenue density based GA. Considering the fairness among clients with the same revenue density, the algorithm first merges the clients with the same class and regroups the clients into new clients, and then executes the GA selection.

The detailed algorithm is depicted in the following Fig. 3.

Algorithm EGA-FRBA:

INPUT: link bandwidth b, the item bandwidth request $\{b_1, b_2..b_k\}$, CoS $\{c_1, c_2..c_k\}$ and revenue $\{r_1, r_2..r_k\}$

OUTPUT: Subset of the items at most revenue

1. Allocate initial bandwidth of ratio R to each client in WRR manner

$$b_{init}(i) = b \times R \times (c_i / \sum_{j \in U} c_j)$$

2. Merge clients with the same revenue densities or CoS (r_i / b_i or c_i) into new set U' with bandwidth request $\{b'_1, b'_2, \ldots, b'_m\}$ and revenue $\{r'_1, r'_2, \ldots, r'_m\}$ and CoS $\{c'_1, c'_2 \ldots c'_m\}$

3. Sort the items in non-increasing order of their revenue densities or CoS (r'_i / b'_i or c'_i) in U'

4. $U'' \leftarrow \Omega$

5. for $i = 1$ to m do begin /*Greedy Algorithm*/

if $\sum_{j \in U''} b'_j + b'_i \le b \times (1 - R)$, then $U'' \leftarrow U'' + i$

6. Calculate the assigned bandwidth for each client

for $i = 1$ to k do begin

$$b_{allocate}(i) = b_{init}(i) + b_{GA}(i)$$

END

Fig. 3. Enhanced Greedy Algorithm for FRBA

The WRR step can be implemented with linear complexity $O(N)$. The regrouping step can be implemented by a standard sorting routine and the best possible complexity of it is $O(N \log N)$. In the final GA step, the time complexity is $O(N)$. Thus, the time complexity of EGA-FRBA is $O(N \log N)$. The space complexity of EGA-FRBA is also $O(N)$.

4 Experiments and Result Analysis

4.1 Experiment Platform

Our testbed is Distributed Extensible sErvices Platform (DEEP), designed for Chinese National High-Tech Project No.2003AA121110. As described in [16], DEEP consists of two routing engines and twelve Network Processor Units (NPUs) based line cards. The routing engine implements control plane functions, while forwarding operations are performed by the NPUs in the line card. DEEP has a whole switch capacity of 128Gbps and could be configured as high-performance ER (Edge Router) and BRAS (Broad Remote Access Server). The processor in routing engine is PowerPC 7410 with PowerPC 604 core embedded. This CPU has 1Mbps level-2 cache, with a clock rate at 450 MHz. The operation system used is Vxworks 5.4 from Windriver Systems and the complier is GNU C complier with level-2 optimization.

Table 1 summarizes the results of our experiments. We measured the execution time of EGA-SRBA and EGA-FRBA in DEEP under BRAS and ER configurations. We measured the client number of 10, 20, 40, 60, 80, 100, 1,000 and 10,000 respectively. All the client request parameters are generated by software randomly. Considering the real applications, the number of service classes is 32. The requesting bandwidth in ER is ranged from 1Mbps to 1024Mbps, while the one in BRAS is ranged from 1Kbps to 8Mbps.Our code was written in ANSI C and the used sorting routine is quick sort algorithm. The listed result is the average value of 1,000 times execution.

Table 1. Measurement Results of RBA

T / N	BRAS-SRBA	BRAS-FRBA	ER-SRBA	ER-FRBA
10	16.0us	14.8us	16.3us	14.8us
20	35.7us	30.7us	35.8us	30.9us
40	76.0us	64.7us	76.0us	64.6us
60	119us	165us	117us	165us
80	165us	140us	166us	142us
100	177us	175us	177us	173us
1,000	2.37ms	2.10ms	2.37ms	2.10ms
10,000	35.67ms	29.83ms	35.05ms	29.83ms

4.2 Result Analysis

From the results above, we analyze three factors that may have an effect on execution time: type of RBA entities (ER or BRAS), RBA type (SRBA or FRBA) and the number of clients. From Fig. 4a and Fig. 4b, we can obviously find that this algorithm is independent from the type of RBA entities, which illustrates that the proposed model and algorithm are logically independent from physical embodiments and underlying technologies. Fig. 4c shows that the execution time of SRBA is longer than FRBA. This is reasonable because that SRBA performs one more GA selection than FRBA.

Regarding the running time, since we adopt the quick sort algorithm, the time complexity should be $O(N \ln N)$, as shown in Fig. 4d.

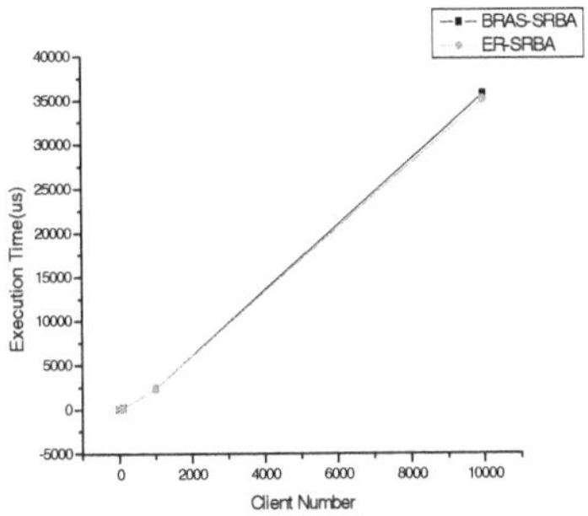

Fig. 4a. SRBA

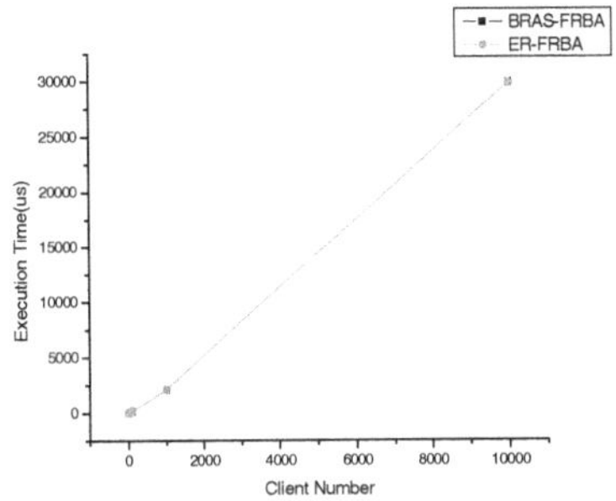

Fig. 4b. FRBA

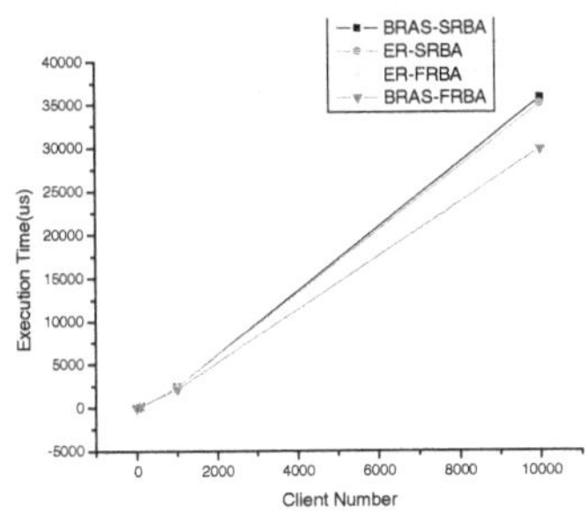

Fig. 4c. SRBA and FRBA

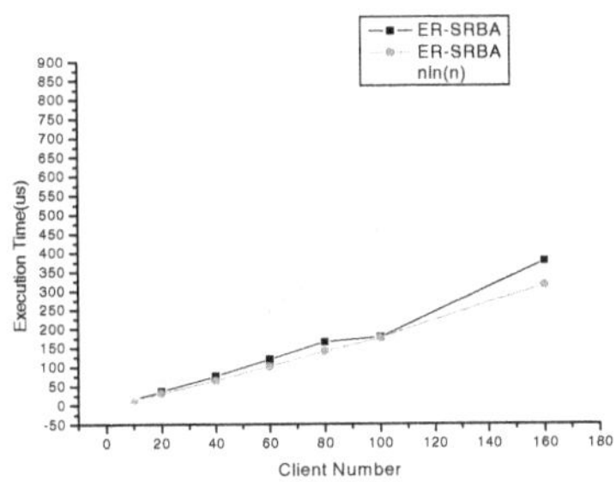

Fig. 4d. ER

Fig. 4. Comparison of Execution Time

5 Conclusions and Future Work

This paper investigates the problem of how to allocate bandwidth efficiently to ensure different QoS requests from different users and maximize the revenue for carriers. This paper describes a generic revenue-aware bandwidth allocation (RBA) model and classifies the RBA problems into SRBA (Strict RBA) and FRBA (Flexible RBA) problems. This paper proves that bandwidth allocation problem is theoretically equivalent to Knapsack problem. Since traditional BKP algorithms are not applicable for real-world embedded systems, this paper proposes an Enhanced Greedy Algorithm (EGA), which can be calculated in $o(N \log N)$ time. EGA has been implemented on our testbed-DEEP. The experiment results show EGA is deterministic and independent from physical embodiments.

We also note that in rigorous applications when the client number is too large ($\geq 10{,}000$), the execution time of this algorithm may be unacceptable. Thus, our future plans include implementing EGA on high performance NPUs or ASICs that may bring nearly an order of magnitude improvement in performance.

References

1. R. Braden, Ed., L. Zhang, S. Berson, S. Herzog and S. Jamin, Resource ReSerVation Protocol, IETF, RFC2205 (1997).
2. S. Blake, D. Black, M. Carlson, E. Davies, Z. Wang and W. Weiss, An Architecture for Differentiated Service, IETF, RFC2475 (1998) .
3. Seddigh N., Nandy B.and Pieda P, Bandwidth assurance issues for TCP flows in a differentiated services network, IEEE GLOBECOM (1999) 1792-1798.
4. Eun-Chan Park and Chong-Ho Choi, Adpative token bucket algorithm for fair bandwidth allocation in diffserv networks, IEEE GLOBECOM (2003) 3176-3180.
5. Eun-Chan Park and Chong-Ho Choi, Proportional Bandwidth Allocation in DiffServ Networks, IEEE INFOCOM (2004) 2038-2049.
6. G. Kramer, G. Pesavento, Ethernet Passive Optical Network (EPON): Building a Next-Generation Optical Access Network, IEEE Communications Magazine (2002) 66-73.
7. IEEE 802.17 Resilient packet ring (RPR) access method & physical layer specifications (2004).
8. Fu-Tai An, Yu-Li Hsueh, Kyeong Soo Kim, Ian M. White, and Leonid G. Kazovsky, A New Dynamic Bandwidth Allocation Protocol with Quality of Service in Ethernet-based Passive Optical Networks, WOC (2003) 383-385.
9. Alharbi, F.and Ansari, N., Low complexity distributed bandwidth allocation for resilient packet ring networks, IEEE HPSR (2004) 277-281.
10. Stewart Byrant and Prayson Pate, PWE3 Architecture, IETF, draft-ietf-pwe3-arch-07.txt (2003).
11. Luca Martini, Nasser El-Aawar and Giles Heron, Encapsulation Methods for Transport of Ethernet Frames Over MPLS Networks, IETF, draft-ietf-pwe3-ethernet-encap-09.txt (2005).
12. ITU-T Workshop on Next Generation Networks: What, When and How?, ITU-T (2003), http://www.itu.int.
13. Garey MJ and Johnson DS., Computers and Intractability: A Guide to the Theory of NP-Completeness, San Franscisco: Freeman (1979).
14. Martello S, Pisinger D and Toth P, Dynamic Programming and strong bounds for the 0-1 knapsack problem, Management Science (1999) 414-424.
15. Martello S, Pisinger D and Toth P, New Trends in exact algorithms for the 0-1 knapsack problem, European Journal of Operational Research (2000) 325-332.
16. Meng Ji, Shao-hua Yu, An innovative packet processing methodology: Policy-based Flow Switching. SPIE proceedings-Volume 5626, Beijing, P.R.China, pp. 730-737, 2004.

Control Flow Error Checking with ISIS

Francisco Rodríguez and Juan José Serrano

Grupo de Sistemas Tolerantes a Fallos - Fault Tolerant Systems Group,
Polytechnical University of Valencia, 46022, Valencia, Spain
{prodrig, jserrano}@disca.upv.es
http://www.disca.upv.es/gstf

Abstract. The Interleaved Signature Instruction Stream (ISIS) is a signature embedding technique that allows signatures to co-exist with the main processor instruction stream with a minimal impact on processor performance, without sacrificing error detection coverage or latency.

While ISIS incorporate some novel error detection mechanisms to assess the integrity of the program executed by the main processor, the limited number of bits available in the signature control word question if the detection mechanisms are effective detecting errors in the program execution flow. Increasing the signature size would negatively impact the memory requirements, so this option has been rejected. The effectiveness of such mechanisms is an issue that must be addressed. This paper details those checking mechanisms included within the ISIS technique that are responsible of the assessment of the integrity of the processor execution flow and the experiments carried out to characterize their coverage.

1 Introduction

With the advent of modern technologies in the field of programmable devices and enormous advances in the software tools used to model, simulate and translate into hardware almost any complex digital system, the capability to design a System-On-Chip (SoC) has become a reality even for small companies. With the widespread use of embedded systems in our everyday life, service availability and dependability concerns for these systems are increasingly important [1].

A SoC is usually modeled using a Hardware Description Language (HDL) like VHDL [2]. It allows a hierarchical description of the system and the designed elements interconnect much the same way as they would in a graphical design flow, but using an arbitrary abstraction level. It also provides IO facilities to easily incorporate test vectors, and language assertions to verify the correct behavior of the model during the simulation.

Efficient error detection is of fundamental importance in dependable computing systems. As the vast majority of faults are transient, the use of a concurrent *Error Detection Mechanism* (EDM) is of utmost interest as high coverage and low detection latency characteristics are needed to recover the system from the error. And as experiments demonstrate [3,4,5], a high percentage of non-overwritten errors results in control flow errors.

L.T. Yang et al. (Eds.): ICESS 2005, LNCS 3820, pp. 659–670, 2005.

The possibility to modify the original architecture of a processor modeled using VHDL gives the SoC designer an unprecedented capability to incorporate EDM's which were previously available at large design companies only.

Siewiorek states in [6] that "To succeed in the commodity market, fault-tolerant techniques need to be sought which will be transparent to end users". A fault-tolerant technique can be considered transparent only if results in minimal performance overhead in silicon, memory size or processor speed. Although redundant systems can achieve the best degree of fault-tolerance, the high overheads imposed limit their applicability in everyday computing elements. The same limitation applies when a software only solution is used, due to performance losses. Siewiorek's statement can be also translated into the SoC world, to demand fault-tolerant techniques that minimize their impact on performance (the scarcest resource in such systems) if those techniques are to be used at all.

The work presented here is structured as follows: The next section is devoted to a minimal background on concurrent EDMs, specifically those using watchdog processors. A section of previous work follows, where the ISIS watchdog technique and its implementation into a SoC is described. The software support for this system is also outlined in this section.

Next section reports how the EDMs associated with the execution flow guarantee it; these are characterized, either theoretically or by means of some experiments. For those requiring experiments, the memory model is described in the corresponding subsection, along with the results obtained. The paper ends with the conclusions obtained and some further research opportunities.

2 Background

A minimal set of basic terms taken from [6] is needed to understand the overall system. A *branch-in* instruction is an instruction used as the target address of a branch or call instruction (for example, the first instruction of a procedure or function). A *branch-out* instruction is an instruction capable to break the sequential execution flow, conditionally or unconditionally (for example, a conditional branch or a procedure call instruction). A *basic block* is a sequence of instructions with no branch-in instructions except the very first one and no branch-out instructions except possibly the last one.

A derived *signature* is a value assigned to each instruction block to be used as reference in the checking process at run-time. The term derived means the signature is not an arbitrarily assigned value but calculated from the block's instructions. Derived signatures are usually obtained xor-ing the instruction opcodes or using the opcodes to feed a Linear Feedback Shift Register (LFSR). These values are calculated at compile time and used as reference by the EDM to verify correctness of executed instructions.

If signatures are interspersed or hashed with the processor instructions the method is generally known as *Embedded Signature Monitoring* (ESM). A watchdog processor is a hardware EDM used to detect *Control Flow Errors* (CFE) and/or corruption of the instructions executed by the processor, usually employing derived signatures and an ESM technique. In this case it performs signature calculations from the instruction opcodes that are actually executed by the main processor, checking these run-time values against their references. If any difference is found the error in the main processor instruction stream is detected and an Error Recovery Mechanism (ERM) is activated.

The percentage of detected error is the error detection *coverage*, and the time from the error being active to the detection is the error detection *latency*. With both values any EDM can be characterized.

A *branch insertion* error is the error produced when the opcode of a non-branch instruction is corrupted and it is transformed into a branch instruction; from a watchdog processor perspective, this error is detected as a too early branch. A *branch deletion* error is the error produced when the opcode of a branch instruction gets corrupted and the instruction becomes a non-branch instruction; the watchdog detects this error condition as a too late branch.

Any error affecting a non-branch instruction other than branch insertion errors, do not affect the execution flow of the program and are not part of the structural integrity checking mechanisms.

3 Previous Work

In [7] a novel technique to embed signatures into the processor's instruction stream is presented. Its main goal is the reduction of the performance impact of the watchdog processor and it is targeted to processors included into embedded systems.

Using this technique, called ISIS (Interleaved Signature Instruction Stream), the watchdog processor signatures are hashed with the application processor's instructions in the same memory area. Signatures are interleaved within instruction basic blocks, but they are never fetched nor executed by the main processor.

Signature control words (or simply signatures) are placed at the beginning of every basic block in the ISIS scheme (see Fig. 1). These references incorporate, among other checking mechanisms, the opcode signature field: a polynomial CRC of the block instruction bits to detect the corruption of any instruction (non-CFE errors and branch insertion and deletion errors as well). Using a polynomial redundancy check 100 % of single bit errors and a large percentage of more complex error scenarios can be detected.

Besides error detection capabilities obtained from the opcode signature, and due to the fact that the block reference word includes the block length, branch insertion and branch deletion errors are detected.

The signature word encoding has been designed in such a way that a main processor instruction can not be misinterpreted as a watchdog signature instruction. This provides an additional check when the main processor executes a branch instruction. This check, called Branch Start, consists in the requirement to find a signature instruction immediately preceding the first instruction of

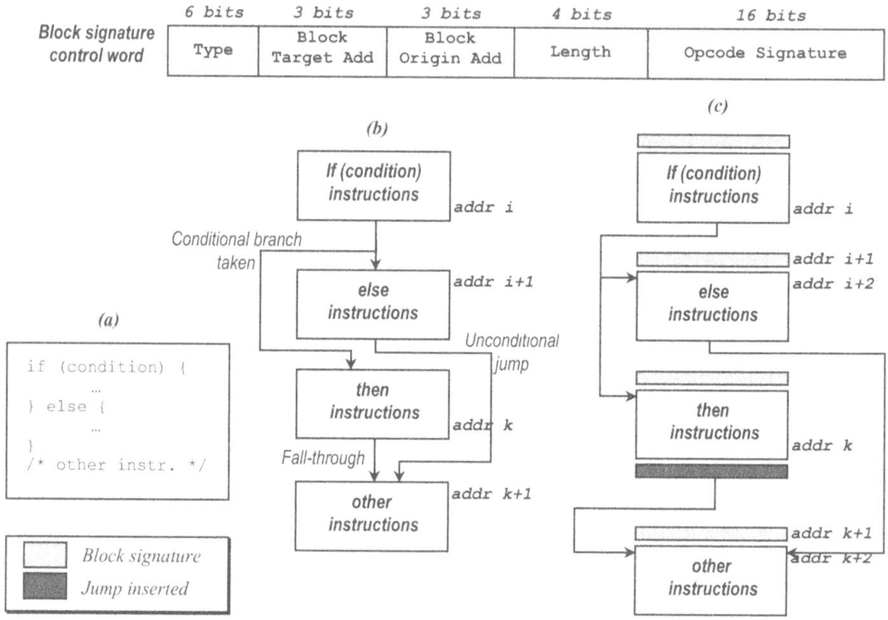

Fig. 1. ISIS signature control word and signature insertion process: (a) high-level language snippet, (b) original blocks at assembly stage, and (c) after code is instrumented with signatures

every block. This also helps to detect a CFE if a branch erroneously targets a signature instruction, because the encoding will force an illegal instruction exception to be raised.

Under the assumption of single bit errors, the block length allows the watchdog processor to detect all branch insertion and branch deletion errors. Additional checking mechanisms related with the signature word instruction type and jump address guard bits are also included.

The Block Address is a check process that uses one of the address check fields in the signature word (Block Origin Address or Block Target Address) to verify the correctness of the address of the target instruction when a branch is taken. The difference between the addresses of the branch instruction and the target instruction is computed at compile time, and a checksum is calculated and stored into the signature word. At run-time, when the processor breaks the execution sequence taking a branch, the actual addresses employed by the processor are used, inside the watchdog processor and following the same algorithm used by the compiler, to calculate another checksum. In the absence of errors, both must match; any mismatch will trigger the watchdog's error detection procedure.

This two EDMs, Block Start and Block Address, form the basic elements used by the watchdog processor to guarantee the integrity of the processor's execution flow. And the work presented in this paper shows their error coverage characteristics, using them separately and combined.

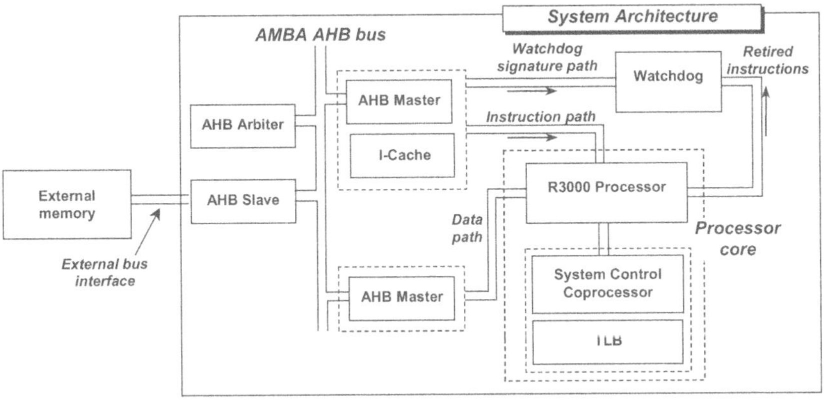

Fig. 2. HORUS processor and overall system architecture

To reduce performance overhead the main CPU should not process signatures in any way. With this objective in mind, the CPU is designed to skip an instruction per basic block while maintaining the normal instruction sequencing. These architectural modifications create word gaps in the main processor instruction stream immediately following branches and calls. A specialized compiler uses these gaps to store watchdog signatures words.

With this arrangement, two completely independent interleaved instruction streams coexist in our system: the application instruction stream, which is divided into blocks and executed by the main processor and the signature stream, used by the watchdog processor.

Isolating the reference signatures from the instructions fed into the processor pipeline results in a minimal performance overhead in the application program. More information about this signature embedding technique can be found in [7].

The ISIS technique has been implemented in the HORUS processor [8], a soft-core clone of the MIPS R3000 [9] RISC processor (see Fig. 2). It is a four stage pipelined processor with a complete Memory Management Unit and instruction cache. The external memory and peripherals are accessed through an AMBA AHB bus [10]. This processor is provided with a Memory Management Unit (MMU) to perform virtual to physical address mapping, isolating memory areas of different processes and checking correct alignment of memory references. The watchdog processor is fed with the instructions from the main processor pipeline as they are retired.

The original processor architecture has been augmented with an ISIS watchdog processor. The instruction cache is modified to include two read ports to provide simultaneous access to both processors (main and watchdog processors).

The watchdog calculates run-time signatures at the same rate of the processor pipeline. When a block ends, these values are stored into a FIFO memory to decouple the checking process. This FIFO allows a large set of instructions to be retired from the pipeline while the watchdog is waiting for the block reference signature word. In a similar way, the watchdog can empty the FIFO while the main processor pipeline is stalled due to a memory operation. When this FIFO memory is full, the main processor is forced to wait for the watchdog checking process to read some data from it.

4 HORUS Compiler Support

The GNU *gcc* compiler already provides a port to target MIPS processors. As its source code is freely available it was the natural starting point to provide the required software support for the HORUS processor. The *gas* program (GNU Assembler) has the responsibility of the assembly stage in the compilation process, after program optimization passes and before the final linker stage.

The gas program and its supporting libraries have been modified to support the architecture of HORUS and its use of the ISIS technique via command line switches. As instructions are assembled,

1. If the current instruction is the target of a branch instruction, a new block starts and so its signature it is inserted.
2. If the current instruction is a branch, the next instruction will fill the branch delay slot and end the current block.

With this information and the opcode bits of the program instructions the assembler can calculate block signatures and insert them at appropriate places. No provisions are needed to modify the target of a branch or call instruction, as all instruction addresses are referenced using symbolic names (labels).

The software splits large sequences of instructions to accommodate the generated blocks to the length field of the signature control word. Reducing the number of instructions in a block increases the memory requirements, but it also reduces the latency from the error activation to its detection. While the length field would allow for blocks of up to 16 instructions, the actual block length could be smaller due to several reasons, most noticeably:

1. One of the instructions in the sequence is the target of a branch instruction. In this case, a signature must precede this instruction, so a new block must be created.
2. The use of variant frags. A variant frag is a combination of two different sequences of instructions generated by the assembler to solve the same task. For example, to store the address of a variable into a register, several sequences of instructions (and with different lengths) are possible using the MIPS instruction set, depending on the availability of a register pointer. If the symbol can not be resolved at assembly time, both sequences are generated. Obviously, only one of these would remain in the final executable, but the decision is delayed until the symbol address is resolvable. As the block size must be determined at the time of instruction generation, the approach taken has been conservative and the assumption that the larger sequence will remain is always followed. By the time the symbol is resolved, the blocks are already formed and their size can not be changed, so if the short sequence is finally selected the block will be shorter than 16 instructions.

5 Error Detection Coverage of CFEs

The Block Start EDM can be theoretically characterized, and its error coverage is 100 % as stated in proposition 1. The Block Address EDM requires some experiments to be carried out, as detailed below.

Proposition 1. *The Block Start checking mechanism ensures that all CFEs targeting an instruction other than the first instruction of a block are detected.*

Proof. A signature precedes the first instruction of a block. The watchdog processor uses the block initial address (being correct or not) as a memory reference to get the block's signature, retrieving it from the memory location immediately preceding this initial address. Given the fact that the bit patterns of signature words are selected not to match any instruction of the main processor, there are no instructions of the main processor that may be misinterpreted by the watchdog processor as a block signature.

So, in the case of a CFE targeting an instruction other than the first instruction of a block, the contents of the immediately preceding memory location is a processor instruction and not a signature word. Its bit pattern will not match any signature type in the watchdog processor, and the mismatch will trigger the error detection. □

Run-time calculation errors inside the main processor are not CFEs except if the incorrect value is an instruction address. Taking a branch or returning from a procedure, where a target instruction address must be calculated or retrieved from memory, are examples of such calculations. The opcode signature can not cover those calculations, as the original instruction is not corrupted.

Assessment of the effectiveness of the Block Address checking mechanism coupled with the Block Start check can only be performed by means of some kind of experimentation.

5.1 Experiment Setup

To determine the error detection coverage of EDMs applicable to CFEs a simulation model of the address calculation process has been created. This model mimics the performed operations of the actual processor at the execution of branches. Injecting faults into the model an erroneous target address is obtained and we are able to determine if the EDMs would detect it.

The simulation model consists of a large array of elements representing the processor's memory. Each element represents a block of sequential instructions with start address, length, signature, type of branch instruction, target address, etc. The type of branch instruction is important, as the address calculation process in the MIPS architecture is completely different if the instruction is a conditional branch or an unconditional jump. The former uses a program counter relative address and the later an absolute address.

Injecting a fault into the address calculation process in this model is as simple as randomly picking up the origin block, and simulating the effect of a single bit error at the branch.

Comparing the new, erroneous target address with the original one the fault masking probability is determined. A fault is masked if the calculation performed produces the same result as if there is no fault.

Using the erroneous address to compute the address guard bits and comparing them to those bits stored into the block signature word, the error detection probability of the Block Address EDM is obtained. The error detection probability of the Block Start EDM is obtained performing a search over the memory model to verify if the erroneous address matches the start of a block or not.

To simulate the effect of a single bit error in the address calculation process, a single bit of one of the operands or a single bit of the result is altered. Which value and which bit are chosen randomly. If it is an operand what is modified, the bit is changed before the target address is calculated. If it is the result, it is modified after the calculation is performed. Thus, a single bit error in the operands may propagate to adjacent bit positions to simulate the effect of a single or multiple bit error.

A synthetic workload is created filling the memory with blocks of random length, following a uniform distribution between 3 and 17 words. While the shortest block in the original MIPS architecture is 2 instructions long (the branch and the instruction at the branch delay slot), this block is augmented with the block signature in HORUS (a signature has the same length of an instruction, it is a 32-bit word). The ISIS-modified gcc compiler limits the block length to accommodate it to the length field of the signature word, so no block larger than 17 words (16 instructions plus the signature) is allowed in our system. These length values match the mean length of sequential instructions, claimed to be between 7 and 8 [11].

Once the memory is filled, for each block the type of instruction at its end and the target block are chosen randomly. With this information, the address guard bits are calculated using the same algorithm internally used by the compiler and stored into the block structure for future reference.

This algorithm starts calculating the address difference between the branch and the target instructions. This 32-bit value is then compressed using a simple xor tree to obtain the address guard bits. Although the original proposal of ISIS reserves 3 bits for such guard, the xor tree is easily expandable to accommodate larger fields if space is available.

Figure 3 shows a representation of the xor tree for a guard fields of bits ($g_2g_1g_0$). Xor-ing alternating bits help the watchdog processor to detect multiple bit errors, where a single bit error into an operand propagates into a sequence of bit errors at the calculated result. Note that the 32-bit value calculated above ($V_{31..0}$) is padded with zeroes where necessary.

5.2 Results

Several fault injection campaigns have been carried out. Each campaign consists in the injection of 50,000 errors, and the experiments have been repeated a number of times with different random seeds to obtain their typical deviation, a statistical dispersion measurement.

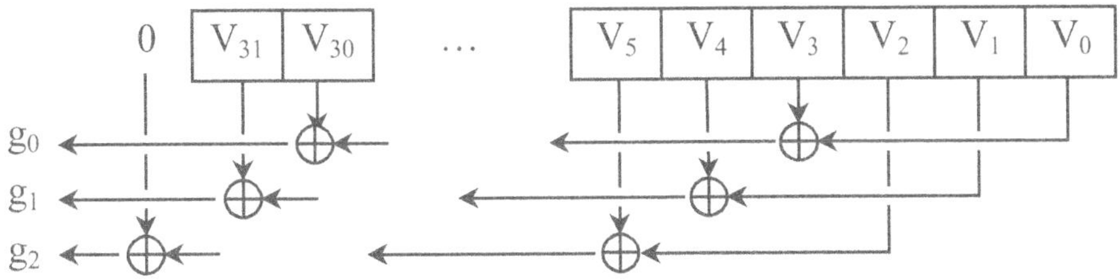

Fig. 3. XOR tree to obtain checksum bits for a 3-bit address guard

Table 1. Block Start error coverage

Memory size	Mean (%)	Typ. deviation
64 Kbytes	45.14	0.287
256 Kbytes	50.44	0.339
1 Mbytes	56.53	0.133
2 Mbytes	59.21	0.212

To analyze the impact of the address guard field size, guards from 2 to 6 bits have been used in each experiment. The memory used by the application program has been changed from 64Kbytes to 2Mbytes. A larger memory size theoretically increases the possibility of an erroneous branch to target the start of a block, and the error being undetected by the Block Start check.

Other elements incorporated into the HORUS processor incorporating checking mechanisms to detect CFEs but not explicitly included into the watchdog processor have not been included into our experiments as they do not characterize the error coverage we're trying to obtain from the inclusion of the watchdog. For example, the Memory Management Unit would trigger an exception if a branch targets a non-used memory area. Another check used by the main processor covering the same type of errors is the alignment check; all instructions fetched from memory must be aligned on a word boundary, or an exception is triggered. This means the results shown do not corresponds to the system error detection coverage, but only the coverage of the aforementioned EDMs.

The Table 1 summarizes the error coverage obtained with the Block Start mechanism alone, for each memory size.

As the results outline, the memory size has the inverse effect of what is theoretically expected. A larger memory increases, although moderately, the error coverage, despite the fact that there are more possibilities to target a block start erroneously. This can be explained by the fact that, at the same time, a larger memory means there are more possibilities the erroneous address fall inside the covered memory area.

The Table 2 shows the error coverage obtained with the Block Address mechanism for different address guard bits and memory sizes, and the combined error coverage is show in Table 3.

Another interesting result from the experiments carried out is the error length distribution, shown in Table 4. This table shows how a single bit error may prop-

Table 2. Block Address error coverage

Guard size Memory size	2 bits Mean (%) Typ. dev	3 bits Mean (%) Typ. dev	4 bits Mean (%) Typ. dev	5 bits Mean (%) Typ. dev	6 bits Mean (%) Typ. dev
64 Kbytes	96.52 0.199	98.31 0.088	98.70 0.094	99.29 0.023	99.37 0.038
256 Kbytes	96.74 0.055	98.42 0.042	99.01 0.042	99.31 0.018	99.37 0.028
1 Mbytes	96.81 0.114	98.48 0.025	99.15 0.056	99.36 0.016	99.40 0.028
2 Mbytes	96.79 0.060	98.49 0.054	99.15 0.020	99.36 0.040	99.40 0.034

Table 3. Block Start and Block Address combined error coverage

Guard size Memory size	2 bits Mean (%) Typ. dev	3 bits Mean (%) Typ. dev	4 bits Mean (%) Typ. dev	5 bits Mean (%) Typ. dev	6 bits Mean (%) Typ. dev
64 Kbytes	97.41 0.139	98.70 0.084	98.73 0.092	99.36 0.023	99.37 0.038
256 Kbytes	97.97 0.032	98.68 0.055	99.31 0.018	99.34 0.016	99.37 0.027
1 Mbytes	97.99 0.070	98.75 0.045	99.34 0.044	99.38 0.013	99.40 0.027
2 Mbytes	98.55 0.038	99.27 0.024	99.35 0.026	99.38 0.045	99.94 0.015

Table 4. Error length distribution

Error length	Mean (%)	Typ. deviation
0 (masked)	16.45	0.149
1	71.45	0.079
2	5.49	0.075
3	2.73	0.089
4	1.45	0.047
5	0.85	0.022
6	0.50	0.016
7	0.39	0.019
8	0.31	0.022
9	0.30	0.020
10	0.01	0.006

agate into a multiple bit error as the address calculation process takes place. Although data shown corresponds to one of the experiments only, the other experiments offer similar results and the data values have been omitted to eliminate the redundancy. Error lengths above 10 bits have been also eliminated by its negligible impact.

As expected, the error length concentrates around single error bits, but percentages of masked errors, and multiple bit errors ranging from 2 to 4 bits are also noticeable.

6 Conclusions

The checking mechanisms to detect CFEs of the ISIS technique have been discussed, and its implementation on the HORUS processor has been outlined. This practical implementation has been complemented by a modified version of the ubiquitous C-language compiler gcc, to automatically insert signatures into the application program, lightening the programmer of most system reliability details.

Although the small number of bits reserved to check branch addresses could have generated some doubts about the effectiveness of the error detection mechanisms, this has been proven in contrary by the injection of faults into a model of the memory subsystem.

The model represents the contents of each block as a sequence of instructions preceded by the block's signature, and the address and length of each block is computed and stored for future reference. Single-bit errors have been injected into the model, and the Block Start and Block Address EDMs have shown their effectiveness detecting CFEs.

Error coverage can be improved using an address guard field larger than the original 3-bit proposal. This requires reducing other checking fields, the opcode signature being the most promising alternative. Reducing this field could also reduce the error coverage of the associated mechanism (not described in this work) so the reduction requires further analysis.

Another interesting result depicted in this paper is the error length distribution in the address calculation process. Although single-bit errors are injected into the model, the arithmetic circuitry used in the address calculation process when a branch is taken helps the error to propagate as a multiple-bit error at the computed value. The error length distribution can be applied to other architectures using absolute or program counter relative addressing modes and would help future researchers to take into account this propagation when designing error detection mechanisms.

Acknowledgements

This work is supported by the Ministerio de Educación y Ciencia of the Spanish Government under project TIC2003-08106-C02-01.

References

1. Avresky, D., Grosspietsch, K. E., Johnson, B. W., Lombardi, F.: Embedded fault tolerant systems. IEEE Micro Magazine, (1998) 18(5):8–11
2. IEEE Std. 1076-1993: VHDL Language Reference Manual. The Institute of Electrical and Electronics Engineers Inc., New York (1995)

3. Gunneflo, U., Karlsson, J., Torin, J.: Evaluation of Error Detection Schemes Using Fault Injection by Heavy-ion Radiation. In Proceedings of the 19th Fault Tolerant Computing Symposium (FTCS-19), Chicago, Illinois (1989) 340–347
4. Czeck, E.W., Siewieorek, D.P.: Effects of Transient Gate-Level Faults on Program Behavior. In Proceedings of the 20th Fault Tolerant Computing Symposium (FTCS-20), NewCastle Upon Tyne, U.K. (1990) 236–243
5. Ohlsson, J., Rimén, M., Gunneflo, U.: A Study of the Effects of Transient Fault Injection into a 32-bit RISC with Built-in Watchdog. In Proceedings of the 22th Fault Tolerant Computing Symposium (FTCS-22), Boston, USA (1992) 316–325
6. Siewiorek, D.P.: Niche Sucesses to Ubiquitous Invisibility: Fault-Tolerant Computing Past, Present, and Future. In Proceedings of the 25th Fault Tolerant Computing Symposium (FTCS-25), Pasadena, USA (1995) 26–33
7. Rodríguez, F., Campelo, J.C., Serrano, J.J.: A Watchdog Processor Architecture with Minimal Performance Overhead. Lecture Notes in Computer Science (LNCS Series), Springer-Verlag ed. (2002) vol. 2434, 261–272
8. Rodríguez, F., Campelo, J.C., Serrano, J.J.: The HORUS Processor. In Proceedings of the XVII Conference on Design of Circuits and Integrated Systems (DCIS 2002), Santander, Spain (2002) 517–522
9. MIPS32 Architecture for Programmers, volume I: Introduction to the MIPS32 Architecture. MIPS Technologies (2001)
10. AMBA Specification rev2.0. ARM Limited (1999)
11. Hennessy, J.L., Patterson, D.A.: Computer Architecture. A Quantitative Approach (2nd edition). Morgan-Kauffmann Publisher (1996)

Support Industrial Hard Real-Time Traffic with Switched Ethernet

Alimujiang Yiming and Toshio Eisaka

Kitami Institute of Technology, Kitami, Hokkaido 090-8507, Japan
alm_ym@mer.cs.kitami-it.ac.jp
eisaka@cs.kitami-it.ac.jp

Abstract. This paper presents a simple and efficient switched Ethernet communication protocol for industrial hard real-time LAN applications. The network is founded with end nodes and a switch, and hard real-time communication is handled by software added between the Ethernet protocols and the TCP/IP suites. We established a virtual link of the source and destination node by applying admission control based upon the requested QoS, and manages hard real-time traffic to bypass the TCP/IP stacks. This bypassing considerably reduces the dwell time in the nodes, and increases the achievable data frame rate. After the bypassing, hard real-time traffic schedule is executed according to dynamic-priority EDF algorithm.

The protocol does not need any modifications in the Ethernet hardware and coexists with TCP/IP suites, therefore, the LAN with the protocol can be connected to any existing Ethernet networks and support both real-time traffic and best-effort traffic. Compared to some conventional hard real-time network protocols, the proposed one has better real-time performances, and meets the requirements of reliability for hard real-time system applications.

1 Introduction

With the increasingly demand for real-time industrial control systems, the ability of computer networks to handle deadline guaranteed "hard" real-time communication is becoming more and more important [1], [2], [3]. High bandwidth and strict deadline guarantee are the critical necessary conditions for hard real-time applications [4]. Unlike traditional, bus-based CSMA/CD Ethernet, the switched Ethernet is a star-based topology which can avoid collision since Data terminal equipment (DTE) connected to a switch communicating in full duplex does not have to use the CSMA/CD access control [5]. Therefore, end node cooperation is needed only for bandwidth control. In addition to this, the full-duplex operation theoretically doubles the bandwidth of the network, and the Ethernet transmission rate and communication reliability have increased over the years. This together with serious attempts to adapt Ethernet hardware to industrial environments, make it an interesting alternative for real-time communication.

Several researches have been done to treat hard real-time communication. MIL-STD-1533 [6] is an early development of the industrial protocol. It is reliable standard interface for token ring LAN. However, bandwidth is one of the main limiting

L.T. Yang et al. (Eds.): ICESS 2005, LNCS 3820, pp. 671 – 682, 2005.

factors for MIL-STD-1533. Another protocol, RTCC (Real-Time Communication Control) [7], is centralized approach that has the disadvantage that failure in the controller will lead to the entire network useless, unless some sort of recovery protocol is implemented. Other researches using switched Ethernet for hard real-time communication is studied in [8], [9], however, these protocols either bring about complex network structures or need Ethernet hardware modifications to implement.

Recently, new schemes have been proposed based on admission control depending upon quality of service (QoS) and choice of the packet service discipline. The common concept of the schemes is establishment of a *Real-time Channel*: a simplex, virtual connection between source nodes and destination nodes, with a priori guarantees for communication performance in switching networks [10], [11], [12].

To support the QoS demands of applications, both the ATM and the IP community have defined service classes that provided per-flow guarantees to applications [13], [14]. In order to provide guaranteed services, resources need to be reserved for every accepted connection. ATM does this at the data-link layer. For every call it reserves a virtual channel over all links on the route/switch from the source to the destination. At the network layer, resource reservation can be done using Diffserv [15] or MPLS [16]. Applications at this level are classified as best-effort, rate sensitive or delay sensitive, therefore, there are no guarantee for strict deadline-sorted real-time communication. RSVP [17] can be used to do reservation at the IP layer. RSVP makes resource reservations for both unicast and multicast applications, therefore, it is more appropriate for multimedia communication in a wide area network such as videoconferencing. Because RSVP is based on IP, there is no guarantee of deadline in application service lifetime, and have large runtime overhead, therefore, there are few applications in industrial control systems.

Based on the knowledge of above mentioned QoS architectures and protocols, in our work, we studied the industrial and embedded application demands on hard real-time communication services, including survey of real-time communication with focus on LAN-technology and switched communication. Then we developed and analyzed a protocol to schedule and control the hard real-time traffic based on the industrial and embedded real-time demands without changing the underlying protocols, while still supporting existing upper protocols for soft real-time and/or non-real-time traffic. We also establish a way (virtual link) between source nodes and destination nodes by applying admission control based upon the requested QoS. However, in our work, a key strategy to realize hard real-time communication is, the proposed protocol manages hard real-time traffic to bypass the TCP/IP stacks. This makes considerably reduce the dwell time in the nodes, and increase the achievable data frame rate by evasion of the non-deterministic behavior inherent in the TCP and IP stacks. This is the main point of our work.

An Ethernet LAN using a switch and several end nodes was constructed, and several experiments have been performed to evaluate the proposed protocol. Comparing with the conventional hard real-time communication protocols, the proposed Ethernet protocol has better real-time performances and meets the requirements of reliability for hard real-time systems.

The rest of the paper is organized as follows. In section 2, outline of the network architecture is introduced. Section 3 describes the RT channel establishment by applying the admission control. Section 4 illustrates the management of hard real-time traffic and best-effort traffic. We elaborate feasibility analysis for RT channel establishment and focus on scheduling of real-time frames in section 5. In section 6, performance evaluation of the proposed protocol is presented. The paper is concluded in section 7.

2 Network Architecture

We applied a full-duplex switched Ethernet LAN which is connected to existing Internet. A switched Ethernet provides some key benefits over traditional Ethernet, such as full duplex and flow control. Therefore, switches enable flexible network configuration of multiple and simultaneous links between various ports.

In our work, a key strategy to realize hard real-time communication is *bypassing* of TCP/IP suites. In order to manage this bypass, both the switch and the end nodes have software --- real-time layer (RT layer) added between the Ethernet protocols and the TCP/IP suite in the OSI reference model. All nodes are connected to the switch and nodes can communicate mutually on the logical real-time channels (RT channel), it is a virtual connection between two nodes of the system respectively (see Fig. 1).

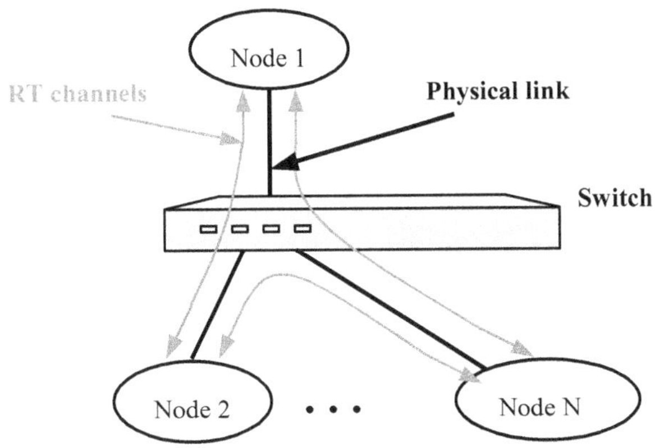

Fig. 1. Network architecture with RT channels

A node can either be real-time node or non real-time node depending on which level QoS is required. Non-real-time node (without RT layer added) can coexist in the network without disturbing the real-time traffic. MAC function, frame buffering and the concentrated transmission arbitration is included in the switch. Therefore, switch has the overall responsibility both for set-up of RT channels and for online control of packets passing through the switch. The RT layer do-nothing to non real-time frames and makes them go through the ordinary circuit with TCP/IP suites.

3 RT Channel Establishment

Before the real-time traffic is transmitted, the RT channel should be established. The establishment of RT channel is including request and recognition communication after the source nodes, destination nodes and switch have agreement with channel establishment. As new real-time requests (channel establishment) are made, they goes through an admission control module that determines if there is sufficient network bandwidth available to satisfy the request of the node. Admission control is the problem of deciding which requests to accept and which to reject based upon the supported QoS, with the goal of maximizing the total profit accrued by the accepted requests. In other words, admission control is the problem of finding a feasible solution with maximum profit.

If the network establishes a transmission request, it first decides on a path from the sending node to the receiving node of that transmission, through which the transmission is being routed. Then it allocates the requested amount of bandwidth and/or buffer space on all links along that path during the time period in which the transmission is active. The allocated resources are released when the connection is completed.

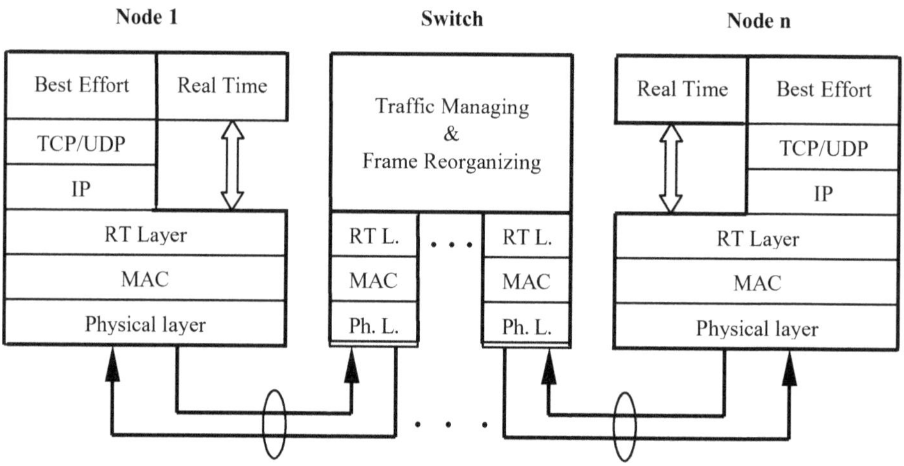

Fig. 2. Real-Time channel establishment

Fig. 2 describes the establishment of an RT channel. When a node wants to send hard real-time frames, it directly accesses the RT layer. The RT layer then sends "RT channel establishment request" to the RT traffic management in the switch. The switch then evaluates the feasibility of traffic schedule of a path from the sending node to the receiving node of that transmission, by applying the admission control. If the schedule is feasible, the switch responses with the network schedule parameters to the sending node. Otherwise, the switch sends out a set of recommended control parameters to the sending node. These control parameters are suggested based on the status of switch queue and the active queue control law.

4 Traffic Management

After RT channel is established, only real-time data traffic from the end node bypasses the TCP/IP stacks. An RT channel should cross two physical links according to the RT layer: one from the source node to the switch, and the other from the switch to the destination node (uploads and downloads, respectively). The RT channel is required to provide real-time guarantees for both the upload and the download.

Besides hard real-time traffic, our Ethernet network protocol should allow for best-effort traffic which does not affect the transmission of hard real-time packets. Namely, best-effort traffic (non real-time or soft real-time traffic) come from best-effort protocols (HTTP, SMTP, FTP, etc.) uses the services of the TCP/IP protocol suites and put in an FCFS-sorted (First Come First Serve) queue in the RT layer. In order to achieve this, best-effort traffic is allowed when no hard real-time packets want to transmit.

When a hard real-time packet becomes ready to transmit again, the RT channel management immediately interrupts the best-effort traffic, and goes to the corresponding node so that the hard real-time traffic may start. According to the RT layer, the last node visited for best-effort traffic should be remembered, so the next round of best-effort traffic packet can start off at that node.

Because there are two different output queues for each port on the switch, "frame recognizing" is necessary. On that account, the switch has two MAC addresses: one is for control traffic (e.g., RT channel request frames); and the other is for hard real-time traffic over RT channels. And then, the switch will be able to recognize the different kinds of frames: control frames, real-time data frames and best-effort data frames that come from TCP/IP stacks.

5 Scheduling of Hard Real-Time Frames

In our star-like network architecture, every end node is connected with a private virtual link to a switch, so that there is a private traffic link for each direction. But congestion may occur when one node is suddenly receiving a lot of packets from the other nodes. Current switches do not provide any guarantees as to which packets will be sent first. We solved this by providing a switch with bandwidth reservation capabilities inside the switch, and we used Earliest Deadline First (EDF) scheduling [18] to make decisions as to which packets are forwarded first. This provides guarantees for both bit rates and strict delivery deadlines.

First, we check the feasibility of the real-time traffic according to calculate the total utilization of all frames. RT channel of the *i*-th task is characterized by $\{T_{pd,i}, C_i, T_{d,i}\}$; where $T_{pd,i}$ is period of the data, C_i is time required to complete the execution of the task per the period, $T_{d,i}$ is the relative deadline used for the end-to-end EDF scheduling.

The task period $T_{pd,i}$ can be described as:

$$T_{pd,i} = T_{n1,i} + T_{n2,i} + T_{ct}, \tag{1}$$

where $T_{n1,i}$ and $T_{n2,i}$ are the deadlines of each real-time frame for upload and download, respectively; and T_{ct} is the delay introduced by the switch. In a fully switched Ethernet there is only one equipment (end node) per each switch port. In case that wire-speed full-duplex switches are used, the end-to-end delay can be minimized by decreasing the message buffering.

According to EDF theory, the total utilization of all frames is then calculated as:

$$U = \sum_i \frac{C_i}{T_{pd,i}} . \tag{2}$$

Suppose $T_{pd,i} \le T_{d,i}$ for simplicity, it is well known that EDF scheduling is feasible if and only if $U \le 1$.

If the test for task *i* succeed and real-time channel is established, hard real-time data frame bypasses the TCP/IP stacks and put in a deadline-sorted queue scheduled by RT layer in the switch and end nodes according to the EDF theory.

The processes of hard real-time traffic and best-effort traffic transmission is shown in Fig. 3, and is summarized as follows:

1. When the switch received a packet from an end-node, it recognizes which application the packet is come from (real-time or best-effort).

2. If the packet come from the real-time application, then the RT layer interrupt transmitting best-effort traffic immediately so that the hard real-time traffic may start. And the information for last transmitted queue of the best-effort traffic should be stored so that the next round of best-effort traffic can start off at that queue.

3-A. The switch will be able to recognize the different kinds of frames: control frames (e.g., RT channel request frames) and real-time data frames. If the received packet is the control frame, then the RT layer must go through an admission control module that determines if there is sufficient network resource (bandwidth and guaranteed time limit) available to satisfy the request of the node.

4-A. If a request is admitted, the switch answers to the requesting nodes with a set of network schedule parameters, and make RT channel virtual connection. And then allocates the requested amount of bandwidth and/or buffer space on this connection link.

4'-A. Otherwise, the switch sends out a set of recommended control parameters to the sending node.

5-B. After RT channel is established, hard real-time data is delivered through the circuit and bypassing the TCP/IP stacks by reading MAC addresses in response parameter.

6-B. The RT layer makes the switch recalculate the Ethernet cyclic redundancy check (CRC) of an incoming hard real-time frame before putting it to the correct deadline-sorted output queue. This will also be useful to increase the reliability of the hard real-time data frames.

7-B. Real-time data passed the above check is then put in a deadline-sorted queue scheduled by RT layer in the switch and end-nodes according to the EDF theory, and then,

8-B. Forward the deadline-sorted data to the destination node. The allocated resources are released when the connection is completed.

3-C. On the other hand, by carrying the final destination MAC address in the Ethernet header when leaving from the source node, non or soft real-time data is delivered through the circuit including the TCP/IP stacks in an FCFS-sorted queue, and transmit the traffics at the idle time of the schedule.

4-C. If a best-effort sender needs to send a large amount of data (for example, a long packet), it tries to make an additional cycling time reservation and transmit its data immediately after reservation. If the time is over and the long packet did not finished yet, it tries to make a reservation again.

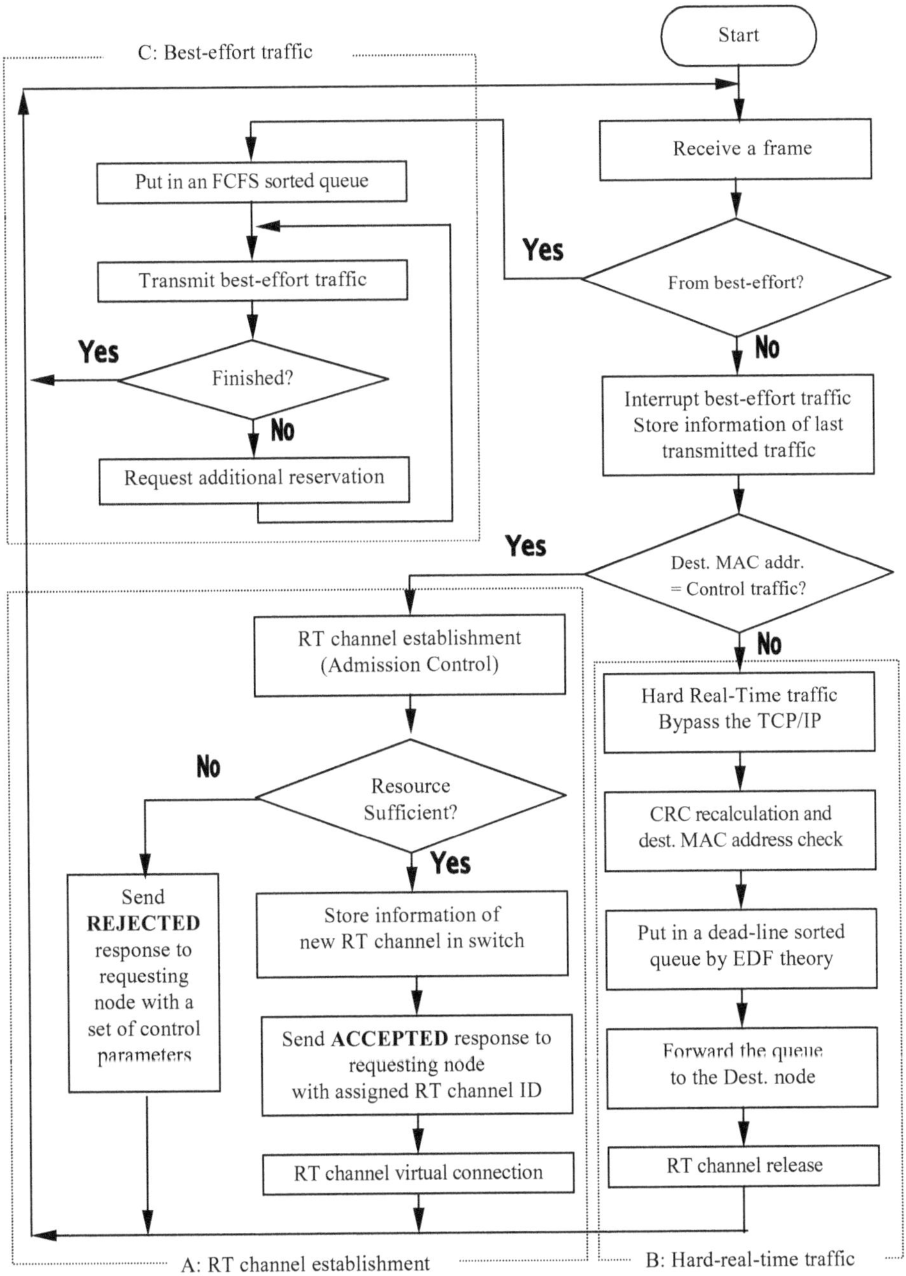

Fig. 3. Processes of traffic transmission

6 Performance Evaluation

In order to evaluate our work, we made a LAN with a full-duplex switched Ethernet and end-nodes, by using desktop computer with AMD-K7(tm) Processor 700MHz and several embedded Ethernet development boards which is produced by YDK Technologies Inc. that provides a hardware platform based on Altera® ACEX™ devices (see Fig. 4).

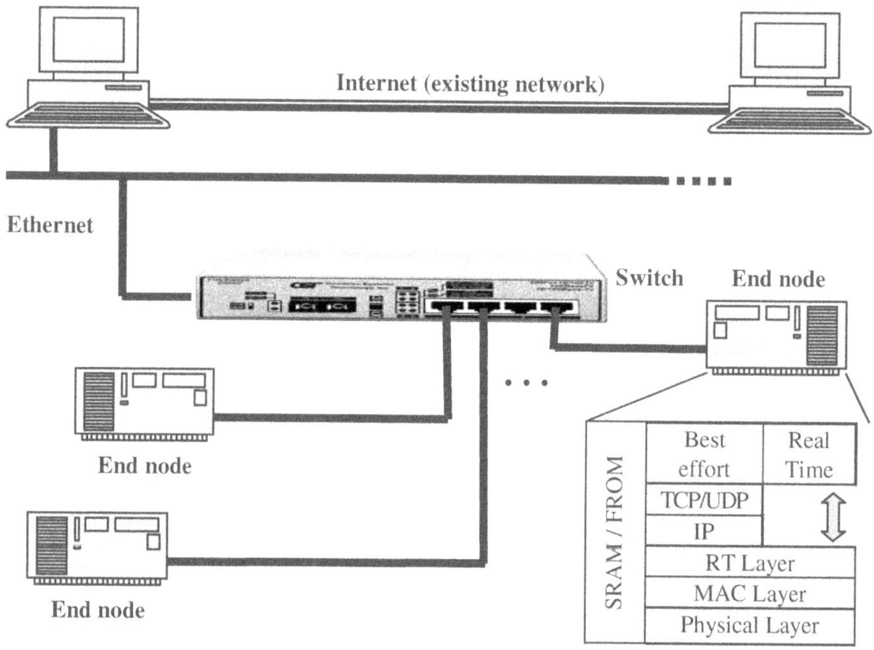

Fig. 4. LAN with full-duplex switched Ethernet

We use a 5-ports Ethernet switch with full-duplex links at 100Mbps. The size of data packet is from 64 bytes to 1538 bytes. There are no modifications in the Ethernet hardware on the NIC (Network Interface Card). Ethernet development board is linked with PC via the Ethernet switch. In order to establish interaction and communication with the Ethernet development board, we downloaded the software (RT layer) to Flash Memory on the board. When download the software to the flash memory, the system module pins are logically connected to pins on the ACEX device. The external physical pins on the ACEX device are in turn connected to other hardware components on the board, allowing the Nios embedded processor to interface with SRAM, FROM, LEDs, LCDs, buttons and switch.

Below we discuss about the transmission latency of the real-time frame in worst-case situation. When all RT-channel starts simultaneously, or all the messages that use all the capability allowances of the RT channel, RT channel equipped with the longest deadline will be scheduled at last so that it may have the worst-case latency. Here for all RT channels, the maximum latency is characterized by:

$$T_{m\_lat} = \max_i \{T_{n1,i} + T_{n2,i} + T_t\}, \tag{3}$$

where $T_{n1,i}$ is the latency from source nodes to switch, $T_{n2,i}$ is the latency from switch to destination nodes, and T_t is the total latency of the switch.

Besides utilization and worst-case latency, another important performance is a runtime overhead: R_i defined as:

$$R_i = \frac{T_{pd,i} - L_i \times 8 / B}{T_{pd,i}}, \tag{4}$$

where L_i is the length of data in a request frame, $L_i \times 8$ is the number of bits in the frame; $T_{pd,\ i}$ represents the period duration from the startup to the end of the frame, and B represents the Ethernet bandwidth.

Utilization, Data frame transmission latency and the frame runtime overhead can be obtained by implementing the proposed protocol to the LAN. Fig. 5 illustrates the utilization on real-time data frame.

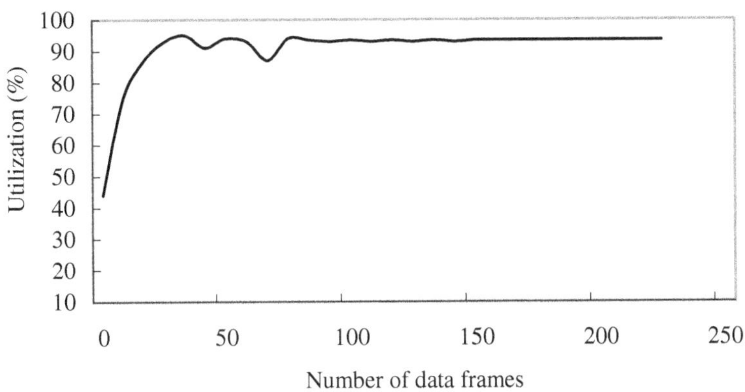

Fig. 5. Utilization on real-time data frame

From the figure we can learn that the trend of utilization is increasing while the traffic increases, until arriving at the peak value that is more than 90%. Sudden decreases happen on the curve sometimes, which is caused by some short frames having pad field whose utilization are lower than longer frames. The utilization curve is always smooth, because we assume the sufficient resources (bandwidth and time specification) have been obtained in our work, when the RT channel is established. Under this circumstance, there should be no overload exists in the real-time channel. The result shows that the deadlines have been met for all data because utilization of all data frames is less than 100% using EDF scheduling. Dynamic priority scheduling with the EDF algorithm has a distinct advantage over fixed priority scheduling: the schedulable bound for EDF is 100% for all task sets [19]. This means that we can fully utilize the computing power of the CPU. Embedded systems are in general fully loaded, as they attempt to get as close to 100% utilization as possible while still maintaining the necessary predictability.

To the best of our knowledge, except a few implementations of hard real-time communication protocols on Ethernet, most of the protocols are generally soft real-time, which means that there are few protocols provides guarantees for both bit rate and strict delivery deadlines, so that it is difficult to compare them with the proposed hard real-time protocol. Therefore, we made performance comparison of the proposed protocol only with the hard real-time communication protocols: MIL-STD-1553B protocol and RTCC protocol. Fig. 6 shows the comparison of the data frame transmission latency of these three kinds of hard real-time communication protocols.

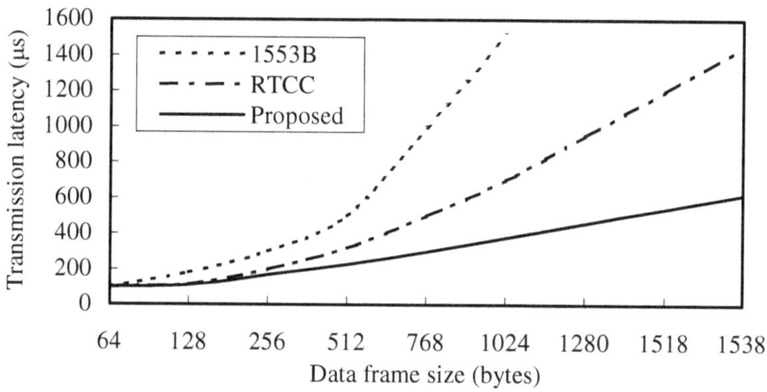

Fig. 6. Transmission latency of data frame

Even for the Ethernet frames that have the data field maximized (1538 bytes in IEEE 802.3 standard), the latency of the proposed protocol is about 620 microseconds. This latency is quite short in a LAN with a full-duplex switched Ethernet at 100 Mbps, and meets the demands of hard real-time communication for industrial distributed control systems. Runtime overhead of data frames are demonstrated in Fig. 7. The figure shows that the runtime overhead of the proposed protocol is higher than the other hard real-time supported protocols at the small-sized data frame. However, as the data frame size become larger (from about 900 bytes), the proposed protocol has better runtime overhead than the other protocols. In both experiments, only MIL-STD-1553B protocol used 1Mbps Ethernet because it is the nominal speed of the protocol.

Furthermore, in order to evaluate the time effectiveness of hard real-time bypassing the TCP/IP stack, we made experiments with ordinary UDP/IP and TCP/IP protocols comparing with the proposed protocol (see Fig. 8). The result shows that by using the proposed protocol to bypass the TCP/IP stacks can reduce 32% of the time comparing with UDP/IP protocol, and more than 50% of the time comparing with TCP/IP protocol even if the proposed protocol needs RT channel establishment and EDF scheduling.

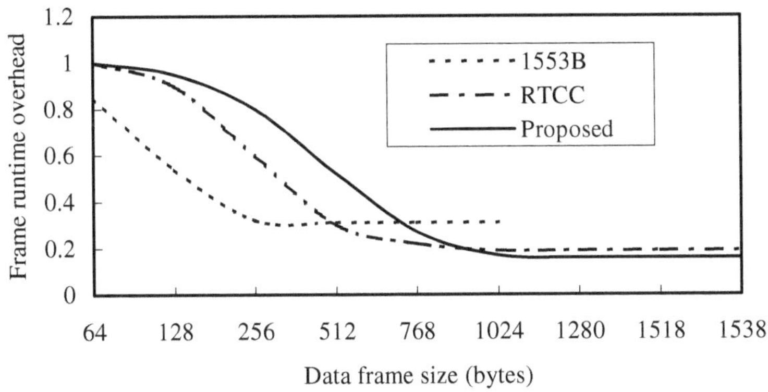

Fig. 7. Runtime overhead of data frame

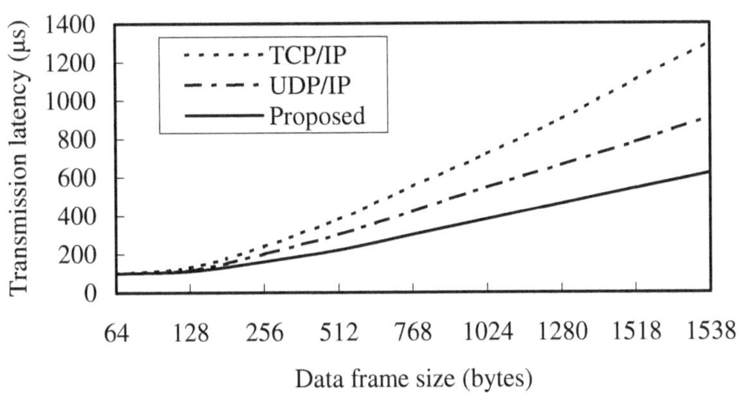

Fig. 8. Transmission latency comparison

7 Conclusion

In this paper, we have presented a simple and efficient switched Ethernet communication protocol for industrial hard real-time applications. The network is set up with nodes and a switch; both switch and end nodes have an RT layer added to support hard real-time traffic. The proposed protocol establishes a virtual link between source nodes and destination nodes by applying admission control based upon the requested QoS. Hard real-time traffic from the end-node bypasses the TCP/IP stacks and thus considerably speed up real-time communication. Real-time traffic scheduling is performed according to dynamic-priority EDF algorithm, therefore it is flexible and efficient.

In the proposed work, there are no modifications in the Ethernet hardware on the NIC. This allows connecting the Ethernet LAN to existing Internet networks. Thus, it can be adopted in industrial hard real-time applications such as embedded systems, distributed control systems and robotics.

We have constructed a simple Ethernet LAN with the proposed protocol and evaluated the protocol. Through the comparison with some conventional hard real-time network protocols, we have shown that the proposed protocol has better real-time performances, and meets the requirements of reliability for hard real-time systems.

One of our further works is to implement the proposed protocol in the multi-layer, many switches real-time communication systems.

References

1. G. Buttazzo: Hard Real-time Computing Systems, Predictable Scheduling Algorithms and Applications - Real-Time Systems Series 2ND Edition, Springer Verlag, (2004)
2. J. Stankovic and K. Ramamritham: Hard Real-Time Systems, IEEE Computer Society Press, (1988)
3. C. Krishna and K.G. Shin: Real-Time Systems, McGraw-Hill International edition, (1997)
4. M. Joseph: Real-Time Systems, Prentice Hall, (1996)
5. IEEE Std. 802.3, 2000 Edition: IEEE Standard for Information technology -- Telecommunications and information exchange between systems -- Local and metropolitan area networks -- Common specifications -- Part 3: Carrier sense multiple access with collision detection (CSMA/CD) access method and physical layer specifications.
6. http://www.condoreng.com/support/downloads/tutorials/MIL-STD-1553Tutorial.PDF
7. Z. P. Wang, G. Z. Xiong, J. Luo, M. Z. Lai and W. Zhou: A hard real-time communication control protocol based on the Ethernet, Proceedings of 7th Australasian Conference on Parallel and Real-Time Systems (PART 2000), pp.161-170, (2000)
8. J. Loeser and H. Haertig: Low-latency hard real-time communication over switched Ethernet, Proceedings of 16th Euromicro Conference on Real-Time Systems (ECRTS'04), pp. 13-22, (2004)
9. S. Ouni and F. Kamoun: Hard and soft real time message scheduling on Ethernet networks, Proceedings of the 2nd IEEE International Conference on Systems, Man and Cybernetics of the twenty-first century, 6, (2002)
10. D. Ferrari and D. Verma: A scheme for real-time channel establishment in wade-area networks, IEEE Jornal of Selected Areas in Communications, vol.8, no.3, pp.368-379, (1990)
11. L. Zhang: Designing a new architecture for packet switching communication networks, IEEE Communications Magazine, vol. 25, n. 9, pp. 5-12, (1987).
12. G. Agrawal, B. Chen, W. Zhao, and S. Davari: Guaranteeing Synchronous Message Deadlines with Time Token Medium Access Control Protocol, *IEEE Transactions on Computers*, Vol. 43, No. 3, pp 327-339, (1994)
13. A. Leon-Garcia and I. Widjaja: Communication Networks - Fundamental Concepts and Key Architectures, McGraw-Hill Osborne, (2001)
14. M. Schwartz & T. E. Stern: Routing Protocols, in Computer Network Architectures and Protocols (Second Ed.), Ed. C.A. Sunshine, Plenum Press, New York / London (1989)
15. S. Blake, D. Black, M. Carlson, E. Davies, Z. Wang, and W. Weiss: An architecture for differentiated service, RFC 2475, 1998.
16. E. Rosen, A. Viswanathan, and R. Callon: Multiprotocol label switching architecture, RFC 2005, 1997.
17. L. Zhang, S. Deering, D. Estrin, S. Shenker, and D. Zappala: RSVP: a new resource reservation protocol, IEEE Network Magazine, 30-9, pp. 8-18, (1993).
18. C. L. Liu and J. W. Layland: Scheduling algorithms for multi-programming in hard real-time traffic environment, Journal of the Association for Computing Machinery, 20-1, pp.46-61, (1973)
19. Phillip A. Laptane: Real-Time System Design and Analysis, IEEE Press, third edition, (2004)

Integer Factorization by a Parallel GNFS Algorithm for Public Key Cryptosystems*

Laurence Tianruo Yang, Li Xu, and Man Lin

Department of Computer Science, St. Francis Xavier University,
Antigonish, NS, B2G 2W5, Canada

Abstract. RSA is a very popular public key cryptosystem for encryption and authentication. The security of RSA mainly relies on the difficulty of factoring large integers. Recent advancement in factoring algorithms have made it possible to factor integers with 150-digits or more. The General Number Field Sieve algorithm (GNFS) is currently the best known method for factoring large numbers over 110 digits. Although the GNFS algorithm is efficient, it still takes a long time to factor a large integer such as an integer with 150-digits or larger. In this paper, we present a parallel GNFS implementation on a SUN-cluster. It can successfully factor integers up to 116 digits very quickly. The experimental results have demonstrated that the algorithm achieves good speedup and can be used for further larger integer factorization.

1 Introduction

RSA [11] is a very popular public-key encryption and decryption algorithm. The security of this algorithm relies on the difficulty of factoring large integers. So far, people have developed many good, fast factoring algorithms. Examples are the Quadratic Sieve (QS) algorithm [4], the Elliptic Curve (ECM) algorithm [9], the Special Number Field Sieve (SNFS) algorithm [2] and the General Number Field Sieve (GNFS) algorithm [3].

The General Number Field Sieve (GNFS) algorithm [3, 5, 7] is derived from the Number Fields Sieve (NFS) algorithm, developed by A. K. Lenstra, H. W. Lenstra, M. S. Manasse and J. M. Pollard [6]. It is the fastest known algorithm for integer factorization. Generally, it is used to factor integer larger than *110* digits.

Sequential GNFS algorithm has been implemented by many researchers. This paper presents an implementation of parallel GNFS algorithm on a SUN cluster. The implementation is based on the sequential code developed by C. Monico [3].

This chapter is organized as follows. We will introduce the GNFS algorithm in section 2. Then we will introduce the detailed parallel algorithm, followed by running results in section 3. The performance analysis will be described in section 4 and the conclusions will be given in section 5.

* The authors' email are {lyang, x2002uwf, mlin}@stfx.ca. The authors would like to thank C. Monico for sharing the serial GNFS code and the help for some technical problems. The authors would also like to thank NSERC for supporting this research.

L.T. Yang et al. (Eds.): ICESS 2005, LNCS 3820, pp. 683–695, 2005.

2 The General Number Field Sieve Algorithm

GNFS is based on the idea of the congruence of squares algorithm [1].

Suppose we are going to factor an integer n (n has two prime factors p and q). Assume there are two integers s and r. Both s^2 and r^2 are perfect squares and satisfy the constraint $s^2 \equiv r^2 \ (mod\ n)$. Since $n = pq$, the following conditions hold [7]:

$$pq|(s^2\text{-}r^2) \Rightarrow pq|(s\text{-}r)(s+r)$$
$$\Rightarrow p|(s\text{-}r)(s+r) \text{ and } q|(s\text{-}r)(s+r)$$

From the number theory we know that, if $c|ab$ and $gcd(b,c) = 1$, then $c|a$. So p, q, r *and* s must satisfy $p|(s\text{-}r)$ or $p|(s+r)$ and $q|(s\text{-}r)$ or $q|(s+r)$. Fig. 1 is a well known table (quoted from [7]) in the area of integer factorization. It shows that there is *2/3* possibilities to factor n by computing the $gcd(n, s+r)$ and $gcd(n, s\text{-}r)$.

The question is: how can we find a congruence of squares? Searching directly for a congruence of squares is certainly inefficient. As many other popular factoring methods, GNFS utilizes the following scheme. It first sieves for relations involving arbitrary powers of numbers from sets called "factor base". Then after collecting enough such relations, it finds a relation whose powers are all even by solving equations defined by a huge matrix. A congruence of squares can then be easily constructed.

There are five major steps (see Fig. 2) in GNFS described in [7].

Step 1: Select Parameters. The theory of GNFS is very sophisticated. The trick is to express the number being factored as a polynomial with small coefficients.

$$n = a_d m^d + a_{d-1} m^{d-1} + \ldots\ldots + a_0. \tag{1}$$

In order to do this, we need to set up two parameters: a polynomial $f(x){:}R \rightarrow R$ with integer coefficients and an integer $m \in N$. These two parameters satisfy the equation $f(m) \equiv 0 \ (mod\ n)$.

Before we set up $f(x)$ and m, we can find the degree d of the polynomial. Table 1 give us some hint of how to choose d [5]. After choosing d, we can choose m to be around $\sqrt[d]{n}$.

Possible Divisibility Scenarios				GCD Results		
$p \mid (s+r)$	$p \mid (s-r)$	$q \mid (s+r)$	$q \mid (s-r)$	$\gcd(pq, s+r)$	$\gcd(pq, s-r)$	Successful Factorization
No	Yes	No	Yes	1	pq	
No	Yes	Yes	No	q	p	⋆
No	Yes	Yes	Yes	q	pq	⋆
Yes	No	No	Yes	p	q	⋆
Yes	No	Yes	No	pq	1	
Yes	No	Yes	Yes	pq	q	⋆
Yes	Yes	No	Yes	p	pq	⋆
Yes	Yes	Yes	No	pq	p	⋆
Yes	Yes	Yes	Yes	pq	pq	

Fig. 1. Possibilities for p and q dividing $s+r$ and $s\text{-}r$

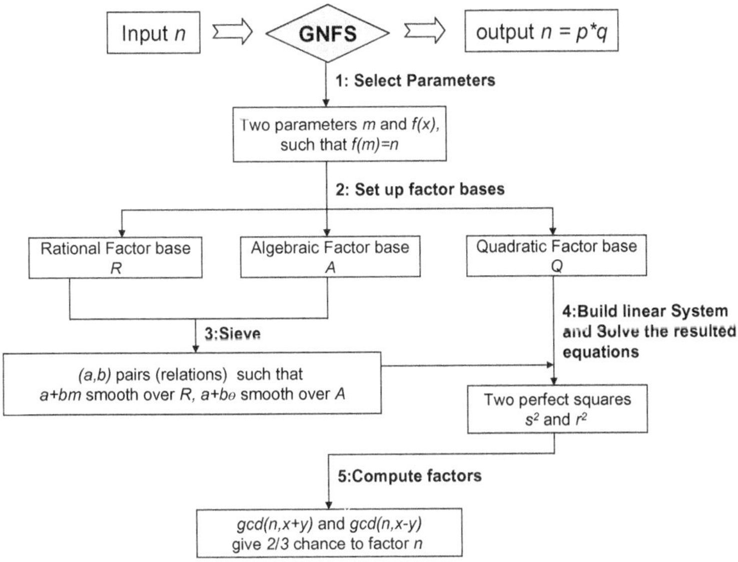

Fig. 2. The 5 major steps of the GNFS algorithm

Table 1. Choosing degree of $f(x)$

Digits of n	< 50	50 - 80	50 - 80	< 110
Degree	2	3	4	5

Step 2: Set Up Factor Bases. After all parameters have been set up, there are three factor bases to be initialized, namely: rational factor base(R), algebraic factor base(A) and quadratic character base(Q). It is easy to verify that each pair (r,p) in A satisfies $f(r) \equiv 0 \ (mod\ p)$. And each (q, s) in Q satisfies $f(s) \equiv 0 \ (mod\ q)$ and q not in A.

Step 3: Sieve. The purpose of sieving is to find pairs (a,b) such that $a+bm$ is R-smooth and $a+b\theta$ is A-smooth [5]. Recall that θ is a root of $f(m)$.

The following shows how the sieving is done.

1. First we set the range of a and b. Let a change from $-N$ and N, b change from $-C$ and C (N and C are integers). For each b, create two arrays: one is set up for $a+bm$ and another is set up for $a+b\theta$. Fig. 3 shows the sieve array [7].
2. For each $p_i \in R$, p_i will divide $a+bm$ if and only if $a = -bm + kp_i$. We check every a for a certain b, mark each value of a that satisfies $a = -bm + kp_i$ and make note of the factor of $a + bm$ in the sieve array. After we check all as for certain b, we increase b by 1, then repeat the checking.
3. For each $(p,r) \in A$, (p,r) divides $a+b\theta$ if and only if $a \equiv -br \ (mod\ p)$. We check every a for a certain b, if $a+b\theta$ can be divided by (p,r), we will make a note for this pair.

$-N + b\theta$	$-N + bm$
$(-N + 1) + \theta$	$(-N + 1) + m$
$\vdots$	$\vdots$
$(N - 1) + b\theta$	$(N - 1) + bm$
$N + b\theta$	$N + bm$

Fig. 3. Structure sieve arrays

Step 4: Build Linear System and Find Perfect Squares. Step 3 already results in a set U: $U = \{(a,b)|a + bm \textit{ and } a + b\theta \textit{ are smooth over } R \textit{ and } A, \textit{ respectively}\}$. In step 4, we need to select a subset of these (a, b) pairs to form two perfect squares. That is, we need to find a set V, such that

$$s^2 = \prod_{(a,b)\in V} (a + bm), \tag{2}$$

and

$$r^2 = \prod_{(a,b)\in V} (a + b\theta). \tag{3}$$

Let the rational factor base R be $\{t_1, t_2, \ldots, t_k\}$. Let the algebraic factor base A be $\{r_1, p_1), (r_2, p2), \ldots (r_l, p_l)\}$ and quadratic character base Q be $\{(s_1, q_1), (s_2, q_2), \ldots,$-$(s_u, q_u)\}$. In order to find two perfect squares, we need to verify the following four conditions:

1. $a + bm$ must be positive.
2. For $\prod_{(a,b)\in V}(a+bm) = t_1^{e_1} t_2^{e_2} \ldots t_k^{e_k}$ to be a perfect square, e_i must be even. That is $e_i \equiv 0\ (mod\ 2)$.
3. For $\prod_{(a,b)\in V}(a + b\theta)) = ((r_1, p_1)^{f_1}(r_2, p_2)^{f_2} \ldots (r_l, p_l)^{f_l}$ to be a perfect square, f_i must be even. That is $f_i \equiv 0\ (mod\ 2)$.
4. Furthermore, by Theorem 6 of [7], the following must also hold for $\prod_{(a,b)\in V}(a + b\theta))$ to be a perfect square: for any $(s, q) \in Q, \prod_{(a,b)\in V} \frac{(a+bs)}{q} = 1$.

We will build a matrix to store the verification information for each pair found in step 3. Each row vector corresponds to one pair. A row vector has *1+k+l+u* entries. The element of the matrix is either 0 or 1. Next, we describe how to construct the *1+k+l+u* entries for a pair (a_j, b_j).

1. the first entry records the sign of $a + bm$; (see condition 1).
2. the next k entries record $e_i\ mod\ 2$ where e_i is the exponent for t_i in R; (see condition 2).
3. the following l entries record $f_i\ mod\ 2$ where f_i is the exponent for (r_i, p_i) in A (see condition 3).
4. the final u entries record $\prod_{(a_j,b_j)\in V} \frac{(a_j+b_j s)}{q}$ for each $(s, q) \in Q$ (see condition 4).

After we build up M, we can solve the equation

$$M^T \begin{pmatrix} X_1 \\ X_2 \\ \vdots \\ \vdots \\ X_y \end{pmatrix} \equiv 0 \ (mod\ 2), \tag{4}$$

for $[X_1, X_2,.....,X_y]^T$. One example of the result could be :

$$[\,0,0,0,1,0,1,0,0,1,1,1,0,0,1,1,0,1,1,1,0,0,0,1,0,1,0,1,0,1,0,0,1,0,0,0,0,0,0]^T.$$

0 means not select and 1 means select. All the entries that have value 1 will be selected to produce perfect squares. Note that this equation has more than one solution because M has more rows then columns.

Next, we show the vector representation for pair *(119,11)* in our example.

$$[0\ (sign\ of\ a{+}bm),$$

$$0,0,1,0,0,0,0,0,1,0\ (exponents\ on\ the\ factors\ of\ a{+}bm),$$

$$0,0,0,0,0,0,1,0,0,0,0,0,1,0,0,0,0,0,1,0\ (exponents\ on\ the\ factors\ of\ a{+}b\theta),$$

$$1,1,0,0,0,0\ (for\ use\ with\ Q)].$$

Step 5: Compute Factors. As we said before, we have *2/3* possibilities to factor n if we get two perfect squares. So *(gcd(s+r),n)* and *(gcd(s-yr),n)* will give us the factors of n.

3 Parallel Implementation Details

3.1 Hardware and Software Programming Environment

Our parallel GNFS program is implemented on a Sun cluster. It consists of 2 dual processor master nodes (*Sun V65*) with hyper-threading enabled and 59 dual processor slaves nodes (*Sun V60*). Each node in the cluster has 2x 3.0 GHz Intel Xeon processors and 3 GB registered DDR-266 ECC SDRAM.

The parallel code is based on the serial code developed by C. Monico in [3]. The program is written in ANSI C and compiled by GNU C compiler (gcc). We adopts MPI as our parallel programming library because it has s rich set of communication routines and is suited for applications implemented on massively parallel processors. The foundation of MPI is a group of functions that can be called by program to achieve parallelism. The message passing functions can be used to transmit data between processors. MPICH1[10] is installed for MPI library. We also use a free library, GMP, for arbitrary precision arithmetic, operating on signed integers, rational numbers, and floating point numbers) 4.x is required to compile and run the program [12].

Table 2. GNFS integer factorization records

Digits	Sieve	Relation	Block Lanczos	Square Root	Total	Sieve/Total
30	26.5s	3.7s	0.1s	2.0s	32.3s	82%
39	15.0s	3.1s	0.1s	1.5s	19.7s	76.1%
45	184.3s	45.9s	4.1s	15.7	250s	74%
51	222.3s	63.9s	7.3s	18	311.5s	71.4%
61	3620.7s	591.7s	32.6s	57.4s	4320.4s	84%
76	26477.9s	8563.5s	1226.3s	904.2s	37171.9s	71.2%
98	17300.6s	2716.8s	504.6s	268.9s	20790.9s	83.2%

3.2 Timing Analysis of GNFS Steps

Before we start the parallel implementation, we perform a timing analysis of the serial code. Table 2 gives the timing results for the steps in GNFS for different chosen n.

From the table we can see that, sieving is the most time consuming step of GNFS algorithm. It takes *70%∼80%* of total execution time. The efficiency of the GNFS algorithm will be improved dramatically if we are able to improve sieving part.

3.3 Serial Sieving

Algorithm 1 gives the details of serial sieving. As we can see, the sieving is done in a two layer **for** loop. In the outer loop, b ranges from Min_b to Max_b. In the inner loop, b is fixed and a changes from -N to N. This process is very time consuming because the range of a and b are usually very large. Generally speaking, the time complexity of sieving increases when the digit of n increases. Table 3 gives the sieve time for some n.

Algorithm 1. Sequential sieving

```
b0 = Min_b;
b1 = Max_b;
a1 = −N;
a2 = N;
for (b=b0;b<b1;b++) do
   for (a=a1;a<a2;a++) do
      if Smooth_R(a,b) and Smooth_A(a,b) then
         save((a,b));
      end if
   end for
end for
```

3.4 Parallel Sieving

Since there are no relations between the generations of different *(a,b)* pairs, the sieving stage of GNFS is ideally suited for parallel implementation. The parallel sieving algo-

Table 3. Sieve time for different n

Digits of n	Range of b	Range of a	Time complexity
39	300	400000	$O(10^8)$
45	500	200000	$O(10^8)$
61	5000	1000000	$O(10^9)$
98	10000	2400000	$O(10^{10})$

rithm is shown in Algorithm 2. The parallel GNFS program uses one master node and a number of slave nodes. There are no communications between slaves in this program. The slave node only communicates with master node. Each slave node has a range partition for bs and generate relations within this b range.

Algorithm 2. Parallel sieving

```
MPI_Init();
MPIcomm_size();
MPI_Comm_rank()();
b0 = Min_b; b1 = Max_b;
a1 = -N; a2 = N;
num_of_bs = ((b1 - b0)/p)
MPI_Bcast(num_of_bs);
for (b=(taskid*num_of_bs+b0);b<(b0+(taskid+1)*num_of_bs); b++) do
   for (a=a1;a<a2;a++) do
      if Smooth_R(a, b) and Smooth_A(a,b) then
         if (master) then
            MPI_Recv((a,b));
            save((a,b));
         else
            MPI_Send((a,b));
         end if
      end if
   end for
end for
```

4 Performance Evaluation

4.1 Test Cases

We have eight test cases. Each of them uses a different n and runs on different number of processors. All test cases and number of processors are listed in Table 4. The eight composite numbers and their factor results can be found in the appendix.

4.2 Timing Results

Table 5 shows the sequential sieve time for each test case. Fig. 4 gives the parallel sieve time for the test cases using different number of processors. We put these test cases in

Table 4. Test cases and number of processors

Test case	Number of processes using
$tst100_{30}$	1, 2, 4, 8, 16, 32
$F7_{39}$	1, 2, 4, 8, 16, 32
$tst150_{45}$	1, 2, 4, 8, 16, 32
$briggs_{51}$	1, 2, 4, 8, 16, 32
$tst200_{61}$	1, 2, 4, 8, 16, 32
$tst250_{76}$	1, 2, 4, 8, 16, 32
$tstS1_{98}$	1, 2, 4, 8, 16, 32
$tstS2_{116}$	1, 2, 4, 8, 16, 32

Table 5. Total sieve time for each test case

Test case	$tst100_{30}$	$F7_{39}$	$briggs_{51}$	$tst200_{61}$	$tst250_{76}$	$tstS1_{98}$	$tstS2_{116}$
Total sieve time	26.5s	184.3s	222.3s	3620.7s	26477.9s	17300.6s	193864.3s

three sub-figures for readability. From these three figures we can see that the total sieve time for large size of n is much longer than small size of n. Fig. 5 gives the parallel execution time for the test cases using different number of processors. From the figure we can see that these curves have the same shape as the curves of parallel sieve time. This is because sieve time takes most of percentage of total execution time ($70\%\sim80\%$).

4.3 Speed-Up

Theoretically, suppose we have n bs and n as, and the sieve time complexity for serial code is $O(n^2)$. If we have p processors and each processor takes care of n/p bs, then the expected sieve time complexity will be $O(n^2/p)$. The speedups for the test cases using different number of processors are presented in Fig. 6.

4.4 Sieving Efficiency

The sieving efficiency is the sieving speed up divided by the number of processors. Fig. 7 gives the sieving efficiency for each test case.

4.5 Discussions

The parallel GNFS achieves good speedup. However, it is still possible to improve the algorithm. Next, we analyze the causes accounting for inefficiency for the current program and possible improvements.

- First, there are many communications between the master nodes and the slaves. Each slave node need to send the sieving results back to the master node for each b. The sieving results include three messages. So the total message passes back to the master node are $3(b_1\text{-}b_0)(p\text{-}1)/p$. The communications time increases when the size of n increases.

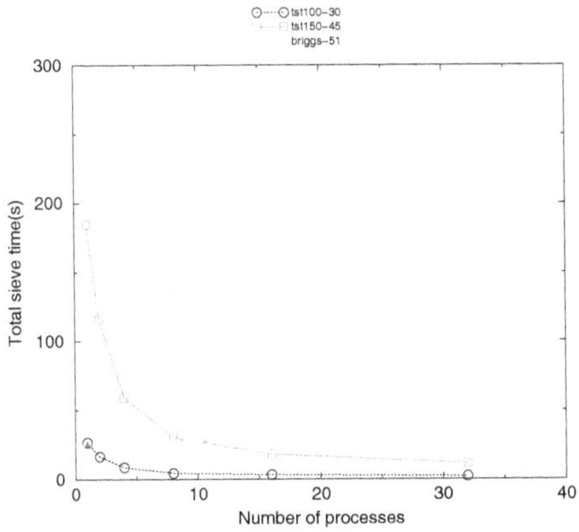

(a) n = 30, 45, 51 digits.

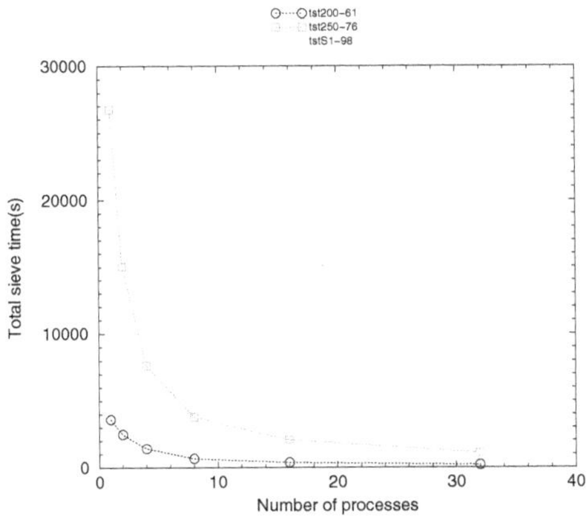

(b) n = 61, 76, 98 digits.

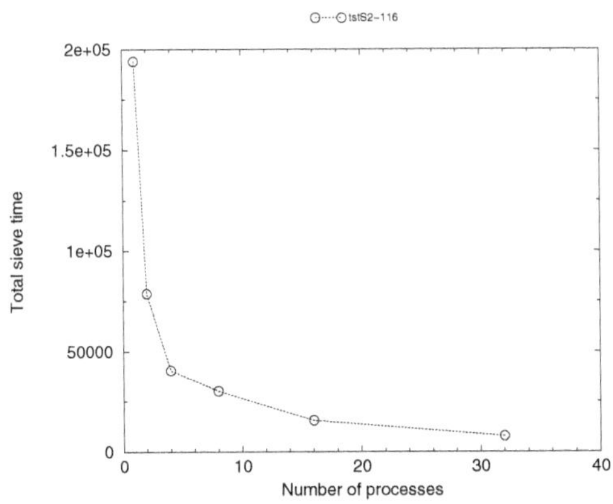

(c) n = 116 digits.

Fig. 4. Parallel sieve time

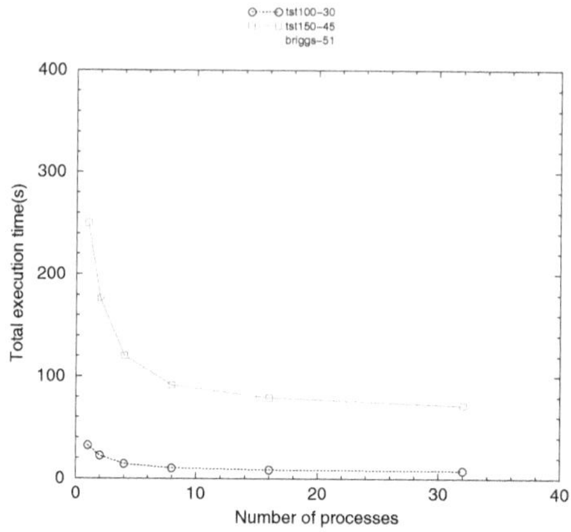

(a) n = 30, 45, 51 digits.

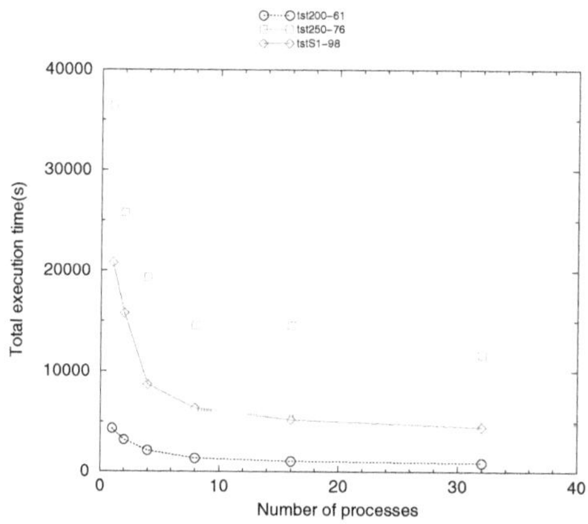

(b) n = 61, 76, 98 digits.

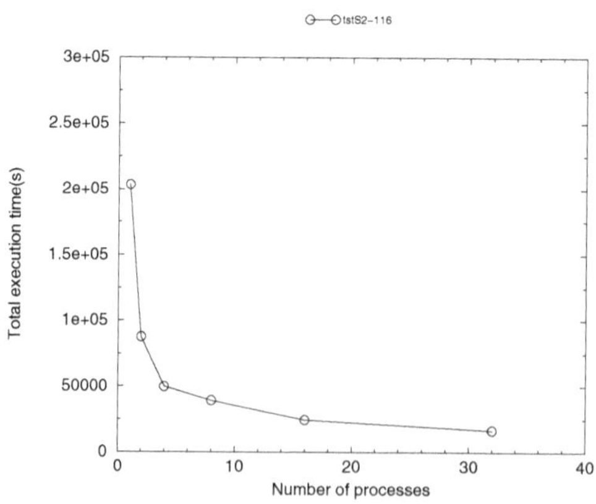

(c) n = 116 digits.

Fig. 5. Parallel execution time

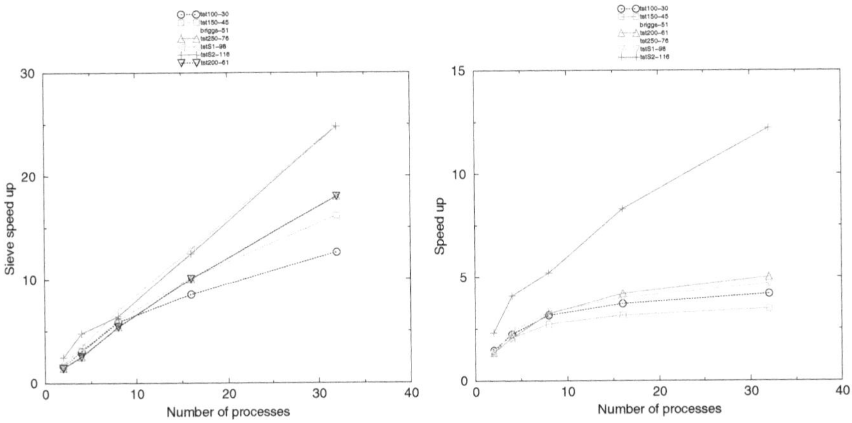

(a) Sieve Speed-up.

(b) Execution Time Speed-up.

Fig. 6. Speed-ups

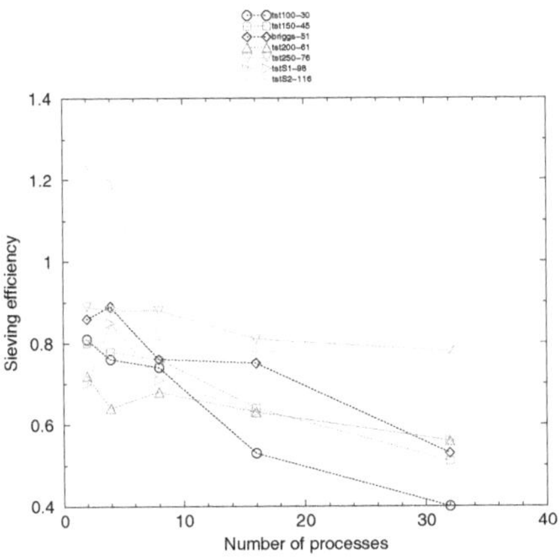

Fig. 7. Sieving efficiency

– Another cause for inefficiency lies in synchronization. Each processor does sieving for different pairs. The sieving time for each processor might be different. The master node can not start the next sieving until all the slave nodes finish their sieving. Processor idle time may occur due to this. Further improvements on better load balance will be investigated in the future work.

Currently, it is difficult to factor integers larger than 116 digits in our cluster. One of the reasons is the memory requirement. In order to factor larger composite numbers, we must sieve a large number of relations. Even for numbers less than 116 digits, we may end up with a linear system whose coefficient matrix has *100,000* entries. To tackle this problem, we need to select good parameters as the parameter selections greatly affect the efficiency of the GNFS algorithm. One hint for for polynomial selection is to reduce the size of the coefficients for *f(x)* as small coefficients tend to give small $\prod(a_i+b_i\theta)$ [8]. We will explore such possibility in our future work.

References

1. A.K.Lenstra. Integer factoring. *Des. Codes Cryptography*, 19(2-3):101–128, 2000.
2. M.S.Manasse, A.K.Lenstra, H.W.Lenstra Jr. and J.M.Pollard. The number field sieve. In *ACM Symposium on Theory of Computing*, pages 564–572, 1990.
3. C.Monico. General number field sieve documentation. Nov 2004.
4. C.Pomerance. The quadratic sieve factoring algorithm. In *Proceeding of the EUROCRYPT 84 Workshop on Advances in Cryptology: Theory and Application of Cryptographic Techniques*, pages 169–182. Springer-Verlag, 1985.
5. J. Dreibelbis. Implementing the general number field sieve. Master of Computer Science, Rochester Institute of Technology, June 2003.
6. H.W.Lenstra Jr., C. Pomerance, and J. P. Buhler. Factoring integers with the number field sieve. In *The Development of the Number Field Sieve*, volume 1554, pages 50–94, New York, 1993. Lecture notes in Mathematics, Springer-Verlag.
7. M.Case. A beginner's guide to the general number field sieve. pages 1–4, Winter 2003.
8. M.E.Briggs. An introduction to the general number field sieve. Master's thesis, Virginia Polytechnic Institute and State University, 1998.
9. N. Koblitz, A. Menezes and S. Vanstone. The state of elliptic curve cryptography. *Des. Codes Cryptography*, 19(2-3):173–193, 2000.
10. MPICH1. http://www-unix.mcs.anl.gov/mpi/mpich/.
11. R.L.Rivest, A.Shamir, and L.M.Adelman. A method for obtaining digital signatures and public-key cryptosystems. Technical Report MIT/LCS/TM-82, 1977.
12. T.Granlund. *The GNU Multiple Precision Arithmetic Library*. TMG Datakonsult, Boston, MA, USA, 2.0.2 edition, June 1996.

Appendix: The Test Cases and the Results

The composite numbers in the eight test cases and their factors are shown in the following table.

Test Cases	Results
tst100-30	727563736353655223147641208603= 978204944528897•743774339337499
tst150-45	799356282580692644127991443712991753990450969= 32823111293257851893153•24353458617583497303673
briggs-51	556158012756522140970101270050308458769458529626977= 449818591141•1236405128000120870775846228354119184397
tst200-61	1241445153765162090376032461564730757085137334450817128010073= 1127192007137697372923951166979•1101360855918052649813406915187
tst250-76	3675041894739039405533259197211548846143110109152323761665377505538520830273= 69119855780815625390997974542224894323•53169119831396634916152282437374262651
tstS1-98	48112675629372767804524219707530062462251150382843481915847109420993527839223554575368891438718253= 2255991822360879425583919003791503• 21326617921435191345914805886616773334390107640406173073760517251
tstS2-116	17880548961179216074249467223995824092950354306282271258584504325872840689417142416998673880521619866825206286597741= 3020063095859586052734248627690201527294469• 5920587879668110479956486319854404483179939902172304914828610258288310089

Localized Energy-Aware Broadcast Protocol for Wireless Networks with Directional Antennas

Hui Xu, Manwoo Jeon, Lei Shu, Wu Xiaoling, Jinsung Cho, and Sungyoung Lee*

Department of Computer Engineering,
Kyung Hee University, Korea
{xuhui, imanoos, sl8132, xiaoling, sylee}@oslab.khu.ac.kr
chojs@khu.ac.kr

Abstract. We consider broadcast protocols in wireless networks that have limited energy and computation resources. The well-known algorithm, DBIP (Directional Broadcast Incremental Power), which exploits "Incremental Power" philosophy for wireless networks with directional antenna to construct broadcasting tree, provides very good results in terms of energy savings. Unfortunately, its computation is centralized, as the source node needs to know the entire topology of the network. Mobility of nodes or frequent changes in the node activity status (from "active" to "passive" and vice-versa) may cause global changes in topology which must be propagated throughout the network for any centralized solution. This may results in extreme and un-acceptable communication overhead. In this paper, we propose and evaluate a localized energy-efficient broadcast protocol, Localized Directional Broadcast Incremental Power Protocol (LDBIP), which employs distributed location information and computation to construct broadcast trees. In the proposed method, a source node sets up spanning tree with its local neighborhood position information and includes certain hops relay information in packet. Directional antennas are used for transmitting broadcast packet, and the transmission power is adjusted for each transmission to the minimal necessary for reaching the particular neighbor. Relay nodes will consider relay instructions received to compute their own local neighborhood spanning tree and then rebroadcasts. Experimental results verify that this new protocol shows similar performance with DBIP in static wireless networks, and better performance in mobile scenarios.

1 Introduction

In wireless networks which have limited resources such as sensor network, communication ranges are limited, thus many nodes must participate to the broadcast in order to have the whole network covered. The most important design criterion is energy and computation conservation, as nodes have limited resources. All the protocols that have been proposed for broadcast can be classified into two kinds of solutions: centralized and localized. Centralized solutions mean that each node should keep global network information and global topology. There exist several centralized energy-aware broadcast algorithms for the construction of broadcast trees with

* Corresponding author.

L.T. Yang et al. (Eds.): ICESS 2005, LNCS 3820, pp. 696 – 707, 2005.

omni-directional antennas in the literature. In addition, the well-known energy-aware algorithm of Broadcast Incremental Power (BIP) [1] is "node-based" algorithm and exploits the "wireless broadcast advantage" property associated with omni-directional antennas, namely the capability for a node to reach several neighbors by using a transmission power level sufficient to reach the most distant one. Applying the incremental power philosophy to network with directional antennas, the Directional Broadcast Incremental Power (DBIP) algorithm [2] has very good performance in energy saving. The problem of centralized approach is that mobility of nodes or frequent changes in the node activity status (from "active" to "passive" and vice-versa) may cause global changes in topology which must be propagated throughout the network for any centralized solution. This may results in extreme and un-acceptable communication overhead for networks. Hence, because of the limited resources of nodes, it is ideal that each node can decide on its own behavior based only on the information from nodes within a constant hop distance. Such distributed algorithms and protocols are called localized [3-7].

In this paper, we propose and implement a localized energy-efficient broadcast protocol which is based on the "Incremental Power" philosophy for wireless networks with Directional Antenna, Localized Directional Broadcast Incremental Power Protocol (LDBIP). Our localized protocol only uses localized and distributed location information and computing to construct broadcast tree. The use of directional antennas can reduce the beam width angle to diffuse the radio transmission to one direction and thus provides energy savings and interference reduction. In our algorithm, source node sets up spanning tree with only position information of its neighbors within certain hops. Directional antennas are used for transmitting broadcast packet, and the transmission power is adjusted for each transmission to the minimal necessary for reaching the particular neighbor. Relay node that receives broadcast packet will consider relay instructions included in received packet to compute its own localized spanning tree and do the same as source node. We compare the performance of our protocol (LDBIP) to those of BIP, DBIP and LBIP [8]. Experimental results show that in static wireless networks, this new protocol has better performance compared to BIP and LBIP, and similar performance to DBIP, and that in mobile wireless networks, LDBIP has better performance even compared to DBIP.

The remainder of the paper is organized as follows: in Section 2, we introduce our system model including the impact of the use of directional antennas on energy consumption; Section 3 presents our localized energy-aware algorithm for broadcast tree construction, which exploits the properties of directional antennas; in Section 4, we compare the performance of our protocol (LDBIP) to those of BIP, DBIP and LBIP; in Section 5, we present our conclusions and future work on this research.

2 System Model

2.1 Network Model

We assume a wireless network consists of N nodes, which are randomly distributed over a specified region. Any node is permitted to initiate broadcast. Broadcast requests are generated randomly at network nodes. In a broadcasting task, a message is to be sent from source node to all the other ones in the network. Some nodes may be used as relays either to provide connectivity to all members in network or to reduce overall energy consumption. The set of nodes and the links of nodes support constructing a broadcast tree. Here, the links are incidental and their existence depends on the transmission power of each node. Thus, it is a set of nodes (rather than links) that are the fundamental units in constructing the tree. The connectivity of the network depends on the transmission power and antenna pattern. We assume that each node can choose its RF power level p^{RF}, such as $p_{\min} \le p^{RF} \le p_{\max}$. The nodes in broadcast tree can adjust their power levels for the various transmission in which it participates.

2.2 Positioning

We assume each node has a low-power Global Position System (GPS [9]) receiver, which provides the position information of the node itself. In every position based broadcast protocol, nodes need position information about neighborhood nodes. The method we used is as following: initially each node emits its position message containing its id, and when a node u receives this kind of special message from a node v, it adds v to its neighborhood table; in mobile network except initialization each node sets timer to check its position, and if mobility happens it will emits his position message again to let other nodes update neighborhood table.

2.3 Propagation Model

We use two kinds of propagation model, free space model [10] and two-ray ground reflection model [11]. The free space model considers ideal propagation condition that there is only one clear line-of-sight path between the transmitter and receiver, while the two-ray ground model takes reality into consideration and considers both the direct path and a ground reflection path.

The following equation to calculate the received signal power in free space at distance d from the transmitter

$$P_r(d) = \frac{P_t G_t G_r \lambda^2}{(4\pi)^2 d^2 L}, \tag{1}$$

where P_t is the transmitted signal power. G_t and G_r are the antenna gains of the transmitter and the receiver respectively. L $(L \ge 1)$ is the system loss, and λ is the wavelength.

The following equation to calculate the received signal power in Two-ray ground model at distance d

$$P_r(d) = \frac{P_t G_t G_r h_t^2 h_r^2}{d^4 L}, \tag{2}$$

where h_t and h_r are the heights of transmit and receive antennas respectively. However, the two-ray model does not give a good result for a short distance due to the oscillation caused by the constructive and destructive combination of the two rays, whereas, the free space model is still used when d is small. Therefore, a cross-over distance d_c is calculated. When $d < d_c$, Eqn. (1) is used. When $d > d_c$, Eqn.(2) is used. At the cross-over distance, Eqns. (1) and (2) give the same result. So d_c can be calculated as

$$(4\pi h_t h_r)/\lambda \quad (3)$$

When considering omni-directional antennas and uniform propagation conditions, it is common to select G_t and G_r as 1.

The use of directional antennas can permit energy savings and reduce interference by concentrating transmission energy where it is needed. We learn from [12] that because the amount of RF energy remains the same, but is distributed over less area, the apparent signal strength is higher. This apparent increase in signal strength is the antenna gain. We use an idealized model in which we assume that all of the transmitted energy is concentrated uniformly in a beam of width θ, as shown in Fig. 1, then the gain of area covered by the beam can be calculated as

$$2\Big/\left(1 - \cos\frac{\theta}{360}\right), \quad (4)$$

while the gain of the other areas is zero. As a consequence of the "wireless broadcast advantage" property of omni-directional systems [13], all nodes whose distance from Node *i* does not exceed r_{ij} will be able to receive the transmission with no further energy expenditure at Node *i*.

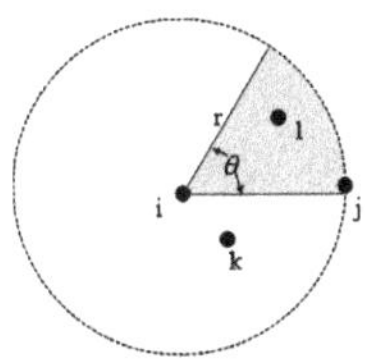

Fig. 1. Use of directional antenna

While using directional antenna, the advantage property will be diminished, since only the nodes located within the transmitting node's antenna beam can receive the signal. In Fig. 1, only *j*, *l* can receive the signal, while *k* cannot receive the signal.

We assume that the beam width θ is fixed beam width and one node can simultaneously support more than one directional antenna. Furthermore, we assume that each antenna beam can be pointed in any desired direction to provide connectivity to a subset of nodes that are within communication range. In addition, we use directional receiving antennas, which have a beneficial impact to avoid background noise and other user interferences.

2.4 Energy Expenditure

In addition to RF propagation, energy is also expended for transmission (encoding, modulation, etc.) and reception (demodulation, decoding, etc.). We define

- p^T = transmission processing power and
- p^R = reception processing power.

The total power expenditure of a node, when transmitting to a maximum range r over a sector of width θ , is

$$p = p^{RF}(r,\theta) + p^T + p^R \tag{5}$$

Where $p^{RF}(r,\theta)$ is RF propagation energy expenditure and the term p^R is not needed for the source node. A leaf node, since it does not transmit but only receives, has a total power expenditure of p^R .

3 Localized Directional Broadcast Incremental Power Protocol

3.1 The Proposed Algorithm

The goal of the localized algorithm is to allow a localized and distributed computation of broadcast tree. We assume every node knows its local neighbors position information.

The principle is as follows: the source node *S* (the one that initiates the broadcast) computes the broadcast tree with its local neighborhood position information and sends the broadcast packet to each of its one hop neighbor, while includes N (integer, N>0) hops computed relay information and the Nth hop relay nodes id in broadcast packet. For each of other nodes, for example, node *U* who receives the packet for the first time, three cases can happen:

- The packet contains both relay instructions for *U* and *U's id*. *U* will use these relay instructions to construct its own local broadcast tree. Then, instead of starting from an empty tree as *S* did, it extends the broadcasting tree based on what source *S* has calculated for it. By this way, the joint neighborhood nodes of *S* and *U* will use the same spanning tree.
- The packet contains only relay instructions for *U*. *U* will just follow these relay instructions to relay the packet.
- There are no relay instructions for *U*. In this case, node *U* does nothing.

After the procedure mentioned above, node *U* will rebroadcast the packet again to its own one hop neighbor and include N hops computed relay information for its own relay nodes and the Nth hop relay nodes id, just like what source node has done. The reason why we use N to refer relay nodes hop number is that the range within which each node manage positional information on other nodes can be changed according to requirement, and the optimal changes according to the application demands and the node's hardware performance.

In this principle, there may be some nodes which will receive this packet more than one time, then at this time, node can simple drop the packet and doesn't rebroadcast again. In order to reduce overlap, we use the neighbor nodes elimination scheme. Source node will include its local N hops neighbor nodes in packet, because these nodes certainly will receive the packet soon. Once the node which is in charge of recalculating local spanning tree receives the packet, except recording the relay information it should also record the nodes which will be covered soon. If the covered node is not used in relay information and also is a neighbor node of this node, then this node will delete it from its neighbor list and after deletion calculate its own broadcast tree. Fig.2 is the pseudo-code of the proposed algorithm.

```
Randomly select source node S
For source node S:
{   /******source node's locale calculation******/
    Computes its local broadcast tree;
    Set up broadcast packet P;
    Include N hops relay instructions in packet P;
    Include N hops neighbors' ID in packet P;
    Include Nth hop relay instructions in packet P;
    Send packet P to each of its one hop neighbor using directional antenna;
}
For any node U (except S):
if (node U receives packet P){
    if ( the first time){
        Inspect packet P;
        if (there is relay instruction for U){
            if (U's id exists in Nth hop relay nodes' id){
                Search and record all relay instructions for U;
                /******Neighbor Nodes Elimination Scheme******/
                Check included covered nodes' ID;
                While ( (ID != U's address)&&( ID∉ relay instruction info) )
                    if (ID⊂U's local neighbors list)
                        delete this node record from U's local neighbors list;
                /******U's local calculation******/
                Refer recorded relay instructions;
                Use U's modified local neighbors list;
                Computes U's local broadcast tree;
                Act as source node;
            }else if (U's id does not exist in Nth hop relay nodes' id)
                Only relay received packet as recorded relay instructions;
        }else if (there is no relay instruction for U)
            Do nothing;
    } else
        Simply drop packet P;
}
```

Fig. 2. Pseudo-code of the proposed algorithm

3.2 Broadcast Tree Calculation

As for how to set up broadcast tree, we have considered two basic approaches with directional antennas:

- Construct the tree by using an algorithm designed for omni-directional antennas; then reduce each antenna beam to our fixed beam width.
- Incorporate directional antenna properties into the tree-construction process.

The first approach can be based on any tree-construction algorithm. The "beam-reduction" phase is performed after the tree is constructed. The second approach which takes directional antenna into consideration at each step of the tree construction process can be used only with algorithms that construct trees by adding one node at a time. In this section, we describe the later approach applied in our algorithm *LDBIP* in detail.

The incremental power philosophy, originally developed for use with omni-directional antennas, can be applied to tree construction in networks with directional antennas as well. At each step of the tree-construction process, a single node is added, whereas variables involved in computing cost (and incremental cost) are not only transmitter power but beam width θ as well. In our simple system model, we use fixed beam width θ_f, that means for adding a new node, we can only have two choices: set up a new directional antenna to reach a new node; raise the length range of beam to check whether there is new node covered or not. A pseudo code of the broadcast tree calculation algorithm can be written as Fig. 3.

Input: given an undirected weighted graph $G(N,A)$, where N: set of nodes, A: set of edges

Initialization: set T:={S} where S is the source node. Set $P(i)$:= 0 for all $1 \le i \le |N|$ where $P(i)$ is the transmission power of node i.

Procedure:

while $|T| \neq |N|$

do find an edge $(i,j) \in T \times (N-T)$ with fixed beam width θ_f such that ΔP_{ij} is minimum; if an edge $(i,k) \in T \times T$ raising the length range of beam can cover a node $j \in (N-T)$, then incremental power $\Delta P_{ij} = d_{ij}^{\alpha} \frac{\theta_f}{2\pi} - P(i)$; otherwise,

$\Delta P_{ij} = d_{ij}^{\alpha} \frac{\theta_f}{2\pi}$.

add node j to T, i.e., $T := T \cup \{j\}$.

set $P(i) := P(i) + \Delta P_{ij}$.

Fig. 3. Pseudo code of broadcast tree calculation algorithm

Fig. 4(a) shows a simple example in which the source node has 4 local neighbor nodes 0, 1, 2, and 3. Node 1 is the closest to 0, so it is added first; in Fig. 4(b), an antenna with beam width of θ_f is centered between 0 and Node 1. Then we must decide which node to add next (Node 2 or Node 3), and which node (that is already in the tree) should be its parent. In this example, the beam from 0 to Node 1 can be extended to include both Node 1 and Node 3, without setting up a new beam. Compared to other choices that setting up a new beam from Node 0 to Node 2, or from Node 1 to Node 2, this method has minimum incremental power. Therefore, Node 3 is added next by increasing the communication range of Node 0 and Node 1. In Fig. 4(c), finally, Node 1 must be added to the tree. Three possibilities are respectively to set up a new beam from Node 0, Node 1, Node 3. Here we assume that Node 3 has minimum distance. Then in Fig. 4 (d) we set up a new beam from Node 3 to Node 2.

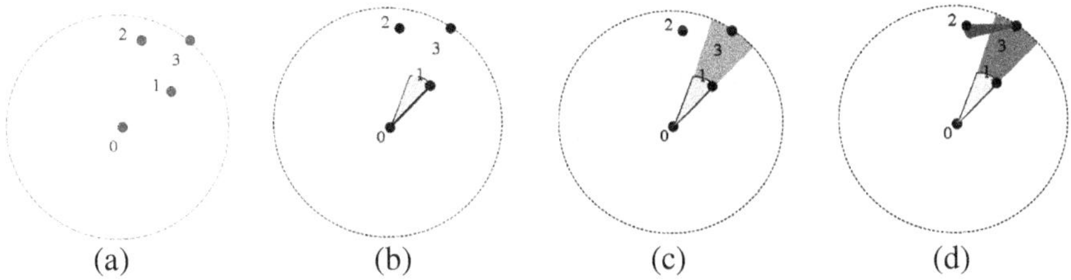

Fig. 4. Nodes addition in LDBIP

3.3 Examples Constructed by the Various Algorithms

Fig. 5 shows the broadcast tree produced by BIP, DBIP, LBIP and LDBIP for a 12-node network, where the source node is shown larger than the other nodes. There broadcast trees are generated in our simulation work, which use the system model mentioned in section 2.

Because DBIP and LDBIP use directional antenna, therefore in our simulation system, according to different θ_f, we can get different broadcast tree; of course, the according energy consumption will also be different. Furthermore, because algorithm LBIP and our LDBIP is distributed, which means every node only calculates its two hops neighborhood broadcast tree, the Fig. 5(c) and (d) in fact is the combination of all local broadcast tree, and the joint parts of those local broadcast trees will not have too much difference because nodes refer relay information from other nodes and apply the neighbor nodes elimination scheme.

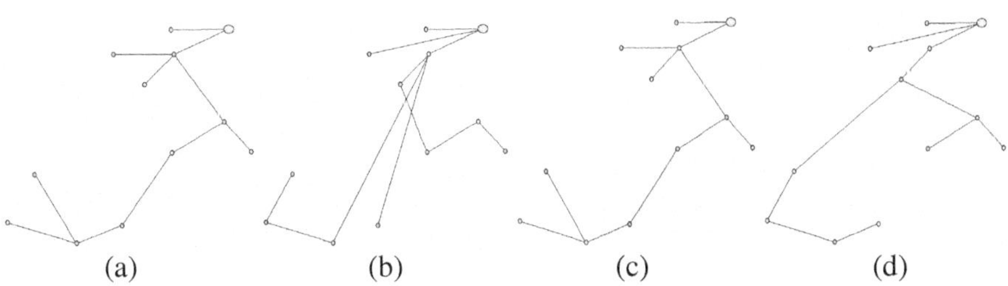

Fig. 5. Broadcast Tree. (a) BIP (b) DBIP (θ_f =30) (c) LBIP (d) LDBIP (θ_f =30)

4 Performance Evaluation

In this section, we present our performance evaluation for our localized algorithm *LDBIP*, and also compare it with two centralized algorithm *BIP* and *DBIP* which are very effective centralized protocols in energy consumption and with another localized algorithm *LBIP*. Especially for *LBIP* and *LDBIP*, we choose the hop number N as 2. We use ns2 as our simulation tool and assume AT&T's Wave LAN PCMCIA card as wireless node model which parameters are listed in table 1. As for system model, we apply the network, propagation, and energy model mentioned in Section 2.

Table 1. Parameters for wireless node model

	AT&T's Wave LAN PCMCIA card
frequency	914MHZ
maximum transmission range	40m
maximum transmit power	8.5872e-4 W
receiving power	0.395 watts
transmitting power	0.660 watts
omni-antenna gain of receiver/transmitter	1db
fixed beam width of directional antennas	30
directional antenna receiver/transmitter gain	58.6955db
MAC protocol	802.11
propagation model	free space / two ray ground

The wireless network is always composed of 100 nodes randomly placed in a square area which size is changed to obtain different network density D defined as the average number of neighbors per each node. The formula can be written as:

$$D = N * \frac{\pi r^2}{A^2}, \tag{6}$$

where A represents the edge length of deployment square area, and r is the maximum transmission range. From Eqn. (6), we can get calculate A by

$$A = r\sqrt{\frac{N\pi}{D}}. \tag{7}$$

For each measure, 50 broadcasts are launched and for each broadcast, a new network is generated.

RAR (Reach Ability Ratio) is the percentage of nodes in the network that received the message. Ideally, each broadcast can guarantee 100% RAR value. While in sparse network since the maximum transmission range of nodes is not big enough to guarantee the network connectivity, RAR may be less than 100%.

To compare the different protocols, we observe the total power consumption over the network when a broadcast has occurred. We compute a ratio named *EER*, that represents the energy consumption of the considered protocol compared to the energy that would have been spent by a Blind Flooding (each node retransmits once with maximum transmission range). The value of *EER* is so defined by:

$$EER = \frac{E_{protocol}}{E_{flooding}} \times 100. \qquad (8)$$

We also observe SRB (Saved Rebroadcast) which is the percentage of nodes in the network that received the message but did not relay it. A Blind Flooding has a SRB of 0%, since each node has to retransmit once the message.

Our simulation work is based on two steps: first we test the performance of our protocol in static wireless ad hoc network, and then we take mobile network into consideration. To compare the performance with those of other protocols, we observe the total power consumption over the network. In mobile simulation environment, the energy consumption includes not only the energy consumption for broadcasting message, but also that for propagation for mobility.

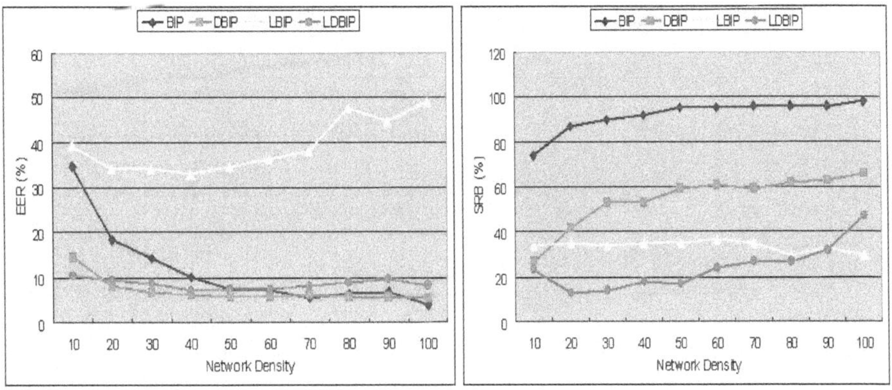

(a) EER comparison (b) SRB comparison

Fig. 6. Performance comparison in static wireless network

Fig.6 shows EER and SRB comparison for *BIP, DBIP, LBIP* and *LDBIP* protocols in static wireless networks with different network density. As for the RAR value, since we choose the network density which can guarantee the network connectivity, so all the RAR results are 100%. From Fig.6 (a) we can find that all the four protocols have much better energy conservation than flooding. Because of employing directional antenna, *DBIP* and *LDBIP* have much less energy consumption compared to *BIP* which uses omni-directional antenna in low network density and similar saving energy performance in high network density. Also benefiting from directional antenna, compared to another localized algorithm *LBIP,* our proposal *LDBIP* has much better performance in energy conservation. In addition, the energy conservation performance of *DBIP* and *LDBIP* is stable despite of network density. Compared to centralized algorithm *DBIP*, our localized algorithm *LDBIP* has a little more energy consumption. That is because our algorithm employs the topology of only local neighbors whereas *DBIP* utilizes the total network topology to calculate energy efficient broadcast tree. From Fig.6 (b) we can observe localized protocols have less SRB compared to centralized protocols, since localized protocols only calculate local broadcasting tree which cause unnecessary relay instructions compared to centralized protocols. In addition, using omni-directional antenna can save more retransmission, since "wireless broadcast advantage" will be decreased by employing directional antenna.

Now we take mobility into consideration. In our simulation we use mobile scenarios to simulate the nodes' mobility in mobile networks. These mobile scenarios are randomly generated by special tool of ns2, "setdest [14]". As we mentioned in section 2.2 positioning, in mobile network except initialization each node should set timer to check whether this node has moved or not. If mobility occurs, node will use its maximum transmission radius to emit its new location information to let other nodes update their neighborhood table. In centralized solution, this information must be propagated throughout the network, In order to compare between different protocols, we use the same mobile scenario in certain network density.

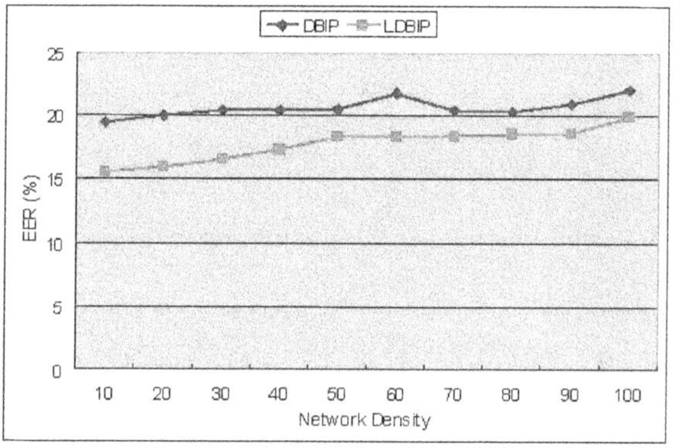

Fig. 7. EER comparison in mobile network

Fig.7 shows EER comparison for *DBIP* and *LDBIP* protocols in mobile networks with different network density. Compared to centralized algorithm *DBIP* in mobile network, our localized algorithm *LDBIP* has better energy saving performance. That is because in centralized solution, e.g. *DBIP*, mobility of nodes need to be broadcasted throughout the network, while in our centralized algorithm *LDBIP*, mobility will be only propagated to that nodes' neighborhood. Therefore *LDBIP* can get better performance. From this, we can infer that as mobility increases in mobile scenarios, *LDBIP* can get much better performance in energy conservation. In addition, as for SRB comparison in mobile network, there is little difference with that in static network.

In summary, our localized protocol *LDBIP* can only use localized location information and distributed computation to complete broadcasting task. Our simulation work verifies that in mobile networks, our localized energy-aware protocol has very good performance in energy conservation.

5 Conclusions

In this paper, we proposed the new localized energy-aware broadcast protocol for wireless networks with directional antennas which have limited energy and computation resources. Our algorithm is based on the localized information and distributed computation method, which means, rather than source node collects all location information of network to calculate broadcast tree, every node collects some part of the whole network's nodes location information and participates calculating broadcast tree. At the cost of a few more information stored in the broadcast packets, our localized algorithm offers better energy saving result than well-known centralized algorithm DBIP in mobile environment. Especially, if mobility of nodes increases in network, our distributed algorithm can get lesser energy consumption and better performance than centralized solution.

In future work, we plan to take realistic facts into consideration for energy consumption and network lifetime.

Acknowledgement

This work was supported by grant No. R01-2005-000-10267-0 from Korea Science and Engineering Foundation in Ministry of Science and Technology.

References

1. J. E. Wieselthier, G. D. Nguyen, A. Ephremides: On the construction of energy-efficient broadcast and multicast trees in wireless networks. Proc. IEEE INFOCOM (2000) 585-594
2. J.E. Wieselthier, G.D. Nguyen, A. Ephremides: Energy-Limited Wireless Networking with Directional Antennas: The Case of Session-Based Multicasting. Proc. IEEE INFOCOM (2002) 190-199
3. P. Bose, P. Morin, I. Stojmenovic, J. Urrutia: Routing with guarantee delivery in ad hoc networks. ACM/Kluwer Wireless Networks (2001) 609-616
4. T. Chu, I. Nikolaidis: Energy efficient broadcast in mobile ad hoc networks. In Proc. Ad-Hoc Networks and Wireless (ADHOC-NOW), Toronto, Canada (2002) 177-190
5. W. Peng, X. Lu: On the reduction of broadcast redundancy in mobile ad hoc networks. In Proc. Annual Workshop on Mobile and Ad Hoc Networking and Computing (MobiHoc'2000), Boston, Massachusetts, USA (2000) 129-130
6. A. Qayyum, L. Viennot, A.Laouiti: Multipoint relaying for flooding broadcast messages in mobile wireless networks. In Proc. 35th Annual Hawaii International Conference on System Sciences (HICSS-35), Hawaii, USA (2002)
7. J. Wu, H. Li: A dominating-set-based routing scheme in ad hoc wireless networks. In Proc. 3rd Int'l Workshop Discrete Algorithms and Methods for Mobile Computing and Comm (DIALM'99), Seattle, USA (1999) 7-14
8. F.Ingelrest, D.Simplot-Ryl: Localized Broadcast Incremental Power Protocol for Wireless Ad Hoc Networks. 10th IEEE Symposium on Computers and Communications (ISCC 2005), Cartagena, Spain (2005)
9. E.D. Kaplan: Understanding GPS: Principles and Applications. Artech House (1996)
10. H.T. Friis: A note on a simple transmission formula. Proc. of the IRE, Vol. 41, May (1946) 254-256
11. H.T. Friis: Introduction to radio and radio antennas. IEEE Spectrum, April (1971) 55-61
12. Joseph J. Carr: Directional or Omni-directional Antenna. Joe Carr's Receiving Antenna Handbook, Hightext (1993)
13. J.E. Wieselthier, G.D. Nguyen, A. Ephremides: Algorithms for Energy-Efficient Multicasting in Static Ad Hoc Wireless Networks. Mobile Networks and Applications (MONET), vol. 6, no. 3 (2001) 251-263
14. Network Simulator - ns-2, http://www.isi.edu/nsnam/ns/.

The Optimal Profile-Guided Greedy Dynamic Voltage Scaling in Real-Time Applications*

Huizhan Yi, Xuejun Yang, and Juan Chen

School of Computer, National University of Defense Technology,
Changsha 410073, Hunan, P.R. China
{huizhanyi, xjyang, juanchen}@nudt.edu.cn

Abstract. Compiler-directed dynamic voltage scaling (DVS) is an effective low-power technique in real-time applications, where compiler inserts voltage scaling points in a real-time application, and supply voltage and clock frequency are adjusted to the relationship between the remaining time and the remaining workload at each voltage scaling point. Greedy dynamic voltage scaling is one of the voltage adjustment schemes, where the slack time of current section is completely used to reduce the clock frequency of next section. In this paper we present the analytical model of the greedy scheme, and by simulations using the analytical model, we find out that the greedy scheme obstructs itself from effectively utilizing the slack times. So we propose a profile-guided greedy voltage adjustment scheme directed by the optimal real-time voltage scheduling in the most frequent execution case. We show by simulations that the new voltage adjustment scheme obtains the largest reduction of energy consumption of all the current representative schemes.

1 Introduction

In the recent years embedded systems for mobile computing, such as hand-held phone and smart sensor, are developing rapidly, and a crucial parameter of mobile systems is the continued time of energy supply. Though the performance of ICs has been steadily growing [1], battery techniques are developed very slowly [2] and it is of substantial importance for battery-powered systems to make use of more effective low-power techniques. At the same time, due attention has been paid to the energy consumption by the facilities from IT industry [3]. Therefore, it is very imperative not only for mobile systems but also for high-performance desktop systems to develop effective low-power techniques.

Dynamic voltage scaling (DVS) [4] [5] is one of the low-power techniques, and it is widely used in embedded systems for mobile computing and desktop systems. In real-time applications, DVS dynamically reduces supply voltage to the lowest possible extent that ensures a proper operation when the required performance is lower than the maximum performance. Since the dynamic energy consumption, the dominant energy consumption in ICs, is in direct proportion to the square of supply voltage, it is possible for DVS to significantly reduce energy consumption.

---

* Supported by the National High Technology Development 863 Program of China under Grant No. 2004AA1Z2210 and Server OS Kernel under Grant No. 2002AA1Z2101.

L.T. Yang et al. (Eds.): ICESS 2005, LNCS 3820, pp. 708–719, 2005.

Directed by software, DVS can save more energy. On the one hand, in a multiple-task real-time environment, real-time operating system (RT-OS) has the global information of the whole system, and based on workload variation, RT-OS reduces energy consumption through inter-task voltage scheduling (InterDVS). On the other hand, there are some practical constrains for InterDVS. Firstly, InterDVS needs OS modification. In addition, in a single-task environment, there are no other tasks to utilize the produced slack times. Even, in a multiple-task environment, if the workload and slack times of one task dominate those of the others, it is impossible for InterDVS to significantly reduce energy consumption. So it is necessary to utilize intra-task voltage scheduling at the same time. Intra-task DVS (IntraDVS) assisted by compiler inserts voltage scaling points in a real-time task and divides the task into some sections, at each voltage scaling point supply voltage and clock frequency are adjusted to the relationship between the remaining time and the remaining workload.

There are many real-time voltage adjustment schemes, and each scheme has to ensure that a task finish before its deadline. Daniel Mosse, et al have summarized three kinds of representative schemes: DPM-P, DPM-G, and DPM-S [6]. In DPM-P, every time a section finishes, the system computes the reclaimed time (the slack time) and allows other sections to slow down proportionally. The large majority of the past works have utilized DPM-P to adjust supply voltage [7] [8] [9]. DPM-G, called a greedy scheme, gives the reclaimed time to next section, and allows next section to utilize the maximum possible amount of the slack, while guaranteeing the feasibility of the real-time execution. DPM-G has nearly used up all the available slack times, and there are some works utilizing DPM-G to adjust supply voltage [9] [15]. In DPM-S, the slack times are distributed to other sections based on the average execution cycle of real-time applications, and some past works have made use of the average execution cycle to set clock frequency [10] [11].

In this paper we present the analytical model of the intra-task greedy dynamic voltage scaling, and then using the analytical model, we investigate the properties of the greedy scheme. Compared with the past assumption that the slack times are distributed evenly, we suppose that the slack times are not evenly distributed in real-time applications, which is much closer to the execution of real-time applications. As a result, we find out that the greedy scheme can aggressively utilize the slack times, but often the aggressive utilization of the slack times cannot lead to the largest energy saving. So we first try to find out an optimal real-time voltage scheduling in the most frequent execution case (sometimes called hot path), and prove that if each voltage scaling point only can make use of the slack times appearing before itself, an optimal voltage scheduling (OPTDVS) minimizes the energy consumption. Then, we present a profile-guided optimizing voltage adjustment scheme directed by OPTDVS, and the simulation results show that the new scheme obtains the largest gain of all the representative schemes. We believe that optimizing the most frequent execution case will lead to more reduction of energy consumption. The contributions of this work are as follows:

1. We present and prove an optimal real-time voltage scheduling in the most frequent execution case (OPTDVS).
2. We propose a new greedy voltage adjustment scheme directed by OPTDVS.
3. The simulations show that the new scheme obtains the largest energy reduction of all the current representative schemes.

The rest of this paper is organized as follows. In Section 2 we review some related works of compiler-directed dynamic voltage scaling. In Section 3 we present the analytical model of the greedy scheme, and investigate the properties of the greedy scheme. In Section 4 we propose a profile-guided greedy scheme directed by OPTDVS, and we show by simulations that the new scheme effectively reduces the energy consumption. Finally, we give the conclusions and the future works.

2 Related Works

Dynamic power consumption, which dominates the total power consumption in ICs, is proportional to the square of supply voltage, and reducing supply voltage can significantly reduce dynamic power consumption. Real-time applications have the dynamic performance requirement, and dynamic voltage scaling is used to exactly meet the performance requirement with the lowest energy consumption by dynamically adjusting supply voltage and clock frequency. Nowadays, the DVS-enabled systems, such as Transmeta Crusoe, Intel Xscale, and AMD K6-IIIE+, are often operated on some discrete voltage levels, and the switch from one level to another has energy and time overhead.

OS-directed dynamic voltage scaling has widely investigated in the past years, and Jacob Rubin Lorch had summarized the OS-based dynamic voltage scaling in detail [12].

In the recent years a lot of works have been published on compiler-directed dynamic voltage scaling, and many algorithms, especially real-time algorithms, have been introduced. Daniel Mosse, et al presented compiler-directed power management and proposed three kinds of real-time dynamic voltage adjustment schemes: DPM-P, DPM-G, and DPM-S [6]. On the assumption that the slack times were evenly distributed in real-time applications, Nevine AbouGhazaleh, et al investigated the optimal number of voltage scaling points in DPM-P and DPM-G [13]. H.Saputra, et al presented a compilation strategy based on integer linear programming, which could accommodate energy/performance constraints [14]. Flavius Gruian employed stochastic data to derive efficient schedules, and took into account the real behavior of real-time systems, which was often better than the worst case [10]. Dongkun Shin, et al proposed a profiled-guided IntraDVS, where they used the average execution cycles to set clock frequency and used the system maximum clock frequency to ensure the real-time execution [11]. Ana Azevedo, et al introduced an intra-task DVS technique under compiler control using program checkpoints [15]. Nevine AbouGhazaleh, et al introduced a collaborative approach between the compiler and operating system that used fine-grained information about the execution time of a real-time application to reduce energy consumption [9]. The idea of Chung-Hsing Hsu, et al was to identify the program regions in which the CPU was mostly idle due to memory stall and slow them down for energy reduction [16]. Dongkun Shin, et al proposed an optimization technique for IntraDVS using data flow information [8].

3 Models and Analyses of IntraDVS

Real-time applications have the timing constraints; a real-time task must finish before its deadline (d) and missing the deadline might lead to a catastrophic result. In order to meet the timing constraints, we need to evaluate the worst-case execution times ($wcet$) or the worst-case execution cycles ($wcec$) in real-time applications, and the worst-case execution time of an application must be less than or equal to its deadline [17]. If the $wcet$ of an application is less than its deadline, we can proportionally reduce supply voltage and clock frequency, and as a result the application can just finish at its deadline. So we obtain a static voltage scheduling, and the initial clock frequency is f_{static}. The static scheduling is the starting point of dynamic voltage scaling.

IntraDVS assisted by a compiler inserts voltage scaling points in a real-time application, and the execution cycle of the application is divided into n sections or subintervals. Suppose that the worst-case execution cycle and the actual execution cycle of each section are respectively denoted by wc_i and ac_i for $i=1,\ldots,n$. At the beginning of each section, we adjust supply voltage (V_i) and clock frequency (f_i) to the relationship between the remaining time and the remaining workload.

Using the greedy scheme, we set the clock frequency of each section to

$$f_i = wc_i /(d - ct_i - rwc_{i+1} / f_{static})$$

where ct_i denotes current time of the ith voltage scaling point, and $rwc_{i+1} = \sum_{l=i+1}^{n} wc_l$. From the above formula, we conclude that the greedy scheme gives all the reclaimed slack time of each section to next section.

In order to utilize the models to analyze the greedy scheme, the above formula becomes

$$f_i = (wc_i /(\sum_{l=1}^{n} wc_l - \sum_{l=1}^{i-1} (ac_l \cdot f_{static} / f_l) - \sum_{l=i+1}^{n} wc_l)) \cdot f_{static} \ , \tag{1}$$

where $ct_i = \sum_{l=1}^{i-1} ac_l / f_l$. After detailed derivation, the formula (1) becomes

$$f_i = cf_i \cdot f_{static} \ , \tag{2}$$

where cf_i is equal to

$$cf_i = wc_i /(wc_i + \sum_{l=1}^{i-1} \left(wc_l \cdot \left(\prod_{k=l}^{i-1} (1 - ac_k / wc_k) \right) \right) \ . \tag{3}$$

Since the dynamic energy consumption dominates the total energy consumption of CMOS, we only take into account the dynamic energy consumption. The dynamic power P of CMOS is defined by

$$P = \alpha \cdot C \cdot V^2 \cdot f \ , \tag{4}$$

where α indicates the average probability of the input node changing on each clock cycle, C is the total capacitance on the gate output node, and V and f respectively denote the supply voltage and clock frequency of CMOS. DVS has divided the execution of an application into multiple sections, and the total energy consumption is

$$E = \sum_{i=1}^{n} P_i \cdot t_i = \alpha \cdot C \cdot \sum_{i=1}^{n} V_i^2 \cdot f_i \cdot t_i \quad . \tag{5}$$

The time t_i of each section is defined by

$$t_i = ac_i / f_i \quad . \tag{6}$$

The formula $f \propto (V - V_T)^2 / V$ has defined the relationship between the clock frequency and supply voltage of CMOS, where V_T denotes the threshold voltage of CMOS. Since V_T is generally much smaller than supply voltage, we can obtain an approximate equation between clock frequency and supply voltage

$$f_i = \beta \cdot V_i \quad , \tag{7}$$

where β is a constant relating to CMOS technology.

Using the formulae from (5) to (7), we can obtain the energy consumption of the static voltage scheduling

$$E_{static} = (\alpha \cdot C / \beta^2) \cdot \sum_{i=1}^{n} f_{static}^2 \cdot ac_i = (\alpha \cdot C / \beta^2) \cdot f_{static}^2 \cdot \mu \cdot wcec \quad , \tag{8}$$

where $wcec = \sum_{i=1}^{n} wc_i = \sum_{i=1}^{n} ac_i / \mu$, $0 \le \mu \le 1$.

Using the formulae from (2) to (7), we can compute the energy consumption of the dynamic voltage scheduling

$$E = (\alpha \cdot C / \beta^2) \cdot \sum_{i=1}^{n} cf_i^2 \cdot f_{static}^2 \cdot ac_i = (\alpha \cdot C / \beta^2) \cdot f_{static}^2 \cdot \sum_{i=1}^{n} cf_i^2 \cdot ac_i \quad . \tag{9}$$

Then the ratio of E to E_{static} is defined by

$$r = E / E_{static} = (1/\mu) \cdot \sum_{i=1}^{n} cf_i^2 \cdot (ac_i / wcec) \quad . \tag{10}$$

Let $ac_i = \mu_i \cdot wc_i$ for $i = 1,...,n$, $wc_i^{'} = wc_i / wcec$ for $i = 1,...,n$, (10) becomes

$$r = (1/\mu) \cdot \sum_{i=1}^{n} cf_i^2 \cdot (\mu_i \cdot wc_i^{'}) \quad , \tag{11}$$

and cf_i is equal to

$$cf_i = wc_i^{'} / (wc_i^{'} + \sum_{l=1}^{i-1} \left(wc_l^{'} \cdot \left(\prod_{k=l}^{i-1} (1 - \mu_k) \right) \right) \quad , \tag{12}$$

where $\sum_{i=1}^{n} wc_i^{'} = 1$, $wc_i^{'} > 0$ for $i = 1,...,n$, $0 \le \mu_i \le 1$ for $i = 1,...,n$.

If we make use of the fixed-length configuration of voltage scaling points (i.e. all wc_i for $i = 1,...,n$ have same value), (11) becomes

$$r^{eq} = (1/n) \cdot \sum_{i=1}^{n} \left(1/(1 + \sum_{l=1}^{i-1} \left(\prod_{k=l}^{i-1} (1 - \mu_k) \right) \right)^2 \cdot (\mu_i / \mu) \quad , \tag{13}$$

where $0 \le \mu_i \le 1$ for $i = 1,...,n$, $0 \le \mu \le 1$.

Finally, we obtain the analytical models of r and r^{eq}.

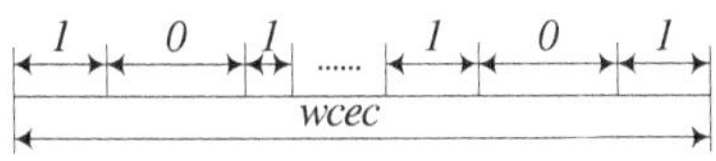

Fig. 1. The execution cycles of an application

```
if (a>b)  [w:100]
...
else      [w:50]
...
end
loop: [w:20*10;b:20*5]
...
end
```

(a)

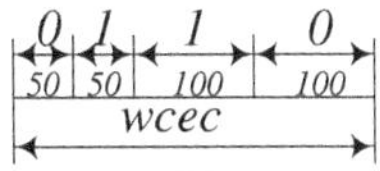

(b)

Fig. 2. An application (a) and its corresponding execution pattern (b)

In real-time applications the slack times are often not evenly distributed, as is shown in Fig. 1. Each section with the tag '1' indicates the actual execution cycle. Since the actual number of loop iterations or the prediction of condition structures could be differentiated from that of the worst case in the execution course, each section with the tag '0' is not executed, i.e. the slack time (cycle). For example, suppose that an application includes a condition sentence and a loop sentence, as is shown in Fig. 2(a), where the condition sentence is executed for 100 cycles if the prediction (a>b) is true, or else 50 cycles. In addition, the worst-case execution cycle and the best-case execution cycle of the loop sentence are 200 and 100 cycles, respectively. If in most cases, the prediction is false and the loop is executed for 100 cycles, then the execution pattern in the most frequent case is shown in Fig. 2(b).

Next we numerically simulate DVS with the model defined by (13). In order to simulate the execution cases that the slack times are not evenly distributed in real-time applications, we divide the execution interval of a task into λ equal subintervals, and call λ simulation precision. In each subinterval, there are two possible values: 1 or 0. The subintervals with the value of 1 are the actual execution cycles, and the subintervals with the value of 0 are not executed. From the knowledge of combinatorics, we draw the conclusion that the number of the total cases is 2^{λ}. In each case we can evaluate parameter μ from the number of the subintervals with the value of 1. For example, there are C_{λ}^{m} cases of m subintervals with the value of 1, and the parameter μ of the cases is equal to m/λ, where C_{λ}^{m} indicates the number of combinations of m elements among λ. We can compute μ_i with the similar method.

Due to space limitation, it is impossible to list all the results, and we just present the typical case. Let $\lambda = 14$, we simulate, for example, the workload pattern like 00010110000000, and the simulation results are shown in Fig. 3, where the horizontal axis and the vertical axis, respectively, represent the number of voltage scaling sections and the percentage of energy consumption.

It is clearly seen that the percentage curve has complex variation with the growth of the number of sections. In the beginning, the percentage has been decreasing with the increase of the number of sections before it reaches the minimum. Subsequently, the percentage has an overall ascending tendency but no monotonicity.

Through analyzing the relationship between the frequency and the workload, we find out the reason for the complex properties. On the one hand, for some configurations of voltage scaling sections, the application has utilized all the available slack times and the whole workload is operated on the lowest frequency. On the other hand, for other configurations of voltage scaling sections, the layout of the frequency has made the earlier part of the workload operated on much lower frequency and consumed all the available slack times; the later part, however, has to be executed on the largest frequency to guarantee the completion before the deadline.

In brief, we come to the conclusion that the greedy scheme cannot effectively utilize the slack times.

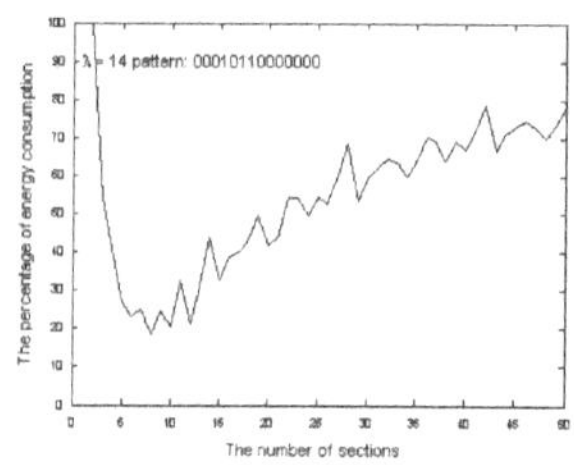

Fig. 3. The percentage of energy consumption using the greedy scheme when $\lambda = 14$ and the pattern: 00010110000000

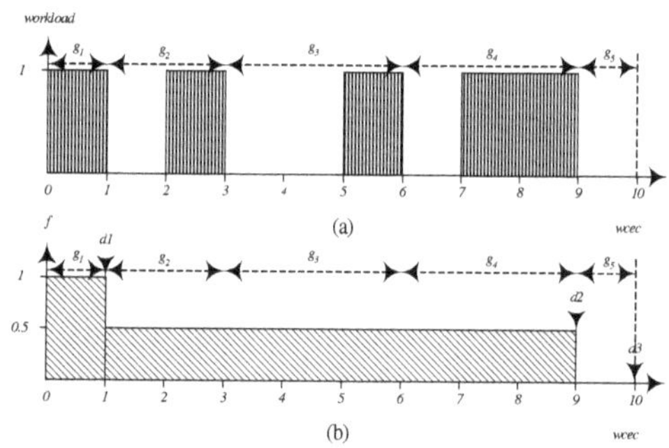

Fig. 4. (a) The most frequent execution case of an application and its grouping. (b) The corresponding frequency configuration.

4 A Profile-Guided Greedy Voltage Adjustment Scheme

In the execution course of an application, there are many possible execution paths, and some paths (called hot paths) are frequently executed. We can obtain the information of the execution path by profile-guided method, and voltage scheduling should minimize the energy consumption of the most frequently executed case. Therefore, we first investigate the optimal real-time voltage scheduling in the most frequent execution case in order to guide the greedy scheme. Suppose that we have known the most frequent execution case of an application, as is shown in Fig. 4 (a). Each section that the workload is 1 represents the executed cycle, and the sections that the workload is 0 are not executed. We form one '0' section and one succeeding '1' section into a group, and all the groups are denoted by g_l for $l = 1,\ldots,n^g$. If the actual execution cycle and the worst-case execution cycle of each group are denoted by $c\_mf_{g_l}$ and wc_{g_l} respectively, then in the most frequent execution case the execution ratio of the i groups at the beginning is defined by

$$r\_mf_i = \sum_{l=1}^{i} c\_mf_{g_l} / \sum_{l=1}^{i} wc_{g_l}$$

Moreover, we can find the maximum of all the execution ratios

$$mr\_mf = \max\{r\_mf_i \mid i = 1,...,n^g\}$$

and the corresponding subscript j (If more than one r_mf_i are equal to the maximum, j corresponds to the maximum subscript). As a result, the frequencies of the j groups at the beginning are set to

$$f = mr\_mf \cdot f_{static}$$

If $j = n^g$, the frequency configuration finishes; otherwise, from the $(j+1)$th group, we continue to utilize the same method to calculate the frequencies of the remaining groups till the frequency of the whole execution interval is solved. We call the produced frequency configuration an optimal real-time dynamic voltage scheduling in the most frequent case (OPTDVS).

For example, suppose that in an application $wcec$ includes 10 cycles, as is shown in Fig. 4 (a). We first divide the whole execution interval into 5 groups, and then calculate all the r_mf_i for $i = 1,...,5$, i.e. $\{1, \ 2/3, \ 1/2, \ 5/9, \ 1/2\}$.

Since $mr\_mf = 1$ and the corresponding subscript is 1, then the frequency of the first group is set to f_{static}. For the remaining 4 groups, we continue to compute the r_mf_i for $i = 1,...,4$, i.e. $\{1/2, \ 2/5, \ 1/2, \ 4/9\}$.

Since $mr\_mf = 1/2$ and its corresponding subscript is 4, then the frequency of the groups from 2 to 4 is set to $f_{static}/2$. The same method sets the frequency of the fifth group to 0. The whole frequency configuration is shown in Fig. 4 (b).

Theorem. *Consider a feasible voltage scheduling set, where each voltage scaling point in each voltage scheduling only utilizes the slack times appearing before itself. If we have known the most frequent execution case of an application, OPTDVS minimizes the energy consumption of the case among the feasible voltage scheduling set.*

Proof. Due to the space limitation, we don't include the proof in this paper.

In each real-time voltage scheduling, each voltage scaling point only utilizes the slack times appearing before itself, then OPTDVS gives the lower limit of all the real-time voltage scheduling in the most frequent execution case. For each voltage adjustment scheme, the ideal result is that the energy consumption reaches or is near the lower limit.

Next we utilize OPTDVS to present a new greedy voltage adjustment scheme. At each voltage scaling point, we must specify the utilization method of the available slack times. Our idea is that the voltage scheduling should be in accord with the OPTDVS in the most frequent execution case as much as possible. After applying OPTDVS to an application, its whole execution interval is divided into some subintervals; each subinterval is operated on a single frequency and has its corresponding deadline. For example, Fig. 4 (b) shows the deadlines of all the subintervals, i.e. d_1, d_2, and d_3. Each subinterval might include some voltage scaling points, and we suppose that the ith voltage scaling point belongs to the mth subinterval. Then the frequency of the ith section approximating to OPTDVS is set to

$$f_i^{opt} = (\sum_{l=i}^{first^{\geq d^m}} mfc_l / (\sum_{l=1}^{first^{\geq d^m}} wc_l - \sum_{l=1}^{i-1} (ac_l \cdot f_{static} / f_l))) \cdot f_{static}$$

where d^m denotes the deadline of the mth subinterval, $first^{\geq d^m}$ indicates the subscript of the first section larger than or equal to d^m, and mfc_l is the actual execution cycle of the lth voltage scaling sections in the most frequent execution case. Apparently, f_i^{opt} cannot ensure the completion of the real-time application before the deadline in worst case. On the contrary, the greedy scheme has aggressively utilized the available slack times. So we utilize the greedy scheme to guarantee the timing constraints. If f_i^g denotes the frequency of the greedy scheme, then the final frequency of the ith section is

$$f_i = \max\{f_i^{opt}, f_i^g\}$$

4.1 The Methodology of Realization

We can implement the new scheme like the greedy scheme, except adding some profile information. For example, the methodology based on the program checkpoints (similar to voltage scaling points) in COPPER project [15] can be used.

As is shown in Fig. 5(a), we present the source code of a program along with the execution cycles of the different branches, where *mf* indicates the cycle of the most frequent execution case, whereas *wc* is the cycle of the worst case. Fig. 5(b) illustrates the source code after checkpoints have been inserted. Notice that a checkpoint CK(5) controlled by condition structure is added in the while loop, and as a result CK(4) can utilize the most frequent execution pattern to make voltage scheduling due to the insertion of CK(5). If the while loop is executed for less than or equal to 200 cycles (most frequent case), then the voltage scheduling of CK(4) makes the frequency near to that of OPTDVS. Otherwise, we will reach the CK(5), where the frequency will be raised up to guarantee the timing constrain. In Fig. 5(c), we give the control flow graph of the checkpoints, where the dashed line indicates the most frequent execution path. Finally, Fig. 5(d) shows the execution pattern and its grouping, where 's' and 'a', respectively, indicate the slack cycle and the actual execution cycle in the most frequent execution case.

If program reaches CK(5), then the application is operated out of the most frequent execution case, and moreover, CK(5) is located on the boundary of the second subinterval of OPTDVS. In order to ensure the completion before the deadline, we utilize the greedy scheme to set clock frequency at CK(5):

$$f_i = wc_i / (d - ct_i - rwc_{i+1} / f_{static})$$

At each checkpoint except CK(5), we utilize the voltage scaling scheme as follows:

$$f_i = \max\left\{ wc_i / (d - ct_i - rwc_{i+1} / f_{static}),\ \ (wc_i + \sum_{l=i+1}^{first^{\geq d^m}} mfc_l) / (d^m - ct_i) \right\}$$

where d^m represents the deadline of the subinterval in OPTDVS that includes the ith checkpoint, $\sum_{l=i+1}^{first \geq d^m} mfc_l$ is the most frequent execution cycle from the $(i+1)$th checkpoint to d^m. For example, suppose that the clock frequency is 1, and then d is 1470 as shown in Fig. 5(d). For CK(1), d^m and $\sum_{l=i+1}^{first \geq d^m} mfc_l$, respectively, are equal to 460 and 250, and wc_i is 100.

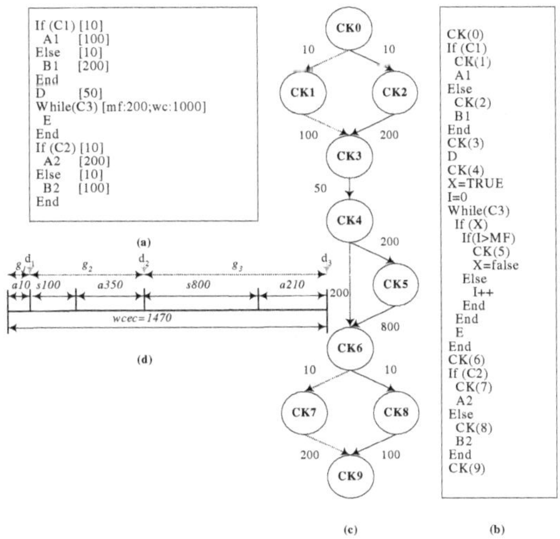

Fig. 5. An example extracting the most frequent execution pattern with program checkpoints: (a) source code; (b) source code added checkpoints; (c) control flow graph of checkpoints; (d) the execution pattern of the most frequent case and the grouping of OPTDVS

To sum up, the methodology has inserted voltage scaling points into the execution interval as shown in Fig. 6, that is, there must be voltage scaling point for every switch from '1' intervals to '0' intervals or from '0' to '1'. The configuration of voltage scaling points guarantees that the energy consumption is equal to that of OPTDVS in most frequent execution case.

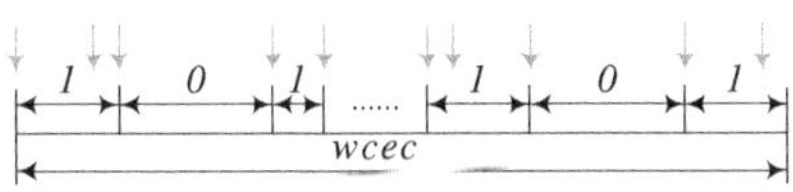

Fig. 6. Insertion of voltage scaling points

4.3 Simulations

By simulations, we compare our voltage adjustment scheme (M) with all the current representative schemes, which include the proportional scheme DPM-P (P) [6] [7], the simple greedy scheme DPM-G (G) [15], and the speculative scheme DPM-S (S) [11].

Utilizing the method of Section 3, we construct the synthetic applications with $\lambda = 20$. In all the cases, our scheme obtains the smallest energy consumption. Due to space limitation, it is impossible to list all the results, and we randomly select some execution patterns in order to interpret some typical cases, as is shown in Fig. 7.

First of all, though the proportional scheme (DPM-P) is the most easily realized, it often cannot effectively utilize the slack times.

Since the simple greedy scheme (DPM-G) can aggressively utilize the slack times, often it can lead to large energy reduction. But due to lack of the information about the application characteristic, aggressive utilization of the slack times could lead to more energy consumption.

Guided by the average execution workload, DPM-S often attains large energy saving. Our voltage adjustment scheme, however, obtains the largest reduction of energy consumption.

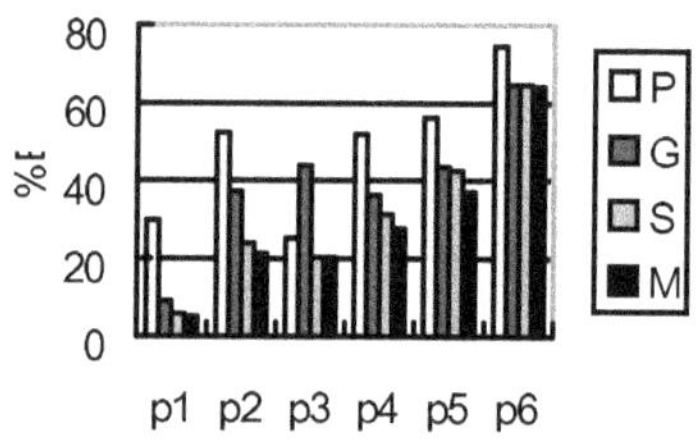

Fig. 7. The energy consumptions of DPM-P (P), DPM-G (G), DPM-S (S), and our scheme (M). (p1) 00001000001010000100, (p2) 00001011101010000000, (p3) 00000001100101111101, (p4) 00101011110010010010, (p5) 00110111110001000101, (p6) 11011101111110110001.

5 Conclusions and Future Works

In this paper we investigate the greedy voltage scheduling, and find out that the greedy scheme can aggressively make use of the slack times, but the aggressive scheme often leads to the ineffective utilization of the slack times. Therefore, we propose a profile-guided greedy voltage adjustment scheme directed by the optimal real-time voltage scheduling in the most frequent execution case of an application. Finally, we show by simulations that the optimizing voltage adjustment scheme obtains the largest gain of all the current representative schemes.

We have given the methodology of the realization about the scheme, and in future, we will integrate the scheme into a real system based on greedy scheme.

References

1. ITRS. International Technology Roadmap for Semiconductors 2003 Edition. Can get from http://public.itrs.net
2. Kanishka Lahiri. Battery-Driven System Design: A New Frontier in Low Power Design. ASP-DAC/VLSI Design 2002, January 07 - 11, 2002, Bangalore, India.

3. Trevor Mudge. Power: A First Class Design Constraint for Future Architectures. HiPC 2000: 215-224.
4. T. Burd, T. Pering, A. Stratakos, and R. Brodersen. A Dynamic Voltage Scaled Microprocess- or System. in Proc. of IEEE International Solid-State Circuits Conference, 2000, pp. 294–295.
5. C.M. Krishna, Yann-Hang Lee. Voltage-Clock-Scaling Adaptive Scheduling Techniques for Low Power in Hard Real-Time Systems. IEEE TRANSACTIONS ON COMPUTERS, December 2003 (Vol. 52, No. 12).
6. Daniel Mosse, H. Aydin, B.R. Childers, R. Melhem. Compiler-Assisted Dynamic Power-Aware Scheduling for Real-Time Applications. Workshop on Compilers and Operating Systems for Low-Power (COLP'00), Philadelphia, PA, October 2000.
7. Dongkun Shin, Seongsoo Lee, Jihong Kim. Intra-Task Voltage Scheduling for Low-Energy Hard Real-Time Applications. In IEEE Design & Test of Computers, Mar. 2001.
8. Dongkun Shin and Jihong Kim. Look-ahead Intra-Task Voltage Scheduling Using Data Flow Information. In Proc. ISOCC, pp. 148-151, Oct. 2004.
9. Nevine AbouGhazaleh, Daniel Mosse, B.R. Childers, R. Melhem, Matthew Craven. Collaborative Operating System and Compiler Power Management for Real-Time Applications. in Proc. of The Real-time Technology and Application Symposium, RTAS, Toronto, Canada (May 2003).
10. Flavius Gruian. Hard Real-Time Scheduling for Low-Energy Using Stochastic Data and DVS Processors. In Proceedings of the International Symposium on Low-Power Electronics and Design ISLPED'01 (Huntington Beach, CA, Aug. 2001).
11. Dongkun Shin, Jihong Kim. A Profile-Based Energy-Efficient Intra-Task Voltage Scheduling Algorithm for Real-Time Applications. In ISLPED'01, August 6-7, Huntington Beach, California, USA.
12. Jacob Rubin Lorch. Operating Systems Techniques for Reducing Processor Energy Consumption [Ph.D. thesis]. UNIVERSITY of CALIFORNIA, BERKELEY, Fall 2001.
13. Nevine AbouGhazaleh, Daniel Mosse, B.R. Childers, R. Melhem. Toward the placement of power management points in real-time applications. Compilers and operating systems for low power, Pages:37-52, 2003. ISBN: 1-4020-7573-1, Kluwer Academic Publishers Norwell, MA, USA.
14. H.Saputra, M. Kandemir, N.Vijaykrishnan, M.J.Irwin, J.S. Hu, C-H.Hsu, U.Kremer. Energy-Conscious Compilation Based on Voltage Scaling. In ACM SIGPLAN Joint Conference on Languages, Compilers, and Tools for Embedded Systems and Software and Compilers for Embedded Systems , June 2002.
15. Ana Azevedo, Ilya Issenin, Radu Cornea. Profile-based Dynamic Voltage Scheduling Using Program Checkpoints. In Proceeding of Design, Automation and Test in Europe Conference (DATE), March 2002.
16. Chung-Hsing Hsu, Ulrich Kremer. The Design, Implementation, and Evaluation of a Compiler Algorithm for CPU Energy Reduction. in Proceedings of the ACM SIGPLAN 2003 conference on Programming language design and implementation, pp. 38--48, June 2003.
17. Peter Puscher, Alan Burns. A Review of Worst-Case Execution-Time Analysis (Editorial). Kluwer Academic Pubilishers, September 24, 1999. USA.
18. Tohru ISHIHARA, Hiroto YASUURA. Voltage Scheduling Problem for Dynamically Variable Voltage Processors. In Proceedings of the 1998 international symposium on Low power electronics and design, Monterey, California, United States, pp. 197-202, 1998, ISBN:1-58113-059-7, ACM Press New York, NY.

A Parallelizing Compiler Approach Based on IXA

Ting Ding and Naiqi Liu

Ting Ding, Naiqi Liu,UESTC-Intel IXA Lab,
Department of Computer Science and Engineering,
University of Electronic Science and Technology of China,
Chengdu, P.R. China 610054
tina_ting915@sina.com, nliu@uestc.edu.cn

Abstract. In this paper, we first analyze the parallel characteristics of both network processor and network application. Our analysis shows that the development using the existed two programming interfaces on IXA is complicated. This suggests that a programming environment which can abstract away architectural details from the developers and can automatically map application to resources is on desire. Thus we introduce a parallelizing compiler developed by Intel called IXP C compiler and analyze its performance on two different mapping forms by compiling packet_processing_pps of ipv4_diffserv-1*10G_Ethernet-egress. Finally we discuss the shortcomings of partition algorithm and also give some suggestions for the future work.

1 Introduction

The architecture of network system has been developed dramatically along with the increasing of the Internet's bandwidth and the diversity of the services. Network processor, in general, is designed to satisfy certain demands to make up the gap between processing rate and line bandwidth, and to meet the requirement of the processors' programmability and flexibility, including efficient parallel processing on network packet, high programmability and extensibility, quick launching etc. Currently, developers have to manage many hardware resources and manually maintain the synchronization, so that it is difficult for them to develop high performance applications at the same time. This paper analyzes the parallel characteristics of both network processor and network application, and introduces a parallelizing compiler based on IXA called IXP C compiler. By analyzing the performance of two different mapping forms of IXP C compiler, we discuss the shortcomings of its partition algorithm and also give some suggestions for the future work.

2 Parallelism of Network Processor Architecture

The conventional network processing method based on ASIC (Application Specific Integrated Circuit) and GPP (General Purpose Processor) is unable to satisfy the demands of the processing rate and flexibility, resulting in the comprehensive development of network processor based on ASIP (Application Specified Instruction Processor). Generally speaking, network processor divides network tasks into control

L.T. Yang et al. (Eds.): ICESS 2005, LNCS 3820, pp. 720 – 725, 2005.

plane and data plane. Take Intel IXP2800 as an example to conclude the parallelism of network processor architecture:

- **Multi-microengine architecture:** IXP2800 has 16 individual RISC engines in frequency of 1.4G.
- **Optimized ALU:** The ME (microengine) instruction set provides network-specialized instructions. ALU and shift operation can be finished in one cycle.
- **Multi-thread supported by hardware:** Every ME independently executes as many as 8 cooperative thread contexts. The swap mechanism is under the instruction control, other than the interrupt, which hides the memory access latency to improve the utilization ratio and processor throughput efficiently.
- **Optimized memory management and DMA unit:** Memory access is always the performance bottle neck. IXP2800 introduces optimized memory controller interface and DMA unit to improve it.
- **Efficient communication mechanisms:** IXP2800 provides inter-thread signaling mechanism, atomic shared memory operations and hardware support for rings and queues.

The features above show that the network processor provides good parallelism on hardware architecture, which is the basis of developing high efficient network applications on it.

3 Characteristics of Network Application

Network services are diverse, but as to the given network service, it can be simply viewed as one application, which processes a continued data units--generally referred to as packets or cells. The whole process of packet-processing application can be divided into three logic phases, receiving, processing and transmitting. Fundamental characteristics of this kind of applications can be concluded as following:

- The logic of packet-processing application can be described using cyclic data-flow graphs. The process functions on the data-flow graph can be represented as M-in, N-out data-flow actors. The actor may act differently for different network services.
- The sequence of functions executed for a packet depends on the packet's type and is triggered by packet arrivals, timers, or other hardware events. Furthermore, most of the functions maintain per-flow state, which is accessed and updated while packet under processing belongs to the flow.
- Functions in packet-processing application are always not compute-intensive but memory-intensive unit. Hence, how to hide the memory access latency is critical to the performance of network application system.
- In most applications, there is little or no dependence between packets belonging to different flows. So the application itself exhibits a high-degree parallelism when processing packets of different flows.

It is obvious that packet-processing applications have the probability to get high performance if mapped to network processor perfectly.

4 Introduction to Existed Programming Interfaces on IXA

Currently, there are two programming interfaces for IXP2800. One is assembly language, with which the assembly code is directly mapped to RISC instructions. Another is microC language, which is an explicitly parallel language interface that provides developers with keywords and extensions to specify multi-thread execution, sleep/wake signaling, inter-process communication, data placement, and manipulation of configuration and status registers. Both require developers to explicitly partition application code onto MEs, and consequently manage threading and synchronization.

It is shown that the developing the above programming interfaces is complicated, and also the key factor restricting the development of network processor. A programming environment, which can abstract away architectural details from the developers and can automatically map application to resources, is on desire. The key factors, which means abstracting and mapping, push the researches of virtual machine and parallelizing compiler based on network processor these years.

5 A Parallelizing Compiler Approach Based on IXA

In this section, we will introduce an incoming parallelizing compiler on network processor developed by Intel as well as the performance analysis and improvement suggestions.

5.1 Introduction to IXP C Compiler

IXPC compiler uses the similar C language as the programming interface with the extensions to support IXP architecture. It hides multithreading, multiprocessing, most of the low-level hardware resources that are unique to IXPs and asynchronous I/O capabilities of IXPs for developers. And it also parallelizes the sequential logic applications according to the performance requirement, then finally map them to hardware resources. Here are some features in detail:

- **IXP C compiler abstracts the network application to a series of function units according to its characteristics mentioned above, which is called PPS (Packet Processing Stage).** A PPS is a logical entity that performs packet processing functionalities in hardware-independent sequential C constructs and libraries, and also un-bound to any hardware resources in IXP. In the whole application system, PPSes which constitute a program run concurrently.
- **In IXP C compiler, the communication channel between PPSes is a data structure called pipe, which provides an implicit synchronization contract of PPSes.** Three pipes are supported, abstract pipe, NN pipe and scratch pipe. The compiler is responsible for realizing pipes. As for abstract pipe, compiler will choose the effective type automatically according to the performance requirement and resources situation, and SRAM rings can also be used when scratch or NN rings are not available.

- **Developers can use a key word *_path* to label the critical path of the program, and set a performance specification for that path.** All of these will guide the compilation because most of the optimization is done for critical path and compiler will try its best to satisfy the given performance on it.
- **In the view of IXP C compiler, the input is c files with PPS, resource description and performance specification on each critical path, and the output is ME allocated uc files and some performance report if needed.**
- **A PPS can be compiled into one or more MEs.** PPSes' mapping to MEs take three kinds of forms:
    - *MTP (multi-threading and multi-processing)*
    With this form, PPSes will be allocated to all threads of several MEs to run concurrently. As shown below:

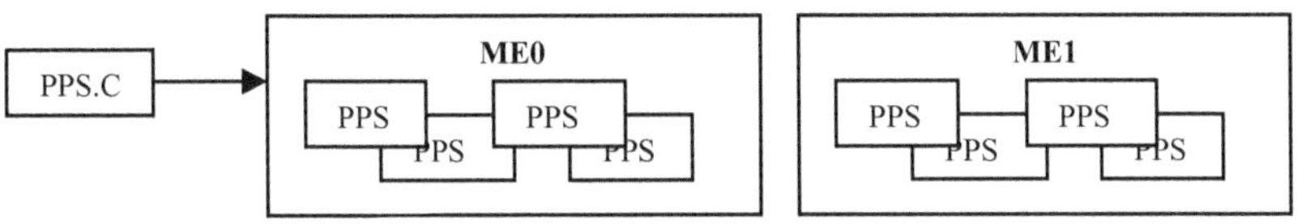

Fig. 1. PPSes in MTP form

- *Pasting*
In this form, thread will be used as the minimal mapping unit instead of ME, which means several PPSes will be allocated to the same ME. This type of compilation is popular in Westport platform because of the limitation of MEs. As shown below:

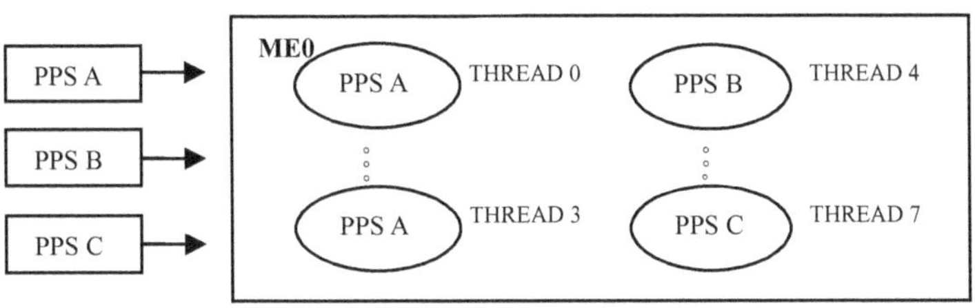

Fig. 2. PPSes in Pasting form

- *CTX (context pipeline)*
In this form, one PPS will be allocated to different MEs to form a pipeline, and each stage of the pipeline will run in multi-threading mode. As shown below (PPS A and PPS B are used as one PPS before partitioning):

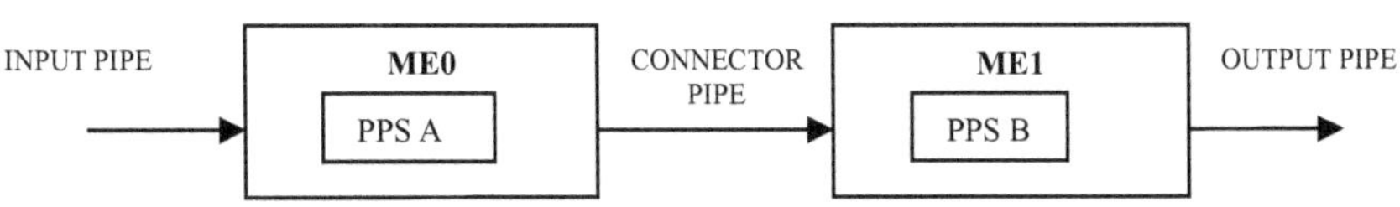

Fig. 3. PPSes in CTX form

In conclusion, developers using IXP C compiler could just focus on the logic of application itself without concerning about the details of network processor architecture. Compiler is responsible to parallelize the sequential logic application and map them to the hardware resources. How to map the program efficiently is a very critical issue during the compilation. On IXP2800, the MTP and CTX are the main map algorithms, with advantages and disadvantages respectively. Here, we will give a brief analysis on the two algorithms of IXP C compiler.

5.2 Performance Analysis on MTP and CTX

We compiled packet_processing_pps of ipv4_diffserv-1*10G_Ethernet-egress both in MTP and CTX forms with the allocation of 3 MEs. Performance data are shown as following:

Table 1. Functional unit utilization-sram

	Sram0(rd)	Sram0(wr)	Sram1(rd)	Sram1(wr)	Sram2(rd)	Sram2(wr)	Sram3(rd)	Sram3(wd)
MTP	27.06%	21.56%	27.06%	3.61%	67.59%	18.01%	9.02%	0.00%
CTX	29.95%	16.61%	19.96%	2.77%	26.47%	8.75%	9.98%	0.00%

Table 2. Functional unit utilization-dram, scratch, pci, and cap

	Dram(rw)	Dram(rd)	Dram(wr)	Scratch(rw)	Scratch(rd)	Scratch(wr)	Pci(rw)	Cap(rw)
MTP	16.50%	6.89%	9.61%	7.19%	3.60%	3.59%	0.00%	0.45%
CTX	15.03%	7.63%	7.41%	6.75%	3.98%	2.76%	0.00%	0.00%

Table 3. Microengine utilization

	ME2	ME3	ME4
MTP	94.83%	94.89%	94.77%
CTX	88.93%	35.65%	100.00%

From these performance data above, we observed:

- In MTP, every ME read the packet descriptor stored in sram for the arrival packet and updated the data structure back to sram when processing finished. On the contrary, in CTX, the packet descriptor was read in when packet arrives and was updated only when the last stage in the pipeline finished processing. That is why the sram read and write in MTP are much more than that is in CTX, which means there is probably much more memory access latency in MTP than that in CTX.
- In CTX, when one PPS was partitioned to several MEs to form a pipeline, the communication channel between each sub-PPS on different MEs was pipe. So the synchronization between MEs was guaranteed by the pipe implementation. In MTP, on the other hand, the communication between MEs was via cap.
- The microengine utilization in MTP was almost equal and high but in CTX, the utilization was obviously not in balance. This should be a critical point of partition algorithm in IXP C compiler and needs to be improved.

5.3 Future Work

As mentioned above, the partition algorithm is not as good as desired. But also note that different application process has different characteristics and may need specialized algorithm. How the application's behavior impact the partition is a hot research. Furthermore, the parallelizing compiler approach as IXP C compiler allocates hardware resources statically. Since the network environment changes every minute, so how to build a dynamic resource allocation environment patched on the compiler will also be our future research work.

6 Conclusion

By relieving developers from managing multi-threading and low-level hardware resources, IXP C compiler makes developing network applications on IXA dramatically easier and faster. It also adds application performance awareness to compilation process and maximizes code reuse across NPU family members. After analyzing its performance on two different mapping forms, we can see that its partition algorithm is not good enough as expected and should be improved based on application behaviors. Also, how to build a dynamic resource allocation environment patched on the compiler to fit the diverse of the realistic network needs further research.

References

1. Douglas E. Comer: Network Systems Design Using Network Processor, Prentice Hall, 2003
2. Intel Corporation: IXP 2800 Hardware Reference Manual, November 2003
3. Intel Corporation: Introduction to the Auto-Partitioning Programming Model, October 2003
4. Intel Corporation: IXP2400/2800 Programmer's Reference Manual, May 2004
5. Eirk J. Johnson and Aaron Kunze: IXP2400/2800 Programming, Intel Press, 2003
6. Uday Naik, Prashant Chandra: IXP2400/2800 Application Design, Intel Press, 2004
7. Bill Carlson: Intel Internet Exchangge Architecture and Applications, Intel Press, 2003
8. B. Hardekopf, T.Riche, J,Mudigonda, M. Dahlin, H.M. Vin, and J. Kaur: Impact of Network Protocols on Programmable Router Architectures, April 2003

The Design of Firewall Based on Intel IXP2350 and Autopartitioning Mode C

Zhang Ke, Liu Naiqi, and Chen Yan

University of Electronic Science and Technology of China, Chengdu 61 00 54, China
Kevin22@126.com, nliu@uestc.edu.cn, carly_chen@126.com

Abstract. This paper introduces a design of firewall based on Intel IXP2350 Network Processor. The functions of this firewall include the packet filtering, state inspection, VPN, NAT/PT and etc. The development language used is Auto-partitioning Mode C (IXP-C). Our development process suggests that IXP-C reduces the development time for the firewall project.

1 Introduction

With the increasing popularization of Internet technology, the global security of network emerges. The technology of firewall separates the private network from the public network and protects the private information and entities. It has been widely applied to the interconnected environments of the dedicated network and public network. The products of firewall are a dark horse just during several years and form an industry soon. The appearance of the firewall restrains the freedom of the data in the network from flowing effectively and improves the security of the network. This paper introduces a design of firewall based on Intel Network Processor IXP2350. The functions of this firewall include the packet filtering, state inspection, VPN, NAT/PT and etc.

2 Intel IXA and IXP2350 Network Processor

The network processor is the core of high speed network devices. Network processors have the merits of ASIC and general processors, such as the Intel IXP2350 network processor, fit network performance requirements and flexibility requirements by highly parallel, programmable architectures.

For the development of next generation network application, Intel created a kind of packet processing architecture based on Intel network processor. Intel calls it IXA (Internet eXchange Architecture). This architecture conform the programmable ability of IXP and the powerful packet processing ability for the fast development of the intelligence network devices. IXA is a kind of network processing architecture and its core is the programmable network processor. It has three key parts: Micro engine technology, XScale technology and the IXA portable architecture.

IXP2350 is the new generation network processor of Intel, which is the base of Intel IXA. It has high performance of packet processing and is suitable for several local networks and remote communications devices. IXP2350 includes four RISC

L.T. Yang et al. (Eds.): ICESS 2005, LNCS 3820, pp. 726–731, 2005.

data processors (MEv2), Intel XScale core, SRAM controllers, DRAM controllers, PCI controller, NPE units and MSF unit, etc. Fig.1 is the diagram of inner structure of IXP2350.

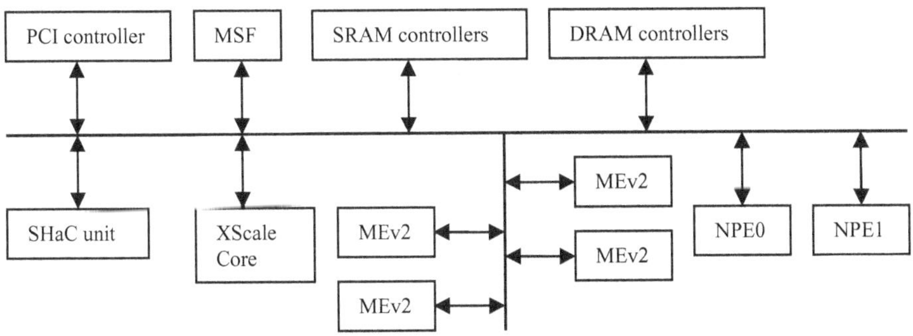

Fig. 1. Diagram of inner structure of IXP2350

3 The Structure of Firewall Based on IXP2350

The hardware structure of firewall based on IXP2350 consists of the following parts: IXP2350 network processor, IA processor, SRAM, DRAM, Flash memory and interface controllers, etc. Fig.2. is the hardware structure diagram.

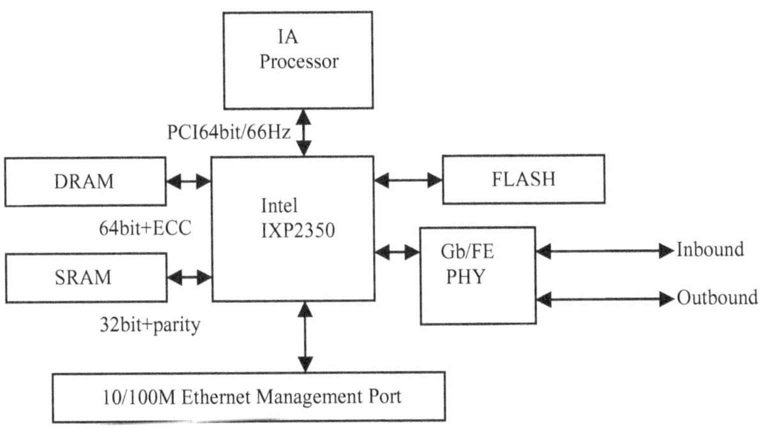

Fig. 2. Firewall based on IXP2350 hardware structure

IXP2350 is the core of this firewall; its functions consist of the following parts: forward the data between two GigE ports, packet filtering, dynamic packet filtering, VPN function and NAT/PT, etc. In IXP2350, the program of hardware interface initialization, tables initialization, inner communications, management run on the XScale core, and the program of packet filtering, dynamic packet filtering, NAT/PT and VPN run on the four MEv2s. And the Network Processor Engine 1 (NPE-1) are dedicated function processors containing hardware coprocessor to support specific features such as Dual 10/100 Ethernet MAC, DES, 3DES, AES, SHA-1, MD-5, etc. These features are software-configurable and controllable.

IA processor can manage the IXP2350, run log module, audit module, proxy module and SNMP management software. Generally, the IA processor is only used for the complicated and unexpected situations. DRAM memories are used for the buffer or store memory of packets. SRAM can be used for the store of some important data structures, such as access control list, SA table and DST, etc. FLASH can be used for solidify the firewall program. The 10/100M Ethernet Management port can be used for the firewall management and configuration, etc.

4 Auto-partitioning Mode C

The Auto-partitioning Mode C language is a subset of ANSI/ISO C with extensions to support the unique hardware features of the Intel IXP2XXX and to support the Auto-partitioning Mode programming model.

An Auto partitioning mode program consists of one or more packet processing stages (PPSes). A PPS is a logical entity expressed using sequential C constructs and libraries and is not bound specifically by the programmer to one or more resources on Intel IXA. As a rough estimate, the maximum compiled code size is around 1500 machine instructions per PPS. One mechanism for PPSes to communicate with other PPSes is called a pipe, which is an abstract, unidirectional channel. Like PPS, a pipe is also a logical entity and not bound to any specific resource. PPSes can communicate through variables in shared memory too. The expression of packets processing application as a set of communicating PPSes represents the logical partitioning of the application into concurrently executing processes. Autopartitioning is the process that maps the set of logical PPSes and pipes onto the processing and communication resources available on a special Intel IXP network processor. In the Autopartitioning programming model, the mapping is performed by the Intel C Compiler and is driven by a performance specification that the programmer provides.

5 The PPSes Run on MEv2

The inbound pipeline of this firewall run on MEv2 consists of the following PPSes: Packet Receive, IP reassembly, inbound packets Processing, NAT/PT, VPN IPSec Dencap, Scheduler, Packet Transmit, Range Match, and HMAC-SHA-1. Fig.3. shows the layout of packet processing stages for the inbound pipeline.

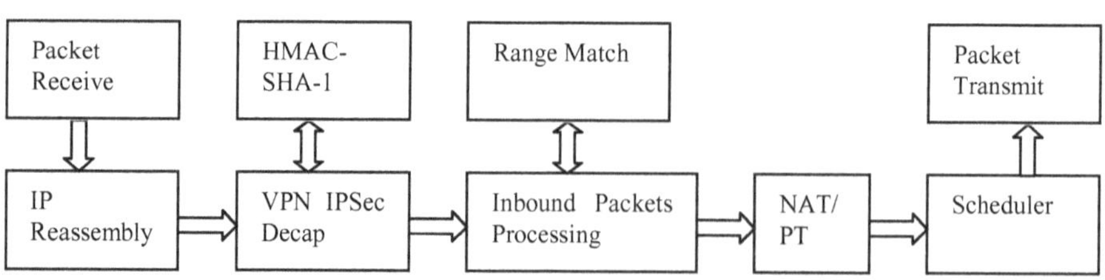

Fig. 3. Inbound Pipeline PPSes Layout

This firewall outbound pipeline run on MEv2 consists of the following PPSes: Packet Receive, NAT/PT, Outbound Packets Processing, VPN IPSec Encap, IP Fragmentation, Scheduler, Packet Transmit, Range Match and HMAC-SHA-1. Fig.4. shows the lay out of packet processing stages for the outbound pipeline.

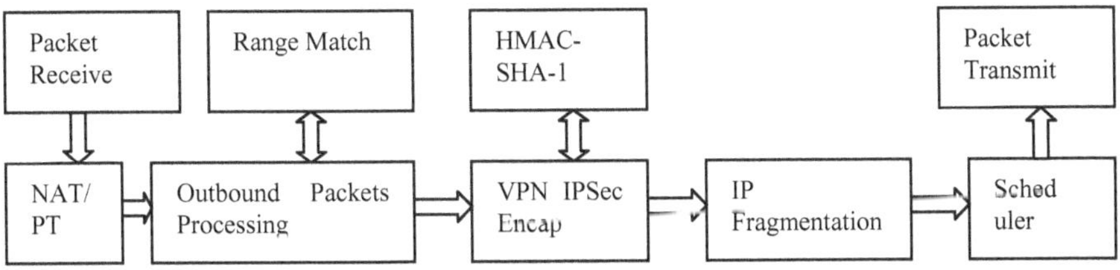

Fig. 4. Outbound Pipeline PPSes Layout

6 Parts of Firewall Implementation and Data Structures

There are some kinds of memory in IXP2350. DRAM (64bit) memories are used for the buffer or store memory of packets. SRAM (32bit) can be used for the store of some important data structures, such as access control list, dialog state table (DST), SA table and global address pool table, etc. Scratchpad can be used for the store of module interfaces information. Fig.5. is the DST data structure for UDP example.

31 ... 16	15 ... 0
Timeout	Ps
SIPP	DIPP
SIPA	
DIPA	

Fig. 5. DST data structure for UDP example

SIPA is the source IP address and DIPA is the destination IP address; SIPP is the source IP port and DIPP is the destination IP port. The Ps field is 16bit, which it is the number of UDP packets that passed the range match. Timeout is the lifetime of this virtual link.

After MEv2 of IXP2350 got a UDP packet from the network, the firewall looks up the DST for related data item. If there isn't any related data item, the packet will be sent to match the firewall access control list (ACL). If this packet can be forwarded, the firewall will add a new item into DST and set the SIPA, DIPA, SIPP and DIPP, and set Ps to1, set Timeout to 50s; If not, it will be dropped. If this item isn't timeout and firewall receives a follow packet belong to the same dialog. Firewall will forward the packet and set Ps to Ps+1, if Ps>=5, firewall will set the Timeout to Timeout+30s. In this way, the firewall can avoid the waste of SRAM and prevent the DOS attack. If the Timeout field of one item is 0, then the firewall releases the resource of this item for other use.

NAPT (Network Address Port Translation) is a kind of effective scheme to solve shortage of network global address and problems of network security, which is a very important part of a firewall, Fig.6.is the two important data structure of firewall design example.

31	16	15 0
Flag		AP
GIPAN		AGIPN
SIPA		
BAGIPA		

Data structure of globe IP address pool

31	16	15 0
Flag		Timeout
Pro		NATPT
IPT		GPT
IIPA		
GIPA		

Data structure of NAPT table

Fig. 6. Two data structure of firewall NAT/PT

In globe IP address pool data structure, the Flag is used for the control of the access to address pool; AP is a pointer that be pointed to the address of last distribution and will be added by the next distribution. GIPAN is used for the number of idle IP addresses in the pool. AGIPN is used for the number of all globe addresses. SIPA is the base address of globe addresses. BAGIPA is the physical location of globe address in SRAM. For the use of these fields, the firewall can distribute globe address and locate the physic location easily.

The NAPT table has eight fields. Flag is used for marking the item static or dynamic. The value of Proc is used for marking TCP or UDP. NATPT is the NAT port, IPT is the inner port and GPT is the globe port. IIPA is the inner network address, and GIPA is the globe address. Timeout is used for the item's life, its default value is 60 (300s), management program run on XScale core check it every 5s. First, if the Flag is 1and the Timeout = 0, this dialog is over, and the related resources will be released. Second, if the Timeout > 0, the firewall will set the Timeout = Timeout – 1. If MEv2 access one item, the related Timeout field will be reset as default value.

7 The Life of a Packet in IXP2350 of Firewall

The life of packet begins when it is received by Gb/FE PHY attached to MSF interface; the packet is fragmentized into m-packets in RBUF. Using the information of THREAD_FREELIST, MSF writes the status words into the thread's registers and signals the thread, and then the thread moves the m-packet into DRAM and put a handle onto a scratchpad ring. MEv2 will check the scratchpad ring and check the packet. For all the tables in SRAM, the MEv2 can check and modify the tables in SRAM and packets in DRAM at high speed, and then the handle of packet will be sending to SRAM for next step. The thread can find the m-packets and move it from DRAM to MSF directly by TBUF. Finally, once MSF receives the EOP m-packet, the Gb/FE PHY transmits the packet, and IXP2350 is going to process the next packet.

8 Conclusion

This paper introduces a design of firewall based on Intel IXP2350 and Auto partitioning Mode C. The IXP-C maps more directly to packet processing pipeline than tradition Micro engine C programming. Users don't have to deal with thread/ME synchronization. So it can reduce the development time for the firewall project. Due to the paper size limitation, this paper only introduces part of the implementation. Further works can be done to improve our design. For examples, we can improve the arithmetic of security, add more function units, and combine it with other security technologies, etc.

References

1. Intel Corp.: Intel IXP23XX Product Line Hardware Reference Manual (2004)
2. Intel Corp.: Intel C Compiler for Intel Network Processors Autopartitioning Mode Reference (2005)
3. Intel Corp.: Intel IXA Software Example Designs for Intel C Compiler Application Note (2005)
4. Douglas E.Comer.: Internetworking with TCP/IP Vol1: Principles, Protocols, and Architectures (Fourth Edition) (2003)
5. Intel Corp.: Intel IXA Software Building Blocks for Intel C Compiler Developers Manual (2005)
6. Intel Corp.: Intel IXP23XX Product Line Programmer's Reference Manual (2004)
7. Intel Corp.: Intel C Compiler for Intel Network Processors Autopartitioning Mode User's Guide (2005)
8. Bill Carlson: Intel Internet Exchange Architecture and Applications (2003)
9. Zhang Ke, Liu Naiqi, Chen Yan: A Design Frame of State Inspection Firewall Based on IXA (2004)

AMT6: End-to-End Active Measurement Tool for IPv6 Network*

Jahwan Koo[1] and Seongjin Ahn[2,**]

[1] School of Information and Communications Engineering, Sungkyunkwan Univ., Chunchun-dong 300, Jangan-gu, Suwon, Kyounggi-do, Korea
jhkoo@songgang.skku.ac.kr

[2] Department of Computer Education, Sungkyunkwan Univ., Myeongnyun-dong 3-ga 53, Jongno-gu, Seoul, Korea
sjahn@comedu.skku.ac.kr

Abstract. Since IPv6 has more benefits over IPv4, the development and deployment of the IPv6 protocol-based products are currently taking place and the migration of IPv4 to IPv6 has also been steadily happen. In these mixed network environment, Network management for both IPv4 and IPv6 is a serious issue. In this paper, we focus on the design and implementation of an active measurement system which can be used for evaluating end-to-end performance of the IPv6/IPv4 network such as end-to-end available bandwidth, one-way delay, and one-way loss. We also describe the procedure of measurement when using AMT6 and some of its features. The IPv6/IPv4 users as well as network operators will be greatly helped to analyze network characteristics using the proposed architectural framework.

1 Introduction

Internet Protocol Version 6 (IPv6) is a critical technology that will help ensure that the Internet can support a rapid growing user base, the increasingly large number of IP-enabled devices such as mobile phones, hand-held devices, and home entertainment, and IP-based services such as online game and voice over IP (VoIP) [2]. Since IPv6 has more benefits over IPv4 in terms of address space, routing infrastructure, security, mobility, and quality of service, the development and deployment of the IPv6 protocol-based products are currently taking place and the migration of IPv4 to IPv6 has also been steadily happen by using various transition mechanisms devised by the Internet Engineering Task Force (IETF). In other words, transition mechanisms such as dual stack, tunneling techniques, and translation have been implemented so that nodes can communicate with each other in IPv6/IPv4 networks. Since it is expected that these mixed network environment will coexist for a long time, network management for both IPv4 and

* This work was supported by grant No. R01-2004-000-10618-0 from the Basic Research Program of the Korea Science and Engineering Foundation.

** Corresponding Author.

L.T. Yang et al. (Eds.): ICESS 2005, LNCS 3820, pp. 732–740, 2005.

IPv6 is a serious issue [1]. This paper focuses on the design and implementation of an active measurement tool which can be used for evaluating end-to-end performance of the IPv6 network.

The rest of the paper is organized as follows. Section 2 presents related work. In section 3, we propose an architecture of active measurement system which can measure IETF's IP Performance Metrics (IPPM) [9] such as end-to-end available bandwidth, one-way delay, and one-way loss in IPv6 network. We named the proposed system Active Measurement Tool for IPv6 (AMT6). In section 4, we also describe the procedure of measurement using AMT6 and some of its features. With measurement data obtained through AMT6, network management for IPv6 can be performed effectively. The final section offers some concluding remarks.

2 Related Work

2.1 Transition Mechanisms

Protocol transitions from IPv4 to IPv6 are not easy because they are typically deployed by installing and configuring the new protocol on all nodes within the network and verifying that all node and router operations work successfully. Many efforts to make rapid protocol transitions on the host have been performed by system software company such as Microsoft [5] (e.g., Microsoft has supported IPv6 transition technologies in the operating system such as Windows server 2003 family and XP) and IETF working group [7] which has devised transition mechanisms as the following categories [8]:

- **Dual stack:** Both IPv4 and IPv6 protocol stacks are in the nodes. This mechanism is used by IPv6/IPv4 nodes in order to communicate with either an IPv4-only node, an IPv6-only node, or another dual stack node.
- **Tunneling:** IPv6 over IPv4 tunneling is the encapsulation of IPv6 packets with an IPv4 header so that IPv6 packets can be sent over an IPv4 network. The IPv4 header contains the IPv4 Protocol field which is set to 41 to indicate an encapsulated IPv6 packet and the Source and Destination fields which are set to IPv4 addresses of the tunnel endpoints. The tunnel endpoints are either manually configured as part of the tunnel interface or are automatically derived from the sending interface, the next-hop address of the matching route, or the source and destination IPv6 addresses in the IPv6 header. While tunneling configurations are manually configured in a configured tunnel, an automatic tunnel does not require manual configuration. The IPv6 protocol for the Windows operating systems supports the automatic tunneling technologies such as 6to4, ISATAP, IPv6 automatic tunneling, and 6over4 [6].
- **Translation:** This is a mechanism that IPv6 packets are converted into IPv4 packets and vice versa. Normally, translation is necessary when the receiver does not understand IPv6 packet sent from the sender in conditions where tunneling does not work.

2.2 IPv6 Management Tools

There are many tools to manage and measure IPv6 networks. The 6NET project group, one of European IPv6 projects, investigated several management tools that currently can be used in IPv6 networks and classified the management tools according to the part of the network they best apply to. Specifically, it recommends *Argus*, *Ethereal*, *Multicast Beacon*, *Pchar*, *Iperf*, and *Ntop* as management tools for LAN and *AS-path-tree*, *Looking glass*, *IPflow*, *Netflow*, *Mping*, *RIPE TT server*, *Cricket*, and *MRTG* as management tools for WAN (For more details, refer to [3]).

On the other hand, the various techniques used by network performance measurement tools can be divided in two categories. One is active measurement, the other is passive measurement. Active measurement means that the tool actively sends some probe packets into the network and measures various performance metrics between end-to-end nodes, and passive measurement means that the tool monitors the packets transmitted over the network for the purpose of fault, configuration, or accounting management. While most tools reported in [3] were implemented by passive measurement technique, only a few tools such as *Pchar* and *Iperf* were based on active measurement. Moreover, *Iperf* [4], only one of all tools presented above can be used to measure performance metrics on an end-to-end path of the IPv6 network.

3 Active Measurement Tool for IPv6 (AMT6)

3.1 Architecture

AMT6 consists of two kinds of systems: (a) Management System (MS) and (b) Agent-based Measurement System (AMS). Figure 1 shows the architecture of AMT6.

The MS system has three components, a management service module (MSM), an agent catalog database (ACD), and a central measurement database (CMD).

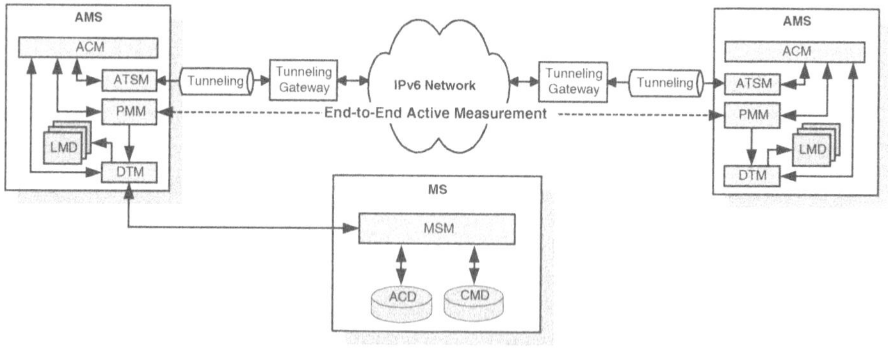

Fig. 1. Architecture of AMT6

The AMS (e.g., sender or receiver in Figure 1) system has five components, an agent control module (ACM), an automatic transition service module (ATSM), a performance measurement module (PMM), a local measurement database (LMD), and a data transmission module (DTM). The functions of modules are the followings:

- **MSM:** The MSM module in the MS system receives agent-related information such as hostname, IP address, and operational status sent from the ACM module in the AMS system when the AMS system is installed in a node, and it stores them in the database ACD. In addition, it receives measurement data come from the ACM module in the AMS system and stores the data in the database CMD.
- **ACM:** The ACM module in the AMS system, which is graphical user interface, receives commands (transition-related or measurement-related pa-

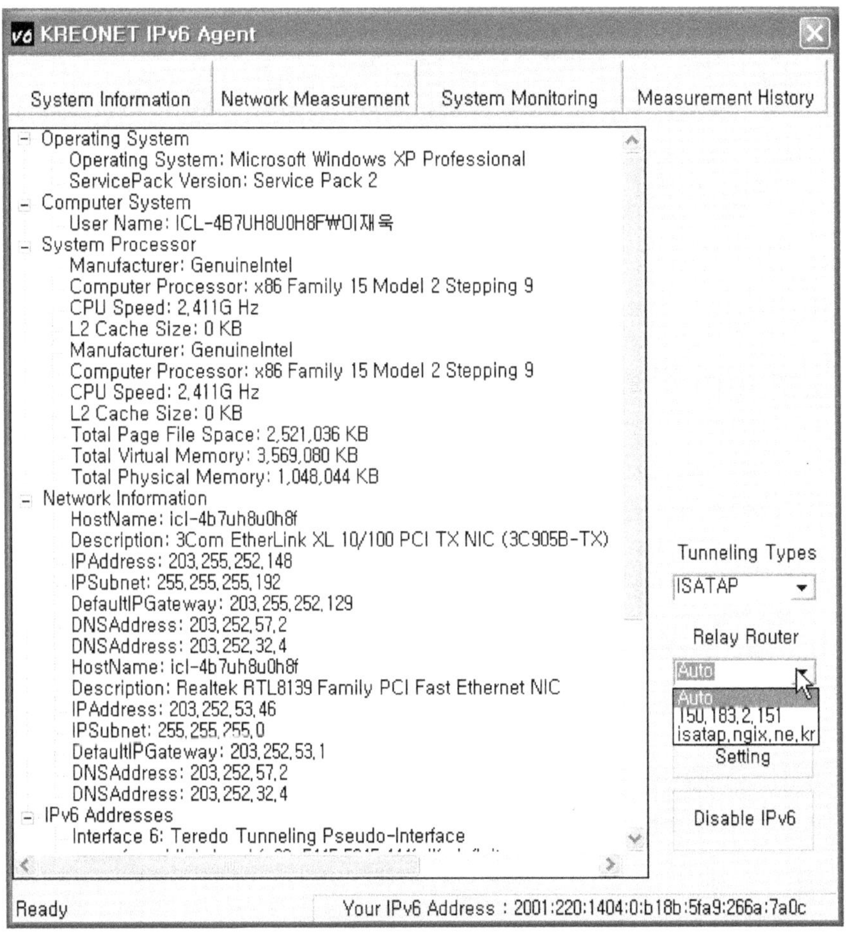

Fig. 2. Visualization of system information and IPv6 transition mechanisms

rameters) from the IPv6 user, parses the commands, and then processes the commands properly. The ACM module also displays the output of result data come from the PMM module.

- **ATSM:** The ATSM module in the AMS system automatically enables or disables protocol transition mechanisms such as 6to4, ISATAP, IPv6 automatic tunneling, and 6over4 on the IPv6 user demands.
- **PMM:** The PMM module in the AMS system measures performance metrics such as available TCP and UDP bandwidth, packet loss, and delay between the sender and the receiver by means of the sender transmitting probe packets to the receiver. The PMM module has two operating modes, server mode and client mode. While it runs as a server if set in server mode, it runs as a client if set in client mode. For example, the sender in client mode generates certain amount of traffic to be sent to the specified receiver, and the receiver in server mode receives the traffic and calculates the effective bandwidth

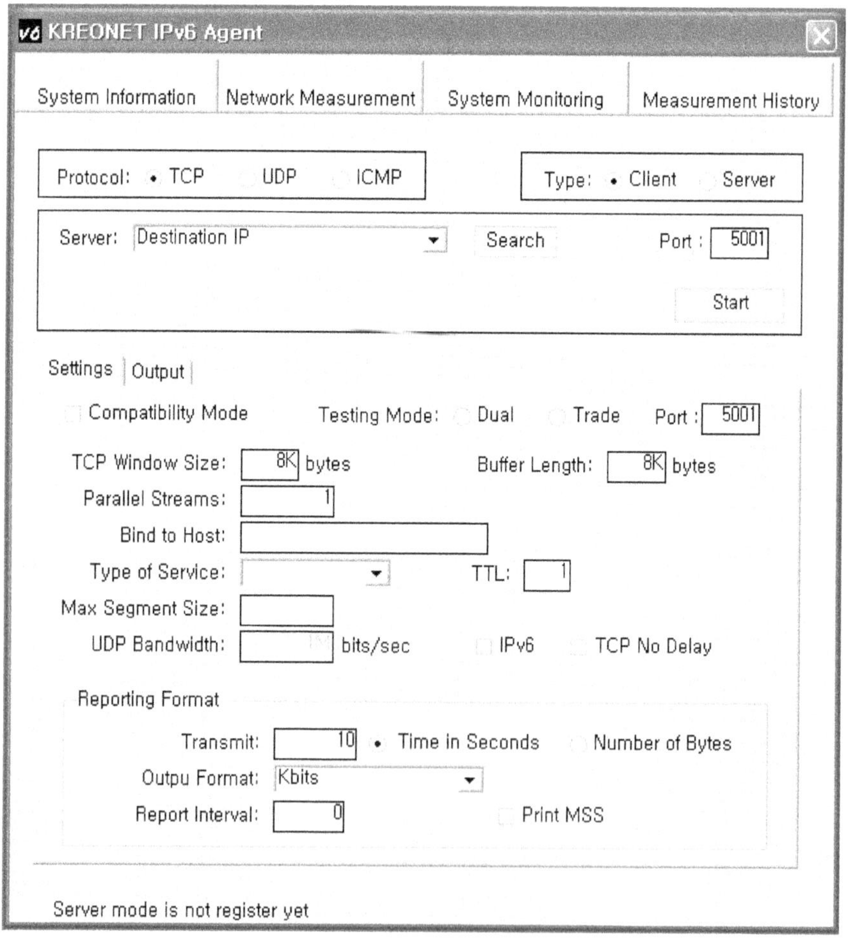

Fig. 3. Graphical user interface for network measurement

between these two nodes. Actually, since the PMM module contains both operating modes, it works as a peer-to-peer system.
- **DTM:** The DTM module sends measurement data to the MSM module in the MS system and stores the data in the local database LMD. The DTM module also receives agent catalog information from the MSM module and transfer that information to the ACM module.

3.2 Graphical User Interface and Features of AMT6

AMT6 is active measurement tool for both IPv4 and IPv6 networks that can be used to measure various aspects of network performance. Similar to *Iperf*, AMT6 measures performance metrics such as available throughput, packet delay, and packet loss between two specified nodes by means of active probing. Figure 2 and 3 show the graphical user interface (GUI) for AMT6 which provides network operator with the measurement method and results.

Major features of AMT6 are the following:

- It can generate different traffic patterns, such as bulk data transfer and interactive data exchange, in order to measure different characteristics of network performance.
- It provides the capability to set the size of the TCP window, and to create multiple TCP data connections in parallel among many different points in the network.
- It can avoid generating non-negligible load on the network by running for specified time, rather than a set amount of data to transfer.
- It provides the graphical user interface easy to use coupled with protocol transition mechanisms directly to active measurement tool.

4 Procedure of Measurement

4.1 Logging into an AMS System

The AMS system of AMT6 provides a graphical user interface called ACM which interprets the options chosen and carries out the corresponding operations. The IPv6/IPv4 user must log in to the AMS system before measuring end-to-end performance as shown in Figure 4. When the user first login to the AMS system, the common management information such as username, hostname, IP address, and operational status have been sent to the MS system automatically. These are stored in the database ACD.

4.2 Measuring End-to-End Performance

The basic steps in measuring a performance metric are as follows:

(1) Setting test parameters. There are many options to set a variety of test parameters, such as TCP window size, buffer length, destination port number, maximum segment size, interval time, and so on. TCP window size

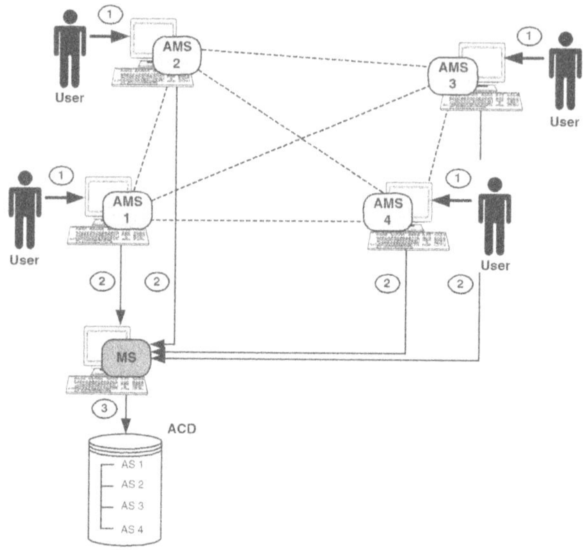

Fig. 4. Logging into an AMS System

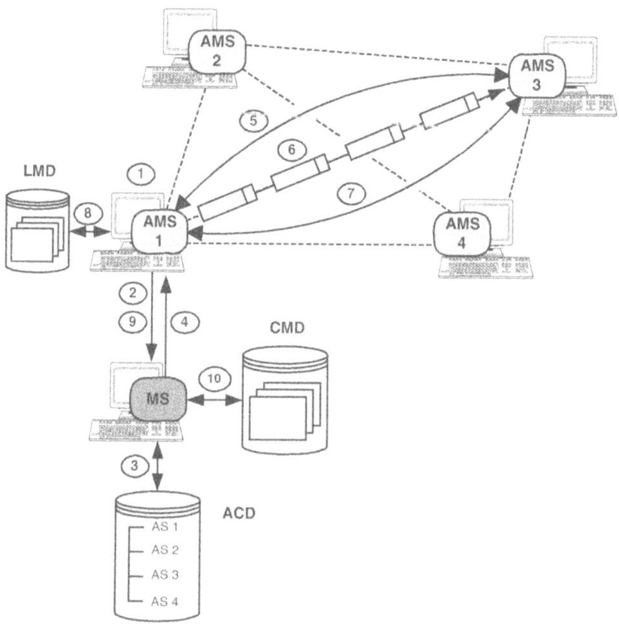

Fig. 5. Measuring end-to-end performance

option means the socket buffer sizes. For TCP, this sets the TCP window size. For UDP, it is just the buffer which datagrams are received in, and so limits the largest receivable datagram size. Buffer length option is the length of buffers to read or write. Default is 8 KB for TCP, 1470 bytes for UDP. Note for UDP, this is the datagram size and needs to be lowered when using IPv6 addressing to 1450 or less to avoid fragmentation. Destination port number option is the server port for the receiver in server mode to listen on and the sender to connect to. Maximum segment size option means the TCP maximum segment size (MSS). The MSS is usually the $MTU - 40$ bytes for the TCP/IP header. For ethernet, the MSS is 1460 bytes. Interval time option is the interval time in seconds between periodic bandwidth, delay, and loss reports. If non-zero, a report is made every interval seconds of the bandwidth since the last report. If zero, no periodic reports are printed.

(2) Connecting AMS1 with MS. The IPv6/IPv4 user who is likely to measure needs to know the network connection status of the specific receiver node. Thus, AMS1 will be connected with MS.

(3) Searching the list of the connection-enabled agents in the database ACD. The ACD database stores agent-related information such as accessible status (login or logout), operation mode (client or server), and current running protocol stack (IPv4 or IPv6).

(4) Sending the list of the connection-enabled agents to AMS1. AMS1 receives the list and represents it on the screen. The user is able to select only one (AMT3 in figure 5) which becomes the receiver to measure.

(5) Configuring test parameters. The sender AMS1 transfers the configuration of test parameters to the receiver AMS3. The receiver AMS3 sets the parameters, otherwise the test will not run properly.

(6) Generating traffic. The sender AMS1 generates certain amount of traffic according to the configuration of test parameters to be sent to the specified receiver.

(7) Reporting test results. For TCP, the results contains TCP window size, destination port number, time interval, the amount of transfer packets, and estimated bandwidth. For UDP, the results contains destination port number, time interval, the amount of transfer packets, estimated bandwidth, delay, and loss.

(8) Storing test results into LMD. At completion of the tests, the user is capable to save the results in the local database LMD. Using the data in this database, the user will be greatly helped to analyze network characteristics.

(9) Connecting AMS1 with MS. It is necessary to replicate the fragmental test results saved in the local database LMD into the central database to clarify more characteristics. Thus, AMS1 will be connected with MS.

(10) Replicating test results into the database CMD. The test results sent from AMS1 stores in the central database CMD, including with the measurement date.

5 Conclusion

In this paper, we proposed an architecture of active measurement system which can measure IETF's IP Performance Metrics (IPPM) [9] such as end-to-end available bandwidth, one-way delay, and one-way loss in IPv6 network. WS also describe the procedure of measurement when using AMT6 and some of its features. With measurement data obtained through AMT6, network management for IPv6 can be performed effectively. AMT6 is expected to be deployed in Korea Research Environment Open NETwork (KREONET) as the end-to-end active measurement tool for IPv6.

References

1. I. Astic and O. Festor, "Current status of IPv6 management," LORIA Techincal Report, available at http://www.inria.fr/rrrt/rt-0274.html, December 2002.
2. S. Deering and R. Hinden, "Internet protocol, version 6 (IPv6)," RFC 2460, December 1998.
3. B. Gajda and W. Procyk, "Final report on IPv6 management tools, developments and tests," 6NET Technical Report, September 2004.
4. A. Tirumala, F. Qin, J. Dugan, J. Ferguson, and K. Gibbs, "Iperf Version 2.0.2," available at http://dast.nlanr.net/Projects/Iperf/, May 2005.
5. "Microsoft windows IPv6 web site," available at http://www.microsoft.com/ipv6.
6. Microsoft Corporation, "IPv6 transition technologies," Windows Server 2003 White Paper, August 2004.
7. "Next generation transition working group web site," available at http://www.ietf.org/html.charters/ngtranscharter.html.
8. R. Gilligan and E. Nordmark, "Transition mechanisms for IPv6 hosts and routers," RFC 2893, August 2000.
9. V. Paxson, "Framework for IP Performance Metrics," RFC 2330, May 1998.

Semantic Web Based Knowledge Searching System in Mobile Environment

Dae-Keun Si, Yang-Seung Jeon, Jong-Ok Choi, Young-Sik Jeong, and Sung-Kook Han

Dept. of Computer Eng. Wonkwang Univ., Korea
{sdk124, skhan}@wonkwang.ac.kr

Abstract. In this paper we propose semantic web-based mobile knowledge searching systems for display Web pages on mobile terminals. The proposed system reduces the time of verification when mobile users search for information to which they want, and ontology-based browsing is possible and the computer can use these resources in mobile environment.

1 Introduction

As the development of Internet technology, people can access and use a huge amount of information through the Web browser. As the number of Internet users and the volume of information increase, users' requirements are getting more diverse and complicated. People are flooded with information and, as a result, it is very important to extract necessary data efficiently, process it, and produce and search accurate and appropriate information [2, 3]. What is the problem is not what we can do with the Web but how effectively we use it to satisfy our needs. Recently the rapid development of mobility has enabled access to an extensive amount of Web information in the mobile environment and mobile terminals are embedded with Web browser. Web access from mobile terminals is not used as much as expected. Of course, because of the increase in the volume of information, mobile users have trouble finding the information that they want [7].

This paper proposes a mobile knowledge searching system to reduce the time of verification when mobile users search for information to which they want.

2 Related Work

Ninety percent of search engines that we use rely on Boolean operations such as AND and OR [5, 6, 8]. However, there are many other search models other than Boolean operations. Representative ones include probability search, weighted search, fuzzy set search and inference search. The performance of Boolean search is high in terms of speed but is lowest in terms of accuracy. However, because other search models are difficult to implement due to problems in expressing complicated logical relations, existing search engines mostly support only Boolean operations. As for the shortcomings of Boolean search, it cannot indicate the relative importance of each concept, cannot show the order of fitness to queries, and cannot find documents that match the

L.T. Yang et al. (Eds.): ICESS 2005, LNCS 3820, pp. 741 – 746, 2005.

keywords partially because it retrieves only those matching the keywords exactly. OR operation produces results more than expected, and AND operation less than expected. The fact that it is not easy to query or modify according to user feedback is another shortcoming of Boolean operation.

The use of Web data through mobile terminals is increasing rapidly, integrated search on the same level as that of Internet search has many practical difficulties. Rather than the existing method with URL input and mobile numeric domains, which has long and complicated connection process, we need a service that can access mobile IP pages just by pressing the number assigned to each service and the mobile IP key. Furthermore, there are problems such as low data compatibility between mobile terminal software and Web contents service providers and low efficiency of process from the production of mobile contents to search service [4, 7, 10].

Mobile searching method is testing mobile search function with mobile communication subscribers. In general, messages are downloaded or sent in the Internet and fees are charged to individual users according to various mobile search services. In the future, there will be no boundary or distinction between platforms in wired/wireless environment, ubiquitous environment. At present, further research needs to be made to overcome the small memory and low power of mobile terminals and to reduce their weight [5].

3 Mobile Knowledge Searching System Based on Semantic Web

The semantic Web is developing standards and technologies for the computer to understand information on the Web, and supporting semantic search, data integration, and navigation. The lowest level is composed of Uniform Resource Identifier, which is an addressing method for indicating resources in Web protocol, and Unicode. The second level is XML, which can define a certain concept in a modular method, and Namespace. The third level is Resource Description Framework (RDF) and RDF schema for describing resources and the fourth level is ontology. The sixth level is technological elements for rules, logic and verification. The seventh level is proof and trust, which are contents related to the reliability of semantic Web information.

The mobile knowledge searching system is composed of four modules - viewer system, Java Web start, ordinary searching engine and knowledge searching system. The viewer system is a client program for mobile users. The Java Web program is to distribute and manage the viewer system on the Web. The searching system provides a table of contents and index service, and the mobile knowledge searching system provides several meaningful data required for keywords. The structure of the mobile knowledge searching system is as in Fig. 1.

User interface is designed to accommodate general applications, Web applications and mobile terminals. Each application is basically based on axis framework, so can use Web services. It is also based on Cocoon framework, supporting WML, so provides expression methods suitable not only for PC but also for mobile terminals. It solves the limits of information expression and information space and differences in the speed and quantity of data transmission.

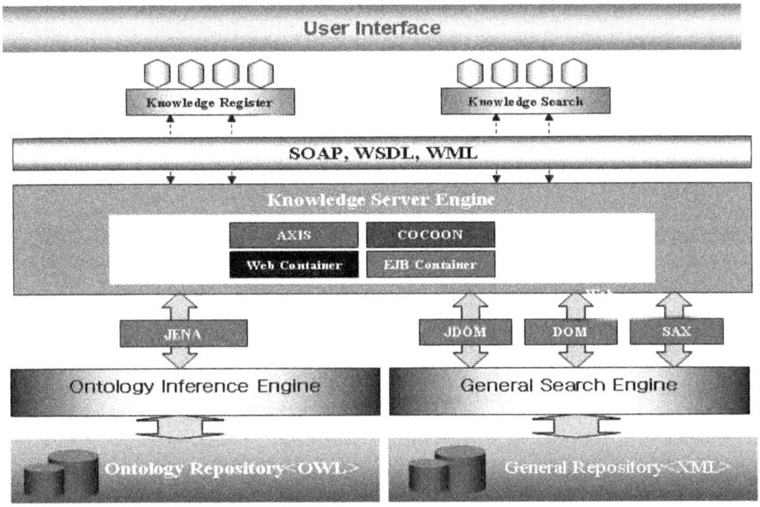

Fig. 1. Structure of mobile knowledge searching system

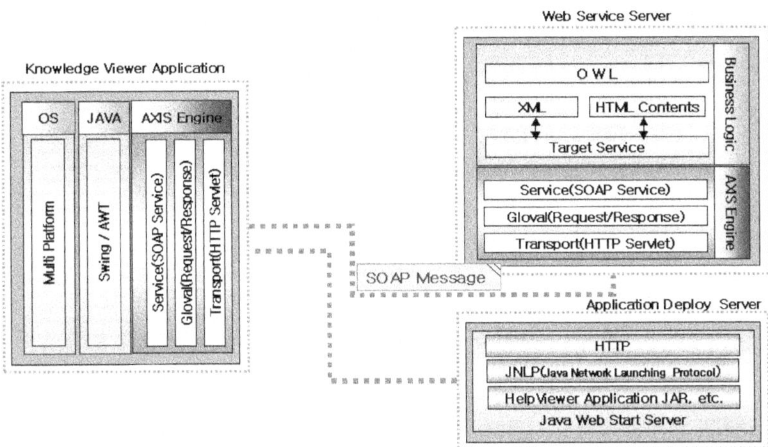

Fig. 2. Mobile knowledge searching system process

We utilize axis framework to support the Web service development environment and Cocoon framework to support mobile environment, and use to pure Java in development. The system uses Java 2 API for process ontology, and makes use of JDOM, DOM and SAX to process basic XML data. The mobile knowledge searching system has JVM, which can be executed regardless of OS as long as the Internet is connected.

In the mobile knowledge searching system, knowledge Web service providers provide index searching service, contents searching service and knowledge searching service. XML is provided as metadata for contents, and ontology is built for

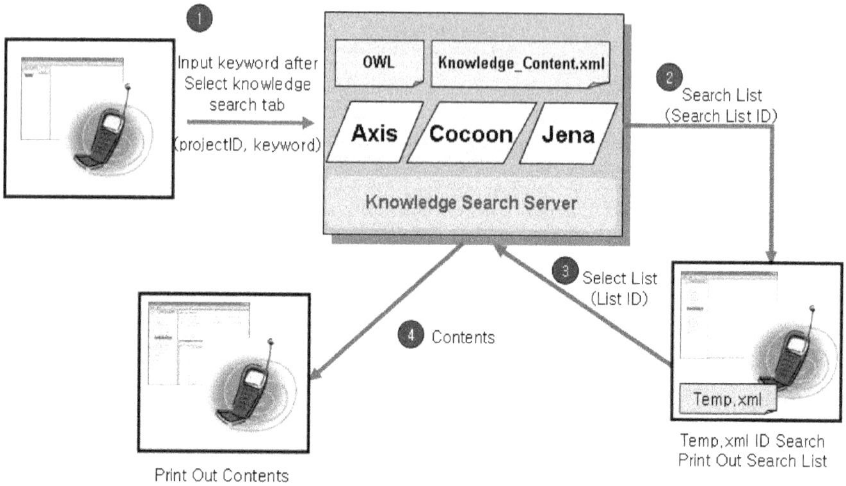

Fig. 3. A scenario of mobile knowledge searching service

knowledge service. Each service has input and output parameters. The process of the mobile knowledge searching system can be expressed as in Fig. 2.

The Web service server provides Web services through the axis engine, and the knowledge viewer application, which is the end user. He receives the services through the axis engine. In addition, the knowledge viewer application is distributed and its version is managed automatically by a separate application server on the Web. Thus, users are provided with the latest knowledge viewer easily without additional installation. Fig. 3 shows a scenario of utilizing the semantic Web-based knowledge search system for mobile environment.

On receiving a search request from the knowledge viewer, the knowledge Web service server run the inference engine from the corresponding ontology, converts the result into XML and return it to the knowledge viewer. The mobile user is provided with the service from the Web service server by clicking the corresponding item. Finally the mobile user can view the desired contents through the knowledge viewer.

4 Performance Analysis

Table 1 shows comparison of functional and technological aspects between the conventional system and the proposed system. The conventional searching system works on the basis of database utilizing stabilized DBMS functions. Its processing speed is fast but the accuracy of searching results is lower than that of proposed researching system. Also, proposed searching system is superior in accuracy more than that of the conventional searching system.

Table 1. Comparison of functions

Item	Conventional System	Proposed System
Knowledge management	• Thesaurus registration through manager's analysis • Hierarchical structure • Directory-based system	• Ontology-based instance registration • Applicable to all applications • Visualization
Searching speed	• Fast using DBMS functions	• Somewhat slow due to the addition of inference step, which is a difference from the current search system
Accuracy	• Low due to simple keyword matching search	• High as semantic interpretation of data is possible
Reusability	• Limitedly reusable	• Reusable according to the international standard of ontology language
User interface	• HTML-based browsing/search	• Ontology-based browsing/search • Browsing/search by topic • Mobile browsing/search
Difficulty in the application of inference technology	• Very difficult	• Easy to apply rule-based inference search
External resource	• Hyperlink • Meta data search	• Link based on Web services • Semantic search based on Web services

5 Conclusions

In the mobile environment, the proposed searching system used to WSDL which is a Web service standard for describing Web services. It can support environment that the computer can understand and process semantically. Our system reduces the time of verification when users search for information that they want. Also, if the system is used in semantic search in semantic Web environment, it can reduce inconveniences. Web service provides environment in which users can use integrated services without the limit of time, place and equipment and, resultantly, it renders diverse services in response to users' demands.

Acknowledgements

This work was supported by the Regional Research Centers Program of the Korean Ministry of Education & Human Resources Development through the Center for Healthcare Technology Development.

References

1. AXIS, http://ws.apache.org/axis/
2. W3C, Simple Object Access Protocol Specification, http://www.w3.org/TR/SOAP
3. UDDI.org, Universal Description, Discovery and Integration 2.0 Data Structure Specification, http://www.uddi.org/pubs/DataStructure-V2.00-Open-20010608.pdf
4. FCC, Annual Report and Analysis of Competitive Market Conditions With Respect to Commercial Mobile Services; English Report, 2003.
5. Tim Berners-Lee, James Hendler, Ora Lassila, "The Semantic Web", Scientific American, 2001.5
6. W3C, Web Service Specification, http://www.w3.org/2002/ws
7. Knowledge Management Metrics Development: A Technical Approach, White Paper No. Ten, http://www.dkms.com/white_papers.htm, June 25, 1998
8. Tim Berners Lee, J. Hendler, and O. Lassilla, "The Semantic Web," Scientific American, Vol.284, No.5, May 2001, pp.34-43.
9. "UDDI Technical White Paper," http://uddi.org/pubs/Iru_UDDI_Technical White_Paper.pdf, UDDI.org, September 2000.
10. W3C Web Services WG, "Web Services Architecture," http://www.w3.org/TR/2004/NOTE-ws-arch-20040211/ , W3C Working Group Note 11, 2004
11. Tim Berners Lee, J. Hendler, and O. Lassilla, "The Semantic Web," Scientific American, Vol.284, No.5, May 2001, pp.34-43.

A General-Purpose, Intelligent RAID-Based Object Storage Device

Fang Wang, Song lv, Dan Feng, and Shunda Zhang

Key Laboratory of Data Storage System, Ministry of Education,
School of Computer, Huazhong University of Science and Technology, Wuhan, China
song8055@163.com, wangfang@mail.hust.edu.cn

Abstract. In this paper we will address the architecture and implementation of an object-based storage system, and describe the design of the intelligent object-based storage device (OSD), which is built on embedded system of RAID. Our OSD is designed for general purpose according to the T10 standard. It not only can be easily added to the massive network storage system over TCP/IP to increase the quantity and quality of the storage system by adding intelligent OSD to the storage, but also can reduce the TCO (total cost of ownership).Also we extend the T10 standard by adding the object physical layout information to help shorten the access latency and to increase the intelligence for our OSD.

1 Introduction

As electronic data is growing continuously and rapidly, the first generation of massive storage system architectures such as NAS, SAN have exposed some of their own advantage and drawbacks [10]. Object-based storage as a much higher level of abstraction for networked storage has combined the advantages of SAN and NAS, thus making the beginning of the next generation of storage designs.

Object storage was first proposed in CMU as an academic research project [1, 2] and is still an active area of research in academia. The first standardization effort [3, 4] of an Object Storage Device specification is embodied in the SCSI protocol and is being implemented as a new set of SCSI commands. The first T10 draft standard was brought to SNIA in 1999.Version 1 of the T10 standard was publicly reviewed and approved in late 2004; the OSD standard has been published as ANSI INCITS 400-2004 [4].

The OSD standard proposes a standard interface of the object-based storage device, by which devices evolve from being relatively unintelligent and externally managed to being intelligent, self-managed, aware of the storage applications they serve and of high compatibility in the objcct-based storage system. Our RAID-based, object-based storage subsystem is designed following the standard to make it a more intelligent OSD with high compatibility.

There are two ways to develop intelligent OSD: embedding the object storage interface into the disk [9](for example, Seagate has designed a prototype disk in this approach) and fulfill the interface by the subsystem [9].

There are several prototype systems designed to provide object storage interface. Lustre developed by Cluster file systems, Inc., demonstrates the concept of object-based storage systems by providing a cluster file system. But the object storage

L.T. Yang et al. (Eds.): ICESS 2005, LNCS 3820, pp. 747 – 756, 2005.

device is not designed according to the T10 standard [12], but managed by their "object storage server" as a file device without intelligent self-management [5]. Panasas storage blade is a wonderful object storage device providing object interface according to the T10 standard. But it is dedicated to its high performance storage cluster with the blade. It is too expensive to be used for general purpose [11].

Our RAID-based, object-based storage subsystem is an embedded system designed following the T10 standard version 10 to make it an intelligent OSD with high compatibility and low cost to be used in our storage system and for commercial use. It is the subsystem of our object-based massive network storage system built over the ISCSI protocol. The OSD is designed based on a RAID system designed by our laboratory, thus equipping the OSD with much more capacity and very high security, while reducing your TCO.

Attributes of the T10 standard do not define the layout information of object, and the current object-based storage systems manage the storage of objects via local file systems, such as XFS used in Lustre [12]. In our OSD subsystem, we add the layout information to the extended attributes for each object, where object data can be accessed only through the attributes. This can make OSD more intelligent as a component of object storage management. We will detail it in Section 3.

The rest of the paper is organized as follows. In Section 2, we will introduce the architecture of our object storage system. Section 3 describes the design of our RAID-based OSD and proposes our extended attributes. Section 4 summarizes the features of our OSD. The paper is concluded in Section 5.

2 Object-Based Storage System Architecture

In OSDs, an object is the basic unit of data stored. An object is a combination of file data and a set of attributes that define various aspects of the data. T These attributes can define on a per-file basis the RAID levels, data layouts, and quality of service. The conventional block storage system must track all of the attributes for each block in the system, whereas in OSDs each object maintains its own attributes to communicate to the storage system and manages this particular piece of data. This simplifies the task of the storage system and increases its flexibility by distributing the task of managing of the data to the data itself.

There are several types of OSD objects: the user object, the collection object, the partition object, the root object. A user object is the carrier for a user file, which contains user data that is referenced by byte offset within the OSD object. Each object is identified by a unique ID (OBID) [7]. A collection object is a logical set of user objects that have some common attributes. A partition object is an OSD object used for creating distinct management domains (e.g., for naming, security, quota management). There is exactly one root object associate with each OSD logical unit which is always present whose attributes contain global characteristics for the OSD logical unit. [7].

Our object-based storage system, shown in Figure 1, consists of Metadata server cluster, RAID-based OSDs, and clients.

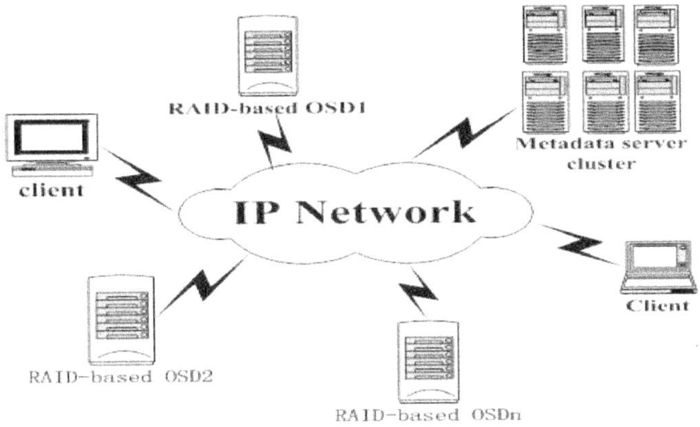

Fig. 1. Object-based, Storage System Architecture

Desirable properties of a storage system include high security, high performance, high scalability, and platform-independent data-sharing. Our proposed architecture attempts to follow this guideline incorporating the notion of object-based storage and following unique characteristics:

1. Complying with the latest T10 standard to provide an object-based storage prototype model and an object storage interface;
2. A scalable metadata server that can dynamically accommodate the joins and departures of OSDs by registering such OBDs, thus allowing the storage system to scale.
3. Extensions of attributes to gain more intelligence and higher performance and security.
4. Both the data path and metadata path are constructed over the TCP/IP network, making it easier to share data across different platforms.

2.1 Metadata Server Cluster

In this architecture, the metadata server (MDS) implements the user component of file system with the following functions:

- Authentication –MDS identifies and authenticates Object-based Storage Devices, provides credentials to new storage system members, and checks/renews those credentials periodically to assure that they are valid members. When a client wants access to the storage system, MDS assures its identity and provides authorization for the access to OSD.
- File interface –MDS provides the client with a virtual file system. When the client requests to perform an operation on a particular file, MDS examines the permissions and access controls associated with the file and converts file operations to object operations on OSDs and provides OSDs's map and a capability to the requesting client. The map consists of the list of OSDs, their IP addresses, and the components of the object in question. The capability is a secure, cryptographic token provided to the client node, which is examined by the OSD with each transaction.

- Capacity management– The MDS must control the balance between the capacity and utilization of the OSDs in the whole system to make sure that the available disk resources are optimally utilized.
- Expandability– MDS is in charge of file/directory management (which is approximately 10% of the workload) [6] and leaves block/sector management (which is approximately 90% of the workload) to OSDs [6] .Because an OSD is easily added to the system, MDS also can expand dynamically to the cluster to guarantee the performance of the system.

As described above, MDS is the bridge between Clients and OSDs and provides a file management interface to clients while keeping track of all OSDs.

2.2 RAID-Based OSD

OSD as an embedded system is the core of the object-based storage system. It is an intelligent self-managed device, which provides an object interface for clients to access data stored in it. Every OSD has its own globally unique ID. The new OSD command set describes the operations available on Object-based Storage Devices. The result is a group of intelligent disks (OSDs) attached to a switched network fabric (ISCSI over Ethernet) providing storage that is directly accessible by the clients. Unlike conventional SAN configurations, the Object Storage Devices can be directly addressed in parallel, allowing extremely high aggregate data throughput rates.

The RAID-based OSD design provides an object interface to every client according to the latest T10 standard, the standard interface focusing on integrating low-level storage, space management, and security functions into OSD from MDS.

Block-based file systems can be roughly divided into two main components namely the user component and the storage component. The former is responsible for presenting user applications with logical data structures, such as files and directories, and an interface for accessing these data structures; whereas the latter maps the data structures to the physical storage. This separation of responsibilities makes it easy to offload management task to the storage device, which is the intended effect of object-based storage. In figure 2, the user component of the file system is unchanged, the storage management component offloaded (approximately 90% of the workload of metadata) to the storage device, and the device interface is changed from blocks to objects.

With the help of MDS, a large file can be divided into more than one object and mapped to different OSDs. The client can communicate with different OSDs in parallel to access the file to make good use of the bandwidth and improve the throughput of the system.

In section 3, we will describe the design of OSD in more details.

2.3 Client Node

The clients work on our FTP-like software to achieve accesses to data stored in our storage system. There two channels of communication: control path to MDS over TCP/IP; data path to OSDs over ISCSI. Though the control path, the storage system provides a virtual system interface to client to hide details of management from the client. Through the data path, the client conducts transfers of data and 90% of the metadata to and from OSDs directly and in parallel after it get the authorization and the OSD's ID, to significantly reduce the MDS's workload, thus removing possible bottlenecks, and enhancing the throughput of the whole storage system.

2.4 System Work Flow

In this section we will use a simple three-node configuration to describe our propose storage system. Each OSO (object Storage Device) is embodied over SCSI, so the system builds on ISCSI protocol over the TCP/IP network.

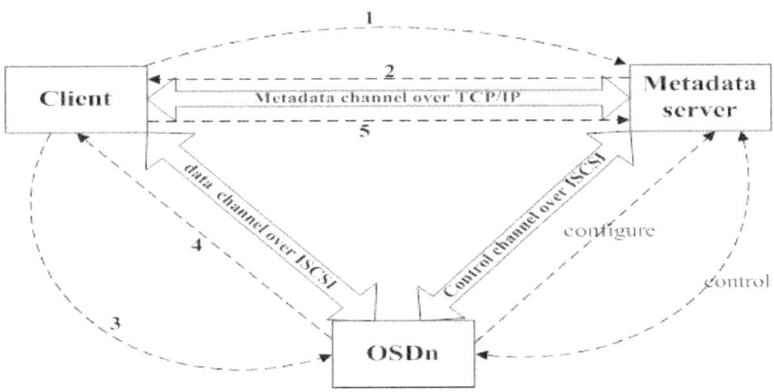

Fig. 2. System work flow

As Figure 2 shows, every OSD must register itself and configure on the metadata server before it can provide service. Metadata server will execute some control object-based storage device commands (e.g., Format OSD, create partition, etc.) through the control channel.

A client request is handled by the system in the following steps, also shown in Figure 2:

1. The Client sends request to the metadata server, which includes file name, file command, and its identification, etc.
2. The metadata server verifies that the identification is legal and translates the file request to corresponding object request on specific OSDs assigned by the metadata server, and returns the object's information, the OSDs's information and access authorization to the client.
3. The client sends the object access request to the designed OSDs with the information provided by MDS.
4. Each request OSD verifies the access authorization information to make sure the object access is legal, then executes the OSD command and begins direct data transfer with client. After finishing the command, the OSD returns the command status to the client.
5. After client receives all the status from all designed OSDs, it sends an acknowledgement to the MDS.

According to the acknowledgement, the MDS will update the file and the OSDs's information stored in MDS.

3 Design of RAID-Based OSD

The RAID-based OSD subsystem is an embedded system built on commodity hardware at a low cost but with a TERABYTE-lever massive storage to make it more cost-effective for general users. We add the ISCSI Target control layer and OSD command interface to the RAID control software to make the EIDE RAID an intelligent OSD. The software is running under the embedded Linux operating system.

3.1 Hardware Architecture

The architecture of the OSD is shown in figure 3. An OSD consists of a processor, RAM memory, disks and Ethernet interface

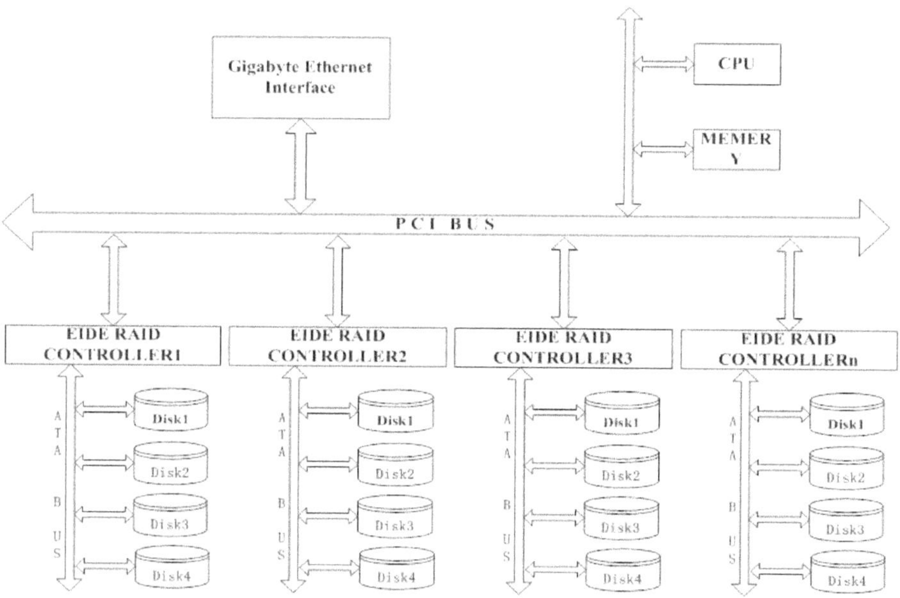

Fig. 3. RAID-based OSD architecture

The OSD is built on the EIDE RAID designed by our laboratory [16].With a high performance, combined with a large quantity IDE disks space, OSD is poised to achieve a TERABYTE-level massive storage at a low cost. More than 16 disks can be added to the main board with the help of an extended RAID card (EIDE RAID CONTROLLER), so an OSD can achieve 1.875TB (16* 120GB/1024=1.875TB) with 120GB each disk.

As an embedded system, OSD has its own CPU and memory to process the control software itself and executes self-managing functions to become an intelligent device.

With the Gigabyte Ethernet interface OSD can provide high throughput as a network storage subsystem to process and store data from the network. Future, it's also very easy to upgrade to serve the next generation of networks by upgrading the network protocol.

3.2 Software Architecture

The software is the heart of the subsystem, it is based on the embedded Linux and consists of server modules including the ISCSI target driver, the OSD command handler, the object storage management, and the RAID control driver. All these components are implemented at Linux kernel level.

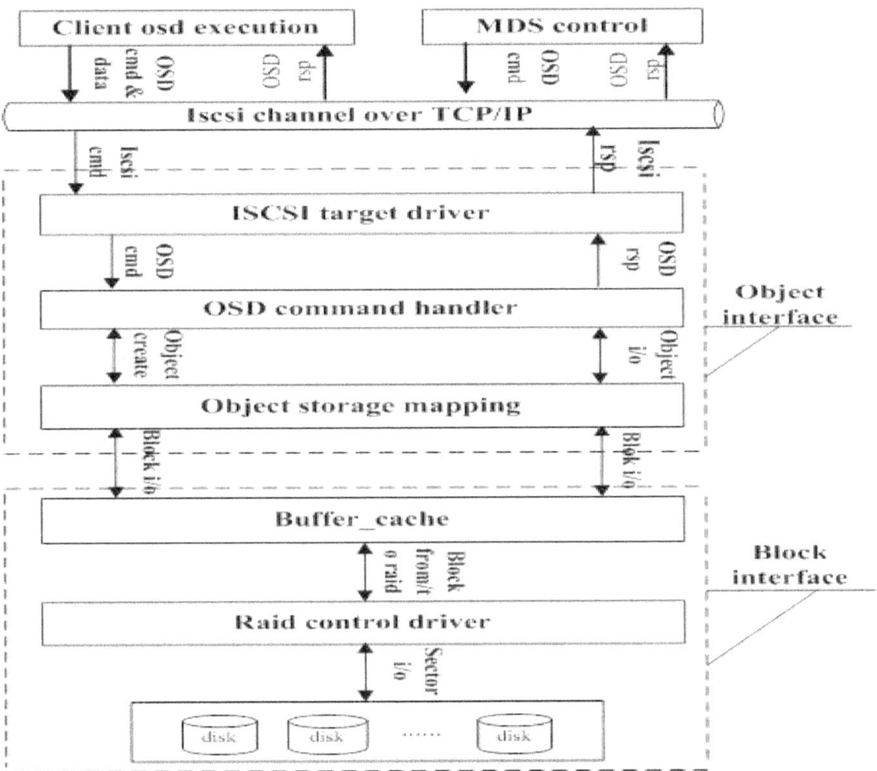

Fig. 4. software architecture

Generally, the software can be divided into two main parts that provide object interface and block interface, respectively, as illustrated in Figure 4.

Object Interface. OSD receives OSD commands and object data from the ISCSI channel initiated by clients or MDS to make sure that they access data as objects. The OSD commands are defined as the extension of the SCSI command in theT10 standard [7]. The ISCSI target driver receives OSD commands and object data encapsulated in

ISCSI PDU, and then unpacks the PDU. The OSD command handler analyzes the command and makes sure the user is legal and then deals with the object command. The object storage manager converts object to blocks in RAID. When an object is created, it is stored in blocks in RAID, and we record the blocks' addresses in the object's extended attribute [7]. The data is not accessible outside the OSD in block format, only via their object OBIDs.

Block Interface. RAID is based on disks, it stores data in blocks in logical. Buffer cache is kernel space memory and is the intermediate repeater to accelerate access blocks in RAID. RAID control driver is in charge of stripping blocks among the disks according to the RAID level configured by the OSD device, and the data as it is laid out into standard tracks and sectors.

3.3 Extended Attributes

Associated with each object is a set of attributes, organized as pages with 2**32 attributes per page and 2**32 attribute pages. But just very few of the attributes are defined, and most of them are in reference to the control information of object. There is not any attribute about the object data layout in OSD.

Currently, the object-based storage systems have not implemented an object-based file system [15]manage the storage of objects for their OSDs. As for Lustre, it storages the file data as object in OST(object storage target), and OSTs are built on existing Linux file system such EXT3 ,XFS, etc[13][14]. So the objects are managed as files in the OSTs, and the file access from Client will map the file to object in MDS, then map object to file in OST. The overhead of accessing an object can superior to the traditional file system.

We define the extended attributes for object data layout information. Object data is stored on disk device as blocks which addressed by block number. The extended attributes are defined as <base block number1, length1>, <base block number2, length2>, …, <base block numbern, lengthn>. Each object will be associated with one 128-bit object id, and the id will map to the attributes for the object. Once the client want to access the object, the OSD will search the extended attributes of the object. With the attributes, OSD can access all the blocks for the object with less overhead. Because the object data cannot be store in all contiguous blocks, we will try to allocate contiguous blocks for it.

4 Intelligence OSD Device Features

As an intelligent embedded system, the OSD has its own hardware and software, so it is able to configure and register itself to the storage system, to manage the storage space as a RAID and all objects in which are in a platform namespace, to handle the OSD command and manage storage spaces for objects, to do the security job.

Configure and register (self-discovery). When the OSD device initiates, it will configure itself (e.g. decide the RAID level, get information from disk to buffer, etc), then send a request with its information to the MDS to register itself. When it success, the OSD is legal member in the storage system and available to all clients.

Self-manage and Extended Attributes. The OSD manage all kinds of objects (root object, partition object, user object, etc.) by their attributes to manage the objects layout in the OSD. Especially for the user object, to shorten the latency of access object it is necessary to buffer the data address. We define the reserved attributes [7], and record all the block address of the object data. And the recently hot object's attributes will be buffered.

Platform Namespace. Objects are on an equal footing with each others, there is not hierarchy relationship (like traditional file system) for objects. We design a platform namespace: once you want to access an object, then the OSD will get the object's attributes by the OBID directly. With the help of attributes, it is easy to get the address of the object data to access the object. The platform namespace shorten the access path and improve the performance.

RAID-Based Device. The RAID configure it RAID level according to the command from MDS, and then strip object data into the RAID. As disk device RAID can make object data much safer in block level with failure recovery. And RAID is easy to enlarge its capacity by adding IDE disks to achieve a TERABYTE-level OSD.

Self-guard. For an intelligent OSD, it is in charge of exchange data between clients directly, so OSD must do security job itself. Both clients and network are not trust for OSD. Every request from the client first will get authorization and a digest of the entire request information (OBID, service_action [7], etc.).And then client will send the request to the OSD includes the command, the client capability, and a digest of the entire request. Upon receipt of a new request, the OSD must first validate the client digest. The OSD will create its own digest of the request and compare this with the digest sent by the client. If they match, the OSD is guaranteed that neither the capability nor any of the arguments in the request were modified. Had either of these changed, the digest generated by the OSD would differ from that sent by the client, and the OSD would reject the request; all responses sent from the OSD to the client can be protected using a digest similar to that sent by the client.

5 Conclusion and Future Work

Our object-based storage system implements a prototype of object interface storage system following the T10 standard. The RAID-based intelligent OSD is an embedded system. As designed on IDE interface RAID, the OSD reduce your TCO of a TERABYTE-level OSD with more security and make the PETABYTE-level object-based storage system comprised of OSDs more acceptable for commercial use, then accelerate the object-based storage industry.

Our OSD implements according to the T10 standard but also extends the standard for its attributes part to make it more intelligent and easier to manage the object data layout one OSD itself. As an intelligent OSD, our OSD has features as self-discovery, self-manage, self-guard, self-configure, and provide a platform name space for objects.

We plan to further explore the object-based attributes and methods, to implement different level security policies for different type of object access, and to define object methods for different application to make OSD much more intelligent and flexible.

Acknowledgements

The authers would like to thank the members of the Key Laboratory of Data Storage System for their hard work and help. This work was supported in part by the National Science Foundation of China under grant 60303032 and the 973 Program of China under Grant No. 2004CB318201.

References

1. G. Gibson, D. Nagle, K. Amiri, F. Chang, E. Feinberg,H. Gobioff, C. Lee, B. Ozceri, E. Riedel, D. Rochberg, and J. Zelenka. File server scaling with network-attached secure disks. *Proceedings of the ACM International Conference on Measurement and Modelling of Computer System, Seattle,WA*, June 1996.
2. G. Gibson, D. Nagle, K. Amiri, F. Chang, H. Gobioff, E. Riedel, D. Rochberg, and J. Zelenka. Filesystems for network-attached secure disks. Technical Report CMU–CS–97–112, CMU, 1997.
3. SNIA-Storage Networking Industry Association. *OSD: Object Based Storage Devices Technical Work Group.* http://www.snia.org/techactivities/workgroups/osd.
4. R. O. Weber. *SCSI Object-Based Storage Device Commands(OSD),Document Number: ANSI/INCITS 400-2004.* InterNational Committee for Information Technology Standards (formerly NCITS), December 2004. http://www.t10.org/drafts.htm.
5. Peter J. Braam. *The Lustre Storage Architecture,* Fall 2003. http://www.clustrfs.com
6. Mike Mesnier, Gregory R. Ganger, Erik Riedel. *Object-Based Storage* IEEE Communications Magazine. August 2003
7. T10/1355-D Working draft reversion 10 *Information technology-SCSI Object-Based Storage Device Commands (OSD)* . 30 July 2004 http://www.t10.org
8. Meth, K.Z., and Satran, J., "Design of the iSCSI Protocol", IEEE/NASA MSST 2003, Apr. 2003.
9. Erik Riedel Seagate Technology, *Object-based storage device (OSD) Basics.* April 2005.
10. Alain Azagury, Vladimir Dreizin, Michael Factor, Ealan Henis, Dalit Naor, Noam Rinetzky, Ohad Rodeh, Julian Satran, Ami Tavory. *Towards an Object Store.*20 th IEEE/11 th NASA Goddard Conference on Mass Storage Systems and Technologies (MSS'03),2003
11. Panasas, WHITE PAPER: Object Storage Architecture: Defining a new generation of storage systems built on distributed, intelligent storage devices
12. Peter J. Braam Lustre: the Intergalactic File System for the National Labs. June. 2001 http://www.clusterfilesystems.com
13. Peter J. Braam and Rumi Zahir, *Lustre, Technical Project Summary – version 2.* Cluster File Systems, Inc. July 29, 2001. http://www.clusterfilesystems.com
14. Peter J. Braam. The Lustre Storage Architecture. Cluster File Systems, Inc. http://www.clusterfs.com. 08/29/2003, HEAD
15. Feng Wang, Scott A. Brandt, Ethan L. Miller, Darrell D. E. Long, *OBFS: A File System for Object-based Storage Devices.* 21st IEEE / 12th NASA Goddard Conference on MSST2004. April 2004.
16. Jiangling Zhang, Dang Feng. Massive Information Storage. Science Press China ,Beijing 2003.

The Design and Implement of Remote Mirroring Based on iSCSI*

Cao Qiang, Guo Tian-jie, and Xie Chang-sheng

Department of Computer, Huazhong University of Science and Technology,
Wuhan 430074, Hubei, China
caoqiang@mail.hust.edu.cn

Abstract. Remote mirroring has become increasingly important as organizations and businesses depending more and more on digital information. Balancing the data availability, access performance and the cost of building and maintaining is essential goal for designing remote mirroring system. This paper presents a novel architecture of remote mirroring based on iSCSI and describes the structure of mirroring log and buffer which can improve performance and keep availability of date synchronously. The experience results show the maximal workload of remote mirroring in 100Mbps and gigabit network environment respectively.

1 Introduction

The majority of today's businesses cannot survive a catastrophic loss of corporate data. Data is growing at exponential rates, forcing businesses to continually examine and enhance the availability, security and efficiency of their data environment. Hardware failures, all kinds of software defects, destruction of vicious virus, buildings fires, electric power broke off and man-made mistake, all of which will lead to the key data being unavailable, even being lost. Though these incidents would not occur frequently, but some preparations have to be made to prevent data lose in these accidents, because the data unavailable penalty is very enormous. In 2001 the investigation showed that 1/4 of the informants estimated that the cost of machine halt was 250,000 dollar per hour, and 8% of them estimate it as to be 1,000,000 dollar per hour[1]. The cost of data loss is even higher. It has been realized recently that the plan for recovery and constancy is necessary, and the key method is to construct the reliable storage system to protect the usability of the data and the ability of unfailing data access.

Data mirroring is a classic technique for tolerating failures by keeping two or more copies of important data. It is widely used inside disk arrays (where it is called RAID1). These copies are distributed across multiple sites, where it is called remote mirroring. Figure 1 shows the basic topological structure of remote-mirroring system, which only includes a single remote-mirroring site, but could naturally expand to multiple ones actually.

* This paper is supported by both National 973 Great Research Project of P R China under the Grant NO 2004CB318203 and National Natural Science Foundation of P R China under the Grant NO 60273073, NO 60303031.

L.T. Yang et al. (Eds.): ICESS 2005, LNCS 3820, pp. 757 – 765, 2005.

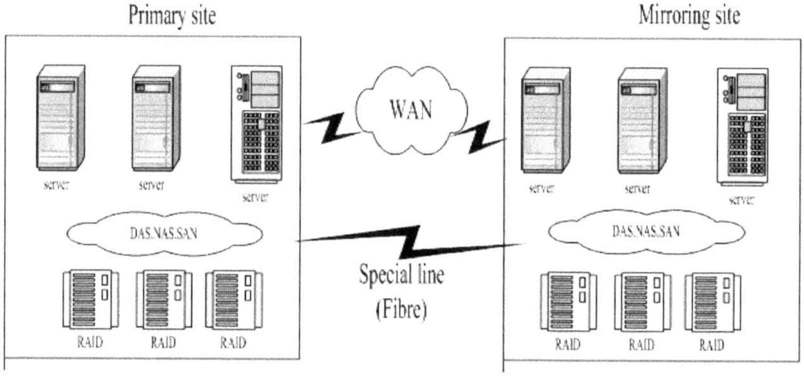

Fig. 1. Classic remote-mirroring system

The design of remote-mirroring systems must have to aim at multiply goals. The first is keeping the copies as closely synchronized as possible to reduce the data loss risk when failures occur. The second is delaying foreground writes as little as possible to reduce the effect on application system. The third is to maintain availability in the face of as many failure types as possible. Finally occupying as little expensive inter-site network bandwidth as possible to reduce the total cost of running and maintenance, because renting dedicated network is very expensive[2]. For example, the rental price of Internet dedicated access bandwidth (the rent per month) for china Unicom, 512K = ￥1024 ; 10M = ￥3012 ; 20M = ￥5700 ; 45M = ￥13190 ; 100M = ￥21200 ; 155M = ￥80000.

From a view of implementation, however, these goals contradict with each other frequently, synchronously updating all copies is the simplest solution, but it has poor write performance and leads to high total costs in remote-mirroring systems. Therefore, the trade-off among data loss risk reduction, performance guarantee and less cost is to be taken into account carefully.

The advent of iSCSI technique offers a practical feasible scheme for high cost-performance rate design for remote mirroring. The iSCSI protocol is perceived as a low cost alternative to the FC protocol for remote storage. iSCSI could be transmitted on common TCP/IP network, and in principle requires no need of dedicated line or hardware supporting. WAN could be even enough. Likewise, iSCSI is based on operational semantics of data block, so it could be applied to remote block mirroring expediently.

Compared with dedicated line such as FC, iSCSI protocol has longer transmission delay. Moreover, if it shares the same network with applications, it would cause transferring shake and even bandwidth shortage, which heavily influences on performance of remote-mirroring system. The solution is to design mirroring buffer for both local system and remote write to keep smooth transmission, improve network efficiency and enhance performance. But the introduction of data buffer would easily cause data loss risk if exceptions occur in local system, such as power's failure or exceptions happen. A feasible method to reduce these risks is using synchronous write between local system and remote system. However it leads to terrible performance. So Design remote mirroring system based on iSCSI is real challenge.

This paper firstly introduces the design principle and presents the architecture of Remote Mirroring Based on iSCSI, then further describes the structure of mirroring LOG and BUFFER, ensuring the availability of data while improving the performance. Finally, our experience results demonstrate that remote-mirroring system could undertake maximum load in 100Mbps and gigabit network environment respectively.

2 The Remote Mirroring Architecture

Remote-mirroring module can be performed in four main places, which are in host OS, HBA (Host Bus Adapter), Fiber Channel switch in SAN, or controller in disk arrays, each with advantages and disadvantages. The benefit of implementation in host is to apply data mirroring to specific application which reduces the volume of data that need be mirrored and support file semantic interface. However, this method may impact on foreground routine and increase additional workload for host. In the other three implementation methods are independent of foreground applications. For large-scale disk array, remote-mirroring function carry out by itself, such as Symmetrix Remote Data Facility (SRDF) [4] of EMC, the price of which is unacceptable for small and medium enterprises. Remote-mirroring function designed in this paper is implemented in host, and also could be easily transplanted into switch or disk array.

The system treats Logic Unit (LU) as entrance of mirroring, which is common used. LU is the basic interface between file system and disk system, and identified as volume for file system. Each LU could be regarded as linear space consisted of many data blocks, accessing corresponding data block by corresponding address. An enterprise-level disk array could contain thousands of LU, and not all the LU need be mirrored. Only mirroring special LU could effectively reduce the needless waste of resource such as disk capacity and network bandwidth, moreover allow file system having different protection level for different data.

Because iSCSI employs TCP/IP network even WAN to connect two sites, the real available bandwidth of network would wave momentarily. Consequently, it would result in shaking in mirroring process[5]. Therefore, it is very important to design special buffer of mirroring to acquire high and stable performance. Mirroring buffers would design in two places, one is mirroring module in local hosts; another one is in remote target. Buffers could smooth network wobble obviously, however it also brings data loss risk. We classify these risks into two levels, the first level is host breakdown and could recovery before long, and the second is local storage devices failover and unavailable in primary site. The former is more frequent than the latter and only could lose data in memory. The latter conduces permanent local data lose, however it is infrequent. In other words, data in local disk have much smaller lost probability than that of failures in host memory. Then, the buffer structure in iSCSI mirroring must conciliate the two sides.

Therefore, we have designed novel structure as mirroring LOG and BUFFER to store all the unfinished remote updating data and operations. Local data buffers have fixed size, and LOG is kept by NVRAM. Local write is absolutely synchronous, which means no returning acknowledgment to upper applications until data really writing to local disk. For the first risk, consequently, there isn't data loss. When there are lots of burst writes and local BUFFER is full, the local disk address of corresponding data should be recorded in log and none of the real data blocks should be reserved in BUFFER. Thus the size of BUFFER could be effectually reduced.

Figure 2 shows the architecture of Remote Mirroring Based on iSCSI. The primary and secondary sites are connected with TCP/IP network. The mirror module is inserted into normal I/O routine between generic device driver and disk drivers, and captures all the write or update requests to forward to remote disk, but is transparent for all read request. To enhance performance, all update data first are stored in data buffer and relevant requests are recorded in command log. After acknowledging from local disk and remote site, data and requests are removed from buffer and log. The remote iSCSI target also comprises its data buffer and command log to reduce response time. Certainly, whether using them is decided by administrator to balance the performance and lost risk in remote site. The primary site includes iSCSI initiator and the remote site includes iSCSI target.

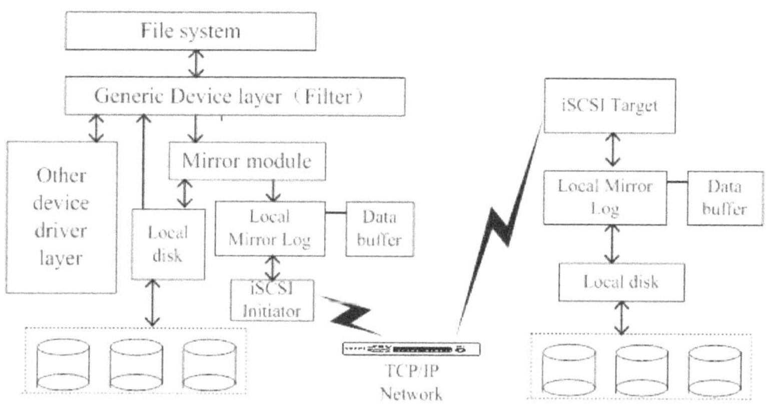

Fig. 2. The architecture of Remote Mirroring Based on iSCSI

The Figure 3 shows the work process of Remote Mirroring Based on iSCSI. When updating data have arrived at the mirroring module, the data flow into two channels, one's target is local disk, which write data to local disk like without mirroring, the other's is writing remote mirroring disk. Local write would be not given more discussion here. The start point of Write routine is local mirroring log and local data buffer in memory. The log merely records writing or updating requests in the same order as FIFO except write coalescing discussed in latter content. The buffer stores updating data until local disk and remote site acknowledging. When receiving acknowledgement, the buffer removes relevant item and data from the log and buffer. More details could be denoted as figure 3. From a view of remote mirroring taxonomy, it is semi-synchronous model.

The object of remote mirroring is data block in LU. Considering that some data blocks will be updated again before long, write coalescing policy could be adopted for enhancing performance. If the last operation of writing the same block still reserves in buffer and has not been executed, then the two operations could be combined together as one, which could save both network bandwidth and log space. The primary effect of write coalescing on fault tolerance is to alter the order in which updates are applied at the secondary site, moreover it could also be applied at the secondary to reduce the amount of work needed for an update. However, write coalescing policy may lead to data inconsistency. To solve this problem, isolated location in mirroring buffer is defined as batch out of which the function of write coalescing could be non-permissible. This scheme explicitly delays sending a batch of updates to the remote site, in the hope that write coalescing will occur, and only one copy need be propagated. Setting accurate isolated locations requires complicated semantic support. To simplify the definition of isolated location, the size of the batch can be selected in the number of updates, or the amount of data written.

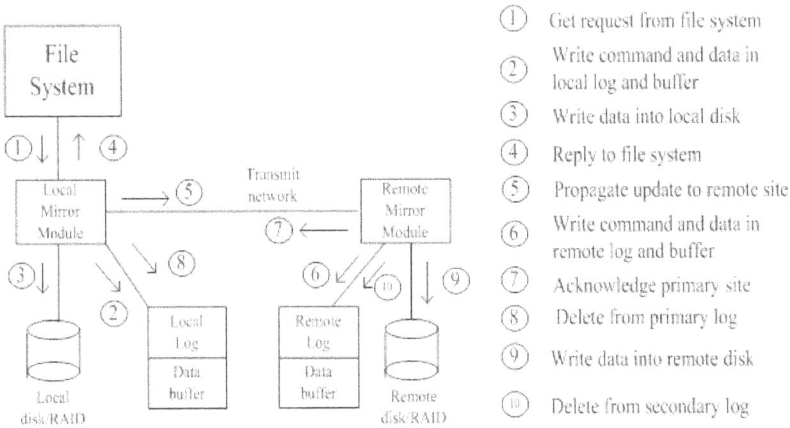

Fig. 3. The flow chart of Remote Mirroring Based on iSCSI

In the case of host faulting over, it is nearly impossible that data don't lose absolutely. Remote-mirroring protect could only reduce amount of data loss in large degree and hardly lose nothing. The data lose is fewer, and its total cost is more. Taking cost, performance and loss risk into consideration, our system could offer two remote-mirroring modes: synchronous mode, semi-synchronous mode. Synchronous mode ensures that all modifications are transferred to the remote site prior to the acknowledgement of each write to the host. Synchronous mirroring guarantees the local copies are consistent with the copies of the data at the remote site and also that the data at the remote site are as up-to-date as possible, but which introduces much latency to synchronize local with remote I/O write. In semi-synchronous mirroring, write commands are propagated to both local and remote storage nodes at the same time, and the application is notified of a completed I/O only when the local write is completed and don't wait for acknowledge from remote site. Our system could support both two modes. The choice for which mode could be decided by configuration before system running.

On Windows platform, the filter could deal with all IRPs before sending them to a lower driver. After the driver processes IRP, the filter get control again, it could connect an I/O fulfilled routine to IRP. After driver calls IoCompleteRequest function, the I/O fulfilled routine is activated. Therefore, mirroring module is designed in filter layer. On Linux platform, it could be realized at device layer. In both ways, mirroring module is fully transparent for application.

Remote iSCSI target also need use data buffer to raise access performance and reduce total latency of remote write. But it is possible that remote target also may break down. So NVRAM is applied instead of DRAM memory to prevent data loss in the first level fault.

We would like to stress that the class/style files and the template should not be manipulated and that the guidelines regarding font sizes and format should be adhered to. This is to ensure that the end product is as homogeneous as possible.

3 The Design of Remote-Mirroring BUFFER

The design for remote mirroring buffer must consider two aspects: buffer size and depth of write coalescing. Buffer size could decide the asynchronous degree between local write and remote write. It is obvious that greater buffer can absorb more delay of remote write, however make more loss in fault. Although NVRAM can prevent partial data loss in the first fault, but all the data the primary site will lose totally such as disaster happening. So the size of buffer is directly relative to the amount of lost data when the host breaks down. Moreover, the size of LOG in the NVRAM could determine the upper bound of data buffer. Furthermore, since mirroring module is lied in host, so the buffer size also could issue host performance for foreground applications. Our system could only provide option for buffer size. Therefore, the buffer size is finally determined by administrator.

The other important hand is how to update data in primary and secondary site, which includes a series of problems, for example, the bound of write coalescing in buffer, choice for asynchronous or semi-synchronous mode, and so on. The bound of write coalescing can be selected in several ways, such as the elapsed time, the number of updates, or the amount of data written, or bytes to transfer. Moreover it would be possible to select the batch size that achieves optimization target data-loss likelihood, taking the WAN link reliability into account However it is hardly to automatically controlled by mirroring and need manual configuration. So in our system, the values of parameters could be adjusted to control running of system.

Write command of SCSI mostly includes five parameters: Operation code, logical device number (SCSI ID and LUN) , logic block address(LBA), data length and control field. The top half of figure 4 is the structure of a log table, in which each row includes eight fields. CDB is command description block defined distinctly in the SCSI protocol. LWC shows the state of local write completion and RWC shows the state of remote write completion, OW shows whether this line could or not implement write coalescing. Data could be stored in three places, local disk, NVRAM or Memory. Unfinished local update data are kept in memory or NVRAM. The data which wait for remote update and have been completed in local disk is always kept in NVRAM if NVRAM has enough capacity; otherwise they are kept in Local disk. Data pointer points to the data address in the BUFFER and data length represents data length for a write command. When the data in the BUFFER exceed threshold defined as local disk record pointer, the data pointer will point to the LBA address of the disk.

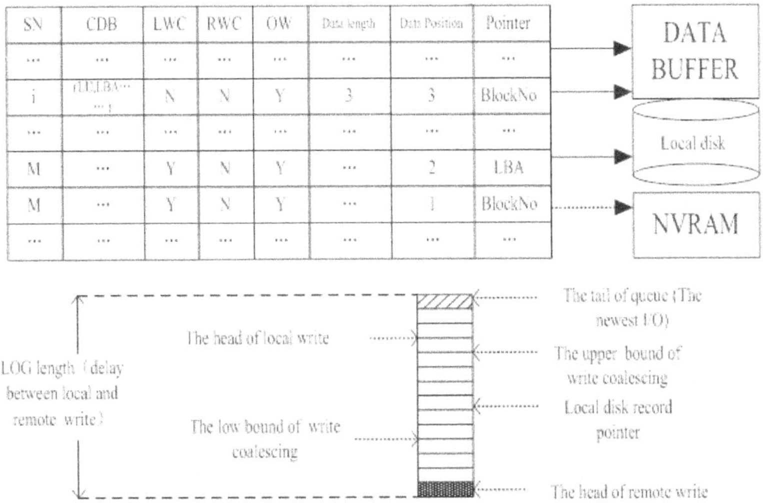

Fig. 4. The structure of mirroring log

The lower half of figure 4 describes several key pointers in mirror log. The running state of system could be controlled by adjusting these values. P_{rw} is defined as the head record of mirroring log, which is waiting for acknowledging from remote site. When remote write has been completed, this line is removed from log, and P_{rw} will be pointed to next record. P_t is the pointer of the tail local operation in log, and it represents the newest I/O request from application. P_{lw} indicates executing local update. If local writes are absolutely synchronous, P_t equal P_{lw}. P_{lwc} and P_{uwc} are the low and upper bound of write coalescing respectively, and they defined as range in which write coalescing could be applied. P_{dr} is the starting point of disk record data, and it represents that latter data blocks couldn't save in memory or NVRAM but local disk. Actually, the length of log is $P_{lw} - P_{rw}$, and it is the delay between local and remote disks write. Threshold D_{rl} could be defined to restrict maximal delay between local and remote write. If D_{rl} equal 0, it is called synchronous mirroring. If the length of reserve record exceeds the threshold, buffer could be congealed compulsively, and system would always wait until remote write has been completed. When the value that P_{lw} subtracts P_{rw} is less than D_{rl}, then write I/O requests could be put into log again, and local write requests would be sent at the same time. In this way, the size of buffer would be controlled to reduce the quantity of data loss in host breakdown.

The structure of log and buffer in remote iSCSI target is similar to those of local, but more simple, write coalescing and disk indexing data policy have no need to be adopted. You will get the best results and your files will be easiest to handle if you use.

4 Performance Evaluation

The test environment includes two servers and LAN devices. HP Proliant 330 simulates remote system and HP G380 is local system. Each server comprises two network cards (network interface card), one is a gigabit fiber NIC as D-Link 550-SX, the other is a self-adapting NIC of RJ45 interface as Intel Pro 100/1000Mbps. The gigabit fiber NIC directly connects to the other counterpart through optical fiber by peer to peer, which forms a gigabit network environment. Two 100Mbps NICs are connected with a CISCO 3524 switch, which makes 100Mbps network environment. Two sets of network environment are used to compare the effect in different network bandwidth on remote mirroring performance. Each server has installed OS of WINDOWS 2000 Advance Server version with the iSCSI Target and initiator modules developed by our lab.

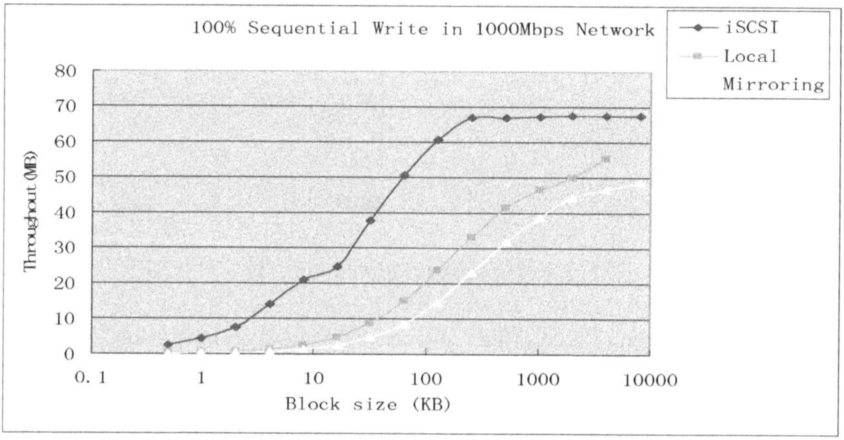

Fig. 5. Test result over the Gigabit network environment

As the experiment is to study the limited load of remote-mirroring system, we use Iometer as our testing tool to produce sequential I/O request, and test three kinds of writing performance including local disk, iSCSI and iSCSI with remote mirroring in the means of 100% sequential writing. Figure 5 and 6 indicate the results of the two sets of network environment respectively. The X-axis indicates the size of I/O request, from 0.5KB to 8MB increased by a multiple of 2, the Y-axis specifies the network data throughout.

In the test, we don't configure the local disks as RAID. Therefore, the local write rate is approximately equal to that of a single disk. Figure 5 indicates that the performance of iSCSI in gigabit network is better than that of the single disk. Since local write is always synchronous, the performance of mirroring is lower than that of local write. In the 100Mbps condition, the performance of local write is better than that of iSCSI when I/O requests are great; When I/O requests are smaller than 64KB, iSCSI has higher performance, which is due to cache. Consequently, the performance of mirroring is close to the lower performance of the two write methods.

The test results indicates the performance of iSCSI with remote mirroring is a little lower than that of pure local disk write and iSCSI write. The experiment only tests the performance of mirroring system in the ultimate load. In practicable, write requests take up a smaller part (generally 33% write request and 67% read request in transaction processing) and not all the requests must be mirrored. 100Mbps and even WAN could be used since iSCSI is not restricted to any specific network. This system would satisfy the requirement of remote-mirroring system with reasonable configuration of LOG parameters combined with practical access pattern.

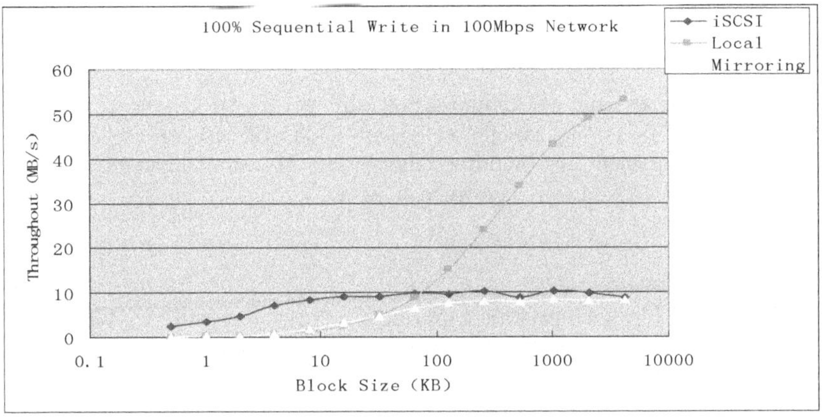

Fig. 6. Test result over 100Mbps network environment

5 Conclusion

Key data must be dependable: the cost of losing it, or even of losing access to it, is simply too high. Remote mirroring is more and more necessary to protect these data. However, its total cost and implement complexity is beyond acceptance of generic enterprise.

Remote mirroring based on iSCSI could use pervasive TCP/IP network and effectively decrease cost. However, it is essential to design solution to improve stability and performance. This paper presents architecture of mirroring LOG and BUFFER to ameliorate system. In the end, our experience shows remote mirroring based on iSCSI could meet practical requirement.

References

[1] Minwen Ji, Alistair Veitch, John Wilkes. Seneca: remote mirroring done write. 2rd USENIX Conference on File and Storage technologies (FAST'03). San Francisco, CA. March-April 2003

[2] Kimberley Keeton, Cipriano Santos. Designing for Disasters. 3rd USENIX Conference on File and Storage technologies (FAST'04). San Francisco, CA. March-April 2004

[3] XIE Chang-Sheng, FU Xiang-Lin, HAN De-Zhi, REN Jin. The Study and Implementation of a New iSCSI-based SAN. JOURNAL OF COMPUTER RESEARCH AND DEVELOPMENT, 2003, Vol 40(5): 746-751

[4] Using EMC SnapView and MirrorView for Remote Backup, Engineering White Paper, EMC Corporation (April 2002).

[5] CAO Qiang, XIE Chang2Sheng. Study of the I/O Request Response Time in Network Storage Systems. JOURNAL OF COMPUTER RESEARCH AND DEVELOPMENT, 40(8),2003:1271-1276

Improvement of Space Utilization in NAND Flash Memory Storages*

Yeonseung Ryu[1] and Kangsun Lee[2]

[1] Department of Computer Software, Myongji University, Nam-dong, Yongin, Gyeonggi-do 449-728, Korea
[2] Department of Computer Engineering, Myongji University,
ysryu@mju.ac.kr

Abstract. Flash Translation Layer (FTL) is the device driver software that makes flash memory device appear to the system like a disk drive. Since flash memory cannot be written over existing data unless erased in advance, the FTL usually employs special address mapping algorithms to avoid having to erase on every data update. In this paper, we propose a new FTL algorithm which considers the access patterns of data blocks. Proposed scheme monitors write access patterns of data blocks and intelligently manages the address mapping to improve the performance. Simulation results show that the proposed scheme improves the space utilization without significant write/update performance degradation.

Keywords: Flash Memory, Flash Translation Layer, Space Utilization.

1 Introduction

Flash memory is becoming important as nonvolatile storages for embedded devices because of its superiority in fast access speeds, low power consumption, shock resistance, high reliability, small size, and light weight [7, 11, 13, 8, 5, 3]. Because of these attractive features, and the decreasing of price and the increasing of capacity, flash memory will be widely used in consumer electronics, embedded systems, and mobile computers. Though flash memory has many advantages, its special hardware characteristics impose design challenges on storage systems. First, flash memory cannot be written over existing data unless erased in advance. Second, erase operations can be performed in a larger unit than the write operation. For an update of even a single byte, an erase operation of a large amount of data would be required. Besides it takes an order of magnitude longer than a write operation. Third, the number of times an erasure unit can be erased is limited (e.g., 10,000 to 1,000,000 times).

To overcome these problems, an software called a *Flash Translation Layer* (FTL) has been employed between host system and flash memory [6, 10, 9, 14, 4].

* This work was supported by the Korea Research Foundation Grant funded by the Korean Government(MOEHRD)(R08-2004-000-10391-0).

L.T. Yang et al. (Eds.): ICESS 2005, LNCS 3820, pp. 766–775, 2005.

Figure 1 shows a typical software organization for NAND-type flash memory. The FTL is usually implemented as the device driver software that works in conjunction with file system to make flash memory device appear to the system like a disk drive. Applications use system calls to access files on the flash memory. The file system then issues read/write commands along with logical block address and the request size to the FTL. Upon receipt of a command, address, and the size, the FTL translates them into a sequence of flash memory intrinsic commands (read/write/erase) and physical addresses.

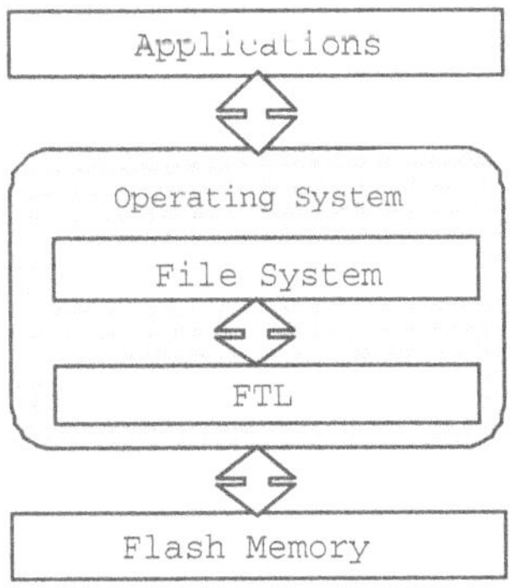

Fig. 1. Software organization for flash memory

In this paper, we study a novel FTL algorithm called *Shared Log Block (SLB)* scheme. The SLB scheme manages the space of flash memory as two types of blocks, data blocks and log blocks. The data blocks hold ordinary data and the log blocks are used as temporary space for update writes to data blocks. When an update to a data block is requested, it is performed to the log blocks allocated for the data block. The SLB classifies data blocks as *hot* or *cold* according to their write access frequencies and intelligently performs log block allocation to the data block. Previous FTL didn't consider data access pattern and may waste the space of flash memory. Proposed SLB scheme can improve the space utilization by sharing the log blocks among several data blocks that are not frequently modified. Performance evaluation based on trace-driven simulation shows that the SLB scheme performs better than previous schemes with respect to the space utilization. Also, by controlling the number of shared log blocks, we can control the performance tradeoff between the space utilization and the write/update operation.

The rest of this paper is organized as follows. In Section 2, we give the overview of previous works. In Section 3, we present a new FTL algorithm called share log block scheme. Section 4 presents the simulation results to show the performance of proposed scheme. The conclusions of this paper are given in Section 5.

2 Background

A NAND flash memory is organized in terms of *blocks*, where each block is of a fixed number of *pages* [8, 5]. There are three basic operations, namely, *read*, *write*, and *erase*. The unit of read and write operations is a page and the size of a page is fixed from 512B to 2KB depending on the product. The unit of erase operaion is a block and the size of block is somewhere between 4KB and 128KB depending on the product. There is a *spare area* appended to every page, which is usually used to store ECC code to detect errors while reading and writing. When the free space on flash memory is written, the space cannot be updated unless it is erased. For an update of even a single byte in a page, a block that contains the page should be erased. A block can be typically erased for 1 million times. A worn-out block could suffer from frequent write errors. Thus, wear leveling activity is needed to erase blocks on flash memory evenly so that a longer overall lifetime could be achieved.

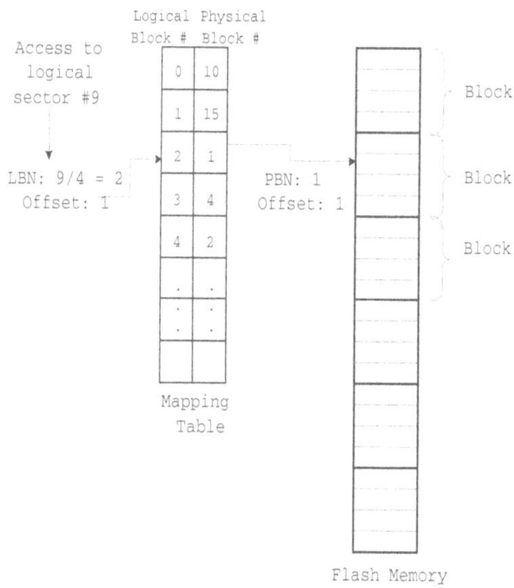

Fig. 2. Block-level mapping

Flash Translation Layer (FTL) is a device driver layer software which performs the address mapping function between the logical address and the physical address. The FTL usually maintains the address mapping table in order to map logical address of I/O requests to physical address in flash memory. The address translation table is indexed by logical block address (LBA), and each entry of the table contains the physical address of the corresponding LBA. In general, the FTL uses *non-in-place update* mechanism to avoid having to erase on every data update. Under this mechanism, the FTL remaps each update request to different location (i.e., data updates are written to empty space) and set obsolete data as garbage, which a software cleaning process later reclaims [3].

The mapping can be maintained either at the page level or at the block level [1, 2]. In the page-level address mapping, a logical page can be mapped to any physical page in flash memory. However, this mapping requires a large amount of space to store the needed mapping table. In the block-level address mapping (see Fig. 2), the logical address is divided into a logical block address and a block offset, and only the logical block address is translated into a physical block address in flash memory. The block address mapping has a restriction that the block offset in the mapped physical block be the same as that in the logical block. When there is an update request to a single page in a block, the physical block that contains the requested page is remapped to a free physical block, the write operation is performed to the page in the new physical block with the same block offset, and all the other page in the same block are copied from the original physical block to the new physical block.

To eliminate expensive copy operation in the basic block scheme, a technique called *log block scheme* was proposed [9] (see Fig. 3). When an update to a page in a data block is requested, a log block is allocated and the update is performed to the log block incrementally from the first page. Once a log block is allocated for a data block, update requests to the data block can be performed in the log block until all the pages in the log block are consumed. When there is no free page in the log block, merge operation is performed with the corresponding data block to reclaim the log block.

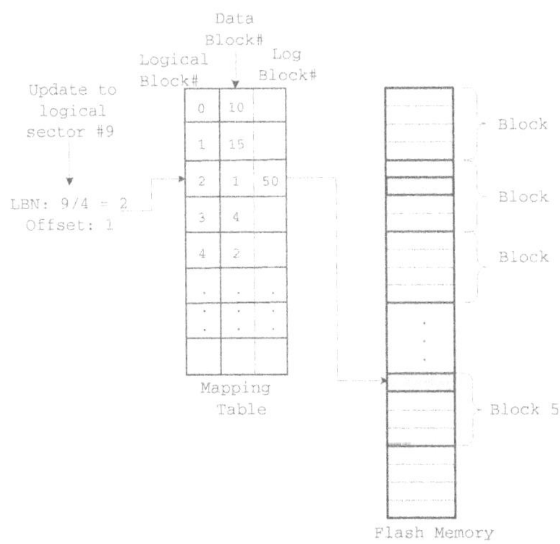

Fig. 3. Log block scheme

The problem of the log block scheme is that it does not consider the space utilization of the log blocks. In [12], authors reported that access locations are highly skewed on disks of an Unix workstation. Roughly one third of all accesses go to the ten most frequently accessed disk blocks. Therefore, we can believe that the access patterns to the flash memory based storages are also likely to be highly skewed. Then it is possible for the log block scheme to waste the space of the dedicated log block when update requests in a data block are not frequent.

3 Shared Log Block Scheme

In this section, we propose a new FTL scheme called *Shared Log Block* scheme. The SLB scheme is based on the log block scheme. It manages the space of flash memory as two types of blocks, data blocks and log blocks. The data blocks hold ordinary data and the log blocks are used to store update writes to data blocks. We define a *log segment* as a set of one or more log blocks. It is the allocation unit of log blocks. The size of a log segment is defined as the number of log blocks in it and is configurable. The log blocks in a log segment are not required to be physically consecutive.

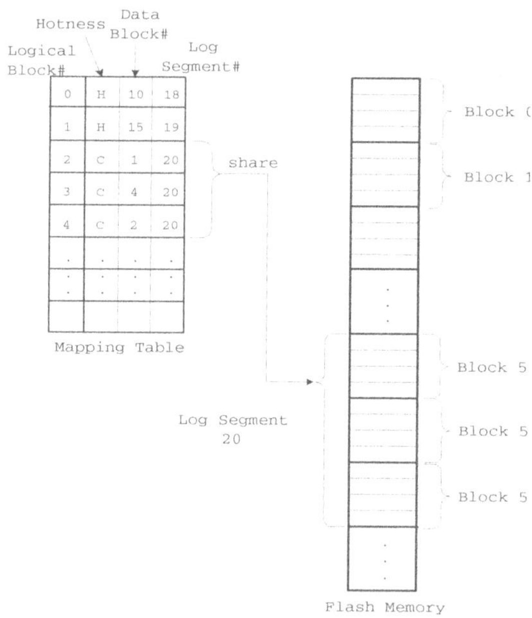

Fig. 4. Shared log block scheme

When a new update to a data block arrives, a log segment is allocated to the data block and the update is performed to the first page of the first log block in the allocated log segment. The SLB can identify the up-to-date copy by scanning the log segment backward from the last valid page. The block mapping table manages the corresponding log segment number for each data block. For a read request, the requested page is serviced either from the data block or from the log segment depending on where the up-to-date copy is present.

Each data block is associated with a state indicating the hotness. Initially all data blocks are defined as the cold block. When a data block is updated frequently, its state is changed to 'hot'. Similarly, hot data block becomes 'cold' block if it is not updated frequently. The degree of hotness of each block is usually determined by the number of times the block has been updated within the specified time interval. We do not describe in detail how to determine the hotness of the data block since there have been many researches about determining the hot and cold blocks.

Because hot blocks are likely to be updated soon and filled up fast, a log segment is allocated and dedicated to the hot block. If the log segemnt becomes full, it is reclaimed by the *merge* operation. The merge operation allocates a free data block and then fills each page with the up-to-date page, either from the log segment if the corresponding page is present, or from the data block otherwise. After copying all the pages, the new block now becomes the data block, and the former data block and the log blocks in the log segment are returned to the pool of free blocks, waiting to be erased by garbage collector.

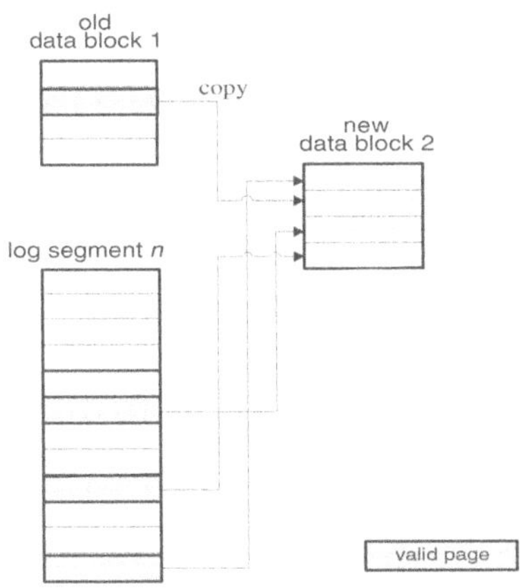

Fig. 5. Merge operation

On the other hand, cold blocks *share* a log segment. When an update to a cold block is newly requested, the SLB allocates either a log segment used by other cold blocks if it exists, or a new log segment from the pool of free blocks otherwise. By sharing the log segment, it avoids wasting the log block space. When the log segment becomes full, it is reclaimed by the *split* operation or *merge* operation. If the log segment is shared with two or more data blocks, the SLB executes split operation. The split operation allocates two log segments and then distributes the up-to-date pages from the former log segment into the new two segments. The pages that belong to the same data block are copied to the same log segment. The log blocks in the former log segment is returned to

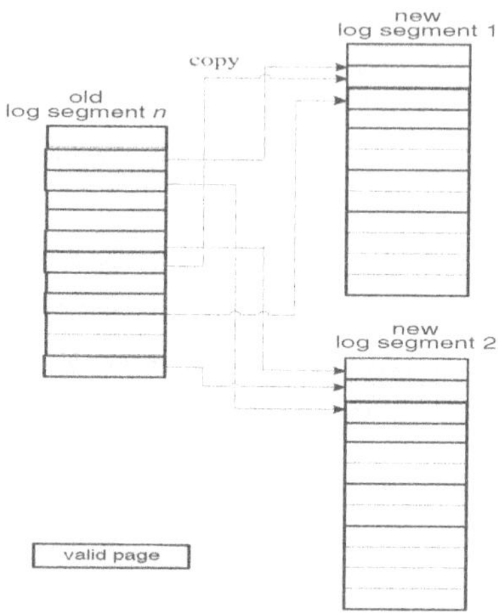

Fig. 6. Split operation

the free blocks, waiting to be erased by garbage collector. In case that the log segment is used by only one data block, the SLB executes merge operation as described before. It allocates a new free block and copies up-to-data pages from the log segment or from the data block depending on where the corresponding page is present. And then the new block becomes the data block. The former data block and the log blocks in the log segment is returned to the free blocks, waiting to be erased by garbage collector.

4 Simulation Studies

To evaluate the proposed scheme, we developed a simulator for the log block scheme [9] and the shared log block scheme. The goal of our performance test is to measure the overwrite performance. To do so, the simulator initially writes data on the entire flash memory space and then overwrites data using one of three access patterns:

- *Uniform* : Each page has equal likelihood of being selected for update.
- *Hot-and-cold*-25 : 60% of the write accesses go to one-eighth of the total pages and other 40% go to another one-eighth. The other three-fourths of the pages are left unmodified. This distribution is intended to simulate meta data write activity on an actual file system. The ratio of writes is bases on the results reported in [12]
- *Hot-and-cold*-10 : Pages are divided into two groups. One group consumes 10% of the space. It is selected for update 90% of the time. The other group consumes 90% of the space but are selected only 10% of the time. The generated traces have very skewed access patterns.

We also performed trace driven simulation using the traces of a digital camera [9]. The workload of the digital cameras are usual operations of the camera such as taking, browsing, and erasing pictures. The traces include many sequential accesses as well as hot spots. Sequential access patterns are usually from storing user data such as image files, while the hot spots are from updates metadata of the file system (Microsoft FAT) due to creation/deletion of files.

We define the number of extra erase operations as the number of erase operations minus the number of erase operations from an ideal scheme. The ideal scheme is defined as a scheme that performs one erase operation for every n-page write requests, where n is the number of pages per block. Similarly, the number of extra write operations is defined as the number of write operations minus the number of writes requested. Performance metrics are the ratio of the number of extra erase operations to the number of erase operations from ideal scheme, the ratio of the number of extra write operations to the number of write requests and the average space utilization of the segment.

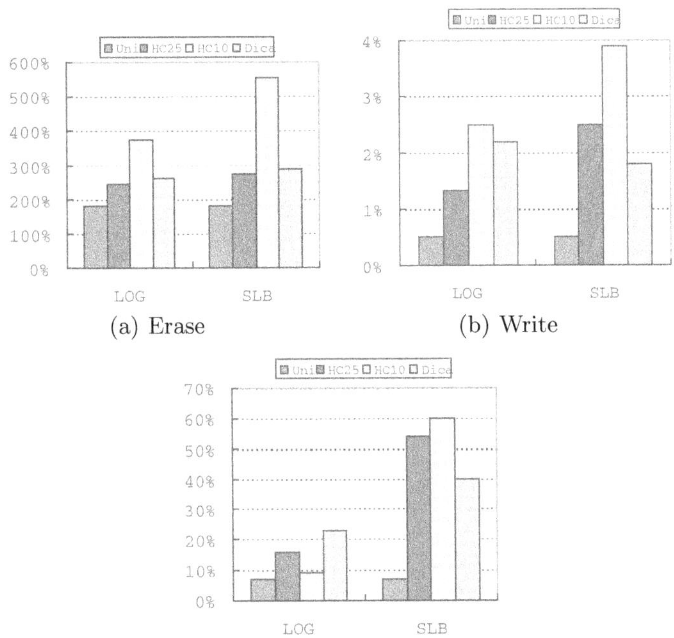

(a) Erase

(b) Write

(c) Average Space Utilization

Fig. 7. SLB-1 vs. log block scheme

In fig. 7, 'Uni' denotes *Uniform* access patterns, 'HC25' denotes *Hot-and-Cold*-25, 'HC10' denotes *Hot-and-Cold*-10, and 'Dica' denotes traces of digital camera. And n of SLB-n denotes the size of a log segment. The proposed scheme significantly improves the space utilization of the log blocks. For example, see fig. 7(c). It increases the average space utilization from 10% to 60% in case of HC10. However, since the shared log blocks will be used frequently like the log blocks for the hot blocks, it could incur more reclamation process and increase

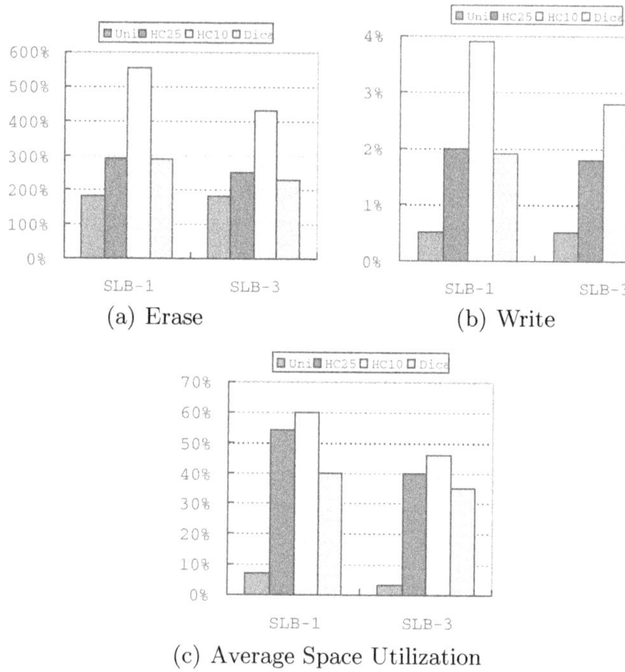

Fig. 8. SLB-1 vs. SLB-3

the number of erase operations and write(i.e., extra data copy) operations. In the log block scheme, on the contrary, since a log block is dedicated to only one data block and a large portion of it remains unused for a long time in case of the cold blocks, it wastes the space but could need fewer erase operations. Simulation results show that there is a tradeoff between the number of erase/write operations and the space utilization.

5 Concluding Remarks

The primary concern in implementing the flash translation layer has been to improve the write and update performance by minimizing the number of erase operations and data copy operations. Previous log block scheme exhibits good performance for the write and the erase operations, but does not consider the space usage of the log blocks. Our approach is to classify data blocks according to their write access frequencies and to share the log blocks in order to improve the space utilization. Simulation results show that the proposed scheme improves the space utilization and there is a tradeoff between the space utilization and the number of erase/write operations. For the future works, we plan to study the garbage collection algorithm used with the proposed shared log block scheme. We also plan to implement proposed scheme in the real system.

References

1. L. Chang and T. Kuo. An adaptive striping architecture for flash memory storage systems of embedded systems. In *Proceedings of the 8th IEEE Real-Time and Embedded Technology and Applications Symposium*, 2002.
2. L. Chang and T. Kuo. An efficient management scheme for large-scale flash memory storage systems. In *Proceedings of ACM Symposium on Applied Computing*, 2004.
3. M. Chiang and R. Chang. Cleaning policies in mobile computers using flash memory. *Journal of Systems and Software*, 48(3):213–231, 1999.
4. T. Chung, D. Park, Y. Ryu, and S. Hong. Lstaff: System software for large block flash memory. *Lecture Notes in Computer Science*, 3398:704–710, 2005.
5. Intel Corporation. Intel strataflash memory product overview. http://www.intel.com.
6. Intel Corporation. Understanding the flash translation layer (ftl) specification. http://developer.intel.com, December 1998.
7. F. Douglis, R. Caceres, F. Kaashoek, K. Li, B. Marsh, and J. Tauber. Storage alternatives for mobile computers. In *Proceedings of the 1st Symposium on Operating Systems Design and Implementation*, 1994.
8. Samsung Electronics. 256m x 8bit / 128m x 16bit nand flash memory. http://www.samsungelectronics.com.
9. J. Kim, S. Noh, S. Min, and Y. Cho. A space-efficient flash translation layer for compactflash systems. *IEEE Trans. on Consumer Electronics*, 48(2):366–375, 2002.
10. M-Systems. Trueffs. http://www.m-systems.com/.
11. B. Marsh, F. Douglis, and P. Krishnan. Flash memory file caching for mobile computers. In *Proceedings of the 27th Hawaii International Conference on Systems Sciences*, 1994.
12. C. Ruemmler and J. Wilkes. Unix disk access patterns. In *Proceedings of 1993 Winter USENIX Conference*, pages 405 – 420, 1993.
13. M. Wu and W. Zwanepoel. envy: A non-volatile, main memory storage system. In *Proceedings of the 6th Internation Conference on Architectural Support for Programming Languages and Operating Systems*, 1994.
14. K. Yim, H. Bahn, and K. Koh. A flash compression layer for smartmedia card systems. *IEEE Trans. on Consumer Electronics*, 50(1):192–197, 2004.

Smart u-Things and Ubiquitous Intelligence

Jianhua Ma

Faculty of Computer and Information Sciences,
Hosei University, Japan
jianhua@k.hosei.ac.jp

Abstract. Smart u-things are real things with attached, embedded or blended computers, networks, and/or some other devices such as sensors, actors, e-tags and so on, and they can sense, compute, communicate and take some adaptive actions/reactions/proactions according to their goals, situated contexts, users' needs, etc. It is envisioned that smart u-thing will be everywhere eventually towards ubiquitous intelligence and smart world. One of the profound implications of such ubiquitous smart u-things is that various kinds and levels of intelligence will exist pervasively in real everyday objects, environments, systems and even ourselves, and possibly be extended from man-made to natural things. The ubicomp/percomp can be regarded, in a sense, as the computing of all these smart/intelligent u-things, which are the basic elements and components of the smart world. After clarifying the essential features and three categories of smart u-things, i.e., smart object, smart space and smart system, the talk is devoted to discuss possible challenges in smart u-things' research in terms of real world complexity. The main intentions are to examine the possible hard issues to suggest some potential research lines; and to let researchers in this field coolhead and being aware of the hardness of these challenges in making real things truly smart.

L.T. Yang et al. (Eds.): ICESS 2005, LNCS 3820, p. 776, 2005.

Author Index

Lecture Notes in Computer Science

For information about Vols. 1–3725

please contact your bookseller or Springer

Vol. 3837: K. Cho, P. Jacquet (Eds.), Technologies for Advanced Heterogeneous Networks. IX, 307 pages. 2005.

Vol. 3835: G. Sutcliffe, A. Voronkov (Eds.), Logic for Programming, Artificial Intelligence, and Reasoning. XIV, 744 pages. 2005. (Subseries LNAI).

Vol. 3833: K.-J. Li, C. Vangenot (Eds.), Web and Wireless Geographical Information Systems. XI, 309 pages. 2005.

Vol. 3826: B. Benatallah, F. Casati, P. Traverso (Eds.), Service-Oriented Computing - ICSOC 2005. XVIII, 597 pages. 2005.

Vol. 3824: L.T. Yang, M. Amamiya, Z. Liu, M. Guo, F.J. Rammig (Eds.), Embedded and Ubiquitous Computing. XXIII, 1204 pages. 2005.

Vol. 3823: T. Enokido, L. Yan, B. Xiao, D. Kim, Y. Dai, L.T. Yang (Eds.), Embedded and Ubiquitous Computing. XXXII, 1317 pages. 2005.

Vol. 3822: D. Feng, D. Lin, M. Yung (Eds.), Information Security and Cryptology. XII, 420 pages. 2005.

Vol. 3821: R. Ramanujam, S. Sen (Eds.), FSTTCS 2005: Foundations of Software Technology and Theoretical Computer Science. XIV, 566 pages. 2005.

Vol. 3820: L.T. Yang, X. Zhou, W. Zhao, Z. Wu, Y. Zhu, M. Lin (Eds.), Embedded Software and Systems. XXVIII, 779 pages. 2005.

Vol. 3818: S. Grumbach, L. Sui, V. Vianu (Eds.), Advances in Computer Science – ASIAN 2005. XIII, 294 pages. 2005.

Vol. 3814: M. Maybury, O. Stock, W. Wahlster (Eds.), Intelligent Technologies for Interactive Entertainment. XV, 342 pages. 2005. (Subseries LNAI).

Vol. 3810: Y.G. Desmedt, H. Wang, Y. Mu, Y. Li (Eds.), Cryptology and Network Security. XI, 349 pages. 2005.

Vol. 3809: S. Zhang, R. Jarvis (Eds.), AI 2005: Advances in Artificial Intelligence. XXVII, 1344 pages. 2005. (Subseries LNAI).

Vol. 3808: C. Bento, A. Cardoso, G. Dias (Eds.), Progress in Artificial Intelligence. XVIII, 704 pages. 2005. (Subseries LNAI).

Vol. 3807: M. Dean, Y. Guo, W. Jun, R. Kaschek, S. Krishnaswamy, Z. Pan, Q.Z. Sheng (Eds.), Web Information Systems Engineering – WISE 2005 Workshops. XV, 275 pages. 2005.

Vol. 3806: A.H. H. Ngu, M. Kitsuregawa, E.J. Neuhold, J.-Y. Chung, Q.Z. Sheng (Eds.), Web Information Systems Engineering – WISE 2005. XXI, 771 pages. 2005.

Vol. 3805: G. Subsol (Ed.), Virtual Storytelling. XII, 289 pages. 2005.

Vol. 3804: G. Bebis, R. Boyle, D. Koracin, B. Parvin (Eds.), Advances in Visual Computing. XX, 755 pages. 2005.

Vol. 3803: S. Jajodia, C. Mazumdar (Eds.), Information Systems Security. XI, 342 pages. 2005.

Vol. 3799: M. A. Rodríguez, I.F. Cruz, S. Levashkin, M.J. Egenhofer (Eds.), GeoSpatial Semantics. X, 259 pages. 2005.

Vol. 3798: A. Dearle, S. Eisenbach (Eds.), Component Deployment. X, 197 pages. 2005.

Vol. 3797: S. Maitra, C. E. V. Madhavan, R. Venkatesan (Eds.), Progress in Cryptology - INDOCRYPT 2005. XIV, 417 pages. 2005.

Vol. 3796: N.P. Smart (Ed.), Cryptography and Coding. XI, 461 pages. 2005.

Vol. 3795: H. Zhuge, G.C. Fox (Eds.), Grid and Cooperative Computing - GCC 2005. XXI, 1203 pages. 2005.

Vol. 3794: X. Jia, J. Wu, Y. He (Eds.), Mobile Ad-hoc and Sensor Networks. XX, 1136 pages. 2005.

Vol. 3793: T. Conte, N. Navarro, W.-m.W. Hwu, M. Valero, T. Ungerer (Eds.), High Performance Embedded Architectures and Compilers. XIII, 317 pages. 2005.

Vol. 3792: I. Richardson, P. Abrahamsson, R. Messnarz (Eds.), Software Process Improvement. VIII, 215 pages. 2005.

Vol. 3791: A. Adi, S. Stoutenburg, S. Tabet (Eds.), Rules and Rule Markup Languages for the Semantic Web. X, 225 pages. 2005.

Vol. 3790: G. Alonso (Ed.), Middleware 2005. XIII, 443 pages. 2005.

Vol. 3789: A. Gelbukh, Á. de Albornoz, H. Terashima-Marín (Eds.), MICAI 2005: Advances in Artificial Intelligence. XXVI, 1198 pages. 2005. (Subseries LNAI).

Vol. 3788: B. Roy (Ed.), Advances in Cryptology - ASIACRYPT 2005. XIV, 703 pages. 2005.

Vol. 3785: K.-K. Lau, R. Banach (Eds.), Formal Methods and Software Engineering. XIV, 496 pages. 2005.

Vol. 3784: J. Tao, T. Tan, R.W. Picard (Eds.), Affective Computing and Intelligent Interaction. XIX, 1008 pages. 2005.

Vol. 3781: S.Z. Li, Z. Sun, T. Tan, S. Pankanti, G. Chollet, D. Zhang (Eds.), Advances in Biometric Person Authentication. XI, 250 pages. 2005.

Vol. 3780: K. Yi (Ed.), Programming Languages and Systems. XI, 435 pages. 2005.

Vol. 3779: H. Jin, D. Reed, W. Jiang (Eds.), Network and Parallel Computing. XV, 513 pages. 2005.

Vol. 3778: C. Atkinson, C. Bunse, H.-G. Gross, C. Peper (Eds.), Component-Based Software Development for Embedded Systems. VIII, 345 pages. 2005.

Vol. 3777: O.B. Lupanov, O.M. Kasim-Zade, A.V. Chaskin, K. Steinhöfel (Eds.), Stochastic Algorithms: Foundations and Applications. VIII, 239 pages. 2005.

Vol. 3775: J. Schönwälder, J. Serrat (Eds.), Ambient Networks. XIII, 281 pages. 2005.

Vol. 3773: A. Sanfeliu, M.L. Cortés (Eds.), Progress in Pattern Recognition, Image Analysis and Applications. XX, 1094 pages. 2005.

Vol. 3772: M. Consens, G. Navarro (Eds.), String Processing and Information Retrieval. XIV, 406 pages. 2005.

Vol. 3771: J.M.T. Romijn, G.P. Smith, J. van de Pol (Eds.), Integrated Formal Methods. XI, 407 pages. 2005.

Vol. 3770: J. Akoka, S.W. Liddle, I.-Y. Song, M. Bertolotto, I. Comyn-Wattiau, W.-J. van den Heuvel, M. Kolp, J. Trujillo, C. Kop, H.C. Mayr (Eds.), Perspectives in Conceptual Modeling. XXII, 476 pages. 2005.

Vol. 3768: Y.-S. Ho, H.J. Kim (Eds.), Advances in Multimedia Information Processing - PCM 2005, Part II. XXVIII, 1088 pages. 2005.

Vol. 3767: Y.-S. Ho, H.J. Kim (Eds.), Advances in Multimedia Information Processing - PCM 2005, Part I. XXVIII, 1022 pages. 2005.

Vol. 3766: N. Sebe, M.S. Lew, T.S. Huang (Eds.), Computer Vision in Human-Computer Interaction. X, 231 pages. 2005.

Vol. 3765: Y. Liu, T. Jiang, C. Zhang (Eds.), Computer Vision for Biomedical Image Applications. X, 563 pages. 2005.

Vol. 3764: S. Tixeuil, T. Herman (Eds.), Self-Stabilizing Systems. VIII, 229 pages. 2005.

Vol. 3762: R. Meersman, Z. Tari, P. Herrero (Eds.), On the Move to Meaningful Internet Systems 2005: OTM 2005 Workshops. XXXI, 1228 pages. 2005.

Vol. 3761: R. Meersman, Z. Tari (Eds.), On the Move to Meaningful Internet Systems 2005: CoopIS, DOA, and ODBASE, Part II. XXVII, 653 pages. 2005.

Vol. 3760: R. Meersman, Z. Tari (Eds.), On the Move to Meaningful Internet Systems 2005: CoopIS, DOA, and ODBASE, Part I. XXVII, 921 pages. 2005.

Vol. 3759: G. Chen, Y. Pan, M. Guo, J. Lu (Eds.), Parallel and Distributed Processing and Applications - ISPA 2005 Workshops. XIII, 669 pages. 2005.

Vol. 3758: Y. Pan, D.-x. Chen, M. Guo, J. Cao, J.J. Dongarra (Eds.), Parallel and Distributed Processing and Applications. XXIII, 1162 pages. 2005.

Vol. 3757: A. Rangarajan, B. Vemuri, A.L. Yuille (Eds.), Energy Minimization Methods in Computer Vision and Pattern Recognition. XII, 666 pages. 2005.

Vol. 3756: J. Cao, W. Nejdl, M. Xu (Eds.), Advanced Parallel Processing Technologies. XIV, 526 pages. 2005.

Vol. 3754: J. Dalmau Royo, G. Hasegawa (Eds.), Management of Multimedia Networks and Services. XII, 384 pages. 2005.

Vol. 3753: O.F. Olsen, L.M.J. Florack, A. Kuijper (Eds.), Deep Structure, Singularities, and Computer Vision. X, 259 pages. 2005.

Vol. 3752: N. Paragios, O. Faugeras, T. Chan, C. Schnörr (Eds.), Variational, Geometric, and Level Set Methods in Computer Vision. XI, 369 pages. 2005.

Vol. 3751: T. Magedanz, E.R. M. Madeira, P. Dini (Eds.), Operations and Management in IP-Based Networks. X, 213 pages. 2005.

Vol. 3750: J.S. Duncan, G. Gerig (Eds.), Medical Image Computing and Computer-Assisted Intervention – MICCAI 2005, Part II. XL, 1018 pages. 2005.

Vol. 3749: J.S. Duncan, G. Gerig (Eds.), Medical Image Computing and Computer-Assisted Intervention – MICCAI 2005, Part I. XXXIX, 942 pages. 2005.

Vol. 3748: A. Hartman, D. Kreische (Eds.), Model Driven Architecture – Foundations and Applications. IX, 349 pages. 2005.

Vol. 3747: C.A. Maziero, J.G. Silva, A.M.S. Andrade, F.M.d. Assis Silva (Eds.), Dependable Computing. XV, 267 pages. 2005.

Vol. 3746: P. Bozanis, E.N. Houstis (Eds.), Advances in Informatics. XIX, 879 pages. 2005.

Vol. 3745: J.L. Oliveira, V. Maojo, F. Martín-Sánchez, A.S. Pereira (Eds.), Biological and Medical Data Analysis. XII, 422 pages. 2005. (Subseries LNBI).

Vol. 3744: T. Magedanz, A. Karmouch, S. Pierre, I. Venieris (Eds.), Mobility Aware Technologies and Applications. XIV, 418 pages. 2005.

Vol. 3742: J. Akiyama, M. Kano, X. Tan (Eds.), Discrete and Computational Geometry. VIII, 213 pages. 2005.

Vol. 3740: T. Srikanthan, J. Xue, C.-H. Chang (Eds.), Advances in Computer Systems Architecture. XVII, 833 pages. 2005.

Vol. 3739: W. Fan, Z. Wu, J. Yang (Eds.), Advances in Web-Age Information Management. XXIV, 930 pages. 2005.

Vol. 3738: V.R. Syrotiuk, E. Chávez (Eds.), Ad-Hoc, Mobile, and Wireless Networks. XI, 360 pages. 2005.

Vol. 3737: C. Priami, E. Merelli, P. Gonzalez, A. Omicini (Eds.), Transactions on Computational Systems Biology III. VII, 169 pages. 2005. (Subseries LNBI).

Vol. 3735: A. Hoffmann, H. Motoda, T. Scheffer (Eds.), Discovery Science. XVI, 400 pages. 2005. (Subseries LNAI).

Vol. 3734: S. Jain, H.U. Simon, E. Tomita (Eds.), Algorithmic Learning Theory. XII, 490 pages. 2005. (Subseries LNAI).

Vol. 3733: P. Yolum, T. Güngör, F. Gürgen, C. Özturan (Eds.), Computer and Information Sciences - ISCIS 2005. XXI, 973 pages. 2005.

Vol. 3731: F. Wang (Ed.), Formal Techniques for Networked and Distributed Systems - FORTE 2005. XII, 558 pages. 2005.

Vol. 3729: Y. Gil, E. Motta, V. R. Benjamins, M.A. Musen (Eds.), The Semantic Web – ISWC 2005. XXIII, 1073 pages. 2005.

Vol. 3728: V. Paliouras, J. Vounckx, D. Verkest (Eds.), Integrated Circuit and System Design. XV, 753 pages. 2005.

Vol. 3727: M. Barni, J. Herrera Joancomartí, S. Katzenbeisser, F. Pérez-González (Eds.), Information Hiding. XII, 414 pages. 2005.

Vol. 3726: L.T. Yang, O.F. Rana, B. Di Martino, J.J. Dongarra (Eds.), High Performance Computing and Communications. XXVI, 1116 pages. 2005.

www.ingramcontent.com/pod-product-compliance
Lightning Source LLC
Chambersburg PA
CBHW071403230926
51846CB00001B/9
9783540308812